INTERNATIONAL ECONOMICS

SIXTH EDITION

DENNIS R. APPLEYARD
DAVIDSON COLLEGE

ALFRED J. FIELD, JR.
UNIVERSITY OF NORTH CAROLINA
AT CHAPEL HILL

STEVEN L. COBB
UNIVERSITY OF NORTH TEXAS

 **McGraw-Hill
Irwin**

Boston   Burr Ridge, IL   Dubuque, IA   New York   San Francisco   St. Louis
Bangkok   Bogotá   Caracas   Kuala Lumpur   Lisbon   London   Madrid   Mexico City
Milan   Montreal   New Delhi   Santiago   Seoul   Singapore   Sydney   Taipei   Toronto

**McGraw-Hill
Irwin**

International Economics

Published by McGraw-Hill/Irwin, a business unit of The McGraw-Hill Companies, Inc., 1221 Avenue of the Americas, New York, NY, 10020. Copyright © 2008, 2006, 2001, 1998, 1995, 1992 by The McGraw-Hill Companies, Inc. All rights reserved. No part of this publication may be reproduced or distributed in any form or by any means, or stored in a database or retrieval system, without the prior written consent of The McGraw-Hill Companies, Inc., including, but not limited to, in any network or other electronic storage or transmission, or broadcast for distance learning.

Some ancillaries, including electronic and print components, may not be available to customers outside the United States.

This book is printed on acid-free paper.

1 2 3 4 5 6 7 8 9 0 DOW/DOW 0 9 8 7

ISBN 978-0-07-337567-0
MHID 0-07-337567-5

Executive editor: *Douglas Reiner*
Editorial coordinator: *Elizabeth Clevenger*
Associate marketing manager: *Kelly Odom*
Project manager: *Dana M. Pauley*
Production supervisor: *Gina Hangos*
Senior designer: *Cara David*
Photo research coordinator: *Lori Kramer*
Senior media project manager: *Susan Lombardi*
Typeface: *10/12 Times Roman*
Compositor: *Laserwords Private Limited*
Printer: *R. R. Donnelley*

Library of Congress Cataloging-in-Publication Data

Appleyard, Dennis R.
   International economics / Dennis R. Appleyard, Alfred J. Field, Jr., Steven L. Cobb. — 6th ed.
      p. cm.
   Includes index.
   ISBN-13: 978-0-07-337567-0 (alk. paper)
   ISBN-10: 0-07-337567-5 (alk. paper)
    1. International economic relations. 2. International trade. 3. International finance.
   I. Field, Alfred J. II. Cobb, Steven L. III. Title.
   HF1359.A77 2008
   337—dc22

                                                          2007026993

www.mhhe.com

The authors dedicate this book to parents, family, and friends whose love and support has sustained us in the writing process over the past 20 years.

ABOUT THE AUTHORS

Dennis R. Appleyard

Dennis R. Appleyard is James B. Duke Professor of International Studies and Professor of Economics at Davidson College, Davidson, North Carolina, and Professor of Economics, Emeritus, University of North Carolina at Chapel Hill. He attended Ohio Wesleyan University for his undergraduate work and the University of Michigan for his Master's and Ph.D. work. He joined the economics faculty at the University of North Carolina at Chapel Hill in 1966 and received the university-wide Tanner Award for "Excellence in Inspirational Teaching of Undergraduate Students" in 1983. He moved to his current position at Davidson College in 1990. At Davidson, he is Chair of the Department of Economics and was Director of the college's Semester-in-India Program in fall 1996 and Semester-in-India and Nepal Program in fall 2000. In 2004 he received Davidson's Thomas Jefferson Award for teaching and service.

Professor Appleyard has taught economic principles, intermediate microeconomics, intermediate macroeconomics, money and banking, international economics, and economic development. His research interests lie in international trade theory and policy and in the Indian economy. Published work, much of it done in conjunction with Professor Field, has appeared in the *American Economic Review, Economic Development and Cultural Change, History of Political Economy, Indian Economic Journal, International Economic Review, Journal of Economic Education,* and *Journal of International Economics,* among others. He has also done consulting work for the World Bank, the U.S. Department of the Treasury, and the Food and Agriculture Organization of the United Nations (in Islamabad, Pakistan). Professor Appleyard derives genuine pleasure from working with students, and he thinks that teaching keeps him young in spirit, since his students are always the same age! He is also firmly convinced that having the opportunity to teach international economics in this age of growing globalization is a rare privilege and an enviable challenge.

Alfred J. Field, Jr.

Alfred J. Field is a Professor of Economics at the University of North Carolina at Chapel Hill. He received his undergraduate and graduate training at Iowa State University and joined the faculty at Carolina in 1967. Field teaches courses in international economics and economic development at both the graduate and undergraduate level, has directed numerous Senior Honors theses and Masters theses, and has served as principal member or director of nearly 100 Ph.D. dissertations. In addition, he has served as Director of Graduate Studies, Associate Chair/Director of the Undergraduate Program in Economics, and Acting Department Chair. In 1966, he received the Department's Jae Yeong Song and Chunuk Park Award for Excellence in Graduate Teaching, and in 2006 he received the University of North Carolina–Chapel Hill John L. Sanders Award for Excellence in Undergraduate Teaching and Service. He is currently serving on the Advisory Board of several university organizations, including the Institute for Latin American Studies.

Professor Field researches in the areas of international trade and economic development. He has worked in Latin America and China, as well as with a number of international agencies in the United States and Europe, primarily on trade and development policy issues. His research interests lie in the areas of trade policy and adjustment and development policy, particularly as they relate to trade, agriculture, and household decision making in developing countries. Another of Field's ongoing lines of research addresses trade and structural adjustment issues in the United States, focusing on the textile and apparel industries and the experience of unemployed textile and apparel workers in North Carolina starting in the 1980s. He maintains an active interest in theoretical trade and economic integration issues, as well as the use of econometric and computable general equilibrium models, in analyzing the effects of trade policy, particularly in developing countries.

Steven L. Cobb

Steven L. Cobb is an Associate Professor in the Department of Economics at the University of North Texas. He currently serves as Director of the Center for Economic Education and is Chair of the Department of Economics. He attended Southwestern University for his undergraduate work in Economics and Political Science. Cobb was a student of Appleyard and Field and received his Ph.D. in Economics in 1987 from the University of North Carolina at Chapel Hill. He joined the faculty at the University of North Texas in 1986 and teaches principles of microeconomics and principles of macroeconomics at the undergraduate level and courses in international economics, comparative economic systems, economic development, and history of economic thought, at both the graduate and undergraduate level. Cobb is a three-time recipient of the Mortar Board Top Prof Award and the 2005 Recipient of the Southern Economic Association's Kenneth G. Elzinga Distinguished Teaching Award. His Center for Economic Education received the 2005 Albert Beekhuis Award for Centers of Excellence in Economic Education from the National Council on Economic Education, and Cobb was presented the 2006 Bessie B. Moore Service Award by the National Association of Economic Educators.

Professor Cobb researches in the areas of economic education, international trade, and economic development. His research interests lie in the areas of internationalization of university curriculum, the impact of attitudes on student performance in economics, cross-cultural training and technology transfer, and U.S.–Mexico trade and immigration. Cobb has also been involved as a consultant and trainer for the National Council on Economic Education's Training of Trainers program in the newly independent states of the former Soviet Union. The program is funded by the U.S. Department of Education and is designed to provide materials and training to allow economists in these nations to teach economics from a market perspective. Cobb has conducted training programs in Russia, Estonia, Latvia, Lithuania, Poland, Belarus, Ukraine, Romania, Bulgaria, Kazakhstan, Uzbekistan, Armenia, Mexico, and South Africa. He enjoys the international aspect of his work and tries to integrate this experience into his teaching.

PREFACE

It is our view that as the new millennium gets under way amid a dramatic increase in globalization, every student must have a conscious awareness of "things international." Whether one is studying, for example, political science, sociology, chemistry, art, history, or economics, developments worldwide impinge upon the subject matter of the chosen discipline. Such developments may take the form of the discovery of a new compound in Germany, an unexpected election result in India, an archeological find in Cyprus, a new awareness of AIDS in Sierra Leone, or a startling new political/terrorist/military development in Afghanistan, Iraq, or Israel. And, because information now gets transmitted instantaneously across continents and oceans, scientists, governments, firms, and households all react quickly to new information by altering behavior in laboratories, clinics, legislative processes, production and marketing strategies, consumption and travel decisions, and research projects. Without keeping track of international developments, today's student will be unable to understand the changing nature of the world and the material that he or she is studying.

In addition to perceiving the need for international awareness on the part of students in general, we think it is absolutely mandatory that students with an interest in economics recognize that international economic events and the international dimensions of the subject surround us every day. As we prepared to launch this sixth edition of *International Economics,* we could not help noting how much had changed since the initial writing for our first edition. The world has economically internationalized even faster than we anticipated nearly 20 years ago, and the awareness of the role of international issues in our lives has increased substantially. Almost daily, headlines focus on developments such as the European Union and the increased economic integration efforts that have fostered monetary union and the euro; policy issues related to reducing trade barriers and the effects of threatened retaliatory actions such as the United States has experienced with its recent steel tariffs; increased integration efforts such as the ongoing negotiations of the Free Trade Agreement for the Americas; and the tensions accompanying growth, structural change, and globalization that surfaced at meetings of international economic organizations such as the World Bank and the World Trade Organization. Beyond these broad issues, headlines also trumpet news of the U.S. trade deficit, rising (or falling) gasoline prices, the value of the Chinese renminbi yuan, and outsourcing to call centers in India.

The growing awareness of the importance of international issues is also in evidence in increased student interest in such issues, particularly those related to employment, international working conditions, and equity. It is thus increasingly important that individuals have a practical working knowledge of the economic fundamentals underlying international actions to find their way through the myriad arguments, emotions, and statistics that bombard them almost daily. Young, budding economists need to be equipped with the framework, the tools, and the basic institutional knowledge that will permit them to make sense of the increasingly interdependent economic environment. Further, there will be few jobs that they will later pursue that will not have an international dimension, whether it be ordering components from a Brazilian firm, traveling to a trade show in Malaysia, making a loan for the transport of Caspian Sea oil, or working in an embassy in Quito or in a medical mission in Burundi.

Thus, the motive for writing this edition is much the same as in earlier editions: to provide a clear and comprehensive text that will help students move beyond simple recognition and interest in international issues and toward a level of understanding of current and future international developments that will be of use to them in analyzing the problem at hand and selecting a policy position. In other words, we seek to help these scholars acquire the necessary human capital for dealing with important questions, for satisfying their intellectual curiosity, and for providing a foundation for future on-the-job decisions.

We have been very flattered by the favorable response to the first five editions of our book. In this sixth edition, we continue to build upon the well-received features to develop a text that is even more attuned to our objectives. We have also, in a number of instances, attempted to clarify our presentation of some of the more difficult concepts and models in order to be more student-friendly.

IMPROVEMENTS

In this edition, as usual, we have attempted to provide current and timely information on the wide variety of international economic phenomena. Further, new boxes have been added to cover emerging issues in the global economy. The text has been updated to include recent developments in U.S. trade policy, major changes in the European Union, progress in the transition from command to market economies, and special issues related to developing nations. We should note that, in the monetary material, we continue to maintain our reliance on the *IS/LM/BP* framework for analyzing macroeconomic policy because we believe that the framework is effective in facilitating student understanding and because that material was favorably received by users of the earlier editions. We also continue to incorporate key aspects of the asset approach into the *IS/LM/BP* model.

Particular mention should be made of the fact that, in this edition, we have introduced Learning Objectives at the beginning of each chapter to orient the reader to the central issues. This text is comprehensive in its coverage of international concepts, and the Learning Objectives are designed to assist the instructor with the choice of chapters to cover in designing the course and to assist the students in focusing on the critical concepts as they begin to read each chapter. Because of the positive response to the addition of the opening vignettes in the fifth edition, we have retained and updated them in this edition to focus on the real-world applicability of the material.

Another improvement introduced throughout the text is a new organization of our pedagogical boxes. The "In the Real World" boxes are designed to provide examples of current international issues and developments drawn straight from the news that illustrate the concepts developed in the chapter. In situations where particularly critical concepts would benefit from further elaboration or graphical representation, we have utilized "Concept" boxes. Finally, there are a number of cases where prominent figures in international economics are profiled. This biographical information is presented in the "Titans of International Economics" boxes.

It is our hope that these changes in the sixth edition will prove beneficial to students as well as to instructors. The improvements are designed to help readers both understand and appreciate more fully the growing importance of the global economy in their lives.

DESCRIPTION OF TEXT

Our book follows the traditional division of international economics into the trade and monetary sides of the subject. Although the primary audience for the book will be students in upper-level economics courses, we think that the material can effectively reach a broad, diversified group of students—including those in political science, international studies, history, and business who may have fewer economics courses in their background. Having taught international economics ourselves in specific nonmajors' sections and Master's of Business Administration sections as well as in the traditional economics department setting, we are confident that the material is accessible to both noneconomics and economics students. This broad audience will be assisted in its learning through the fact that we have included separate, extensive review chapters of microeconomic (Chapter 5) and macroeconomic (Chapter 24) tools.

International Economics presents international trade theory and policy first. Introductory material and data are found in Chapter 1, and Chapters 2 through 4 present the Classical model of trade, including a treatment of pre-Classical Mercantilism. A unique feature is the *devotion of an entire chapter to extensions of the Classical model* to include more than two countries, more than two goods, money wages and prices, exchange rates, and transportation costs. The analysis is brought forward through the modern Dornbusch-Fischer-Samuelson model including a treatment of the impact of productivity improvements in one country on the trading partner. Chapter 5 provides an *extensive review of microeconomic tools* used in international trade and can be thought of as a "short course" in intermediate micro. Chapters 6 through 9 present the workhorse neoclassical and Heckscher-Ohlin trade theory, including an examination of the assumptions of the model. Chapter 6 focuses on the traditional production possibilities–indifference curve exposition. We are unabashed fans of the offer curve because of the nice general equilibrium properties of the device and because of its usefulness in analyzing trade policy and in interpreting economic events, and Chapter 7 extensively develops this concept. Chapter 8 explores Heckscher-Ohlin in a theoretical context, and Chapter 9 is *unique in its focus on testing the factor endowments approach,* including empirical work on the trade-income inequality debate in the context of Heckscher-Ohlin.

Continuing with theory, Chapters 10 through 12 treat extensions of the traditional material. Chapter 10 *discusses various post–Heckscher-Ohlin trade theories* that relax standard assumptions such as international factor immobility, homogeneous products, constant returns to scale, and perfect competition. An important focus here is upon imperfect competition and intra-industry trade. Chapter 11 explores the comparative statics of economic growth and the relative importance of trade, and it includes material on endogenous growth models and on the effects of growth on the offer curve. Chapter 12 examines causes and consequences of international factor movements, including both capital movements and labor flows.

Chapters 13 through 17 are devoted to trade policy. Chapter 13 is *exclusively devoted to presentation of the various instruments of trade policy.* Chapter 14 then explores the welfare effects of the instruments, including discussion of such effects in a "small-country" as well as a "large-country" setting. Chapter 15 examines various arguments for protection, including strategic trade policy approaches. Chapter 16 begins with a discussion of the political economy of trade policy, followed by a review of various trade policy actions involving the United States as well as issues currently confronting the WTO. Chapter 17 is a separate chapter on *economic integration.* We have updated the discussion of the transition economies, the European Union, and the North American Free Trade Agreement. The trade part of the book concludes with Chapter 18, which provides an overview of how international trade influences growth and change in the developing countries as well as a discussion of the external debt problem.

The international monetary material begins with Chapter 19, which introduces balance-of-payments accounting. In contrast to the approach in some texts, *balance-of-payments accounting is discussed prior to the foreign exchange market,* which is considered in Chapter 20. We think this sequence makes more sense than the reverse, since the demand and supply curves of foreign exchange reflect the debit and credit items, respectively, in the balance of payments. A differentiating feature of the presentation of the foreign exchange market is the *extensive development of various exchange rate measures,* for example, nominal, real, and effective exchange rates. Chapter 21 then describes character-istics of "real-world" international financial markets in detail, and discusses a (we hope not-too-bewildering) variety of international financial derivative instruments. Chapter 22 presents in considerable detail *the monetary and portfolio balance (or asset market) approaches to the balance of payments and to exchange rate determination.* The difficult discussion of empirical testing of these approaches is in an appendix. The chapter con-cludes with an examination of the phenomenon of *exchange rate overshooting.* In Chapters 23 and 24, our attention turns to the more traditional price and income adjustment mecha-nisms. Chapter 24 is in effect a *review of basic Keynesian macroeconomic analysis.*

Chapters 25 through 27 are concerned with macroeconomic policy under different exchange rate regimes. As noted earlier, we continue to utilize the *IS/LM/BP* Mundell-Fleming approach rather than employ exclusively the asset market approach. The value of the *IS/LM/BP* model is that it can embrace both the current and the capital/financial accounts in an understandable and perhaps familiar framework for many undergraduates. This model is presented in Chapter 25 in a manner that does not require previous acquain-tance with it but does constitute review material for most students who have previously taken an intermediate macroeconomic theory course. The chapter concludes with an analy-sis of monetary and fiscal policy in a fixed exchange rate environment. These policies are then examined in a flexible exchange rate environment in Chapter 26, and the analysis is broadened to the *aggregate demand–aggregate supply framework* in Chapter 27. The con-cluding chapters, Chapters 28 and 29, focus on particular topics of global concern. Chapter 28 considers various issues related to the choice between fixed and flexible exchange rates, including material on currency boards. Chapter 29 then traces the historical development of the international monetary system from Bretton Woods onward and examines proposals for reform such as target zone proposals.

Because of the length and comprehensiveness of the *International Economics* text, it is not wise to attempt to cover all of it in a one-semester course. For such a course, we recommend that material be selected from Chapters 1 to 3, 5 to 8, 10, 13 to 15, 19 and 20, 22 to 26, and 29. If more emphasis on international trade is desired, additional material from Chapters 17 and 18 can be included. For more emphasis on international monetary economics, we suggest the addition of selected material from Chapters 21, 27, and 28. For a two-semester course, the entire *International Economics* book can be covered. Whatever the course, occasional outside reading assignments from academic journals, current popular periodicals, a readings book, and Web sources can further help to bring the material to life. The "References for Further Reading" section at the end of the book, which is organized by chapter, can hopefully give some guidance. If library resources are limited, the text contains, both in the main body and in boxes, summaries of some noteworthy contributions.

PEDAGOGICAL DEVICES

To assist the student in learning the material, we have included a variety of pedagogical devices. We like to think of course that the major device in this edition is again clear expo-sition. Although all authors stress clarity of exposition as a strong point, we continue to be pleased that many reviewers praised this feature. Beyond this general feature, more specific devices are described herein.

Learning Objectives

Virtually every chapter begins with a set of explicit learning objectives to help students focus on key concepts. The learning objectives can also be useful to instructors in selecting material to cover in their respective classes.

Opening Vignettes

These opening vignettes or cases were mentioned earlier. The intent of each case is to motivate the student toward pursuing the material in the forthcoming chapter as well as to enable the student to see how the chapter's topics fit with actual applied situations in the world economy.

Boxes

There are three types of material that appear in boxes (more than 100 of them) in *International Economics*. Some are analytical in nature (Concept Boxes), and they explain further some difficult concepts or relationships. We have also included several biographical boxes (Titans of International Economics). These short sketches of well-known economists add a personal dimension to the work being studied, and they discuss not only the professional interests and concerns of the individuals but also some of their less well-known "human" characteristics. Finally, the majority of the boxes are case studies (In the Real World), appearing throughout chapters and supplemental to the opening vignettes. These boxes serve to illuminate concepts and analyses under discussion. As with the opening vignettes, they give students an opportunity to see the relevance of the material to current events. They also provide a break from the sometimes heavy dose of theory that permeates international economics texts.

Concept Checks

These are short "stopping points" at various intervals within chapters (about two per chapter). The concept checks pose questions that are designed to see if basic points made in the text have been grasped by the student.

End-of-Chapter Questions and Problems

These are standard fare in all texts. The questions and problems are broader and more comprehensive than the questions contained in the concept checks.

Lists of Key Terms

The major terms in each chapter are boldfaced in the chapters themselves and then are brought together at the end of the chapter in list form. A review of each list can serve as a quick review of the chapter.

References for Further Reading

These lists occur at the end of the book, organized by chapter. We have provided bibliographic sources that we have found useful in our own work as well as entries that are relatively accessible and offer further theoretical and empirical exploration opportunities for interested students.

Instructor's Manual and Test Bank

This companion work offers instructors assistance in preparing for and teaching the course. We have included suggestions for presenting the material as well as answers to the end-of-chapter questions and problems. In addition, sample examination questions are provided, including some of the hundreds of multiple-choice questions and problems that we have used for examining our own students. Access this ancillary, as well as the online version of the test bank, through the text's Online Learning Center.

Online Learning Center

The sixth edition of *International Economics* is accompanied by a comprehensive Web site, www.mhhe.com/appleyard6e. The Instructor's Manual and Test Bank exist in Word format on the password protected portion. Additionally, the password protected site includes the link to EZ Test Online, answers to the Graphing Exercises, and a Digital Image Library containing all of the images from the text. Students also benefit from visiting the Online Learning Center. Chapter-specific graphing exercises and interactive quizzes serve as helpful study materials.

ACKNOWLEDGMENTS

Our major intellectual debts are to the many professors who taught us economics, but particularly to Robert Stern of the University of Michigan and Erik Thorbecke of Cornell University. We also have found conversations and seminars over the years with faculty colleagues at the University of North Carolina at Chapel Hill to have been extremely helpful. We particularly wish to thank Stanley Black, Patrick Conway, William A. Darity, Jr., Richard Froyen, and James Ingram. Thanks also to colleagues at Davidson College, especially Peter Hess, Vikram Kumar, David Martin, Lou Ortmayer, and Clark Ross; and colleagues at the University of North Texas, especially Michael McPherson, David Molina, and Margie Tieslau; and to the many students at Chapel Hill and Davidson who were guinea pigs for the material. We also express our appreciation to Barbara Carmack for her cheerful and very extensive help with the mechanics of manuscript preparation. Timely assistance was also provided by Christoph Pross.

We are also indebted to the entire staff at McGraw-Hill/Irwin, especially Dana Pauley, Gina Hangos, Cara David, Lori Kramer, Susan Lombardi, Douglas Reiner, Elizabeth Clevenger, and Kelly Odom. We thank them for their cooperation, patience, encouragement, and guidance in the development of this sixth edition.

In addition, we are grateful to the following reviewers; their thoughtful, prescriptive comments have helped guide the development of these six editions:

Mohsen Bahmani-Oskooee	University of Wisconsin–Milwaukee
Michael Barry	Mount St. Mary's University
Scott Baier	Clemson University
Bruce Blonigen	University of Oregon
Eric Bond	Pennsylvania State University
Harry Bowen	University of California–Irvine
Victor Brajer	California State University–Fullerton
Drusilla Brown	Tufts University
Geoffrey Carliner	Babson College
Roman Cech	Longwood University
Winston Chang	State University of New York at Buffalo
Charles Chittle	Bowling Green State University
Bienvenido Cortes	Pittsburg State University
Kamran Dadkhah	Northeastern University
Joseph Daniels	Marquette University
William Davis	University of Tennessee at Martin
Alan Deardorff	University of Michigan
Khosrow Doroodian	Ohio University–Athens
Mary Epps	University of Virginia
Jim Gerber	San Diego State University
Norman Gharrity	Ohio Wesleyan University
Animesh Ghoshal	DePaul Univesity
James Hartigan	University of Oklahoma
Stephen Haynes	University of Oregon

Pershing Hill	University of Alaska
William Hutchinson	Vanderbilt University
William Kaempfer	University of Colorado
Mitsuhiro Kaneda	Georgetown University
Patrick Kehoe	University of Pennsylvania
Frank Kelly	Indiana University–Purdue University Indianapolis
David Kemme	Wichita State University
Madhu Khanna	University of Illinois–Champaign
Yih-Wu Liu	Youngstown State University
Thomas Love	North Central College
Judith McDonald	Lehigh University
Thomas McGahagan	University of Pittsburgh at Johnstown
Joseph McKinney	Baylor University
Thomas McKinnon	University of Arkansas
Michael McPherson	University of North Texas
William G. Mertens	University of Colorado at Boulder
Thomas Mondschean	DePaul University
Michael Moore	The George Washington University
Sudesh Mujumdar	University of Southern Indiana
John Pomery	Purdue University
Michael Quinn	Bentley College
James Rakowski	University of Notre Dame
James Rauch	University of California–San Diego
Simran Sahi	University of Minnesota
Jeff Sarbaum	University of North Carolina–Chapel Hill
W. Charles Sawyer	University of Southern Mississippi
Don Schilling	University of Missouri
Modiful Shumon Islam	Columbia Southern University
John N. Smithin	York University
Richard G. Stahl	Louisiana State University
Jeffrey Steagall	University of North Florida
Edward Tower	Duke University
John Wilson	Michigan State University

We also wish to thank David Ball (North Carolina State University), David Collie (Cardiff University), David Cushman (University of Saskatchewan), Guzin Erlat (Middle East Technical University–Ankara), J. Michael Finger (World Bank, retired), Dan Friel (Bank of America), Art Goldsmith (Washington and Lee University), Monty Graham (The Peterson Institute of International Economics), Michael Jones (Bowdoin College), Joseph Joyce (Wellesley College), and Joe Ross (Goldman Sachs) for their helpful comments on this and earlier editions. Appreciation is also extended to the many other individuals who have contacted us over the years regarding our book. Of course, any remaining shortcomings or errors are the responsibility of the authors (who each blame the other two). A special note of thanks goes to our families for their understanding, support, and forbearance throughout the time-absorbing process required to complete all six editions.

Finally, we welcome any suggestions or comments that you may have regarding this text. Please feel free to contact us at our e-mail addresses. And thank you for giving attention to our book!

Dennis R. Appleyard
deappleyard@davidson.edu

Alfred J. Field, Jr.
afield@email.unc.edu

Steven L. Cobb
scobb@unt.edu

BRIEF CONTENTS

CONTENTS

PART 2

NEOCLASSICAL TRADE THEORY   63

PART 3

ADDITIONAL THEORIES AND
EXTENSIONS   171

CHAPTER 10
**Post–Heckscher-Ohlin Theories of Trade and
Intra-Industry Trade, 173**

PART 5

──────────────────◉──────────────────

FUNDAMENTALS OF INTERNATIONAL MONETARY ECONOMICS   453

1

THE WORLD OF INTERNATIONAL ECONOMICS

INTRODUCTION

Welcome to the study of international economics. No doubt you have become increasingly aware of the importance of international transactions in daily economic life. When people say that "the world is getting smaller every day," they are referring not only to the increased speed and ease of transportation and communications but also to the increased use of international markets to buy and sell goods, services, and financial assets. This is not a new phenomenon, of course: In ancient times international trade was important for the Egyptians, the Greeks, the Romans, the Phoenicians, and later for Spain, Portugal, Holland, and Britain. It can be said that all the great nations of the past that were influential world leaders were also important world traders. Nevertheless, the importance of international trade and finance to the economic health and overall standard of living of a country has never been as clear as it is today.

Signs of these international transactions are all around us. The clothes we wear come from production sources all over the world: the United States to the Pacific Rim to Europe to Central and South America. The automobiles we drive are produced not only in the United States but also in Canada, Mexico,

Japan, Germany, France, Italy, England, Sweden, and other countries. The same can be said for the food we eat, the shoes we wear, the appliances we use, and the many different services we consume. In addition, in the United States, when you call an 800 number about a product or service, you may be talking to someone in India. Further, products manufactured in the United States often use important parts produced in other countries. At the same time, many U.S. imports are manufactured with important U.S.–made components.

This increased internationalization of economic life is made even more complicated by foreign-owned assets. More and more companies in many countries are owned partially or totally by foreigners. Further, in the 1990s, foreigners purchased U.S. government bonds and corporate stocks in record numbers, partly fueling the stock market boom of those years. The overall heightened presence of foreign goods, foreign producers, and foreign-owned assets causes many to question the impact and desirability of international transactions. It is our hope that after reading this text you will be better able to understand how international trade and payments affect a country and that you will know how to evaluate the implications of government policies that are undertaken to influence the level and direction of international transactions.

You will be studying one of the oldest branches of economics. People have been concerned about the goods and services crossing their borders for as long as nation-states or city-states have existed. Some of the earliest economic data relate to international trade, and early economic thinking often centered on the implications of international trade for the well-being of a politically defined area. Although similar to regional economics in many respects, international economics has traditionally been treated as a special branch of the discipline. This is not terribly surprising when one considers that economic transactions between politically distinct areas are often associated with many differences that influence the nature of exchanges between them rather than transactions within them. For example, the degree of factor mobility between countries often differs from that within countries. Countries can have different forms of government, different currencies, different types of economic systems, different resource endowments, different cultures, different institutions, and different arrays of products.

The study of international economics, like all branches of economics, concerns decision making with respect to the use of scarce resources to meet desired economic objectives. It examines how international transactions influence such things as social welfare, income distribution, employment, growth, and price stability and the possible ways public policy can affect the outcomes. In the study of international trade, we ask, for example: What determines the basis for trade? What are the effects of trade? What determines the value and the volume of trade? What factors impede trade flows? What is the impact of public policy that attempts to alter the pattern of trade? In the study of international monetary economics we address questions such as: What is meant by a country's balance of payments? How are exchange rates determined? How does trade affect the economy at the macro level? Why does financial capital flow rapidly and sizably across country borders? Should several countries adopt a common currency? How do international transactions affect the use of monetary and fiscal policy to pursue domestic targets? This chapter provides an overview of the subjects and issues of international economics that will be discussed throughout the rest of this text.

THE NATURE OF MERCHANDISE TRADE

Before delving further into the subject matter of international economics, however, it is useful to take a brief look at some of the characteristics of world trade today. The value of world merchandise exports was $10.2 trillion in 2005, a figure that is dramatic when one realizes that the value of goods exported worldwide was less than $2 trillion in 1985.

TABLE 1   Growth in Volume of World Goods Production and Trade, 1963–2005 (average annual percentage change in volume)

	1963–1973	*1970–1979*	*1980–1985*	*1985–1990*	*1990–1998*	*1995–2000*	*2000–2005*	*2004*	*2005*
Production									
All commodities	6.0%	4.0%	1.7%	3.0%	2.0%	4.0%	2.0%	4.0%	2.5%
Agriculture	2.5	2.0	2.9	1.9	2.0	2.5	2.0	4.0	0.5
Mining	5.5	2.5	−2.7	3.0	2.0	2.0	2.0	4.0	1.0
Manufacturing	7.5	4.5	2.3	3.2	2.0	4.0	2.5	4.0	3.5
Exports									
All commodities	9.0%	5.0%	2.1%	5.8%	6.5%	7.0%	4.5%	9.5%	6.0%
Agriculture	14.0	4.5	1.0	2.2	4.0	3.5	3.5	3.5	5.5
Mining	7.5	1.5	−2.7	4.8	5.5	4.0	2.5	5.5	2.5
Manufacturing	11.5	7.0	4.5	7.0	7.0	8.0	5.0	11.0	7.0

Sources: General Agreement on Tariffs and Trade, *International Trade 1985–86* (Geneva: GATT, 1986), p. 13; GATT, *International Trade 1988–89,* I (Geneva: GATT, 1989), p. 8; GATT, *International Trade 1993: Statistics* (Geneva: GATT, 1993), p. 2; GATT, *International Trade 1994: Trends and Statistics* (Geneva: GATT, 1994), p. 2; World Trade Organization, *Annual Report 1999: International Trade Statistics* (Geneva: WTO, 1999), p. 1; WTO, *International Trade Statistics 2003* (Geneva: WTO, 2003), p. 19 and WTO, *International Trade Statistics 2006* (Geneva: WTO, 2006), p. 15, both obtained from www.wto.org.

TABLE 2   Exports and Imports by Region, 2005 (billions of dollars and percentage of world totals)

	Exports		*Imports*	
	Value ($, billions f.o.b.*)	*Share (%)*	*Value ($, billions c.i.f.*)*	*Share (%)*
North America[†]	$ 1,478	14.5%	$ 2,285	21.7%
South and Central America	355	3.5	298	2.8
Europe	4,372	43.0	4,543	43.2
(European Union[‡])	(4,001)	(39.4)	(4,135)	(39.3)
Commonwealth of Independent States (CIS)[§]	340	3.3	216	2.1
Africa	298	2.9	249	2.4
Middle East	538	5.3	322	3.1
Asia	2,779	27.4	2,599	24.7
Total	$10,159	100.0%	$10,511	100.0%

Note: Components may not sum to totals because of rounding.

*Exports are recorded f.o.b. (free on board) and imports are recorded c.i.f. (cost, insurance, and freight).

[†]Includes Mexico.

[‡]Austria, Belgium, Cyprus, Czech Republic, Denmark, Estonia, Finland, France, Germany, Greece, Hungary, Ireland, Italy, Latvia, Lithuania, Luxembourg, Malta, Netherlands, Poland, Portugal, Slovak Republic, Slovenia, Spain, Sweden, and United Kingdom.

[§]Armenia, Azerbaijan, Belarus, Georgia, Kazakhstan, Kyrgyz Republic, Moldova, Russian Federation, Tajikistan, Turkmenistan, Ukraine, and Uzbekistan.

Source: World Trade Organization, *International Trade Statistics 2006* (Geneva: WTO, 2006), p. 16, Table I.3, obtained from www.wto.org.

Throughout the past four decades, international trade volume has, on average, outgrown production (see Table 1), illustrating how countries are becoming more interdependent.

The Geographical Composition of Trade

In terms of major economic areas, the industrialized countries dominate world trade. Details of trade on a regional basis are provided in Table 2. The relative importance of Europe, North America, and Asia is evident, as they account for more than 85 percent of trade. Asia has become increasingly important in developing countries' imports and exports.

TABLE 3   Regional Structure of World Merchandise Exports, 2005 (percentage of each origin area's exports going to each destination area)

Origin	Destination							
	North America	South and Central America	Europe	CIS	Africa	Middle East	Asia	World
North America	55.8%	5.9%	16.1%	0.5%	1.2%	2.3%	18.3%	100.0%
South and Central America	33.2	24.3	19.1	1.6	2.7	1.8	13.4	100.0
Europe	9.1	1.3	73.2	2.5	2.6	2.8	7.6	100.0
CIS	5.7	2.0	52.3	18.1	1.4	3.1	11.8	100.0
Africa	20.2	2.8	42.9	0.3	8.9	1.7	16.3	100.0
Middle East	12.3	0.6	16.1	0.6	2.9	10.1	52.2	100.0
Asia	21.9	1.9	17.9	1.3	1.9	3.2	51.2	100.0
World	20.6	3.0	43.3	2.2	2.4	3.2	24.0	100.0

Note: Destination percentages for any given origin area do not sum to 100.0% because of rounding and/or incomplete specification.

Source: Data contained in World Trade Organization, *International Trade Statistics 2006* (Geneva: WTO, 2006), p. 37, Table III.3, obtained from www.wto.org.

To obtain an idea of the geographical structure of trade, look at Table 3, which provides information on the destination of merchandise exports from several regions for 2005. The first row, for example, indicates that 55.8 percent of the exports of countries of North America went to other North American countries, 5.9 percent of North American exports went to South and Central America, and so forth. From this table it is clear that the major markets for all regions' exports are in North America, Europe, and Asia. This is true for these three areas themselves, especially for Europe, which sends 73.2 percent of its exports to itself. In addition, the table makes it evident that the countries in Africa and the Middle East trade relatively little with themselves.

At the individual country level (see Table 4), the relative importance of Europe, North America, and Asia in 2005 is again quite evident. The largest country exporter is Germany (which displaced the United States in 2003). The 6 largest traders (exports plus imports) are the United States, Germany, China, Japan, France, and the United Kingdom, and they account for more than 40 percent of world trade. Also noteworthy has been the spectacular growth in the trade of Hong Kong, the Republic of Korea (South Korea), Taiwan, China (especially), and Singapore. Finally, the 10 largest trading countries account for almost 55 percent of world trade. World trade thus tends to be concentrated among relatively few major traders, with the remaining, almost 200 countries accounting for about 45 percent.

The Commodity Composition of Trade

Turning to the 2005 commodity composition of world trade (Table 5), manufactures account for 72 percent of trade, with the remaining amount consisting of primary products. Among primary goods, trade in fuels is the largest (13.8 percent), followed by food products (6.7 percent). Trade in raw materials, ores and other minerals, and nonferrous metals accounts for 5.2 percent. In the manufacturing category, machinery and transport equipment account for 37.9 percent of world trade. Office and telecom equipment and automotive products are major subcategories, accounting for 12.6 percent and 9.0 percent of exports, respectively. Other important categories of manufactures include trade in chemicals (10.9 percent) and in textiles and clothing (4.7 percent).

TABLE 4   Leading Merchandise Exporters and Importers, 2005 (billions of dollars and percentage share of world totals)

Exports			Imports		
Country	Value	Share	Country	Value	Share
1. Germany	$ 969.9	9.3%	United States	$ 1,732.4	16.1%
2. United States	904.4	8.7	Germany	773.8	7.2
3. China	762.0	7.3	China	660.0	6.1
4. Japan	594.9	5.7	Japan	514.9	4.8
5. France	460.2	4.4	United Kingdom	510.2	4.7
6. Netherlands	402.4	3.9	France	497.9	4.6
7. United Kingdom	382.8	3.7	Italy	379.8	3.5
8. Italy	367.2	3.5	Netherlands	359.1	3.3
9. Canada	359.4	3.4	Canada	319.7	3.0
10. Belgium	334.3	3.2	Belgium	318.7	3.0
11. Hong Kong (China)	292.1	2.8	Hong Kong (China)	300.2	2.8
12. Korea, Republic of	284.4	2.7	Spain	278.8	2.6
13. Russia	243.6	2.3	Korea, Republic of	261.2	2.4
14. Singapore	229.6	2.2	Mexico	231.7	2.1
15. Mexico	213.7	2.0	Singapore	200.0	1.9
16. Taiwan	197.8	1.9	Taiwan	182.6	1.7
17. Spain	187.2	1.8	India	134.8	1.3
18. Saudi Arabia	181.4	1.7	Switzerland	126.5	1.2
19. Malaysia	140.9	1.4	Austria	126.2	1.2
20. Switzerland	130.9	1.3	Russia*	125.3	1.2
21. Sweden	130.1	1.2	Australia*	125.3	1.2
22. Austria	124.0	1.2	Thailand	118.2	1.1
23. Brazil	118.3	1.1	Turkey	116.6	1.1
24. United Arab Emirates	115.5	1.1	Malaysia	114.6	1.1
25. Thailand	110.1	1.1	Sweden	111.2	1.0
26. Ireland	109.9	1.1	Poland	101.0	0.9
27. Australia	105.8	1.0	United Arab Emirates	80.7	0.7
28. Norway	103.8	1.0	Brazil	77.6	0.7
29. India	95.1	0.9	Czech Republic*	76.7	0.7
30. Poland	89.3	0.9	Denmark	76.0	0.7
Total†	$ 8,741.0	83.8%		$ 9,031.7	83.8%
World†	$10,431.0	100.0%		$10,783.0	100.0%

Note: Components may not sum to totals because of rounding.

*Imports valued f.o.b.

†Includes significant re-exports and imports for re-export. The "World" figures thus differ from the totals in Table 2.

Source: World Trade Organization, *International Trade Statistics 2006* (Geneva: WTO, 2006), p. 17, Table I.5, obtained from www.wto.org.

What is especially notable is the current importance of trade in manufactures and the declining importance of primary products. Comparison of the last column of Table 5 with the next-to-last column illustrates the relatively sluggish growth of primary products in world trade compared with the growth in manufactured goods. For example,

TABLE 5   Commodity Composition of World Exports, 2005 and 1980

Product Category	Value in 2005 ($, billions)	Share in 2005	Share in 1980
Agricultural products	**$ 852**	**8.4%**	**14.7%**
Food	683	6.7	11.0
Raw materials	169	1.7	3.7
Mining products	**1,748**	**17.2**	**27.7**
Ores and other minerals	149	1.5	2.1
Fuels	1,401	13.8	23.0
Nonferrous metals	199	2.0	2.5
Manufactures	**7,311**	**72.0**	**53.9**
Iron and steel	318	3.1	3.8
Chemicals	1,104	10.9	7.0
Other semimanufactures	711	7.0	6.7
Machinery and transport equipment	3,851	37.9	25.8
Office and telecom equipment	1,275	(12.6)	(4.2)
Automotive products	914	(9.0)	(6.5)
Other machinery and transport equipment	1,663	(16.4)	(15.2)
Textiles	203	2.0	2.7
Clothing	276	2.7	2.0
Other consumer goods	848	8.3	5.8
Total	$10,159	100.0%	100.0%

Note: Components may not sum to category totals because of rounding. The three aggregate categories do not sum to $10,159 and 100.0% because of incomplete specification of products.

Sources: World Trade Organization, *International Trade 1995: Trends and Statistics* (Geneva: WTO, 1995), p. 77; WTO, *International Trade Statistics 2006* (Geneva: WTO, 2006), pp. 210 and 215 of Table A10, obtained from www.wto.org.

food products accounted for 11.0 percent of world exports in 1980 but only 6.7 percent in 2005; fuels, which constituted 23.0 percent in 1980, fell in importance to 13.8 percent in 2005; and the share of primary products in total dropped from 42.4 percent in 1980 to 25.6 percent in 2005. These developments are of particular relevance to many developing countries, whose trade has traditionally been concentrated in primary goods. Specialization in commodity groups that are growing relatively more slowly makes it difficult for them to obtain the gains from growth in world trade accruing to countries exporting manufactured products. The demand for primary products not only tends to be less responsive to income growth but is also more likely to demonstrate greater price fluctuations.

U.S. International Trade

To complete our discussion of the current nature of merchandise trade, we take a closer look at the geographic and commodity characteristics of the 2005 U.S. international trade (see Tables 6 and 7). Geographically, Canada is the most important trading partner for the United States, both in exports and imports. NAFTA partners (Canada and Mexico) are the largest multi-country unit, followed by the EU. The third-largest individual trading partner country of the United States, behind Canada and Mexico, is China, followed by Japan, Germany, the United Kingdom, South Korea, Taiwan, and France. Of note is the fact that a major portion (47.0 percent) of the trade deficit of the United States in 2005 could be traced to China, Japan, and Canada.

TABLE 6   **U.S. Merchandise Trade by Area and Country, 2005 (millions of dollars)**

	Exports	*Imports*	*Balance*
Total	$894,631	$1,677,371	$−782,740
Europe	207,891	354,269	−146,378
European Union	183,466	307,909	−124,443
Belgium	18,563	13,018	5,545
France	22,255	33,767	−11,512
Germany	33,584	84,588	−51,004
Ireland	9,323	28,744	−19,421
Italy	11,245	30,966	−19,721
Netherlands	26,288	14,802	11,486
United Kingdom	37,570	50,536	−12,966
Non-European Union	24,425	46,360	−21,935
Canada	212,192	293,314	−81,122
Latin America and Other Western Hemisphere	192,387	294,993	−102,606
Brazil	15,174	24,434	−9,260
Mexico	120,264	172,110	−51,846
Venezuela	6,410	33,978	−27,568
Asia and Pacific	237,515	607,148	−369,633
China	41,799	243,472	−201,673
Hong Kong (China)	16,319	8,925	7,394
Japan	53,264	138,008	−84,744
Korea, Republic of	27,135	43,781	−16,646
Malaysia	10,386	33,686	−23,300
Singapore	20,259	15,091	5,168
Taiwan	21,453	34,827	−13,374
Thailand	7,192	19,889	−12,697
Middle East	29,760	62,437	−32,677
Saudi Arabia	6,526	27,192	−20,666
Africa	14,886	65,210	−50,324
Nigeria	1,625	24,239	−22,614
(Members of OPEC)	(31,308)	(124,939)	(−93,631)

Note: Aggregate group percentages may not sum to 100.0% because of rounding.

Source: Renee M. Sauers and Matthew J. Argersinger, "U.S. International Transactions: First Quarter of 2006," *Survey of Current Business,* July 2006, pp. 73–75, obtained from www.bea.gov.

Turning to the commodity composition of U.S. trade (Table 7), agricultural products (foods, feeds, and beverages) are an important source of exports. The capital goods category is the largest single export category and is dominated by nonelectric machinery. Industrial supplies, importantly consisting of chemicals and metal/nonmetallic products, is also an important export category for the United States, although imports are larger than exports in the entire category (even excluding energy products). Sizable net imports occur in consumer goods, autos, and energy products. The largest import category is industrial supplies and materials, followed by consumer goods. Currently, energy products account for 17.6 percent of total imports. It is not surprising that the United States is a major importer of several primary products, such as petroleum, and also of products that traditionally rely relatively heavily on labor in production such as textiles and apparel.

TABLE 7   Composition of U.S. Trade, 2005 (billions of dollars and percentage shares)

	Value of Exports	Share (%)	Value of Imports	Share (%)
Total	**$894.6**	**100.0%**	**$1,677.4**	**100.0%**
Foods, feeds, and beverages	**59.0**	**6.6**	**68.1**	**4.1**
Fish and shellfish	4.2	0.5	11.9	0.7
Grains and preparations	15.6	1.7	—	—
Meat products and poultry	7.2	0.8	7.5	0.4
Soybeans	6.6	0.7	—	—
Vegetables, fruits, nuts, and preparations	11.6	1.3	13.9	0.8
Wine, beer, and related products	—	—	6.9	0.4
Industrial supplies and materials	**233.1**	**26.1**	**524.6**	**31.3**
Building materials, except metals	9.6	1.1	34.4	2.1
Chemicals, excluding medicinals	76.0	8.5	51.0	3.0
Energy products	32.2	3.6	295.8	17.6
Metals and nonmetallic products	53.7	6.0	83.8	5.0
Iron and steel products	11.3	1.3	30.8	1.8
Nonferrous metals	20.8	2.3	31.8	1.9
Paper and paper-base stocks	15.1	1.7	13.6	0.8
Textile supplies and related materials	12.9	1.4	12.8	0.8
Capital goods, except automotive	**362.7**	**40.5**	**379.2**	**22.6**
Civilian aircraft, engines, and parts	60.8	6.8	25.8	1.5
Electric generating machinery, electric apparatus, and parts	33.4	3.7	43.1	2.6
Nonelectric machinery, including parts and attachments	264.9	29.6	308.0	18.4
Computers, peripherals, and parts	45.5	5.1	93.3	5.6
Industrial engines, pumps, and compressors	14.9	1.7	12.7	0.8
Machine tools and metalworking machinery	7.7	0.9	8.3	0.5
Measuring, testing, and control instruments	16.7	1.9	12.2	0.7
Oil drilling, mining, and construction machinery	19.0	2.1	15.6	0.9
Scientific, hospital, and medical equipment and parts	27.0	3.0	24.4	1.5
Semiconductors	47.2	5.3	25.8	1.5
Telecommunications equipment	25.7	2.9	37.0	2.2
Automotive vehicles, parts, and engines	**98.6**	**11.0**	**239.5**	**14.3**
(to/from Canada)	(53.6)	(6.0)	(70.8)	(4.2)
Passenger cars, new and used	30.5	3.4	123.4	7.4
Trucks, buses, and special-purpose vehicles	13.5	1.5	22.7	1.4
Engines and engine parts	11.3	1.3	19.8	1.2
Other parts and accessories	43.3	4.8	73.7	4.4
Consumer goods (nonfood), except automotive	**115.7**	**12.9**	**407.3**	**24.3**
Consumer durable goods, manufactured	53.6	6.0	201.2	12.0
Household and kitchen appliances and other household goods	23.4	2.6	97.1	5.8
Radio and stereo equipment, including records, tapes, and disks	—	—	12.2	0.7
Television and video receivers	—	—	35.1	2.1
Toys, shooting, and sporting goods, including bicycles	—	—	27.1	1.6
Consumer nondurable goods, manufactured	52.8	5.9	186.1	11.1
Footwear of leather, rubber, and other materials	—	—	13.7	0.8
Medical, dental, and pharmaceutical preparations, including vitamins	27.6	3.1	—	—

TABLE 7   Composition of U.S. Trade, 2005 (billions of dollars and percentage shares) *(continued)*

Textile apparel and household goods, except rugs	—	—	79.7	4.8
Unmanufactured consumer goods (gemstones, nursery stock)	9.2	1.0	20.0	1.2
Goods, not elsewhere classified (including U.S. import goods returned)	**25.6**	**2.9**	**58.6**	**3.5**

Notes: (a) Major category figures may not sum to totals because of rounding; (b) — = not available or negligible

Source: Renee M. Sauers and Matthew J. Argersinger, "U.S. International Transactions: First Quarter of 2006," *Survey of Current Business,* July 2006, pp. 76–77, obtained from www.bea.gov.

WORLD TRADE IN SERVICES

The discussion of world trade has to this point focused on merchandise trade and has ignored the rapidly growing trade in services, estimated to be more than $2 trillion in 2005 (one-sixth of the total trade in goods and services). The rising importance of services in trade should not be unexpected since the service category now accounts for the largest share of income and employment in many industrial countries including the United States. More specifically, services account for 77 percent of gross domestic product (GDP) in France, 69 percent in Germany, 77 percent in the United States, 73 percent in the United Kingdom, and 68 percent in Japan.[1] In this context, services generally include the following categories in the International Standard Industrial Classification (ISIC) system: wholesale and retail trade, restaurants and hotels, transport, storage, communications, financial services, insurance, real estate, business services, personal services, community services, social services, and government services.

International trade in services broadly consists of commercial services, investment income, and government services, with the first two categories accounting for the bulk of services. Discussions of trade in "services" generally refer to trade in commercial services. During the 1970s this category grew more slowly in value than did merchandise trade. However, since that time, exports of commercial services have outgrown merchandise exports, and the relative importance of commercial services is roughly the same today as it was in the early 1970s. A word of caution is in order, however: The nature of trade in "services" is such that it is extremely difficult to obtain accurate estimates of the value of these transactions. This results from the fact that there is no agreed definition of what constitutes a traded service, and the ways in which these transactions are measured are less precise than is the case for merchandise trade. Estimates are obtained by examining foreign exchange records and/or through surveys of establishments. Because many service transactions are not observable (hence, they are sometimes referred to as the "invisibles" in international trade), the usual customs records or data are not available for valuing these transactions. Thus, it is likely that the value of trade in commercial services is underestimated. However, there may also be instances when firms may choose to overvalue trade in services, and reported figures must be viewed with some caution.

In terms of the geographical nature of trade in services, this trade is also concentrated among the industrial countries (see Table 8). The principal world traders in merchandise are generally also the principal traders in services. It is notable that both exports and imports of services are important for emerging economies such as Thailand, Taiwan, Singapore, India, and South Korea.

The nature of trade in services is such that until the 1980s they were virtually ignored in trade negotiations and trade agreements. However, because of their increasing importance,

---

[1] World Bank, *World Development Indicators 2007* (Washington, DC: World Bank, 2007), pp. 194–96.

TABLE 8   Leading Exporters and Importers of Commercial Services, 2005 (billions of dollars and percentage share of world totals)

| | Exports | | | Imports | |
Country	Value	Share	Country	Value	Share
1. United States	$ 354.0	14.7%	United States	$ 281.2	12.0%
2. United Kingdom	188.7	7.8	Germany	201.4	8.6
3. Germany	148.5	6.2	United Kingdom	154.1	6.6
4. France	115.0	4.8	Japan	132.6	5.6
5. Japan	107.9	4.5	France	104.9	4.5
6. Italy	93.5	3.9	Italy	92.4	3.9
7. Spain	92.7	3.8	China	83.2	3.5
8. Netherlands	76.7	3.2	Netherlands	70.9	3.0
9. China	73.9	3.1	Ireland	66.1	2.8
10. Hong Kong (China)	62.2	2.6	Spain	65.2	2.8
11. India	56.1	2.3	Canada	64.2	2.7
12. Ireland	53.3	2.2	Korea, Republic of	57.7	2.5
13. Belgium	53.3	2.2	India	52.2	2.2
14. Austria	52.6	2.2	Belgium	50.3	2.1
15. Canada	52.2	2.2	Austria	48.5	2.1
16. Singapore	45.1	1.9	Singapore	44.0	1.9
17. Switzerland	44.0	1.8	Russia	38.5	1.6
18. Korea, Republic of	43.9	1.8	Denmark	36.0	1.5
19. Sweden	42.8	1.8	Sweden	35.0	1.5
20. Denmark	41.2	1.7	Hong Kong (China)	32.4	1.4
21. Luxembourg	40.0	1.7	Taiwan	31.4	1.3
22. Greece	34.1	1.4	Australia	28.9	1.2
23. Norway	28.5	1.2	Thailand	27.5	1.2
24. Australia	27.7	1.1	Norway	27.2	1.2
25. Taiwan	25.6	1.1	Switzerland	25.2	1.1
26. Turkey	25.6	1.1	Luxembourg	24.8	1.1
27. Russia	24.3	1.0	Indonesia	23.2	1.0
28. Thailand	20.5	0.8	Brazil	22.3	0.9
29. Malaysia	19.0	0.8	Malaysia	21.6	0.9
30. Israel	16.8	0.7	Mexico	20.9	0.9
Total	$2,059.7	85.3%		$ 1,963.8	83.7%
World	$2,415.0	100.0%		$ 2,345.0	100.0%

Note: Components may not sum to totals because of rounding.

Source: World Trade Organization, *International Trade Statistics 2006* (Geneva: WTO, 2006), p. 19, Table I.7, obtained from www.wto.org.

there has been a growing concern for the need to establish some general guidelines for international transactions in services. Consequently, discussions regarding the nature of the service trade and various country restrictions that may influence it were included in the last completed round of trade negotiations (the Uruguay Round) conducted under the auspices of the General Agreement on Tariffs and Trade (GATT), which became the World Trade Organization in 1995. Clearly, with the rapid advances that have already been made in communications, it is likely that trade in services will continue to grow. It is important that guidelines for trade in services be established so that country restrictions on trade in services and information flows do not impede their movement and the benefits that occur because of them.

THE CHANGING DEGREE OF ECONOMIC INTERDEPENDENCE

It is important not only to recognize the large absolute level of international trade but also to recognize that the relative importance of trade has been growing for nearly every country and for all countries as a group. The relative size of trade is often measured by comparing the size of a country's exports with its gross domestic product (GDP). Increases in the export/GDP ratio indicate that a higher percentage of the output of final goods and services produced within a country's borders is being sold abroad. Such increases indicate a greater international interdependence and a more complex international trade network encompassing not only final consumption goods but also capital goods, intermediate goods, primary goods, and commercial services. The recent increase in international interdependence is evident in the various export/GDP ratios for selected countries for 1970 and 2005 shown in Table 9.

TABLE 9   International Interdependence for Selected Countries and Groups of Countries, 1970 and 2005 (exports of goods and nonfactor services as a percentage of GDP)

	1970	*2005*
Industrialized countries:		
Australia	14%	18%
Belgium	52	87
Canada	23	39
France	16	26
Germany	NA	40
Italy	16	26
Japan	11	13
Netherlands	42	71
United Kingdom	23	26
United States	6	10
Developing countries:		
Argentina	9	25
Chile	15	42
China	3	38
Czech Republic	NA	72
India	4	21
Iran	24	39
Kenya	30	27
Korea, Republic of	14	43
Mexico	6	30
Nigeria	8	53
Russian Federation	NA	35
Singapore	102	243
Low- and middle-income countries:		
Sub-Saharan Africa	21	33
East Asia and Pacific	7	46
South Asia	5	20
Europe and Central Asia	NA	41
Middle East and North Africa	29	37
Latin America and Caribbean	13	26

Notes: (a) NA = not available; (b) some of the figures are for a slightly different year.

Sources: World Bank, *World Development Report 1993* (Oxford: Oxford University Press, 1993), pp. 254–55; World Bank, *World Development Indicators 2007* (Washington, DC: World Bank, 2007), pp. 218–20.

Although the degree of dependence on exports varies considerably among countries, the relative importance of exports has increased in almost all individual cases and for every country grouping where data are available. This means not only that individual countries are experiencing the economic benefits that accompany the international exchange of goods and services but also that their own economic prosperity is dependent upon economic prosperity in the world as a whole. It also means that competition for markets is greater and that countries must be able to facilitate changes in their structure of production consistent with changes in relative production costs throughout the world. Thus, while increased interdependence has many inherent benefits, it also brings with it greater adjustment requirements and greater needs for policy coordination among trading partners. Both of these are often more difficult to achieve in practice than one might imagine, because even though a country as a whole may benefit from relative increases in international trade, individual parties or sectors may end up facing significant adjustment costs.

Even though the United States is less dependent on exports than most of the industrialized countries, the relative importance of exports has increased substantially since 1960, when the export/GDP ratio was about 4 percent. Thus, the United States, like most of the countries of the world, is increasingly and inexorably linked to the world economy. This link will, in all likelihood, grow stronger as countries seek the economic benefits that accompany increased economic and political integration. Such movements have been evident in recent years as Europe has pursued greater economic and monetary union and the North American Free Trade Agreement was implemented by Canada, Mexico, and the United States.

SUMMARY

International trade has played a critical role in the ability of countries to grow, develop, and be economically powerful throughout history. International transactions have been becoming increasingly important in recent years as countries seek to obtain the many benefits that accompany increased exchange of goods, services, and factors. The relative increase in the importance of international trade makes it increasingly imperative that we all understand the basic factors that underlie the successful exchange of goods and services and the economic impact of various policy measures that may be proposed to influence the nature of international trade. This is true at both the micro level of trade in individual goods and services and the macro level of government budget deficits/surpluses, money, exchange rates, interest rates, and possible controls on foreign investment. It is our hope that you will find the economic analysis of international transactions helpful in improving your understanding of this increasingly important type of economic activity.

Appendix   A GENERAL REFERENCE LIST IN INTERNATIONAL ECONOMICS

The various books, articles, and data sources cited throughout this text will be useful for those of you who wish to examine specific issues in greater depth. Students who are interested in pursuing international economic problems on their own, however, will find it useful to consult the following general references:

Specialized Journals

European Economic Review

Finance and Development (World Bank/IMF)

Foreign Policy

International Economic Journal

The International Economic Review

The International Economy

International Monetary Fund Staff Papers

The International Trade Journal

Journal of Common Market Studies

Journal of Economic Integration

The Journal of International Economics

Journal of International Money and Finance

Review of International Economics

The World Economy

General Journals

American Economic Review

American Journal of Agricultural Economics

Brookings Papers on Economic Activity

Canadian Journal of Economics

Challenge: The Magazine of Economic Affairs

The Economic Journal

Economic Letters

Economic Policy Review (Federal Reserve Bank of New York)

Journal of Economic Literature

Journal of Economic Perspectives

Journal of Finance

Journal of Political Economy

Kyklos

Quarterly Journal of Economics

Review of Economics and Statistics

Sources of International Data

Balance of Payments Statistics Yearbook (IMF)

Bank for International Settlements Annual Report

Direction of Trade Statistics (IMF, quarterly and annual yearbook)

Federal Reserve Bulletin

International Financial Statistics (IMF, monthly and annual yearbook)

OECD Main Economic Indicators

Survey of Current Business (Bureau of Economic Analysis, U.S. Department of Commerce)

UN International Trade Statistics Yearbook

UN Monthly Bulletin of Statistics

US Economic Report of the President

World Development Report and World Development Indicators (World Bank)

World Economic Outlook (IMF)

General Current Information

The Economist

Financial Times

IMF Survey

The International Herald Tribune

The Los Angeles Times

The New York Times

The Wall Street Journal

The Washington Post

Internet Sources

www.bea.gov (Bureau of Economic Analysis, U.S. Department of Commerce)

www.bis.org (Bank for International Settlements)

www.imf.org (International Monetary Fund)

www.cia.gov/cia/publications/factbook (Central Intelligence Agency's *World Factbook*)

www.unctad.org (United Nations Conference on Trade and Development)

www.usitc.gov (U.S. International Trade Commission)

www.ustr.gov (U.S. Trade Representative)

www.worldbank.org (World Bank)

www.wto.org (World Trade Organization)

www.intracen.org (International Trade Centre)

part 1

THE CLASSICAL THEORY OF TRADE

> The ordinary means therefore to increase our wealth and treasure is by foreign trade, wherein we must ever observe this rule; to sell more to strangers yearly than we consume of theirs in value.
>
> Thomas Mun, 1664

The continued expansion of world trade, coupled with political events in Europe and North America related to the liberalizing of international economic relations, indicates that we are entering a unique period in the long history of international trade and exchange. It has never been more important to understand the underlying basis for trade, the policies that governments propose to influence it, and how current ideas have evolved and developed over several centuries.

Because several early views about international trade form the foundation for present-day analysis and other less viable views still influence trade policy from time to time, it is important to trace briefly their origins to evaluate their appropriateness in today's world.

Part 1 reviews the early contributions of the Mercantilist and the Classical schools of thought. Chapter 2, "Early Trade Theories," provides a brief overview of Mercantilist views on international trade and the early Classical response of David Hume and Adam Smith. Chapter 3, "The Classical World of David Ricardo and Comparative Advantage," provides a more extensive discussion of Ricardo's idea of comparative advantage and is followed by a discussion of several extensions of the basic Ricardian model in Chapter 4, "Extensions and Tests of the Classical Model of Trade." Together these three chapters provide an introduction to the basics underlying international trade and a foundation on which to construct contemporary theory. ●

> Two men can both make shoes and hats, and one is superior to the other in both employments, but in making hats he can only exceed his competitor by one-fifth or 20 per cent, and in making shoes he can excel him by one-third or 33 per cent:—will it not be for the interest of both that the superior man should employ himself exclusively in making shoes, and the inferior man in making hats?
>
> David Ricardo, 1817

EARLY TRADE THEORIES

Mercantilism and the Transition to the Classical World of David Ricardo

LEARNING OBJECTIVES

- ■ To learn the basic concepts and policies associated with Mercantilism.

- ■ To understand Hume's price-specie-flow mechanism and the challenge it posed to Mercantilism.

- ■ To grasp Adam Smith's concepts of wealth and absolute advantage as foundations for international trade.

INTRODUCTION

The Oracle in the 21st Century

When the ancient Greeks faced a dilemma, they consulted the Oracle at Delphi. If we were to ask the Oracle the secret to wealth, what would she say? Work hard? Get an education? Probably not. Diligence and intelligence are strategies for improving one's lot in life, but plenty of smart, hard-working people remain poor.

No, the Oracle's advice would consist of just a few words: *Do what you do best. Trade for the rest.* In other words, specialize and then trade.[1]

When did the idea of gains from trade first emerge? How did the views on trade change in the 18th century? It has long been perceived that nations benefit in some way by trading with other nations. Although the underlying basis for this belief has changed considerably over time, it is surprising how often we encounter ideas about the gains from trade and the role of trade policy that stem from some of the earliest views of the role of international trade in the pursuit of domestic economic goals. Some of these early ideas are found in the writings of the Mercantilist school of thought. Later, these ideas were challenged both by time and by writers who subsequently were identified as early Classical economic thinkers. This challenge to Mercantilism culminated in the work of David Ricardo, which to this day lies at the heart of international trade theory. To render a sense of the historical development of international trade theory and to provide a basis for evaluating current trade policy arguments that are clearly Mercantilist in nature, this chapter briefly examines several of the more important ideas of these Mercantilist writers, the problems associated with Mercantilist thinking, and the emergence of a different view of trade offered by Adam Smith. By the end of this chapter, you should be able to recognize that Mercantilist notions still exist even though their shortcomings were ascertained long ago.

MERCANTILISM

Mercantilism refers to the collection of economic thought that came into existence in Europe during the period from 1500 to 1750. It cannot be classified as a formal school of thought, but rather as a collection of similar attitudes toward domestic economic activity and the role of international trade that tended to dominate economic thinking and policy during this period. Many of these ideas not only were spawned by events of the time but also influenced history through their impact on government policies. Geographical explorations that provided new opportunities for trade and broadened the scope of international relations, the upsurge in population, the impact of the Renaissance on culture, the rise of the merchant class, the discovery of precious metals in the New World, changing religious views on profits and accumulation, and the rise of nation-states contributed to the development of Mercantilist thought. Indeed, Mercantilism is often referred to as the *political economy of state building.*

The Mercantilist Economic System

Central to Mercantilist thinking was the view that national wealth was reflected in a country's holdings of precious metals. In addition, one of the most important pillars of Mercantilist thought was the static view of world resources. Economic activity in this setting can be viewed as a **zero-sum game** in which one country's economic gain was at the expense of another. (A zero-sum game is a game such as poker where one person's winnings are

---

[1]"The Fruits of Free Trade," *2002 Annual Report,* reprint, Federal Reserve Bank of Dallas, p. 6.

matched by the losses of the other players.) Acquisition of precious metals thus became the means for increasing wealth and well-being and the focus of the emerging European nation-states. In a hostile world, the enhancement of state power was critical to the growth process, and this was another important Mercantilist doctrine. A strong army, strong navy and merchant marine, and productive economy were critical to maintaining and increasing the power of a nation-state.

Mercantilists saw the economic system as consisting of three components: a manufacturing sector, a rural sector (domestic hinterland), and the foreign colonies (foreign hinterland). They viewed the merchant class as the group most critical to the successful functioning of the economic system, and labor as the most critical among the basic factors of production. The Mercantilists, as did the Classical writers who followed, employed a **labor theory of value,** that is, commodities were valued relatively in terms of their relative labor content. Not surprisingly, most writers and policymakers during this period subscribed to the doctrine that economic activity should be regulated and not left to individual prerogative. Uncontrolled individual decision making was viewed as inconsistent with the goals of the nation-state, in particular, the acquisition of precious metals. Finally, the Mercantilists stressed the need to maintain an excess of exports over imports, that is, a **favorable balance of trade** or **positive trade balance.** This doctrine resulted from viewing wealth as synonymous with the accumulation of precious metals (specie) and the need to maintain a sizable war chest to finance the military presence required of a wealthy country. The inflow of specie came from foreigners who paid for the excess purchases from the home country with gold and silver. This inflow was an important source of money to countries constrained by a shortage in coinage. Crucial to this view was the implicit Mercantilist belief that the economy was operating at less than full employment; therefore, the increase in the money supply stimulated the economy, resulting in growth of output and employment and not simply in inflation. Hence, the attainment of a positive trade balance could be economically beneficial to the country. Obviously, an excess of imports over exports— an **unfavorable balance of trade** or a **negative trade balance**—would have the opposite implications.

The Role of Government

The economic policies pursued by the Mercantilists followed from these basic doctrines. Governments controlled the use and exchange of precious metals, what is often referred to as **bullionism.** In particular, countries attempted to prohibit the export of gold, silver, and other precious metals by individuals, and rulers let specie leave the country only out of necessity. Individuals caught smuggling specie were subject to swift punishment, often death. Governments also gave exclusive trading rights for certain routes or areas to specific companies. Trade monopolies fostered the generation of higher profits through the exercise of both monopoly and monopsony market power. Profits contributed both directly and indirectly to a positive trade balance and to the wealth of the rulers who shared the profits of this activity. The Hudson Bay Company and the Dutch East India Trading Company are familiar examples of trade monopolies, some of which continued well into the 19th century.

Governments attempted to control international trade with specific policies to maximize the likelihood of a positive trade balance and the resulting inflow of specie. Exports were subsidized and quotas and high tariffs were placed on imports of consumption goods. Tariffs on imports of raw materials that could be transformed by domestic labor into exportables were, however, low or nonexistent, because the raw material imports could be "worked up" domestically and exported as high-value manufactured goods. Trade was fostered with the colonies, which were seen as low-cost sources of raw materials and agricultural products and as potential markets for exports of manufactures from the parent country. Navigation policies aimed to control international trade and to maximize the inflow (minimize the outflow) of specie for shipping services. The British Navigation Acts, for example, excluded foreign ships from engaging in coastal trade and from carrying merchandise to Britain or its colonies. Trade policy was consistently directed toward controlling the flow of commodities between countries and toward maximizing the inflow of specie that resulted from international trade.

Mercantilism and Domestic Economic Policy

The regulation of economic activity also was pursued within the country through the control of industry and labor. Comprehensive systems of regulations were put into effect utilizing exclusive product charters such as those granted to the royal manufacturers in France and England, tax exemptions, subsidies, and the granting of special privileges. In addition to the close regulation of production, labor was subject to various controls through craft guilds. Mercantilists argued that these regulations contributed to the quality of both skilled labor and the manufactures such labor helped produce—quality that enhanced the ability to export and increased the wealth of the country.

Finally, the Mercantilists pursued policies that kept wages low. Because labor was the critical factor of production, low wages meant that production costs would be low and a country's products would be more competitive in world markets. It was widely held that the lower classes must be kept poor in order to be industrious and that increased wages would lead to reduced productivity. Note that, in this period, wages were not market determined but were set institutionally to provide workers with incomes consistent with their traditional position in the social order. However, because labor was viewed as vital to the state, a growing population was crucial to growth in production. Thus, governments stimulated population growth by encouraging large families, giving subsidies for children, and providing financial incentives for marriage.

Mercantilist economic policies resulted from the view of the world prominent at that time. The identification of wealth with holdings of precious metals instead of a nation's productive capacity and the static view of world resources were crucial to the policies that were pursued. While these doctrines seem naive today, they undoubtedly seemed logical in the period from 1500 to 1750. Frequent warfare lent credibility to maintaining a powerful army and merchant marine. The legitimization of and growing importance of saving by the merchant class could easily be extended to behavior by the state, making the accumulation of precious metals seem equally reasonable. However, the pursuit of power by the state at the expense of other goals and the supreme importance assigned to the accumulation of precious metals led to an obvious paradox: Rich nations in the Mercantilist sense would comprise large numbers of very poor people. Specie was accumulated at the expense of current consumption. At the same time, the rich nations found themselves expending large amounts of their holdings of precious metals to protect themselves against other nations attempting to acquire wealth by force.

CONCEPT CHECK

1. Why were Mercantilist thinkers concerned with the acquisition of specie as opposed to overall productive capacity?

2. Why was regulation of economic activity critical to this line of thinking?

3. If one is referred to as a Mercantilist, what types of trade policy does one favor? Why?

IN THE REAL WORLD:

MERCANTILISM IS STILL ALIVE

On April 30, 1987, the U.S. House of Representatives passed the Trade and International Economic Policy Reform Act, which became known as the Omnibus Trade Bill. Prior to its passing, Rep. Richard A. Gephardt (D–MO) offered an amendment "to require the U.S. trade representative to enter into negotiations with countries running excessive unwarranted trade surpluses with the United States and mandate retaliatory action against such countries if negotiations fail."

Under the proposed amendment, countries with "excessive" trade surpluses with the United States were to be placed on a list, and each country's trading practices would be scrutinized by the U.S. trade representative, a cabinet-level member of the executive branch. A six-month negotiation period would begin with those countries. Successful negotiations would lead to no action by the United States, but the trading practices of the country in question were to be reexamined at yearly intervals. In the case of unsuccessful negotiations, the United States was to retaliate on a dollar-for-dollar basis against the value of the unfair trading practices that the country in question maintained. If the country failed to eliminate its unfair trading practices and maintained a huge trade surplus with the United States, it would be faced with a bilateral surplus reduction requirement of 10 percent for each of four years. The president could reduce or eliminate the surplus-reduction requirement under special circumstances, for example, if the country was experiencing a debt problem or if it was not in the best interests of the United States to require the reduction. One supporter of the amendment, Rep. Bill Richardson (D–NM), now the governor of New Mexico, indicated that "Our national security is at stake and the standard of living for future generations. The time to act is long overdue." The amendment passed by a vote of 218 to 214. It was later enacted into law in a slightly relaxed form (as the "Super 301" provision) in the Omnibus Trade and Competitiveness Act of 1988. Thankfully (for economists), Super 301 is no longer a part of U.S. trade policy.

Other comments and examples abound with respect to the initiation of policy measures to restrict trade so as seemingly to benefit the trade-restricting nation. For example, Canada and the United States have "cabotage" laws. The Canadian law states that ships carrying merchandise between Canadian ports must be owned and crewed by Canadians; the United States law adds to the ownership and crew provisions that the ship must have been built in the United States. Such laws are "justified" as providing for national defense because they give rise to a strong merchant marine. Of course, they also add to export receipts because of this legislated use of domestic shipping services.

Mercantilist notions regarding trade were echoed by Patrick J. Buchanan in his 1996 and 2000 campaigns for presidential nomination. For example, during a speech in August 1996, referring to the U.S. trade deficits that he attributed to the 1993 North American Free Trade Agreement (NAFTA) and the 1994 worldwide trade-liberalizing pact signed by members of the General Agreement on Tariffs and Trade (GATT), he noted, " . . . that is 4 million lost jobs for America's working men and women."

Finally, the Mercantilist balance-of-trade doctrine was verbalized beautifully by the head of a local chapter of presidential candidate Ross Perot's United We Stand organization in 1993 when, in reference to the U.S. trade deficit of the time, he said, "If we just stopped trading with the rest of the world, we'd be $100 billion ahead." *The Economist* summarized the situation when it stated, in 2004, that "Mercantilism has been defunct as an economic theory for at least 200 years, but many practical men in authority remain slaves to the notion that exports must be promoted and imports deterred."

Sources: *Congressional Digest,* June–July 1987, pp. 169, 184, 186, 192; Bob Davis, "In Debate over Nafta, Many See Global Trade as Symbol of Hardship," *The Wall Street Journal,* Oct. 20, 1993, p. A9; "Jones Act," obtained from www.mctf.com/jones_act.shtml; "The Jones Act," obtained from www.geocities.com/The Tropics/1965/jones.htm; "Liberating Trade," *The Economist,* May 13, 2004, obtained from www.Economist.com; " 'No Triumph without Tears' in the Buchanan Party," *Congressional Quarterly Weekly Report,* Aug. 17, 1996, p. 2338; United States Trade Representative, *1999 Trade Policy Agenda and 1998 Annual Report of the President of the United States on the Trade Agreements Program,* p. 254, obtained from www.ustr.gov/reports/tpa/1999/viii.pdf.

THE CHALLENGE TO MERCANTILISM BY EARLY CLASSICAL WRITERS

In the early 18th century, ideas regarding the nature of economic activity began to change. Bullionism and bullionists began to be thought of as naive. National political units had already emerged under the pressure of peasant wars and kingly conquest, and feudalism began to give way to centralized monarchies. Technological developments coupled with the strengthening of the profit motive supported the development of market systems, and state monopolies began to disappear. New ideas and new philosophies (particularly the skeptical inquiry of the humanist viewpoint), fostered in part by the Italian Renaissance, contributed to the continuing spirit of change. By the late 18th century, ideas concerning international trade began to change when early Classical writers such as David Hume and Adam Smith challenged the basic tenets of Mercantilism.

David Hume—The Price-Specie-Flow Mechanism

One of the first attacks on Mercantilist thought was raised by David Hume (in his *Political Discourses,* 1752) with his development of the **price-specie-flow mechanism.** Hume challenged the Mercantilist view that a nation could continue to accumulate specie without any repercussions to its international competitive position. He argued that the accumulation of gold by means of a trade surplus would lead to an increase in the money supply and therefore to an increase in prices and wages. The increases would reduce the competitiveness of the country with a surplus. Note that Hume is assuming that changes in the money supply would have an impact on prices rather than on output and employment. At the same time, the loss of gold in the deficit country would reduce its money supply, prices, and wages, and increase its competitiveness (see Concept Box 1). Thus, it is not possible for a nation to continue to maintain a positive balance of trade indefinitely. A trade surplus (or deficit) automatically produces internal repercussions that work to remove that surplus (or deficit). The movement of specie between countries serves as an automatic adjustment mechanism that always seeks to equalize the value of exports and imports (i.e., to produce a zero trade balance).

Today the Classical price-specie-flow mechanism is seen as resting on several assumptions.

CONCEPT BOX 1

CAPSULE SUMMARY OF THE PRICE-SPECIE-FLOW MECHANISM

Given sufficient time, an automatic trade balance adjustment would take place between a trade surplus country and a trade deficit country by means of the following steps:

	Italy (Trade Surplus) vis-à-vis *Spain (Trade Deficit)*	
	Exports > Imports	Exports < Imports
Step 1	Net inflow of specie	Net outflow of specie
Step 2	Increase in the money supply	Decrease in the money supply
Step 3	Increase in prices and wages	Decrease in prices and wages
Step 4	Increase in imports and decrease in exports	Decrease in imports and increase in exports
	UNTIL	UNTIL
	Exports = Imports	Exports = Imports

CONCEPT BOX 2

CONCEPT REVIEW—PRICE ELASTICITY AND TOTAL EXPENDITURES

You learned in previous economics courses that *price elasticity of demand* refers to the ratio between the percentage change in quantity demanded of a given product and the percentage change in its price, that is, $\eta = (\Delta Q/Q)/(\Delta P/P)$. (Because quantity demanded varies inversely with price, price elasticity of demand will have a negative sign. Economic convention often ignores the negative sign, but it is understood that η's value will be less than 0, that is, negative.) When this ratio (ignoring the negative sign) is greater than 1.0, indicating that the percentage change in quantity demanded for a given price change is greater than the percentage change in price, demand is said to be *elastic*. When the ratio has a value of 1.0, demand is said to be

unit-elastic, and when the ratio is less than 1.0, demand is said to be *inelastic.* Because the relative change in quantity is greater than the relative change in price when demand is elastic, total expenditures on the product will increase when the price falls (quantity demanded increases) and fall when the price increases (quantity demanded falls). When demand is inelastic, the exact opposite happens: Total expenditures rise with a price increase and decline with a price decrease. In the case of unit elasticity, total expenditures are invariant with changes in price. Thus, for trade balances to change in the appropriate manner in the price-specie-flow mechanism, it is sufficient to assume that demand for traded goods is price elastic. ●

1. There must be some formal link between money and prices, such as that provided in the **quantity theory of money** when full employment is assumed:

$$M_S V = PY$$

where: M_S = the supply of money

V = the velocity of money, or the rate at which money changes hands

P = the price level

Y = the level of real output

If one assumes that the velocity of money is fixed by tradition and institutional arrangements and that Y is fixed at the level of full employment, then any change in the supply of money is accompanied by a proportional change in the level of prices.

2. Demand for traded goods is price elastic (see Concept Box 2). This is necessary to ensure that an increase in price will lead to a decrease in total expenditures for the traded goods in question and that a price decrease will have the opposite effect. If demand is price inelastic, the price-specie-flow mechanism will tend to worsen the disequilibrium in the trade balance. However, demand elasticities tend to be greater in the long run than in the short run as consumers gradually adjust their behavior in response to price changes. Hence, even though the price-specie-flow mechanism may be "perverse" in the short run, Hume's result is likely to occur as time passes.

3. Perfect competition in both product and factor markets is assumed in order to establish the necessary link between price behavior and wage behavior, as well as to guarantee that prices and wages are flexible in both an upward and a downward direction.

4. Finally, it is assumed that a **gold standard** exists. Under such a system, all currencies are pegged to gold and hence to each other, all currencies are freely convertible into gold, gold can be bought and sold at will, and governments do not offset the impact of the

gold flows by other activities to influence the money supply. This is sufficient to establish the link between movements of specie and changes in a nation's money supply.

If all of these assumptions are satisfied, the automatic adjustment mechanism will, allowing time for responses to occur, restore balanced trade any time it is disrupted. Balance-of-payments adjustment mechanisms and the gold standard are still prominent in discussions of international monetary economics.

Adam Smith and the Invisible Hand

A second assault on Mercantilist ideas came in the writing of Adam Smith. Smith perceived that a nation's wealth was reflected in its productive capacity (i.e., its ability to produce final goods and services) not in its holdings of precious metals. Attention thus turned from acquiring specie to enlarging the production of goods and services. Smith believed that growth in productive capacity was fostered best in an environment where people were free to pursue their own interests. Self-interest would lead individuals to specialize in and exchange goods and services based on their own special abilities. The natural tendency "to truck, barter, and exchange" goods and services would generate productivity gains through the increased division and specialization of labor. Self-interest was the catalyst and competition was the automatic regulation mechanism. Smith saw little need for government control of the economy. He stressed that a government policy of **laissez faire** (allowing individuals to pursue their own activities within the bounds of law and order and respect for property rights) would best provide the environment for increasing a nation's wealth. The proper role of government was to see that the market was free to function in an unconstrained manner by removing the barriers to effective operation of the "invisible hand" of the market. In *The Wealth of Nations,* Smith explained not only the critical role the market played in the accumulation of a nation's wealth but also the nature of the social order that it achieved and helped to maintain.

Smith applied his ideas about economic activity within a country to specialization and exchange between countries. He concluded that *countries* should specialize in and export those commodities in which they had an **absolute advantage** and should import those commodities in which the trading partner had an absolute advantage. Each country should export those commodities it produced more efficiently because the absolute labor required per unit was less than that of the prospective trading partner. Consider the two-country, two-commodity framework shown in Table 1. Assume that a labor theory of value is employed (meaning that goods exchange for each other at home in proportion to the relative labor time embodied in them).

In this situation, with a labor theory of value, 1 barrel of wine will exchange for 4 yards of cloth in England (or 1C for $^1/_4$W); on the other hand, 1 barrel of wine will exchange for $1^1/_2$ yards of cloth in Portugal (or 1C for $^2/_3$W). These exchange ratios reflect the relative quantities of labor required to produce the goods in the countries and can be viewed as opportunity costs. These opportunity costs are commonly referred to as the *price ratios in autarky.* England has an absolute advantage in the production of

TABLE 1   **Labor Requirements and Absolute Advantage**

	Cloth	*Wine*	*Price Ratios in Autarky*
England	1 hr/yd	4 hr/bbl	1W:4C
Portugal	2 hr/yd	3 hr/bbl	1W:1.5C

TITANS OF INTERNATIONAL ECONOMICS:

ADAM SMITH (1723–1790)

It is more than 200 years since the death of this Scottish social philosopher, yet his ideas on economic organization and economic systems continue to be fashionable worldwide, especially with the recent spread of the market system in Central and Eastern Europe and the former Soviet Union. Smith was born in 1723 in Kirkcaldy, County Fife, Scotland, a town of 1,500, where nails were still used for money by some residents. Smith demonstrated intellectual ability early in life, and he received a sound Scottish education. At 17 he went to Oxford University where he studied for six years. He returned to Edinburgh and gave lectures on political economy that contained many of the principles he later developed in *The Wealth of Nations.* (The actual full title is *An Inquiry into the Nature and Causes of the Wealth of Nations,* which is commonly shortened to *The Wealth of Nations.*) In 1751 he accepted the Chair of Logic at the University of Glasgow, and two years later, the Chair of Moral Philosophy, which he held until 1764. During those years he wrote his first book, *The Theory of Moral Sentiments* (1759), an inquiry into the origin of moral approbation and disapproval, which attracted immediate attention in England and on the Continent.

Work on *The Wealth of Nations* began in the late 1760s in France, where he was serving as a tutor to the young duke of Buccleuch. Although an initial draft of the masterpiece was apparently completed by 1770, he continued to work on it for six more years, finally publishing it in 1776. Little did he know the impact that his work, often referred to as the most influential book on economics ever written, would have for years to come.

It is remarkable that this writer of moral philosophy was able to envision some sort of order and purpose in the world of contrasts with which he was confronted daily. There hardly seemed a moral purpose to the contrast between the opulence of the leisured classes and the poverty, cruelty, and danger that existed among the masses and which Smith deplored. Production occurred in diverse situations such as the Lombe textile factory (consisting of 26,586 water-driven wheels and 97,746 movements working 221,178 yards of silk thread each minute—and staffed by children working 12- to 14-hour days), mines with degrading human conditions, simple cottage industries, and bands of roaming agricultural laborers from the Welsh highlands. The brilliant man who saw some central purpose to this hostile world was the epitome of the "ivory tower" professor. He not only was notoriously absentminded but also suffered from a nervous disorder throughout his life, which often caused his head to shake and contributed to his odd manner of speech and walking gait. A true intellectual, his life was his writing and discourse with students and thinkers such as David Hume, Benjamin Franklin, François Quesnay, and Dr. Samuel Johnson. A confirmed bachelor, Smith lived out the rest of his life in Edinburgh, where he served as commissioner of customs and took care of his mother. Smith died at the age of 67 on July 17, 1790.

Sources: Robert L. Heilbroner, *The Worldly Philosophers: The Lives, Times, and Ideas of the Great Economic Thinkers,* rev. ed. (New York: Simon and Schuster, 1961), chap. 3; "The Modern Adam Smith," *The Economist,* July 14, 1990, pp. 11–12.

cloth and Portugal has an absolute advantage in the production of wine because less labor time is required to produce cloth in England and wine in Portugal. According to Smith, there is a basis for trade because both nations are clearly better off specializing in their low-cost commodity and importing the commodity that can be produced more cheaply abroad.

For purposes of illustrating the gains from trade, assume that the two countries, rather than producing each good for themselves, exchange goods at a rate of 1 barrel of wine for 3 yards of cloth. For England this means obtaining wine in Portugal for only 3 yards of cloth per barrel instead of 4 yards at home. Similarly, Portugal benefits from acquiring cloth for a cost of only $1/3$ barrel of wine instead of $2/3$ barrel of wine at home. It is important to note (as will be discussed in Chapter 3) that gains from trade can occur over a wide range of barter prices. Smith's argument was especially significant at the time because it indicated that both countries could benefit from trade and that trade was not a zero-sum game as the Mercantilists had believed.

The fact that trade was mutually beneficial and was a **positive-sum game** (i.e., all players can receive a positive payoff in the game) was a powerful argument for expanding trade and reducing the many trade controls that characterized the Mercantilist period. Smith saw the source of these absolute advantages as the unique set of natural resources (including climate) and abilities that characterized a particular nation. He also recognized that certain advantages could be acquired through the accumulation, transfer, and adaptation of skills and technology.

Smith's ideas were crucial for the early development of Classical thought and for altering the view of the potential gains from international trade. David Ricardo expanded upon Smith's concepts and demonstrated that the potential gains from trade were far greater than Adam Smith had envisioned in his concept of absolute advantage.

CONCEPT CHECK

1. Is there a basis for trade in the following case, according to Smith's view? Why or why not? If there is, which commodity should each country export?

	Cutlery	*Wheat*
Germany	50 hr/unit	30 hr/bu
Sweden	40 hr/unit	35 hr/bu

2. Suppose that Germany has a trade surplus with Sweden. Explain how the price-specie-flow mechanism would work to bring about balanced trade between the two countries, given sufficient adjustment time.

SUMMARY

Immediately prior to Adam Smith, the Mercantilists' views on the role and importance of international trade were dominant. They emphasized the desirability of an export surplus in international trade as a means of acquiring specie to add to the wealth of a country. Over time, this concept of wealth, the role of trade, and the whole Mercantilist system of economic thought were challenged by writers such as David Hume and Adam Smith. Smith's concept of absolute advantage was instrumental in altering views on the nature of and potential gains from trade. The realization that all countries could benefit simultaneously from trade had great influence on later Classical thought and trade policy.

KEY TERMS

absolute advantage
bullionism
favorable balance of trade (or
    positive trade balance)
gold standard

labor theory of value
laissez faire
Mercantilism
positive-sum game
price-specie-flow mechanism

quantity theory of money
unfavorable balance of trade (or
    negative trade balance)
zero-sum game

QUESTIONS AND PROBLEMS

1. Why did the Mercantilists consider holdings of precious metals so important to nation-state building?
2. What were the pillars of Mercantilist thought? Why was regulation of the economy so important?
3. What is meant by the "paradox of Mercantilism"? How was this reflected in Mercantilist wage and population policies?
4. What are the critical assumptions of the price-specie-flow mechanism? What happens to the trade balance in a surplus country if the demand for traded goods is price inelastic? Why?

5. Briefly explain why the ideas of Smith and Hume were so devastating to Mercantilist thinking and policy.
6. The following table shows the hours of labor required to produce 1 unit of each commodity in each country:

	Wheat	*Clothing*
United States	3 hr	9 hr
United Kingdom	4 hr	4 hr

Which country has an absolute advantage in wheat? In clothing? Why? If trade takes place between the United States and the United Kingdom at a barter price of 1 clothing for 2 wheat (or 1 wheat for $^1/_2$ clothing), why does each country gain from trade? Explain.

7. (*a*) Suppose that, in the situation in Question 6, the United Kingdom has 500 hours of labor available to it. Prior to trade, the country is using 300 of those labor hours to produce clothing and the remaining 200 labor hours to produce wheat. How much wheat and how much clothing will the United Kingdom be producing in this pretrade situation? (Because there is no trade, your answers will also indicate the amounts of wheat and clothing *consumed* in the United Kingdom prior to trade.)

(*b*) Now suppose that the United Kingdom enters into trade with the United States at the previously indicated barter price of 1 clothing for 2 wheat (or 1 wheat for $^1/_2$ clothing). The United Kingdom now devotes all of its labor hours to clothing production and hence produces 125 units of clothing and 0 units of wheat. Why is this so? Suppose that the country exports 40C (and therefore receives 80W in exchange) and keeps the remaining 85C for its own consumption. What will be the U.K. *consumption* of wheat and clothing in the trading situation? By how much has the United Kingdom, because of trade, been able to increase its consumption of wheat and its consumption of clothing?

8. (*a*) Continuing with the numerical example in Question 6, now assume that the United States has 600 hours of labor available to it and that, prior to trade, it is using 330 of those hours for producing wheat and the remaining 270 hours for producing clothing. How much wheat and how much clothing will the United States be producing (and therefore consuming) in this pretrade situation?

(*b*) Assume that trade between the United Kingdom and the United States takes place as in Question 7(*b*). With trade the United States devotes all of its labor hours to

wheat production and obtains 200 units of wheat. Consistent with the United Kingdom's trade in Question 7(*b*), the United States then exports 80W and imports 40C. What will be the U.S. consumption of wheat and clothing in the trading situation? By how much has the United States, because of trade, been able to increase its consumption of wheat and its consumption of clothing? Looking at your answers to this question and to Question 7(*b*), can you conclude that trade is indeed a positive-sum game? Why or why not?

9. China has had an overall trade surplus in recent years. Economists suggest that this continuing phenomenon is due to several things, including an inappropriate exchange rate. How would a Mercantilist view this surplus? Why might David Hume argue that the surplus will disappear on its own?

10. Suppose that, in the context of the price-specie-flow mechanism, Switzerland currently exports 5,000 units of goods to Spain, with each export unit having a price of 100 Swiss francs. Hence, Switzerland's total value of exports to Spain is 500,000 Swiss francs. At the same time, Switzerland imports 410,000 francs' worth of goods from Spain, and thus has a trade surplus with Spain of 90,000 Swiss francs (=500,000 francs − 410,000 francs). Because of this trade surplus, suppose that all prices in Switzerland now rise uniformly by 10 percent, and assume that this rise in price of Swiss goods causes its imports from Spain to rise from their initial level of 410,000 francs to a level of 440,000 francs. (For purposes of simplicity, assume that the price level in Spain does not change.)

Suppose now that the elasticity of demand of Spanish consumers for Swiss exports is (ignoring the negative sign) equal to 2.0. With the 10 percent rise in the price level in Switzerland, the Swiss export price for each unit of its exports thus rises to 110 francs. With this information, calculate the resulting change in quantity and the new total value of Swiss exports. Has the price rise in Switzerland been sufficient to eliminate its's trade surplus with Spain? Why or why not?

3

THE CLASSICAL WORLD OF DAVID RICARDO AND COMPARATIVE ADVANTAGE

LEARNING OBJECTIVES

■ To understand comparative advantage as a basis for trade between nations.

■ To identify the difference between comparative advantage and absolute advantage.

■ To quantify the gains from trade in a two-country, two-good model.

■ To recognize comparative advantage and the potential gains from trade using production-possibilities frontiers.

INTRODUCTION

Some Common Myths

We hear that trade makes us poorer. It's just not so. Trade is the great generator of economic well-being. It enriches nations because it allows companies and workers to specialize in doing what they do best. Competition forces them to become more productive. In the end, consumers reap the bounty of cheaper and better goods and services. . . .

We hear that exports are good because they support U.S. industry, but imports are bad because they steal business from domestic producers. Actually, imports are the real fruits of trade because the end goal of economic activity is consumption. Exports represent resources we don't consume at home. They are how we pay for what we buy abroad, and we're better off when we pay as little as possible. Mercantilism, with its mania for exporting, lost favor for good reason. . . .

We need to understand what's at stake. Being wrongheaded on trade increases the risk of making bad choices that will sap our economy and sour our relations with other nations.[1]

The underlying basis for these words is comparative advantage. Unfortunately, it remains a widely misunderstood concept, even today—more than 190 years since it was introduced by the Classical economist David Ricardo in *The Principles of Political Economy and Taxation* (1817), who stressed that the potential gains from international trade were not confined to Adam Smith's absolute advantage. We begin this chapter by focusing on the basic assumptions that underlie the modern expositions of the Ricardian model. Several of these assumptions are very restrictive and unrealistic, but they will be relaxed later and do not invalidate the basic conclusions of the analysis. The chapter then provides a rigorous demonstration of the gains from trade according to the Classical model. The overriding purpose of the chapter is to show that, contrary to Mercantilist thinking, trade is a positive-sum game (i.e., all trading partners benefit from it).

ASSUMPTIONS OF THE BASIC RICARDIAN MODEL

1. Each country has a fixed endowment of resources, and all units of each particular resource are identical.

2. The factors of production are completely mobile between alternative uses within a country. This assumption implies that the prices of factors of production also are the same among these alternative uses.

3. The factors of production are completely immobile externally; that is, they do not move between countries. Therefore, factor prices may be different between countries prior to trade.

4. A labor theory of value is employed in the model. Thus, the relative value of a commodity is based solely on its relative labor content. From a production standpoint, this implies that (*a*) no other inputs are used in the production process, or (*b*) any other inputs are measured in terms of the labor embodied in their production, or (*c*) the other inputs/labor ratio is the same in all industries. In simple terms, this assumption means that a good embodying two hours of labor is twice as expensive as a good using only one hour.

5. The level of technology is fixed for both countries, although the technology can differ between them.

---

[1]"The Fruits of Free Trade," *2002 Annual Report*, reprint, Federal Reserve Bank of Dallas, p. 5. (Emphasis added.)

TITANS OF INTERNATIONAL ECONOMICS:

DAVID RICARDO (1772–1823)

David Ricardo was born in London on April 18, 1772, the son of wealthy Jewish immigrants. He received private instruction as a child and was exceedingly bright. At age 14 he started work in his father's stockbroker's office, but this association with his family ended seven years later when he became a Unitarian and married a Quaker. Ricardo then began his own immensely successful career in securities and real estate. A most important factor in his financial success was his purchase of British government securities only four days before the Duke of Wellington defeated Napoleon at Waterloo in 1815. The subsequent boom in British securities alone made him a wealthy man.

While on vacation in 1799, Ricardo read Adam Smith's *The Wealth of Nations.* (Don't we all read economics books while on vacation?) Fascinated, he gradually made economics his avocation and wrote pamphlets and newspaper articles on the subject. Ricardo's opposition to the government's gold policies and to the Corn Laws (the restrictive laws on the importation of grain into England) attracted widespread attention, and he soon broadened his inquiries to questions of profits and income distribution. In 1817, Ricardo's landmark book, *The Principles of Political Economy and Taxation,* was published, bringing him fame even though he himself thought that few people would understand it. He became a member of Parliament in 1819. An excellent debater, despite a voice once described as "harsh and squeaky," he was influential in educating the House of Commons on economic questions, although the Corn Laws were not repealed until long after his death.

Ricardo is usually credited with originating the concept of comparative advantage. In addition, Ricardo built an entire model of the economic system in which growth rests on capital accumulation and profits and the law of diminishing returns eventually leads to a stationary state with zero profits and affluent landlords. Ricardo was a paradox through his condemnation of the landlord class, even though he himself was a member of that class. After a remarkable career as a businessman, scholar, and politician, Ricardo died unexpectedly at age 51 on September 11, 1823. He was survived by his wife and seven children.

Sources: Robert B. Ekelund, Jr., and Robert F. Hebert, *A History of Economic Theory and Method,* 3rd ed. (New York: McGraw-Hill, 1990), chap. 7; Robert L. Heilbroner, *The Worldly Philosophers: The Lives, Times, and Ideas of the Great Economic Thinkers,* 3rd ed. (New York: Simon and Schuster, 1967), chap. 4; G. de Vivo, "David Ricardo," in John Eatwell, Murray Milgate, and Peter Newman, eds., *The New Palgrave: A Dictionary of Economics,* Vol. 4 (London: Macmillan, 1987), pp. 183–86.

6. Unit costs of production are constant. Thus, the hours of labor per unit of production of a good do not change, regardless of the quantity produced. This means that the supply curve of any good is horizontal.

7. There is full employment.

8. The economy is characterized by perfect competition. No single consumer or producer is large enough to influence the market; hence, all are price takers. All participants have full access to market information, there is free entry to and exit from an industry, and all prices equal the marginal cost of production.

9. There are no government-imposed obstacles to economic activity.

10. Internal and external transportation costs are zero.

11. The analysis is confined to a two-country, two-commodity "world" to simplify the presentation. This simplification will be dropped later to make the model more realistic.

RICARDIAN COMPARATIVE ADVANTAGE

Ricardo began by noting that Smith's idea of absolute advantage determined the pattern of trade and production internal to a country when factors were perfectly mobile. Using the example of Yorkshire and London, he noted that industry locates where the greatest

TABLE 1   Ricardian Production Conditions in England and Portugal

	Wine	*Cloth*	*Price Ratios in Autarky*
Portugal	80 hr/bbl	90 hr/yd	1W:$^8/_9$C (or 1C:$^9/_8$W)
England	120 hr/bbl	100 hr/yd	1W:$^6/_5$C (or 1C:$^5/_6$W)

absolute advantage exists and that labor and capital move to the area where productivity and returns are the greatest. This movement would continue until factor returns were equalized. Internationally, however, the story is different. While international trade can take place on the basis of absolute advantage (e.g., trade between tropical and temperate zones), given the international immobility of the factors of production, gains from trade on the basis of **comparative advantage** can occur as well. To make his point, Ricardo presented a case describing the production of two commodities, wine and cloth, in England and Portugal. The labor requirements per unit of production, given in Table 1, reflect the technologies in each country and imply the relative value of each commodity.

In this example, Portugal has an absolute advantage in the production of both commodities. From Adam Smith's perspective, there is no basis for trade between these countries because Portugal is more efficient in the production of both goods. England has an absolute disadvantage in both goods. Ricardo, however, pointed out that Portugal is relatively more efficient in the production of wine than of cloth and that England's relative disadvantage is smaller in cloth. The figures show that the relative number of hours needed to produce wine (80 in Portugal, 120 in England) is less than the relative number of hours needed to produce cloth (90 in Portugal, 100 in England). Because of these relative cost differences, both countries have an incentive to trade. To see this, consider the **autarky (pretrade) price ratios** (i.e., the price ratios when the country has no international trade). Within England, 1 barrel of wine would exchange for $^6/_5$ yards of cloth (because the same labor time is embodied in each quantity), while in Portugal, 1 barrel would exchange for only $^8/_9$ yard of cloth. Thus, Portugal stands to gain if it can specialize in wine and acquire cloth from England at a ratio of 1 barrel:$^6/_5$ yards, or 1W:$^6/_5$C. Similarly, England would benefit by specializing in cloth production and exporting cloth to Portugal, where it could receive $^9/_8$ barrel of wine per yard of cloth instead of $^5/_6$ barrel per yard at home. Even though trade is unrealistically restricted to two goods in this basic analysis, similar potential gains also occur in more comprehensive analyses (as developed in Chapter 4, "Extensions and Tests of the Classical Model of Trade"). The main point is that the basis for and the gains from trade rest on comparative, not absolute, advantage.

To examine the gains from trade, let us explore the price ratios further. With England in autarky, 1 barrel of wine exchanges by the labor theory of value for 1.2 ($^6/_5$) yards of cloth, so any price ratio in which *less* than 1.2C have to be given up for 1W is desirable for England. Similarly, the autarkic price ratio in Portugal is 1W:$^8/_9$C, or 0.89C. Thus, Portugal will gain if its wine can command in trade *more* than 0.89 unit of cloth. With an international price ratio between these two autarkic price ratios, both countries will gain.

Ricardo did not examine the precise determination of the international price ratio or the **terms of trade.** But the important point is that, after trade, there will be a *common* price of wine in terms of cloth in the two countries. To see this point, consider what is happening in the two countries with trade. Because wine is coming into England (new supply from Portugal) and Portugal is now demanding English cloth (new demand), the relative price of English cloth in terms of wine will rise. This means that *less* cloth will exchange for a unit of wine than the previous 1.2C. In Portugal, the relative price of wine will rise because cloth is arriving from England and the English are demanding Portuguese wine. Thus the price will rise above 1W:0.89C toward *more* cloth being given up to obtain a unit of wine. The pretrade ratios of 1W:1.2C in England and 1W:0.89C in Portugal thus converge toward each other through trade. This is simply the economic phenomenon of two separate markets (autarky) unifying into a single market (trade). A single price will then prevail rather than two different prices. With trade, prices are no longer determined solely by the labor theory of value but also by relative demands in the two trading countries.

To illustrate the gains from trade, Ricardo arbitrarily assumed that the terms-of-trade ratio was 1W:1C. At these terms, consider the gain for England. With trade, England could devote 100 hours of labor to producing cloth, its comparative-advantage good, and get 1C. This 1C could then be exchanged with Portugal for 1W. Thus, 100 hours of labor in England have *indirectly* produced 1 unit of wine. If England had chosen to produce 1W at home *directly,* the cost involved would have been 120 hours of labor. However, trade saves England 20 hours (120 − 100) of labor for each unit of its imported good. Ricardo expressed the gains in terms of labor time saved because he viewed trade essentially as a mechanism for reducing the outlay of labor necessary for obtaining goods, for such labor implied work effort and "real costs." Another way to state the same result is that with trade more goods can be obtained for the same amount of labor time than is possible in autarky.

There is also obviously a gain for Portugal in terms of labor time saved. Portugal can take 80 hours of labor and produce 1 unit of wine. With this 1W, Portugal can obtain 1 unit of cloth through trade. Direct production of 1C in Portugal would have required 90 hours of labor; trade has enabled the country to gain or save 10 hours of labor per unit of its imported good. Thus, unlike the zero-sum game of the Mercantilists, international trade is a *positive-sum game.*

The precise terms of trade reflect relative demand and will be considered in later chapters. However, the terms of trade are important for the distribution of the gains between the two countries. Suppose that we specify the terms of trade as 1W:1.1C instead of 1W:1C. Intuitively, we expect Portugal to gain more in this case because its export good is now commanding a greater volume of the English good. In this case, Portugal could take 80 hours of labor, get 1W, and then exchange that 1W for 1.1C; in effect, Portugal is obtaining 1.1C for 80 hours of labor. To produce 1.1C at home would have required 99 hours (90 hours × 1.1), so Portugal gains 19 hours (99 − 80) per each 1.1C, or 17.3 hours per each 1C (19/1.1 = 17.3).

England experiences smaller gains in the second case. If England devotes 110 hours to cloth production, it will get 1.1C, which can then be exchanged for 1W. Because 1W produced directly at home would have required 120 hours of labor, England saves 10 hours rather than 20 hours per unit of wine. *Clearly, the closer the terms of trade are to a country's internal autarky price ratio, the smaller the gain for that country from international trade.* At the limits (1W:1.2C for England and 1W:0.89C for Portugal), the country whose prices in autarky equaled the terms of trade would get no gain and would be indifferent to trade. The other country would obtain all the gains from trade.

The **equilibrium terms of trade** are those that bring about balanced trade (exports = imports in total value) for each country. If the Ricardian 1W:1C ratio left Portugal with a balance-of-trade surplus, the terms of trade would shift toward relatively more expensive wine, say, 1W:1.1C. This shift occurs because the price-specie-flow mechanism raises prices and wages in the surplus country, Portugal, and depresses them in the deficit country, England.

IN THE REAL WORLD:

EXPORT CONCENTRATION OF SELECTED COUNTRIES

In the Classical model presented in this chapter, a country exports only one good. This is an unrealistic situation, so multiple exports are incorporated into the model in Chapter 4. Nevertheless, some countries broadly resemble the single-export situation, and there is no doubt that trade moves production in all countries toward a more specialized production pattern than would be the case in autarky. Table 2 presents data on the degree of commodity export concentration for several countries based on the most aggregated categories in the Standard International Trade Classification (SITC) system of the United Nations. The types of goods exported differ, reflecting the underlying comparative advantage of each country.

The degrees of export concentration in this sample indicate that developing countries tend to have comparative advantages in food products (e.g., Comoros and El Salvador), crude materials and materials-based basic manufactured products, or natural resource products (e.g., Brunei, Jamaica, and Zambia). Developed countries (e.g., Japan and the United States) specialize in machinery and transport equipment (capital goods). However, there are exceptions. Note that the Republic of Korea (South Korea) and Mexico export machinery and transport equipment.

TABLE 2   Extent of Export Concentration, Selected Countries

Country	Export Categories (SITC No.)	Percentage of Total Export Value
Brunei (2003)	Mineral fuels, etc. (3)	87.7%
	Miscellaneous manufactured articles (8)	5.4
Comoros (2000)	Food and live animals (0)	88.4
	Chemicals and related products (5)	5.8
El Salvador (2003)	Food and live animals (0)	30.5
	Manufactured goods classified chiefly by material (6)	25.3
Gabon (2004)	Mineral fuels, etc. (3)	76.2
	Manufactured goods classified chiefly by material (6)	4.5
Ireland (2004)	Chemicals and related products (5)	44.6
	Machinery and transport equipment (7)	27.0
Jamaica (2002)	Crude materials, inedible, except fuels (2)	64.8
	Food and live animals (0)	17.6
Japan (2004)	Machinery and transport equipment (7)	65.6
	Manufactured goods classified chiefly by material (6)	10.6
Korea, Republic of (2004)	Machinery and transport equipment (7)	63.0
	Manufactured goods classified chiefly by material (6)	14.6
Malawi (2004)	Beverages and tobacco (1)	45.8
	Food and live animals (0)	30.1
Mexico (2004)	Machinery and transport equipment (7)	55.6
	Miscellaneous manufactured articles (8)	13.3
United States (2004)	Machinery and transport equipment (7)	48.1
	Chemicals and related products (5)	13.8
Zambia (2004)	Manufactured goods classified chiefly by material (6)	63.8
	Crude materials, inedible, except fuels (2)	15.6

Note: "Manufactured goods classified chiefly by material" refers to products such as rubber, wood, and textile yarn and fabrics; "Miscellaneous manufactured articles" refers to a wide variety of consumer products.

Source: United Nations, 2004 *International Trade Statistics Yearbook,* Vol. I (New York: United Nations, 2006), various pages.

COMPARATIVE ADVANTAGE AND THE TOTAL GAINS FROM TRADE

The essence of Ricardo's argument is that international trade does not require different absolute advantages and that it is possible and desirable to trade when comparative advantages exist. A comparative advantage exists whenever the relative labor requirements differ between the two commodities. This means simply that, when the relative labor requirements are different, the internal opportunity cost of the two commodities is different in the two countries; that is, the internal price ratios are different between the two countries prior to trade. The gain from different relative prices was demonstrated for England and Portugal in terms of labor time saved per unit of the imported good acquired.

We now turn from the gain per unit of the imported good to the total gains from trade for the country. Table 3 provides information that can be used to increase familiarity with the type of numerical examples used in Ricardian analysis.

Country A has a comparative advantage in the production of cloth, and country B has a comparative advantage in the production of wine. Country A's comparative advantage clearly lies in cloth, inasmuch as the relative labor cost ($^1/_2$) is less than that in wine ($^3/_4$). The basis for trade is also evident in the fact that the autarky price ratios in each country are different.

When trade is initiated between the two countries, it will take place at international terms of trade that lie within the limits set by the price ratios for each country in autarky. If trade takes place at one of the limiting autarky price ratios, one country reaps all the benefits. For example, if trade commences at international terms of trade of 1W:3C, then country B gains 1 yard of cloth per each 1 barrel of wine exchanged, while country A gains nothing because it pays the same relative price that it faces in autarky. Thus, for both countries to gain, the international terms of trade must lie somewhere between the autarky price ratios. *The actual location of the equilibrium terms of trade between the two countries is determined by the comparative strength and elasticity of demand of each country for the other's product.* This is often referred to as *reciprocal demand,* a concept developed by John Stuart Mill in 1848 (see Chapter 7, "Offer Curves and the Terms of Trade").

Resource Constraints   To demonstrate the total gains from trade between these two countries, it is necessary to first establish the amount of the constraining resource—labor—available to each country. Suppose that country A has 9,000 labor hours available and country B has 16,000 labor hours available. These constraints, coupled with the production information in Table 3, permit us to establish the production possibilities open to these two countries in autarky. Country A can produce 9,000 yards of cloth and no wine, or 3,000 barrels of wine and no cloth, or any combination of these two goods that absorbs 9,000 hours of labor. Country B, on the other hand, can produce 8,000 yards of cloth and no wine, 4,000 barrels of wine and no cloth, or any combination of these two goods that exactly absorbs 16,000 hours of labor. Assume that country A produces 6,000 yards of cloth and 1,000 barrels of wine prior to trade and that country B produces 3,000 yards of cloth and 2,500 barrels of wine. Suppose that the two countries exchange goods at the terms of trade of 1W:2.5C. Suppose also that

TABLE 3   Ricardian Production Characteristics

	Cloth	*Wine*	*Price Ratios in Autarky*
Country A	1 hr/yd	3 hr/bbl	1W:3C
Country B	2 hr/yd	4 hr/bbl	1W:2C

country A exchanges 2,500 yards of cloth for 1,000 barrels of wine from country B, but the two countries do not alter their production. How will the posttrade and pretrade scenarios compare?

In keeping with Ricardo's emphasis on labor time, we examine the equivalent quantity of domestic labor services consumed before and after trade for each country. We will use the common yardstick of labor hours because wine and cloth cannot be added meaningfully without weighting for relative importance (the old "apples and oranges" problem). Prior to trade, country A produced and consumed 6,000C and 1,000W, reflecting the 9,000 labor hours available to it. After trade, country A consumes 3,500C (6,000 yards produced − 2,500 yards exported to country B) and 2,000W (1,000 barrels produced at home + 1,000 barrels imported from country B), a combination that would have required 9,500 labor hours if produced at home (3,500 hours for cloth, because each cloth unit would require 1 hour, and 6,000 hours for wine, because each of the 2,000 wine units would require 3 hours). Country A has thus gained the equivalent of 500 labor hours (9,500 − 9,000) through trade. What about country B? Prior to trade, it produced and consumed 3,000 yards of cloth and 2,500 barrels of wine, reflecting the 16,000 labor hours available to it. After trade, country B consumes 5,500 yards of cloth (3,000 yards of domestic production + 2,500 yards of imports) and 1,500 barrels of wine (2,500 barrels of domestic production − 1,000 barrels of exports to country A), a combination that would have required 17,000 labor hours if produced at home (11,000 hours for cloth, because each of the 5,500 cloth units would require 2 hours, and 6,000 hours for wine, because each of the 1,500 wine units would require 4 hours). Country B has gained the equivalent of 1,000 labor hours (17,000 − 16,000) through trade.

Complete Specialization

In the previous example, both countries gained from trade even though *neither altered its production* of cloth or wine. But this is an incomplete picture. With the new prices determined by trade, producers will necessarily increase the production of the good that has a comparative advantage because this good gets a relatively higher price on the world market than it did in autarky. **Complete specialization** means that all resources are devoted to the production of one good, with no production of the other good. Both countries now alter their production patterns and engage in complete specialization in the commodities in which they have a comparative advantage. Each experiences even greater gains from trade.

Assume that with country A producing only cloth and country B producing only wine, they exchange 2,000 barrels of wine for 5,000 yards of cloth. In this instance, country A would consume 4,000C (9,000 yards produced − 5,000 yards exported) and 2,000W (all imported). This combination has a labor value in country A of 10,000 hours (4,000 hours for cloth, because each cloth unit would require 1 hour, and 6,000 hours for wine, because each of the 2,000 wine units would require 3 hours), which is greater than the labor value of consumption in either autarky or in the case of trade with no production change. Country B is also better off because it now consumes 5,000 yards of cloth (all imported) and 2,000 barrels of wine (4,000 barrels produced − 2,000 barrels exported) with a labor value of 18,000 hours (10,000 hours for cloth, because each of the 5,000 cloth units would require 2 hours, and 8,000 hours for wine, because each of the 2,000 wine units would require 4 hours). This contrasts with a labor value of 16,000 in autarky and 17,000 in trade with incomplete specialization of production. The Classical writers concluded that if there is a basis for trade, it automatically leads a country toward complete specialization in the commodity in which it has the comparative advantage. Consumption remains diversified across goods as dictated by consumer preferences.

CONCEPT CHECK

1. In a Ricardian model, suppose that the United States can produce 1 unit of wheat in 3 days of labor time and 1 unit of clothing in 4 days of labor time. What is the autarky price ratio in the United States? If the world price ratio (terms of trade) is 1 wheat:1 clothing, which good will the United States export and which will it import? Why? Suppose that the world price ratio is 1 wheat:0.5 clothing. Which good will the United States export and which will it import? Why?

2. When a country has a comparative advantage in a good, must it also have an absolute advantage in that good? Why or why not?

3. If a country has an absolute advantage in a good, must it also have a comparative advantage in that good? Why or why not?

REPRESENTING THE RICARDIAN MODEL WITH PRODUCTION-POSSIBILITIES FRONTIERS

The basis for trade and the gains from trade can also be demonstrated with the **production-possibilities frontier (PPF)** concept. The production-possibilities frontier reflects all combinations of two products that a country can produce at a given point in time given its resource base, level of technology, full utilization of resources, and economically efficient production. Because all of these conditions are met in the list of assumptions presented early in this chapter, it is clear that the Classical model assumes the participating countries to be producing and consuming on their production-possibilities frontiers in autarky. Furthermore, the constant-cost assumption implies that the opportunity cost of production is the same at the various levels of production. The production-possibilities frontier is thus a straight line whose slope represents the opportunity cost of economywide production.

The shift into this framework presents not only a graphical picture of the Ricardian model. It also provides a means for escaping from the limitations of the labor theory of value while retaining the comparative-advantage conclusions about the basis for trade. Because the slope (ignoring the negative sign) of the production-possibilities frontier indicates the amount of production of one commodity that must be given up to obtain one additional unit of the other commodity, the values that lie at the basis of this calculation can reflect the cost of all inputs, not only labor, that go into the production of the commodities. This realization not only makes the concept of comparative advantage more realistic and interesting but also implies that the basic idea is sufficiently general to cover a wide range of production scenarios, among which a labor theory of value is only one possibility.

Production Possibilities—An Example

The figures on labor hours and production for countries A and B (see Table 3) make it possible to display the production-possibilities frontiers for each country. A production-possibilities schedule can be calculated and the respective production-possibilities curves can be inferred from those schedules (see Figure 1). Because constant costs are assumed, we need merely to locate the intercepts on each product axis and connect these points with a straight line. The result is a constant-cost production-possibilities frontier whose slope reflects the opportunity cost in autarky—what we have called the autarky price ratio. Country A had a pretrade combination of 6,000 yards of cloth and 1,000 barrels of wine. With the initiation of trade, country A was able to obtain 1 barrel of wine for only $2\frac{1}{2}$ yards of cloth compared with 3 yards at home. This produces for country A a new, flatter **consumption-possibilities frontier (CPF)** with trade, which begins at the initial production point and lies outside the production-possibilities frontier.

FIGURE 1   Ricardian Production-Possibilities Schedules and Frontiers

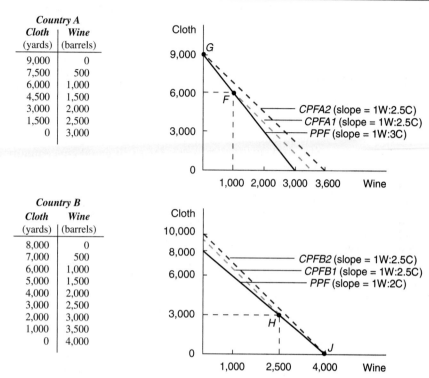

Country A	
Cloth	**Wine**
(yards)	(barrels)
9,000	0
7,500	500
6,000	1,000
4,500	1,500
3,000	2,000
1,500	2,500
0	3,000

Country B	
Cloth	**Wine**
(yards)	(barrels)
8,000	0
7,000	500
6,000	1,000
5,000	1,500
4,000	2,000
3,000	2,500
2,000	3,000
1,000	3,500
0	4,000

Country A produces and consumes 6,000 cloth and 1,000 wine in autarky (point *F*) at its opportunity cost ratio of 1W:3C. When exposed to international terms of trade of 1W:2.5C, country A can, even without a change in production, consume along consumption-possibilities frontier *CPFA1,* which enables it to consume combinations impossible in autarky. If country A completely specializes in cloth (its comparative-advantage good), it produces at point *G* and can consume even greater quantities of the two goods (on *CPFA2*). For country B, initial production at point *H* can yield consumption combinations along *CPFB1,* and complete specialization (with production at point *J*) permits consumption with trade to be on *CPFB2*.

This new consumption-possibilities frontier is indicated by *CPFA1*. (Note that the consumption-possibilities frontier under autarky is the same as the production-possibilities frontier.) By participating in trade with country B, country A can now choose to consume a combination of goods that clearly lies outside its own production possibilities in autarky, thus demonstrating the potential gains from trade. In other words, trade permits consumption combinations that are unattainable without trade. The farther the new consumption-possibilities curve lies outside the PPF, the larger the potential gains. The CPF moves out when country A begins to specialize in the production of cloth—in which it has a comparative advantage—and reduces its production of wine. The largest set of consumption possibilities for given terms of trade occurs when country A produces only cloth and no wine. To consume on this consumption-possibilities frontier *(CPFA2)* means that country A *must* export cloth to country B in exchange for wine if it wishes to consume any wine at all. [For example, at the maximum, if country A exports all 9,000 yards of cloth it could obtain 3,600 barrels of wine (9,000/2.5 = 3,600).] More favorable terms of trade for country A would yield a flatter consumption-possibilities frontier, further enlarging the potential gains from trade.

The situation is similar for country B. Production and consumption in autarky was initially 3,000 yards of cloth and 2,500 barrels of wine. With trade, country B can now obtain 2.5C for 1W, instead of obtaining only 2C at home. Country B faces a consumption-possibilities frontier through trade *(CPFB1)* that is steeper and, with no production changes, begins at the initial level of production. This trading possibility allows country B to consume outside its consumption-possibilities frontier in autarky, reflecting again the potential gains from trade with country A. The set of consumption possibilities can be made even larger the more country B specializes in the production of wine, its comparative-advantage good. The largest potential consumption combinations for given terms of trade occur when country B produces only wine and imports all of its cloth. [For example, at the maximum, if country B exports all 4,000 barrels of wine, it could conceptually obtain 10,000 yards of cloth $(4,000 \times 2.5 = 10,000)$.]

Maximum Gains from Trade

In the Classical model, production generally takes place at an *end point* of the production-possibilities frontier of each country. We first indicated the potential gain from trade without changing the production point purely as an expositional device. Our procedure showed that trade could benefit a country even if all of its resources were "frozen" into their existing production patterns. However, economic incentives cause production to tend to move to an endpoint of the frontier, where the maximum gain for the given terms of trade will be realized. For example, the new international price ratio of 1W:2.5C, compared with the price ratio of 1W:2C in autarky, indicates that country B has an incentive to expand the production of wine because 2.5 units of cloth can be obtained for 1 unit of wine *even though the opportunity cost of 1W is only 2C.* This opportunity cost stays the same even with additional wine production because of the constant-cost technology. Thus, there is no reason to stop at any point on the production-possibilities frontier until the maximum amount of 4,000 barrels is reached. In simple terms, the "cost" of producing 1 wine is 2 yards of cloth, but the "return" from producing 1 barrel of wine is 2.5 yards of cloth. A similar conclusion applies to *any* price ratio where more than 2C are obtained in the world market for 1W. In country A, the incentive is to expand cloth production by exactly the same cost versus benefit reasoning.

An exception to this complete specialization can occur. Suppose that in the previous example (see Figure 1) total demand of both countries A and B for cloth is larger than the maximum 9,000 yards of available supply from country A. In this case, country B will continue to produce both cloth and wine on its PPF at country B's opportunity cost of 1W:2C, somewhere between point *H* and point *J.* Trade will take place at country B's autarkic price ratio, and country A will therefore attain maximum gains from trade. Country B, however, will continue to consume at the autarkic consumption point *H* on its own PPF because prices are the same in both international trade and in autarky. All benefits from trade will accrue to country A as it trades at the opportunity cost prevailing in country B. In the Classical world, a country whose production capacity of its comparative-advantage good is incapable of meeting total world demand for that good will experience substantial gains from trade. The price of wool blankets exported from Nepal to the United States, for example, is likely to be dominated by U.S. rather than Nepali market conditions.

1. In the Ricardian analysis, why does each trading partner have an incentive to produce at an endpoint of its production-possibilities frontier?
2. Use a diagram to defend this statement: The greater the difference between the terms of trade and prices under autarky, the greater the gains from trade.
3. When might the consumption-possibilities frontier with trade *not* be outside the consumption-possibilities frontier under autarky? Why?

COMPARATIVE ADVANTAGE—SOME CONCLUDING OBSERVATIONS

Up to this point, nothing has been said about the basis for the comparative advantages that a country might have in trade. Indeed, the Classical theory does not offer a satisfactory explanation of why production conditions differ between countries. This is perhaps not surprising given the nature of production at that time. Resource and cost differences were taken as given and as part of the environment in which the economic system functioned. The underlying cost differences were viewed as being determined outside the economic system for the most part, governed by the natural endowment of a country's resources. For Smith and his successors, this endowment included the quantity of usable land, the quality of the soil, the presence of natural resources, and the climate, as well as cultural characteristics influencing such things as entrepreneurship, labor skills, and organizational capacity. Thus, for any or all of these reasons, production conditions were assumed to vary across countries. The theory does, however, make it clear that even if a country is absolutely more or less efficient in the production of all commodities, a basis for trade still exists if there is a difference in the degree of relative efficiency across commodities.

The Classical economists thought that participation in foreign trade could be a strong positive force for development. Adam Smith argued that export markets could enable a country to use resources that otherwise would remain idle. The resulting movement to full employment would increase the level of economic activity and allow the country to acquire foreign goods to enhance consumption and/or investment and growth. Ricardo and subsequent Classical economists argued that the benefits from trade resulted not from the employment of underused resources but from the more efficient use of domestic resources which came about through the specialization in production according to comparative advantage. Besides the static gains resulting from the reallocation of resources, economists such as John Stuart Mill pointed out the dynamic effects of trade that were of critical importance to a country's economic development. These included the ability to acquire foreign capital and foreign technology and the impact of trade and resource reallocation on the accumulation of savings. In addition, the benefits associated with increased contact with other countries and cultures could help break the binding chains of tradition, alter wants, and stimulate entrepreneurship, inventions, and innovations.

Economic growth and development propelled by trade can of course generate some undesirable consequences. Specialization in the production of goods that have few links to the rest of the economy can lead to a lopsided pattern of growth and do little more than produce an export enclave, a result that often negates the dynamic effects of trade. These more complex trade issues are examined in Chapter 18, "International Trade and the Developing Countries."

Thus, the Classical writers have made us aware that trade not only produces static gains but also can be a positive vehicle for economic growth and development and that it should be encouraged. Any country can benefit from trade in which some foreign goods can be purchased at prices that are *relatively* lower than those at home, even if it is absolutely less efficient in the production of all goods compared to a more developed trading partner.

SUMMARY

This chapter has developed the basic Ricardian comparative advantage model. This model demonstrates that gains from trade occur even if a country is absolutely more or absolutely less efficient in the production of all of its goods than other countries. The source of these gains lies in the fact that relative prices with trade differ from relative prices in autarky. The gains were shown through numerical examples and through the use of production-possibilities frontiers. While the principle of comparative advantage as it applies to countries is the focus of international trade, the basic principle also applies to individuals and to regions within a country. Specialization according to comparative advantage enhances the efficiency of resource use and increases the well-being of all.

In the next chapter, some of the assumptions of the Ricardian model are relaxed, and the analysis will take into account more real-world characteristics, including the introduction of more than two countries, more than two goods, transportation costs, prices in monetary terms, and exchange rates.

KEY TERMS

autarky (pretrade) price ratios
comparative advantage
complete specialization

consumption-possibilities frontier (CPF)
equilibrium terms of trade

production-possibilities frontier (PPF)
terms of trade

QUESTIONS AND PROBLEMS

1. The following table shows the number of days of labor required to produce 1 unit of output of computers and wheat in France and Germany:

	Computers	*Wheat*
France	100 days	4 days
Germany	60 days	3 days

   (a) Calculate the autarky price ratios.

   (b) Which country has a comparative advantage in computers? Explain why. Which has a comparative advantage in wheat? Explain why.

   (c) If the terms of trade are 1 computer:22 wheat, how many days of labor does France save per unit of its import good by engaging in trade? How many days does Germany save per unit of its import good?

   (d) If the terms of trade are 1 computer:24 wheat, how many days of labor do France and Germany each save per unit of their respective import good?

   (e) What can be said about the comparative distribution of the gains from trade between France and Germany in part (d) and part (c)? Why?

2. The following table shows the number of days of labor required to produce a unit of textiles and autos in the United Kingdom and the United States:

	Textiles	*Autos*
United Kingdom	3 days	6 days
United States	2 days	5 days

   (a) Calculate the number of units of textiles and autos that can be produced from *1 day* of labor in each country.

   (b) Suppose that the United States has 1,000 days of labor available. Construct the production-possibilities frontier for the United States.

   (c) Construct the U.S. consumption-possibilities frontier with trade if the terms of trade are 1 auto:2 units of textiles.

   (d) Select a pretrade consumption point for the United States, and indicate how trade can yield a consumption point that gives the United States greater consumption of both goods.

3. In the example in Question 2, suppose that the United States always wishes to consume autos and textiles at the ratio of 1 auto to 10 textiles. What quantity of each good would the United States consume in autarky? What combination would the United States consume with trade and complete specialization? What would be the gains from trade?

4. In the light of the Ricardian model, how might you evaluate the claim by developing countries that they are at a disadvantage in trade with powerful industrialized countries?

5. Suppose that Portugal requires 4 days of labor to produce 1 unit of wine and 6 days of labor to produce 1 unit of clothing, while England requires 8 days of labor to produce 1 unit of wine and 12 days of labor to produce 1 unit of clothing. Which country has absolute advantages and why? What is the situation with respect to comparative advantages?

6. How can a country gain from trade if it is unable to change its production pattern?

7. During the debate prior to the passage of the North American Free Trade Agreement (NAFTA), opponents argued that given the relative size of the two economies, the income

gains resulting from the agreement would likely be smaller for the United States than for Mexico. Comment on this position in view of what you have learned about the distribution of the benefits of trade in the Classical model.

8. "If U.S. productivity growth does not keep up with that of its trading partners, the United States will quickly lose its international competitiveness and not be able to export any products, and its standard of living will fall." Critically evaluate this statement in light of what you have learned in this chapter.

9. Suppose that country A and country B both have the same amount of resources and that A has an absolute advantage in both steel and wheat and a comparative advantage in steel production. Draw production-possibilities frontiers for countries A and B (on the same graph) that reflect these characteristics, and explain why you drew them in the manner you did.

4

EXTENSIONS AND TESTS OF THE CLASSICAL MODEL OF TRADE

LEARNING OBJECTIVES

- To grasp how wages, productivity, and exchange rates affect comparative advantage and international trade patterns.

- To understand the implications of extending the basic model of comparative advantage to more than two countries and/or commodities.

- To make the reader aware that real-world trade patterns are consistent with underlying comparative advantages.

INTRODUCTION

Trade Complexities in the Real World

North Carolina textile manufacturers complain about the "undervalued" Chinese renminbi yuan and the "unfair" impact it has on their industry. At the same time, analysts ponder whether the currently depreciating dollar will lead to a reduction in the current U.S. trade deficit, and U.S. producers continue to worry about the impact of cheap foreign labor on their competitiveness and ability to remain in business. In addition, the recent upturn in transportation costs is raising concerns about a possible slowdown in growth in world trade. In light of ongoing structural changes taking place in the increasingly integrated trading world and changes in demand for certain kinds of labor, international competitiveness of certain key regional industries has taken center stage in the current political arena, and the effect of reduced trade barriers is often cited as the cause of these industry problems.

Our discussion of Classical comparative advantage and the basis for gains from trade presented in the previous chapter did not incorporate information on variables such as those mentioned in the vignette above and the possible effect they could have on the basis for trade and the commodity composition between countries. It is important to note that the usefulness of the simple labor-based Ricardian model is not restricted to the basic barter framework that was the focus of Chapter 3. Indeed, incorporating several of these important monetary/cost/price considerations into the analysis can provide helpful insights into the underlying basis for trade across a range of goods. Thus, in this chapter we show how the basic Ricardian model can be made more realistic by incorporating wage rates and an exchange rate. This exercise then permits us to analyze trade in terms of money and prices and to examine rigorously the role of wages, productivity, and the exchange rate in influencing trade patterns. The realism of the model is further extended by including a larger number of commodities, transportation costs, and more than two countries. Relaxing the restrictive assumptions used in the discussion of the Classical model provides helpful insights into the forces that influence international trade.

THE CLASSICAL MODEL IN MONEY TERMS

The first extension of the Classical model changes the example from one of labor requirements per commodity to a monetary value of the commodity. This is a logical extension because most economic transactions, even in Ricardo's time, were based on money prices and not barter. This monetization will be accomplished by assigning a wage rate to each country. The domestic value of each good is then found by multiplying the labor requirement per unit by the appropriate wage rate. This valuation procedure does not change the internal prices under autarky because the relative labor content—the underlying basis for relative value—is still the same. It does, however, provide a set of money prices in each country that can be used to determine the attractiveness of buying or selling abroad. Because each country's price is now stated in its own currency, however, money prices cannot be used until a link between the two currencies is established. The link is provided by specifying an **exchange rate,** which is the number of units of one currency that exchange for one unit of a second currency. Once the exchange rate is established, the value of all goods can be stated in terms of one currency.

To demonstrate comparative advantage in a monetized Ricardian model, let us examine the production of cloth and wine in Ricardo's original example countries of England and Portugal. In this example, England has the absolute advantage in both goods. Table 1 contains data on wages per hour and the money price of each commodity based on the labor needed to produce 1 unit of each good in each country. Assume that the *fixed* exchange rate is 1 escudo (esc) = £1. The pattern of trade now responds to money-price differences.

TABLE 1   Labor Requirements and Money Prices in a Ricardian Framework

		Cloth		*Wine*	
	Wage/Hour	*Labor/Unit*	*Price*	*Labor/Unit*	*Price*
(1) England	£1/hr	1 hr/yd	£1	3 hr/bbl	£3
(2) Portugal	0.6 esc/hr	2 hr/yd	1.2 esc	4 hr/bbl	2.4 esc

Cloth will be purchased in England because the price of cloth in either currency is less in England than in Portugal. Wine, however, is cheaper in Portugal, so consumers will buy Portuguese wine. This result is the same as that reached in the examination of relative labor efficiency between the two countries (i.e., England should export cloth and import wine because $\frac{1}{2} < \frac{3}{4}$).

The monetizing of the model produces an additional piece of information: Once prices and an exchange rate are specified, the international commodity terms of trade are uniquely specified. Table 1 shows that the low price of cloth (in England) is £1/yd or 1 esc/yd, while the low price of wine (in Portugal) is £2.4/bbl or 2.4 esc/bbl. As trade takes place, England will export cloth and import wine at a rate of 2.4 yards of cloth per each barrel of wine. The price ratio, P_{wine}/P_{cloth} (2.4/1), yields the quantity of cloth that exchanges for 1 barrel of wine. These are clearly viable international terms of trade because they lie within the limits imposed by the prices under autarky in the two countries. As under barter, both countries will benefit from trade on these terms. If for some reason the terms of trade do not produce balanced trade, then gold will move to the country with an export surplus and away from the country with a trade deficit. When this occurs, the price-specie-flow mechanism will cause prices (and wages) in the surplus country to rise and prices (and wages) in the deficit country to fall (see Chapter 2). These adjustments will take place until the international terms of trade bring about balanced trade.

WAGE RATE LIMITS AND EXCHANGE RATE LIMITS

In the monetized version of the Classical model, a country exports a product when it can produce it the most inexpensively, given wage rates and the exchange rate. The **export condition**—the cost conditions necessary for a country to export a good—can be stated in the following manner for any country 1 (England in our example):

$$a_{1j}W_1e < a_{2j}W_2$$

where: a_{1j} = the labor requirement/unit in country 1 for commodity j
  W_1 = the wage rate in country 1 in country 1's currency
  e = the country 2 currency/country 1 currency exchange rate, or the number of units of country 2's currency required to purchase 1 unit of country 1's currency
  a_{2j} = the labor requirement/unit in country 2 for commodity j
  W_2 = the wage rate in country 2 in country 2's currency

It is clear that England (country 1) should export cloth since (1 hr) × (£1/hr) × (1 esc/£1) < (2 hr) × (0.6 esc/hr). This condition does not, however, hold for wine, since (3 hr) × (£1/hr) × (1 esc/£1) > (4 hr) × (0.6 esc/hr). Thus, England should export cloth and import wine. In a two-country, two-commodity framework, once the export and import goods are known for one country, the import and export pattern for the trading partner is also determined: England's exports are Portugal's (country 2's) imports, and England's imports are Portugal's exports.

The export condition is a useful way to examine potential trade flows; it makes it clear that, in a monetized world, the ability to export depends not only on relative labor efficiency but also on relative wage rates and the exchange rate. Shifts in wage rates and/or the exchange rate can affect trade. This possibility is apparent if one rewrites the export condition in the following manner:

$$a_{1j}/a_{2j} < W_2/(W_1 \times e)$$

A fall in W_2 reduces the relative cost competitiveness of country 1, whereas a fall in W_1 enhances its cost competitiveness. Similarly, if the pound rises in value relative to the escudo (a rise in e), English goods cost more in Portugal, thus offsetting some of England's initial relative labor efficiency. If the escudo rises in value relative to the pound (a fall in e), England's cost advantage in cloth increases or its cost disadvantage in wine decreases.

Because changes in the wage rate can alter the degree of cost advantage to a country, changes that are too severe could eliminate a country's ability to export or its willingness to import a good. A country would lose the ability to export if wages rose sufficiently to cause the domestic price to exceed the foreign price. The same country would have no desire to import a good if its wage rate fell to the point that the price of the import good was now cheaper at home than abroad. Thus, given a fixed exchange rate and a fixed wage in the second country, the wage rate must lie within a certain range if trade is to take place by comparative advantage. If we adopt the Portuguese wage rate and the exchange rate from the example, and if the English wage rises to £1.2/hr, then prices for cloth are equalized between England and Portugal, and England loses its guaranteed export market. If wages in England fall to £0.8/hr, then the cost of wine is equalized between both countries, and England has no incentive to import wine from Portugal. Given the English wage and the exchange rate, the **wage rate limits**—the endpoints of the range within which the wage can vary without eliminating the basis for trade—for Portugal are 0.5 esc/hr and 0.75 esc/hr. At 0.5 esc/hr, the prices of cloth are equal, and at a wage rate of 0.75 esc/hr, the prices of wine are equal.

Similarly, there are **exchange rate limits.** Using the wage levels in the England–Portugal example (see Table 1), it is obvious that an exchange rate of 1.2 esc/£1 will cause the price of cloth to be the same in both countries. On the other hand, an exchange rate of 0.8 esc/£1 will cause wine prices to be the same in both countries. For trade to take place, the exchange rate must lie within these limits. The closer it lies to 1.2 esc/£1, the more the terms of trade benefit England. The closer the exchange rate lies to 0.8 esc/£1, the more the terms of trade benefit Portugal. For a summary, see Concept Box 1.

The limits to wages and the exchange rate can also be determined by using the export condition explained earlier. Because the export condition indicates when a country has a cost advantage in a particular product, that condition can be used to determine the wage that will cause prices to be the same in the two countries. Replace the $<$ sign with an $=$ sign; then solve for the single unknown wage, given the wage rate in the other country, labor requirements, and the exchange rate. For example, suppose that you want to know what wage would cause Portugal to lose its price advantage over England for wine. You would set the wine labor requirements ratio equal to the wage ratio, or

$$a_{1j}/a_{2j} = W_2/(W_1 \times e)$$
$$3/4 = W_2/(1 \times 1/1)$$
$$W_2 = 3/4 = 0.75 \text{ esc/hr}$$

CONCEPT BOX 1

WAGE RATE LIMITS AND EXCHANGE RATE LIMITS IN THE MONETIZED RICARDIAN FRAMEWORK

The wage rate and exchange rate limits related to Table 1 can be summarized in the following manner.

In England, with a Portuguese wage rate of 0.6 esc/hr and an exchange rate of 1 esc/£1, the following wage limits hold:

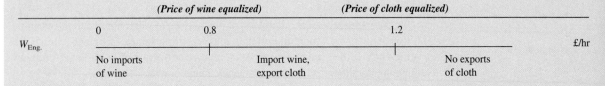

In Portugal, with an English wage rate of £1/hr and an exchange rate of 1 esc/£1, the following wage limits hold:

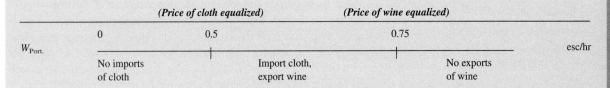

Finally, with $W_{Port.}$ = 0.6 esc/hr and $W_{Eng.}$ = £1/hr, the following exchange rate limits hold:

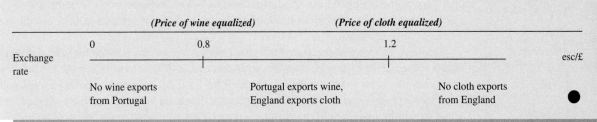

To find the other wage limit, you proceed in the same manner, except that you use the relative labor requirements for cloth instead of wine:

$$1/2 = W_2/(1 \times 1)$$

$$W_2 = 1/2 = 0.5 \text{ esc/hr}$$

To locate the limits to England's wages, you solve for W_1, given wages in Portugal and the exchange rate. For example, for the upper limit to England's wages,

$$1/2 = 0.6/W_1(1)$$

$$W_1 = £1.2/\text{hr}$$

whereas for the lower limit,

$$3/4 = 0.6/W_1(1)$$

$$W_1 = £0.8/\text{hr}$$

The limits to the exchange rate are found by setting up the same relationships and then solving for e, given the wage levels in the two countries. Work this out by yourself to demonstrate that the limits are indeed 0.8 esc/£1 and 1.2 esc/£1.

You may have noticed that the range of English wages is above the range of Portuguese wages. This is no accident: the higher-productivity country will have more highly paid workers. If Portuguese workers sought wages equal to those in England, Portugal would be unable to export either good and would import both. The price-specie-flow mechanism would then operate to reduce Portuguese wages until they fell within the specified range.

CONCEPT CHECK

1. Once prices are brought into the Ricardian framework, what is the export condition that determines the basis for trade?
2. Suppose that the exchange rate in the example in Table 1 had been 0.9 esc/£1. What would the English wage limits be?
3. Is there a basis for trade in the following case if the exchange rate (using the historical currencies) is 1 franc/1.25 marks? If so, what commodity will each country export? What are the terms of trade? What are the wage limits in each country? What are the limits to the exchange rate?

	Wage Rates	Cutlery	Wheat
Germany	2 marks/hr	60 hr/unit	30 hr/bu
France	3 francs/hr	30 hr/unit	20 hr/bu

MULTIPLE COMMODITIES

Up to this point, it has been assumed that trade was taking place within a two-country, two-commodity world, but in the real world countries produce and trade more than two products. What, if anything, can Ricardian comparative advantage say about the nature of trade in a multicommodity world? As it turns out, the concept of comparative advantage can be extended into a larger group of products using the export condition discussed in the previous section. Suppose that two countries have labor requirements per unit of production and wages as described in Table 2 and that the exchange rate is 0.8 pounds/1 euro or £0.8/€1. In this situation, the relative labor requirements, a_{1j}/a_{2j}, must be less than $W_2/(W_1 e)$ in order for Spain (country 1) to export the good. If Spain's relative labor requirements are greater than the relative wage cost (expressed in a common currency), then Spain should import the good from the United Kingdom. With only two countries, once imports and exports are determined for one country, they are automatically determined for the other. The way to solve this problem is to place the commodities in ascending order according to their relative labor requirements (a_{1j}/a_{2j}) and

TABLE 2   Unit Production Conditions in a Two-Country, Multicommodity Ricardian Framework

	Wage Rate	Wine	Cutlery	Cloth	Hardware	Wheat	Cheese
Spain	€2/hr	4 hr	12 hr	6 hr	15 hr	5 hr	7 hr
United Kingdom	£3.2/hr	3 hr	4 hr	5 hr	6 hr	2.8 hr	3 hr

then position the relative wage cost in the appropriate place in the goods spectrum. The following array of goods will then appear:

Cloth		Wine		Wheat		$W_2/(W_1 \times e)$		Cheese		Hardware		Cutlery
6/5	<	4/3	<	5/2.8	<	3.2/[(2)(0.8/1)]	<	7/3	<	15/6	<	12/4
						= 2.0						
{_____Spain exports_____}								{_____Spain exports_____}				
{_____U.K. imports_____}								{_____U.K. imports_____}				

The pattern of trade is thus clear: Spain should specialize in and export cloth, wine, and wheat while importing cheese, hardware, and cutlery from the United Kingdom. (In this example, each country exports three goods, but there is no a priori reason for two trading partners to import and export the same *number* of goods, as we shall see later.)

To verify that indeed each country's exports are in fact the lowest price goods, the array of goods prices is as follows:

	Wine	Cutlery	Cloth	Hardware	Wheat	Cheese
Spain	€8	€24	€12	€30	€10	€14
United Kingdom	£9.6	£12.8	£16	£19.2	£ 8.96	£ 9.6
Spain	£6.4	£19.2	£ 9.6	£24	£ 8	£11.2

When the prices are all stated in one currency (e.g., pounds) using the exchange rate, it is clear that the array of exports (imports) based on price alone is the same as previously demonstrated. That is, Spain exports cloth, wine, and wheat, and the United Kingdom exports cutlery, hardware, and cheese.

A final observation is important: Should the ratio of relative labor requirements equal exactly the ratio of relative wages, the good in question will cost the same in both countries. Hence, it may or may not be traded because consumers will be indifferent to the source of the good: home or foreign (and no transportation costs are assumed).

The Effect of Wage Rate Changes

Expanding the number of commodities is a useful extension of the basic Classical model because it permits an analysis of the effects of exogenous changes in relative wages or the exchange rate on the pattern of trade. (In the two-country, two-commodity model, sufficiently large wage or exchange rate movements can remove the basis for trade, but if trade takes place, it is always the same trade pattern.) To drive this point home, suppose that an increased preference for leisure causes the U.K. wage rate to increase from £3.2/hr to £4.2/hr. With the new, higher wage rate, the relative labor wage ratio is now 2.6— 4.2/[(2)(0.8/1)] = 2.6—instead of 2.0. This means that the dividing point between exports and imports has now shifted to the right and lies to the right of both cheese and hardware, as shown below:

Cloth		Wine		Wheat		Cheese		Hardware		$W_2/(W_1 \times e)$		Cutlery
6/5	<	4/3	<	5/2.8	<	7/3	<	15/6	<	4.2/[(2)(0.8/1)]	<	12/4
{_____Spain exports_____}										{Spain imports}		
{_____United Kingdom imports_____}										{United Kingdom exports}		

This shift in relative wages means that Spain will now export cheese and hardware, instead of importing them from the United Kingdom. The pattern of trade has shifted markedly because the United Kingdom's cost advantage has been eroded by the increase in its wage rate, which has eliminated its ability to export two products. If trade takes place, however, cloth will always be exported by Spain and cutlery by the United Kingdom.

The Effect of Exchange Rate Changes

Changes in the exchange rate also can alter a country's trade pattern. A shift in tastes and preferences toward foreign goods, which leads to an increase in the domestic price of foreign currency, will make domestic products cheaper when measured in that foreign currency, thereby increasing the competitiveness of a country in terms of exports. A decrease in the domestic cost of foreign currency will make foreign goods cheaper and act as a stimulus to imports. In the Classical model, this means that changes in the exchange rate can cause goods not at the endpoints of the spectrum to change from exports to imports. In the example with the original wage rates, an increase in the pound/euro exchange rate to £1/€1 from £0.8/€1 will cause the relative wage ratio to become $1.6 [= 3.2/(2 \times 1/1)]$. Wheat becomes an import instead of an export for Spain. A decrease in the pound/euro rate would have the opposite effect, potentially increasing Spain's exports and reducing its imports.

What determines the equilibrium relative wage ratio in this two-country, multiple-commodity analysis? In this single-factor approach, the relative size of the labor force will clearly be critical from the supply perspective. Holding other considerations constant, the larger the labor force in one country, the smaller is its relative wage rate and, other things being equal, the larger the number of goods it will export. Reciprocal demand will also play a role in determining the ultimate relative wage rate in equilibrium. As John Stuart Mill (1848) pointed out, the equilibrium terms of trade will reflect the size and elasticity of demand of each country for each other's products, given the initial production conditions determined by the resource endowments and technology. Appropriate adjustment to demand conditions is provided in the Classical model by the price-specie-flow mechanism if trade is not balanced between the two trading partners. The equilibrium terms of trade are thus realized by adjustments in the relative wage rates because of the movement of gold between the two countries. A country with a trade surplus will find gold flowing in, resulting in an increase in prices and wages. This will continue until wages have risen sufficiently to reduce its exports and increase its imports and trade is balanced between the two countries. The reverse will occur in the deficit country. The mechanism ensures that each country will export at least one good.

The general equilibrium nature of the Classical approach is formally presented in a well-known model by Rudiger Dornbusch, Stanley Fischer, and Paul Samuelson (1977). They construct a multicommodity model between two countries that captures the relative supply conditions between the two countries and incorporates total (both countries) relative demand for the commodities under consideration. This enables them to demonstrate the simultaneously determined links between relative wage rates, prices, and exchange rates and to show clearly that wages and prices are jointly determined with trade when balanced trade between the two countries is achieved. The original model also incorporated transportation costs, tariffs, and nontraded goods.[1] Using this model, Dornbusch, Fischer, and

---

[1] Appleyard, Conway, and Field (1989) extended this model to a three-country framework.

Samuelson explain how exogenous changes in productivity and relative demand can affect the structure of trade, wages, and prices in the trading partners. For a more complete description of this model, see the appendix at the end of this chapter.

TRANSPORTATION COSTS

Our discussion of the Classical explanation of international trade has so far assumed no transportation costs. The incorporation of transport costs alters the results covered to this point, because the cost of moving a product from one country's location to another affects relative prices. To examine the effect of transportation costs, it is assumed that (1) all transportation costs are paid by the importer and (2) transportation costs are measured in terms of their labor content, in keeping with the labor theory of value. Transportation costs are perceived as increasing the amount of relative labor required per unit of output *in the exporting country.* The labor cost of transportation is added to the production labor requirement in that country. In the first Spain–United Kingdom multiple-commodity example, the transportation costs to export cloth, wine, and wheat would be added to Spain's labor requirements in production, while the transportation costs for cheese, hardware, and cutlery would be added to those of the United Kingdom. With transportation costs, Spain's (country 1's) export condition becomes $(a_{1j} + tr_j)/a_{2j} < W_2/(W_1 \times e)$ and the import condition becomes $W_2/(W_1 \times e) < a_{1j}/(a_{2j} + tr_j)$. The symbol tr_j reflects the transportation cost per unit for commodity j measured in labor hours. Taking account of transportation costs in this manner allows for the possibility that certain commodities might not be imported by either country because the transportation cost makes them more expensive than the domestically produced alternative. This will be true any time $(a_{1j} + tr_j)/a_{2j} > W_2/(W_1 \times e)$ and $W_2/(W_1 \times e) > a_{1j}/(a_{2j} + tr_j)$.

To illustrate this point numerically, consider again the Spain–United Kingdom example (page 47). In addition, assume that the transportation cost per unit of each of the products is 1 labor hour. The relative labor cost of each product delivered in the importing country is now:

Cloth	Wine	Wheat	$W_2/(W_1 \times e)$	Cheese	Hardware	Cutlery
(6 + 1)/5	(4 + 1)/3	(5 + 1)/2.8	3.2/[(2)(0.8)]	7/(3 + 1)	15/(6 + 1)	12/(4 + 1)

When these additional costs are taken into consideration, wheat becomes a nontraded good for Spain since (5 + 1)/2.8 = 2.1 > 3.2/(2)(0.8) = 2, while the United Kingdom is no longer cost competitive in cheese since 7/(3 + 1) = 1.75 < 2. Each of these goods is produced for domestic use in both countries. Both are tradeable goods, but they are not traded because the comparative advantage in each case is overcome by the cost of transportation. The incorporation of transportation costs is important because it produces a third category of goods, **nontraded goods,** that will not enter into international trade, even though one of the countries may have a comparative advantage in production. Given relative labor requirements, goods that lie close to the wage ratio are thus likely to be nontraded. Consideration of transportation costs also illustrates that products subject to high transportation costs must have a relatively large production cost advantage if a country is to sell them to another country. It is not surprising that many bulky, heavy products are not traded.

IN THE REAL WORLD:

THE SIZE OF TRANSPORTATION COSTS

The cost of shipping a product from one point to another is determined by a number of factors, including distance, size, weight, value, and the overall volume of trade between the two points in question. To get an idea of the average impact of shipping costs on trade in general, a *freight and insurance factor (FIF)* is estimated by the International Monetary Fund. This factor is calculated by dividing the value of a country's imports, including freight and insurance costs (the c.i.f. value) by the value of its imports excluding shipping expenses, the f.o.b. (free-on-board) value (i.e., FIF = $\text{imports}_{CIF}/\text{imports}_{FOB}$). If, for example, the FIF has a value of 1.08, it indicates that shipping and insurance costs added an additional 8 percent to the cost of imports. The value of this ratio thus reflects not only the composition of a country's imports but also the shipping distances involved as well as the other factors. Some examples of this measure are given in part (a) of Table 3 for several countries for 1975, 1985, 1995, and 2005. (The 2005 figures and all figures for individual developing countries were calculated by the authors.)

To get some idea of the relative importance of transportation costs for specific goods, some freight rates as a percentage of price for selected commodities and shipping routes are given in Table 3(b). The United Nations Conference on Trade and Development has estimated that freight costs as a percentage of world import value declined from 6.64 percent in 1980 to 5.25 percent in 1995/1996. Recently, however, ocean-shipping rates surged as demand for shipping services skyrocketed. As a result, the price of shipping commodities such as coal, iron, and soybeans nearly tripled, raising concern about the effect on commodity prices and inflation. (See Robert Guy Matthews, "A Surge in Ocean-Shipping Rates Could Increase Consumer Prices," *The Wall Street Journal,* November 4, 2003, pp. A1, A13.) (For a useful discussion of long-term shipping costs, see "Schools Brief: Delivering the Goods," 1997.)

TABLE 3   (a) Freight and Insurance Factors
1975, 1985, 1995, 2005

	1975	1985	1995	2005
Industrialized countries	**1.065**	**1.048**	**1.044**	**NA**
United States	1.066	1.047	1.037	1.037
Canada	1.027	1.025	1.027	1.036
Australia	1.070	1.118	1.067	1.038
Japan	1.132	1.082	1.090	1.087
France	1.049	1.039	1.034	1.025
Germany	1.041	1.028	1.028	1.017
United Kingdom	1.072	1.045	1.025	NA
Switzerland	1.026	1.010	1.010	NA
Developing countries	**1.128**	**1.118**	**1.114**	**NA**
China	NA	1.105	1.173	1.050
Republic of Korea	1.044*	1.168	1.047	1.022
Argentina	NA	1.084	1.070	1.062
Colombia	1.111	1.110	1.072	1.055
Kenya	1.116	1.131	1.119	1.070**
Saudi Arabia	NA	1.160	1.095	1.091

*1976 figure.
**2004 figure.

TABLE 3   (b) Freight Rates as a Percentage of
Commodity Price

Commodity: Route	1970	1980	1990	2000	2005
Rubber: Singapore/ Malaysia to Europe	10.5%	15.5%	13.9%	15.0%	8.0%
Jute: Bangladesh to Europe	12.1	21.2	15.5	37.0	30.5
Cocoa Beans: Ghana to Europe	2.4	6.7	4.1	4.8	4.0
Coconut Oil: Sri Lanka to Europe	8.9	NA	15.5	25.9	12.7
Tea: Sri Lanka to Europe	9.5	10.0	5.3	5.9	9.2
Coffee: Brazil to Europe	5.2	10.0	6.9	4.4	5.7

NA = not available.

Sources: International Monetary Fund (IMF), *1996 International Financial Statistics Yearbook* (Washington, DC: IMF, 1996), pp. 122–25; IMF, *International Financial Statistics Yearbook 2006* (Washington, DC: IMF, 2006), pp. 83–84; IMF, *International Financial Statistics,* December 2006, various pages; United Nations Conference on Trade and Development (UNCTAD), *Review of Maritime Transport 1998* (New York: UNCTAD, 1999), p. 7; UNCTAD, *Review of Maritime Transport 2001* (New York: UNCTAD, 2002), p. 61; UNCTAD, *Review of Maritime Transport 2006* (New York: UNCTAD, 2006), p. 72.

MULTIPLE COUNTRIES

In a two-country framework, the pattern of trade has always been unambiguous. With two commodities, the pattern of trade was determined by comparative advantage based on relative unit labor requirements. In the monetized, multicommodity model, the trade pattern was uniquely determined by relative labor costs and relative wages. When several countries are taken into account, however, the specification of the trade pattern is less straightforward.

Returning to our two-good world to simplify the analysis, let us examine the case for trade between three countries in order to make generalizations about the pattern of trade. Table 4 shows a clear basis for trade because the autarky prices are different among the potential trading partners. The incentive for trade will be greatest between the two countries with the greatest difference in autarky prices. The potential gains from trade initially are the greatest between Sweden and France; that is, the autarky price ratios are the most different. The equilibrium terms of trade will settle somewhere between 1C:2.5F and 1C:4F. Sweden has the comparative advantage in the production of cutlery $10/20 < 4/5$, France has the comparative advantage in fish, and the trade pattern between the two countries is determined as in the two-country model. But what of Germany? Will there be a reason for Germany to trade? If so, in which commodity will it have a comparative advantage?

Like "middle goods" in the example of multiple commodities, there is no single answer about the middle country's (Germany's) trade role. Germany's participation will be dependent on the international terms of trade. Three possibilities exist within the 1C:2.5F–1C:4F range. The terms of trade may be 1C:3F, 1C: > 3F, or 1C: < 3F. In the first instance (1C:3F), where the terms of trade are exactly equal to Germany's own domestic price ratio in autarky, Germany would have no potential gains from trade. In the second category, 1C:3.5F, Germany stands to gain from trade because the terms of trade are different from its own autarky prices. This gain will come about if Germany exports cutlery and imports fish, receiving 3.5 pounds for each unit of cutlery instead of only 3 pounds at home. The world pattern of trade in this case would consist of Germany and Sweden exporting cutlery and importing fish from France. If, on the other hand, the terms of trade settled in the third category, for example, 1C:2.8F, Germany would again find it profitable to trade since the terms of trade again differ from its own autarkic price ratio. The pattern of trade would not, however, be the same as in the second case. At these terms of trade, Germany would find it advantageous to produce and export fish and import cutlery, since 1 unit of cutlery can be obtained for only 2.8 pounds of fish with trade as opposed to 3 pounds of fish at home. The world pattern of trade would consist of France and Germany exporting fish and importing cutlery from Sweden.

Introducing multiple countries into the analysis results in an ambiguity in the trade pattern for all but the end-of-spectrum countries until the ultimate equilibrium terms of trade are specified. Once an international terms-of-trade ratio is specified, then the trading status

TABLE 4   Labor Requirements in a Two-Good,
Three-Country Ricardian Framework

Country	Fish	Cutlery	Autarky Price Ratio
Sweden	4 hr/lb	10 hr/unit	1 cut:2 $1/2$ lb fish
Germany	5 hr/lb	15 hr/unit	1 cut:3 lb fish
France	5 hr/lb	20 hr/unit	1 cut:4 lb fish

of the "middle" countries can be determined. Little can be said about the trade pattern of a middle country beyond noting the international terms of trade at which it would not gain from trade and the pattern of trade that would emerge if the world price ratio is less than or greater than its own autarkic price ratio. More advanced analysis exploring many countries and many goods is beyond the scope of this text.

CONCEPT CHECK

1. What determines the basis for trade in a two-country, multicommodity Ricardian framework?
2. What happens to the pattern of trade if the level of wages in one country increases, other things being equal? If the price of foreign currency rises for the same country (i.e., its home currency depreciates in value)?
3. Briefly explain under what conditions the "middle countries" will trade in a two-good, multicountry Ricardian framework. Why can you not say, a priori, which commodity these countries will export?

EVALUATING THE CLASSICAL MODEL

Although the Classical model seems limited in today's complex production world, economists have been interested in the extent to which its general conclusions are realized in international trade. In particular, economists have focused on the link between relative labor productivity, relative wages, and the structure of exports. One of the earliest empirical studies was conducted by G. D. A. MacDougall in 1951. In this classic study, the relative export performance of the United States and the United Kingdom was examined, using the export condition utilized throughout this chapter. MacDougall wanted to see if export performance was consistent with relative labor productivities and wage rates in the two countries. He argued that, relative to the United Kingdom, the United States should be more competitive in world markets whenever its labor was more productive than that of the United Kingdom, after taking into account wage rate differences. Another way to state this is that the value of U.S. commodity exports should be greater than that of U.K. commodity exports whenever the ratio of labor productivity in the United States to that in the United Kingdom in that industry is greater than the ratio of wages between the United States and the United Kingdom (i.e., the ratio of labor input/unit in the United States to that in the United Kingdom is less than W_{UK}/W_{US}). Whenever the ratio of U.S. to U.K. productivity in a given industry is less than the ratio of U.S. to U.K. wages, the United Kingdom should dominate in exports of the good.

The early results of MacDougall and later studies by Stern (1962) and Balassa (1963) confirmed the initial hypothesis. Some of MacDougall's early findings are conceptually represented in Figure 1. The relative productivity of more than 20 exporting industries in each of the two countries is plotted on the vertical axis; the relative volume of individual industry exports is plotted on the horizontal axis. In 1937, U.S. wages were on average twice those of the United Kingdom. A horizontal line is drawn intersecting the vertical axis at the value of 2. If a vertical line is now drawn intersecting the horizontal axis at a value of 1 (as a dividing line between U.S. dominance of exports and U.K. dominance of exports), four quadrants are formed. If the basic thrust of the Classical model holds, U.K. dominant exports should lie in the lower left-hand quadrant and U.S. dominant exports should lie in the upper right-hand quadrant. You can see that the empirical results tend to confirm the Classical prediction.

The MacDougall general framework has been applied to 1990 data in work by Stephen S. Golub (1996; see also "Not So Absolutely Fabulous," 1995). He focused on U.S. trade with various countries, primarily in the Asia-Pacific region, and constructed

FIGURE 1   Labor Productivity, Relative Wages, and Trade Patterns in the MacDougall Study

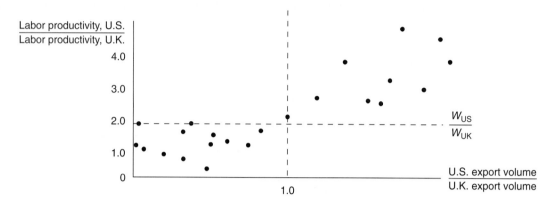

Some Commodity Examples Represented in the Above Graph

	(Pre-World War II) **U.S. Output/Worker** ——————— **U.K. Output/Worker**	*(1938)* **U.S. Weekly Wages ($)** ——————— **U.K. Weekly Wages ($)**	*(1937)* **U.S. Export Quantity** ——————— **U.K. Export Quantity**
Pig iron	3.6	1.5	5.1
Motor cars	3.1	2.0	4.3
Machinery	2.7	1.9	1.5
Glass containers	2.4	2.0	3.5
Paper	2.2	2.0	1.0
Beer	2.0	2.6	0.056
Hosiery	1.8	1.9	0.30
Cigarettes	1.7	1.5	0.47
Woolens and worsteds	1.35	2.0	0.004

Source: G. D. A. MacDougall, "British and American Exports: A Study Suggested by the Theory of Comparative Costs, Part I," *The Economic Journal* 61, no. 244 (December 1951), pp. 703, 707.

useful measures of **unit labor costs** in manufacturing in the various countries. In general, unit labor cost for an industry is defined as the labor cost per unit of output, and it is calculated by dividing the total wage bill (including fringe benefits) by the industry's output. Noting that manufacturing wages, for example, in Malaysia were about 10 percent of wages in the United States in 1990, an observer unfamiliar with the Classical model would wonder how U.S. industries could ever compete with Malaysian industries. However, Golub calculated that Malaysian productivity in manufacturing was also about 10 percent of the U.S. productivity level. Hence, unit labor costs would be similar in general in the two countries. This finding recalls our earlier numerical examples, where the higher-wage country was also the higher-productivity country. Golub also examined several other countries and found that unit labor costs were slightly higher in the manufacturing sectors in India, Japan, and the Philippines than in the United States and were somewhat lower in Mexico and South Korea. The main point, however, is that unit labor costs are much more clustered around U.S. unit labor costs than are the wage levels of those countries around the U.S. wage level.

Working within this unit-labor-cost framework, Golub then examined the possible association of comparative unit labor costs by individual *industries* (not for manufacturing as a whole) with trade performance. Although unit labor costs may be roughly similar across countries for the manufacturing sector in the aggregate, they differ by specific industries across countries, reflecting comparative advantages in production. For example, Golub found that labor productivity in Japan was about 60 percent below the U.S. level in the food industry but about 20 percent above the U.S. level in the automobile industry and 70 percent above in steel. And, indeed, the United States had a trade surplus with Japan in food products and deficits with Japan in automobiles and steel. In similar comparisons across individual industries in other countries, relative productivity, unit labor costs, and bilateral trade patterns did appear to be consistent with Classical theory. Hence, the Ricardian/MacDougall results tended to be confirmed for 1990.

A recent, more ambitious paper has also provided empirical support for the Classical model. Carlin, Glyn, and Van Reenen (2001) utilized data pertaining to the export patterns in 12 aggregate manufacturing categories of 14 developed countries from 1970 to the early 1990s. They calculated unit labor costs à la Golub but then calculated the *relative* unit

IN THE REAL WORLD:

LABOR PRODUCTIVITY AND IMPORT PENETRATION IN THE U.S. STEEL INDUSTRY

Although the Classical model is deficient in many respects, there is a clear relationship in practice between relative improvements in labor productivity and import competitiveness. This is demonstrated in the experience of the U.S. steel industry in recent decades. As U.S. productivity and wage changes led to a relative increase in the unit cost of steel compared with other world producers in the 1970s and early 1980s (see Table 5), the penetration of imports in the U.S.

market generally increased. Parts (a) and (b) of Figure 2 show absolute U.S. productivity and the import penetration ratio (i.e., the share of imports in U.S. consumption), respectively, for the 1973–2005 period. Labor productivity rose in the late 1980s and continued to do so through the 1990s. The import penetration ratio declined in the late 1980s and then leveled off, but it climbed again in the mid- to late 1990s. It then declined slightly in the last few years shown in the second graph.

TABLE 5   Indexes of Unit Labor Costs in Iron and Steel (1964 = 100)

	United States	Japan	France	Germany	United Kingdom
Output/hour:					
1972	116.1	219.8	157.1	157.7	130.0
1977	116.0	290.7	172.4	178.6	117.5
1982	107.0	315.7	222.2	212.0	156.9
Hourly labor cost:					
1972	160.7	277.4	214.8	210.9	206.1
1977	277.0	645.1	529.1	362.3	507.6
1982	496.3	887.0	1,076.2	495.7	1,035.0
Unit labor cost (U.S. dollars):					
1972	138.4	150.8	132.7	166.6	142.5
1977	238.7	300.3	305.8	347.2	271.0
1982	463.7	408.7	360.5	382.6	414.6

(continued)

IN THE REAL WORLD: *(continued)*

LABOR PRODUCTIVITY AND IMPORT PENETRATION IN THE U.S. STEEL INDUSTRY

FIGURE 2   Trends in U.S. Industry Labor Productivity—The Steel Industry (1987 = 100)

(a)

U.S. Steel Industry Import Penetration Ratios, 1973–2005 (imports as percentage of U.S. market)

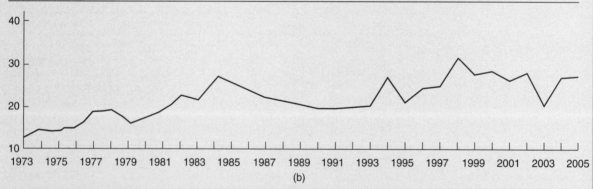

(b)

Sources: B. Eichengreen, "International Competition in the Products of U.S. Basic Industries," in M. Feldstein, ed., *The United States in the World Economy* (Chicago: University of Chicago Press for the National Bureau of Economic Research, 1988), p. 311; B. Eichengreen and L. H. Goulder, "The U.S. Basic Industries in the 1980s: Can Fiscal Policies Explain Their Changing Competitive Position?" in S. W. Black, ed., *Productivity Growth and the Competitiveness of the American Economy* (Boston: Kluwer Academic Publishers, 1989), pp. 15, 17; Michael O. Moore, "The Rise and Fall of Big Steel's Influence on U.S. Trade Policy," in Anne O. Krueger, ed., *The Political Economy of Trade Protection* (Chicago: University of Chicago Press for the National Bureau of Economic Research, 1996), p. 19; American Metal Market, *Metal Statistics 1995* (New York: Chilton Publications, 1995), p. 39; American Metal Market, *Metal Statistics 1999* (New York: Cathers Business Information, 1999), p. 267; Gary Clyde Hufbauer and Ben Goodrich, "Time for a Grand Bargain in Steel?" Policy Brief 02-1, obtained from the Institute for International Economics website, www.usii.net/iie; International Iron and Steel Institute, *Steel Statistical Yearbook 2006,* pp. 75, 84, obtained from www.worldsteel.org. The index of labor productivity for all years was obtained from www.bls.gov.

labor costs of the 14 countries in any given industry category. Thus, for example, in "transport equipment," they ranked countries in unit labor costs for each of the various years. Each industry's unit labor cost was divided by the 14-country industry average and then ranked from lowest to highest. This set of data was then paired with export market share data—that is, the percentage that each country's industry had of the 14 countries' total exports in the product category (again, from lowest to highest) in each of the given years.

With these series in hand, statistical tests were run to see if the export market shares were correlated with the relative unit labor costs by industry across the countries across the years. If labor costs were important in determining market shares, a negative relationship would be expected—higher relative unit labor costs would be associated with lower shares of exports of the 14-country total. Carlin, Glyn, and Van Reenen then estimated determinants of market shares and indeed found a statistically significant negative relationship. When they disaggregated the 12 industries into 26 categories, they obtained a virtually identical result. Thus, Classical comparative advantage theory does seem to be supported by this comprehensive recent study.

While these various findings suggest that the Classical model may be generally consistent with observed trading patterns, they in no way suggest that this model is sufficient for understanding the basis for trade. In today's complex trading world, the Classical model has several severe limitations that restrict its usefulness. Among the most limiting assumptions are the labor theory of value and constant costs, which are at odds with what can be observed in the present-day world. In addition, as countries grow and develop, relative resource endowments, including labor, change. Consequently, a richer paradigm is needed to better grasp the underlying basis for international trade. This richer paradigm is presented in Part 2, "Neoclassical Trade Theory."

The Classical model examined in this part, however, gives some suggestions for the direction of policy. Free trade is a means for a country and the world to enhance well-being. Further, in order to realize the full benefits of specialization and exchange through increased labor efficiency, resources need to be mobile within countries. Finally, government restraints and taxes on industry reduce economic competitiveness and the gains from trade.

SUMMARY

This chapter has focused on several of the more common extensions of the Classical Ricardian model of trade that contribute to a fuller understanding of the forces influencing the pattern of trade in the world. By monetizing the model, the critical roles of relative wages and the exchange rate were observed. The inclusion of these variables not only led to a specific estimate of the international commodity terms of trade but also provided a vehicle by which the price-specie-flow adjustment mechanism would work if trade is unbalanced. This analysis also indicated that wages and/or the exchange rate could change only within certain limits without removing the basis for trade and setting the adjustment mechanism into operation. Extending the analysis to include multiple commodities and transportation costs not only made the

model more realistic but also provided an explanation for the presence of nontraded goods. The multicommodity framework allowed us to see that changes in relative wages or the exchange rate can cause a country to change from being an exporter to an importer (or vice versa) of certain, but not *all,* commodities. These extensions also permitted the examination of the link between relative wages and the exchange of goods and services. The consideration of multiple countries indicated that, while comparative advantage would permit the determination of the trade pattern for the end-of-spectrum countries, the trade pattern of "middle countries" was dependent on the world terms of trade that emerged. Finally, empirical tests have given support to the relationships between relative productivities, unit labor costs, and trade patterns suggested by the Classical economists.

KEY TERMS

exchange rate	export condition	unit labor costs
exchange rate limits	nontraded goods	wage rate limits

QUESTIONS AND PROBLEMS

1. Suppose that France has a trade surplus with the United Kingdom. What would you expect to happen to prices, wages, and commodity prices in France? Why? What would happen to the terms of trade between the two countries?

2. Consider the following Classical labor requirements:

	Shoes	**Wine**
Italy	6 hr/pr	4 hr/gal
Switzerland	8 hr/pr	4 hr/gal

   (*a*) Why is there a basis for trade?

   (*b*) With trade, Italy should export _____ and Switzerland should export _____ because _____.

   (*c*) The international terms of trade must lie between _____ and _____.

   (*d*) If the wage rate in Italy is €4/hr, the wage rate in Switzerland is 3.5 francs/hr, and the exchange rate is 1 franc/€1, what are the commodity terms of trade?

3. In the example in Question 2, what are the limits to the wage rate in each country, other things being equal? What are the exchange rate limits?

4. If the following three commodities are included in the example in Question 2, what will the export and import pattern be? Will your answer change if a transportation charge of 1 hour/commodity is taken into consideration? Why or why not?

	Clothing	**Fish**	**Cutlery**
Italy	9 hr/unit	3 hr/unit	16 hr/unit
Switzerland	10 hr/unit	2.5 hr/unit	15 hr/unit

5. In the following two-good, multicountry example of labor requirements, do all the countries stand to gain from trade if the international terms of trade are 1 lb fish:0.5 bu potatoes? If so, what commodities will each country export and import? If these commodities are not exported or imported, why not?

	Fish	**Potatoes**
Poland	3 hr/lb	5 hr/bu
Denmark	1 hr/lb	4 hr/bu
Sweden	2 hr/lb	2 hr/bu

6. During the debate on the North American Free Trade Agreement (NAFTA), *The Economist* (September 11,

1993, p. 22) noted that average wages and fringe benefits in Mexican manufacturing industries were about one-fifth those in U.S. manufacturing and that U.S. output per worker was about five times that of Mexican manufacturing. Based on your understanding of this chapter and of the Classical model, is there any causal relationship between these two facts? Explain.

7. You are given the following Classical-type table showing the number of days of labor input required to obtain 1 unit of output of each of the five commodities in each of the two countries:

	Bread	**VCRs**	**Lamps**	**Rugs**	**Books**
United Kingdom	2 days	8 days	4 days	3 days	2 days
United States	2 days	6 days	2 days	2 days	3 days

   (*a*) Assume that the wage rate in the United Kingdom (W_{UK}) is £8/day, the wage rate in the United States (W_{US}) is $20/day, and the exchange rate (*e*) is $2/£1. With this information, determine the goods that will be U.K. exports and the goods that will be U.S. exports.

   (*b*) Keeping W_{US} at $20/day and keeping the exchange rate at $2/£1, calculate the upper and lower limits (in pounds per day) to the U.K. wage rate that are consistent with two-way trade between the countries.

   (*c*) With W_{UK} at £8/day and W_{US} at $20/day, calculate the upper and lower limits (in $/£) to the exchange rate that are consistent with two-way trade between the countries.

8. Suppose that, starting from your initial W_{UK}, W_{US}, *e*, and the resulting trading pattern in part (*a*) of Question 7, there is now a uniform 20 percent improvement in productivity in all of the U.K. industries (i.e., the labor coefficients for the five industries in the United Kingdom all fall by 20 percent).

   (*a*) In this new situation, determine the goods that will be U.K. exports and the goods that will be U.S. exports.

   (*b*) In this new situation, and keeping W_{US} at $20/day and *e* at $2/£1, calculate the upper and lower limits (in pounds per day) to the U.K. wage rate.

9. What do you regard as the main weaknesses of the Ricardian/Classical model as an explanation of trade patterns? Why do you regard them as weaknesses?

10. (Requires appendix material) Explain what would happen in the DFS model to relative wages and the pattern of trade if there is a uniform increase in productivity in all industries in the *foreign* country. What will happen to real income in each of the two countries? Why?

Appendix   THE DORNBUSCH, FISCHER, AND SAMUELSON MODEL

The interaction of supply and demand in the Classical model and the determination of relative wages and the trade pattern between two countries, given their initial endowments of labor, has been demonstrated by Rudiger Dornbusch, Stanley Fischer, and Paul Samuelson (1977), hereafter called the *DFS model*. Assuming a large number of goods, they rank the goods from the one with the smallest relative labor requirement to the one with the largest from the home country perspective (country 1). All commodities are indexed by $A = a_2/a_1$, where a_2 is the labor requirement for a unit of output in country 2 and a_1 the unit labor requirement in country 1 for any particular good in the continuum. The good with the lowest relative labor requirement for country 1 (lowest a_1/a_2 or highest a_2/a_1) is ranked first and the good with the highest relative labor requirement for country 1 (highest a_1/a_2 or lowest a_2/a_1) is ranked last. This is equivalent to ranking goods starting with those in which country 1's relative productivity is the greatest (i.e., relative labor time is the smallest). The question of which goods will be produced in which country is approached by using the general export condition in this chapter. The location of production (country 1 or country 2) for any good will depend on relative wages and the exchange rate. The home country will export those commodities

where $\dfrac{a_1}{a_z} < \dfrac{W_2}{W_1 e}$, or $a_2/a_1 > W_1 e/W_2$, and import those products where $\dfrac{a_1}{a_2} > \dfrac{W_2}{W_1 e}$, or $a_2/a_1 > W_1 e/W_2$.

With this framework in mind, one can graph the home production and export goods at various relative wage rates and a fixed exchange rate. If the array of commodities is plotted on the horizontal axis and relative wages on the vertical axis, the two will have a downward-sloping relationship because the number of goods exported from country 1 will rise as $W_1 e/W_2$ falls. For a large number of commodities, this downward-sloping relationship can be drawn as the continuous A curve in Figure 3. The commodities supplied by the home country reflect those goods whose relative labor time (a_2/a_1) is greater than the ratio of relative wages, $W_1 e/W_2$ [or $a_1/a_2 < W_2/W_1 e$]. The condition $a_2/a_1 = W_1 e/W_2$ separates the goods produced and exported by the home country from those imported, given the relative wages.

The A curve reflects supply conditions. On the demand side, national income (which equals the wage rate times the amount of labor) and the wage rate in the home country will depend, other things being equal, on the number of commodities that it produces based on world demand. The greater the number of goods demanded from the home country (i.e., moving to the right on the horizontal axis), the higher will be its wage rate relative to the other country, since the greater demand for the goods of country 1 will lead to a greater demand for country 1's labor and therefore drive up country 1's wage. This relationship is shown in Figure 3 as the upward-sloping curve C, which plots relative wages against the array of goods.

A more thorough explanation of the upward-sloping C curve involves interpreting that curve as reflecting alternative balanced-trade positions between the two countries. For any good on the horizontal axis, designate the *cumulative* fraction of income spent on country 1's goods up through that particular good (by the world as well as by each country, since tastes are assumed to be identical everywhere) as θ_1. Also, let the *cumulative* fraction of income spent on country 2's goods at that particular good (which are all goods other than country 1's goods) be represented by θ_2. Because the fraction of income spent on country 1's goods plus the fraction of income spent on country 2's goods must add up to 100 percent of income (or 1), the term θ_2 is therefore equal to $(1 - \theta_1)$.

Consider a situation of balanced trade between the two countries. The income spent on *imports* by country 1 from country 2 is equal to country 1's income multiplied by the fraction of income spent on country 2's goods; that is, it is (when expressed in terms of country 2's currency)

$$\theta_2 \times W_1 L_1 \times e$$

where W_1 = wage rate in country 1 and L_1 = labor force in country 1. Likewise, the income spent on imports by country 2 from country 1 is country 2's income multiplied by the fraction of income spent on country 1's goods; that is,

$$\theta_1 \times W_2 L_2$$

FIGURE 3   Determination of Equilibrium in the Dornbusch-Fischer-Samuelson Model

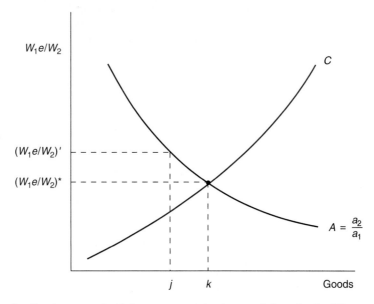

The A curve describes the pattern of trade between country 1 and country 2 that exists for different sets of relative wages, given the exchange rate e. For example, if relative wages were equal to $(W_1e/W_2)'$, country 1 would export all commodities whose relative labor requirements, a_2/a_1, are greater than $(W_1e/W_2)'$ (i.e., goods to the left of good j) and would import all commodities lying to the right of j.

The demand side of the DFS model, represented by the upward-sloping C curve, demonstrates that, as a greater number of home country (country 1) goods are demanded and therefore produced (i.e., a movement to the right on the horizontal axis), the home country wage rate will be bid up relative to the foreign country wage rate (i.e., a movement upward on the vertical axis). The intersection of the C curve and the A curve yields the equilibrium set of relative wages and the accompanying actual pattern of trade.

where W_2 = wage rate in country 2 and L_2 = labor force in country 2.

With balanced trade, the amount spent on imports by country 1 equals the amount spent on its exports by country 2 (i.e., the amount spent on imports by country 2). Hence, in a balanced-trade situation,

$$\theta_2 W_1 L_1 e = \theta_1 W_2 L_2$$

or

$$(1 - \theta_1) W_1 L_1 e = \theta_1 W_2 L_2$$

or

$$\frac{W_1 e}{W_2} = \frac{\theta_1 L_2}{(1 - \theta_1) L_1}$$

From this expression note that, as we move to the right on the horizontal axis in Figure 3, more goods are being exported from country 1, and therefore the cumulative fraction of income spent on country 1's goods increases. With this increase, other things being equal, the fraction $\theta_1 L_2/(1 - \theta_1)L_1$ rises, since the numerator gets larger and the denominator gets smaller. With balanced trade, this means that W_1e/W_2 rises and thus a movement to the right on the horizontal axis is associated with a movement upward on the vertical axis in Figure 3. The C curve is therefore upward sloping.

When the A curve and the C curve are in place, observe in Figure 3 how the patterns of trade and relative wages are determined simultaneously, given the size of the labor force in each country,

FIGURE 4   **Demand and Productivity Shifts in the DFS Model**

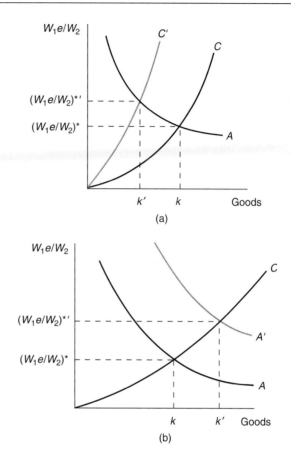

(a)

(b)

preferences for commodities, the exchange rate, and the level of technology. The equilibrium relative wage and the trade pattern are indicated by the intersection of the two curves at relative country wage $(W_1e/W_2)^*$ and good k. All goods to the left of good k are produced and exported by the home country because country 1's relatively low labor time compared with country 2 more than offsets the wage rate in country 1 relative to country 2's wage rate. That is, country 1 has lower unit labor costs in all goods to the left of good k. All goods to the right are produced and exported by the foreign country because country 1's unit labor costs are higher than unit labor costs in country 2 in all goods to the right of good k.

This Classical-like framework can also be used to demonstrate the effects of changes in technology, the relative size of labor forces, and changes in preferences. For example, suppose that preferences in both countries shift toward the goods lying nearest the origin. Because these goods are exported by the home country, this change in preferences will lead to an increase in demand for country 1's goods, causing an increase in its relative wages. Each of the goods is therefore associated with a higher W_1e/W_2, meaning that the C curve has shifted to C' in Figure 4(a). Consequently, the range of goods produced and exported by country 1 is reduced because labor is shifted to the production of those goods for which demand is growing. An increase in the size of the foreign country relative to the home country would have a similar effect on equilibrium because of the impact on demand for country 1's products.

On the other hand, suppose that there is an improvement in technology in country 1 that uniformly reduces the labor requirements (a_1) for producing every good there. This means that a_2/a_1 rises for each good, so the A curve shifts to A' as shown in Figure 4(b). Compared with the initial equilibrium level, there will be an increase in country 1's export goods. The result is that both the range of goods exported and the relative wage of the home country will rise.

A very important result of this technological improvement that is often overlooked should be stressed here. This result is that, even though country 1, because of its increase in productivity, is exporting more goods and therefore country 2 is exporting fewer goods, *country 2 still benefits from country 1's technological advance because country 2's real income rises due to that advance.*

To elaborate, consider real income in country 2. Real income is nominal income (W_2L_2) divided by goods prices, and it can be expressed in terms of any particular set of goods chosen. For example, real income in country 2 can be measured in terms of any of its own goods as $W_2L_2/(a_2 \times W_2)$, where the denominator $a_2 \times W_2$ is the price of a good (since it is labor time multiplied by the wage rate per unit of that labor time). Real income in country 2 can also be measured in terms of country 1's goods as $W_2L_2/(a_1 \times W_1e)$.

If productivity uniformly increases in country 1's industries (i.e., a_1 falls), then the real income of country 2 measured in terms of any of country 2's goods does not change. This is so because

$$\frac{W_2L_2}{a_2W_2} = \frac{L_2}{a_2}$$

and L_2 and a_2 are unaffected by country 1's productivity improvement. However, when the real income of country 2 is measured in terms of any of country 1's goods, that is,

$$\frac{W_2L_2}{a_1eW_1} = \frac{L_2}{a_1 \times (W_1e/W_2)}$$

there is an improvement in country 2's real income. How do we know this? L_2 is constant, so the right-hand numerator does not change. In the denominator, a_1 falls because of the productivity improvement in country 1, but W_1e/W_2 rises. However, W_1e/W_2 does not rise by as much as a_1 falls since, in Figure 4(b), a_1 falls by the vertical distance between curve A and curve A' but W_1e/W_2 rises by the vertical distance from $(W_1e/W_2)^*$ to $(W_1e/W_2)^{*\prime}$, which is a smaller amount than the vertical distance between A and A'. Thus the denominator of $L_2/[a_1 \times (W_1e/W_2)]$ falls, and the whole expression rises. This indicates that, since some of country 2's consumption bundle consists of imported goods from country 1, there is an increase in real income in country 2. In other words, the benefits of technological progress get transmitted across country borders, and country 2's real income goes up as a result of an improvement in productivity in country 1's industries.

By using the same general technique, you should be able to demonstrate that country 1's real income rises from its own productivity increase. This result occurs both when real income is measured in terms of country 1's own goods and when country 1's real income is measured in terms of country 2's goods.

part 2

NEOCLASSICAL TRADE THEORY

The recent developments in analysis of international trade have made it difficult to handle all the various theoretical cases by the traditional means of numerical examples. The following graphic application of indifference curves may provide a comparatively simple and handy tool of representation and analysis for the problem involved.

Wassily W. Leontief, 1933

Although basic propositions regarding the nature and impact of international trade were developed by economists in the Classical school in the late 18th and 19th centuries, the Classical economists were limited considerably in their analysis by the labor theory of value and the assumption of constant costs. The development of neoclassical economic theory in the late 19th and early 20th centuries provided tools for analyzing the impact of international trade in a more rigorous and less restrictive manner. The application of neoclassical theory to international trade issues and later refinements of these ideas constitute the basic contemporary theory of trade.

Part 2 will focus on the central elements of the neoclassical-based trade theory. Chapter 5, "Introduction to Neoclassical Trade Theory: Tools to Be Employed," provides a review of microeconomic concepts critical to the ideas developed in subsequent chapters. Chapter 6, "Gains from Trade in Neoclassical Theory," presents the analysis of the gains from trade, while Chapter 7, "Offer Curves and the Terms of Trade," focuses on the determination of the international terms of trade. The underlying basis for differences in international relative prices as developed by Heckscher and Ohlin is presented in Chapter 8, "The Basis for Trade: Factor Endowments and the Heckscher-Ohlin Model," followed by a summary of empirical work on the Heckscher-Ohlin model in Chapter 9, "Empirical Tests of the Factor Endowments Approach." ●

Australia has an abundant supply of agricultural land but a scanty population. Land is cheap and wages are high in comparison with most other countries; therefore, production of goods that require vast areas of land but little labor is cheap.

Bertil Ohlin, 1933

INTRODUCTION TO NEOCLASSICAL TRADE THEORY

Tools to Be Employed

LEARNING OBJECTIVES

- To review the microeconomic principles of consumer and producer behavior.

- To understand the concept and limitations of a community indifference curve.

- To recognize the underlying basis for a production-possibilities frontier with increasing opportunity costs.

INTRODUCTION

The principal changes in trade theory since Ricardo's time have centered on a fuller development of the demand side of the analysis and on the development of the production side of the economy in a manner that does not rely on the labor theory of value. To set the stage for this analysis, this chapter presents basic microeconomic concepts and relationships employed in analyzing trade patterns and the gains from trade. Although these tools will be familiar to readers who have studied intermediate microeconomics, this chapter should prepare the reader for the way the tools are employed in trade theory. We first present the theoretical analysis of decision making by consumers as they seek to maximize their satisfaction by proper allocation of their spending among final goods and services. Next, we describe a similar kind of process that occurs when producers allocate expenditures among factors of production in order to maximize efficiency. Finally, the meaning of efficient production in the entire economy is developed. The systematic application of the concepts and relationships in the context of international trade begins with Chapter 6, "Gains from Trade in Neoclassical Theory."

THE THEORY OF CONSUMER BEHAVIOR

Consumer Indifference Curves

Traditional microeconomic theory begins the analysis of individual consumer decisions through the use of the **consumer indifference curve.** The originator of the concept of the consumer indifference curve was F. Y. Edgeworth. This curve shows, in an assumed two-commodity world, the various consumption combinations of the two goods that provide the same level of satisfaction to the consumer. A typical indifference curve diagram is shown in Figure 1.

Adopting the basic postulate that more of any good is preferred to less, the S_1, S_2, and S_3 curves illustrate different levels of satisfaction, with level S_3 being greater than level S_2, which in turn is greater than level S_1. Economists recognize that it is impossible to measure an individual's levels of satisfaction precisely; for example, we cannot say that S_1 represents 20 units of welfare while S_2 represents 35 units of welfare. Such a numbering of the indifference curves would indicate **cardinal utility;** that is, actual numerical values can be attached to levels and changes of welfare. Instead, micro theory uses the concept of **ordinal utility,** which means

FIGURE 1   Consumer Indifference Curves

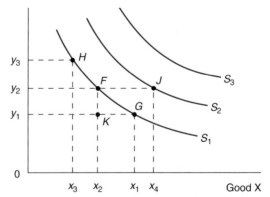

Indifference curve S_1 shows the various combinations of good X and good Y that bring equivalent welfare to the consumer. Curves S_2 and S_3 represent successively higher levels of welfare. If, from point F, the consumer gives up FK of good Y, he or she must receive amount KG of good X in order to be restored to the welfare level S_1. The (negative of the) slope at any point on an indifference curve is called the marginal rate of substitution (MRS).

TITANS OF INTERNATIONAL ECONOMICS:

FRANCIS YSIDRO EDGEWORTH (1845–1926)

F. Y. Edgeworth was born in Edgeworthstown, County Long-ford, Ireland, on February 8, 1845. He was educated at home by tutors and then entered Trinity College, Dublin, in 1862, where he specialized in the classics. He then went on to Oxford University where he earned the highest distinction in his field. Possessed of a prodigious memory, he supposedly could recite complete books of Homer, Milton, and Virgil. At his final oral examination at Oxford, he is said to have responded to a particularly difficult question by asking, "Shall I answer briefly, or at length?" Subsequently, Edgeworth studied mathematics and law, and he was admitted to the bar.

Edgeworth lectured for a number of years on English language and literature at London's Bedford College. The scholarly Edgeworth used vocabulary seldom heard in conversational English. The poet Robert Graves (quoted in Creedy, 1986, p. 11) tells the story that when Edgeworth met T. E. Lawrence (Lawrence of Arabia) upon Lawrence's return from a visit to London, he asked, "Was it very caliginous in the metropolis?" Lawrence replied, "Somewhat caliginous, but not altogether inspissated." (To save you a trip to the dictionary, *caliginous* means "misty or dim; dark," and *inspissated* means "thickened; dense.") In 1891, Edgeworth became professor of political economy at Oxford University. There he remained for the rest of his career. In addition, he served as editor of the prestigious *Economic Journal* from 1890 to 1911, when he was succeeded by John Maynard Keynes. Edgeworth died at the age of 81 on February 13, 1926.

Today students are familiar with Edgeworth through his box diagram (see pages 78–81), sometimes called the Edgeworth-Bowley box diagram, in joint recognition of the contribution of Professor A. L. Bowley. Edgeworth first formulated the concept of the consumer indifference curve in *Mathematical Psychics* (1881). His work in microeconomic theory and mathematical economics has been widely recognized, particularly his forceful demonstration of the application of mathematics to economics. He argued that mathematics can assist "unaided" reason, as is reflected in the following quotation (*Mathematical Psychics*, p. 3):

> He that will not verify his conclusions as far as possible by mathematics, as it were bringing the ingots of common sense to be assayed and coined at the mint of the sovereign science, will hardly realise the full value of what he holds, will want a measure of what it will be worth in however slightly altered circumstances, a means of conveying and making it current.

Sources: John Creedy, *Edgeworth and the Development of Neoclassical Economics* (Oxford: Basil Blackwell, 1986), chap. 1; F. Y. Edgeworth, *Mathematical Psychics* (London: C. Kegan Paul, 1881); John Maynard Keynes, *Essays in Biography* (London: Macmillan, 1933), part II, chap. 3; Peter Newman, "Francis Ysidro Edgeworth," in John Eatwell, Murray Milgate, and Peter Newman, eds., *The New Palgrave: A Dictionary of Economics,* Vol. 2 (London: Macmillan, 1987), pp. 84–98.

that we can say only that welfare or utility on curve S_2 is *greater* than welfare on curve S_1. *How much* greater cannot be determined, but the concept of ordinal utility reflects the assumption that a consumer can rank different levels of welfare, even if he or she cannot specify precisely the degree to which welfare is different. It is also important to note that consumers are assumed to have **transitivity** in their preferences. Transitivity means that if a bundle of goods B_2 is preferred (or equal) to a bundle of goods B_1 and if a bundle of goods B_3 is preferred (or equal) to B_2, then bundle B_3 must be preferred (or equal) to bundle B_1.

Given this indifference curve map, it is instructive to focus next on a given curve, S_1 (see Figure 1). The definition of the curve indicates that this consumer is indifferent among all points on the curve. Thus, possession of quantity $0x_1$ of good X and quantity $0y_1$ of good Y (at point G) brings the same level of satisfaction as does possession of quantity $0x_2$ of good X and quantity $0y_2$ of good Y (at point F). Note that point J (on curve S_2) is preferred to point F because the consumer has the same amount of good Y at the two points but more of good X ($0x_4 > 0x_2$). The consumer is better off at point J than at point F in terms of well-being. By applying the concept of transitivity, it is also clear that J is preferred to G and H, because the latter two points provide the same welfare as F.

Another feature of the indifference curve is its shape. First, we know that the curve must be downward sloping because, since goods are substitutes, less of one good must be compensated with more of the other good to maintain the same satisfaction level. But we can make an even stronger statement. The indifference curve is not only downward sloping but also *convex to the origin,* as are the curves in Figure 1. The reason for this convexity lies in the economic principle of the **diminishing marginal rate of substitution,** reflecting the law of diminishing marginal utility. The marginal rate of substitution (MRS) is the name given to reflect the slope of the indifference curve. (It is actually the slope, which is negative, multiplied by a minus sign, which gives a positive number.) In economic theory, the MRS is defined as the quantity of good Y that must be taken away from a consumer to keep that individual at the same level of welfare when a specified additional amount of good X is given to the consumer. Along any indifference curve in Figure 1, successive additional units of X are associated with successively smaller reductions in Y. This is because each additional unit of X brings less utility than did the previous unit; likewise, a reduction in the number of units of Y brings a higher utility for the last unit consumed. Hence, the MRS is diminishing as we move toward consumption of a greater number of units of good X along any given indifference curve.

The MRS can be expressed in useful economic terms. If we reduce the amount of good Y consumed, the change in *utility* (ΔU, where Δ indicates a small change) is equal to the change in Y (ΔY) multiplied by the marginal utility associated with the amount of Y lost (MU_Y), or $\Delta U = (\Delta Y) \times (MU_Y)$. If we offset this loss by giving additional X to the consumer, the change in utility from this additional X is equal to the amount of new X (ΔX) times the marginal utility associated with that X (MU_X). Hence,

$$(\Delta Y) \times (MU_Y) + (\Delta X) \times (MU_X) = 0$$
$$(\Delta Y) \times (MU_Y) = -(\Delta X) \times (MU_X)$$
$$\Delta Y/\Delta X = -MU_X/MU_Y$$
$$-\Delta Y/\Delta X = MU_X/MU_Y$$

This expression indicates that the (negative of the) slope of the indifference curve equals the ratio of the marginal utilities of the two goods. Note that we do not need the actual marginal utilities—for example, 5 units of satisfaction for MU_Y and 4 units of satisfaction for MU_X—in order to measure the MRS. All that is required is a knowledge of the ratio—for example, $^5/_4$—of the marginal utilities.

One final property associated with an indifference curve is the obvious one that indifference curves cannot intersect for the individual consumer. If they did, then one combination of X and Y (at the intersection) would yield two different levels of satisfaction, and this makes no economic sense.

The nonintersecting indifference curves are important to the study of international economics, because in Chapter 6, "Gains from Trade in Neoclassical Theory," indifference curves will be used to represent welfare not for an individual consumer but for a *country.* The **community indifference curve** (or **country indifference curve**) drawn in Figure 2 shows the combinations of goods X and Y that yield the same level of well-being for the community (or country) as a whole. To obtain this curve, we do *not* add together individual consumer indifference curves; economists do not believe that utilities of different consumers can be compared. Rather, the following question is answered as we plot the community indifference curve: If a given quantity of good Y is taken away from the community so that each person's consumption of good Y is reduced in proportion to that person's share of the country's total consumption of good Y, how much of

FIGURE 2   A Community Indifference Curve

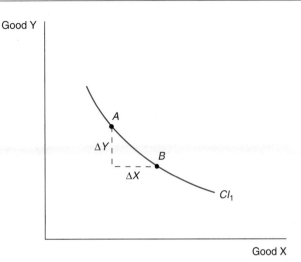

A community indifference curve shows the various consumption combinations of good X and good Y that yield equivalent satisfaction for the "community" or country. Removal of amount ΔY of good Y requires that amount ΔX of good X be provided to the community in order to yield the original welfare for each person in the community (at point B) as at starting point A.

good X must be given to consumers so that each consumer is brought back to his or her original level of utility? When the total amount of good Y removed from all consumers (ΔY immediately below point A) is replaced by the total of good X necessary to bring all consumers back to each consumer's original utility level (ΔX), we have traced out the movement from point A to point B. The entire curve CI_1 can be plotted when this exercise is done for each point on the curve.

If consumers differ in their tastes, a crucial point is that a community indifference curve for one distribution of income in the country *can* intersect a community indifference curve for another possible income distribution in the country. In Figure 3, curve CI_1 represents the community indifference curve for a given income distribution, and curve CI'_1 is a more preferred curve for the same income distribution. Community indifference curve CI_2 represents a curve for another income distribution, one in which consumers with less relative preference for good X have a greater weight in the income distribution. (Curve CI'_2 is a less preferred curve for this second income distribution.) If we start at point A, the removal of ΔY would require that ΔX be given to consumers in the first income distribution (moving to A' on curve CI_1) to keep community welfare the same as at point A. However, with the second income distribution, *more* of good X (amount $\Delta X'$) must be given to consumers to compensate for the loss of ΔY (moving consumers to point A''). More of good X must be provided because it does not bring as much marginal utility as in the first income distribution; thus, more units of X are needed to offset the loss of Y. In other words, because consumers who have a greater preference for good Y at the margin and a smaller preference for good X at the margin have a greater proportion of the income in this second distribution, they require more X to be compensated for a loss of good Y.

What is the point of this discussion? Very simply, suppose that some economic event moves the country from point A to point B. This event can change the income distribution so that curve CI_1, for example, is relevant before the event but curve CI'_2 is relevant *after*

FIGURE 3   Intersecting Community Indifference Curves

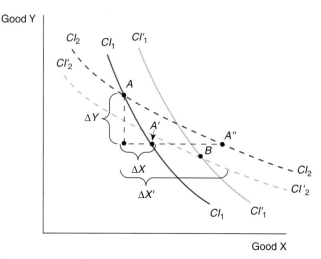

Curves CI_1 and CI'_1 are community indifference curves for one distribution of income in the country. If ΔY is removed from the total of all consumption bundles, then amount ΔX must be provided in order to keep each consumer at his or her original level of welfare. Curves CI_2 and CI'_2 represent a second income distribution, one in which income is distributed more heavily toward consumers who have a higher preference at the margin for good Y and a lower preference at the margin for good X than in the first income distribution. Hence, when aggregate amount ΔY is proportionately removed from total consumption, aggregate amount $\Delta X'$ must be provided to keep all consumers at their initial levels of welfare. In the graph as drawn, point B is preferred to point A on the basis of the first income distribution, but point A is preferred to point B on the basis of the second income distribution.

the event. What can be said about welfare change for the community? On the basis of the first income distribution, the community is better off since point B on curve CI'_1 is preferred to point A on curve CI_1. However, on the basis of the second income distribution, the community is *worse* off, because B on curve CI'_2 is inferior to A on curve CI_2. Thus, the possibility that changes in income distribution may alter the community indifference map must be kept in mind when employing this concept. Although this presents a potential problem when the community indifference map is employed in the analysis of the impact of international trade, community indifference curves will be employed in subsequent chapters assuming that the community indifference map, like those for individuals, does not change within the period of analysis. Further discussion of the intersecting indifference curve problem will be presented in subsequent chapters but the point should be clear: The use of indifference curves to represent *community* welfare is a more complex phenomenon than the use of indifference curves to represent welfare for an individual consumer.

CONCEPT CHECK

1. What is the distinction between *cardinal utility* and *ordinal utility?*
2. Why is the marginal rate of substitution along an indifference curve "diminishing" as more of the good on the horizontal axis is consumed and less of the good on the vertical axis is consumed?

3. If consumers differ in their tastes, why does a change in the income distribution within a country lead potentially to a differently shaped community indifference curve, one that can intersect a community indifference curve reflecting the "old" income distribution?

FIGURE 4   Consumer Budget Constraints

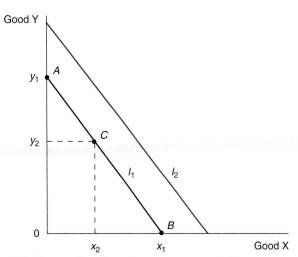

With income level I_1 and fixed commodity prices, the consumer can spend all income on good X (at point B) or on good Y (at point A) or some income on Y and some on X (such as at point C). Higher income level I_2 permits higher consumption levels. The (negative of the) slope of the budget line is P_X/P_Y.

The Budget Constraint

To determine actual consumption on the individual consumer's indifference curve, we need to examine the income level of the consumer. The income level is represented by the **budget constraint** (or **budget line**) as shown in Figure 4. This line shows the various combinations of goods X and Y that can be purchased with a given level of income at fixed commodity prices. Income level I_1 gives this constraint for one level of income (say, $500 per week), and income level I_2 (say, $600 per week) shows the constraint for a higher level of income. Consider income level I_1. If all income is spent on good X, then quantity $0x_1$ (at point B) can be purchased, but none of good Y. Alternatively, quantity $0y_1$ (at point A) can be purchased, but there is no income remaining with which to purchase any X. It is assumed that an infinite number of such combinations could be selected, and thus a straight line can be drawn connecting all feasible consumption combinations, given income level I_1. Hence, an intermediate position such as point C can also be attained.

The slope of the budget line can be determined in the following way: If all income were spent on good X (at point B), then the quantity purchased of X is simply the income I_1 divided by the price of good X, that is, $0x_1 = I_1/P_X$. Similarly, if all income were spent on good Y (at point A), the quantity purchased is the income divided by the price of Y, that is, $0y_1 = I_1/P_Y$. The slope of the curve as movement occurs from point B to point A is the change in Y divided by the change in X, or

$$\text{Slope (or } \Delta Y/\Delta X) = (0y_1)/(-0x_1)$$
$$= (I_1/P_Y)/(-I_1/P_X)$$
$$= -P_X/P_Y$$

The (negative of the) slope of the budget line is thus simply the price of X divided by the price of Y. An increase in the price of X (or a decrease in the price of Y) would yield a steeper budget line, and a decrease in the price of X (or an increase in the price of Y) would yield a flatter budget line.[1]

Consumer Equilibrium

With the concepts of the consumer indifference curve and the budget constraint in mind, it is a straightforward matter to indicate **consumer equilibrium.** The objective of the consumer is to maximize satisfaction, subject to the income constraint. Because the individual indifference curves show (ordinal) levels of satisfaction, and the budget line indicates the income constraint, the consumer maximizes satisfaction when the budget line just touches the highest indifference curve attainable. The point of maximum satisfaction with budget line FG is shown as point E on indifference curve S_2 in Figure 5. Clearly, the consumer would not settle at point B because B is on a lower indifference curve (curve S_1), or welfare level, than point E. Also, although the consumer would like to be at point A (on higher indifference curve S_3), this point is not possible given the

FIGURE 5   Consumer Equilibrium

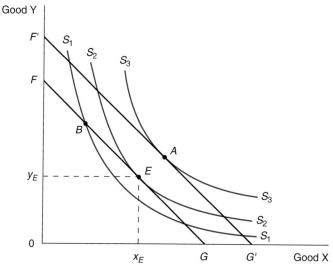

The consumer maximizes satisfaction for budget constraint FG by settling at point E, at which quantity $0x_E$ of good X and quantity $0y_E$ of good Y are consumed. Point A on indifference curve S_3 is unattainable unless higher income reflected in budget constraint $F'G'$ becomes available. Point B would not be chosen with budget constraint FG because MU_X/MU_Y is greater than P_X/P_Y at that point and welfare level S_1 is lower than welfare level S_2, which can be attained by consuming less of good Y and more of good X.

---

[1]The slope of the budget line can also be determined through algebraic examination of the consumer's budget constraint. If the consumer spends all income on the two goods (no saving takes place), then the expenditures on good X (the price of X times the quantity of X purchased) plus expenditures on good Y (the price of Y times the quantity of Y purchased) must equal the consumer's entire income. Thus,

$$(P_X)(X) + (P_Y)(Y) = I_1$$
$$Y = (I_1)/(P_Y) - (P_X/P_Y)(X)$$

This expression gives the equation of the budget line, with I_1/P_Y as the intercept (point A in Figure 4) and $-(P_X/P_Y)$ as the slope.

income level of the consumer. If income rises so that the consumer faces budget constraint $F'G'$, then point A could be attained and more of both goods could be consumed. (For a look at consumer allocation of expenditures among various categories of goods in the United States, see page 74.)

It is important to grasp the economic meaning of consumer equilibrium point E in Figure 5. Because budget line FG is tangent to indifference curve S_2 in equilibrium, the slope of S_2 at point E is therefore equal to the slope of budget line FG at point E. Thus, in consumer equilibrium,

$$MU_X/MU_Y = P_X/P_Y$$

or

$$MU_X/P_X = MU_Y/P_Y$$

This last expression indicates that, *at the margin,* the utility obtained from spending \$1 on good X is equal to the utility obtained from spending \$1 on good Y. If this were not the case, the consumer could increase welfare by reallocating purchases from one good to the other.

For example, consider a position such as point B. The consumer will not wish to remain at B because

$$MU_X/MU_Y > P_X/P_Y$$

or

$$MU_X/P_X > MU_Y/P_Y$$

In this situation, the marginal utility obtained from spending the last dollar on good X exceeds the marginal utility obtained from spending the last dollar on good Y. The consumer can increase total utility by switching a dollar spent on good Y to good X. The consumer will continue to reallocate expenditures until this difference in marginal utility per dollar of the two goods disappears, at point E.

CONCEPT CHECK

1. Suppose that, in Figure 5, the consumer is situated at the point where indifference curve S_1 crosses budget constraint FG just above point G. Use economic reasoning to explain why the consumer will move from this point to point E.

2. Students often ask why the (negative of the) slope of the budget line is P_X/P_Y and not P_Y/P_X. How would you answer these students?

PRODUCTION THEORY

Having examined consumer behavior, we now turn to producers. Our focus is not on every aspect of production—for example, we do not examine the producer's decision of what price to charge for a product—but on input choice and production efficiency within the firm.

Isoquants

In considering producer choice of inputs, assume that there are two factors of production, capital (K) and labor (L), employed in generating output. An **isoquant** is the concept that relates output to the factor inputs. An isoquant shows the various combinations of the two inputs that produce the same level of output; a typical production isoquant is illustrated in

IN THE REAL WORLD:

CONSUMER EXPENDITURE PATTERNS IN THE UNITED STATES

The tangencies of consumer indifference curves (reflecting tastes) with budget lines (reflecting incomes and relative prices) determine household expenditure patterns. Table 1 indicates the percentages of personal consumption expenditures in the United States devoted to broad categories of goods and services in 1960, 1970, 1980, 1990, 2000, and 2005.

These figures show that, as incomes have grown over time, U.S. families have chosen to devote a roughly similar percentage of their consumption expenditures to durable

goods and a much smaller percentage to nondurable goods. Particularly important declines in spending shares occurred in food, clothing and shoes. A dramatic rise in expenditure share has occurred in services, and 59.1 percent of consumer expenditures were devoted to this category in 2005. Within services, the greatest growth has occurred in purchases of medical care, where the share rose from 5.3 percent in 1960 to 17.1 percent in 2005.

TABLE 1   U.S. Consumer Expenditure Patterns, 1960–2005

Item	1960	1970	1980	1990	2000	2005
Durable goods	13.1%	13.1%	12.2%	12.3%	12.8%	11.8%
Motor vehicles and parts	5.9	5.5	5.0	5.5	5.7	5.1
Furniture and household equipment	5.4	5.5	4.9	4.5	4.6	4.3
Nondurable goods	46.1	41.9	39.6	32.6	28.9	29.0
Food	24.8	22.2	20.3	16.6	13.7	13.7
Clothing and shoes	8.1	7.4	6.1	5.3	4.4	3.9
Gasoline, fuel oil, and other energy goods	4.8	4.1	5.8	3.2	2.8	3.5
Services	40.9	44.9	48.2	55.1	58.3	59.1
Housing (including imputed rents for owner-occupied housing)	14.5	14.5	14.6	15.6	14.9	14.9
Household operation (including electricity and gas)	6.1	5.8	6.5	5.9	5.8	5.5
Transportation	3.4	3.7	3.7	3.8	4.3	3.7
Medical care	5.3	8.0	10.5	14.5	15.2	17.1

Note: Major category totals may not sum to 100 percent because of rounding.

Sources: *Economic Report of the President,* February 2006 (Washington, DC: U.S. Government Printing Office, 2006), p. 302; U.S. Department of Commerce, Bureau of Economic Analysis, *Survey of Current Business,* January 2007, p. D-11 (obtained from www.bea.gov.).

Figure 6. For example, output Q_0 (say, 75 units) could be produced with the quantity $0k_1$ of capital and the quantity $0l_1$ of labor (point A). Alternatively, that level of output could be produced by using $0k_2$ of capital and $0l_2$ of labor (point B).

The exact shape of an isoquant reflects the substitution possibilities between capital and labor in the production process. Curves Q_0, Q_1, and Q_2 in Figure 6 illustrate how capital and labor can be relatively easily substituted for each other. If substitution were difficult, the curve would be drawn more like a right angle. If substitution were easier, the isoquant would have less curvature. A precise measure of the curvature, and thus of the substitution possibilities, is the elasticity of substitution (see Chapter 8, "The Basis for Trade: Factor Endowments and the Heckscher-Ohlin Model").

A major feature of isoquants is that they, unlike consumer indifference curves, have cardinal properties rather than simply ordinal properties. Thus, in Figure 6 the three isoquants

FIGURE 6   Production Isoquants

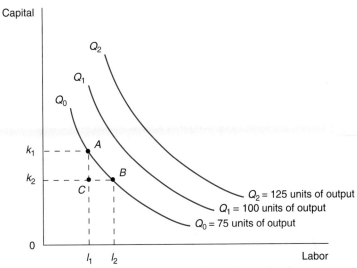

An isoquant shows the various combinations of the two factor inputs that produce the same output. Isoquant Q_1 represents a greater amount of output than does isoquant Q_0 since, for a given amount of any input, a greater amount of the other input is being used. Thus, isoquants that are "farther out" from the origin represent greater quantities of output. By definition, isoquants cannot intersect, since the intersection point would imply that one combination of inputs is producing two different levels of output. In addition, starting at point A on isoquant Q_0 and moving to point C, the removal of k_2k_1 of capital will decrease output by the amount of capital removed ($\Delta K = k_1k_2$) multiplied by the marginal physical product of capital (MPP_K). The subsequent addition of l_1l_2 of labor to move to point B will increase output by the amount of labor added ($\Delta L = l_1l_2$) multiplied by the marginal physical product of labor (MPP_L). Because the output level at B is the same as at A, the (negative of the) slope of an isoquant ($\Delta K/\Delta L$) can be expressed as MPP_L/MPP_K.

represent different absolute levels of output, with isoquants farther from the origin representing higher levels of output. Clearly, isoquants are downward sloping, but not vertical or horizontal or upward sloping, because reducing usage of one input requires greater usage of the other to maintain the same level of output. In addition, isoquants cannot intersect. If they could intersect, doing so would mean that, at the intersection point, the same quantity of capital and labor would be producing two different levels of output. Because an assumption behind isoquants is that maximum technical or engineering efficiency is achieved along each curve, an intersection makes no sense.

Finally, consider the slope of the isoquant. Suppose that the producer reduces the amount of capital used in production and offsets the effect on output by adding labor. The loss in output from the removal of capital is the change in the amount of capital employed (ΔK) multiplied by the marginal physical product of that capital (MPP_K), or $\Delta Q = (\Delta K) \times (MPP_K)$. The addition to output (ΔQ) from the extra labor is equal to the amount of that additional labor (ΔL) multiplied by the marginal physical product of that labor (MPP_L), or $\Delta Q = (\Delta L) \times (MPP_L)$. Hence, since output remains unchanged after the substitution of labor for capital:

$$(\Delta K) \times (MPP_K) + (\Delta L) \times (MPP_L) = 0$$
$$(\Delta K) \times (MPP_K) = -(\Delta L) \times (MPP_L)$$
$$-\Delta K/\Delta L = MPP_L/MPP_K$$

Because the slope at any point on the isoquant is $\Delta K/\Delta L$, this last expression states that the (negative of the) slope of the isoquant at any point is equal to the ratio of the marginal productivities of the factors of production (MPP_L/MPP_K). The ratio of marginal productivities is often referred to as the **marginal rate of technical substitution** (MRTS). The MRTS is defined economically as the amount of capital that must be removed to keep output constant when one unit of labor is added. Clearly, the MRTS declines as more labor and less capital are used. This decline reflects the fall of MPP_L as we use more labor and the *rise* of MPP_K as we use *less* capital (because of the law of diminishing marginal productivity).

A final point needs to be made about isoquants as they relate to international trade theory. The assumption usually employed in trade theory is that the production function is characterized by **constant returns to scale.** This means that if *all* the inputs are changed by a given percentage, then output will change in the same direction by the same percentage. Thus, in Figure 7, a doubling of the inputs (labor from 20 to 40 units and capital from 10 to 20 units) will double the output (from 100 to 200 units). If **increasing returns to scale** existed, then isoquant Q_2 would have an output value *greater* than 200, as the doubling of the inputs would more than double the output. Analogously, **decreasing returns to scale** means that output Q_2 would be less than 200 units.

Isocost Lines

In making the decision of how many units of each factor of production to employ, the firm must know not only the technical relationship between inputs and output but also the relative *cost* of those inputs. The costs of the factors of production are illustrated by isocost lines. An **isocost line** shows the various combinations of the factors of production that can be purchased by the firm for a given total cost at given input prices. Thus, if the given wage rate is $10 per hour and the rental rate on machinery is $50 per hour, then a "budget" or "cost" of $500 per hour means that the firm could hire 25 workers and 5 pieces of machinery. (If machinery is owned rather than rented, there is still an "opportunity cost" equal to the rental rate on machinery.) Alternatively, the firm could use 8 machines and 10 workers. Clearly, there are many such possibilities; these possibilities are reflected in an isocost or budget line, such as line B_1 in Figure 8.

FIGURE 7   Isoquants with Constant Returns to Scale

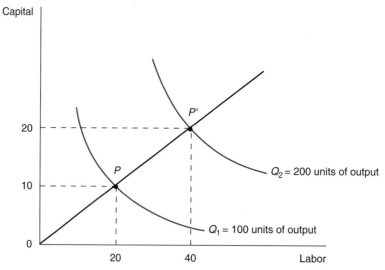

The term *constant returns to scale* means that a given percentage increase in all inputs will lead to the same percentage increase in output. Thus, the doubling of the quantity of inputs used at point P (from 10 to 20 units of capital and from 20 to 40 units of labor) will mean that, at point P', twice as much output (200 units) is obtained as at point P (100 units).

FIGURE 8   Producer Equilibrium

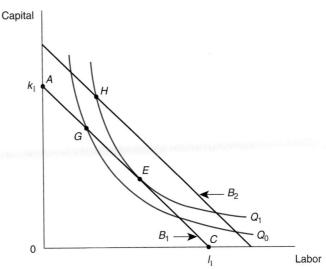

An isocost line such as B_1 shows the combinations of the two inputs that can be purchased by the firm for the same cost. At point C, quantity $0l_1$ of labor can be hired but no capital can be employed; at point A, $0k_1$ of capital can be used but no labor can be employed. For the budget B_1, the firm obtains the most output (Q_1) by producing at point E, where the (negative of the) slope of the isoquant (MPP_L/MPP_K) is equal to the (negative of the) slope of the isocost line (w/r). Production at point G obtains less output (Q_0) for budget B_1 than production at point E. Production at point H provides the same output as production at point E, but at a higher cost.

Before indicating the optimal choice of how much of each factor to employ, consider the slope of an isocost line. In Figure 8, if all of budget B_1 were spent on capital, then $0k_1$ units could be purchased but no labor could be employed (point A). Or $0l_1$ of labor could be hired but no capital could be used (point C). If we imagine a movement from point C to point A, the slope is simply $\Delta K/\Delta L$ or $(0k_1)/(-0l_1)$. The distance $0k_1$ can be restated as the size of the budget (B_1) divided by the rental rate on capital or price of capital (r); the distance $0l_1$ can be restated as the size of the budget divided by the wage rate (w):

$$(\Delta K)/(\Delta L) = (0k_1)/(-0l_1)$$
$$= -(0k_1)/(0l_1)$$
$$= -(B_1/r)/(B_1/w)$$
$$-(\Delta K)/(\Delta L) = w/r$$

Thus, the (negative of the) slope of the isocost is equal to the ratio of the wage rate to the rental rate on capital; and, for this reason, the isocost line is often referred to as the *factor price line*. A steeper isocost line reflects a rise in the wage rate relative to the rental rate on capital, while a flatter factor price line indicates the opposite.[2]

---

[2] Another way to look at the isocost line is to obtain the equation of the line. The producer's budget, or amount spent for the factors of production, is simply the rental rate on capital times the amount of capital used plus the wage rate times the amount of labor used:

$$B = rK + wL$$
$$rK = B - wL$$
$$K = (B/r) - (w/r)L$$

This equation indicates that the isocost line has a vertical intercept of B/r and a slope of $-(w/r)$.

Producer Equilibrium   The choice of the combination of factors of production to employ involves consideration of factor prices and technical factor requirements. Point E in Figure 8 indicates the
producer equilibrium position for a given cost B_1. At this point the isoquant is tangent
to the isocost, and the firm is obtaining the maximum output for the given cost (i.e.,
production efficiency). The firm would not settle at a point like G because this point
yields less output for the given cost than does point E. Alternatively, the producer equilibrium can be viewed as the point where the given output (Q_1) is obtained for the lowest cost. Isocost line B_2 (e.g., at point H) also could be used to get Q_1 of output, but B_2
involves greater cost than B_1.

In straightforward economic terms, it is clear why point E would be chosen but point G
would not. Because the isoquant is tangent to the isocost at point E, this means that
$MPP_L/MPP_K = w/r$, or that $MPP_L/w = MPP_K/r$. In other words, producer equilibrium
obtains when the marginal productivity of \$1 spent on labor is equal to the marginal pro-
ductivity of \$1 spent on capital. It is clear that point G is not an efficient production point
since MPP_L/MPP_K is greater than w/r (or MPP_L/w is greater than MPP_K/r). Thus, the
entrepreneur has an incentive to employ more labor services and fewer capital services—
which decreases MPP_L and increases MPP_K—and the firm moves down the isocost line
from point G to point E.

CONCEPT CHECK

1. Why are isoquants drawn as convex to the origin?
2. Briefly explain what happens to the intercepts and the slope of an isocost line for a given budget size if the rental rate on capital (r) falls at the same time that the wage rate (w) rises.

3. If MPP_L/MPP_K in production of a good is less than w/r, why is the firm not in producer equilibrium? Explain how, with a given budget for the firm, output can be increased by changing input combinations.

THE EDGEWORTH BOX DIAGRAM AND THE PRODUCTION-POSSIBILITIES FRONTIER

From the standpoint of understanding international trade theory, two other concepts need
to be introduced in this chapter. Both concepts look at the entire economy, not simply individual consumers and producers.

**The Edgeworth Box
Diagram**
This diagram is useful for discussion of a number of economic concepts and relationships. It will be used in this book to study efficient economywide production. (It can
also be used to discuss economywide consumption.) Construction of a typical **Edgeworth
box diagram** begins by considering firms in two separate industries, industry X and
industry Y (see Figure 9). Part (a) shows the isoquants for firms in industry X, and part
(b) shows the isoquants for firms in industry Y. Because ray $0_X A$ is flatter than ray $0_Y B$,
the X industry is the more labor-intensive industry and the Y industry is the more capital-
intensive industry.[3] It should be remembered that, in a competitive economy with factor
mobility between industries, the relative factor prices $(w/r)_1$ facing the two industries will
be identical.

---

[3]The slope of a ray from the origin to the production point for any industry gives the ratio of capital to labor (K/L)
used in the industry. A steeper ray implies a greater K/L and thus greater capital intensity. Fuller discussion of relative factor intensity is provided in Chapter 8, "The Basis for Trade: Factor Endowments and the Heckscher-
Ohlin Model."

FIGURE 9   Isoquants for Two Industries with Different Factor Intensities

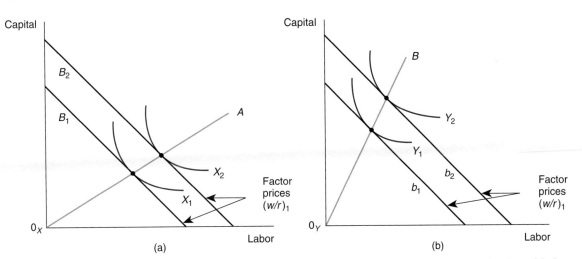

The X industry in panel (a) and the Y industry in panel (b) both face factor prices $(w/r)_1$, as indicated by the (negative of the) slope of the isocost lines. In producer equilibrium the X industry employs, for the given factor prices, a ratio of capital to labor (reflected by the slope of the ray $0_X A$) that is lower than the ratio of capital to labor employed in the Y industry (reflected by the slope of the ray $0_Y B$). The X industry is designated as *the relatively labor-intensive industry* and the Y industry is designated as the *relatively capital-intensive industry.*

The Edgeworth box diagram takes the isoquants of these two industries (assumed to be the only two industries in the economy) and puts them into one diagram as in Figure 10. The isoquants of industry X are positioned as in part (a) of Figure 9. However, the Y isoquants of part (b) of Figure 9 are positioned differently in Figure 10. The origin for the Y industry, 0_Y, is positioned so that increased use of capital is indicated by *downward* movements from 0_Y and increased use of labor is indicated by *leftward* movements from 0_Y. Hence, from 0_Y, increased output of the Y industry is indicated by moving to isoquants that are further downward and to the left of 0_Y. An important feature of the Edgeworth box diagram is that its dimensions measure the total labor and total capital available in the *economy as a whole.* Thus, horizontal distance $0_X F$ and horizontal distance $0_Y G$ each indicate the *total* labor available, while vertical distance $0_X G$ and vertical distance $0_Y F$ each measure the *total* capital available. The total labor and the total capital in the economy will be divided between the two industries.

The economy can produce at any point within the confines of the Edgeworth box. However, some points of production are better (i.e., yield more total output) than other points. The points of "best" production are those where isoquants of the two industries are tangent, such as point Q (isoquants x_1 and y_5) or point R (isoquants x_2 and y_4). The line connecting these points of tangency is called the **production efficiency locus,** or the "contract curve." It is evident that this efficiency locus runs from 0_X through Q, R, S, T, W to 0_Y. At any given point on the locus, MPP_L/MPP_K is identical in both industries (and equal to w/r if the economy chooses to produce at that particular point).

Why do efficiency locus points represent the points of best production? To illustrate, consider point V off the locus. At V, the X industry is producing quantity x_3 of output and is using quantity $0_X l_1$ of labor and $0_X k_1$ of capital. The Y industry is producing y_1 of output and is using $0_Y l_2 (=l_1 F)$ of labor and $0_Y k_2 (=k_1 G)$ of capital. Note also that the labor used in the two industries adds up to the total labor available in the economy because $0_X l_1 + 0_Y l_2 = 0_X l_1 + l_1 F = 0_X F$ (or $=l_2 G + 0_Y l_2 = 0_Y G$). By similar analysis, the sum of the capital used in the two industries is the total capital available in the economy.

FIGURE 10   The Edgeworth Box Diagram and Economywide Production Efficiency

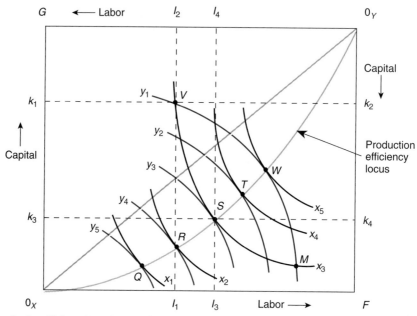

The production efficiency locus $0_X QRSTW 0_Y$ shows points where more of one good can be produced only by producing less of the other good. If the economy is off the efficiency locus (such as at point V), more output can be obtained of at least one good with no less output of the other good by moving to the efficiency locus (as to point S). Alternatively, more output can be obtained of both goods (as in moving from point V to point T) by producing on the efficiency locus.

But consider point S, which is *on* the efficiency locus. This production point yields x_3 of X output, the same as point V because the two points are on the same isoquant. However, point S yields y_3 of Y output, which is *greater* than the Y output at point V because S is on a Y isoquant with greater production. Hence, point S is a superior point to V because S has the same amount of X output but a larger amount of Y output. From point V, point S could be reached by shifting $l_4 l_2 (= l_1 l_3)$ of labor from Y production to X production and shifting $k_3 k_1 (= k_2 k_4)$ of capital from X production to Y production. These shifts move labor out of the capital-intensive industry into the labor-intensive industry, and they move capital out of the labor-intensive industry into the capital-intensive industry. By a similar argument, point W is superior to point M because W has the same Y output as M but more X output. Finally, a point such as T has greater X output *and* greater Y output than either points V or M. The important conclusion is that, for each point *not* on the efficiency locus, some point *on* the efficiency locus involves greater production of at least one good and no less production of the other good.

What comparisons can be made of points along the production efficiency locus itself? From the production standpoint alone, no judgments can be made about the relative desirability of these points because movement from one point to another leads to greater output of one good and *less* output of the other. Thus, for example, point S has more Y output but less X output than point W. Only when demand in the economy is brought into the analysis (see Chapter 6, "Gains from Trade in Neoclassical Theory") can we indicate the relative desirability of points along the locus and the output combination that will actually be chosen. Nevertheless, we can conclude that points off the locus are inefficient for the economy

FIGURE 11   Increasing Opportunity Costs on the PPF

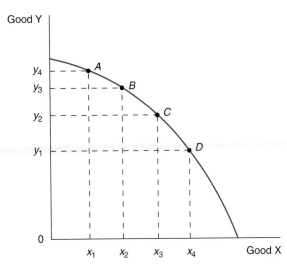

As production is shifted from point *A* to point *B,* the additional x_1x_2 of output of good X requires that output of good Y be reduced by amount y_3y_4. For a subsequent move from point *B* to point *C,* additional good X output of x_2x_3 (which is equal to x_1x_2) requires that amount y_2y_3 of good Y, which is greater than y_3y_4, be given up. Thus, the opportunity cost of getting more X rises as more X is produced. This conclusion holds for any movement *along* the PPF. Similarly, moving in the direction of greater output of good Y requires that increasing amounts of good X be given up *for each additional* unit of Y output.

as a whole because any such point can be improved upon by moving to the production effi-ciency locus. Points on the locus are efficient, because moving along the locus *requires* giving up output of one good in order to get more output of the other good. The econo-mist's term for this trade-off characterizing the efficiency locus is called **Pareto efficiency,** after Vilfredo Pareto (1848–1923).

The Production-Possibilities Frontier

A typical production-possibilities frontier (PPF) is drawn in Figure 11. Unlike the PPF used by the Classical economists, however, this PPF demonstrates **increasing opportu-nity costs.** If the economy is located at point *A,* it is producing $0x_1$ of the X good and $0y_4$ of the Y good. If movement takes place to point *B,* then x_1x_2 of the X good is being added, but y_3y_4 of Y is being given up. If we add an additional amount of X, x_2x_3, which is equal to x_1x_2, the amount y_2y_3 of the Y good must be forgone. *Increasing* amounts of Y must be given up in order to get the same additional amount of X because $y_1y_2 > y_2y_3 > y_3y_4$, and so on. Similarly, if the economy moves in the other direction (say, from point *D*), increasing opportunity costs occur because giving up equal amounts of good X (e.g., x_3x_4, then x_2x_3, then x_1x_2) yields smaller increments of good Y (y_1y_2, then y_2y_3, then y_3y_4). With increasing opportunity costs, the shape of the PPF is thus concave to the origin or bowed out, as in Figure 11.

The formal name for the (negative of the) slope of the PPF is the **marginal rate of transformation** (MRT), which reflects the change in Y (ΔY) associated with a change in X (ΔX). Because the slope itself ($\Delta Y/\Delta X$) is negative, the negative of the slope or $-\Delta Y/\Delta X$ is a positive number (the MRT). It can be shown mathematically [which we will not do here, thankfully for you (?)] that MRT $= MC_X/MC_Y$, or the ratio of the marginal costs in the two industries. Because firms incur rising marginal costs when they expand output, movement toward more X production means that MC_X will rise; similarly, as *less* Y production is undertaken, MC_Y will *fall*. As more X and less Y production is undertaken, the ratio MC_X/MC_Y will rise. In other words, the PPF gets steeper as we produce relatively more X.

There are several other ways to explain the concave shape of the PPF. The earliest explanation (given by Gottfried Haberler in 1936) involved "specific factors" of production. Suppose we move from point D to point C in Figure 11. In Haberler's view, the factors of production in the X industry that will move into Y production are the more mobile and adaptable factors. Their adaptability enables them to contribute a good deal to Y output. As we continue to shift resources from X to Y (e.g., from C to B), however, the factors being shifted are less adaptable. They contribute less to Y production than the previous factors. It is evident that the additional output of Y attained for given reductions in X output is declining. Thus, increasing opportunity costs are occurring. Another way to explain the shape of the PPF has been offered by Paul Samuelson (1949, pp. 183–87). Suppose that each industry is characterized by constant returns to scale suppose, too, that the industries have different factor intensities: the X industry is relatively labor intensive and the Y industry is relatively capital intensive. Then, in Figure 12, assume that all factors (only capital and labor in this discussion) are devoted to Y production, so that the economy is located at point R and is producing $0y_1$ of good Y and none of good X. Now assume that one-half of the economy's labor and capital are removed from Y production and devoted to X production. Where would the economy then be situated? With constant returns to scale, Y production will be cut in half because one-half the factors have been removed, and X production will reach one-half of its maximum amount. Thus, the economy will be located at point M, where $0x_1/2$ and $0y_1/2$ are being produced. If various proportions of the factors were switched in this fashion, the straight line RMQ would be traced.

However, as Samuelson has indicated, this switching of factors in proportionate fashion from one industry to the other does not make economic sense (the technical term for this is "dumb"). Because X is the labor-intensive industry and Y is the capital-intensive industry, it

FIGURE 12   An Increasing-Opportunity-Cost PPF with Constant Returns to Scale

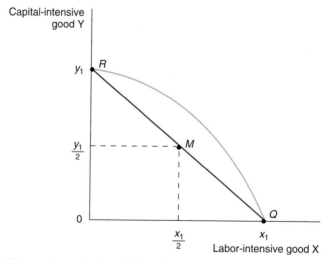

If all capital and all labor are devoted to the production of capital-intensive good Y, production in the economy occurs at point R. With constant returns to scale, allocation of one-half of each factor to X production and one-half of each factor to Y production yields production point M, where one-half the maximum output of each good is produced. Other proportionate allocations of the factors would trace the straight line RMQ. However, if relatively more of the labor supply is allocated to production of labor-intensive good X and relatively more of the capital stock is allocated to capital-intensive good Y, the economy can produce on the concave line connecting R and Q. That is, it can produce combinations of output that are superior to those on straight line RMQ.

makes more sense to switch *relatively more labor* from Y to X and *relatively less capital.* The industries will then be using factors in greater correspondence with their optimum requirements than in the equiproportional switching strategy, and the economy can do better than straight line *RMQ.* Thus, the PPF will be *outside RMQ* except at endpoints *R* and *Q,* and the concave line connecting *R* and *Q* is the PPF, which clearly has increasing opportunity costs.

Finally, a useful way to look at the PPF and its slope is to examine the relationship between the PPF and the Edgeworth box diagram, since the Edgeworth box diagram is the analytical source of the PPF. To demonstrate this point, consider Figure 13. The

FIGURE 13   The Edgeworth Box and the Production-Possibilities Frontier

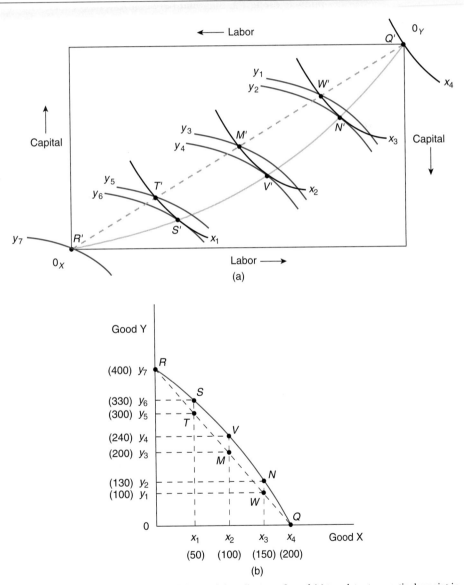

As discussed in the text, any point in the Edgeworth box diagram of panel (a) translates to a particular point in the production-possibilities diagram in panel (b). If production moves along the diagonal $R'T'M'W'Q'$ in panel (a), these output combinations follow straight line *RTMWQ* in panel (b). Points on the production efficiency locus $R'S'V'N'Q'$ in panel (a) translate to the production-possibilities frontier *RSVNQ* in panel (b).

Edgeworth box in panel (a) has the properties discussed earlier, while panel (b) shows an increasing-cost PPF.

In the Edgeworth box, suppose that production is taking place at the X industry origin, also labeled as point R'. At this point, maximum Y production and *zero* X production are occurring. We can thus transfer this point R' onto Figure 13(b) as point R, with $0y_7$ of good Y and none of good X being produced. Similarly, point Q' in the box (with maximum X production and zero Y production) translates in Figure 13(b) as point Q, with $0x_4$ of good X and none of good Y being produced. To facilitate the discussion, we have placed illustrative output numbers on the axes of the PPF diagram in Figure 13(b).

What about points where some production of both goods occurs? Keeping in mind the assumption of constant returns to scale, move along the diagonal of the box. If M' is midway along the diagonal between R' and Q', then one-half of the economy's capital and one-half of the economy's labor is devoted to each industry. Thus, isoquant x_2 is one-half the output level of isoquant x_4, and isoquant y_3 is one-half the output level of isoquant y_7. Point M' in the Edgeworth box is then plotted as point M in Figure 13(b). Further, suppose that point T' in the box involves one-quarter of the economy's labor and capital being used in the X industry and three-quarters in the Y industry. Point T' will then be plotted as point T in panel (b), where $0x_1$ is one-quarter of $0x_4$ and $0y_5$ is three-quarters of $0y_7$. A similar analysis yields point W in panel (b) if point W' in the box in panel (a) represents employment of three-quarters of the economy's labor and capital in the X industry and one-quarter of the economy's labor and capital in the Y industry. Hence, the dashed line $RTMWQ$ in panel (b) represents the plotting of the diagonal $R'T'M'W'Q'$ in panel (a). Clearly, *any* point in the Edgeworth box—not only those on the diagonal—has a corresponding point in panel (b).

However, the PPF indicates the *best* that the economy can do in terms of production of the two goods. Does $RTMWQ$ in panel (b) represent *maximum* production points? Certainly not. As you recall, maximum production points in the Edgeworth box were located on the production efficiency locus. Hence, plotting these *production efficiency points* in panel (b) will generate the PPF; any point on the efficiency locus will be on the PPF, and any point on the PPF must necessarily have been derived from a point on the production efficiency locus.

To demonstrate that points on the efficiency locus are maximum production points, consider points T', M', and W' on the Edgeworth diagonal in Figure 13(a) and their analogues T, M, and W in Figure 13(b). Point T' is associated with $0x_1$ of good X (50X) and $0y_5$ of good Y (300Y). However, the isoquants indicate that we can get *more* Y output by moving to isoquant y_6 and still *maintain the same amount of X output*. Thus, we can move to point S' in the box to get the *most* Y output compatible with $0x_1$ of X output. Point S' translates into point S on the PPF (50X, 330Y). An identical procedure can be done with points M' and V' in the box, as well as with points W' and N'. Hence, the maximum production points on the efficiency locus in Figure 13(a) are all represented in Figure 13(b) as points on the PPF, which shows maximum production combinations for the economy.[4]

Finally, remember that on the production efficiency locus, increases in output of one good require that output of the other good be decreased. This same property is also

---

[4]Note that if the production efficiency locus is the diagonal, then the accompanying production-possibilities frontier will exhibit constant opportunity costs; that is, it will be a straight line. When this happens, both goods have the same capital/labor ratio throughout the production range, meaning that the two industries cannot be distinguished by relative factor intensity.

applicable to the PPF due to its construction from the efficiency locus. On the PPF, increases in the output of one good *must* involve decreases in the output of the other. This is not true, however, for points inside the PPF (i.e., off the production efficiency locus). *On* the PPF, all resources are fully employed and are utilized in their most efficient manner given the technology reflected in the isoquants. In addition, the shape and position of the PPF will also reflect the endowments of labor and capital in the economy.

| CONCEPT CHECK | 1. Why do points on the production efficiency locus in the Edgeworth box diagram show "production efficiency" in the economy?
 2. If a production combination in a country's production-possibilities diagram is *inside* the | production-possibilities frontier, can the country be producing on its production efficiency locus in the Edgeworth box diagram? Why or why not? |

SUMMARY

This chapter has reviewed and developed basic tools of microeconomic analysis that will be used in international trade theory in later chapters. In micro theory, individual consumers are interested in maximizing satisfaction subject to their budget constraints, and the indifference curve-budget line analysis sets forth the principles involved in this maximization. Individual firms are interested in the most efficient use of production inputs (i.e., in obtaining the maximum output for a given cost),

and the isoquant-isocost analysis provides basic principles for realizing this efficient production. Finally, examination of economic efficiency from the standpoint of the economy as a whole was undertaken through development of the Edgeworth box diagram and the production-possibilities frontier. All the analytical material of this chapter will be employed in our presentation of international trade theory. The next chapter begins this application of the tools.

KEY TERMS

budget constraint
   (or budget line)
cardinal utility
community indifference curve (or
   country indifference curve)
constant returns to scale
consumer equilibrium
consumer indifference curve

decreasing returns to scale
diminishing marginal rate of
   substitution
Edgeworth box diagram
increasing opportunity costs
increasing returns to scale
isocost line
isoquant

marginal rate of technical
   substitution
marginal rate of transformation
ordinal utility
Pareto efficiency
producer equilibrium
production efficiency locus
transitivity

QUESTIONS AND PROBLEMS

1. Suppose that, from an initial consumer equilibrium position, the price of one good falls while the price of the other good remains the same. Using indifference curve analysis, explain how and why the consumer's *relative* consumption of the two goods will change.

2. Explain why a change in the distribution of income in a country can change the shapes of the community indifference curves for the country.

3. If the MPP_L/MPP_K in the production of a good is less than w/r, why is the producer not in producer equilibrium? Explain how, with no change in budget size for the firm and with the given factor price ratio, output of the firm can be increased.

4. Suppose that, from an initial producer equilibrium position, the rental rate of capital rises and the wage rate of labor falls. Can it be determined unambiguously whether the quantity of output of the firm will rise or fall as a result of this change in relative factor prices? Why or why not?

5. Suppose that a firm has a budget of $30,000, that the wage rate is $10 per hour, and that the rental rate of capital is $100 per hour. If the wage rate increases to $15 per hour and the rental rate of capital rises to $120 per hour, what happens to the producer budget or isocost line? What will happen to the equilibrium level of output because of this change in factor prices? What will happen to the *relative* usage of labor and capital because of the change in factor prices? Explain.

6. If the production efficiency locus in the Edgeworth box diagram were the diagonal of the box, what would be the shape of the production-possibilities frontier, assuming constant returns to scale in both industries?

7. Evaluate the statement: If a country's production-possibilities frontier demonstrates increasing opportunity costs, this means that each of the industries within the country must be operating in a context of decreasing returns to scale.

8. In Figure 13, as one moves from S' to V', is the country producing more or less of the capital-intensive good and less or more of the labor-intensive good? What should happen to the demand for labor and the demand for capital as this movement takes place? What will happen to relative factor prices? Will the slope of the isoquants at the point of tangency on the contract curve be the same at V' as it was at S'? Why or why not?

9. Suppose that the country experiences an increase in its capital stock. How would the Edgeworth box change? How would the production-possibilities frontier change as a result? Could the country now obtain more of both goods than before the increase in capital stock or more of only the capital-intensive good? Explain.

10. Suppose that the price or rental rate of capital rises. Explain how producers would respond, using the isocost/isoquant framework. What would happen to the capital/labor ratio in production?

GAINS FROM TRADE IN NEOCLASSICAL THEORY

LEARNING OBJECTIVES

- ■ To understand economic equilibrium in a country that has no trade.

- ■ To grasp the welfare-enhancing impact of opening a country to international trade.

- ■ To realize that either supply differences or demand differences between countries are sufficient to generate a basis for trade.

- ■ To appreciate the implications of key assumptions in the neoclassical trade model.

INTRODUCTION

The Effects of Restrictions on U.S. Trade

In 1999, economist Howard J. Wall of the Federal Reserve Bank of St. Louis investigated the extent to which trade barriers restricted U.S. trade and the size of the welfare costs of U.S. interferences with free trade.[1] He focused his attention on U.S. trade with countries other than Mexico and Canada since the United States had been removing barriers to trade with those countries due to the start of the North American Free Trade Agreement (NAFTA) in 1994. Wall indicated that the United States imported $723.2 billion of goods from non-NAFTA countries in 1996, but it would have had imports that were $111.6 billion greater than that if there had been no U.S. import restrictions. Hence, U.S. imports would have been 15.4 percent larger ($111.6 billion ÷ $723.2 billion = 15.4%) but for the restrictions. He also calculated that U.S. exports to non-NAFTA countries, which were $498.8 billion in 1996, would have been $130.4 billion or more than 26 percent larger ($130.4 billion ÷ $498.8 billion = 26.1%) if foreign countries had not had barriers to U.S. exports. Hence, interferences with free trade substantially reduce the amount of U.S. trade. Wall then calculated that the reduction in U.S. imports imposed a welfare cost on the United States of $97.3 billion in 1996, equivalent to 1.4 percent of U.S. gross domestic product at the time. Although he was unable to estimate the welfare cost of the restrictions on U.S. exports, it is nevertheless clear that sizable welfare losses in general can occur because of interferences with free trade.

In this chapter we use the microeconomic tools developed in Chapter 5 to present the basic case for participating in trade and thus for avoiding these welfare costs of trade restrictions. This case is essentially an updating of the Ricardian analysis to include increasing opportunity costs, factors of production besides labor, and explicit demand considerations. We first describe the autarky position of any given country in the neoclassical theoretical framework, then explain why it is advantageous for the country to move from autarky to trade, and finally discuss qualifications that can be made to the analysis. Comprehending the nature of the gains from trade in this more general framework not only will facilitate your grasp of material in later chapters but also should provide an intuitive understanding of the welfare costs that result from the imposition of trade restrictions.

AUTARKY EQUILIBRIUM

To the economist, *autarky* means total absence of participation in international trade. In this situation—as well as one with trade—the economy is assumed to be seeking to maximize its well-being through the behavior of its economic agents. Crucial assumptions made throughout this chapter include the following: (1) Consumers seek to maximize satisfaction, (2) suppliers of factor services and firms seek to maximize their return from productive activity, (3) there is mobility of factors within the country but not internationally, (4) there are no transportation costs or policy barriers to trade, and (5) perfect competition exists.

In autarky, as in trade, production takes place on the production-possibilities frontier (PPF). The particular point at which producers operate on the PPF is chosen by considering their costs of inputs relative to the prices of goods they could produce. Producer equilibrium on the PPF is illustrated in Figure 1. The equilibrium is at point *E*, where the PPF is tangent to the price line for the two goods.

---

[1]Howard J. Wall, "Using the Gravity Model to Estimate the Costs of Protection," Federal Reserve Bank of St. Louis *Review*, January/February 1999, pp. 33–40.

FIGURE 1   Producer Equilibrium in Autarky

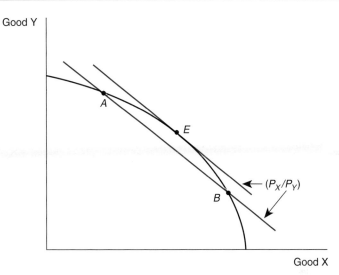

Production equilibrium in autarky is at point E, where the domestic price line is tangent to the PPF. At point E, $P_X/P_Y = MC_X/MC_Y$ and there is thus no incentive for producers to alter production. At point A, however, P_X/P_Y $< MC_X/MC_Y$, and at point B, $P_X/P_Y < MC_X/MC_Y$, indicating that greater profits can be obtained in both instances by moving to point E.

Why is point E the equilibrium point? You will remember from Chapter 5 that the (negative of the) slope of the budget line or relative price line for goods X and Y is P_X/P_Y. It was also pointed out that the (negative of the) slope of the PPF is the marginal rate of transformation (MRT) of the goods, which in turn is equal to the ratio of the marginal costs of production in the two industries, MC_X/MC_Y. Thus, in production equilibrium on the PPF, $P_X/P_Y = \text{MRT} = MC_X/MC_Y$. Alternatively, $(P_X/MC_X) = (P_Y/MC_Y)$, which indicates that, at point E, producers have no incentive to change production because the price received in the market for each good relative to the marginal cost of producing that good is the same. Only if these price/cost ratios were different would there be an incentive to switch production. (Remember also that with perfect competition, price equals marginal cost in equilibrium.)

Suppose that the economy is not at point E, but at point A (again, see Figure 1). Would this be an equilibrium point for the economy? Clearly not. At point A, because the given price line is steeper than the PPF, $(P_X/P_Y) > (MC_X/MC_Y)$ or, restating, $(P_X/MC_X) > (P_Y/MC_Y)$. Hence, point A cannot be an equilibrium production position for the economy because the price of good X relative to its marginal cost exceeds the price of good Y relative to its marginal cost. Producers have an incentive to produce *more X* and *less Y* because X production is relatively more profitable at the margin than Y production. As resources consequently move from Y to X, the economy slides down the PPF toward point E, and it will continue to move toward more X production and less Y production until point E is attained. As the movement from A to E takes place, the expanded X production raises MC_X and the reduced Y production lowers MC_Y. Therefore, the ratio (P_X/MC_X) is falling and the ratio (P_Y/MC_Y) is rising; because (P_X/MC_X) was originally greater than (P_Y/MC_Y)—at point A—this means that the two ratios are converging toward each other. They will continue to converge until point E is reached, where $(P_X/MC_X) = (P_Y/MC_Y)$. Movement to E would also occur from point B, where $P_X/P_Y < MC_X/MC_Y$.

FIGURE 2   General Equilibrium in Autarky

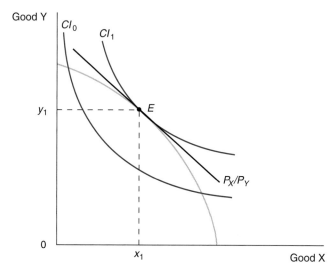

The autarky equilibrium for a country, taking account of both supply and demand, is at point E. At that point, the country is on the highest community indifference curve possible, given production constraints described by the PPF. Neither producers nor consumers can improve their situation, because, at point E, $MU_X/MU_Y = P_X/P_Y = MC_X/MC_Y$.

Next, consumers are brought into the picture and the economy is portrayed in autarky equilibrium at point E in Figure 2. The attainment of this point is the result of the country attempting to reach its highest possible level of well-being, given the production constraint of the PPF. Note that the resulting price line is tangent not only to the PPF but also to the (community) indifference curve CI_1. The tangency between an indifference curve and the price line reflects the fact that the relative price ratio (P_X/P_Y) is equal to the ratio of marginal utilities (MU_X/MU_Y), which in turn is defined as the marginal rate of substitution (MRS). Thus, in *autarky equilibrium* for the economy as a whole,

$$\text{MRT} = MC_X/MC_Y = P_X/P_Y = MU_X/MU_Y = \text{MRS}$$

With equilibrium at point E and given prices (P_X/P_Y), production of good X is $0x_1$ and production of good Y is $0y_1$. Note that equilibrium consumption under autarky is *also* $0x_1$ of good X and $0y_1$ of good Y. Without trade, production of each good in a country must equal the consumption of that good because none of the good is exported or imported. If the good were exported, then home production of the good would exceed home consumption because some of the production is being sent out of the country. If the good were imported, then home consumption would exceed home production because some of the consumption demand is met from production in other countries.

INTRODUCTION OF INTERNATIONAL TRADE

Suppose international trade opportunities are introduced into this autarkic situation. The most important feature to keep in mind is that the opening of a country to international trade means *exposing the country to a new set of relative prices.* When these different prices are available, the home country's producers and consumers will adjust to them by reallocating their production and consumption patterns. This reallocation leads to gains

FIGURE 3   Single (Home) Country Gains from Trade

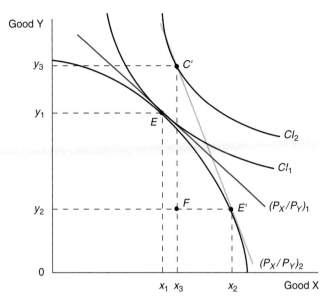

In autarky, the home country is in equilibrium at point E. With the opening of trade, it now faces the international terms of trade, $(P_X/P_Y)_2$. Given the relatively higher international price of the X good, production moves to E', the point of tangency between the international terms of trade and the PPF. At the same time, the Y good is relatively less expensive at international prices, so consumers increase their relative consumption of it and begin consuming at point C', where the terms of trade are tangent to the highest community indifference curve possible. C' lies outside the PPF and is obtained by exporting the amount $x_3 x_2$ of the X good and exchanging it for $y_2 y_3$ imports of the Y good. The country is clearly better off because trade permits it to consume on the higher indifference curve CI_2.

from trade. *The ultimate source of gain from international trade is the difference in relative prices in autarky between countries.*

The reallocation of production and consumption and the gains from trade are illustrated in Figure 3. (This figure will be used extensively in this book, so it is important to understand it now.) Under autarky the optimal point for the economy is at E, producing and consuming $0x_1$ of the X good and $0y_1$ of the Y good. The welfare level is indicated by indifference curve CI_1, and prices in autarky are $(P_X/P_Y)_1$. Suppose that the country now faces international prices of $(P_X/P_Y)_2$. This new set of prices is steeper than the prices in autarky, reflecting the assumption that relative prices in the home market are lower for X and higher for Y than in the international market. Thus, the home country has a *comparative advantage in good X* and a *comparative disadvantage in good Y*. The difference between relative prices in the home country and the set of international prices indicates that the home country is relatively more efficient in producing X and relatively less efficient in producing Y.

With producers now facing a relatively higher price of X in the world market than in autarky, they will want to shift production toward X and away from Y because they anticipate greater profitability in X production. Thus, production will move from point E to point E'. The stimulus for increasing X production and decreasing Y production is that the new relative price ratio $(P_X/P_Y)_2$ exceeds the ratio MC_X/MC_Y at E and will continue to exceed MC_X/MC_Y until equality between relative prices and relative marginal costs is restored at point E'. At E', production of good X has risen from $0x_1$ to $0x_2$, and production of good Y has fallen from $0y_1$ to $0y_2$.

Thus, production in the home country will move to point E'. What about the country's consumption? In tracing consumption geometrically, the key point is that the relative price line tangent to E' is also the country's **trading line,** or consumption-possibilities frontier. With production at E', the country can exchange units of good X for units of good Y at the new prevailing prices, $(P_X/P_Y)_2$. Thus, the country can settle anywhere on this line by exchanging some of its X production for good Y in the world market. Consumer theory tells us that consumers will choose a consumption point where an indifference curve is tangent to the relevant price line. *With trade,* this point is C' in Figure 3. The well-being of the country's consumers is maximized at C', and the consumption quantities are $0x_3$ of good X and $0y_3$ of good Y. Thus, with trade and the new relative prices, production and consumption adjust until MRT $= MC_X/MC_Y = (P_X/P_Y)_2 = MU_X/MU_Y =$ MRS.

Note that point C' is beyond the PPF. Like the Classical model discussed in Chapter 3, international trade permits consumers to consume a bundle that lies beyond the production capabilities of their own country. Without trade, consumption possibilities were confined to the PPF, and the PPF was also the CPF (consumption-possibilities frontier). With trade, the CPF differs from the PPF and permits consumption combinations that simply cannot be reached by domestic production alone. The CPF is represented by the given international price line, since the home country could choose to settle at any point along this line. Access to the new CPF can benefit the country because consumption possibilities can be attained that previously were not possible. The gains from trade in Figure 3 are reflected in the fact that the new CPF allows the country to reach a higher community indifference curve, CI_2.

Trade has thus enabled the country to attain a higher level of welfare than was possible under autarky. The trade itself also is evident in Figure 3. Because production of good X is $0x_2$ and consumption of good X is $0x_3$, the difference between these two quantities—x_3x_2—represents the *exports* of good X by this country. Similarly, because $0y_2$ is production of good Y and $0y_3$ is consumption of good Y, the difference between these two quantities—y_2y_3—measures the *imports* of good Y by the country. Further, the trade pattern is summarized conveniently in **trade triangle** $FC'E'$. This triangle for the home country has the following economic interpretation: (a) The base of this right triangle (distance FE') represents the exports of the country, since $FE' = x_3x_2$; (b) the height or vertical side of the triangle (distance FC') represents the imports of the country, since $FC' = y_2y_3$; and (c) the hypotenuse $C'E'$ of the triangle represents the trading line, and (the negative of) its slope indicates the world price ratio or terms of trade.

The Consumption and Production Gains from Trade

As discussed, the home country has gained from trade. Economists sometimes divide the total gains from trade into two conceptually distinct parts—the **consumption gain** (or **gains from exchange**) and the **production gain** (or **gains from specialization**).

The consumption gain from trade refers to the fact that the exposure to new relative prices, *even without changes in production,* enhances the welfare of the country. This gain can be seen in Figure 4, where points E, E', and C' are analogous to E, E', and C' in Figure 3, as are the autarky prices $(P_X/P_Y)_1$ and the trading prices $(P_X/P_Y)_2$. When the country has no international trade, it is located at point E. Now suppose that the country is introduced to the trading prices $(P_X/P_Y)_2$ but that, for the moment, production does not change from point E. A line representing the new price ratio is then drawn through point E; production remains at E, and the new, steep price line with slope $(P_X/P_Y)_2$ is the trading line. With this trading line, consumers can do better than at point E, so they move to a tangency between the new prices and an indifference curve. If consumers remained at E, the price of good X divided by the price of good Y would be greater than the marginal utility of good X divided by the marginal utility of good Y. In

FIGURE 4   Gains from Exchange and Specialization with Trade

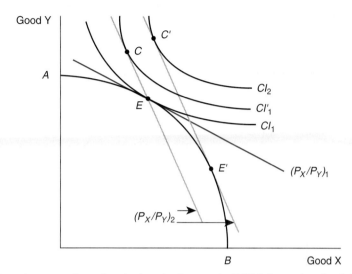

In autarky, domestic consumption and production take place at point E. With the opening of trade but without any change in domestic production, consumers can consume along the international terms-of-trade line, $(P_X/P_Y)_2$, passing through point E. Because the relative price of good Y is lower internationally, consumers will begin to consume more Y and less X, choosing point C. The increase in well-being represented by the difference between CI_1 and CI'_1 is referred to as the consumption gain or "gains from exchange." Given enough time to adjust production, domestic producers will begin producing more of the relatively more valuable good X and less of good Y, maximizing profits at point E'. The increase in welfare brought about through the specialization in good X allows consumers to reach CI_2 and C'. The increase in well-being represented by the movement from C to C' (CI'_1 to CI_2) is referred to as the production gain or "gains from specialization."

other words, the marginal utility of good Y per dollar spent on Y would exceed the marginal utility of good X per dollar spent on X. The consumers would hence change their consumption bundle toward consuming more of good Y and less of good X. Maximizing welfare with this production constraint thus places consumers at point C. Because point C is on a community indifference curve (CI'_1) that is higher than the community indifference curve (CI_1) in autarky, the country has gained from trade even though production has not changed. The gain reflects the fact that, with new prices, consumers are switching to greater consumption of import good Y, now priced lower, and away from export good X, now priced higher. Thus, even if a country has an absolutely rigid production structure where no factors of production could move between industries, there are still gains from trade.

A further welfare gain occurs because production changes rather than remains fixed at E in Figure 4. With the new relative prices, there is an incentive to produce more of good X and less of good Y since X is now relatively more profitable to produce than is Y, and the production switch from E to E' is in accordance with comparative advantage. Moving production toward the comparative-advantage good thus increases welfare, permitting consumers to move from point C to point C'. In sum, the **total gains from trade** attained by moving from point E to point C' (and correspondingly from CI_1 to CI_2) can be divided conceptually into two parts: (1) the consumption gain, involving movement from point E to point C (and correspondingly from CI_1 to CI'_1); and (2) the production gain, involving movement from point C to point C' (and correspondingly from CI'_1 to CI_2).

FIGURE 5   Partner Country Gains from Trade

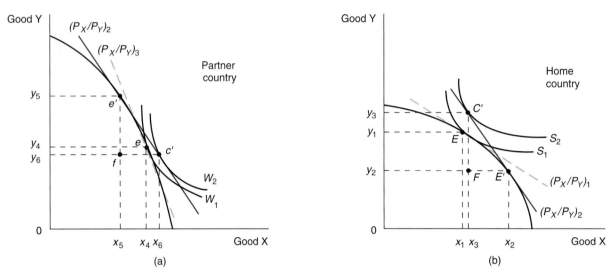

As indicated in panel (a), in autarky the partner country produces and consumes at point e. With trade it now faces the international price ratio $(P_X/P_Y)_2$, which is flatter than its internal relative prices in autarky. Consequently, production of the relatively more expensive good Y expands and production of good X contracts, until further adjustment is no longer profitable at point e'. Consumers now find good X relatively less expensive and adjust their consumption expenditures by moving from point e to point c'. The opening of trade allows the country to consume outside the PPF on the higher indifference curve W_2, thus demonstrating the gains from trade (the difference between W_1 and W_2). Note that, with trade, both countries face the same set of relative product prices, $(P_X/P_Y)_2$.

Trade in the Partner Country

If we assume a two-country world, the analysis for the trading partner is analogous to that employed for the home country, although the trade pattern is reversed. Figure 5(a) is the basic graph. The discussion of it can be brief because no new principles are involved. For purposes of contrast, panel (b) illustrates the home country situation discussed earlier.

In Figure 5(a), the trading partner's equilibrium in autarky is at point e, where the country faces autarky prices $(P_X/P_Y)_3$. The partner is producing quantity $0x_4$ of good X and quantity $0y_4$ of good Y, and the welfare level for the country is indicated by indifference curve W_1. With international trade, international relative prices $(P_X/P_Y)_2$ will be *less* than autarky prices $(P_X/P_Y)_3$. (The exact determination of trading prices will be explored in considerably more detail in Chapter 7.) Thus, this partner country has a comparative advantage in good Y and a comparative disadvantage in good X.

Because of the new relative prices available through international trade, producers in the partner country have an incentive to produce more of good Y and less of the X good. The production point moves from e to e', where there is a tangency of the PPF with $(P_X/P_Y)_2$ and where production of good X is $0x_5$ and production of good Y is $0y_5$. From point e', the country can move along the trading line until consumers are in equilibrium, represented by a point of tangency of the price line $(P_X/P_Y)_2$ to an indifference curve. The consumption equilibrium is point c' with trade, and consumption is $0x_6$ of good X and $0y_6$ of good Y.

As in the case of the home country, the difference between production and consumption of any good reflects the volume and pattern of trade. Because production of good X is $0x_5$ and consumption of good X is $0x_6$, the country *imports* x_5x_6 of good X. Because production of good Y is $0y_5$ and consumption of good Y is $0y_6$, the country thus *exports* y_6y_5 of good Y. Trade triangle *fe′ c′* represents the same phenomenon as earlier, but in this case horizontal side *fc′* indicates imports and vertical side *fe′* represents exports. Note that in a two country world, the partner country trade triangle *fe′ c′* is congruent to home country trade triangle *FC′ E′*. This must be so because, by definition, the exports of the home country are the imports of the partner country, and the imports of the home country are the exports of the partner country. In addition, the trading prices $(P_X/P_Y)_2$ are the same for each country.

It is obvious that the partner country also gains from trade. With trade, the country's consumers are able to reach indifference curve W_2, whereas in autarky the consumers could reach only lower indifference curve W_1. The "gains from trade" for this country could also be split into the "production gain" and the "consumption gain" as was done for the home country, but this is an exercise left for the reader.

CONCEPT CHECK

1. What is necessary for a country to gain from trade in neoclassical theory? How does one know if a country has gained from trade?
2. Explain the difference between the "gains from exchange" (consumption gain), the "gains from specialization" (production gain), and the "total gains from trade."
3. What is meant by the trade triangle? Why must the trade triangles of the partner and the home country be congruent in a two-country analysis?
4. Within what range must the international terms of trade lie?

MINIMUM CONDITIONS FOR TRADE

The discussion in the previous section demonstrated that there is a basis for trade whenever the relative prices of goods in autarky of the two potential trading partners are different. It is important to address briefly conditions under which this could come about. If the generation of relative price differences in autarky seems highly unlikely, then the total potential gains from trade would be limited and trade theory largely irrelevant. On the other hand, if there seems to be a considerably broad set of circumstances that could generate relative price differences, there would be a strong underlying basis for believing that potential gains from trade are present.

Theoretically, there are two principal sources of relative price variation between two countries: differences in supply conditions and differences in demand conditions. To establish *minimum* conditions for generating relative price differences in autarky, we look first at the role of demand, assuming identical production conditions. Second, we address the role of supply under identical demand conditions.

Trade between Countries with Identical PPFs

This case could not possibly have been handled in the Classical analysis. In Ricardian analysis, if the production conditions were the same for the trading partners in all commodities (i.e., identical PPFs), then the pretrade price ratios in the two countries would be the same; there would be no incentive for trade and of course no gains from trade.

According to neoclassical theory, two countries with identical production conditions *can* benefit from trade. Different demand conditions in the two countries and the presence of increasing opportunity costs are the two principal conditions. The latter condition—increasing opportunity costs—plays the more important role, but the recognition of how different demand conditions influence trade is also necessary to update the Classical analysis.

FIGURE 6   The Basis for Trade between Two Countries with Identical PPFs and
Different Demand Conditions

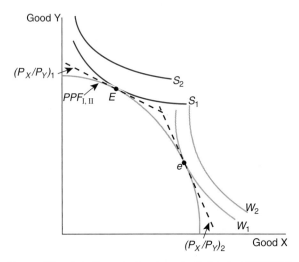

With identical production conditions in both country I and country II, the same PPF (*PPF*$_{I, II}$) exists for both. If demand conditions differ between the two countries, then their respective community indifference maps are different. If this is the case, points of tangency between the two different community indifference curves and the common PPF will occur at different points on the PPF (i.e., *E* and *e*) and hence reflect different sets of relative prices in autarky. There is thus a basis for trade.

Figure 6 illustrates this special case. The two countries have identical production conditions, so we need to draw only one PPF because it can represent either country. The different tastes in the two countries are shown by different indifference maps. Suppose that country I has a relatively strong preference for good Y; this preference is indicated by curves S_1 and S_2, which are positioned close to the Y axis. On the other hand, country II has a relative preference for the X good, so its curves W_1 and W_2 are positioned close to the X axis. The autarky equilibrium points are point *E* for country I and point *e* for country II. Given these autarky positions, it is evident that the autarky price ratio in country I is $(P_X/P_Y)_1$ and that the autarky price ratio in country II is $(P_X/P_Y)_2$.

Because $(P_X/P_Y)_1$ is less than $(P_X/P_Y)_2$, country I has the comparative advantage in good X, and country II has the comparative advantage in good Y. The price ratios show that the preference for good Y in country I has bid up P_Y relative to P_X and that the preference for good X in country II has bid up P_X relative to P_Y. With the opening of trade between the two countries, country I will export X and expand the production of X in order to do so and it will decrease production of good Y as good Y is now imported. Similarly, country II will have an incentive to expand production of and to export good Y and an incentive to contract production of and to import good X. The countries will trade at a price ratio (not shown) somewhere between the autarky price ratios, a price ratio that is tangent to the identical PPFs at a point between *E* and *e*. Both countries will be able to attain higher indifference curves. The common sense of the mutual gain from trade is that each country is now able to consume more of the good for which it has the greater relative preference. Thus, trade between identical economies with different demand patterns can be a source of gain and can be interpreted easily by neoclassical trade theory, while the Classical model cannot explain why trade would take place

FIGURE 7   The Basis for Trade between Two Countries with Identical Demands and Different Production Structures

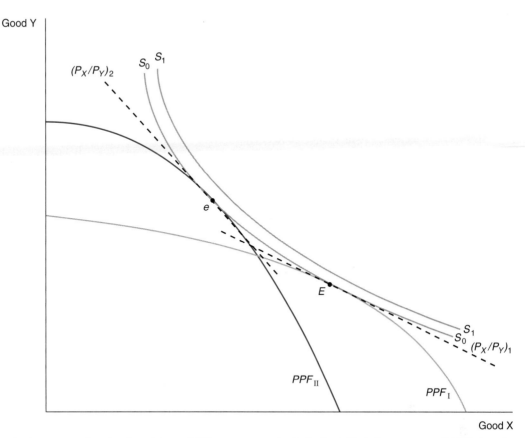

Different production structures based on the existence of different country technologies (but with similar resource availabilities) are demonstrated in the two differently shaped PPFs. Country I has a technical advantage in the production of good X and country II has a technical advantage in production of good Y. Given identical demand structures (i.e., a common community indifference map), the tangencies between the PPFs and the highest indifference curve will occur at different points E and e. Because the slopes at those points are different, the relative prices in autarky are different. With international terms of trade somewhere between the two sets of autarky prices, both countries can gain by trading.

since, with identical constant-opportunity-cost PPFs, relative prices in the two countries would not differ.

Trade between Countries with Identical Demand Conditions

We now turn to the situation in which two countries have the same demand conditions but different production conditions. Production conditions may differ because different technologies are employed in two countries with the same relative amounts of the two factors, capital and labor, because similar technologies exist in both countries but the relative availability of factors differs, or because the two countries have a combination of different technologies and different relative factor availabilities.

Let us assume for the present discussion that production conditions differ between the two countries because the technologies are different. Each country is employing a different technology, so there will be different production possibilities and different PPFs (see Figure 7). Assuming that the relative amounts of factors are similar between the two countries, PPF_I demonstrates a technology that is relatively more efficient in the production of good X, and PPF_{II} a technology that is relatively more efficient in the production of good Y.

With demand conditions assumed to be identical in both countries, an identical community indifference map can be used to represent tastes and preferences. The existence of different production conditions is sufficient to produce different domestic price ratios in autarky, even in the presence of identical demand conditions. Country I, which is relatively more efficient in producing good X, will find itself producing and consuming relatively more of this product in autarky, for example, at point E. Similarly, country II, which has the technological advantage in good Y, will find itself producing and consuming more of good Y in equilibrium (point e). As relative prices are different in autarky, there is a basis for trade because $(P_X/P_Y)_I < (P_X/P_Y)_{II}$. Country I will export good X and import good Y at terms of trade (not shown) that are between the two autarky price ratios, and it will increase production of good X and decrease production of good Y. Country II will do the reverse— it will expand production of and export good Y and will contract production of and import good X. Each country can then attain a higher indifference curve. We conclude that a second possible minimal condition for gains from international trade is a difference in supply conditions, even with identical demand in the two countries.

Conclusions

We have seen that relative prices in autarky reflect underlying supply and demand conditions, thus depending jointly on the relative amounts and quality of available resources, the characteristics of the production technologies employed, and the nature of demand in a country. Different relative prices can therefore exist between countries as long as *one or more* of these factors are different. Such a minimal condition suggests that the likelihood of a basis for trade between the many countries of the world is great. It also makes it clear that the underlying basis for trade can change as technology changes, as factors grow within countries, as factors move between countries, and as individual country demand patterns change in response to economic development and/or the increased exposure to different products and cultures.

SOME IMPORTANT ASSUMPTIONS IN THE ANALYSIS

This section briefly discusses three important assumptions used in the previous analysis that may need to be taken into account when examining the "real world." The intent is to introduce an element of caution rather than doubt concerning neoclassical theory. Indeed, few principles are so universally accepted by economists as comparative advantage and the gains from international trade.

Costless Factor Mobility

One important assumption is that factors of production can shift readily and without cost along the PPF as relative prices change and trade opportunities present themselves. In practice, however, it may not be possible to adjust immediately to the changed relative prices. Movement from the autarky production point to the trade production point may first involve a movement *inside* the PPF as workers and equipment are no longer used in the import-competing industry but have yet to be fully absorbed in the export industry. Perhaps labor must be retrained, factors must be moved from one section of the country to another, or depreciation allowances for plant and equipment must accumulate before capital can be reinvested elsewhere. Only after time passes will the export industry be able to employ the unused factors and move the economy to the PPF. These kinds of mobility problems are assumed away in the theory presented earlier.

When factor movement does occur slowly or experiences an adjustment cost so that the production point does not slide easily along the PPF but moves inside it, many economists argue that some type of government assistance is required. Many countries have set up such assistance programs. For example, beginning in 1962 and continuing to the present, the United States has had a program of **trade adjustment assistance** in place (although the nature and funding of the program have varied over the years) to help in the transition following tariff reductions through trade negotiations. (The program of such assistance in the United States is discussed further in Chapter 16, "Political Economy and U.S. Trade Policy.")

Full Employment of Factors of Production

This assumption is related to the problem of adjustment, but it merits separate treatment because of its application to a more general context. The assumption that all of a country's factors of production are fully employed (or experience a given level of unemployment owing to institutional characteristics, e.g., a "natural level of unemployment"), combined with their efficient use in the competitive market, means that the country is operating on the PPF. Thus, because of this assumption, we have not previously analyzed situations where trade moved the country from somewhere inside the PPF to a point on the PPF.

The "full-employment" assumption is a general one in microeconomic theory as well as in trade theory. In micro, it is assumed that the *macroeconomic* question of unemployment has been solved. The solution to the problem of unemployment might lie, for example, with effective monetary and fiscal policies. Given this solution, the subject of microeconomics looks at questions of efficiency and welfare.

Of course, the real world does not always reach full employment. The assumption of full employment is not made to ignore real-world problems, however, but to separate conceptually the problem of efficiency and welfare from that of idle capacity. The internal problem of unemployment may not present itself any differently when the country is in autarky than in a trading situation; policies that are not necessarily "international" in dimension can be used in either case. By moving to a higher indifference curve, there are gains from trade even if the country has unemployment; the opening of the country to trade will lead to different prices facing consumers and producers than was the case with autarky. Gains from exchange and specialization still occur.

The Indifference Curve Map Can Show Welfare Changes

In Chapter 5, the possibility that *community* indifference curves might intersect was raised. If intersections occur, there might be a problem in interpreting welfare changes when a country moves from autarky to trade. In this chapter, however, no intersecting community indifference curves have so far been drawn. It is useful to comment on this disparity.

A number of somewhat restrictive assumptions can be used to construct nonintersecting community indifference curves. These assumptions can guarantee that welfare changes can be interpreted as they have been in this chapter (see Tower 1979). The explanation of the conditions necessary for concluding that welfare will improve when autarky gives way to trade is straightforward. Two general conditions are pertinent: (1) that individuals within the economy have reasonably similar tastes and (2) that the opening of the economy to trade does not radically alter the distribution of income. The underlying rationale for these conditions is that, without them, our earlier analysis would suggest that community indifference curves could intersect. By assuming that redistribution is not large and that people have similar tastes, we thus minimize the possibility of not being able to tell whether actual welfare has changed.

However, even with these general conditions, we cannot be sure that the direction of the actual welfare change can be meaningfully ascertained, as the phrases "have reasonably similar tastes" and "radically alter the distribution of income" do not lend themselves to precise interpretation. Because of this uncertainty, advanced trade theory has gone well beyond the use of indifference curves to other modes of demonstrating

IN THE REAL WORLD:

INCOME DISTRIBUTION CHANGES WITH INCREASED TRADE IN THE UNITED STATES

The initiation of trade can influence the distribution of income by means of changes in both production and consumption conditions. With the opening of trade, the relative price of export goods increases and the relative price of import substitute goods decreases. On the supply side, this will lead to an expansion of production of export goods and a contraction of production of import-substitute goods. Consequently, there will be an increase in the demand for inputs used in export production and a reduction in demand for inputs used in the domestic production of the import good. In the adjustment process, the price of certain factors or inputs will likely increase and the price of others will likely decline, leading to a change in income distribution. Estimates of such supply-side impacts will be discussed in Chapters 8 and 9, which deal with production and income distribution in the context of the supply-oriented theory of the determination of comparative advantage known as the Heckscher-Ohlin theorem. However, a study by Spilimbergo, Londoño, and Székely (1999) examined 34 countries from 1965 to 1992 and suggested that, while relative factor endowments go a long way in explaining personal income distribution, distribution is also influenced by the degree of general openness of a country to international trade. The study concluded that reductions in trade barriers (becoming more "open") decreased income inequality in capital-abundant countries but increased income inequality in skill-abundant countries. These provocative conclusions reinforce the notion that trade can influence income distribution, although the mechanisms are likely much more complicated than suggested by the simple Heckscher-Ohlin framework.

In addition, distribution effects occur in consumption. Because the price of export goods is rising with trade and that of import goods is falling, individuals who spend relatively more of their income on export goods will find their real income relatively smaller compared to that of individuals who spend relatively more on import goods, other things being equal. To give an example of the magnitude of possible consumption-related income distribution effects, consider Susan Hickok's (1985, p. 11) estimates of the impact of the higher domestic prices caused by U.S. import restrictions on automobiles, sugar, and clothing in 1984. The protection-induced increases in expenditure on these products were equivalent to an income tax surcharge of 66 percent for low-income earners ($7,000–$9,350 annually), 33 percent for those in the $14,050–$16,400 range, 20 percent for those earning $23,400–$28,050, and only 5 percent for individuals earning $58,500 and above. Because these products absorb a higher percentage of individual expenditures of low-income earners than of high-income earners, increasing international trade by removing those tariff and quota barriers would clearly have had the effect that low-income groups would benefit relatively more than high-income groups.

the gains from trade. The **compensation principle** summarizes the general conclusion of these extensions. The advanced literature demonstrates that *potential* gains from trade exist in the sense that, within the country, the people who gain from trade can compensate the losers and still be better off (or at least no worse off). This must mean, therefore, that there is a larger "pie"—or at least the same-size pie—to split up after trade has been introduced. If the compensation is paid, then society is better off because the gainers have benefited even after compensating the losers. Everyone is at least as well off as in autarky, and some people are better off. In the limiting case of no change in welfare, trade would still be preferred to autarky because trade involves the possibility of higher welfare than autarky, but the reverse is never true. If the compensation is not actually paid, then society is described as being only "potentially" better off. It is potential because some people could be made better off and everyone else no worse off, but this would not happen without the transfer. Further consideration of this principle using our familiar community indifference curves is given in the appendix to this chapter.

CONCEPT CHECK   1. Briefly describe the minimum conditions for trade to take place between two countries, that is, for there to be a difference in their respective price ratios in autarky.
2. Why do different demand conditions influence the basis for trade in neoclassical theory but not in Classical theory?
3. How can opening a country to trade influence income distribution? How does this affect our ability to demonstrate the gains from trade?

SUMMARY

Neoclassical trade theory's demonstration of the gains from international trade uses the analytical tools of the production possibilities frontier and the community indifference curve. In autarky, a country reaches its highest indifference curve when the marginal rate of transformation (MRT) in production equals the price ratio of goods, which in turn equals the marginal rate of substitution (MRS) in consumption. When the country is opened to international trade, it faces a new set of relative prices. The adjustment by producers and consumers to this new set of prices and the resulting trade enables the country to attain a higher indifference curve. A preliminary inquiry into the minimal conditions necessary to produce different autarky prices showed that autarky price ratios can differ as long as there is a difference in either demand or supply conditions. For example, two countries with identical (increasing-opportunity-cost) PPFs

can both gain from trade if tastes differ between the countries. Or a basis for trade can exist if different technologies are employed by countries that are otherwise identical. The important role played by the relative availability of factors in influencing relative prices in autarky will be discussed in Chapter 8, "The Basis for Trade: Factor Endowments and the Heckscher-Ohlin Model."

The neoclassical theory of trade makes use of some special assumptions involving adjustment to change, full employment, and indifference curves. These assumptions were discussed briefly in this chapter and will be referred to again. In addition, we frequently utilized an assumption that, when a country is opened to trade, the country takes the new set of world prices as *given*. Forces influencing the determination of the new price ratio will be covered in more detail in the next chapter.

KEY TERMS

compensation principle	production gain (or gains from	trade adjustment assistance
consumption gain (or gains from	specialization)	trade triangle
exchange)	total gains from trade	trading line

QUESTIONS AND PROBLEMS

1. Indicate the equilibrium production and consumption point in autarky, using a PPF and a community indifference curve under increasing-opportunity-cost conditions. Why is this an equilibrium? What must occur for this country to gain from trade?

2. Assume that a country produces and consumes two goods, cloth and machines, and is in equilibrium in autarky. It now finds that it can trade at international prices where $(P_{cloth}/P_{machines})$ on the world market is greater than $(P_{cloth}/P_{machines})$ in the domestic market. Should it trade? If so, what commodity should it export? Why? Will it gain from trade? How do you know?

3. Explain the difference between the "gains from exchange" (consumption gain) and the "gains from specialization" (production gain).

4. Suppose a country that is producing within its production-possibilities frontier in autarky experiences an 8 percent

rate of unemployment. Is it possible for it to gain from trade if the rate of unemployment remains approximately the same?

5. "The inability of factors to move from one use to another in production will completely take away any possible gains from trade." Agree? Disagree? Explain.

6. What general conditions must hold for one to be able to use community indifference curves to represent consumer well-being in a country and demonstrate gains from international trade?

7. The United States has had an embargo on trade with Cuba for almost 50 years, but pressure is increasing to relax it. Opponents of ending the embargo argue that opening trade between the United States and Cuba would benefit Cuba and hurt the United States by injuring U.S. producers of goods that compete with potential Cuban exports. Evaluate this position utilizing what you have learned in this chapter.

8. If the production conditions in the United States and Japan were to become essentially the same, would the neoclassical model suggest that trade between the two countries would cease? Why or why not?

9. Ms. Jones, one of your neighbors, spends the majority of her income on food. She complains to you that, after your country became more open to trade and began exporting a variety of food products, her real income was reduced. She therefore maintains that the country has obviously been hurt by the new, expanded trade and that trade restrictions should be imposed. How would you respond to Ms. Jones?

10. (Requires appendix material) "If trade should cause income distribution to change such that there was a shift in the indifference map, it would be impossible to reach a conclusion regarding any possible gains from international trade." Discuss.

Appendix

"ACTUAL" VERSUS "POTENTIAL" GAINS FROM TRADE

You have seen in Chapter 5 an illustration in which a change in income distribution yielded new community indifference curves that intersected previous community indifference curves. Figure 8 shows this situation in the context of trade (see Samuelson 1962, pp. 826–27). In autarky, the country is at point E on indifference curve CI_1. Suppose that the introduction of trade moves production to point P and consumption to point C, a tangency point to community indifference curve CI_2 associated with the *new* income distribution that has resulted from trade. Clearly, point C is preferred to point E on the basis of the new income distribution (CI_2 represents a higher level of welfare than does CI'_2), but C is inferior to E on the basis of the autarky income distribution (CI'_1 represents a lower level of welfare than does CI_1).

Do we conclude that trade has not improved the welfare of the country? No! With trading line $(P_X/P_Y)_T$, the amount of trade could be altered to move to consumption at point F, which has larger quantities of both goods X and Y than does point E. This is the essence of the compensation principle: Trade provides the means to make at least some people better off and no one worse off, enabling society to gain. With consumption at point F, the quantities of X and Y are sufficient to compensate fully any losers (i.e., to reproduce the consumption bundle at autarky position E) and still have some of both goods left over. If the country remains at point C and no compensation is paid, it still has gained welfare in the "potential" sense that trade has made it possible to have gainers and no losers. Furthermore, even at C, the country is consuming at a point that was impossible under autarky, and trade has thus opened up possibilities that were previously unattainable.

FIGURE 8   Gains from Trade with Intersecting Community Indifference Curves

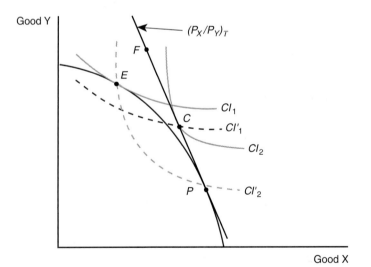

Trade moves the country from production (and consumption) point E to production point P and consumption point C. On the basis of the income distribution under autarky, C is "worse" than E (CI'_1 represents a lower level of welfare than does CI_1); on the basis of the income distribution with trade, C is "better" than E (CI_2 represents a higher level of welfare than does CI'_2). However, trade makes possible a movement to a point such as F, where the consumption bundle in autarky at point E can be reproduced (that is, there would be no losers from trade) and some additional quantities of goods X and Y would still remain available for consumption by the "gainers" from trade.

OFFER CURVES AND THE TERMS OF TRADE

LEARNING OBJECTIVES

- To understand a country's offer curve and how it is obtained.

- To learn how the equilibrium international terms of trade are attained.

- To identify and determine how changes in both supply and demand conditions influence a country's international terms of trade and volume of trade.

- To appreciate the usefulness of different concepts of the terms of trade.

INTRODUCTION

**Terms-of-Trade
Shocks**

Changes in the terms of trade of a country—the price of the country's exports divided by the price of its imports—can be sizable, and they can have major economic effects on the country. For example, economists Paul Cashion and Catherine Pattillo[1] of the International Monetary Fund (IMF) calculated that, in 1986–1987, a drop in the price of coffee, a main export from Ethiopia, caused a 40 percent drop in Ethiopia's terms of trade and a decline of about 6 percent in Ethiopia's real income. And such shocks may last for some time, too: In their study of sub-Saharan countries, Cashion and Pattillo estimated that a typical shock's duration for Mozambique is from six months to three years, while the duration for a typical shock for Gambia could be up to 12.2 years. Estimates were also made of the size of the shocks. For example, in Côte d'Ivoire in any given year, there is a one-in-three chance that the country's terms of trade will change by more than 9 percent; for Nigeria, there is a one-in-three chance that the movement in its terms of trade in any given year will be more than 20 percent.

A second IMF study[2] looked at movements of the terms of trade during 1998, 1999, and January–June 2000 for countries exporting mainly primary products. These movements were then compared with the terms-of-trade average level for the base period 1995–1997. For almost 30 countries, their terms of trade fell during the January 1998–June 2000 period by more than 10 percent in comparison with the base period, and in 11 countries the fall exceeded 20 percent. For three countries (Burundi, Ethiopia, and Uganda), the decline was greater than 30 percent. The losses due to the terms-of-trade movements were estimated to be equivalent to more than 8 percent of total domestic spending for some countries and, on average for the countries examined in the study, about 4 percent of total domestic spending.

Clearly terms-of-trade movements can occur, can last for a long time, and can have important economic effects. This chapter introduces and explains the factors that determine the terms of trade or posttrade prices. In the discussion in previous chapters, an important simplification was made: World prices with trade were assumed to be at a certain level. Thus, for example, in the Ricardo model we assumed that one barrel of wine would exchange for one yard of cloth in international trade and did not investigate the factors that determined this relative price ratio. Similarly, in Chapter 6, a given P_X/P_Y was drawn in the PPF–indifference curve diagram, and no attention was paid to the reason for this price ratio. An important analytical concept employed to explain the determination of the terms of trade is known as the offer curve. We first present this basic analytical tool and then use it to demonstrate how equilibrium prices are attained in international trade. Then the offer curve framework is used to explain the price and trade volume effects of phenomena such as economic growth and changes in consumer tastes. This concept is helpful in the interpretation and understanding of ongoing, complex economic events in the international arena.

A COUNTRY'S OFFER CURVE

The **offer curve** (or **reciprocal demand curve**) of a country indicates the quantity of imports and exports the country is willing to buy and sell on world markets at all possible relative prices. In short, the curve shows the country's willingness to trade at various possible terms of trade. The offer curve is a combination of a demand curve (the

---

[1]This paragraph draws on Paul Cashion and Catherine Pattillo, "The Duration of Terms of Trade Shocks in Sub-Saharan Africa," *Finance and Development* 37, no. 2 (June 2000), pp. 26–29.

[2]International Monetary Fund, *World Economic Outlook,* October 2000 (Washington, DC: International Monetary Fund, 2000), pp. 78–79.

demand for imports) and a supply curve (the supply of exports). The two-pronged nature of the curve distinguishes it from most graphic devices in economics. An offer curve is easy to understand, and we are great fans of the concept because it usefully portrays the net result of a wide variety of reactions and activities by consumers and producers.

There are several methods of deriving an offer curve, but we will concentrate on the method that builds directly upon the PPF–indifference curve diagram. This method is called the *trade triangle approach.* Consider Figure 1(a), which shows the equilibrium trading position for a country at world prices $(P_X/P_Y)_1$. Free trade is occurring, and the country is producing $0x_2$ of good X and $0y_2$ of good Y (at point P). Consumption is $0x_1$ of good X and $0y_1$ of good Y (at point C). With these amounts of production and consumption, x_1x_2 of good X is exported and y_2y_1 of good Y is imported. This trade pattern is reflected in trade triangle RCP, with line RP representing the exports and line RC representing the imports the country is willing to undertake at the terms of trade $(P_X/P_Y)_1$.

Consider Figure 1(b). The country now faces a steeper world price line than it did in panel (a), and its production and consumption have correspondingly adjusted. Because $(P_X/P_Y)_2$ in panel (b) is greater than $(P_X/P_Y)_1$ in panel (a), producers have responded to the relatively higher price of X (and to the relatively lower price of Y) by increasing their production of X and decreasing their production of Y. Production now takes place at P', with $0x_4$ of good X and $0y_4$ of good Y being produced. At prices $(P_X/P_Y)_2$ consumption takes place at point C' with $0x_3$ of good X and $0y_3$ of good Y consumed. Exports of this country are now x_3x_4 of good X, and imports are y_4y_3 of good Y. This volume of trade is represented by trade triangle $R'C'P'$.

It is clear from Figure 1 that different trade volumes exist at the two different sets of relative commodity prices. The offer curve diagram takes the information from panels (a) and

FIGURE 1   Trade Triangles at Two Possible Terms of Trade

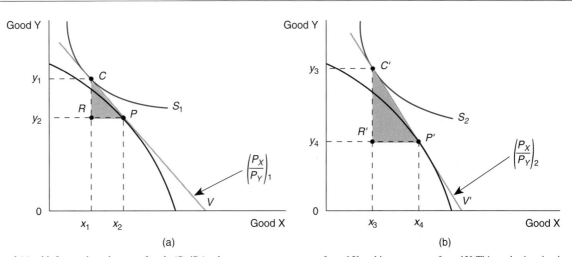

In panel (a) with free trade and terms of trade $(P_X/P_Y)_1$, the country exports x_1x_2 of good X and imports y_2y_1 of good Y. This trade situation is summarized by trade triangle RCP, with length RP representing exports of good X and length RC representing imports of good Y. In panel (b), a higher relative price for good X (and therefore a lower relative price for good Y) is indicated by terms-of-trade line $(P_X/P_Y)_2$, which is steeper than $(P_X/P_Y)_1$ in panel (a). With the terms of trade of panel (b), the country exports x_3x_4 of good X and imports y_4y_3 of good Y. This trade pattern is summarized by trade triangle $R'C'P'$, with exports equal to length $R'P'$ and imports equal to length $R'C'$.

FIGURE 2   Alternative Terms of Trade and Export-Import Combinations on the Offer Curve

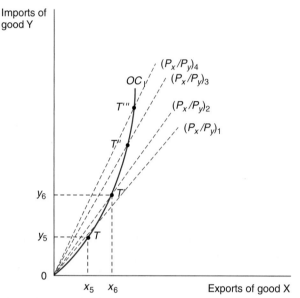

Relative prices $(P_X/P_Y)_1$ are the same as in Figure 1(a). At these terms of trade, the country exports quantity $0x_5$ of good X [equal to x_1x_2 in Figure 1(a)] and imports quantity $0y_5$ of good Y [equal to y_2y_1 in Figure 1(a)], yielding point T. At the higher relative price ratio $(P_X/P_Y)_2$, which is equal to $(P_X/P_Y)_2$ in Figure 1(b), the country exports $0x_6$ of good X and imports $0y_6$ of good Y [equal to x_3x_4 and y_4y_3 in Figure 1(b), respectively], yielding point T'. Additional possible trade points (such as T'' and T''') are then joined with T and T' to form the offer curve for country I, OC_I. At its pretrade prices in autarky (prices not shown), country I would be situated at the origin with zero exports and zero imports.

(b) of Figure 1 and plots it onto a new curve (see Figure 2). This figure does not show production or consumption but presents only the *quantities of exports and imports* at the two sets of prices. The key geometrical difference between the two figures is that the P_X/P_Y price ratios are upward sloping in Figure 2 rather than downward sloping. Thus, $(P_X/P_Y)_1$ in Figure 2 is the same price ratio as $(P_X/P_Y)_1$ in Figure 1(a). Angle $0VC$ in Figure 1(a), where the price line hits the x-axis, is the same size as the angle formed at the origin in Figure 2 between the $(P_X/P_Y)_1$ line and the x-axis. At this set of prices, the country exports quantity $0x_5$, which is equal to distance x_1x_2 in Figure 1(a). Similarly, the country imports quantity $0y_5$, which is equal to distance y_2y_1 in Figure 1(a). With the exports and imports thus plotted, point T represents the volume of trade associated with the $(P_X/P_Y)_1$ price ratio. Point T is a *point* that corresponds to the volume of trade indicated by the horizontal and vertical sides of trade triangle RCP in Figure 1(a).

The higher relative price ratio $(P_X/P_Y)_2$ of Figure 1(b) is represented by a steeper price line in Figure 2, as it was in panel (b) of Figure 1. A higher price for X on the world market means that greater quantities of it are exported. Quantity of exports $0x_6$ in Figure 2 corresponds to quantity of exports x_3x_4 in Figure 1(b). At this new, higher relative price for good X, good Y is relatively lower priced. Therefore, quantity of imports $0y_6$ in Figure 2, which equals quantity y_4y_3 in Figure 1(b), is greater than quantity of imports $0y_5$. The volume of trade at prices $(P_X/P_Y)_2$ is thus represented by point T'.

We have now obtained two points on this country's offer curve. You can conceptualize the remainder of the curve by mentally constructing trade triangles in Figure 1 for every set of possible prices. The sides of these trade triangles would be plotted in Figure 2 as indicated by illustrative points T'' and T'''. The construction of the offer curve is completed by connecting all possible points at which a country is willing to trade, with the resulting curve labeled OC_I, designating our country as country I. The exact shape of this offer curve will be discussed later. Concept Box 1 provides another method of deriving an offer curve.

The most useful feature of the offer curve diagram is that it can bring two trading countries together in one diagram. To accomplish this, the offer curve of country I's trading partner, country II, needs also to be developed. There is nothing new analytically about country II's offer curve. The trade triangles for that country are plotted in the same manner as those for country I. The only difference is that country II exports good Y and imports good X. Thus, country II's offer curve appears as curve OC_{II} in Figure 4. This curve reflects country II's willingness to trade at alternative relative prices. Of course, a *lower* P_X/P_Y means that country II has a *greater* willingness to trade, because a lower relative price for good X means a greater incentive for country II's consumers to import it. Similarly, a lower P_X/P_Y means a relatively higher price for good Y, leading to a greater willingness by country II to export it.

CONCEPT BOX 1

THE TABULAR APPROACH TO DERIVING AN OFFER CURVE

An alternative approach to the use of trade triangles for deriving an offer curve is the *tabular approach,* which simply uses a numerical example. This approach (see Haberler 1936, pp. 145–48) is demonstrated by development of a hypothetical country A's offer curve from the information contained in Table 1. Column (1) lists possible terms of trade on the world market. Column (2) illustrates the demand side of an offer curve by listing country A's assumed quantity demanded of imports of good Y at the various prices indicated by the terms of trade in column (1). Moving down column (1), good Y gets relatively cheaper because more of it exchanges for one unit of good X. Corresponding to the law of demand, greater quantities of good Y are demanded as we move down column (2).

Column (3) indicates the supply side of the offer curve and illustrates the link between exports and imports.

Exports are supplied to the world market so that the country can purchase imports. In the first row of the table, 10 units of good Y are being demanded on the world market and the price of 1Y is 1X; therefore, 10 units of X must be supplied to the world market. Similarly, in row 2, 44Y are demanded at a price that requires one unit of X be given up for every two units of Y and 22X must thus be "given up" or exported. The figures in column (3) are obtained by dividing the numbers in column (2) by the relative prices in column (1).

From the information in this table, the offer curve is obtained by plotting the quantities exported and imported at each relative price on the familiar set of axes, as in Figure 3. If you imagine an infinite number of such combinations, then you have plotted the offer curve of country A.

TABLE 1   Country A's Exports and Imports at Various Terms of Trade

(1) Terms of Trade (assumed)	(2) Quantity Demanded of Imports of Y (assumed)	(3) Quantity Supplied of Exports of X = (2) [P_X/P_Y in (1)]
1X:1Y or $P_X/P_Y = 1$	10 units	10 units
1X:2Y or $P_X/P_Y = 2$	44 units	22 units
1X:3Y or $P_X/P_Y = 3$	81 units	27 units
1X:4Y or $P_X/P_Y = 4$	120 units	30 units

(continued)

CONCEPT BOX 1 *(continued)*

THE TABULAR APPROACH TO DERIVING AN OFFER CURVE

FIGURE 3   Country A's Offer Curve

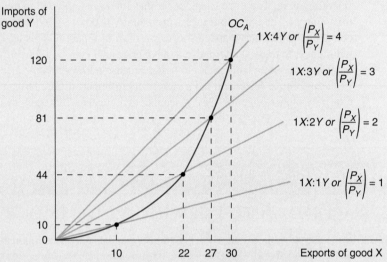

Row 1 of Table 1 indicates that, at a P_X/P_Y ratio of 1, country A wants to import 10 units of good Y. Therefore, 10 units of good X would be exported to obtain that quantity of imports. At $P_X/P_Y = 2$, the country wants 44 units of imports of good Y and therefore would export 22 units of good X to obtain them. The plotting of the other two import-export combinations, plus a tracing of other possible combinations of imports, exports, and terms of trade, yields offer curve OC_A.

TRADING EQUILIBRIUM

With the two countries' offer curves brought together in one figure (see Figure 4), we can indicate the trading equilibrium and show the **equilibrium terms of trade.** The horizontal axis indicates exports of good X for country I and imports of good X for country II. Similarly, the vertical axis indicates country I's imports of good Y and country II's exports of good Y. Trading equilibrium occurs at point *E,* and the *equilibrium terms of trade,* TOT_E, *are indicated by the slope of the ray from the origin passing through* E.

Why is point *E* the trading equilibrium? At point *E,* the quantity of exports that country I wishes to sell ($0x_E$, on OC_I) exactly equals the quantity of imports that country II wishes to buy (also $0x_E$, on OC_{II}). In addition, the quantity of imports that country I wishes to buy ($0y_E$, on OC_I) equals exactly the quantity of exports that country II wishes to sell (also $0y_E$, on OC_{II}). Thus, relative prices $(P_X/P_Y)_E$ are market-clearing prices because the demand for and supply of good X on the world market are equal, as are the demand for and supply of good Y.

Let us explore economically why TOT_E is the market-clearing (equilibrium) price ratio. Suppose in Figure 4 that world prices are not at TOT_E but at some lower relative price for good X of TOT_1. At this set of prices, country I would like to trade at point *A;* that is, it would like to sell $0x_1$ of good X and buy $0y_1$ of good Y. However, at this lower relative price for good X, country II would like to trade at point *B.* It would like to buy $0x_2$ of good

FIGURE 4   Trading Equilibrium

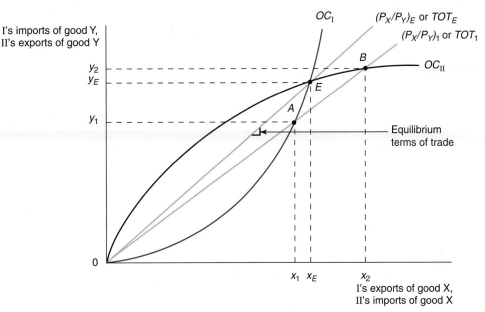

Relative prices $(P_X/P_Y)_E$ (or terms of trade TOT_E) are market-clearing prices since the quantity of good X $(0x_E)$ that country I wishes to export equals the quantity of good X that country II wishes to import and the quantity of good Y that country I wishes to import $(0y_E)$ equals the quantity of good Y that country II wishes to export. Thus, point E is the trading equilibrium position, and the equilibrium terms of trade are equal to the slope of the ray from the origin through point E. If relative prices $(P_X/P_Y)_1$ or TOT_1 prevailed in the market instead of $(P_X/P_Y)_E$ or TOT_E, there would be excess demand for good X of amount x_1x_2 and excess supply of good Y of amount y_1y_2. Therefore, $(P_X/P_Y)_1$ or TOT_1 would rise until the excess demand and excess supply were eliminated at $(P_X/P_Y)_E$ or TOT_E.

X and sell $0y_2$ of good Y. Therefore, at TOT_1, there is excess demand for good X of the amount x_1x_2 and excess supply of good Y of the amount y_1y_2. The excess demand for good X will bid up its price on the world market, while the excess supply of good Y will bid down its price. With these changes in price, the relative price ratio $(P_X/P_Y)_1$ will *rise,* which means that the price line becomes steeper. As it does, both the excess demand for good X and the excess supply of good Y will be reduced. The price line will continue to rise until the excess demand and the excess supply are eliminated at equilibrium point E. It should be noted that in this two-commodity model an excess demand for one good means that there must be an excess supply of the other; equilibrium in one good's market means that equilibrium exists in the other good's market also.

CONCEPT CHECK

1. Why does a point on a country's offer curve represent the country's willingness to trade at those particular terms of trade? In other words, what motivates the country to export and import those particular quantities at that relative price ratio? (Hint: Remember what a "trade triangle" implies about the level of well-being of the country.)

2. Why would a country exporting good X be willing to import greater quantities of good Y as P_X/P_Y rises?

3. Suppose that in Figure 4 a terms-of-trade line TOT_2 appears that is *steeper* than TOT_E. In terms of excess supply and excess demand, explain why the terms of trade will fall from TOT_2 to TOT_E.

SHIFTS OF OFFER CURVES

The determination of the equilibrium relative prices in the last section was carried out under the assumption that offer curves are fixed for each country. What we have done is develop a "snapshot" of the trading situation at a particular point in time. In practice, however, offer curves do not stay fixed. Over time, changes in the two countries lead to changes in the offer curves—and a new "snapshot" will emerge.

Suppose that, after reaching equilibrium as shown in Figure 4, the consumers in country I change their tastes and decide that they would like to purchase more of good Y. Because Y is the import, this means an increase in demand for imports. Country I now has greater willingness to trade and its offer curve will shift to indicate this change. The shift is analogous to an "increase in demand" in the ordinary demand-supply diagram. An increased willingness to trade in the offer curve analysis means that, *at each possible terms of trade,* the country is willing to supply more exports and demand more imports. (Back in Figure 1, this change in tastes toward good Y would shift the indifference curves toward the y-axis. Hence, the trade triangles for each relative price line would be larger.) In Figure 5, the offer curve shifts or pivots to the right from OC_I to OC'_I. Note that the shift is accomplished by plotting a point "farther out" on each potential price line than was originally plotted (such as point F' instead of point F, point G' instead of point G, and so on). A shift could occur of course for reasons other than a change in tastes for the imported good. Other reasons could include a rise in income that led to an increased demand for imports or an improvement in productivity in country I's export industries that caused an increased supply of exports. Similarly, a decrease in willingness to trade or a decrease in reciprocal demand is indicated by offer curve OC''_I, where the curve has shifted or pivoted inward to the left. This decrease could

FIGURE 5   Shifts in Country I's Offer Curve

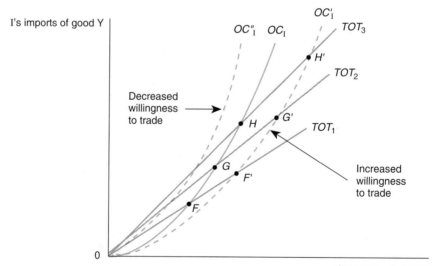

If country I changes its tastes toward relatively greater preference for the (imported) Y good, or for any other reason wants to increase its international trade, offer curve OC_I shifts diagonally or pivots to the right to become offer curve OC'_I. This new curve indicates a greater willingness to trade at all possible terms of trade. A decreased willingness to trade (such as would result, for example, from the imposition of a tariff by country I) would shift OC_I diagonally leftward to OC''_I.

FIGURE 6   Shifts in Country II's Offer Curve

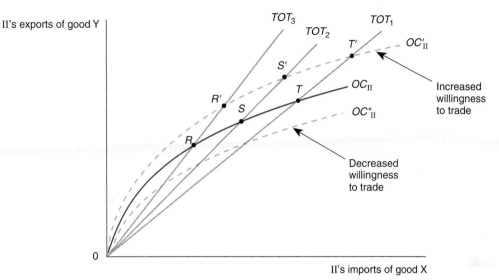

If country II increases its willingness to trade, its offer curve OC_{II} shifts diagonally or pivots to OC'_{II}, indicating a greater desire to trade at each possible terms of trade. For example, point R with TOT_3 becomes point R', point S with TOT_2 becomes point S', etc. Similarly, a decreased willingness to trade on the part of country II shifts OC_{II} diagonally downward to OC''_{II}.

reflect a change in tastes away from the imported good, a decline in national income, or, of particular importance, the imposition of a tariff by country I.

An analogous procedure applies to country II. Because an increased willingness to trade represents a desire to export and import greater quantities at all terms of trade, the original OC_{II} in Figure 6 shifts or pivots *upward* to OC'_{II}. Note again that, on each price line, the willingness-to-trade points are plotted farther out than they were originally. Country II's decreased willingness to trade is reflected in offer curve OC''_{II}.

When offer curves shift, the equilibrium terms of trade and volume of trade change. These changes reflect the alteration of underlying market conditions. Suppose that country I and country II are in initial equilibrium in Figure 7 at TOT_E and at trading volumes $0x_E$ of good X and $0y_E$ of good Y. Now suppose that there is a shift in tastes by country I toward its import good Y. As noted earlier, this change in tastes will cause offer curve OC_I to shift to OC'_I. With the increase in country I's willingness to trade, the previous terms of trade, TOT_E, are no longer sustainable. TOT_E results in excess demand for good Y and, correspondingly, excess supply of good X. Country I is willing to buy $0y_2$ of good Y and offer $0x_2$ of good X in exchange. However, country II has experienced no change in its offer curve, and it is still willing to supply only $0y_E$ of good Y and to demand $0x_E$ of good X at TOT_E. With excess demand of y_Ey_2 for good Y and excess supply of x_Ex_2 for good X, the price of Y will rise on the world market and the price of X will fall. This change in relative prices will continue until the excess demand for Y and the excess supply of X are eliminated at new equilibrium point E′ with terms of trade TOT_1.

The change in the terms of trade means that the price of the good that country I sells (good X) has fallen relative to the price of the good that it buys (good Y); alternatively, the price of the good that country I buys has risen relative to the price of the good that it sells. (See Concept Box 2 on the measurement of changes in a country's terms of trade in practice.) The economic explanation for this rise in the relative price of the import good is that

FIGURE 7   An Increased Demand for Imports by Country I

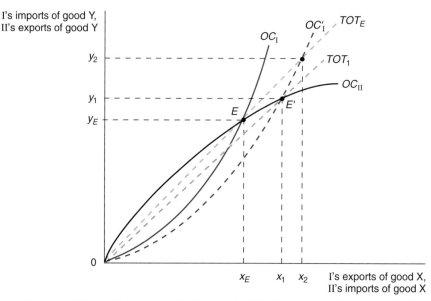

If country I's tastes shift toward its import good Y, OC_I shifts to OC'_I. At original equilibrium point E with TOT_E, there is now an excess demand of $y_E y_2$ for good Y and an excess supply of $x_E x_2$ of good X. The resulting movement in the terms of trade from TOT_E to TOT_1 eliminates the excess demand and supply. The new equilibrium position is point E', with quantities $0x_1$ of good X and $0y_1$ of good Y being traded.

the increased demand for the good by country I's consumers indicates that they value good Y more highly than before and are willing to give up more of good X to get each unit of good Y. Thus, with an unchanged supply schedule of exports from country II, the price of the good has been bid up. The increased desire for imports has raised the volume of imports from the original $0y_E$ to $0y_1$, and the quantity of exports exchanged for the new import quantity is $0x_1$, a larger amount than the original $0x_E$.

We have illustrated the effect of an increased willingness to trade by country I. Obviously, other shifts could take place. For example, a decreased willingness to trade by country I would shift its offer curve to the left and lead to a higher P_X/P_Y and a smaller volume of trade. Further, an increased willingness to trade by country II would shift its offer curve upward and, with no change in country I's offer curve, also would lead to higher equilibrium P_X/P_Y but with a greater volume of trade than prior to the shift. A decreased willingness to trade by country II would shift its offer curve downward and produce a fall in P_X/P_Y and a reduction in the volume of trade. (A discussion of recent movements in the terms of trade of major trading areas—movements that reflect the continuing shifts of offer curves in the real world—can be found on pages 115–16).

The conclusion that shifts in a country's offer curve can affect its terms of trade has an important exception in a country that is a **small country.** A small country is defined in international economics as a country that is *unable to influence its terms of trade* by its own actions. On the other hand, a **large country** *can* influence its terms of trade by its own actions, and most of the offer curve diagrams in this book portray this case. The inability of a small country to influence the terms of trade means that, no matter how many units of its import good the country buys or how many units of its export good the country sells on the world market, the country will have no effect on world prices. The small country is a "price

CONCEPT BOX 2

MEASUREMENT OF THE TERMS OF TRADE

The relative price ratio P_X/P_Y in the offer curve diagram is called the **commodity terms of trade,** or **net barter terms of trade,** but usually, and most simply, the terms of trade (TOT). (Other concepts of the terms of trade are discussed later in this chapter.) The commodity terms of trade for any particular *country* are defined as the price of that country's exports divided by the price of its imports. Thus, in our previous examples, the TOT for country I would be P_X/P_Y, while the TOT for country II would be P_Y/P_X. The economic interpretation of the terms of trade is that, as the price of exports rises relative to the price of imports, each unit of a country's exports is able to purchase a larger quantity of imports. Thus, more imports, which like any other goods bring utility to consumers, can be obtained with a given volume of exports, and the country's welfare on the basis of these price relations alone has improved.

In calculating the terms of trade for any given country, because a country trades many goods, a **price index** must be calculated for exports and for imports. A price index is a weighted average of the prices of many goods, calculated for comparison with a base year. A base year for the export price (P_X) and import price (P_M) indexes must be chosen. The base-year price indexes are then set at values of 100, and other years can be compared with them. For example, the International Monetary Fund (IMF), in its January 2007 issue of *International Financial Statistics,* used 2000 as its base year in calculating the terms of trade for the United States (and other countries); thus $P_{XUS}^{2000} = 100$ and $P_{MUS}^{2000} = 100$. Suppose we then consider 2005. According to the IMF (pp. 68–69), the price index for U.S. exports in 2005 was 106.9 (that is, export prices were 6.9 percent above the 2000

base-year prices), and the price index for U.S. imports was 110.0 (that is, import prices were 10.0 percent above the 2000 base-year values). The index of the terms of trade for the United States in 2005 would be calculated as follows:

$$TOT_{US}^{2005} = \frac{P_{XUS}^{2005}}{P_{MUS}^{2005}} \times 100$$

$$= (106.9/110.0) \times 100$$

$$= 97.2$$

The multiplication by 100 is carried out to put the result into the usual index-number form. The figure 97.2 means that each unit of U.S. exports in 2005 exchanged for 2.8 percent $(2.8 = 100 - 97.2)$ fewer units of imports than in the base year.

Calculations of the commodity terms of trade have been carried out extensively in empirical work in economics. Indeed, an ongoing controversy concerns the claim by spokespersons for developing countries that, over the long run, developing countries have been damaged by a decline in their commodity terms of trade. If the world is divided into only two groups—developing countries and the developed countries—then a decline in the terms of trade for developing countries must be associated with a *rise* in the terms of trade of the developed countries. (This rise would occur because, with only two trading groups, one group's exports must be the other group's imports and vice versa.) Such behavior of the terms of trade would imply that real income is being transferred *from* developing countries *to* developed countries! This controversy is covered more fully in Chapter 18.

taker" in the same sense as is the individual consumer as a buyer and the individual firm as a seller in perfect competition in microeconomic theory. In the offer curve context, the offer curve *facing* the small country is a straight line from the origin. Thus, back in Figure 7 on page 112, if the offer curve of (*small*) country I (OC_I) shifted outward to OC'_I, the terms of trade would remain at TOT_E. (The TOT_E line in effect would be the offer curve of the rest of the world that is facing country I.) Country I, if small, would be unable to influence its terms of trade no matter where its offer curve were located (although the location of the offer curve would affect the volume of trade).

Whether a country is large or small is an empirical question. Increased demand by Chad for machinery imports or increased export supply by Grenada of textiles is unlikely to affect either world prices or the terms of trade of those countries. However, some countries whose land area or GDP is small may be large in the economic sense because they export large quantities of goods that are in strong demand and they therefore have significant impact on world prices (e.g., Ghana in cocoa, Thailand in rice, Colombia in coffee).

ELASTICITY AND THE OFFER CURVE

A feature previously neglected in this chapter is the precise shape of the offer curve, and the shape is important because it influences the impacts of shifts in offer curves. The shape can be discussed in terms of the general concept of elasticity. The elasticity of an offer curve at various points can be defined in several ways, but we shall present the most common definition. It deals with the **elasticity of demand for imports** along the curve, which is the percentage change in the quantity of imports demanded divided by the percentage change in the relative price of imports. This definition is analogous to the usual definition of price elasticity of demand, except that it refers to the *relative* price of the good instead of to an absolute price.[3]

Geometrically, the import-demand elasticity can be measured as follows. (The proof involves mathematical manipulation shown in Appendix A at the end of this chapter.) On the offer curves OC_I in Figure 8, consider any point P. From this point, drop a perpendicular line to the horizontal axis and draw a tangent to P that also hits the horizontal axis. The elasticity is measured as the horizontal distance from origin 0 to the intersection of the perpendicular line, divided by the horizontal distance from the origin to the intersection of the tangent line. In Figure 8, the import-demand elasticity is thus $0R/0S$. (Technically, a negative sign is in front of this measure, which we will disregard in our discussion.) The three parts of Figure 8 illustrate the three classifications associated with elasticity. In panel (a), $0R/0S > 1$ because

FIGURE 8   The Elasticity of Demand for Imports along an Offer Curve

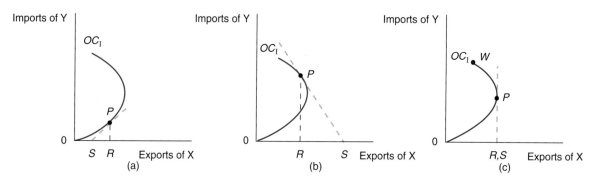

The import-demand elasticity of the offer curve at any point is measured by the distance $0R$ divided by the distance $0S$. In panel (a) the curve is "elastic" at point P because $0R > 0S$ and therefore $0R/0S > 1$. In panel (b) the offer curve is "inelastic" at point P because $0R < 0S$ and therefore $0R/0S < 1$. In panel (c) the offer curve is "unit-elastic" at point P since $0R = 0S$ and therefore $0R/0S = 1$.

---

[3]Two other definitions of elasticity used in offer curve analysis are (*a*) the *elasticity of supply of exports,* which is the percentage change in the quantity of exports supplied divided by the percentage change in the relative price of exports (which recognizes the "dual" nature of an offer curve as showing a supply of exports as well as a demand for imports), and (*b*) the *elasticity of the offer curve* itself, which is the percentage change in imports divided by the percentage change in exports as movement occurs along the offer curve. To avoid the confusion of multiple definitions and to conform to standard practice, we employ only the elasticity of demand for imports in this text. We also refer to the elasticity of demand for imports along the offer curve as "elasticity of the offer curve," although this usage is not strictly correct.

OR is a longer distance than OS and the offer curve is referred to as "elastic" at points on this upward-sloping range. In panel (b), distance OR is shorter than distance OS; thus the fraction $OR/OS < 1$. The offer curve in this downward-sloping or backward-bending portion is "inelastic." In panel (c), $OR = OS$ (the perpendicular and the tangent are the same line), so the offer curve is "unit-elastic" at point P.

The total offer curve as usually drawn has three ranges like those in panels (a), (b), and (c) in Figure 8. In panel (c), the offer curve is "elastic" at all points from the origin to point P. This is the way offer curves have been drawn heretofore in this chapter. From point P to point W (in the limiting case, W could be on the vertical axis), the offer curve is "inelastic." The offer curve at point P itself is "unit-elastic." The use of elastic-inelastic-unit-elastic in this offer curve context parallels its use in ordinary demand curve analysis. When a country is located in the "elastic" range of its offer curve, a given percentage change in the relative price of that country's import good will induce a greater percentage change in the quantity of imports purchased. When the country is located in the "inelastic" range, a given percentage change in the relative price of imports will induce a smaller percentage change

IN THE REAL WORLD:

TERMS OF TRADE FOR MAJOR GROUPS OF COUNTRIES, 1972–2005

A country's terms-of-trade movements over time reflect shifts in underlying demand and supply conditions ("willingness to trade" in the offer curve context). In Table 2 export and import price data published by the IMF have been used to construct terms-of-trade indexes for particular groups of countries over the period 1972–2005. The indexes have been constructed with a base year of 1995 = 100.

The industrial countries experienced a terms-of-trade decline of 19 percent (from an index value of 105 to 85) during the 1972–1980 period—when imported oil prices were increasing rapidly—and a rise of 18 percent from 1980 to 1995, when oil and other imported primary-product prices were generally falling. The non–oil-exporting developing countries faced a deterioration of 20 percent in their terms of trade (from an index of 116 to 93) from 1972 to 1980 and had variable TOT but no real trend from 1980 to 2005. Sufficient data for the oil-exporting countries are not available for calculating their terms of trade for the 1972–1990 period, but a sharp fall from 1990 to 1995 and a large rise after 1995 occurred. However, the terms of trade for the Middle East can be used as a rough proxy in the earlier years for the terms of trade of the oil-exporting countries, and the Middle East terms of trade *rose by 389 percent* (from an index of 37 to an index of 181) between 1972 and 1980. A substantial decline then occurred as the index fell to 100 in 1995. The dramatic rise reflected the oil embargo of 1973–1974, when the Organization of Petroleum Exporting

Countries (OPEC) restricted oil exports, and a second oil shock in 1979–1980, when supplies were disrupted by the Iranian revolution and prices were forced up further by OPEC. These developments can be thought of as large leftward shifts in the OPEC offer curve on the offer curve diagram, when OPEC exports are placed on the horizontal axis. The subsequent decline in the terms of trade from 1980 to 1995 can be interpreted as reflecting a downward shift in the collective OPEC trading partners' offer curve as demand for OPEC oil was reduced through events such as increased energy conservation, the emergence of substitute energy sources (e.g., solar energy), and the rise of alternative oil sources (the North Slope in Alaska, the North Sea).

The indexes in the table for developing countries as a whole mix together oil-exporting countries and non-oil-exporting countries and are less meaningful than separate indexes would be. Nevertheless, the indexes show a dramatic rise from 60 to 105 over the 1972–1980 period and a very slight decline to 101 in 2005. Note that performance differs by geographical grouping—the Asian countries demonstrated remarkable stability throughout most of the 1972–2000 period, while Latin American (Western Hemisphere) countries experienced little change in the 1970s, an increase in the 1980s, and a large decline from 1990 to 1995. There was a doubling of oil-exporting countries' terms of trade from 1995–2005, as one might suspect from the behavior of energy product prices in recent years.

(continued)

IN THE REAL WORLD: *(continued)*

TERMS OF TRADE FOR MAJOR GROUPS OF COUNTRIES, 1972–2005

TABLE 2   Terms-of-Trade Indexes, Selected Years, 1972–2005 (1995 = 100)

Country Group	1972	1973	1974	1979	1980
Industrial countries	105	104	93	93	85
Developing countries	60	63	85	95	105
Africa	NA	NA	NA	NA	NA
Asia	97	99	98	100	98
Europe	106	103	96	68	65
Middle East	37	41	103	138	181
Western Hemisphere	137	134	109	138	131
Oil-exporting countries	NA	NA	NA	NA	NA
Non–oil-exporting developing countries	116	115	105	98	93

Country Group	1985	1990	1995	2000	2005
Industrial countries	84	95	100	97	98
Developing countries	99	101	100	102	101
Africa	NA	98	100	95	104
Asia	95	100	100	94	86
Europe	60	65	100	103	106
Middle East	177	121	100	156	218
Western Hemisphere	117	159	100	99	103
Oil-exporting countries	NA	137	100	139	201
Non–oil-exporting developing countries	88	100	100	95	87

NA = not available.
Sources: International Monetary Fund (IMF), *International Financial Statistics Yearbook 2002* (Washington, DC: IMF, 2002), pp. 138–41; IMF, *International Financial Statistics Yearbook 2003* (Washington, DC: IMF, 2003), pp. 87–88; IMF, *International Financial Statistics Yearbook 2006* (Washington, DC: IMF, 2006), pp. 86–87; IMF, *International Financial Statistics,* January 2007, pp. 68–69. A linking procedure was used to convert data with 2000 = 100 to 1995 = 100.

in the quantity of imports purchased. Finally, in the "unit-elastic" range, a given percentage change in the relative price of imports will induce an equal percentage change in the quantity of imports.

These elasticity ranges give a clue to the reason for the shape of the offer curve. Recall that an "elastic" demand means that if the price of a good falls, total spending (or total revenue, price times quantity) will rise because the percentage increase in quantity is greater than the percentage decrease in price. In the "inelastic" demand situation, a fall in price is associated with a fall in total spending on the good (total revenue) because the percentage increase in quantity is less than the percentage decrease in price. Finally, if demand is "unit-elastic," then a fall in price will produce no change in total revenue because the percentage increase in quantity matches the percentage decrease in price.

The relationship of total spending or revenue change to elasticity is relevant to the shape of the offer curve. The important point is that *a country gives up its export good to be able*

FIGURE 9   Elasticity Ranges and Export Quantities Given Up to Acquire Imports

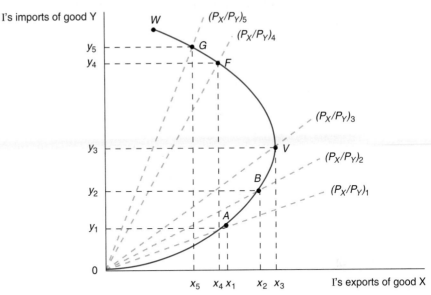

In the elastic range of the offer curve, when the relative export price rises (relative import price falls) from $(P_X/P_Y)_1$ to $(P_X/P_Y)_2$, the quantity of exports increases from $0x_1$ to $0x_2$ as more imports (y_1y_2) are demanded; in the inelastic range of the curve, when the relative export price rises (relative import price falls) from $(P_X/P_Y)_4$ to $(P_X/P_Y)_5$, the quantity of exports decreases from $0x_4$ to $0x_5$ as more imports (y_4y_5) are demanded; and at unitary point V on the offer curve, an infinitesimal rise in the relative export price (fall in relative import price) from $(P_X/P_Y)_3$ would yield no change in the quantity of exports supplied by the country. These export quantity responses are analogous to the total spending (revenue) responses of consumers to a fall in the price of a good when demand is elastic, inelastic, and unit-elastic.

to purchase its import good. In the offer curve diagram, the quantity of exports is analogous to total spending or total revenue in the ordinary demand curve analysis. The export quantity plays this role because it shows what a country is willing to part with to obtain imports, just as in ordinary demand analysis the total amount spent on the good is what consumers are willing to part with to obtain the good.

Because exports are analogous to total spending, the shape of the offer curve can be related to elasticity in a straightforward manner. Consider Figure 9. In range $0V$, a change in the terms of trade from $(P_X/P_Y)_1$ to $(P_X/P_Y)_2$ indicates a relative decline in the price of good Y. Consequently, country I is willing to spend more on good Y because demand for Y is elastic, so country I's willingness to export rises from $0x_1$ to $0x_2$. The upward-sloping portion of the offer curve is the elastic portion because declines in the price of the import good are associated with giving up more exports ($0x_2$ rather than $0x_1$) in order to purchase more imports; that is, the country moves from a point like A to a point like B.

It is clear why the inelastic portion of the offer curve is downward sloping. Suppose that prices are $(P_X/P_Y)_4$ at point F but then rise to $(P_X/P_Y)_5$. Country I's willingness to trade—as shown by its offer curve—indicates that because the relative price of the import has fallen, country I is willing to purchase more imports of good Y (an increase from quantity $0y_4$ to quantity $0y_5$). However, because demand is inelastic, country I is willing to spend less on Y or, in this offer curve context, to *give up fewer exports.* Thus, exports fall from $0x_4$ to $0x_5$.

Finally, the unit-elastic case at point V is the borderline case between elastic and inelastic. For an infinitesimal price change at V, or a larger price change if a vertical offer curve segment had been drawn for some distance above V, there would be some increase in the quantity of imports but no change in the quantity of exports $0x_3$ if prices rose above $(P_X/P_Y)_3$. Thus, no change in spending on imports is associated with a relative price change at this point, a characteristic of unit-elastic demand.

This discussion has used the concept of elasticity to identify and explain the shape of the offer curve. The unusual feature that emerges in the offer curve is the downward-sloping or backward-bending portion of the curve. Several explanations can be given for the economic behavior behind these various sizes of elasticity, and we briefly present one explanation to provide a better impression of what takes place as the terms of trade change and the country moves along its offer curve.

When the price of good X rises relative to the price of good Y—that is, P_X/P_Y rises and the terms-of-trade line gets steeper—let's consider what will happen to the quantity of exports supplied. (We know from Figure 9 that the quantity of imports demanded will increase as P_X/P_Y rises.) First, country I's consumers will tend to shift their purchases away from good X and toward good Y. Thus, out of any given production of good X by country I, more of X will be available for *export* because home consumers do not wish to consume as much of it. This **substitution effect** makes the offer curve upward sloping because, other things equal, the higher price of X results in a rise in the quantity of desired exports of X.

When the price of good X rises relative to the price of good Y, country I's producers will also have an incentive to produce more X and less Y because the higher price of good X indicates potentially higher profitability in X production relative to Y production. This **production effect** will reinforce the substitution effect because the greater production of X means that a greater quantity of X is available for export. Thus, the production effect, other things being equal, tends to yield an upward-sloping offer curve since the relatively higher price of X is inducing a greater quantity of exports of X.

Finally, when the price of good X rises relative to the price of good Y, it is clear that country I's real income has risen because the good it is sending abroad (good X) is commanding a relatively higher price while the good being purchased from abroad (good Y) is now relatively cheaper. With the rise in real income because of the relative price change, country I purchases more of both X and Y.[4] Other things being equal, the greater domestic purchases of good X because of higher real income reduce the amount of good X available for export. This **income effect** or **terms-of-trade effect** on exports works in the opposite direction from the substitution and production effects.

When the combined substitution and production effects on exports are stronger than the income effect on exports, the offer curve will be upward sloping or "normal" in shape, such as in range OV of Figure 9. However, if the income effect dominates the other two effects, the offer curve will have a downward-sloping or backward-bending portion like range VW. Obviously, if the income effect just matches the other two effects, the offer curve would be vertical and would be unit-elastic. Ultimately, the shape of the offer curve is an empirical question. For a discussion of how offer curve elasticities, can influence the stability of an equilibrium position, see Appendix B at the end of this chapter.

---

[4]We are assuming the absence of inferior goods. An "inferior good" is a good purchased in smaller quantities as real income rises. For example, as your real income rises, you may buy less hamburger because you are switching to higher-quality meats. This assumption of "no inferior goods" seems reasonable if we think of good X as country I's entire bundle of export goods and of good Y as country I's entire bundle of import goods.

CONCEPT CHECK

1. From an initial trading equilibrium position in the offer curve diagram, suppose that a country's consumers change their tastes so that they have a relatively stronger preference for the good their country *exports*. What will happen to the willingness to trade and the terms of trade of this country? Illustrate and explain.

2. Assume that a single offer curve represents the willingness to trade of a group of oil-exporting countries (such as OPEC). What effect would the group's collusive agreement to demand a higher price for oil exports have on this collective offer curve and on the terms of trade of the oil-exporting countries, other things equal? Explain.

3. In what respect is the shape of a country's offer curve analogous to the relationship between price changes and total revenue changes along an ordinary straight-line demand curve for a commodity?

OTHER CONCEPTS OF THE TERMS OF TRADE

We conclude this chapter with a brief discussion of three other meanings of the phrase *terms of trade* that exist in the literature. These meanings differ from the price of exports/price of imports (P_X/P_M) or commodity terms-of-trade concept (the P_X/P_Y of country I) that is most frequently used in this chapter. It is important to keep the various concepts distinct because they are not interchangeable in their implications.

Income Terms of Trade

A country's **income terms of trade** (TOT_Y)—sometimes judged to be more useful than the commodity terms of trade from an economic development perspective—are the commodity terms of trade multiplied by a quantity index of exports, that is, $TOT_Y = (P_X/P_M) \times Q_X$ or $(P_X \times Q_X)/P_M$. They are thus an index of total export earnings or value ($P_X \times Q_X$) divided by the price index of imports (P_M). This measure attempts to quantify the trend of a country's export-based capacity to import goods, as opposed to only the price relations between exports and imports. A rise in TOT_Y indicates that the country's export earnings now permit the country to purchase a greater quantity of imports. For developing countries, capital- and technology-intensive imports yield a stream of output in the future and can be critical for the development effort. A rise in TOT_Y can be very beneficial.

The commodity terms of trade and the income terms of trade do not have to move in the same direction over time, because a decline in P_X/P_M, for example, could be more than offset by a rise in the quantity of exports (Q_X). It is also true that a decline in the commodity terms of trade for a country can be reinforced by a decline in the quantity of exports, so that the income terms of trade fall to a greater extent than the commodity terms of trade.

Single Factoral Terms of Trade

The **single factoral terms of trade** (TOT_{SF}) relate import price trends to productivity growth of the factors of production. The TOT_{SF} concept is the commodity terms of trade multiplied by an index of productivity in the export industries, that is, $TOT_{SF} = (P_X/P_M) \times O_X$, where O_X is the productivity index. If the single factoral terms of trade rise, the economic interpretation is that a greater quantity of imports can be obtained for a *given unit of work effort* in producing exports. In other words, a rise means that more imports can be purchased for a given amount of employment time of the factors of production in the export industries. There have been some calculations of TOT_{SF}, but a major difficulty involves generating accurate productivity indexes. The TOT_{SF} will usually show a more favorable (or less unfavorable) trend for any given country than will the commodity terms of trade because productivity usually increases over time.

IN THE REAL WORLD:

INCOME TERMS OF TRADE OF MAJOR GROUPS OF COUNTRIES, 1972–2005

Table 3 portrays income terms-of-trade indexes for 1972–2005, calculated by dividing the index of export value in each year ($P_X \times Q_X$, with 1995 = 100) by the index of import prices. Compare this table with the commodity terms of trade in Table 2, noting that movements in the income terms of trade do not necessarily mirror movements of the commodity terms of trade. Furthermore, *all* groups of countries have shown improvement in their income terms of trade over time (although the Middle East had marked deterioration in the early 1980s), a result that is conceptually impossible with the commodity terms of trade because an improvement in the commodity terms of trade of some groups *must* mean a deterioration for at least one other group. The most dramatic improvement in income terms of trade over the entire period occurred for the developing economies in Asia, which importantly reflects the strong demand in world markets for the products of China, Hong Kong, South Korea, Singapore, and Taiwan.

TABLE 3   Income Terms-of-Trade Indexes, Selected Years, 1972–2005 (1995 = 100)

Country Group	1972	1973	1974	1979	1980
Industrial countries	34	38	36	47	45
Developing countries	18	22	28	39	39
Africa	NA	NA	NA	NA	NA
Asia	10	11	11	18	19
Europe	NA	NA	NA	NA	NA
Middle East	44	55	125	163	147
Western Hemisphere	28	32	36	53	56
Oil-exporting countries	NA	NA	NA	NA	NA
Non–oil-exporting developing countries	16	19	18	25	26

Country Group	1985	1990	1995	2000	2005
Industrial countries	50	75	100	143	170
Developing countries	38	57	100	167	269
Africa	NA	96	100	154	225
Asia	27	53	100	156	253
Europe	NA	NA	100	213	389
Middle East	78	104	100	203	357
Western Hemisphere	60	79	100	163	209
Oil-exporting countries	NA	120	100	181	315
Non–oil-exporting developing countries	32	52	100	162	260

NA = not available.
Sources: International Monetary Fund (IMF), *International Financial Statistics Yearbook 2002* (Washington, DC: IMF, 2002), pp. 126–31, 140–41; IMF, *International Financial Statistics Yearbook 2003* (Washington, DC: IMF, 2003), pp. 81–83, 88; IMF, *International Financial Statistics Yearbook 2006* (Washington, DC: IMF, 2006), pp. 80–82, 87; IMF, *International Financial Statistics,* January 2007, pp. 62–64, 69. A linking procedure was used to convert data with 2000 = 100 to 1995 = 100.

Double Factoral Terms of Trade

The final terms of trade concept adjusts the single factoral terms of trade for productivity trends in a country's trading partners. Thus, the **double factoral terms-of-trade** ratio (TOT_{DF}) is the single factoral terms of trade divided by the index of productivity in the export industries of the trading partners, that is, $TOT_{DF} = (P_X/P_M) \times (O_X/O_M)$, where O_M

represents the foreign productivity index for the home country's imports. A rise in TOT_{DF} indicates that given quantities of the services of the home country's factors of production in its export industries are being exchanged for a greater quantity of the services of the factors of production in export industries in trading partner countries. In this sense, the "exchange of factors" between the partners has become more favorable for the home country. The TOT_{DF} have been occasionally calculated in practice, but the empirical difficulty of obtaining data on the productivity of foreign factors of production must be added to the difficulty of obtaining data on the productivity of home factors of production.

In overview, the selection of the appropriate terms-of-trade concept to emphasize depends upon the purpose the analyst has in mind. Each concept is designed to interpret a different aspect of relative price changes. In the remainder of this text, *terms of trade* will refer to the commodity or net barter terms of trade unless otherwise indicated. However, keep in mind that this concept is not necessarily appropriate for examination of many trade issues.

CONCEPT CHECK

1. If demand increases for the export good of country A, how does the elasticity of country A's offer curve influence the extent to which its terms of trade will improve?

2. If demand for a country's export good rises, other things being equal, will both the commodity terms of trade and the income terms of trade improve? Explain.

SUMMARY

This chapter has developed the concept of the offer curve. The offer curve demonstrates a country's willingness to participate in international trade at various terms of trade and provides a vehicle for illustrating the determination of the equilibrium terms of trade in the world market. Economic growth, changes in tastes, and commercial policy actions are among the events that will shift a country's offer curve and can influence the volume and terms of trade. Finally, the chapter discussed the elasticity of an offer curve and several concepts of the terms of trade.

KEY TERMS

commodity terms of trade (or net barter terms of trade)
double factoral terms of trade
elasticity of demand for imports
equilibrium terms of trade

income effect (or terms-of-trade effect)
income terms of trade
large country
offer curve (or reciprocal demand curve)

price index
production effect
single factoral terms of trade
small country
substitution effect

QUESTIONS AND PROBLEMS

1. Discuss several economic events that would increase a country's willingness to trade.
2. Assume that demand increases for a country's export good. Will there be a different qualitative effect on the country's terms of trade if the country is "large" rather than "small"? Why or why not?
3. Suppose that country I increases its willingness to trade at the same time that trading partner country II *decreases* its willingness to trade. What can be said about the resulting impact on the terms of trade and on the volume of trade?

(Note: You will not be able to say anything concrete about one of these two impacts. Why not?)

4. Suppose that country I and trading partner country II decrease their willingness to trade at the same time. What will be the impact on the terms of trade and on the volume of trade? (Note: You will not be able to say anything concrete about one of these impacts. Why not?)
5. In the offer curve analysis, why must an excess supply of one good be associated with an excess demand for the other good?

6. In August 1990, many countries decided to retaliate against Iraq for its invasion of Kuwait by refusing to trade with Iraq (except in food and humanitarian goods). With such an "embargo" in place, what conceptually would happen to Iraq's terms of trade and volume of trade? Illustrate and explain your answer using offer curves.

7. Suppose that an offer curve diagram has developed countries' exports on one axis and developing countries' exports on the other axis. Explain the predicted impact, other things equal, on the terms of trade of developing countries of relatively slow growth in demand for developing countries' goods by developed countries combined with relatively rapid growth in demand by developing countries for developed countries' goods.

8. In the past, the members of OPEC have been able to raise the relative price of petroleum by a large amount with a relatively small decrease in export volume, thereby increasing substantially the revenues they received from the buyers of their petroleum exports. Describe the likely shapes of the offer curves of the importing countries—shapes that enabled the OPEC countries to pursue their trade strategy successfully.

9. "If countries are behaving rationally, they should always be willing to export more at a higher export price. Thus, one would not expect to see 'backward-bending' offer curves." Discuss.

10. You have the following information for a country for 2005, with all price indexes utilizing 1995 as the base year: The export price index is 120, the import price index is 130, the quantity index of exports is 115, and the quantity index of imports is 100. Calculate the commodity terms of trade and the income terms of trade for this country for 2005. Interpret your results.

Appendix A   DERIVATION OF IMPORT-DEMAND ELASTICITY ON AN OFFER CURVE

To derive the import-demand elasticity on the offer curve at any point P in the standard fashion, consider Figure 8(a) on page 114. The import-demand elasticity (ε) is the percentage change in the quantity demanded of the import good Y divided by the percentage change in the relative price of Y. The relative price of Y is the amount of export good X given up to obtain 1 unit of good Y. Using the calculus,

$$\varepsilon = \frac{dY/Y}{\dfrac{d(X/Y)}{X/Y}} = \frac{(dY/Y)(X/Y)}{d(X/Y)}$$

Hence,

$$\varepsilon = \frac{(XdY/Y^2)}{d(X/Y)} = \frac{(XdY)/Y^2}{\dfrac{YdX - XdY}{Y^2}}$$

$$\varepsilon = \frac{XdY}{YdX - XdY} = \frac{1}{\dfrac{YdX}{XdY} - 1}$$

Geometrically, in Figure 8(a), $Y/X = RP/OR$ and $dX/dY = SR/RP$. Therefore,

$$\varepsilon = \frac{1}{\dfrac{RP}{OR} \times \dfrac{SR}{RP} - 1} = \frac{1}{\dfrac{SR}{OR} - 1}$$

$$= \frac{1}{\dfrac{SR - OR}{OR}} = \frac{1}{-\dfrac{OS}{OR}} = -\frac{OR}{OS}$$

Ignoring the negative sign, the import-demand elasticity ε is thus OR/OS, or the distance from the origin to the point where the perpendicular from P hits the x-axis divided by the distance from the origin to the point where the line tangent to P hits the x-axis.

Appendix B   ELASTICITY AND INSTABILITY OF OFFER CURVE EQUILIBRIA

In this chapter and in the rest of this book, unless otherwise noted, we assume that equilibrium positions are stable. This means that a deviation from an equilibrium will set forces into motion to move to the equilibrium. This kind of equilibrium is the type familiar, for example, from ordinary demand and supply diagrams. A price of a good above (below) the equilibrium price is associated with excess supply (demand), and the price therefore falls (rises) to the equilibrium price. However, in the offer curve diagram, it is possible for an equilibrium position to be an unstable one. This means that a deviation from equilibrium will push the relative price P_X/P_Y farther away from the original equilibrium relative price rather than toward that price.

Recall that an offer curve can be drawn with an elastic range, a unit-elastic turning point, and an inelastic range. It is theoretically possible for the interaction of two countries' curves to yield multiple equilibrium positions (see Figure 10). In this unusual-looking graph, which resembles a poorly tied bow tie, there are three equilibrium positions—E_1, E_2, and E_3—with offer curves OC_I and OC_{II}. The existence of multiple equilibria makes it unclear where the world economy will settle, since the resting place could be a matter of historical accident rather than of any particular economic forces.

Points E_1 and E_3 are stable equilibrium positions because small deviations from those points set forces in motion to move to those points. For example, at point E_1 and TOT_1, it is clear that terms of trade TOT_2 are associated with excess supply of good X and excess demand for good Y. Hence, TOT_2

FIGURE 10   Multiple Equilibria in International Trade

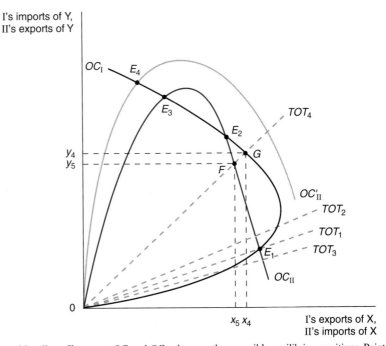

With backward-bending offer curves OC_I and OC_{II}, there are three possible equilibrium positions. Point E_1 is a stable equilibrium, since terms of trade TOT_2 and TOT_3 will be associated with excess demands and supplies of the goods that will move the terms of trade to TOT_1. However, terms of trade at TOT_4 will not move to equilibrium position E_2 because, at TOT_4, there is excess supply of good X (of amount x_5x_4) and excess demand for good Y (of amount y_5y_4). The terms of trade will thus move from TOT_4 downward to TOT_1. Analogously, a terms-of-trade line slightly above E_2 would move up to stable equilibrium position E_3. In addition, if the initial equilibrium position is E_1, a shift in OC_{II} to OC'_{II} would cause equilibrium to move to position E_4.

are not sustainable and relative prices fall to TOT_1. Similarly, relative prices TOT_3 are associated with excess demand for good X and excess supply of good Y, so the terms of trade move to TOT_1. An identical analysis with point E_3 would show that E_3 is also a stable equilibrium position.

However, in Figure 10, point E_2 is an unstable equilibrium position. Consider terms of trade TOT_4. With the trading partners in disequilibrium at TOT_4, will trade move to E_2? Clearly *not!* At TOT_4, country I wishes to trade at point G, where it will be supplying quantity $0x_4$ of exports and demanding quantity $0y_4$ of imports. However, country II, at point F on its offer curve, wishes to supply quantity $0y_5$ of exports and to demand quantity $0x_5$ of imports. At TOT_4, there is excess supply of good X (of x_5x_4) and excess demand for good Y (of y_5y_4). This situation will cause the P_X/P_Y ratio to *fall;* thus, TOT_4 will give way to a flatter price line. The trading partners under the forces of the market will not go to E_2, but to E_1, where the excess supply of good X and the excess demand for good Y are eliminated. A similar analysis can show why a terms-of-trade line slightly above E_2 will set forces in motion to drive the trading equilibrium to point E_3. Incidentally, the mathematical condition for an unstable equilibrium, such as E_2, to exist is that the *sum* of the absolute values of the two countries' import elasticities of demand at that point be less than 1.0. The relevant empirical question to be investigated concerns whether the sum of the absolute values of the elasticities is high enough (such as $0.4 + 1.5 = 1.9$) to generate a stable equilibrium or whether it is so low ($0.5 + 0.3 = 0.8$) that an equilibrium position is unstable.

A main point is that if elasticities in international trade are such that countries are operating on the inelastic portion of their offer curves, then it is possible that countries can experience large movements of prices in one direction (such as from immediately below E_2 to E_1). Further, suppose that the two countries are initially at E_1 but that the offer curve of country II (OC_{II}) now shifts upward to OC'_{II}. The new equilibrium position will be E_4, with a considerably different set of prices and volume of trade than at E_1. Such large changes could engender risk for many firms and individuals engaged in international trade. Risk-averse participants might then be less willing to expose themselves to the world economy altogether and would sacrifice gains from trade.

THE BASIS FOR TRADE

Factor Endowments and the
Heckscher-Ohlin Model

LEARNING OBJECTIVES

- To understand how relative factor endowments affect relative factor prices.

- To recognize how different relative factor prices generate a basis for trade.

- To learn how trade affects relative factor prices and income distribution.

- To understand how real-world phenomena can modify Heckscher-Ohlin conclusions.

INTRODUCTION

Do Labor Standards
Affect Comparative
Advantage?

The role of labor standards in fostering international trade has been in the forefront of the trade policy agenda in recent years. It has attracted the interest of humanitarian organizations, governments, and international organizations as production of labor-intensive goods has continued to move to developing countries with increased globalization. In a recent article, Matthias Busse analyzes econometrically whether different categories of labor standards do, in fact, have an effect on comparative advantage in developing countries.[1] He addresses the question of whether a developing country can derive comparative advantage in unskilled-labor-intensive goods by employing low labor standards and thus increase its world exports. A number of different groups believe that this is happening and thus are urging the implementation of import barriers against countries with notably lower standards for both humanitarian reasons and to ensure a more "level playing field."

Busse distinguished between "core" labor standards (important human rights such as union rights, freedom from forced labor, abolition of child labor, equal opportunity) and labor standards often referred to as "acceptable conditions of work" (for example, minimum wages, safety and health standards). He focused on the effect of core standards on comparative advantage and exports utilizing the Heckscher-Ohlin theoretical framework developed in this chapter to provide the underpinnings for his empirical work. Because comparative advantage is determined by relative factor endowments, he hypothesized that lower core labor standards would lead to a relative increase in unskilled labor and thus increase relative exports of unskilled-labor-intensive goods. Five indicators of core labor standards [discrimination against women, presence of child labor, use of forced labor, basic union rights, and number of ratifications of the eight International Labour Office (ILO) conventions of core labor standards] were key variables used to explain the share of unskilled-labor-intensive goods in total exports in an 83-country cross-section regression analysis. Several of the more interesting conclusions were that greater discrimination against women weakened comparative advantage, whereas weaker union rights, greater child labor, and greater use of forced labor increased export share. Interestingly, the number of ratifications of the ILO conventions appeared to have no significant effect. It is, however, important to note that in all cases educational attainment and the overall relative labor endowment had relatively stronger influences on the trade patterns than did the labor standard variables.

Interesting and useful policy analysis such as that contained in the Busse paper necessitates the use of a more formal structure in which the complexities of international comparative advantage can be sorted out in a consistent way. In the previous chapter, we demonstrated that a country will gain from trade any time that the terms of trade differ from its own relative prices in autarky. The country gains by expanding production of and exporting the commodity that is relatively more valuable in the foreign market and reducing production of and importing the good that is relatively less expensive in the foreign market. These adjustments permit the consumption of a combination of goods that lies outside the production-possibilities frontier at a higher level of consumer well-being. It was further demonstrated that the underlying basis for the relative price differences that led to international trade could be traced to differences in supply and/or demand conditions in the two countries. This chapter will examine in greater detail the factors that influence relative prices prior to international trade, focusing on differences in supply conditions. We first examine how different relative quantities of the factors of production can influence product prices and produce a basis for trade. We then discuss how the resulting trade will in turn affect factor prices and the distribution of income within the trading countries. Finally, the implications of various assumptions employed in the analysis are presented. The purpose

---

[1]Matthias Busse, "Do Labor Standards Affect Comparative Advantage in Developing Countries?" *World Development* 30, no. 11 (November 2002), pp. 1921–32.

of this chapter is to provide you with a deeper understanding of the critical factors underlying relative cost differences and therefore comparative advantage.

SUPPLY, DEMAND, AND AUTARKY PRICES

You will recall that the source of differences in pretrade price ratios between countries lies in the interaction of aggregate supply and demand as represented by their respective production-possibilities frontiers and community indifference curves. Thus, there is a basis for trade whenever supply conditions or demand conditions vary between countries. For example, where two countries are identical in all supply aspects but have different tastes and preferences (see Figure 6 in Chapter 6, page 96), it is clear that relative product prices will differ in autarky. A similar result occurs if demands in the two countries are identical but supply conditions vary, as reflected in differently shaped production-possibilities frontiers (see Figure 7 in Chapter 6, page 97). In this case, the different autarky price ratios could be the result of different technologies in the two countries, different relative factor availabilities, or a combination of the two. Whatever the reason, the different prices in autarky again indicate that there is a basis for gainful trade between these two countries.

It is safe to conclude that differences in either demand or supply conditions are sufficient to provide a basis for trade between two countries. This of course assumes that there is no intervention in the markets to alter prices from these general equilibrium results. Clearly, taxes and subsidies can cause autarky prices to be more or less different prior to trade. The policy implications of price-distorting policies will be covered in Chapter 14, "The Impact of Trade Policies." We now turn to a more rigorous examination of the role of factor availabilities in international trade.

FACTOR ENDOWMENTS AND THE HECKSCHER-OHLIN THEOREM

The effects of factor endowments on international trade were analyzed early in the twentieth century by two Swedish economists, Eli Heckscher (in 1919) and Bertil Ohlin (in 1933). As employed by modern economists, this analysis makes a number of simplifying assumptions, specifically that:

1. There are two countries, two homogeneous goods, and two homogeneous factors of production whose initial levels are fixed and assumed to be relatively different for each country.

2. Technology is identical in both countries; that is, production functions are the same in both countries.

3. Production is characterized by constant returns to scale for both commodities in both countries.

4. The two commodities have **different relative factor intensities,** and the respective commodity factor intensities are the same for all factor price ratios.

5. Tastes and preferences are the same in both countries. Further, for any given set of product prices, the two products are consumed in the same relative quantities at all levels of income; that is, there are homothetic tastes and preferences.[2]

---

[2]It can be shown in more advanced discussions that, with identical and homothetic tastes and preferences, changes in income distribution will not cause the indifference map to change. Thus, the possibility that pretrade and posttrade community indifference curves might intersect due to trade-induced changes in income distribution is precluded.

6. Perfect competition exists in both countries.

7. Factors are perfectly mobile within each country and not mobile between countries.

8. There are no transportation costs.

9. There are no policies restricting the movement of goods between countries or interfering with the market determination of prices and output.

Most of these assumptions are already familiar to you, but the two that are especially critical to the Heckscher-Ohlin (H-O) explanation of the emergence and structure of trade are (assumption 1) that factor endowments are different in each country and (assumption 4) that commodities are always intensive in a given factor regardless of relative factor prices. The two assumptions need to be examined in greater detail prior to discussing the H-O theorem.

Factor Abundance and Heckscher-Ohlin

It is important to understand that the phrase *different factor endowments* refers to **different relative factor endowments,** not different absolute amounts. Crucial to the H-O analysis is that factor proportions are different between the two countries. Relative factor abundance may be defined in two ways: the **physical definition** and the **price definition.** The physical definition explains factor abundance in terms of the physical units of two factors, for example, labor and capital, available in each of the two countries. Country I would be the capital-abundant country if its ratio of capital to labor exceeded the ratio of capital to labor in country II [$(K/L)_\mathrm{I} > (K/L)_\mathrm{II}$]. It must be stressed that the relative amount of the factors is critical, not country size. A country with fewer absolute units of physical capital than a larger country could still be the capital-abundant country as long as the amount of capital relative to labor was greater than the same ratio in the larger country. Finally, in the two-country, two-factor case, if country I is the capital-abundant country, then country II must by definition be the labor-abundant country.

The price definition relies on the relative prices of capital and labor to determine the type of factor abundance characterizing the two countries. According to this definition, country I would be the capital-abundant country as long as $(r/w)_\mathrm{I} < (r/w)_\mathrm{II}$; that is, the ratio of the price or rental rate of capital (r) to the price or wage of labor (w) in country I is less than in country II. This definition views relative abundance in terms of the factors' relative scarcity prices. The greater the relative abundance of a factor, the lower its relative price.

One definition focuses on physical availability (supply), and the other focuses on factor price. What is the link, if any, between the two? On the surface, there does not seem to be a problem because the greater or smaller the supply of a factor, the lower or higher its price tends to be. In countries with large populations such as India and China, the price of labor is relatively low while that of capital is relatively high. The converse tends to be true in a country such as Germany or the United States. However, the problem is that the factor price reflects not only the supply of available factors but also the demand. Because factors of production are not consumed directly but are used to produce final goods and services that are consumed, demand for the factors results from the structure of demand for final goods and services. Demand for a factor of production is thus often referred to as a derived demand resulting from producers meeting final consumption needs. Factor prices reflect not only the physical availability of the factors in question but also the structure of final demand and the production technology employed. Fortunately, because the H-O model assumes that technology and tastes and preferences are the same in both countries, the two definitions will produce the same result. With technology and demand influences neutralized between the two countries, the country with the relatively larger K/L ratio also will have the relatively smaller r/w ratio. The link between the two definitions is unambiguous

IN THE REAL WORLD:

RELATIVE FACTOR ENDOWMENTS IN SELECTED COUNTRIES, 1992

Relative factor endowments differ considerably across countries. Three factor ratios are given below for a number of selected countries to provide some indication of the degree of difference in endowments in 1992. The wide variety of relative factor endowments supports the idea that underlying factor supply conditions continue to vary from country to country, as Heckscher and Ohlin posited many years ago.

Country	Capital/Labor ($/worker)	Capital/Land ($/sq. kilometer)	Labor/Land (worker/sq. kilometer)
Australia	$ 38,729	$ 40,162	1.08
Austria	36,641	1,744,478	47.61
Bolivia	5,355	24,274	4.55
Canada	44,970	62,958	1.40
Chile	11,306	74,733	6.61
Denmark	33,814	2,359,203	69.77
Finland	47,498	421,782	8.88
France	37,460	1,764,366	47.10
Germany	41,115	4,491,403	109.24
Greece	23,738	719,261	30.30
Hong Kong	14,039	42,117,000	3,000.00
India	1,997	204,073	102.19
Ireland	22,171	633,425	28.57
Italy	33,775	2,580,748	76.41
Japan	41,286	6,881,138	166.67
Madagascar	1,750	14,910	8.52
Mexico	13,967	223,809	16.34
Norway	47,118	290,718	6.17
Philippines	3,598	287,840	80.00
Spain	30,888	917,682	29.71
Sweden	41,017	364,641	8.89
Switzerland	76,733	5,614,554	73.17
Turkey	7,626	244,718	32.09
United Kingdom	22,509	2,572,554	114.29
United States	35,993	476,187	13.23
Venezuela	18,296	140,513	7.68

Note: Capital is valued at 1985 prices.

Sources: Capital/labor: Penn World Tables, obtained from datacentre.chass.utoronto.ca; capital/land: (capital/labor) (labor/land); labor/land: World Bank, *World Development Report 1994* (New York: Oxford University Press, 1994), pp. 162–63, 210–11.

unless technology or demands differ between the two countries. When this happens, the price definition may differ from the physical definition; for example, physically abundant capital may be relatively high priced. We will refer to this possibility later in the chapter.

Commodity Factor Intensity and Heckscher-Ohlin

A commodity is said to be factor-x-intensive whenever the ratio of factor x to a second factor y is larger when compared with a similar ratio of factor usage of a second commodity. For example, steel is said to be capital intensive compared with cloth if the K/L ratio in steel production is larger than the K/L ratio in cloth production. H-O assumes not only that the two commodities have different factor intensities at common factor prices but also that the difference holds for all possible factor price ratios in both countries. This means that at all possible factor prices, the isoquants reflecting the technology used in steel production are more oriented toward the capital axis, compared with the isoquants reflecting cloth production, so that the capital/labor ratio for steel will always be larger than that for cloth (see Figure 1). It is important to note that this assumption does not preclude substituting labor for capital if capital becomes relatively more expensive, or substituting capital for labor if the relative price of labor rises. While such price changes would indeed change the capital/labor ratios in both commodities, they would never cause cloth to use more capital relative to labor compared with steel. This is a strong assumption and it is critical to the H-O analysis. We will later examine some possible conditions when it would not hold and the resulting implications for international trade.

The Heckscher-Ohlin Theorem

The set of assumptions about production leads to the conclusion that the production-possibilities frontier will differ between two countries solely as a result of their differing factor endowments. With identical technology in both countries, constant returns to scale, and a given factor-intensity relationship between final products, the country with abundant capital will be able to produce relatively more of the capital-intensive good,

FIGURE 1   Factor-Intensity Relationships

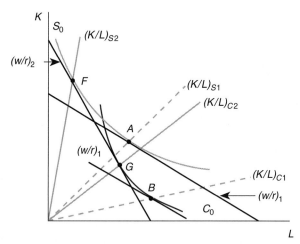

A critical assumption of the H-O analysis is that commodities are intensive in a given factor regardless of relative factor prices. This assumption is met in the above case for steel (isoquant S_0) and cloth (isoquant C_0). Given the nature of the isoquant map for each commodity, steel will always have a higher K/L ratio than cloth whatever the relative factor prices, and thus it is the capital-intensive product. If steel is relatively capital intensive, it follows that cloth must necessarily be labor intensive; that is, it will always have a relatively smaller K/L ratio compared with steel. This is evident if one compares the K/L ratios of the two goods when labor is relatively cheap [$(w/r)_1$] with ratios when labor is relatively expensive [$(w/r)_2$]. The K/L ratio used in production at any point on an isoquant is given by the slope of a ray from the origin through the production point. Thus, at $(w/r)_1$ production of steel (at A) is more K intensive than production of cloth (at B); at $(w/r)_2$, production of steel (at F) is again more K intensive than production of cloth (at G).

IN THE REAL WORLD:

RELATIVE FACTOR INTENSITIES IN SELECTED PRODUCTS, 1992

Heckscher-Ohlin assumed that relative factor intensities were different across commodities and that these differences were consistent across countries. To provide an indication of the degree of variation within a country, we calculated the following capital-labor ratios for a selected group of SIC (Standard Industrial Classification) commodities for the United States for 1992. As can be observed, there are huge variations in *K/L* ratios; the range is from $468,000 per worker (petroleum and coal products) to about $8,000 per worker (apparel and other textile products).

Commodity	SIC	K/L ($/employee)
Food and kindred products	20	$ 74,875.76
Tobacco products	21	167,636.84
Textile mill products	22	44,051.59
Apparel and other textile products	23	8,274.03
Lumber and wood products	24	39,134.64
Furniture and fixtures	25	21,735.51
Paper and allied products	26	171,729.68
Printing and publishing	27	37,691.24
Chemicals and allied products	28	192,593.45
Petroleum and coal products	29	468,085.66
Rubber and miscellaneous plastics products	30	52,122.09
Leather and leather products	31	12,465.88
Stone, clay, and glass products	32	84,056.74
Primary metal industries	33	123,594.93
Fabricated metal products	34	43,408.40
Industrial machinery and equipment	35	49,949.85
Electronic and other electric equipment	36	54,582.36
Transportation equipment	37	67,846.68
Instruments and related products	38	47,725.27
Miscellaneous manufacturing industries	39	22,638.58

Source: Underlying data are from U.S. Department of Commerce, Bureau of the Census, *1992 Census of Manufactures: General Summary,* tables 1-3b and 1-4, obtained from www.census.gov/prod/1/manmin/92sub/mc92-s-1.pdf. ⬤

while the country with abundant labor will be able to produce relatively more of the labor-intensive good. The shape and position of the production-possibilities frontier is thus determined by the factor intensities of the two goods and the amount of each factor available. This is obvious if one compares the Edgeworth boxes for two countries with different factor endowments (see Figure 2). The two boxes show that country I is the capital-abundant country. This is evident since the height of the box (amount of capital) is greater for country I, whereas the length of the box (physical amount of labor) is greater for country II. In more general terms, the slope of the diagonal reflects the *K/L* ratio and therefore the relative endowment of the country. This slope is greater in country I, making it clearly the capital-abundant country. The analysis in Chapter 5, which discussed how the PPF was obtained from the Edgeworth box, leads us to conclude that the production-possibilities frontier for

FIGURE 2   Different Relative Factor Endowments and the Nature of the Edgeworth Box

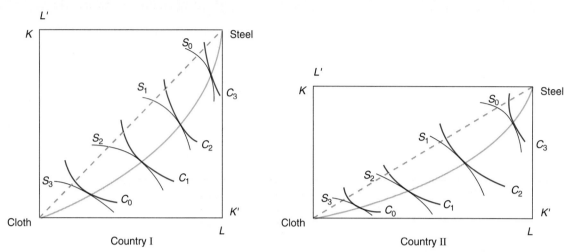

The different shapes of the Edgeworth boxes reflect the relative factor endowments in the two countries. The relatively taller box for country I— the steeper diagonal reflects a higher K/L ratio—indicates that it is the capital-abundant country, whereas the relatively longer box for country II (flatter diagonal) indicates that it is the labor-abundant country. If technology is the same in both countries, the different relative factor endowments will lead to differently shaped PPFs. Because country I has relatively more capital than country II, it will be able to produce relatively more of the capital-intensive good. Consequently, its PPF will reflect a greater relative ability to produce steel, whereas country II's PPF will reflect a greater relative ability to produce cloth.

each country will be different. Country I's PPF is oriented more toward steel, and country II's PPF is oriented more toward cloth.

If these two differently shaped production-possibilities frontiers are now combined with the same set of tastes and preferences, two different sets of relative prices will emerge in autarky, as shown in Figure 3(a). The relative price of steel will be lower in country I (the capital-abundant country) as reflected in a steeper autarky price line, while the relative price of cloth will be lower in country II (the labor-abundant country) as evidenced by a flatter autarky price line. Because relative prices in autarky are different between the two countries, a clear basis for trade results from the different factor endowments.

The trade implications of this situation can be seen in Figure 3(b). The international terms of trade must lie necessarily between the two internal price ratios, being flatter than the autarky price line in country I and steeper than the autarky price line in country II. In this situation, country I will export steel to and import cloth from country II, reaching a higher community indifference curve in the process. Country II also will find itself better off by exporting cloth and importing steel.

The common equilibrium international terms of trade that produce this result are drawn between the autarky prices of both of the countries. A single international terms-of-trade (TOT) line, $(P_C/P_S)_{int}$, tangent to both PPFs, is used in panel (b) for convenience, although all that is required is an equally sloped TOT line, not necessarily a common line. For equilibrium to occur, country I's desired exports of steel (S_1S_0) and imports of cloth (C_2C_1) must equal exactly country II's desired exports of cloth (C_1C_0) and imports of steel (S_2S_1) at the prevailing international terms of trade. When this occurs, both countries find themselves on the higher indifference curve, IC_1, indicating the mutual gain from trade.

The previous discussion used the physical definition of factor abundance. A similar result would have occurred if we had used the price definition. Because country I is the

FIGURE 3   Gains from Trade in Two Countries with Identical Technology and Demands but Different Relative Factor Endowments

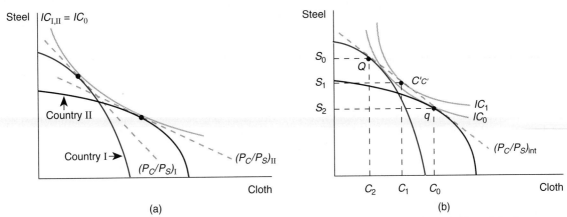

(a)   (b)

The two graphs demonstrate the basis for trade when demand conditions and technology are assumed to be identical but relative factor endowments are different for countries I and II. Country I is assumed to be the capital-abundant country and has a PPF skewed toward the production of the capital-intensive good, steel. The PPF for country II, the labor-abundant country, is skewed toward the labor-intensive good, cloth. With identical demand structures, indicated by the common community indifference curve, $IC_{\mathrm{I,II}}$, we see that the relative price of cloth $(P_C/P_S)_{\mathrm{II}}$ in country II is going to be less (a flatter relative price line) than that in country I, $(P_C/P_S)_{\mathrm{I}}$. There is thus a basis for trade between the two countries. For both to benefit from trade, they must settle at an international terms of trade that lie between the two domestic price ratios in autarky, $(P_C/P_S)_{\mathrm{int}}$ in panel (b). Both countries will now wish to consume at $C'c'$, which lies outside their respective PPFs. At the same time, production will move to Q in country I and to q in country II. Country II will therefore export C_1C_0 of cloth and import S_2S_1 of steel. Country I will export S_1S_0 of steel and import C_2C_1 of cloth. In equilibrium, C_1C_0 of country II exports is the same as C_2C_1 of country I imports, and S_1S_0 of country I exports is the same as S_2S_1 of country II imports.

capital-abundant country, $(r/w)_{\mathrm{I}} < (r/w)_{\mathrm{II}}$ [or $(w/r)_{\mathrm{I}} > (w/r)_{\mathrm{II}}$]. With identical technology and constant returns to scale, country I will be able to produce steel relatively more cheaply than country II, and country II can produce cloth relatively more cheaply than country I.

This relationship between relative factor prices and relative product prices can be developed more formally through isoquant-isocost analysis. Consider Figure 4(a). Given isocost line MN in country I, whose slope reflects $(w/r)_{\mathrm{I}}$, steel would be produced at point X and cloth at point Y. Thus, the same factor cost in the two industries yields S_1 units of steel and C_1 units of cloth. On the other hand, $(w/r)_{\mathrm{II}} < (w/r)_{\mathrm{I}}$, so a flatter isocost line is present in country II $(M'N')$. Given this isocost line, country II's producers would select points Q and T. Hence, in country II, C_2 units have the same cost as S_1, while in country I only C_1 units (a smaller quantity than C_2) could be produced for the same cost as S_1. Thus, cloth is relatively cheaper in country II and steel is relatively cheaper in country I [$(P_{\mathrm{cloth}}/P_{\mathrm{steel}})_{\mathrm{II}} < (P_{\mathrm{cloth}}/P_{\mathrm{steel}})_{\mathrm{I}}$]. The conclusion is that a higher w/r leads to a higher relative price of cloth. The H-O relationship is illustrated in Figure 4(b). Note that if steel had been the relatively labor-intensive good rather than cloth, the relationship would be reflected in a downward-sloping line.

It is now clear that different relative factor prices will generate different relative commodity prices in autarky. Consequently, there is a basis for trade, and each country will export the product it can produce less expensively: steel in country I and cloth in country II. This same conclusion was reached in the graphical PPF analysis that utilized the physical definition of factor abundance. In both cases, each country expanded production of and exported the good that made the more intensive use of its relatively abundant factor of production.

With this H-O analysis in mind, one of its major conclusions, commonly referred to as the **Heckscher-Ohlin theorem,** can be stated: *A country will export the commodity that*

TITANS OF INTERNATIONAL ECONOMICS:

PAUL ANTHONY SAMUELSON (BORN 1915)

Paul A. Samuelson is one of the most widely known economists in the United States, due not only to his prodigious research for the last half-century but also for the success of his principles book, *Economics,* which introduced millions of students to the subject and which has been in print for more than 50 years. He was born in Gary, Indiana, in 1915 and later attended some 14 different secondary schools, eventually entering the University of Chicago at age 17. Upon graduation in 1935, he studied economics at Harvard University for five years. Samuelson published his first article in 1937 as a 21-year-old graduate student and averaged more than five articles a year during his career. His 1941 doctoral dissertation is still regarded as the seminal work on the mathematical foundations of theoretical economics. He accepted a position on the economics faculty at the Massachusetts Institute of Technology in 1940 and has remained there ever since. He has written on microeconomic theory, consumer theory, and welfare economics; capital theory, dynamics, and general equilibrium; public finance; macroeconomics; and international trade.

Samuelson once said, "Our subject puts its best foot forward when it speaks out on international trade," and his own contributions in the area have had a lasting impact. In the study of trade, he is well known for his seminal work on Heckscher-Ohlin (sometimes referred to as the Heckscher-Ohlin-Samuelson model), focusing on factor price equalization and the Stolper-Samuelson theorem on the distributional effects of trade (discussed later in this chapter). He was awarded the Nóbèl Prize in economics in 1970 and has received all the major honors in the economics profession. His many mathematical and theoretical contributions have had a profound effect on the discipline and the profession.

Sources: Stanley Fischer, "Paul Anthony Samuelson," in John Eatwell, Murray Milgate, and Peter Newman, eds., *The New Palgrave: A Dictionary of Economics,* Vol. 4 (London: Macmillan, 1987), pp. 234–41; Adrian Kendry, "Paul Samuelson and the Scientific Awakening of Economics," in J. R. Shackleton and Gareth Locksley, eds., *Twelve Contemporary Economists* (London: Macmillan, 1981), chap. 12. ●

FIGURE 4   Relative Factor Prices and Relative Product Prices

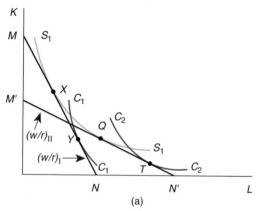
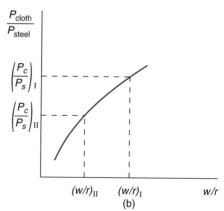

(a)   (b)

Relative factor prices $(w/r)_I$ are represented in panel (a) by isocost line MN. Country I will produce S_1 units of steel at point X and C_1 units of cloth at point Y. Because labor is relatively more abundant in country II, its relative factor prices $(w/r)_{II} < (w/r)_I$; that is, its isocost line $M'N'$ is flatter than that of country I. It will therefore produce at point Q and at point T. Because C_2 represents a larger quantity of cloth for the same opportunity cost of steel, S_1, the relative price of cloth must be cheaper in country II than in country I. This link between relative factor prices and relative product prices is shown more directly in panel (b). An increase in the wage rate relative to the price of capital will lead to an increase in the price of the labor-intensive good, cloth, relative to the price of the capital-intensive good, steel. If relative factor prices are placed on the horizontal axis and relative product prices on the vertical axis, this relationship takes the form of an upward-sloping line.

uses relatively intensively its relatively abundant factor of production, and it will import the good that uses relatively intensively its relatively scarce factor of production. This conclusion follows logically from the initial assumptions. While the Heckscher-Ohlin theorem seems to be consistent in a general way with what we observe, violations of H-O assumptions can lead to different behavior by a nation in terms of the commodity structure of its trade. The extent to which the H-O theorem is supported by empirical tests is discussed in the next chapter.

The Factor Price Equalization Theorem

Different relative prices in autarky are sufficient to generate a basis for trade in trade theory. Further, as trade takes place between two countries, prices adjust until both countries face the same set of relative prices. Our discussion of H-O demonstrated that this convergence of product prices takes place as the price of the product using the relatively abundant factor increases with trade and the price of the product using the country's relatively scarce factor falls. This change in final product prices has implications for the prices of factors in both of the participating countries as well, as was rigorously pointed out by Paul A. Samuelson in 1949.

Let's again consider the two countries producing cloth and steel, with cloth the labor-intensive good and steel the capital-intensive good. Country I is the capital-abundant country and country II the labor-abundant country. With the opening of trade, the price of cloth rises and the price of steel falls in country II, signaling producers to produce more cloth and less steel. Assuming perfect competition, production will shift along the PPF toward more output of cloth and less of steel. For this to happen, resources must be shifted from the production of steel to cloth. However, the bundle of resources released from steel production is different from the bundle desired for increased cloth production because the relative factor intensities of the two goods differ. As the capital-intensive good, steel uses a bundle of resources that contains relatively more capital than the bundle of resources desired by cloth producers at the initial factor prices. Alternatively, the bundle released from steel production does not contain the desired amount of labor relative to capital to satisfy the expanding cloth production. There is thus an increase in the demand for labor and a decrease in the demand for capital as this adjustment takes place. Assuming fixed factor supplies (see Figure 5), these market changes will lead to an increase in the price of labor

FIGURE 5   Factor Price Adjustments with Trade

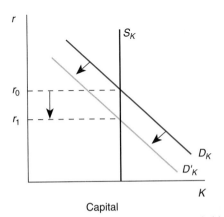 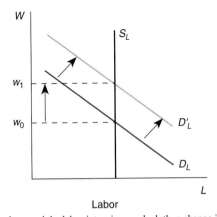

With the shift in production in country II away from the capital-intensive good, steel, toward the labor-intensive good, cloth, a change in the demand for both capital and labor occurs. The expansion of cloth production will lead to an increase in overall demand for labor because cloth is labor-intensive relative to steel. At the same time, the reduction in steel production leads to a decline in the overall demand for capital. These shifts in demand result in a fall in the price of capital and a rise in the price of labor.

FIGURE 6   Producer Adjustment to Changing Relative Factor Prices Accompanying International Trade

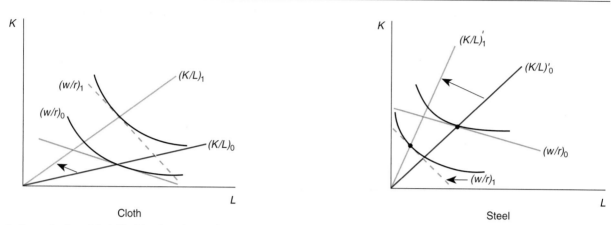

As the production of cloth (the labor-intensive good) expands and the production of steel (the capital-intensive good) declines in country II, the price of labor increases and the price of capital declines. This change in relative prices is depicted here as the change from $(w/r)_0$ to $(w/r)_1$. The relative increase in the cost of labor leads producers to substitute some capital for labor, that is, to move along the relevant production isoquant in both industries. This factor substitution results in a rise in the K/L ratio from $(K/L)_0$ to $(K/L)_1$ in cloth production and from $(K/L)'_0$ to $(K/L)'_1$ in steel production. Because of the increase in cloth production, this factor-use adjustment takes place along a higher isoquant, while the reduction in steel production causes this adjustment to take place along a lower isoquant.

and a decrease in the price of capital. The change of factor prices will cause the factor price ratio, $(w/r)_{II}$, to rise and induce producers to move to a different equilibrium point on each respective isoquant (see Figure 6). Note that these price and production adjustments lead to a higher K/L ratio in *both* industries in this labor-abundant country.

In country I, a similar adjustment takes place. With the initiation of trade, the relative price of steel rises, signaling producers to produce more steel and less cloth. The expansion of steel production and the contraction of cloth production lead to an increase in the overall demand for capital and a decrease in the overall demand for labor. With factor supplies fixed, an increase in the price of capital and a decrease in the price of labor will occur. The resulting decline in the factor price ratio, $(w/r)_I$, means that producers will substitute labor for capital in both industries until the ratio of factor prices is again equal to the slope of the production isoquants. As a result of this change in relative prices, the K/L ratio in country I will fall in both industries.

Combining the general equilibrium results of country I and country II reveals an interesting phenomenon. Prior to trade, $(w/r)_I > (w/r)_{II}$. However, with trade the factor price ratio in country I falls while that of country II rises. Trade will expand until both countries face the same set of relative factor prices. The result is what is known as the **factor price equalization theorem,** often referred to as the second important contribution of the H-O analysis (the first being the H-O theorem): *In equilibrium, with both countries facing the same relative (and absolute) product prices, with both having the same technology, and with constant returns to scale, relative (and absolute) costs will be equalized. The only way this can happen is if, in fact, factor prices are equalized.* Trade in final goods essentially substitutes for movement of factors between countries, leading to an increase in the price of the abundant factor and a fall in the price of the scarce factor among participating countries until relative factor prices are equal (see Figure 7).

Although the implications of trade for factor prices seem logically correct, we do not observe in practice the complete factor price equalization suggested by H-O. This is not

FIGURE 7   Factor Price Equalization with Trade

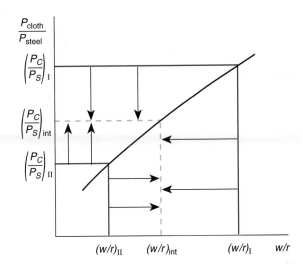

Country II is assumed to be labor-abundant and country I capital-abundant. Prior to trade $(P_C/P_S)_{II} < (P_C/P_S)_I$, and $(w/r)_{II} < (w/r)_I$. With the initiation of trade, $(w/r)_I$ begins to fall and $(w/r)_{II}$ begins to rise. These movements will continue until each country's factor prices are consistent with the new international terms of trade, $(P_C/P_S)_{int}$. This will occur only when $(w/r)_{II} = (w/r)_I = (w/r)_{int}$, that is, when relative factor prices are equalized between the two countries. Given the assumptions of the H-O model, absolute prices for given factors are also equalized.

surprising because several of the assumptions of H-O are not realized, or not realized as fully as stated in the model. Transportation costs, tariffs, subsidies, or other economic policies contribute to different product prices between countries. If product prices are not the same, then relative factor prices certainly cannot be expected to be the same although the *tendency* to equalize can still be present.

In addition to the failure of goods prices to equalize, imperfect competition, nontraded goods, and unemployed resources also cause problems for factor price equalization. In addition, the factors of production are not homogeneous. If one acknowledges that the relative structure and quality of factors can vary between countries, the equalization of factor prices—in the sense that they are discussed here—is much less likely to come about. Further, technology is not everywhere identical, so that the rewards given the factors of production may well vary from country to country and inhibit the equalization of factor prices.

Despite these limitations, the H-O model provides some helpful insights into the likely impact of trade on relative factor prices. Trade based on comparative advantage should tend to increase the demand for the abundant factor and ultimately exert some upward pressure on its price, assuming that the presence of unemployed resources does not entirely absorb the price pressure. Thus, for the labor-abundant country, trade can offer a way to employ more fully the abundant factor and/or to increase its wages, and at the same time earn scarce foreign exchange necessary to import needed capital goods. The experiences of economies such as Taiwan support this view and demonstrate that in a general way, the factor price movements described above do occur. Finally, as economist Robert Mundell (1957) noted, the same result would obtain with respect to commodity prices and factor prices if factors were mobile between countries and final products were immobile internationally. In this instance, the relatively abundant factors would move from relatively low-price countries to high-price countries, causing factor price movements similar to those described. These factor movements would continue until factor (and commodity) prices are equalized, assuming that such movement of factors is costless. Thus, concerning their impact on prices, goods movements and factor movements are indeed substitutes for each other.

The Stolper-Samuelson Theorem and Income Distribution Effects of Trade in the Heckscher-Ohlin Model

Wolfgang Stolper and Paul Samuelson developed the Stolper-Samuelson theorem in an article published in 1941. The initial article focused on the income distribution effects of tariffs, but the theorem was subsequently employed in the literature to explain the income distribution effects of international trade in general. The argument builds upon the changes in factor prices that accompany the opening of trade, which were discussed in the previous section. The argument proceeds as follows: Assume that a labor-abundant country initiates trade. This will lead to an increase in the price of the abundant factor, labor, and a decrease in the price of the scarce factor, capital. Assuming that full employment takes place both before and after trade, it is clear that labor's total nominal income has increased, because the wage has increased and the labor employed remains the same. Similarly, the nominal income share of capital will have fallen since the price of capital has fallen and the capital employed remains the same at full employment.

To this point the argument seems very straightforward. However, it is important to remember that the ability to obtain goods and services, that is, real income, depends not only on changes in income but also on changes in product prices. Thus, workers who consume only the cheaper, imported capital-intensive good are clearly better off, because their nominal income has increased and the price of the capital-intensive good has fallen. Their absolute and relative command over this product has increased. But what about those workers who consume only the labor-intensive export good? This case is not so clear, since both their nominal income and the price of the good they consume have increased. If their income has increased relatively more (less) than the price of the labor-intensive good, then their real income has increased (decreased). Is it possible to reach a definitive conclusion about the real income of this group with trade?

Using the equilibrium condition that comes about in competitive factor markets, we can demonstrate that the wage rate in the labor-abundant country will rise relatively more than the price of the export good. Remember that, in equilibrium, labor's wage equals the marginal physical product of labor (MPP_L) times the price of the export good. Because both the wage and the price of the export good are increasing, the answer to the question, "Which is rising relatively more?," rests on the nature of changes in MPP_L. If labor is becoming more productive, then wages will be rising more than the price of the export good, and real income will be rising. If labor is becoming less productive, then wage increases will be outpaced by rising export-good prices.

With trade, the labor-abundant country will find the price of capital falling and the wage rate increasing (as noted earlier), and its producers will respond by using relatively more capital and relatively less labor in production; that is, the capital/labor ratio in production will rise. This will increase the productivity of labor at the margin (that is, MPP_L increases), resulting in an unambiguous increase in the real income of labor. We can therefore conclude that the real income share of the owners of the abundant factor increases with trade. Because a similar argument can be used to demonstrate that the price of capital is *falling* relatively more than the price of the capital-intensive import (because with an increase in the capital/labor ratio the marginal product of capital is *falling,* since each unit of capital has less labor to work with), it is clear that the real income of the owners of the scarce factor is decreasing with trade. This result—that the price of a factor changes relatively more than the price of the good intensive in that factor—is often referred to as the *magnification effect.*

Thus, the third aspect of the Heckscher-Ohlin analysis regarding the income distribution effects of trade is explained in the following more formal way by the **Stolper-Samuelson theorem:** *With full employment both before and after trade takes place, the increase in the price of the abundant factor and the fall in the price of the scarce factor because of trade imply that the owners of the abundant factor will find their real incomes rising and the owners of the scarce factor will find their real incomes falling.* Given these conclusions, it is not surprising that owners of the relatively abundant resources tend to be "free traders" while owners of relatively scarce resources tend to favor trade restrictions. For example, within the United States, agricultural producers and owners of technology and capital-intensive industries have tended to support expanding trade and/or dismantling trade restrictions, while organized labor has tended to oppose the expansion of trade.

Finally, we may not see the clear-cut income distribution effects with trade because relative factor prices in the real world do not often appear to be as responsive to trade as the H-O model implies. In addition, personal or household income distribution reflects not only the distribution of income between factors of production but also the ownership of the factors of production. Since individuals or households often own several factors of production, the final impact of trade on personal income distribution is far from clear.

Conclusions

The initial work by Heckscher and Ohlin has had a profound effect on the theory of international trade. This seminal work led not only to the famous H-O theorem but also to three additional propositions. Two of these, the factor price equalization theorem and the Stolper-Samuelson theorem, have been discussed. The final theorem, the Rybczynski theorem, which focuses on changes in factor endowments and the accompanying changes in final products produced, will be developed in Chapter 11, "Economic Growth and International Trade."

CONCEPT CHECK

1. What is the basis for trade according to Heckscher-Ohlin? What products should a country export? Why?
2. Explain why the K/L ratio in each industry will rise with the initiation of trade in a labor-abundant country and will fall in a capital-abundant country.
3. What happens to the functional (factor-based) distribution of income with trade?

THEORETICAL QUALIFICATIONS TO HECKSCHER-OHLIN

Several of the assumptions in the H-O model are not always applicable to the real world. For that reason, it is useful to examine several assumptions that seem especially critical to the results of the model and to determine the impact of their absence on the H-O result.

Demand Reversal

A strong assumption in the H-O model is that tastes and preferences are identical in the trading countries. If this is not true, it is no longer possible to predict the pretrade autarky prices and thus the structure of trade. The reason is that each country's tastes and preferences could cause it to value the products in very different ways. An extreme example of this is often referred to as **demand reversal.** In Figure 8, demands in the two countries are so different that in country I the price of the good (steel) that intensively uses the relatively abundant factor is actually higher than its price in the trading partner, country II. With the opening of trade, country I would find itself exporting cloth and importing steel from country II because steel is relatively cheaper at international prices. This is illustrated in Figure 8 by the international terms-of-trade line, $(P_C/P_S)_{int}$, which is steeper than autarky

FIGURE 8   Demand Reversal

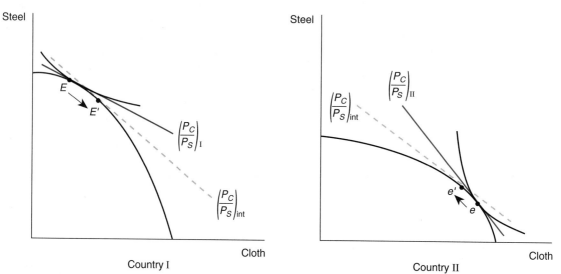

Demand in country I is so oriented toward steel, the commodity using relatively intensively its relatively abundant factor, that the relative pretrade price of steel is greater than that in country II. Consequently, $(P_C/P_S)_I < (P_C/P_S)_{II}$. With trade, country I expands production of cloth, contracts production of steel, exports cloth, and imports steel. Country II does the opposite, and a pattern of trade emerges that is directly opposite to that predicted by H-O. Because this is the result of a particular set of demand conditions, it is referred to as *demand reversal*.

prices in country I and flatter than autarky prices in country II. This pattern of trade is, of course, the opposite of that predicted by H-O. It will cause the relative price of capital to fall in country I and that of labor to fall in country II. The difference in the nature of demand between these two countries, with each tending to prefer the good intensive in its physically abundant factor, has caused them to trade in a manner opposite to that antici- pated by the H-O analysis.

While demand patterns seem to be similar throughout the world, especially among sim- ilar socioeconomic income classes, differences in tastes and preferences certainly exist. If the differences are sufficiently strong, they can reduce the ability of the H-O model to pre- dict trade and the movement of factor prices. Note, however, that the H-O model would still hold even in this instance if the analysis is restricted to the price definition of relative factor abundance. This occurs because home demand for the product using the abundant factor intensively leads to such a high price for that product and the factor used intensively in its production that the physically abundant factor is the scarce factor from the standpoint of the price definition.

Factor-Intensity Reversal

A second assumption crucial to the H-O conclusions is that a commodity is always relatively intensive in a given factor regardless of relative factor prices (the strong-factor-intensity assumption). Critical to this exercise is drawing the curvature of the isoquants so that each possible pair intersected only once (see Figure 1, page 130). Without this assumption, the H-O model cannot always accurately predict the structure of trade, even if technology is the same between countries.

A violation of the assumption appears in Figure 9. The degree of substitution between the two factors is sufficiently different between industries (labor and capital can be substituted for each other more easily in cloth production than in steel production) so that we cannot guarantee

FIGURE 9   Factor-Intensity Reversal

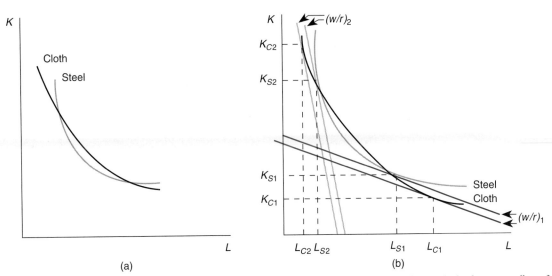

The isoquants for steel and cloth violate the H-O assumption that steel and cloth would each be intensive in a particular factor regardless of relative factor prices. The pair of isoquants crossing twice indicates that the nature of factor substitution for each product is sufficiently different so that the relative factor intensities can change as factor prices change. This is demonstrated in panel (b), where we see that when labor is relatively cheap [flatter isocost lines with slope $(w/r)_1$], cloth is the labor-intensive good (lower K/L ratio). But when labor is relatively expensive [steep isocost lines with slope $(w/r)_2$], cloth is the capital-intensive good (higher K/L ratio). If the relative factor intensity is different at different relative factor prices, it is impossible to predict the nature of trade based on the H-O proposition without relative more information.

that a given product will always be relatively intensive in the same factor. To see why this is so, look at panel (b). At $(w/r)_1$, capital is relatively expensive; that is, the price of capital is high and the price of labor is low. With relatively flat isocost lines, producers will minimize costs by using K_{S1} amounts of capital and L_{S1} amounts of labor in steel production and K_{C1} amounts of capital and L_{C1} of labor in cloth production. The K/L ratio in steel production is greater than that in cloth production, suggesting that steel is the capital-intensive product.

Next, suppose that labor is relatively more expensive. This results in a higher w/r ratio, $(w/r)_2$, and a steeper isocost line. Producers attempting to minimize cost will employ K_{S2} amounts of capital and L_{S2} amounts of labor in steel production and K_{C2} amounts of capital and L_{C2} amounts of labor in cloth production. With this set of relative prices, the K/L ratio for cloth is now larger than the K/L ratio for steel. The factor-intensity comparison between steel and cloth has reversed with this large change in relative factor prices. These commodities are thus not always relatively intensive in the same factor. The H-O model may no longer be able to predict the export good based on relative factor abundance. ·

Suppose that $(w/r)_1$ applies to country I and $(w/r)_2$ to country II. From H-O, we expect country I (the labor-abundant country in this example) to export cloth (the labor-intensive good) and country II (the capital-abundant country) to export steel (the capital-intensive good). However, when capital is abundant (country II), cloth is the capital-intensive good. We would expect cloth to be country II's export as well. Predicting trade flows in this two-country case is problematic because **factor-intensity reversal** exists. Factor-intensity reversal occurs when a commodity has a different relative factor intensity at different relative factor prices. With one country exporting cloth and the other exporting steel in actual trade, one of them will match the H-O prediction, but the other will not.

FIGURE 10   The Impact of Transportation Costs on Trade

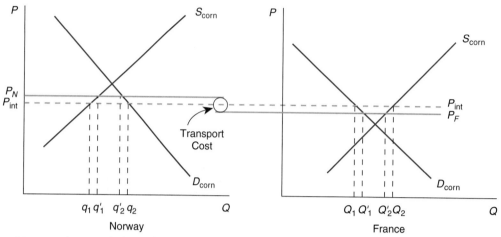

In the absence of transportation costs, the international price will settle at P_{int}, where Norway's desired imports (q_1q_2) are equal to France's desired exports (Q_1Q_2). With the introduction of transport costs, the price in Norway rises (the quantity of imports demanded falls) and the price in France decreases (the quantity of exports falls) until the difference between the two prices is exactly equal to the amount of the transportation charge. At the new equilibrium the amount of France's desired exports ($Q'_1Q'_2$) is exactly equal to Norway's desired imports ($q'_1q'_2$).

Factor-intensity reversal could also interfere with factor price equalization, because one of the two countries can end up exporting the good that intensively uses its relatively scarce factor. For example, in Figure 9, country I might end up exporting steel and importing cloth. This will produce upward pressure on the price of capital and downward pressure on wages in country I, much like that occurring in country II. If this happens, relative factor prices in both countries (w/r) will move in the same direction (both will be falling) instead of converging toward each other. In the larger context, factor-intensity reversal helps us understand why it might be possible for a labor-abundant country such as India and a capital-abundant country such as the United States to export the same commodity, steel, for example. The question remains open as to whether factor-intensity reversals actually exist to any important degree, but most economists doubt that these reversals alone are likely to explain trade patterns that appear to be inconsistent with H-O.

Transportation Costs   A third assumption that is not valid in the real world is that of no transportation costs. Product prices will differ between two locations by the cost of transportation. This is demonstrated by the two-country market graphs for corn in Figure 10. The market price in autarky for corn is lower in France than in Norway. Consequently, Norway has an incentive to buy corn from France. Ignoring transportation costs, these two countries should trade at a common (international) price for corn that will be lower than the price in Norway and higher than the autarky price in France. That will cause the amount of excess supply available for export in France (Q_1Q_2) to be exactly equal to the excess demand for imports (q_1q_2) in Norway.

Suppose that we now include transportation costs. If France attempts to pass the entire transportation cost on to Norway, the price of corn in Norway will rise and Norway's excess demand (and imports) will fall. This leaves France with an inventory of corn it does not want. France will lower its price and, thus, the price including transportation costs in Norway. As this happens, France will find that it now has a smaller amount of corn available for export, an amount more in line with the new quantity demanded in Norway at the higher transportation-inclusive price. Ultimately, the price in Norway will rise above the original international equilibrium price, and the price in France will fall below that price until the amount of France's desired exports is exactly equal to the amount of Norway's desired imports. The difference between the price of corn in the two countries will equal exactly the transportation costs involved.

Another point is that the participating countries will not necessarily share the transportation costs equally. Ultimately, the incidence of the transportation cost will depend on the elasticities of supply and demand in each country. The more inelastic supply and demand are in the importing country and the more elastic demand and supply are in the exporting country, the larger the relative amount of transportation costs paid by the importing country. Similarly, the more inelastic market conditions are in the exporting country and the more elastic in the importing country, the greater the amount of transportation costs borne by the exporting country.

The costs associated with moving goods between countries have been undergoing change in recent years because of new transport technologies and emerging marketing concerns. Until recently, transportation costs had demonstrated a downward trend because of the use of larger ocean vessels, new cargo handling techniques, and an expanded use of air transport. However, in the new globalized world where "quick response" is replacing the holding of large inventories, increased attention is being directed to transport time as well as distance. David Hummels estimated that each day of increased ocean transit time between two countries reduced the probability of trade by 1.5 percent for manufacturers.[3] Further, exporters appeared to be willing to pay for time savings equal to 0.8 percent per day. This implies that the opportunity cost of a 20-day ocean voyage compared to a 1-day air shipment is equivalent to a 16 percent ad valorem tariff. His empirical results suggested that the advent of fast air transport and faster ocean vessels resulted in an average saving of 29.5 transport days between 1950 and 1998 and, thus, was equivalent to reducing tariffs on manufactured goods from 32 percent to 9 percent. With respect to Figure 10, the transport cost "circle" is thus being reduced in size, contributing to the growth in world trade.

The implications of transportation costs do not alter H-O conclusions about the composition of trade, although the amount of trade and specialization of production will be reduced. However, because relative product prices do not equalize between countries, relative factor prices will not equalize and complete factor price equalization cannot be attained. Finally, if transportation costs are sufficiently large, they can prevent trade from taking place, even though commodity autarky prices are clearly different between countries; that is, transportation costs can lead to the presence of nontraded goods.

Imperfect Competition

A fourth assumption important to the H-O analysis has been the presence of perfect competition. This assumption was necessary to guarantee that product prices and factor prices would equalize with trade. Again, we know in the real world that imperfect information, barriers to entry (both natural and contrived), and so forth, lead to *imperfect* competition of many different forms. Let's examine briefly how imperfect competition such as monopoly can alter the H-O conclusions about several of the effects of trade.

A first case is a variant of the traditional domestic monopoly model. The monopolist maintains the monopoly position at home but at some point chooses to export at world prices. In other words, the monopolist continues to act as a price setter at home but becomes a price taker on the world market. This can occur only if imports are prevented

---

[3]David Hummels, "Time as a Trade Barrier," unpublished manuscript, Purdue University, July 2001.

FIGURE 11   Domestic Monopoly and Exports

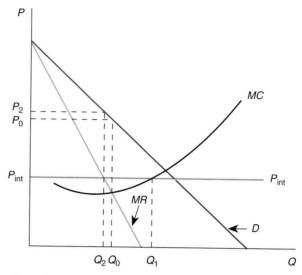

The domestic monopolist maximizes profits by producing where $MC = MR,(Q_0)$, and charging P_0 in the domestic market. However, by exporting, the monopolist's MR beyond Q_2 becomes P_{int} and profits are maximized by producing where $MC = P_{int}$, that is, at Q_1. Because the monopolist need not accept a lower MR than P_{int}, the quantity sold in the domestic market is lowered to Q_2 and the domestic price is raised to P_2. Participating in international trade thus leads to a widening of prices between the domestic and the foreign markets, not a narrowing as was the case under perfect competition.

from coming into the country. Assume that the monopolist is maximizing profits at the quantity of output where marginal cost (MC) equals marginal revenue (MR), that is, at P_0 and Q_0 in Figure 11. If it now becomes possible to export as much as desired at the world price, P_{int}, what should the monopolist do to maximize profits? Profits are still maximized by equating MC with MR. However, the MR curve now consists of the domestic MR curve down to the P_{int} curve, and the P_{int} curve beyond that point. Because the monopoly firm can sell all that it wishes at the international price, it has no reason ever to sell at a lower MR. Consequently, production is Q_1, where $MC = P_{int}$. The quantity Q_2 is sold in the domestic market at price P_2, and $Q_1 - Q_2$ is exported. Because the international price puts a floor on the marginal revenue at all quantities to the right of Q_2, the monopolist actually reduces the amount sold in the local market and charges a higher price. In this case, international trade leads to an increased difference between the domestic price and the world price, not a convergence to a single commodity price. The production and factor price effects tend to approach the H-O result as the monopolist acts as a price taker in the world market. However, the domestic market distortion that permits the monopolist to sell with trade at a higher price at home than in autarky inhibits product price equalization and thus factor price equalization.

A second case is simply the application of pure monopolistic price discrimination to international trade. In this case, we have a single world supplier faced with how to distribute output among several countries and what price to charge in each. It is assumed that the monopolist is a profit maximizer, that the markets in the various countries can be kept separate (i.e., arbitrage cannot take place between markets), and that the elasticities of demand differ between the various markets.

FIGURE 12   Market Price Discrimination in International Trade

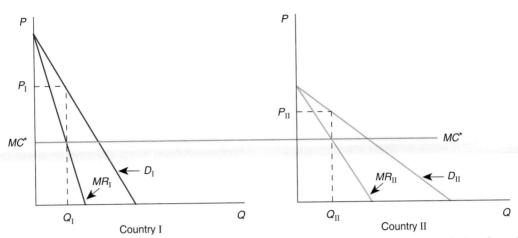

The price-discriminating monopolist is faced with the question of what quantity to sell in each of the above markets and what price to charge in each. The monopolist will determine the amount to sell in each market by equating MC to MR in each respective market. To maximize profits, the monopolist will sell Q_I in country I and charge P_I, while Q_{II} will be sold in country II at P_{II}. As long as the markets are kept separate and the elasticity of demand is different in each, the product prices in the two countries will not tend to equalize. A move to perfect competition would lead to an expansion of output and a common price in both markets.

Assume that the monopolist is faced with two markets (see Figure 12). Assume also that the marginal cost of the monopolist is constant. What is the optimal amount to sell in each market? The level of total output is equal to the sum of the optimal amount of sales in each market. To maximize profits, the monopolist locates the quantity in each market at which $MC = MR$. The profit maximization criterion thus indicates that at a marginal cost of MC^*, the quantity Q_I should be sold in country I at P_I, and Q_{II} in country II at P_{II}. A higher price will be charged in the market where demand is less elastic.

Pure price discrimination leads to the charging of different prices in different markets and tends to reduce the degree of factor price equalization that takes place. (Remember that this type of discrimination exists only as long as there is no arbitrage between markets.) Although the presence of a single world supplier of a product is very rare, it is not uncommon for several major suppliers to band together and form a cartel. This arrangement allows them to behave economically as a single world supplier and to price-discriminate between markets.

Immobile or Commodity-Specific Factors

It has been assumed up to this point that factors are completely mobile between different uses in production within a country. This assumption permits production adjustments to move smoothly along the PPF in response to changes in relative product prices. Often, however, it is not easy or even possible for factors to be moved from the production of one product to another (e.g., from wheat to automobile production). With some degree of factor immobility, at least in the short run, the nature of the adjustment to international trade is altered from that suggested in the H-O framework. Adjustment to trade has been analyzed in this instance through the use of the specific-factors model.

The **specific-factors model** (SF model) is an attempt to explore the implications of short-run factor immobility between sectors in an H-O context. In the short run, it assumes that there are *three* factors of production, not two. The three factors in industries X and Y are (*a*) labor, which is mobile and can be used to produce either good X or

IN THE REAL WORLD:

THE EFFECTS OF INTERNATIONAL CARTELS

Economists know from their theoretical understanding of market behavior that imperfect competition leads to a reduction in the quantity sold and an increase in the price. This conclusion can be supported by examples. In the mid-1920s tungsten carbide sold in the United States at $50 per pound. However, in 1927, the General Electric Company was given control over the U.S. market by means of an agreement with the German company, Krupp, which was the principal world supplier. The price of tungsten in the United States rose immediately to $453 per pound, and it remained in the $255–$453 range throughout the 1930s. In 1942, GE's monopoly was broken by antitrust action and the price fell to a range of $27 to $45.

In addition, the adoption of severe discriminatory pricing practices by a cartel was historically documented by the U.S. Tariff Commission in 1939 in a study of the incandescent electric lamp cartel. The accompanying table indicates the different prices charged for light bulbs in the Netherlands, Germany, Japan, and the United States. The cartel clearly kept prices from equalizing across countries, inhibiting the factor price equalization that normally would accompany trade.

In more recent times, OPEC was successful in raising prices dramatically through production controls and the exercise of market power in the two oil shocks of 1973–1974 and 1979–1980. The average price for crude oil was $2.89 per barrel in 1972, $3.24 in 1973, and $11.60 in 1974 (more than four times the 1972 level). By 1978 the price was $13.39 per barrel, and it rose to $30.21 in 1979 and $36.68 in 1980 (2.7 times the 1978 level and 12.7 times the 1972 level). Oil prices then fell because of consumer conservation; new sources of supply from Mexico, the North Sea, and Alaska; and switches to alternative fuels. By 1986 oil prices had fallen to $14.17; they then fell, after some increase in the early 1990s, to $13.07 in 1998. OPEC then attempted to restrict output, and the price averaged $28.23 per barrel in 2000. There were somewhat lower prices in 2001 and 2002, but the price was roughly $30.00 at the end of 2003. The decision by OPEC to cut output by 10 percent in early 2004, as well as growth in demand, led to an average price of $53.35 in 2005. In early 2007, the average price was about $60.00 per barrel.

Country	25 Watts	45 Watts	60 Watts
Netherlands	$0.32	$0.59	$0.70
Germany	0.30	0.36	0.48
United States	0.15	0.15	0.15
Japan	—	—	0.07

Sources: Franklin R. Root, Roland L. Kramer, and Maurice Y. d'Arlin, *International Trade and Finance,* 2nd ed. (Chicago: Southwestern Publishing, 1966), p. 319; U.S. Tariff Commission, "Incandescent Electric Lamps," Report no. 133, 2nd series (Washington, DC: U.S. Government Printing Office, 1939), p. 49; International Monetary Fund (IMF), *International Financial Statistics Yearbook 2002* (Washington, DC: IMF, 2002), pp. 184–85; IMF, *International Financial Statistics Yearbook 2003* (Washington, DC: IMF, 2003), p. 121; IMF, *International Financial Statistics* December 2006, p. 70.

good Y; (*b*) capital in industry X, K_X, which can be employed in that industry but *not* in industry Y; and (*c*) capital in industry Y, K_Y, which cannot be used in industry X. The SF model acknowledges that, in practice, it takes time for capital to be depreciated in one industry and reemployed in another.

The contrast between the assumptions of the SF model and those of the H-O model can be shown in an Edgeworth box diagram (see Figure 13). In panel (a) the factors are freely mobile between sectors, and the production contract curve has smooth curvature and connects the lower-left and upper-right origins of the box. This is the typical Edgeworth box. Panel (b) illustrates the Edgeworth box in the context of the SF model. Because capital is fixed in industry X, that amount of fixed capital is shown by the vertical distance $0_x \bar{K}_x$. No matter what amount of good X is produced, quantity $0_x \bar{K}_x$ of capital is used in industry X. Similarly, the fixed capital used in industry Y is shown by the vertical distance $0_y \bar{K}_y$. Hence, in the SF model, the contract curve is the horizontal line $\bar{K}_x A \bar{K}_y$. This contract curve coincides with the "normal" contract curve only at point *A*.

FIGURE 13   Capital Immobility in the Edgeworth Box Diagram

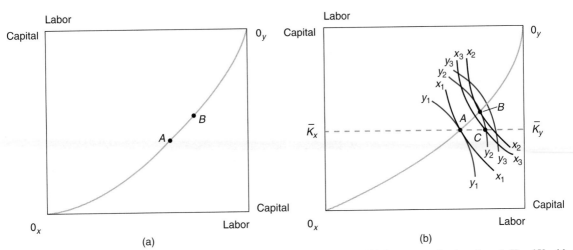

(a)   (b)

In panel (a), the smooth contract curve reflects the fact that both factors are perfectly mobile between production of goods X and Y, with A and B both being possible efficient-production points. In panel (b), it is assumed that capital cannot move in the short run from the amounts $0_x \bar{K}_x$ and $0_y \bar{K}_y$ that are used to produce the two products at A. Thus, any attempt to produce more of the X good can be accomplished only by acquiring labor previously used in the production of Y. This will lead to a movement along the $\bar{K}_x A \bar{K}_y$ line to, for example, point C. This production point is off the perfect-mobility contract curve, and it represents a smaller amount of production of the X good than exists on the perfect-mobility contract curve for the new quantity of Y (represented by y_2) being obtained. It thus represents a production point inside the PPF that is constructed when factors are completely mobile.

The different contract curves in the two situations will be associated with different production-possibilities frontiers (PPFs), because PPFs are derived from contract curves (see Chapter 5). In Figure 14, the PPF labeled $RA'S$ is the PPF associated with the normal contract curve of both panels of Figure 13. The PPF labeled $TA'V$ represents the PPF associated with the specific-factors contract curve $\bar{K}_x A \bar{K}_y$. This "new" PPF is coincident with the "normal" PPF only at point A'. A movement from point A to point B on the normal contract curve in Figure 13(b) yields a movement from point A' to point B' on the normal PPF in Figure 14, while a movement from A to C on the specific-factors contract curve results in a movement from point A' to point C'. But the output of good Y at B or B' (amount y_2) in the normal situation will be associated with less output of good X under the specific-factors situation than under the normal or mobile-factors situation. This difference in output of X reflects the fact that isoquant y_2 in Figure 13(b) is associated with isoquant x_2 on the normal contract curve but only with the smaller quantity of X on isoquant x_3 (at point C) on the specific-factors contract curve. Because analogous contrasts can be made with all other points on the two different contract curves in Figure 13(b), it follows that the specific-factors PPF in Figure 14 will lie inside the normal PPF except at point A.

The implication of the immobility of capital in an H-O context can be seen by comparing the impact on the rates of return to the factors of production when a country moves from autarky to trade. Suppose we have the normal situation of a country with full mobility of all factors of production. If the country is located at point A in Figure 13(b) in autarky, then an opening of the country to trade involving specialization in the labor-intensive good X will result, for example, in a movement from A to B in Figure 13(b) or from A' to B' in Figure 14. This movement will bid up the price of labor and reduce the price of capital as expanding industry X seeks to acquire relatively more labor and contracting industry Y is releasing relatively more capital. After the adjustment, at point B in

FIGURE 14   Production Adjustment When Capital Is Immobile

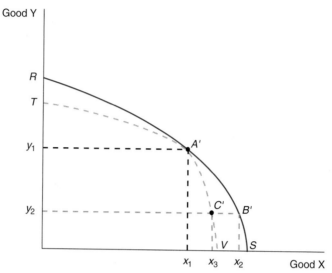

The PPF represented by the solid line $RA'S$ is drawn under the assumption that factors are completely mobile. Thus, points A′ and B′ correspond to points A and B, respectively, in Figure 13(b). If both factors were completely immobile, the production-possibilities frontier would be represented by $y_1A'x_1$. If only capital is immobile, the production possibilities will lie somewhere between these two extremes. Such a possibility is represented by the dashed PPF $TA'V$. Assuming that only labor is mobile, the attempt to produce more of the X good will force the economy to use resources less efficiently, thus moving to a new point on $TA'V$ inside the normal PPF. Point C' represents a possible new production point consistent with point C in Figure 13(b).

Figure 13(b), the ratio of capital to labor in each industry has risen. With the rise in the K/L ratio in each industry, each worker in each industry has relatively more capital to work with, so the worker is more productive; thus, productivity and wages rise. The flip side of the rise in wages is the fall in the real return to capital.

The important policy implication in the traditional Heckscher-Ohlin, full-factor mobility situation is that the country's abundant factor prefers free trade to autarky and that the country's scarce factor prefers autarky to free trade. Even though the country as a whole gains from trade, some part of the economy (the scarce factor) will have an incentive to argue for protection.

What is the consequence of trade for factor returns in the specific-factors model? With autarky at point A in Figure 13(b) and the opening of the country to trade, labor-intensive industry X expands because of the higher price of X and capital-intensive industry Y contracts because of the lower price of Y. Production tends to move to the right from point A in the direction of a point such as point C on the SF contract curve. The increased demand for labor will bid up the money wage of all labor. However, the direction of movement of the return to capital depends on which industry is being considered. Industry X has increased its demand for capital, but the supply of capital is fixed at $0_x\bar{K}_x$. Hence, the return to capital in X rises with the opening of the country to trade. However, the demand for capital in industry Y falls because some of good Y is now imported rather than produced at home. Thus, the demand for capital in industry Y decreases, while its supply of capital is fixed. The return to capital in Y therefore falls. These income distribution effects of trade are obviously different from those of the traditional H-O model. There, capital as a whole suffered a decline in its return, but in the SF model capital in X gains and capital in Y loses. The scarce factor of production will not be unanimously opposed to moving from autarky to trade. Owners of capital in industry Y will argue against free trade, while those in industry X will argue in favor of it. This situation may indeed be more realistic than the traditional H-O type of model, especially in the short run, where all of one factor was opposed to trade and all of the other factor favored it.

A final note is necessary about the return to labor. Saying that the *money* wage for labor has risen does not mean that labor's *real* wage has risen. Consider the money wage in industry X, which equals the money wage in industry Y with competition. Remember that the money wage equals the price of the product times the marginal physical product of labor, thus, $w = (P_X)(MPP_{LX})$. With trade, MPP_{LX} falls, because more labor is being used with the fixed amount of capital $0_x\bar{K}_x$. In other words, each worker has less capital to work with. Because $w = (P_X)(MPP_{LX})$, this means that w/P_X has fallen because $(w/P_X) = MPP_{LX}$. The fall in w/P_X simply indicates that money wages have not risen as much as the price of good X. Workers who consume only good X are worse off because their real wages have declined. Analogously, w/P_Y rises; thus, if workers consume only good Y, their real wages have risen. The direction of the real return for a worker therefore depends on the bundle of goods being consumed. The SF model yields conclusions on the winners and losers from free trade that may be more consonant than traditional H-O trade theory with what we observe in the real world.

Other Considerations   It is evident that several other assumptions, such as constant returns to scale, identical technology, and the absence of policy obstacles to trade, also are not always applicable to the real world. To the extent that they are not, the conclusions of the H-O model are compromised. Several of these conditions will be examined further in Chapter 10, "Post-Heckscher-Ohlin Theories of Trade and Intra-Industry Trade" and in later chapters on trade policy.

CONCEPT CHECK

1. Explain the difference between factor-intensity reversal and demand reversal. Do they have similar effects on the validity of the H-O theorem?
2. Can factor-intensity reversal occur if the two industry isoquants do not cross each other but are tangent to one another? Explain.

3. What are the conditions necessary for imperfect competition to cause prices to be further apart after trade than before trade?
4. Explain how the opening of trade can lead to an increase in money wages in a *capital-abundant* country if capital is immobile between sectors. Does this mean that labor is necessarily better off with trade?

SUMMARY

This chapter first examined the underlying basis for differences in relative prices in autarky. Country differences in demand, technology, and factor abundance contribute to possible differences in relative prices in autarky. Attention then focused on the Heckscher-Ohlin explanation of trade, factor price equalization, and income distribution effects of trade.

Building on a rigorous set of assumptions, Heckscher-Ohlin demonstrated that differences in relative factor endowments are sufficient to generate a basis for trade, even if there are no country differences in technology or demand conditions. Their model allowed them not only to predict the pattern of trade based on initial factor endowments but also to demonstrate that trade would lead to an equalization of factor prices between trading countries. Stolper-Samuelson pointed out that the same relative factor price movements would lead to an improvement in real income for owners of the abundant factor and a worsening position for owners of the scarce factor.

Several theoretical qualifications on the role of tastes and preferences, factor intensity of products, transportation costs, imperfect competition, and factor immobility were briefly discussed. Reflection on the limitations imposed by these assumptions helps one to understand why the pattern and effects of international trade are not always what we might expect from the H-O theory. These limitations do not destroy the basic link between relative factor abundance and the pattern of trade. They do, however, influence the degree to which these links hold and are observed. Chapter 9 examines the validity of the factor endowments approach in the real world.

KEY TERMS

demand reversal
different relative factor
   intensities
different relative factor
   endowments

factor-intensity reversal
factor price equalization theorem
Heckscher-Ohlin theorem
physical definition of factor
   abundance

price definition of factor abundance
specific-factors model
Stolper-Samuelson theorem

QUESTIONS AND PROBLEMS

1. Explain the difference between the price and the physical definitions of factor abundance. When could they give conflicting answers about which factor is the abundant factor?

2. If the K/land ratio for Belgium is higher than that for France, what kind of products might Belgium export to France? Why?

3. Suppose that the K/L ratio is higher in France than in Spain. What would you expect to happen to wages in France as trade took place between the two countries? Why?

4. You read in a newspaper that the owners of capital in a particular country are urging their government to restrict trade through import quotas. What might you infer about the relative factor abundance in that country? Why?

5. It has been argued that opening a country to international trade is a great "antitrust" policy. What impact would the threat of imports have on a monopolist who had never before been faced with foreign competition? How would the monopolist respond concerning the quantity produced and the price charged in the domestic market?

6. How does the existence of demand reversal complicate the predictions of Heckscher-Ohlin?

7. Using the specific-factors model, explain why you might expect to see certain capital owners and labor groups arguing against expanding trade in a capital-abundant country.

8. Given your knowledge of the basis for trade, would you be surprised or not to learn that the composition of the exports and imports of a former "Soviet bloc" country such as Hungary or Poland changed with the dissolution of the Soviet Union and the opening of trade with the West? Explain your answer.

9. In Figure 14, suppose the country is producing in equilibrium at A'. If P_x then increases such that it would lead to production at B' on the "normal" PPF, would the same change in relative prices lead to production precisely at C' in the specific-factors case? Why or why not?

10. "Within the Heckscher-Ohlin framework, complete factor price equalization cannot be achieved in the presence of transportation costs." Agree? Disagree? Explain.

11. Even though their relative factor abundances differ widely, both India and the United States export similar agricultural products such as rice. What might explain this apparent contradiction of the Heckscher-Ohlin model?

12. "Increasing the mobility of labor and/or capital within a country not only will reduce the internal opposition to the expansion of the country's international trade but also will lead to greater gains in real income for the country." Comment on this statement.

EMPIRICAL TESTS OF THE FACTOR ENDOWMENTS APPROACH

LEARNING OBJECTIVES

■ To learn about the failure of U.S. trade patterns to conform to Heckscher-Ohlin predictions.

■ To understand possible explanations for the U.S. trade paradox.

■ To become acquainted with issues arising from multi-country Heckscher-Ohlin tests.

■ To grasp the role of trade in generating growing income inequality in developed countries.

INTRODUCTION

Theories, Assumptions, and the Role of Empirical Work

It is common to hear trade theories criticized for not being "relevant to the real world" or for having "unrealistic assumptions." This has led researchers such as Leamer and Levinson (1995) to assert that empirical work on trade has had very little influence on trade theories and to encourage their colleagues to "Estimate, don't test." They propose that researchers should attempt to learn from real-world data rather than simply accepting or rejecting an abstract hypothesis.

Rather than using the lack of relevance to the real world as a reason to ignore trade theory, it should serve as a motivation for empirical testing. Davis and Weinstein (1996) offer a more encouraging view of empirical work.

. . . a second approach to testing is to look for ways of weakening the strict assumptions of the theory in sensible directions in order to find a version that does in fact work. By successive approximation, we should learn which of the assumptions of the model are most crucial, and to which types of data sets one can sensibly apply the various versions of the theory.[1]

This chapter will follow the second approach by examining the empirical tests of the Heckscher-Ohlin predictions in an attempt to find which of the often strict assumptions are crucial. You will see that there is not a consensus among economists on the degree to which relative factor endowments explain international trade flows and the consequences of trade flows.

As you recall, the Heckscher-Ohlin theorem states that a country will export goods that use relatively intensively the country's relatively abundant factor of production and will import goods that use relatively intensively the country's relatively scarce factor of production. In this chapter, we review some empirical tests of this seemingly straightforward and commonsense hypothesis. The literature has produced some conflicting results on the real-world validity of the H-O theorem. The most surprising result of one early test was that the world's largest trader, the United States, did not trade according to the Heckscher-Ohlin pattern. Explanations are given on why this surprising result might have occurred. We then review tests for other countries and more recent work on trade patterns. In addition, we survey the current controversy regarding the extent to which H-O-type trade has contributed to the increasing income inequality in developed countries in recent years, especially in the United States.

THE LEONTIEF PARADOX

The first major test of the H-O theorem was conducted by Wassily W. Leontief and published in 1953. This comprehensive test has influenced empirical research in this area ever since. Leontief made use of his own invention—an **input-output table**—to test the H-O prediction. An input-output table provides details, for all industries in an economy, of the flows of output of each industry to all other industries, the purchases of inputs from all other industries, and the purchases of factor services. In addition, the table can be used to indicate not only the "direct factor requirements" of any given industry—the capital and labor used with intermediate goods in the particular stage of production—but also the **total factor requirements.** The total requirements include the direct requirements as well as the

---

[1]For a more extensive review of the relevant literature see Edward E. Leamer and James Levinsohn, "International Trade Theory: The Evidence" in *Handbook of International Economics,* vol. III, ed. Gene M. Grossman and Kenneth Rogoff (Amsterdam: Elsevier, 1995), pp. 1339–94; Donald R. Davis and David E. Weinstein, "Empirical Tests of the Factor Abundance Theory: What Do They Tell Us?" *Eastern Economic Journal* 22, no. 4 (Fall 1996), pp. 433–40.

capital and labor used in the supplying industries of all inputs to the industry (the "indirect factor requirements"). The table is very useful for calculating the aggregate *country* requirements of capital and labor for producing a bundle of goods such as exports and import substitutes.

To evaluate the H-O prediction for the United States, Leontief imagined a situation where, using 1947 data, the United States simultaneously reduced its exports and imports proportionately by a total of $1 million each. The input-output table made it possible to determine how much capital (K) and labor (L) would be released from producing exports and how much capital and labor would be required to produce at home the $1 million of goods no longer being imported. (Leontief confined his analysis to "competitive imports," meaning that he did not include goods that the United States did not produce at home, such as bananas.)

Given the estimates of the K and L released from reducing exports and required to reproduce imports, a comparison could be made between them. Because the United States was thought to be a relatively capital-abundant country, the expectation from the statistical analysis was that the K/L ratio of the released factors from the export reduction would be greater than the K/L ratio of the factors required to produce the forgone imports. This expectation could be evaluated as to its validity through the concept of the **Leontief statistic,** which is defined as

$$\frac{(K/L)_M}{(K/L)_X}$$

where $(K/L)_M$ refers to the capital/labor ratio used in a country to produce import-competing goods and $(K/L)_X$ refers to the capital/labor ratio used to produce exports. According to the H-O theorem, a relatively capital-abundant country would have a Leontief statistic with a value less than 1.0 (since the denominator would be larger than the numerator) and a relatively labor-abundant country would have a Leontief statistic greater than 1.0.

Leontief's results were startling. He found that the hypothesized reduction of U.S. exports would release $2.55 million worth of capital and 182.3 years of labor-time, for a $(K/L)_X$ of approximately $14,000 per labor-year. On the import side, to produce the forgone imports would require $3.09 million worth of capital and 170.0 years of labor-time, yielding a $(K/L)_M$ of approximately $18,200 per labor-year. Thus, the Leontief statistic for the United States was 1.3 ($= \frac{\$18,200}{\$14,000}$), totally unexpected for a relatively capital-abundant country. A disaggregated analysis of his results also supported these findings. The most important export industries tended to have lower K/L ratios and higher labor requirements and lower capital requirements per dollar of output than did the most important import-competing industries. Thus, the seemingly commonsense notion that a country abundant in capital would export capital-intensive goods and import labor-intensive goods was seriously called into question. The doubt cast on the widely accepted Heckscher-Ohlin theorem by this study became known as the **Leontief paradox.**

SUGGESTED EXPLANATIONS FOR THE LEONTIEF PARADOX

Leontief's results have produced many studies seeking to explain why these unexpected findings might have occurred. In this section, we briefly discuss the more well-known "explanations."

Demand Reversal   The concept of demand reversal was introduced in Chapter 8. In demand reversal, demand patterns across trading partners differ to such an extent that trade does not follow the H-O pattern when the physical definition of relative factor abundance is used.

The relative preference of a country for goods made with its physically abundant factor (called "own-intensity preference") offers one explanation for the Leontief paradox if we hypothesize that the United States has relative preference for capital-intensive goods and that U.S. trading partners have relative preference for labor-intensive goods. The U.S. demand for capital-intensive goods bids up the price of those goods until the U.S. comparative advantage lies in labor-intensive goods. A similar process occurs in trading partners, giving them a comparative advantage in capital-intensive goods.

The validity of demand reversal as an explanation of the Leontief paradox is an empirical question. However, considerable dissimilarity (which seems unlikely in practice) is required for the demand reversal explanation to be of value in understanding the paradox. Further, the presence of demand reversal would imply that demand within the United States for labor-intensive goods would be relatively low and therefore *U.S. wages also would be relatively low*—hardly consistent with observed wage rates across countries! Thus, other reasons for the Leontief result need to be explored.

Factor-Intensity Reversal

As noted in Chapter 8, factor-intensity reversal (FIR) occurs when a good is produced in one country by relatively capital-intensive methods but is produced in another country by relatively labor-intensive methods. It is not possible to specify unambiguously which good is capital intensive and which is labor intensive, and the Heckscher-Ohlin theorem cannot be valid for both countries. In the context of the Leontief paradox, the reversal suggests that, although U.S. import goods might have been produced labor intensively overseas, the production process of these goods in the United States was relatively capital intensive. The trading partners (being labor-abundant) were conforming to H-O when they exported the goods, but the United States was not conforming to H-O.

The validity of this explanation for the occurrence of the Leontief paradox is also an empirical question. The literature is somewhat divided on the matter of whether factor intensity reversals occur with any frequency, and we cannot rule them out altogether.

The most famous test was conducted by B. S. Minhas (1962) for the United States and Japan using 1947 and 1951 data for 20 industries. Suppose that we consider the same 20 industries, that we have the K/L ratio employed in each country in each of the 20 industries, and that we rank the 20 industries in descending order according to K/L ratios (as Minhas did). For example, in the United States (using total capital and labor requirements) petroleum products constituted the most capital-intensive industry (it had the highest K/L ratio), coal products ranked number 2, iron and steel ranked number 8, textiles ranked number 11, shipbuilding ranked number 15, leather ranked number 19, and so forth. *If there are no factor-intensity reversals,* then the rankings for Japan would be the same as those for the United States. Statistically, this means that the rank correlation coefficient between the U.S. ranking and the Japanese ranking would be 1.0. (Note: If two rankings are identical, the correlation coefficient between them is 1.0; if they are perfectly opposite to each other, the coefficient is -1.0; and if there is no association between the two rankings whatsoever, the rank correlation coefficient is 0.)

When Minhas calculated this correlation coefficient using total factor requirements, he obtained a rank correlation coefficient of only 0.328. (This reflects that in Japan iron and steel was number 3 instead of 8, shipbuilding was number 7 instead of 15, etc.) For "direct" requirements only, the coefficient was higher but still only 0.730. Thus, doubt can be cast on the "no factor-intensity reversals" assumption of Heckscher-Ohlin. Later, economists such as G. C. Hufbauer (1966) and D. S. Ball (1966) pointed out that if the differences in land availability and agriculture in the two countries and the influence of these differences on the relative employment of K and L are allowed for, then the rank correlation coefficients are much closer to 1.0. Thus, while there is some suggestion of factor-intensity reversals in the real world, FIRs may not be as important as Minhas suggested.

IN THE REAL WORLD:

CAPITAL/LABOR RATIOS IN LEADING EXPORT AND IMPORT INDUSTRIES—LEONTIEF TEST

The Leontief test produced the surprising result that the capital per worker embodied in U.S. exports was less than the capital per worker embodied in U.S. imports. This result reflects the relative factor intensities of the individual industries. Table 1 lists, from 167 industrial categories, the 10 largest net export and import categories (where exports exceeded imports and imports exceeded exports, respectively, by the greatest dollar amounts) per $1 million of total exports and competitive imports, respectively, in Leontief's data for the 1947 test year. Also listed are the capital/labor ratios for each of the industries in dollars of capital required per person-year of labor. These K/L ratios are total or direct-plus-indirect factor requirements.

Looking at the table, it is evident that 7 of the 10 net import industries have larger K/L ratios than their corresponding net export industries. Also, the average (mean) K/L ratio of the 10 net importers is $18,287 per worker, while the average K/L ratio for the net exporters is $14,788 per worker.

Figure 1 presents the data for Table 1 in another way. The horizontal axis measures the labor requirements per $1 million of final output in the leading net export and net import industries, while the vertical axis measures the capital requirements per $1 million of final output for these same industries. The points on the graph show the capital

and labor requirements for each of the 20 industries. The rays from the origin indicate capital/labor ratios. The industries marked with an X are the 10 largest net export industries; those marked with an M are the 10 largest net import industries. The Heckscher-Ohlin theorem would lead us to expect that the export industries would be located toward the upper left-hand portion of the diagram (at the higher K/L ratios), while the import industries would be located toward the lower right-hand portion of the diagram (at the lower K/L ratios). However, these results do not seem to hold. There appears to be a slight tendency for the net import industries, not the net export industries, to be located toward the upper left-hand portion of the diagram.

An interesting sidelight is that several leading net exporters in 1947 (motor vehicles; textile mill products: spinning, weaving and dyeing; steelworks and rolling mills; and petroleum products) are now net *import* categories for the United States. In addition, agriculture and fisheries and paper are generally net exports. Comparative advantages do change over time. However, these changes do not seem to have influenced the general tendency for Leontief paradoxes to occur, because later tests (without allowing for natural resources and human capital or skills) have seldom shown a reversal of the paradox. Later in this chapter, we discuss labor skills and natural resources as they pertain to the Leontief paradox.

TABLE 1   Leading Net Export and Net Import Industries and Capital/Labor Ratios, 1947

Net Exporters	K/L	Net Importers	K/L
1. Wholesale trade	$ 7,638	Agriculture and fisheries	$29,689
2. Motor vehicles	10,447	Paper and paperboard mills	11,123
3. Grain mill products	20,752	Rubber	17,848
4. Textile mill products: spinning, weaving, and		Pulp mills	12,180
dyeing	10,738	Food products: canning, preserving, and freezing	15,635
5. Railroad transportation	21,022	Other nonferrous mining (i.e., not copper,	16,205
6. Ocean transportation	15,945	lead, zinc, bauxite)	
7. Steelworks and rolling mills	15,273	Crude petroleum and natural gas	29,508
8. Coal mining	8,491	Furs (hunting and trapping)	14,259
9. Special industrial machinery	10,439	Primary copper	20,080
10. Petroleum products	27,139	Other primary metals (i.e., not lead, zinc,	16,344
		copper, aluminum)	

Source: Derived from data in W. W. Leontief, "Domestic Production and Foreign Trade: The American Capital Position Re-examined," in Jagdish Bhagwati, ed., *International Trade: Selected Readings* (Middlesex, England: Penguin, 1969), table 2, pp. 102–21.

(continued)

IN THE REAL WORLD: *(continued)*

CAPITAL/LABOR RATIOS IN LEADING EXPORT AND IMPORT INDUSTRIES—LEONTIEF TEST

FIGURE 1   Capital and Labor Requirements in Leading Net Export and Net Import Industries—Leontief Test

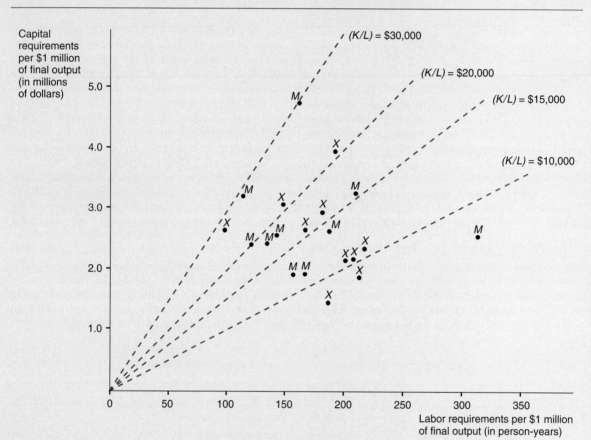

The points labeled *X* indicate the U.S. capital-labor combinations used in producing output in the 10 largest net export industries, while the points labeled *M* indicate the U.S. capital-labor combinations used in producing output in the 10 largest net import industries. The Heckscher-Ohlin analysis would suggest that the *X* points would be located toward the upper left and that the *M* points would be situated toward the lower right. The diagram indicates a slight tendency for the opposite results to occur.

U.S. Tariff Structure   This explanation for the Leontief paradox focuses on the factor intensity of the goods that primarily receive tariff (and other trade barrier) protection in the United States. From Heckscher-Ohlin and the accompanying Stolper-Samuelson theorem we learned that the opening of a country to trade increases the real return of the abundant factor and decreases the real return of the scarce factor. This suggests that, in the United States, labor will be more protectionist than will owners of capital (which is the case). Therefore, U.S. trade barriers tend to hit hardest the imports of relatively labor-intensive goods. With these goods restricted, the hypothesis is that the composition of the U.S. import bundle is relatively more capital intensive than would otherwise be the case because labor-intensive goods are kept out by protection. Thus, the Leontief result might be in part a reflection of the tariff structure of the United States and not an indication of the free-trade pattern that might conform to Heckscher-Ohlin.

Can this argument account for the occurrence of the Leontief paradox? In a 1971 study, Robert Baldwin recognized the possible role of tariffs and estimated that the K/L ratio in U.S. imports would be about 5 percent lower if this effect were incorporated. While allowance for the tariff structure works toward reducing the extent of the paradox, it seems unable to remove it fully.

Different Skill Levels of Labor

In this explanation of the Leontief paradox, the basic point is that the use of "labor" as a factor of production may involve a category that is too aggregative, because there are many different kinds and qualities of labor. A test involving this approach was conducted by Donald Keesing (1966). Keesing divided labor into eight different categories. For example, category I (scientists and engineers) was regarded as the most skilled labor (we have unsuccessfully searched for a listing of economists in this category!), while category II (technicians and draftsmen) was regarded as the second most skilled. This listing continued through category VIII (unskilled and semiskilled workers). Keesing then compared U.S. labor requirements in export- and import-competing industries with those of 13 other countries for 1962. He found that U.S. exports embodied a higher proportion of category I workers and a lower proportion of category VIII workers than the exports of other countries. Similarly, on the import side, the United States used the smallest fraction of category I workers and the largest fraction of category VIII workers.

This type of test suggests that the Leontief paradox may have occurred because a two-factor test was employed instead of a test with a larger number of factors (with each skill category of labor regarded as a distinct factor of production). Perhaps the United States is skilled labor abundant (as well as capital abundant) and unskilled labor scarce in its factor endowments. If so, the U.S. trade pattern conformed to Heckscher-Ohlin because the United States was exporting goods that were relatively intensive in skilled labor and importing goods that were relatively intensive in unskilled labor.

Other tests have confirmed the general impressions from the Keesing analysis. For example, Robert Baldwin's study (1971) found that, compared with import-competing industries, export industries had a higher proportion of workers with 13 or more years of schooling. On the other hand, compared with export industries, import-competing industries had a higher proportion of workers with eight years of schooling or less. Using data from the 1970s and early 1980s, Staiger, Deardorff, and Stern (1988) estimated that a move to free trade by the United States would lead to a reduction in demand for operatives and an expansion of demand for scientists, engineers, and physical capital. These results of eliminating trade restrictions are also consistent with an H-O multifactor explanation of trade that has no Leontief paradox. Indeed, many tests of this type have suggested that it is necessary to go beyond a two-factor model to test whether the U.S. trade pattern conforms to Heckscher-Ohlin.

The Role of Natural Resources

This explanation also builds around the notion that a two-factor test is too restrictive for proper assessment of the empirical validity of the Heckscher-Ohlin theorem. In this case, the additional factor is "natural resources." In the context of the Leontief paradox, many of the import-competing goods labeled as "capital intensive" were really "natural resource intensive." Leontief was assessing the factor requirements for producing imports at home and found that this production required the use of capital-intensive production processes; but in industries such as petroleum products, coal products, and iron and steel, domestic production of the goods involves a great deal of natural resources as well as capital. For Leontief, production of these import-competing goods involved capital-intensive production [raising $(K/L)_M$ in the calculation of the Leontief statistic] because his was a two-factor test. However, the "true" intensity of the goods produced might not be in capital but in natural resources. If we were able to identify the true factor intensity, we might conclude that the United States was importing natural-resource-intensive products. If the United States is relatively scarce in its endowment of natural resources, then there is no paradox with Heckscher-Ohlin.

The importance of natural resources has been confirmed in some empirical tests. For example, James Hartigan (1981) performed Leontief-type tests for U.S. trade for 1947 and 1951. A paradox existed in general, but *not* when natural-resource-intensive industries were deleted from the tests. Without natural-resource industries, U.S. trade yielded a Leontief statistic of 0.917 for 1947 and 0.881 for 1951. These results are not "paradoxical." Leontief himself (1956) also discovered that adjustment for natural resources could reverse the paradox. On the other hand, Robert Baldwin (1971) found that accounting for natural resources reduced the paradox but did not eliminate it. Thus, there is uncertainty about the relative importance of the "natural resources as a third factor" explanation of the Leontief paradox.

OTHER TESTS OF THE HECKSCHER-OHLIN THEOREM

The paradox found by Leontief has spawned many, many investigations into the question of the validity of the Heckscher-Ohlin theorem in predicting trade patterns. We will mention only a few of these studies here, but even our limited discussion should suffice to indicate that the question of the empirical validity of H-O continues to be an unanswered one. This ambiguity was established early on when some tests utilizing Leontief's approach—Tatemoto and Ichimura (1959) for Japan, Stolper and Roskamp (1961) for East Germany, and Rosefielde (1974) for the Soviet Union—found support for the theorem, because factor intensities of trade flows matched expectations from factor endowments, while other studies—Wahl (1961) for Canada and Bharadwaj (1962) for India—yielded "surprising," unexpected results. (For example, India's exports to the United States were found to be relatively capital intensive and India's imports from the United States were found to be relatively labor intensive!)

With respect to the United States, Robert Baldwin (1971, p. 134) found, for 1962 trade, a Leontief statistic of 1.27; when agriculture was excluded, the figure rose to 1.41, and when natural resource industries were excluded, the Leontief statistic fell to 1.04. Thus, in all cases (although only barely so when natural resource industries were excluded), the paradox still existed. However, utilizing a different approach, Harkness and Kyle (1975) found that, if natural resource industries are excluded, a U.S. industry had a greater probability of being a positive net exporter (where net exports = exports minus imports of the industry's product) if, among other characteristics, it utilized a *higher* ratio of capital to labor in production. This does *not* suggest a paradox because the United States was thought to be relatively capital abundant and relatively labor scarce. In addition, an industry had a higher probability of being a positive net exporter if it had a higher ratio of scientists and engineers in its labor force, which lends support to a "labor skills" or "human capital" explanation of the U.S. trade pattern. An important role for human capital was also uncovered by Stern and Maskus (1981). They attempted to explain the net export position of U.S. industries over the years 1958–1976, and they found the size of net exports of an industry to be positively correlated with the amount of human capital used in the industry. They also found the size of net exports to be negatively correlated with the amount of labor in the industry and sometimes, although not always, negatively correlated with the amount of physical capital used in the industry. (In affirmation of the traditional H-O prediction, positive net exports were in fact positively associated with physical capital in some years.)

Factor Content Approach with Many Factors

Other studies have moved beyond calculating Leontief statistics and often beyond examining only the United States. Many factors of production in many countries have been included. Calculations are first made (using input-output tables) of the quantity of any given factor needed to produce the goods contained in any given country's aggregate output bundle (i.e., the supply of the factor's services embodied in production). This requirement is then compared with the demand for the given factor embodied in the country's existing aggregate consumption bundle. If the total production requirement for any given factor exceeds the total consumption requirement, then (with assumed full employment of the factor) the country must, on balance, be exporting the services of that factor; if the total consumption requirement exceeds the total production requirement, then the country must, on balance, be importing the services of the given factor. In effect, then, a country with positive net exports of the services of a given factor must be relatively abundant in that factor, and a country with negative net exports (that is, positive net imports) of the services of a given factor must be relatively scarce in that factor.[2]

As an example of this "factor-content" type of study, Keith Maskus (1985) attempted to ascertain the implied factor endowments in the United States by examining the net exports and net imports of the services of five broad categories of factors of production. For the year 1958, he determined that the factor-abundance rankings were (1) scientists and engineers (most abundant because largest net export), (2) nonproduction workers except scientists and engineers, (3) human capital (reflecting mainly education), (4) production labor, and (5) physical capital (least abundant because largest net import). For 1972, the rankings for the first three factors were the same, but physical capital and production labor switched positions.

Along the same line, a very ambitious study of factor abundance and net export of factor services was carried out in 1987 by Harry Bowen, Edward Leamer, and Leo Sveikauskas. This study examined 12 different factors of production in 27 different countries to predict the implied factor abundances (and hence the implied Heckscher-Ohlin trade flows). Their general qualitative results for six countries are given in Table 2. A plus sign indicates that, through trade, the country was a net exporter of the services of that factor and thus was "revealed" to be abundant in that factor (because more of the factor's services were supplied in production than were demanded by the country through its consumption pattern); a minus sign indicates that the country was a net importer of a factor service and therefore that the country was relatively scarce in that factor (since more of the services of the factor were demanded through the country's consumption pattern than were supplied in domestic production).

For the United States in 1967 (the test year), the Leontief paradox did not seem to exist when allowance was made for factors other than capital and labor. The United States exported the services of capital (as general intuition would expect), as well as the services of professional/technical workers, agricultural workers, and arable land. Eight other services were imported and thus scarce in the United States. With respect to other countries, Table 2

---

[2]Technically, this relationship is known as the *Heckscher-Ohlin-Vanek theorem*, in recognition of the work of Jaroslav Vanek in the 1960s. The theorem basically states that a country's relative factor abundances are revealed by the country's trade flows.

TABLE 2   Net Export (+) and Net Import (−) of Factor Services through Trade, Selected Countries, 1967

Factor of Production	U.S.	Canada	Fed. Rep. of Germany	Japan	Mexico	Philippines
Capital stock	+	+	−	−	−	−
Total labor force	−	−	−	+	+	−
Professional/technical workers	+	−	+	+	+	−
Managerial workers	−	−	+	+	+	−
Clerical workers	−	−	+	+	+	−
Sales workers	−	−	−	−	+	+
Service workers	−	−	−	−	+	+
Agricultural workers	+	+	−	−	+	+
Production workers	−	−	+	+	−	−
Arable land	+	+	−	−	+	+
Forest land	−	+	−	−	+	−
Pasture land	−	+	−	−	+	−

Source: Derived from Harry P. Bowen, Edward E. Leamer, and Leo Sveikauskas, "Multicountry, Multifactor Tests of the Factor Abundance Theory," *American Economic Review* 77, no. 5 (December 1987), p. 795.

indicates that Canada exported the services of capital, agricultural workers, and various kinds of land while importing different kinds of labor services. Germany and Japan imported capital and land services while exporting the services of professional/technical workers and managerial workers. (The latter two worker categories had the largest net exports for Germany and Japan in the underlying data for Table 2.) For the developing countries in the table, Mexico was a net exporter of land-based factor services and various labor services while a net importer of the services of capital (these results are not surprising and thus are not paradoxical), while the Philippines imported capital and skilled-labor services and exported some "lower-skilled" labor services (again, results that are not surprising).

A recent addition to the list of factors that may serve as a source of comparative advantage is the financial sector. Svaleryd and Vlachos (2005) propose that underlying technological and organizational differences among industries cause them to differ in their need for external financing. Given that the services provided by the financial sector are relatively immobile across national boundaries, patterns of industrial specialization should be influenced by the relative endowments of financial development. Using a broad group of developed countries for their empirical analysis, Svaleryd and Vlachos find that countries with well-functioning financial systems tend to specialize in industries highly dependent on external financing. In fact, their results show that differences in financial systems are more important than differences in human capital. Their results support the Heckscher-Ohlin-Vanek model.

Comparisons of Calculated and Actual Abundances

Even the seemingly more friendly results for the Heckscher-Ohlin theorem (such as the Bowen-Leamer-Sveikauskas type) have been called into question, however. Remember the nature of factor-content tests—they are calculating whether a factor's services, on balance, are being exported or imported by a country, and, if exported (imported), the conclusion is drawn that the country is abundant (scarce) in that factor. Then a judgment is rendered as to whether this abundance or scarcity fits with our general intuition and thus whether H-O generally seems to have been validated. But a point of attack with respect to these more recent studies is that the *calculated* relative abundance (scarcity) of a factor may not match the *actual* relative abundance (scarcity) that can be ascertained by the use of different, independent data. In other words, for example, a factor might be calculated as being "relatively abundant" in a country because there is positive net export of the factor's services, but independent data on actual endowments of the factor in that country and other countries would show the factor to be relatively scarce in that country. The independent data in these comparisons would consist of measures such as a country's share of the world's actual endowments of capital and labor. Indeed, Maskus (1985) found that, in tests comparing the United States with other countries, the actual U.S. relative abundances and scarcities matched the predicted abundances and scarcities two-thirds of the time in one test, one-third of the time in another test, and only one-sixth of the time in a third test. These results are hardly reassuring. Bowen, Leamer, and Sveikauskas also examined their 12 factors in 27 countries to see if the predicted relative abundances and scarcities matched the actual data. Only in 4 of the 12 factors was there a predictive success rate of 70 percent or more across the countries, and only 7 of the 12 factors were successfully predicted for the United States.

Productivity Differences and "Home Bias"

In more recent work, Daniel Trefler (1995) examined, for the year 1983, data for 33 countries that accounted, at the time, for 76 percent of world exports and 79 percent of world GNP. Nine factors of production were considered: (1) capital; (2) cropland; (3) pasture land; (4) professional and technical workers; (5) clerical workers; (6) sales workers; (7) service workers; (8) agricultural workers; and (9) production, transport, and unskilled workers. His first test of the data with respect to whether net factor flows through trade matched the expectation from actual endowments produced disappointing results. However, he noted that, while the Heckscher-Ohlin theorem and the usual H-O tests assume that technology/productivity in any given industry is identical across countries, this assumption is very unrealistic. In fact, he found that, across countries, there tended to be systematic differences in productivity levels. For example, Panama's industries tended to be about 28 percent as productive as U.S. industries, and Finland's about 65 percent as productive as U.S. industries. Thus the United States had close to four times as much "effective" labor ($1/0.28 = 3.6$) in comparison with Panama as standard labor force measures would indicate [or, alternatively, Panama had only about one-quarter (0.28) as much "effective" labor relative to the United States as standard labor force measures would indicate]. Hence, Trefler adjusted his data to reflect these differences. Panama's factor endowments, when compared with those of the United States, were thus only 28 percent of the actual level, Finland's only 65 percent of the actual level, and so on. These adjusted factor endowments were then used in the comparison of factor endowments with the flows of factor services through trade. This type of adjustment was also accompanied by another adjustment—Trefler felt that, for whatever reason, consumers in any given country had a preference for home goods over foreign goods, and this preference needed to be incorporated into the examination of trade flows. (This adjustment was necessitated in Trefler's view because standard Heckscher-Ohlin tests seemed to predict a much larger volume of trade than actually occurred—Trefler's "home bias" was designed to account for this difference.)

With both of these adjustments in place, Trefler more satisfactorily "explained" the existing trade patterns than he had done without the adjustments and than had been done with regard to explaining trade in the various previous studies. The thrust of his work, then, is that actual trade differs from Heckscher-Ohlin-predicted trade because technology/productivity levels differ across countries and because consumers have a general preference for home goods. These two factors should be taken account of in considering the determination of trade flows, because H-O by itself does not do a very good job of explaining the flows. In 2002, Conway confirmed Trefler's conclusion regarding these mysteries but suggested alternate explanations. Feenstra and Hanson (2003) indicate that it is standard in Heckscher-Ohlin models to assume that exports are produced entirely by combining domestic factors of production with domestically produced intermediate inputs. They suggest that this assumption is wrong and that accounting for trade in intermediate inputs can help resolve the mystery of the missing trade.

In a survey of the relevant literature, Helpman (1999) strongly questioned the home-bias assumption of Trefler. However, Helpman and others have increasingly explored the notion of productivity/technology differences across countries, with the view that such differences are important becoming more generally accepted. Helpman notes (1999, p. 133) that recent work suggests that "allowing for differences in techniques of production can dramatically improve the fit of factor content equations. Now economists need to identify the forces that induce countries to choose different techniques of production." Further, Reeve (1998, cited in Helpman 1999) and Davis, Weinstein, Bradford, and Shimpo (1997) have found, in different settings, that factor endowments do a decent job of predicting the location of particular types of industries, if not of predicting trade itself. That is, while a country that is relatively abundant in a particular factor may not have been found by existing estimation techniques to be exporting the services of that factor, the country's production structure emphasizes goods that are relatively intensive in that factor. This finding would be consistent with the Heckscher-Ohlin general notion that a country will specialize in the production of goods utilizing the country's abundant factors, even if the next step of linking production to trade has not been empirically established.

In a more recent look at the issue of productivity/technology differences across countries, Schott (2003) looks beyond the traditional industry-based data to examine the actual subsets of goods produced in a country. His contention is that too many traditional attempts to find empirical support for the Heckscher-Ohlin idea that a country's endowments determine production and trade has used the overly restrictive assumption that all countries produce a given category of goods using the same technology. Schott argues that within the category of electronics, for example, the more labor-abundant Philippines may be producing portable radios while the more capital-abundant Japan is manufacturing semiconductors and satellites. The Schott approach permits a given sector's output to vary with a country's endowments, allowing countries to move in and out of sectors as they develop. The estimation focuses on finding the capital per labor cutoffs, where changes in the subset of output produced take place and using this to group countries according to the subset of goods they produce.

Schott's technique highlights the potential differences in the choices of output within industries across countries and suggests that moving beyond the standard, industry-level data is necessary to test Heckscher-Ohlin hypotheses. By designating products within the category of manufacturing by the relative capital intensity of their production, Schott finds strong support for the idea that country product mix varies with relative endowments. In addition to pointing out the need to move beyond industry-level data to test international specialization, this analysis suggests that the technique can be used to explore violations of Heckscher-Ohlin assumptions assigned to home bias in trade (e.g., Trefler 1995).

In overview, while the Heckscher-Ohlin theorem is logical, straightforward, and seemingly a commonsense hypothesis, there have been difficulties in demonstrating the validity of the theorem in practice. As empirical work continues, however, we are beginning to get a better picture of what the analysis does and does not seem to explain. Supplementary forces besides factor endowments and factor intensities increasingly need to be considered, however, and some of these factors are dealt with in the next chapter.

This chapter began with Leamer and Levinsohn's call for a reorientation of empirical work in international trade. Their call was summarized in the statement "Estimate, don't test." In other words, draw on relevant empirical evidence to improve understanding of a phenomenon rather than trying to devise a perfect, yes-or-no test of a theorem explaining the phenomenon. A review of empirical work on the H-O-V model by Davis and Weinstein

IN THE REAL WORLD:

CASE OF THE MISSING TRADE AND OTHER MYSTERIES

Daniel Trefler (1995) provides an excellent examination of observed patterns and volumes of trade. He identifies the the-oretical predictions of the Heckscher-Ohlin-Vanek (H-O-V) model and suggests that four "mysteries" arise from empirical testing. Trefler reports these divergences between the theory and empirical record using data from 33 countries for nine factors of production in the year 1983. The first two mysteries identified by Trefler are referred to as "missing trade" and "predictive error." The missing trade designation comes from the fact that the predicted volume of trade is larger than the actual volume in the sample. The predictive error is a result of the correlation between trade volumes and factor endow-ments being quite small.

The remaining mysteries are referred to as the "sign–H-O-V" and the "endowments paradox." In Trefler's empirical analysis, the estimations of the model resulted in the signs of the parame-ters linking trade volume and relative factor endowments being the same in less than 50 percent of the 297 observations (sign–H-O-V). Another puzzle was that there was a strong neg-ative correlation between the number of factors in which a country is abundant and country per capita gross domestic product (GDP). In other words, it seems to Trefler, with his measures of factor abundance, that "Rich countries tend to be scarce in most factors, and poor countries tend to be abundant in all factors"(!) (Trefler, p. 1032). He calls this the endowment paradox. After considering a variety of alternatives, Trefler con-cludes that there are two causes for the mysteries. The first involved country-specific productivity differences. Allowing a country-specific productivity adjustment has the potential to address both pattern of trade and volume of trade mysteries. A preference for home-country goods in consumption is the sec-ond reason cited for the missing trade. Trefler's results suggest

that correcting for country-specific productivity differences and the preference for home-country goods in consumption improves the performance of the H-O-V model in predicting both the pattern and the volume of trade.

Conway (2002) confirms Trefler's insight that the rela-tive size of endowments and expenditure is at the heart of the H-O-V prediction problems. He found that the missing trade and predictive error mysteries are related to poor pre-dictive power of the H-O-V theory on the volume of trade. The sign–H-O-V and the endowments paradox are evidence of the poor predictive power of the H-O-V theory on the pat-tern of trade. Separating the mysteries into two distinct groups is the first contribution by Conway. Although he agrees that there are problems with the classical H-O-V model, Conway also offers alternative explanations of the mysteries that Trefler identified. In the case of mysteries related to the pattern of trade, Conway found them best addressed through an adjustment that could be either a restatement of relative purchasing power or a restatement of relative productivity. In terms of the predictions of the vol-ume of trade, Conway found that a sluggishness in reallocat-ing productive factors within each country is an alternative hypothesis for explaining the lower-than-predicted volume of trade. While the Trefler corrections improve the perfor-mance of the H-O-V specification, Conway's results show an even greater gain in explanatory power when compared with the usual H-O-V model.

Sources: Daniel Trefler, "The Case of the Missing Trade and Other Mysteries," *American Economic Review* 85, no. 5 (December 1995), pp. 1029–46; Patrick Conway, "The Case of the Missing Trade and Other Mysteries," *American Economic Review* 92, no. 1 (March 2002), pp. 394–404.

(1996) suggested that the accumulation of results is more influential than any individual study. Each study sheds new light on the circumstances under which a particular theory is useful. Davis and Weinstein suggested that researchers should both estimate and test. Their suggested criterion: Does the test narrow the range of sensible application of the theory? An affirmative reply indicates that the test is useful.

HECKSCHER-OHLIN AND INCOME INEQUALITY

In recent years, a debate has been taking place in the United States and in Western Europe over a phenomenon that is associated with the Heckscher-Ohlin analysis. While the debate is not always couched in H-O terms (the average person on the street, unlike you, is not an expert on Heckscher-Ohlin!), it involves an important implication of that analysis and has also been the subject of empirical tests. The phenomenon is the growing income inequality that has been occurring in the developed countries.[3]

That income inequality in the United States has been increasing is rather clear. For example, the share of household income received by the lowest 20 percent of households has fallen from a high of 4.3 percent in 1975 to only 3.4 percent in 2005, while the top 20 percent of households experienced an increase in their share of income from 43.6 percent in 1975 to 50.4 percent in 2005. During the same period, the middle 20 percent of households experienced a drop from 17.3 percent of income to 14.6 percent. While real incomes have been rising over the entire 30-year period, the rates of increase have varied substantially. Between 1975 and 2005, the lowest 20 percent of households experienced an increase in mean household income (in 2005 dollars) from $9,304 to $10,655 (an increase of 14.5 percent), the middle 20 percent experienced an increase from $37,494 to $46,301 (an increase of 23.5 percent), and the top 20 percent of households experienced an increase from $96,188 to $159,583 (an increase of 66 percent). In addition to disparity in income growth, mean real income for the lowest 20 percent peaked at $11,614 in 1999 and fell consistently until it reached $10,587 in 2004 (U.S. Census Bureau, *Income, Poverty, and Health Insurance Coverage in the United States, 2005*).

Looking at other data, in 1963 the weekly wage of a male in the 90th percentile of the U.S. earnings distribution was 2.91 times the wage of a male in the 10th percentile; this ratio rose to 3.00 by 1969, to 3.47 by 1979, and to 4.42 by 1989 (Burtless 1995, p. 802). Another study indicated that, for all workers, the ratio of the real wage of the 90th percentile worker to the 10th percentile worker rose from 3.48 in 1979 to 4.42 in 1995 before receding slightly to 4.32 in 2000 and then rising to 4.51 in 2005 (Mishel, Bernstein, and Allegretto 2007, p. 121). Meanwhile, in Western Europe, where wage rates are less flexible than in the United States due to institutional factors such as strong labor legislation and prominent unions, the increased inequality has registered itself not so much through widening wage differentials as through increased unemployment rates (with consequent loss of income). In 1973, the unemployment rate for developed countries in Europe was 2.9 percent, but unemployment averaged 9.3 percent from 1983 to 1991 (Freeman 1995, p. 18) and in mid-1999 was at double-digit levels in Belgium (12.7 percent), France (14.2 percent), Germany (10.5 percent), Italy (12.0 percent), and Spain (16.1 percent) (*The Economist,* September 11, 1999, p. 114). For the same five countries, the January 2007 figures were 11.7 percent, 8.6 percent, 9.5 percent, 6.8 percent, and 8.5 percent, respectively (*The Economist,* February 17, 2007, p. 101).

To many observers, a disturbing factor about this rise in inequality is that it has been occurring at the same time that the United States and the world as a whole have been becoming more open to international trade. In 1970, the ratio of U.S. exports to U.S. gross domestic product (GDP) was 5.5 percent, while that of imports to GDP was 5.4 percent; by 1980 these ratios had reached 10.0 percent for exports and 10.6 percent for imports; and in 2006 the figures were 10.85 percent and 16.6 percent, respectively (*Economic Report of the President,* February 1999, pp. 326–27; U.S. Department of Commerce, Bureau of Economic Analysis, *Survey of Current Business,* February 2007, pp. D-6, D-58). And, in particular, rapid growth has been occurring in imports into the United States and Western Europe from developing countries. These imports into the United States were 14 percent of all imports in 1970 but rose

---

[3]There has also been growing inequality of the same general nature in developing countries. It should be noted that Slaughter (1999, p. 612) maintains that, among developed countries, the growing inequality has mainly occurred only in the United States and the United Kingdom.

to 35 percent by 1990 and 55 percent by 2005. For the European Union countries, the figures were 5 percent of all imports in 1970, 12 percent in 1990, and 30 percent in 2002.[4] These kinds of increases in trade in general and especially in imports from developing countries suggest that there may be a link between them and the rising inequality.

Clearly, the Heckscher-Ohlin and Stolper-Samuelson theorems can provide such a link. As you remember from Chapter 8, the H-O theorem postulates that a country will export goods intensive in the country's relatively abundant factor of production and will import goods intensive in the country's relatively scarce factor of production. Extending this pattern of trade to income distribution considerations, the Stolper-Samuelson theorem indicates that, with trade, the real return to the abundant factor rises and the real return to the country's scarce factor falls. In the context of an expanded H-O framework for the United States where labor is divided into relatively skilled labor and relatively unskilled labor, such as the framework utilized in empirical tests discussed earlier in this chapter, the implication is that the real incomes of highly skilled workers (who tend to be in the upper portions of the income distribution) will increase with expanded trade and the real incomes of less skilled workers (who tend to be in the lower portions) will decrease. And, indeed, probing further into factor income data for the United States, supporting evidence can easily be found. For example, in 1979 full-time male workers aged 25 years and older who had at least a bachelor's degree had earnings 49 percent higher than those of similar workers who had no degree above a high school diploma; by 1993 this "premium" had risen to 89 percent (*Economic Report of the President,* February 1996, p. 191).With a somewhat different grouping, U.S. Census Bureau data indicated that, in 2001, annual earnings of individuals with a bachelor's degree as the highest degree were 89 percent above the earnings of individuals with a high school degree but no college attendance; however, by 2004, the figure had fallen to 80 percent.[5]

The critical question facing trade economists concerns the extent to which the rising imports are the *cause* of the increased wage inequality.[6] Most studies of the relationship have found trade to be a factor accounting for the increased inequality but not a major factor. For example, Borjas, Freeman, and Katz (1992, discussed in Burtless 1995, p. 808) calculated that from 8 to 15 percent of the 1980–1988 rise in the wage differential between college and high school graduates in the United States was attributable to the combined effects of trade and immigration into the United States, with most of this 8 to 15 percent due to the trade component. Other studies also found modest effects, and Richard Freeman (1995, p. 25) summarizes by stating that "factor content analysis studies indicate that trade can account for 10–20 percent of the overall fall in demand for unskilled labor needed to explain rising wage differentials in the United States or rising joblessness in Europe."

---

[4]The 1970 and 1990 figures are from Freeman (1995, pp. 16, 19). The 2005 figures were obtained from data in International Monetary Fund, *Direction of Trade Statistics Quarterly,* March 2007, pp. 26, 379.

[5]U.S. Census Bureau, *Statistical Abstract of the United States: 2003* (123rd Edition), Washington, DC, 2003, p. 154; U.S. Census Bureau, *Statistical Abstract of the United States: 2007* (126th Edition), Washington, DC, 2006, p. 144.

[6]It should be reiterated that the increased wage inequality occurred only since the late 1970s. In a useful article, Robert E. Baldwin and Glen G. Cain note that the time period in the United States from 1968 through 1996 can be divided into four subperiods with differing characteristics regarding wages and wage equality: (1) 1968–1973, when average real wages increased and there was also a movement toward greater wage equality; (2) 1973–1979, when average real wages decreased slightly and there continued to be a movement toward greater wage equality; (3) 1979–1987, when average real wages increased slightly and there was a sizable increase in wage inequality; and (4) 1987–1996, when average real wages fell somewhat and the trend toward greater inequality generally continued. See Robert E. Baldwin and Glen G. Cain, "Shifts in Relative U.S. Wages: The Role of Trade, Technology, and Factor Endowments," *Review of Economics and Statistics* 82, no. 4 (November 2000), pp. 580–95.

The findings on this relatively minor role for trade have been disputed by other economists.[7] The most ardent advocate of the view that the increased trade with the developing countries has led to the increased income inequality in developed countries has been Adrian Wood of the University of Sussex (see Wood 1991, 1994), who contends that the usual estimates of the decrease in demand for unskilled labor in the developed countries are significant underestimates. In essence, he claims that replacing labor-intensive imports from developing countries with developed-country production would require considerably more low-skilled labor than is generally thought to be the case.

As a response to these arguments, economists have usually made several major points, which we summarize here:

1. A major consideration brought out in the discussion is that if trade is operating in accordance with the Stolper-Samuelson theorem to generate the increased inequality, then the prices of low-skill-intensive *goods* would also be falling. This follows because factor prices in the Heckscher-Ohlin analysis move in the same direction as the prices of the goods that the factors are used to produce. However, studies of relative goods' price movements in recent years do not find a pronounced decline in the prices of unskilled-labor-intensive goods relative to skilled-labor-intensive goods. Thus, the trade explanation for the increased inequality lacks a mechanism that is consistent with trade theory.

2. The rise in the demand for skilled labor relative to unskilled labor in the developed countries has not been confined to the *traded* goods industries—indeed, it has occurred across almost all industries. If the increased inequality were purely a *trade* phenomenon, the fall in the relative price of unskilled labor would cause the nontraded goods industries to substitute toward the use of relatively more unskilled labor,which is the opposite of what has happened. Rather, the use of skilled labor relative to unskilled labor has risen across industries, whether the industries are producing traded goods or nontraded goods. Consequently, the general rise in demand for skilled labor in all industries is likely to have occurred because of the nature of *technological change* in this age of increased use of computers, robots, and so on.

3. There are other reasons for the decline in the relative earnings of unskilled labor besides trade and the above-mentioned technological change. In regard to the United States, some such reasons are the increased immigration of relatively unskilled labor, the decline in the importance and influence of organized labor, and the fall in the real minimum wage (since the nominal minimum wage has not kept pace with the price level). Indeed, in an informal survey of economists attending a conference at the Federal Reserve Bank of New York, the average respondent attributed 45 percent of the rising wage inequality in the United States to technological change, 11 percent to trade, and less than 10 percent each to the decline in the real minimum wage, the decline in unionization, and the increased immigration of unskilled labor (with the remainder attributed to various other reasons). (See Burtless 1995, p. 815, and *Economic Report of the President,* February 1997, p. 175.)

Despite these strong points, however, the matter of the causes of the inequality is an unsettled one. For example, Wood has countered the technological-change argument by strongly suggesting that the adoption of the unskilled-labor-saving type of new

---

[7]See, for example, Mishel, Bernstein, and Allegretto (2007, pp. 171–77). In addition, the entire January 1995 issue of the Federal Reserve Bank of New York's *Economic Policy Review* was devoted to the rising wage inequality in the United States. Also, four papers (by Peter Gottschalk; George E. Johnson; Robert H. Topel; and Nicole M. Fortin and Thomas Lemieux) in the Spring 1997 issue of the *Journal of Economic Perspectives* address the increase in wage inequality.

technology is occurring as a response to the threat of imports and thus that this reduction in the demand for unskilled labor should also be attributed to trade.[8] Further, it could be said that the weakening of unions is also a result of new trade pressures. In addition, other potential causes for the increased inequality have been suggested. For example, Robert Feenstra and Gordon Hanson (1996) suggest that an important factor in reducing the demand for unskilled labor is the rise in "outsourcing" by U.S. firms. The point here is that firms are increasingly shipping abroad their component and intermediate-input production that is relatively unskilled-labor-intensive in nature, and this can also put downward pressure on the wages of U.S. low-skilled laborers. Hence, another route by which trade can increase inequality has entered the debate. In Feenstra's view (1998, p. 41), outsourcing and the shifting of activities abroad lead to the result that "the whole distinction between 'trade' versus 'technology' becomes suspect." This muddling of trade and technology occurs because outsourcing can importantly be a response to technological change (e.g., improvements in communications, enhanced use of computers for inventory and monitoring purposes), and then trade responds to the outsourcing. Hence, in this view, the most important cause of increasing inequality is not to be identified as trade *or* technology—rather, both trade *and* technology are involved together in the increasing-wage-inequality process.

To conclude this discussion, it is difficult in empirical analysis to sort out the specific impact on inequality of trade by itself in a complex, dynamic economy undergoing continuous structural change. Economists in general tend to doubt that trade is the dominant factor in the rising wage inequality, but needed work continues on this important issue.

---

[8]Responses to this argument would be that firms in nontraded goods industries have also adopted skill-intensive technological change and that firms will adopt new technology in order to pursue profit maximization regardless of whether the threat comes from imports or from purely domestic competitors.

IN THE REAL WORLD:

OUTSOURCING AND WAGE INEQUALITY IN THE UNITED STATES

Robert Feenstra and Gordon Hanson (1996) maintain that outsourcing has played an important causal role in the increasing wage inequality that has occurred in the United States in recent decades. To test this hypothesis, they constructed a measure of outsourcing and a measure of the trend in wage inequality for the years 1972–1990 for 435 U.S. industries and ran statistical tests to see if there was a significant association between the two constructed data series.

Feenstra and Hanson measured outsourcing for an industry as the share of imported intermediate inputs in the purchases of total nonenergy materials by the industry. Hence, if $30 worth of inputs were imported and the industry's total nonenergy input purchases were $1,000, outsourcing would be calculated for this industry as 0.03 (=$30/$1,000). Energy inputs generally cannot be outsourced since the geographical location

of such supplies cannot be shifted, but this measure in effect treats all other imported inputs as fitting into the "outsourced" category. This is a very broad measure of outsourcing. To some observers, *outsourcing* intuitively implies something more narrow, as in Hummels, Rapoport, and Yi (1998, p. 82), who define it as "the relocation of one or more stages of the production of a good from the home country"; or, as in current discussions in the United States, the sending of particular jobs abroad, such as staffing call centers in India rather than in the United States (see Chapter 16). In contrast, the Feenstra-Hanson measure counts goods that have nothing to do with relocated production from a home firm. Nevertheless, using their measure (which they called S_O), Feenstra and Hanson indicated increasing interdependence between the United States and other countries, since S_O for the 435 industries in the aggregate doubled

(continued)

IN THE REAL WORLD: *(continued)*

OUTSOURCING AND WAGE INEQUALITY IN THE UNITED STATES

from 1972 (5.34 percent) to 1990 (11.61 percent). Feenstra and Hanson also examined another measure of interdependence (which they called S_M), which was the share of imports in final U.S. consumption of the products of the various industries. This figure for the 435 industries as a whole also doubled from 1972 (5.02 percent) to 1990 (10.65 percent). Feenstra and Hanson (1996, p. 242) took the fact that S_O and S_M moved together over the period as "consistent with the idea that outsourcing is a response to import competition." In other words, when final goods imports as a percentage of U.S. consumption rose, U.S. firms responded by seeking lower costs through obtaining intermediate inputs from foreign locations.

As a measure of wage trends, Feenstra and Hanson calculated, for each of the 435 industries, the share of the industry's wage bill that is paid to nonproduction workers. This is used as a proxy for the relative demand for skilled labor. As payments to nonproduction workers (e.g., executives, scientists, computer technicians) rise relative to payments to production workers, this measure (which they called S_N) will rise. This rise is interpreted by Feenstra and Hanson to be a relative increase in the demand for skilled labor and hence an indication of greater wage inequality. Again, this measure is clearly a broad one, and it ignores differing skills and wage trends within the nonproduction-worker category, as well as within the production-worker category.

With the S_O, S_M, and S_N figures in hand for the 435 industries, Feenstra and Hanson then conducted statistical tests for the years 1972–1990. They divided the period into two parts (1972–1979 and 1979–1990), in recognition of the fact that the increasing-inequality phenomenon had basically begun only at about the end of the 1970s. Their results were that, for 1972–1979, the annual changes in S_N were not related to the annual changes in S_O (after allowing for other influences on the wage share besides the annual changes in S_O); for 1979–1990, however, there was a highly significant positive association between S_N and S_O. Changes in S_N were also positively related to changes in S_M in a highly significant manner in the later period, whereas that had not been the case in the earlier period. In view of these statistical associations and the differing results for the later period as compared with the earlier period, Feenstra and Hanson concluded (1996, p. 243) that their research suggests, for the 1979–1990 period, "that outsourcing has contributed substantially to the increase in the relative demand for nonproduction labor." Indeed, they estimated that the outsourcing could account for from 30.9 to 51.3 percent of the increase that had occurred in the share of the wage bill going to nonproduction workers.

In a followup study, Feenstra and Hanson (2003) presented evidence of a direct link between trade and wage inequality. By using data on changes in industry behavior over time, they showed that foreign outsourcing is associated with increases in the share of wages paid to skilled workers in the United States, Japan, Hong Kong, and Mexico. In several cases, outsourcing can account for half or more of the observed skill upgrading. In the case of the United States, Feenstra and Hanson present evidence that during the 1980s and 1990s outsourcing contributed to changes in industry productivity and product prices that, in turn, mandated increases in the relative wage of skilled labor.

In view of this study (and others), outsourcing is clearly a phenomenon that needs to be given serious attention when considering the increasing inequality that has been occurring in the United States. Such attention needs to address questions of how best to measure outsourcing and relative labor demand, as well as the matter of whether or not the relationships in the United States also exist in other countries. ●

SUMMARY

The seemingly straightforward and intuitively appealing Heckscher-Ohlin theorem has been subjected to a large number of empirical tests. However, the theorem has not had a particularly high success rate. An early and extensive test for the United States resulted in the famous Leontief paradox. Various explanations for the occurrence of this paradox have been offered, but none of them has been judged to be entirely convincing. The most promising avenues for further testing of Heckscher-Ohlin seem to lie in the incorporation of a larger number of factors of production by disaggregating labor into different skill categories and by adding natural resources. Nevertheless, tests for other countries besides the United States have sometimes shown success in the standard two-factor framework. In addition, tests of a significant implication of the Heckscher-Ohlin analysis—that a country's scarce factor loses from trade—have been conducted in the context of examining the importance of trade as a cause of rising income inequality (especially in the United States); these tests have also yielded mixed results.

Particularly given the frustrations which have emerged with respect to successful verification of the Heckscher-Ohlin predictions on trade patterns, two questions pose themselves to economists: (1) Should we look for better ways of testing Heckscher-Ohlin? or (2) Should we search for other theoretical explanations of trade patterns and the composition of trade, as H-O has not been particularly successful? The literature has moved in both directions in response to these questions. The "better-testing" approach has focused importantly on extending the analysis to a greater number of factors than the original two, capital and labor. This approach runs the risk that, in disaggregating into more factors, we lose generality and meaningful understanding of the forces influencing a country's trade pattern. As Paul Samuelson has suggested, we may end up concluding that Switzerland exports Swiss watches because Switzerland is well endowed with Swiss watchmakers! The second approach of searching for alternative trade theories to Heckscher-Ohlin has generated a great deal of activity in recent years. These newer theories are the subject of the next chapter.

KEY TERMS

input-output table
Leontief paradox

Leontief statistic

total factor requirements

QUESTIONS AND PROBLEMS

1. What was the "Leontief paradox," and why was it a paradox?
2. What do you think is the major defect in the Leontief test that might have caused the paradox to occur? Why?
3. If you have traveled in a foreign country, would your observations confirm the view that the country's demand patterns reflect consumer preferences in that country for goods produced with the country's relatively abundant factor of production?
4. If U.S. tariffs and other trade barriers are placed more heavily on labor-intensive goods than on capital-intensive goods because of the H-O suggestion that the scarce factor of production gains from protection, how do you explain why many developing countries also have relatively high import barriers on labor-intensive goods?

5. Should economists discard the Heckscher-Ohlin theorem as a practical explanation of trade patterns and search for other theories of trade? Or should they seek better ways of testing Heckscher-Ohlin? Explain.
6. Build a case for the view that increasing openness of the U.S. economy has been the primary factor causing increased income inequality in recent decades.
7. Build a case against the view that increasing openness of the U.S. economy has been the primary factor causing increased income inequality in recent decades.

part 3

ADDITIONAL THEORIES AND EXTENSIONS

> The classical theory assumes as fixed, for purposes of reasoning, the very things which, in my view, should be the chief objects of study if what we wish to know is the effects and causes of international trade, so broadly regarded that nothing of importance in the facts shall fail to find its place in the analysis.
>
> John H. Williams, 1929

Although it had long been acknowledged that several important factors influencing the nature and direction of international trade were ignored by both Classical and neoclassical trade theorists, the Leontief paradox proved to be a catalyst stimulating new inquiry into the underlying bases for international trade flows. While some of these endeavors centered on relaxing certain restrictive assumptions normally employed in general theoretical analysis, others looked more closely at economic variables that could clearly change over time and often did as a consequence of international trade flows.

Part 3 provides an overview of work that has expanded the theory of international trade to take into account the impact of other influences on trade flows that had been ignored before. In Chapter 10 we first introduce theories that go beyond the Heckscher-Ohlin analysis in explaining the basis for trade. Next, in Chapter 11, we examine the impact of economic growth on trade and the implications for social well-being in the open economy. Finally, Chapter 12 looks briefly at the importance of factor movements in the world today and discusses the implications of capital and labor mobility for international trade and general social well-being. In Part 3 we get directly at some of the dynamic considerations concerning the underlying basis for trade that are so critical when taking into account the possible costs and benefits of alternative economic policies. ●

> Most students of international trade have long had at least a sneaking suspicion that conventional models of comparative advantage do not give an adequate account of world trade. . . . [I]t is hard to reconcile what we see in the manufactures trade with the assumptions of standard trade theory.
>
> Paul Krugman, 1983

10

POST–HECKSCHER–OHLIN THEORIES OF TRADE AND INTRA-INDUSTRY TRADE

LEARNING OBJECTIVES

- To understand explanations for the basis of trade in manufactures beyond Heckscher-Ohlin.

- To appreciate the roles of technology dissemination, demand patterns, and time in affecting trade.

- To grasp how the presence of imperfect competition can affect trade.

- To understand the phenomenon known as intra-industry trade.

INTRODUCTION

A Trade Myth

Roy J. Ruffin of the University of Houston and Federal Reserve Bank of Dallas points out that, contrary to popular belief, the top U.S. imports from Mexico are not clothing, fruits, and vegetables. These represent only 10 percent of the U.S. imports. Electrical machinery and equipment (and related parts) rank first, representing 27 percent of U.S. imports from Mexico. Vehicles rank second, and nuclear reactors, boilers, and related items are third. Interestingly, the United States's top three exports to Mexico are these same three categories. Not only are Mexico's exports to the United States quite similar to its imports, but Mexico's exports are more concentrated in those big items.[1]

These empirical challenges to the predicted trade patterns of traditional models of international trade will be the focus of this chapter. The chapter reviews several of the more recent theories on the causes and consequences of trade. These newer approaches depart from trade theory as presented earlier by relaxing several assumptions employed in the basic trade model. Some of the implications of this relaxation will be presented in theories that incorporate differences in technology across countries, an active role for demand conditions, economies of scale, imperfect competition, and a time dimension to comparative advantage. Finally, intra-industry trade—a common element in several theories—will be discussed in detail, because it is a prominent feature in international trade of manufactured goods. It is important to recognize that the causes of trade are more complex than those portrayed in the basic Heckscher-Ohlin model.

POST–HECKSCHER-OHLIN THEORIES OF TRADE

The Imitation Lag Hypothesis

The **imitation lag hypothesis** in international trade theory was formally introduced in 1961 by Michael V. Posner. This theory is discussed here only to the extent that it paves the way for a better-known theory—the product cycle theory.

The imitation lag theory relaxes the assumption in the Heckscher-Ohlin analysis that the same technology is available everywhere. It assumes that the same technology is *not* always available in all countries and that there is a delay in the transmission or diffusion of technology from one country to another. Consider countries I and II. Suppose that a new product appears in country I due to the successful efforts of research and development teams. According to the imitation lag theory, this new product will not be produced immediately by firms in country II. Incorporating a time dimension, the **imitation lag** is defined as the length of time (e.g., 15 months) that elapses between the product's introduction in country I and the appearance of the version produced by firms in country II. The imitation lag includes a learning period during which the firms in country II must acquire technology and know-how in order to produce the product. In addition, it takes time to purchase inputs, install equipment, process the inputs, bring the finished product to market, and so on.

In this approach, a second adjustment lag is the **demand lag,** which is the length of time between the product's appearance in country I and its acceptance by consumers in country II as a good substitute for the products they are currently consuming. This lag may arise from loyalty to the existing consumption bundle, inertia, and delays in information flows. This demand lag also can be expressed in a number of months, say, four months.

A key feature in the Posner theory is the comparison of the length of the imitation lag with the length of the demand lag. For example, if the imitation lag is 15 months, the **net lag**

---

[1]Roy J. Ruffin, "The Nature and Significance of Intra-Industry Trade," *Economic and Financial Review,* Fourth Quarter 1999, Federal Reserve Bank of Dallas.

is 11 months, that is, 15 months less 4 months (demand lag). During this 11-month period, country I will export the product to country II. Before this period, country II had no real demand for the product; after this period, firms in country II are also producing and supplying the product so the demand for country I's product diminishes. Thus, the central point of importance in the imitation lag hypothesis is that trade focuses on new manufactured products.[2] How can a country become a continually successful exporter? By continually innovating! This theory has considerable relevance for present-day concerns about the global competitiveness of U.S. firms. Further, it seems to be more capable of handling "dynamic" comparative advantage than are the Heckscher-Ohlin and Ricardo models.

| The Product Cycle Theory | The **product cycle theory (PCT)** of trade builds on the imitation lag hypothesis in its treatment of delay in the diffusion of technology. However, the PCT also relaxes several other assumptions of traditional trade theory and is more complete in its treatment of trade patterns. This theory was developed in 1966 by Raymond Vernon. |

The PCT is concerned with the life cycle of a typical "new product" and its impact on international trade. Vernon developed the theory in response to the failure of the United States—the main country to do so—to conform empirically to the Heckscher-Ohlin model. Vernon emphasizes manufactured goods, and the theory begins with the development of a new product in the United States. The new product will have two principal characteristics: (1) It will cater to high-income demands because the United States is a high-income country; and (2) it promises, in its production process, to be labor-saving and capital-using in nature. (It is also possible that the product itself—e.g., a consumer durable such as a microwave oven—will be labor saving for the consumer.) The reason for including the potential labor-saving nature of the production process is that the United States is widely regarded as a labor-scarce country. Thus, technological change will emphasize production processes with the potential to conserve this scarce factor of production.

The PCT divides the life cycle of this new product into three stages. In the first stage, the **new-product stage,** the product is produced and consumed only in the United States. Firms produce in the United States because that is where demand is located, and these firms wish to stay close to the market to detect consumer response to the product. The characteristics of the product and the production process are in a state of change during this stage as firms seek to familiarize themselves with the product and the market. No international trade takes place.

The second stage of the life cycle is called the **maturing-product stage.** In this stage, some general standards for the product and its characteristics begin to emerge, and mass production techniques start to be adopted. With more standardization in the production process, economies of scale start to be realized. This feature contrasts with Heckscher-Ohlin and Ricardo, whose theories assumed constant returns to scale. In addition, foreign demand for the product grows, but it is associated particularly with other *developed* countries, because the product is catering to high-income demands. This rise in foreign demand (assisted by economies of scale) leads to a trade pattern whereby the United States exports the product to other high-income countries.

Other developments also occur in the maturing-product stage. Once U.S. firms are selling to other high-income countries, they may begin to assess the possibilities of producing abroad in addition to producing in the United States. If the cost picture is favorable (meaning that production abroad costs less than production at home plus transportation costs),

---

[2]The imitation lag hypothesis can also be applied in the case of new, lower-cost processes for producing an existing product. The demand lag in such a situation, however, is less meaningful than in the case of a new product.

then U.S. firms will tend to invest in production facilities in the other developed countries. If this is done, export displacement of U.S.-produced output occurs. With a plant in France, for example, not only France but other European countries can be supplied from the French facility rather than from the U.S. plant. Thus, an initial export surge by the United States is followed by a fall in U.S. exports and a likely fall in U.S. production of the good. This relocation-of-production aspect of the PCT is a useful step because it recognizes—in contrast to H-O and Ricardo—that capital and management are not immobile internationally. This feature also is consistent with the very large amount of direct investment by U.S. firms in Western Europe during the 1960s and 1970s and, in a more recent context, by Japanese firms in rapidly growing countries in Asia (such as China, South Korea, and Taiwan).

Vernon also suggested that, in this maturing-product stage, the product might now begin to flow from Western Europe to the United States because, with capital more mobile internationally than labor, the price of capital across countries was unlikely to diverge as much as the price of labor. With relative commodity prices thus heavily influenced by labor costs, and with labor costs lower in Europe than in the United States, Europe might be able to undersell the United States in this product. (Remember that Vernon was writing in 1966; it is less true today that Europe's labor costs are lower than those of the United States.) Relative factor endowments and factor prices, which played such a large role in Heckscher-Ohlin, have not been completely ignored in the PCT.

The final stage is the **standardized-product stage.** By this time in the product's life cycle, the characteristics of the product itself and of the production process are well known; the product is familiar to consumers and the production process to producers. Vernon hypothesized that production may shift to the developing countries.[3] Labor costs again play an important role, and the developed countries are busy introducing other products. Thus, the trade pattern is that the United States and other developed countries may import the product from the developing countries. Figure 1 summarizes the production, consumption, and trade pattern for the originating country, the United States.

In summary, the PCT postulates a **dynamic comparative advantage** because the country source of exports shifts throughout the life cycle of the product. Early on, the innovating country exports the good but then it is displaced by other developed countries—which in turn are ultimately displaced by the developing countries. A casual glance at product history yields this kind of pattern in a general way. For example, electronic products such as television receivers were for many years a prominent export of the United States, but Europe and especially Japan emerged as competitors, causing the U.S. share of the market to diminish dramatically. More recently, Japan has been threatened by South Korea and other Asian producers. The textile and apparel industry is another example where developing countries (especially China, Taiwan, Malaysia, and Singapore) have become major suppliers on the world market, displacing in particular the United States and Japan. Automobile production and export location also shifted relatively from the United States and Europe to Japan and later still to countries such as South Korea and Malaysia. This dynamic comparative advantage, together with factor mobility and economies of scale, makes the product cycle theory an appealing alternative to the Heckscher-Ohlin model.

There is no single all-encompassing test (such as the Leontief test of Heckscher-Ohlin) to verify empirically the product cycle theory. Instead, researchers have examined particular features of the PCT to see if they are consistent with real-world experience. For example,

---

[3]Theoretical models investigating developed-countries–developing-countries trade in a PCT context have been offered by Dollar (1986), Krugman (April 1979), and Flam and Helpman (1987).

FIGURE 1   The Trade Pattern of the United States in the Product Cycle Theory

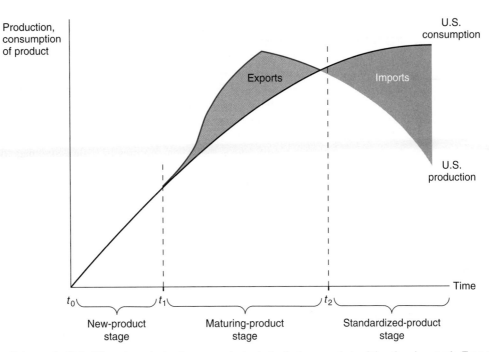

From time t_0 until time t_1, the United States is producing the new product only for the home market and thus there is no trade. From time t_1 until time t_2, the United States exports the good to other developed countries (exports = production minus consumption) and may even begin importing the good from those countries (imports = consumption minus production). From time t_2 onward, imports arrive into the United States from other developed countries and, increasingly, from developing countries.

new product development is critical to the PCT, and it is often the result of research and development (R&D) expenditures. Therefore, economists hypothesize that, in the U.S. manufacturing sector, there should be a positive correlation between R&D expenditures and successful export performance by industry. A number of early tests indicated this result, including those by Donald Keesing (1967) and William Gruber, Dileep Mehta, and Vernon (1967). Kravis and Lipsey (1992) found that high R&D intensity was positively associated with large shares of exports by U.S. multinational companies (MNCs). Furthermore, over the past 25 years, greater shares of exports from U.S. MNCs have come from overseas production, which is consistent with the direct-investment and export-displacement features of the PCT. In addition, in 1969, Louis Wells examined the income elasticity of demand of the fastest-growing U.S. exports and found that trade in "high-income"-type products indeed grew more rapidly than other products—again, an occurrence consistent with the PCT.

Among the many other empirical works is Gary Hufbauer's (1966) study of trade in synthetic materials. Hufbauer found that the United States and other developed countries tended to export new products while developing countries tended to export older products. Gruber, Mehta, and Vernon (1967) also discovered that research-intensive U.S. industries had a high propensity to invest abroad. This is consistent with the maturing-product stage of the theory. In 1972, John Morrall found that U.S. industries that were successful exporters also tended to have relatively high expenditures on non-payroll costs such as advertising, sales promotion, and so forth. This finding is consistent with the product cycle theory because production of new products involves such spending. Many other studies of PCT features have shown consistency between real-world experience and aspects of the theory.

Raymond Vernon (1979) later suggested that the PCT might need to be modified. The main alteration concerns the location of the production of the good when the good is first introduced. Multinational firms today have subsidiaries and branches worldwide, and knowledge of production conditions outside the United States is more complete than it was at the time of Vernon's original writing in 1966. Thus, the new product may be produced first not in the United States but outside the country. In addition, per capita income differences between the United States and other developed countries are not as great now as in 1966, so catering to high-income demands no longer implies catering to U.S. demands alone. Even with this modification, the salient features of scale economies, direct investment overseas, and dynamic comparative advantage still distinguish the product cycle theory from the Heckscher-Ohlin model.

One hesitates, however, to distinguish the product cycle theory so clearly from the Heckscher-Ohlin model. Elias Dinopoulos, James Oehmke, and Paul Segerstrom (1993) constructed a theoretical model that has PCT-type trade emerging as a *result* of differing factor endowments across countries. The model utilizes three production sectors in each country: an innovating high-technology sector, an "outside-goods" sector that engages in no product innovation, and a sector that supplies R&D services to the high-technology sector. Like H-O, there are only two factors (capital and labor), identical production functions across countries, and constant returns to scale. Assuming that the R&D sector is the most capital-intensive sector, a capital-abundant country produces a great deal of R&D. This enables a firm in the high-technology sector in that country to obtain a temporary monopoly in a new product—with patent protection—and then to export the product. After the patent expires, production occurs abroad with some export from that location. While a complete explanation is beyond the scope of this book, Dinopoulos, Oehmke, and Segerstrom's model generates PCT-type trade as well as intra-industry trade (a concept discussed later) and a role for MNCs. Thus, Heckscher-Ohlin and the product cycle theory may well be complementary, not competing, theories.

In similar fashion, James Markusen, James Melvin, William Kaempfer, and Keith Maskus (1995, p. 209) introduced the idea of a life cycle for new technologies containing elements of both the Dinopoulos, Oehmke, and Segerstrom model and the product cycle model. Noting the growing importance of technology in the trade of industrialized countries, Markusen et al. suggest that, just as there is a product cycle for consumer goods, there increasingly appears to be a cycle for techniques of production and machinery, as techniques and machines developed in industrialized countries eventually find their way into labor-abundant developing countries.

This **technology cycle** is driven by the capital-abundant, high-wage countries where there is both a cost incentive and a sufficient market demand to warrant new labor-saving technology and new-product development. The capital-abundant countries thus produce a flow of new products and innovations, with firms often protected by a temporary monopoly via patents to produce for the home market. Because the new labor-saving technologies are not consistent with the relative factor abundances in the labor-abundant developing countries, those countries initially have little economic incentive to acquire the innovations. Consequently, capital-abundant countries export the new products utilizing the new technology. Eventually, however, as incomes start to rise in developing countries and even newer technologies are produced in the developed countries, the machines embodying the original "new" technology are exported by capital-abundant countries and the final products start being produced in the labor-abundant countries. Later, as in the product cycle theory, the machines themselves may be produced in the developing countries and exported from them.

The Linder Theory

This theory explaining the composition of a country's trade was proposed by the Swedish economist Staffan Burenstam Linder in 1961. The **Linder theory** is a dramatic departure from the Heckscher-Ohlin model because it is almost exclusively demand oriented. The H-O approach was primarily supply oriented because it focused on factor endowments and factor intensities. The Linder theory postulates that tastes of consumers are conditioned strongly by their income levels; the per capita income level of a country will yield a particular pattern of tastes. (Note that Linder is concerned only with manufactured goods; he regards Heckscher-Ohlin as fully capable of explaining trade in primary products.) These tastes of "representative consumers" in the country will in turn yield demands for products, and these demands will generate a production response by firms in that country. Hence, the kinds of goods produced in a country reflect the per capita income level of that country. This set of particular goods forms the base from which exports emerge.

To illustrate the theory, suppose that country I has a per capita income level that yields demands for goods A, B, C, D, and E. These goods are arrayed in ascending order of product "quality" or sophistication, with goods A and B, for example, being low-quality clothing or sandals while goods C, D, and E are farther up the quality scale. Now suppose that country II has a slightly higher per capita income. Because of its higher income, it may demand and therefore produce goods C, D, E, F, and G. Goods F and G may be quality products (such as silks or fancy shoes) not purchased by country I's lower-income consumers. Each country is therefore producing goods that cater to the demands and tastes of its own citizens.

Given these patterns of production, what happens if the two countries trade with each other? Which goods will be traded between them? Trade will occur in goods that have **overlapping demand,** meaning that consumers in both countries are demanding the particular items. In our example, goods C, D, and E will be traded between countries I and II.

The determination of the trading pattern by observing overlapping demands has an important implication for the types of countries that will trade with each other. Suppose that we introduce country III, which has an even higher per capita income than country II. Country III's consumer demand may be for goods E, F, G, H, and J. Which goods will country III trade with the other two countries? It will trade goods E, F, and G with country II but will trade only good E with country I. For all three countries I, II, and III, Figure 2 portrays the income-trade relationships, recognizing that there is a representative range of individual incomes around each country's per capita income level.

Looking at the Linder model as a whole, the important implication is that *international trade in manufactured goods will be more intense between countries with similar per capita income levels than between countries with dissimilar per capita income levels.* The Linder conclusion is consistent with aspects of the product cycle theory and fits with the observation that the most rapid growth in international trade in manufactured goods in the post–World War II period has been between developed countries.

The Linder theory has been subjected to a number of empirical tests. A common type of test is formulated as follows: Suppose that we have figures on the *absolute value* of the per capita income differences between a given country I and its trading partners. Then we get information on the intensity of trade between country I and each of its trading partners. The Linder theory would hypothesize that the relationship between these two series is negative

FIGURE 2   **Overlapping Demands in the Linder Model**

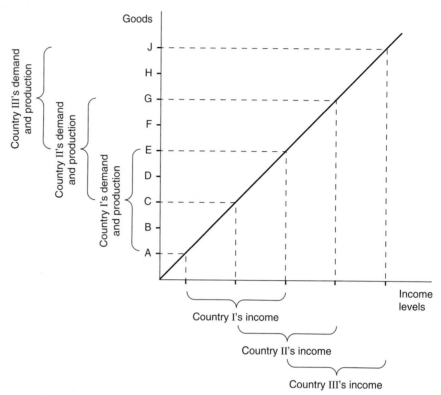

In the preceding three-country example, the level of per capita income in country I yields a demand for goods A, B, C, D, and E. Country II's higher per capita income yields a demand for goods C, D, E, F, and G, and country III's even higher per capita income is associated with demands for goods E, F, G, H, and J. According to the Linder hypothesis, there will be an interest in trade only where socio-income-induced product demands are similar or "overlap." Thus, we would expect to see countries I and II trading goods C, D, and E with each other and countries II and III exchanging goods E, F, and G. Because their respective income levels do not generate common demands for any good except good E, countries I and III will trade with each other only in that good.

because the greater the difference between the per capita incomes of country I and a trading partner, the less intensely the two countries will trade with each other. Studies, such as that by Joel Sailors, Usman Qureshi, and Edward Cross (1973), have indeed found a negative correlation. However, a complicating factor is that countries with similar per capita incomes often tend to be near one another geographically, so that the intense trade may also reflect low transportation costs and cultural similarity. After correcting for geographic proximity and other shortcomings, studies by Hoftyzer (1975), Greytak and McHugh (1977), Qureshi et al. (1980), and Kennedy and McHugh (1980) found little or no evidence in support of the Linder theory. At this point, the primary tool employed in these studies was simple correlation analysis.

More recently, gravity models in a multiple regression context have been used in the testing of the Linder theory. (The gravity model framework is discussed later in this chapter). The gravity models focus on the interaction between the resistance (geographic distance) and attraction (similar demand patterns). The expectation is that controlling for geographic factors, countries with similar demand patterns will trade more intensively with each other. Two early tests using gravity models found little or no evidence to support the Linder theory [Hoftyzer (1984), Kennedy and McHugh (1983)]. However, using a gravity model to control for distance between countries and other determinants of trade, Jerry and Marie Thursby (1987, p. 493) found that support for Linder's hypothesis was overwhelming in their study of the manufactured goods trade of 13 European developed countries, Canada, Japan, the United States, and South Africa. Only Canada and South Africa failed to have a significantly negative regression coefficient for per capita income differences with a trading partner on the volume of trade with that given partner. Additional studies by Hanink (1988, 1990), Greytak and Tuchinda (1990), Bergstrand (1990), and McPherson et al. (2000) found evidence supporting Linder's hypothesis using a gravity model. Several studies have also indicated that a problem with omitted countries may have created a bias rejecting the Linder hypothesis.

Finally, we need to make one very important point concerning the Linder theory. In our example of countries I, II, and III, the theory identified the goods that would be traded between any pair of countries. However, the Linder theory did *not* identify the direction in which any given good would flow. When we said that countries I and II would trade in goods C, D, and E, we did not say which good or goods would be exported by which country. This was not a slip in the model; Linder made it clear that a good might be sent in *both* directions—both exported and imported by the same country! This phenomenon was not possible in our previous models of trade, for how could a country have a comparative advantage *and* a comparative disadvantage in the same good?

The answer to this question will be pursued later (see the final section of this chapter), but this type of trade could clearly occur, for example, because of **product differentiation.**

IN THE REAL WORLD:

A REEXAMINATION OF THE LINDER HYPOTHESIS

A common practice in the attempts to empirically test the Linder hypothesis has been to exclude data from countries that receive zero dollars' worth of goods and services from the country under investigation. As a result, potentially important information on potential trading partners is being omitted, and this omission may have affected the results. Specifically, excluded data may create a bias toward *acceptance* or *rejection* of the hypothesis. If the countries excluded have per capita incomes *similar* to the country under investigation, then the resulting bias will increase the chance of *accepting* the hypothesis. If the countries omitted have per capita incomes that are *different* from the country under investigation, there will be a bias toward *rejecting* the hypothesis. A recent analysis by McPherson, Redfearn, and Tieslau (2000) has utilized a technique that avoids the bias.

McPherson et al. (2000) tested the validity of the Linder hypothesis for each of the 19 countries of the Organization for Economic Cooperation and Development (OECD). By

using an estimation technique known as a random effects tobit, they were able to include the data for potential partners that did not trade with a given country in the year analyzed. In their sample, the (per capita) incomes of the potentially "excluded" countries were only about 30 percent of that of the potentially included countries on average. In this case, exclusion of the data would have incorrectly cast the Linder hypothesis in a pessimistic light.

Using the random effects tobit model, McPherson et al. were able to use the data from 161 potential trading partners for the 19 OECD nations. By avoiding the unnecessary exclusion of countries, they found empirical support for the Linder hypothesis in 18 of the 19 countries. These results indicate that countries do tend to trade more intensely with economies similar to their own. In addition, their results imply that the inability of previous studies to find support for the Linder hypothesis may have been a result of the exclusion of potential trade partners. ●

This term refers to products that are seemingly the same good but which are perceived by the consumer to have real or imagined differences. Clearly two different makes of automobiles are not the same in the consumer's mind. Nor does the consumer regard as equivalent two different brands of beer, tennis rackets, or word-processing programs. Linder's theory can incorporate this notion of product differentiation, because country II might be exporting Hyundais to country III and country III might be exporting Ford Fusions to country II.

Another probable cause of this two-way flow of a product is that producers in any one country are producing for the mass market of consumers in their country. Consumers with specialty tastes or at income levels well above or below the per capita income level of the country may find their wants unsatisfied by home producers and will import their desired varieties of the good. Thus, low-income consumers in higher-income country II may purchase the good from country I, which has a lower per capita income, and high-income consumers in country I may purchase the good from country II.

Countries that export and import items in the same product classification are engaging in **intra-industry trade.** The topic of intra-industry trade, covered later in this chapter, is an aspect of Linder's theory that has generated considerable theoretical and empirical work.

CONCEPT CHECK

1. If the imitation lag for a new product is nine months and the demand lag is two months, why will there be no trade in the product in the first month after the innovating country introduces it?
2. If firms in innovating country A build new plants in similar high-income country B during the maturing product stage of the product cycle theory, why might A's exports to another high-income country, C, decline along with A's exports to country B?
3. Suppose that country F has a per capita income of $3,000. Using the Linder theory, what is its relative intensity of trade with country G ($1,000 per capita income) compared with country H ($6,000 per capita income)? Explain.

Economies of Scale

Some alternative trade theories are based on the existence of economies of scale. In several of these models, the economies of scale are external economies pertaining to the industry rather than the firm. In such industries, as output increases firms experience cost reductions per unit of output because, for example, the industry growth is attracting a pool of qualified labor.

In a two-country world where the countries have identical PPFs and demand conditions, there is normally no incentive to trade. If the two industries experience economies of scale, the model generates a potentially new reason for trade. In spite of the fact that both countries begin with identical autarky positions, a shock that results in each country moving to specialization in different goods and trading would lead both countries to experience gains from trade. See Appendix A at the end of this chapter for the complete development of this model.

While the gains from trade are clearly a result of the cost reductions that come from specialization that exploit the economies of scale, there are a number of uncertainties in this model. First, there is no way to know which country will specialize in each good. Second, something unusual is needed to jolt production away from the autarky point, but there is no way to predict the cause of the shock. In spite of these uncertainties, the analysis opens up new possibilities for gains that do not exist in traditional models. Whether the introduction of increasing returns is more realistic than the constant-returns assumption is a debated question, but increasingly, economists do think that scale economies can be important.

IN THE REAL WORLD:

PRODUCT DIFFERENTIATION IN AUTOMOBILES

An obvious prominent example of an industry with substantial product differentiation is the automobile industry. Table 1 lists the 308 different car models available to U.S. consumers in 2007. The list includes minivans, sport-utility vehicles, and pickup trucks because these vehicles are basically substitutes for passenger automobiles. (Note: The list of 308 models is shorter than the true list because there are different models within categories, such as the Honda Accord EX and Honda Accord LX.)

TABLE 1   Car Models in the United States in 2007

Acura MDX	Cadillac CTS-V	Dodge Durango	GMC Savana
Acura RDX	Cadillac DTS	Dodge Grand Caravan	GMC Sierra
Acura RL	Cadillac Escalade	Dodge Magnum	GMC Yukon
Acura TL	Cadillac Escalade EXT	Dodge Nitro	GMC Yukon XL 1500
Acura TSX	Cadillac SRX	Dodge Ram 1500	GMC Yukon XL 2500
Aston Martin DB9	Cadillac STS	Dodge Ram 2500	Honda Accord
Aston Martin Vantage	Cadillac STS-V	Dodge Ram 3500	Honda Civic
Audi A3	Cadillac XLR	Dodge Sprinter 2500	Honda CR-V
Audi A4	Cadillac XLR-V	Dodge Sprinter 3500	Honda Element
Audi A6	Chevrolet Avalanche	Dodge Viper	Honda Fit
Audi A8	Chevrolet Aveo	Ford Crown Victoria	Honda Odyssey
Audi Q7	Chevrolet Cobalt	Ford E-150	Honda Pilot
Audi RS4	Chevrolet Colorado	Ford E-250	Honda Ridgeline
Audi S4	Chevrolet Corvette	Ford E-350	Honda S2000
Audi S6	Chevrolet Equinox	Ford Edge	Hummer H2
Audi S8	Chevrolet Express	Ford Escape	Hummer H3
Audi TT	Chevrolet HHR	Ford Expedition	Hyundai Accent
Bentley Arnage	Chevrolet Impala	Ford Explorer	Hyundai Azera
Bentley Continental	Chevrolet Monte Carlo	Ford Explorer Sport Trac	Hyundai Elantra
BMW 3-series	Chevrolet Silverado	Ford F-150	Hyundai Entourage
BMW 5-series	Chevrolet Suburban	Ford F-250	Hyundai Sante Fe
BMW 6-series	Chevrolet Tahoe	Ford F-350	Hyundai Sonata
BMW 7-series	Chevrolet Trailblazer	Ford Five Hundred	Hyundai Tiburon
BMW M5	Chevrolet Uplander	Ford Focus	Hyundai Tucson
BMW M6	Chrysler 300	Ford Freestar	Infiniti FX35
BMW X3	Chrysler Aspen	Ford Freestyle	Infiniti FX45
BMW X5	Chrysler Pacifica	Ford Fusion	Infiniti G35
BMW Z4	Chrysler PT Cruiser	Ford GT	Infiniti QX56
Buick Enclave	Chrysler Sebring	Ford GT500	Infiniti M35
Buick LaCrosse	Chrysler Town & Country	Ford Mustang	Infiniti M45
Buick Lucerne	Dodge Avenger	Ford Ranger	Isuzu Ascender
Buick Rainier	Dodge Caliper	GMC Acadia	Isuzu I-280
Buick Rendezvous	Dodge Caravan	GMC Canyon	Isuzu I-290
Buick Terraza	Dodge Charger	GMC Envoy	Isuzu I-350
Cadillac CTS	Dodge Dakota	GMC Envoy XL	Isuzu I-370

(continued)

IN THE REAL WORLD: *(continued)*

Jaguar S-Type	Maserati Quattroporte	Nissan 350Z	Subaru Legacy
Jaguar X-Type	Maybach 57	Nissan Altima	Subaru Outback
Jaguar XJ-Series	Maybach 62	Nissan Armada	Suzuki Aerio
Jaguar XK-Series	Mazda B-2300	Nissan Frontier	Suzuki Forenza
Jeep Commander	Mazda B-3000	Nissan Maxima	Suzuki Forenza Wagon
Jeep Compass	Mazda B-4000	Nissan Murano	Suzuki Grand Vitara
Jeep Grand Cherokee	Mazda CX-7	Nissan Pathfinder	Suzuki Reno
Jeep Liberty	Mazda CX-9	Nissan Quest	Suzuki SX4
Jeep Patriot	Mazda MAZDA3	Nissan Sentra	Suzuki XL-7
Jeep Wrangler	Mazda MAZDA5	Nissan Titan	Toyota 4Runner
Kia Amanti	Mazda MAZDA6	Nissan Versa	Toyota Avalon
Kia Optima	Mazda MAZDASPEED3	Nissan Xterra	Toyota Camry
Kia Rio	Mazda MAZDASPEED6	Pontiac G5	Toyota Camry Solara
Kia Rio5	Mazda Miata	Pontiac G6	Toyota Corolla
Kia Rondo	Mazda RX-8	Pontiac Grand Prix	Toyota FJ Cruiser
Kia Sedona	Mazda Tribute	Pontiac GTO	Toyota Highlander
Kia Sorento	Mercedes-Benz C-Class	Pontiac Montana	Toyota Highlander Hybrid
Kia Spectra	Mercedes-Benz CL-Class	Pontiac Solstice	Toyota Land Cruiser
Kia Spectra5	Mercedes-Benz CLK-Class	Pontiac Torrent	Toyota Matrix
Kia Sportage	Mercedes-Benz CLS-Class	Pontiac Vibe	Toyota Prius
Land Rover LR2	Mercedes-Benz E-Class	Porsche 911	Toyota RAV4
Land Rover LR3	Mercedes-Benz G-Class	Porsche Boxster	Toyota Sequoia
Land Rover Range Rover	Mercedes-Benz GL-Class	Porsche Cayenne	Toyota Sienna
Land Rover Range Rover Sport	Mercedes-Benz M-Class	Porsche Cayman	Toyota Tacoma
Lexus ES350	Mercedes-Benz R-Class	Rolls Royce Phantom	Toyota Tundra
Lexus GS350	Mercedes-Benz S-Class	Saab 9-2X	Toyota Yaris
Lexus GS430	Mercedes-Benz SL-Class	Saab 9-3	Volkswagen Beetle
Lexus GS450H	Mercedes-Benz SLK-Class	Saab 9-5	Volkswagen Eos
Lexus GX470	Mercury Grand Marquis	Saab 9-7X	Volkswagen Golf
Lexus IS250	Mercury Mariner	Saturn Aura	Volkswagen GTI
Lexus LS460	Mercury Milan	Saturn ION	Volkswagen Jetta
Lexus LX470	Mercury Montego	Saturn ION Quad Coupe	Volkswagen Passat
Lexus RX350	Mercury Monterey	Saturn Outlook	Volkswagen Rabbit
Lexus RX400H	Mercury Mountaineer	Saturn Relay	Volkswagen Touareg
Lexus SC430	MINI Cooper	Saturn Sky	Volvo C70
Lincoln Mark LT	Mitsubishi Eclipse	Saturn VUE	Volvo S40
Lincoln MKX	Mitsubishi Eclipse Spider	Scion TC	Volvo S60
Lincoln MKZ	Mitsubishi Endeavor	Scion Xa	Volvo S80
Lincoln Navigator	Mitsubishi Galant	Scion Xb	Volvo V50
Lincoln Town Car	Mitsubishi Lancer Evolution	Subaru B9 Tribeca	Volvo V70
Lotus Elise	Mitsubishi Outlander	Subaru Forester	Volvo XC70
Lotus Exige	Mitsubishi Raider	Subaru Impreza	Volvo XC90

Source: Autoweb.com.

The Krugman Model

This theory of trade represents a family of newer trade models that has emerged since Heckscher-Ohlin. While Paul Krugman has developed other models, we refer to this widely cited model (November 1979) as the **Krugman model.** This model rests on two features that are sharply distinct from those of traditional models: economies of scale and monopolistic competition.

In the Krugman model, labor is assumed to be the only factor of production. The scale economies (which are *internal* to the firm) are incorporated in the equation for determining the amount of labor required to produce given levels of output by a firm, as shown here:

$$L = a + bQ \qquad [1]$$

L stands for the amount of labor needed by the firm, a is a constant (technologically determined) number, Q represents the output level of the firm, and b specifies the relation at the margin between the output level and the amount of labor needed. The equation works as follows: If $a = 10$ and $b = 2$, this means that when the firm's output level is 20 units, then the labor required to produce that level of output is $L = 10 + (2)(20)$, or 50 units of labor. However, suppose that output doubles to 40 units. The labor required to produce 40 units is $L = 10 + (2)(40)$, or 90 units. What does this equation imply? It means that a doubling of output requires less than a doubling of input; that is, economies of scale in production exist. All firms in the economy are assumed to have this type of labor requirement equation. It should be evident that this equation is not applicable to a Ricardian model, because constant costs of production would make the relevant labor-usage equation $L = bQ$; that is, the labor input has a constant relation to the amount of output.

The second main characteristic of the Krugman model is the existence of the market structure of **monopolistic competition.** In monopolistic competition, there are many firms in the industry and easy entry and exit. In addition, there is zero profit for each firm in the long run. However, unlike the perfect competition of traditional trade theory, the output of firms in the industry is not a homogeneous product. The products differ from each other, and each firm's product possesses a certain amount of consumer brand loyalty. Product differentiation leads to advertising and sales promotion as firms attempt to differentiate their products in the minds of consumers. (For a review of monopolistic competition and the effect of changes in the price elasticity of demand, see Appendix B at the end of this chapter.)

The Krugman model is most easily portrayed through Krugman's basic graph (see Figure 3). On the horizontal axis, we place consumption of a typical good by any representative consumer in the economy, that is, per capita consumption, c. The vertical axis indicates the ratio of the price of the good to the wage rate, P/W. The basic notions of the model are illustrated in this figure and through explanation of the PP and ZZ curves.

The upward-sloping PP curve reflects the relationship of the price of the good to marginal cost. As consumption increases, demand becomes less elastic. This is like the ordinary straight-line demand curve studied in the introductory economics course—at lower prices and larger quantities, demand is less elastic than at higher prices and smaller quantities. Thus, the expression $[e_D/(e_D + 1)]$, which is developed in Appendix B, increases and, with constant marginal cost, profit maximization dictates a higher price. Thus, P/W rises as c increases, and the PP curve is upward sloping.

The ZZ curve in Figure 3 reflects the phenomenon in monopolistic competition that economic profit for the firm is zero in long-run equilibrium. (Ignore the $Z'Z'$ curve for the moment.) To arrive at the downward slope, remember that zero profit means that price is equal to average cost at all points on the ZZ curve. From any given point on the curve, if per capita consumption (c) increases (a horizontal movement to the right), average cost is reduced because of the economies-of-scale phenomenon specified in this model. Hence, to

FIGURE 3   Basic Krugman Diagram

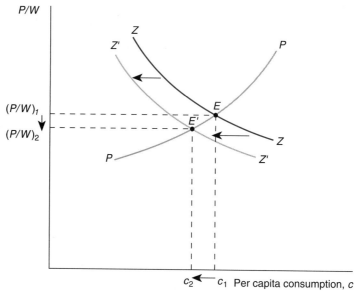

The upward-sloping *PP* curve indicates that as per capita consumption (c) of the good rises, the price of the good will rise. The reason is that demand is assumed to become less elastic as consumption increases, and thus the profit-maximizing price $P = MC[e_D/(e_D + 1)]$ increases. The downward-sloping *ZZ* curve reflects the fact that profit in the long run is zero. A greater amount of consumption brings the realization of scale economies, which in turn leads to price reductions and eventually to zero economic profit. Equilibrium occurs at the intersection point E.

With the introduction of international trade, the size of the market facing the firm is increased; this is represented by a shift of the *ZZ* curve to the left or downward to $Z'Z'$. The consequence is that per capita consumption of the good falls but total consumption of each good increases. In addition, the fall in P/W means that the real wage (W/P) has increased.

maintain the zero profit and to move back to the *ZZ* curve, price must be reduced (a vertically downward movement); this yields a downward slope for the curve.

Clearly, when the downward-sloping *ZZ* curve is put together with the upward-sloping *PP* curve in Figure 3, there is an equilibrium position. (We're assuming that you've been able to figure out where it is!) At point E, the representative monopolistically competitive firm is in equilibrium because it is charging its profit-maximizing price (and hence is on the *PP* curve), and this is a long-run equilibrium position because economic profit is zero (because the firm is on the *ZZ* curve). In Figure 3, the firm thus settles at $(P/W)_1$, and the per capita consumption level of the product is c_1.

To introduce international trade, suppose that we designate the home country of this representative firm as country I. Let's now introduce another country, country II, which is identical to country I in tastes, technology, and characteristics of the factors of production. (Country II could also be identical in size, although that is not necessary.) Traditional trade theory would conclude that, with these same general supply and demand conditions (and hence relative prices), the two countries would have no incentive to trade with each other. However, Krugman (and Linder) would disagree.

When the two countries are opened to trade, the important point to note is that the *market size is being enlarged* for each representative firm in each country, because there are now more potential buyers of any firm's good. And, when market size is enlarged, economies of scale can come into play and production costs can be reduced for all goods. In Figure 3, if the firm being considered is in country I, the opening of the country to trade with country II means that consumers in *both* countries are now consuming this product (as well as all other products)—country II's consumers now add country I products to their consumption bundle, just as country I's consumers add country II products to their consumption bundle. If the firm's total output is momentarily held constant, there is thus, with the larger consuming population but with the spreading out of consumption to other, newly available products, less *per capita* consumption of this firm's product at each P/W than was previously the case. This is equivalent to a leftward shift of the ZZ curve, represented by the $Z'Z'$ curve in Figure 3. [For example, if country II's population is identical in size to country I's population, then the size of the consuming population has doubled—this would lead to a shift to the left of ZZ by 50 percent (per capita consumption would be one-half of its previous value); if country II's population were 25 percent of that of country I, the ZZ curve would shift to the left by 20 percent, because per capita consumption would now be 80 percent ($=1/1.25$) of its previous value.]

Given the shift of ZZ to $Z'Z'$, there is thus disequilibrium at the old equilibrium point E, and movement takes place to the new equilibrium position E'. As movement from E to E' occurs, P/W falls from $(P/W)_1$ to $(P/W)_2$ and per capita consumption of this firm's good falls from c_1 to c_2. Notice that, although per capita consumption at the new equilibrium has declined in comparison with per capita consumption at the old equilibrium, it has not declined proportionately to the extent by which the size of the consuming population increased. [If it had, per capita consumption would be at the level on the $Z'Z'$ curve that is associated with $(P/W)_1$.] Because per capita consumption has not decreased proportionately with the increase in the size of the consuming population, this means that *total* consumption of the firm's product has increased; with this increased output by the firm, the scale economies have come into play and have reduced unit costs (and hence the price of the firm's output).

As noted, the opening of trade has reduced P/W in this country (and has done so in the other country, too) because economies of scale have been realized. However, if P/W has decreased, obviously its reciprocal W/P has increased. The significance of an increase in W/P is that *real income has risen* because W/P is the real wage of workers. Thus, trade causes an improvement in real income and a corresponding increase in output of all goods. Also, there is a less tangible but nevertheless very real additional benefit from trade—consumers now have foreign products available to them as well as home-produced products. This increase in product variety and consumer choice should also be counted as a gain from trade. Further, the trade between the countries in this model is trade of similar but differentiated products. As in the Linder theory, an exchange of similar goods emerges, that is, intra-industry trade, a result that conforms with the nature of much of international trade in the present-day world. Consequently, this model can explain trade between similar countries. Krugman has noted elsewhere (1983) that factor endowments can determine the broad range of types of goods a country will export and import; within that broad range, however, product differentiation and scale economies play a very important role in generating trade and the gains from trade.

Finally, another potential result of the Krugman model's trade is also important. The increased well-being from trade is available to *all* consumers. Thus, even if a person is a "scarce factor of production" in a Heckscher-Ohlin context and would tend to lose from trade, the gains for that person in the Krugman model both from a higher real wage due to the scale economies and from the increased variety of goods due to product differentiation can more than offset the loss from being a scarce factor. Hence, the "gainer-loser" income distribution aspects of trade do not necessarily occur if trade consists of an exchange of differentiated manufactured goods produced under conditions of economies of scale.

Other Post–Heckscher-Ohlin Theories

We conclude this examination of post–Heckscher-Ohlin theories of trade by summarizing two other approaches—one model known as the "reciprocal dumping" model of trade and the other model known as the "gravity" model of trade. As with previous theories, we are simplifying the approaches for the purposes of this textbook but at the same time trying to get across the essential elements.

The **reciprocal dumping model** was first developed by James Brander (1981) and was then extended by Brander and Paul Krugman (1983). (See also Krugman 1995, pp. 1268–71.) To begin to understand this model, remember from Chapter 8 of this textbook that a monopoly firm may charge a different (lower) price in the export market than in the home market. This price discrimination phenomenon in the context of international trade is called **dumping,** and it usually arises because demand is more elastic in the export market than in the domestic market. (Remember that, with price discrimination, markets are separated and the same good is sold in the different markets at different prices, with the lower price being charged in the market where demand is more elastic.)

In the Brander-Krugman model, there are two countries (a home country and a foreign country) and two firms (a home firm and a foreign firm) producing a homogeneous (standardized) good. An important feature is that there is a transportation cost of moving the good (in either direction) between the home country and the foreign country, so this is a barrier that can keep the markets separated. Suppose first that the transportation cost of moving the good between the countries is very high—each firm then may well produce only for its own home market, and each will have a monopoly position in that market. In such a situation, each firm will follow the usual criterion of producing at the output level where marginal revenue equals marginal cost, and of marking up price over marginal cost in accordance with the markup formula $P = MC [e_D/(e_D + 1)]$ developed in Appendix B. Thus, each of the two firms is maximizing profit and is selling in only one market (the home firm in the home country and the foreign firm in the foreign country).

Suppose, however, that the transportation cost is not so high, and the home firm notes that the price charged by the foreign firm in the foreign market exceeds the home firm's marginal cost of producing a unit of output plus the transportation cost of moving that unit of home output to the foreign market. If this is so, then the home firm will want to sell in the foreign market as well as in the home market, since there will be some additional profit that can be made by doing so. Analogously, if the foreign firm notices that the price in the home market exceeds the foreign firm's marginal cost plus the transportation cost of sending the good from the foreign market to the home market, then it will want to sell in the home country's market, too. Thus, there clearly are possibilities for international trade to emerge in this model.

Once the two firms start selling in each other's country as well as in their own home countries, we enter a market structure of **duopoly** (two sellers in a market), and the price in each country will change from the previous monopoly situation because of the new rivalry. This duopoly structure gives rise to a situation where each firm must take account of the behavior of the other firm when choosing its own price and output. The recognized interdependence between the firms and the manner in which price and output decisions are made in this context are best addressed by **game theory,** a complicated subject about which we will have more to say in Chapter 15. In general, each firm determines an array of various profit-maximizing positions, one for each possible output level of the other firm. The two firms then interact with each other in accordance with these arrays; for the purposes of this present chapter, suffice it to say that an equilibrium price and output level will be determined in each market for each firm. There will be this one outcome which is satisfactory to both firms, and, in this equilibrium position, each firm will be maximizing its profit for the given output level of the other firm.

An additional aspect of the situation can also be usefully mentioned. Each firm is maximizing profit in each market ($MR = MC$ in each market), but note the nature of the marginal cost of selling in the foreign country's (home country's) market for the home (foreign) firm. That cost will include not only production cost but also the transportation cost. If demand structures are similar in the two countries, then, using the home firm as an example, the *net* price received in the foreign market (price in the foreign market less transportation cost) is likely to be lower than the price received in the home market (where there is no transportation cost). It is in this rather particular sense that "dumping" is occurring in the model—the price received in the foreign market is less than the price received in the home market.

Note, however, what the main point of the model is from the standpoint of trade theory. *International trade in a homogeneous product is occurring, with each country both exporting and importing the product.* This result emerges importantly because of the imperfectly competitive market structure, and it could never emerge with perfect competition. We clearly have intra-industry trade here, and the model may help us to understand real-world trade flows consisting of the movement of similar products between countries.

Finally, Brander and Krugman discuss welfare implications of the model. On one hand, welfare tends to increase for each country and for the world because previously monopolistic sellers in each country are now faced with a rival and this pro-competitive effect will put downward pressure on price. On the other hand, a negative welfare aspect exists in that there clearly is waste involved in sending identical products past each other on transportation routes! (It would be better from a transportation cost perspective by itself to have each country supplying exclusively its own market.) Hence, in general, we cannot say whether this two-way trade in a homogeneous product is on balance welfare enhancing or welfare reducing—the result will depend on the particulars of the actual situation being considered.

Another model that has attracted the attention of researchers is known as the **gravity model** of trade. This model has a relatively long history. (For early formulations, see Tinbergen 1962, Pöyhönen 1963, and Linnemann 1966; for more recent discussion, see Deardorff 1984, Leamer and Levinsohn 1995, and Helpman 1999.) It differs from most other theories (including traditional theory) in that it is trying to explain the *volume* of trade and does not focus on the composition of that trade.

The model itself uses an equation framework to predict the volume of trade on a *bilateral* basis between any two countries. (The particular equation form need not concern us—the form has some similarity to the law of gravity in physics, which has resulted in the term *gravity model* being applied.) It is concerned with selecting economic variables that will produce a "good fit," that is, that will explain at least in a statistical sense a substantial portion of the size of trade that occurs. The variables that are nearly always used in the equation as causes of, say, the flow of exports from a country I to a country II are:

1. A national income variable for country II (GNP or GDP), which is expected to have a positive relationship with the volume of exports from I to II because higher income in II would cause II's consumers to buy more of all goods, including goods from country I.

2. A national income variable for country I (GNP or GDP), reflecting that greater income in I means a greater capacity to produce and hence to supply exports from I to II.

3. Some measure of distance between country I and country II (as a proxy for transportation costs), with the expectation being that greater distance (greater transportation costs) would reduce the volume of exports from country I to country II.

Sometimes other variables are introduced, such as population size in the exporting and/or importing country (to get at large market size and thus perhaps to economies of scale) or a variable to reflect an economic integration arrangement (such as a free-trade area) between the two countries.

Empirical tests using the gravity model have often been remarkably successful, meaning that the volume of trade between pairs of countries has been rather well "explained." In addition, by selecting different pairs of countries, other interesting questions can be addressed. For example, Helpman (1999, p. 138) discussed work in the literature that indirectly sought to distinguish between factor endowments and product differentiation as underlying causes of trade. The gravity equation worked best for similar countries that had considerable intra-industry trade with each other, better than it did for countries with different factor endowments and a predominance of traditional trade rather than intraindustry trade. At the minimum, these findings suggest that product differentiation is indeed a phenomenon to be considered above and beyond factor endowments.

Gravity models are thus useful in that they help us to understand influences on the volume of trade, and they can also cast some light on underlying causes of trade. They play a useful role in focusing on the volume of trade and in relating that volume to important economic variables. It is important to do so if we are to make headway in understanding the world economy, and the volume of trade is not considered by many trade theories. Further discussion of the gravity model and its testing and theoretical foundation is provided in Appendix C at the end of this chapter.

Finally, another avenue of research that has been explored concerns **vertical specialization-based trade** (see Hummels, Rapaport, and Yi 1998). In this research it is recognized that, increasingly, various stages in the production process of any particular good are taking place in different countries. Thus, some components of an automobile engine may be made in Germany and then sent to the United Kingdom where the engine is assembled, and the engine itself is then sent to the United States for placement in the automobile. Such *outsourcing* or *offshoring* of components by the U.S. auto firm, rather than making or having the components made domestically, has been growing noticeably in recent years. There is no new "theory" of trade here, but there is a recognition that comparative advantage may pertain to a portion of the production process of a good rather than to the entire good itself (as in traditional theory).

Concluding Comments on Post–Heckscher-Ohlin Trade Theories

From the preceding discussion, it is clear that trade theory is moving in directions neglected by traditional trade theory. The newer approaches enhance our understanding of the causes and consequences of trade beyond the insights provided early on by the Heckscher-Ohlin model. We have looked principally at theories that allow for lags in diffusion of technology, demand considerations, economies of scale, international capital mobility, dynamic comparative advantage, and imperfect competition. There is considerable theoretical analysis in this area, much of which we have not discussed. For example, there is a growing literature on government policy and how it can generate comparative advantage and alter the distribution of the gains from trade between countries. Examples from this literature will be given in Chapter 15. Further, yet another approach (by Paul Krugman) explores the role of location of production in the determination of comparative advantage and consequent trade patterns.

What are the implications of the newer theories for the developing countries? The imitation lag hypothesis and the product cycle theory do not lead to particularly optimistic conclusions about the future export performance of developing countries because they suggest that developing countries may be confined to exporting older products rather than new high-technology goods. On the other hand, these theories suggest that a potential exists for moving away from exporting principally primary products toward exporting more manufactured goods, as Taiwan and South Korea and other developing countries have now done. However, theories such as those of Linder and Krugman imply that trade will increasingly take place between countries of similar income levels. This forecast may not bode so well for developing countries who wish to break into developed-country markets, although the analyses suggest that they may beneficially trade more among themselves in the future. Finally, economies-of-scale models indicate the difficulty of predicting future trade patterns but suggest potentially large gains from trade.

IN THE REAL WORLD:

GEOGRAPHY AND TRADE

In a series of lectures at the Catholic University of Leuven, Belgium, in 1990, later published under the title *Geography and Trade* (1991), Paul Krugman examined various economic issues that arise when firms make interdependent spatial decisions regarding the location of production. He dubbed this exercise "economic geography" because the concept of "location" seemed too narrow and restrictive. Assuming the presence of economies of scale, transportation costs, and imperfect competition, he examined possible reasons for the concentration of manufacturing production, the localization of production across a broad spectrum of goods within the United States, and the role played by nations in interregional and international trade.

In these lectures, Krugman introduced a new perspective (although geographers might say "reintroduced an old perspective") on the basis for trade in manufactured goods which rests on the observation that trade often takes place as a result of more-or-less "arbitrary specialization based on increasing returns, rather than an effort to take advantage of exogenous differences in resources or productivity" (p. 7). This strong accidental or serendipitous component of international specialization sets off cumulative processes that throughout history have tended to be pervasive. Thus whether one looks at Catherine Evans's interest in tufting bedspreads in 1895 and the manner in which it generated a local handicraft industry that evolved into the center of the U.S. carpet industry in Dalton, Georgia, or the classic examples of Eastman Kodak in Rochester, New York, the giant Boeing Corporation in Seattle, or Silicon Valley in California, dynamic comparative advantage in manufactures often

appears to have its roots in a quirk of fate which sets off important cumulative processes. Critical to these developments are, of course, economies of scale and transportation cost considerations. In addition, Krugman (p. 62) also points to Alfred Marshall's belief that the pooling of labor and the readily available supply of specialized inputs also play a crucial role in promulgating specialized local production and regional and international comparative advantage.

The existence of potential economies of scale is a crucial element in this approach in that firms have reason to concentrate their production activities as long as the cost advantages related to larger size are not offset by transportation costs associated with either inputs or final products. Thus, production locates both with regard to the size of the market and the availability of inputs, given the objective of concentrating production. Once established, production generates a dynamic of its own and tends to be self-sustaining. Nations are important from this perspective primarily because they adopt policies that influence economic decision making and the evolution of the critical cumulative processes. While policies are often enacted to inhibit the flow of goods and/or factors, government policies can also stimulate these critical processes, as was the case with the state government's decision to provide financial support for the Research Triangle Park in North Carolina. In the context of international trade policies, Krugman and Livas Elizondo (1996) hypothesized that protectionist policies in developing countries may lead to heavy concentration of production and linkages in a particular geographic region of the protectionist country. ●

CONCEPT CHECK

1. If two countries have identical PPFs and demand conditions, how do external economies of scale generate potential gains from trade for both countries?

2. In the Krugman model, why does the opening of a country to a larger market (world market rather than domestic market alone) lead to lower product prices?

3. What is meant by "reciprocal dumping," and why might it occur?

INTRA-INDUSTRY TRADE

A characteristic of a country's trade that has appeared in many new theories and is increasingly recognized as important in the real world is intra-industry trade (IIT). IIT occurs when a country is both exporting and importing items in the same product classification category. This trade differs from **inter-industry trade,** where a country's exports and imports are in *different* product classification categories. Traditional trade theory dealt only with inter-industry trade, but intra-industry trade clearly constitutes an important segment of international trade. Table 2 indicates magnitudes and trends in the intra-industry trade in manufactured goods of selected countries. (IIT is more important in manufactured goods than in nonmanufactured goods.) It can also be noted that other data (not shown in Table 2) indicate that IIT is typically the highest for more sophisticated manufactured goods such as chemicals, machinery, transport equipment, and electronics, where scale economies and product differentiation can be important (*OECD Economic Outlook* 71, pp. 160–61).

Reasons for Intra-Industry Trade in a Product Category

Unfortunately, comparative advantage based on factor endowments is of little or no help in predicting intra-industry trade. In fact, intra-industry trade will be relatively greater (compared with inter-industry trade) the more similar are the capital and labor endowments of the countries being examined. In view of this deficiency of the Heckscher-Ohlin model, we now look at several possible explanations for the occurrence of intra-industry trade. (For an extensive seminal discussion of reasons for intra-industry trade, see Herbert Grubel and P. J. Lloyd 1975.)

TABLE 2   Manufacturing Intra-Industry Trade as a Percentage of Total Manufacturing Trade

	1992–1995	*1996–2000*
High and increasing intra-industry trade		
Czech Republic	66.3	77.4
Slovak Republic	69.8	76.0
Mexico	74.4	73.4
Hungary	64.3	72.1
Germany	72.0	72.0
United States	65.3	68.5
High and stable intra-industry trade		
France	77.6	77.5
Canada	74.7	76.2
United Kingdom	73.1	73.7
Switzerland	71.8	72.0
Spain	72.1	71.2
Ireland	57.2	54.6
Low and increasing intra-industry trade		
Korea	50.6	57.5
Japan	40.8	47.6
Low and stable intra-industry trade		
New Zealand	38.4	40.6
Turkey	36.2	40.0
Norway	37.5	37.1
Greece	39.5	36.9
Australia	29.8	29.8
Iceland	19.1	20.1

Note: Countries are classified as having a "high" or "low" level of intra-industry trade according to whether intra-industry trade is above or below 50 percent of total manufacturing trade on average over all periods shown and "increasing" or "stable" according to whether intra-industry trade increased by more than 5 percentage points over a specified time period.

Source: OECD calculations, based on OECD International Trade Statistics, adapted from *OECD Economic Outlook* 71.

Product differentiation

This explanation for IIT was outlined earlier. Briefly, many varieties of a product exist because producers attempt to distinguish their products in the minds of consumers to achieve brand loyalty or because consumers themselves want a broad range of characteristics in a product from which to choose. Thus, U.S. firms may produce large automobiles and non-U.S. producers may produce smaller automobiles. The consequence is that some foreign buyers preferring a large car may buy a U.S. product while some U.S. consumers may purchase a smaller, imported car. Because consumer tastes differ in innumerable ways, more so than the varieties of products manufactured by any given country, some intraindustry trade emerges because of product differentiation.

Transport costs

In a physically large country such as the United States, transport costs for a product may play a role in causing intra-industry trade, especially if the product has large bulk relative to its value. Thus, if a given product is manufactured both in the eastern part of Canada and in California, a buyer in Maine may buy the Canadian product rather than the California product because the transport costs are lower. At the same time, a buyer in Mexico may purchase the California product. The United States is both exporting and importing the good. Another mechanism by which transport costs can lead to intra-industry trade is as specified in the reciprocal dumping model discussed earlier in this chapter.

Dynamic economies of scale

This reason is related to the product differentiation reason. If IIT has been established in two versions of a product, each producing firm (one in the home country, one in the foreign country) may experience "learning by doing" or what has been called **dynamic economies of scale.** This means that per-unit cost reductions occur because of experience in producing a particular good. Due to these cost reductions, sales of each version of the product may increase over time. Because one version was an export and the other an import for each country, intra-industry trade is enhanced over time because of this production experience.

Degree of product aggregation

This explanation rests on the observation that IIT can result merely because of the way trade data are recorded and analyzed. If the category is broad (such as beverages and tobacco), there will be greater intra-industry trade than would be the case if a narrower category is examined (such as beverages alone or, even more narrowly, wine of fresh grapes). Suppose a country is exporting beverages and importing tobacco. The broad category of "beverages and tobacco" [a category in the widely used Standard International Trade Classification (SITC) System of the United Nations] would show IIT, but the narrower categories of "beverages" and "tobacco" would not. Some economists think that finding IIT in the real world may be mainly a statistical artifact because of the degree of aggregation used, even though actual calculations use less broad categories than "beverages" and "tobacco." Nevertheless, most trade analysts judge that IIT exists as an economic characteristic of trade and not primarily as a result of using aggregative classification categories.

Differing income distributions in countries

This explanation for intra-industry trade was offered by Herbert Grubel (1970). Even if two countries have similar per capita incomes, differing distributions of total income in the two countries can lead to intra-industry trade. Consider the hypothetical income distributions plotted in Figure 4. Country I has a heavy concentration of households with lower incomes, while country II has a more "normal" or less skewed distribution. Producers in country I will be concerned primarily with satisfying the bulk of country I's population, so they will produce a variety of the product that caters to consumers with incomes, for example, between y_1 and y_2. Producers in country II will cater to the bulk of country II's households, say, those households between y_3 and y_4. Therefore, country II's firms produce a

FIGURE 4   Intra-industry Trade from Differing Distributions of Income

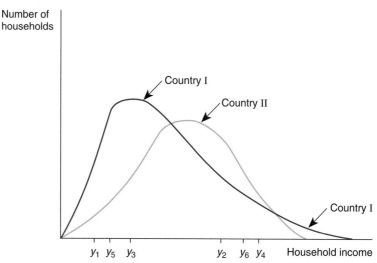

Country I's producers supply varieties of the product catering to households with incomes between y_1 and y_2, while country II's firms produce varieties to satisfy households with income levels between y_3 and y_4. A household in country I with income y_6 and a household in country II with income y_5 will therefore each consume an imported variety of the good. Intra-industry trade in this general product thus exists.

variety of the good with characteristics that satisfy that group. What about a household in country I with a high income such as y_6? And what about a household in country II with a low income such as y_5? These consumers will purchase the good from the producers in the *other* country because their own home firms are not producing a variety of the good that satisfies these consumers. Hence, both countries have intra-industry trade in the product. This explanation can be applied in the context of the Linder model to help in predicting the pattern of intra-industry trade.

Differing factor endowments and product variety

In work that attempts to marry intra-industry trade with the Heckscher-Ohlin approach, Falvey (1981) and Falvey and Kierzkowski (1987) developed a model in which different varieties of a good are exported by countries with different relative factor endowments. Assuming that the higher-quality varieties of a good require more capital-intensive techniques, the model produces the result that higher-quality varieties are exported by capital-abundant countries and lower-quality varieties are exported by labor-abundant countries. Thus Heckscher-Ohlin can, in this framework, yield intra-industry trade. In related work, and building on the assumption that the higher-quality varieties require greater capital intensity in production, Jones, Beladi, and Marjit (1999) hypothesized that a labor-abundant country (such as India) may export capital-intensive varieties of a good to high-income countries (such as the United Kingdom or the United States) and keep the lower-quality, labor-intensive varieties for the home market. A further complication for trade theory!

The Level of a Country's Intra-Industry Trade

Work on intra-industry trade has gone beyond examination of reasons for IIT in any particular product. Attempts have been made to determine if the levels of intra-industry trade differ systematically by *country,* such as is suggested by Table 2. A study by Bela Balassa (1986) is an example of this research.

Using a standard measure of intra-industry trade (see Appendix D to this chapter), Balassa examined a sample of 38 countries (18 developed and 20 developing countries) to test various hypotheses on factors associated with IIT. He hypothesized that a higher level of per capita income for a country is associated with a greater amount of intra-industry trade. Balassa's reasoning followed Linder's suggestion that, at higher levels of development, trade consists increasingly of differentiated products. Second, a positive association was postulated between IIT and *total* income of a country, because a larger national income permits greater realization of economies of scale. In his regression equations, Balassa also used independent variables representing items such as distance from trading partners, a common border with principal trading partners, and degree of "openness," or degree of absence of trade restrictions, of countries.

In general, the various hypotheses were essentially confirmed. Greater per capita income, greater national income, greater openness, and the existence of a common border with principal trading partners were positively correlated with the extent of intra-industry trade. Distance from trading partners (a proxy for transportation costs) was negatively associated with IIT. Thus, commonsense intuitions on IIT seem to be statistically supported. Another finding was that developing countries had their intra-industry trade better "explained" by the analysis than developed countries.

A final comment is necessary. Intra-industry trade is an economic phenomenon that reflects the complexity of production and trade patterns in the modern world. This complexity is not fully captured by previous international trade models. Intra-industry trade can bring with it greater gains than might be surmised from traditional literature; in particular, the product differentiation that is so important to the rise of intra-industry trade provides consumers with a wider variety of goods. The additional choice available to consumers also should be counted as a gain from international trade.

SUMMARY

This chapter has surveyed theories that introduce new considerations beyond factor endowments and factor intensities into the examination of the underlying causes of international trade. The theories relax assumptions contained in the traditional approaches, and they can be thought of as complementary to Heckscher-Ohlin and not necessarily as "competing" with H-O. The imitation lag hypothesis examines the implications of allowing for delays in the diffusion of technology across country borders. The product cycle theory relaxes several traditional assumptions and emerges with a picture of dynamic comparative advantage. The Linder theory focuses on overlapping demands and on trade between countries with similar per capita income levels. It also has led to substantial investigation of intra-industry trade in the literature. The presence of economies of scale can create a basis for trade, even when countries have identical production possibilities and tastes. The focus on trade among similar countries has been carried further by Krugman, who incorporated scale economies but also introduced imperfect competition and product differentiation. Imperfect competition in conjunction with transportation costs can result in reciprocal dumping being a cause of intra-industry trade. Because many newer theories incorporate intra-industry trade, the chapter also examined other possible causes of such trade. In a different vein and ignoring intra-industry considerations, the gravity model has been used by economists to analyze the determinants of the volume of trade between countries.

KEY TERMS

demand lag	imitation lag hypothesis	new-product stage
dumping	inter-industry trade	overlapping demand
duopoly	intra-industry trade	product cycle theory (PCT)
dynamic comparative advantage	Krugman model	product differentiation
dynamic economies of scale	Linder theory	reciprocal dumping model
game theory	maturing-product stage	standardized-product stage
gravity model	monopolistic competition	technology cycle
imitation lag	net lag	vertical specialization-based trade

QUESTIONS AND PROBLEMS

1. What factors are important in determining the length of the imitation lag and the length of the demand lag? Explain.

2. What products might be examples of goods that are currently going through or have gone through the various stages outlined in the product cycle theory?

3. What would the Linder theory suggest about the prospects of developing countries in exporting goods to developed countries? Do you think that this is a realistic suggestion? Why or why not?

4. While the recognition of economies of scale may make trade theory more "realistic," what does this recognition do to the ability of trade theory to predict the commodity trade patterns of countries? Explain.

5. Ignoring the mathematics, explain the operation of the Krugman model in economic terms, and indicate the principal lessons of it.

6. Why is an increase in the number of varieties of a good regarded as a gain from trade? Can you think of economic disadvantages associated with greater product variety? Explain.

7. Is the existence of product differentiation a necessary condition for the existence of intra-industry trade? Why or why not?

8. Is the distinction between "intra-industry trade" and "inter-industry trade" a useful distinction? Why or why not?

9. In recent years, U.S. firms have become very concerned about the increasing production of "pirated" and "counterfeit" goods abroad, especially in Asia. Successful U.S. export products are copied by foreign producers without payment of royalties and/or adherence to patent or copyright protection. How might this phenomenon affect the product cycle and new product research and development in the United States?

10. How is it possible that reciprocal dumping can be beneficial for aggregate welfare if identical commodities are moving between countries and transportation costs are being incurred?

11. In the late 1970s, a large part of athletic shoe production shifted from plants in the United States to plants in South Korea. In late 1993, it was reported that South Korean shoe firms had suffered a large reduction in jobs and sales because, due to rising wages, shoe production had shifted to Indonesia and China. (See Steve Glain, "Korea Is Overthrown as Sneaker Champ," *The Wall Street Journal,* October 7, 1993, p. A14.) How might these moves in product location fit the product cycle theory? Could Heckscher-Ohlin also be of value in explaining these developments? Why or why not?

12. (From Appendix D material) The exports and imports of country A in year 1 are listed below. These are the only goods traded by country A.

Good	Value of Exports	Value of Imports
T	$100	$ 20
X	300	80
Y	100	300
Total	$500	$400

Calculate country A's index of intra-industry trade for year 1.

Appendix A   ECONOMIES OF SCALE

We present in this appendix a representative economies-of-scale model that draws upon early work of Murray C. Kemp (1964). Such models are discussed in more detail in Bhagwati and Srinivasan (1983, chap. 26) and Bhagwati, Panagariya, and Srinivasan (1998, chap. 11).

Assume a two-commodity world where both industries experience economies of scale. Further, the economies of scale are such that the PPF is drawn as *convex* to the origin, as in Figure 5. (It is to be noted that the presence of economies of scale in both industries does not necessarily generate a convex PPF; the shape depends on the relative degree of the economies of scale in the two industries.) Suppose that the economy is initially located at point E, where the PPF is tangent to the price line reflecting autarky prices (P_X/P_Y). An immediate difference between this autarky equilibrium and the traditional autarky equilibrium with a concave PPF is that the autarky equilibrium is an *unstable* equilibrium. Thus, slight departures from E will not produce a return to E. Consider a point to the right and downward from E, such as point G, which has the same goods prices (P_X/P_Y) as E. Because the (negative of the) slope of the PPF is (MC_X/MC_Y), it is evident at point G that $(P_X/P_Y) > (MC_X/MC_Y)$ or, alternatively, that $(P_X/MC_X) > (P_Y/MC_Y)$.[4] There is thus an incentive to

---

[4]We follow Kemp in assuming that the extent of external economies of scale is identical in the two industries. This assumption permits the ratio of private marginal costs to equal the ratio of social marginal costs, and thus the term *marginal cost* can be used without further qualification.

FIGURE 5   A Convex-to-the-Origin Production-Possibilities Frontier (PPF)

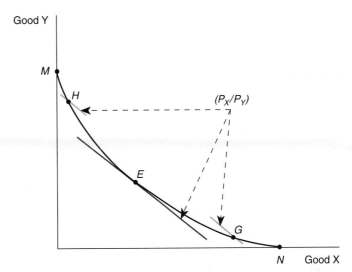

The existence of economies of scale in the production of both good X and good Y can yield a PPF that is convex to the origin. In this situation, point E is an unstable equilibrium, since the production location at point $G(H)$ will generate incentives to shift production to point $N(M)$ rather than to point E.

produce more of good X and less of good Y, and the economy will move from point G to point N (with complete specialization in good X), not to point E. If the economy were located instead at point H with given prices P_X/P_Y, production would move from point H to point M (with complete specialization in good Y) instead of to point E.

Assuming that this country, call it country I, has somehow reached the autarky equilibrium point E, what are the implications of introducing international trade? As with many increasing-returns-to-scale models, there is some uncertainty as well as some new results. Consider this country again in Figure 6, where it is in autarky equilibrium at point E with the internal price ratio $(P_X/P_Y)_I$. With the opening of the country to trade, suppose that the terms of trade TOT_W [steeper than $(P_X/P_Y)_I$] represent world prices. The country can specialize in the production of good X, and, as we have just seen, the consequent movement downward and to the right from point E will, because E was an "unstable" equilibrium, cause production to go to the complete specialization point N. Obviously, gains from trade occur because country I can export good X along a trading line associated with TOT_W and reach a higher indifference curve than was reached during autarky. (Indifference curves have not been drawn in Figure 6, but you should be able to picture them in your mind!) And, because country I has gone all the way to an endpoint of the PPF, the indifference curve attained will be "farther out" than would be the case without complete specialization, other things equal.

But now consider another country, country II, which has an *identical* PPF to that of country I. In addition, suppose that demand conditions in country II *are also identical* to demand conditions in country I. Certainly, in the Classical model of Chapters 3 and 4, there were no incentives for trade and no gains from trade in the situation of identical production possibilities; indeed, even in the neo-classical, Heckscher-Ohlin model of Chapters 6 through 8 there were no incentives for trade and no gains from trade when production possibilities *and* demand conditions were identical. (In both models, the autarky relative prices would be identical.) But, in this economies-of-scale framework, both countries *could* gain from trade with each other. Note that, in Figure 6, terms of trade TOT_W could also be associated with production at endpoint M of this PPF, where the complete specialization is in good Y and not in good X. Hence, even if both countries have the same PPF and identical demands, country I can specialize in good X by producing at point N and country II can specialize in good Y by

FIGURE 6   The Convex PPF and Gains from Trade

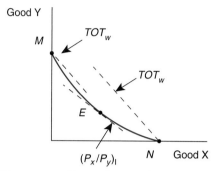

With a convex-to-the origin PPF, a country could move from autarky equilibrium point E [with relative prices $(P_X/P_Y)_1$] to complete specialization point N. It could then export good X and import good Y along a trading line associated with TOT_W, and it would experience gains from trade. Another country with identical production possibilities and identical tastes (tastes are not shown in the diagram) could move from point E to complete specialization point M. This second country could then export good Y and import good X along a trading line associated with TOT_W and also gain from trade. Hence, unlike the situation in traditional models, two countries can engage in mutually beneficial trade even though their supply and demand conditions are alike.

producing at point M, and there can be mutually beneficial trade since both countries can attain higher indifference curves than was the case under autarky.

Appendix B   MONOPOLISTIC COMPETITION AND PRICE ELASTICITY OF DEMAND IN THE KRUGMAN MODEL

Two features of the Krugman model in the chapter are briefly explained in this appendix: (1) the short run and long run in monopolistic competition and (2) the relationship between price elasticity, demand facing a firm, and the firm's product price.

With respect to (1), analytically, the demand curve facing the monopolistically competitive firm is not the horizontal demand curve of perfect competition. Rather, the demand curve is downward sloping, and marginal revenue (MR) is less than price. The firm produces where MR equals marginal cost (MC) rather than where price equals MC. In Figure 7, the profit-maximizing output level is Q_1 and the price charged is P_1. We have drawn the marginal cost curve MC as horizontal, reflecting Krugman's assumption that marginal cost is constant. (MC in the Krugman model is equal to the b coefficient in equation [1] times the wage rate.) At this equilibrium output position, with price P_1 and average cost AC_1, the total profit for the firm is the area of the shaded rectangle $(AC_1)(P_1)FB$.

Figure 7 refers to a short-run situation because there is positive profit for this firm and, with easy entry into the industry, new firms will begin to produce this type of product. The demand curve facing existing firms will shift down and will become more elastic because of the presence of more substitutes. Price and profit will be reduced for existing firms, and in the long run there will be zero economic profit, as in perfect competition. In a long-run equilibrium diagram (not shown) for the monopolistically competitive firm, the demand curve is tangent to the declining portion of the AC curve immediately above the MR/MC intersection—meaning no economic profit.

Regarding (2), the relationship between demand elasticity and price, the price elasticity of demand for a good (e_D) is the percentage change in quantity demanded divided by the percentage change in price. Thus, if Δ stands for "change in,"

$$e_D = \frac{\Delta Q/Q}{\Delta P/P} = \frac{P\Delta Q}{Q\Delta P}$$

FIGURE 7   **Short-Run Profit Maximization for the Firm in Monopolistic Competition**

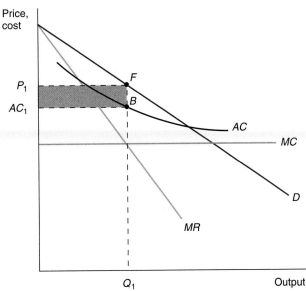

The monopolistically competitive firm maximizes profit at the output level Q_1, where $MR = MC$. The price charged is P_1, and the firm's economic profit in the short run is indicated by the shaded rectangle. In the long run, D would shift downward, as would MR, until D was tangent to AC immediately above the MR/MC intersection and the firm would make a normal (zero economic) profit.

Total revenue (TR) is equal to $P \times Q$. If price changes by ΔP, this will change quantity demanded by ΔQ, so that total revenue after a price change (and subsequent quantity change) is $(P + \Delta P) \times (Q + \Delta Q)$. Therefore, the change in total revenue that occurs because of a price change (and subsequent quantity change) is

$$\Delta TR = (P + \Delta P) \times (Q + \Delta Q) - P \times Q$$
$$= PQ + P\Delta Q + Q\Delta P + \Delta P\Delta Q - PQ$$
$$= P\Delta Q + Q\Delta P + \Delta P\Delta Q$$

For a small price and quantity change, the term $\Delta P\Delta Q$ is very small and can be neglected. Thus, the change in total revenue is $P\Delta Q + Q\Delta P$.

Marginal revenue (MR) is the change in total revenue divided by the change in quantity; that is,

$$MR = \frac{P\Delta Q + Q\Delta P}{\Delta Q}$$
$$= P + Q\Delta P/\Delta Q$$
$$MR/P = 1 + Q\Delta P/P\Delta Q$$

However, $Q\Delta P/P\Delta Q$ in the last expression is simply the reciprocal of $P\Delta Q/Q\Delta P$; that is, it is the reciprocal of the elasticity of demand. Thus,

$$MR/P = 1 + 1/e_D = (e_D + 1)/e_D$$

Therefore,

$$MR = P[(e_D + 1)/e_D]$$

or

$$P = MR\frac{e_D}{e_D + 1}$$

[2]

For example, if the elasticity of demand is -2 and MR is \$20, then price equals $(\$20)[(-2)/(-2 + 1)] = (\$20)[(-2)/(-1)] = (\$20)(2) = \$40$. If the firm is in profit-maximizing equilibrium, that is, marginal revenue = marginal cost ($=\$20$ in this example), then the profit-maximizing price equals $MC[(e_D)/(e_D + 1)]$. This equation plays an important role in the Krugman model. Krugman assumes that e_D becomes *less elastic* as individuals buy more units of the good. (Remember from microeconomic theory that this is consistent with a straight-line demand curve—as more units are consumed, demand becomes less elastic.) Thus, as consumption rises, the expression $[(e_D)/(e_D + 1)]$ becomes larger. For example, if $e_D = -1.5$, the value is $[(-1.5)/(-1.5 + 1)]$ or $[(-1.5)/(-0.5)] = 3$. The price in the above example would be \$60.

Appendix C   DIFFERENTIATING AMONG ALTERNATIVE TRADE THEORIES USING THE GRAVITY EQUATION

The gravity equation has been used successfully by a number of researchers to explain bilateral trade flows, but its theoretical foundations are much less clearly understood. Feenstra, Markusen, and Rose (2001) were especially intrigued by the wide empirical success of the gravity equation for both OECD and developing countries. The equation arises from a model in which countries are fully specialized in differentiated goods. While this may fit well with manufactured goods, it is not thought to fit particularly well with homogeneous primary goods. Given that developing countries are usually presumed to sell more homogeneous goods, the success of the model in these countries deserves a closer examination.

In an attempt to reconcile the specialized nature of the theory with the general success of the empirical applications, Feenstra, Markusen, and Rose argue that a wider range of theories is consistent with the gravity-type equation. The alternative theories can be distinguished by subtle differences in parameter values that emerge in the estimates. They begin with product differentiation (and therefore complete specialization). In the empirical work, the distinction is seen in the relative size of the export elasticities. In the case of free entry, the export elasticity with respect to the exporter's income is larger than that with respect to the importer's income. The reverse is true for restricted entry. Empirical work for differentiated goods produced results consistent with the theoretical predictions of the monopolistic competition model with free entry.

The second focus of the Feenstra, Markusen, and Rose empirical work was on homogeneous goods. As the analysis moves from differentiated goods to homogeneous goods, the elasticity of exports with respect to the exporter's income falls. Their finding is consistent with theoretical predictions of the reciprocal dumping model with restricted entry or even with a model with national product differentiation. Feenstra, Markusen, and Rose argued that a gravity-type equation can arise from a wide range of theoretical models, and this appears to be the case. The models differ in their implications of the "home-market" effect (the importance of the exporter's income on exports), depending on whether goods are homogeneous or differentiated and whether or not there are barriers to entry. Feenstra, Markusen, and Rose began with a puzzle related to the wide-ranging empirical success of gravity models in contrast to the seemingly restrictive theoretical basis. Their work suggests that the theoretical foundations of the gravity equation are actually quite general.

Appendix D   MEASUREMENT OF INTRA-INDUSTRY TRADE

Given that intra-industry trade takes place within a commodity category, how can it be measured for a country as a whole? A country measure is useful because it allows the tracing of the development of IIT for a country through time or permits the comparison of different countries at a particular point in time. The following measure has been developed. If we designate commodity categories by i, represent exports and imports in each category by X_i and M_i, respectively, total exports and imports by X and M, respectively, and call our index of intra-industry trade I_I, the formula for calculating the degree of country intra-industry trade is

$$I_I = 1 - \frac{\Sigma|(X_i/X) - (M_i/M)|}{\Sigma[(X_i/X) + (M_i/M)]}$$ [3]

In this formula, X_i/X (or M_i/M) is the percentage of the country's total exports (or imports) in category i and $|(X_i/X) - (M_i/M)|$ indicates the absolute value of the difference between the share of exports and imports in the category. The $[(X_i/X) + (M_i/M)]$ indicates the sum of the export and import shares in the category. The Σ sign means that we are summing over all the commodity categories, and the denominator must have a value of 2 because 100 percent of exports are being added to 100 percent of imports.

This measure of IIT is best illustrated by example. Suppose that country A has only three categories of traded goods and that exports and imports in each category are as follows:

Good	Value of Exports	Value of Imports
W	$500	$ 200
X	200	400
Y	100	400
Total	$800	$1,000

This country's index of intra-industry trade is

$$I_I = 1 - \frac{|500/800 - 200/1,000| + |200/800 - 400/1,000| + |100/800 - 400/1,000|}{(500/800 + 200/1,000) + (200/800 + 400/1,000) + (100/800 + 400/1,000)}$$

$$I_I = 1 - \frac{|0.625 - 0.200| + |0.250 - 0.400| + |0.125 - 0.400|}{(0.625 + 0.200) + (0.250 + 0.400) + (0.125 + 0.400)}$$

$$= 0.575$$

This country has a moderate amount of intra-industry trade. The index would equal 1.0 ("total" intra-industry trade) if exports were equal to imports in each category. The index would be zero if, in each category, there were exports or imports but not both.

ECONOMIC GROWTH AND INTERNATIONAL TRADE

LEARNING OBJECTIVES

■ To understand the different ways growth can affect trade.

■ To grasp how the source of growth affects the nature of production and trade.

■ To see how growth and trade affect welfare in the small country.

■ To understand how growth in a large country can have different welfare effects than growth in a small country.

INTRODUCTION

China—A Regional
Growth Pole

There is a common misconception that China's growth is taking place at the expense of its many trading partners. This is prompting threats of trade policy retaliation on the part of many of the trading partners, not the least of which is the United States. A useful overview of the Chinese role in regional growth and development was provided by Phillip Day.[1] He correctly points out that even though exports of other Asian countries to the United States have fallen as those of China have increased, the total exports of those other countries are growing in a complementary fashion through increased trade with each other. The reason is that China is already the largest importer of South Korean and Taiwanese goods as well as a substantial importer from Japan (if exports into Hong Kong are taken into account). Interestingly, as China grows, it finds itself on the midpoint of a supply chain in that it imports high-tech components from East Asia, assembles them into final commodities, and exports them to final end-markets throughout the world. Thus, instead of hurting other countries in the region, China's rapid growth and emergence as an export power-house in the world economy has had a positive impact on other East Asian countries. Unfortunately, the politicians, trade groups, and companies that are critical of China's export success are also ignoring the fact that it is often foreign investment and foreign companies that are underpinning the Chinese export locomotive. For example, China's top exporter of color televisions—owned by South Korea's LG Group and Taiwan's Lite-On Technology Corporation—employs 300,000 people at 18 factories in China. The immense size of foreign investment (more than $50 billion in foreign direct investment) flowing annually into China is importantly driving its production machine and high rate of growth.

China's notable rate of growth in recent years and its growing impact on world trade and globalization reflect the fact that the production possibilities for a country do not remain fixed and are often fostered by the country's economic policies. Growth in output potential is represented by outward shifts in the PPF, which enable the country to reach a higher level of real income (a consumption-possibilities frontier further to the right) and presumably a higher level of well-being. Growth comes about by means of change in technology or through the acquisition of additional resources such as labor, physical capital, or human capital. Inasmuch as international trade affects and is affected by economic growth, it is important to examine several of the more important economic implications of growth. This chapter begins by pointing out how growth influences trade through changes in both production and consumption. This is followed by a discussion of the sources of growth and the manner in which they influence changes in the economy. The chapter concludes by looking briefly at the effect of growth on the country's economic well-being when the country is participating in international trade.

CLASSIFYING THE TRADE EFFECTS OF ECONOMIC GROWTH

As real income increases, it affects both producers and consumers. Producers need to decide how to alter production, given the increase in resources or the change in technology. Consumers, on the other hand, are faced with how to spend the additional real income. Both of these decisions have implications for the country's participation in international trade and thus for determining whether countries become more or less open to trade as economic growth occurs. We begin this analysis by categorizing the alternative production and consumption responses that accompany economic growth in terms of their respective implications for international trade.

---

[1]Phillip Day, "China's Trade Lifts Neighbors," *The Wall Street Journal,* August 8, 2003, p. A9.

FIGURE 1   Production Effects of Growth

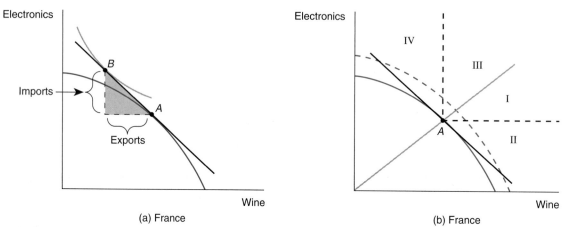

(a) France   (b) France

Assume that France is a (small) country and is in equilibrium as demonstrated in panel (a), producing at point A, consuming at point B, exporting wine and importing electronics. With growth the PPF will shift outward, permitting the country to choose different production combinations of the two goods in question [panel (b)]. The various new production possibilities are located within the regions fixed by the mini-axes drawn through the original production point A and the straight line drawn through the origin and point A. If the new production point lies on the straight line passing through point A, growth is product neutral. If the new point lies in region I, it is protrade biased; in region II it is ultra-protrade biased; in region III it is antitrade biased; and in region IV it is ultra-antitrade biased.

Trade Effects of Production Growth

Let us assume that a small country is characterized by increasing opportunity costs and is currently in equilibrium at a given set of international prices (see Figure 1), remembering that a small country cannot influence world prices.[2] In panel (a), France is producing at point A and consuming at point B. To do this, France exports wine and imports electronics. As growth occurs, the production-possibilities frontier shifts outward, and French producers have the opportunity to select a point on the new PPF that will maximize their profits. In general terms, they have the possibility of producing (1) more of both commodities in the same proportion as at point A, (2) more of both commodities but *relatively* more of one than the other, or (3) absolutely more of one commodity and absolutely less of the other. These possibilities can be demonstrated on our figure and will form the basis for categorizing the various production trade effects that can accompany growth.

To establish the classification of the trade effects of growth, return to point A. This will become the origin for new mini-axes, shown as dashed lines in panel (b). Points lying to the left of the dashed vertical line reflect cases where the new production of wine is less than at point A. Points to the right of this vertical line indicate cases where the new production of wine is greater than at point A. Similarly, points lying above the dashed horizontal mini-axis reflect greater production of electronics, whereas points below this line indicate less production of electronics. Points lying above and to the right of point A thus represent larger production of both goods. Production points lying on the straight line passing through the origin and point A reflect outputs of electronics and wine that are proportionally the same as at A; that is, the ratio of electronics to wine production is a constant. Points beyond point A that fall on this line demonstrate a **neutral production effect** because production of the export good and the import-competing good have grown at the same rate.

---

[2]An alternative assumption to that of a small country is that prices are held constant to focus exclusively on real income effects (regardless of country size).

The remaining production possibilities with growth conveniently fall into four regions, which are isolated by the neutral ray from the origin and the mini-axes at point *A*. Region I represents possible new production points that reflect increased production of both commodities, but where the change in the production of wine is relatively greater than the change in the production of electronics. Because wine is the export good, this type of growth has a **protrade production effect,** reflecting the relatively greater availability of the export good. Region II contains production-possibilities points that demonstrate increased production of wine but a decrease in production of electronics. New production points lying in this region as a result of growth fall in the **ultra-protrade production effect** category, suggesting an even greater potential effect on the desire to trade. New production points lying in region III reflect higher production levels of both goods but relatively greater increases in electronics than in wine. Because electronics are the import-competing good, growth reflecting this production change has an **antitrade production effect.** Finally, new production points lying in region IV, with increased production of electronics and less of wine, are placed in the **ultra-antitrade production effect** category. The actual point of production after growth will be the point where the new enlarged PPF is tangent to the international price line. This point will necessarily fall in one of the aforementioned regions.[3]

Trade Effects of Consumption Growth

A similar technique can be used to describe the various consumption effects of growth. In this case, we analyze the nature of consumer response to growth relative to the original equilibrium at point *B* [Figure 1, panel (a)]. Figure 2 focuses on this initial equilibrium point, which serves as the origin for new mini-axes.

FIGURE 2   Consumption Effects of Growth

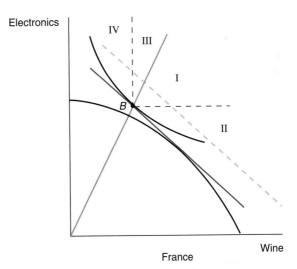

With growth there is an increase in real income indicated by the rightward shift in the consumption-possibilities line (the international terms-of-trade line). This allows consumers to choose combinations of electronics and wine previously not possible. The consumption effects of growth on trade can be isolated by the mini-axes whose origin is at pregrowth consumption point *B*. If the new consumption point is on the straight line from the origin through *B*, consumption of both goods will increase proportionally and the consumption trade effect will be neutral. Should the new consumption point fall in region I, it is an antitrade consumption effect; if it falls in region II, it is an ultra-antitrade consumption effect; if it falls in region III, it is a protrade consumption effect; and if it falls in region IV, it is an ultra-protrade consumption effect.

---

[3]We disregard the two borderline cases where production settles on either the vertical or horizontal dashed line.

FIGURE 3   The Effect of Growth on the Size of Trade

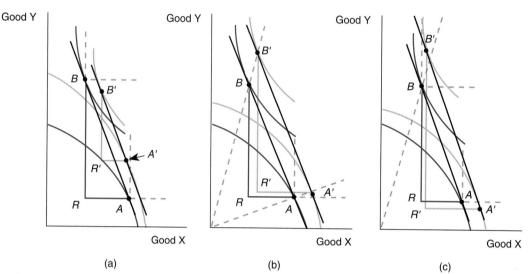

(a)   (b)   (c)

The effects of growth on trade reflect both the consumption and production effects. In panel (a) an ultra-antitrade production effect coupled with an ultra-antitrade consumption effect leads to a reduction in trade, that is, a smaller trading triangle after growth compared with before growth. In panel (b), a protrade production effect is combined with a neutral consumption effect, leading to a slight relative expansion of trade when compared with income growth. In panel (c) an ultra-protrade production effect is combined with a protrade consumption effect, producing an even larger relative expansion of trade compared with income growth.

Points lying to the left of the dashed vertical axis reflect less consumption of wine, while points to the right indicate greater consumption. Points lying below the dashed horizontal axis reflect less electronics consumption, while points above that line indicate more. Points lying beyond B on the straight line passing through point B and the origin of the original axes indicate cases where goods are consumed in the same proportion as at point B. Points so situated reflect a **neutral consumption effect,** since consumers have not changed their relative consumption pattern with growth.

The remaining effects will be isolated in a manner similar to that used in the production analysis. New consumption points lying in region I as a result of growth in real income reflect a relatively larger increase in the consumption of wine than in that of electronics. Because wine is the export good, the change in consumption reduces the country's relative willingness to export. This effect is called an **antitrade consumption effect.** An even more extreme case of this type of behavior is found in region II, where the consumption of wine increases and that of electronics falls. This response is called an **ultra-antitrade consumption effect.** If growth causes consumption to move into region III, where consumption of both goods increases but consumption of electronics (the import good) increases relatively more than wine, a **protrade consumption effect** occurs. Finally, if consumption of electronics increases and consumption of wine actually falls with growth (region IV), an **ultra-protrade consumption effect** exists.[4]

The ultimate impact of economic growth on trade depends on the effects on both production and consumption. The expansionary impact of growth on trade is larger whenever both the production and the consumption effects are in the "pro" or "ultra-pro" regions. The total effect of growth on trade is demonstrated with three different cases in Figure 3. In

---

[4]Again, consumption could settle on the dashed axes themselves, but we ignore these cases.

panel (a), both production and consumption effects are in the ultra-antitrade category. With growth, production moves from point A to point A' and consumption from point B to point B'. Note that commodity prices are fixed, because this is a small country. The result of growth is a reduction in trade, reflected in the new trade triangle, A'R'B', which is smaller than the original triangle, ARB.

In panel (b), the production effect is a protrade effect and the consumption effect is neutral. These effects can be observed in the position of point A' and point B' with respect to point A and point B. The result is a relative expansion of trade (trade triangle A'R'B'). In panel (c) an ultra-protrade production effect is coupled with a protrade consumption effect. Again, trade expands relatively (from ARB to A'R'B'). As we move from panel (a) to panel (c) in Figure 3, the new trading triangle gets successively larger. While the volume of trade generally increases with growth, this is not always true. For example, growth leading to ultra-antitrade consumption and production effects actually causes trade to decline.

A useful way to summarize the net result of production and consumption effects on the growing country's trade is through the concept of the **income elasticity of demand for imports** (*YEM*). This measure is the percentage change in imports divided by the percentage change in national income. If *YEM* = 1.0, then trade is growing at the same rate as national income, and the net effect is neutral. If 0 < *YEM* < 1, trade is growing in absolute terms but at a slower rate than income; the net effect is antitrade. If *YEM* < 0, trade is actually falling as income grows (ultra-antitrade effect). Finally, if *YEM* > 1.0 (imports or trade growing more rapidly than national income), there is a protrade or ultra-protrade net effect. (The algebraic distinction between protrade and ultra-protrade is more complex and need not concern us.) As a general rule, if both the production effect and the consumption effect are of the same type (e.g., both "protrade"), then the net or overall effect will be of the same type as the two individual effects. If one effect is protrade (antitrade) and the other is neutral, the net effect will be protrade (antitrade). There are obviously various other combinations, and some of them require more information on the precise size of each of the two effects before the net result can be determined, such as with a protrade production effect that is coupled with an antitrade consumption effect.

SOURCES OF GROWTH AND THE PRODUCTION-POSSIBILITIES FRONTIER

In the introduction to this chapter, we mentioned that growth can result from changes in technology or the accumulation of factors such as capital and labor. Because they affect the production-possibilities frontier in different ways, we will examine the two kinds of changes individually.

The Effects of Technological Change

Technological change alters the manner in which inputs are used to generate output, and it results in a larger amount of output being generated from a fixed amount of inputs. Let us assume that we are dealing with two inputs, capital and labor. The new technology may be **factor neutral;** that is, it results in the same relative amounts of capital and labor being used as before the technology changed (at constant factor prices). However, smaller amounts of inputs are used per unit of output. On the other hand, the new technology might be **labor saving** in nature. In this instance, fewer factor inputs are required per unit of output, but the relative amount of capital used rises at constant factor prices (i.e., the *K/L* ratio increases). Finally, the technological change could lead to a decrease in the *K/L* ratio at constant factor prices. In this instance, we say that the technological change is **capital saving.** In effect, a labor-(capital-)saving technological change has an effect equivalent to increasing the relative amount of labor (capital) available to the economy. It is easy to see why a technological change that reduces the relative labor requirement per unit of output (labor-saving technological change) is not necessarily thought desirable in a relatively labor-abundant developing country. We limit our analysis of technological change to the factor-neutral type.

On the production-possibilities frontier, a factor-neutral change in technology that affects one commodity means that the country is able to produce more of that commodity for all possible levels of output of the second commodity. Thus, this commodity-specific change in technology causes the PPF to move outward except at the intercept for the nontechnology-changing commodity (see Figure 5). In panel (a) of Figure 5, if the change in technology occurs in autos, this is shown by the PPF that is the farthest out

IN THE REAL WORLD:

LABOR AND CAPITAL REQUIREMENTS PER UNIT OF OUTPUT

Figure 4 indicates the changes in the relative use of capital and labor that took place in six countries from the mid-1960s to the mid-1980s. The changes are measured per unit of output. The three points on each graph show the actual level of capital and labor used, and the isoquants demonstrate the nature of substitution between capital and labor in the country for each year. Although the nature of the adjustment has been different in the six countries, the use of capital relative to labor has clearly increased in all of them. Japan and Germany experienced the greatest increase in the *K/L* ratio, and the U.S. ratio appears to have increased the least.

FIGURE 4   Input of Capital and Labor Required per Unit of Output—Capital-Labor Isoquants

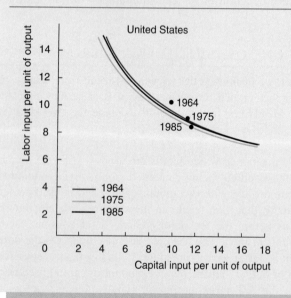
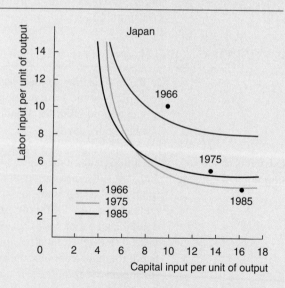

(continued)

IN THE REAL WORLD: *(continued)*

LABOR AND CAPITAL REQUIREMENTS PER UNIT OF OUTPUT

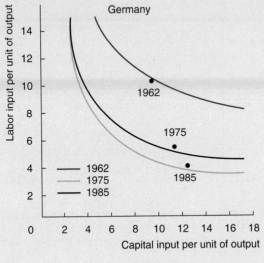

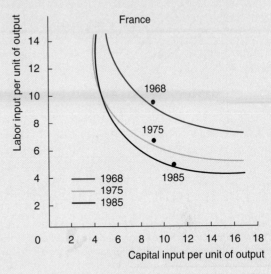

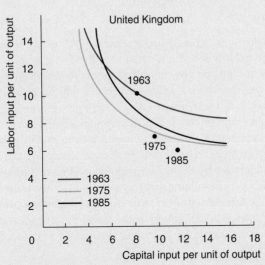

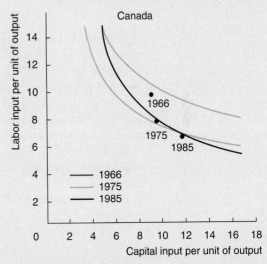

Source: Organization for Economic Cooperation and Development, *Economic Studies,* no. 10 (Spring 1988), p. 44. Used with permission.

along the autos axis. On the other hand, the PPF that is the farthest out along the food axis indicates what happens if the technological change occurs only in food production. Finally, if the change in technology affects both commodities in the same relative manner, the PPF shifts outward in an equiproportional fashion, as demonstrated in panel (b) of Figure 5. This is **commodity-neutral technological change.**

FIGURE 5   The Effects of Technological Change on the PPF

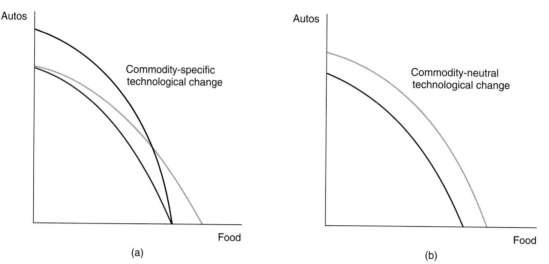

If technological change takes place only in automobile production, the PPF pivots upward, intersecting the auto axis at a higher point, as indicated by the highest PPF along the autos axis in panel (a). If the change in technology affects only food production, the PPF intersects the food axis at a higher point, as indicated by the PPF farthest out on that axis. If the change in technology affects both products equally, the PPF shifts outward in an equidistant manner, as shown in panel (b).

Traditionally, technological change has been treated exogenously (i.e., as an independent event from outside) in the growth literature, often at a fixed rate of growth.[5] However, in the late 1980s a series of long-run growth models began to appear in which the rate of technological change was determined endogenously, or within the system, instead of being imposed from outside. In these newer models, the rate of technological change is determined by such factors as the growth in physical capital and the increase in human capital. New investment fosters and/or embodies new innovations and inventions which can, in turn, stimulate additional technological change as experience with the new capital leads to more change in a "learning-by-doing" environment. Similar "spillover" effects are also linked to the acquisition of human capital as well as to expenditures on research and development. These models, generally referred to as **endogenous growth models,** reflect the basic idea that change in technology is the result of things that people do, not something produced outside a particular economic system.[6] In so doing, they

----

[5]A typical way of incorporating technical change is demonstrated in the following traditional Cobb-Douglas production function from micro theory:

$$Y = Ae^{gt}K_t^{\alpha}L_t^{\beta}$$

where Y refers to GDP, A is an initial technology level, e is the base of natural logarithms, g represents the exogenous rate of growth of technology, K_t is the level of capital stock at time t, and L_t refers to the labor force at time t. The exponents α and β are the respective elasticities of output with respect to capital and labor.

[6]In this framework, following Paul Romer (1989), the production function takes on the general form of $Y = f(K_t, L_t, A_t)$, where A_t refers to the economy's level of technology at time t and now appears inside the production function as an endogenous input. A_t is influenced, for example, by research and development, growth in capital, acquisition of skills, and various spillover effects associated with increased capital and labor.

have provided an explanation of how rapid sustainable growth can take place, avoiding the traditional neoclassical conclusion that economic growth would ultimately converge to the natural rate of population growth due to the declining productivity of capital. Work by Grossman and Helpman (1991) not only added to the burgeoning literature on endogenous growth but also examined the implications of endogenous technological change on international issues including dynamic comparative advantage, trade and growth, product cycles, and the international transmission of policies.[7] We do not pursue these developments in this book, however. For our purposes, whether technological change is exogenous or endogenous, it still results in an outward shift of the production-possibilities frontier.

The Effects of Factor Growth

The second source of economic growth is increased availability of the factors of production. We consider the impact of factor growth in terms of two homogeneous inputs, capital and labor. In the real world, there are other primary inputs such as natural resources, land, and human capital, and factors do not tend to be homogeneous. Labor and capital remain, however, two of the most important inputs, and the insights gained from examining K and L can be extended to the more general case. Estimates for the growth in capital and labor for selected countries for 1966–2004 are presented in Table 1.

An increase in factor abundance can take place through increases in capital stock, increases in the labor force, or both. The capital stock of a country grows as domestic and foreign investment occurs in the country. The labor force expands through increases in population (including immigration), increases in the labor force participation rate, or both. If both labor and capital grow at the same rate, the PPF will shift out equiproportionally, as in the case of commodity-neutral technological change. This **factor-neutral growth effect** is demonstrated in panel (a) in Figure 6 with the new PPF that is farther out than the old.

The matter is more complex if one of the factors grows and the other does not. Suppose that the capital stock increases but the size of the labor force remains constant. How will the production-possibilities frontier change? In answering this question, remember the production assumptions from neoclassical theory and the Heckscher-Ohlin analysis. Assume that cutlery is capital intensive and cheese is labor intensive. If the capital stock grows, it has the greatest relative impact on the capital-intensive product. Think of this as an expansion of the Edgeworth box (see Chapter 5) along the capital side, with the labor side remaining the same size. If all the country's resources are devoted to the production of cutlery, the expansion of the capital stock permits the country to reach a higher output level (higher isoquant) than that reached prior to the growth of capital. The growth in capital also permits a larger amount of cheese to be produced for any level of cutlery because capital can be substituted to some degree for labor. However, because cheese is the labor-intensive good, the potential impact on production is less than it is for the capital-intensive good. Consequently, the PPF shifts outward asymmetrically in the direction of the capital-intensive good. This shift is demonstrated in panel (b) of Figure 6. An analogous argument can be made for growth in labor when the capital stock is held constant. Then the production-possibilities frontier shifts outward in an asymmetrical manner, with the labor-intensive product showing

---

[7]For an excellent overview of the literature on endogenous technological change, see the symposium on "New Growth Theory" (with papers by Paul M. Romer, Gene M. Grossman and Elhanan Helpman, Robert M. Solow, and Howard Pack) in the *Journal of Economic Perspectives* 8, no. 1 (Winter 1994), pp. 3–72.

TABLE 1 Factor Endowments in Selected Countries, 1966, 1985, and 2004

Country	1966		1985	2004	Annual Average Growth Rate, 1966–2004
United States:					
Capital	$785,933		$1,020,600	$4,053,237	4.32%
Labor	76,595		107,150	153,700	1.83
Land		—742,400—			
Japan:					
Capital	$165,976		$ 438,631	$2,774,907	7.42
Labor	49,419		58,070	67,000	0.80
Land		—31,396—			
Canada:					
Capital	$ 76,537		$ 150,587	$ 341,990	3.94
Labor	7,232		11,311	17,400	2.31
Land		—386,632—			
Australia:					
Capital	$ 35,053		$ 47,761	$ 241,424	5.08
Labor	4,727		6,646	10,200	2.82
Land		—521,973—			
France:					
Capital	$146,052		$ 233,089	$ 717,488	4.19
Labor	21,233		21,193	26,900	0.62
Land		—46,560—			
Mexico:					
Capital	$ 21,639		$ 72,753	$ 242,546	6.36
Labor	12,844		22,066	42,400	3.20
Land		—176,100—			

Note: The estimates of real capital stock are in millions of 1966 U.S. dollars, labor is in thousands of economically active individuals, and land is in thousands of hectares.

Sources: The 1966 figures are from Harry P. Bowen, Edward E. Leamer, and Leo Sveikauskas, "Multicountry, Multifactor Tests of the Factor Abundance Theory," *American Economic Review* 77, no. 5 (December 1987), pp. 806–07. Capital figures for 1985 through 1994 were estimated by summing annual real gross domestic investment flows (from annual issues of the World Bank's *World Tables*) starting in 1975 and using an annual depreciation rate of 10 percent. For 1995–2004, foreign exchange rates and real gross investment figures were obtained from the IMF's *International Financial Statistics Yearbook 2000* and *International Financial Statistics,* December 2006. Price indexes for gross fixed investment, taken from the *Economic Report of the President,* February 1999 and February 2006, were used. Labor endowments for 1985 are from issues of the International Labor Organization's *Yearbook of Labor Statistics,* and land endowments are from annual issues of the Food and Agriculture Organization's *Production Yearbook.* The 2004 labor figures are from the World Bank's *World Development Indicators 2006.*

a greater relative response. The effect of growth in the labor force is demonstrated in Figure 6(c).

CONCEPT CHECK

1. What is the difference between a protrade production effect and a protrade consumption effect? What is the net effect on trade?
2. What is the difference between an ultraprotrade production or consumption effect and a protrade production or consumption effect?
3. How does the change in the PPF resulting from growth in capital differ from that resulting from growth in labor? Why do they each shift the PPF outward on both axes?

FIGURE 6   The Effects of Factor Growth on the PPF

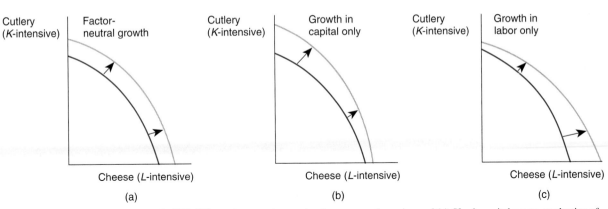

If both factors grow at the same rate, the PPF shifts out in an equiproportional manner as shown in panel (a). If only capital grows, production of both goods can potentially increase, but the increase is relatively larger in the capital-intensive good. The impact of growth in capital only is shown in panel (b). If only labor grows, the impact on production is relatively greater in the labor-intensive good, as shown in panel (c).

FACTOR GROWTH, TRADE, AND WELFARE IN THE SMALL-COUNTRY CASE

A nonneutral growth in factors will shift the production-possibilities frontier in an asymmetrical manner and alter the relative factor abundance in the country. The economic response to this change depends on relative commodity prices. Let us continue to assume that the country is a small country and cannot influence world prices, which remain constant. What happens to production in this case when one factor, labor, for example, grows and capital stock remains fixed? We already know that the PPF will shift outward relatively more along the axis of the labor-intensive commodity. When this occurs, production takes place at the point of tangency between the new PPF and the same set of relative prices (see Figure 7). This new tangency occurs at a level of production that represents an increase in output of the labor-intensive good and a decrease in output of the capital-intensive good. If the labor-intensive good is the export good, this is an ultra-protrade production effect; if the labor-intensive good is the import good, growth in labor produces an ultra-antitrade production effect. The conclusion that growth in one factor leads to an absolute expansion in the product that uses that factor intensively and an absolute contraction in output of the product that uses the other factor intensively is referred to as the **Rybczynski theorem** after the British economist T. M. Rybczynski. The economics that lie behind the Rybczynski theorem is straightforward. Because, by the small-country assumption, relative product prices cannot change, then relative factor prices cannot change because technology is constant. If relative factor prices are unchanged in the new equilibrium, then the K/L ratios in the two industries at the new equilibrium are the same as before the growth. The only way this can happen, given the increased amount of labor, is if the capital-intensive sector releases some of its capital to be used with the new labor in the labor-intensive sector. When this transfer of capital occurs, output of the capital-intensive good falls and output of the labor-intensive good expands.

What effect does factor growth have on trade in the small-country case? The production impact of factor growth on trade depends on whether the growing factor (labor in our example) is the abundant or the scarce factor. If it is the abundant factor, there is an ultra-protrade production effect, assuming the country is exporting the commodity that

FIGURE 7   Factor Growth and Production: The Small-Country Case

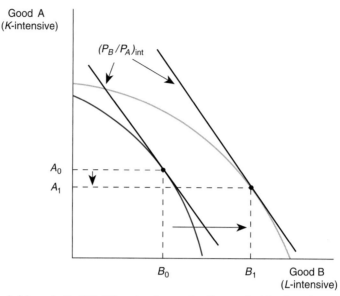

With an increase in labor only, the PPF shifts outward proportionally more for labor-intensive good B than it does for capital-intensive good A. Because this does not affect relative world prices in the small-country case, the increased availability of labor leads to an expansion of output of the labor-intensive good. Because some capital is required to produce the additional output of B and this can be acquired only by attracting it from the capital-intensive good, the production of A must decline as the production of B increases. Both production points represent tangencies between $(P_B/P_A)_{int}$ and the old PPF and new PPF, respectively.

is intensive in the abundant factor, in the manner of Heckscher-Ohlin. If it is the scarce factor, there is an ultra-antitrade production effect. Other things being equal, therefore, the expansionary impact on trade is greater with growth in the abundant factor than in the scarce factor. The total effect on trade depends on both production and consumption effects, however. As a general rule, if the consumption effect is protrade, then the country will participate more heavily in trade if the abundant factor grows. If the scarce factor grows, the total effect can be less participation in trade. A full assessment of the impacts of factor growth on the country's participation in trade requires estimation of both supply and demand effects.

Consider the effect of growth on welfare. If capital grows or there is technological change, there is an increase in well-being, because either of those changes will increase real per capita income and permit the country to reach a higher community indifference curve. It is assumed that the social benefits resulting from the increased output are not offset by negative income distribution effects. However, if there is growth in the labor force, the welfare implications of growth are less straightforward. The community indifference curve map that existed prior to growth is no longer relevant, because the new members of the labor force may have different tastes than the original members. It is therefore not possible to use the two different indifference curve maps to make welfare comparisons. In practice, economists use levels of per capita income to approximate changes in country welfare. While this measure has deficiencies, it appears to correlate well with many other variables indicative of welfare. It does not, however, take explicit account of changes in income distribution.

CONCEPT BOX 1

LABOR FORCE GROWTH AND PER CAPITA INCOME

Under the assumption of constant returns to scale, a 20 percent growth in the labor force leads to a 20 percent growth rate in the output of a particular commodity only if all other inputs also grow at 20 percent. If all inputs grow by a fixed percentage, the PPF *MN* shifts out to PPF *M'N'* in an equidistant manner by a similar percentage, as shown in Figure 8. However, if only labor grows, the PPF shifts out relatively more for the labor-intensive good than for the capital-intensive good, as indicated by the dashed PPF *M''N''*. But, because only labor is growing, the outward shift from *MN* to *M''N''* must be less for all combinations of the two final goods than was the case when all inputs and output increased by the same percentage. It follows that whatever the combination of the country's two products, the increase in income represented by *M''N''* is always less than that represented by *M'N'*, other things being equal. Thus, a 20 percent increase in the labor force leads to an increase in income that is less than 20 percent, and per capita income therefore declines.

FIGURE 8   Changes in the PPF under Different Factor Growth Assumptions

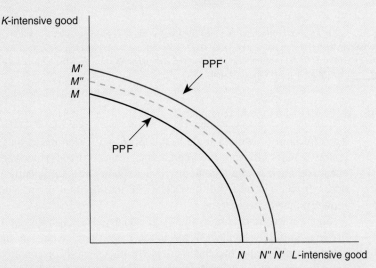

If all factors grow by the same percentage, the PPF shifts outward in an equidistant manner as indicated by *M'N'*. If only labor grows, the PPF changes in the manner indicated by the dashed PPF, *M''N''*. Because *M''N''* necessarily lies inside *M'N'* for a given level of growth in the labor force, the percentage increase in income associated with only labor force growth is necessarily less than the percentage increase in the labor force. Thus, per capita income falls if only the labor force grows.

If we adopt per capita income as the measure of welfare in the case of labor force growth, what can be concluded about the impact of such growth on welfare? We have assumed that our production is characterized by using two inputs and that there are constant returns to scale. The definition of constant returns to scale states that if all inputs increase by a given percentage, output will increase by the same percentage. If, however, only one input expands, output will expand by a smaller percentage than the increase in the single factor. (See Concept Box 1 for additional discussion of this point.) Thus, if we use per capita income as our measure of well-being, we conclude that an increase in population (labor) will lead to a fall in per capita income and hence in country well-being, other things being equal.

FIGURE 9   Large-Country Growth and Terms-of-Trade Effects

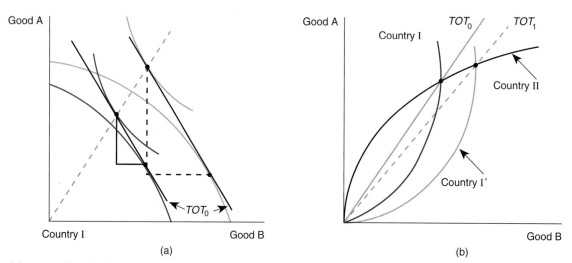

Growth in country I [panel (a)] leads to an ultra-protrade production effect and a neutral consumption effect, which enlarges country I's desired amount of trade (the dashed trading triangle) at initial world prices TOT_0. This causes country I's offer curve to pivot outward [panel (b)], lowering international relative prices to TOT_1. This terms-of-trade effect reduces the gains from growth compared with what would have happened if world prices had not been altered by growth (see Figure 11).

GROWTH, TRADE, AND WELFARE: THE LARGE-COUNTRY CASE

The effects of growth on trade to this point have been based on the assumption that the country cannot influence the international terms of trade. However, a country could influence world prices of a commodity if the country is a sufficiently large consumer or producer. In that instance, we must also take into account the possible effects of economic growth on the terms of trade.

Suppose we are dealing with a large country that can influence international prices and that growth of the abundant factor, in this case capital, causes an ultra-protrade production effect. Assume further that this is coupled with a neutral consumption effect. The total effect on trade is that this country demands more imports and supplies more exports at the current set of international prices [see panel (a) of Figure 9]. As a result of growth, this country alters its "offer" at that particular set of prices on the world market. The increased supply of the export good (good B) and the increased demand for the import good (good A) reduce the international terms of trade [see panel (b) of Figure 9]. (For a discussion of how the different types of growth affect the offer curve of a growing country, see Concept Box 2.) The increase in the relative price of imports effectively reduces the possible gains from growth and trade, because the country now receives fewer imports per unit of exports (see Figure 11). Graphically, the international terms-of-trade line TOT_1 is flatter now than before growth (TOT_0), and it is tangent to a lower indifference curve (IC_2) than would be the case if prices had not been affected (IC_1). Thus, some of the gains of growth are effectively offset by the deterioration in the terms of trade. For growth to be beneficial to the large trading country, these negative terms-of-trade effects must not completely offset the positive effects of growth.

Growth can result in declining well-being in two ways in the large-country case. First, if labor is the abundant and growing resource, the loss in welfare linked to the resulting decline in per capita income is further augmented by the deterioration in the international terms of trade (increase in the relative price of imports). The result is essentially the same

CONCEPT BOX 2

ECONOMIC GROWTH AND THE OFFER CURVE

When a country experiences economic growth, its offer curve will shift. However, the extent and even the direction of the shift depend on the type of growth that takes place. (See Meier 1968, p. 18.) In Figure 10, the pregrowth offer curve of country I is OC_I. If the net effect of country I's production and consumption effects is ultra-protrade growth, its offer curve shifts rightward to OC_{UP}, with a consequent increase in the volume of trade and a deterioration of the terms of trade with trading partner country II. If the net effect is pro-trade growth, the offer curve of country I shifts to OC_P, with a smaller increase in the volume of trade and a smaller deterioration in the terms of trade than with OC_{UP}. But, perhaps

surprisingly, even with neutral growth, country I's offer curve still shifts to the right (to OC_N). This result occurs because, even though trade in relation to national income for country I has remained constant (since the income elasticity of demand for imports, YEM, equals 1.0), the absolute willingness to trade increases. That the absolute amount of trade increases is also true even with antitrade-biased growth (offer curve OC_A), despite the fact that trade is falling relative to national income ($0 < YEM < 1$). Finally, a net effect of ultra-antitrade-biased growth shifts the offer curve of country I leftward to OC_{UA}. Only in this case, other things equal, will the volume of trade decrease and the terms of trade improve.

FIGURE 10   Offer Curve Shifts with Different Types of Growth

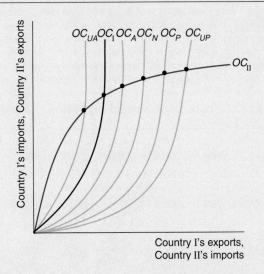

Starting with pregrowth offer curve OC_I for country I, the four growth types of ultra-protrade, protrade, neutral, and antitrade all make country I more willing to trade. Its offer curve shifts rightward in these cases to OC_{UP}, OC_P, OC_N, and OC_A, respectively; the volume of trade with country II increases and country I's terms of trade deteriorate. Only with ultra-antitrade-biased growth will country I's offer curve shift to the left (to OC_{UA}) and lead to less trade and an improvement in country I's terms of trade.

as in the small-country case except it is intensified by the negative terms-of-trade effect. Second, even if capital is the growing abundant factor (or there is technological change in the export commodity) and the negative terms-of-trade effects are sufficiently strong, the country could be worse off after growth (see Figure 12). In this case, the deterioration in the terms of trade is so great that the new, flatter international terms-of-trade line (TOT_1) is tangent to a lower community indifference curve (IC_2 at point C_2) than it was prior to

FIGURE 11   Large-Country Growth, Terms-of-Trade Effects, and Welfare

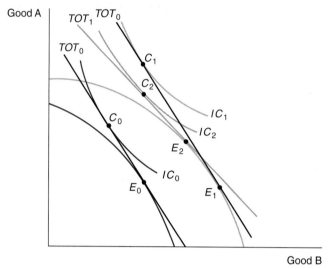

The decline in the terms of trade for country I from TOT_0 to TOT_1 after growth causes country I to produce less of export good B and more of import good A (the movement from E_1 to E_2) compared with what it would have done had relative prices not changed. At the same time, the relatively higher price of good A leads consumers to shift consumption from C_1 to C_2. The combined effect of these responses to the growth-induced change in the terms of trade is a reduction in the degree of specialization and trade, leading to a fall in well-being (represented by the shift from IC_1 to IC_2) compared with what it would have been had the terms of trade not changed. However, in this case country I is still better off with price changes and growth compared with the pregrowth situation (IC_0).

FIGURE 12   The Case of Immiserizing Growth

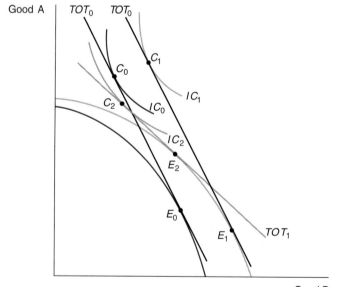

It is possible that the change in the terms of trade associated with growth of the large country can be large enough to leave the country less well-off compared with conditions before growth. Postgrowth TOT_1 is so much smaller than pregrowth TOT_0 that, after producers and consumers respond to the new set of relative prices (E_2 and C_2), country I finds itself less well-off than before it grew. Consumers are now attaining a lower indifference curve compared with the pregrowth situation ($IC_2 < IC_0$). This large-country growth effect is referred to as *immiserizing growth*.

FIGURE 13   Growth in the Scarce Factor in the Large-Country Case

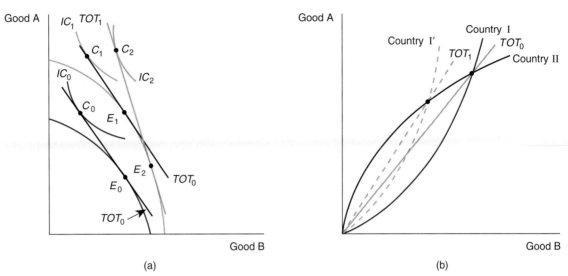

(a)   (b)

Following the Rybczynski theorem, growth in the scarce factor leads to an expansion of output of the import good (good A) and a contraction of production of the export good (good B). If this ultra-antitrade production effect is not offset by a very strong consumption effect toward more trade, the desired level of trade at the initial level of prices, TOT_0, falls. Should this happen, country I's offer curve shifts inward, demonstrating the reduced willingness to trade after growth. This leads to an improvement in the terms of trade for country I ($TOT_1 > TOT_0$) and to production and consumption adjustments. Postgrowth production shifts from E_1 to E_2, consumption from C_1 to C_2, and the level of well-being from IC_1 to IC_2. The change in the terms of trade thus leads to greater specialization and trade and additional gains from growth compared with what would have taken place at the original terms of trade.

growth (IC_0 at point C_0). When the negative terms-of-trade effects outweigh the positive growth effects in this manner, the situation is referred to as **immiserizing growth,** first pointed out by Jagdish N. Bhagwati (1958).

We need to discuss briefly the effects of growth in the scarce factor for a large country. According to the Rybczynski theorem, growth in the scarce factor leads to an increase in output of the import-competing good and a decrease in output of the export good. Ignoring any offsetting consumption effects, for the large country this leads to a reduction in the "offer" of exports for imports by the expanding country since growth is ultra-antitrade biased [see panel (b) of Figure 13]. The growth phenomenon leads to an improvement in the terms of trade faced by this country, as the reduced amount of exports places upward pressure on the price of the export good and the reduced import demand produces downward pressure on the price of the import good. The positive effects of growth are enhanced by the terms-of-trade effects, causing the country to reach an even higher indifference curve. This effect is shown in panel (a) of Figure 13, as consumer welfare rises from IC_0 before growth to IC_1 with growth alone to IC_2 after the terms-of-trade effects are taken into account. Finally, if labor is the growing scarce factor, the positive terms-of-trade effects can offset, at least in part, some of the loss in well-being due to declining per capita income.

CONCEPT CHECK

1. How does growth affect production according to the Rybczynski theorem? Is country size ("small" or "large" in trade) important for this result?
2. How can growth lead to a deterioration in the terms of trade for the large country? Can growth ever improve a country's terms of trade? If so, when?
3. Explain how the change in the terms of trade accompanying growth can leave a country worse off after growth compared with its state of well-being prior to growth.

GROWTH AND THE TERMS OF TRADE: A DEVELOPING-COUNTRY PERSPECTIVE

The preceding analysis of growth, trade, and welfare provides a useful background for examining the interaction between growth, trade, and economic development. The importance of technological change and the accumulation of capital in improving country welfare is certainly clear. In countries where population and thus labor is growing at a relatively high rate, some stimulus to production in addition to labor must occur if per capita incomes are to improve steadily.

It is also important to consider the possible effect of growth on the international terms of trade. Although most developing countries are not large in an overall economic sense, many are sufficiently important suppliers of individual primary commodities to be able to influence world prices. Several important observations need to be made. First, economic growth based on expansion of production of these goods may well lead to adverse terms-of-trade movements. Although immiserizing growth does not appear to be common in the real world, adverse terms-of-trade movements clearly reduce the benefits of growth and trade to the developing countries. This observation provides strong support for considering product diversification in the development strategy to reduce the likelihood of growth contributing to negative terms-of-trade movements and the reliance on only one main product for export earnings. A major world supplier of an export good such as coffee, cocoa, or groundnuts that relies heavily on the particular commodity for its export proceeds could find itself in difficult economic and financial straits if a bumper crop drives down world prices.

Second, keep in mind that growth may lead to changes in relative demand for final products. We allowed this possibility in the discussion of the trade effects that accompany growth. In general, various classes of commodities tend to behave in a predictable way when income grows, and the different behavior patterns can be described by using the income elasticity of demand (income elasticity of demand in general, not just the income elasticity of demand for imports). For example, primary goods such as minerals and food products tend to have income elasticities less than 1.0, while manufactures tend to be characterized by an income elasticity greater than 1.0. To the extent that developing countries export labor- and land-intensive primary goods and import manufactured goods, growth in traditional export industries tends to generate protrade or ultra-protrade consumption effects that may well generate balance-of-trade deficits in fixed exchange rate economies or a depreciation of the home currency if the exchange rate is flexible.

Finally, from a broader perspective, countries that rely on exports of primary goods for export earnings may find that the international prices of these goods do not rise as rapidly as the prices of the manufactured goods they import due in part to the differences in their income elasticities. This deterioration in the terms of trade certainly lowers the gains from growth in the short run and reduces the future growth rate by diminishing the ability to import needed capital goods. Economists such as Raul Prebisch (1959), Hans Singer (1950), and Gunnar Myrdal (1956) have argued that the terms of trade of the developing countries have declined over a long period of time, much to their disadvantage. These arguments are based not only on the different demand characteristics of the two categories of products but also on the price effects of technological change. Technological advances in developing countries are assumed to lead to decreases in the prices of developing-country products, whereas in the industrialized countries, technological advances lead to increased payments to the factors of production (instead of reduced prices for manufactured goods). While it is not clear that a long-term decline in the international terms of trade of developing countries has taken place, it is fairly clear that there have been periods of marked short-run deterioration and improvement, often in response to unanticipated supply effects. Since primary goods tend to be less elastic than manufactures with respect to both price and income, relative price instability is potentially a more serious problem for the developing countries than for industrialized countries. For this reason price stabilization proposals such as commodity agreements with buffer stocks and export controls have been relatively common for developing countries (see Chapter 18).

IN THE REAL WORLD:

TERMS OF TRADE OF BRAZIL, JORDAN, KENYA, AND THAILAND, 1980–2005

The terms-of-trade behavior of four developing countries—Brazil, Jordan, Kenya, and Thailand—during recent decades is presented in Figure 14. The graph indicates that the greatest deterioration in the terms of trade over this time period occurred for Thailand. There was rather steady downward movement from the initial 1980 value of 130 (1995 = 100) to a 2005 value of 75. Thailand's gross domestic product (GDP) growth was 7.6 percent per year from 1980–1990, 4.2 percent per year from 1990–2000, 5.4 percent from 2000–2004, and 4.5 percent in 2005. As is suggested in this chapter, a rapidly growing country (such as Thailand to a great extent from 1980–1990 and a lesser extent from 1990–2005) may well experience a deterioration in its terms of trade.

For Jordan, there was some terms-of-trade improvement from 1980–1995 but then some deterioration. Jordan's GDP grew at 2.5 percent from 1980–1990, 5.0 percent from 1990–2000, 5.5 percent from 2000–2004, and 7.5 percent in 2005. In general, it appears that there may have been a tendency for Jordan's terms of trade to improve somewhat during years of slower growth and to fall during the years of somewhat more rapid growth.

For Brazil, the terms of trade experienced a cyclical rise from 1980–1988 and then a decline in cyclical fashion until 1995. There was then a cycle with no real trend through 2005. Brazil's average GDP growth rate per year was 2.7 percent

from 1980–1990 and 2.9 percent for 1990–2000, 2.0 percent from 2000–2004, and 2.5 percent in 2005. No clear terms of trade/growth relationship appears evident for Brazil.

Finally, Kenya experienced terms-of-trade deterioration for 1980–1990 and some slight cyclical rise after that time. (The relevant price data for Kenya are not available after 2000.) Kenya's GDP growth rate averaged 4.2 percent for 1980–1990 and 2.2 percent for 1990–2000. Again, the period of faster growth tended to have less favorable terms-of-trade behavior and the period of slower growth to have more favorable terms-of-trade behavior.

In overview, in these decades of increased globalization, there is some general tendency in this sample of countries (except for the case of Brazil) for more rapid (less rapid) growth to be associated with some improvement (some deterioration) in a country's terms of trade. However, a much more detailed and systematic investigation is needed in order to derive firm conclusions.

Sources: International Monetary Fund (IMF), *International Financial Statistics Yearbook 2002* (Washington, DC: IMF, 2002), pp. 138–41; IMF, *International Financial Statistics Yearbook 2003* (Washington, DC: IMF, 2003), pp. 87–88; IMF, *International Financial Statistics,* February 2007, pp. 86–87; World Bank, *World Development Indicators 2002* (Washington, DC: World Bank, 2002), pp. 204–07; World Bank, *World Development Indicators 2006* (Washington, DC: World Bank, 2006), pp. 192–96. ●

FIGURE 14 Terms of Trade of Brazil, Jordan, Kenya, and Thailand, 1980–2005

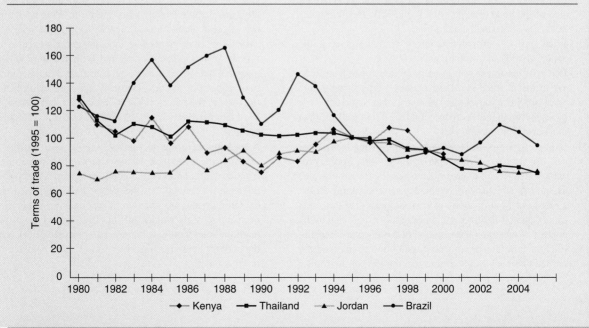

SUMMARY

This chapter focused on how growth in a country's real income influences its international trade. Growth in output has an effect on a country's trade through both consumption and production effects, which do not necessarily work in the same direction. The chapter focused on technological change and factor growth as the underlying bases for growth, and it explained the differences between the two in terms of their impact on the production-possibilities frontier. The effect of growth of a single factor is an expansion of production of the commodity that uses it relatively intensively and a contraction in production of the second good. The welfare effects of factor growth and technological change were positive in all small-country cases with the exception of population growth. In that case, population growth led to a fall in per capita income. The large-country case was introduced to point out the implications of growth that yields changes in the international terms of trade. Output growth in the export good generates negative terms-of-trade effects that offset some of the gains from growth. In the extreme case, a country's welfare can decline if the effects of negative terms-of-trade changes more than offset the gains from growth. Growth in production of the import-competing good can produce terms-of-trade effects that enhance the normal growth effects. Finally, this theoretical framework was used to discuss some implications of growth for the trade and development prospects of developing countries.

KEY TERMS

antitrade consumption effect
antitrade production effect
capital-saving technological change
commodity-neutral technological change
endogenous growth models
factor-neutral growth effect

factor-neutral technological change
immiserizing growth
income elasticity of demand for imports
labor-saving technological change
neutral consumption effect
neutral production effect

protrade consumption effect
protrade production effect
Rybczynski theorem
ultra-antitrade consumption effect
ultra-antitrade production effect
ultra-protrade consumption effect
ultra-protrade production effect

QUESTIONS AND PROBLEMS

1. In a small country, why does growth in only one factor lead to either an ultra-protrade or an ultra-antitrade production effect?

2. Can growth in the abundant factor ever lead to an expansion of the trade triangle if the Rybczynski theorem holds in the case of a small country?

3. What type of consumption effect will take place if the export good is an inferior good?

4. Is it possible for growth in the scarce factor to lead to an expansion of trade in a large country? Why or why not?

5. Why might a developing country that experiences a bumper crop in its export good find itself less well-off than in a normal production year?

6. Explain why growth based only on a growing labor force can on average leave people less well-off. Would your answer be different if there were increasing returns to scale?

7. There was sluggishness in the Japanese economy in the 1990s, and Japan's terms of trade improved at the same time. Can you interpret and analyze this experience in the context of what you have studied in this chapter? Explain.

8. Explain how the production-possibilities frontier of the unified Germany might differ from the PPF of the former Federal Republic of Germany (West Germany), keeping in mind that West Germany, in the two-factor context, was generally considered relatively capital abundant and the German Democratic Republic (East Germany) was generally considered relatively labor abundant. What would theory suggest about the differences in relative output of capital-intensive goods and labor-intensive goods of the former West Germany compared with the unified Germany? What would theory suggest, if anything, about the trade pattern of the new Germany compared with that of the former West Germany if it is assumed that the former West Germany was capital abundant relative to its trading partners?

9. New manufacturing technologies are often viewed as labor saving in nature. Using a production-possibilities frontier with manufactured goods on one axis and (labor-intensive) services on the other axis, illustrate and explain how the introduction of labor-saving innovations in manufacturing would shift the PPF. What type of production effect would occur at constant world prices (with the country being assumed to be an exporter of manufactured goods)?

10. In a two-good world (goods X and Y), consider the following information for (small) country I, which is engaged in trade:

	1995	*2000*	*2005*
Production of good X	100 units	120 units	140 units
Production of good Y	60 units	66 units	86 units
Consumption of good X	80 units	92 units	110 units
Consumption of good Y	70 units	80 units	101 units

(a) What is the volume of trade and the trade pattern for country I in 1995? In 2000? In 2005?

(b) What type of production effect occurs between 1995 and 2000? Between 2000 and 2005? Explain.

(c) What type of consumption effect occurs between 1995 and 2000? Between 2000 and 2005? Explain.

(d) What is the "net effect" on trade of this country's growth between 1995 and 2000? Between 2000 and 2005? Explain.

11. If a small country cannot influence its terms of trade, why is it that small developing countries may have experienced a decline in their terms of trade over time?

CHAPTER

12

INTERNATIONAL FACTOR MOVEMENTS

LEARNING OBJECTIVES

- ■ To learn about the different types of foreign investment and the welfare effects of capital movements.

- ■ To understand the determinants of foreign direct investment and the associated costs and benefits.

- ■ To grasp the motivation for labor migration and its effects on participating countries.

- ■ To appreciate the size and importance of international remittances.

INTRODUCTION

In this chapter, we step away from international trade in goods and services to examine the international movements of factors of production—capital and labor. The theoretical literature has long assumed that factors of production are mobile within countries, but it has also traditionally assumed that factors of production do not move between countries. This second assumption is patently false in today's world, as we are constantly made aware of the movement of investment and labor from one country to another. We need only to note, for example, that the alleged threat of domination of the Canadian economy by American firms operating within Canada was an issue in Canadian parliamentary elections, or that controversies continue on the effect on U.S. workers of capital flows from the United States to Mexico following the 1994 implementation of the North American Free Trade Agreement (NAFTA). In addition, the constant concern in the United States about illegal immigrants from Mexico reflects the anticipated impact of large-scale labor mobility. Further, developing countries are seeking ways to restrain the outflow of skilled labor (the "brain drain"). This chapter seeks to provide an economic overview of causes and consequences of capital and labor flows. We first describe the current nature of international capital movements, discuss the principal factors that influence international investment decisions, and analyze the various effects of such investment. This is followed by a discussion of the causes and impacts of labor migration between countries.

INTERNATIONAL CAPITAL MOVEMENTS THROUGH FOREIGN DIRECT INVESTMENT AND MULTINATIONAL CORPORATIONS

Foreign Investors in China: "Good" or "Bad" from the Chinese Perspective?[1]

Few, if any, countries have ever experienced the kind of rapid economic growth that China has achieved from the end of the 1970s until the present time. World Bank data indicate that the annual average rate of increase in gross domestic product was 10.6 percent from 1990 to 2000 and 9.4 percent from 2000 to 2004. These are growth rates that yield a doubling of GDP in every seven or eight years! While China's 2005 per capita income level of $1,740 was still very low compared with that in high-income countries (e.g., per capita income in the United States in 2005 was $43,740), the growth rate was extraordinarily impressive. When allowance is made for the actual internal purchasing power of the Chinese yuan in terms of goods and services and then converting to dollars, China's per capita income in 2005 was $6,600 rather than $1,740 and the country's *total* GDP in 2005 was $8.6 trillion. This total GDP was the second largest in the world, after the United States. (Note: The data refer to mainland China, exclusive of Taiwan and also exclusive of the separate high-income administrative region of Hong Kong.)

While there have been many causes of this rapid growth, the general emphasis by economists has been placed on the liberalization of the economy that began in 1978 and featured the continuous introduction of market-oriented reforms, including greater participation in international trade. Also included in the liberalization has been the permitted entry of more foreign investors into manufacturing; such foreign direct investment has increased dramatically. The foreign investment has been especially important in the emergence of the strong export sector—China has moved into the top five merchandise exporting countries in the world in recent years—because about one-half of Chinese exports come from firms in which foreign investors have at least some ownership share.

---

[1]This discussion draws on material from the following sources: Lee G. Branstetter and Robert C. Feenstra, "Trade and Foreign Direct Investment in China: A Political Economy Approach," *Journal of International Economics* 58, no. 2 (December 2002), pp. 335–38; "Out of Puff: A Survey of China," *The Economist,* June 15, 2002, p. 13 (survey follows p. 54); "The Real Leap Forward," *The Economist,* November 20, 1999, pp. 25–26, 28; "Troubles Ahead for the New Leaders," *The Economist,* November 16, 2002, pp. 35–36; World Bank, *World Development Indicators 2006* (Washington, DC: World Bank, 2006), p. 194; World Bank, *World Development Report 2007* (Washington, DC: World Bank, 2006), p. 288.

Should China have allowed foreign investment to come into the country in such large volume? In this chapter we analyze general economic causes and consequences of flows of capital and labor across country borders, but the Chinese case has an unusual twist that illustrates that the decision to allow foreign investment cannot be entirely economic. In an article entitled "Trade and Foreign Investment in China: A Political Economy Approach" in the December 2002 *Journal of International Economics,* economists Lee Branstetter and Robert Feenstra examined determinants of foreign direct investment (FDI) into China during the years 1984–1995. Policies played a critical role in attracting FDI, and the policies varied by province (of which China has 30). In 1979, Guangdong and Fujian provinces on the southeast coast became sites of "special economic zones" that gave favorable tax and administrative treatment to foreign firms (more favorable treatment than to domestic Chinese firms). This favorable treatment successfully enticed foreign investors but, because the authorities did not want to endanger already-existing Chinese heavy industry, these zones were not located in China's developed industrial areas of that time. In 1984, other areas along the coast were also permitted to give special treatment to foreign investors. In 1986, further rules permitting special tax treatment throughout China were adopted, although local regions still had regulatory powers of their own.

Branstetter and Feenstra were concerned with ascertaining the factors that influenced the Chinese, by province, in their decisions regarding the allowance of greater foreign investment. In particular, the Chinese planners were hypothesized to be trading off the benefits of increased foreign direct investment (as well as increased international trade) against the losses that would be incurred by state-owned enterprises (SOEs) if foreign investment enters and, by competition against the SOEs, made the latter nonviable. To test the relevant determinants of FDI in this context, Branstetter and Feenstra looked at the provincial consumption levels of products that are provided by multinational firms who had undertaken FDI. They related the consumption levels of these FDI products to the consumption levels of similar goods produced by SOEs as well as to the levels of goods supplied as imports. An additional determinant in their testing equation was a term incorporating the wage premium paid by foreign investors, with the hypothesis being that if foreign investors pay higher wages than domestic firms, this would be an enticement for the authorities to permit more FDI so that Chinese workers would be better off. There was also a tariff revenue term, which was comprised of tariff rates (which were and still are high) times the value of imports—if tariff revenue is high, it means that potential foreign investors are supplying the Chinese market by sending in imports rather than by producing within China.

What seemed to be the relationships between these various terms and production by foreign investors? The general results were that less spending on the output of Chinese state enterprises was associated with greater spending on the output of foreign investors (there was a trade-off between the two types of output), as was a higher wage premium. Higher tariff revenue collections, as expected, were associated with less foreign investor output (because foreign investors would, other things equal, be supplying from outside rather than within the country). Thus, there was a clear threat posed by FDI to production by state firms, and FDI was "bad" in that sense. Further, the fact that higher imports and consequently tariff revenues were associated with lower FDI meant that the government got the revenues ("good" from the state's standpoint), but the presence of high tariff rates was "bad" for consumer welfare. The higher wages paid by the foreign firms constituted "good" results from the standpoint of worker/consumer welfare.

Branstetter and Feenstra then tried, in a complicated way, to integrate these results into a mathematical function that would express the government's relative desires to promote consumer utility (by raising consumption levels and promoting higher wages), collect revenues from multinational firms (such as by imposing taxes and various fees), earn profits from production by state firms, and collect tariff revenues for the government's coffers. The most significant finding was that, although the authorities wanted to promote both state-owned production and consumer welfare, they seemed to place four to seven times as much weight on encouraging output by the state-owned enterprises as they did on promoting consumer utility. There was indeed a trading off of benefits from foreign investment against the threat of loss of viability of the state-owned production units. The politics of communism clearly played a role in this result; the populace gained in the roles of consumers and workers from having foreign investment present, but the government greatly worried that state-owned firms would take a hit from the presence of the foreign competitors. Thus, in the 1980–1995 period, China seemed to want foreign investors, but there were strong political restraining forces.

Definitions

When speaking of the international movement of "capital," we need to distinguish two types of capital movements: **foreign direct investment** and **foreign portfolio investment.** This chapter covers foreign direct investment; foreign portfolio investment is covered in international monetary economics. Foreign direct investment (FDI) refers to a movement of capital that involves ownership and control, as in the preceding Chinese example, where foreign ownership of production facilities took place. For example, when U.S. citizens purchase common stock in a foreign firm, say, in France, the U.S. citizens become owners and have an element of control because common stockholders have voting rights. For classification purposes, this type of purchase is recorded as FDI if the stock involves more than 10 percent of the outstanding common stock of the French firm. If a U.S. company purchases more than 50 percent of the shares outstanding, it has a controlling interest and the "French" firm becomes a **foreign subsidiary.** The building of a plant in Sweden by a U.S. company is also FDI, because clearly there is ownership and control of the new facility—a **branch plant**—by the U.S. company. Foreign direct investment is usually discussed in the context of the **multinational corporation (MNC),** sometimes referred to as the **multinational enterprise (MNE),** the **transnational corporation (TNC),** or the **transnational enterprise (TNE).** These terms all refer to the same phenomenon—production is taking place in plants located in two or more countries but under the supervision and general direction of the headquarters located in one country.

Foreign portfolio investment does not involve ownership or control but the flow of what economists call "financial capital" rather than "real capital." Examples of foreign portfolio investment are the deposit of funds in a U.S. bank by a British company or the purchase of a bond (a certificate of indebtedness, not a certificate of ownership) of a Swiss company or the Swiss government by a citizen or company based in Italy. These flows of financial capital have their immediate effects on balances of payments or exchange rates rather than on production or income generation.

Some Data on Foreign Direct Investment and Multinational Corporations

A recent estimate by the United Nations Conference on Trade and Development (in its *World Investment Report 2006,* p. 9, available at www.unctad.org) indicates that the stock of accumulated FDI inflow to countries of the world was $10,130 billion as of 2005. This $10.1 trillion stock reflected very rapid growth; the stock had grown at an average annual rate of 16.8 percent from 1986 to 1990, 9.3 percent from 1991 to 1995, 17.3 percent from 1996 to 2000, and as rapidly as 20.6 percent in 2003 and 16.1 percent in 2004. These growth rates outstripped the growth rates of international trade during the corresponding time periods.

To get a general picture of the size of foreign direct investment with respect to the United States, we present information on the amount of U.S. foreign direct investment in

TABLE 1   U.S. Direct Investment Position Abroad, December 31, 2005
(Historical-Cost Basis)

	Value ($, billions)	Share (%)
(a) By Industry		
Manufacturing (chemicals $109.4; computers and electronic products $58.8; transportation equipment $48.9; food $31.5; machinery $29.2; primary and fabricated metals $21.7; electrical equipment, appliances, and components $13.1)	$ 451.4	21.8%
Finance (except depository institutions) and insurance	393.7	19.0
Wholesale trade	143.0	6.9
Mining	114.4	5.5
Depository institutions	70.3	3.4
Information	55.5	2.7
Professional, scientific, and technical services	49.2	2.4
Holding companies (nonbank)	623.1	30.1
Other industries	169.4	8.2
Total	$2,070.0	100.0%
(b) By Region or Country		
Europe (United Kingdom $323.8; Netherlands $181.4; Germany $86.3; Switzerland $83.4; Luxembourg $61.6; Ireland $61.6; France $60.9)	$1,059.4	51.2%
Asia and Pacific (Australia $113.4; Japan $75.4; Singapore $48.1; Hong Kong $37.9)	376.8	18.2
Latin America and other Western Hemisphere (Bermuda $90.4; United Kingdom islands in the Caribbean $85.3; Mexico $71.4; Brazil $32.4)	353.0	17.1
Canada	234.8	11.3
Africa	24.3	1.2
Middle East	21.6	1.0
Total	$2,070.0	100.0%

Note: Major components may not sum to totals because of rounding.

Source: Jeffrey H. Lowe, "U.S. Direct Investment Abroad: Detail for Historical-Cost Position and Related Capital and Income Flows, 2003–2005," U.S. Department of Commerce, Bureau of Economic Analysis, *Survey of Current Business,* September 2006, p. 106, available at www.bea.gov.

other countries in Table 1 and on the size of foreign direct investment in the United States in Table 2. These figures represent the total book value of accumulated FDI at the end of 2005; they are *stock* figures and not the *flow* of new investment that occurred in 2005 alone. *Book value* means that the numbers are basically the balance sheet figures recorded when the investments were made. Older investments are thus substantially understated relative to current value because of inflation since the time of purchase.

The data indicate that the largest portion of U.S. direct investments abroad is in manufacturing (21.8 percent) and finance and insurance (19.0 percent). Geographically, European countries are the **host countries** (i.e., recipients) of more than one-half of U.S. FDI. Overall, the three largest recipients of U.S. direct investment in the world are the United Kingdom (15.6 percent), Canada (11.3 percent), and the Netherlands (8.8 percent).

For foreign investments in the United States in Table 2, note that investments held by foreign citizens or institutions in the United States ($1,635.3 billion) are $434.7 billion less than investments held abroad by U.S. citizens and institutions in Table 1 ($2,070.0 billion).

TABLE 2   Foreign Direct Investment Position in the United States, December 31, 2005
(Historical-Cost Basis)

	Value ($, billions)	Share (%)
(a) By Industry		
Manufacturing (chemicals $151.6; transportation equipment $76.0; machinery $48.7; computers and electronic products $47.0; primary and fabricated metals $28.7; food $19.8; electrical equipment, appliances, and components $14.2)	$ 538.1	32.9%
Wholesale trade	230.1	14.1
Finance (except depository institutions) and insurance	207.6	12.7
Information	142.6	8.7
Depository institutions	130.9	8.0
Professional, scientific, and technical services	41.9	2.6
Real estate and rental and leasing	41.0	2.5
Retail trade	29.7	1.8
Other industries	273.4	16.7
Total	$1,635.3	100.0%
(b) By Region or Country		
Europe (United Kingdom $282.5; Germany $184.2; Netherlands $170.8; France $143.4; Switzerland $122.4; Luxembourg $116.7)	$1,143.6	69.9%
Asia and Pacific (Japan $190.3)	252.6	15.4
Canada	144.0	8.8
Latin America and other Western Hemisphere	82.5	5.0
Middle East	10.0	0.6
Africa	2.6	0.2
Total	$1,635.3	100.0%

Note: Major components may not sum to totals because of rounding.

Source: Jeffrey H. Lowe, "Foreign Direct Investment in the United States: Detail for Historical-Cost Position and Related Capital and Income Flows, 2002–2005," U.S. Department of Commerce, Bureau of Economic Analysis, *Survey of Current Business,* September 2006, p. 59, available at www.bea.gov.

The manufacturing sector easily accounts for the largest portion of FDI in the United States. About 70 percent of the investments have been made by Europeans. By country, the United Kingdom is the largest source of the FDI (17.3 percent), followed by Japan (11.6 percent), Germany (11.3 percent), and the Netherlands (10.4 percent).

Table 3 lists the 10 largest corporations in the world (measured by dollar value of revenues in 2005). Table 4 then lists the 10 largest banks in the world (measured by total 2006 assets), a type of corporation of special interest to us because of banks' involvement in the financing of international trade and payments. The home country or "nationality" of each firm is given in both tables following the name of the firm.

U.S. firms represent 6 of the largest 10 companies. If the table were extended further, the United States would be found to have 18 of the top 50 firms, Japan 6 of the 50, and Germany and France 5 each of the 50. Some large multinational companies now have "parentage" in developing countries—China has 3 firms in the top 50, and South Korea, Mexico, and Venezuela each have 1 firm in the top 50. The United States is clearly not the dominant country in banking, as only Citigroup and Bank of America are in the top 10. Three British banks, two Japanese banks, and two French banks are on the list.

TABLE 3   World's Largest Corporations by Revenues, 2005 (billions of dollars)

Company	Home Country	Revenues ($, billions)
1. ExxonMobil	United States	$339.9
2. Wal-Mart Stores	United States	315.7
3. Royal Dutch Shell	Netherlands	306.7
4. BP	United Kingdom	267.6
5. General Motors	United States	192.6
6. Chevron	United States	189.5
7. DaimlerChrysler	Germany	186.1
8. Toyota Motor	Japan	185.8
9. Ford Motor	United States	177.2
10. Conoco Phillips	United States	166.7

Source: "Global 500: World's Largest Corporations," *Fortune,* July 24, 2006, p. 113.

TABLE 4   World's Largest Banks by Total Assets, 2006 (billions of dollars)

Bank	Home Country	Value of Assets ($, billions)
1. Barclays Bank	United Kingdom	$1,591.5
2. UBS	Switzerland	1,567.6
3. Mitsubishi UFJ Financial Group	Japan	1,508.5
4. HSBC Holdings	United Kingdom	1,502.0
5. Citigroup	United States	1,494.0
6. BNP Paribas	France	1,484.1
7. Crédit Agricole Groupe	France	1,380.6
8. Royal Bank of Scotland	United Kingdom	1,337.5
9. Bank of America Corporation	United States	1,291.8
10. Mizuho Financial Group	Japan	1,226.6

Source: "The Top 1000 World Banks 2006," *The Banker,* July 3, 2006, obtained from www.thebanker.com.

Reasons for International Movement of Capital

It should be clear that there is considerable mobility of capital across country borders in the world economy today. We cannot make a full examination of the reasons for this mobility, but brief mention can be made of possible causes. Above all, economists view the movement of capital between countries as fundamentally no different from movement between regions of a country (or between industries), because the capital is moved *in response to the expectation of a higher rate of return* in the new location than it earned in the old location. Economic agents seek to maximize their well-being. Although many additional reasons for capital movements have been suggested, all imply the seeking of a higher rate of return on capital over time. We list and comment briefly on several hypotheses, many of which have found empirical support.

1. Firms will invest abroad in response to large and rapidly growing *markets* for their products. Empirical studies have attempted to support this general hypothesis at the aggregative level by seeking a positive correlation between the gross domestic product (and its rate of growth) of a recipient country and the amount of foreign direct investment flowing into that country.

2. Similarly, because manufacturing and services production in developed countries is catering increasingly to high-income tastes and wants (recall the product cycle theory from Chapter 10), it can be hypothesized that developed-country firms will invest overseas if the recipient country has a *high per capita income*. This suggestion leads us to expect that there would be little manufacturing investment flowing from developed countries to developing countries. However, per capita income must be kept distinct from total income (GDP), because firms in developed countries are eager to move into China because of its sheer market size and despite its relatively low per capita income.

3. Another reason for direct investment in a country is that the foreign firm can secure access to *mineral or raw material deposits* located there and can then process the raw materials and sell them in more finished form. Examples would be FDI in petroleum and copper.

4. *Tariffs and nontariff barriers* in the host country also can induce an inflow of foreign direct investment. If trade restrictions make it difficult for the foreign firm to sell in the host-country market, then an alternative strategy for the firm is to "get behind the tariff wall" and produce within the host country itself. It has been argued that U.S. companies built such **tariff factories** in Europe in the 1960s shortly after the European Economic Community (Common Market) was formed, with its common external tariff on imports from the outside world. Such U.S. investment continued in the 1990s as Europe pressed for even closer economic integration and adopted a common currency for 11 countries in 1999.

5. A foreign firm may consider investment in a host country if there are *low relative wages* in the host country, although studies indicate that low wages per se are not as much an enticement for FDI as envisioned by the general public. Clearly, the existence of low wages because of relative labor abundance in the recipient country is an attraction when the production process is labor intensive. In fact, the production process often can be broken up so that capital-intensive or technology-intensive production of components takes place within developed countries while labor-intensive assembly operations that use the components take place in developing countries. This division of labor is facilitated by offshore assembly provisions in the tariff schedules of developed countries (see Chapter 13, "The Instruments of Trade Policy").

6. Firms also argue that they need to invest abroad for *defensive purposes to protect market share.* Firm A, for example, reasons that it needs to begin production in the foreign market location in order to preserve its competitive position because its competitors are establishing plants in the foreign market currently served by A's exports or because firms in the host country are producing in larger volume and competing with A's goods.

7. It has also been suggested that firms may want to invest abroad as a means of *risk diversification.* Just as investors prefer to have a diversified financial portfolio instead of holding their assets in the stock of a single company, so firms may wish to distribute their real investment assets across industries or countries. If a recession or downturn occurs in one market or industry, it will be beneficial for a firm not to have all its eggs in one basket. Some of the firm's investments in other industries or countries may not experience the downturn or may at least experience it with reduced severity.

8. Finally, foreign firms may find investment in a host country to be profitable because of some firm-specific knowledge or assets that enable the foreign firm to outperform

the host country's domestic firms (see Graham and Krugman 1995, chap. 2, and Markusen 1995). Superior management skills or an important patent might be involved. At any rate, the opportunity to generate a profit by exploiting this advantage in a new setting entices the foreign firm to make the investment.

A considerable amount of further empirical research is needed to determine the most important causes of international capital mobility, and different reasons will apply to different industries, different periods, and different investors.

Analytical Effects of International Capital Movements

The existence of substantial international capital mobility in the real world has various implications for the output of the countries involved, for world output, and for rates of return to capital and other factors of production. The economist employs a straightforward microeconomic apparatus to examine these effects, and this section presents this analytical

IN THE REAL WORLD:

DETERMINANTS OF FOREIGN DIRECT INVESTMENT

Numerous econometric studies have attempted to ascertain the factors that cause foreign direct investment flows between countries. Reinhilde Veugelers (1991) examined data for 1980 on FDI from developed countries to other developed countries to determine why some recipient countries were chosen over others. The dependent variable in Veugelers's regression analysis was the number of foreign affiliates (plants abroad with at least some home firm control) of any country *i* located in recipient country *j* as a percentage of the total foreign affiliates of country *i*. With respect to the independent variables, a statistically significant positive relationship was found with the GDP of the recipient country, weighted by the degree of openness of the recipient. This finding reflects the importance of market size and possible economies of scale. The weight for openness was included in recognition of the engagement of foreign affiliates in export and in recognition that a recipient country's greater openness to trade would permit greater exports from any affiliate. Veugelers also found a positive relationship with FDI when the sending and receiving countries shared a common language or common boundaries. However, a negative relationship was found with the ratio of fixed investment to GDP in the recipient country; this was surprising because Veugelers had expected that a high fixed-investment ratio would mean a relatively large amount of infrastructure and thus an inducement for foreign investors. Finally, labor productivity in the recipient country, distance between the sending and receiving countries, and tariff rates in both sets of countries had insignificant impacts.

In another study, Franklin Root and Ahmed Ahmed (1979) examined possible influences on the inflow of FDI into the manufacturing sector in a sample of 58 developing countries. Six variables seemed to be most important. Other things being equal, the amount of FDI was greater,

a. The higher the per capita GDP of the host country. Higher per capita GDP obviously indicates greater ability to purchase manufactured goods on the part of consumers.

b. The greater the growth rate in total GDP of the host country. Greater GDP growth indicates greater potential future market expansion for the output of the foreign investing firm.

c. The greater the degree of recipient country participation in economic integration projects such as customs unions, free-trade areas, and so forth. Participation suggests a larger potential market size and encourages tariff factories.

d. The greater the availability of infrastructure facilities (e.g., transport and communications networks) in the recipient country. These facilities provide assistance to firms in serving markets and obtaining inputs and information.

e. The greater the extent of urbanization of the recipient country. This variable reflects concentration of markets in central locations.

f. The greater the degree of political stability in the host country. Political stability was measured by the number

(continued)

IN THE REAL WORLD: *(continued)*

DETERMINANTS OF FOREIGN DIRECT INVESTMENT

of changes in government during the period, with a smaller number of changes indicating greater stability. Stability provides firms with greater assurance that the rules of the game on the treatment of foreign investors will not be changed.

A later study by Ray Barrell and Nigel Pain (1996) examined possible determinants of U.S. direct investment abroad during the 1970s and 1980s. In their econometric work, they found that world market size (as measured by the combined GNPs of the seven largest industrialized countries) was a stimulant to U.S. FDI, with a 1 percent rise in the combined GNPs leading to an increase of 0.83 percent in the stock of U.S. investment facilities abroad. In addition, they found a positive relationship between U.S. FDI and the level of U.S. labor costs relative to labor costs in Canada, Japan, Germany, France, and the United Kingdom. The statistical estimate was that an increase of 1 percent in relative U.S. labor costs raised U.S. FDI by 0.49 percent. A positive association was also evident between U.S. FDI and U.S. relative capital costs. Further, there was some positive relation between U.S. FDI and domestic profits in the United States—suggesting an "availability of funds" cause. Besides these findings regarding the role of market size, relative labor and capital costs, and profits, an interesting result pertained to the exchange rate. An expected rise in the value of the dollar relative to other currencies led to some temporary postponement of U.S. foreign direct investment, suggesting that payments abroad associated with making the investment are delayed in anticipation of the greater command

over foreign currencies that the dollar will have when the appreciation eventually takes place.

Finally, a paper by Romita Biswas (2002) examined econometrically the determinants of U.S. foreign direct investment in 44 countries from 1983 to 1990. In particular, Biswas focused on the influence of compensation paid per employee, infrastructure in the receiving country (with infrastructure being measured by installed capacity of electric generating plants per capita and by the number of main telephone lines per capita), and total GNP. Further, political variables such as type of regime in place (autocracy or democracy), regime duration, rule of law, property rights (such as extent of protection from expropriation by the government), and amount of corruption in government were also included in the empirical analysis. (Obviously, some of these variables would be difficult to measure!) In general, infrastructure was found to contribute positively and significantly to the receipt of FDI, higher wages meant less FDI (although not in all tests), and democracies were more attractive to FDI than were autocracies. Greater protection of property rights also enhanced FDI. Curiously, a longer duration of a regime significantly reduced FDI. Biswas hypothesizes that this result might have occurred because the longer a regime is in place, the greater the chance that interest groups will form—groups that decrease the flexibility and efficiency of government.

In overview, there are clearly many different possible influences leading to foreign direct investment. Important attention is being paid, and rightfully so, to political variables in addition to traditional economic variables. ●

approach. We return to this apparatus in our discussion of the international movement of labor later in the chapter.

Figure 1 portrays the marginal physical product of capital (MPP_K) schedules for countries I and II. The analysis assumes that they are the only two countries in the world, that there are only two factors of production—capital and labor—and that both countries produce a single, homogeneous good that represents the aggregate of all goods produced in the countries. In microeconomic theory, a marginal physical product of capital schedule plots the additions to output that result from adding 1 more unit of capital to production when all other inputs are held constant. With constant prices, this schedule constitutes the demand for capital inputs derived from the demand for the product. Schedule AB shows the MPP_K in country I (MPP_{KI}) for various levels of capital stock measured in a rightward direction from origin 0. Analogously, schedule $A'B'$ indicates the MPP_K in country II (MPP_{KII}), with the levels of capital stock measured *leftward* from origin $0'$.

FIGURE 1   Capital Market Equilibrium—The Two-Country Case

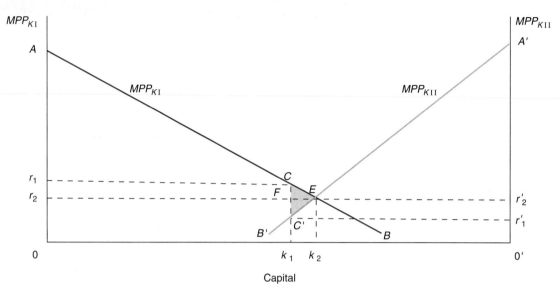

The demand (MPP_{KI}) for capital in country I is plotted from the left, and the demand for capital in country II (MPP_{KII}) is plotted from the right. The total available supply of capital in the two countries is demonstrated by the length of the horizontal axis from 0 to 0'. If markets are working perfectly, the productivity of capital (and thus the return) should be equal in both countries. Otherwise, there will be an incentive to shift capital from lower- to higher-productivity uses. The equality condition occurs where the two demand curves intersect (point E). If E is attained, the return to capital is the same in both countries ($0r_2 = 0'r'_2$) and $0k_2$ capital is employed in country I and $0'k_2$ capital is employed in country II, exhausting the total supply of capital jointly available.

Assume in the initial (pre-international-capital-flow) situation that the capital stock in country I is measured by the distance $0k_1$ and capital in country II is measured (in the leftward direction) by the distance $0'k_1$. The total world capital stock is fixed and equal to the distance $00'$, or the sum of $0k_1$ and $0'k_1$. With the standard assumption of perfect competition, capital in country I will be paid at the rate equal to its marginal product ($0r_1$), which is associated with point C on schedule AB. Similarly, capital in country II will be paid at the rate equal to its marginal product ($0'r'_1$), which is associated with point C' on schedule $A'B'$. Remembering that total product is equal to the area under the marginal product curve at the relevant size of capital stock, the total output (or GDP) in country I is equal to area $0ACk_1$ and the total output (GDP) in country II is equal to area $0'A'C'k_1$. (World output is of course equal to the sum of these two areas.) The total output in country I is divided between the two factors such that the rectangle $0r_1Ck_1$ is the total return (or profit) of capital (i.e., the rate of return $0r_1$ multiplied by the amount of capital $0k_1$), and workers receive the remaining output (or income) consisting of triangle r_1AC. In country II, by similar reasoning, capital receives total return (or profit) of area $0'r'_1C'k_1$ and labor receives the area of triangle $r'_1A'C'$.

This situation will change if capital is permitted to move between countries because the rate of return to capital in country I ($0r_1$) exceeds that in country II ($0'r'_1$). If capital mobility exists between the two countries, then capital will move *from* country II *to* country I as long as the return to capital is greater in country I than in country II. (We are assuming that the same degree of risk attaches to investments in each country or that the rates of return have been adjusted for risk. We are also assuming that there is no international movement of labor.) In Figure 1, the amount of capital k_2k_1 in country II moves to country I to take

IN THE REAL WORLD:

HOST-COUNTRY DETERMINANTS OF FOREIGN DIRECT INVESTMENT INFLOWS

The United Nations Conference on Trade and Development (UNCTAD), in its *World Investment Report 1998,* categorized types of FDI and the general characteristics of host countries that are considered by investors deciding whether to undertake a project in any given country. These factors have also been elaborated on in the context of developing countries in a 1999 article in *Finance and Development* (Mallampally and Sauvant 1999).

The particular economic determinants of FDI, according to the UNCTAD staff, depend on whether the FDI project falls into one of three categories: (1) *market-seeking FDI,* that is, firms that are attempting to locate facilities near large markets for their goods and services; (2) *resource-seeking and asset-seeking FDI,* that is, firms that are in search of particular natural resources (e.g., copper in Chile) or particular human skills (e.g., computer literacy and skills in Bangalore, a city in southern India often referred to as the "Second Silicon Valley"); and (3) *efficiency-seeking FDI,* that is, firms that can sell their products worldwide and are in search of the location where production costs are

the lowest. These general economic determinants are listed in the left-hand column of Table 5.

Beyond economic factors, foreign firms considering investment in any given country will also be influenced by various policies and attitudes of the host country's government. In addition, broader, more general characteristics of the business environment (called "business facilitation" by UNCTAD) will play a role in the investment decision. These policy and business environment considerations, as presented by UNCTAD, are listed in the right-hand column of Table 5. In general, the table gives us a framework for viewing the decision to undertake FDI in any given case. Of course, the weights to be applied to each factor will differ from potential host country to potential host country, and different weights will also be applied by different foreign firms.

Source: Padma Mallampally and Karl P. Sauvant, "Foreign Direct Investment in Developing Countries," *Finance and Development* 36, no. 1 (March 1999), p. 36. Originally appeared in United Nations Conference on Trade and Development, *World Investment Report 1998: Trends and Determinants* (Geneva: UNCTAD, 1998), p. 91.   ●

TABLE 5   **Host-Country Determinants of Foreign Direct Investment**

Economic Determinants	Policy Framework
Market-seeking FDI:	Economic, political, and social stability
Market size and per capita income	Rules regarding entry and operations
Market growth	Standards of treatment of foreign affiliates
Access to regional and global markets	Policies on functioning and structure of markets (e.g., regarding
Country-specific consumer preferences	competition, mergers)
Structure of markets	International agreements on FDI
Resource- or asset-seeking FDI:	Privatization policy
Raw materials	Trade policies and coherence of FDI and trade policies
Low-cost unskilled labor	Tax policy
Availability of skilled labor	**Business Facilitation**
Technological, innovative, and other created assets	Investment promotion (including image-building and
(e.g., brand names)	investment-generating activities and investment-facilitation
Physical infrastructure	services)
Efficiency-seeking FDI:	Investment incentives
Costs of above physical and human resources and assets	"Hassle costs" (related to corruption and administrative efficiency)
(including an adjustment for productivity)	Social amenities (e.g., bilingual schools, quality of life)
Other input costs (e.g., intermediate products, transport costs)	After-investment services
Membership of country in a regional integration agreement,	
which could be conducive to forming regional corporate	
networks	

advantage of the higher rate of return. This foreign direct investment by country II in country I bids down the rate of return in country I to $0r_2$. On the other hand, because capital is leaving country II, the rate of return in country II rises from $0'r'_1$ to $0'r'_2$. In equilibrium, the MPP_K in the two countries is equal, and this is represented by point E, where the two marginal physical product of capital schedules intersect. At this equilibrium, the rate of return to capital is equalized between the countries (at $0r_2 = 0'r'_2$), and there is no further incentive for capital to move between the countries.

What has been the effect of capital flow k_2k_1 from country II to country I on output in the two countries and on total world output? As expected, total output has risen in country I because additional capital has come into the country to be used in the production process. Before the capital flow, output in country I was area $0ACk_1$, but output has now increased to area $0AEk_2$. Thus, output in country I has gone up by the area k_1CEk_2. In country II, there has been a decline in output. The before-capital-flow output of $0'A'C'k_1$ has been reduced to the after-capital-flow output of $0'A'Ek_2$, a decrease by the amount $k_1C'Ek_2$. However, *world output and thus efficiency of world resource use has increased* because of the free movement of capital. World output has increased because the increase in output in country I (area k_1CEk_2) is greater than the decrease in output in country II (area $k_1C'Ek_2$). The extent to which world output has increased is indicated by the triangular shaded area $C'CE$. Thus, just as free international *trade* in goods and services increases the efficiency of resource use in the world economy, so does the free movement of capital—and of factors of production in general. In addition, free movement of factors can equalize returns to factors in the two countries, just as free international trade in the Heckscher-Ohlin model could lead to factor price equalization between the countries. In recognition of these parallel implications of trade and factor mobility for efficiency of resource use and returns to factors, economists often stress that free trade and free factor mobility are substitutes for each other.

Some comments also can be made about the total return to each of the factors of production in the two countries. The total return to country I's owners of capital was $0r_1Ck_1$ before the capital movement, but it has now fallen to the amount $0r_2Fk_1$ (a decline by the amount r_2r_1CF). The return to country II's owners of capital has increased from $0'r'_1C'k_1$ to $0'r'_2Fk_1$, an increase by the amount $r'_1r'_2FC'$. While we know that owners of capital in country I have been injured and those in country II have gained from the capital flow, we cannot say anything about the sum of the two returns (and thus of world profits) unless more information is available on the slopes of the MPP_K schedules and the size of the capital flow. However, because world output has increased, it is theoretically possible to redistribute income so that both sets of capital owners *could* be better off than they were prior to the capital movement. A similar conclusion applies to labor. Workers in country I have received an increase in their total wages, because before-capital-flow wages consisted of area r_1AC while after-capital-flow wages are indicated by area r_2AE (an increase in wages by the amount r_2r_1CE). In country II, wages have fallen because workers now have less capital with which to work. The wage bill in country II prior to the capital flow was area $r'_1A'C'$, and it has decreased to $r'_2A'E$ after the capital flow (a decrease by the amount $r'_1r'_2EC'$). Again, no a priori statement can be made about the impact of the capital flow on total wages in the world without more information, but the increase in world output (and income) suggests that all workers *could* be made better off by income redistribution policies.

Finally, we can make unambiguous statements about the impact of the capital flow on national income [or gross national product (GNP)—the product of a country's nationals or citizens] in both countries. The income of country I's citizens consists of total wages plus total profits. We have seen that the capital flow has increased total wages by area r_2r_1CE and has decreased the returns to the owners of capital by area r_2r_1CF. Comparison of these two areas indicates that the income of workers rises by *more* than the income of capital owners falls in country I; we conclude that national income or GNP—the income of the factors of production —in country I increases because of the capital inflow (by triangular area FCE). (GDP—the total output produced within a country—for country I has risen by k_1CEk_2. However, area k_1FEk_2 of that amount accrues to country II's investors.) Analogously, the capital outflow in country II causes total wages to fall by area $r'_1r'_2EC'$ and the total returns to owners of capital to rise by area $r'_1r'_2FC'$. National income (GNP) in country II thus increases by amount $C'FE$. Country II thus has higher income (GNP) despite the fact that the output produced in II (its GDP) has fallen from area $O'A'C'k_1$ to area $O'A'Ek_2$. Hence, both countries gain from international capital mobility. Restrictions on the flow of foreign direct investment have an economic cost of lost efficiency in the world economy and lost income in each of the countries.

Potential Benefits and Costs of Foreign Direct Investment to a Host Country

In this section, we cover some of the alleged benefits and costs of a direct capital inflow to a host country. (For an expanded discussion of many of these points, see Meier 1968, 1995.) While there are also benefits and costs to the home country from capital outflow, we focus only on host-country effects. The focus on impacts to the host country particularly permits us to discuss developing countries more prominently.

Potential benefits of foreign direct investment

A wide variety of benefits may result from an inflow of foreign direct investment. These gains do not occur in all cases, nor do they occur in the same magnitude. Several of the potential gains are listed below.

Increased output.   This impact was discussed earlier. The provision of increased capital to work with labor and other resources can enhance the total output (as well as output per unit of input) flowing from the factors of production.

Increased wages.   This was also discussed earlier. Note that some of the increase in wages arises as a redistribution from the profits of domestic capital.

Increased employment.   This impact is particularly important if the recipient country is a developing country with an excess supply of labor caused by population pressure.

Increased exports.   If the foreign capital produces goods with export potential, the host country is in a position to generate scarce foreign exchange. In a development context, the additional foreign currency can be used to import needed capital equipment or materials to assist in achieving the country's development plan, or the foreign exchange can be used to pay interest or repay some principal on the country's external debt.

Increased tax revenues.   If the host country is in a position to implement effective tax measures, the profits and other increased incomes flowing from the foreign investment project can provide a source of new tax revenue to be used for development projects. However, the country must spend such revenue wisely and refrain from imposing too high a rate of taxation on the foreign firm, as this high taxation might cause the firm to leave the country.

Realization of scale economies.   The foreign firm might enter into an industry in which scale economies can be realized because of the industry's market size and technological features. Home firms might not be able to generate the necessary capital to achieve the cost reductions associated with large-scale production. If the foreign investor's activities realize economies of scale, consumer prices might be lowered.

Provision of technical and managerial skills and of new technology.   Many economists judge that these skills are among the scarcest resources in developing countries. If so, then a crucial bottleneck is broken when foreign capital brings in critical human capital skills in the form of managers and technicians. In addition, the new technology can clearly enhance the recipient country's production possibilities.

Weakening of power of domestic monopoly.   This situation could result if, prior to the foreign capital inflow, a domestic firm or a small number of firms dominated a particular industry in the host country. With the inflow of the direct investment, a new competitor is provided, resulting in a possible increase in output and fall in prices in the industry. Thus, international capital mobility can operate as a form of antitrust policy. A recent example of the potential for this is the effort by U.S. telecommunications firms to gain greater access to the Japanese market. In addition, a World Trade Organization–sponsored multilateral telecommunications agreement in early 1997 opened the way for weakening of domestic monopolies and for reduction of consumer prices in this important sector.

Potential costs of foreign direct investment

Some alleged disadvantages to the host country from a foreign capital inflow are listed and briefly discussed.

Adverse impact on the host country's commodity terms of trade.   As you will recall, a country's commodity terms of trade are defined as the price of a country's exports divided by the price of its imports. In the context of FDI, the allegation is sometimes made that the terms of trade will deteriorate because of the inflow of foreign capital. This could occur if the investment goes into production of export goods and the country is a large country in the sale of its exports. Thus, increased exports drive down the price of exports relative to the price of imports.

Transfer pricing is another mechanism by which the host country's terms of trade could deteriorate. The term *transfer prices* refers to the recorded prices on *intra*firm international trade. If one subsidiary or branch plant of a multinational company sells inputs to another subsidiary or branch plant of the same firm in another country, no market price exists; the firm arbitrarily records a price for the transaction on the books of the two subsidiaries, leaving room for manipulation of the prices. If a subsidiary in a developing country is prevented from sending profits home directly or is subject to high taxes on its profits, then the subsidiary can reduce its *recorded* profits in the developing country by understating the value of its exports to other subsidiaries in other countries and by overstating the value of its imports from other subsidiaries. What happens is that the country's recorded terms of trade are worse than they would have been if a true market price were used for these transactions.

Decreased domestic saving.   The allegation, in the context of a developing country, is that the inflow of foreign capital may cause the domestic government to relax its efforts to generate greater domestic saving. If tax mechanisms are difficult to put into place, the local government may decide there is no need to collect more taxes from a low-income population for the financing of investment projects if a foreign firm is providing investment capital. The forgone tax revenues can be used for consumption rather than saving. This is only one of several possible mechanisms for achieving the same result.

Decreased domestic investment.   Often the foreign firm may partly finance the direct investment by borrowing funds in the host country's capital market. This action can drive up interest rates in the host country and lead to a decline in *domestic* investment through a "crowding-out" effect. In a related argument, suppliers of funds in the developing country may provide financial capital to the MNC rather than to local enterprise because of perceived lower risk. This shift of funds may divert capital from uses that could be more valuable to the developing countries.

Instability in the balance of payments and the exchange rate.   When the foreign direct investment comes into the country, it usually provides foreign exchange, thus improving the balance of payments or raising the value of the host country's currency in exchange markets. However, when imported inputs need to be obtained or when profits are sent home to the country originating the investment, a strain is placed on the host country's balance of payments and the home currency can then depreciate in value. A certain degree of instability will exist that makes it difficult to engage in long-term economic planning.

Loss of control over domestic policy.   This is probably the most emotional of the various charges levied against foreign direct investment. The argument is that a large foreign investment sector can exert enough power in a variety of ways so that the host country is no longer truly sovereign. For example, this charge was levied forcefully against U.S. direct investment in Western Europe in the 1960s and it is often raised against U.S. FDI into developing countries.

Increased unemployment.   This argument is usually made in the context of developing countries. The foreign firm may bring its own capital-intensive techniques into the host country; however, these techniques may be inappropriate for a labor-abundant country. The result is that the foreign firm hires relatively few workers and displaces many others because it drives local firms out of business.

Establishment of local monopoly.   This is the converse of the presumed "benefit" that FDI would break up a local monopoly. On the "cost" side, a large foreign firm may undercut a competitive local industry because of some particular advantage (such as in technology) and drive domestic firms from the industry. Then the foreign firm will exist as a monopolist, with all the accompanying disadvantages of a monopoly.

Inadequate attention to the development of local education and skills.   First propounded by Stephen Hymer (1972), this argument has the multinational company reserving the jobs that require expertise and entrepreneurial skills for the head office in the home country. Jobs at the subsidiary operations in the host country are at lower levels of skill and ability (e.g., routine management operations rather than creative decision making). The labor force and the managers in the host country do not acquire new skills.

Overview of benefits and costs of foreign direct investment

No general assessment can be made regarding whether the benefits outweigh the costs. Each country's situation and each firm's investment must be examined in light of these various considerations, and a judgment about the desirability of the investment can be clearly positive in some instances and negative in others. These considerations get us beyond the simple analytical model discussed earlier in this chapter, where the capital flow was always beneficial in its impact.

Developed and developing countries often try to institute policies that will improve the ratio of benefits to costs connected with a foreign capital inflow. Thus, **performance requirements** are frequently placed on the foreign firm, such as stipulating a minimum percent of local employees, a maximum percent of profits that can be repatriated to the home country, and a minimum percent of output that must be exported to earn scarce foreign exchange. In addition, the output of the firm may be subject to domestic content requirements on inputs, or foreign firms may be banned altogether from certain key industries. Some progress toward eliminating such distortionary performance requirements was made in the Uruguay round of trade negotiations in the 1990s.

Finally, brief mention can be made of the fact that clearly there are impacts of FDI on the sending or home country of the investment as well as on the receiving or host country. As noted in the discussion of Figure 1, the sending country (country II in the figure) experiences a reduction in its GDP (although an increase in its national income or gross *national* product), a reduction in total wages, and an increase in the total return to its investors. The country could also undergo such effects as a loss of tax revenue from the investing firms (depending on tax treaty arrangements between the sending and the receiving country of the FDI) and a loss of jobs. International trade could also be affected—for example, exports from the FDI-sending country could rise if the new plants abroad obtained inputs from home sources. Alternatively, exports from the sending country could fall if the new plant was set up abroad to supply the foreign market from the foreign country itself rather than through export from the home country (as in the product cycle theory in Chapter 10). On the import side, imports into the home country could increase if the new FDI plant assembles or produces relatively labor-intensive products in a relatively labor-abundant host country and the home country is a relatively capital-abundant country. Other effects in practice, of course, depend on the particular investment project being considered.

CONCEPT CHECK

1. What is the difference between foreign direct investment and foreign portfolio investment?
2. Suppose that there is an increase in the productivity of capital in country II. What happens to the location of capital between country I and country II?
3. What are the principal costs and benefits of foreign direct investment to the host country? What might be the principal costs and benefits of foreign direct investment to the investing country?

LABOR MOVEMENTS BETWEEN COUNTRIES

Seasonal Workers in Germany[2]

The Winkelmann farming group, headed by two brothers, has grown, over the last 10 to 15 years, from a local asparagus farm in Germany to a position where it is one of the top 10 white asparagus suppliers in the country. The firm relies heavily on temporary immigrant workers for harvesting its crops—from a situation of owning 2.5 acres and using two migrant workers in 1989, the Winkelmanns expanded into the former Democratic Republic of Germany (East Germany) after German reunification in 1990 and, in 2002, owned 2,500 acres of land and employed almost 4,000 migrant workers. These workers, 80 percent of whom are Polish, are hired after a thorough recruitment process that includes extensive background checks and training in the workers' home country. The workers are employed for three months per year, and they are then sent home, with transportation for the trip home paid for by the Winkelmanns. (The Winkelmanns hire only workers who have a job at home, a job to which they can return after the three months' employment in Germany has been completed.) While in Germany, the temporary migrants receive housing and insurance from the Winkelmanns, and Polish workers can earn wages in the three months that are equivalent to 150 percent of a year's pay in Poland.

This temporary migration system is of considerable value to the Winkelmanns and to other farms like theirs, but it also appears to benefit Germany in its agricultural production. Germany gains because it has been difficult to recruit Germans to harvest the asparagus, apparently because the work is physically demanding and pays relatively low wages (relatively low for the Germans but not for the Poles).

Permanent Migration: A Greek in Germany

Hasan Touzlatzi is a mid-fiftyish Muslim from West Thrace, Greece, who now lives in Espelkamp, a small town in Germany. He grew up in a poor family in Greece, and he left West Thrace at age 20 in 1970 to go to Germany for temporary work. Hasan traveled to Germany with other temporary "guest workers," and the trip had been organized by the German government. He was provided with a job in a firm in Espelkamp, and, at least partly because he began learning the German

---

[2]This discussion as well as the next one, "Permanent Migration: A Greek in Germany," are drawn from chapter 4 of Scott Reid, "Germany and the Gastarbeiterfrage: A Study of Migration's Legacy in Germany, 1815–2003," senior thesis, Center for Interdisciplinary Studies, Davidson College, April 2003. We thank Scott Reid for permission to utilize his material.

language as soon as he arrived in the country, he advanced quickly with the firm. When the firm later folded, Hasan decided on several successive occasions, although planning only for a short extension on each occasion, to stay on in his new country. His wife joined him and, after children were born, the Touzlatzis became permanent residents so that their children could benefit from the German education system.

Hasan Touzlatzi has become a respected and prominent member of the Espelkamp community, where he has now lived for more than 30 years. He owns a flower shop, is active in a local club of immigrants from West Thrace, and participates regularly in the Espelkamp Muslim prayer room and mosque. He and his family and other fellow migrants are solid parts of the German community and economy, although ties continue with their homeland. (For example, two of Hasan's sons went to Greece to serve in the Greek army, and Hasan has kept his Greek citizenship.) The Touzlatzis are permanent immigrants who have become integrated into their host country, although they retain identification with their homeland.

These two vignettes offer examples of temporary migration and permanent migration between countries. Just as capital moves in large volume across country borders, so too does labor. As of 1999, for example, 24.6 percent of Australia's force was born outside the country; for Canada, the figure was 19.2 percent, and foreign-born labor constituted 11.7 percent of the U.S. labor force.[3] In addition, *The Economist* magazine estimated that, between 1989 and 1998, about 1 million people per year entered the United States legally and 500,000 per year did so illegally; for the European Union, the figures were 1.2 million per year legally and perhaps 500,000 entering illegally.[4] Indeed, the magazine stated that "In both America and Europe, immigration has been the main driver of population growth."[5] In fact, in 2004, the number of foreign-born people in the United States was more than 30 million, with Mexican immigrants totaling 10.5 million (Hanson 2006, p. 869). While there are many different reasons for such large-scale migration, including economic, political, and familial ones, we focus mainly on the economic causes and consequences in this chapter.

Technically, the desire to migrate on the part of an individual depends on the expected costs and benefits of the move. Expected income differences between the old and new location, costs of the move, cost-of-living differences between the two locations, and other nonpecuniary net benefits in the new location such as health facilities, educational opportunities, or greater political or religious freedom figure into the decision to migrate. Even within this more general framework, expected wage or income differences are an important factor. At the same time, the movement of labor can influence the average wage in both the old and the new locations. For both countries, the movement of labor thus has welfare implications similar to capital movements and trade in goods and services.

Economic Effects of Labor Movements

The economic implications of labor movements between countries can be observed most readily by using a figure similar to that used for capital. Assuming that labor is homogeneous in the two countries and mobile, labor should move from areas of abundance and lower wages to areas of scarcity and higher wages. This movement of labor causes the wage rate to rise in the area of out-migration and to fall in the area of in-migration. In the absence of moving costs, labor continues to move until the wage rate is equalized between the two regions (see Figure 2). The labor force of both countries is represented by the length of the horizontal axis. The demand (the marginal physical product) for labor in each

---

[3]"The Longest Journey: A Survey of Migration," *The Economist,* November 2, 2002, p. 4. (The original source for the figures was the Organization for Economic Cooperation and Development.)

[4]Ibid., p. 5.

[5]Ibid.

FIGURE 2   Labor Market Equilibrium—The Two-Country Case

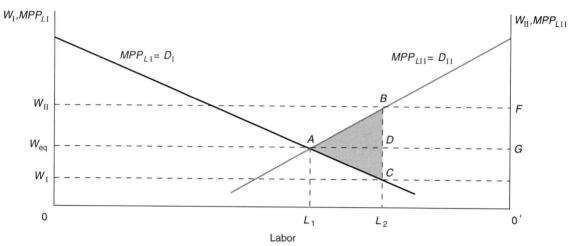

The demand for labor in country I (the $MPP_{LI} = D_I$) is graphed from the left, and the demand for labor in country II (the $MPP_{LII} = D_{II}$) is graphed from the right. The total supply of labor available in both countries is indicated by the length of horizontal axis $00'$. If labor markets are working perfectly and there are no barriers to labor movements, labor will move between countries until the MPP of labor (and thus the wage) is everywhere the same. This occurs at point A with the resulting equilibrium wage, $0W_{eq}$; $0L_1$ labor is employed in country I, and L_10' labor is employed in country II.

country is denoted by demand curves D_I and D_{II}. If markets are working perfectly and labor is mobile, the wage in both countries should settle at $0W_{eq}$, and $0L_1$ labor will be employed in country I and L_10' in country II. Suppose that the markets have not jointly cleared and that the wage in country I remains below that of country II. This would be the result if $0L_2$ existed in country I and country II had only L_20' labor. If labor now responds to the wage difference, labor should move from country I to country II. As this takes place, the wage in country I should rise while that in country II should fall until $0W_{eq}$ exists in both countries. As these adjustments occur, output falls in country I and rises in country II. The remaining laborers in country I are better off both absolutely (due to the higher wage) and relatively, as the productivity of the other factors falls with the reduced labor supply. In country II, the opposite takes place. With the fall in the wage rate in country II, labor is less well-off. Productivity of the other factors, however, has risen with the increased use of labor, so owners of these factors are better off. The other factors in country II gain area $ABFGD$, while country II's labor loses area $DBFG$. The amount of income earned by the new migrants is L_1ADL_2.

What can be said about the change in overall well-being in country I, country II, and the world as a result of the labor movement? Given the existence of diminishing marginal productivity of labor in production, other things being equal, output (GDP) in country I falls at a slower rate than the decrease in the labor force, leading to an increase in per capita output. In country II, output (GDP) grows more slowly than the increase in the labor force, leading to a decrease in per capita output. Finally, the world as a whole gains from this migration since the fall in total output in country I (area L_1ACL_2) is more than offset by the increase in output in country II (area L_1ABL_2) by the shaded area ABC.

An even clearer case of world gains from migration occurs if it is assumed that market imperfections within country I lead to an initial excess supply of labor. Now not only do wages differ between country I and country II, but some labor remains unemployed in

FIGURE 3   The Effect of Labor Migration in the Case of Surplus Labor

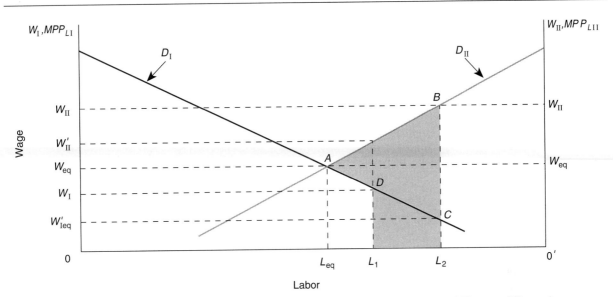

An initial state of market disequilibrium exists with a wage rate of $0'W_{II}$ in country II and of $0W_I$ in country I. The wage difference is accompanied by unemployment of L_1L_2 workers in country I (I's initial labor force is $0L_2$). The movement of these unemployed workers to country II causes output to increase in country II and the wage in country II to decline to $0W'_{II}$. Because these workers were not employed in country I prior to migrating, output in country I remains unchanged, and per capita income increases. Complete market adjustment (equalization of labor productivity and wages) requires that $L_{eq}L_1$ additional workers migrate from country I to country II. This movement causes the wage in country II to fall even further (to $0W_{eq}$) while at the same time causing the wage in country I to increase to $0W_{eq}$.

country I at the institutional (traditional) wage rate. This above-equilibrium wage could be the result of minimum wage laws and labor union–induced downward wage rigidity in manufacturing or of the existence of an agricultural sector where families simply divide up farm output among all members (workers thus receive their average product, not their marginal product). This excess supply is often called **surplus labor** in the economic development literature. Figure 3 shows distance L_20' as the amount of labor available in country II, and distance $0L_2$ as the amount of labor in country I. The labor in country II is employed at the domestic equilibrium wage of $0'W_{II}$ while in country I the prevailing wage rate is $0W_I$ (instead of the lower, market-clearing $0W'_{Ieq}$), leading to only $0L_1$ people being employed. L_1L_2 people are thus currently unemployed at the prevailing wage rate. Migration of unemployed workers L_1L_2 from country I to country II in this case leads to an expansion of output in country II without any reduction in output in country I. Complete equalization of wages requires that additional $L_{eq}L_1$ workers move from country I to country II so that $L_{eq}0'$ workers are employed in country II. If this additional migration occurs, output in country I declines because previously employed labor, $L_{eq}L_1$, leaves the country. The effect of migration resulting from surplus labor, while similar in direction to that in the earlier full-employment case, produces different magnitudes of results. The gain in per capita output in country I caused by the migration is clearly greater because the loss of unemployed workers, L_1L_2, does not affect country I's total output. The increase in total output and the decline in per capita output in country II is the same as before (see Figure 2), and the net world gain (area ABC plus area L_1DCL_2—the shaded area) is larger by L_1DCL_2, that is, the value of production forgone in country I as a result of the unemployment. This example points out that the greater the number of market imperfections—in this case a domestic

FIGURE 4   The Growth Effects of Labor Market Adjustment and Migration

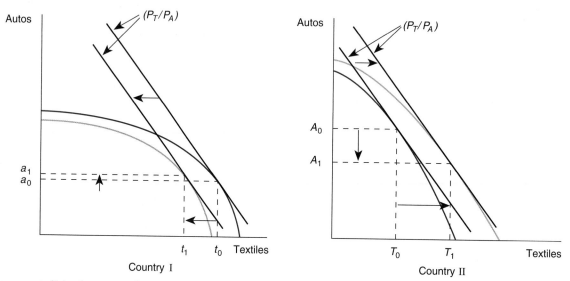

The movement of labor from country I to country II is indicated by the outward shift of the PPF for country II and the inward shift of the PPF for country I. Assume that country I is the labor-abundant country exporting the labor-intensive good (textiles) and importing the capital-intensive good (autos) prior to the labor migration and that the two countries in question are small countries. The Rybczynski theorem indicates that this change in relative labor supplies will lead country I to contract production of textiles (the labor-intensive good) from t_0 to t_1 and expand production of autos from a_0 to a_1. Country II, on the other hand, will expand production of textiles from T_0 to T_1 with the newly acquired labor and reduce the production of autos from A_0 to A_1. Both production adjustments are ultra-antitrade in nature since factor flows have in effect substituted for trade flows.

market distortion (failure of the domestic labor market in country I to clear) and an international distortion (differential wage rates across countries)—the greater the potential gains from removing these distortions.

Migration of labor (or capital) also affects the composition of output and structure of trade in the countries involved. The inflow of labor into country II is similar in effect to growth in the labor force discussed in Chapter 11 (see Figure 4). Given full employment, at constant international prices the increase in the labor force in country II leads, according to the Rybczynski theorem, to an expansion of output of the labor-intensive good (textiles) and a contraction in output of the capital-intensive good (autos). Assuming that country I is the labor-abundant country, that country II is the capital-abundant country, and that trade between the two follows the Heckscher-Ohlin pattern, the effect of the labor movement between the two can be examined. Output of the export good in country II declines and output of the import good increases. Thus, the production trade effect is an *ultra-antitrade effect.*

In a similar fashion, the reduction in labor in country I causes production of the labor-intensive good to fall and production of the capital-intensive good to rise. The production effects in both countries are symmetric and are ultra-antitrade in nature. The total effect of the labor movement on the volume and structure of trade will ultimately depend not only on the production effects but also on the consumption effects, which reflect the income changes and the income elasticity of demand for the two products in both countries. Finally, this analysis assumes the absence of any price distortions in either country and assumes that international prices do not change as a result of the factor movements. Price distortions and changes in international prices could alter these conclusions. The analysis of factor movements with price distortions and world price changes is beyond the scope of this text.

Additional Considerations Pertaining to International Migration

The previous models help us understand some of the basic issues that affect the politics of labor migration. It is not surprising that labor in country II wants restrictions against immigration because new workers lower the wage rate. On the other hand, owners of other resources such as capital favor immigration because it increases their returns. At the same time, labor in country I favors out-migration (emigration), while capital owners tend to discourage the labor movement. While the simple models are useful in providing an understanding of the basic economics involved, several extensions of this analysis are important to discuss briefly.

First, the new immigrant might transfer some income back to the home country. When this happens, the reduction in income (from home production) in country I is at least partly offset by the amount of the transfer, while the increase in income resulting from the increased employment in country II is reduced by the amount of the transfer. Assuming that the transfer is between labor in the two countries, labor income in country I is enhanced and total income (and per capita income) available to the labor force in country II is further reduced. In fact, a study of remittances submitted by Greek emigrants indicated that the income, employment, and capital formation benefits to Greece from these remittances were substantial, while the costs of the emigration itself to Greece were limited (see Glytsos 1993). In other examples, in the year 2000 India received $9.0 billion in remittances from its citizens abroad, Morocco $2.2 billion, and Bangladesh $2.0 billion.[6] More recent estimates from the Inter-American Development Bank and USAID suggest that in 2001 more than $23 billion in remittances flowed from the United States to Latin America and the Caribbean ($9.2 billion into Mexico). Further, in July 2004 *The Economist* cited a World Bank study that indicated that remittances to developing countries amounted to $93 billion in the year 2003. In general these remittances more than exceeded the amount of foreign aid received by these countries. More specifically, these payments were equivalent to more than a quarter of GDP for several countries and more than 5 percent for many others.[7]

A second issue is the nature of the immigration. We have assumed so far that the immigration is permanent, not temporary. A temporary worker, such as a Polish asparagus worker in Germany in the earlier vignette, is often called a **guest worker.** In the preceding analysis, all workers were assumed to be identical and the new immigrant thus received the same wage-benefit package as the domestic worker. This is not an unrealistic assumption because many countries do not permit employers to discriminate against permanent immigrants. A two-tier wage structure is thus not possible. However, these restrictions do not often hold for guest workers or seasonal migrants.

If migrant labor is not perceived as homogeneous with domestic labor, it is possible for the owners of capital in the recipient country to gain without reducing the income of domestic labor (see Figure 5). If employers can discriminate against the migrant worker, they will hire L_1L_2 short-term guest workers at the new market-clearing wage, $0W_2$, subsidize the initial level of domestic workers by the amount of the total wage difference, W_2W_1AB, and gain area ABC. In this instance, country II clearly benefits since the permanent domestic labor force is no worse off and the owners of capital are clearly better off. It is not surprising that there is less opposition to temporary immigration than permanent migration, and there seemed to be none in the earlier asparagus example. It also

---

[6]"The Longest Journey: A Survey of Migration," *The Economist,* November 2, 2002, p. 11.

[7]See Kasey Q. Maggard, "The Role of Social Capital in Remittance Decisions of Mexican Migrants," Economics Honors Thesis, Department of Economics, University of North Carolina-Chapel Hill, 2004; "Monetary Lifeline," *The Economist,* July 31, 2004, p. 66.

IN THE REAL WORLD:

IMMIGRANT REMITTANCES

A neglected economic feature in the immigration debate (both with respect to legal immigration and illegal immigration) is the flow of funds that occurs from the immigrants to their relatives back in their home countries. These flows can have significant effects on the countries from which the migrants originated.

A recent set of estimates offered by Dilip Ratha of the World Bank suggests the magnitude and impact of these flows. Immigrant remittances were projected to be greater than $232 billion during 2005 alone, with $167 billion of that amount going to developing countries. However, these were only the recorded flows. In fact, unrecorded flows were thought to be at least 50 percent larger than the recorded flows, which implies a total annual flow of well over half a *trillion* dollars [$232 billion + (1.50)($232 billion) = $580 billion]. In fact, even using only the recorded flows, the remittances were the second largest item in external funds received by developing countries (behind foreign direct investment). The funds were double the amount of foreign aid received from developed countries. For specific countries as examples, *The Economist* magazine indicated that in 2000, Bangladesh received $2.0 billion in remittances and $1.2 billion in aid, Brazil received $1.1 billion in remittances and $322 million in aid, and the Dominican Republic received $1.7 billion in remittances and only $62 million in aid. It has also been estimated that remittances to Mexico from migrants to the United States were equivalent to 2.2 percent of Mexico's GDP in 2004. (Interestingly, illegal immigrants to the United States from Mexico seemed more likely to send funds back to their families than did legal immigrants to the United States from Mexico.)

Remittances of this size can clearly benefit the recipient countries. An estimate by the World Bank is that such remittances have reduced the poverty rate by almost 11 percentage points in Uganda, 6 percentage points in Bangladesh, and 5 percentage points in Ghana. Such funds help the recipients purchase consumer goods, housing, education, and health care. The effect also seems to be countercyclical—

when the fund-receiving countries go into recession, for example, the inflow of remittances seems to increase (in contrast to regular private capital flows, which would decrease in that instance). In addition, when substantial labor migrates abroad, this out-migration can relieve some of a labor surplus in the sending country and put upward pressure on wage rates.

The sizable level of remittances does not necessarily imply that the migrant outflow from the home countries is therefore a positive force for those countries, however. When the migrants leave, they often take substantial human capital with them because the migrants can be high-skilled workers. The tax base in the labor-sending countries is also being eroded when the workers leave—one estimate was that in 2001, immigrant Indians in the United States were equivalent to 0.1 percent of India's population but equivalent to 10 percent of the national income of India. This fact meant that India's lost tax revenue was perhaps equal to 0.5 percent of its GDP. In addition, large remittances into a country can lead to a rise in the value of that country's currency and thus to a reduction in the country's ability to export. Further, the inflow of funds may have an adverse impact on the work effort of the family members receiving the funds and thus reduce economic growth.

In summary, the size of immigrant remittances presently being transmitted is substantial. There are positive and negative effects associated with the migration flow and with the remittances, and the net impacts on the home countries receiving the funds will vary from case to case. In any event, in today's world, these flows and their impacts clearly need to be included in any analysis of labor migration.

Sources: Dilip Ratha, "Remittances: A Lifeline for Development," *Finance and Development* 42, no. 4 (December 2005), pp. 42–43; "Sending Money Home: Trends in Migrant Remittances," *Finance and Development* 42, no. 4 (December 2005), pp. 44–45; "The Longest Journey: A Survey of Migration," *The Economist,* November 2, 2002, pp. 11–12; Gordon H. Hanson, "Illegal Migration from Mexico to the United States," *Journal of Economic Literature* 44, no. 4 (December 2006), p. 872.

is not surprising to see home labor discourage even seasonal labor immigration if it perceives that short-term migration keeps average wage rates fixed in the presence of rising production and product prices.

We need to make some final observations about the nature of the migrant and the implications of migrant characteristics on both countries. The assumption that workers are homogeneous is certainly not true in the real world, and the welfare implications that

FIGURE 5   The Effects of Migrant Wage Discrimination

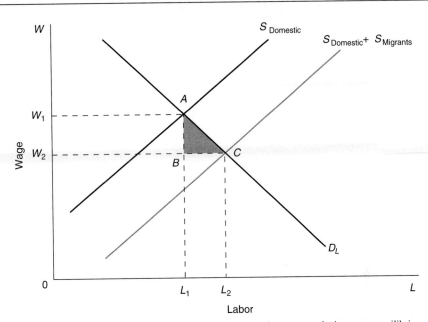

The immigration of labor leads to a rightward shift in the labor supply curve, producing a new equilibrium wage, $0W_2$. By paying all labor the market wage $0W_2$ and then subsidizing each of the initial $0L_1$ domestic workers by amount W_1W_2, domestic labor is left no worse off and the producer gains a net surplus of area ABC. This gain can take place only if the producer can effectively discriminate between domestic and guest workers.

accompany migration can vary as a result. The labor force in each country possesses an array of labor skills ranging from the untrained or unskilled to the highly trained or skilled. For this discussion, let us assume that each country has only two types of labor, skilled and unskilled. The implications of out-migration on the home country vary according to the level of skill of the migrants.

The traditional migrant responding to economic forces tends to be the low-skilled worker who is unemployed or underemployed in the home country and who seeks employment in the labor-scarce country with the higher wage. The motive for the migration is not only the higher wage in the host country but also the greater probability of obtaining full-time work, along with other considerations. The movement of low-skilled workers based on expected income differentials has effects on the two countries that are consistent with our previous analysis. Total world output rises, output falls and average low-skilled labor income rises both absolutely and relatively in the home country, and output rises and average income of low-skilled labor falls both absolutely and relatively in the host country. It is important to note that the return to skilled labor in the host country, like capital, is likely to rise.

The host country may also experience increased social costs through larger expenditures for human safety-net programs (unemployment transfers, education, housing and health subsidies, etc.) as the number of unskilled workers increases relatively and absolutely. Because the unskilled worker tends to suffer greater employment instability, an increase in the relative number of unskilled workers is generally linked to higher social maintenance costs. An increase in these indirect costs results in higher taxes, therefore reducing the net gain for owners of other factors such as capital. The reduction in average

IN THE REAL WORLD:

IMMIGRATION INTO THE UNITED STATES AND CANADA

To learn more about the determinants of labor flows between countries, Michael Greenwood and John McDowell (1991) studied migration flows from 18 different countries (14 developed countries and 4 developing countries) to the United States and Canada from 1962 to 1984. The regression results for the United States indicated that higher wages in the source country, other things being equal, were negatively related to migration into the United States. However, a higher GDP growth rate in the source country did *not* seem to reduce migration into the United States. In addition, immigration was negatively associated with source country distance from the United States, and positively associated with fluency in English and higher education levels of the migrants. There was also a positive association of migration with the source country's degree of urbanization and proportion of labor engaged in the manufacturing sector, presumably reflecting some similarity in industrial and skill structure with the United States. There was a negative association between the degree of "political rights" in the source country and the amount of migration to the United States; that is, less political freedom was associated with a greater propensity to migrate. Finally, the source country's involvement in an international crisis or clash with another country brought a greater chance of migration to the United States.

The results for immigration to Canada were generally the same as those for the United States except higher education levels played no role in Canadian immigration, and "political rights" and the degree of urbanization in the source country were insignificant. However, involvement of the source country in an international crisis or clash seemed to be more important in Canadian than in U.S. immigration. In summary of Greenwood and McDowell's paper, economic factors play a role in the decision to migrate to both the United States and Canada, but other influences are also of importance.*

More recently, evidence suggests another disparity between immigrants arriving in the United States and those arriving in Canada. The United States has increasingly been accepting immigrants on the basis of the existence of ties to family members already in the United States, and hence decreasingly on the basis of the potential migrant's particular job skills. On the other hand, Canada has been very willing to allow immigrants with particular skills that match those needed in Canada. The consequence of this disparate treatment is that many foreign citizens seeking to migrate to North America are now not even seriously considering the United States but are applying for entry into Canada instead. Indeed, Canada has been encouraging the immigration of workers, and in 2000 it increased its target of 200,000 permanent immigrants per year (which the country had actually been falling short of attaining) to 300,000 per year. The number of immigration officials to process applications has been increased, and recruiters have been sent to fairs in Europe and in Latin America. The Immigration Minister also expressed a desire to use family reunification criteria more heavily in decisions regarding immigration permits as a way to increase the inflow of workers.

*In their various tests, Greenwood and McDowell made allowances for changes in U.S. immigration laws over the 1962–1984 period.

Sources: Michael J. Greenwood and John M. McDowell, "Differential Economic Opportunity, Transferability of Skills, and Immigration to the United States and Canada," *Review of Economics and Statistics,* November 1991, pp. 612–23; Barry Newman, "In Canada, the Point of Immigration Is Mostly Unsentimental," *The Wall Street Journal,* December 9, 1999, pp. A1, A12; Julian Beltrane, "Canada's Yawning Need for Immigrants Grows," *The Wall Street Journal,* July 10, 2000, p. A24.

low-skilled wages, including the concomitant increased taxes, is thus greater than suggested by the fall in the market wage alone. It is not surprising that most countries attempt to control the inmigration of low-skilled workers. In an attempt to avoid some of the indirect social costs of this immigration, several European countries such as Switzerland have in the past adopted guest worker policies that allow low-skilled labor to immigrate for short periods of time, but the workers do not qualify for citizenship and can be required to leave the country at the government's request.

The movement of skilled labor, especially between developing and industrialized countries, is a relatively recent phenomenon. However, an increasing number of highly educated people [economists(?), physicians, research scientists, university professors, and other skilled professionals] are leaving the developing countries for the United States, Canada, and Western Europe—a movement often referred to as the **brain drain.** Higher salaries, lower taxes, greater professional and personal freedom, better laboratory conditions, and access to newer technologies, professional colleagues, and the material goods and services found in these countries explain this movement of labor. In many cases, the person had received formal training in the industrialized country and found it difficult to readjust, at least professionally, to life in the home country.

From an economic standpoint, if markets are working and labor is paid its marginal product in both countries, the analysis of skilled-labor movements is similar to that of unskilled labor, except for the differences in magnitude connected to the difference in marginal products. It is possible, however, that skilled labor is in such short supply in the home country that the loss of these workers leads to a fall in per capita income, not an increase. The opportunity cost to the home country may be even larger than indicated by the market wage if the skilled worker generates other positive benefits (externalities) for the home country such as a general improvement in the level of technology. In addition, to the extent that the home country has subsidized the education of these people (i.e., invested in their accumulation of human capital) the out-migration represents a loss of scarce capital on which a reasonable social rate of return was expected. Finally, the cost to the home country is even greater if markets are distorted by government regulation in a way that the individual was receiving something less than the free-market wage. In that event, the wage formerly received by the worker understated the true market value of the worker.

The opposite is true in the recipient country. The productivity of the immigrant skilled worker is relatively higher, the possibility of positive externalities is greater, and expected indirect social costs are lower than with the low-skilled migrant. In addition, the inflow of the skilled professional reduces the domestic price of nontraded services such as medical care. In this case, the pressure against immigration will come from professional labor groups, not from the overall labor force. In general, however, most industrialized countries have done little to restrict the immigration of skilled workers, and in some cases have made it easier for skilled workers to obtain work visas than is the case for unskilled workers.

The developing countries are in a quandary. The migration of skilled labor often represents a substantial static and dynamic cost to them. Because the combination of externalities, market wage distortions, and the opportunity cost of the human capital investment frequently exceeds the income paid to the skilled worker, countries are often inclined to restrict the out-migration of skilled labor. Until recently, for example, restrictions of this kind were common in Eastern Europe. However, the loss in personal freedom associated with labor movement restrictions makes such restrictions unappealing. Restriction of personal freedoms may also lead to lower productivity and a loss of professional leadership and entrepreneurship, which is important to these countries as they undergo economic reforms. Several policies can be directed toward removing market imperfections: (1) paying skilled labor its marginal product, (2) subsidizing professionals so that their income reflects their true social value including externalities, (3) taxing out-migrants or requiring remittances from them to cover at least part of the investment in human capital, (4) guaranteeing employment and high-quality jobs to those who return home following training abroad, and (5) appealing to the nationalism of the skilled worker. These policies may be more attractive than the restriction of free movement between countries.

While the movement of skilled labor from developing countries to the industrialized countries may lead to an increase in efficiency and world output in the static sense, it contributes to increased divergence of income between low-income and high-income countries. In addition, the loss of this very scarce resource alters the dynamics of change in the developing countries. Thus, the correct policy response is not clear. The answer to the

IN THE REAL WORLD:

IS THERE A LICENSING BIAS AGAINST FOREIGN MEDICAL GRADUATES?

As of 1990, about 130,000 physicians in the United States had received their medical training abroad. This number represented approximately 21 percent of the profession and contained about 20,000 Americans who received their medical training in a foreign medical school. Approximately one-half of these physicians practiced in five states—New York, New Jersey, California, Florida, and Illinois—and many played an important role in caring for the low-income populations in major cities such as New York and Chicago.

A 1990 article in *The Wall Street Journal* noted that, increasingly, members of this professional group claim that they are being discriminated against by licensing agencies. Because medical facilities, training, and technology vary considerably around the world, most medical licensing agencies rely on certification tests and procedures to ensure that medical practitioners have some basic level of knowledge and expertise. Many procedures are attacked because they are used to discriminate against foreign-trained physicians in order to protect jobs for U.S.-trained physicians. According to one foreign-trained physician, "Discrimination against graduates in the areas of jobs, promotions, hospital privilege, licensing, reciprocity and other facets of medical practice is common. . . . Under false pretense of quality patient care the authorities are clandestinely eliminating the foreign medical graduates from the practice of medicine." Although the licensing agencies adamantly deny these charges, the International Association of American Physicians has pressed Congress to pass a bill to prevent state licensing boards from discriminating against physicians who were educated abroad. Such efforts have been opposed by the American Medical Association, which is worried about increasing federal control over the practice of medicine and the quality of health care in general.

Foreign-trained physicians must pass tests demonstrating proficiency in English and medicine, complete one to three years of training in a residency program, and pass a nationwide exam before being licensed to practice by a state board. While it is necessary to make certain that foreign-trained physicians are qualified to practice medicine in the United States, it is easy to see how this testing system could be used by the domestic profession to control the supply of physicians in the country. Not surprisingly, the pressures seem to be coming from the profession itself and not from the general population being served, including those in the inner cities and rural areas, whose access to professional medical care would be more restricted without these doctors.

Restrictions on entry extend beyond the medical profession: Other foreign professionals often face obstacles as well. For example, in 1995 the U.S. government issued new rules to, among other things, make it more difficult for U.S. companies to pay lower wages to workers in the "H-1B" category of immigrants, the category under which certain foreign specialty workers are granted visas for employment for up to six years in the United States. It had been alleged by domestic labor groups that, prior to these new rules, the H-1B professionals (such as physical therapists and engineers) were hired at wage rates lower than prevailing U.S. rates, at the expense of domestic workers. Clearly, U.S. employers have been opposed to these rules. In addition, events such as the September 11, 2001, terrorist attacks have made it even more difficult to obtain appropriate work visas in the United States.

Sources: Kenneth H. Bacon, "Foreign Medical Graduates Claim Licensing Bias," *The Wall Street Journal,* September 18, 1990, pp. B1, B4; G. Pascal Zachary, "Curbs on Foreign Professionals Assailed," *The Wall Street Journal,* January 13, 1995, p. A2.

question, Which is larger?—the social cost reflected in the loss in personal freedoms caused by emigration restrictions or the social cost associated with free outward movement of labor—must be sought beyond economic paradigms. In the end, individual freedom of movement may well dominate any economic considerations.

Immigration and the United States— Recent Perspectives

We cannot leave this analysis of international labor movements without a brief discussion of the large volume of research related to the economic impact of immigration on host countries in general and the United States in particular.[8] Inasmuch as this research is directed toward an examination of immigrant performance, impact on host-country

---

[8]Much of this research is nicely summarized in Borjas (1994).

IN THE REAL WORLD:

IMMIGRATION INTO THE UNITED STATES AND THE BRAIN DRAIN FROM DEVELOPING COUNTRIES

Between 2 and 3 million people in the world emigrate from their homelands every year, with the majority of them going to four countries—Australia, Canada, Germany, and the United States.[*] Several recent studies have shed light on the type of labor that decides to emigrate to the United States and the impact of immigrants on the U.S. economy. While there is considerable debate regarding the Borjas claim that current U.S. immigrants are relatively less skilled than their earlier counterparts (and thus that current migrants are less likely to have a positive impact on the economy than their predecessors),[†] it appears clear that the typical person who has emigrated from most developing countries in the past is relatively skilled.

In 1999 William J. Carrington and Enrica Detragiache presented the results, using 1990 census data, of an examination of the educational background of the *stock* of developing-country emigrants (not the *flow* of migrants, which Borjas was examining) over 25 years of age who now reside in the United States.[‡] The first striking result in the study was that individuals with no more than a primary education (zero to eight years of schooling) accounted for only about 7 percent of the total immigrants (i.e., about 500,000 of the total of 7 million immigrants). Approximately 53 percent (3.7 million of the 7 million) were persons from other North American countries (which included Central American and Caribbean countries in the Carrington and Detragiache definition) who had at most a secondary education. Most of these individuals were from Mexico. Almost 1.5 million immigrants (21 percent) were highly educated individuals with a tertiary level of schooling (more than 12 years) from Asia and Pacific countries. (Note: This "highly educated" measure does not include international students in the United States, who were excluded from the "immigrant" definition.) In addition, although small in number (128,000), 75 percent of immigrants into the United States from Africa consisted of highly educated individuals. More than 60 percent of migrants from Egypt, Ghana, and South Africa had a tertiary education, as did 75 percent of migrants to the United States from India. Immigrants from China and South American countries were about equally divided between the secondary and tertiary education levels. Mexico and Central American countries thus appeared to be an exception in that most of the migrants from those countries had education only through the secondary level.

An important point to make is that, in general, individuals who emigrate to the United States tend to be better educated than the average person in their home countries. Further, the migrants often represent a sizable portion of the similarly skilled workforce in their own countries. Carrington and Detragiache present some truly startling statistics in this regard. They calculated the stock of immigrants of a given education level in the United States from any given country and then divided that number by the size of the population of the same education level who remained in the home country. For example, at the tertiary-education level, the number of Jamaican immigrants in the United States divided by the size of the Jamaican population with tertiary education gave a figure of *70 percent.* While the number of Jamaican immigrants is relatively small in absolute terms and the percentage of the Jamaican population with tertiary education is likewise small, this figure gives concrete force to the notion of brain drain from developing countries. Other (small) developing countries also had high numbers with regard to the tertiary-education level—Guyana (70 to 80 percent), The Gambia (60 percent), and Trinidad and Tobago (50 to 60 percent). El Salvador, Fiji, and Sierra Leone had ratios greater than 20 percent. For many countries in Latin America, the ratios that were the highest were those with respect to secondary education rather than tertiary education [e.g., Mexico (20 percent), Nicaragua (30 percent)], but, even so, their magnitude indicates a substantial outflow of skill.

Thus, regardless of how the characteristics of the flow of immigrants to the United States at the present time compare with those of earlier-period flows, it appears obvious that U.S. immigrants originating in developing countries represent a relatively large loss to the developing world in terms of scarce human capital. This loss of tertiary-level (and secondary-level) individuals cannot help but impede the economic and social progress of source countries spread throughout the world.

[*]World Bank, *World Development Report 1999/2000* (Oxford: Oxford University Press, 2000), pp. 37–38.

[†]See George Borjas, *Heaven's Door* (Princeton, NJ: Princeton University Press, 1999); Jagdish Bhagwati, "Bookshelf: A Close Look at the Newest Newcomers," *The Wall Street Journal,* September 28, 1999, p. A24; Spencer Abraham, "Immigrants Bring Prosperity," *The Wall Street Journal,* November 11, 1997, p. A18; "Immigrants to U.S. May Add $10 Billion Annually to Economy," *The Wall Street Journal,* May 19, 1997, p. A5; "The Longest Journey: A Survey of Migration," *The Economist,* November 2, 2002, p. 13 (where an estimate is presented that first-generation migrants to the United States impose an average net fiscal loss of $3,000 per person while the second generation yields an $80,000 net fiscal gain per person).

[‡]William J. Carrington and Enrica Detragiache, "How Extensive Is the Brain Drain?" *Finance and Development* 36, no. 2 (June 1999), pp. 46–49.

labor markets, and the likely impact of immigration policy, a brief presentation of some key findings is a fitting way to conclude our discussion of the economic implications of international labor movements. What emerges very clearly in the case of the United States is that the economic characteristics of immigration have been changing in recent years both with respect to initial migrant earning performance and the broader, longer-term implications for the economy in general. Up through the 1970s, based on the stylized facts regarding immigration in the first half of the century, it was widely accepted that although immigrants as a group were initially in an economically disadvantaged position, their earnings soon caught up with the earnings of those domestic workers with similar socioeconomic backgrounds and *eventually surpassed them*. What was interesting was that this adjustment took place in a relatively short time, within 10 to 20 years on average, and appeared to have little or no adverse impact on the domestic labor market.

Research by George Borjas (1992; 1994, p. 1686), however, indicates that the origin of U.S. immigrants has changed significantly from this pattern, with a marked increase in the proportion coming from developing countries. Concomitant with this change in country of origin, there has also been a decline in the immigrants' skill levels over much of the postwar period. Borjas therefore concludes that it is not likely that the more recent wave of immigrants will continue to obtain wage parity with domestic workers of similar socioeconomic backgrounds.[9] This suggests not only that they will likely have a heavier participation rate in U.S. welfare programs but also that this differential will carry over into second-generation wage and skill differences, which will be reflected in widening ethnic income differences within the overall labor market.[10] There is also weak evidence that the increasing numbers and declining skill levels of immigrants may have contributed to the relative decline of domestic unskilled wages in the 1980s. For example, Borjas, Richard Freeman, and Lawrence Katz (1992) conclude that perhaps one-third of the 10 percent decline in the relative wage of high school dropouts from 1980 to 1988 could be explained by immigration flows. If these trends are indeed the case and continue into the twenty-first century, there will likely be far-reaching and long-lasting effects on the labor force, net welfare costs, and income distribution in the United States. Countries which are able to effectively control the skill characteristics of the new migrants will be able to negate some of the aforementioned negative effects. It is thus not surprising that immigration policy is a "hot topic" in government circles in Washington, DC. Adding to the discussion is the emerging view that, without continued immigration, the United States may soon see a marked slowdown in the growth of its labor force as its population gets older. This slowdown likely would have negative implications for the rate of U.S. economic growth in the future.[11]

CONCEPT CHECK

1. Could labor movements between countries ever have a protrade effect? If so, under what circumstances?

2. How could temporary migration movements be encouraged by producers and not be objected to by domestic workers?

3. From the standpoint of country per capita income, does it make a difference whether a high-skilled or a low-skilled person migrates? Why or why not?

---

[9]Similar results have been observed by Wright and Maxim (1993) for Canada.

[10]See Borjas (1993) for analysis of intergenerational characteristics of migrants.

[11]See Robert Dunn, "The Economic Need for Immigration," *Financial Times*, July 31, 2000, p. 14.

SUMMARY

This chapter discussed various aspects of international factor movements between countries. Causes and consequences of international mobility of capital and of labor have been examined, and particular attention has been devoted to some implications for international trade and relative factor prices. Movements of factors of production have received relatively little attention in the literature on international economics compared with movements of goods and services, and a systematic and comprehensive framework incorporating the many facets of these movements remains to be formulated. In addition, judgments on the welfare and development implications of factor flows differ according to who is making the assessment and to the weights placed on various objectives. As capital and labor mobility become more prominent in the world economy in the future, it will increasingly become necessary to investigate further the causes, the consequences, and the policy implications of the international movements of factors of production.

KEY TERMS

brain drain
branch plant
foreign direct investment
foreign portfolio investment
foreign subsidiary
guest worker

host countries
multinational corporation (MNC)
[or multinational enterprise (MNE), transnational corporation (TNC), or transnational enterprise (TNE)]

performance requirements
surplus labor
tariff factories
transfer pricing

QUESTIONS AND PROBLEMS

1. Describe the current net direct investment position of the United States. In which countries is U.S. investment the greatest? In which industries? What are the five largest investor countries in the United States? In what industries is foreign investment concentrated?

2. Compare and contrast the country ownership of the largest industrial corporations with that of the largest banking firms.

3. What are principal reasons often cited for foreign direct investment?

4. Explain how real capital investment in a developing country affects trade, using the Heckscher-Ohlin model and the Rybczynski theorem.

5. What happens to output and the relative sizes of capital stock if controls over foreign ownership keep the marginal productivity of capital from equalizing between two countries?

6. Would the migration of highly skilled labor from a developing country to the United States have the same trade impact as the migration of less-skilled production workers? Why or why not?

7. Why might voters have a very different economic perspective on the immigration of skilled labor such as physicians than would professional groups such as the American Medical Association? What should the role of Congress be in this dispute?

8. If two countries form a common market (no trade barriers or barriers to factor movements), why is it difficult to predict the nature and level of trade between them in the long run?

9. During the heated discussions in the United States about the North American Free Trade Agreement (NAFTA), many observers stated that adoption of the agreement would lead to a surge of investment from the United States into Mexico because of Mexico's much lower wages. From the standpoint of tariff elimination alone, how might NAFTA *reduce* the amount of U.S. investment in Mexico?

10. Briefly explain why there is increasing concern about immigration policy in the United States in recent years. What effects might reducing the inflow of migrants, both legal and illegal, have on the economy?

part 4

TRADE POLICY

Second only in political appeal to the argument that tariffs increase employment is the popular notion that the standard of living of the American worker must be protected against the ruinous competition of cheap foreign labour. Equally prevalent abroad is its counterpart that European industry cannot compete with the technically superior American system of production.

Wolfgang F. Stolper and Paul A. Samuelson, 1941

Free enterprise made this country. Free trade will destroy it. For five years, I've been advocating a 20 percent tariff on all imports. We can either do that, or our industrial base will erode to the point that we can't build products to defend ourselves even in case of war. Our people will walk the streets because we are exporting jobs and importing welfare.

June M. Collier, President, National Industries, Inc., 1985

In spite of the persuasive theoretical arguments pointing out the net welfare gains that result from unobstructed international trade, individuals and organizations continue to pressure government policymakers to restrict imports or artificially enhance the size of a country's exports. Because the expansion or contraction of international trade has implications for income distribution, it is important to understand who the "winners" and "losers" are from trade interferences in order to assess the economic and political desirability of alternative trade policies. Because the impact of restrictions varies with the particular trade instrument employed, the political economy of trade policy can become very complex. This is particularly true when the dynamic effects of trade policy are taken into account, along with strategic behavior on the part of governments.

Part 4 provides a general background for understanding the issues associated with trade policy. Chapter 13 provides an overview of the various instruments of trade policy available to government policymakers, followed by a discussion of welfare implications in Chapter 14. An analysis of frequently employed potential justifications for interference with free trade is presented in Chapter 15. Chapter 16 covers U.S. trade policy and the General Agreement on Tariffs and Trade (GATT) and World Trade Organization (WTO) rounds of trade liberalization. Chapter 17 examines issues surrounding economic coalitions of countries and takes a brief look at recent developments in Europe and North America. Finally, Chapter 18 surveys trade and trade policy issues facing developing countries.

Free trade can be shown to be beneficial to the universe as a whole but has never been proved to be the best policy also for a single country.

Tibor de Scitovszky, 1942

International trade seems to be a subject where the advice of economists is routinely disregarded. Economists are nearly unanimous in their general opposition to protectionism. . . . [T]he increase in U.S. protection in recent years . . . demonstrates that economists lack political influence on trade policy.

Robert E. Baldwin, 1989

THE INSTRUMENTS OF TRADE POLICY

LEARNING OBJECTIVES

- To learn about the different tax instruments employed to influence imports.

- To become familiar with policies used to affect exports.

- To grasp the problems encountered in measuring the presence of protection.

- To understand the different nontariff policies used to restrict trade.

INTRODUCTION

In What Ways Can I Interfere with Trade?

Vignettes from various news articles . . .

In April 2001, Japan restricted imports of agricultural goods from China; two months later, China returned the "favor" by putting 100 percent tariffs on Japanese autos, cell phones, and air conditioners. Japan then considered limiting imports of Chinese towels.[1]

In May 2000, the United States complained that Japan, in giving aid to developing countries, set the terms of the aid so that most of the procurement and consulting contracts associated with the aid went to Japanese firms. In addition, the United States claimed that, despite earlier anti-subsidy agreements, Canadian and German exporting firms were obtaining loans at commercial rates but with government backing and hence were receiving unfair export subsidies.[2]

In November 2003, the European Union threatened to slap retaliatory tariffs on over $2 billion of U.S. exports because of tariffs that the United States had placed on steel imports in 2002. In addition, the EU threatened to put sanctions on over $4 billion of U.S. exports because of the U.S. policy of providing tax relief to U.S. companies that exported goods under a special arrangement known as Foreign Sales Corporations, even though such tax relief had been declared illegal by the supervising body for trade rules, the World Trade Organization.[3]

In the late 1990s and the early years of the new century, Mississippi Delta catfish farmers found themselves subject to considerable competition from catfish being imported from Vietnam. To their surprise, even some of the frozen catfish being served in Mississippi, the state that is the heart of the U.S. catfish industry, came from Vietnam. In 2002, Congress therefore passed an amendment to an appropriations bill that stipulated that, of the 2,000 types of catfish in existence, only the American-born family could be called "catfish"—the Vietnamese could sell their catfish in the United States only under the names "basa" and "tra."[4]

Clearly, countries can use a number of different measures to cause trade to diverge from the comparative advantage pattern. A glance at any daily newspaper makes it clear that governments do not adhere to free trade despite the strong case for the efficiency and welfare gains from trade that has been developed in earlier chapters. Policymakers have proven very resourceful in generating different devices for restricting the free flow of goods and services. In this chapter, we describe some of the most important forms of interference with trade.

The first section discusses import tariffs and their measurement. Several of the more common policy instruments used to influence exports are presented in the next section, followed by an examination of various nontariff barriers that are commonly used to reduce imports. The material in this chapter serves as background to the analysis of policy-induced trade and welfare effects that follows in subsequent chapters.

IMPORT TARIFFS

Specific Tariffs

A **specific tariff** is an import duty that assigns a fixed monetary (dollar) tax per physical unit of the good imported. Thus, a specific duty might be $25 per ton imported or 2 cents per pound. The total import tax bill is levied in accordance with the number of units

---

[1]Peter Wonacott, "Trade Row between China, Japan Is Likely to Spread," *The Wall Street Journal,* June 25, 2001, p. A14; Masayoshi Kanabayashi, "China's Punitive Tariffs Hit Home in Japan," *The Wall Street Journal,* June 29, 2001, p. A9.

[2]Michael M. Phillips, "U.S. Is Out to Curb Export Subsidies by Other Countries," *The Wall Street Journal,* May 17, 2000, p. A10.

[3]Neil King, Jr., and Michael Schroeder, "EU Trade Chief Warns of Sanctions," *The Wall Street Journal,* November 5, 2003, pp. A2, A15.

[4]"The Great Catfish War," *The New York Times,* July 22, 2003, obtained from www.nytimes.com.

coming into the importing country and not according to the price or value of the imports. Tax authorities can collect specific tariffs with ease because they need to know only the physical quantity of imports coming into the country, not their monetary value. However, the specific tariff has a fundamental disadvantage as an instrument of protection for domestic producers because its protective value varies inversely with the price of the import. If the import price from the foreign producer is $5 and the tariff is $1 per unit, this is equivalent to a 20 percent tariff. However, if inflation occurs and the price of the import rises to $10, the specific tariff is now only 10 percent of the value of the import. Domestic producers could rightly feel that this tariff is not doing the job of protection (after inflation) that it used to do. The inflation that took place during and after World War II and again in dramatic form in the late 1970s and early 1980s led countries to turn away from specific tariffs, but they still exist on many goods.

Ad Valorem Tariffs

The ***ad valorem* tariff** makes it possible for domestic producers to overcome the loss of protective value that the specific tariff was subject to during inflation. The *ad valorem* tariff is levied as a constant percentage of the monetary value of 1 unit of the imported good. Thus, if the *ad valorem* tariff rate is 10 percent, an imported good with a world price of $10 will have a $1 tax added as the import duty; if the price rises to $20 because of inflation, the import levy rises to $2.

Although the *ad valorem* tariff preserves the protective value of the trade interference for home producers as prices increase, there are difficulties with this tariff instrument because customs inspectors need to make a judgment on the monetary value of the imported good. Knowing this, the seller of the good is tempted to undervalue the good's price on invoices and bills of lading to reduce the tax burden. On the other hand, customs officials may deliberately overvalue a good to counteract undervaluation or to increase the level of protection and tariff revenue. (Of course, the importer may further undervalue to offset the overvaluation that is offsetting the undervaluation, and so on—you get the idea!) Nevertheless, *ad valorem* tariffs have come into widespread use.

Finally, **import subsidies** also exist in some countries. An import subsidy is simply a payment per unit or as a percent of value for the importation of a good (i.e., a negative import tariff).

Other Features of Tariff Schedules

Other aspects of tariff legislation also deserve attention. This section briefly covers some common features and concepts pertinent to tariff instruments and policy.

Preferential duties

Preferential duties are tariff rates applied to an import according to its geographical source; a country that is given preferential treatment pays a lower tariff. A historical example of this phenomenon was Commonwealth or imperial preference, whereby Great Britain levied a lower rate if the good was coming into Britain from a country that was a member of the British Commonwealth, such as Australia, Canada, or India. At the present time, preferential duties in the European Union (EU) enable a good coming into one EU country (such as France) from another EU country (such as Italy) to pay zero tariff. The same good usually would pay a positive tariff if arriving from a country outside the EU unless some other special arrangement were in effect. An analogous situation applies in the North American Free Trade Agreement (NAFTA) among Canada, Mexico, and the United States. (Economic unions are discussed in Chapter 17.) Another prominent example is the **Generalized System of Preferences (GSP),** a system currently in place where a large number of developed countries permit reduced duties or duty-free entry for a selected list of products if those products are imported from particular developing countries. This duty-free entry exists even though a positive tariff is levied if those products come in from developed countries or other, richer developing countries. The important point about preferential duties is that they are geographically discriminatory in nature—with the term *discriminatory* implying not necessarily undesirable treatment but simply different treatment.

Most-favored-nation
treatment

Another feature of tariff legislation in widespread use is **most-favored-nation (MFN) treatment** or, as now called in U.S. legislation, **normal trade relations (NTR).** The *MFN* term is misleading because it implies that a country is getting special, favored treatment over all other countries. However, the term means the opposite—it represents an element of *non*discrimination in tariff policy. The new term *normal trade relations* reflects the concept more satisfactorily.

Suppose that the United States and India conclude a bilateral tariff negotiation whereby India reduces its tariffs on U.S. computers and the U.S. reduces its tariffs on Indian clothing. Most-favored-nation treatment, or normal trade relations, states that any third country with which the United States has an MFN/NTR agreement (such as Kenya) will get the same tariff reduction on clothing from the United States that India received. Further, Kenya will, if it has an MFN/NTR agreement with India, also get the same tariff reduction from India on computers (if Kenya exported any computers to India) that the United States received. These reductions for Kenya occur even though Kenya itself did not take part in the bilateral tariff negotiations. In effect, they make the U.S. tariff on clothing and the Indian tariff on computers nondiscriminatory by country of origin. In practice, MFN/NTR treatment has been a hallmark of post–World War II multilateral tariff negotiations under the auspices of the General Agreement on Tariffs and Trade [the international sponsoring organization known as GATT, which was superseded by the World Trade Organization (WTO) in 1995].

Offshore assembly
provisions

This feature of tariff legislation exists in several developed countries, including the United States. Under **offshore assembly provisions (OAP),** now referred to as **production-sharing arrangements** by the U.S. International Trade Commission, the tariff rate in practice on a good is lower than the tariff rate listed in the tariff schedules. Suppose that the United States imports cell telephones from Taiwan at $80 per phone. If the tariff rate on phones is 15 percent, then a $12 import tax must be paid on each phone brought into the country, and (assuming the small-country case) the price to the U.S. consumer would be $92. However, suppose that U.S. components used in the product made by the Taiwanese firm have a value of $52. Under OAP, the 15 percent U.S. tariff rate is applied to the value of the final product *minus* the value of the U.S. components used in making that final product, that is, to the value added in the foreign country. Thus, when a cell phone arrives at a U.S. port of entry, the "taxable value" for tariff purposes is $80 less $52, or $28, and the duty is 15 percent times $28, or only $4.20. The price to the U.S. consumer after the tariff has been imposed is $84.20. The consumer is better off with OAP because the tariff rate as a percentage of the import price is only 5.25 percent ($4.20/$80.00 = 5.25%) rather than the 15 percent of the tariff schedule.

Despite the consumer benefits, OAP legislation is controversial. Workers in the protected industry in the United States (telephones) will object because assembly work that might otherwise have remained in the United States is sent overseas to Taiwanese workers. On the other hand, workers in the U.S. *components* industry will favor this legislation because foreign firms have an incentive to use U.S. components to become more competitive in selling their product in the United States.

IN THE REAL WORLD:

U.S. TARIFF RATES

Table 1 lists the tariffs for the year 2007 on selected goods imported into the United States. The column headed "MFN/NTR" shows the tariffs applicable to goods coming from most U.S. trading partners. These rates apply to countries with which the United States has normal trade relations (NTR), formerly referred to as most-favored-nation (MFN) treatment—see the discussion on page 260. [There are, of course, special exceptions to these rates in situations such as the North American Free Trade Agreement (NAFTA) and U.S. free-trade agreements with individual

countries.] The "Non-MFN/NTR" column refers to the higher tariffs applicable to the remaining trade partners. In 2007, the two countries facing these higher rates were Cuba and North Korea.

The U.S. tariff schedule maintains very fine divisions of products and contains different degrees of restriction for different goods. Note that some rates are specific tariffs (e.g., grapefruit), some are *ad valorem* tariffs (e.g., music synthesizers), and some are a combination of specific and *ad valorem* tariffs (e.g., wristwatches).

TABLE 1   Selected Tariffs in the United States, 2007

	MFN/NTR	*Non-MFN/NTR*
Live goats	68¢/head	$3.00/head
Roquefort cheese, grated or powdered	8%	35%
Spinach:		
Fresh or chilled	20%	50%
Frozen	14%	35%
Grapefruit:		
If entered August 1–September 30	1.9¢/kg	3.3¢/kg
If entered during October	1.5¢/kg	3.3¢/kg
If entered at any other time	2.5¢/kg	3.3¢/kg
Chewing gum, whether or not sugar-coated	4%	20%
Irish and Scotch whiskies	Free	$1.99/proof liter
Chloromethane (methyl chloride)	5.5%	125%
Dental floss	Free	88¢/kg + 75%
New pneumatic rubber tires:		
Of a kind used on motor cars, buses, or trucks, if radial	4%	10%
Of a kind used on motor cars, buses, or trucks, if not radial	3.4%	10%
Of a kind used on aircraft	Free	30%
Of a kind used on motorcycles	Free	10%
Dog leashes	2.4%	35%
Handbags:		
With outer surface of reptile leather	5.3%	35%
With outer surface of other leather, composition leather, or patent leather:		
Valued not over $20 each	10%	35%
Valued over $20 each	9%	35%
Woven fabrics of cotton, containing 85 percent or more by weight of cotton, weighing more than 200g/m², of yarns of different colors: denim	8.4%	20.9%
Round wire of stainless steel	Free	34%
Plywood, not of tropical wood, each ply not exceeding 6 mm. in thickness, with at least one outer ply of nonconiferous wood, not surface covered or surface covered with a clear or transparent material which does not obscure the grain, texture, or markings of the face ply:		
With a face ply of birch	Free	50%
With a face ply of Spanish cedar or walnut	5.1%	40%
With other face ply	8%	40%

(continued)

IN THE REAL WORLD: *(continued)*

	MFN/NTR	Non-MFN/NTR
Men's or boys' suit-type jackets and blazers, knitted or crocheted:		
Of wool or fine animal hair	38.6¢/kg + 10%	77.2¢/kg + 54.5%
Of cotton	13.5%	90%
Men's or boys' suit-type jackets and blazers, not knitted or crocheted:		
Of cotton containing 36 percent or more by weight of flax fibers	2.8%	35%
Of other cotton	9.4%	90%
Women's or girls' dresses, not knitted or crocheted, of wool or fine animal hair:		
Of cotton containing 36 percent or more by weight of flax fibers	2.8%	35%
Of other cotton	9.4%	90%
Women's or girls' blouses and shirts, knitted or crocheted: cotton	19.7%	45%
T-shirts, singlets, tank tops, and similar garments, knitted or crocheted, of cotton	16.5%	90%
Sunglasses	2%	40%
Files, rasps:		
Not over 11 cm in length	Free	47.5¢/dozen
Over 11 cm but not over 17 cm in length	Free	62.5¢/dozen
Over 17 cm in length	Free	77.5¢/dozen
Household- or laundry-type washing machines, of a dry-linen capacity not exceeding 10 kg, fully automatic	1.4%	35%
Cash registers	Free	35%
Electronic calculators	Free	35%
Electric sound amplifier sets	4.9%	35%
Automatic teller machines	Free	35%
Nuclear reactors	3.3%	45%
Military rifles	4.7% on the value of the rifle plus 20% on the value of the telescopic sight, if any	65%
Telephone answering machines	Free	35%
Motor cars, principally designed for the transport of persons (nine persons or less, including the driver)	2.5%	10%
Motor vehicles for the transport of goods, except dumpers, with spark-ignition internal combustion engine	25%	25%
Wristwatches, with case of precious metal or of metal clad with precious metal: electrically operated, whether or not incorporating a stopwatch facility, with mechanical display only, having no jewels or only one jewel in the movement	51¢ each + 6.25% on the case & strap, band, or bracelet + 5.3% on the battery	$2.25 each + 45% on the case + 80% on the strap, band, or bracelet + 35% on the battery
Music synthesizers	5.4%	40%
Playing cards	Free	10¢/pack + 20%
Refills for ball point pens	0.4¢ each + 2.7%	6¢ each + 40%
Snow skis:		
Cross-country	Free	33⅓%
Other	2.6%	33⅓%
Paint rollers	7.5%	50%

Source: U.S. International Trade Commission, *Harmonized Tariff Schedule of the United States (2007)*, effective February 3, 2007, (Washington, DC: U.S. Government Printing Office, 2007), obtained at www.usitc.gov.

IN THE REAL WORLD:

THE U.S. GENERALIZED SYSTEM OF PREFERENCES

The United States currently gives GSP treatment to 113 developing countries. In general, GSP imports coming into the United States from these countries consist of a specified list of goods that are permitted duty-free entry up to a certain maximum for each country. The developing countries themselves maintain that the list of eligible goods is rather restrictive; for example, textiles and clothing are ineligible for GSP. In addition, some developing countries feel that the countries eligible for GSP can change rather arbitrarily. For example, the United States decided some time ago that Malaysia, Taiwan,

South Korea, and Hong Kong had "graduated" from the list of countries needing this special trade assistance.

Table 2 lists the 113 countries currently receiving GSP treatment. Besides these countries and not listed are 19 nonindependent countries and territories (such as Anguilla, Gibraltar, and the Falkland Islands) that also receive GSP treatment.

Further, 42 of the countries on the GSP list are designated "least developed" countries and are given an additional benefit (see Table 3). GSP-eligible products from these countries have no ceiling on the quantities permitted duty-free entry.

TABLE 2   Countries Receiving GSP Treatment from the United States, 2007

Afghanistan	Dominica	Liberia	São Tomé and Principe
Albania	Dominican Republic	Macedonia, former Yugoslav	Senegal
Algeria	East Timor	Republic of	Serbia and Montenegro
Angola	Ecuador	Madagascar	Seychelles
Argentina	Egypt	Malawi	Sierra Leone
Armenia	Equatorial Guinea	Mali	Solomon Islands
Bangladesh	Eritrea	Mauritania	Somalia
Belize	Ethiopia	Mauritius	South Africa
Benin	Fiji	Moldova	Sri Lanka
Bhutan	Gabon	Mongolia	Suriname
Bolivia	Gambia, The	Mozambique	Swaziland
Bosnia and Herzegovina	Georgia	Namibia	Tanzania
Botswana	Ghana	Nepal	Thailand
Brazil	Grenada	Niger	Togo
Burkina Faso	Guinea	Nigeria	Tonga
Burundi	Guinea-Bissau	Oman	Trinidad and Tobago
Cambodia	Guyana	Pakistan	Tunisia
Cameroon	Haiti	Panama	Turkey
Cape Verde	India	Papua New Guinea	Tuvalu
Central African Republic	Indonesia	Paraguay	Uganda
Chad	Iraq	Peru	Ukraine
Colombia	Jamaica	Philippines	Uruguay
Comoros	Jordan	Russia	Uzbekistan
Congo (Brazzaville)	Kazakhstan	Rwanda	Vanuatu
Congo (Kinshasa)	Kenya	St. Kitts and Nevis	Venezuela
Costa Rica	Kiribati	Saint Lucia	Yemen, Republic of
Côte d'Ivoire	Kyrgyzstan	Saint Vincent and	Zambia
Croatia	Lebanon	the Grenadines	Zimbabwe
Djibouti	Lesotho	Samoa	

Source: U.S. International Trade Commission, *Harmonized Tariff Schedule of the United States (2007),* effective February 3, 2007, (Washington, DC: U.S. Government Printing Office, 2007), obtained from www.usitc.gov.

(continued)

IN THE REAL WORLD: *(continued)*

TABLE 3   Countries Receiving "Least Developed" Status in the U.S. GSP, 2007

Afghanistan	Equatorial Guinea	Nepal
Angola	Ethiopia	Niger
Bangladesh	Gambia, The	Rwanda
Benin	Guinea	Samoa
Bhutan	Guinea-Bissau	São Tomé and Principe
Burkina Faso	Haiti	Sierra Leone
Burundi	Kiribati	Somalia
Cambodia	Lesotho	Tanzania
Cape Verde	Liberia	Togo
Central African Republic	Madagascar	Tuvalu
Chad	Malawi	Uganda
Comoros	Mali	Vanuatu
Congo (Kinshasa)	Mauritania	Yemen, Republic of
Djibouti	Mozambique	Zambia

Source: U.S. International Trade Commission, *Harmonized Tariff Schedule of the United States (2007)*, effective February 3, 2007, (Washington, DC: U.S. Government Printing Office, 2007), obtained from www.usitc.gov.

Measurement of Tariffs

The "height" of tariffs

A prominent issue in tariff discussions concerns the height of a country's average tariff or, in other words, how much price interference exists in a country's tariff schedule. The problem arises because all countries have a large number of different tariff rates on imported goods. How do we determine the average tariff rate from this great variety?

One measure of a country's average tariff rate is the **unweighted-average tariff rate.** Suppose that we have only three imported goods with the following tariff rates: good A, 10 percent; good B, 15 percent; and good C, 20 percent. The unweighted average of these rates is

$$\frac{10\% + 15\% + 20\%}{3} = 15\%$$

The problem with this technique is that it does not take into account the relative importance of the imports: if the country imports mostly good A, this unweighted average would tend to overstate the height of the country's average tariff.

The alternative technique is to calculate a **weighted-average tariff rate.** Each good's tariff rate is weighted by the importance of the good in the total bundle of imports. Using the tariff rates from the unweighted case, suppose that the country imports $500,000 worth of good A, $200,000 worth of good B, and $100,000 worth of good C. The weighted average tariff rate is

$$= \frac{(10\%)(\$500,000) + (15\%)(\$200,000) + (20\%)(\$100,000)}{\$500,000 + \$200,000 + \$100,000}$$

$$= \frac{\$50,000 + \$30,000 + \$20,000}{\$800,000}$$

$$= \frac{\$100,000}{\$800,000}$$

$$= 0.125, \text{ or } 12.5\%$$

The weighted rate of 12.5 percent is lower than the unweighted rate of 15 percent, indicating that relatively more low-tariff imports than high-tariff imports are coming into the country. Nevertheless, the weighted-average tariff rate has a disadvantage related to the law of demand. Assuming demand elasticities are similar across all goods, purchases of goods with relatively high tariffs tend to decline because of the imposition of the tariff, while those of goods with relatively low tariffs tend to decline to a lesser degree. Thus, the tariff rates themselves change the import bundle, giving greater weight to low-tariff goods. The weighted-average tariff rate is therefore biased downward.

The weighting problem can be illustrated in an extreme form with prohibitive tariffs. A **prohibitive tariff** has a rate that is so high that it keeps imports from coming into the country. In the preceding example, a prohibitive tariff would exist if a good D had a tariff rate of 200 percent, but there are zero imports of D because of this rate. The weighted-average tariff rate for the country would still be 12.5 percent, because the 200 percent tariff has zero weight. In the extreme, a country that imports a few goods with zero tariffs but has prohibitive tariffs on all other potential imports will have a weighted-average tariff rate of 0 percent, and the country would look like a free-trade country!

In practice, the unweighted-average tariff rate may be as useful as the weighted-average rate. A way to avoid some of the bias of the weighted-average rate is to calculate it by using weights of the goods in world trade, not the particular country's trade. This procedure reduces the bias associated with using the importing country's own weights, because the world weights are less influenced by the importing country's tariff schedule.

"Nominal" versus "effective" tariff rates

An additional issue in recent decades concerns the choice of the appropriate tariff rate when evaluating the impact of tariffs. This matter is important when countries are negotiating tariff rate reductions because the negotiation requires focusing on an appropriate rate. The issue involves the distinction between the **nominal tariff rate** on a good and the **effective tariff rate,** more commonly known as the **effective rate of protection (ERP).** The nominal rate is simply the rate listed in a country's tariff schedule (as discussed earlier), whether it is an *ad valorem* tariff or a specific tariff that can be converted to an *ad valorem* equivalent by dividing the specific tariff amount per unit by the price of the good. The ERP can best be illustrated by a numerical example.

Economists employing the nominal rate are concerned with the extent to which the price of the good to domestic consumers is raised by the existence of the tariff. However, economists are concerned, when using the ERP, about the extent to which "value added" in the domestic import-competing industry is altered by the existence of the whole tariff structure (i.e., the tariff rate not only on the final good but also on the intermediate goods that go into making the final good). Indeed, the ERP is defined as the percentage change in the value added in a domestic import-competing industry because of the imposition of a tariff structure by the country rather than the existence of free trade. Consider a situation in which good F is the final good and goods A and B are intermediate inputs used in making F. Assume that A and B are the only intermediate inputs and that 1 unit each of A and B is used in producing 1 unit of final good F. Goods A and B can be imported goods *or* domestic goods that compete with imports and thus have their prices influenced by the tariffs on the competing imports. Suppose that, under free trade, the price of the final good (P_F) is $1,000 and the prices of the inputs are $P_A = \$500$ and $P_B = \$200$. In this free-trade situation, the value added is $1,000 − ($500 + $200) = $1,000 − $700 = $300.

Now consider a situation where protective tariffs exist; a prime mark next to a price (P') indicates a tariff-protected price. Suppose that the tariff rate (t_F) on the final good is 10 percent and that the tariff on input A (t_A) is 5 percent and on input B (t_B) is 8 percent. If we assume that the country is a small country—remember, it takes world prices as given and cannot influence them—then the domestic prices of the goods with the tariffs in place are

$$P'_F = \$1{,}000 + 0.10(\$1{,}000) = \$1{,}000 + \$100 = \$1{,}100$$
$$P'_A = \$500 + 0.05(\$500) = \$500 + \$25 = \$525$$
$$P'_B = \$200 + 0.08(\$200) = \$200 + \$16 = \$216$$

The value added in industry F under protection is $\$1{,}100 - (\$525 + \$216) = \$1{,}100 - \$741 = \$359$. The industry has experienced an increase in its value added because of the tariffs, and therefore the factors of production (land, labor, and capital) working in industry F are able to receive higher returns than under free trade. There is thus an economic incentive for factors of production in other industries to move into industry F. Because the effective rate of protection is the percent change in the value added when moving from free trade to protection, the ERP in this example is

$$\text{Value added under protection} - \text{value added with free trade}$$
$$\overline{\text{Value added with free trade}}$$
$$= \frac{\text{VA}' - \text{VA}}{\text{VA}} = \frac{\$359 - \$300}{\$300} = 0.197, \text{ or } 19.7\%$$

Thus, the factors of production in industry F have benefited from the tariffs, although consumers have lost. A more common formula for calculating the ERP for any industry j utilizing inputs designated as i is

$$ERP_j = \frac{t_j - \Sigma_i a_{ij} t_i}{1 - \Sigma_i a_{ij}}$$

where a_{ij} represents the free-trade value of input i as a percentage of the free-trade value of the final good j, t_j and t_i represent the tariff rates on the final good and on any input i, respectively, and the Σ_i sign means that we are summing over all the inputs. In the example, the a_{ij} for input A is $\$500/\$1{,}000$ or 0.50, and the value of the a_{ij} for input B is $\$200/\$1{,}000$ or 0.20. The ERP in the example is the same as in the preceding calculation:

$$ERP_F = \frac{0.10 - [(0.50)(0.05) + (0.20)(0.08)]}{1 - (0.50 + 0.20)}$$
$$= \frac{0.10 - (0.025 + 0.016)}{1 - 0.70}$$
$$= \frac{0.10 - 0.041}{0.30} = \frac{0.059}{0.30} = 0.197, \text{ or } 19.7\%$$

This second method of calculating the ERP has the advantage of illustrating three general rules about the relationship between nominal rates and effective rates of protection. These rules are (1) if the nominal tariff rate on the final good is higher than the weighted-average nominal tariff rate on the inputs, then the ERP will be higher than the nominal rate on the final good; (2) if the nominal tariff rate on the final good is lower than the weighted-average nominal tariff rate on the inputs, then the ERP will be lower than the nominal rate on the final good; and (3) if the nominal tariff rate on the final good is equal to the weighted-average nominal tariff rate on the inputs, then the ERP will be equal to the nominal rate on the final good.

IN THE REAL WORLD:

NOMINAL AND EFFECTIVE TARIFFS IN THE UNITED STATES AND JAPAN

Estimates of nominal and effective tariff rates were calculated for the United States and Japan by Alan Deardorff and Robert Stern (1986), who aggregated all traded goods industries in the two countries into 22 categories and calculated the aggregated-industry-average rates and the weighted-average rates for each country. Table 4 provides the results for the top 10 industries by degree of restrictiveness in the United States and Japan. The figures do not reflect the cuts agreed to in the Uruguay Round (see Chapter 16). While the levels of the various tariff rates are thus lower than those shown here, the point that effective rates are above nominal rates remains valid.

Within each country, the 10 industries with the highest nominal rates were also the 10 industries with the highest effective rates. Also, 7 of these highest-protection industries

in the United States also appeared in Japan's "top 10" list. The rankings according to nominal protection and ERPs were similar but not identical within each country, and some differences also exist in the comparative industry rankings of the two countries.

Note that the ERPs are roughly 50 percent higher than the nominal rates, both within an industry and for each country as a whole, meaning that substantial escalation exists. Also, Japan was approximately 50 percent more protective than the United States (8.4 percent versus 5.2 percent on nominal rates, 13.2 percent versus 8.1 percent on ERPs). However, a full assessment of the degree of protection in both countries also must consider nontariff barriers to trade, as is done later in this chapter.

TABLE 4   Highest 10 Industries' Nominal and Effective Tariff Rates, United States and Japan

	Nominal Rate (%)		Effective Rate (%)
United States			
1. Wearing apparel	27.8%	1. Wearing apparel	50.6%
2. Textiles	14.4	2. Textiles	28.3
3. Glass and glass products	10.7	3. Glass and glass products	16.9
4. Nonmetallic mineral products	9.1	4. Nonmetallic mineral products	15.9
5. Footwear	8.8	5. Food, beverages, and tobacco	13.4
6. Furniture and fixtures	8.1	6. Footwear	13.1
7. Miscellaneous manufactures	7.8	7. Metal products	12.7
8. Metal products	7.5	8. Furniture and fixtures	12.3
9. Electrical machinery	6.6	9. Miscellaneous manufactures	11.1
10. Food, beverages, and tobacco	6.3	10. Electrical machinery	9.4
22-industry average	5.2	22-industry average	8.1
Japan			
1. Food, beverages, and tobacco	25.4%	1. Food, beverages, and tobacco	51.1%
2. Agriculture, forestry, and fisheries	18.4	2. Footwear	33.6
3. Footwear	16.4	3. Agriculture, forestry, and fisheries	27.7
4. Wearing apparel	13.8	4. Wearing apparel	27.1
5. Nonelectrical machinery	9.1	5. Furniture and fixtures	15.1
6. Furniture and fixtures	7.8	6. Nonelectrical machinery	13.8
7. Glass and glass products	7.5	7. Metal products	12.0
8. Electrical machinery	7.4	8. Glass and glass products	11.5
9. Metal products	6.9	9. Electrical machinery	11.0
10. Chemicals	6.2	10. Chemicals	9.8
22-industry average	8.4	22-industry average	13.2

Source: Alan V. Deardorff and Robert M. Stern, *The Michigan Model of World Production and Trade: Theory and Applications* (Cambridge: MIT Press, 1986), pp. 90, 94.

IN THE REAL WORLD:

EFFECTIVE TARIFF RATES IN BANGLADESH

The actual level of effective rates of protection (ERPs) in the real world can be rather high, and this is particularly true in developing countries' tariff structures. However, trade liberalization in recent years has also occurred in developing countries. Table 5 indicates calculations by the World Trade Organization (WTO), for Bangladesh, of the average ERP across 40 sectors during the period from 1992/1993 to 1999/2000. As is evident, the level of effective protection fell by two-thirds over these years, from 75.7 percent to 24.5 percent.

TABLE 5   Effective Protection in
             Bangladesh, 1992–2000

Year	Average Sectoral ERP
1992/1993	75.7%
1993/1994	56.7
1994/1995	40.6
1995/1996	33.0
1996/1997	32.4
1997/1998	28.6
1999/2000[*]	24.5

*Provisional estimate.

Source: World Trade Organization (WTO), Trade Policy Review, *Bangladesh,* presented in David Greenaway and Chris Milner, "Effective Protection, Policy Appraisal and Trade Policy Reform," *The World Economy* 26, no. 4 (April 2003), p. 448.

Rule (1) incorporates an **escalated tariff structure** and reflects the situation in most countries. It means that nominal tariff rates on imports of manufactured goods are higher than nominal tariff rates on intermediate inputs and raw materials. This situation has particular relevance to trade between developed countries and developing countries. Because the developed countries have escalated tariff structures with correspondingly heavier protection for manufactured goods industries than for intermediate goods and raw materials industries, developing countries judge that this discriminates against their attempts to develop manufacturing and that it consigns the developing countries to exporting products at an early stage of fabrication. The developing countries are thus forced to continue to be suppliers of raw materials to and importers of manufactured goods from the developed countries when they would like to supply manufactured goods. The developing countries claim that the existing *pattern* of protection should be altered in addition to a lowering of the level of protection in developed countries. Some progress has been made in changing the pattern and level of developed-country tariff protection against the developing countries through the Generalized System of Preferences.

As a final note on the "nominal" versus "effective" tariff distinction, remember that an industry does not always have an ERP higher than its nominal rate. Further, an ERP can be *negative,* meaning that the tariffs on inputs are considerably higher than the tariff on the final good. Thus, the structure of tariffs in this latter situation works to drive factors of production out of the industry rather than draw resources in.

In overview, the nominal tariff rate is useful for assessing the price impact of tariffs on consumers. For producers, however, the effective rate is more useful because factors tend to flow toward industries with relatively higher ERPs. The nominal rate concept is used in Chapter 14, "The Impact of Trade Policies," because the focus is on consumer welfare; nevertheless, the effective rate concept also should be kept in mind in evaluating the full impact of protection. In the assessment of development prospects and economic planning in the developing countries, a strong case can be made for ERPs as analytical tools, even more so than nominal rates of protection.

CONCEPT CHECK

1. Why might consumers of an imported good prefer a specific tariff to an *ad valorem* tariff on the good?

2. Suppose that a friend tells you that the United States should not give most-favored-nation treatment to France because the French do not deserve to be treated better than all our other trading partners. How is your friend misinterpreting the MFN concept?

3. Why and how does the existence of prohibitive tariffs distort the weighted-average tariff rate of a country?

4. Explain how the value added in a domestic industry is enhanced if the nominal tariff rate on imports of the industry's final product is increased while the nominal tariff rates on the industry's inputs are left unchanged.

EXPORT TAXES AND SUBSIDIES

In addition to interfering on the import side of trade by means of import tariffs, countries also interfere with their free flow of exports. An **export tax** is levied only on home-produced goods that are destined for export and not for home consumption. The tax can be specific or *ad valorem*. Like an import tax or tariff, an export tax reduces the size of international trade. An **export subsidy,** which is really a negative export tax or a payment to a firm by the government when a unit of the good is exported, attempts to increase the flow of trade of a country. Nevertheless, it distorts the pattern of trade from that of the comparative-advantage pattern and, like taxes, interferes with the free-market flow of goods and services and reduces world welfare.

The export subsidy has been the subject of a great deal of discussion over the years. For example, the United States and the European Community, after heated discussion and threatened retaliatory tariff actions, agreed in November 1992 to reduce their agricultural export subsidies 36 percent in value over a six-year period (see *Economic Report of the President,* January 1993, pp. 19–20). In addition, U.S. manufacturers have often maintained that partner country export subsidies are an important element of "unfair trade" in the world economy. Indeed, as of February 15, 2007, U.S. manufacturers had succeeded in getting 35 "countervailing duties" in place against foreign export-subsidized goods coming into the United States. The duties were levied against goods from 15 different countries.[5]

NONTARIFF BARRIERS TO FREE TRADE

Besides the use of tariffs and subsidies to distort the free-trade allocation of resources, government policymakers have become very adept at using other, less visible, forms of trade barriers. These are usually called **nontariff barriers (NTBs)** to trade, and they have become more prominent in recent years. Economists have noted that as tariffs have been

---

[5]United States International Trade Commission, "Antidumping and Countervailing Duty Orders in Place as of February 15, 2007, by Country," obtained from www.usitc.gov.

reduced through multilateral tariff negotiations during the past 40 years, the impact of this reduction may have been importantly offset by the proliferation of NTBs. Our purpose now is to describe some of these NTBs.

Import Quotas

The **import quota** differs from an import tariff in that the interference with prices that can be charged on the domestic market for an imported good is *indirect,* not direct. It is indirect because the quota itself operates directly on the quantity of the import instead of on the price. The import quota specifies that only a certain physical amount of the good will be allowed into the country during the time period, usually one year. This is in contrast to the tariff, which specifies an amount or percentage of tax but then lets the market determine the quantity to be imported with the tariff in existence. Nevertheless, the quota can be specified in "tariff equivalent" form. For example, the United States International Trade Commission estimated that, while the average U.S. tariff rate on apparel coming from countries subject to apparel import quotas by the United States in 2002 was 11.3 percent, the quotas themselves, by restricting supply, acted like an *additional* 9.5 percent tariff. In dairy products, the existing 10.0 percent average tariff was supplemented by another 27.8 percent tariff equivalent due to quotas.[6]

"Voluntary" Export Restraints (VERs)

An alternative to the import quota is the **"voluntary" export restraint (VER).** It originates primarily from political considerations. An importing country that has been preaching the virtues of free trade may not want to impose an outright import quota because that implies a legislated move away from free trade. Instead, the country may choose to negotiate an administrative agreement with a foreign supplier whereby that supplier agrees "voluntarily" to refrain from sending some exports to the importing country. The inducement for the exporter to "agree" may be the threat of imposition of an import quota if the VER is not adopted by the exporter. There are also some possible direct benefits to the exporter from the VER (see Chapter 14).

Besides quotas and VERs, there are other types of NTBs. We discuss several of them below, with the main purpose of strengthening the point that governments employ many different types of devices that prevent a free-trade allocation of resources.

Government Procurement Provisions

An object of discussion in recent years, as well as an object of an international code of behavior in the 1979 Tokyo Round of trade negotiations, is legislation known as **government procurement provisions.** In general, these provisions restrict the purchasing of foreign products by home government agencies. For example, the "Buy American" Act stipulated that federal government agencies must purchase products from home U.S. firms unless the firm's product price was more than 6 percent above the foreign supplier's price. This figure was 12 percent for some Department of Defense purchases, and, for a time a 50 percent figure was used. (See Balassa 1967, and Cooper 1968.) Many state governments in the United States also have such restrictions. As another example, the European Community announced in 1992 that EC public utilities would be required to purchase inputs from EC suppliers with a 3 percent price preference—which set off threatened retaliation by the United States and an eventual compromise. Such preferences are clearly similar to an *ad valorem* tariff in that the domestic producer is given a certain "percentage of price" protection. A World Trade Organization–sponsored agreement on government procurement

---

[6]United States International Trade Commission, *The Economic Effects of Significant U.S. Import Restraints: Fourth Update 2004,* USITC Publication 3701 (Washington, DC: USITC, June 2004), p. xvii, obtained from www.usitc.gov.

designed to put foreign and domestic purchases on an equal footing went into effect on January 1, 1996, but not all purchases or all WTO members are included. In addition, government procurement provisions are increasingly being expanded to include nonprice considerations. This is a growing trend in the European Union and in Europe in general. For example, Danish government agencies are required to apply environmental and energy criteria in addition to normal market considerations in their purchases. In practice, this means that government agencies will likely be able to purchase only those products which are eco-safe (carrying an "eco-label" or produced by a firm with a satisfactory "eco-audit"). Therefore, firms in countries without such labeling practices may be prevented from selling to Danish government agencies.

Domestic Content Provisions

Domestic content provisions attempt to reserve some of the value added and some of the sales of product components for domestic suppliers. For example, this kind of policy would stipulate that a given percentage of the value of a good sold in the United States must consist of U.S. components or U.S. labor. A restrictive policy of this sort appeared in trade bills (not enacted) before the U.S. Congress. These provisions can also appear in developing countries. For instance, the attempt to produce automobiles in Chile during the "import-substituting industrialization" phase of development in the 1960s contained increasingly restrictive domestic content provisions. (See Leland Johnson 1967.) More recently, under the North American Free Trade Agreement (NAFTA), members do not permit duty-free entry of automobiles from other members unless 62.5 percent of the value of the automobile originates in the NAFTA countries of Canada, Mexico, and the United States. These provisions clearly interfere with the international division of labor according to comparative advantage, as domestic or NAFTA-wide sources of parts and labor may not be the low-cost sources of supply.

European Border Taxes

A controversial NTB from the standpoint of U.S. firms concerns the European tax system. The value-added tax (VAT) common in Western Europe is what economists call an "indirect" tax. The United States puts more reliance on direct taxes such as the personal income tax and the corporate income tax. Direct taxes are taxes levied on income per se, while indirect taxes are levied on a base other than income.

International trade implications arise from the different tax systems because the WTO permits different treatment for indirect taxes than for direct taxes. With the value-added tax, any firm that works on components at any stage of the production process, adds value to them, and then sells them in a more finished form must pay a tax on the value added. This tax is passed on to the buyer of the more finished good. Ultimately, the final price to the consumer incorporates the accumulation of value-added taxes paid through the production process. Under WTO rules, any import coming into the country must pay the equivalent tax because it too is destined for consumption, and both goods will then be on an equal footing. To U.S. firms trying to sell to Europe, this border tax that matches the value-added tax looks suspiciously like a tariff, even though it is not labeled as such.

European exporters, however, will have paid the accumulation of the VAT through the prior production stages. But because the good is not destined for final use within its country of manufacture, the exporter can collect a *rebate* for the accumulated VAT paid. To U.S. competitors, this looks suspiciously like an unfair export subsidy. The whole indirect-direct tax controversy arises because such border taxes and rebates are not permitted for direct taxes. The reasoning comes from public finance literature on the ability of each type of tax to be "passed on" to consumers. This is the source of the controversy over the U.S. tax treatment of separately established Foreign Sales Corporations referred to at the beginning of this chapter. The WTO regards the favorable tax treatment as akin to a rebate of a *direct* tax, the corporate income tax. This procedure is not permitted, as a direct tax is not the same as an indirect tax such as the value-added tax. Another point to consider is that the European countries' exchange rates against the dollar may negate the effects of border taxes and subsidies. For example, if the tax on imports reduces imports from the United States and thus reduces European demand for the dollar, the dollar will depreciate. This depreciation thereby lowers the price of the U.S. good to European consumers. We do not need to get into these issues, but it is clear that a potential distortion of free-trade patterns exists.

Administrative Classification

The point here is straightforward. Because tariffs on goods coming into a country differ by type of good, the actual tax charged can vary according to the category into which a good is classified. There is some leeway for customs officials, as the following example makes clear: In August 1980, the U.S. Customs Service raised the tariff rate on imported light trucks by simply shifting categories. Before then, unassembled trucks (truck "parts") were shipped to the West Coast and assembled in the United States. The tariff rate was 4 percent. However, the Customs Service ruled that the imports were not "parts" but the vehicle itself. The applicable duty to the vehicle was 25 percent. Arbitrary classification decisions clearly can influence the size of trade.

Restrictions on Services Trade

This is a widely discussed area at the present time, and we will cover it in greater extent in Chapter 16. In short, many nontariff regulations restrict services trade. For example, foreign insurance companies may be restricted in the types of policies they can sell in a home country, foreign ships may be barred from carrying cargo between purely domestic ports (as is the case in the United States), landing rights for foreign aircraft may be limited, and developing countries may reserve data processing services for their own firms. As further examples, Canada, to protect "Canadian culture," requires that 50 percent of prime-time television programs be Canadian programs; in addition, Canada permits U.S. magazine publishers to sell Canadian editions but only if a certain percentage of advertising space is reserved for Canadian firms. These kinds of restrictions are less visible or transparent than many restrictions on goods. However, because services are growing in world trade, restrictions on them are becoming more serious as sources of departure from comparative advantage.

Trade-Related Investment Measures

Trade-related investment measures (TRIMs) consist of various policy steps of a trade nature that are associated with foreign investment activity within a country. Examples would be "performance requirements," whereby the foreign investor must export a certain percentage of output (and thus earn foreign exchange for the host country), and requirements mandating that a specified percentage of inputs into the foreign investor's final product be of domestic origin. These measures occur frequently in developing countries, and they distort trade from the comparative-advantage pattern.

Additional Restrictions

Developing countries facing a need to conserve on scarce foreign exchange reserves may resort to generalized exchange control. In the extreme, exporters in the developing countries are required to sell their foreign exchange earnings to the central bank, which in turn parcels out the foreign exchange to importers on the basis of the "essentiality" of the import purchases. Thus, free importation cannot take place because foreign exchange is rationed. This form of restriction can result in a severe distortion of imports from the free-trade pattern. In addition, **advance deposit requirements** are sometimes used by developing countries. In this situation, a license to import is awarded only if the importing firm deposits funds with the government equal to a specified percentage of the value of the future import. The deposit is refunded when the imports are brought into the country, but in the meantime the firm has lost the opportunity cost of the funds.

IN THE REAL WORLD:

IS IT A CAR? IS IT A TRUCK?

In early 1989, the U.S. Customs Service proposed that some imported minivans and sport-utility vehicles (such as the Suzuki Samurai and the Isuzu Trooper) be reclassified from "cars" to "trucks." This administrative change would have raised the *ad valorem* tariff rate to 10 times its previous value, because the U.S. tariff rate on automobiles is 2.5 percent but that on trucks is 25 percent. Then-Chairman Lee Iacocca of Chrysler (now DaimlerChrysler) declared that the reclassification was desirable because it would bring in more tax revenue—$500 million per year, which would help to reduce the U.S. federal government budget deficit. (It would be unseemly for him to praise it for giving Chrysler a greater level of protection.)

The reaction to the proposed reclassification was a howl of protest from imported car dealers and consumer interests. In response, the Customs Service reconsidered the matter, then issued rulings on which of the vehicles would be classified as cars and trucks. For example, if a particular sport-utility vehicle had four doors, it was a car; if two doors, a truck. If a minivan had windows on the side and back, and rear and side doors and seats for two or more persons behind the front seat, it was a car; if it lacked any of these features, it was a truck.

Oddly enough, the proposed reclassification occurred partly because of pressure from Suzuki Motors. Suzuki had a small share of the Japanese VER of 2.3 million automobiles annually, and it believed that the reclassification would help its sales in the United States because trucks were not subject to the VER. Despite the higher tariff rate, Suzuki judged that it could be more successful in the U.S. market if it was not limited to its small VER share. Another sidelight is that the 25 percent truck tariff itself had originated from retaliation by the United States in 1963 against import duties placed by the European Community on U.S. poultry exports (the infamous "Chicken War").

The classification controversy reappeared in 1993, when the U.S. automobile industry pushed (unsuccessfully) for a move of some minivans from the car to truck category. Chrysler pledged to limit its own minivan price increases if the reclassification step was undertaken. Chrysler's advocacy of the higher duties on minivans occurred despite the fact that Chrysler's share of the minivan market increased substantially from 1992 to 1993.

Sources: "A Bad Trade Rule Begets Another," *The New York Times,* January 24, 1989, p. A20; Eduardo Lachica, "Imports Ruling for Vehicles Is Eased by U.S.," *The Wall Street Journal,* February 17, 1989, pp. A3, A9; idem, "Suzuki Samurai, Others to Be Treated as Truck Imports with Higher Tariffs," *The Wall Street Journal,* January 5, 1989, p. C9; Eduardo Lachica and Walter S. Mossberg, "Treasury Rethinks Increased Tariffs on Vehicle Imports," *The Wall Street Journal,* January 13, 1989, p. 85; Neal Templin and Asra Q. Nomani, "Chrysler to Curb Minivan Price Rises if Japanese Vehicles Get a 25% Tariff," *The Wall Street Journal,* March 25, 1993, p. A3.

| Additional Domestic Policies That Affect Trade

Several types of policies aimed at the domestic market also have direct implications for trade flows. Health, environmental, and safety standards are applied by governments to both domestic and foreign products. Surely, domestic consumers of foreign goods should be protected from impurities and sources of disease, but some economists claim that restrictions are excessive in some instances and contain an element of protectionism. An example is the controversial European restriction on the import of U.S. genetically engineered products. This restriction has been ruled illegal by the World Trade Organization, but it remains in place as of this writing. Similarly, governments may require that all products, foreign and domestic, meet certain packaging and labeling requirements. In addition, inconsistent treatment of intellectual property rights (through patents, copyrights, etc.) across countries can distort international trade flows. In the Uruguay Round of trade negotiations, completed in 1994, agreement was reached on harmonization of such practices, commonly known as trade-related intellectual property rights (TRIPs). See Chapter 16.

Subsidies to domestic firms also have direct implications for trade. Although a particular subsidy may not be intended to affect trade, a subsidy that reduces a firm's cost may stimulate exports. For example, U.S. lumber producers have long felt that the Canadian provincial governments sell timber rights (stumpage fees) to Canadian firms at subsidized

IN THE REAL WORLD:

EXAMPLES OF CONTROL OVER TRADE

Countries have differing degrees of interference with free trade. As examples, we summarize below some regulations imposed by Australia, Pakistan, and El Salvador. The material is drawn from the International Monetary Fund's *Annual Report on Exchange Arrangements and Exchange Restrictions 2006*. The regulations for Australia and Pakistan are those in effect on December 31, 2005; those for El Salvador are as of January 31, 2006.

AUSTRALIA

In Australia there is a tariff quota (whereby the tariff rate changes after a specified quantity of imports comes into the country) on certain cheeses and curd. For some goods, written authorization is required from relevant authorities before imports are allowed—these are products such as narcotics, firearms, some chemicals, and certain glazed ceramic ware. Most imports of agricultural goods do not face any tariffs. There is a general tariff rate of 5 percent on many manufactured goods, but the tariff on automobiles is 10 percent (but is scheduled to fall to 5 percent by 2010). Textiles, clothing, and footwear have tariff rates ranging from 0 to 17.5 percent; the upper limit will be reduced to 5 percent to 10 percent by 2010 and to 5 percent by 2015. Australia has free-trade agreements with New Zealand, Singapore, Thailand, and the United States, with the Thailand and U.S. agreements being phased in over a 10-year period that began in 2005. All goods arriving from the least-developed countries are imported free of duties and quotas.

On the export side, there are export controls on products such as uranium and related nuclear materials, and controls also exist on some exports of food and agricultural products. Licenses are needed to export unprocessed wood, including wood chips. There is also a ban on the export of merino ewes to any country other than New Zealand, and there are controls on the export of rams (except to New Zealand).

PAKISTAN

There is a "negative list" of import products banned for religious and health reasons, and imports from Israel are prohibited. There is also a "positive list" stating the goods that can be imported from India. Advance payments (i.e., payments to foreign exporters before the goods have actually arrived) of up to 50 percent of the value of the imports are permitted for certain capital goods. Imports in general face five possible tariff rates—5 percent, 10 percent, 15 percent,

20 percent, and 25 percent—although higher rates apply to beverages, liquor, motor vehicles, and vinegar. Allowances for foreign exchange for students' tuition and fees abroad are permitted without prior approval. The sending of profits out of the country by branches of foreign companies (except for banks, insurance and shipping companies, and airlines) is freely permitted.

Export licenses are not required. There is an "export development surcharge" of 0.25 percent on almost all exports. Various income tax rates are applied to earnings from exports (0.75 percent, 1 percent, 1.25 percent, and 1.5 percent). Exporters must sell their export proceeds in the Pakistan banks' foreign exchange market within three days of receipt, although up to 10 percent of the proceeds may be retained for specified purposes.

EL SALVADOR

Licenses are required for the import of ethyl alcohol, refined or raw sugarcane, corn, wheat flour, and rice. There are prohibitions on the import of "subversive material or teachings contrary to the political, social, and economic order," lightweight motor vehicles more than 8 years old, heavy motor vehicles more than 15 years old, and a few other items. Imported sugar is required to have been fortified with vitamin A. The schedule of tariff rates ranges from 0 percent on capital goods to 25 percent to 30 percent on automobiles, cigarettes, textiles, clothing, shoes, and a few other categories; to 40 percent on meat, rice, and sugar; and to 45 percent on alcoholic beverages. Virtually all goods coming from other Central American countries are free of duty. Most products arriving from Chile, the Dominican Republic, Mexico, and the United States also have no tariff applied.

All exports must be registered. Special authorization is required for the export of, among other goods, meat, coffee, machinery, diesel fuel, and wildflowers and plants. There are no export taxes, and some exporters to markets outside of Central America get reimbursed for tariffs that were paid on imported raw materials. An interesting aspect of the El Salvador situation is that "foreign exchange," the U.S. dollar, is legal tender, and dollars circulate within the country as well as the local colones (at a fixed rate of 8.75 colones = $1).

Source: International Monetary Fund, *Annual Report on Exchange Arrangements and Exchange Restrictions 2006* (Washington, DC: IMF, 2006), pp. 95, 97–99, 406–09, 890, 893–95.

IN THE REAL WORLD:

THE EFFECT OF PROTECTION INSTRUMENTS ON DOMESTIC PRICES

In an attempt to ascertain the effects of tariffs, government procurement provisions, import quotas, VERs, and other such trade restrictions, economist Scott Bradford in 2003 calculated some revealing estimates. His guiding hypothesis was that such barriers will cause differences between the world price (landed import price) of a final good and its domestic price in the importing country. This makes good economic sense—a tariff will clearly generate a difference between the two prices, with the domestic price being higher, and nontariff barriers will do the same thing.

Bradford utilized consumer price data from the Organization for Economic Cooperation and Development on 124 basic categories of final goods (103 household consumption goods and 21 capital goods) for the period 1991–1993. He adjusted the data so that they became producer price data rather than retail price data because margins for wholesale and retail trade and transportation costs differ across countries. In his view, prices at the producer level are more relevant for examining the impact of trade restrictions per se than are consumer prices.

The end result of Bradford's work was a set of protection estimates that report the ratio of the domestic price to the world price for eight different countries for 29 aggregated industries. The extent to which the ratio exceeds 1.000 is a measure of the protection afforded to the industry. We present a sample of the industry results in Table 6 as well as a measure of country averages. As is evident, the United States has the lowest protection level at 11.8 percent (ratio of domestic prices to world prices of 1.118), while Japan has the highest protection at 56.7 percent (ratio of 1.567). Belgium (1.555), the Netherlands (1.541), Germany (1.539), and the United Kingdom (1.480) are close to Japan's level, while Canada (1.270) and Australia (1.266) are closer to the U.S. level than to the other countries' levels. Looking at the table as a whole, protection varies by industry and by country, with some remarkably high rates such as 194.4 percent for leather and products in Australia, 234.9 percent for drugs and medicines in the Netherlands, 210.5 percent for drugs and medicines in the United States, and 128.9 percent for footwear in Japan. It is clear that these Bradford estimates of protection are a good bit higher than the protection that would be suggested by looking at existing nominal rates (such as were given in Table 1 earlier in this chapter) and effective rates (such as in Table 4 of this chapter).

Source: Scott Bradford, "Paying the Price: Final Goods Protection in OECD Countries," *Review of Economics and Statistics* 85, no. 1 (February 2003), pp. 24–37.

TABLE 6   Ratios of Domestic Prices to World Prices

	Australia	*Belgium*	*Canada*	*Germany*	*Japan*	*Netherlands*	*United Kingdom*	*United States*
Agriculture, fisheries, forestry	1.067	1.157	1.112	1.529	1.584	1.080	1.648	1.158
Textiles	1.111	1.218	1.163	1.101	1.478	1.140	1.237	1.051
Apparel	1.264	1.569	1.175	1.457	1.384	1.280	1.074	1.158
Leather and products	2.944	1.777	1.236	1.437	1.329	1.658	1.168	1.143
Footwear	1.657	1.823	1.415	1.328	2.289	2.239	1.027	1.111
Drugs and medicines	1.001	1.692	2.680	2.643	1.217	3.349	1.845	3.105
Chemical products	1.092	1.137	1.064	1.107	1.555	1.075	1.064	1.037
Metal products	1.430	1.622	1.328	1.770	1.977	1.837	1.602	1.165
Office and computing machinery	1.008	1.513	1.234	1.446	1.000	2.101	1.666	1.015
Motor vehicles	1.224	1.351	1.197	1.315	1.000	1.648	1.680	1.106
Country Means	**1.266**	**1.555**	**1.270**	**1.539**	**1.567**	**1.541**	**1.480**	**1.118**

Source: Scott Bradford, "Paying the Price: Final Goods Protection in OECD Countries," *Review of Economics and Statistics* 85, no. 1 (February 2003), p. 31.

and unfairly low prices, putting U.S. firms at a competitive disadvantage, and countervailing duties have been imposed. The controversy continues, however. In the case of an import-competing firm, the lowering of a firm's own costs through government subsidies can make the domestic firm more cost competitive, leading to an expansion of output and employment and a reduction in imports. A low-interest U.S. government loan to the Chrysler Corporation in the Carter administration can also be thought of as a government subsidy program that had clear trade implications. Similarly, government-provided managerial assistance, retraining programs, R&D financing, investment tax credits or special tax benefits to domestic firms that are producing traded goods can have a direct impact on relative cost competitiveness and international trade.

In addition, spillovers from government-financed defense, space, and nonmilitary expenditures can influence the international competitiveness of affected firms by their impact on relative costs or product characteristics. The effect of such government programs or policies on trade flows will be even greater when such programs or policies allow firms to experience economies of scale and be even more cost competitive.

In general, we see the presence of many forms of control that affect international trade. We have mentioned only the most widely discussed instruments; information on a particular country can be obtained only by studying that particular country. However, it is clear that *free* trade in the pure sense does not exist in the real world, and the various interferences can severely distort prices and resource allocation.

CONCEPT CHECK	1. How can government procurement provisions act like a tariff?	2. Which instrument does the use of domestic content provisions resemble, a tariff or an import quota? Why?

SUMMARY

The various instruments of trade policy have been discussed to make the point that there are many different devices for altering trade from its pattern of comparative advantage. Special attention was given to specific tariffs, *ad valorem* tariffs, export taxes and subsidies, import quotas, and voluntary export restraints. In addition, a number of the wide variety of nontariff barriers to the free-trade allocation of resources were briefly examined.

Departures from free trade are common because so many trade-distorting instruments are in place. But what are the welfare effects of these distortions? Can these policies really be good for the world as a whole, for a country, or for particular groups within a country given our conclusions on the virtues of unrestricted trade? The next chapters attempt to answer these important questions in detail.

KEY TERMS

ad valorem tariff
advance deposit requirements
domestic content provisions
effective tariff rate [or effective rate of protection (ERP)]
escalated tariff structure
export subsidy
export tax
Generalized System of Preferences (GSP)

government procurement provisions
import quota
import subsidies
most-favored-nation (MFN) treatment [or normal trade relations (NTR)]
nominal tariff rate
nontariff barriers (NTBs)

offshore assembly provisions (OAP) [or production-sharing arrangements]
preferential duties
prohibitive tariff
specific tariff
unweighted-average tariff rate
"voluntary" export restraint (VER)
weighted-average tariff rate

QUESTIONS AND PROBLEMS

1. Explain why a country's use of preferential duties is inconsistent with MFN treatment of trading partners by that country.
2. Why do you suppose that there has been such a proliferation of different instruments of protection?
3. Suppose, in a small country, that under free trade a final good F has a price of $1,000, that the prices of the *only* two inputs to good F, goods A and B, are $P_A = \$300$ and $P_B = \$500$, and that 1 unit each of A and B is used in producing 1 unit of good F. Suppose also that an *ad valorem* tariff of 20 percent is placed on good F, while imported goods A and B face *ad valorem* tariffs of 20 percent and 30 percent, respectively. Calculate the ERP for the domestic industry producing good F, and interpret the meaning of this calculated ERP.
4. Do you think that it is ever possible to obtain a good indication of the precise degree of protection accorded by a country to its import-substitute industries? Why or why not? (Remember that, in addition to tariffs, protection is also provided by various nontariff barriers.)
5. Suppose that a country announces that it is moving toward free trade by reducing its tariffs on intermediate inputs while maintaining its tariffs on final goods. What is your evaluation of the announced "free-trade" direction of the country's policy?
6. The nominal tariff rates on the 10 imports into the fictional country of Tarheelia, as well as the total import value of each good, are listed below:

	Nominal Rate	Value		Nominal Rate	Value
Good A	10%	$400	Good F	2.5%	$400
Good B	5%	$600	Good G	15%	$100
Good C	Free	$500	Good H	$0.50/unit	$400 (100 units)
Good D	30%	$300	Good I	40%	$200
Good E	2%	$200	Good J	$2.50/unit	$100 (10 units)

(a) Calculate the unweighted-average nominal tariff rate for Tarheelia.
(b) Calculate the weighted-average nominal tariff rate for Tarheelia.

7. Suppose that recent inflation has resulted in an increase in world prices and that all of the import values in Question 6 are increased by 25 percent (that is, $400 becomes $500, $600 becomes $750, and so forth). Given these new values, and assuming that the quantities of each import do not change:
(a) Calculate the unweighted-average nominal tariff rate for Tarheelia.
(b) Calculate the weighted-average nominal tariff rate for Tarheelia.
8. Why can a case be made that the difference between the domestic producer price of an import-competing good and the world price of the good is a reasonable indicator of the amount of domestic interference with free trade in the good?
9. In the early stages of the Kennedy Round of multilateral trade negotiations in the 1960s, U.S. officials claimed that the European Economic Community (EEC) had higher average tariff rates than did the United States, and EEC officials claimed that the United States had higher average tariff rates than did the EEC. It so happened that both claims were correct. How is this possible?

THE IMPACT OF TRADE POLICIES

LEARNING OBJECTIVES

- To understand how tariffs, quotas, and subsidies affect domestic markets.

- To identify the winners, losers, and net country welfare effects of protection.

- To clarify how the effects of protection differ between large and small countries.

- To grasp how protection in one market can affect other markets in the economy.

INTRODUCTION

Gainers and Losers from Steel Tariffs[1]

In March 2002 President George W. Bush, following a recommendation by the U.S. International Trade Commission, an independent federal agency that investigates trade matters, imposed a variety of tariffs on imports of steel into the United States. *Ad valorem* tariffs were imposed for three years, with some of them having a downward-sliding scale over the years, and the maximum tariff rate was 30 percent. The stated intent of the tariffs was to provide the U.S. steel industry with "breathing room" so that it could upgrade its equipment and reduce labor costs in order to become more competitive. Clearly, competitiveness had been slipping. Imports of steel products had risen from 18 percent of U.S. steel consumption in 1990 and 1991 to 31.4 percent in 1998, 27.7 percent in 1999, 28.7 percent in 2000, and 25.5 percent in 2001. The steel industry applauded the decision, but some politicians didn't think that the import restrictions went far enough. For example, Senator Richard Durbin (D–IL) likened the actions to throwing a 30-foot rope to someone who was "drowning 40 feet offshore." Foreign exporting countries protested the action. British Prime Minister Tony Blair said that the import restrictions were "unacceptable and wrong," and Germany and China in particular registered strong objections. In addition, U.S. steel consumers faced sharply rising prices because of the tariffs, and they undertook such actions as hiring public relations firms and organizing protests. One firm in Illinois saw its steel input costs rise by more than 50 percent, and it had cut production by 15 percent. The objections by consumers are understandable in view of an estimate by Gary C. Hufbauer of the Peterson Institute for International Economics that, over the previous 30 years, various U.S. import protections had cost steel consumers $120 billion. The objections became so heated that the Bush administration soon implemented a number of exceptions to the tariff impositions and later repealed the tariffs.

As with all tariffs, the steel case discussed here indicates that there are gainers and losers from actions that restrict international trade. The purpose of this chapter is to explore the effects of the tools of trade policy that were discussed in Chapter 13 on the nation that uses the tools. We thus examine the winners and losers when trade-distorting measures are undertaken and the net effects on the country.

The initial or direct impact of a trade restriction takes place in the market of the commodity that is the focus of the specific instrument. When the analysis of a policy effect is confined to only one market and the subsequent or secondary effects on related markets are ignored, a **partial equilibrium analysis** is being conducted. While the most immediate and, very likely, the strongest effects are felt in the specific market for which the instrument is designed, it is important to remember the secondary effects. Because these secondary, or indirect, effects are often important, economists try to examine the effects of economic policy in a **general equilibrium model.** In this framework, the markets for all goods are analyzed simultaneously and the total direct and indirect effects of a particular policy are determined. Because both partial and general equilibrium impacts are useful for policy analysis, we will use both approaches to examine the effects of trade policy instruments. The first two sections are devoted to the analysis of trade restrictions in a partial equilibrium context, and the third section to an analysis in a general equilibrium framework. The central thrust of the chapter is that there is generally a net social cost to the country that employs trade restrictions, regardless of the type of instrument employed or the framework of analysis.

---

[1]This summary of the steel tariff situation draws from the following sources: Robert Guy Matthews and Neil King, Jr., "Imposing Steel Tariffs, Bush Buys Some Time for Troubled Industry," *The Wall Street Journal,* March 6, 2002, pp. A1, A8; Neil King, Jr., and Geoff Winestock, "Bush's Steel-Tariff Plan Could Spark Trade Battle," *The Wall Street Journal,* March 7, 2002, pp. A3, A8; "Free Trade Over a Barrel," *The Wall Street Journal,* July 9, 2002, p. A18; Neil King, Jr., and Robert Guy Matthews, "So Far, Steel Tariffs Do Little of What President Envisioned," *The Wall Street Journal,* September 13, 2002, pp. A1, A12; "Steel Consumption and Imports," obtained from www.steelnet.org, the Web site of the Steel Manufacturers Association.

TRADE RESTRICTIONS IN A PARTIAL EQUILIBRIUM SETTING: THE SMALL-COUNTRY CASE

The Impact of an Import Tariff

First, let us examine the market in which an economically small (price-taker) country imports a product because the international price is less than the domestic equilibrium price in autarky (see Figure 1).[2] Because the country can import all that it wishes at the international price (P_{int}), the domestic price (P_0) equals the international price. If the small country imposes an import tariff, the domestic price of the foreign good increases by the amount of the tariff. With an *ad valorem* tariff, the domestic price now equals $P_{int}(1 + t) = P_1$, where P_{int} is the international price and t is the *ad valorem* tariff rate. (With a specific tariff, the domestic price equals $P_{int} + t_{specific}$.) With the increase in domestic price from P_0 to P_1, domestic quantity supplied increases from Q_{S0} to Q_{S1}, domestic quantity demanded falls from Q_{D0} to Q_{D1}, and imports decline from $(Q_{D0} - Q_{S0})$ to $(Q_{D1} - Q_{S1})$. What is the net impact of these changes? Because the adoption of this policy involves both winners and losers, we must turn to a device that allows us to evaluate the costs and the benefits accruing to all those affected.

To measure the effect of a tariff, we employ the concepts of consumer and producer surplus. The concept of **consumer surplus** refers to the area bounded by the demand curve on top and the market price below. It reflects the fact that all buyers pay the same market price regardless of what they might be willing to pay. Consequently, all those consumers who pay less (the market price) than they would be willing to pay (as represented by the height of the demand curve) are receiving a surplus [see Figure 2, panel (a)]. As market price rises, this consumer surplus falls; as price falls, consumer surplus increases.

FIGURE 1   The Single-Market Effect of a Tariff in a Small Country

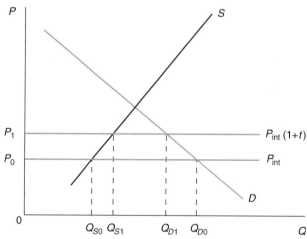

In the small country, the imposition of tariff rate t causes the domestic price to rise by amount tP_0; that is, the new price is equal to $P_{int}(1 + t)$. The increase in price from P_0 to P_1 causes the quantity demanded to fall from Q_{D0} to Q_{D1}, the domestic quantity supplied to rise from Q_{S0} to Q_{S1}, and imports to decline from $(Q_{D0} - Q_{S0})$ to $(Q_{D1} - Q_{S1})$.

---

[2]This chapter deals with the case where the domestic good and the imported good are homogeneous, or identical. For a treatment of the more complex situation where the goods are close substitutes, but not identical, see Appendix A to this chapter.

FIGURE 2   The Concepts of Consumer and Producer Surplus

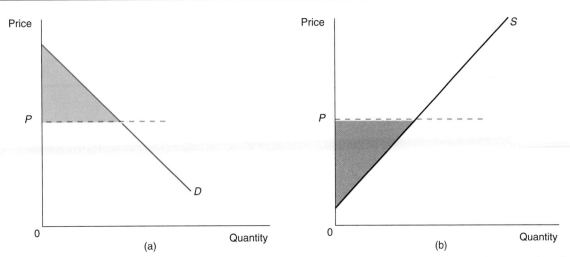

The amount of consumer surplus in a market is defined as the area bounded on top by the demand curve and on the bottom by the market price, indicated by the shaded area in panel (a). Producer surplus is shown as the shaded area in panel (b). It is equal to the area bounded on top by the market price and on the bottom by the supply curve.

In a similar vein, the concept of **producer surplus** refers to the area bounded on top by the market price and below by the supply curve. Because all producers receive the same market price, a surplus occurs for all units whose marginal cost of production (represented by the supply curve) is less than the market price received [see panel (b) of Figure 2]. Consequently, as price increases, producer surplus increases, and as market price falls, producer surplus decreases. A change in market price thus leads to a transfer of surplus between producers and consumers. With an increase in price, producer surplus is increased and consumer surplus is decreased. For a price decrease, surplus is transferred from producers to consumers. For our purposes, the *changes* in producer and consumer surplus that result from the tariff-induced price change are of interest.

Let us now isolate the effects of a tariff on a market and estimate conceptually the various effects accruing to the winners and losers. The two actors who gain from the imposition of a tariff are producers and the government. In Figure 3, a 20 percent *ad valorem* tariff imposed on the market causes the domestic price to rise from $5 to $6, increasing producer surplus by trapezoid area *ABCJ*. At the same time, the government collects the tariff ($1) on each unit of the new level of imports; total receipts are represented by rectangular area *KCFG*. The losers from this policy are consumers who have to pay a higher price and consequently reduce their quantity demanded. This leads to a loss in consumer surplus equal to trapezoid area *ABFH*. What is the net effect of this tariff? Part of the loss in consumer surplus is transferred to the government (area *KCFG*) and part to producers (area *ABCJ*). This leaves two triangular areas, *JCK* and *GFH*, which reflect losses in consumer surplus that are not transferred to anyone. These areas are the **deadweight losses** of the tariff and represent the net cost to society of distorting the domestic free-trade market price. They can be viewed as efficiency losses resulting from the higher cost of domestic production on the margin (area *JCK*) and the loss in consumer surplus accompanying the tariff (area *GFH*) on the units consumers no longer choose to purchase. Because of the higher product price resulting from the tariff, consumers switch to alternative goods that bring lower marginal satisfaction per dollar.

FIGURE 3   The Welfare Effects of a Tariff in a Small Country

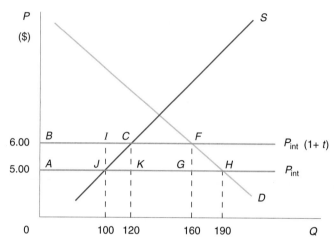

The 20 percent *ad valorem* tariff causes the domestic price to increase from $5 to $6. This causes a loss in consumer surplus equal to area *ABFH*. Because of the increase in price, producers gain a surplus equal to area *ABCJ*. The government collects revenue equal to area *KCFG*, the product of the tariff ($1.00) times the new quantity of imports (40) existing with the new tariff. Lost consumer surplus that is not transferred either to producers or to the government is equal to the sum of the areas of triangles *JCK* and *GFH*. These are referred to as the deadweight efficiency losses of the tariff and reflect the net welfare effect on the country of the imposition of the tariff.

These changes in consumer and producer surplus allow us to place a value on the impact of the tariff. For example, area *ABFH* (loss in consumer surplus with the tariff) is equal to the area of rectangle *ABFG* plus the area of triangle *GFH*. Similarly, the value of the gain in producer surplus is equal to the area of rectangle *ABIJ* plus the area of triangle *JIC* (which, because the lines are straight lines, equals the area of triangle *JCK*). The value of government revenue received is equal to the area of rectangle *KCFG*. Using the quantities and prices from Figure 3, the various effects are

$$\text{Change in consumer surplus} (-) = (\$1)(160) + (1/2)(\$1)(190 - 160)$$
$$= (-)\$175$$
$$\text{Change in producer surplus} (+) = (\$1)(100) + (1/2)(\$1)(120 - 100)$$
$$= (+)\$110$$
$$\text{Change in government revenue} (+) = (\$1)(160 - 120)$$
$$= (+)\$40$$
$$\text{Deadweight losses} = (1/2)(\$1)(120 - 100) + (1/2)(\$1)(190 - 160)$$
$$= \$25$$

There is thus a net cost to society of $25 due to the tariff ($-$$175 + $110 + $40). Care must be taken, however, in interpreting these precise values in a welfare context. Since one dollar of income may bring different utility to different individuals, it is difficult to determine the exact size of the welfare implications when real income is shifted between two parties, in this case from consumers to producers. In addition, part of the loss in consumer surplus may be offset by government use of the revenue, which affects consumers in a positive way. However, it is clear that there is a net efficiency cost to society whenever prices are distorted with a policy such as a tariff. From Chapter 6, we know that free trade benefits society because the losers could be paid compensation and some income could still be "left over." In reverse, the departure from free trade has reduced country welfare.

The Impact of an Import Quota and a Subsidy to Import-Competing Production

The preceding analysis suggests that a tariff produces a net efficiency (welfare) loss, so the question arises, What are the effects of alternative trade policies such as quotas or producer subsidies? Might they be preferred to tariffs on economic efficiency and welfare grounds?

The import quota

As explained in Chapter 13, a quota operates by limiting the physical amount of the good or service imported. This reduces the quantity available to consumers, which in turn causes the domestic price to rise. The domestic price continues to rise until the quantity supplied domestically at the higher price plus the amount of the import allowed under the quota exactly equals the reduced quantity demanded. The quota thus restricts quantity supplied, causing *price* to adjust, in contrast to a tariff, which induces a quantity adjustment by fixing a higher domestic price. The market effects in the two cases are exactly the same. Return to Figure 3. The imposition of a 20 percent tariff caused the domestic price to rise to $6 and the quantity of imports to decline from 90 units to 40 units, as domestic quantity supplied increased and domestic quantity demanded decreased. The imposition of a quota of 40 units would have produced the very same result! With imports restricted to 40 units, the domestic price will rise and continue to rise until the combination of domestic quantity supplied and the quota-restricted imports equals quantity demanded. Thus, every quota has an **equivalent tariff** that produces the same market result, just as every tariff has an **equivalent quota.**[3]

While the market effects of tariffs and quotas are identical, the welfare implications are not. Since the price and quantity adjustments are the same under both instruments, the changes in producer surplus, consumer surplus, and the consequent deadweight efficiency losses are also the same. The government revenue effect is, however, not the same. With a tariff, the government receives revenue equal to the amount of the tariff per unit times the quantity of imports. No such tax is collected under a quota. In effect, the difference between the international price and the domestic price of the import good is an economic **quota rent,** which may accrue to the domestic importer/retailer, the foreign supplier/foreign government, or the home government or may be distributed among the three. Domestic importers/retailers will receive the rent if foreign suppliers do not organize to raise the export price or if the home government does not require that everyone importing the good buy a license from the government in order to do so. Foreign suppliers receive the quota rent if they behave in a noncompetitive, monopolistic manner and force up the price they charge the importing country's buyers. However, it is also possible that the foreign government might step in and devise a scheme for allocating the supply of exports whereby it receives the quota rent; for example, the foreign government sells export licenses at a price equal to the difference between the international price and the domestic price in the quota-imposing country. If either foreign suppliers or the foreign government captures the rent, then the welfare loss to the home country is greater than it is with an equivalent home country tariff, since the previous tariff revenue now accrues to the foreign country.

The mystery of what happens to the quota rent can be resolved to the quota-imposing government's benefit if it sells licenses to those who wish to import the good at a price

---

[3]This is not true over time after any initial equivalence. For example, if home consumer demand rises, no larger quantity of imports can come into the country with the quota (assuming no change in the size of the quota), but a tariff permits more imports as the demand curve shifts out. Also, any price rise caused by an increase in demand is greater with the fixed quota than with the tariff.

equal to the difference between the international price and the higher (quota-distorted) domestic price. This generates government revenue equal to that achieved with the equivalent tariff. One way this might be accomplished is to have a competitive auction of import licenses. Potential importers should be willing to pay up to the difference between the international price and the expected domestic price to have the right to import. However, this kind of system, often called an **auction quota system,** will incur administrative costs that absorb productive resources and become additional deadweight losses. Again, the country welfare cost of the quota will likely exceed the welfare cost of the equivalent tariff, because these administrative costs are likely to be greater than those of the tariff.

Subsidy to an import-competing industry

The static impact of a tariff and that of a quota on a market and welfare are essentially the same, except for the distribution of the quota rent. This conclusion does not hold for government subsidies paid to the import-competing domestic supplier. If the intent of the tariff or quota is to provide an incentive to increase domestic production and sales in the domestic market, then an equivalent domestic production result could be achieved by paying a sufficient per-unit subsidy to domestic producers, who are thereby induced to supply the same quantity at international prices that they were willing to provide at the higher tariff inclusive domestic price (see Figure 4). In effect, the subsidy shifts the domestic supply curve down vertically (in a parallel fashion) until it intersects the international price line at the same quantity that would occur were the tariff (or equivalent quota) in effect.

With an **equivalent subsidy,** producers are equally as well off as when the tariff was in place. The subsidy not only provides them with an increase in producer surplus equal to

FIGURE 4   The Single-Market Effects of a Subsidy to Home Producers

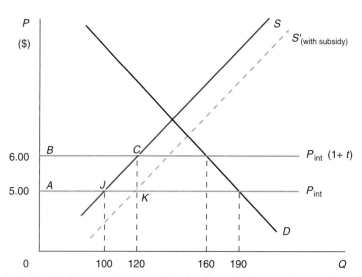

A government subsidy of $1 for every unit produced has the effect of shifting supply curve S down vertically by $1 at each quantity to S'. Producers will now produce 120 units instead of 100 units at the international price of $5. The combination of the $5 international price and the $1 subsidy leaves the producers in a position equivalent to that with the imposition of a 20 percent tariff. The welfare effects, however, are different. Because consumers continue to pay the international price, there is no loss in consumer surplus in this market. Producers receive a transfer of area $ABCK$ from the government, of which $ABCJ$ represents a gain in producer surplus and JCK represents a deadweight efficiency loss. The taxpayer cost of the subsidy is equal to the amount of the subsidy transfer, that is, $ABCK$.

that under the tariff or quota but also compensates them for the higher production cost on the additional production. The cost to the government (area *ABCK*) is equal to the quantity produced domestically (120 units) times the amount of the subsidy ($1) or $120. Note, however, that there is no change in the domestic market price; it remains equal to the international price in the case of a domestic producer subsidy. There is no loss in consumer surplus and no deadweight loss for consumers. The increased domestic production at a resource cost that exceeds international price on the margin leads, however, to a production-efficiency loss. This is equal to area *JCK* and is the amount by which the subsidy cost (*ABCK*) exceeds the increase in producer surplus (*ABCJ*). It can be viewed as the cost of moving from a lower-cost foreign supply to a higher-cost domestic supply on the margin.

From a welfare standpoint, the production subsidy certainly is more attractive than a tariff or quota. If the consumers are also the taxpayers, the cost of the subsidy ($120) is less than the loss in consumer surplus ($175) that results from either a tariff or a quota. To the extent that the consumers of the specific product are not the only taxpayers, then a subsidy is more equitable. From a cost-benefit perspective, the cost of protection of a domestic industry should be borne by those who receive the benefits of its larger output. If the protection of the industry is judged desirable for the public at large (for example, because the industry is deemed to be valuable for national security), then the burden of the policy should be borne by the public at large and not by the subset of the public that consumes this product.

Regardless of these last considerations, the subsidy to domestic import-competing producers has a lower welfare cost to the country as a whole than does the import tariff. In our numerical example, the net loss to society from the use of the subsidy is only $10 (triangle *JCK*) rather than the $25 associated with the tariff (triangle *JCK* plus triangle *GFH* in Figure 3). It is $10 because the increase in producer surplus of $110 (area *ABCJ* in Figure 4) is $10 less than the subsidy cost of $120 (area *ABCK* in Figure 4). Thus, in the steel example with which we began this chapter, the United States would have imposed upon itself a lower welfare cost if the domestic steel industry were further subsidized (which, in fact, it has been already by a mixture of federal as well as state and local government policies)[4] rather than protected by the import tariffs.

In practical terms, the welfare effects of tariffs and other import restrictions can be substantial. Two economists from the Peterson Institute for International Economics, a Washington, DC, "think tank," estimated (for 1990) the impact on U.S. consumers of tariff and quota restrictions on a number of products.[5] Selected results for the annual loss of U.S. consumer surplus were as follows: benzenoid chemicals, $309 million; frozen concentrated orange juice, $281 million; softwood lumber, $459 million; dairy products, $1.2 billion; sugar, $1.4 billion; apparel, $21.2 billion; and textiles, $3.3 billion. Taking into account offsetting producer surplus and tariff revenue gains, the "net" welfare losses from the trade restrictions were smaller—"only" $10 billion in benzenoid chemicals, $35 million in frozen concentrated orange juice, $12 million in softwood lumber, $104 million in dairy products, $581 million in sugar, $7.7 billion in apparel, and $894 million in textiles. Nevertheless, welfare gains could clearly be realized by reducing import barriers, and the barriers obviously have substantial distributional transfers from consumers to domestic producers. Another set of findings was generated in 1999 by Howard Wall of the Federal Reserve Bank of St. Louis.[6]

---

[4]See Robert Guy Matthews, "U.S. Steel Industry Itself Gets Billions in Public Subsidies, Study Concludes," *The Wall Street Journal,* November 29, 1999, p. B12.

[5]Gary Clyde Hufbauer and Kimberly Ann Elliott, *Measuring the Costs of Protection in the United States* (Washington, DC: Institute for International Economics, 1994), pp. 8–9.

[6]Howard J. Wall, "Using the Gravity Model to Estimate the Costs of Protection," Federal Reserve Bank of St. Louis *Review,* January/February 1999, pp. 33–40.

FIGURE 5   The Effect of an Export Tax

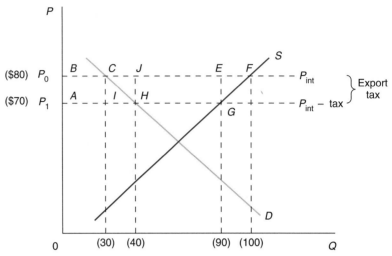

The imposition of an export tax (a $10 per-unit tax in this example) reduces the price received for each unit of export by the amount of the tax. This causes the domestic price to fall from P_0 to P_1 as domestic producers expand sales in the home market to avoid paying the export duty. The fall in the domestic price leads to a loss in producer surplus equal to area *ABFG*, an increase in consumer surplus of *ABCH*, an increase in government revenue of *HJEG*, and deadweight losses to the country of *CJH* and *GEF*.

He estimated that U.S. imports from non–North American Free Trade Agreement (NAFTA) countries (i.e., from countries other than Canada and Mexico) were 15.4 percent smaller than would otherwise have been the case because of U.S. tariffs and other import restrictions. The restriction had an associated net welfare loss for the United States of 1.43 percent of U.S. gross domestic product. In addition, U.S. exports to non–NAFTA countries were 26.2 percent less than they would have been without foreign import restrictions on U.S. goods. (He was unable to estimate the welfare impact of these restrictions.) Hence, existing trade restrictions definitely have nonnegligible impacts.

CONCEPT CHECK	**1.** How does a tariff affect consumer surplus? Producer surplus?	**3.** How do the effects of a tariff differ from those of a quota? Of a production subsidy?
	2. Who gains from a tariff? Who loses? What are the net effects for society?	

The Impact of Export Policies

The impact of an export tax

We examine here the impact of three types of export policies—an export tax, export quota, and export subsidy—on the well-being of the country that is exporting the good. The imposition of an export tax, a levy on goods exported, leads to a *decrease* in the domestic price as producers seek to expand domestic sales to avoid paying the tax on exports. The domestic price (P_0) falls until it equals the international price (P_{int}) minus the amount of the tax (see Figure 5). (Note that in the export situation the given international price is *above* the intersection of the home demand and supply curves.) When this occurs, gains and losses can again be measured using producer and consumer surplus.

As domestic price falls and quantity supplied contracts, there is a reduction in producer surplus equal to the area of trapezoid *ABFG*. Part of this loss is transferred to domestic consumers through the lower price, producing an increase in consumer surplus equal to area *ABCH*. In addition, the government acquires tax revenue equal to area *HJEG*. Finally, areas *CJH* and *GEF* reflect deadweight efficiency losses that result from the price distortion. These areas represent losses in producer surplus that are not transferred to anyone in the economy.

After summing up the effects of the export tax policy on the winners and the losers, the net effect on the economy is negative. It should be emphasized that the domestic supply and demand responses lead to a smaller level of exports (distance *HG*) after tax than before the tax (distance *CF*). Governments will thus overestimate the export tax revenue that will be received if they form their revenue expectation without fully accounting for the reduction in export quantity. The less elastic domestic supply and demand are, the smaller the impact of the tax on the quantity of exports and the greater the revenue earned by the government. The less elastic producer and consumer responses are, the smaller the deadweight efficiency losses. With the numbers indicated in the parentheses in the graph, producer surplus would thus fall by [($80 − $70)(90 − 0) + (1/2)($80 − $70)(100 − 90)] = $900 + $50 = $950; consumer surplus would rise by [($80 − $70)(30 − 0) + (1/2)($80 − $70)(40 − 30)] = $300 + $50 = $350; tax revenue would rise by ($80 − $70)(90 − 40) = $500; and the net result is (−)$950 + $350 + $500 = (−)$100. This $100 loss is equal to triangle *CJH* ($50) plus triangle *GEF* ($50).

The impact of an export quota

If an export quota instead of an export tax is employed, the effects are similar to those of the export tax. However, the welfare impact of the two instruments may differ because, as with the import quota, no government revenue is necessarily collected. The recipient of the quota rent is unclear. The government in the exporting country can acquire the revenue by auctioning off export quotas. In a competitive market, exporters should be willing to pay up to the difference in price in the importing and exporting countries for the privilege to export (assuming no transaction costs). If this occurs, the revenue from the auction quota system will be equivalent to the revenue from an export tax. If this does not occur, exporters can organize and act like a single seller to acquire the quota rent by charging the importing country the market-clearing price. If foreign importing firms are organized, they have the potential to acquire the quota rent by buying the product at the market-clearing price in the exporting country and selling it at the higher market-clearing price at home. In our numerical example in Figure 5, the area *HJEG* ($500) would then be an additional loss to the exporting country.

The effects of an export subsidy

The final instrument considered is the export subsidy. Its use and the interest that it has sparked make it important to examine its effects. In Chapter 13, we noted that an export subsidy is in effect a negative export tax. Consequently, the effects of this instrument can be analyzed in a manner similar to that used with the export tax.

In a small country, the imposition of the subsidy directly raises the price received by the producer for exported units of the product. For every unit exported, the producer receives the international price *plus* the subsidy. Producers are thus given the incentive to shift sales from the domestic to foreign markets to receive the government subsidy. The end result is that the export subsidy reduces the quantity sold in the domestic market, increases the price in the domestic market to where it equals the international price plus the subsidy, and increases the quantity supplied by producers as they respond to the higher price, leading finally to increased exports.

FIGURE 6   The Effects of an Export Subsidy

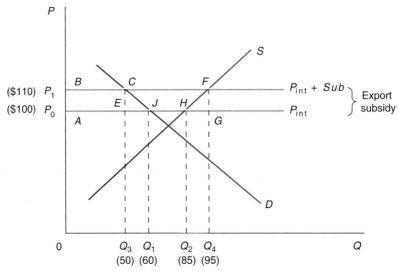

The availability of the export subsidy leads to an increase in the domestic price from P_0 to P_1. With the increase in the domestic price, there is a loss in consumer surplus of *ABCJ*, a gain in producer surplus of *ABFH*, and deadweight losses to society of *ECJ* and *HFG*. The taxpayer cost of the subsidy program is *ECFG*. The subsidy expands production from Q_2 to Q_4 and increases exports from distance Q_1Q_2 to distance Q_3Q_4.

These demand and supply responses are evident in the partial equilibrium analysis for a small country (see Figure 6). The imposition of the export subsidy raises the domestic price, which was equal to $P_0 = P_{int}$ ($100) without the subsidy, to $P_1 = P_{int} + Sub$ ($100 + $10 = $110). The increase in price causes domestic quantity demanded to fall from Q_1 (60 units) to Q_3 (50 units), the quantity supplied to rise from Q_2 (85 units) to Q_4 (95 units), and the quantity of exports to increase from distance Q_1Q_2 (25 units) to distance Q_3Q_4 (45 units). These market adjustments to the export subsidy lead to a fall in domestic consumer surplus equal to area *ABCJ* and an increase in domestic producer surplus equal to area *ABFH*. Assuming that taxes pay for the subsidy program, the taxpayer cost of the subsidy program equals the amount of the per-unit subsidy times the new quantity of exports, area *ECFG*. Finally, the net social cost of the export subsidy is equal to the two deadweight triangles, *ECJ* and *HFG*. Area *ECJ* represents part of the transfer to producers, which is paid for twice—once by a loss in consumer surplus and once by the cost of the subsidy—and recaptured only once (by home producers). It can be thought of as a deadweight consumer/taxpayer loss. Triangle *HFG* is the usual production-efficiency loss that results from the less efficient domestic production shown by the movement from Q_2 to Q_4.[7] Using the numbers in parentheses in Figure 6, consumer surplus falls by [($110 − $100)(50 − 0) + (1/2)($110 − $100)(60 − 50)] = $500 + $50 = $550; producer surplus rises by [($110 − $100)(85 − 0) + (1/2)($110 − $100)(95 − 85)] = $850 + $50 = $900; the cost of the subsidy is ($110 − $100)(95 − 50) = $450; and the net social cost is −$550 + $900 − $450 = −$100. This loss is equal to the sum of triangles *ECJ* ($50) and *HFG* ($50).

[7]It is important to note that this analysis assumes that domestic consumers cannot turn to the world market to import the good at $P_0 = P_{int}$. If they could, the domestic price would not rise above P_0 and the only loss to the country would be the deadweight loss of area *HFG*.

CONCEPT CHECK   1. In the case of an export quota, why is the dis-   2. How does an export tax differ from an export
                     position of the quota rent important for wel-   subsidy? Which policy would domestic con-
                     fare analysis?   sumers prefer? Why?

TRADE RESTRICTIONS IN A PARTIAL EQUILIBRIUM SETTING: THE LARGE-COUNTRY CASE

Framework for Analysis

To this point, we have been using the already familiar demand and supply curves for a good in a small country whose trade policies have no impact on the world price. We now turn to an examination of the effects of trade policies in the large-country setting, where an impact on world price does occur.

To facilitate this discussion, we need to introduce a special demand curve and a special supply curve: (*a*) the **demand for imports schedule,** as distinct from the total demand curve for a good, and (*b*) the **supply of exports schedule,** as distinct from the total supply curve of a good. The demand for imports schedule applies to a particular segment of the entire market for a good that is produced and consumed at home as well as imported, and the supply of exports applies to a particular segment of the entire market for a good that is produced and consumed at home as well as exported. The impact of trade policy hits directly on these particular market segments, which in turn have an impact on the entire market.

Demand for imports schedule

Figure 7, panel (a), portrays the demand and supply for a homogeneous good within a particular country. The good might be shirts and the country the United States. Demand curve D_h shows the quantity of shirts (whether made at home or abroad) that home consumers

FIGURE 7   **The Derivation of a Country's Demand for Imports Schedule of a Good**

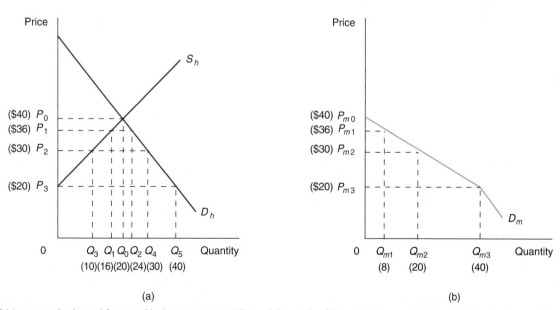

Panel (a) portrays the demand for a good by home consumers (D_h) and the supply of the good by home producers (S_h). At price P_0, quantity demanded (Q_0) by consumers equals quantity supplied by home producers, so the quantity of imports demanded [shown in panel (b)] at P_{m0} ($=P_0$) is zero. At a lower price, P_2, home consumers demand Q_4 units and home producers supply only Q_3 units, so the quantity demanded of imports (excess demand) is ($Q_4 - Q_3$). This amount is shown as Q_{m2} in panel (b) at the price P_{m2} ($=P_2$). By plotting the excess of D_h over S_h at all other prices below P_0, the country's demand for imports schedule, D_m, is generated.

are willing to purchase at each particular price during a time period. Supply curve S_h shows the various quantities that *domestic* producers are willing to deliver to the market during this period at various possible prices. Remember that imports are simply home demand minus home supply. Thus, if the price of shirts is P_0 ($40), consumers and domestic producers are both satisfied with quantity Q_0 (20 units), so there is no need for imports. In deriving the demand for *imports* schedule in panel (b), the quantity of imports demanded at price $P_0 (=P_{m0})$ is thus zero. However, suppose that the price in the United States is P_1 ($36). At this price, home consumers want to purchase quantity Q_2 (24) in panel (a), but home producers are only willing to supply quantity Q_1 (16) at this lower and less profitable price. Thus, there is excess demand of $(Q_2 - Q_1)$ over home supply, which yields a demand for imports of Q_{m1} $(=Q_2 - Q_1 = 24 - 16 = 8)$, as plotted in panel (b) at price P_{m1} $(=P_1 = \$36)$. Similarly, at price P_2 ($30), there is excess home demand of $(Q_4 - Q_3 = 30 - 10)$, which translates into a demand for imports of Q_{m2} ($20) at price P_{m2} ($30). Finally, note that at price P_3 ($20) in panel (a), all domestic production ceases. The quantity demanded of Q_5 (40) is all excess demand, and Q_5 equals Q_{m3} in panel (b). Note that the resulting D_m schedule is flatter than the D_h schedule. This means that the demand for imports schedule generally will be more elastic than the demand for the good itself, although it should be remembered that slope and elasticity are not identical terms. The greater elasticity reflects the response of both domestic supply and demand to the change in price. Finally, observe that D_m is identical to D_h at and below the price at which domestic production ceases.

Supply of exports schedule

The simple rule to remember when deriving the supply of exports schedule for a country is that exports are equal to home production *minus* home consumption. The technique for obtaining the home supply of exports schedule for any good is analogous to that of the demand for imports schedule. Thus, schedule S_h in Figure 8, panel (a), shows the quantity of the good supplied by domestic producers at various market prices, while schedule D_h shows the quantities of the good home consumers are willing to buy at those prices. At $P_0 (=P_{x0} = \$40)$, there is no export supply since consumers are willing to purchase all of the good produced by domestic firms. However, at higher price P_1 ($46), there is excess supply at home, because the higher price has caused home consumers to purchase smaller quantities and home producers to offer more in the market. The excess supply at price P_1 is $(Q_2 - Q_1 = 26 - 14)$, which translates in panel (b) into quantity Q_{x1} (12) at price P_{x1} ($46). At the next-higher price, P_2 ($52), there is a larger excess supply $(Q_4 - Q_3 = 32 - 8)$; this amount is supplied to the world market as exports Q_{x2} (24) because home consumers are not purchasing that excess supply. Finally, all home production is supplied as exports at P_3 ($60). Export supply schedule S_x is identical to home supply schedule S_h at and above P_3. Note that S_x is flatter or more elastic than S_h up to price P_{x3} (which equals price P_3), because an increase in price affects the quantity of exports supplied both through increased quantity supplied domestically and decreased quantity demanded. With these schedules now in hand, we can examine various trade policy instruments.

The Impact of an Import Tariff

Having explained how the import demand curve and export supply curve for large trading partners are obtained, we can now use these curves to demonstrate market equilibrium between two large countries. Market equilibrium is indicated by the international price where home import demand equals foreign export supply, that is, $D_m = S_{fx}$ in panel (a) of Figure 9. Equilibrium quantity (exports = imports) is measured on the horizontal axis. Given this large-country equilibrium, let us examine how an import tariff affects the market.

In Chapter 13, you learned that tariffs can be specific or *ad valorem* in nature. The imposition of a specific duty is illustrated in Figure 9(b) and the *ad valorem* tariff in Figure 9(c).

FIGURE 8   The Derivation of a Country's Supply of Exports Schedule of a Good

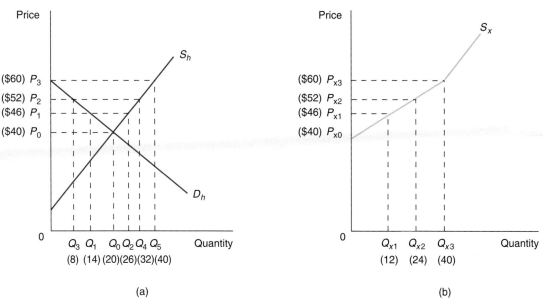

(a)   (b)

Panel (a) shows the demand for a good by home consumers (D_h) and the supply of the good by home producers (S_h). At price P_0, the quantity supplied by home producers (Q_0) equals the quantity demanded by home consumers, so the quantity of exports supplied [shown in panel (b)] at price P_{x0} (=P_0) is zero. At a higher price, P_2 for example, home producers supply Q_4 units but home consumers demand only Q_3 units, so the quantity supplied of exports (excess supply) is ($Q_4 - Q_3$). This amount is shown as Q_{x2} in panel (b) at price P_{x2} (=P_2). By plotting the excess of S_h over D_h at all other prices above P_0, the country's supply of exports schedule, S_x, is generated.

FIGURE 9   Large-Country Market Equilibrium and the Imposition of a Specific and an *Ad Valorem* Tariff

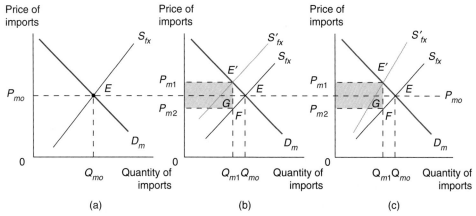

(a)   (b)   (c)

In all three panels, the free-trade equilibrium is at E—the intersection of the home demand for imports schedule (D_m) and the supply of foreign exports schedule (S_{fx}). With the imposition of a specific tariff in panel (b), S_{fx} shifts up vertically by the amount of the specific tariff per unit of the imported good. S'_{fx} is thus above and parallel to S_{fx}. The imposition of the *ad valorem* tariff in panel (c) causes S_{fx} also to shift up to S'_{fx}. However, S'_{fx} is not parallel to S_{fx} in panel (c) since, for each given quantity, the price of imports on S_{fx} is raised by a constant percentage of that price rather than by a constant dollar amount. Thus, S'_{fx} "pulls away" from S_{fx} at the higher prices and quantities. The new equilibrium is at E' in both panels (b) and (c). Consumers pay higher price P_{m1} per unit rather than P_{m0}, and foreign suppliers receive lower price P_{m2} per unit rather than P_{m0}. The tariff revenue collected is indicated by the shaded areas.

Curve D_m in each panel is the demand for imports schedule for this good, and the S_{fx} schedule is the supply schedule of foreign exports to this country. Prior to the imposition of the tariff, the equilibrium price is located at the intersection of these curves, at price P_{m0}, and the equilibrium quantity sold is quantity Q_{m0}. When the specific tariff is imposed (for example, \$1 per unit of the good imported) in panel (b), the relevant supply of exports curve becomes S'_{fx} instead of S_{fx}, as the schedule shifts up vertically at each quantity by \$1 per unit. (Each quantity of exports supplied has a price that is \$1 higher on S'_{fx} than on S_{fx}.) Thus, the new supply of foreign exports schedule is parallel to the old schedule but above it at each quantity by the amount of the tax. As a consequence of the import tax, the market equilibrium is E' rather than E. Consumers are now paying the higher price, P_{m1}, and purchasing the smaller quantity, Q_{m1}. The foreign supplier of the good receives a lower price per unit—P_{m2} rather than P_{m0}. The lower price is received by the foreign firm because, with the tax in place, there is a smaller quantity purchased from the foreign firm and the price is bid down in this large-country setting, where the importing country can affect world prices by imposing the tariff. Finally, the difference between the price paid by consumers, P_{m1}, and the price received by the foreign producers, P_{m2}—or the distance $(P_{m1} - P_{m2})$—represents the tariff per unit of the goods imported.

In this example, the total tariff revenue collected by the importing country's government is represented by shaded area $P_{m2}P_{m1}E'F$. Part of this tariff revenue is paid economically by domestic consumers, area $P_{m0}P_{m1}E'G$, in that a higher price is paid over the free-trade price for each unit of the good imported. The other part of the tariff revenue is paid economically by the foreign exporter, area $P_{m2}P_{m0}GF$, in that the exporter receives a lower price than that under free trade for each unit exported. The extent to which the tariff is paid by one party or the other, the **incidence of the tariff,** depends importantly on the slope of the S_{fx} schedule. If this supply of exports schedule were flatter or more elastic, more of the tax burden would be borne by the domestic consumer and less by the foreign producer. In the extreme case where the home (importing) country is a small country, S_{fx} would be represented by a *horizontal* line reflecting the given world price. S'_{fx} would be parallel to and above S_{fx} by the vertical amount of the tariff per unit of the import. In this case, the tariff burden would be borne entirely by home consumers, since the world price (the price received by exporters) would not change with the imposition of the tariff. It can also be noted that the division of the tariff between the two parties depends on the slope of the D_m schedule. The flatter (or more elastic) the schedule, the more the tariff is paid by the foreign producer rather than by the home consumer.

The imposition of an *ad valorem* tariff is shown in Figure 9(c). The only difference in construction from the specific tariff in Figure 9(b) is that the new supply curve, S'_{fx}, is no longer parallel to the free-trade supply curve S_{fx}. The new curve "pulls away" from the old curve at the higher prices because a constant percentage of a higher price is a larger absolute amount, and thus the new curve is plotted at greater distances above the old curve as we go up the vertical axis. In all other respects, the qualitative impacts in Figure 9, panel (c), are the same as in panel (b)—the new price paid by consumers is P_{m1}, the new price received by foreign producers is P_{m2}, the new quantity purchased in equilibrium is Q_{m1}, and the tariff revenue collected is area $P_{m2}P_{m1}E'F$.

In the small country, the entire negative welfare impact of the tariff is borne by consumers in the imposing-country market. In the large country, however, the impact of the tariff can be potentially shifted, at least in part, to the exporting country through a reduction in international price. The reduction in international price means of course that the domestic price inclusive of the tariff in the imposing (large) country is less than it would be if the international price had remained the same, the loss in consumer surplus is less, and the net cost of protection is less than that for a small country.

FIGURE 10   The Effects of a Tariff in a Single Market in the Large-Country Setting

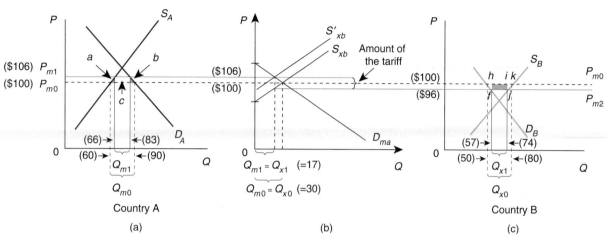

Country A   Country B

(a)   (b)   (c)

The initial international equilibrium price is determined by the demand for imports and the supply of exports at P_{m0} [panel (b)]. The imposition of a specific tariff by the importing country A shifts the export supply curve from S_{xb} to parallel curve S'_{xb}. The tariff reduces A's purchases of the import good, leading to a reduction in world demand and in the export price from country B. The world price falls until the amount of exports supplied by country B at the new price equals the amount of imports demanded by country A at the international price *plus* the tariff, P_{m1}. The reduction in the world price means that the price in country A does not rise by the full amount of the tariff. As a result, the deadweight losses in country A, areas *a* and *b*, are less than they would be in a small country where the world price remains unchanged when a tariff is imposed. Further, the fall in the world price due to the imposition of the tariff means that the exporting country is paying part of the tariff, shown by area *fhij* in country B. Country A can benefit from the imposition of the tariff if area *fhij* is larger than the sum of the deadweight losses ($a + b$).

To see why the welfare cost is less, let us turn to a two-country framework similar to that used with transportation costs in a large-country setting in Chapter 8 (page 142). Figure 10 depicts this situation, in which two large countries are engaged in trade. Because country A [panel (a)] is the higher-cost producer of this commodity in autarky, it has an incentive to import the product, resulting in the import demand curve D_{ma} in panel (b). Country B [panel (c)] is the low-cost producer and has an incentive to export the product, resulting in the supply of exports curve S_{xb} in panel (b). When they trade, countries A and B will arrive at an equilibrium international price, P_{m0} (=$100 in our numerical example), which causes the desired quantity of imports into country A to be equal to the desired quantity of exports from country B ($Q_{m0} = Q_{x0} = 30$ units).

If country A now imposes a specific tariff of $10 on this product [a shift of S_{xb} to S'_{xb} in panel (b)], the effect will be a rise in the price of the good above P_{m0} by the amount of the tariff. When this happens, there will be an increase in the quantity supplied domestically by A's producers, a decrease in the quantity demanded in country A, and a decrease in desired imports. As the quantity of imports desired by country A begins to fall, country B finds itself with an excess supply at P_{m0} and begins to lower its domestic price. The new price in B leads to an increase in domestic quantity demanded, a decrease in quantity supplied, and a decrease in available exports. The reduction in country B's export price means that the domestic tariff-inclusive price in country A begins to decline, stimulating greater purchases of imports. Ultimately, price will adjust concomitantly in both markets until the quantity of desired imports, Q_{m1} (17 units), in country A at the tariff-inclusive price, P_{m1} ($106), is equal to the desired level of exports of country B, Q_{x1} (17 units), at its export (non-tariff-inclusive) price, P_{m2} ($96). Prices in the two markets will always differ by the amount of the tariff (assuming no transportation costs).

We can now analyze the welfare implications of the tariff.[8] To the extent that the domestic price rises in tariff-imposing country A, there will be a loss in consumer surplus, a gain in producer surplus, a gain in government revenue, and the usual deadweight efficiency losses (triangles a and b in Figure 10). The deadweight losses will be less than they would have been if the domestic price in country A had risen by the full amount of the tariff, as it did in the small-country case. Notice also that the tariff revenue is now represented not by area c alone but by area c—paid by home consumers through a higher domestic price—plus area *fhij* in panel (c)—paid by the exporting country's producers, who receive a lower price for the good. In addition, the net effect of the tariff on country A's welfare depends on the relative size of triangles $a + b$ (deadweight losses) and rectangle *fhij* (a gain to A transferred from B because of the lower export price). If losses $(a + b)$ are greater than the gain transferred from country B (area *fhij*), country A loses from the tariff. However, if losses $(a + b)$ are smaller than the gain from area *fhij,* large country A *can actually gain* from the imposition of the tariff. This is more likely to occur when domestic demand and supply are more elastic in country A (the importing country) and demand and supply are less elastic in the exporting country. Similarly, a large country is less able to shift the cost of the tariff to the exporting country when domestic demand and supply are less elastic and the exporting country's demand and supply are more elastic.

In our numerical example in Figure 10, the deadweight loss area a has a value of 0.5($106 − $100)(66 − 60) = (1/2)($6)(6) = $18, and the deadweight loss area b has a value of 0.5($106 − $100)(90 − 83) = (1/2)($6)(7) = $21. The total deadweight loss is thus $18 + $21 = $39. However, area *fhij* of the tariff revenue (total tariff revenue equals area c plus area *fhij*) is acquired as a transfer from the exporting country B. This area *fhij* has a value of ($100 − $96)(74 − 57) = ($4)(17) = $68. Hence, the imposition of the tariff by large country A, with these particular numbers, has led to a net *gain* in welfare for A by the amount of $68 (the transfer from country B) − $39 (the deadweight losses) = $29. Another way to look at this result is through observing, in country A, the changes in consumer surplus, producer surplus, and tariff revenue. The change in consumer surplus in A because of the imposition of the tariff is −[($106 − $100)(83 − 0) + (1/2)($106 − $100)(90 − 83)] = −[$498 + $21] = −$519. The gain in producer surplus in country A is [($106 − $100)(60 − 0) + (1/2)($106 − $100)(66 − 60)] = $360 + $18 = $378. Finally, the total tariff revenue is area c [=($106 − $100)(83 − 66)] plus area *fhij* [=($100 − $96)(74 − 57)], or [$102 + $68] = $170 (that is, the specific tariff of $10 per unit multiplied by the 17 units imported). Hence, the sum of the change in consumer surplus, the change in producer surplus, and the tariff revenue, is −$519 + $378 + $170 = +$29 (a gain). Keep in mind, though, that this gain is achieved at the expense of the trading partner country B, and subsequently there might well be retaliatory tariffs placed by B on products coming into B from country A. Also, the numbers easily could have been set up so that there was a *loss* for country A rather than a gain—a gain is by no means a certainty.

CONCEPT CHECK

1. Why is a country's demand curve for imports of a good more elastic (or flatter) than the consumers' total demand curve for the good?
2. Why is a country's supply curve of exports of a good more elastic (or flatter) than the supply curve of the home producers of the good?
3. Is it ever possible for a large country to gain net welfare by the imposition of a tariff? Explain.

4. Other things being equal, why does greater elasticity in the supply of foreign exports of a good mean that the importing country's consumers of the good are more likely than the foreign suppliers of the good to bear the burden of an import tariff?

---

[8]For an analysis of the welfare effects of the tariff and other policy instruments that uses only the import demand and export supply curves, see Appendix B to this chapter.

The Impact of an Import Quota

Just as in the small-country situation, an import quota in a large-country situation leads to price adjustments because of the reduced quantity of imports purchased by the importing country. Because the importing country is a large country, however, it has a noticeable effect on world demand for the product and hence reduces world price. The impact of the quota on the large importing country and the large exporting country (or the rest of the world) is illustrated in Figure 11. Graphically, the impact of the quota looks exactly like the impact of the tariff discussed in the previous section. The imposition of the import-reducing quota leads to an increase in price in the importing country from P_{m0} to P_{m1} and to a decrease in price in the exporting country from P_{m0} to P_{m2}. These are the prices at which the level of desired exports by country B is equal to the import quota in country A. The impact of an "equivalent" quota on price and the level of trade is thus the same as the impact of the tariff discussed previously.

Turning to the welfare effects, there is a major difference between the tariff and the quota because no tariff revenue is collected with a quota. Thus, the question of what happens to the "quota rent" must be addressed before a welfare analysis can be completed. As in the small-country case, the quota rent can be captured (1) by the home government through the auctioning of import licenses, (2) by domestic importers/retailers that buy at the new international price (P_{m2}) and sell at the home price (P_{m1}), (3) by organized foreign producers that sell at the new price in the importing country (P_{m1}), (4) by exporting-country governments that auction off export licenses to their firms, or (5) by any combination of the first four. In a situation where the entire quota rent ends up in the importing country (the first two cases listed), the welfare impact is exactly the same as under the import tariff. The importing country incurs deadweight losses of triangles a and b and a positive transfer from abroad of rectangle *fhij* due to the reduced world price of the imports. The net effect

FIGURE 11   **The Effects of an Import Quota in a Single Market in the Large-Country Setting**

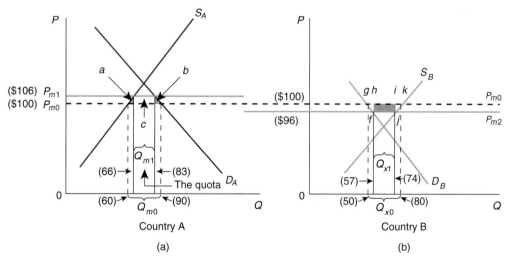

The imposition of an import quota, Q_{m1} (17 units), by large country A reduces its purchases of the import good. This leads to a fall in world demand for the good and to a fall in the export price in country B. The world price declines until the amount of exports supplied from B, Q_{x1}, is equal to the quota amount, Q_{m1}. If country A is able to keep the quota rent, then its welfare improves if area *fhij* is greater than the sum of areas a and b; if country A is unable to obtain any of the quota rent, its welfare declines by areas a, b, and c. Exporting country B has deadweight losses from A's quota of area *ghf* and area *ikj;* country B will also lose area *fhij* if country A obtains the quota rent. If country B itself is able to get the quota rent, the net welfare effect of the quota on B is positive if area c is greater than the sum of areas *ghf* and *ikj*.

of the quota is thus the sum of these two effects and can be positive or negative depending on their relative size; that is, the importing country can possibly benefit from the imposition of the quota because of the ability to influence world price. In the cases where the entire quota goes abroad (the third and fourth cases listed), the importing country not only incurs the deadweight losses a and b but also loses the rectangle c, which is effectively sent abroad through higher domestic import prices (P_{m1} instead of P_{m0}). The impact of the quota on the importing country is thus clearly negative and equal to the sum of the three areas. Using the numbers in Figure 11 (the same as in Figure 10), the loss for country A would thus be area a ($18) plus area b ($21) plus area c ($102), a total loss of $18 + $21 + $102 = $141.

The impact of the import quota on the *exporting* country can also be identified. In the cases where the entire quota rent goes to the importing country, the exporting country incurs deadweight losses of triangles *ghf* and *ikj* as well as the transfer rectangle *fhij*. The net welfare effect in this case is clearly negative. In the cases where the exporting country captures the entire quota rent, the deadweight losses are offset, at least in part, by the transfer from the importing country of rectangle c. Hence, should the exporting country be able to capture the quota rent, the net welfare effects will be positive whenever rectangle c is greater than the sum of the triangles *ghf* and *ikj*.

Possible results for exporting country B can be illustrated by using the numbers in Figure 11. If the entire quota rent goes to importing country A, country B loses deadweight loss triangles *ghf* and *ikj* as well as the rectangle *fhij*. Area *fhij* was earlier calculated in Figure 10 to be $68. Area *ghf* has a value of $(1/2)($100 − $96)(57 − 50) = (1/2)($4)(7) = 14. Area *ikj* has a value of $(1/2)($100 − $96)(80 − 74) = (1/2)($4)(6) = 12. Thus, if the importing country captures the quota rent, the exporting country loses welfare of the amount ($68 + $14 + $12) = $94. Alternatively, this loss can be thought of, for the exporting country, as the amount by which country B's loss of producer surplus (from the lower price and the smaller quantity sold) outweighs country B's gain of consumer surplus (from the lower domestic price and greater domestic quantity consumed). The loss of producer surplus in panel (c) of Figure 10 is $[($100 − $96)(74 − 0) + (1/2)($100 − $96)(80 − 74)] = $296 + $12 = 308. The gain in consumer surplus in exporting country B is $[($100 − $96)(50 − 0) + (1/2)($100 − $96)(57 − 50)] = $200 + $14 = 214. Hence, the loss in producer surplus of $308 exceeds the gain in consumer surplus of $214 by $94, the net loss for country B. However, if exporting country B were able to capture the quota rent, it would *not* lose area *fhij* and it would *gain* area c from country A. Triangles *ghf* ($14) and *ikj* ($12) are still lost, but area c is a gain to be offset against those losses. With the numbers in Figure 11, area $c = ($106 − $100)(83 − 66) = ($6)(17) = 102, and, hence, if B captures the quota rent, the country *gains* $102 (area c) − $14 (area *ghf*) − $12 (area *ikj*) = $76.

To minimize any adverse welfare effect of foreign import protection on their economies, exporting countries have employed *voluntary export restraints* (VERs) to avoid the importing country's actively utilizing tariffs or quotas to reduce imports. (VERs are often adopted at the behest of the importing country under the threat of an import quota if the VER is not used. This might occur if the importing country did not want to look like it was openly restricting trade by imposing an import quota—the VER looks less like the "fault" of the importing country.) The effect of an equivalent VER is graphically the same as that of the import quota described in Figure 11. The only difference is that the VER definitely allows the exporting country to capture the quota rent associated with the reduced trade. It thus results in an unambiguous welfare loss for the importing country and a possible welfare gain for the exporting country if the positive transfer effect from the importing country more than offsets the deadweight losses in the exporting country, as it did in our immediately preceding numerical example.

FIGURE 12   The Effects of an Export Tax in a Single Market in the Large-Country Setting

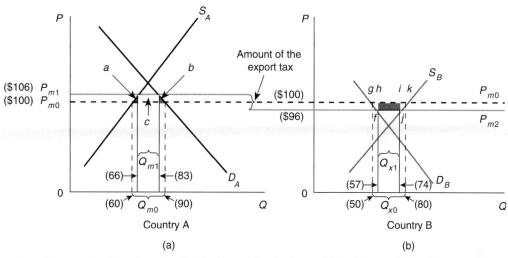

With the imposition of the export tax, firms in country B attempt to avoid paying the tax ($10 in this example) by selling more at home. To do this, they lower price until the price in B, P_{m2}, plus the export tax is equal to the international price. The resulting reduction in exports reduces world supply and leads to an increase in the international price to P_{m1}. At this point, the desired amount of country A imports is reduced to where it is equal to the desired amount of exports of country B, and the difference between P_{m1} and P_{m2} is equal to the amount of the export tax. Because of the increase in the international price, part of the export tax is passed on to country A's consumers and the domestic price in country B falls by less than the amount of the entire tax. Country B can actually benefit from the tax if the sum of the two deadweight loss triangles, *ghf* and *ikj*, is less than the amount of tax paid by consumers in country A (rectangle *c*). Welfare in country A clearly declines, as that country incurs not only deadweight losses of triangles *a* and *b* but also the transfer to country B of rectangle *c*.

The Impact of an Export Tax

The impact of a tax imposed by an exporting country is demonstrated in Figure 12 for two large countries. Graphically, it appears the same as the impact of a tariff and/or quota, discussed in the previous two sections, and we will use the same illustrative numbers as in Figures 10 and 11. The mechanism by which the export tax operates (a $10 per-unit export tax in our example) and the welfare effects on the two countries are, however, quite different.

With the imposition of the export tax, producers in the exporting country B are induced, as in the small-country case, to lower their domestic price and sell more at home to avoid paying the tax. This will take place until the difference between the price of the good in country B and the world price is equal to the export tax. As a result of the tax, exports decline due to both the increased local consumption and the reduced quantity supplied of the export good. Because this is a large-country setting, the reduced supply of exports on the world market results in an increase in the international price. Thus, the import price for country A rises from the initial nondistorted price of P_{m0} ($100) to P_{m1} ($106), and the price of the good in exporting country B falls from P_{m0} to P_{m2} ($96). Desired exports Q_{x1} (17 units) are then equal to desired imports Q_{m1}, and the difference between P_{m1} and P_{m2} equals the export tax ($10). The government revenue received by the *exporting* country is equal to the amount of the tax ($P_{m1} - P_{m2}$) times the quantity of exports (Q_{x1}), and this is represented by the sum of rectangles *c* and *fhij* in Figure 12.

From a welfare standpoint, the export tax results in deadweight losses of triangle *ghf* plus triangle *ikj* in the exporting country and an inward transfer of rectangle *c* from the importing country because of the higher world price. In this instance, the importing country effectively "pays" part of the export tax through the higher import price, and the exporting country can benefit if the inward transfer from the importing country more than offsets

IN THE REAL WORLD:

WELFARE COSTS OF U.S. IMPORT QUOTAS AND VERs

Robert Feenstra (1992) assembled a variety of industry estimates and information to arrive at an overall figure of the costs of protection related to major U.S. import quotas and VER arrangements negotiated with trading partners. He examined restrictions under U.S. import quotas and VERs on automobiles, sugar, textiles and apparel, dairy products, and steel products, and incorporated the effects of U.S. tariffs on these goods that were also in place.

Feenstra's welfare analysis framework was the large country situation represented in Figure 11. As a general rule, the quota rents in these products are captured by foreign exporters because the quotas are administered abroad and not by the United States. We discussed in the text the welfare cost of such restrictions. Feenstra (p. 163) estimated a welfare cost range (for years centering around 1985) of $7.9 billion to $12.3 billion to the United States for areas a and b of Figure 11. He estimated a U.S. loss range of approximately $7.3 billion to $17.3 billion for area c of Figure 11. Thus the total U.S. welfare cost of the restrictions ranged from $15.2 billion ($7.9 billion + $7.3 billion) to $29.6 billion ($12.3 billion + $17.3 billion). Other costs associated with the quotas and VERs were not contained in the estimates. These would include the waste of resources by U.S. firms in lobbying for protection and the neglect of modernization of equipment by U.S. firms in order to show the need for continued protection.

An interesting feature of Feenstra's analysis was his calculation of the welfare impact on the world as a whole. Because, in Figure 11, area c and area *fhij* are simply transfer areas between countries, the world as a whole loses the sum of the four areas a, b, *ghf*, and *ikj*. Feenstra estimated this "world loss" to be in the range of $12.2 billion to $31.1 billion. Because this range was very close to the U.S. loss range by itself, the U.S. restrictions on balance did not help or injure foreign suppliers because the quota rents were nearly equal to the losses from reduced export sales.

It should be noted that the VERs on autos and the import quotas on textiles and apparel no longer exist. A U.S. International Trade Commission (USITC) estimate (2007, p. xxi) indicates that liberalization of significant U.S. import restraints would lead to a U.S. welfare gain of $3.7 billion, an amount well below the Feenstra estimates. Hence, relatively, the earlier VERs and import quotas appear to have imposed sizable welfare losses on the U.S. economy.   ●

the deadweight losses resulting from the tax (i.e., if area c is greater than the sum of triangles *ghf* and *ikj*). For the *importing* country, the imposition of the export tax leads not only to deadweight losses of a and b but also to the transfer abroad of rectangle c. The potential gains (losses) for the exporting (importing) country are greater the more inelastic are supply and demand in the importing country and the more elastic are supply and demand in the exporting country. With our numerical example and the calculations done earlier, we see that the exporting country gains in this example from the export tax, although this does not have to be the case conceptually. Rectangular area c ($102) exceeds the sum of triangles *ghf* ($14) and *ikj* ($12) by $76. The importing country loses areas a ($18) + b ($21) + c ($102) = $141.

If the exporting country could lose from the export tax, however, why would it want to impose the tax?[9] We can briefly indicate some reasons, noting that export taxes are common in developing countries. A very important reason for the use of export taxes by developing countries is to generate government revenue, because it is more difficult to implement other forms of taxation such as income or property taxes. Another reason to impose export taxes is to combat domestic inflationary pressures. Because the price of the good on the domestic market falls, this could dampen the rise in the home price level. (However, the export tax by itself is unlikely to be a successful anti-inflationary device

---

[9]In the United States, the use of export taxes is prohibited by the U.S. Constitution.

FIGURE 13   The Effects of an Export Subsidy in a Single Market in the Large-Country Setting

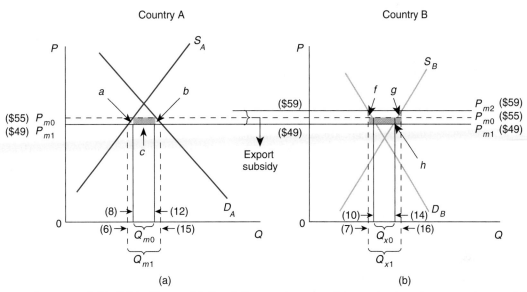

(a)   (b)

In the presence of an export subsidy ($10 in this example), firms in the exporting country B have a clear incentive to export because of the higher revenues received per unit. Assuming that there is no possibility of importing the good at the international price, this leads to an increase in the domestic price in country B to where it is equal to the international price plus the subsidy. However, at the same time, the resulting increase in both domestic quantity supplied and exports by B leads to a fall in the international price. These price movements continue until the difference between the domestic price in country B and the import price in country A, $(P_{m2} - P_{m1})$, is equal to the export subsidy and desired exports by B (Q_{x1}) equal desired imports by A (Q_{m1}). The lower import price results in welfare gains for country A of deadweight triangles a and b and the rectangle c. On the other hand, country B experiences welfare losses of the deadweight triangles f and g as well as the transfer abroad of rectangle h through the lower world price.

unless a contractionary domestic macroeconomic policy is also employed.) Further, export taxes can be used to redistribute domestic income. If the exported good is an agricultural product grown by large and wealthy landowners and consumed by low-income urban dwellers, then the lowering of the domestic price by means of the export tax can alter the income distribution toward greater equality. (See Leff 1969.) In addition, of course, if an export tax is imposed and *import* prices do not change, the country's terms of trade will improve.

The Impact of an Export Subsidy

We now turn to the last policy to be examined in the large-country setting, the case of the export subsidy. This case is depicted in Figure 13. Starting with an illustrative no-subsidy price of $55, suppose firms now receive a per-unit payment of $10 when they export the good. Thus, domestic suppliers will sell to their own home market only if they receive a price equal to the revenue per unit (price plus subsidy) received by exporting. Assuming that no imports are allowed, the domestic price in the exporting country B rises, leading to a reduction in B's consumption, an increase in B's production, and an increase in B's exports. Because country B is a large country, the increase in exports will lead to a fall in the world price. The price movements will continue until an import price $(P_{m1} = \$49)$ in country A is reached at which the quantity of desired imports Q_{m1} $(=15 - 6 = 9$ units$)$ is equal to the quantity of desired exports Q_{x1} of country B. The difference between P_{m2} $(\$59)$ and P_{m1} $(\$49)$ is the amount of the per-unit export subsidy, and the cost of the subsidy to the government of country B is $(P_{m2} - P_{m1}) \times (Q_{x1})$. In our example, this cost is

($59 − $49)(16 − 7) = $90. Note that the presence of the export subsidy leads to a fall in the international price (from P_{m0} to P_{m1}) and to an increase in imports (from Q_{m0} to Q_{m1}) into country A as A's production of the good declines and consumption of the good increases.

Turning to the welfare effects in both countries, we observe that there is a net gain in the importing country A, which experiences net gains of triangles a and b as well as the rectangle c due to the fall in the international price. These three areas represent the amount by which the gain in consumer surplus in country A exceeds the loss of producer surplus in A. In the exporting country, the resulting increase in the domestic price from P_{m0} to P_{m2} leads to deadweight losses of unshaded triangles f and g, if we assume that consumers are also the taxpayers who pay for the subsidy (just as in the small-country case). However, there is an *additional cost* to the exporting country associated with the fall in the international price. Even though the per-unit subsidy amounts to $(P_{m2} − P_{m1})$, or $10, prices received by country B's producers rise by only $(P_{m2} − P_{m0})$, or $4, and the remainder of the subsidy, $(P_{m0} − P_{m1})$, or $6, is transferred abroad to country A through lower prices. The total amount transferred is $(P_{m0} − P_{m1}) \times (Q_{x1})$ and is depicted by the shaded rectangle h in panel (b) of Figure 13. The net welfare effect on the exporting country is thus the two deadweight losses coupled with the transfer abroad (also negative), or areas f, g, and h [=($55 − $49)(9) = $54]. Thus, in the case of an export subsidy, being a large country results in an additional welfare loss that would not occur if the country were small. With our numbers, importing country A thus gains area a [=(1/2)($55 − $49)(8 − 6) = $6] plus area b [=(1/2)($55 − $49)(15 − 12) = $9] plus area c [=($55 − $49)(12 − 8) = $24], or a total of $39. The exporting country B loses area f [=(1/2)($59 − $55)(10 − 7) = $6] plus area g [=(1/2)($59 − $55)(16 − 14) = $4] plus area h [=($55 − $49)(16 − 7) = $54], for a total loss of $64.

CONCEPT CHECK

1. Is it ever possible for a large country to gain from the imposition of an import quota? If so, when?

2. How do the impacts of an export subsidy in the large-country case differ from those in the small-country case?

TRADE RESTRICTIONS IN A GENERAL EQUILIBRIUM SETTING

The discussion of the effect of trade restrictions has to this point focused largely on the market of the particular good that is the target of the restriction in question. While this is a useful exercise, remember that as this market adjusts to the policy, other parts of the economy are also affected. Increased protection leads producers to reallocate resources to the protected industry and consumers to find substitutes for the now more expensive good. These economywide reverberations need to be taken into account if one is to assess fully the welfare impact of the trade restriction.

Protection in the Small-Country Case

To demonstrate the usefulness of the broader analysis of trade restrictions, let us return to the general equilibrium framework to demonstrate the gains from trade. This framework was discussed in Chapter 6, "Gains from Trade in Neoclassical Theory." Assume that a small country is engaged in free trade (see Figure 14). Initially, consumers are consuming at point C_0, producers are producing at point B_0, the country is exporting X_0 of agricultural goods, and imports of textiles are equal to M_0. Due to successful lobbying by the textile industry, an *ad valorem*

IN THE REAL WORLD:

THE U.S. EXPORT ENHANCEMENT PROGRAM FOR WHEAT

Under the lead of Senator Robert Dole (R–KS) and with the strong support of the ranking Democrat on the Agricultural Committee (Senator Edward Zorinsky, D–NE) and budget director David Stockman, the Export Enhancement Program (EEP) for Wheat was enacted in December 1985, being codified in the Food Security Act. This act consisted of enabling legislation which defined both what the executive branch was "required to do" and what it had "discretionary authority to do." The act "required the secretary of agriculture to provide Commodity Credit Corporation (CCC) commodities at no cost 'to United States exporters, users and processors and foreign purchasers,' and required that a total of $2 billion in CCC commodities be used for this purpose during the three fiscal years ending September 30, 1988. The purposes the subsidized exports were to serve are broadly stated: In addition to combating other countries' subsidies and the high value of the dollar, export subsidies may be used to offset 'the adverse effects of U.S. agriculture price support levels that are temporarily above the export prices offered by overseas competitors in export markets' " (Gardner 1996, pp. 62–63; the inset quotations are from "The Food Security Act of 1985," *U.S. Statutes at Large* 19, p. 1483). The guidelines for this program were set out by the Economic Policy Council of the White House and included the following four criteria: (1) The subsidized exports must result in an increase in exports and not just in a replacement of existing exports— a concept often referred to as "additionality"; (2) the exports should be directed toward displacing competing foreign exporters that are being subsidized by their own governments; (3) the subsidies should result in a net gain to the U.S. economy; and (4) the subsidies should be "neutral" with respect to their impact on the budget.

In addition to subsidizing wheat producers directly, the act also authorized wheat stocks to be used for cross subsidization; that is, wheat stocks could be used to subsidize other producers of exports, such as egg producers and pork producers. U.S. millers also benefited by receiving wheat subsidies in the case of flour exports. The losers were, of course,

domestic buyers of wheat and foreign producers, whereas wheat farmers gained through higher domestic prices and the government gained through a reduction in the cost of the wheat price support program since farm prices rose concomitantly with the increase in exports. The following figures summarize the annual estimated costs and benefits of the EEP, assuming that the resulting increase (additionality) in exports of wheat was somewhere between a low of 2 million metric tons and a high of 6 million metric tons:

Costs and Benefits	Amount ($, millions)
Direct cost of EEP subsidies	$1,000(−)
Reduction in cost of price supports	$350 to $1,050(+)
Domestic wheat farmers' gain	$120 to $300(+)
Livestock feeders' loss	$40 to $100(−)
Domestic consumers' loss	$200 to $500(−)
Estimated net welfare effects	(−)$250 to (−)$770

Thus, even though some of the costs of the EEP subsidies were offset by a reduction in cost of the price support program, the program appears to have generated a net loss to the U.S. economy and to have failed to meet the third initial guideline. It is also questionable whether the program turned out to be budget-neutral (i.e., the reduction in the cost of price supports probably did not offset the direct cost of the EEP subsidies). In spite of these results, the program has proved to be a political winner as its implementation failed to stimulate any opposition from losing groups in the country. In addition, a projection by the Food and Agricultural Policy Institute (Meyers 1997) indicated that exports with the EEP were 10 percent to 15 percent larger (the additionality) than they would have been without the EEP. Further, average wheat prices on the world market may have been $0.05 to $0.15 per bushel lower because of the program.

Source: Based on the paper by Bruce Gardner (1996).

import tariff is now imposed. In the small-country case, this increases the domestic price of textiles by t percent, and the domestic price of textiles becomes $P_{\text{tex}}(1 + t)$. Domestic relative prices now become $P_{\text{ag}}/[P_{\text{tex}}(1 + t)]$, which are less than $P_{\text{ag}}/P_{\text{tex}}$, the international relative prices. Producers see the increase in the relative price of textiles as a signal to produce more textiles (and consequently fewer agricultural goods) and adjust production until $MC_{\text{ag}}/MC_{\text{tex}}$ equals $P_{\text{ag}}/[P_{\text{tex}}(1 + t)]$. This occurs when the flatter domestic price line is

FIGURE 14   The General Equilibrium Effects of a Tariff in the Small-Country Case

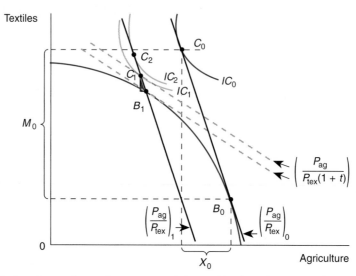

Under free trade, the country produces at B_0, consumes at C_0, imports M_0 units, and exports X_0 units. With an *ad valorem* import tariff (t), the domestic price of textiles rises to $P_{tex}(1 + t)$, causing the domestic relative price ratio $[P_{ag}/P_{tex}(1 + t)]$ to be smaller than the international terms of trade P_{ag}/P_{tex}. Producers now see a greater incentive to produce textiles, and domestic production moves to B_1, where the domestic relative price line is tangent to the PPF. The new level of real income measured at international prices (or the consumption-possibilities frontier) is now represented by $(P_{ag}/P_{tex})_1$, which passes through new production point B_1. Consumers, facing the same set of domestic relative prices as producers, move to C_1, where the slope of community indifference curve IC_1 is just tangent to the farther out of the $[P_{ag}/P_{tex}(1 + t)]$ lines, and are clearly less well-off than with free trade. Finally, if an equivalent subsidy had been used to attain B_1, consumers would still face international prices and would choose C_2 instead of C_1. The equivalent subsidy would leave them strictly better off than with the tariff but less well-off than with free trade.

tangent to the production-possibilities frontier at point B_1. This adjustment by producers represents a movement away from specialization and reduces the consumption possibilities available to the country from line $(P_{ag}/P_{tex})_0$ to parallel line $(P_{ag}/P_{tex})_1$. The adjustment in production thus leads to a *reduction in real income* and a consequent loss in welfare as consumers are forced to choose from smaller consumption possibilities along $(P_{ag}/P_{tex})_1$ instead of $(P_{ag}/P_{tex})_0$ and must therefore be on a lower indifference curve.

Consumers must make a new consumption choice, given their lower level of real income. What point on the new consumption-possibilities frontier, $(P_{ag}/P_{tex})_1$, will maximize their well-being in this tariff-distorted world? Because they face the same tariff-distorted prices as producers, they will try to find a point on the new consumption-possibilities line that represents an optimal consumption choice, given relative domestic prices. This will occur at a combination of agricultural goods and textiles that lies on $(P_{ag}/P_{tex})_1$ and that results in $MU_{ag}/MU_{tex} = P_{ag}/[P_{tex}(1 + t)]$. This choice is indicated by point C_1 in Figure 14. At C_1 the slope of lower indifference curve IC_1 is equal to the domestic price ratio that contains the tariff on textiles, $P_{ag}/[P_{tex}(1 + t)]$. This is indicated by the tangency of IC_1 to the dashed line at point C_1. The tariff thus has a negative welfare impact on the country, represented by the shift from point C_0 on indifference curve IC_0 to point C_1 on the community indifference curve IC_1.[10]

[10]This analysis ignores the complications linked to the use of the tariff revenue. It is assumed that tariff revenue is simply redistributed to individuals in the country. Indeed, it is equal to the vertical distance between the two distorted domestic price ratio lines if measured in units of textiles. Note also that, if the tariff were high enough to be a prohibitive tariff, consumers would settle at B_1, and there would be no tariff revenue to redistribute.

The general equilibrium effects of a quota (not shown in Figure 14) are similar to those of the tariff as long as the quota rent remains in the country. This would be the case if the government auctions the quotas or if importers receive the quota rent. Because every tariff has an equivalent quota that produces the same change in relative domestic prices, the imposition of a quota leads to the same producer and consumer adjustments. The only static difference in the two instruments is that quotas fix quantities and let prices adjust to clear the market, whereas a tariff alters prices and lets quantities adjust. If, however, the exporting country receives the quota rent, for example, through the efforts of organized exporters or the imposition of a voluntary export restraint (VER), the result is different. The imposition of a VER has the impact of raising the price of the restricted good to the importing country, thus worsening the importing country's terms of trade and leading to a position on an even lower indifference curve than did the tariff.

It is useful at this juncture to contrast the effect of a tariff with that of a production subsidy to the import-competing industry. You will recall that for every tariff, there is an equivalent production subsidy that causes domestic production to be the same as that under the tariff (see Figure 4 earlier in this chapter). The subsidy leads to the same reduction in the gains from specialization and loss in real income. What is different, however, is that consumers continue to consume at international prices. The loss in real income means that consumers have to reduce consumption so that they are consuming on the new consumption-possibilities curve in Figure 14 $(P_{ag}/P_{tex})_1$. However, because they continue to face international prices, they attempt to find the consumption point where an indifference curve is tangent to the new consumption-possibilities frontier. This tangency is indicated by point C_2, which is on a higher indifference curve than C_1. Again, if the government wishes to encourage production in the import-competing sector, it is preferable to do so by direct subsidization of producers rather than through price-distorting mechanisms such as tariffs. The smaller the negative effects of government intervention, the fewer the number of economic actors that are affected. With the subsidy, the distortion directly affects only producers, and the principal social cost of the subsidy is the loss in real income resulting from decreased specialization along the lines of comparative advantage.

Protection in the Large-Country Case

In the large-country case, the welfare impact of protection is less clear and concise. Because the large country can influence international prices by its own actions, the impact of a tariff is felt not only domestically but also internationally. With its tariff, the tariff-imposing country reduces both its import demand and export supply; that is, it is less willing to trade. Consequently, both the international demand for the import good and the world supply of the export good are reduced. Both effects cause the international terms of trade to change, increasing the price of the export good relative to the import good and improving the terms of trade of the tariff-imposing country. The overall reduction of welfare in the tariff-imposing country resulting from the smaller amount of trade is thus offset, at least in part, by improved terms of trade. It is possible that the effects of the terms of trade could more than offset the effect of the reduction in trade and leave the tariff-imposing country better off, assuming, of course, that its trading partners do not retaliate. (See the later discussion of the "optimum tariff rate" on pages 321–23 in Chapter 15).

The general equilibrium effects of trade restrictions in the large-country case can be usefully examined through the use of offer curves. The offer curve concept was introduced in Chapter 7. To illustrate the impact of a tariff in such a framework, consider first the manner in which the curve shifts when a tariff is imposed. Figure 15 illustrates the offer curve for country I, which is exporting good B and importing good A. Remember that the curve was derived by plotting the willingness of the country to trade at alternative terms of trade. Curve 0*I* shows that country I is willing to export quantity

FIGURE 15   The Imposition of a Tariff in the Offer Curve Diagram

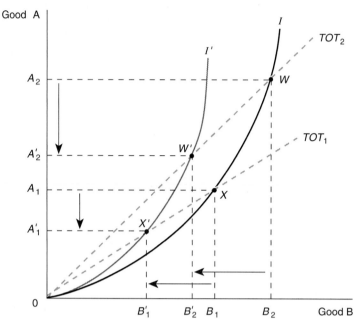

Free-trade offer curve $0I$ shows country I's willingness to trade at various terms of trade (e.g., it will export quantity $0B_1$ of good B in exchange for $0A_1$ of good A at TOT_1). When country I imposes an import tariff, it is less willing to trade at each terms of trade. Thus, for example, the country will then export only $0B'_1$ of good B in exchange for $0A'_1$ of good A at TOT_1. The offer curve $0I$ shifts inward to $0I'$.

$0B_1$ of good B and to import quantity $0A_1$ of good A at TOT_1. Similarly, at TOT_2, the country is willing to export $0B_2$ and import $0A_2$. When a tariff is imposed, the country is less willing to trade at each terms of trade. At TOT_1 on new offer curve $0I'$, the country is willing to export only amount $0B'_1$ and to import only $0A'_1$. The willingness to trade at TOT_2 is indicated in corresponding fashion. Thus, the offer curve "shifts inward" with the imposition of a tariff. The same shift can also represent an export tax as well as an import tariff, because both instruments indicate less willingness to trade at any terms of trade.

Consider the comparative impacts of tariffs and quotas. Figure 16 portrays the imposition of an import tariff along with the foreign offer curve. (Both countries I and II are large countries in these diagrams.) Prior to the tariff, the free-trade equilibrium is at point E with quantity $0B_1$ of good B exported from country I (and imported by country II) and quantity $0A_1$ imported by country I (and exported by country II). With the imposition of the tariff, offer curve $0I'$ rather than $0I$ becomes the relevant curve. The quantity of exports of country I falls to $0B_2$, and this quantity is exchanged for $0A_2$ of imports. Note also that the terms of trade improve for the tariff-imposing country, since TOT_2 is steeper than TOT_1.

The offer curve analysis of import quotas and VERs is contained in Figure 17. In panel (a), the offer curve of country I with an import quota is identical to free-trade offer curve $0I$ until quota amount $0A_2$ is reached (equal to $0A_2$ in Figure 16). Then the offer curve ceases rising because no greater quantity of imports will be permitted, and the curve in its entirety becomes $0RI'$ (horizontal line RA_2 after point R). Like the import tariff, the quantity imported of good A is $0A_2$ at the new equilibrium E', the quantity exported of good B is $0B_2$, and the terms of trade are TOT_2.

FIGURE 16   The Impact of a Tariff

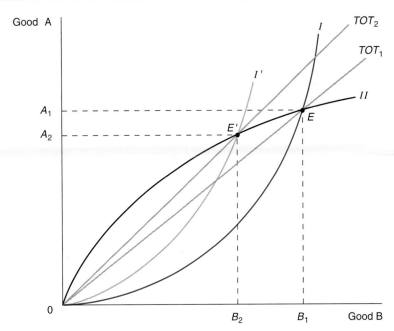

With the imposition of the tariff, country I's offer curve $0I$ shifts inward to $0I'$. The equilibrium quantity of exports falls from $0B_1$ to $0B_2$, and the quantity of imports falls from $0A_1$ to $0A_2$. Country I's terms of trade improve from TOT_1 to TOT_2. An export tax by country I would be portrayed in the same fashion.

FIGURE 17   An Import Quota and a VER

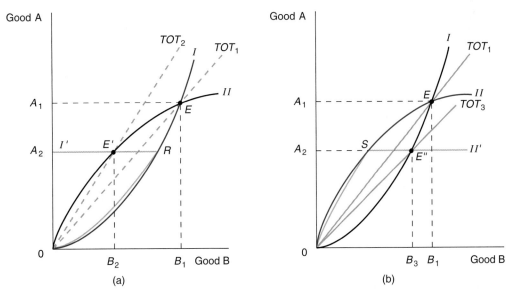

(a)   (b)

The use of an import quota by country I is shown in panel (a). The free-trade offer curve $0I$ becomes $0RI'$, indicating that country I is willing to import up to quantity $0A_2$ of good A but no more than that quantity. The equilibrium position moves from point E to point E', and country I's terms of trade improve from TOT_1 to TOT_2.

Panel (b) illustrates the use of a voluntary export restraint (VER) by country II to limit exports to country I to quantity $0A_2$. Country II's offer curve changes from $0II$ to $0SII'$, indicating that it will send up to $0A_2$ of good A to country I. With the shift in the equilibrium position from E to E'', country I's terms of trade deteriorate from TOT_1 to TOT_3.

The VER is shown in Figure 17, panel (b). Because it is the foreign country that is undertaking the measure, country II's offer curve is the curve affected, not the offer curve of country I. Because country II can now export no more than $0A_2$, country II's curve becomes horizontal at that quantity. Its offer curve in its entirety is $0SII'$ rather than the free-trade curve $0II$. The new equilibrium is at point E''. Country I still imports $0A_2$ of good A, but it now exports the larger amount (compared with the import tariff and the import quota) $0B_3$ of good B. Note also that the terms of trade have *deteriorated* for country I compared with the free-trade situation: They are now TOT_3 rather than the original TOT_1. In this two-country graph, the deterioration of country I's terms of trade constitutes an improvement in those of country II. Clearly, country II prefers the VER to the import quota and the import tariff if the terms-of-trade impact is the only consideration.

OTHER EFFECTS OF PROTECTION

We have examined the effect of protection from a direct static perspective using partial and general equilibrium analyses. Now we need to mention several other possible effects of protection. First, we need to reemphasize that restriction of imports is likely to lead to a reduction in exports of the tariff-imposing country. This takes place as soon as domestic resources are withdrawn from export production and used in the production of domestic import substitutes at the higher relative domestic price of these goods. Further, there is likely to be foreign country tariff and nontariff retaliation against the tariff-imposing country's exports. Protection thus not only lowers real income in the imposing country but also redistributes it from export industries to import-competing industries. These shifts take place in the short run and reduce the incentive to invest in the affected export industries, contributing to reduced ability to export in the future. A reduced ability to export could be deadly to industries that rely on today's investment in research and development to be competitive in the future. The subsequent slowing down of technological change in the comparative-advantage industries could be critical to efficiency and welfare in our increasingly interdependent world.

Second, you will recall that trade restrictions have an impact on the distribution of income among the factors of production. With the imposition of a tariff in the Heckscher-Ohlin model, the scarce factor gains and the abundant factor loses. Or in the specific-factors model, the fixed factor in the import-competing industry (export industry) gains (loses), while the impact on the variable factor depends on consumption patterns. Income distribution effects are discussed further in Chapter 15, "Arguments for Interventionist Trade Policies."

Third, the effect of protection in certain industries on total imports may be less than it appears if only the change in imports of the protected goods is examined. This would be the case if the increase in domestic production of the import-competing products required intermediate inputs that have to be imported. Then, while protection reduces imports of the targeted products, increased domestic production leads to increased importation of the required intermediate products. This is an often-ignored aspect of protection that turned out to be critical for a number of developing countries that were pursuing an import-substitution policy to reduce their total imports by producing the previously imported goods at home. Ignoring the indirect import requirement of the expanding import-competing sector contributed to serious mistakes in estimating the potential effectiveness of import-substitution strategies.

It is also important not to ignore the possible effects of protection on foreign supply. History demonstrates that foreign suppliers will attempt to find ways to circumvent any kind of trade restriction, whether it be a tariff or nontariff barrier. Faced with the import

IN THE REAL WORLD:

DOMESTIC EFFECTS OF THE SUGAR QUOTA SYSTEM

The U.S. sugar industry has received protection since 1934. From 1934 to 1974, sugarcane and sugar beet growers were protected through import quotas, subsidy programs, and acreage restrictions. Since 1976, import tariffs, import fees, and quotas have been used fairly extensively. The effect of these restrictions on the industry has been substantial, causing the domestic U.S. price to be considerably above the world price. For example, in 1988 the average domestic price was $0.2212/pound and the world price was $0.1178/pound; that is, there was an equivalent tariff rate of 88 percent. In 1989, the world price was $0.1445/pound, and the average U.S. price was $0.2281/pound, an equivalent tariff rate of 58 percent. This protection cost consumers an estimated $1.2 billion in 1988, $1.1 billion in 1989, and $1.4 billion in 1990. The related net social losses from the program in those years were estimated at $242 million, $150 million, and $185 million, respectively. These estimates do not include any of the indirect or "downstream" effects on industries that use sugar as an input and whose costs of production were consequently higher as a result of sugar protection. A 2003 study (Beghin et al.) indicated that in 1998 sugarcane growers gained $307 million, sugar beet growers $650 million, and processors $89 million because of the program. Further, users of sugar lost $1.9 billion, and the dead weight losses associated with the program were put at $532 million. More recently the USITC in 2007 estimated the net welfare cost of the sugar program to be $811 million.[*]

The impact of protection, however, goes beyond the efficiency and distribution effects reflected in the above estimates. A 1990 *Wall Street Journal* article (see the sources for this box) focused on the state and local effects of the sugar program in a sugar beet–growing region of Minnesota. The higher prices for sugar gave farmers an incentive to shift land from other uses to the production of sugar beets, where they could earn up to four times what they could growing corn or wheat. However, the administration of the sugar program does not give everyone the opportunity to grow sugar beets. The sugar beet program is essentially administered through sugar processors. These sugar refiners are guaranteed a target price as long as they pay growers the support price.

Because there are no other restrictions, the amount of sugar beets that can be grown depends on the processing capacity of the local plant and the access of growers to the plant. In southern Minnesota, growers gained access to refining facilities by buying shares in the Southern Minnesota Beet Sugar Cooperative, which was founded in 1974. Without membership in the cooperative, growers had no place to sell sugar beets. Consequently, the benefits of the program accrued only to those few farmers who were members of the cooperative, and the program generated sizable impacts on local income distribution, land use, and consequently the entire social fabric of the community. Tensions rose every day as the "Beeters" sought to acquire more land from non–sugar beet growers and the evidence of their economic gains became even more visible. (It was estimated that large farmers reaped $100,000 to $200,000 in annual benefits from the sugar program.)

Rural communities were wrenched apart. Families split over the issue, formerly good friends no longer met for coffee or spoke, churches and community organizations became divided, and vandalism against supporters and nonsupporters of the program occurred. The noneconomic social costs of price distortions like those introduced by the sugar program are too often ignored in policy analysis. They are, however, very real in communities such as Maynard, Minnesota.

Removal of such price distortions would eventually lead to a return to land use consistent with unrestricted supply and demand considerations and would remove the source of the distribution distortion and community stress. Of course, new stresses would be introduced with changes in the distribution. The noneconomic personal and community costs that have already been incurred may, however, never be recouped. Nevertheless, the program continues to receive strong support in Congress, even though the Bush Administration has proposed reductions in the program, noting the high cost to consumers.

[*]It can be noted that, in April 2007, the U.S. domestic price was about twice the world price. This implies an equivalent tariff rate of about 100 percent.

Sources: U.S. International Trade Commission, *The Economic Effects of Significant U.S. Import Restraints, Phase II: Agricultural Products and Natural Resources*, USITC Publication 2314 (Washington, DC: U.S. Government Printing Office, September 1990), chap. 2, *Fourth Update, 2004*, USITC Publication 3701 (Washington, DC: June 2004), p. xvii, and *Fifth Update, 2007*, USITC Publication 3906 (Washington, DC: February 2007), p. xxi, obtained from www.usitc.gov; Bruce Ingersoll, "Small Minnesota Town Is Divided by Rancor over Sugar Policies," *The Wall Street Journal*, June 26, 1990, pp. A1, A12; Gary C. Hufbauer and Kimberly A. Elliott, *Measuring the Costs of Protection in the United States* (Washington, DC: Institute for International Economics, 1994), pp. 79–81; John Beghin, Barbara El Osta, Jay R. Cherlow, and Samarendu Mohanty, "The Cost of the U.S. Sugar Program Revisited," *Contemporary Economic Policy* 21, no. 1 (2003), p. 106, obtained from www.econpapers.repec.org; Bruce Odessey, "Bush Advisers View Sugar Program as Hurting U.S. Consumers," obtained from www.usinfo.state.gov.

barrier, foreign firms may devote even more time and resources to reducing costs of production in order to compete with domestic producers. The ultimate irony occurs when a portion of a quota rent is transferred to the foreign producer (either directly or indirectly through its government), which then uses it to make technological innovations and become an even stronger competitor. This took place in the U.S. textile and apparel industry and the automobile industry. Too often, protection seems to impair the pursuit of cost-reducing innovations in the imposing country while increasing the cost-reducing incentives in the exporting country. Unfortunately, this scenario leads over time to pleas for greater and greater protection from the already-protected industry. The increased levels of protection bring greater and greater net welfare losses to the trade-restricting country.

CONCEPT CHECK

1. How does protection of the import good affect production of the export good in the general equilibrium framework?

2. How can tariffs on the import good lead to a decline in consumption of both the import and export good?

SUMMARY

This chapter has looked at the ways trade-restricting policies affect a country. Both the partial and general equilibrium approaches indicate that in the small-country case, restricting trade leaves the country less well-off. In the large-country case, trade restrictions can under certain conditions lead to an improvement in well-being for the country imposing the restrictions as long as the partner country does not retaliate. Retaliation and the resulting trade war leave everyone worse off. From the perspective of both cost and international policy, domestic subsidies remain the more desirable alternative if countries wish to assist import-competing industries. The subsidies also produce a domestic production distortion, but because they affect only producers, they are less costly to subsidy-financing consumers and have a smaller impact on the level of imports coming into the country than either tariffs or quotas.

KEY TERMS

auction quota system
consumer surplus
deadweight losses
demand for imports schedule
equivalent quota

equivalent subsidy
equivalent tariff
general equilibrium model
incidence of the tariff
partial equilibrium analysis

producer surplus
quota rent
supply of exports schedule

QUESTIONS AND PROBLEMS

1. Suppose that the free-trade price of a good is $12 and a 10 percent *ad valorem* tariff is put in place. As a result, domestic production in a small country rises from 2,000 units to 2,300 units and imports fall from 600 units to 200 units. Who are the winners and losers? What is the size of their gains and losses? What is the net effect on society?

2. Using the example in Question 1, how does an equivalent subsidy to the import-competing producer affect the market? What is the cost to the government of this subsidy? Which policy would consumers prefer, the tariff or a subsidy?

3. How does an import quota differ from a tariff? Can the government ever capture the quota rent? If so, how?

4. If you were an import-competing producer in a growing market, which trade instrument would you prefer—a tariff, an import quota, or a subsidy? Why?

5. What is the difference between an export tax and an export subsidy? Which instrument are domestic consumers likely to prefer? Why?

6. Why might a large country like the United States have a greater incentive than a small country to use trade restrictions?

7. Using a general equilibrium approach, point out the real income loss from a tariff to a country. What is the consumer welfare loss? Why might consumers prefer a production subsidy rather than a tariff?

8. Explain why an export subsidy is more costly in the case of a large country than in the case of a small country, other things being equal.

9. It has been said that U.S. consumers/taxpayers ended up paying "twice" for the wheat subsidy program. Is there any basis for such a claim?

10. Suppose that a (small) country is an importer of good X, for which the current world price is $8. At that price with free trade, home producers are supplying 500 units of good X and the country is importing 300 units. It is now rumored that a 10 percent import duty will be imposed on good X. Estimate the welfare impacts that would occur with such a tariff, given that the elasticity of demand by consumers for good X is −2.0 and that the elasticity of home supply is 1.6.

Appendix A

THE IMPACT OF PROTECTION IN A MARKET WITH NONHOMOGENEOUS GOODS

The analysis to this point has examined the welfare impact of trade policy–induced price distortions, assuming that the product on which the tariff is placed is a homogeneous good that can be represented with a single demand curve and price. However, if imperfect substitution exists between the foreign- and domestic-produced good, then the pretariff prices of the two products can be different and the single-market approach is inappropriate. With nonhomogeneous goods, the increase in the price of the foreign import resulting from the tariff causes consumers to increase their demand for the domestic substitute. This increase in demand leads in turn to an increase in price of the domestic good and a subsequent loss in consumer surplus, even though the tariff does not apply directly to it. An analysis of the impact of a tariff must take into account the indirect effects of the tariff both on related goods and the good upon which it is levied. This idea is developed in this appendix. (For elaboration, see U.S. International Trade Commission 1989, chap. 2.)

In the case of close but not perfect substitutes, we need to analyze the impact of the tariff in two markets, not just one. See Figure 18, where panel (a) describes the situation in the market for the domestic good and panel (b) describes the market for the imported good in this small-country case. Because the two goods are assumed to be close substitutes, the demand for each good is linked positively (the cross-price elasticity is positive) to the price of the other. Consequently, when the domestic price of one good changes, it leads to a change in demand for the other in the same direction.

In Figure 18, panel (b), the imposition of a tariff on the foreign good raises its price on the domestic market from P'_0 to $P'_1 = P_{int}(1 + t)$, simultaneously reducing the quantity demanded of the foreign good and causing the demand for the domestically produced good [panel (a)] to increase (a shift to the right of the demand curve D_{dom} to D'_{dom}). With a normal upward-sloping domestic supply curve, the price of the domestic substitute increases, triggering an increase in demand for the foreign good (a rightward shift in the demand curve for the foreign product). The imposition of the initial tariff thus sets off demand shifts as the markets adjust to the price distortion. When the repercussions of the tariff have worked through the two demand curves, both curves will have shifted to the right, and the country will import an amount such as Q_4 in panel (b), and there will be a higher price of the domestic good, P_1, as shown in panel (a). Because the price has increased in both markets, two groups of consumers find that their consumer surplus has declined, not just one as with the homogeneous good.

Because both demand curves have shifted in the adjustment process, calculating the effects of the tariff distortion is not as straightforward as with homogeneous goods. The measure of the loss in consumer surplus differs according to the use of the pretariff demand curves or the after-tariff demand curves. Because of the joint market adjustments, measuring the loss in consumer surplus of the import good along pretariff demand curve D_f ignores the cost to consumers who choose to switch to the import good because of the higher cost of the domestic substitute. Similarly, measuring the loss in consumer surplus along the tariff-ridden demand curve D'_f overstates the loss in consumer surplus because it includes individuals who chose not to consume the

FIGURE 18   Tariff Effects on Nonhomogeneous Goods

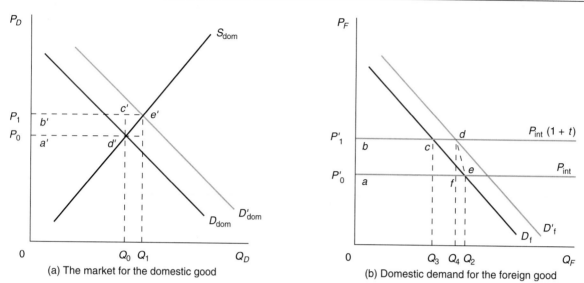

(a) The market for the domestic good

(b) Domestic demand for the foreign good

The tariff raises the domestic price of the import good from P'_0 to $P'_1 = P_{int}(1 + t)$ as indicated in panel (b). At the same time, the increase in the price of the foreign good leads to an increase in the demand for the substitute domestic product and a higher price. The increase in price of the domestic substitute then leads to a subsequent outward shift in the demand for the foreign good. These simultaneous adjustments take place until the markets are again in equilibrium. The outward shift of the demand curve for the domestic good [panel (a)] from D_{dom} to D'_{dom} leads to a higher domestic price (P_0 to P_1) and quantity supplied (Q_0 to Q_1). The average loss of consumer surplus in the domestic market is $a'b'e'd'$, which is transferred to domestic producers. The demand adjustments cause the reduction in imports in the import market to be less than the initial reduction, that is, from Q_2 to Q_4 instead of to Q_3. There is an average reduction of consumer surplus equal to the area $abde$ in this market, where $abdf$ represents the tariff revenue received by the government and area fde the deadweight consumer loss. The total consumer loss from the tariff is the sum of the losses in both the domestic substitute market and the import market.

import good—or to consume less of it—at the free-trade price but who would do so now. It is common practice to use an average of the estimates under each demand curve—that is, area $abde$ in panel (b)—when measuring the loss in consumer surplus in the import market. A similar argument in the domestic market leads to the use of area $a'b'e'd'$ as the estimate of loss in consumer surplus due to the tariff on the foreign substitute. (It can be demonstrated theoretically that these are the appropriate measures of the loss in consumer surplus, assuming that the demand curves are linear and that there are no income effects, i.e., that the demand curves are "compensated" demand curves.)

The effects of the tariff are a government revenue gain of $abdf$ and a consumer deadweight loss of fde in the import good market. In the domestic market the consumer surplus loss $a'b'e'd'$ is equal exactly to the gain in producer surplus.

An example of this kind of calculation with nonhomogeneous goods was provided by economist William R. Cline in 1990. For the U.S. textile industry in 1986, using the technique of this appendix, he calculated that the consumer welfare loss in the import market from import restrictions was $1,275 million (or $1.3 billion). Further, the consumer welfare loss in the market for domestically produced goods from those same import restrictions was $1,513 million (or $1.5 billion). In the domestic goods market, however, the transfer to producers was of course also $1,513 million, so there was no net social effect in the domestic goods market. In the import market, there was a tariff revenue gain of $488 million, and thus the net welfare effect in the import market (and therefore the net welfare effect for the United States as a whole) was a loss of $787 million (= $1,275 million − $488 million).

Appendix B   THE IMPACT OF TRADE POLICY IN THE LARGE-COUNTRY
SETTING USING EXPORT SUPPLY AND IMPORT DEMAND CURVES

This appendix demonstrates the price, quantity, and welfare effects of trade policies using only the export supply/import demand diagram developed in the chapter. Thus, the demand and the supply curves within each country are not portrayed, although they are the bases for the export supply and import demand curves. We examine below the four basic instruments of trade policy—an import tariff, an import quota, an export tax, and an export subsidy.

THE IMPACT OF AN IMPORT TARIFF

Figure 19 reproduces panel (b) of Figure 10 in this chapter with the relevant illustrative numbers. Recall that the imposition of this specific tariff causes the free-trade price, P_{m0} ($100) to increase to P_{m1} ($106) in the importing country and the quantity imported to fall from Q_{m0} (30 units) to Q_{m1} (17 units). The importing country's government collects tariff revenue represented by the rectangle $P_{m2}P_{m1}E'F$ [=($106 − $96)(17) = $170], and the foreign supplier now receives price P_{m2} ($96).

Consider the welfare effects on the tariff-imposing country. The sum of areas a and b in Figure 10 conceptually equals the area of triangle $GE'E$ in Figure 19 because the base of triangle $GE'E$ (Q_{m0} − Q_{m1} = 30 − 17 = 13) equals the sum of the bases of triangles a and b in Figure 10; that is, the change in imports is the sum of the reduction in home consumption (base of triangle b = 7) and the increase in home production (base of triangle a = 6). The height of triangle $GE'E$ in Figure 19 (P_{m1} − P_{m0} = $106 − $100 = $6) is the height of each of the triangles a and b in Figure 10. Further, the part of the tariff revenue paid by home consumers (area c in Figure 10) equals area $P_{m0}P_{m1}E'G$ in Figure 19 [both are equal to ($106 − $100)(17) = $102], while the part of the tariff paid by the exporting country (area $fhij$ in Figure 10) equals area $P_{m2}P_{m0}GF$ in Figure 19 [both are equal to ($100 − $96)(17) = $68]. Thus, the net welfare effect in Figure 19 for the importing country is negative if deadweight loss triangle $GE'E$ is greater than rectangle $P_{m2}P_{m0}GF$, and the net welfare effect is positive if the area $GE'E$ is less than area $P_{m2}P_{m0}GF$. In our numerical example, because area $GE'E$ = [(1/2)($106 − $100)(30 − 17)] = [(1/2)($6)(13)] = $39, and area $P_{m2}P_{m0}GF$ = [($100 − $96)(17)] = [($4)(17)] = $68, there is a gain to the tariff-imposing country of ($68 − $39) = $29, just as occurred back in Figure 10.

FIGURE 19   The Imposition of a Specific Import Tariff

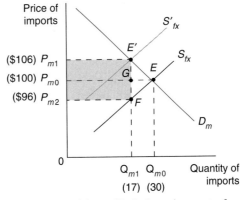

The imposition of the tariff raises the price of the good in the importing country from P_{m0} to P_{m1} and reduces the quantity imported from Q_{m0} to Q_{m1}. Tariff revenue of area $P_{m2}P_{m1}E'F$ is generated. The country's welfare increases if area $P_{m2}P_{m0}GF$ is larger than area $GE'E$.

THE IMPACT OF AN IMPORT QUOTA

To illustrate the imposition of an import quota in the demand for imports (D_m)–supply of foreign exports (S_{fx}) diagram, consider Figure 20. In free-trade equilibrium, quantity Q_{m0} (30 units) is imported at price P_{m0} ($100). Now the government, under pressure from domestic import-competing suppliers, specifies that only amount Q_{m1} (17) of the good can be imported into the country. The effect of the quota is that, at quantity Q_{m1}, a vertical line is erected (line $Q_{m1}FS'_{fx}$). The supply of exports schedule thus becomes RFS'_{fx}, which is the normal supply of exports schedule from R to F (with point F occurring at quota amount Q_{m1}) followed by the vertical segment indicating that no more imports can come in beyond quantity Q_{m1}. The equilibrium position in the market with the quota in place is point E' at equilibrium price P_{m1} ($106). Thus, as with the tariff, the domestic price has been increased and the quantity has been decreased compared with equilibrium under free trade. The domestic consumer pays a higher price than that under free trade—the increase in price is represented by distance $(P_{m1} - P_{m0} = \$6)$—and the foreign supplier receives a lower price than that under free trade; the decrease is represented by the distance $(P_{m0} - P_{m2} = \$4)$. Because there is a price divergence between what the consumer pays and what the producer receives for each unit of the import, the rectangle (quota rent) $P_{m2}P_{m1}E'F$ in Figure 20 is available for someone (as discussed in the chapter).

What are the welfare effects of the import quota? In Figure 20 (as in Figure 19), triangle $GE'E$ is the sum of the deadweight losses related to decreased home consumption and increased inefficient home production. However, if the government captures quota rent area $P_{m2}P_{m1}E'F$ as revenue by selling import licenses, or if domestic importing firms capture it when the government does not sell licenses, then area $P_{m2}P_{m0}GF$ is a transfer to the home country from foreign exporters. If this area is larger (smaller) than $GE'E$, the country will gain (lose) from the import quota. (Remember that we

FIGURE 20   The Imposition of an Import Quota

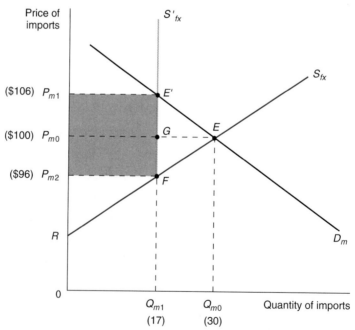

The free-trade equilibrium position is at point E, the intersection of RS_{fx} and D_m. If an import quota of size Q_{m1} is imposed, the supply of exports schedule becomes RFS'_{fx} and the quantity of imports falls from the free-trade level, Q_{m0}. The price to the importing country's consumers rises from P_{m0} to P_{m1} because of the artificial scarcity, while the price on the world market falls to P_{m2}. The shaded area represents the quota profit or rent. The welfare impact of the quota importantly depends on who receives this rent.

are assuming that trading partner countries do not retaliate.) In our numerical example, area $GE'E$ = $39 and area $P_{m2}P_{m0}GF$ = $68. But if the entire quota rent area, $P_{m2}P_{m1}E'F$, is captured by foreign suppliers or foreign governments with a rise in price of the good, the rent is captured by the exporting country. The net welfare effect of the quota would then be unambiguously worse than that of the tariff for the home (importing) country. The net welfare effect of the *tariff* was gain area $P_{m2}P_{m0}GF$ ($68) minus loss area $GE'E$ ($39); the net welfare effect of the *quota* if the foreign country captures the quota rent is a loss of *both* areas $GE'E$ ($39) and $P_{m0}P_{m1}E'G$ [($106 − $100 × 17) = $102]. (Note: Area $P_{m2}P_{m0}GF$ is not a loss from the departure from free trade because that area accrued to the foreign country under free trade as part of export receipts.)

A VER is illustrated like the import quota in Figure 20 because the impact on domestic price and quantity of the import is the same. However, the important difference between the two instruments is that the quota rent area is now virtually certain to be captured by the foreign supplier or government. With the restricted quantity in place and under control of the exporting country, that country can raise the price up to P_{m1}. The welfare effect for the importing country from the VER is thus a loss equal to the loss from the import quota when the foreign exporters captured the quota rent. If foreign exporters do not capture the import quota rent, the loss to the importing country from the VER exceeds the loss from the import quota, which in turn could not be a loss smaller than that with a tariff.

THE IMPACT OF AN EXPORT TAX

The impact of an export tax by the foreign country can be analyzed in parallel fashion to an import tariff. (Hopefully this discussion is not getting too taxing!) Again, the tax can be specific or *ad valorem* in nature, but the basic principles are the same. Figure 21 illustrates the imposition of a specific export tax. The supply of exports schedule, S_{fx}, slopes upward and the demand schedule for imports, D_m, slopes downward in the usual fashion. Before the imposition of the tax, the market equilibrium

FIGURE 21   The Imposition of an Export Tax

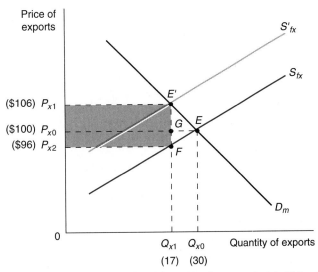

The free-trade position is at E, the intersection point of the supply of exports schedule (S_{fx}) and the demand for imports schedule (D_m). With a specific export tax, S_{fx} shifts up to S'_{fx}. With the tax in place, importing-country buyers pay the higher price P_{x1} per unit rather than free-trade price P_{x0}, and suppliers of the export receive lower amount P_{x2} per unit (rather than P_{x0}). The quantity of exports falls from Q_{x0} to Q_{x1} because of the imposition of the tax. The export tax revenue is indicated by the shaded area. The tax-imposing country improves its welfare if area $P_{x0}P_{x1}E'G$ is greater than area FGE.

is at point E with price P_{x0} and quantity Q_{x0}. When the tax is levied, the supply of exports schedule shifts upward (a decrease in supply) to become S'_{fx}. With the tax in place, the price of the export on the *world* market is P_{x1} ($106) and the quantity sold is Q_{x1} (17) at the new equilibrium point E'. The large, exporting country has thus been able to force up the world price to some extent because of the decrease in supply. However, the price that exporters receive after paying the tax falls to P_{x2} ($96) because, with less of the good exported, more is sold on their home market, driving down the domestic price. The exporting country's government collects revenue of shaded area $P_{x2}P_{x1}E'F$[($106 − $96)(17) = $170] from the tax. Some of the revenue is economically paid by the importing-country buyer (area $P_{x0}P_{x1}E'G$ [($106 − $100)(17) = $102]), and the remainder is paid by the producer (area $P_{x2}P_{x0}GF$) through receipt of lower revenues. The export tax hurts the exporting country's producers, but its consumers gain through a reduced domestic price. This is opposite to the case of an import tariff by a country, where the importing country's producers gain through the higher domestic price and its consumers are hurt.

Let us now examine the welfare effects of this tax on the country imposing the tax. In Figure 21, the exporting country's export price rises from P_{x0} to P_{x1}. If import prices remain the same, then the terms of trade ($P_{\text{exports}}/P_{\text{imports}}$) will rise because of the export tax. Because of the improvement in the terms of trade, the welfare effect for the exporting country can be positive. In Figure 21, triangle FGE is the deadweight loss associated with the export tax; it corresponds conceptually to triangles ghf and ikj in Figure 12 in this chapter. It corresponds because the combined base of the two triangles in Figure 12 was the fall in exports, as is ($Q_{x0} − Q_{x1} = 13$) in Figure 21, and the price reduction was the old, pretax price minus the new domestic, after-tax price ($P_{x0} − P_{x2} = $100 − 96), which equals ($P_{m0} − P_{m2}$) in Figure 12. Potentially offsetting the deadweight losses from the export tax in Figure 21 is rectangular area $P_{x0}P_{x1}E'G$, the transfer of welfare as tax revenue to the government from importing country buyers of the export good. The large country will gain (lose) from the export tax if area $P_{x0}P_{x1}E'G$ is larger (smaller) than area FGE. In our example, area $P_{x0}P_{x1}E'G = $($106 − $100)(17) = $102 and area $FGE = [(1/2)($100 − $96)(30 − 17)] = $26 so the exporting country gains ($102 − $26) = $76.

THE IMPACT OF AN EXPORT SUBSIDY

An export subsidy is in effect a negative export tax, and the analytics of the two devices are similar. In Figure 22, the equilibrium in the export supply–import demand graph is initially at point E, with price P_{x0} ($55) and quantity exported Q_{x0}. When the exporting-country government provides an export subsidy, say, of $10 per unit, the S_{fx} schedule shifts vertically *downward* (an increase in supply) to S'_{fx}, which is shown as a parallel shift since we assume that a subsidy of a fixed monetary amount per unit exported is paid. The new price at which the exporter can sell the good is P_{x2} ($49), and the new equilibrium is at point E' with quantity Q_{x1} (9). Because there is now a relatively greater incentive for the producer of the good to export rather than to sell in its domestic market, the reduced amount of the good in the exporting country causes the domestic price to rise to P_{x1}. (With price P_{x1}, the firm receives the same total amount per unit of sales in each market, because price P_{x1} equals export price P_{x2} plus the subsidy per unit received for exporting the good.) Thus, domestic consumers are injured when their producers receive an export subsidy. An additional possible source of injury to the exporting country is that the export subsidy (unlike the export tax or the import tariff) does not bring in revenue to the government. Rather, the subsidy requires government expenditure. The amount of subsidy required for export quantity Q_{x1} (9 units) in Figure 22 is shaded area $P_{x2}P_{x1}FE'$, which is the amount of the subsidy per unit of exports [vertical distance $E'F$—equal to distance ($P_{x1} − P_{x2}$)] times the number of units of the export (the horizontal distance from the origin to export quantity Q_{x1}). Hence, the total subsidy cost is ($59 − $49)(9) = $90.

Finally, regarding welfare in the large-country case of an export subsidy for the country employing the subsidy, triangle EFG represents the deadweight losses. This area is conceptually equivalent to triangles f and g in earlier Figure 13. In that figure, the sum of the bases of the two triangles was increased exports due to the export subsidy, as is length EG or ($Q_{x1} − Q_{x0} = 5$) in Figure 22. Similarly, the height of triangles f and g in Figure 13 indicated the difference between the market price in the exporting country with the export subsidy and the international market

FIGURE 22   An Export Subsidy

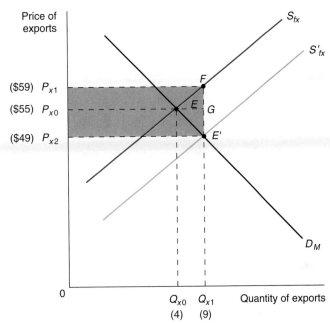

The free-trade equilibrium position is at point E. With an export subsidy, the supply of exports schedule S_{fx} shifts down vertically (to S'_{fx}) by the amount of the subsidy per unit of exports. Because the producer can now sell the good for the lower price, P_{x2}, on the world market (rather than P_{x0}), the quantity exported rises from Q_{x0} to Q_{x1}. The price to domestic buyers rises from P_{x0} to P_{x1} because less of the good is available for consumption in the exporting country. The shaded area represents the total expenditure by the government in the form of the subsidy to exporting firms. Welfare unambiguously declines in the exporting country.

price without the subsidy—as does length FG or $(P_{x1} - P_{x0})$ in Figure 22. For welfare purposes, the country *also* loses area $P_{x2}P_{x0}GE'$, the amount of price reduction to the foreign buyers (because of the export subsidy) times the quantity of exports. Thus, the export subsidy has *a loss* in the large-country case on the country that uses it, a loss that did not occur in the small-country case. In this example, the total loss is thus area EFG [$\frac{1}{2}(\$59 - \$55)(9 - 4) = \$10$] plus area $P_{x2}P_{x0}GE'$ [($\$55 - \$49)(9) = \$54$], or a total loss of \$64.

15

ARGUMENTS FOR INTERVENTIONIST TRADE POLICIES

LEARNING OBJECTIVES

- To understand why trade policy instruments are often part of broader social policy and why other policy instruments might be less costly.

- To evaluate the effectiveness of trade policy in the presence of market imperfections.

- To recognize invalid economic arguments for protection.

- To grasp the role of trade policy in promoting strategic industries and dynamic comparative advantage.

INTRODUCTION

On almost a daily basis, there are articles in newspapers in which someone or some group is arguing for the imposition of protection against imports of goods and services. Many of these arguments have a long and colorful history and, surprisingly, continue to influence policymakers and the general public. The following statements provide examples of the kind of arguments one continues to encounter on a regular basis:

A 15 percent revenue tariff on all imported manufactures and goods in competition with American-made goods would be a fitting way to declare our economic independence. (Patrick J. Buchanan, 1998)

I do not know much about the tariff, but I know that when we buy our own products we get both the goods and the money, but when we import goods we get the goods and the exporting country gets the money. (A statement often attributed to Abraham Lincoln)

We should subsidize smokestacks and erect tariffs to protect our manufacturers from foreign competitors. (Eamonn Fingleton, *In Praise of Hard Industries*)

We need to impose tariffs and quotas to protect our manufacturers from cheap foreign labor.

It is important to restrict imports in order to stop the hemorrhaging of employment and the exports of U.S. jobs to the rest of the world.

Which of these arguments have economic merit? Which do not? Obviously the public and its representative elected officials are prone to be influenced on this matter because various groups in the United States spend millions of dollars each year in an attempt to influence policymakers to enact legislation that will restrict international trade. Given that, in principle, most economists at least agree that trade increases the overall well-being of a country, it is striking to note how much individual interests are willing to spend to reduce international trade. In this chapter we present a number of these arguments for protection and then evaluate the validity of each from an economic perspective. As a usual final step in each case, we ask whether an alternative policy instrument might do a better job of achieving the objective of the restrictive trade policy. Because economists think in terms of alternatives and benefits versus costs, our procedure is essentially to ask, "Given the objective, what are the benefits and costs of a restrictive trade policy compared with those of another policy?"

Finally, bear in mind (as nicely put in Ingram 1986, p. 341) that the perspective from which an argument for protection is put forth is important. For that reason, we have chosen to organize the presentation of these arguments in terms of the nature of the policy question being addressed. The presentation begins by looking at a number of arguments that tend to be proposed from a national perspective, where trade policy instruments are part of a broader social policy package that affects the nation as a whole. We then turn to proposals for protection that are suggested as ways of offsetting various kinds of market imperfections such as those arising from imperfect competition and externalities of varying kinds. The third category looks at arguments for protection that are undertaken as a response to policy distortions arising from the actions of our trading partners. This is followed by a brief overview of several miscellaneous arguments that reappear from time to time but that have little or no economic basis. Finally, the last category contains some of the key arguments that focus on temporarily restricting trade as a strategy to foster comparative advantages over time, particularly in manufacturing. The chapter concludes with a brief summary and conclusions.

TRADE POLICY AS A PART OF BROADER SOCIAL POLICY OBJECTIVES FOR A NATION

Trade policy is often conducted as a component of a policy package that is directed toward improving the well-being of different groups in society or reaching certain national and international objectives. From this perspective, trade restrictions are promoted to the public at large in terms of, for example, influencing income distribution, strengthening national defense, maintaining global power, and fostering international equity. In this section we review a number of the more common arguments for protection that come into play as part of a policy package directed toward broader social policy objectives.

Trade Taxes as a Source of Government Revenue

For many countries, consumption taxes are an important source of government revenue. This is particularly true in those cases in which it is difficult for governments to effectively use taxes on income and property to generate the needed revenue to finance public expenditures. In this instance, governments often turn to trade taxes along with other domestic sales taxes to generate needed revenue. The decision to use trade taxes, as opposed to other forms of taxation, to fund government expenditures in this broader social context turns on issues of tax efficiency and equity. In certain large-country settings, it is also possible that countries may be able to shift some of the incidence of the tax to trading partners. This case clearly illustrates how the broader social policy objective of earning revenue dominates and might well result in the imposition of trade taxes as a part of a set of broad government revenue policies. In the longer term, however, changes in the institutional setting that will permit the inclusion of a broader tax base (including property and income) will likely prove to be more beneficial to the country. In the case of the United States, trade taxes provide an extremely small portion of total government revenue today, whereas prior to a century ago, trade and consumption taxes were the principal source of government revenue and income and property taxes were considerably less important. It is worth noting, however, that trade taxes continue to be an important source of government revenue for many countries in the world. Not surprisingly, the majority of these countries are in the developing world.

National Defense Argument for a Tariff

The **national defense argument** for a tariff assumes that an industry is vital to a country's security because its product or the skills it develops are invaluable to the country during wartime or periods of national emergency. If, during normal times, free trade is permitted in the product of this industry, imports may capture the lion's share of the market and either drive domestic producers from the industry or reduce the size of the industry. However, in times of national emergency or world conflict, normal trade patterns might be disrupted and import supplies cut off. If a cutoff occurs, the country is left without adequate supplies of the product and national security is threatened. To prevent this threat from becoming a reality in the future, the industry must be protected now. With tariff protection, the industry will thrive, and national security will not be undermined should world conflict or disruption occur.

What are we to make of this argument? The important point to recognize is that it is not easy to identify which industries are vital to national defense. Indeed, in petitions for protection, almost all industries put forth some claim concerning their importance for the security of the country. For example, the U.S. watch industry successfully obtained protection using this argument, and (see Ingram and Dunn 1993, p. 154) even the garlic and clothespin industries petitioned for protection using the national defense argument. The determination of which industries are truly vital is extraordinarily difficult and ultimately must be made by the political process.

Once an industry has been determined vital to national security, the task of the economist is to point out that policies other than the tariff may have a lower welfare cost for the country. For example, the good could be stockpiled, like U.S. oil with the Strategic Petroleum Reserve, and thus be available when foreign supplies are cut off. Or, as in the U.S. semiconductor industry, a joint business-government research and development firm (Sematech) was set up to assist the industry. A production subsidy also could be given to keep domestic firms in operation; as was noted in Chapter 14, a subsidy has a lower deadweight loss than

IN THE REAL WORLD:

THE RELATIVE IMPORTANCE OF TRADE TAXES AS A SOURCE OF GOVERNMENT REVENUE

Trade taxes continue to be an important part of government financing in many countries of the world. This is particularly the case in countries that do not have the institutional tradition of financing government expenditures with income, wealth, and property taxes. They thus rely on transaction taxes, most often of a consumption nature, to finance government programs. A number of countries rely on trade taxes because they are more easily collected upon import or export and, in the large-country case, can be passed on in part to countries that are importing the good. This is particularly true in the case of countries that are exporting goods for which foreign demand is relatively inelastic. In Table 1, the relative importance of trade taxes is indicated for selected countries. (We follow the World Bank's classification of countries in this table.) It is not surprising to note that trade taxes are generally relatively unimportant for the high-income countries, but they are extremely important for a number of low-income and middle-income countries.

TABLE 1   Trade Taxes as a Percentage of Central Government Revenue

Country	Year	Percentage	Country	Year	Percentage
High-Income Countries					
Bahrain	2005	8.98%	Switzerland	2002	1.22%
Rep. of Korea	2005	3.35	United States	2005	1.11
Australia	2005	2.22	Iceland	2002	0.96
Kuwait	2005	1.89	Netherlands	2005	0.81
Canada	2005	1.27	Norway	2005	0.19
Middle-Income Countries					
Swaziland	2003	47.66%	Peru	2005	5.69%
Lesotho	2004	45.16	Georgia	2005	5.61
Russia	2005	24.19	Moldova	2005	5.50
Mauritius	2005	19.86	Costa Rica	2005	5.07
Guatemala	2005	15.00	Kazakhstan	2005	3.63
Algeria	2002	12.94	Indonesia	2004	3.02
Jordan	2005	11.46	Colombia	2005	3.01
Thailand	2005	7.48	Estonia	2004	0.22
El Salvador	2005	6.56	Slovak Republic	2005	0.11
Iran	2005	5.93			
Low-Income Countries					
Bangladesh	2004	32.56%	Nepal	2005	19.04%
Ghana	2004	28.51	India	2002	14.85
Democratic Republic of Congo	2002	27.40	Kenya	2004	11.17
Sierra Leone	2004	26.96	Burkina Faso	2005	10.83

Note: Some 2005 data are preliminary.
Source: International Monetary Fund, *Government Finance Statistics Yearbook 2006* (Washington, DC: International Monetary Fund, 2006), various pages.

a tariff. In addition, the burden of protection of the industry would be borne by all taxpayers (who all benefit from the "defense") and not just by the consumers of the particular product. Further, each year Congress reviews the merits of continuing a subsidy, so there is ample opportunity to reassess the value of the protection. On the other hand, a tariff tends to remain in the tariff structure because no regular policy review is required. Economists thus can suggest other instruments superior to the tariff.

Tariff to Improve the Balance of Trade

The argument for a **tariff to improve the balance of trade** claims that the imposition of the tariff will reduce imports. Assuming that exports are not affected, the obvious result is that the balance of trade improves, because the balance of trade (the value of exports minus the value of imports) becomes less negative (i.e., the trade deficit is reduced) or a deficit turns into a surplus.

The economist responds to this argument by saying that it fails to recognize the economic and political repercussions of this Mercantilistic action, and the end result when these repercussions are taken into account may be no improvement in the trade balance and a reduction in country (and world) welfare.[1] Examples of these repercussions include the following:

1. Retaliation by trading partners.
2. A reduction in national income abroad and a reduced ability of foreign countries to buy the home country's products.
3. A reduction in exports of the home country if the imports now excluded were inputs into the production process of the home country's exports.
4. A reduction in exports and an increase in imports of the home country because of a rise in the value of the home currency.
5. A reduction in exports and an increase in imports of the home country because of inflationary pressures in the home country. Because the application of a tariff has the effect of turning demand inward to home-country products, this new demand could generate upward price pressures if the home country is close to full employment. If inflationary tendencies appear, then home country firms become less competitive in world markets and in the domestic market against the goods of other countries.

Thus, the use of a tariff is no guarantee that the balance of trade will improve. In addition, considerable discussion in recent years has centered on the trade deficit as essentially a macroeconomic phenomenon and on the tariff by itself as having virtually no effect on the balance of trade because it does not address the relevant macroeconomic variables. The point concerning the **macroeconomic interpretation of a trade deficit** can be simply made. In macroeconomic equilibrium in a simple national income model,

$$Y = C + I + G + (X - M)$$

where: Y = national income
C = consumption
I = investment
G = government spending on goods and services
X = exports
M = imports

---

[1] The myopic view of the balance-of-trade argument was ridiculed beautifully by Henry George (1911, originally 1886, p. 117) when he stated that "on the same theory the more ships sunk at sea the better for the commercial world. To have all the ships that left each country sunk before they could reach any other country would, upon protectionist principles, be the quickest means of enriching the whole world, since all countries would then enjoy the maximum of exports with the minimum of imports."

Rearranging this expression, we obtain

$$Y - (C + I + G) = (X - M)$$

Because $(C + I + G)$ indicates domestic spending (by consumers, business, and government), the conclusion is that if a trade deficit exists (i.e., if $X < M$), it occurs because $Y < (C + I + G)$ or income is less than domestic spending. In other words, the country is spending beyond its means. The only way to reduce the deficit is to increase Y, to reduce spending, or to undertake some combination of the two. If the deficit is a macroeconomic problem, a tariff is unlikely to be of much help, especially if the economy is close to full employment and income therefore cannot be increased to any significant extent.

Even ignoring the macroeconomic interpretation of the deficit, another policy besides a tariff might eliminate or reduce a trade deficit. Less welfare loss could be incurred if the country adopted a policy that operates on the balance of trade in its entirety, namely, a devaluation or depreciation of the currency (assuming some fixed currency value was initially in place). The point to be made here is that policies other than a tariff may be able to accomplish the particular objective.

The Terms-of-Trade Argument for Protection

The **terms-of-trade argument** for protection maintains that national welfare can be enhanced through a restrictive trade policy instrument. It acknowledges that world welfare will decline with a departure from free trade because the home country's gains in welfare are more than offset by the losses of welfare occurring in other countries. In gaining at the expense of foreign countries, the terms-of-trade argument resembles many other arguments for protection in that the protectionist policy is thus a **beggar-my-neighbor policy.**

The terms-of-trade argument states that restrictive trade policy can raise the ratio of $P_{exports}/P_{imports}$ (P_X/P_M) and thus enhance a country's welfare. Economically, the use of a tariff by the home country reduces demand for the foreign good on the world market. Consequently, the world price of the imported good will fall and P_X/P_M will rise. The use of a tariff therefore has the potential to increase home welfare, although foreign welfare will fall as the commodity terms of trade of foreign countries decline. We emphasize that only a large country can employ the terms-of-trade argument with any success because the tariff-imposing country must be able to influence its terms of trade.

The terms-of-trade argument is best understood with an offer curve diagram. In Figure 1, OC_I represents the offer curve of the home country (country I), while OC_{II} is the offer curve of the foreign country (country II). In free trade, the terms of trade are TOT_1. If country I imposes a tariff, its offer curve shifts to OC'_I, establishing the new equilibrium at point E'. While country I's exports are reduced from $0x_1$ to $0x_2$ and its imports from $0y_1$ to $0y_2$, the terms of trade have improved from TOT_1 to TOT_2. Thus, there is potential for increased well-being for country I because it is receiving more imports for each unit of its exports. Alternatively, it is giving up fewer exports for each unit of imports obtained. In a welfare sense, this means that country I is potentially "better off."

The terms-of-trade argument is not yet complete, however. What has not been taken into account in a welfare sense is that the quantity of imports has fallen with the imposition of the tariff. This quantity reduction, other things being equal, reduces the level of country I's welfare because the country's consumption of low-cost imports, for which home production is at a comparative disadvantage, has been reduced. In sum, country I gains because of a lower world price of the imported good but loses because of a smaller import quantity of that good. This additional consideration of forgone quantities is brought into the analysis through the concept of the optimum tariff rate. The **optimum tariff rate** is the rate that maximizes the country's welfare. Conceptually, it is the tariff rate at which the positive difference between the gain from better prices and the loss from reduced quantity of imports

FIGURE 1   A Tariff to Improve the Terms of Trade

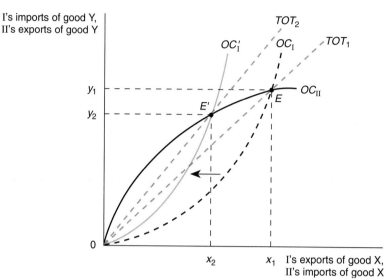

The initial free-trade equilibrium is at point E, the intersection of country I's free-trade offer curve OC_I and country II's free-trade offer curve OC_{II}. Country I's imposition of a tariff shifts its offer curve from OC_I to OC'_I, as the country is now less willing to trade at the previous terms of trade, TOT_1. Because of the tariff, the new equilibrium is at point E'. Country I's exports of good X fall from $0x_1$ to $0x_2$ and its imports of good Y fall from $0y_1$ to $0y_2$. However, the terms of trade for country I improve from TOT_1 to TOT_2, and each unit of country I's exports now commands a greater quantity of imports.

is at a maximum. If the tariff rate is higher than this optimum rate, then welfare is below the maximum, because the additional gain from better terms of trade is more than offset by the additional loss from the reduced quantity of imports. Similarly, at a tariff rate below the optimum, the unexploited gains from improving the terms of trade exceed the losses from the additional reduction in quantity of imports.

What characterizes the optimum tariff rate of a country? First, the optimum tariff for country I involves the intersection of I's offer curve with country II's offer curve in the *elastic* portion of II's curve. If country I's offer curve with a tariff intersected in the inelastic portion of the foreign offer curve, the tariff rate could not be "optimum" for I because an even higher tariff would improve country I's terms of trade *and* increase I's quantity of imports. (Remember that the inelastic portion of country II's offer curve is downward sloping.) If country I's offer curve with a tariff intersected in the unit-elastic portion of II's curve, the tariff rate also could not be "optimum" because an even higher tariff would improve I's terms of trade and still yield the same quantity of I's imports. (Remember that a unit-elastic portion of II's offer curve would be horizontal.) We do not pursue further the matter of the optimum tariff here, and in fact such a rate is extremely difficult to calculate. The most important point to remember is that improving the terms of trade does not necessarily mean that welfare will improve for the tariff-imposing country.

How valid is the terms-of-trade argument as a guide for policy? Economists agree that the argument logically leads to the conclusion that the imposition of the tariff, other things equal, might enhance the tariff-imposing country's welfare. If a country's objective is solely to improve its terms of trade, no domestic policy instrument, such as a subsidy to import-competing production, is superior to the tariff for doing so. However, the terms-of-trade argument is a beggar-my-neighbor argument because the welfare of the partner country falls. Because the partner country is injured by the tariff, it will likely retaliate with a tariff of its own. In that event, both countries will end up with reduced welfare compared with their situations under free trade. If continual retaliation occurs, trade shrinks dramatically in the offer curve diagram, and neither country may end up with terms of trade better than during the initial free trade. The potential retaliation and other consequences (such as injury to other countries) may partly explain why large countries such as the United States and Japan do not have frequent large-scale tariff wars. (See, e.g., Petri 1984, chap. 7.)

Tariff to Reduce Aggregate Unemployment

The argument for a **tariff to reduce aggregate unemployment** runs as follows: Given that a country has unemployment in slack times, the imposition of a tariff will result in a shift in demand by domestic consumers from foreign goods to home-produced goods. With this increase in demand, home industries will expand their output and, in the process, will hire more labor and thus contribute to the reduction of unemployment in the country. The new labor hired will also be earning spendable income and, by the familiar Keynesian multiplier process, other industries will then expand and add new jobs. Therefore, the tariff has accomplished its stated objective.

In assessing this argument, the economist raises several points, most of which center around the possibility that very few new jobs will be created by the tariff. The home country might lose jobs in *export* industries to such an extent that the net effect on employment is negligible or even negative. The loss of jobs in the home export industries can occur for several reasons:

1. Expanded employment in the import-substitute industries in the domestic country comes about in a beggar-my-neighbor manner because jobs are lost in foreign countries. When the home country reduces its imports by the tariff, there is an equivalent loss of exports and attendant job losses in other countries. To avert this job loss, those countries may impose retaliatory tariffs that reduce *export* jobs in the home country.

2. Even without any retaliation, exports of the home country may decline because the reduction in exports in the foreign countries has lowered their national income. This causes a cut in spending on the home country's export goods and reduces employment in the export industries in the home country.

3. If the home country has an exchange rate that is free to vary, then foreign currencies will depreciate when the home country imposes the tariff and buys fewer foreign goods. The purchase of fewer foreign goods implies that there is less demand for foreign currency with which to purchase those goods. The depreciation, or fall in value, of foreign currencies is equivalent to a rise in value of the home currency, which serves to reduce home exports (because it takes more units of the foreign currency to buy the home goods) and to increase home country imports (which are now relatively cheaper to home residents). The net effect of the rise in the value of the home currency is to reduce jobs in the home export and import-substitute industries.

We could cite other repercussions to the imposition of the tariff, but the main point should be clear: There is no certainty that the tariff will accomplish the objective. In addition, economists stress that if the goal is to increase employment, why use the tariff when other policies might accomplish the goal more directly and with more certainty? The other policies—the macroeconomic instruments of monetary and fiscal policy—could be used in an expansionary way to increase employment. Employment in foreign countries might also increase as the home country uses its expanded income to buy more imports and transmit some of its expansion to other countries. Thus, welfare everywhere could rise instead of fall as it would do with a tariff. If a problem such as aggregate unemployment exists, then the appropriate policies to use are those aimed specifically at dealing with that problem. This notion is known as the **specificity principle,** and we shall employ it in several other arguments for protection.

Tariff to Increase Employment in a Particular Industry

The **tariff to increase employment in a particular industry** takes a microeconomic view of the employment question, arguing that if protection is granted to a given industry, demand shifts from the import to the home product because the price of the imported good rises relative to the price of the home good. This shift in purchases then bids up the price of the home good, inducing domestic producers to supply a greater quantity. The production of these additional units results in the hiring of more domestic labor, thus increasing employment in the home industry. However, new jobs in the protected industry may be filled at the expense of employment in other industries. Thus, an addition to total employment in the country may not take place, but this is not the objective of the tariff. Rather, the goal is to increase employment in the particular industry, and the tariff has succeeded in accomplishing this objective.

Economists do not dispute that the tariff can augment employment in this industry. However, their interest in efficiency leads them to question whether the tariff is the best method of increasing employment. If the goal of adding to employment in this industry is accepted—even given that employment is being reduced elsewhere—a subsidy to production or employment is a welfare-superior way to attain the goal compared with using a tariff. (Chapter 14 discussed the superiority of a subsidy over a tariff.) Thus, while this argument for protection may be valid theoretically from its particular perspective, this validity does not mean that tariff protection should be granted. An alternative instrument for providing jobs in the industry—a subsidy by the home government—can do the job (pun intended) at lower cost in a welfare sense.

Tariff to Benefit a Scarce Factor of Production

The **tariff to benefit a scarce factor of production** is a more sophisticated and rigorous argument than many arguments for protection. It makes no claim that the country as a whole benefits from the protection; it is instead an argument for protection from the perspective of an individual factor of production. Although the country as a whole suffers reduced welfare from the trade policy, the country's scarce factor gains. This analysis was developed in Chapter 8 and will not be repeated here.

Two points can be made in assessing the argument, however. First, the country as a whole loses welfare from the imposition of a tariff; a political decision to redistribute income to labor (or the scarce factor) by a tariff does reduce national well-being. If politicians wish to make this redistribution, economists will respond that a more efficient way to accomplish the objective is to undertake (if the political process permits) a direct transfer by taxing capital (or the abundant factor) and awarding the tax revenues to labor. This direct process does not lead to the welfare loss associated with reducing the country's participation in international trade.

Second, it may be that countries do not have the complete factor mobility implied in the argument. Recall the specific-factors model (see Chapter 8). If the assumptions of the specific-factors model are more relevant in the real world than those of the Heckscher-Ohlin model, the scarce-factor conclusion does not hold. If protection is adopted, the return to capital in the import-competing industry will rise, the return to capital in the export industry will fall, and the money wage will rise. However, the impact on real wages of workers depends on their consumption patterns. A gain occurs if a worker's consumption pattern is tilted toward consumption of the export good, but the worker suffers a reduced real wage if the consumption pattern is tilted toward the import good. No a priori judgment can be made on the impact on the scarce factor. Further, if economies of scale and greater product

IN THE REAL WORLD:

COSTS OF PROTECTING INDUSTRY EMPLOYMENT

Tariffs can have an impact on employment in particular industries because the imposition of a tariff stimulates output of import-substitute industries as consumers turn away from the now higher-priced imports toward domestic goods. However, the costs to consumers and to the country as a whole can be large, and an appropriate question is whether the large costs are justified in view of the amount of employment created by tariff.

Economists Gary C. Hufbauer and Kimberly A. Elliott (1994) attempted to quantify the costs of employment

protection. Table 2 provides a sampling of the effects in 12 industries of a variety of import restraints in the United States. The figures pertain to 1990. Estimates of this sort require many assumptions and are subject to a large margin of error; nevertheless, some of the costs are staggering!

It is clear from the table that if a worker's job is to be protected, the consumer cost of doing so considerably exceeds worker wages in the listed industries. It would be cheaper to make a direct monetary transfer of the annual wage from consumers to workers (if this were politically possible!)

TABLE 2   Consumer Costs per Job Saved and Welfare Costs to the United States of Protection of Various Industries, 1990

Industry with Import Restraint	Jobs Saved	Consumer Cost per Job Saved	Annual Welfare Cost to the U.S.
Ball bearings	146	$ 438,356	$ 1,000,000
Benzenoid chemicals	216	> 1,000,000	10,000,000
Costume jewelry	1,067	96,532	5,000,000
Dairy products	2,378	497,897	104,000,000
Frozen concentrated orange juice	609	461,412	35,000,000
Glassware	1,477	180,095	9,000,000
Luggage	226	933,628	26,000,000
Machine tools	1,556	348,329	35,000,000
Polyethylene resins	298	590,604	20,000,000
Rubber footwear	1,701	122,281	12,000,000
Softwood lumber	605	758,678	12,000,000
Woman's footwear, except athletic	3,702	101,567	11,000,000

Source: Gary Clyde Hufbauer and Kimberly Ann Elliott, *Measuring the Costs of Protection in the United States* (Washington, DC: Institute for International Economics, 1994), pp. 12–13, appendixes I and II.

variety are relevant (as discussed in Chapter 10), all residents of a trading country can gain regardless of scarce-factor status.

Fostering "National Pride" in Key Industries

Pride in your country can clearly be thought of as a legitimate social objective. Countries often take pride in being able to produce particular products in that such production serves as an indication that they are as "modern" or capable or creative as other countries to which they might be comparing themselves. This can, in a sense, be viewed as a social externality that is not captured in the price of the domestically produced product. If it is the physical production itself that produces this pride, then it may warrant a policy intervention. However, as is often the case, a production subsidy will be a more cost-effective way of achieving this end. Only when it is necessary to keep out all foreign goods to achieve the desired objective would blocking all imports through the use of a prohibitive tariff or product embargo be a logical policy choice.

Differential Protection as a Component of a Foreign Policy/Aid Package

Countries often have complex sets of targets or objectives that involve many different policy instruments. This is especially true in the area of global objectives. Thus, it is not uncommon to see a country adopt policy positions that may differ across its trading partners. For example, a country can generally be in favor of reducing barriers to trade and yet, at the same time, place a trade embargo on one or more countries for reasons linked to other social or hegemonic objectives. We must always take care to acknowledge the social costs of incorporating trade restrictions to meet the objective. Such differentiated policy treatment can also work in a positive fashion. For example, a number of industrial countries have adopted the Generalized System of Preferences (GSP) in dealing with some particular goods coming from the poorer nations of the world. This policy is one that substantially reduces the barriers to trade with respect to goods coming in from certain developing countries. It can, in essence, be viewed as part of a broader foreign aid package that might involve bilateral and multilateral aid. While removing protection on all imports would be preferable, this inconsistent policy treatment could be viewed as providing a short-term advantage for the poor country so that country can become competitive. It is critical, of course, that the GSP provision be applied to products for which the recipient country has a potential comparative advantage. Otherwise, it will simply provide an incentive to misallocate scarce resources in the developing country.

CONCEPT CHECK

1. Why is it difficult to assess the relevance of the national defense argument for any particular industry?
2. Why might a tariff not affect a country's balance of trade?
3. The terms of trade for a large country improve with every successive increase in a tariff, so why is the optimum tariff rate for the country not infinite, even assuming no retaliation by a trading partner?
4. Why does a tariff-induced increase in employment in a given sector not necessarily increase aggregate employment in a country?

PROTECTION TO OFFSET MARKET IMPERFECTIONS

The Presence of Externalities as an Argument for Protection

The externality argument is based on the notion that the social costs or benefits of a given production or consumption process differ from the private costs or benefits of that production or consumption process. As discussed in introductory courses, in such a situation, there is *market failure* in that even a perfectly competitive market will not maximize social welfare.[2] For example, if a production process generates air pollution, or a "negative externality," the producing firm itself may not bear the full "cost" of its production because the pollutants (rather than having to be cleaned up by the firm) can simply be passed into the atmosphere for the society at large to deal with. Hence, the private cost to the firm of the production process is less than the social cost of the production process (which would equal the private cost plus the pollution cost). Because the cost paid by the firm is less than the "true" cost, the price paid by the consumer (based on the private cost) is lower than it would be if all costs were included, and hence more of the good will be produced than would otherwise be the case. Because this price

---

[2]For an excellent critique of the presence of market failures as an argument for protection, see Jagdish Bhagwati, *Free Trade Today* (Princeton, NJ: Princeton University Press, 2002), pp. 11–33.

(a reflection of the benefit received by the consumer from purchasing one more unit) is less than the true cost of producing that unit, society's welfare actually declines because of the production of that last unit. A "solution" to the problem is to tax the production process in this case, and to tax to the extent of the difference between private cost and social cost. With this tax in place, price will rise, fewer units of the good will be produced because of the decline in quantity demanded, and welfare will rise since the units of the good where social cost exceeds benefits are no longer produced.

Consider now how such externality situations can form the basis for an argument for protection against imports. We will discuss two different types of externality from the one previously mentioned—a situation of a *negative externality in consumption* and a situation of a *positive externality in production*. Following this discussion, an assessment of the case for protection will be made.

A negative externality in consumption involves a situation in which the process of consuming a good can generate adverse externality effects. For example, if a person consumes Scotch whisky, the person may do damage to society if he or she subsequently injures other persons or damages property by driving an automobile while intoxicated. With respect to consumption of this good, then, the economist would say that the private benefit to the individual from consuming the last unit of the good is greater than the social benefit from consuming that last unit because the social benefit is equal to the private benefit less the utility lost because of the injury or the property damage. Further, because the price paid for the good (which is assumed to reflect production costs and, in market equilibrium, also to reflect the marginal benefit of consumption to the private individual) is greater than the marginal benefit to society of the consumption of the last unit, welfare has been reduced for society as a whole by the consumption of that unit. Hence, in terms of protection, the argument is that, if an imported good has this negative consumption externality feature, a way to increase social welfare would be to put a tariff on the imported good. This would reduce consumption of the good, and the units no longer consumed are ones that would have reduced social welfare. Hence, society has experienced an increase in its well-being because of the imposition of the tariff.

A second situation involving externalities and protection involves a positive externality in production. Suppose, for example, that a firm, when it employs workers, provides those workers with skills that can be useful beyond the setting of this particular firm. The particular firm, of course, cannot prevent some of those workers from moving to other jobs at some future time. If a worker does leave and go to work for another firm, the worker will take with him or her the skills acquired at the first firm, and the second firm will therefore not have to bear the costs of training this worker. Hence, costs at the second firm are lower than they otherwise would have been—the first firm is reducing costs of production elsewhere in the economy. This means that the private costs being incurred by the first firm are actually greater than the total social costs that should properly be allocated to it (because some of those costs should be absorbed by the second and other firms). Hence, in the market, where the price of the first firm's product covers that firm's private costs, price (or marginal benefit to consumers) exceeds the true cost to society of that particular firm's output. Output by the first firm should therefore be expanded, and the consequent expansion to units of output where benefits exceed social cost would add to society's welfare. In the context of this chapter, a way to encourage expansion would be to put a tariff on imported goods that compete with the first firm's product. With this tariff in place, the firm would expand its production and would therefore add to society's well-being.

What are we to make of these cases for protection? In general, economists would respond with two main points. First, even if it is granted that a logical case for protection can be built in these two scenarios, there would remain the difficulty of actually estimating the size of the externalities and deciding upon the appropriate tariff rate to apply. It is highly unlikely that the concepts involved permit any precise estimate of what rate to use. Second, and more importantly, we should ask why *imports* are being singled out as the target for policy. For example, in the case of the imported whisky, an equal case can be made that all whiskies (or all alcoholic beverages for that matter) have the same negative externalities, *whether they are imported or produced domestically.* The appropriate policy, therefore, would be to tax the consumption of all such goods, whether foreign-made or domestically produced. There is no case for discriminating on the basis of the location of production. In the case of the positive externality in production, the appropriate remedy for the externality and its distortion is to provide a general production subsidy for the good produced by the first firm. The use of the import tariff would not be the welfare-maximizing device because it distorts consumption (with consequent welfare losses) at the same time that it stimulates domestic production. What is needed is the stimulus to domestic production (only), *without* any reduction in consumer surplus because of a tariff (and which can be accomplished by the production subsidy to the domestic firm). In sum, in these cases, as well as in a variety of other externality cases, the policies needed are those dictated by the previously discussed specificity principle. Choose the policy that gets directly to the problem, which in the first case above would be a tax on consumption of the good (and not just on consumption of the imported variety of the good) and in the second case would be a subsidy to production of the domestic good.

Tariff to Extract Foreign Monopoly Profit

The analysis of a **tariff to extract foreign monopoly profit**[3] was originated by James Brander and Barbara Spencer (1981). In their framework, the home country faces a foreign monopoly supplier of a good. The restrictive assumption is made that the foreign firm is the *only* supplier of this product in the world market, and thus there is no home production—the home country is entirely dependent on the foreign monopoly firm for the product.

Figure 2 illustrates the basic analysis. The demand curve represents the home country's demand for the foreign monopoly firm's product. Because the firm faces a downward-sloping demand curve (unlike the case in perfect competition, where the demand curve facing an individual firm is horizontal), marginal revenue is less than price. Assume for the sake of simplicity that marginal cost is constant (i.e., that each additional unit of output is produced at the same cost as previous units) and that there are no fixed costs and no transportation costs. Because of this, the marginal cost (MC) curve is horizontal and equals the average cost (AC) curve. With free trade, the firm will set MR equal to MC to maximize profit, and the quantity shipped to the home country will be $0q_1$. The price charged will be $0p_1$ and the (economic) profit of the firm will be the rectangle, $c_1 p_1 RF$. Because the producing firm is a monopolist, no competitive pressure is forcing price to become equal to MC (or AC).

Now suppose that the home country wishes to obtain some of this foreign monopoly profit. To do so could mean an increase in home-country welfare at the expense of the foreign monopolist. If a tariff is imposed that must be paid on each unit by the foreign firm before it is allowed to sell the good in the home country, then the marginal cost curve shifts up vertically to $MC + t$, where t is the amount of tax per unit. To the foreign firm, this tax is simply another "cost" associated with selling each additional unit of output in the home country, so profit maximization now equates marginal revenue with "new" marginal cost $MC + t$. Quantity produced for the home country drops to $0q_2$, and the price charged per unit is $0p_2$.

---

[3]This theory is usually called the *tariff to extract foreign monopoly rent* because the economic profit of the monopolist is also a rent (i.e., a return above opportunity cost due to restricted supply). We use the *profit* terminology because it may be more familiar to students who have taken only introductory courses.

FIGURE 2   A Tariff to Extract Foreign Monopoly Profit

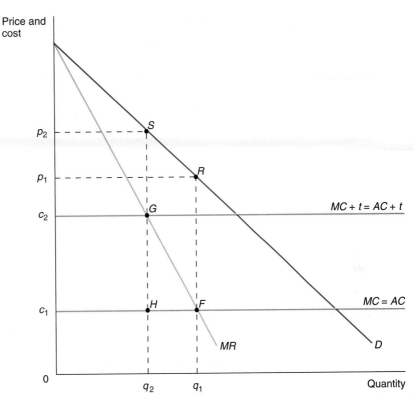

Without the tariff by the home country, the foreign monopoly firm sells quantity $0q_1$ to the home market at price $0p_1$, determined by the intersection of MR and MC. With the tariff in place, the foreign monopolist's marginal cost of selling in the home market is $MC + t$, where t is the amount of the tariff per unit. The new profit-maximizing quantity is $0q_2$ (where $MR = MC + t$). Consumers in the home country now pay price $0p_2$ and have their consumer surplus reduced by the trapezoid p_1p_2SR. However, the home country gains tariff revenue of the amount c_1c_2GH, which was formerly part of the foreign monopolist's economic profit.

To consider the welfare change in the tariff-imposing country, examine the profit of the monopoly firm. Profit after the imposition of the tariff is rectangular area c_2p_2SG. What about area c_1c_2GH? This area represents the tariff revenue, and it also represents *former profit of the monopolist that has been transferred to the home country.* This gain for the home country must be set against the lost consumer surplus by home-country consumers in the amount of trapezoid p_1p_2SR, then the home country has succeeded in enhancing its welfare at the expense of the foreign producer. Clearly, this intervention can be desirable for the home country.

While some economic profit has been transferred to the home country, the economist does not necessarily conclude that the protectionist action was beneficial even if the transfer of profit outweighed the loss in consumer surplus. Due to the tariff, world efficiency and welfare are reduced because, in a monopoly situation, efficiency and welfare are enhanced if actions cause the monopolist to reduce price and to increase output—and the opposite has happened with the imposition of this tariff on the monopolist's product! Thus, a home-country welfare gain can occur while the world as a whole loses (a beggar-my-neighbor situation). A full analysis of whether or not to undertake the action also requires examining matters such as the prospects for retaliation by the foreign country on goods coming from the home country.

FIGURE 3   The Effect of an Export Tax on a Domestic Monopolist

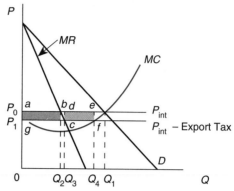

The monopolist initially maximizes profits where MC equals MR, that is, P_{int}, thus producing Q_1, selling Q_2 in the home market and exporting $Q_1 - Q_2$. With the imposition of an export tax, the monopolist lowers domestic price to (P_{int} − export tax) and increases domestic sales to Q_3. With the lower after-tax marginal revenue, (P_{int} − export tax), the firm reduces production to Q_4, and the new level of exports is $Q_4 - Q_3$. In the process, consumers gain $abcg$ of consumer surplus and the government receives $cdef$ of tax revenue.

The Use of an Export Tax to Redistribute Profit from a Domestic Monopolist

For the situation in which a domestic monopolist is both selling in the domestic market and exporting at the international price (as a price taker), it is clearly possible for the country to transfer well-being from a domestic monopolist to consumers and the government by imposing an export tax. Note that in this case we are considering a policy restriction on exports rather than on imports. Figure 3 shows how the presence of a foreign alternative essentially forces the monopolist to become a price taker. In this instance the firm produces at Q_1, where P_{int} is equal to the firm's MC. The firm sells Q_2 in the home market (where $P_{int} = P_0$ crosses the marginal revenue curve) and exports the remainder, $Q_1 - Q_2$. The imposition of an export tax lowers the after-tax export price to the firm, leading it to reduce quantity supplied and exports, and increases the quantity sold in the home market. As a result, there is a transfer from the monopoly to consumers and the government as seen in the increase in consumer surplus with the lower price and increased sales in the home market ($abcg$) and the tax revenue ($cdef$) captured by the government. The presence of the export tax thus offsets some of the monopoly leverage of the firm as it drives the domestic price downward closer to MC, expanding domestic consumption and generating government revenue. However, the country as a whole still experiences deadweight losses.

PROTECTION AS A RESPONSE TO INTERNATIONAL POLICY DISTORTIONS

Many countries have provisions in place that provide a way for them to respond quickly to the actions of foreign governments and or firms that are perceived to be trade distorting in nature and very costly to domestic firms. These are distortions that are seen to reduce not only country welfare in the short and medium run but also world welfare to the extent they foster less efficient production from the world perspective. These are often referred to as "trigger-price" mechanisms that, upon substantiation of the distortion, provide a tariff response to offset the initial distortion. In this section, arguments for protection are provided for distortions related to foreign dumping, foreign subsidies, and apparent non-tariff barriers to trade.

Tariff to Offset Foreign Dumping

This argument, usually known as the **antidumping argument** for a tariff, has been used prominently in the United States in recent years. It is first necessary to define *dumping*. To the economist, **dumping** occurs when a firm sells its product at a lower price in the export market than in the home-country market. This definition says nothing about "selling below cost"—the popular meaning of dumping. Rather, to the economist, dumping is simply a form of price discrimination. As you recall, price discrimination occurs when a firm sells the same product in different markets at different prices.

The argument for protection is that dumping by foreign firms into the home country is in some sense unfair and constitutes a threat to domestic producers because of the low import price; therefore, a tariff can offset the foreign firm's unfair price advantage. The argument was buttressed by the U.S. Trade Act of 1974, which added a second definition of dumping distinctly different from that used by economists. In addition to recognizing the traditional definition, the act also allowed "dumping" to be a situation in which the foreign firm is "selling below cost" or "fair value." Given this definition, the argument indeed takes on the implication that this "unfair" behavior should be prevented through the imposition of a tariff, that is, an **antidumping duty.**

How should we assess the validity of this argument for protection? In any assessment, economists usually distinguish three types of dumping. In **persistent dumping,** the good is continually sold at a lower price in the importing country than in the home country. This situation is one in which the import good is simply being sold in different markets for different prices under profit-maximizing conditions. This is the price-discrimination phenomenon discussed at the end of Chapter 8. Any trade barrier would result in a higher price for consumers in the importing country, and the welfare effects discussed in Chapter 14 apply. (This behavior could not persist in the long run under the selling-below-cost definition because of producer losses, unless government provided a subsidy.)

However, the dumping may be not persistent but intermittent. Intermittent dumping can be of two types: **predatory dumping** and **sporadic dumping.** In predatory dumping, a foreign firm sells at a low price until home producers are driven out of the market; then the price is raised because a monopoly position has been established. Domestic firms may then be attracted back into the market, only to have the price reduced again to a low level. There is a valid argument for protection with predatory dumping because of the associated wasteful resource movements. As factors of production move in and out of the industry because of fluctuating import prices, real costs and waste are generated for society.

Sporadic dumping occurs when a foreign producer (or government) with a temporary surplus of a good exports the excess for whatever price it will command. This type of dumping may have temporary adverse effects on competing home suppliers (as in agriculture) by adding to the uncertainty of operating in the industry. This uncertainty, as well as the welfare losses from possible temporary resource movements, can be avoided by the imposition of protection, although other welfare effects (also applicable in predatory dumping) should be brought into the analysis when considering trade restrictions. However, sporadic dumping does not seem to justify protection when it is short-term.

The difficulty in practice is determining whether persistent, predatory, or sporadic dumping is occurring. No policymaker has yet been truly able to identify the immediate motivation behind dumping. The general procedure followed in the United States in response to alleged dumping is discussed in the box that follows.

IN THE REAL WORLD:

ANTIDUMPING ACTIONS IN THE UNITED STATES

The first U.S. antidumping law was the Antidumping Act of 1916, which was superseded by the more-enforceable Antidumping Act of 1921. The 1921 act served as the basis for antidumping investigations by the Department of the Treasury until 1979, when the investigations were transferred from the Treasury to the Department of Commerce. Since 1979, U.S. antidumping law has been amended to make it consistent with GATT and WTO agreements. The underlying specification of illegal action incorporated into U.S. legislation is that imports are being dumped or sold at "less than fair value" when a foreign producer sells a good in the U.S. market at a price lower than the price in the foreign producer's home market, or at a price judged to be below the cost of production. The comparison with the price in the exporter's home market is replaced by a comparison in a "third country" if there aren't many sales in the producer's home market; if no "third country" market has sufficient sales, either, a value is constructed that is based on a cost-plus-profit approach. The investigation of whether or not dumping is occurring can occur only if a petition has been filed that is supported by producing firms or workers that account for at least 25 percent of the domestic import-competing industry's output, among other criteria. As indicated in the main body of this text, if dumping is determined by the Department of Commerce to have occurred and if material injury or threat of material injury to the U.S. import-competing industry is determined by the U.S. International Trade Commission (USITC) to have taken place, then an antidumping duty equal to the difference between the U.S. price and the foreign or constructed price is imposed.

At the behest of U.S. import-substitute firms, the U.S. authorities have very frequently undertaken antidumping investigations in recent years; indeed, antidumping duties are often said to be the recent "instrument of choice" of protectionists. From 1980 through 2003 (fiscal years), there were *1,058* antidumping petitions brought to the Department of Commerce/U.S. International Trade Commission. In the 1,058 cases, an affirmative finding was indicated by both Commerce and the USITC (i.e., dumping was determined to have taken place and injury or threat of injury was a consequence) in 441 instances, or 41.7 percent of the cases [(441/1,058) = 41.7 percent]. A negative finding was indicated by the USITC (i.e., no finding of injury or threat of injury occurred even though dumping had taken place) in 410 cases, or 38.8 percent of the total cases [(410/1,058) = 38.8 percent]. Finally, in the remaining 207 cases (19.6 percent of the total), the Department of Commerce terminated or

suspended the investigations or determined that dumping had not occurred (see Figure 4). Termination or suspension can occur before conclusion of the investigation in any given case if the exporters of the good to the United States agree to eliminate the dumping, to stop exporting the good to the United States, to raise the price to eliminate the dumping, or to work out some other arrangement (such as a VER) that will reduce the quantity of imports. Indeed, the mere threat of an antidumping investigation may cause foreign firms to raise their export prices and thus to cease any dumping they were practicing. Termination can also be done by Commerce (as it did with respect to a petition against imported oil in 1999) if the majority of domestic U.S. firms in the import-competing industry do not indicate agreement with the antidumping petition. In the case of a suspended agreement, the investigation can be reinstituted if the dumping begins again.

To get a feel for the frequency with which antidumping findings have been affirmative, note that, according to the USITC, there were, on February 15, 2007, 248 antidumping orders in effect on goods coming from 41 different countries. These totals reflected the cumulative number of affirmative findings still in effect since their earlier implementation. Some of the antidumping orders dated back to the 1970s. With respect to countries, China had the most antidumping orders in effect on its products (61), covering goods such as barium chloride, axes, carbon steel plate, and honey. Japan ranked second with 22 antidumping orders applied to its goods—products such as ball bearings, polyvinyl alcohol, cement, and polychloroprene rubber. Other countries with sizable numbers of antidumping orders in effect were South Korea (16), Taiwan (15), India (14), Italy (12), and Brazil (11).

An additional aspect of the antidumping scene recently has been the controversy over a 2000 U.S. congressional action, the Byrd Amendment, which permitted the funds collected from antidumping duties (as well as countervailing duties), to be channeled to the U.S. firms claiming injury from the dumping. Hence, dumping continues to be a contentious political issue.

Sources: U.S. International Trade Commission, *Antidumping and Countervailing Duty Handbook,* USITC Publication 3750 (Washington, DC: USITC, January 2005); *The Year in Trade 2005,* USITC Publication 3875 (Washington, DC: USITC, August 2006), "Antidumping and Countervailing Duty Orders in Place as of February 15, 2007, by Country"; and "Trade Remedy Investigations: Byrd Amendment," all obtained from www.usitc.gov; and "Commerce Department Rejects Oil-Dumping Inquiry," *The Wall Street Journal,* August 10, 1999, pp. A2, A6.

IN THE REAL WORLD: *(continued)*

FIGURE 4   Antidumping Case Summary (by number of cases), Fiscal Years 1980–2003

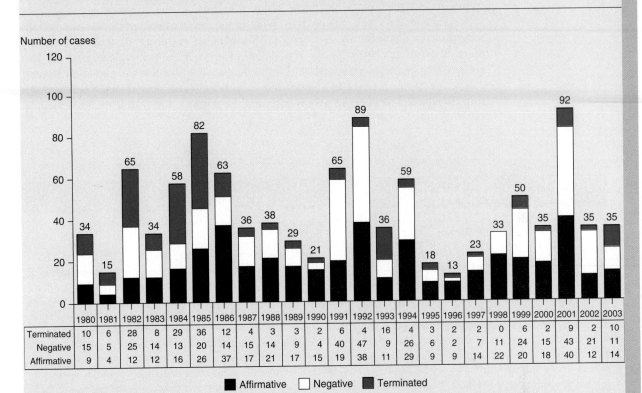

	1980	1981	1982	1983	1984	1985	1986	1987	1988	1989	1990	1991	1992	1993	1994	1995	1996	1997	1998	1999	2000	2001	2002	2003
Terminated	10	6	28	8	29	36	12	4	3	3	2	6	4	16	4	3	2	2	0	6	2	9	2	10
Negative	15	5	25	14	13	20	14	15	14	9	4	40	47	9	26	6	2	7	11	24	15	43	21	11
Affirmative	9	4	12	12	16	26	37	17	21	17	15	19	38	11	29	9	9	14	22	20	18	40	12	14

■ Affirmative   □ Negative   ■ Terminated

Source: U.S. International Trade Commission, *Antidumping and Countervailing Duty Handbook,* USITC Publication 3750 (Washington, DC: USITC, January 2005), Appendix E, obtained from www.usitc.gov.

1. Upon receipt of a petition from a domestic import-competing firm or industry, the Department of Commerce determines from price and cost data (which may be difficult to obtain) whether dumping is occurring. If so, then:

2. The U.S. International Trade Commission (USITC), an independent federal agency, determines from a study of the recent history of the industry whether this dumping has been an important source of injury to the industry. If so, then:

3. Antidumping duties are imposed on the imported good. The size of the duties is designed to offset the extent of the dumping.

Similar procedures exist in other countries that belong to the World Trade Organization (WTO).

Tariff to Offset a Foreign Subsidy

The basic point of the argument for a **tariff to offset a foreign subsidy** is that a foreign government subsidy awarded to a foreign import supplier constitutes unfair trade with the home country and that the amount of foreign subsidy should be matched by a home tariff to restore equal footing to the home and the foreign industry.

In principle, an economist should have no difficulty in supporting the imposition of a tariff to offset a foreign subsidy under certain conditions, despite the recognition that domestic consumers will pay higher prices. If the subsidy allows the foreign firm to be an exporter of the product *when the foreign country does not have a comparative advantage in this good,* then the subsidy generates a distortion from the free-trade allocation of resources. World welfare is reduced because of the distortion—although the *importing* country's welfare may rise owing to the lower consumer price—and the offsetting of the distortion by an import tariff can aid in restoring the trade pattern to a more efficient one. Note that the application of this general principle is difficult. It is not an easy task to determine whether a foreign subsidy is occurring, and many import-competing firms are quick to assert that a subsidy exists because they are being undersold. In addition, conceptual issues surround the definition of a subsidy. For example,

IN THE REAL WORLD:

COUNTERVAILING DUTIES IN THE UNITED STATES

The first U.S. countervailing-duty (CVD) law was passed in 1897, when duties were authorized against subsidized imports of sugar. The current provisions of the law differ somewhat from the original legislation. Originally, duties were to be assessed on goods that benefited from an export subsidy, but the U.S. Congress in 1922 extended the application of the duties to subsidies on manufacture as well as subsidies on export. Also, prior to 1974, there was no injury test necessary to have CVDs imposed—a finding of the existence of the subsidy was sufficient. In addition, since 1979, the Department of Commerce has conducted the investigations on the existence of subsidies (previously done by the Department of the Treasury), and the U.S. International Trade Commission (USITC) has conducted the injury investigations (analogous to the injury investigations regarding dumping). These injury investigations are not generally required as a condition for imposing a countervailing duty if the offending country is not a member of the World Trade Organization (WTO, which has 150 members as of this writing).

As with the antidumping investigations discussed earlier, there have been a large number of industry petitions, which have to meet certain criteria to be accepted, and subsequent investigations in recent years. From 1980 to 2003, there were 452 petitions, of which 117 cases, or 25.9 percent [(117/452) = 25.9 percent], were decided in the affirmative. Hence, in each of these 117 cases, the Department of Commerce judged that a subsidy had been given by the exporting country's government and the USITC determined that material injury or threat of material injury had occurred. In 196 of the cases, or 43.4 percent [(196/452) = 43.4 percent], the

result was negative, meaning that the USITC found no injury or threat of injury even though the Department of Commerce had found that a subsidy had taken place. Finally, in the remaining 139 cases (30.8 percent), the investigation was terminated or suspended or Commerce did not find a subsidy (see Figure 5). Termination can occur if a petition is withdrawn (perhaps because some solution, such as the negotiation of a VER, is worked out). A suspension can occur if the subsidizing country or countries agree to eliminate the subsidy, to stop exporting the product to the United States, or in some way to eliminate any injurious effects on the domestic industry. If these conditions are violated, the investigation can begin again or the previously determined countervailing duty can then be imposed. It should also be noted that, in either an antidumping case or a countervailing-duty case, the foreign exporter must put up funds equal to the potential value of the duty even before the case is finally decided. If the ultimate decision is not to put on antidumping duties or countervailing duties, then these funds are refunded (but of course the foreign firm has lost the use of the funds in the meantime).

As with antidumping duties, the number of CVD orders in effect (the accumulation over the years that are still operative) gives a sense of the importance of this trade policy instrument. As of February 15, 2007, there were 35 CVDs in place against 15 countries. While not nearly as large in number as the 248 antidumping orders in effect at that time, the CVD number does indicate substantial use of the antisubsidy mechanism. The countries facing the most CVDs were India (7) and South Korea (5). There was some diversity

(continued)

the United States and Canada have been embroiled in a dispute for more than 10 years as to whether Canadian exports of softwood lumber to the United States are subsidized. The United States maintains that the stumpage fees paid by Canadian firms for the right to cut logs on government-owned land are "too low" and constitute a subsidy and unfair competition for U.S. firms cutting logs on private U.S. land. Canadians deny that their firms are subsidized.

Despite these uncertainties, the United States has a well-defined procedure, similar to the antidumping procedure, for implementing a tariff to offset a foreign subsidy. Upon receipt of a petition from a U.S. importing firm or industry, the

IN THE REAL WORLD: *(continued)*

regarding type of product (e.g., honey, pasta, softwood lumber), but there was a rather heavy concentration on iron and steel products (more than one-half of the total).

Sources: U.S. International Trade Commission, *Antidumping and Countervailing Duty Handbook,* USITC Publication 3750 (Washington, DC: USITC, January 2005); *The Year in Trade 2005,* USITC Publication 3875 (Washington, DC: USITC, August 2006); and "Antidumping and Countervailing Duty Orders in Place as of February 15, 2007, by Country," all obtained from www.usitc.gov; and U.S. Trade Representative, *2007 Trade Policy Agenda and 2006 Annual Report of the President of the United States on the Trade Agreements Program* (Washington, DC: Office of the U.S. Trade Representative, 2007), obtained from www.ustr.gov.

FIGURE 5   Countervailing Duty Case Summary (by number of cases), Fiscal Years 1980–2003

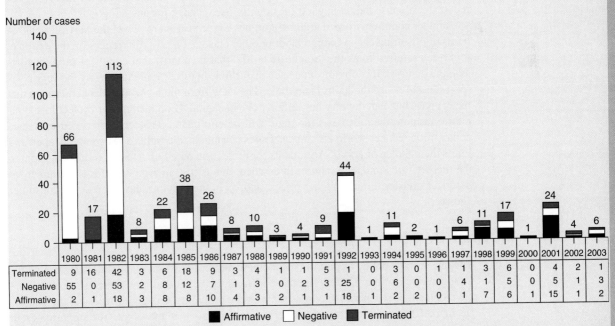

	1980	1981	1982	1983	1984	1985	1986	1987	1988	1989	1990	1991	1992	1993	1994	1995	1996	1997	1998	1999	2000	2001	2002	2003
Terminated	9	16	42	3	6	18	9	3	4	1	1	5	1	0	3	0	1	1	3	6	0	4	2	1
Negative	55	0	53	2	8	12	7	1	3	0	2	3	25	0	6	0	0	4	1	5	0	5	1	3
Affirmative	2	1	18	3	8	8	10	4	3	2	1	1	18	1	2	2	0	1	7	6	1	15	1	2

■ Affirmative   □ Negative   ■ Terminated

Source: U.S. International Trade Commission, *Antidumping and Countervailing Duty Handbook,* USITC Publication 3750 (Washington, DC: USITC, January 2005), Appendix E, obtained from www.usitc.gov.

Department of Commerce determines whether or not a foreign supplier has been given a subsidy. If the answer is yes, the USITC applies the "injury test." If injury is occurring, then a **countervailing duty (CVD)** is imposed to offset the price impact of the foreign subsidy.

CONCEPT CHECK	1. Will a tariff designed to capture foreign monopoly profit necessarily increase domestic welfare in the importing country? 2. Why do markets have to be kept separate by artificial or natural barriers for dumping to occur?	3. How can an export subsidy by a country actually reduce world welfare?

MISCELLANEOUS, INVALID ARGUMENTS

Various arguments are continually encountered that, on the surface, seem logical but, upon close examination, make little sense. Several examples of these arguments are discussed briefly herein. One common argument is that a country should use protection to reduce imports and "keep the money at home." First, this is a pure Mercantilist argument that seemingly places emphasis on holdings of money as central to the decision as opposed to productivity, economic efficiency, and higher consumer well-being. Because money is of value only in its ability to be used as a claim for desired goods and services, the money that flows out of a country to acquire imports will ultimately return to the country in terms of a claim on home exports. Because trade allows both countries to get goods cheaper, the movement of money has increased the overall welfare of the countries involved, not reduced it because the money left the country in exchange for desired goods.

Another commonly heard argument argues for protection to "level the playing field" in terms of offsetting cheap foreign labor or other reasons for cost differences. In the extreme, it is often referred to as the "scientific tariff," that is, a tariff that equalizes product costs among countries. It is obvious that such distortions in the extreme take away the very basis for trade and hence the gains from trade. The view from the labor-abundant country is that the capital-abundant country has unfairly cheap capital. If both countries protect in a symmetric fashion, the cost basis for trade will be eliminated. Protection imposed to reduce competition reduces world efficiency, denies consumers the right to get goods cheaper, and limits their choice of goods. Arguments for protection based on a local producer's "right to the market" are similar in nature. In essence, this is just an argument for a consumer-to-producer transfer through higher prices, and, as in the previous case, it reduces consumer choice.

STRATEGIC TRADE POLICY: FOSTERING COMPARATIVE ADVANTAGE

The use of trade policy as part of development and/or industrial policy has been around for a long period of time. Underlying these ideas is the belief that governments can foster the development of comparative cost advantages by providing firms with access to the domestic market for a reasonably short period of time so that they have the opportunity to develop the underlying comparative cost advantage through economies of scale and improved production efficiency. One of the earliest approaches, which has endured over the years, is the now-famous infant industry argument introduced by Alexander Hamilton and Frederick List in the late 18th century. Although it was a little-used strategy earlier on, it became much more popular during the 20th century, particularly in Latin America. This section begins with a discussion of this still-present argument and then moves on to some of the newer theories for protection, often referred to as **strategic trade policy** theories, which suggest how a country can benefit over time from the active use of trade policy instruments, usually at the expense of trading partners. A distinguishing feature of the approach in these more recent theories is that **imperfect competition** exists in the industries under consideration—a departure from the competitive industries commonly employed in traditional trade analysis. Other critical elements of this approach include recognized interdependence of firms in a given industry and the presence of **economies of scale.** Within this framework it can be demonstrated that policies that seek to expand exports or reduce imports can potentially lead to the realization of dynamic, long-run cost advantage. In the latter part of this section, we summarize several of these new theories to provide an insight as to how trade policy might, in fact, be used to foster dynamic comparative advantages.

The Infant Industry Argument for Protection

Economists generally agree that this long-standing argument for protection is valid from the standpoint of enhancing the welfare of the world as a whole. The **infant industry argument** rests on the notion that a particular industry in a country may possess, for various reasons, a long-run comparative advantage even though the country is an importer of the good at the present time. Suppose that the growth of the industry in a country is inhibited by low-cost imports from a foreign country. Production in the foreign country may be occurring because of historical accident, and the home-country industry is getting a "late start." If protection could temporarily be given to the industry in the home country, the argument goes that firms in this industry will be able to achieve a reduction in unit costs through realizing economies of scale or through learning by doing. The economies of scale could be internal to firms, which are now each producing a larger volume of output; that is, producers in the home country will be moving down their downward-sloping long-run average cost curves. Or the knowledge acquired by producing the good could lead workers and managers to devise more cost-efficient methods, which would shift cost curves downward. Or the economies could be external to the firm but internal to the industry, in which case greater *industry* output would reduce costs for the individual firm due, for instance, to the attraction of a pool of skilled labor to an area. In any event, per-unit costs eventually fall to such an extent that the industry in the home country becomes an exporter of the good. At this point, protection can be removed as it is no longer needed. The home industry has a comparative advantage that it cannot realize in the short run but can in the long run if temporary protection is imposed. The consumers of the home country are asked to finance the long-run expansion of the industry, but they will be more than "repaid" when the industry "grows up." Indeed, with a new comparative-advantage producer in the world market, the world as a whole benefits.

In practice, the infant industry argument is put forth more frequently in developing countries than in developed countries. Developing countries often propound the argument in the context of an import-substitution program, whereby reliance on the world market for a good is to be replaced by home production, whether or not export potential is envisioned. This application of the infant industry argument is a variant of the traditional version, but it can be evaluated on similar grounds.

What are we to make of the infant industry argument? Even though economists generally agree that it is theoretically valid, not every industry that claims to be an infant should automatically be granted protection. The difficulty in making this argument operational centers around the identification of industries that are likely to become low-cost producers.

If an industry protected by this argument is not a true infant, then the country (and the world) may be saddled with permanent protection of a high-cost industry and less efficient resource use. This was noted long ago by American economist Henry George, who wrote (1911, p. 97, originally 1886), "Nothing could better show the futility of attempting to make industries self-supporting by tariff than the confessed inability of the industries that we have so long encouraged to stand alone."

IN THE REAL WORLD:

U.S. MOTORCYCLES—A SUCCESSFUL INFANT INDUSTRY?

A modern variant of the infant industry argument is found in U.S. motorcycle production. The industry itself is hardly an infant since the first motorcycle was manufactured commercially in the United States in 1901, and there have been about 150 U.S. producers since then. By 1978, however, largely because of imports, Harley-Davidson was the *only* remaining U.S.–owned producer.

Until the early 1980s, Harley-Davidson had produced mostly heavyweight motorcycles with a piston displacement of more than 1,000 cubic centimeters. Imports were of smaller displacement and were rapidly increasing their market share. Harley-Davidson petitioned the U.S. International Trade Commission (USITC) for import relief in 1982. A USITC investigation found that imports were a substantial cause of injury to Harley-Davidson, and in 1983, higher tariff rates were imposed for a five-year period on imports above already existing quota levels. One reason that the USITC granted the increased protection was that Harley-Davidson planned to improve its efficiency and introduce a new line of smaller motorcycles (800 to 1,000 cubic centimeters); the USITC wanted to give the firm an opportunity to implement these plans. It is in the context of a new line of production (the smaller cycles) that the Harley-Davidson case has infant industry characteristics.

After the new tariffs were imposed, the import share in the U.S. motorcycle market fell from 60 to 70 percent in the early 1980s to 31 percent by 1984. In response, Japanese companies Kawasaki and Honda increased their production within the United States. Harley-Davidson itself changed management strategy, reduced costs, and improved quality. Domestic production increased, but the estimated cost to U.S. consumers (Hufbauer, Berliner, and Elliott 1986, p. 268) was $400 to $600 per motorcycle and, in 1984, $150,000 per job saved in the motorcycle industry. Nevertheless, employment and output increased in the mid-1980s, and Harley-Davidson's share of the domestic market rose.* The value of shipments from U.S.–based firms has been estimated to have risen by 75

percent in real terms from 1987 to 1993, importantly due to the popularity of the cycle with engine capacity above 700 cubic centimeters and to perceived greater safety in motorcycles. In addition, exports from the United States increased at an annual rate of 37 percent from 1987 to 1991, although this growth slowed thereafter. Some of the increase in exports was also attributed to the falling dollar, especially against the yen. Exports of motorcycles and parts continued to grow at about a 12 percent annual rate from 2000 to 2005. Harley-Davidson continued to be profitable in the 1990s and into the new century. As an example, a share of Harley-Davidson common stock bought in March 1997 for $35.00 split twice and was worth more than $240 in March 2007.

How does the motorcycle industry fit the infant industry argument? A domestic firm had sought temporary protection with the hope of gaining time to move into a new product. The temporary protection was granted, the firm expanded production, and eventually it became an exporter. The consumer cost was high, however, and some of the export performance was perhaps due to other factors (the exchange rate, improved safety perceptions).

*In fact, Harley-Davidson in 1987 concluded that it was then able to compete with the Japanese and asked for removal of the higher tariffs one year ahead of schedule.

Sources: "Harley Asks ITC to End Tariffs Firm Sought in '83," *The Wall Street Journal,* March 18, 1987, p. 46; Gary Clyde Hufbauer, Diane T. Berliner, and Kimberly Ann Elliott, *Trade Protection in the United States: 31 Case Studies* (Washington, DC: Institute for International Economics, 1986), pp. 263–69; "Reagan Rebuffs Trade Bill in Motorcycle-Plant Tour," *The Wall Street Journal,* May 7, 1987, p. 6; U.S. Department of Commerce, *U.S. Industrial Outlook 1990,* pp. 40–10 and 40–11; U.S. Department of Commerce, *U.S. Industrial Outlook 1993,* pp. 37–7 and 37–8; U.S. Department of Commerce, *U.S. Industrial Outlook 1994,* p. 37–9; International Trade Administration of the U.S. Department of Commerce, "Top 20 U.S. Export Destinations for Motorcycles and Parts," obtained from www.ita.doc.gov.

A century later, Gerald Meier (1987) reviewed empirical evidence on the infant industry argument in developing countries. He noted (p. 830) that Krueger and Tuncer (1982) concluded that Turkey's protected industries did not experience decreasing costs more than less protected industries did; further, the protected industries might well have grown without the protection. Martin Bell, Bruce Ross-Larson, and Larry Westphal (1984, p. 114) found that few protected firms in a number of developing countries increased productivity sufficiently to attain international competitiveness. Meier also cites the point by Westphal (1981, p. 12) that the initial costs in terms of domestic resources for infant industry protection in developing countries might be twice the amount of foreign exchange saved or earned by the protection.

Beyond the problem of identification, the economist should also ask whether the tariff or another form of protection is the relevant policy—even if the industry is a qualifying infant. For example, a case might be made, for attaining both internal and external economies and stimulating learning by doing, that a subsidy to the industry by the home-country government is superior to a tariff. As noted in Chapter 14, a subsidy has a lower welfare cost to the country than a tariff. A subsidy also comes up for reevaluation every year when a government authorizes expenditure, so its benefits and costs are analyzed more frequently than is possible with a tariff, which is placed in the schedules and does not need to be brought up for annual review.

More fundamentally, however, the economist asks why the industry in the country is unable to proceed on its own and why it needs protection. If internal economies of scale and/or learning by doing could be realized from expansion, entrepreneurs in a market economy presumably know this and would undertake expansion on their own. They would borrow funds from financial institutions, invest in plant expansion, and use the profits from the new dominance in the market to repay the loans. (However, this entrepreneurial expansion would not necessarily occur in the case of external economies of scale.) If this process does not get under way on its own, capital markets are probably operating inefficiently in allocating funds. Therefore, a proper focus of policy should be on taking measures to improve the operation of capital markets, perhaps through deregulation or government guarantees for the loans. The focus on the capital market as the culprit is especially relevant for developing countries, because their financial institutions are often cited as biased toward making short-term rather than long-term loans. An important cause of this bias in developing countries may be the uncertainty surrounding the repayment of long-term loans.

Economies of Scale in a Duopoly Framework

An important contribution to the strategic trade policy literature came from economist Paul Krugman (1984). In his model, Krugman assumes there are two firms in an industry, a **duopoly** (a home firm and a foreign firm), that compete with each other in markets throughout the world (including in each other's markets). Krugman's intention is to demonstrate how import protection for one firm leads to an increase in *exports* for the protected firm in any foreign market in which that firm operates. Two assumptions are particularly critical: (1) Marginal cost declines with an increase in output—that is, economies of scale are associated with producing output; and (2) each firm takes the actions of the other firm into account when making its own price and output decisions. The last point means, for example, that the home firm perceives that its revenue depends positively on its own output but negatively on the foreign firm's output. This **recognized interdependence** does not exist in a perfectly competitive model.

With recognized interdependence, we can conceive of **reaction functions** for each firm in each market (see Figure 6). The symbol X_i on the horizontal axis refers to the sales of the home firm in any market i, while X_i^* on the vertical axis refers to the sales of the foreign firm in the same market. HH is the reaction function for the home firm. The reasoning

FIGURE 6   Home-Firm and Foreign-Firm Sales in a Third-Country Market

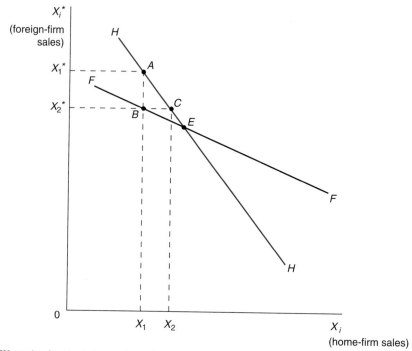

The *HH* reaction function indicates the profit-maximizing level of sales in a third-country market for the home firm, given various levels of foreign firm sales in that market. *HH* slopes downward because increased foreign sales will depress price and profit for the home firm, so that firm will contract sales. The *FF* reaction function shows the profit-maximizing level of sales for the foreign firm, given various sales levels of the home firm, and it slopes downward for analogous reasons. At points such as *A, B,* and *C,* sales levels are altered until equilibrium point *E* is attained.

behind this function is that if the foreign firm increases sales in the market (an increase in X_i^*), the demand for the home firm's product will fall and the price of its good will be depressed. Thus, profit opportunities for the home firm are lessened so that the amount sold by the home firm (X_i) will decrease. The reaction function for the home firm is downward-sloping, and similar reasoning yields a downward-sloping reaction function, *FF,* for the foreign firm. These reaction functions show the most profitable level of sales in market *i* for each firm, given various levels of sales of the other firm. Note that these functions are drawn for a *given* marginal cost, implying that each firm's total output is constant but the sales in any given market can vary. Finally, the equilibrium position is at point *E,* where each firm is selling its profit-maximizing quantity, given the behavior of the other firm.

To see why point *E* is attained, consider point *A.* If the two firms are producing for this market at *A,* then the home firm is satisfied with its sales of $0X_1$ but the foreign firm is not satisfied with its sales of $0X_1^*$. To maximize profit, the foreign firm cuts production to $0X_2^*$ because the firm was producing "too much" at *A* for maximum profit. With this change in foreign sales, point *B* is reached. However, *B* is not a profit-maximizing point for the home firm, and the firm expands production to $0X_2$ so that it achieves point *C.* This process will continue until point *E* is attained. This movement to *E* occurs because we have drawn *HH* steeper than *FF.* If *FF* were the steeper of the two lines, the equilibrium point would be unstable and forces would drive the firms farther away from *E* if they were not at *E.* Because continual movements away from an equilibrium involving radical changes in market shares are not usually observed in oligopoly markets, Krugman regards the slopes in Figure 6 as more relevant than the reverse case.

　　Now let us examine the total output level of each firm rather than the sales level in each of the markets the firm serves. Remember the assumption that marginal cost decreases as output increases. In addition, remember that a shift downward or decrease in the marginal cost schedule leads to an increase in output, given the demand and marginal revenue curves. With these relationships in mind, consider Figure 7(a). The horizontal axis measures the total output of the home firm, which in turn is the sum of the sales in all markets served by the home firm. The vertical axis represents home firm marginal cost. Curve MM reflects the assumption that an increase in output (along the horizontal axis) causes marginal cost to decrease; curve QQ reflects the reverse relationship, namely, that a decrease in marginal cost (along the vertical axis) will cause an increase in output.[4] Equilibrium for the firm will be at point T, where there is no incentive for the firm to change its output level. Of course, a similar graph (not shown), could portray the foreign firm, with that firm's total output occurring where an M^*M^* curve (analogous to MM) intersects a Q^*Q^* curve (analogous to QQ).

FIGURE 7   Home-Country Protection and Home-Firm Sales through Economies of Scale

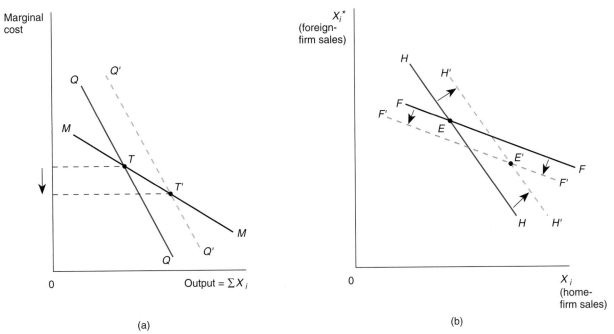

In panel (a), curve QQ indicates that a fall in marginal cost will induce a larger total output for the home firm, where total output is the sum of the firm's sales in all markets i. Curve MM indicates the presence of economies of scale, because larger output levels lead to lower marginal cost. Equilibrium for the firm occurs at point T, where the firm has no incentive to change its output level. An import tariff by the home government shifts the home firm's QQ schedule to $Q'Q'$, because the firm can sell more output in the home market at each level of marginal cost. With $Q'Q'$ in effect, the home firm's marginal cost falls. The consequence of this decline in marginal cost is that, in panel (b), the home firm's reaction function in any export market i shifts outward from HH to $H'H'$. Further, because the home-country protection has reduced sales by the foreign firm in the home market, the foreign firm's marginal cost rises and its reaction function in panel (b) shifts inward from FF to $F'F'$. Equilibrium therefore shifts from E to E', with the home firm gaining sales in each market at the expense of the foreign firm.

---

[4]For reasons of stability of equilibrium, Krugman draws curve QQ steeper than curve MM. Support for this assumption is empirical—firms do not experience the continually falling or rising marginal cost and output levels implied when MM is steeper than QQ.

Given this setup, consider the impact of protection. Suppose the home-country government imposes a tariff or import quota on imports of the good of the foreign firm, which has the effect of reserving some of the home-country market for the home firm. The initial impact of this protection is on the home firm's output [Figure 7, panel (a)]. Because home-firm output has increased for any given level of marginal cost, curve QQ shifts to the right to $Q'Q'$, causing the firm's equilibrium position to move to T', where *lower* marginal cost is incurred. In the analogous graph for the foreign firm (not shown), the Q^*Q^* curve of the foreign firm would shift to the *left*. Less output is associated with each level of marginal cost because some of the home-country market is now being denied the foreign firm. The result would be an *increase* in marginal cost for the foreign firm.

Because marginal costs have changed for each firm, there is a feedback onto the reaction functions because those functions were each drawn with a given marginal cost. In Figure 7, panel (b), the decrease in marginal cost for the home firm causes home-firm sales to increase for each given level of foreign firm sales in each export market; that is, HH shifts to the right to $H'H'$. Similarly, the increase in marginal cost for the foreign firm causes FF to shift down vertically to $F'F'$, because the foreign firm will sell a smaller amount of the good for each given level of home firm sales. Thus, equilibrium in the duopoly situation in each market is now at point E' rather than E, and the home firm has gained sales in all markets at the expense of the foreign firm. This theory of protection can be called the **tariff to promote exports through economies of scale** because these new sales in all the i markets are exports from the home country.

Krugman advanced the economies-of-scale analysis not as a recommendation for protection per se but as an explanation for phenomena such as Japan's emergence in the 1970s and 1980s as a leading exporter of several products whose domestic producers had initially been protected (e.g., automobiles). In that light, it makes sense. However, when considering it as a basis for recommending protection, the foreign country would probably retaliate by imposing its own tariff. Note that the end result would be market shares that are relatively unaffected but a volume of trade that is greatly reduced. In addition, as in many of these "new protectionist" arguments, the resources used to expand the protected industry mean that output in other industries is given up, and these opportunity costs definitely need to be considered. (See Krugman, "Is Free Trade Passé?" 1987.)

Research and Development and Sales of a Home Firm

This approach to protection was also developed by Paul Krugman (1984). It has some similarities to the economies-of-scale approach but emphasizes a different route by which protection generates an increase in exports by a home firm. In considering this **tariff to promote exports through research and development,** assume again that a duopoly market structure of a home firm and foreign firm exists and that the firms are competing in many markets. However, assume that marginal costs for each firm are constant with respect to output (that is, marginal cost curves are horizontal) but that, for any given level of output, marginal cost depends on investment in research and development (R&D). The relationship is negative, meaning that a greater amount of R&D expenditure (on new product characteristics, new production processes, and so on) will lead to a reduction in marginal cost. In turn, the amount of R&D expenditure is a positive function of the level of output, as larger current output generates greater profits that can be used to finance additional R&D.

The key relationships in this R&D model are illustrated in Figure 8. The amount of R&D spending by the home firm is measured on the vertical axis, while the home firm's output is measured on the horizontal axis as the sum of the firm's sales in all the i markets. The upward-sloping line MM indicates that, as output increases, the amount of R&D spending increases because of greater profits. The upward-sloping line QQ indicates the

FIGURE 8   Home-Country Protection and Home-Firm R&D Spending and Output

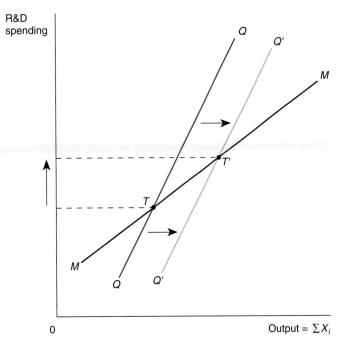

The *MM* line indicates that, with an increase in total output by the home firm, R&D spending rises due to greater profit. The *QQ* line reflects the fact that, as R&D spending increases, the firm's marginal cost falls and greater output is produced. The initial equilibrium point for the firm is at point *T*. With the imposition of a tariff by the home-country government, the home firm can produce more output for the home market at each level of R&D; that is, *QQ* shifts to the right to *Q′Q′*. This increase in output permits greater R&D spending as the equilibrium moves to *T′*, and the greater R&D generates larger sales for the firm in all markets *i*.

dependence of output on R&D: As R&D increases, marginal cost falls, which, in turn, enables the firm to sell a larger quantity of output. Mutual consistency of the two relationships occurs when the firm is located at equilibrium point *T*.[5] Analogous to this graph would be a similar graph for the foreign firm (not shown), with an *M*M** line plotted against a *Q*Q** line and with location of the firm at a *T*** analogous to *T* in Figure 8.

The consequences of protection in this model are similar to those in the economies-of-scale model. Suppose the home-country government imposes a tariff to reserve some of the home market for the home firm. The effect of this protection is that line *QQ* in Figure 8 shifts to the right to *Q′Q′*. This shift indicates that a greater amount of output is now linked to each amount of R&D spending. But notice that the new equilibrium position *T′* yields a greater amount of R&D spending, which will bring lower marginal cost so that the firm is able to take sales away from the foreign firm in *all* markets. The gain in sales at the expense of the foreign firm is reinforced when we remember that the opposite process takes place for the foreign firm. For that firm, there has been a decrease in output associated with each level of R&D. The end result is a decline in R&D spending and a relative *rise* in marginal cost for the foreign firm—leading to a decrease in sales by that firm in each of the markets served by the duopoly.

---

[5]The *QQ* line is assumed to be steeper than the *MM* line for stability reasons.

In assessing this argument, we must point to the possibilities of retaliation and the forgone opportunity costs of inducing more resources into the R&D–oriented industry. In addition, the argument assumes that the firm's sales are the primary determinant of R&D, but factors other than sales, such as patent protection, may also be important. Further, much R&D may be directed toward new-product development rather than toward reducing the cost of producing existing goods.

The basic point concerning economies of scale and research and development in relation to protection in these two sections of this chapter is that import protection can potentially generate exports, whether the mechanism operates by way of economies of scale, generation of R&D spending, or other possible routes.

Export Subsidy in Duopoly

The **export subsidy in duopoly** approach to government intervention was originally advanced by Barbara Spencer and James Brander (1983) and is presented in a less technical and more accessible form by Gene Grossman and David Richardson (1985). The analysis again assumes a duopoly context of a home firm and a foreign firm. The firms are competing for sales in the market of a third country, that is, in a market that is not the domestic market of either of the two duopolists; and it is assumed that they do not sell any output in their own domestic markets. The basic diagram is Figure 9, which reproduces the reaction functions of Figure 6 in this chapter.

FIGURE 9   The Effect of a Home-Country Export Subsidy in a Third-Country Market

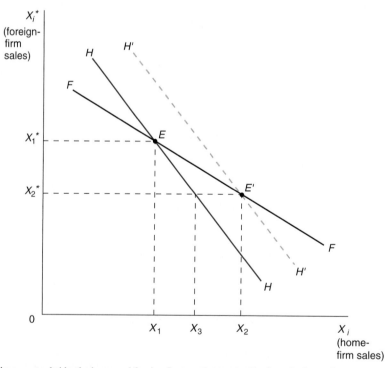

Without the export subsidy, the home and foreign firms settle at point E, where the home firm sells quantity $0X_1$ and the foreign firm sells quantity $0X_1^*$. If the home-country government gives an export subsidy to the home firm, the home firm's reaction function shifts from HH to $H'H'$ because costs of production paid by the firm itself have decreased and more output is produced. The new equilibrium is at point E'; the home firm's sales rise to $0X_2$, while the foreign firm's sales fall to $0X_2^*$.

Given this duopoly framework and the equilibrium position at point E, suppose that the home firm wishes to enlarge its market share and profits by moving to point E'. (Ignore the dashed $H'H'$ line for the moment.) Hence, the home firm threatens to expand sales to $0X_2$ from the current level of $0X_1$. If this expansion did occur, the foreign firm would reduce its sales along its reaction function FF from $0X_1^*$ to $0X_2^*$, a contraction of foreign sales that does indeed give up market share to the home firm. However, given that the firms are aware of each other's operations, the foreign firm would *not* contract sales in response to the home-firm threat to move to E'. The reason for this lack of response is that the foreign firm knows that the threat is not believable because the home firm will always choose to operate on the HH line to maximize profits. The foreign firm knows that if it continues to produce $0X_1^*$, the home firm would make a greater profit by producing $0X_1$ units rather than $0X_2$ units.

In this situation, Spencer and Brander indicate that there is a potential role for an *export subsidy* to the home firm by the home government. If this subsidy is granted and announced ahead of time (a precommitment by the home government), then the home firm will be willing to undertake expanded sales for each level of foreign firm sales. Line HH shifts to the right to line $H'H'$ because of the subsidy. The shift in the home firm's reaction function makes the threat to increase export sales to $0X_2$ *credible*. The foreign firm now realizes that it must reduce its own sales to level $0X_2^*$ because it wishes to stay on its reaction function. The end result of the use of the export subsidy is that the equilibrium position becomes point E'. The increased sales and profitability of the home firm enhance the home country's producer surplus, and the home country can, other things equal, consequently gain welfare if the increase in producer surplus outweighs the cost of the subsidy. (In the model, there is no reduced home-country consumer surplus because the good is not consumed at home. If it were, the analysis would be more complicated, but a gain could still occur.) Of course, the increased home-country welfare is at the expense of the foreign country, which has lower producer surplus because of the fall in sales.

It should also be noted that the foreign-country government could respond to the home country's export subsidy by implementing its own export subsidy to the foreign firm. This would shift FF upward and to the right in Figure 9, and the foreign firm would regain market share. David Collie (1991) hypothesized a different response to the subsidy, although his model is different in that he has the firms selling in each other's markets. In his model, the foreign country responds to the home country's export subsidy by imposing a countervailing duty rather than implementing its own export subsidy. This allows the foreign country to recapture as tariff revenue some of the foreign firm's profit—a profit that was transferred to the home firm by the original export subsidy. In a large-country case, the countervailing duty worsens the terms of trade of the home country, and the home country loses welfare from its export subsidy. Collie concludes that the potential use of the countervailing duty by the foreign country is likely to deter the home country from subsidizing the home firm's exports in the first place. In a later extension of Collie, Slotkin (1995, chap. 3) considered, among other things, the fact that some home firms may be at least partly owned by the foreign country's investors. In this framework, some of the original benefits (with no foreign-country countervailing duty) to the home country from the home country's export subsidy now accrue to the foreign country and its investors, and thus the optimal export subsidy is smaller than would otherwise be the case.

The use of a subsidy for enhancing exports can be shown in a more concrete fashion by a numerical example of a type that has become standard in the literature. Suppose that home firm H and foreign firm F contemplate production for the world market of a good with substantial economies of scale. Figure 10 shows a "payoff matrix" for the four possible situations. The upper-left portion of the matrix indicates that, if both firms produce the

FIGURE 10   Hypothetical Payoff Matrix for Home Firm and Foreign Firm

Firm F

		Produces	Does not produce
Firm H	Produces	−$20 / −$20	$0 / $200
	Does not produce	$200 / $0	$0 / $0

It is assumed that substantial economies of scale exist in the production of the good. If both firms produce the good, they each lose $20 million; if neither firm produces the good, no losses are incurred (and no profits are received). If one firm produces and the other does not, the producing firm earns $200 million while the other firm earns no profit. There is no certain outcome to this "game."

FIGURE 11   Hypothetical Payoff Matrix for Home Firm and Foreign Firm with a $50 Million Subsidy to the Home Firm

Firm F

		Produces	Does not produce
Firm H	Produces	−$20 / $30	$0 / $250
	Does not produce	$200 / $0	$0 / $0

With the home-government subsidy, the home firm will always choose to produce the good because a profit is guaranteed. The foreign firm will lose $20 million if it also produces the good, so it will choose not to produce. Thus, the outcome of this game is determinate.

good, each will lose $20 million because the market is not large enough for both of them to produce the good economically. The upper-right portion of the diagram indicates that production by firm H and *no* production by firm F would yield $200 million profit for the home firm while the foreign firm would earn no profit. The lower-left part of the matrix is opposite to the upper-right part, with producing firm F obtaining $200 million profit and nonproducing firm H receiving no profit. Finally, if neither firm produces the good, profits are zero for each firm, as shown in the lower-right portion of the matrix.

In Figure 10, the outcome of the "game" is uncertain. However, suppose that the home firm's government announces that it will grant a $50 million subsidy to firm H if it produces for the world market. With this commitment, the payoff matrix now appears as shown in Figure 11. The upper-left and upper-right portions of the matrix reflect the $50 million subsidy to the home firm. The home firm will produce the good no matter what the foreign firm does because the home firm has a guaranteed profit. The subsidy ensures that firm H will dominate the market; firm F will not produce because it never earns a profit when the home

FIGURE 12   A Tariff Game by Governments

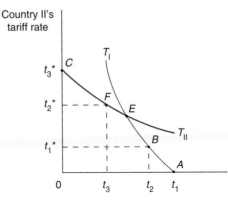

Curve T_1 shows the various tariff rates by country I that maximize its welfare, given various tariff rates by country II. Curve T_{II} shows the opposite—the various tariff rates by country II that maximize its welfare, given various tariff rates by country I. Point E is the equilibrium position; at E, each country is maximizing its own welfare given the tariff rate of the other country. However, the universal free-trade point at the origin of the axes is the point of maximum world welfare, and this point cannot be reached without negotiations between the countries.

firm produces. Note also that the government subsidy of $50 million generates a $250 million profit for the home producer, which can increase the home country's welfare. Of course, there is no guarantee that the foreign government will not retaliate with its own subsidy. In addition, if home consumption exists, an export subsidy by a home government raises prices to home consumers and thereby decreases consumer welfare. The chances of the country improving its overall welfare through the subsidy are thereby reduced.

Strategic Government Interaction and World Welfare

We now turn away from government trade policy designed to capture market share, rents, or profit for particular firms to a more general model of government behavior with respect to trade policy. An important result of this forthcoming analysis is that country governments each can be maximizing their own country's well-being, given the behavior of other governments, and yet world welfare as a whole is definitely *not* being maximized.

Consider first an analysis based upon the terms-of-trade or optimum-tariff analysis of Chapter 14.[6] Assume that there are two *large* countries—country I and country II. In Figure 12, we construct a **tariff reaction function** for each country. The horizontal axis indicates possible tariff rates for country I's government to adopt, and the vertical axis indicates the same for country II's government. Suppose now that country II has a zero tariff rate; that is, country II is practicing free trade. Because country I is a large country, it can influence its terms of trade, and, with the objective of maximizing its own welfare, it will apply tariff t_1 (point A). Remember from Chapter 14 that the optimum tariff is the one that results in the enhanced welfare from the improved terms of trade more than offsetting the welfare loss from a reduced quantity of imports by the maximum amount. Next, suppose country II did not practice free trade but instead had tariff rate t_1^* in place. *Given this tariff rate,* country I would choose a tariff rate that would maximize its welfare in this new

---

[6]See Grossman and Richardson (1985, pp. 24–26); for the original article, see Johnson (1953–1954, especially pp. 146–50).

IN THE REAL WORLD:

AIRBUS INDUSTRIE

An example of government subsidization to stimulate international competitiveness is the European airplane firm Airbus Industrie. Formed in 1970, Airbus is a consortium project by firms from France (38 percent of ownership), Germany (38 percent), Great Britain (20 percent), and Spain (4 percent). The governments of all four countries have provided funds to the consortium project; although there is no precise way to measure the extent of subsidization, the U.S. Department of Commerce estimated in 1993 that the amount received by Airbus as of that time was about $26 billion (cited in Coleman 1993). In 1996 a strengthening of Airbus occurred when the partner companies agreed to convert the firm from a loose consortium to a centralized, integrated company in order to keep better control of costs and to enable Airbus to seek funds from outside investors for financing a new and larger jumbo jet. As a result of these measures, Airbus Industrie's market share reached 45 percent in 1997, a significant gain from the 30 percent share attained in the early 1990s. By 2003, Airbus and its U.S. competitor, the Boeing Company, each had one-half of the passenger aircraft market, and Airbus had more pending orders than Boeing. However, troubles began to develop for Airbus when it devoted massive resources to building and marketing a huge jumbo jet, the A380, which was reputed to be the most spacious civilian airplane in history but that did not sell well. Scandal also was involved, and senior executives lost their jobs. In the meantime, Boeing became more competitive by outsourcing some work to China and Japan and by streamlining its Seattle assembly plant. Airbus itself had become 80 percent owned by a Dutch company, European Aeronautic Defense and Space Company (EADS), in 2000. EADS is publicly owned and has included DaimlerChrysler among its shareholders.

Boeing and other U.S. producers complain about the subsidies received by Airbus Industrie, although it was estimated that by 1993 Boeing, General Dynamics, and McDonnell Douglas had received $41 billion in "indirect subsidies" through U.S. government military and space contracts. In an attempt to control subsidies, the United States and the European Community signed an accord in 1992 limiting the subsidies to 33 percent of airplane development costs. However, by 1997, dissatisfaction was evident in Europe, as European Union trade officials felt that the 1993 restrictions placed on Europe's direct subsidies posed a greater burden than did the restrictions on the indirect subsidies in the United States. Tensions continued, and a January 2005 U.S.–EU meeting tried to resolve differences. By early 2007, the World Trade Organization had become involved.

Finally, Richard Baldwin (cited in "A Survey of World Trade," 1990, pp. 20–21) estimated that because of the Airbus subsidies, Europe probably lost welfare and that the United States also lost because Boeing's profits were reduced by more than the gain experienced by aircraft users from price reductions. The only winners appear to have been other countries, where the airlines and their passengers have gained from lower aircraft prices. Perhaps "strategic trade policy" benefits only the countries who don't engage in it!

Sources: "Airbus Pins Itself Down," *The Economist,* January 30, 1988, pp. 50–51; Jeff Cole and Helene Cooper, "U.S., EU Open Aircraft-Subsidy Talks as Europe Weighs Status of Boeing Deal," *The Wall Street Journal,* April 28, 1997, p. A20; Jeff Cole and Charles Goldsmith, "Rivalry between Boeing, Airbus Takes New Direction," *The Wall Street Journal,* April 30, 1997, p. B4; Brian Coleman, "Airbus Subsidies Are Invisible to Radar," *The Wall Street Journal,* March 4, 1993, p. A10; Bob Davis, "U.S. Presses EC to Renegotiate Aircraft Accord," *The Wall Street Journal,* February 26, 1993, pp. A2, A4; Charles Goldsmith, "Airbus Consortium Plans to Centralize to Compete Better," *The Wall Street Journal,* July 9, 1996, p. A8; "A Survey of World Trade," *The Economist,* September 22, 1990, following p. 60; U.S. Department of Commerce, *U.S. Industrial Outlook 1994* (Washington, DC: U.S. Department of Commerce, January 1994), p. 20–6; Charles Goldsmith, "After Trailing for Years, Airbus Aims for 50% of the Market," *The Wall Street Journal,* March 16, 1998, p. A1; Jeff Cole, "Airbus Prepares to 'Bet the Company' as It Builds a Huge New Jet," *The Wall Street Journal,* November 3, 1999, p. A1; Daniel Michaels and Jeff Cole, "Airbus Beats Boeing in Jet Orders for First Time," *The Wall Street Journal,* January 13, 2000, p. A17; Daniel Michaels, "Airbus Partners Meet Boeing Head-On," *The Wall Street Journal,* June 26, 2000, p. A28; J. Lynn Lunsford, "With Airbus on Its Tail, Boeing is Rethinking How It Builds Planes," *The Wall Street Journal,* September 5, 2001, pp. A1, A16; J. Lynn Lunsford, "Boeing, Losing Ground to Airbus, Faces Key Choice," *The Wall Street Journal,* April 21, 2003, pp. A1, A8; "How Airbus Lost Its Bearings," *The Wall Street Journal,* May 24, 2006, p. A15; "The Airbus Debacle," *The Wall Street Journal,* June 20, 2006, p. A20; "Airbus Problems Lead to Ouster of Key Executives," *The Wall Street Journal,* July 3, 2006, pp. A1, A2; "Hard Landing," *The Economist,* February 17, 2007, p. 68; www.eads.net; www.ustr.gov; www.airbus.com.

situation. Because trade has already been restricted to some extent by II's tariff, country I will find that its new optimum tariff rate will be somewhat lower than the original t_1 because import quantity has already been somewhat reduced compared with that under free trade by II's reduced willingness to trade. Hence, we suppose that tariff rate t_2 is the optimum tariff for country I when country II has tariff rate t_1^* in place (point B). Following the same reasoning, we can trace out schedule T_1, country I's tariff reaction schedule showing the various levels of its tariff that would maximize I's welfare, given various tariff rates by country II.

Now consider country II. By an identical procedure to that used above for country I, we can specify that optimum tariff rate t_3^* will be selected when country I has free trade (point C), t_2^* will be selected when I has t_3 in place (point F), and so forth. We thus delineate the resulting schedule T_{II} as country II's tariff reaction function—it shows the various tariff rates that maximize country II's welfare, given various tariff levels by country I.

Clearly, point E is the point where the two countries will settle. Similar to our discussion of Figure 6 in this chapter, but presented in terms of country welfare rather than firms' profits, movement will take place to E from any other position in the diagram. However, the important point is that E is *not* the world's welfare-maximizing point, even though each country is maximizing its own welfare given the behavior of the other country. Point E has been attained by inward shifts of offer curves, and trade has correspondingly been reduced from the free-trade level. Both countries have lost welfare in comparison with the free-trade situation, and we know from trade theory that free trade maximizes world welfare. In fact, the most desirable point on the graph from the standpoint of world welfare is at the *origin* of the diagram, where each country has a zero tariff. Unfortunately, neither country has an incentive to take unilateral action to move to the origin. If either country unilaterally moved away from E, it would be moving away from its welfare maximization, *given* the tariff rate of the other country.

The same general point can be made with the game theory payoff matrix shown in Figure 13. In this matrix, we simply pose for each country's government the choice of free trade versus protection without permitting varying degrees of protection (varying degrees such as were available in Figure 12). Nevertheless, the same general conclusion about world welfare will emerge as the one that emerged from Figure 12.

FIGURE 13   **Two-Country Trade Policy Payoff Matrix**

		Country II	
		Free trade	Protection
Country I	Free trade	$100 / $100	$120 / $50
	Protection	$50 / $120	$60 / $60

If country I engages in free trade, it will realize well-being of $100 if country II also engages in free trade but only $50 of welfare if II practices protection. Likewise, if country II engages in free trade, it will attain welfare of $100 if I also engages in free trade but only $50 of welfare if I practices protection. Each country has a dominant strategy of protection, and so the outcome of the game is in the lower-right cell of the payoff matrix. This location is inferior to universal free trade as represented by the upper-left cell of the matrix.

With the matrix in Figure 13, note that if country I pursues free trade while country II does also, they end up in the upper left cell, where country I's welfare is $100 (somehow measured) and country II's welfare is also $100. If country I engages in free trade but II adopts protection, country I has welfare of $50 while II has welfare of $120. These results in the upper-right cell differ from those in the upper-left cell because II has applied its optimum tariff, which has led to a gain at the expense of country I. Alternatively, in the lower-left cell of the matrix, country I has adopted its optimum tariff (generating $120 of welfare), while country II has free trade (and $50 of welfare). Finally, in the lower-right cell, both countries have their optimum tariffs in place (analogous to point E in Figure 12), and both have welfare of $60.

Where will the two participating governments in the game end up? Note that country I has what is called a **dominant strategy.** A dominant strategy occurs when following one of the two possible strategies always produces a superior outcome to following the other possible strategy. For country I, if it pursues protection, it will obtain $120 of welfare if country II pursues free trade and $60 of welfare if country II pursues protection. These outcomes are superior to the comparative respective results of $100 and $50 for country I if it always pursues free trade. Hence, protection is the dominant strategy for country I. Because the matrix has been constructed with identical numbers for the two countries, country II also has a dominant strategy—the strategy of protection rather than free trade. Clearly, with both countries pursuing protection, the game ends up in the lower right cell, with $60 of welfare being attained for each country.

Both in Figure 12 and in Figure 13, therefore, we find the two countries, when each is pursuing its own self-interest, arriving at a predictable end result (point E in Figure 12 and the lower right cell in Figure 13). But, in both situations, there is a result that would be superior for both of them as well as for the world as a whole (the origin in Figure 12 and the upper left cell in Figure 13). The strategic game will not get the countries to these best positions. The only way to achieve these best positions is to have *tariff negotiations* between the countries, and successful negotiations could bring each country's tariff level down to zero and thus maximize welfare. We discuss such negotiations in practice in the next chapter.

Concluding Observations on Strategic Trade Policy

The increase in globalization in trade and finance in recent years has been accompanied by considerable dialogue on country competitiveness and the role of government policy in promoting success in an ever-smaller economic world. Within the industrialized countries, the increased importance of international transactions has been accompanied by relative changes in economic structure as the service sector has expanded at a very fast rate. The relative growth in services, accompanied by a decline in the share of the workforce in manufacturing, has produced considerable concern that deindustrialization is taking place and that "good" manufacturing jobs are being shipped abroad through rapidly growing imports of manufactures. Bolstered by writings by prominent individuals such as then–MIT School of Management dean Lester Thurow, White House policy adviser Ira Magaziner, and Harvard professor and later secretary of labor Robert Reich, policy discussions often centered on ways in which governments could mitigate this trend by enacting industrial policies which would promote high-wage, high-labor value-added or high-technology industries. It was argued that, if successful, these policies would result in the evolvement of new comparative-advantage products which would keep the country competitive in the emerging global marketplace.

Not surprisingly, a number of economists, including Paul Krugman (1993, 1996), were highly critical of these kinds of policies. It was quickly pointed out that while competitiveness is relevant for individual firms, comparative advantage and not competition is what is relevant for countries. Further, it is extremely difficult to determine which products might have a potential comparative advantage and hence be the focus of such strategic trade policy.

Focusing on high-wage or high-labor value-added industries certainly does not provide a useful guideline, since these industries tend to be very capital-intensive and expansion of them may not be an efficient use of resources. Further, it is not clear why government policy-makers will have a better insight than the market with respect to which products should be fostered and developed. The case for government intervention in the form of strategic indus-trial policy thus appears to be the strongest when market failures result in the presence of positive social externalities that result in insufficient private investment and product develop-ment. While such may be the case in terms of certain high-technology products, the problem still arises regarding identification of these goods. Caution regarding the active use of strate-gic trade policy is indicated by the high social cost of Airbus Industrie and the failure of U.S. policy to promote the flat-screen technology into a comparative-advantage good. In sum, while there certainly may be instances when strategic trade policy can be useful in stimulat-ing dynamic comparative advantage and/or in providing an environment within which a domestic firm may have a greater likelihood of being successful in an increasingly firm-competitive world, it remains extremely difficult to identify likely candidates for support. There is, however, ample evidence of the high social cost associated with making the wrong guess and supporting goods where comparative advantage does not emerge.

CONCEPT CHECK

1. In the Krugman research and development model, what role does the positive depend-ence of R&D spending on the level of the home firm's total output play in making a case for protection?

2. In Figure 9, why is the threat by the home firm to sell at level $0X_2$ without a government subsidy not believable to the foreign firm?

3. In the payoff matrix in Figure 10, is a subsidy to the home firm (assuming no retaliation) beneficial to the home country if both the home firm and the foreign firm could make a positive profit when there is no government intervention; for example, if the numbers in the upper left were +$20 and +$20? Explain.

4. Explain what is meant by a country's tariff reaction function.

5. Why do the reaction functions in Figure 6 slope downward?

SUMMARY

This chapter has presented and examined many of the most com-mon arguments for protection. In the first part of the chapter, tra-ditional arguments were grouped into several key categories organized around the objectives of the action in question. It was noted that protection could be undertaken as part of a broader social objectives package, as a way of dealing with market imper-fections, and as a response to policy actions of a country's trading partners. We focused attention on the possibility of using welfare-superior alternatives to reach specific objectives, the beggar-my-neighbor character of several of the arguments, and the difficulty of applying the arguments in practice. In the last part of the chap-ter we examined several of the arguments that focus on the dynamic benefits of protection. These theories build on the imperfect nature of competition in many industries and stress that unilateral action can bring potential gains such as a transfer of foreign monopoly profit and the realization of economies of scale that will lead to greater exports. An increase in research and development spending, with subsequent enhanced exports, can also be attained through home-market protection. Further, export subsidies can be used to enhance the share of home firms in overseas markets, thereby improving, in some circumstances, home welfare. However, protection based on these analyses does not necessarily guarantee an improvement in home well-being because, among other things, foreign retaliation is ignored. In addition, the originators of the theories are not necessarily rec-ommending protection but are attempting to show possible implications of departing from the perfect competition assump-tion of traditional trade theory. Further, successful implementa-tion of strategic trade policy is not an easy or straightforward matter. Attempts by trading partners to implement such policy can easily leave all the countries less well-off if noncooperative trade "strategy" dominates cooperation and trade negotiations. In addition, experience has shown that identification of potential candidates for government intervention is far from easy and that "betting on the wrong horse" can be a costly wager for the gov-ernment policymaker.

KEY TERMS

antidumping argument
antidumping duty
beggar-my-neighbor policy
countervailing duty (CVD)
dominant strategy
dumping
duopoly
economies of scale
export subsidy in duopoly
imperfect competition
infant industry argument
macroeconomic interpretation of a
   trade deficit
national defense argument

optimum tariff rate
persistent dumping
predatory dumping
reaction functions
recognized interdependence
specificity principle
sporadic dumping
strategic trade policy
tariff reaction function
tariff to benefit a scarce factor of
   production
tariff to extract foreign monopoly
   profit

tariff to improve the balance of
   trade
tariff to increase employment in a
   particular industry
tariff to offset a foreign subsidy
tariff to promote exports through
   economies of scale
tariff to promote exports through
   research and development
tariff to reduce aggregate
   unemployment
terms-of-trade argument

QUESTIONS AND PROBLEMS

1. You are analyzing a tariff for extracting foreign monopoly profit. Will the transfer of profit become greater or less, for a given tariff amount, when the demand curve facing the foreign monopolist becomes more elastic? Will the loss in home consumer surplus become greater or less, for a given tariff amount, when the demand curve becomes more elastic? What can be concluded, if anything, about the relationship between the elasticity of demand and the net welfare gains to the home country from the tariff? Explain.

2. Suppose that the firm obtaining protection in a Krugman-type framework has marginal costs that *increase* rather than decrease with greater production. Would Krugman's results follow if this were true? Why or why not?

3. Suppose that the production technology of a self-proclaimed "infant industry" permits economies of scale. Suppose also that the same technology is available to foreign producers. Is there a valid argument for protection in this situation from the perspective of the world as a whole? Why or why not?

4. Why might the use of a tariff to decrease aggregate unemployment in a country eventually generate an *increase* in aggregate unemployment in that country?

5. You have learned that a subsidy is preferable to a tariff if the objective is to generate a given amount of employment in an individual industry. Explain this point in language understandable to someone untrained in economics.

6. Does persistent dumping into the domestic country necessarily mean that a foreign government is subsidizing the foreign exporting firm? Why or why not?

7. Evaluate this statement: If a tariff is imposed to reduce imports, the balance of trade will surely improve as it is safe to assume that exports will be unaffected by the tariff.

8. In Figure 6, suppose that the home firm's reaction function is flatter than that of the foreign firm. Use a diagram to explain why a point away from equilibrium will lead the firms farther away from the equilibrium position.

9. Suppose that a payoff matrix analogous to Figure 10 looks as follows:

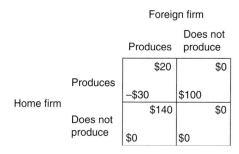

Will the foreign firm produce the good? Why or why not? Assuming no subsidy, will the home firm produce the good? Why or why not?

10. In Question 9, suppose that a subsidy of $50 is given to the home firm. (No subsidy is given to the foreign firm.) Will this subsidy change the production pattern from that of Question 9? If so, why? If not, why not? Is the subsidy of benefit to the home country? Explain.

11. The following graph shows the demand curve (*D*) of a home country facing the foreign monopoly supplier of a good to the home country, the associated marginal revenue curve (*MR*), the foreign firm's horizontal marginal cost curve when there is no tariff imposed by the home country

(*MC*), and the foreign firm's marginal cost curve plus the cost of the tariff when a specific tariff is imposed by the home country (*MC + t*):

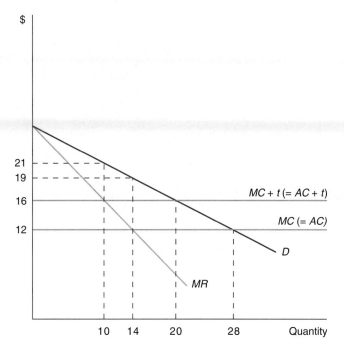

Assuming that average cost (*AC*) equals marginal cost:

(*a*) Indicate the price charged to home-country consumers by the foreign-monopoly supplier when there is no home-country tariff.

(*b*) Indicate the price charged to home-country consumers by the foreign-monopoly supplier when the home-country tariff is in place.

(*c*) Calculate the loss in consumer surplus in the home country because of the imposition of the tariff.

(*d*) Calculate the amount of former foreign-monopoly profit that is transferred as tariff revenue to the home country when the home country imposes the tariff.

(*e*) Does the home country gain or lose because of the imposition of the tariff? What is the dollar value of the gain or loss?

12. In Figure 12, suppose the countries are located at point *F.* Explain why movement will take place to point *E*.

16

POLITICAL ECONOMY AND U.S. TRADE POLICY

LEARNING OBJECTIVES

■ To comprehend several basic concepts of the political economy of economic policy.

■ To understand critical developments in the history of multilateral trade negotiations.

■ To become familiar with recent trade policy issues.

■ To increase awareness of ongoing U.S. trade policy developments.

INTRODUCTION

Contrasting Vignettes on Trade Policy

In January 2004, U.S. Trade Representative Robert Zoellick proposed that all agricultural export subsidies by countries be eliminated and that all tariffs on food and other agricultural imports be cut dramatically. These and other proposals were made in a letter to the 148 member countries of the World Trade Organization. The intent of the letter and the proposed measures was to put new life into multilateral trade negotiations to reduce trade barriers worldwide. . . .[1]

In November 2003 the chief trade official of the European Union (EU), Pascal Lamy, threatened that the EU would impose steep tariffs on $6 billion of U.S. exports to the EU unless the United States altered two of its trade policies. First, the World Trade Organization (WTO) had ruled that U.S. tariffs imposed in March 2002 on imported steel were illegal. Second, the WTO had also ruled that favorable U.S. tax treatment of special divisions of U.S. companies set up to promote exports was illegal, since the treatment constituted an export subsidy not permitted by international trade rules. Lamy indicated that the EU was seeking "compliance" with agreed rules, and that the EU intended to carry out its threat if no U.S. changes were made. . . .[2]

These contrasting vignettes indicate that a country, in these cases the United States, can be pushing for freer trade, as in the first vignette, but at the same time be, as in the second vignette, employing policies that depart from free trade according to comparative advantage. Trade policy can involve conflicting and complex economic and political forces, and outcomes are not so clear-cut as traditional trade theory would suggest. This chapter first addresses the question of how the setting of trade policy is influenced by institutions and the political process and then summarizes U.S. and multilateral trade policy developments during the last several decades. We begin with a brief discussion of some common analyses of the interaction between citizens and their elected representatives/policymakers in the process of policy formulation and of the concerns reflected in a country's trade stance. As will be seen, a minority of the population is often successful in procuring policies that benefit that minority at the expense of general social welfare. We then present an overview of U.S. trade policy since the 1930s. A central point is that the past approximately 70 years have seen a dramatic liberalization of trade in the United States and other industrial countries.

THE POLITICAL ECONOMY OF TRADE POLICY

As has often been pointed out, the one issue on which economists are in almost unanimous agreement is the social gains to be made by specializing and trading on the basis of comparative advantage and, correspondingly, opposition to protectionism. In spite of this view, the world continues to experience pressures to restrict the movement of goods, services, and factors between countries. Indeed, countries seem to continue to find new and novel ways to restrict these economic activities. Too often as one trade-restricting instrument falls into disfavor and is reduced or eliminated, new trade-restricting provisions seem to pop up. It is little wonder, then, that one is often asked, "If free trade is so beneficial to a country, why are so many groups or individuals trying their best to reduce trade?" Why is it that, as Robert Baldwin (1989, p. 119) so aptly pointed out, "international trade seems to be a subject where the advice of economists is routinely disregarded"?

The answer to this question lies in what is referred to as "the political economy of trade policy." In reality, trade policy takes place within a political-social milieu and is influenced

---

[1]Neil King, Jr., and Scott Miller, "U.S. Trade Chief Moves to Revive Global Parleys," *The Wall Street Journal,* January 13, 2004, p. A2.

[2]Neil King, Jr., and Michael Schroeder, "EU Trade Chief Warns of Sanctions," *The Wall Street Journal,* November 5, 2003, pp. A2, A15. Note that the United States did remove the March 2002 steel tariffs.

by individuals and groups who feel that they will be better off with restricted trade even though the country as a whole may be worse off. As we have noted in previous chapters, reducing the barriers to trade may make the country better off, but as the corresponding structural adjustments are made, some individuals will be made better off and some worse off. Politicians thus find themselves confronted with a vast array of groups attempting to influence trade policy, and, consequently, they often ignore the advice of economists when establishing the country's trading regime. In the past three decades, an area of research has emerged that focuses on analyzing the actual determinants of trade policy in the political environment within which it is developed. We now turn to a brief discussion of several of the more important strands of research on this topical issue.

The Self-Interest Approach to Trade Policy

The study of the political factors influencing trade policy has proceeded along two major fronts. The first, and perhaps the most pervasive, focuses on the economic self-interest of the political participants.[3] Much of this literature is embedded in **public-choice economics,** which essentially uses economic models to analyze governmental decision-making behavior. In this approach, government decision makers are essentially utility maximizers whose level of satisfaction is dependent upon being reelected and who act in a manner that maximizes the probability that this will in fact take place.[4] An immediate implication of this approach is that the majority of the public will be served by public decision makers who enact legislation to maximize their chances of remaining in office. This is the focus of the **median-voter model,** which holds that the decision maker who votes in such a way as to satisfy the median voter will maximize his or her reelection possibilities. In this approach each individual voter is assigned a position along an array based on the expected costs or benefits of a particular policy. The median voter is in the center of this array, that is, the middle voter. Should the majority expect to benefit from a particular policy, the median voter will be in favor of the policy and support the politician who favors it. Should the majority feel that they will be harmed by a particular action, the median voter will not favor the policy and will not support a political candidate who attempts to make a case for it. This is a natural model to use in studying international trade policy because, as we have noted in previous theory chapters, trade policy inevitably results in different welfare effects for different groups in the economy.

In the median-voter framework, should a greater number of voters expect to benefit from a particular trade policy than incur a loss, the median voter would be in favor of the proposed legislation and the policymaker would presumably vote in favor of the policy measure. Should the policymaker not support the legislation in this case, the median voter is likely to vote against the legislator in the next election. This approach would thus seem to ensure that the will of the majority would be followed. Unfortunately, however, there are a number of practical problems, which, if they arise, can circumvent the preferences of the median voter and result in policies that are inconsistent with majority benefits. The median-voter model rests on the assumptions that the voters have full information regarding any gains or losses resulting from a particular policy and that they will actually vote consistent with their preferences. Inasmuch as neither of these two assumptions always holds in the real world, it is clearly possible that the preferences of the median voter do not win out. For example, a tariff benefiting only a small group of individuals may end up being supported by a voting majority.

---

[3]The early background literature on this approach was nicely reviewed by Hillman (1989).

[4]While a number of things such as political ideology, place in history, personal gain, etc., undoubtedly influence the policymaker, nonetheless, remaining in office is central to what the politician hopes to accomplish.

There are a number of situations that can produce these seemingly contradictory results. In the case where there are information-gathering costs as well as opportunity costs associated with actually voting, some potential voters may simply choose not to participate, particularly if expected gains are small and hence the expected net benefits negative. If, in addition, the voter feels that one vote will not actually influence or "swing" the result, he or she may simply accept the outcome without actually engaging in the political process. In this case, voters are acting as "free riders," that is, accepting the outcome without expending any effort or costs. Although this would not be a problem if every voter had an equal probability of not participating, in reality, the differences in the amount of expected benefits and costs (asymmetric gains and losses) strongly suggest that individuals will have different degrees of incentive and that interest groups will form. A particular policy action such as sugar quotas may have only a minor individual or per capita impact on a large group in society (e.g., consumers) but a large per capita impact on a minority (e.g., sugar producers).

Interest groups can influence political outcomes in a variety of ways. Because the costs (benefits) of a policy are relatively great to these groups, they have an incentive to influence political action and are more likely to overcome the free-rider problem of their relatively small number of members. A small group of individuals who stand to gain much from a policy intervention in the market thus obtain a certain group solidarity, participate in the political process, and vote for the candidate who supports their position on protection. At the same time, however, the larger group of diverse consumers who stand to lose with protectionism expect to gain little *individually* by making the effort to acquire information and/or vote; consequently they do not participate. As a result, there is a small voter turnout and the candidate espousing the views of the solid minority block wins. This phenomenon can lead to a **status quo bias** against liberalizing trade policy through lower levels of protection even though doing so carries the promise of improving aggregate welfare. For a large number of people the net personal gains are so small (perhaps even negative) or uncertain that they choose not to participate actively in the political process, and the minority interest group gets its way. There is no doubt that groups such as this are very influential in the conduct of trade policy formation. As Vousden (1990, p. 198) points out, interest or pressure groups tend to be more successful if they are large enough to be visible but small enough to control the free riding of their members, there is a well-defined commonality of interest, and the per capita organizational and information-gathering costs are relatively low.

A second way in which special interest groups can influence political outcomes is through the funding of political campaigns. Funding of campaigns not only contributes to candidate visibility but also can be a relatively low cost way of providing interest-group-centered information to potential voters to motivate them to participate in the political process. In a similar vein, withholding campaign funding or making implied threats to fund an opposition candidate also are effective in getting a politician's attention and support for a particular policy position. Groups that attempt to influence policy in their favor through the use of campaign contributions are said to be carrying on **rent-seeking activity** because the group is committing resources to the pursuit of benefits from protection. Note that the group would not rationally expend resources in excess of the expected benefits that it would receive from the policies in question. Rent-seeking activity can, of course, extend beyond simple campaign contributions to the use of corruptive practices such as bribes to political decision makers to influence their votes. Because the resources used in this type of activity are not producing any good or service but are merely influencing the distribution of income, these actions are often referred to as **directly unproductive activity.**

Rent-seeking activity can be further complicated when an interest group tacitly agrees to support continued protection in other sectors, even if it means a loss in welfare for its

IN THE REAL WORLD:

POLITICS PUTS THE SQUEEZE ON TOMATO IMPORTS

Actions by the Clinton administration in the 1990s to negotiate a floor price on tomato imports from Mexico constitute an excellent example of how the political process can result in a protectionist measure that circumvents the median-voter principle and rewards a small vocal minority (a small number of large Floridian growers) at the expense of the large mass of unorganized free-riding tomato consumers. Led by producer Paul J. DiMare, the Florida tomato producers, who are controlled by a handful of wealthy growers, had argued for years for protection from cheap foreign imports that "are driving Florida farmers out of business." Interestingly, however, the Florida tomato industry has not collapsed even though hurricanes, cold snaps, and other weather-related woes have hindered production. Of concern to the growers was the increase in imports from Mexico, which they feared would become even larger as the North American Free Trade Agreement (NAFTA, discussed in Chapter 17) accords came into place. Even though the tariff on Mexican tomatoes was low (1.4 cents/pound) prior to NAFTA, DiMare and others argued that the resulting increase in Mexican tomato imports endangered thousands of U.S. jobs and that without help the Florida tomato industry was "going down the tubes." The Florida growers got little sympathy from their counterparts in California, whose summer crop competes directly with Mexico's crop. According to Ken Moonie, vice president of the tomato operations of California-based Calgene Inc., "All this is about protecting four big guys . . . it is not like corn or any other agricultural commodity where thousands of growers are involved."

Imports of tomatoes from Mexico have increased in the past several years, cutting into Florida's share of the winter market. Some of this market penetration reflects the simple fact that the taste of the hand-picked, vine-ripened Mexican tomatoes surpasses that of the Florida tomatoes, which are picked green and then gas-ripened prior to shipping. DiMare did not see that consumer preference for the juicier, more tasty vine-ripened fruit had anything to do with the increase in imports, allowing that "it really doesn't matter" how tomatoes taste since they are condiments, seldom eaten alone.

Under the accord reached in October 1996, Mexican growers agreed not to sell tomatoes in the United States below a certain price. The U.S. Department of Commerce stated that this price would be the lowest average price during a recent period when there was a clear absence of any "price suppression" on the part of Mexican producers. This accord was negotiated by Commerce Secretary Mickey Kantor and the Clinton administration because Florida was considered essential in the November 1996 elections. According to one Clinton strategist, "It's not that we're afraid that the farmers won't vote for us—there aren't enough tomato farmers down there. The fear is they'll hit us with a negative advertising campaign." The result of the administration's concern regarding campaign funding and possible negative campaigning was that the median voter/consumer ended up with a less tasty, more expensive tomato and U.S. exporters such as pork producers in the Midwest feared that the negotiated tomato settlement might lead to Mexican retaliation against their products.

Sources: Helene Cooper and Bruce Ingersoll, "Playing Catch-Up: With Little Evidence, Florida Growers Blame Tomato Woes on NAFTA," *The Wall Street Journal,* April 3, 1996, p. A1; Robert S. Greenberger, "Mexico Agrees to Temporary Floor on Price of Tomatoes Sold in U.S.," *The Wall Street Journal,* October 14, 1996, p. B3; George Anthan, "Politics Put Squeeze on Tomato Imports; U.S. Growers Prevail," *The Des Moines Register,* October 29, 1996, p. 3A. ●

own members, in exchange for support for one's own protection. The idea here is that the combined support of several groups for protection provides a sufficient political critical mass to get the protectionist candidates elected and the trade restrictions maintained. For example, textile and apparel workers (along with sector-specific capital owners in textiles and apparel) might well support the status quo on sugar and steel protection in exchange for the sugar and steel sectors' support of protection in the textile and apparel industry. In this instance, the loss to their membership through higher prices for sugar and steel-using products might well be small compared with the gains obtained through the continued protection of textiles and apparel. This is another example, often called "logrolling," of status quo bias in which a group (or several groups) benefits at the expense of society as a whole.

The median voter has again been supplanted in terms of the policy action undertaken because of a large uninvolved free-riding majority and the efforts of an interest-centered pressure group.

Before leaving this discussion, it is important to note that while the self-interest approach has proved quite useful in better understanding the trade policy issue, it ignores the fact that people do things that do not appear to be in their pure economic self-interest. No one would dispute the fact that, although it may be relatively small, individuals have often demonstrated the willingness to sacrifice some of their real income to improve over-all welfare, whether it be in their community, their country, or even the world. It is for this reason that we turn to other approaches to political economy.

The Social Objectives Approach

From this perspective, trade policy is conducted taking into account the well-being of different groups in society along with various national and international objectives. In this environment, trade policy is promoted to the public at large in terms of broader social goals such as income distribution, increased productivity, economic growth, national defense, global power and leadership, and international equity. With regard to domestic income distribution, Corden (1974, p. 107) suggests that trade policy appears to have a conservative bias in that governments often seem to give more weight to avoiding real income losses in a particular segment of the economy and assign less weight to increasing the real income of a particular group. Other social objectives which have been discussed in the literature involve minimizing consumer loss, improving the real income of the lowest-income groups, minimizing or delaying adjustment costs for particular industries, and protecting the relative income level of specific socioeconomic groups.[5]

Such a macro approach does, however, create problems. If a country talks a "free-trade talk" and then proceeds *not* to "walk the free-trade walk" by protecting certain import competing sectors for reasons such as those given earlier, it quickly loses credibility with the voters. Once pressure groups learn that the government is concerned about income distribution, the verbalized commitment to free trade and structural adjustment is compromised and structural adjustment by both labor and capital slows. The expectation of trade policy relief thus reduces the outward movement of factors from any given declining industry, economic conditions in the industry continue to worsen, and greater and greater pressures are put on the government to intervene to maintain relative income levels and the status quo. The expectation and likely realization of government support of the threatened industry thus results in slowing down the necessary structural change, a loss in overall economic efficiency, and little or no change in equity. The inability to commit to a free-trade policy hence forces the country whose trade policy is influenced by income distribution concerns to maintain protection. It is often argued that this type of analysis is useful in explaining the high level of protection offered to textiles and apparel over time. Deardorff (1987) also suggests that such concerns help explain why governments prefer VERs to tariffs. Finally, Baldwin (1989, p. 129) argues that income distribution concerns can also help explain why governments use protection instead of domestic subsidies to help import-competing firms. With a tariff, quota, or VER, consumers who use the product essentially bear the burden of the policy through higher prices. Inasmuch as they were the group that initially benefited from the import-induced lower prices, an increase in domestic price that returns them more-or-less to the initial higher price leaves them no worse off than they were previously—even if the tariff revenue is not returned to them. Were a production subsidy used to support the affected industry, the burden of the tax (to pay for the subsidy)

---

[5]See Baldwin (1989, pp. 126–30) for an excellent overview of these studies.

would presumably fall on all taxpayers, thus reducing the relative income of those who do not consume the product and were not affected by the lower product price.

Foreign trade policy has also been used as part of the total foreign policy package. As such, foreign policy concerns have been used to support both increased protection and increased trade liberalization. Since World War II, the United States has been the major hegemonic power in the world. During much of that time, U.S. foreign policy was directed toward limiting the spread of communism and strengthening the noncommunist world economically. U.S. trade and aid policy was clearly influenced by these concerns, and they perhaps explain why the United States chose not to use its hegemonic power to improve its international terms of trade. In addition to hegemonic concerns, there is also evidence that a number of countries have concerns about the international distribution of income that go beyond their own self-interest. Examples of this include the amount of untied foreign aid (i.e., aid that can be spent on goods from any country, not just from the donor country) that has been given to the developing countries as well as the reduced trade restrictions that have been granted both unilaterally and multilaterally through such programs as the Generalized System of Preferences (GSP). Analysis of this type has been relatively common among political scientists in recent years. We therefore turn to a brief discussion of that line of research with respect to trade policy.

An Overview of the Political Science Take on Trade Policy[6]

Political scientists have taken several tacks in examining the trade policy issue. One tack, similar to the economic self-interest approach, views trade policy as the result of a political process involving competition between various domestic interest groups. A second approach focuses on trade policy as the result of the distribution of economic and political power among trading partners. Building on this focus, others have suggested that the size and/or degree of hegemonic power strongly influences the nature of trade policy. More specifically, writers have argued that the larger the hegemon's international finance and trade interests, the more it will stand to gain from freer trade and the more likely it will work to liberalize international transactions. This proposition has been strongly contested by other political scientists, especially in situations in which a few large nation-states tend to dominate world transactions. Others have questioned the logic of such a conclusion, given that a large country can potentially gain from imposing trade restrictions as it has the ability to pass on part of the domestic costs through changes in international prices (its terms of trade).

From an international relations perspective, it has been tempting for political scientists to focus on the role of the chief executive of a country in influencing not only international policy relating to national security but also policy relating to trade. However, this "unitary actor" approach has been criticized for ignoring the microfoundations of policy formulation that underlie the process by which various pressure groups influence the setting of policy. A perhaps more satisfying approach, also state centered, focuses on the institutional and ideological structures within a country that lead to the setting of government policy, including trade policy. Again, however, the microfoundations are too often not sufficiently developed.

Baldwin's Integrative Framework for Analyzing Trade Policy

All the previously discussed approaches have enhanced our understanding of various aspects of the policy-setting phenomenon. At the same time, all have certain deficiencies. As economist Robert Baldwin (1996, p. 156) has suggested, a general framework is needed that explains not only how policies are set and changed in the presence of "shocks" to the system but also "how the institutions, values and ideologies, and distribution of international economic and political power that shape a country's response to these shocks are themselves determined." Baldwin set

---

[6]This subsection draws heavily on Baldwin (1996).

out a general framework that would address the issue at hand. It is built around four major sets of actors: individual citizens, common-interest groups, the domestic government, and foreign governments/international organizations. The domestic government would be viewed as the key actor because it ultimately sets policy. Without going into more detail about Baldwin's approach at this time, it is clear that this broader framework would incorporate such diverse factors as the role of the chief executive, the social concerns of citizens, the domestic impact of the policy in question, and the role of relative hegemonic power of the country in question. While we are still far from the formal specification and application of such a model, it does provide an organizational structure which can be useful in directing and coordinating further work in this area by both economists and political scientists.

With this general background of how interest group behavior and social concerns influence the making of trade policy, we now turn to a summary of both historical and recent U.S. trade policy.

CONCEPT CHECK

1. Explain theoretically why the median-voter principle should result in the will of the majority being revealed in policy decisions.

2. What are the critical assumptions underlying the median-voter model?

3. What is the underlying basis for the social objectives rationale for public policy decisions?

A REVIEW OF U.S. TRADE POLICY

The liberalization of trade can be divided into several stages beginning after the **Tariff Act of 1930,** usually called the **Smoot-Hawley Tariff,** which established extremely high protection in the United States (an average tariff level of about 50 percent). Other countries retaliated with their own stiff tariffs, and world trade shrank dramatically. An estimate by Jakob Madsen (2001, p. 865) is that 41 percent of the decline in world trade was due to the imposition of the new trade barriers and 59 percent was due to falling incomes that resulted in less purchasing power to buy imports. Recognizing that there is imprecision in such estimates and that tariffs and income are interrelated (higher tariffs can reduce national income and falling national income can increase the calls for more protection from imports), Madsen concluded (p. 867) that "the contribution of the imposition of the discretionary trade barriers was about as important as the output decline in explaining the contraction in world trade." In any event, economists and policymakers generally agree that this tariff worsened the Great Depression of the 1930s. The tariff legislation since that time has occurred largely in response to this impact on the Great Depression and the increasing economic interdependence of countries. We now give a brief overview of trade agreements from 1934 to 1960, followed by examination of the Kennedy Round (1960s) and the Tokyo Round (1970s) of trade negotiations. We then discuss the most recent round that has been completed (1994), the Uruguay Round. We close the chapter with a look at prospects for the current round of trade negotiations, the Doha Development Agenda, and with a review of several recent trade policy actions.

Reciprocal Trade Agreements and Early GATT Rounds

The long process of tariff reduction began with the passage by Congress of the **Reciprocal Trade Agreements Act of 1934.**[7] This act authorized the executive branch to engage in **bilateral negotiations** with individual trading partners on tariff reductions. The act was renewed every three years until the end of World War II. A particular feature of

---

[7]For a good review of tariff policy from 1934 into the 1960s, see "Some Aspects of United States Foreign Trade and the Kennedy Round," Federal Reserve Bank of Cleveland, *Economic Review,* September 1967, pp. 179–82.

the negotiation process was its employment of an **item-by-item approach,** meaning that rate reductions on goods were bargained individually rather than uniformly agreed upon for a broad range of categories. While significant reductions were made on many goods and on the overall U.S. tariff level, the item-by-item approach does not permit smooth and quick negotiation when many goods are encompassed by the proceedings.

At the end of World War II, tariff bargaining took the form of **multilateral negotiations**, meaning that many countries took part simultaneously. The **General Agreement on Tariffs and Trade (GATT)** took effect in 1947. Under this agreement, countries committed themselves to multilateral bargaining for the purpose of easing trade restrictions in all of the participating countries. GATT became an ongoing organization that sponsored regular negotiations of this type. From 1947 until 1962, five **GATT rounds of trade negotiations** were held, in which the participating countries hammered out mutually acceptable reductions of various barriers. The first round, held in Geneva in 1947, was reasonably successful. However, economists did not judge the next four rounds in 1949, 1951, 1956, and 1962, as having attained much success. Nevertheless, some multilateral tariff reductions were achieved, and all these early rounds embodied the most-favored-nation (MFN) principle (discussed in Chapter 13), as did those that followed.

The Kennedy Round of Trade Negotiations

To put new life into the trade negotiation process and to avoid being shut out by the newly forming European Economic Community, the United States led the way into a new round of negotiations from 1962 to 1967. The key stimulus for the round was the U.S. **Trade Expansion Act of 1962.** This legislation authorized the president to negotiate tariff reductions of up to 50 percent, and these reductions could be negotiated through an **across-the-board approach** rather than an item-by-item approach. Broad categories of goods could be discussed all at once and a given rate reduction could apply to the whole group—a more streamlined approach. The Trade Expansion Act also introduced a feature of trade policy known as **trade adjustment assistance (TAA),** which means that, if a tariff reduction injures workers or industries by causing an inflow of imports, displaced workers can, for example, petition for additional unemployment compensation or for help in retraining for other types of jobs. To most economists, this was a marked step forward for public policy, because previously the only alternative considered was to reimpose the tariff (the "escape clause"). Thus, TAA in a broad sense tries to promote internal adjustment to changing international conditions and reduction in protection. It is an attempt to facilitate the movement of the economy along the production-possibilities frontier. Without this assistance, a country's production point might initially move inside the PPF and get back onto the frontier only after a considerable period of time has passed. Recently, the Trade Adjustment Assistance Reform Act of 2002 created an additional program for a health coverage tax credit and added a new benefit for older workers. Workers who lost their jobs because their companies shifted production abroad to countries that were part of a free trade agreement with the United States, or to some African and Western Hemisphere countries, were also made eligible for TAA.[8]

With the passage of the Trade Expansion Act, the United States moved into multilateral negotiations in Geneva in what became known as the **Kennedy Round of trade negotiations.** Seventy countries participated, and tariffs on manufactured products were reduced by an average of 35 percent, with at least some reduction occurring in 64 percent of manufactured goods with tariffs. (See Ellsworth and Leith 1984, p. 230.) Note that this success

---

[8]"Labor Department Certifies Pillowtex Workers for Trade Adjustment Assistance," www.dol.gov; "Trade Adjustment Assistance Reform Act of 2002: Free Trade Agreement and Trade Beneficiary Countries," www.doleta.gov.

was in terms of cuts achieved in manufactured goods; the Kennedy Round achieved little progress in reducing barriers on agricultural products. In addition, the Kennedy Round did little to ease nontariff barriers.

The Tokyo Round of Trade Negotiations

With the completion of the Kennedy Round of tariff cutting in 1967, no further steps were taken until 1973, when preliminary moves were initiated at a multilateral meeting in Tokyo toward beginning another round of negotiations. A main impetus for the new round was that, while tariff rates had been moving downward, NTBs had been rising and had offset some of the benefits of the tariff reductions.

The **Trade Act of 1974** enabled the United States to participate in this new round, the **Tokyo Round of trade negotiations.** This act of Congress authorized the president to enter into trade negotiations for the purpose of reducing tariff and nontariff barriers. Reductions of up to 60 percent were authorized on existing duties greater than 5 percent, and tariffs could be eliminated altogether on goods whose existing duties were less than 5 percent. In addition, authorization was granted to enter into individual-sector negotiations to work for the liberalization of NTBs. Other features of interest in this bill were the provision for introduction of the U.S. Generalized System of Preferences (GSP) for the products of developing countries (see Chapter 13) and the provision for more generous treatment of claims for trade adjustment assistance.

Finally, the Trade Act of 1974 attempted to systematize procedures on claims for import relief by import-competing firms. Prominent provisions of the act in this respect (some of which predate 1974) were as follows:

1. *Section 201:* This part of U.S. legislation permits import-competing firms to petition for relief from rapidly increasing imports (or "surges" in imports). The U.S. International Trade Commission (USITC) then investigates whether the rapid increases in imports are causing "substantial injury" to the U.S. industry and, if so, makes a recommendation for protection to the president. The president may or may not accept the recommendation.

2. *Section 232:* The president is authorized to restrict any good that "is being imported into the United States in such quantities or under such circumstances as to threaten to impair the national security." This provision has seldom been used (principally on petroleum in earlier years). In 1986, it was used to limit machine tool imports, which resulted in voluntary export restraints (VERs) with Japan and Taiwan.[9]

3. *Section 301:* This unfair-trade portion of U.S. law permits the president to take retaliatory action in response to unjustifiable, unreasonable, or discriminatory restrictions on U.S. exports by foreign countries. *Unjustifiable* refers to any action that violates the international legal rights of the United States; *unreasonable* refers to unfair and inequitable practices, although these are obviously hard to define; and *discriminatory* means actions that deny national or MFN treatment to the United States.[10] The range of U.S. possible actions is broad, and includes (among others) suspending trade agreement concessions, imposing duties or other import restrictions, and entering into agreements with the other country to eliminate the behavior or to provide compensation to the United States.

In addition to this Section 301 provision, there is a *Special 301* provision of U.S. trade law whereby the U.S. Trade Representative (USTR), a cabinet-level officer in the executive

---

[9]William J. Long, "National Security versus National Welfare in American Foreign Economic Policy," *Journal of Policy History* 4, no. 3 (1992), pp. 288–91.

[10]*Economic Report of the President,* February 1988 (Washington, DC: U.S. Government Printing Office, 1988), p. 156.

IN THE REAL WORLD:

THE DETERMINANTS OF TRADE ADJUSTMENT ASSISTANCE

An article by Christopher Magee (2001) investigated empirically the determinants of any given worker's chances of being certified by the U.S. Department of Labor to receive trade adjustment assistance (TAA). The actual statutory procedure for seeking TAA is that a group of three or more workers from a firm first files a petition with the Department of Labor. Then the Department of Labor ascertains whether a significant percentage of the workers in the petitioners' firm has become partly or wholly separated from the firm or is under a potential threat of being separated, whether sales or production (or both) of the firm have declined in absolute terms, and whether increases in imports of the petitioners' firm's product contributed in an important way to the separation or threat of separation. If the petition is approved, workers receive unemployment compensation for 12 months (rather than for the 6 months in normal unemployment situations), or 18 months if the workers are enrolled in a retraining program. Between 1975 and 1994, the percentage of applicants who were certified annually ranged from more than 70 percent to 10 percent, depending on the year.

Magee's empirical tests attempted to ascertain the actual variables over the 1975–1992 period that seemed to yield a good chance for workers to be certified to receive TAA. His first result was that a higher level of tariff protection for the industry in which the workers have been engaged yields a greater chance of approval of petitions. His reasoning for this finding is that industries with higher tariffs are causing more of a production distortion than are industries with low tariffs. With greater protection and distortion, therefore, there is an incentive for officials to look more favorably upon providing TAA because the TAA might facilitate the removal of the distortion. This is an efficiency-type argument for TAA. Another way that Magee states this reasoning is that more TAA must be given to get tariff reductions in the industries with high tariffs; that is, "higher tariff industries require a greater payoff in order to reduce protection" (p. 119).

Empirically, and as expected, there was a negative relationship between TAA certification and the tariff change in an industry. In other words, a greater tariff reduction (a more negative tariff change) was associated with a greater positive chance of receiving TAA. This is common sense because the greater tariff change will, other things equal, lead to more workers being displaced.

Four further results can be mentioned: (1) The fraction of petitions certified rises as an industry's unemployment rate rises—there is more social concern for the laid-off workers in this industry. (2)Workers in high-wage industries are less likely to get TAA, or, alternatively, workers in low-wage industries are more likely to get TAA—suggesting some equity concerns in the decisions to certify workers. (3) A worker was more likely to receive TAA if the worker was a member of a union, as unions can exercise political power. (4) The share of the domestic market supplied by imports was positively related to certification. Hence, a large import share of the market in and of itself seemed to indicate a threat and consequently to lead to certification. Magee expresses surprise that *changes* in imports, *changes* in industry employment, and *changes* in domestic shipments do not seem to be related to the certification for TAA, as changes in such variables are the principal criteria put forth in the TAA statute.

All in all, this paper indicated that separated workers likely to receive trade adjustment assistance come from high-tariff industries, from industries in which tariff reductions have been great, and from industries with high unemployment rates. Also, workers are more likely to receive certification if they belong to a union, if they are laid off from a low-wage industry, and if the industry's market has a large import component.

Source: Christopher Magee, "Administered Protection for Workers: An Analysis of the Trade Adjustment Assistance Program," *Journal of International Economics* 53, no. 1 (February 2001), pp. 105–25.

branch, identifies countries that are denying adequate or effective intellectual property rights to U.S. industries or persons. Such identification leads to a designation of the offending countries as "Priority Foreign Countries" and can be followed by USTR initiation of Section 301 action.[11]

---

[11]United States Trade Representative, *2007 Trade Policy Agenda and 2006 Annual Report* (Washington, DC: USTR, 2007), p. 215, obtained from www.ustr.gov.

4. *Section 701:* This covers subsidies to exports by foreign countries. Petition is made by import-competing firms to the Department of Commerce to ascertain the existence of the subsidy; if affirmed, the USITC determines whether or not injury is occurring.

5. *Section 731:* This portion of trade law consists of the antidumping provisions summarized in Chapter 15, pages 331–33.

With this enabling legislation in hand, U.S. negotiators took part in the multilateral negotiations in Geneva between 1974 and 1979, which resulted in agreement (see Allen 1979) that (1) tariff rates on manufactured goods were to be reduced by an average of about one-third in a phase-in process over eight years, and (2) new codes of behavior concerning several NTBs were to be adhered to with respect to, for example, government procurement procedures, subsidies and countervailing duties, and valuation of goods for customs duties purposes. In addition, agreement was reached that tariff preferences should be given by developed countries to various manufactured exports from the developing countries and that the **nonreciprocity principle** should apply to developing countries. This principle holds that, even though developed countries may reduce barriers on exports from developing countries, no corresponding behavior is required by developing countries on exports to them from developed countries. By embracing tariff preferences and nonreciprocity, the world community basically affirmed the value judgment that the plight of the developing countries in the international economy and the relatively low levels of their per capita income required special, discriminatory measures in favor of these countries.

After the implementation of the Tokyo Round tariff cuts, it was estimated that the average tariff level in the United States on manufactured products had been reduced to 4.3 percent. Other countries appeared to have relatively similar average tariff levels: Canada 5.2 percent, France 6.0 percent, Japan 2.9 percent, United Kingdom 5.2 percent, and West Germany 6.3 percent.[12] Except for Japan, all of these rates were slightly higher than the rate in the United States, but the differences were minor. The low Japanese rate points out one difficulty with these calculations, because they do not adequately include nontariff barriers. Nevertheless, the broad level of tariff rates was substantially lower than the levels existing at the time of Smoot-Hawley.

The Uruguay Round of Trade Negotiations

The first four years, 1986–1990

Despite the presence of relatively low tariff rates in the industrialized world, a new round of trade negotiations began in September 1986 and was to be completed by December 1990. These talks were initiated in Punta del Este, Uruguay, and became known as the **Uruguay Round of trade negotiations.** Major objectives of this new round included a continuation of the attempt to reduce NTBs, an enlargement of the negotiations to embrace trade in services in addition to the traditional emphasis on trade in goods, and a determination to deal with restrictions on agricultural trade.

The Uruguay Round set forth an ambitious agenda. Members established 15 groups to work on reducing restrictions in the following areas: (1) tariffs, (2) NTBs, (3) tropical products, (4) natural resource–based products, (5) textiles and clothing, (6) agriculture, (7) safeguards (against sudden "surges" in imports), (8) subsidies and countervailing duties, (9) trade-related intellectual property restrictions, (10) trade-related investment restrictions, and (11) services, as well as four other areas dealing with GATT itself (e.g., dispute-settlement procedures and implementation of the NTB codes of the Tokyo Round, especially on dumping).[13] The biggest controversies in the negotiations involved services, intellectual property, and agriculture.

---

[12]Alan V. Deardorff and Robert M. Stern (1986), p. 49. Note that the nominal rates for Japan and the United States differ from those in Chapter 13, page 267, reflecting different weights and procedures.

[13]"GATT Negotiations Essential to Maintain Strong Multilateral Trading System," *IMF Survey,* December 12, 1988, pp. 386–89.

The most heated controversy by far concerned agriculture. Most countries use a wide variety of policies to assist the agriculture sector: price supports, direct production subsidies, export subsidies, quotas on imports, acreage restrictions to raise commodity prices, and others. These interventions lead away from the free-market and free-trade allocation of resources, since they introduce price distortions. The United States initially proposed a 10-year phaseout of all subsidies that affect agricultural trade and of all agricultural import barriers. The proposal was similar to one made by the Cairns Group, a collection of 14 developing and developed countries with agricultural interests (e.g., Argentina, Australia, Brazil, Canada, New Zealand). The European Community (EC) wanted to go more slowly and to moderate the extent of reduction in agriculture support.[14] By 1990, the wide disparity in subsequent proposals overshadowed all other aspects of the negotiations, and the four-year effort had seemingly ended with no signed agreement on the liberalization of trade.

Continued negotiations lead to success, 1993

Despite the failure of the Uruguay Round talks to meet the originally scheduled completion deadline of December 1990, negotiations continued. President Bush requested and received from Congress in 1991 a two-year extension to continue the talks under the **fast-track procedure,** also known as the **Trade Promotion Authority.** Under this procedure, which has characterized past trade negotiations, Congress must simply vote yea or nay on a negotiated agreement. No amendments can be made. The debate over fast-track was heated because the authorization also applied to the negotiations for the North American Free Trade Agreement (NAFTA), which is discussed in Chapter 17.

Hope of success for the Uruguay Round began to reappear at the end of 1992 owing to a trade policy threat. The United States had been concerned about a European Community agricultural support program that harmed U.S. exports of oilseeds (e.g., soybeans) and had twice received backing from GATT that the EC program should be modified. In retaliation for the EC subsidy, the United States threatened to impose 200 percent tariffs on EC exports to the United States, valued at $300 million; if the EC in turn retaliated against this tariff, the United States was ready to impose a second round of tariffs on $700 million of manufactured exports from the EC to the United States.[15] With this stimulus to renewed negotiations on agriculture, an accord was eventually reached by which the oilseeds export subsidies were to be reduced 36 percent by value and 21 percent by quantity over a six-year period. This positive development then set off activity to work again on many other aspects of the Uruguay Round. Finally, after intense discussions, the 117 participating countries in the Uruguay Round reached agreement on December 15, 1993 (the deadline date), and the signing took place on April 15, 1994, in Marrakech, Morocco. After ratification by participating countries, the agreement took effect on January 1, 1995.

Provisions of the Uruguay Round agreement

Only a brief look is provided here of the features of this broad agreement.[16] First, tariffs on average were cut by 34 percent (39 percent by developed countries) and were dropped altogether in the developed countries on a variety of products such as pharmaceuticals, construction and agricultural equipment, furniture, paper, and scientific instruments. Second,

---

[14]"GATT Negotiations on Agriculture," *IMF Survey,* December 12, 1988, p. 388; "The General Disagreement," *The Economist,* November 26, 1988, p. 81.

[15]Bob Davis, "Tough Trade Issues Remain as EC, U.S. Agree on Agriculture," *The Wall Street Journal,* November 23, 1992, p. A6.

[16]For fuller discussion, see Bob Davis and Lawrence Ingrassia, "After Years of Talks, GATT Is at Last Ready to Sign Off on a Pact," *The Wall Street Journal,* December 15, 1993, pp. A1, A7; idem, "Trade Pact Is Set by 117 Nations, Slashing Tariffs, Subsidies Globally," *The Wall Street Journal,* December 16, 1993, pp. A3, A11; "Trade Agreement Mandates Broad Changes," *IMF Survey,* January 10, 1994, pp. 2–4. See also Deardorff (1994), pp. 10–11.

IN THE REAL WORLD:

WELFARE EFFECTS OF PRICE DISTORTIONS IN SELECTED COUNTRIES

Two analytical measures used to assess the impact of policy and price distortions in agriculture are the **producer subsidy equivalent (PSE)** and the **consumer subsidy equivalent (CSE)**. For a given good, the PSE (CSE) indicates the monetary benefit to producers (consumers) because of transfers through government expenditures and price distortions in the economy, stated as a percentage of the value of production (consumption) if these transfers did not occur. Thus, if a farmer would have received $100,000 from a crop with no transfers but actually received $120,000 because of a price support program and subsidized inputs (e.g., water), then the farmer's PSE would be 20 percent [= ($120,000 − $100,000)/$100,000]. Analogously, if consumers would have paid $200 for a good without government intervention but pay $250 because of price support programs and higher taxes to finance agriculture subsidies, the CSE would be *minus* 25 percent [= ($200 − $250)/$200]. The CSE is negative in this case because it is defined as the "benefit" from intervention, and the benefit (the transfer) is negative. If consumer subsidies were provided (e.g., for food in urban areas in some developing countries), the CSE would be positive.

The presence of distortions as reflected in nonzero PSEs and CSEs can have important implications for the welfare effects of policy changes. For example, if there is a positive PSE for a given product in a given country, production is distorted in that too much production of the good is taking place compared to the competitive, efficient allocation of resources. If some policy change in the economy then leads to an expansion of that good's production, welfare is injured because the distortion is being given even more importance in the economy than previously; if production had contracted instead, that would lead to a "gain" because the distortion was being accorded less importance in the economy.

James Anderson (1998) carried this matter of the effects of policy changes on economies with CSE and PSE distortions further in the context of the effects of trade policy. Specifically, he examined estimates of the price changes in agricultural products that were predicted to follow from the Uruguay Round's steps toward worldwide liberalization of agricultural trade. Given the expected price changes (increases for some goods such as basic foods, decreases for others such as cotton), he calculated a terms-of-trade effect of the liberalization on each of nine developing countries.

Then, utilizing a computable-general-equilibrium model for each country—a model that attempts to capture statistically the structure and the many relationships that occur in an economy—he estimated the production and consumption effects of the terms-of-trade changes, incorporating the fact that these effects were taking place in a CSE- and PSE-distorted environment.

Anderson's results are important for emphasizing the detrimental effects of distortions on an economy's well-being. For his nine countries, the terms-of-trade effect per se indicated small improvements in welfare for four countries and slight declines in welfare for the five others. However, because of the existing PSE and CSE distortions, the production and consumption changes often took place in such a fashion either to work against the terms-of-trade benefits or to augment the terms-of-trade losses. For Thailand and Tunisia, welfare gains from improved terms of trade were partly offset by the new welfare losses from the production and consumption changes associated with CSE and PSE distortions; for India and Turkey, the terms-of-trade gains were *more than offset* by the additional CSE and PSE distortion losses; for Colombia, Indonesia, and (especially) Pakistan, welfare losses from the terms-of-trade changes were supplemented by the losses from domestic agricultural distortions. Only for Bangladesh and Morocco did the PSE and CSE distortions get lessened in their severity because of the production and consumption changes associated with the Uruguay Round agricultural trade policy changes.

The important point of this discussion is not that the Uruguay Round per se can injure some countries' welfare (and such a conclusion would be unwarranted because the preceding discussion pertains only to agriculture and developing countries are likely to gain from the Uruguay Round changes made with respect to manufactured products). Rather, the point is that *domestic* distortions such as indicated by PSEs and CSEs can often make the welfare effects of *trade* policies less beneficial than would otherwise be the case. Because the domestic and trade parts of economies are interrelated, policy reforms should be pursued internally as well as internationally.

Source: James E. Anderson, "The Uruguay Round and Welfare in Some Distorted Agricultural Economies," *Journal of Development Economics* 56, no. 2 (August 1998), pp. 393–410. ●

the value of agricultural export subsidies was to be cut by 36 percent and most domestic support for agriculture by 20 percent, and average developed-country agricultural tariffs would be reduced by 36 percent over a six-year period. Third, textiles and apparel trade were to be moved from the existing quota framework of the Multi-Fiber Arrangement into the GATT framework, with tariffs to be phased out over 10 years. In fact, the quotas were ended on January 1, 2005, but tariffs remain. In addition, Japan and South Korea promised to open their markets to some extent for rice imports. Revised rules were also adopted regarding dumping and export subsidies, and voluntary export restraints (VERs) were to be eliminated. Further, action on trade-related intellectual property rights (TRIPs) provided for minimum standards for trademarks, patents, and copyrights. (For example, patents are now in force for 20 years. In the United States, the previous length had been 17 years.) Some trade-related investment measures (TRIMs), such as local content requirements for foreign investors, were to be eliminated within two years by developed countries, five years by developing countries, and seven years by "least developed" countries.

Considerable friction prevented attainment of some of the goals for services. An important controversy involved France's refusal to permit the import of U.S. motion pictures on the scale the United States wanted. Nevertheless, a general agreement on trade in services (GATS) calls for "national treatment" in services, meaning that any country is to treat foreign service providers in the same fashion as domestic service providers, as well as for MFN treatment for services. New procedures were also adopted for the settlement of disputes. Finally, GATT itself was replaced by a new organization, the **World Trade Organization (WTO),** which supervised the implementation of the Uruguay Round agreement and is handling trade disagreements.

Trade Policy Issues after the Uruguay Round

With the successful conclusion of the Uruguay Round, governments in the next several years centered on the implementation of the measures that had been adopted. In addition, further sectoral agreements were pursued (such as completed agreements in telecommunications and financial services) that would put specifics into the broad general framework that had been laid out in the Uruguay Round for particular sectors. However, as the 1990s drew to a close, there emerged a desire on the part of many countries to begin a new round of multilateral trade deliberations. Many countries wished to attain further relaxation of trade-restricting measures in agriculture and services, to reduce remaining tariffs further, and to consider a variety of other matters pertaining to areas such as antidumping procedures, procedures within WTO, and intellectual property rights. Further, there was a desire by developed countries—but decidedly *not* by developing countries—to discuss the broad general area known as "labor standards." In addition, and again mainly by developed countries, there was pressure to include consideration of the environmental impact of trade and international shifts in production location by firms.

The labor standards question has been one of intense debate in the last several years. The debate revolves around several issues—most importantly child labor, health and safety features of the workplace, and hours of work per day and days of work per week. For example, campus groups in the industrial countries have protested the use of child labor (often children in the lower-teen years or younger) in assembly plants in developing countries. Out of humanitarian concern, these groups demand that their universities and colleges not deal with companies that employ such labor. Similar protests are made, including objections by labor union groups and their employers, in industrial countries regarding the dangerous work environments in developing countries, where little attention is paid to safety procedures, properly operated equipment, and sanitary conditions in the plants. Developed-country labor and employers in labor-intensive industries, of course, claim that it is "unfair" that they have to compete with goods made under such "sweatshop" conditions. The view is

IN THE REAL WORLD:

TARIFF REDUCTIONS RESULTING FROM THE URUGUAY ROUND

Given the broad guidelines of the Uruguay Round with respect to tariff reductions, it is useful to examine the actual differences between pre-Uruguay and post-Uruguay Round tariffs at both the country/region level and the commodity group level. WTO estimates of the pre- and post-Uruguay Round weighted-average tariff levels are found in Table 1. Note that developing countries have substantially higher protection (both pre- and post-Uruguay Round) than developed countries and that, among products, textiles and clothing have the highest weighted-average tariff rates.

TABLE 1   Average Tariffs on Industrial Products

	Pre-Uruguay Round	*Post-Uruguay Round*
(a) By Country/Region		
Developed countries' imports from		
World	6.2%	3.7%
North America	5.1	2.8
Latin America	4.9	3.3
Western Europe	6.4	3.5
Central/Eastern Europe	4.0	2.4
Africa	2.7	2.0
Asia	7.7	4.9
Developing countries' imports from		
World	20.5%	14.4%
North America	23.2	15.7
Latin America	27.6	18.5
Western Europe	25.8	18.3
Central/Eastern Europe	18.4	15.1
Africa	12.3	8.0
Asia	17.8	12.7
(b) By Product		
All industrial products*	6.3%	3.8%
Fish and fish products	6.1	4.5
Wood, pulp, paper, and furniture	3.5	1.1
Textiles and clothing	15.5	12.1
Leather, rubber, and footwear	8.9	7.3
Metals	3.7	1.4
Chemicals and photographic supplies	6.7	3.7
Transport equipment	7.5	5.8
Nonelectric machinery	4.8	1.9
Electric machinery	6.6	3.5
Mineral products and precious stones	2.3	1.1
Manufactured articles, not elsewhere specified	5.5	2.4
Industrial tropical products	4.2	2.0
Natural resource–based products*	3.2	2.1

*Excluding petroleum products.

Source: Report on "The Uruguay Round" obtained from the WTO website, www.wto.org.

that, were developing-country firms forced (by threat of sanctions against their goods by developed countries) to provide a safe, healthful environment and to adhere to the length of workday and workweek adhered to by developed-country firms, this would yield "fair" trade since all firms would be competing on an equal basis.

Generally speaking, economists are very skeptical of this line of thinking. As a prominent example, Alan Greenspan, chairman of the Board of Governors of the Federal Reserve, told Congress in March 2004 that tying labor standards to trade agreements would hurt the United States and that worries over job loss would be better handled by improved education.[17] Often the preceding arguments are being put forth by developed-country labor under the mantle of humanitarian concerns when in fact the real motivation for the "concern" is protection. The Heckscher-Ohlin and Stolper-Samuelson theorems from Chapter 8 would lead us to expect that the scarce factor of production in the United States and other developed countries (labor and, more specifically, relatively unskilled or low-tech labor) would be injured by an expansion of trade and would gain from protection. Further, the specific-factors model in Chapter 8 also indicated that capital owners in import-competing industries in capital-abundant countries lose from trade as well, which can explain the desire of developed-country firms in import-besieged sectors to seek these new, potentially persuasive arguments for protection. With regard to the child labor issue per se, a case can be made that, without the work of children in developing countries, a typical family might find itself in considerably greater economic difficulty. Children can be economic assets in a developing-country setting, and production is also often carried out by the family unit as a whole, such as in carpet weaving in parts of India.[18] Finally, there is a certain uncomfortableness (arrogance?) about developed countries specifying what working conditions should be in developing countries and what should be the organization of production. Imposition of rules from the outside is not behavior that developing countries, many of which have an unhappy history of colonialism, will want to accept with open arms.

Along with the issue of labor standards, concern has been expressed with regard to the role of environmental standards. The reservations expressed here are that freer trade and investment has meant that companies, and therefore production, have been encouraged to locate where environmental protection is the most lax. The upshot is that because lax environmental standards mean that pollution-control equipment and the like does not have to be installed, firms in the weak-standard countries (usually developing countries) will be able to undercut firms (usually in developed countries) that must pay such costs. Because of the differing environmental standards, firms in developed countries are thus faced with "unfair" competition because their governments have tougher environmental standards in place. Further, world pollution problems worsen because production centers where environmental protection is weakest. In addition, because of the trade disadvantage for firms in the less polluted countries, there is a tendency for those firms to press their governments for a relaxation of standards. The argument then concludes that there is a "race to the bottom" in terms of environmental protection. An alternative, of course, is for developed-country governments to pressure developing-country governments for tighter standards or to simply impose protection on the products coming from the developing countries.

Obviously environmental concerns are worthy of attention. But a response of economists to these views is that the problem is essentially one of environmental protection per se, not a matter of trade. The specificity principle of Chapter 15 applies in this context—the solution

---

[17]Greg Ip, "Greenspan Warns Trade Standards Will Harm U.S.," *The Wall Street Journal,* March 12, 2004, p. A2.

[18]As a potentially useful alternative to child labor, developed countries or international organizations could provide education grants to offset income losses as well as to enhance the skill levels of the younger members of the labor force (such as has been done in Brazil).

to pollution problems lies in measures that reduce pollution, not in measures that restrict trade. In addition, especially if multinational companies are engaged in exporting from developing countries, the exporting companies often adhere to higher environmental standards than do domestic firms within the developing countries. If protection in the developed countries restricts developing countries' exports, then factors of production will be forced to move to domestic firms, where even less attention to the environment is paid. Finally, as noted in *The Economist* (October 9, 1999, p. 17), if trade indeed makes countries better off, the countries will want a cleaner environment as they get wealthier, and they will be able to devote more resources to that objective than was previously the case (a point that has been supported by empirical studies). In other words, expansion of trade rather than restriction of trade may be in order.

Besides these debates on labor standards and environmental protection, other matters were proposed for inclusion in a new round of trade negotiations.[19] In a series of meetings, many countries expressed a desire to broaden and deepen trade rules regarding market access for services, as well as a desire to consider foreign investment rules in more detail. The European Union and Japan emphasized the need to include antitrust and competition policy in the negotiations, as such differences across countries can yield different pricing and behavior by firms. There was also concern by some developing countries about the phase-out schedule of the old Multi-Fiber Agreement on textiles and clothing, and some developing countries as well as developed countries urged full integration of agricultural goods into the WTO framework on the same comprehensive basis as manufactured goods. Further issues related to treatment of electronic commerce and progress on elimination of abuses of intellectual property rights.

At the end of November and beginning of December 1999, trade ministers from the 134 WTO member countries met in Seattle, Washington, to discuss and agree upon the agenda for a next round of multilateral trade negotiations. It was widely anticipated that the sessions would be contentious, but what was underestimated was the contentiousness of various groups of non-WTO people opposing further relaxation of trade barriers worldwide. The week of the ministerial conference was marked by large and noisy demonstrations, and in fact by some violence, in Seattle. The groups demonstrating against the WTO were a diverse lot—trade unionists concerned about the threat to their jobs and wages from greater imports of labor-intensive goods from developing countries, "greens" concerned about the environmental damage associated with trade expansion, and opponents of child labor, among others. Also prominent were individuals and groups who (incorrectly) viewed the WTO as an agency with massive power, in effect as an agency of supranational status that could dictate all sorts of rules to its member nations.

The end result of the disagreements over the agenda, together with the disruptive demonstrations, was that the conference ended with no agreement for a new round of negotiations. This failure had, in addition, been facilitated by President Clinton, who, though wanting a new round of negotiations, had spoken in Seattle of the desirability of incorporating labor standards into the WTO, a viewpoint which angered developing countries.[20]

The Doha Development Agenda

After the failure of the ministerial meeting in Seattle, many observers were pessimistic about the chances for a new round of trade negotiations, and multilateral trade matters lay dormant for some time (although activity continued on bilateral and regional agreements, see Chapter 17). The general gloom was lifted within two years, however. Trade ministers

---

[19]For discussion of some of these issues, see Edward Wilson, "Preparation for Future WTO Trade Negotiations," USITC *International Economic Review,* May/June 1999, pp. 15–21.

[20]In fact, Dartmouth economist Douglas Irwin entitled an opinion piece in *The Wall Street Journal,* "How Clinton Botched the Seattle Summit" (December 6, 1999, p. A34).

IN THE REAL WORLD:

NATIONAL SOVEREIGNTY AND THE WORLD TRADE ORGANIZATION

Much of the recent publicity surrounding the World Trade Organization (WTO) conveys the idea that the WTO has sovereignty over its member nations. Nothing is further from the truth. The WTO is an international institution comprised of member nations whose objective is to facilitate agreements between member countries to reduce barriers to trade and mediate any disagreements between countries which may arise in carrying out the agreements in question. All rules, principles, and agreements are made by or between WTO members, not by the WTO itself. If there is any loss of sovereignty in a given agreement, it is essentially a swap in that access to the home market is exchanged for equally valuable access to the foreign market. Further, any country is free to abandon an agreement in question at any time. However, it will likely lose its foreign access right in the process, because it is unlikely that other members will maintain their side of the agreement if the one participant reneges on its end. One objective of the WTO is to provide a mediating mechanism so that agreements are applied in a nondiscriminatory manner and challenges to trade agreements do not lead to trade wars and an unraveling of the world trading system as happened in the 1930s.

Economists at the Organization for Economic Cooperation and Development (OECD) in Paris have usefully clarified what WTO membership rules *do not* require:*

- WTO rules do not prevent member countries from establishing their own policy objectives or applying regulatory measures required to achieve those objectives.
- WTO rules do not require that member countries eliminate all barriers to imports.
- WTO rules do not require that member countries adopt a uniform set of trade regulations or trade procedures but require only that the regulations or procedures be applied in a nondiscriminatory (MFN)

manner. However, even here, exceptions are permitted for regional trade agreements as well as for measures which may relate to a legitimate national or international public policy objective.

- WTO rules do not require that member countries reduce tariffs or barriers to foreign services. They do, however, provide a mechanism for binding participants to an agreement in order to provide predictability and market access when there is a freely negotiated agreement.
- WTO rules do not prevent member countries from providing public funds to support domestic policies and regulatory objectives.
- WTO rules do not require that member countries accept each other's product-quality, service, or safety standards. Rather, the WTO membership has adopted rules pertaining to the preparation, adoption, and application of such standards as they relate to legitimate country social objectives. WTO also encourages, but does not mandate, regulatory cooperation directed toward the harmonization of standards or the development of mutual recognition agreements pertaining to each member country's standards.

In sum, the WTO is not a sovereign authority but, rather, an institution made up of and controlled by member nations for the purpose of facilitating the flow of goods and services between members. It is an institutional mechanism for assisting countries in making mutually acceptable agreements to facilitate international transactions, carrying them out in a nondiscriminatory manner, and holding each other to the bargains to which they have agreed.

*Organization for Economic Cooperation and Development, *Open Markets Matter: The Benefits of Trade and Investment Liberalisation* (Paris: OECD, 1998), pp. 125–27.   ●

---

met in Doha, Qatar, in November 2001 under the auspices of the WTO to attempt to put in place a new multilateral trade negotiation round. (Some cynics maintained that remote Doha was selected for the WTO meeting so that the number of protesters would be kept to a minimum.) And indeed, on November 14, 2001, the 142 WTO members announced that a new round would begin,[21] to be called the **Doha Development Agenda.** Promises were made to reduce trade barriers further, including those in the agricultural sector. A particular

---

[21]Much of the rest of this paragraph is drawn from "Seeds Sown for Future Growth," *The Economist,* November 17, 2001, pp. 65–66.

focus of trade liberalization was to be on making clearer and stricter the rules for imposing antidumping duties (a focus to which many U.S. members of Congress objected). Several of the plans for the round were of considerable potential benefit to developing countries, such as the intent to give developing countries cheaper access to pharmaceuticals (e.g., for combating HIV/AIDS in Africa). In the words of *The Economist,* "In a sign of their increasing clout, poor countries won a clear victory over the drug makers."[22] Other potential benefits to developing countries may come from some special trade preferences and from promised improved access for agricultural exports to developed countries' markets. Also, the fact that there were *no* commitments made in regard to labor standards and trade was also regarded as a victory for the developing countries.

Overall, the plans for liberalization were ambitious, as they could, for example, lead to a future elimination of agricultural export subsidies as well as a reduction in domestic agricultural support programs. In nonagricultural goods, no sectors or products were to be excluded from the negotiations. Further, broad statements were made regarding commitments to promote sustainable development, eliminate environmentally harmful trade policy measures, and make all border procedures more transparent and efficient. A statement to strive for greater discipline in government procurement was made, with the intent of fighting corruption, and a working group was to be established to examine the relationships among trade, debt, and finance. Further, the ministers agreed to make the WTO dispute settlement procedures more transparent and to attempt to identify core principles regarding policy within countries toward anticompetitive practices and competition.[23]

The ultimate results of a successful trade negotiation round on these issues could be important. One estimate has been made that world GDP would be $355 billion larger in the year 2015 than otherwise if the round is successful. Another estimate was that U.S. GDP would increase by $144 billion per year greater than otherwise (or an additional $2,000 for a U.S. family of four).[24]

After this ambitious beginning, however, there were many disappointments. Various negotiating groups met in 2002 and 2003 to discuss areas of contention, but not much progress was made. The groups were to establish "negotiating modalities," meaning to reach agreement on the terms and structure of the specific individual negotiations. The modalities were to be formulated by March 31, 2003, in agriculture and by May 31, 2003, in nonagriculture market access, but agreements were not reached. The services area group agreed by March 2003 on part of the negotiating agenda, but the negotiations dealing with special treatment for developing countries reached an impasse after several extensions of deadlines. Disagreements were not resolved in 2002 and 2003 on whether to even include such areas as competition policy, investment, and government procurement in the trade negotiating round.[25]

A bright spot on the negotiating front, as previewed earlier, was the agreement reached on provision of pharmaceuticals to developing countries. On August 30, 2003, the WTO members agreed that developing countries could import generic copies of drugs used against diseases of a substantial threat (e.g., AIDS and malaria) and that the drugs could also be produced in developing countries with the capability to do so, as long as the drugs

[22]Ibid., p. 65.

[23]United States Trade Representative, "USTR Fact Sheet Summarizing Results from WTO Doha Meeting," November 14, 2001, obtained from www.ustr.org.

[24]*Economic Report of the President,* February 2004 (Washington, DC: U.S. Government Printing Office, 2004), p. 236.

[25]Edward Wilson, "WTO Trade Negotiations after Cancun," U.S. International Trade Commission, *International Economic Review,* January/February 2004, pp. 9–10.

were then exclusively exported to developing countries that needed them. There were several specific, detailed procedural provisions to be followed before the drug shipments could occur, but this agreement constituted substantive progress.[26]

Following these various developments and *non*developments, trade ministers met September 10–14, 2003, in Cancun, Mexico. However, this meeting proved to be a substantial setback for progress toward multilateral liberalization of trade. Disagreements were very prominent on agriculture, and particularly on developed-country export subsidies (especially on cotton exports). Developing countries pushed hard for developed countries to remove these subsidies, because those subsidies undercut developing-country production and exports. Complaints were also registered against domestic agricultural support measures within the developed countries. But there were also disputes on nonagricultural market access and on whether to include matters such as investment and competition policy in the negotiations. Finally, the Cancun talks essentially broke down, and the conference ended with little progress.[27] There was considerable disappointment, and Pascal Lamy, the chief trade negotiator for the European Union, said, "We all could have gained here and now we have all lost."[28] The diplomatic language of the concluding ministerial statement covered over the discouragement and the resentments that were present.[29]

> All participants have worked hard and constructively to make progress as required under the Doha mandates. We have, indeed, made considerable progress. However, more work needs to be done in some key areas to enable us to proceed towards the conclusion of the negotiations in fulfilment of the commitments we took at Doha.

After the breakdown of the Cancun Ministerial, attempts were made by head WTO officials to reach agreement on major issues through consultations with various WTO members. However, substantial disagreement remained, and Edward Wilson of the U.S. International Trade Commission (USITC) wrote, in the January/February 2004 issue of the USITC's *International Economic Review,* that "Although members agreed in principle to resume negotiations, there appears little readiness among participants to alter negotiating stances that could resolve the current stalemate over how to restart negotiations."[30] One method for circumventing the deadlock that is being considered is an "opt-out clause." In this arrangement, the WTO could conclude an agreement even if some countries refused to sign (unanimity had previously been sought).A country could refuse to agree to undertake a particular tariff reduction, for example, but then it wouldn't receive tariff reductions from other countries on its exports. Other proposals were to limit the scope of the talks so that contentious issues such as government procurement and competition policy would not be included.[31]

Another development with some promise that was and is being considered by economists, the World Bank, the IMF, and the WTO is the concept of **Aid for Trade.** This is the notion that developing countries may not be able to gain from trade if they lack the

---

[26]Scott Miller, "WTO Drug Pact Lifts Trade Talks," *The Wall Street Journal,* September 2, 2003, p. A2; ibid., pp. 10–11.

[27]Neil King, Jr., and Scott Miller, "U.S. Races to Break WTO Impasse," *The Wall Street Journal,* September 12, 2003; Wilson, "WTO Trade Negotiations after Cancun," pp. 11–12.

[28]Elizabeth Becker, "Delegates from Poorer Nations Walk Out of World Trade Talks," *The New York Times,* September 15, 2003, p. A1.

[29]WTO, "Day 5: Conference Ends without Consensus," obtained from www.wto.org.

[30]Wilson, "WTO Trade Negotiations after Cancun," p. 14.

[31]Scott Miller, "After Cancun, WTO Panel Seeks an End to Gridlock," *The Wall Street Journal,* September 29, 2003, p. A16.

infrastructure (ports, roads, power, etc.) for exporting, and, hence, trade liberalization measures may need to be accompanied by assistance from the developed countries to increase their ability to trade. Thus, developing countries might be more willing to engage in multilateral negotiations if trade barrier reductions were paired with assistance from developed countries that could help to generate greater exports.[32] Nevertheless, in July 2006, the WTO agreed to the suspension of the Doha negotiations[33] and the situation had not basically changed by the time of this writing. Efforts have continued to revive the talks, but Pascal Lamy, current director-general of the WTO, indicated that there would be major problems even if the agricultural policy issues were somehow resolved.[34]

Recent U.S. Actions   In this subsection we summarize several important policy matters in recent U.S. trade policy. First, in 1993, the European Union put in place trade rules that provided preference to Western Europe's former colonies in the Caribbean and Africa with respect to the purchase of bananas. The United States objected to this policy because it constituted explicit discrimination against the sale of bananas to the EU from Central and South America by two U.S. firms, Chiquita Brands and Dole Foods. The United States appealed the European Union rules to the WTO, which, including its predecessor agency, GATT, ruled against the EU policy five times in six years. Attempts at compromise were unsuccessful. Ultimately, in April 1999, the United States levied retaliatory tariffs of *100 percent* against 15 EU products, including candles, specialty pork, cashmere sweaters and pullovers, electrothermic coffee or tea makers, and feta and other sheep's milk cheeses. This tariff action received the support of the WTO. An ironic outcome was that some of the tariffs fed back to injure U.S. firms, such as a Rhode Island company that owned a cashmere-processing plant in Mongolia that in turn supplied goat's hair to EU cashmere sweater manufacturers. Finally, in April 2001, the United States and the EU reached an understanding when the EU agreed to give greater market access to the exports of U.S. banana firms with a new system of import licenses and a revised quota/tariff system. The United States then ended the 100 percent *ad valorem* duties that it had imposed in 1999.[35]

Another area of contention in U.S. trade policy also pitted the United States against the European Union. Specifically, since 1989 the EU has had a ban in place on the import of hormone-treated beef from the United States. This particular instance of genetic engineering poses, in the minds of many Europeans, unacceptable health risks in the form of increasing the probability of developing cancer. (Can we say the EU "beefs about beef," or would you not put much "stock" in that remark?) In the beef situation, as with bananas, the WTO has ruled against the EU policy several times. Supporting the WTO and the U.S. position is the fact that many scientists have given the opinion that the hormone-treated beef is safe for consumption. Nevertheless, the EU had not removed its ban as of this writing in 2007 and, just as in the banana dispute, the United States took

---

[32]See, for example, "Aid for Trade," South Centre *T.R.A.D.E. Policy Brief*, November 2005, available at www.uneca.org, and various materials available at the Web site of the Centre for Trade and Development, www.centad.org.

[33]"Doha Doldrums Carry a High Price Tag," *IMF Survey*, August 21, 2006, p. 254.

[34]Greg Hitt and Deborah Solomon, "White House Tussles on Doha," *The Wall Street Journal*, March 5, 2007, p. A8.

[35]See James Cox, "Punitive Actions by U.S. Felt Worldwide," *USA Today*, March 11, 1999, p. 3B; idem, "U.S. Importers Decry Duties," *USA Today*, March 5, 1999, p. 3B; Michael M. Phillips, "WTO Supports U.S. in Dispute over Bananas," *The Wall Street Journal*, April 7, 1999, pp. A3, A8; *Federal Register*, July 6, 2001, p. 35689.

retaliatory commercial policy action. In July 1999, tariffs of 100 percent had been levied on a number of EU products, including French mustard, Roquefort cheese, and truffles.[36]

A policy of the United States has also been in dispute. For a number of years, the United States has attempted to give tax relief to U.S. firms engaged in exports to increase the profitability and therefore the amount of those exports. However, repeatedly, the favorable tax treatment has been ruled illegal because it constitutes an "unfair" export subsidy. Under the latest incarnation of the tax package, U.S. firms could export goods through offshore subsidiaries and receive a partial exemption from taxes on the profits earned from the exports if the exports contain substantial U.S. components. This tax relief helped some companies immensely—for example, Boeing and General Electric received benefits from this "extra-territorial income exclusion" of more than $1 billion each during the period 1997–2002. The WTO has ruled that such treatment is illegal, and the U.S. Congress has been attempting, without success, to come up with an alternative.[37]

Another controversial U.S. policy action was the imposition of steep tariffs on steel imports in March 2002. The WTO ruled against these tariffs, and the European Union threatened to retaliate. The tariffs were then canceled in December 2003.

In late 2003, the Bush administration took another unilateral policy action. Temporary import quotas were placed on several textile items imported from China—brassieres, bathrobes, and knit fabrics (which had recently totaled $645 million of imports for the three items).[38] There has been long-simmering resentment in the United States against Chinese imports in general and textile imports in particular because of the resulting large numbers of job losses in manufacturing in general and in textiles that are claimed to be attributable to the Chinese imports. We say "claimed" because many economists think that, at least for manufacturing as a whole, sizable productivity increases have played a more important role in leading to job losses than have imports. The Bush administration indicated that the quotas were used to protect against "surges" in imports, and China had agreed that such surges could be protected against when China joined the WTO in 2001. In general, there has been substantial feeling in the United States that China has been "unfair" in its trade with the United States, such as with pirating of software and with keeping the Chinese currency "too low" in value to stimulate exports.[39]

U.S.–Chinese relations were further aggravated when the long-standing Multi-Fiber Agreement in textiles and clothing, which controlled such imports into developed countries from developing countries, expired on January 1, 2005. Chinese exports to the United States then increased at a very rapid rate. China, after pressure, imposed taxes on the export of such goods to the United States but later rescinded them after restrictive U.S. "safeguard" action occurred. The United States then placed quotas on 34 apparel products from China in an agreement that was to run from January 1, 2006, to December 31, 2008. In addition, China agreed to allow more beef and medical equipment imports from the United States and to permit greater competition by U.S. firms for Chinese government

---

[36]See Helene Cooper, "U.S. Imposes 100% Tariffs on Slew of Gourmet Imports in War over Beef," *The Wall Street Journal,* July 20, 1999, p. A6; United States Trade Representative, "Snapshot of WTO Cases Involving the United States, March 9, 2004," obtained from www.ustr.gov.

[37]See Geoff Winestock, "WTO Rules Against U.S. on Tax Break," *The Wall Street Journal,* July 27, 1999, p. A19; Shailagh Murray, "Congress Stalls on Lifting Illegal Export Tax," *The Wall Street Journal,* February 13, 2004, p. A4.

[38]Neil King, Jr., and Dan Morse, "Bush Sets Quotas on Some Imports of Chinese Goods," *The Wall Street Journal,* November 19, 2003, pp. A1, A4.

[39]"Bush Sets Quotas on Some Imports of Chinese Goods," pp. A1, A4.

IN THE REAL WORLD:

RESTRAINTS ON U.S. STEEL IMPORTS

In 1984, the Reagan administration granted protection to the U.S. steel industry in the form of negotiated, "temporary" voluntary restraint agreements (VRAs)* with major exporters of steel to the United States. These VRAs were designed to keep overall steel imports to about 20 percent of the domestic market. The 18 separate country agreements were considered an election-year response to calls for import restraint by the domestic industry and to the recommendation for restraints by the 1984 Democratic presidential candidate, Walter Mondale. It was understood that if the VRAs were adopted, the domestic industry would take steps to improve its productivity and competitiveness.

After the 1984 VRAs were put into place, total imports were reduced from 24 percent of the U.S. market in 1983 to 20.8 percent in 1988, and imports from the 29 countries covered by 1989 accounted for 14.7 percent of the market. Productivity increased rapidly in the domestic industry, work practices were streamlined, specialty steel minimills expanded, and the industry increased its profits. Foreign steel exporters also benefited by getting a guaranteed market share and by obtaining higher profits. However, consumers of steel faced higher prices because of the restraints. In addition, opponents of the VRAs indicated that more than 5 million workers were employed in the steel-*using* industries—30 times greater than the number employed in steel production itself—and these workers are injured when steel prices rise.

The five-year 1984 accords were due to expire in September 1989, and a debate ensued over whether they should be renewed. The debate was complicated by George H. W. Bush's 1988 election promise in steel-producing Pennsylvania to continue the protection. The U.S. industry wanted a five-year extension, while steel users wanted the program ended. The result was a compromise—a two-and-a-half year extension. When this extension expired in March 1992, U.S. steel firms filed antidumping petitions against 19 countries and countervailing-duty petitions to combat foreign subsidies against 12 others. In response, tariffs were adopted in June 1993 that averaged 36.5 percent (with duties ranging up to 109 percent in dumping cases and up to 73 percent in the subsidy cases).

Well into the late 1990s, pressure continued for protection because of the virtually continual rise in steel imports. A major strategy of the domestic industry has been the constant filing of antidumping petitions and petitions for countervailing duties against allegedly subsidized imports. (Note: The U.S. steel industry itself imports steel, although it claims that such steel is not part of the "unfair" trade.) Some duties have been imposed, and some countries such as Russia and Brazil signed agreements to limit their steel exports to the United States to avoid punitive duties. In 1999 the protectionist efforts resulted in a quota bill that passed the U.S. House of Representatives but died in the U.S. Senate.

In the ensuing years, a major move toward greater protection of the U.S. steel industry was made. President George W. Bush (the second President Bush) imposed tariffs in March 2002 in the face of surging steel imports, tariffs that ranged up to 35 percent (see Chapter 14). However, in November 2003, the WTO ruled that these tariffs were illegal in an answer to the U.S. appeal of a similar March 2003 WTO decision. The European Union then reiterated its earlier threat to place high tariff duties on a number of U.S. exports (such as orange juice, motorboats, sunglasses, clothing), and these tariffs were especially designed to inflict injury on U.S. states that had supported George W. Bush in the 2000 presidential election. The Bush administration responded that it had imposed the tariffs to give the domestic steel industry an opportunity to restructure itself and to become stronger. Nevertheless, in December 2003, the administration eliminated the steel tariffs that it had imposed. The European Union then canceled its plans to retaliate against the United States. Thus, this latest episode in the steel saga indicates that there was again, after a long period of time and at least for some time into the future, hope for freer trade in steel for the United States. This hope was buttressed by the fact that, in late 2006, the U.S. International Trade Commission decided not to renew antidumping duties on some steel imports from Australia, Canada, France, and Japan.

*It is totally unclear to us why the export restraints were called VERs for automobiles and VRAs for steel!

Sources: Chris Adams, "Steelmakers Complain about Foreign Steel; They Also Import It," *The Wall Street Journal,* March 22, 1999, p. A1; American Iron and Steel Institute, *AISI Newsletter,* December 1999, obtained from www.steel.org; Stuart Auerbach, "Bush Signs Steel Quota Extension,"*Washington Post,* July 26, 1989, pp. D1, D3; "Big Cartel," *The Wall Street Journal,* March 22, 1989, p. A14; James Bovard, "Steel Rulings Dump on America," *The Wall Street Journal,* June 23, 1993, p. A14; "Brazil to Reduce Exports of Steel, in Pact with U.S.," *The Wall Street Journal,* July 8, 1999, p. A10; Helene Cooper, "Russia Agrees to Limit Steel Shipments, Avoiding Antidumping Duties by U.S.," *The Wall Street Journal,* February 23, 1999, p. A4; idem, "Senate Thwarts Bill to Curb Steel Imports," *The Wall Street Journal,* June 23, 1999, p. A2; Asra Q. Nomani and Dana Milbank, "U.S. Increases Tariffs on Steel by Large Margin," *The Wall Street Journal,* June 23, 1993, pp. A5; Art Pine, "U.S. Seeks Reduced Exports of Steel by Three Countries," *The Wall Street Journal,* September 5, 1986, p. 40; Peter Truell, "U.S. Agrees to Quotas on Steel Imports with EC and 16 Other Major Suppliers," *The Wall Street Journal,* December 13, 1989, p. A2; Neil King, Jr., and Carlos Tejada, "Bush Abandons Steel Tariff Plan," *The Wall Street Journal,* December 5, 2003, p. A3; Neil King, Jr., Scott Miller, and Carlos Tejada, "U.S. Steel Tariffs Ruled Illegal, Sparking Potential Trade War," *The Wall Street Journal,* November 11, 2003, p. A1; Don Evans, "Victory," *The Wall Street Journal,* December 5, 2003, p. A12; Greg Hitt, Paul Glader, and Mike Spector, "Trade Ruling on Steel May Boost Auto Industry," *The Wall Street Journal,* December 15, 2006, p. A3.

contracts, among other actions.[40] In addition, in March 2007, the U.S. Department of Commerce changed its policy regarding the use of countervailing duties (to offset foreign subsidies) with respect to China. Previously, antidumping duties could be levied against imports from state-controlled economies, but countervailing duties were not assessed because of the difficulty in identifying the subsidies. The Commerce Department decided that countervailing duties could now be imposed, and it levied preliminary duties on a variety of paper products from China.[41] It seems clear that trade disagreements and tensions between China and the United States will persist for some time.

Briefly, two other noteworthy recent developments can be mentioned. First, agreement was reached in 2006 pertaining to a long dispute between the United States and Canada with respect to U.S. imports of Canadian softwood lumber. As mentioned in Chapter 15 (p. 335), the dispute centered on the U.S. allegation of subsidies by Canada to such exports. The U.S. duties had been 27 percent in 2002 but had decreased to an average of 11 percent in 2006 because of various reviews and rulings. In the new agreement, Canada will impose taxes on its exports if the lumber price falls below a certain level. In return, U.S. tariffs and quotas will be removed, and refunds of some penalty tariff revenues earlier collected by the United States would be given to Canadian producers.[42]

Second, the U.S. Congress in 2006 repealed the Byrd Amendment. This amendment (see Chapter 15, p. 332), officially labeled the Continued Dumping and Subsidy Offset Act of 2000, had authorized the distribution of the revenues from antidumping and countervailing duties to the U.S. import-competing producers who were being protected by the duties. The amendment had been challenged at the WTO, and the WTO in 2004 had authorized retaliation against it by U.S. trading partners. Four economic units (Canada, the European Union, Japan, and Mexico) had done so by 2006. The repeal of the amendment meant that, after October 1, 2007, the duties collected will again go to the U.S. Treasury.[43]

In summary fashion, we can mention a prominent additional aspect of U.S. trade policy. This aspect is that the United States has, in recent years, been negotiating bilateral and regional trade agreements. As far back as 1985, a U.S.–Israel free trade agreement went into effect. This was followed by the North American Free Trade Agreement (NAFTA), which began in 1994 and is discussed in the next chapter. In addition, free-trade agreements with 10 countries went into effect from 2001–2007, and agreements had been negotiated and talks were underway with still others.[44] This recent step-up in bilateral/regional trade negotiation activity is partly attributable to the fact that fast-track (Trade Promotion Authority) was restored to the president in 2002 (with a one-vote margin in the House of Representatives) and partly attributable to the slow going in the Doha Round multilateral negotiations. The lack of multilateral progress suggests to officials that freer trade may be achieved more quickly on a selective basis. However, Trade Promotion Authority was to

---

[40]Charles Hutzler, "Beijing Rescinds Textile Duties, Slams U.S., EU on Import Limits," *The Wall Street Journal,* May 31, 2005, pp. A3, A6; Office of the United States Trade Representative, "Facts on Textiles: Benefits from Establishing Quotas on Certain Chinese Apparel Exports to the United States," obtained from www.ustr.gov; Greg Hitt and Andrew Batson, "U.S., China Set Some Trade Deals, But Thorny Piracy Issues Persist," *The Wall Street Journal,* April 12, 2006, p. A4.

[41]Mark Drajem, "Commerce Department Applies New Duties against China (Update 7)," March 30, 2007, obtained from www.bloomberg.com.

[42]"U.S., Canada Sign Lumber Agreement," *The Wall Street Journal,* July 3, 2006, p. A7.

[43]Office of the United States Trade Representative, "Congress Takes Important Action: Byrd Repeal Brings U.S. into Compliance with WTO Ruling," February 1, 2006, obtained from www.ustr.gov.

[44]*Economic Report of the President,* February 2004, p. 236; Office of the United States Trade Representative, "Trade Promotion Authority Delivers Jobs, Growth Prosperity and Security at Home," January 31, 2007, obtained from www.ustr.gov.

expire in mid-2007, and there were doubts as to whether it would be renewed, especially with a Democratically controlled Congress in existence.

Finally, a phenomenon that has caught the attention of the American public in the last few years is the phenomenon of **outsourcing** (or **offshoring**). Outsourcing was discussed in Chapter 9 in the context of U.S. firms purchasing materials inputs from abroad. The "new" outsourcing refers to the U.S. firms' purchases of services abroad, services that would otherwise be provided in the United States. The classic example referred to is the use of Indian personnel in call centers, whereby a U.S. service call via a toll-free telephone number is answered or dealt with by someone in an Indian city such as Bangalore or Bombay (Mumbai). (These services utilize capital inputs as well as the foreign labor inputs— capital inputs that are often put in place by U.S. firms operating abroad.) These service jobs are usually white-collar jobs, not blue-collar jobs, and thus the domestic group being hurt is not the import-competing manufacturing industries' relatively less-skilled labor à la an application of Heckscher-Ohlin to the United States. Outsourcing seems to have "taken off" in the 1990s when the U.S. economy was booming and firms were seeking to reduce costs in a labor market that was close to or at full employment. Outsourcing has grown so much that one estimate made in 2003 was that 3.3 million white-collar service jobs and $136 billion in wages would go abroad in the 15 years after 2003. And, in 2007, Alan Blinder, a Princeton economist and former vice chair of the Board of Governors of the Federal Reserve, thought that up to 40 million U.S. jobs might be at risk in the next 10 to 20 years.[45] The hue and cry has led some states to attempt to implement explicit legislation against outsourcing, and there has also been pressure on the federal government to do likewise.

Economists in general, however, do not regard outsourcing or offshoring as a cause for alarm. There is absolutely no question that there are severe short-run dislocations from outsourcing. Workers lose their source of income, and retraining for or physical movement to a new job takes time. In the long run, however, the economy benefits from this free trade in white-collar services, but the long run may take a good while to arrive. But people may be skeptical of waiting for the long run—there was considerable consternation within the Bush administration and some congressional calls for resignation when N. Gregory Mankiw, chairman of the president's Council of Economic Advisers, said in early 2004 that outsourcing "is probably a plus for the economy in the long run."[46]

Another point is that there is increasing mention being made of the fact that outsourcing may also lead to *more* jobs in the United States. For example, one (U.S. industry-sponsored) study indicated that the use of service labor abroad reduces U.S. labor costs, leads to increased productivity for U.S. firms, and hence yields greater profits that can lead to companies' expansion at home and abroad. The estimate was that 90,000 jobs were created in the United States in 2003 because of this scenario.[47] As an example, another *Wall Street Journal* article featured a firm in New Jersey that sent work abroad to Bombay, which reduced costs so much that the firm obtained a sizable number of new customers and expanded its operations in the United States.[48] Further, another benefit to the country sending jobs offshore is that the country can experience a rise in real income because of the

[45]Clare Ansberry, "Outsourcing Abroad Draws Debate at Home," *The Wall Street Journal,* July 14, 2003, p. A2; David Wessel and Bob Davis, "Pain from Free Trade Spurs Second Thoughts," *The Wall Street Journal*, March 28, 2007, p. A1.

[46]Bob Davis, "Some Democratic Economists Echo Mankiw on Outsourcing," *The Wall Street Journal,* February 12, 2004, p. A4.

[47]Michael Schroeder, "Outsourcing May Create U.S. Jobs," *The Wall Street Journal,* March 30, 2004, p. A2.

[48]Craig Karmin, "'Offshoring' Can Generate Jobs in the U.S.," *The Wall Street Journal,* March 16, 2004, pp. B1, B7.

lower prices of the final output embodying the outsourced services as well as, indirectly, an increase in corporate profits and dividends for the companies doing the outsourcing. One estimate is that perhaps 70 percent to 80 percent of the income gains from the off-shoring/outsourcing phenomenon go to the outsourcing country and the remaining 20 percent to 30 percent to the country performing the outsourced services.[49] Finally, business writer Robert Samuelson pointed out that most estimates of annual U.S. job loss because of outsourcing are around 300,000 to 500,000 jobs, and this is a very small percentage of 138 million U.S. jobs.[50]

As should be evident from these policy examples and the debate over outsourcing, international trade policy continues to be controversial in the United States. As has been stated many times in this book, there are gainers and losers from a policy of moving to freer trade, and, though a country gains overall, compensation is not generally paid to the people who lose. Hence, income distribution is affected by trade, and there will always be controversy over policies in this area.

CONCLUDING OBSERVATIONS ON TRADE POLICY

International negotiations, both multilateral and bilateral, have clearly reduced the level of trade restrictions over the long run in industrialized countries. Any continued advance along these lines requires that countries remain willing to sit down at the bargaining table to negotiate trade policies in their mutual interest. Chapter 15 discussed various arguments for protection which indicate that sometimes an individual country can gain from the imposition of a trade restriction, even though the welfare of the world is reduced. But a gain under these circumstances tenuously depends on the absence of retaliation from adversely affected trading partners. International negotiations serve the critical purpose of keeping countries from unilaterally imposing new barriers. Historically, these negotiations have demonstrated that it is in a country's interest to reduce barriers rather than raise them. Cooperation, not unilateral action, plays a vital role in enhancing both the welfare of the world and the interests of individual countries.

The Conduct of Trade Policy

Disputes regarding trade policy reveal an underlying broad conflict on the relative extent to which the conduct of trade policy should be rules based or results based. A **rules-based trade policy** is one that adheres to commonly accepted international guidelines and codes of behavior on trade, such as those embodied in the World Trade Organization. This type of policy embraces MFN treatment, preference for tariffs as the instrument of choice rather than import quotas and VERs (which are more distortionary for resource allocation than tariffs and also discriminatory by country), common procedures on antidumping and countervailing duties, multilateral negotiations on trade barrier reductions, and so forth.

On the other hand, a **results-based trade policy** stresses that policy should seek, through aggressive, unilateral action or threat of action, to achieve carefully specified objectives, such as the penetration of a particular foreign market for a particular good by x percent, the limitation of imports of a particular good to y percent of the domestic market, special protection and incentives to particular industries, and attainment of balanced trade with specified trading partners. Or, the policy might be for a home country to treat each individual trading partner country exactly as that partner treats the home country with

---

[49]David Smith, "Offshoring: Political Myths and Economic Reality," *The World Economy* 29, no. 3 (March 2006), pp. 251–52.

[50]Robert Samuelson, "Threat of Outsourcing Overstated," *The Charlotte Observer,* January 17, 2004, p. 13A.

respect to trade—sometimes called the **new reciprocity approach to trade policy.** (See Cline 1983.) This more direct, results-based approach to the guidance of resource allocation is also sometimes known as a form of **industrial policy** or as **managed trade.**

Many observers of recent U.S. trade patterns feel that since other countries are more interventionist in trade than the United States, the United States should respond by according a stronger role to government. These observers advocate the results-based approach. On the other hand, other observers (including most economists) indicate that allocation of resources by government will be inferior to allocation of resources by the market. The superior market allocation is best attained in an environment of an established set of "rules."

Empirical Work on Political Economy	A final observation needs to be made. A number of empirical studies have focused on the role of the political economy factors discussed at the beginning of this chapter in influencing U.S. trade policy. In this work, an attempt is made, for example, to ascertain the characteristics of particular industries or sectors that cause those industries or sectors to be more or less protectionist and to ascertain how elected public officials are influenced in their voting on trade legislation. It has been found (Cheh 1974) that U.S. industries in which large labor adjustment costs would be incurred through tariff reduction are likely to be granted relatively high levels of protection (or relatively smaller reductions of protection) in tariff negotiations. In addition, in the congressional voting on the Trade Act of 1974, the percentage of workers in a representative's district employed in import-substitute industries was associated with a negative vote on that trade bill, as was the size of contributions to individual congressional campaigns by labor unions (Baldwin 1981). In general, a survey of various empirical tests for the United States (Baldwin 1984) indicated that a statistically significant positive relationship exists between the degree of industry protection and, for example, (*a*) the number of workers in an industry; (*b*) the labor/output ratio in the industry [both (*a*) and (*b*) reflect labor intensity but also voting strength that politicians wish to court]; (*c*) the percentage of unskilled workers in an industry, reflecting social concern as well as the relative scarcity of U.S. unskilled labor (remember the Stolper-Samuelson theorem from Chapter 8); and (*d*) the extent to which the product is a consumption good rather than an intermediate good (reflecting the fact that lower prices for intermediate goods are desired by domestic firms). Negative associations have been found between the degree of industry protection and, for example, (*a*) the number of firms in an industry, reflecting less ability to organize for protection, and (*b*) the average wage in an industry, again reflecting lower skills. More recently, Magee (2001, p. 115) found that a higher industry concentration ratio, a lower capital-labor ratio in the industry, and a higher fraction of an industry's labor force that consisted of scientists and engineers all were associated with a higher tariff rate. The first two of these results are what would be expected, but the third is not. In a paper by Scott Bradford (2003), an important result is that the amount of protection given to an industry is a strong positive function of the number of workers in the industry. In addition, the presence of a large number of firms in an industry seemed to be positively associated with lobbying effort, which in turn was positively associated with protection. Finally, an interesting result was that "politicians place about 15 percent more weight on a dollar of campaign contributions than on a dollar of consumer surplus" (Bradford 2003, p. 35).

Noteworthy in this discussion is the role of income distributional factors in trade policy, a role that is clearly what we would expect from our earlier presentation of trade theory. Although countries and the world as a whole gain from participation in international trade, not all citizens of all countries experience these gains. Remember that the consumption bundle after trade is large enough so that the "losers" from trade can be fully compensated by the "gainers," but this doesn't mean that compensation necessarily takes place in practice. The debates about trade policy therefore center importantly around struggles on income distribution.[51]

The political economy literature has developed specific hypotheses about the determinants of the general level of protection in different time periods. For example, Magee and Young (1987) examined the average level of protection in the United States during 16 presidential administrations from 1905 to 1980, focusing on macroeconomic influences. They found a strong positive association between the average tariff rate and the unemployment rate. Clearly, in slack times, there is greater political pressure for higher tariffs because of the workers' belief that higher tariffs provide greater job and wage security. This pressure is stronger than antiprotectionist sentiment by consumers, who are usually passive on trade policy. Magee and Young also found a significant positive association between the average tariff level and the ratio of the prices of U.S. manufactured goods exports to the prices of U.S. manufactured goods imports. With the assumption that the United States imports labor-intensive (especially unskilled-labor-intensive) manufactured goods, a decline in the relative prices of those goods will lead to greater demands for protection on the part of labor. Finally, they found a *negative* association between the U.S. inflation rate and the average level of tariffs. While one might think that the greater imports induced by inflation would stimulate a net increase in protectionist pressure because of lobbying by import-competing industry groups, Magee and Young hypothesized that consumers are indeed aroused by high inflation and are more effective in keeping import barriers low during inflationary periods, thus permitting the downward pressure on the price level that imports exert. Further, the possible depreciation of the dollar during inflationary periods raises the domestic price of imported goods and reduces pressure for protection by domestic import-competing firms.

A National Bureau of Economic Research empirical study (Krueger 1996) of seven different U.S. industries raised several interesting questions regarding the political economy of U.S. trade policy. General conclusions[52] were the following: First, there is no persuasive evidence that protection was, in general, important in turning an industry around economically. Second, the negative impact or costs of protection are often underestimated because of failure to consider secondary effects outside the affected industry. Third, protection will more likely be granted when there is unanimity within the industry regarding the desirability of it and when there is a well-organized and effective special-interest group to promote it. Finally, there was evidence that the existence of current protection increases the ease with which protection can be maintained in a given industry.

A general point that has emerged in the political economy literature is that, while economists traditionally investigate how protection affects imports, the reverse sequence should also be taken into account—that is, the level of imports affects the degree of protection. Thus, if tariffs and NTBs are reduced, the intensity of lobbying for protection by the affected import-competing industries will increase. If this lobbying is successful and leads to new protectionist devices being put into place, imports may not increase very much on balance. This scenario suggests that trade liberalization efforts face greater obstacles in actually getting freer trade in the world economy than would otherwise be the case. Working in this line

---

[51]It can also be noted that the literature has generally found a negative association between protection for an industry and the amount of intra-industry trade in that industry. This can partly be explained by the influence of exporters of the product lobbying against import barriers in general due to fears of retaliation. But it can also partly be explained by the fact that, as noted in Chapter 10, intra-industry trade based on economies of scale may not have the potentially large income distribution impacts that inter-industry trade has. That is, realization of economies of scale means that everyone can potentially gain from trade. See Rodrik 1995, pp. 1481–83.

[52]Anne O. Krueger, "Implications of the Results of Individual Studies," in Krueger (1996), pp. 99–103.

of thought, Daniel Trefler (1993) estimated that the "feedback" impact of import penetration had, in the case of nontariff barriers in the United States, reduced imports by almost $50 billion (in 1983) over the situation without the feedback.

The political economy area of research obviously has potential for broadening the scope of trade policy discussions. Students interested in pursuing trade policy further will find this topic a fruitful one for investigation.[53]

---

[53]For an interesting descriptive and quantitative analysis of the history of trade politics in six nations over the past two centuries, see Michael J. Hiscox, *International Trade and Political Conflict* (Princeton, NJ: Princeton University Press, 2002).

SUMMARY

This chapter examined political economy influences, such as interest groups and social concern, on trade policy, and considered related empirical work in the context of the United States. This was accompanied by a review of U.S. trade policy which highlighted the long-term trend of liberalization of trade, first through bilateral and then through multilateral negotiations. After the disastrous effects of the Smoot-Hawley Tariff of 1930, the United States began a long process of reducing tariff barriers. The Reciprocal Trade Agreements Act of 1934 initiated a series of bilateral, item-by-item negotiations that achieved some success. These procedures were superseded by the emergence of GATT at the end of World War II, and GATT sponsored eight rounds of multilateral negotiations that brought tariffs on manufactured goods to relatively low levels. Although recent years witnessed the rise of many nontariff barriers and of difficulties in the Uruguay Round with respect to services and agriculture, nevertheless the Uruguay Round was successfully concluded. Attempts to continue the path of long-term liberalization of trade are obviously desirable from the standpoint of increasing world welfare, but lack of significant progress in the negotiations on the Doha Development Agenda tentatively suggests that further important multilateral liberalization is not highly likely in the near future. However, there has been substantial progress in bilateral and regional negotiations, as discussed further in the next chapter.

KEY TERMS

across-the-board approach	Kennedy Round of trade	rent-seeking activity
Aid for Trade	negotiations	results-based trade policy
bilateral negotiations	managed trade	rules-based trade policy
consumer subsidy equivalent (CSE)	median-voter model	Smoot-Hawley Tariff (Tariff Act of
directly unproductive activity	multilateral negotiations	1930)
Doha Development Agenda	new reciprocity approach to trade	status quo bias
fast-track procedure (or Trade	policy	Tokyo Round of trade negotiations
Promotion Authority)	nonreciprocity principle	Trade Act of 1974
GATT rounds of trade negotiations	outsourcing (or offshoring)	trade adjustment assistance (TAA)
General Agreement on Tariffs and	producer subsidy equivalent (PSE)	Trade Expansion Act of 1962
Trade (GATT)	public-choice economics	Uruguay Round of trade
industrial policy	Reciprocal Trade Agreements Act	negotiations
item-by-item approach	of 1934	World Trade Organization (WTO)

QUESTIONS AND PROBLEMS

1. Explain two reasons a minority in a median-voter model is able to obtain net benefits through a restrictive trade policy that clearly harms the majority group and the country as a whole.

2. In what respects might bilateral trade negotiations be superior to multilateral trade negotiations? In what respects might multilateral trade negotiations be superior to bilateral trade negotiations?

3. The number of consumers in the United States far exceeds the number of workers in textiles and apparel, for example, so why do we see import restrictions on textiles and apparel despite the obvious losses to consumers?

4. Explain why a government's commitment to income distribution issues can cause policy to be protectionist. Is such policy inevitable if income distribution is a key target?

5. (*a*) Why might an economist see virtue in the concept of trade adjustment assistance (TAA)? What difficulties might be encountered in practice in the implementation of TAA?

   (*b*) Some economists think that TAA is discriminatory because special assistance is given to workers displaced by imports while workers displaced by domestic competition receive no such special favors. Do you think this observation rules out TAA as a desirable policy? Why or why not?

6. Why have tariff reductions been substantial over the years while reductions in nontariff barriers have been minimal?

7. (*a*) Build a case in favor of the use of the nonreciprocity principle for developing countries.

   (*b*) Build a case against the use of the nonreciprocity principle for developing countries.

8. If all interventions in agriculture were removed, what would happen to food prices? To the incomes of farmers? To world welfare? Might your answer be different for some developing countries than for developed countries?

9. Some observers have noted that by adopting VERs (or VRAs) instead of tariffs in recent years, the United States has injured itself "twice" rather than only "once." What does this statement mean?

10. What factors explain the considerable variation in the degree of trade restriction across U.S. industries?

17

ECONOMIC INTEGRATION

LEARNING OBJECTIVES

■ To understand the differences between the four basic levels of economic integration.

■ To identify the static and dynamic effects of economic integration.

■ To grasp the real-world impact of economic integration on countries in the European Union and the North American Free Trade Agreement.

■ To increase awareness of current economic integration efforts in the world.

INTRODUCTION

EU: Two New Members, More Economic Growth?

Tuesday, January 2, 2007 (The Guardian) The fireworks seemed brighter than elsewhere in Romania and Bulgaria at midnight on Sunday as the Black Sea neighbors celebrated 2007 and their historic entry into the European Union. The accession of these two former communist countries creates a club of 27 states that embraces 490 million people. That's an extraordinary achievement to reflect on now and again in March, the 50th anniversary of the signing of the Treaty of Rome, which set up the original six-member EEC. The excitement in Bucharest and Sofia is a reminder that the jaded citizens of older EU members have long lost their enthusiasm for integration, although prosperity and stability have come with every successive enlargement. Greece, Spain, and Portugal were helped to consolidate democracy after decades of dictatorship. Ireland made huge advances thanks to the growth and confidence generated by Europe. Slovenia, one of the 10 "big bang" entrants of May 2004, adopted the euro Monday.

In our previous discussions of trade policy, we generally conducted the analysis in a framework whereby a country was raising or lowering trade barriers against all trading partners simultaneously and uniformly. Increasingly, however, as suggested in the European Union news clipping, much international trade is taking place in a context where countries accord differential treatment to their trading partners. This treatment usually occurs by way of economic integration, where countries join together to create a larger economic unit with special relationships among the members. What precisely is economic integration? What are the benefits that cause all these nations to want to join an economic union? Are there costs involved? In this chapter, we discuss several different types of economic integration, present a framework for analyzing the welfare impacts of these special relationships, and examine recent integration efforts in the world economy.

TYPES OF ECONOMIC INTEGRATION

When countries form economic coalitions, their efforts represent a partial movement to free trade and an attempt by each participating country to obtain some of the benefits of a more open economy without sacrificing control over the goods and services that cross its borders and hence over its production and consumption structure. Countries entering special trade arrangements soon realize that the more they remove restrictions on the movement of goods and services between members of the group, the more domestic control of the economy is lost. Consequently, actions taken to integrate economies often take place in stages, and the first preferential agreement is potentially less threatening to the loss of control than the later stages. Four basic types of formal regional economic arrangements are usually distinguished.

Free-Trade Area

The most common integration scheme is referred to as a **free-trade area (FTA).** Characteristics: All members of the group remove tariffs on each other's products, while at the same time each member retains its independence in establishing trading policies with nonmembers. In other words, the members of an FTA can maintain individual tariffs and other trade barriers on the "outside world." This scheme is usually assumed to apply to all products between member countries, but it can clearly involve a mix of free trade in some products and preferential, but still protected, treatment in others. Potential concerns: When each member country sets its own external tariff, nonmember countries may find it profitable to export a product to the member country with the lowest level of outside protection and then through it to other member countries whose protection levels against the outside world are higher. Without **rules of origin** by members regarding the source country of a product, there is nothing to preclude nonmember countries from using this **transshipment** strategy to escape some of the trade restrictions in the more highly protected member countries. The most prominent free-trade area at present is, of course, the free-trade area set up in 1994 by Canada, Mexico, and the United States under the **North American Free Trade Agreement** (**NAFTA**) discussed later in this chapter.

Customs Union	The second level of economic integration is a **customs union.** Characteristics: All tariffs are removed between members and the group adopts a common external commercial policy toward nonmembers. Furthermore, the group acts as one body in the negotiation of all trade agreements with nonmembers. The existence of the **common external tariff** takes away the possibility of transshipment by nonmembers. The customs union is thus a step closer toward economic integration than the FTA. Potential concerns: Member nations give up independence in setting tariff rates. An example of a customs union is that of Belgium, the Netherlands, and Luxembourg (Benelux), which was formed in 1947 and absorbed into the European Community in 1958.
Common Market	The third level of economic integration is referred to as a **common market.** Characteristics: All tariffs are removed between members, a common external trade policy is adopted for nonmembers, *and* all barriers to factor movements among the member countries are removed. The free movement of labor and capital between members represents a higher level of economic integration and, at the same time, a further reduction in national control of the individual economy. Potential concerns: Members give up sovereignty in immigration and capital flows. In addition, factor integration has proven to be very difficult. The Treaties of Rome in 1957 established a common market within the **European Community** (**EC**), which officially began on January 1, 1958, and which became the **European Union** (**EU**) on November 1, 1993. (The EU is discussed later in this chapter.)
Economic Union	The most comprehensive of the four forms of economic integration is an **economic union.** Characteristics: Includes all features of a common market but also implies the unification of economic institutions and the coordination of economic policy throughout all member countries. While separate political entities are still present, an economic union generally establishes several supranational institutions whose decisions are binding upon all members. When an economic union adopts a common currency, it has become a **monetary union** as well. Potential concerns: While this level of economic integration is often aspired to, member countries find it extraordinarily difficult to give up the domestic sovereignty the scheme requires. Giving up autonomy in monetary policy is also a concern.

Thus, there are several different forms of economic integration. Existing integration units exhibit a wide variety of differing characteristics.

THE STATIC AND DYNAMIC EFFECTS OF ECONOMIC INTEGRATION

Static Effects of Economic Integration	Economic integration implies differential treatment for member countries as opposed to nonmember countries. Because this type of integration can lead to shifts in the pattern of trade between members and nonmembers, the net impact on a participating country is, in general, ambiguous and must be judged on the basis of each individual country. While integration represents a movement to free trade on the part of member countries, at the same time it can lead to the diversion of trade from a lower-cost nonmember source (which still faces the external tariffs of the group) to a member-country source (which no longer faces any tariffs). These two **static effects of economic integration,** meaning that they occur directly on the formation of the integration project, are called **trade creation** and

FIGURE 1   Trade Creation and Welfare

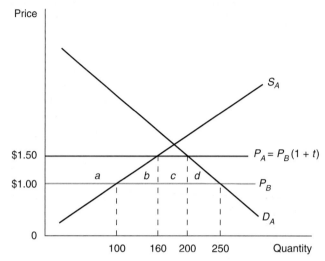

Before the economic integration, the price of the good in country A is $1.50 (= the $1.00 price in country B plus the 50 percent tariff). With integration between A and B, the tariff is removed, and A now imports 150 units (250 units − 100 units) rather than 40 units (200 units − 160 units) from B. Sixty units (160 − 100) of the increased imports displace previous home production, and 50 units (250 − 200) reflect the greater consumption at the new $1.00 price facing country A's consumers. The net welfare impact is the sum of areas b and d, or (1/2)(60)($0.50) + (1/2)(50)($0.50) = $27.50.

trade diversion. These terms were coined by Jacob Viner (1950), who defined trade creation as taking place whenever economic integration leads to a shift in product origin from a domestic producer whose resource costs are higher to a member producer whose resource costs are lower. This shift represents a movement in the direction of the free-trade allocation of resources and thus is presumably beneficial for welfare. Trade diversion takes place whenever there is a shift in product origin from a nonmember producer whose resource costs are lower to a member-country producer whose resource costs are higher. This shift represents a movement away from the free-trade allocation of resources and could reduce welfare. Because both trade creation and trade diversion are clearly possible with economic integration, we find ourselves in the world of **second best** because economic integration represents only a partial movement to free trade. Whether or not it produces a net benefit to participating countries is an empirical issue.

Let us approach this second-best problem ("first best" being completely free trade) by examining the impact of economic integration in a market for a single good in one of the member countries, country A. In Figure 1, D_A is the demand curve by country A's consumers for the good and S_A is the supply curve of country A's home producers. Assume that country A is importing the good from country B as well as producing it domestically prior to the formation of the economic integration unit (e.g., a customs union). If country A is a price taker in the world market at $1.00 per unit from country B and there is a 50 percent tariff on the good, the domestic price in A is $1.50,[1] the quantity consumed is 200 units, and the quantity supplied domestically is 160 units. The quantity imported by A from B is 40 units. When the tariff is removed on country B's good because of the union,

---

[1]Throughout the analysis of this chapter, we are assuming no transportation costs between trading countries.

IN THE REAL WORLD:

ECONOMIC INTEGRATION UNITS

Table 1 lists some of the regional economic groups in the world today. The units differ in the extent of integration desired or formed and in the degree to which they have actually carried out the intended integration. You can see that a large number of the world's more than 200 nations have undertaken economic integration projects, and the impact on trade can be significant. For example, the EU comprises about 40 percent of world trade.

TABLE 1   Economic Integration Units in the World Economy

Andean Community of Nations (CAN)
Bolivia
Colombia
Ecuador
Peru
Venezuela

Arab Cooperation Council (ACC)
Egypt
Iraq
Jordan
Yemen

Arab Maghreb Union (AMU)
Algeria
Libya
Mauritania
Morocco
Tunisia

Association of Southeast Asian Nations (ASEAN)
Brunei
Cambodia
Indonesia
Laos
Malaysia
Myanmar (Burma)
Philippines
Singapore
Thailand
Vietnam

Benelux Economic Union (Benelux)
Belgium
Luxembourg
Netherlands

Caribbean Community and Common Market (CARICOM)
Antigua and Barbuda
Bahamas, The
Barbados
Belize
Dominica
Grenada
Guyana
Haiti
Jamaica
Montserrat
St. Kitts and Nevis
St. Lucia
St. Vincent and the Grenadines
Suriname
Trinidad and Tobago

Central American Common Market (CACM)
Costa Rica
El Salvador
Guatemala
Honduras
Nicaragua

Common Market for Eastern and Southern Africa (COMESA)
Angola
Burundi
Comoros
Congo, Democratic Republic of
Djibouti
Egypt
Eritrea
Ethiopia
Kenya
Libya

Madagascar
Malawi
Mauritius
Rwanda
Seychelles
Sudan
Swaziland
Uganda
Zambia
Zimbabwe

Economic Community of the Great Lakes Countries (CEPGL)
Burundi
Congo, Democratic Republic of
Rwanda

Economic Community of West African States (ECOWAS)
Benin
Burkina Faso
Cape Verde
Côte d'Ivoire
Gambia, The
Ghana
Guinea
Guinea-Bissau
Liberia
Mali
Mauritania
Niger
Nigeria
Senegal
Sierra Leone
Togo

European Free Trade Association (EFTA)
Iceland
Liechtenstein

Norway
Switzerland

European Union (EU)
Austria
Belgium
Bulgaria
Cyprus
Czech Republic
Denmark
Estonia
Finland
France
Germany
Greece
Hungary
Ireland
Italy
Latvia
Lithuania
Luxembourg
Malta
Netherlands
Poland
Portugal
Romania
Slovakia
Slovenia
Spain
Sweden
United Kingdom

Latin American Integration Association (LAIA)
Argentina
Bolivia
Brazil
Chile
Colombia
Cuba
Ecuador

(continued)

IN THE REAL WORLD: *(continued)*

Mexico	**North American Free Trade**	Pakistan	Paraguay
Paraguay	**Agreement (NAFTA)**	Sri Lanka	Uruguay
Peru	Canada		Venezuela
Uruguay	Mexico	**Southern African Customs**	
Venezuela	United States	**Union (SACU)**	**West African Economic and**
		Botswana	**Monetary Union (WAEMU)**
Monetary and Economic	**South Asian Association for**	Lesotho	Benin
Community of Central Africa	**Regional Cooperation**	Namibia	Burkina Faso
(CEMAC)	**(SAARC)**	South Africa	Côte d'Ivoire
Cameroon	Bangladesh	Swaziland	Guinea-Bissau
Central African Republic	Bhutan		Mali
Chad	India	**Southern Cone Common**	Niger
Congo, Republic of	Maldives	**Market (MERCOSUR)**	Senegal
Equatorial Guinea	Nepal	Argentina	Togo
Gabon		Brazil	

Source: Central Intelligence Agency, *The World Factbook 2007* (Washington, DC: CIA, 2007), obtained from www.odci.gov.

IN THE REAL WORLD:

TRADE CREATION AND TRADE DIVERSION IN THE EARLY STAGES OF EUROPEAN ECONOMIC INTEGRATION

There have been numerous attempts to estimate trade creation and trade diversion in the real world. Many of them have dealt with the European Community (EC) or the "European Common Market" as it was traditionally called. Estimates are difficult to make because the researchers are comparing actual trade flows with trade flows that hypothetically would have existed without the integration.

Bela Balassa was a leader in making creation-diversion estimates. His approach (Balassa 1974) utilizes the concept of the *ex post* **income elasticity of import demand (YEM)**—the average annual percentage change in observed imports divided by the average annual percentage change in observed GNP, with both changes evaluated at constant prices (that is, adjusting for inflation). For Balassa, after integration occurs, (*a*) a *rise* in the YEM for imports *from partner countries* (intra-area imports) is denoted as gross trade creation, or increased imports from the partners whether or not this new trade represents displacement of home production or displacement of outside world production; (*b*) trade diversion is indicated by a *fall* in the YEM for imports *from the outside world* (extra-area imports); and (*c*) trade creation proper is indicated by a *rise* in the YEM for

imports *from all sources* (partners and the outside world). A rise in the last YEM suggests that the formation of the integration unit made the EC more receptive to imports overall, meaning that there was a relative turning away from domestic production. Underlying the use of all three YEMs is the important assumption that the YEMs would have remained constant if the formation of the economic integration unit had not occurred.

Table 2 presents Balassa's results, comparing the YEMs before the EC took effect (1953–1959) with those of roughly the first decade of the EC (1959–1970). It is clear that there was substantial overall gross trade creation, since the YEM for intra-area imports rose from 2.4 to 2.7. This means that, before integration, each 1 percent rise in GNP yielded a 2.4 percent rise in intra-area imports, but after integration, each 1 percent rise in GNP yielded a 2.7 percent increase in these imports. Marked increases in this YEM took place in fuels (from 1.1 to 1.6, an almost 50 percent increase), chemicals, machinery, and transport equipment (all with increases of over 20 percent). There was no overall trade diversion because the total YEM for extra-area imports remained at 1.6. However, diversion occurred in nontropical food, beverages, and tobacco; chemicals; and

IN THE REAL WORLD: *(continued)*

other manufactured goods. The fall in nontropical food, beverages, and tobacco reflected the adoption of import restrictions on the outside world in connection with the EC's Common Agricultural Policy. Finally, overall trade creation proper of about 10 percent occurred because of a rise in the YEM for total imports from 1.8 to 2.0. Major increases occurred in fuels, machinery, and transport equipment.

It should be pointed out that these estimates involve more than the static effects discussed in the text. The measures in this table can move in unexpected directions (such as a rise in the YEM for extra-area imports and a fall in the YEM for intra-area imports) because of dynamic effects such as increased economic growth and changes in tastes, or because of the failure to allow for a change in the YEMs that would have occurred even without integration. Finally, these estimates do not directly address welfare impacts of the formation of the EC. Nevertheless, they strongly suggest that welfare rose in the EC with economic integration.

TABLE 2   *Ex Post* Income Elasticities of Import Demand (YEMs), European Community, 1953–1959 and 1959–1970

	YEMs, 1953–1959	YEMs, 1959–1970
Intra-area imports (gross trade creation):		
Chemicals	3.0	3.7
Fuels	1.1	1.6
Machinery	2.1	2.8
Nontropical food, beverages, tobacco	2.5	2.5
Raw materials	1.9	1.8
Transport equipment	2.9	3.5
Other manufactured goods	2.8	2.7
Total of above categories	2.4	2.7
Extra-area imports (trade diversion):		
Chemicals	3.0	2.6
Fuels	1.8	2.1
Machinery	0.9	2.4
Nontropical food, beverages, tobacco	1.4	1.0
Raw materials	1.0	1.0
Transport equipment	2.2	2.5
Other manufactured goods	2.5	2.1
Total of above categories	1.6	1.6
Total imports (trade creation proper):		
Chemicals	3.0	3.2
Fuels	1.6	2.0
Machinery	1.5	2.6
Nontropical food, beverages, tobacco	1.7	1.5
Raw materials	1.1	1.1
Transport equipment	2.6	3.2
Other manufactured goods	2.6	2.5
Total of above categories	1.8	2.0

Source: Bela Balassa, "Trade Creation and Trade Diversion in the European Common Market: An Appraisal of the Evidence," *The Manchester School of Economic and Social Studies* 42, no. 2 (June 1974), p. 97.

the price of the good in A falls to $1.00, the quantity consumed rises to 250, the quantity produced at home falls to 100, and the quantity imported rises to 150 (= 250 − 100).

This is a trade-creating union in Viner's sense because 60 units (160 − 100) have been switched from home production in country A to lower-cost production in B. In addition to the switch in the source of production, consumers gain from a larger quantity consumed. (Viner neglected the consumption effect.) The welfare impact on country A is clearly positive. Consumers have received the additional consumer surplus of areas $a + b + c + d$. Of this amount, a is a transfer of producer surplus from country A's suppliers, while c formerly was tariff revenue that now accrues to A's consumers. Therefore, the net welfare gain for the country consists of areas $b + d$. In terms of the example, $b = (1/2)(60 \text{ units})(\$0.50/\text{unit}) = \$15.00$, while $d = (1/2)(50 \text{ units})(\$0.50/\text{unit}) = \$12.50$. Country A as a whole has increased its welfare by $\$15.00 + \$12.50 = \$27.50$. The effect is unambiguous because this trade creation represents a movement in the direction of comparative advantage.

The ambiguity concerning the welfare effect of economic integration arises when trade diversion occurs. This possibility is illustrated in the partial equilibrium analysis in Figure 2. Suppose that we are examining three countries—A, B, and C. Let A be the home country, B the potential union partner, and C the nonmember country. The production cost in C is $1.00 and the cost in B is $1.20, but the product price in home country A is $1.50 because A has a 50 percent tariff in place. In this instance, country A will buy from country C since C's price, including the tariff, is lower than the tariff-inclusive price of country B, which equals $1.20 + 50% ($1.20), or $1.80 (not shown in Figure 2). Suppose now that country A forms a customs union with country B and drops its protection against B's good as part of the integration agreement, while at the same time maintaining its protection against country C.

FIGURE 2   Trade Diversion and Welfare

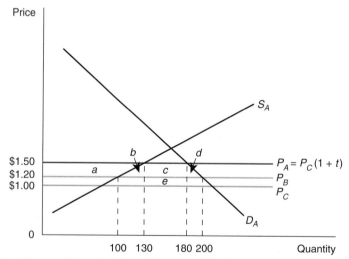

Before the union with country B, country A has a 50 percent tariff on imports of the good. Thus country C's tariff-inclusive price in A's market is $1.50, and country B's tariff-inclusive price is $1.80 (not shown). Before the union, A imports 50 units (180 units − 130 units) from C. When the union is formed with B, country A imports 100 units (200 − 100), all coming from partner B, which no longer faces a tariff. The net welfare change for A is the difference between areas $b + d$ (a positive effect due to the lower price in A) and area e (a negative effect due to lost tariff revenue by A that is not captured by A's consumers). In this example, welfare is reduced since $b + d = (1/2)(30)(\$0.30) + (1/2)(20)(\$0.30) = \$4.50 + \$3.00 = \$7.50$, while $e = (50)(\$0.20) = \$10.00$.

Country A can now purchase the product for $1.20 from country B, compared with the tariff-inclusive price of $1.50 from C. Even though C is still the low-cost supplier in terms of real resource costs, C is no longer competitive in A's market because of A's preferential treatment of country B. Consequently, country A shifts from C to B as a source of this product. The impact in A is to reduce the domestic price from $1.50 to $1.20, a change that produces a welfare gain equal to the two deadweight triangles b and d.

The welfare gain in areas b and d is not the total welfare effect, however. Because country A is now importing from country B and charging no tariff, the government in A no longer collects any revenue. The revenue that was previously collected was equal to the difference between the low-cost supply price ($1.00) in country C and the previous domestic price ($1.50) for each unit imported. The value of this revenue is equal to the area of rectangles c and e. Rectangle c reflects that part of the government revenue given up after integration, which is transferred to domestic consumers through the reduction in the domestic price. Rectangle e represents the difference in cost between the nonmember source and the new higher-cost member source, and as such it is the cost of moving to the less efficient producer in terms of lost government revenue. The net effect of economic integration between country A and country B in this case depends on the sum $(b + d - e)$. There is no certainty that the sum of $b + d$ will be larger than area e.

In Viner's terms, area e represents the difference in cost per unit between country B and country C ($1.20 − $1.00 = $0.20) times the amount of trade diverted—the original 50 units (180 units − 130 units). This trade diversion has a value of ($0.20)(50) = $10.00. Areas b and d again represent the consumer surplus gain that is not a transfer from domestic producers and the government. Area b is actually a trade-creating (improved efficiency) effect because 30 units of the good (130 units − 100 units) are now produced at a lower cost in country B than they were in country A. This effect has a value of (1/2)(30)($0.30) = $4.50. Area d represents the remaining consumer surplus gain from the lower price to country A's consumers, and is equal to (1/2)(20 = 200 − 180)($0.30) = $3.00. Consequently, the net effect of integration between A and B in this market is a loss of $2.50 ($4.50 + $3.00 − $10.00). If the customs union involves some trade diversion, it is certainly possible that welfare can be reduced for country A. This conclusion can also be derived in a general equilibrium context with the PPF and community indifference curves. (See Concept Box 1.)

General Conclusions on Trade Creation/Diversion

There are four general conclusions that can be make regarding trade creation/diversion: (1) The more closely the price in the partner country approaches the low-cost world price, the more likely the effect of integration on the market in question will be positive. (2) The effect of the integration is more likely to be positive the higher the initial tariff rate, as areas b and d will be larger. (At the extreme, if the tariff were initially prohibitive so that country A's imports were zero, there would be no welfare loss at all from trade diversion.) (3) The more elastic the supply and demand curves, the greater the quantity response by both consumers and producers; thus, the larger are b and d. (4) Integration is more likely to be beneficial when there is a greater number of participating countries, because there is a smaller group of countries from which trade can be diverted. (The extreme case occurs when all countries in the world embrace integration because there could be no trade diversion.)

In addition to the creation/diversion effects, there are other static, more institutional effects of economic integration that may accompany the formation of a union. First, economic integration can lead to administrative savings by eliminating the need for government officials to monitor the partner goods and services that cross the borders. Providing around-the-clock customs surveillance at all possible crossover points can be costly. Second, the economic size of the union may permit it to improve its collective terms of trade vis-à-vis the rest of the world compared with the average terms previously obtained by

CONCEPT BOX 1

TRADE DIVERSION IN GENERAL EQUILIBRIUM

The trade diversion impact of integration in the two-commodity general equilibrium graphical approach is presented in Figure 3. We begin with the country already protecting its import good and consuming on indifference curve IC_t at point b. [Free-trade prices $(P_w/P_a)_{ft}$ are shown to provide a basic reference point; consumption with free trade would be at point a on indifference curve IC_{ft}.] If this country now forms a customs union with a country that cannot produce autos as cheaply as reflected in $(P_w/P_a)_{ft}$, economic integration will lead to terms of trade in the union that are greater than the tariff-distorted domestic prices $(P_w/P_a)_d$ but less than $(P_w/P_a)_{ft}$. If the prices in the new partner country, $(P_w/P_a)_{u1}$, for example, are sufficiently close to world prices, the

formation of the union generates a consumption possibilities frontier that allows consumers to reach point c on a higher indifference curve such as IC_{u1}. If prices in the new partner country do not involve sufficiently low auto prices, for example, $(P_w/P_a)_{u2}$, consumers may find themselves restricted to a new consumption-possibilities line that leaves them less well-off (such as at point f on IC_{u2}). Consequently, we again see that the static welfare effect of economic integration that involves trade diversion is ambiguous. Only by examining a specific country and determining the extent to which the effects of trade diversion offset the gains from the partial movement to free trade can any conclusion be reached about the effect of integration.

FIGURE 3   Trade Diversion in General Equilibrium

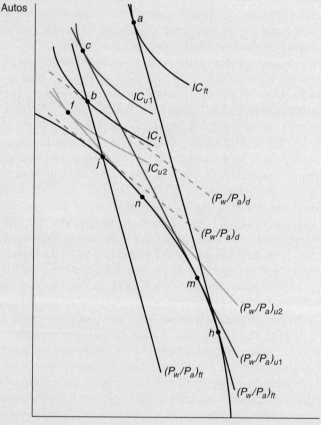

With free trade, the country produces at point h and consumes at point a on indifference curve IC_{ft}. With a tariff in place on all auto imports, production is at point j and consumption is at point b on IC_t. If a trade-diverting union is formed so that the union partner's prices are $(P_w/P_a)_{u1}$, production takes place at point m and consumption at point c on indifference curve IC_{u1}. Because IC_{u1} represents a higher welfare level than IC_t, the country has gained. However, if the union partner's prices are $(P_w/P_a)_{u2}$ rather than $(P_w/P_a)_{u1}$, production takes place at point n and consumption at point f on indifference curve IC_{u2}. Because IC_{u2} represents a lower welfare level than IC_t, welfare falls with the formation of the union.

individual member countries. Finally, the member countries will have greater bargaining power in trade negotiations with the rest of the world than they would have had negotiating on their own.

CONCEPT CHECK	1. Why is the formation of an economic integration project regarded as a second-best situation? 2. In Figure 2, what would be the welfare impact of the union on country A if the	partner were country C rather than country B? Explain. 3. Why is there an incentive for transshipment in a free-trade area but not in a customs union or a common market?

Dynamic Effects of Economic Integration

In addition to the static effects of economic integration, it is likely that the economic structure and performance of participating countries may evolve differently than if they had not integrated economically. The factors that cause this to come about are the **dynamic effects of economic integration.** For example, reducing trade barriers brings about a more competitive environment and possibly reduces the degree of monopoly power that was present prior to integration. In addition, access to larger union markets may allow economies of scale to be realized in certain export goods. These economies of scale may result internally to the exporting firm in a participating country as it becomes larger, or they may result from a lowering of costs of inputs due to economic changes external to the firm. In either case, they are triggered by market expansion brought about by membership in the union. The realization of economies of scale may also involve specialization on particular types of a good, and thus (as has been observed with the European Community) trade may increasingly become intra-industry trade rather than inter-industry trade. (See Chapter 10 for a discussion of intra-industry trade.)

It is also possible that integration will stimulate greater investment in the member countries from both internal and foreign sources. For example, massive U.S. investment occurred in the EC in the 1960s. Investment can result from structural changes, internal and external economies, and the expected increases in income and demand. It is further argued that integration stimulates investment by reducing risk and uncertainty because of the large economic and geographic market now open to producers. Furthermore, foreigners may wish to invest in productive capacity in a member country in order to avoid being frozen out of the union by trade restrictions and a high common external tariff.

Finally, economic integration at the level of the common market may lead to dynamic benefits from increased factor mobility. If both capital and labor have the increased ability to move from areas of surplus to areas of scarcity, increased economic efficiency and correspondingly higher factor incomes in the integrated area will result.

Summary of Economic Integration

Let us briefly summarize the conditions under which *economic integration is more likely to have overall beneficial effects.* The higher the level of preunion tariffs and the lower the common external tariff, the more likely the net effects will be positive. Along this same line, the more elastic supply and demand in the member countries are, the more likely the net results will be positive. The net positive effects will likely be larger the greater the number of participating members and the larger the economic size of the group. Also, the greater the ease of switching from a higher-cost domestic source to a lower-cost member source, the greater the preunion per-unit cost differences between the two sources, and the greater the scope for experiencing economies of scale and attracting foreign investment, the larger the potential gains from integration. Finally, if transportation costs are considered, the closer the member countries are geographically, the more likely there will be static and dynamic gains from integration.

With all the possible ways of gaining from integration, it seems logical to inquire why economic integration has often failed. We have focused on the economic consequences of integration in a representative country and have ignored two important issues. *The first relates to the distribution of benefits between member countries, and the second to the issue of national sovereignty.* Our static analysis pointed out the internal distribution effects on consumers and producers, but it told us nothing about the distribution of benefits between member countries. This issue has been a stumbling block to putting integration schemes into place, as economic integration has often been viewed as a zero-sum game by potential members. Each country wants access to other countries' markets but is often unwilling to give access to its own. The distribution problem has been enhanced by the unwillingness of individual countries to give up the control of their economies required by joining an economic integration plan.

It is not surprising that economic integration schemes have had a spotty record as an economic policy strategy. This is particularly true historically in the developing countries where integration experiments such as the East African Common Market failed. In the case of the developing countries, one not only encounters country distribution and sovereignty problems, but the potential gains are not always obvious because potential member countries often trade little with each other and are not very large economically. Their respective economies sometimes produce different (not similar) goods destined for the markets of industrialized countries. Finally, their domestic demand and supply curves appear to be less elastic than those in similar markets in industrialized countries. Consequently, the static gains do not appear great and the success of the economic integration scheme rests on the realization of dynamic gains resulting from the increased investment and the new industries that come into being to serve the larger group market. This, of course, leads to controversies about location of new industries and the distribution of the benefits of structural change among the member countries. Thus, while economic integration offers advantages of larger markets and possible economies of scale to developing countries, the ability to take advantage of these dynamic development effects depends on the countries' willingness to give up some national economic control and on solving the basic problem of how to distribute the benefits among member countries.

THE EUROPEAN UNION

History and Structure   With this conceptual background, we now turn to the most ambitious and best-known integration unit in the world economy—the European Community (EC), which, since November 1993, has been officially called the European Union. The formation of this unit[2] formally began in 1951 when the Treaty of Paris was signed by Belgium, France, West Germany, Italy, Luxembourg, and the Netherlands. This treaty established the European Coal and Steel Community for coordination of production, distribution, and other matters concerning these two industries within the six countries. The countries then advanced their cooperation much further by signing two Treaties of Rome in 1957; one treaty established the European Economic Community (EEC) and the other formed the European Atomic Energy Commission (Euratom) for joint research, cooperation, and management in that field. The two treaties went into effect on January 1, 1958, and with the earlier Treaty of Paris became the constitution of the European Community. The ultimate objective was the

---

[2]See Gary Clyde Hufbauer, "An Overview," in Hufbauer (1990), pp. 1–64.

IN THE REAL WORLD:

THE EAST AFRICAN COMMUNITY

The East African countries of Kenya, Tanzania, and Uganda established the East African Community (EAC) in 1967. The EAC was a step toward a considerable amount of integration. The enabling agreement, the Treaty for East African Cooperation, created the East African Common Market (EACM) with a common external tariff, free trade among the members, harmonization of monetary and fiscal policies, fixed exchange rates, and coordination of development planning efforts. However, the EACM did not permit free movement of labor and capital and did not extend the free-trade provisions to agricultural products. In addition, a transfer tax was implemented on some trade between members to protect less industrialized Tanzania and Uganda from more industrialized Kenya.

The treaty also established the East African Development Bank (with equal contributions from each of the three members) to distribute investment funds among the countries. In addition, common service organizations operated railways, ports, telecommunications, and airways. Overseeing all activities was the East African Authority, a board consisting of the three country presidents—Kenyatta of Kenya, Nyerere of Tanzania, and Obote of Uganda—with unanimity required for decisions.

The three countries had cooperated with one another since the time they were ruled as British colonies. Kenya and Uganda had formed a customs union in 1917 and Tanganyika (as Tanzania was known before the addition of Zanzibar) had joined in 1923. There had been a common income tax and a joint provision of some services, and a common currency (the East African shilling) had been in use from 1936 until the mid-1960s. It was thought that, with the attainment of independence in the early 1960s, the new East African Community of sovereign states had great promise.

The bright promise of the EAC soon faded, however. It became evident that the gains from integration were unevenly distributed. Kenya grew more rapidly than the other two partners. Its average annual real GDP growth was 7.5 percent from 1967 to 1977, while Tanzania's was 6.3 percent and Uganda's 2.0 percent (Eken 1979, p. 39). In addition, new firms located in Kenya because of its better industrial base. The East African Development Bank's funds were also distributed disproportionately toward Kenya in comparison with the planned distribution. Further, trade diversion toward Kenya's products meant that Tanzania and Uganda were

potentially losing from the union, because a considerable amount of tariff revenue (an important source of government financing) was given up. It has been suggested (Eken 1979, p. 39) that the union could not really "create" trade between Tanzania and Uganda because previous tariffs were not a factor that inhibited trade between them. Both countries specialized in the same primary products and were highly dependent on trade with developed countries; exports to developed countries were 90 percent of total exports for both Tanzania and Uganda. Finally, Tanzania and Uganda each had large intra-union trade deficits with Kenya because of their heavy importation of manufactured goods.

Political and ideological factors also caused difficulty. The East African Authority never met after 1971 because Julius Nyerere refused to deal with Uganda's new president, General Idi Amin, who had seized power from Milton Obote. Amin was also displeased that Tanzania had offered a safe haven to Obote. Ideologically, Tanzania was trying to create a socialist state and deplored Kenya's strong emphasis on capitalism. Kenya's emphasis on the market also contributed to its receiving the lion's share of investment from the outside world, which exacerbated the distribution of benefits problem.

With all of these political, ideological, and economic difficulties, the East African Community collapsed in 1977 after several years of disintegrating events (e.g., expulsion of each other's citizens, imposition of exchange and import controls). The integration experiment that had been so promising ended after only 10 years of operation. Later, in the 1990s and at present, the countries are again members of trading groups both among themselves and with other countries, but the overlapping arrangements were not always consistent with each other and little success was attained.

Sources: "Combustious Community," *The Economist,* September 20, 1975, pp. 64, 66; Sena Eken, "Breakup of the East African Community," *Finance and Development* 16, no. 4 (December 1979), pp. 36–40; Arthur Hazlewood, "The End of the East African Community: What Are the Lessons for Regional Integration Schemes?" *Journal of Common Market Studies* 18, no. 1 (September 1979), pp. 40–58; Joseph Kakoza, "The Common External Tariff and Development in the East African Community," *Finance and Development* 9, no. 1 (March 1972), pp. 22–29; "Three Fall Out," *The Economist,* January 4, 1975, pp. 38–39; Robert Sharer, "Trade: An Engine of Growth for Africa," *Finance and Development* 36, no. 4 (December 1999), pp. 26–29. ●

formation "of an integrated market for the free movement of goods, services, capital, and people. These are known as the 'four freedoms' . . . "[3] The EC subsequently expanded from 6 to 15 countries with the addition of Denmark, Ireland, and the United Kingdom in 1973, Greece in 1981, Portugal and Spain in 1986, and Austria, Finland, and Sweden in 1995. In a vote on April 19, 2003, the European Parliament voted to accept the accession treaties of Cyprus, the Czech Republic, Estonia, Hungary, Latvia, Lithuania, Malta, Poland, Slovakia, and Slovenia, in 2004. On January 1, 2007, Bulgaria and Romania joined, bringing the total to 27 nations.

To facilitate the attainment of the broad objective and to obtain greater political cohesion, various supranational institutions were established. The European Commission, the executive body, is charged with implementing the treaties and with general leadership. The Council of Ministers is the decision-making unit on communitywide matters. The European Council, comprised of the political leaders of the individual member countries, sets broad policy guidelines. The European Parliament is elected by voters in the member countries (with a specified number of seats allocated to each country), and it makes proposals to the Commission. Finally, the Court of Justice interprets the constitution and settles disputes.

Growth and Disappointments

The newly formed EC eliminated tariffs on intra-EC trade and adopted the common external tariff by July 1968. Trade among the member states grew rapidly in the 1960s as did world trade in general. In addition, the average annual growth rate of real GNP for the Community as a whole from 1961 to 1970 was 4.8 percent, and the growth rate in GNP per capita was 4.0 percent. This compared with a U.S. growth rate of 3.8 percent for GNP and 2.5 percent for per capita GNP.[4] Many attributed this impressive early growth performance to the establishment of the EC itself, although some had doubts whether this was the cause. Impressive growth was also associated during the late 1960s and early 1970s with the implementation of 35 percent tariff cuts under the Kennedy Round. Indeed, the origination of the Kennedy Round itself can be linked with the formation of the EC. U.S. officials viewed a new round of tariff cutting as a way to offset some of the discrimination against U.S. goods caused by the removal of tariffs within the EC and the erection of the common external tariff. The U.S.–EC bargaining within the round was critical for the success of the negotiations.[5]

The successful EC growth experience in the 1960s gave way to disappointments in the 1970s and 1980s. The oil crises of 1973–1974 and 1979–1980, accompanied by periods of simultaneous recession and inflation, led to slow growth and rising unemployment in Europe. Annual EC real GNP growth fell to 1.4 percent during the 1981–1985 period; in contrast, the U.S. real GDP growth rate for 1981–1985 was 2.3 percent, and Japan grew at a rate of 3.7 percent.[6] Because of these relatively and absolutely low growth rates in the EC and high European unemployment rates (sometimes above 10 percent), the term **"Eurosclerosis"** was coined.[7]

---

[3]Ibid., p. 1.

[4]Central Intelligence Agency, Directorate of Intelligence, *Handbook of Economic Statistics, 1990: A Reference Aid* (Washington, DC: CIA, 1990), pp. 39–40.

[5]See Bela Belassa, *Trade Liberalization among Industrial Countries: Objectives and Alternatives* (New York: McGraw-Hill, 1967), p. 13; and Hufbauer, "An Overview," pp. 3–4.

[6]Central Intelligence Agency, Directorate of Intelligence, *Handbook of International Economic Statistics 1992* (Washington, DC: CIA, 1992), pp. 26–27.

[7]Hufbauer, "An Overview," p. 6. The originator of the term is thought to be Herbert Giersch of Germany's Kiel Institute.

**Completing the
Internal Market**

Economic disappointments and the perception of a Europe "falling behind" the United States and Japan became a concern to the members of the Community. Some thought that the continued existence of internal barriers to fuller economic integration within the Community itself was an important retardant to better European performance. Although tariffs had been removed by 1968 on intra-EC trade, a variety of nontariff hindrances to free trade remained. Therefore, in 1985 the European Commission issued a policy paper, *Completing the Internal Market: White Paper from the Commission to the European Council,* prescribing changes to eliminate these various hindrances and restrictions. These internal market barriers essentially consisted of

(*i*) differences in technical regulations between countries, which impose extra costs on intra-EC trade;

(*ii*) delays at frontiers for customs purposes, and related administrative burdens for companies and public administrations, which impose further costs on trade;

(*iii*) restrictions on competition for public purchases through excluding bids from other Community suppliers, which often result in exclusively high costs of purchase;

(*iv*) restrictions on freedom to engage in certain service transactions, or to become established in certain service activities in other Community countries. This concerns particularly financial and transport services, where the costs of market entry barriers also appear to be substantial. (Emerson et al. 1988, p. 1)

The European Community's members were receptive to this call for completing the removal of internal barriers, and in February 1986 the Council of Ministers adopted the **Single European Act** to implement the various recommendations. The date set for the removal of all the internal market restrictions was December 31, 1992—the term **EC92** came into existence to indicate the target for complete integration of the Community. There were 282 different directives issued for implementation,[8] and many (but by no means all) were accomplished by or shortly after the deadline.

Prospects

What were the expected consequences of the increased economic integration in the European Union? The European Commission calculated that the annual GDP over the medium term would be from 3.2 to 5.7 percent greater than it would have been without the increased economic integration, with much of the increase coming from the liberalization of financial services and from supply-side effects. The supply-side effects reflect phenomena such as realization of economies of scale, greater efficiencies brought about by the heightened competition between producers, and the reduction of direct costs due to former technical barriers such as the lack of standardization of product inputs. Consumer prices were expected to be from 4.5 to 7.7 percent lower than otherwise, and employment was to rise by 1.3 million to 2.3 million jobs (Emerson et al. 1988, p. 208). However, the immediate situation in the EC in the early 1990s was not optimistic. The worldwide recession of 1990–1991 hit the EC hard, and economic performance was poor. Real GDP growth in the European Community was 1.7 percent in 1991, 1.2 percent in 1992, and *negative* 0.4 percent in 1993. Growth then picked up and was in the 1.7 percent to 3.0 percent range annually through 1999. In 2000, EU real GDP grew 3.9 percent, but growth fell to 2.1 percent in 2001, 1.4 percent in 2002, 1.5 percent in 2003, 2.6 percent in 2004, and 1.9 percent in 2005. However, the unemployment rate averaged 10.8 percent from 1995 to 1997 before falling steadily to 7.4 percent in 2001 and rising to 7.7 percent in 2002 and 8.2 percent in 2003. The figure (Euro area only) was 8.8 percent in 2004 and 8.6 percent in 2005. The EU's

---

[8]Tony Horwitz, "Europe's Borders Fade, and People and Goods Can Move More Freely," *The Wall Street Journal,* May 18, 1993, p. A10.

inflation performance was good, with the rise in the GDP deflator falling steadily from 5.4 percent in 1991 to 1.4 percent in 1999, before rising to 1.5 percent in 2000, 2.4 percent in 2001, 2.6 percent in 2002, 2.3 percent in 2003, and 1.9 percent (Euro area) in both 2004 and 2005. (IMF, *World Economic Outlook*, various issues.)

A very important step in the European integration process was the task of undertaking the adjustments necessary to move toward the goal of full monetary union by January 1, 1999. A series of macroeconomic criteria involving such matters as maximum ratio of public debt to GDP and permissible inflation rates, exchange rates, and interest rates were set for nations to qualify for participation. (We discuss the monetary aspects of European integration in our chapters on international monetary economics.) In May 1998, the European Council confirmed that 11 nations had fulfilled the necessary criteria to adopt the euro on January 1, 1999, which was also the date when the exchange rates of the participating currencies were irrevocably set. Greece was a late qualifier (June 2000) and was included on January 1, 2002, when the new euro banknotes and coins were introduced as the common European currency. The 12 participating members were Belgium, Germany, Greece, Spain, France, Ireland, Italy, Luxembourg, Netherlands, Austria, Portugal, and Finland. Denmark, Sweden, and the United Kingdom are members of the European Union but do not, as of this writing, participate in the single currency.[9]

Ten mostly Central and Eastern European countries joined the European Union in May 2004. As noted earlier, the accession treaties were accepted by the European Parliament in April 2003. The national parliaments of all 15 EU member states approved the expansion; in addition, each candidate country voted for membership in a referendum. All new entrants are expected to be net beneficiaries of the EU structural adjustment funds and Common Agricultural Policy subsidies. The lower per capita incomes of the accession countries could make them eligible for the highest level of subsidies, and this is very controversial because it can result in substantial redistribution away from current members.[10] The cost of the deal for the current EU states between 2004 and 2006 stands at 40.8 billion euros, 15 billion of which it will receive back as budget contributions from the new members.[11] Resistance to enlargement of the EU has been pronounced in some current member countries. The focus of the debate has long been centered on whether the organization should become "deeper" through closer integration of its existing members or whether it should get "wider" by taking in new members. On January 1, 2007, the widening continued. Bulgaria and Romania became the 26th and 27th members of the European Union. On the same day, Slovenia became the first of the Central and Eastern European nations to qualify as a euro participant. The accession of these new members creates an unprecedented "widening" eastward and will turn the EU into a totally different institution.

In overview, the integration of Europe has proceeded rapidly in historical terms since its formation by the Treaties of Rome in 1957, and there are imposing challenges facing it in the future. In viewing the process and the future prospects, it is important to realize that the increasing integration of Europe involves more than economics. There are political implications of establishing supranational institutions and of sacrificing some autonomy and sovereignty by member states. There are also cultural and social dimensions associated with the increased mobility of labor and capital and the "four freedoms" declared at the EC's formation. "Economic integration" is really much more than just "economic," and the scale of the already-attained integration in this broader sense in Europe is impressive.

---

[9]European Central Bank, *Background to the Euro,* www.euro.ecb.

[10]Rajendra K. Jain, "Eastward Enlargement of the European Union: Issues, Problems, and Challenges," presented at *The European Union in a Changing World,* September 2001, Jawaharlal Nehru University, New Delhi, India.

[11]Radio Free Europe/Radio Liberty, *EU: Enlargement Approved for 2004,* www.rterl.org, December 16, 2002.

ECONOMIC DISINTEGRATION AND TRANSITION IN CENTRAL AND EASTERN EUROPE AND THE FORMER SOVIET UNION

Two dramatic recent events with important implications for the world economy were (1) the pervasive movement beginning in early 1990 in Central and Eastern Europe away from socialism and central planning and toward capitalism and the market, and (2) the breakup of the Union of Soviet Socialist Republics (Soviet Union) into 15 independent republics in late 1991, accompanied by a move away from central planning and government resource allocation toward decentralized market economies. The precise causes of these changes will be debated for years, and they clearly involve political, sociological, psychological, and religious dimensions as well as economics. Nevertheless, low growth rates, slow rates of modernization and technological change, and generally poor economic performance under the old order were important factors.

Council for Mutual Economic Assistance

In foreign trade, the Central and Eastern European countries and the Soviet Union (with Cuba, Mongolia, and Vietnam) had been integrated through the Council for Mutual Economic Assistance (CMEA, often called Comecon). This was a markedly different form of economic integration from the other types of units we have studied in this chapter.[12] The CMEA was begun in 1949 to promote economic cooperation among the member countries as a Soviet counterpart to the Marshall Plan. For most of the CMEA's history, the greater part of its members' trade had been with other members. Table 3 shows that this was still generally true at the time of the dramatic political and economic changes. With the exception of Romania, the percent of total trade of the Central and Eastern European countries with other members of the CMEA in 1989 was high. For 1990, the percent of total trade of the 15 now independent republics of the former Soviet Union with each other indicated a pronounced interdependence among them. In addition, because about one-half of the total trade of the unified Soviet Union was with the countries of Central and Eastern Europe at the end of the CMEA in 1991, the CMEA countries were indeed somewhat independent of or insulated from the rest of the world economy.

Trade under the CMEA, in which the USSR chiefly supplied raw materials to Central and Eastern Europe in exchange for manufactured goods, was not of the general "free trade among partners" variety of typical economic integration units. Rather, the CMEA set rules for undertaking *bilateral* trading agreements. Further, within an agreement between any two countries, balanced trade was sought *within* category groupings, as well as balanced trade as a whole between the countries. A common currency for accounting for the trade flows—the "transferable ruble"—was used. Prices for goods were determined by a formula in which a world market average over a five-year period was employed and then translated into rubles (the Soviet monetary unit) at an official CMEA exchange rate. However, it appears that bargaining and bureaucratic intervention also played a role. Historically, the CMEA countries regarded trade as simply a vehicle for obtaining goods that were unavailable at home, and this made the countries relatively closed. It is also thought that the planning agencies in the countries paid little attention to any cost versus benefit aspects of trade, so the gains from open trade using comparative advantage were not realized.

Moving toward a Market Economy

The impact of the market fervor on trade flows in Central and Eastern Europe and in the republics of the former Soviet Union is difficult to assess. There has been some "disintegration" in former CMEA countries and greater integration with the rest of the world. This

---

[12]For elaboration, see Paul R. Gregory and Robert C. Stuart, *Soviet Economic Structure and Performance,* 4th ed. (New York: Harper & Row, 1990), pp. 329–32; Martin Schrenk, "Whither Comecon?" *Finance and Development* 27, no. 3 (September 1990), pp. 28–31.

TABLE 3   Shares of Internal Trade in Total Trade of Central and Eastern European
Countries and Republics of the Former Soviet Union

Central and Eastern European Countries (1989)	Trade with CMEA Countries as Percentage of Total Trade
Bulgaria	53.4%
Czechoslovakia*	47.2
Hungary	40.3
Poland	43.1
Romania	21.0

Republics of Former Soviet Union (1990)	Trade with Other Republics of Former Soviet Union as Percentage of Total Trade
Armenia	90.1%
Azerbaijan	87.7
Belarus	86.8
Estonia	91.6
Georgia	85.9
Kazakhstan	88.7
Kyrgyz Republic	85.7
Latvia	88.6
Lithuania	89.7
Moldova	87.7
Russia	60.6
Tajikistan	86.5
Turkmenistan	92.5
Ukraine	82.1
Uzbekistan	89.4

*Became the Czech Republic and the Slovak Republic (Slovakia) in 1993.
Source: Constantine Michalopoulos and David Tarr, "Energizing Trade of the States of the Former USSR," *Finance and Development* 30, no. 1 (March 1993), p. 23.

integration with the rest of the world not only can help the former CMEA members but also can be beneficial to world welfare if it improves the world's allocation of resources.

The challenges for these **transition economies** of moving into the world trading system begin with the need for a generally acceptable and convertible currency. The issue of product quality is also a major concern. Competition within the CMEA was weak to nonexistent, but opening markets to international competition is forcing domestic producers to increase the quality of their output. In addition, exporters must produce output with a combination of price and quality that can be competitive with U.S. and Western European products. Trade balances fell quickly into deficit in many transitional economies as the demand for Western imports and capital exceeded export demand. Finally, a change in system does not automatically open export markets. Decades of tension must be overcome, customers must be educated about the existence and quality of new products, and trade routes must be reopened.

The process of moving from a centrally planned economy to a market economy proved to be difficult and costly. The transition experience demonstrated that many of the costs of the transition are experienced immediately, while the benefits come much later. Three immediate problems to be dealt with are inflation, unemployment, and budget

IN THE REAL WORLD:

IMPACTS ON TRADE OF BLACK SEA REGIONAL ECONOMIC COOPERATION

The Black Sea Economic Cooperation (BSEC) zone was formed in July 1992. The BSEC was one of the first formal initiatives that sought to develop economic cooperation between countries that were once in adversarial alliances (NATO and the Warsaw Pact). The 11 members include Albania, Armenia, Azerbaijan, Bulgaria, Georgia, Greece, Moldova, Romania, Russia, Turkey, and Ukraine.

The partnership was an unusual pre-FTA that was needed to overcome some of the barriers created by the decades of in-bloc self-sufficiency and barter trade that had been encouraged by the CMEA. In 1992, only Greece and Turkey had market economies, and the other nine were in the early stages of their transition. The goal of the BSEC was to facilitate the growth of "natural" (as opposed to diverted) trade between the member nations. Rather than focusing on the reduction of tariffs and quotas, the BSEC aimed to relax structural and ideological constraints that prevented large volumes of trade between members.

Professor Sayan of Bilkent University in Turkey conducted an empirical analysis of the BSEC utilizing a "gravity model"

(discussed earlier in Chapter 10). The analysis was based on the argument that trade flows between two countries must be positively related to their economic "masses" represented by the GDP and inversely related to the distance between them. Data problems forced Sayan to limit his analysis to Greece, Romania, and Turkey over the period 1992–1994. There was no liberalization of trade policy between members and/or harmonization of policies toward third parties during this period.

The empirical results reveal that the total actual value of trade by these BSEC members to nonmembers in the sample exceeded the normally expected values over the 1993–1994 period. This suggests that the formation of the BSEC led to new trade with the outside world. All three countries enjoyed higher values of exports to/imports from other BSEC members in both 1993 and 1994 (see Table 4).

While additional study is certainly necessary, the BSEC appears to have encouraged cooperation and improved market access. It has helped its members improve their ability to link up with the global economy and create welfare gains through increased trade for its members.

TABLE 4   Estimates of Trade Creation (millions of U.S. dollars)

	New Trade with Outside World	
	Exports	*Imports*
Turkey	$317.9	$60.2
Romania	462.8	930.1
Greece	29.8	1,402.6
	Gross Trade Creation	
	Additional Exports	*Additional Imports*
Turkey	$389.1	$760.0
Romania	317.2	438.8
Greece	374.5	256.1

Source: This material is drawn from S. Sayan, "Could Regional Economic Cooperation Generate Trade Creation and Trade Diversion Effects without Altering Trade Policies of Members? Preliminary Results from a Gravity Application to BSEC," Discussion Paper No. 98-10, Bilkent University Department of Economics, Ankara, Turkey, 1998.

deficits. Under central planning, prices on many necessities were kept intentionally low, and shortages resulted in long lines and empty shelves rather than price increases. Guaranteed employment and centralized resource allocation resulted in firms with

TABLE 5   Inflation Experience in Transition Economies, 1995–2005 (Annual Percentage Change in Consumer Prices)

European Union Members

	1995	*1996*	*1997*	*1998*	*1999*	*2000*	*2001*	*2002*	*2003*	*2004*	*2005*
Bulgaria	62.1	123.0	1,061.2	18.8	2.6	10.4	7.5	5.8	2.3	6.1	5.0
Czech Republic	9.1	8.8	8.5	10.6	2.1	3.9	4.8	1.8	0.1	2.8	1.8
Estonia	29.0	23.1	11.2	8.2	3.3	4.0	5.8	3.6	1.3	3.0	4.1
Hungary	28.3	23.5	18.3	14.3	10.0	9.8	9.2	5.3	4.7	6.8	3.6
Latvia	25.2	17.6	8.4	4.6	2.4	2.6	2.5	1.9	2.9	6.2	6.8
Lithuania	39.5	24.7	8.8	5.1	0.8	1.0	1.3	0.3	−1.2	1.2	2.7
Poland	27.9	27.9	19.9	14.9	11.8	7.3	10.1	5.5	1.9	0.8	2.1
Romania	32.3	38.8	154.8	59.1	45.8	45.7	34.5	22.5	15.3	11.9	9.0
Slovak Republic	9.9	5.8	6.1	6.7	10.7	12.0	7.3	3.3	8.5	7.5	2.7
Slovenia	13.5	9.9	8.4	7.9	6.2	8.9	8.4	7.5	5.6	3.6	2.5
Remaining Transition Countries											
Albania	7.8	12.7	32.1	20.9	0.4	—	3.1	5.2	2.3	2.9	2.4
Armenia	176.7	18.7	14.0	8.6	0.6	−0.8	3.1	1.1	4.8	7.0	0.6
Azerbaijan	411.8	19.8	3.7	−0.8	−8.5	1.8	1.5	2.8	2.2	6.7	9.7
Belarus	709.3	52.7	63.8	73.0	293.7	168.6	61.1	42.6	28.4	18.1	10.3
Bosnia/Herzegovina	3.8	−11.5	5.6	−0.4	2.9	5.0	3.2	0.3	0.1	0.3	1.9
Croatia	2.0	3.5	3.6	5.7	4.1	6.2	4.9	2.3	1.5	2.1	3.3
Georgia	162.7	39.3	7.0	3.6	19.1	4.0	4.7	5.6	4.8	5.7	8.3
Kazakhstan	176.3	39.1	17.4	7.3	8.4	13.3	8.3	5.9	6.4	6.9	7.6
Kyrgyz Republic	43.5	32.0	23.4	10.5	35.9	18.7	6.9	2.1	2.7	4.1	4.3
Macedonia	15.8	2.3	2.6	−0.1	−0.7	5.8	5.3	2.4	1.2	0.1	0.5
Moldova	30.2	23.5	11.8	7.7	39.7	31.3	9.8	5.3	11.7	12.5	11.9
Mongolia	56.8	46.8	36.6	9.4	7.6	11.6	6.3	0.9	5.0	7.9	12.5
Russia	198.0	47.9	14.7	27.8	85.7	20.8	21.6	15.8	13.7	10.9	12.8
Tajikistan	610.0	418.2	88.0	43.2	27.5	32.9	38.6	12.2	16.4	7.1	7.1
Turkmenistan	1,005.2	992.4	83.7	16.8	23.5	8.0	11.6	—	—	5.9	10.7
Ukraine	376.4	80.2	15.9	10.6	22.7	28.2	12.0	0.8	5.2	9.0	13.5
Uzbekistan	304.6	54.0	70.9	16.7	44.6	49.5	47.5	44.3	14.8	8.8	21.0

— = not available

Source: International Monetary Fund (IMF), *World Economic Outlook,* database 1995–2006 (Washington, DC: IMF, 2007).

excess labor. Federal governments that were dependent on the turnover tax[13] were forced to develop new systems of income and consumption taxes.

In the early stages of the transition, several notable events occurred. For example, the freeing of prices from government control resulted in serious inflation. As seen in Table 5, many of the transitional nations experienced annual rates of inflation rates of more than 100 percent. Further, the pressure to cover costs of production and be profitable that comes with the movement to a market system forced firms to release their unnecessary workers. This resulted in unemployment rate in excess of 20 percent in nations that had no history of dealing with unemployment. The need to provide a safety net for newly unemployed workers and pensioners; cover the losses of unprofitable, state-owned enterprises; and meet the continuing obligations of the state with a shrinking tax base results in budget deficits. In addition, tremendous

---

[13]In a centrally planned economy with one national bank, a percentage of every transaction is allocated to the government. This was known as a turnover tax.

TABLE 6   Real GDP Experience in Transition Economies, 1995–2005 (Annual Percentage Change in Real GDP)

	1995	1996	1997	1998	1999	2000	2001	2002	2003	2004	2005
EU Members											
Bulgaria	−1.8	−8.0	−5.6	4.0	2.3	5.4	4.1	4.8	4.3	5.0	5.2
Czech Republic	5.9	4.3	−0.8	−1.0	0.5	3.3	3.1	2.0	2.9	3.0	3.4
Estonia	4.3	3.9	9.8	4.6	−0.6	7.3	6.5	6.0	4.7	5.5	5.0
Hungary	1.5	1.3	4.6	4.9	4.2	5.2	3.8	3.5	2.9	3.2	3.4
Latvia	−0.8	3.7	8.4	4.8	2.8	6.8	7.9	6.1	6.7	6.0	6.0
Lithuania	3.3	4.7	7.0	7.3	−1.7	3.9	6.4	6.8	9.0	6.7	6.3
Poland	6.8	6.0	6.8	4.8	4.1	4.0	1.0	1.4	3.7	4.7	4.0
Romania	7.3	3.9	−6.1	−4.8	−1.2	2.1	5.7	5.0	4.9	5.0	5.0
Slovakia	6.5	6.1	4.6	4.2	1.5	2.0	3.8	4.4	4.2	3.9	4.9
Slovenia	4.9	3.8	4.4	3.7	5.9	4.1	2.9	2.9	2.3	3.5	4.1
Remaining Transition Countries											
Albania	8.9	9.1	−10.2	12.7	10.1	7.3	7.6	4.7	6.0	6.0	6.0
Armenia	6.9	5.9	3.3	7.3	3.3	6.0	9.6	12.9	12.0	7.0	6.0
Azerbaijan	−11.8	1.3	5.8	10.0	7.4	11.1	9.9	10.6	11.2	8.1	13.2
Belarus	−10.4	2.8	11.4	8.4	3.4	5.8	4.7	5.0	6.8	4.8	3.5
Bosnia/Herzogovina	16.4	61.9	30.0	15.8	9.6	5.5	4.4	5.5	5.5	3.0	4.0
Croatia	6.8	5.9	6.8	2.5	−0.9	2.9	3.8	5.2	4.4	3.4	3.8
Georgia	2.6	10.5	10.6	2.9	3.0	1.9	4.7	5.5	3.5	6.0	5.0
Kazakhstan	−8.3	0.5	1.6	−1.9	2.7	9.8	13.5	9.5	9.5	8.0	7.5
Kyrgyz Republic	−5.8	7.1	9.9	2.1	3.7	5.4	5.3	−0.5	3.2	4.1	4.5
Macedonia	−1.1	1.2	1.4	3.4	4.3	4.5	−4.5	0.9	3.1	4.0	4.5
Moldova	−1.4	−5.9	1.6	−6.5	−3.4	2.1	6.1	7.8	6.3	5.0	4.0
Mongolia	6.3	2.4	4.0	3.5	3.2	1.1	1.0	3.9	5.0	5.3	5.5
Russia	−4.2	−3.6	1.4	−5.3	6.3	10.0	5.1	4.7	7.3	6.0	5.3
Tajikistan	−12.5	−4.4	1.7	5.3	3.7	8.3	10.2	9.1	10.2	8.0	4.0
Turkmenistan	−7.2	−6.7	−11.3	7.0	16.5	18.0	20.5	—	—	3.0	3.0
Ukraine	−12.2	−10.0	−3.0	−1.9	−0.2	5.9	9.2	5.2	9.3	6.0	4.0
Uzbekistan	−0.9	1.6	2.5	2.1	3.4	3.2	4.1	3.2	0.3	2.0	2.0

— = not available

Sources: International Monetary Fund (IMF), *World Economic Outlook,* March 2007 (Washington, DC: IMF, 2007).

problems have been encountered as state enterprises are privatized by sale to citizens in an environment lacking well-developed capital markets and a modern banking system.[14]

A detailed look at the two important macroeconomic variables, the growth rate of real GDP, and the inflation rate of consumer prices is provided in Tables 5 and 6. In Table 5, the effect of price decentralization can be seen. In many nations, the initial inflation was compounded by excessive money growth (monetary issues will be discussed later in the international monetary economics chapters). Most of the nations began to get inflation under control by the mid- to late 1990s. Table 6 indicates that the declines in the level of real GDP that were associated with the early stages of transition had ceased in the EU accession countries by 1995, and they had begun positive growth. The remaining transitional economies, particularly Russia and Central Asia,

---

[14]For a useful discussion of early problems, see "Rediscovering the Wheel," *The Economist,* April 14, 1990, pp. 19–21.

TABLE 7   GDP per Capita in Transition Economies, 2005 (U.S. dollars, PPP)

Country	GDP		Country	GDP
Slovenia	$22,160		Belarus	$7,890
Czech Republic	20,140		Kazakhstan	7,730
Hungary	16,940		Macedonia	7,080
Slovak Republic	15,760		Ukraine	6,720
Estonia	15,420		Albania	5,420
Lithuania	14,220		Armenia	5,060
Poland	13,490		Azerbaijan	4,890
Latvia	13,480		Georgia	3,270
Croatia	12,750		Mongolia	2,190
Russian Federation	10,640		Moldova	2,150
Romania	8,940		Uzbekistan	2,020
Bulgaria	8,630		Kyrgyz Republic	1,870
Turkmenistan*	8,098		Tajikistan	1,260

*2004; obtained from www.imf.org
Source: World Bank, *World Development Indicators 2007* (Washington, DC: World Bank, 2005, pp.14–16.)

were a little slower to return to positive growth. An important point is often missed when examining the changes in real GDP for transitional nations: The declines in real GDP associated with the early stages of the transition involved the privatization (and, in many cases, closing) of formerly state-owned enterprises. When the economies returned to positive growth and eventually reached their 1988–1989 levels of real GDP, the output produced was of a higher quality, and it was produced in a more efficient manner.

Clearly, there have been important improvements in macroeconomic performance since the dismal early 1990s, when the transition economies first began the adoption of market-economy institutions and practices. Table 7 lists GDP per capita for transition economies in 2005. (Note: The figures in Table 7 are given in *purchasing-power-parity* dollars, meaning that cost-of-living differences across countries have been adjusted for and the results have been expressed in U.S. dollars. Purchasing power parity is discussed in later chapters covering international monetary economics.)

Finally, in examining the comparative performances of the transition economies the World Bank (1996, pp. 142–45) indicated some general conclusions. These conclusions emphasized that success is more likely (1) when consistent policies regarding liberalization of markets, trade, and new business entry are followed; (2) when private property rights are clearly defined; and (3) when social policy reform with respect to poverty programs, education, and health care takes place. However, we emphasize that the process is not easy and that there are many short-run difficulties. Assurances by economists of long-run benefits despite short-run costs sound hollow if poor economic performance continues and the "short run" never seems to end. In overview, the ongoing transitions in the economies of Central and Eastern Europe and the former Soviet Union constitute a tumultuous event in the world economy that will be continuing for years. These transitions to market economies have implications for world trade, welfare, and stability, but the timing and precise nature of those implications are uncertain at the present time.

NORTH AMERICAN ECONOMIC INTEGRATION

Greater Integration

A widely hailed movement toward economic integration occurred when the **Canada–U.S. Free Trade Agreement** went into effect on January 1, 1989. It called for the elimination of all bilateral tariffs between the two countries either immediately or in 5 or 10 equal annual steps. The momentum toward greater regional free trade continued soon after the Canada–U.S. accord. The executive branches of the governments of Canada, Mexico, and the United States signed the North American Free Trade Agreement (NAFTA) in August 1992, agreeing to create a free-trade area with a combined GDP comparable to that of the EU and EFTA combined which, at the time, had a GDP of $7.5 trillion and a population of 372 million.[15] This agreement took effect on January 1, 1994, and established free trade between the United States and its first- and third-largest trading partners.[16] NAFTA eliminates tariffs among the three member countries over a 15-year period and at the same time substantially reduces nontariff barriers. Because the United States and Canada already had established a free-trade area, this discussion will focus on U.S.–Mexican policy steps. Several of the more important sector agreements involved automobiles, textiles and apparel, agriculture, energy/petrochemicals, and financial services (Kehoe and Kehoe 1994, p. 21). In the case of automobiles, Mexican tariffs were immediately reduced from 20 to 10 percent and were scheduled to decline to zero over the next 10 years. In addition, tariffs on auto parts were to be reduced to zero, and rules of origin specified that to qualify for preferential tariff treatment, vehicles must contain 62.5 percent North American content. Further, the requirement that autos supplying the Mexican market be produced in Mexico was to be gradually eliminated over a 10-year period. There was also additional easing of export restrictions on Mexican-produced vehicles and on Mexican imports of U.S. or Canadian produced buses and trucks.

In the textile and apparel industry, trade barriers were eliminated on 20 percent of U.S.–Mexican trade, and barriers on an additional 60 percent were removed over a 6-year period. In addition, rules of origin required that to receive NAFTA tariff preferences, apparel must be manufactured in North America from the yarn-spinning stage forward. In agriculture, tariffs were immediately reduced from initial levels of 10 to 20 percent to zero for one-half of U.S. exports to Mexico, with the understanding that the tariffs on the remaining agricultural products will be reduced to zero over the 15-year adjustment period. Mexico's licensing requirements for grain, dairy, and poultry were immediately eliminated. Similarly, trade and investment restrictions were eliminated immediately on most petrochemicals.

With respect to foreign investment and financial services in general, all barriers to the movement of capital were immediately dropped. In addition, Mexico's restrictions on Canadian and U.S. ownership and provision of commercial banking, insurance, securities trading, and other financial services were to be removed. Finally, U.S. and Canadian financial firms are now permitted to establish wholly owned subsidiaries in Mexico and to operate them in the same manner as Mexican firms operate. In like manner, Canada, Mexico, and the United States are to extend "national treatment" in services to each other, meaning that foreign-owned service firms are treated exactly like domestic firms, and to guarantee

---

[15]*Facts on File,* January 13, 1994, p. 12.

[16]Canada was and is the largest U.S. trading partner. Mexico was third behind Japan at the time NAFTA began; it is now third behind China.

IN THE REAL WORLD:

POLAND AND RUSSIA IN TRANSITION: A STUDY IN CONTRASTS

Both Poland and Russia have been involved in a transition from a centrally planned economy to a more market-oriented economic system for more or less the past 15 years. In Poland, the first major reform, known as the Balcerowicz Plan, was initiated in January 1990. This was a major movement toward a market-directed economy in that it abolished price controls, removed foreign exchange restrictions, devalued the Polish zloty and pegged it to the U.S. dollar, legalized private ownership of businesses and assets, reduced subsidies, and taxed firms where wages rose by more than 30 percent above the rate of inflation.* In the process, inflation soared, GDP declined, unemployment rose, and the exchange rate depreciated in 1990. Unemployment continued to rise through 1994 to 16 percent and then began to decline. Other economic variables began to improve in one or two years, and economic conditions continued to improve throughout the 1990s. If one considers sustainable recovery or growth in output as an indicator of success of economic transition, Poland has done relatively well. As indicated in Table 8, GDP grew at an average annual rate of 4.5 percent for the critical period from 1990 to 1998, gross domestic investment by 10.6 percent, and exports by 12.3 percent. Strong export growth resulted in part from the depreciation of the zloty from 9,500 zloty per U.S. dollar in 1990 to 34,754 zloty per U.S. dollar in 1998. Although the average annual growth rate of inflation (27 percent) appears high, it must be emphasized that the highest rate of inflation occurred in 1990 (586 percent) and that after that time the rate of inflation steadily declined to only 13 percent in 1997. New economic reforms, designed to complete the process that began in 1990, were announced in 2002. The package was designed to prepare the Polish economy for entry into the European Union by improving the investment climate. The government is also trying to improve public finances in preparation for adoption of the euro as early as 2009.

A similar story cannot be told for Russia. The Russians initiated a "shock therapy" program in January 1992 under the direction of the minister of finance, Yegor Gaidar. Prices on nearly all basic commodities were decontrolled, state subsidies and military spending were cut to reduce the government budget deficit, a privatization program was implemented, and the ruble was made partially convertible. The result was difficult at best for Russia. GDP *declined* at an annual average rate of 7 percent during the comparable 1990–1998 period when Poland was growing by an average 4.5 percent per year. The annual rate of inflation over the 1990–1998 period was 235.3 percent, and gross domestic investment declined at an annual rate of 14.8 percent. Only exports demonstrated a positive rate of growth over that period, due in large part to the depreciation of the ruble from 1.7 rubles per U.S. dollar in 1990 to 20,650 rubles per U.S. dollar in 1998.

Not surprisingly, observers have questioned why the transition from a centrally planned economic system to a more market-oriented system triggered such different initial responses in these two countries. Economically, repressive financial policies in Russia (and former Soviet economies in general) have been blamed for many of the transition problems. However, much of the answer seemed to lie in institutional characteristics of the two countries during this time of change. As Yeager suggested, "Poland has managed to create an environment in which the rules of the game are adequately spelled out, in which most people follow the rules so that uncertainty is manageable, and in which transaction costs are reasonably low. Russia has an economy plagued by crime, corruption, and high transaction costs."† In Russia, people appeared to feel that the *operating rules* were unfair and consequently tried to cheat the system. The Russian economy began to recover in 1999. From 1999 to 2005, Russian GDP grew by an average of 6.7 percent (see Table 6), assisted by higher oil prices and a weaker ruble. By 2004, the Russian economy had become the ninth largest in the world and the fifth largest in Europe. Russia appears to have overcome many of the earlier obstacles to transition.

TABLE 8   Key Average Annual Growth Rates for Poland and Russia in the 1990–1998 Transition Period

	Real GDP	GDP Deflator	Exchange Rate	Exports	Gross Domestic Investment
Poland	4.5%	27.0%	16.2%	12.3%	10.6%
Russia	−7.0	235.3	117.6	2.0	−14.8

*Timothy J. Yeager, *Institutions, Transition Economies, and Economic Development* (Boulder, CO: Westview Press, 1999), p. 88.
†Ibid., p. 105.
Sources: Timothy J. Yeager, *Institutions, Transitional Economies, and Economic Development* (Boulder, CO: Westview Press, 1999); Yegor Gaidar, "Lessons of the Russian Crisis for Transition Economies," *Finance and Development* 36, no. 2 (June 1999), pp. 6–9; International Monetary Fund, *International Financial Statistics,* January 2000, pp. 616, 634; The World Bank, *World Development Report 1999/2000* (Oxford: Oxford University Press, 2000), pp. 231, 251; International Monetary Fund, *World Economic Outlook: May 2000* (Washington, DC: IMF, 2000), p. 213; Patrick Conway, "Financial Repression in Transition: Output Reduction and Hyperinflation in the Former Soviet Economies," unpublished working paper, University of North Carolina, at Chapel Hill, 2000.

MFN treatment in services. Agriculture is also an important part of the agreement. (See Aguilar 1993, pp. 14–15.) NAFTA was the first regional agreement among countries with such diverse income levels, and an important aspect of the agreement was the anticipated reinforcement that it would give to the strong growth that Mexico had achieved at the time of NAFTA formation since adopting structural, market-oriented reforms in the mid-1980s.

Worries over NAFTA   The impact of NAFTA on the three participating economies has been hotly debated, and there have been widely varying estimates of the potential effects. A study by the U.S. International Trade Commission (USITC) concluded that NAFTA would cause Mexico's real GDP to increase by anywhere from 0.1 to 11.4 percent (a wide range!), while Canadian and U.S. real GDPs would each rise by less than 0.5 percent.[17] Drusilla Brown (1992, p. 47) surveyed the estimates of various models that had increasing returns to scale incorporated into the estimates. NAFTA would raise Canadian GNP in a range from 0.7 to 6.75 percent, Mexican GNP from 1.6 to 5.0 percent, and U.S. GNP from 0.5 to 2.55 percent.

Estimates of the employment effects also varied. A study by Gary Clyde Hufbauer and Jeffrey J. Schott (1992, p. 58) estimated that NAFTA would create 609,000 jobs in Mexico and 130,000 jobs in the United States, and Mickey Kantor, the Clinton administration's trade representative at the time, predicted that the United States would gain 200,000 industrial jobs by 1995.[18] However, even though the most pessimistic forecasts for the United States had been for a job loss of 500,000, presidential candidate Ross Perot created a stir in 1993 by saying that almost 6 million U.S. jobs would be put at risk.[19] One reason for widely differing employment estimates is that the effects of NAFTA on foreign investment flows from the United States to Mexico are very uncertain. U.S. firms have invested extensively in Mexico in the past in connection with the ***maquiladora* program,** and many think NAFTA gave a stimulus to further investment because of lower wages in Mexico. In addition, the agreement provided various other incentives for U.S. firms to invest in Mexico. However, recall from Chapters 8 and 12 that goods movements and factor movements can be substitutes for each other; if so, with freer trade, U.S. investment flows, other things equal, could theoretically *decrease.*

The precise size of other impacts of NAFTA is also questionable. Sectoral impacts on Mexican–U.S. trade and changes in U.S. regional employment have occurred. While the USITC estimated a positive impact on wages in all three countries (0.7 to 16.2 percent for Mexico, 0.5 percent or less in Canada, 0.3 percent or less in the United States),[20] there has been considerable concern that lower wages in the United States may result. Without dynamic effects such as faster economic growth and technological change, of course, the factor price equalization theorem (see Chapter 8) would lead us to expect some general narrowing of the wage differentials (fall in wages in the labor-scarce country, rise in labor-abundant country). The process can be more complicated, however, when three countries rather than two are involved. Finally, although NAFTA is now in place, it is too early to evaluate the long-term effects. Nevertheless, it is without question that NAFTA has led to a shift of unskilled jobs from the United States to Mexico. In the low-unemployment period in the late 1990s and again in more recent years (less than 5 percent in 2007), however, jobs were available for many (though not all) of the displaced workers.

---

[17]Cited in Asra Q. Nomani, "Mexico Is Viewed as the Clear Winner from Free Trade Pact in Study by ITC," *The Wall Street Journal,* February 3, 1993, p. A2.

[18]"Kantor Predicts Jobs Gain from Mexico Trade Pact," *The Wall Street Journal,* May 7, 1993, p. A11.

[19]Ross Perot (with Pat Choate), *Save Your Job, Save Our Country: Why NAFTA Must Be Stopped Now!* (New York: Hyperion, 1993), p. 56.

[20]Nomani, "Mexico Is Viewed as the Clear Winner," p. A2.

IN THE REAL WORLD:

THE MEXICAN MAQUILADORAS

In 1965, Mexico inaugurated the idea of industrial parks *(maquiladoras)* on the U.S.–Mexican border that were permitted to contain plants *(maquilas)* that were partly or totally foreign owned. (Foreign ownership of industry in Mexico other than in the *maquiladoras* was severely restricted at that time.) Many of these plants initially served as assembly operations for U.S. firms, allowing them to take advantage of lower-cost Mexican labor. The components coming into these plants from the United States entered Mexico duty free, and the finished goods that were reexported to the United States faced only a customs duty on the value added in Mexico, falling under the offshore assembly provisions. Originally, all production had to be located on the border and all goods had to be exported from Mexico, but these requirements have now been relaxed. The removal of barriers to trade by NAFTA has also reduced the need to rely on offshore assembly provisions for goods to move more freely between the United States and Mexico. Consequently, it has been expected that there will be increased movement away from the border areas to plant locations deeper inside Mexico. This has already started happening, and areas such as Aguascalientes, northwest of Mexico City, and Hermosillo are showing rapid expansion of foreign investment and manufacturing in autos and auto parts, semiconductors, electronics, and apparel.

Initially focusing on basic assembly operations, the *maquilas* now assemble complex finished products, and the production workers are some of the most skilled in Mexico. The *maquilas* are owned by medium and small firms as well as large firms such as Ford, General Motors, Chrysler, Sony, GE, and Hitachi; most *maquilas* are of U.S. origin, but there are some Canadian, Japanese, and European firms. Since 1994, dozens of Asian manufacturers have also initiated some $2 billion in direct investment in massive assembly plants along the 700-mile U.S.–Mexican border between Tijuana and Ciudad Juarez. The sources of these funds include China, the Republic of Korea, and Taiwan, and the investments reflect not only the perceived benefits of access to U.S. and Canadian markets provided in NAFTA but also the advantages associated with the convenient assembly/market location and lower labor costs. In addition, European Union investors have shown interest in Mexico since the concluding of an EU–Mexico free trade agreement in 1999.

The *maquiladoras* construct and maintain the physical facilities, recruit, train and pay the Mexican labor, and deal with all relationships between the *maquilas* and state and local governments. The foreign owner takes care of the production and business aspects of the operation. The *maquiladora* facilitates operation of production in Mexico chiefly for small- to medium-sized firms that otherwise might find it difficult to operate in a different cultural milieu. As a result of these industrial parks, Mexico has obtained a much larger amount of foreign investment and considerable domestic employment. U.S. firms that might have gone out of business are able to stay competitive because of the lower *maquila* assembly costs, thus maintaining or increasing the demand for U.S. component parts and the skilled and semiskilled labor that produce them. For example, more than $1 billion of the jeans that U.S. companies such as Levi Strauss and VF Corporation market in a year will be assembled in Mexico in Torreon or Puebla, with denim woven in North Carolina or Georgia using U.S.-grown cotton. It has been estimated that, early in 1999, manufactures accounted for 90 percent of Mexican exports and that more than half were produced in foreign-owned assembly plants. These ventures were so successful that it has been estimated that the *maquiladoras* were running a $1 billion surplus per month with the United States alone. This helps to explain partly how Mexican exports to the United States more than doubled from 1994 to 1998. Overall, employment at *maquiladora* plants also more than doubled from 1993 to 2000, although wages in the plants rose hardly at all.

The 2001 recession in the United States had a serious impact on Mexico's *maquiladora* industry. From a high point in 2000, the industry's contraction included a loss of almost 260,000 jobs. While reductions in U.S. demand and increases in the cost of doing business (due to wage and exchange rate fluctuations) explain a considerable portion of this downturn, other factors were at work. The low wages and tax incentives that were advantages of operating in Mexico are now offered in a number of developing countries. In addition, a new NAFTA rule went into effect in 2001 that made *maquiladora* operations more difficult, costly, and uncertain in Mexico. NAFTA Article 303 outlawed tariff rebates for imports from non-NAFTA countries. For firms that imported from Asia for assembly in Mexico and subsequent export to the United States, Article 303 made Mexican operations more expensive overnight. The resulting incentives to take jobs elsewhere appear to have been strongest in electronics and textiles.

IN THE REAL WORLD: *(continued)*

In general, the success of the *maquiladora* program raised some new issues. While grasping the importance of the *maquiladora* as a vehicle for stimulating foreign investment, employment, and exports, Mexico has felt pressure on its domestic infrastructure of the rapid growth in these manufacturing endeavors. Strains are also being experienced in education, public safety, water treatment, and other components of social infrastructure in the border areas and other urban areas where the new assembly plants and satellite industries are springing up.

Sources: Linda M. Aguilar, "NAFTA: A Review of the Issues," Federal Reserve Bank of Chicago, *Economic Perspectives* (January/February 1993), p. 16; Peter F. Drucker, "Mexico's Ugly Duckling—the Maquiladora," *The Wall Street Journal,* October 4, 1990, p. A20; Joel Millman, "Asian Investment Floods into Mexican Border Region,"

The Wall Street Journal, September 6, 1996, p. A10; Matt Moffett, "Along Its U.S. Border, Mexico Experiences North's Economic Ills," *The Wall Street Journal,* January 14, 1991, pp. A1, A9; Julien Beltrame and Joel Millman, "U.S. Trade Gap's New Culprits: Canada, Mexico," *The Wall Street Journal,* July 20, 1999, p. A16; Joel Millman, "Mexico, U.S. Near Tax Deal on Foreign Plants," *The Wall Street Journal,* October 29, 1999, p. A15; "EU and Mexico Reach Free-Trade Pact," *The Wall Street Journal,* November 26, 1999, p. A9; Joel Millman, "Mexico Replaces Investments Lost to U.S. Slowdown," *The Wall Street Journal,* March 2, 2001, p. A9; Joel Millman, "Mexican Workers Along U.S. Border Grow Restive with Low Wages," *The Wall Street Journal,* June 13, 2001, p. A17; Roberto Coronado, Jesus Canas, and Robert W. Gilmer, "Maquiladora Downturn: Structural Change or Cyclical Factors?" *International Business and Economics Journal,* August 2004; William C. Gruben, "Beyond the Border Have Mexico's Maquiladoras Bottomed Out?" *Southwest Economy* (January/February 2004) (Federal Reserve Bank of Dallas).

In addition, it has been noted that not only have U.S. companies benefited from shifting their unskilled work outside the country with consequent lower labor costs but such a shift has also freed up funds for new technology as well as freed up U.S. labor to take on more skilled work.[21] Finally, although more time may be needed to evaluate many of NAFTA's effects, some attempts have been made to determine the impact of the agreement's implementation on the trade flows among the partner countries. After 10 years under the agreement, Russell L. Frisbie of the U.S. Department of State has the following views on the impact of NAFTA:

> The results are impressive in trade, investment, job creation and improved standards of living. Trade among the three NAFTA nations expanded quickly, more than doubling between 1993 and 2002. At the end of last year, U.S. two-way trade (merchandise exports plus imports) with its NAFTA partners amounted to more than $600 billion, or about $1.6 billion each day. Trade growth was particularly strong between the U.S. and Mexico, almost tripling from $81 billion in 1993 to $232 billion in 2002 . . . Canada and Mexico together take 37 percent of all worldwide U.S. exports and supply 30 percent of all U.S. imports.[22]

A prominent objection to NAFTA is that it pays insufficient attention to the environmental damage that may occur as production increases in Mexico with its lower environmental standards and enforcement than those in the United States or Canada. However, there is no consensus on this point; several studies suggest that negative environmental externalities might be less under NAFTA than under a continuation of the pre-NAFTA trading arrangements. Other objections occurred over lower labor standards in Mexico

---

[21]See Joel Millman, "Job Shift to Mexico Lets U.S. Firms Upgrade," *The Wall Street Journal,* November 15, 1999, p. A28.

[22]Russell L. Frisbie, "The Impact of NAFTA—A U.S. Perspective," speech delivered on March 12, 2003, and obtained from www.usembassy.at/en/embassy/photo/nafta_frisbie.htm.

IN THE REAL WORLD:

THE EFFECTS OF NAFTA ON NORTH AMERICAN TRADE

Although a long time has not elapsed since the formation of NAFTA at the beginning of 1994, and in fact the tariff reductions have not all been fully implemented yet, a persistent question among observers has been, "What have been the economic effects of NAFTA?" In response, attempts have been made to ascertain the impacts, attempts that either utilize the limited data on actual events since NAFTA or forecast effects on the basis of pre-NAFTA information. In this case study, we focus on two papers that attempted to determine the impact on trade flows of that free-trade agreement; only when the effects on trade flows are clear can economists begin to address the larger questions of the impacts on such variables as production, employment, income distribution, and welfare.

David M. Gould (1998) of the Federal Reserve Bank of Dallas tried to provide quantitative figures on the actual effects of NAFTA on trade during the first three years of operation of the agreement. He developed equations to explain exports and imports among the three countries. For example, imports of one of the countries from each of the two others were made a function of country price levels, real GDPs, and the relevant exchange rate. Additional terms were then introduced into the equations to represent the initiation of NAFTA. (Note: Gould's equations were of the gravity-model type discussed at the end of Chapter 10.) The intent of the particular formulation of the equations was to determine whether or not the growth rates of the six trade flows were altered during the first three years of NAFTA in comparison with the rates in pre-NAFTA years. (The six trade flows are U.S. imports from Canada, U.S. imports from Mexico, Canadian imports from the United States, Canadian imports from Mexico, Mexican imports from the United States, and Mexican imports from Canada.) Gould's statistical estimating equations covered the years 1980–1996, with the last three years being the NAFTA period.

In his statistical work, Gould estimated that, on average, U.S. exports to Mexico grew 16.3 percent faster per year with NAFTA in place as compared to what would have happened without NAFTA; U.S. imports from Mexico had a figure of 16.2 percent faster growth per year. Further, Gould noted that there was high statistical significance associated with these figures. With respect to U.S.–Canada trade, he estimated that U.S. exports to Canada grew 8.6 percent faster with NAFTA than they would have done without NAFTA, and U.S. imports from Canada grew 3.9 percent

faster. However, in his estimations, these results were not statistically significant, meaning that there was no demonstrated effect of NAFTA on U.S.–Canada trade. This is not surprising, because the United States and Canada have had a free-trade agreement with each other in effect since the beginning of 1989. Finally, there was no noticeable effect of NAFTA on trade between Canada and Mexico, probably because trade between the two countries is a small share of their total trade. Gould even suggests that the effect of NAFTA might have been negative, meaning that the agreement might have caused some Canadian imports from Mexico to now be purchased from the United States.

Another study, by David Karemera and Kalu Ojah (1998), carried the investigation of trade effects further by looking specifically at possible trade creation and trade diversion. Unlike Gould's approach, however, this study was anticipatory—indicating, on the basis of past information, what *might* happen with NAFTA rather than what had already happened in the brief history of NAFTA. The Karemera and Ojah study was carried out at the microeconomic industry level. They first estimated trade creation in any given industry by utilizing pre-NAFTA trade values, import-demand elasticities (which they calculated from import-demand equations that they constructed), and the size of NAFTA tariff reductions in the particular industry being examined. The trade diversion equations in general utilized data on imports of any given product from non-NAFTA countries, import-competing home production, import-demand elasticities, and the tariff rate reductions with NAFTA. These creation and diversion calculations were done for various industries in the six NAFTA trade flows, with the particular commodities being used depending on which trade flow was being examined. The selected products accounted (in 1990–1992) for 20 percent of U.S. imports from Canada, 23 percent of U.S. imports from Mexico, 6 percent of Canadian imports from the United States, 24 percent of Canadian imports from Mexico, 7 percent of Mexican imports from the United States, and 12 percent of Mexican imports from Canada.

Table 9 presents the results of the estimations by Karemera and Ojah of what might be expected from NAFTA. The column "Trade Expansion" is the total expected impact on the trade of the selected products; this, in turn, as will be recalled from customs union theory earlier in this chapter, can be divided into "trade creation" and "trade diversion." For example, in the table, the flow of U.S. imports from

IN THE REAL WORLD: *(continued)*

Canada is expected to expand by $1.074 billion, with $690 million of that trade expansion representing trade creation and $384 million representing trade diversion—imports that previously came into the United States from other countries but now will come from Canada. U.S. imports from Mexico are expected to rise by $335 million, and again trade creation is larger than trade diversion. Further, Canadian imports from the United States in the selected commodities will also undergo greater creation than diversion, as will

Mexican imports from the United States. Note, however, that NAFTA is expected to have a *substantial* excess of trade diversion over trade creation in the cases of Canadian imports from Mexico and Mexican imports from Canada. Clearly, if such estimates are anywhere near the mark, outside-world suppliers of the goods involved (e.g., paper and paperboard, automatic data processing equipment, internal-combustion piston engines) will not be pleased with the effects of NAFTA.

TABLE 9   Estimated Effects of NAFTA on Trade Flows (thousands of U.S. dollars)

Trade Flow	Trade Expansion	Trade Creation	Trade Diversion
U.S. imports from Canada	$1,074,186	$689,997	$384,189
U.S. imports from Mexico	334,912	284,774	50,138
Canadian imports from the United States	63,656	38,444	25,212
Canadian imports from Mexico	167,264	3,321	163,943
Mexican imports from the United States	77,687	50,036	27,651
Mexican imports from Canada	28,001	902	27,099

Source: David Karemera and Kalu Ojah, "An Industrial Analysis of Trade Creation and Diversion Effects of NAFTA," *Journal of Economic Integration* 13, no. 3 (September 1998), pp. 419–20.
Sources: David M. Gould, "Has NAFTA Changed North American Trade?" Federal Reserve Bank of Dallas *Economic Review,* First Quarter 1998, pp. 12–23; David Karemera and Kalu Ojah, "An Industrial Analysis of Trade Creation and Diversion Effects of NAFTA," *Journal of Economic Integration* 13, no. 3 (September 1998), pp. 400–25.

(e.g., less restrictive workplace safety laws) and the possibilities of large "import surges" as the agreement was implemented. Because of these labor-standard and environmental objections, two side agreements accompanied NAFTA. The North American Agreement on Labor Cooperation created an atmosphere of cooperation among NAFTA's members on labor issues, and it has provided for oversight and enforcement of labor laws. Violations of labor laws, such as in two cases where Mexican firms did not allow Mexican unions to vote by secret ballot, are now brought out into the open, thereby permitting correction. In addition, in the 1990s, Mexico increased its financing for the enforcement of labor laws. With respect to environmental protection, the environmental side agreement has facilitated certification and financing of infrastructure projects that will improve the environment along the 2,000-mile Mexican–U.S. border. Further, the NAFTA Commission for Environmental Cooperation has led to greater cooperation on various issues, such as illegal trade in hazardous wastes, endangered wildlife, and elimination of pesticides and some toxic chemicals.[23]

---

[23]U.S. Trade Representative, "Executive Summary" of *Study on the Operation and Effect of the North American Free Trade Agreement* (Washington, DC: U.S. Government Printing Office, 1997), obtained from www.ustr.gov.

OTHER MAJOR ECONOMIC INTEGRATION EFFORTS

MERCOSUR

In 1991 Argentina, Brazil, Paraguay, and Uruguay formed the Southern Cone Common Market **(MERCOSUR),** which is a customs union that eliminates tariffs on goods and services between member countries and establishes a common external tariff. In addition, the MERCOSUR countries established a separate reciprocal investment promotion and protection agreement (the January 1994 Colonia Protocol) "that guarantees nondiscriminatory treatment, prohibits performance criteria such as minimum exports or local inputs, bans restrictions on capital repatriation and profit remittances, and prohibits expropriation" (USITC, *International Economic Review,* October/November 1996, p. 23). Further, an August 1995 protocol provides limited terms of reference on intellectual property rights, and all member countries have accepted the intellectual property rules negotiated as part of the Uruguay Round. There is no provision, however, for government procurement because this activity is regulated in Brazil under its constitution. Venezuela signed a membership agreement on June 17, 2006, and became a full member on July 4. The addition of Venezuela gives MERCOSUR a total population of more 260 million and a combined GDP of more than $1.4 trillion. The four original members have adopted a common set of customs tariffs and free transit of goods and services and, at the time of this writing, are waiting for Venezuela to present its schedule for meeting the requirements of membership. Bolivia, Chile, Colombia, Ecuador, and Peru currently have associate member status.[24] MERCOSUR officials also have held talks with representatives from other Andean countries and Mexico regarding possible FTA arrangements.

CAFTA–DR

The **U.S.–Central America Free Trade Agreement–Dominican Republic (CAFTA–DR),** signed August 5, 2004, is a historic agreement that creates the second-largest free trade zone in Latin America for U.S. exports. Under this agreement, the Dominican Republic joins the Central American Free Trade Agreement (CAFTA) signed earlier in 2004 with Costa Rica, El Salvador, Guatemala, Honduras, and Nicaragua.[25] The United States exports more than $15 billion annually to the region, making it second behind Mexico in Latin America and America's 10th-largest export market worldwide. CAFTA–DR is a larger U.S. export market than Russia, India, and Indonesia combined. Upon entry into force, the CAFTA–DR agreement will eliminate 80 percent of the tariffs immediately, with the remaining tariffs phased out over 10 years.[26]

The implementing legislation was signed by the United States in August 2005. The CAFTA–DR entered into force for El Salvador on March 1, 2006; for Honduras and Nicaragua on April 1, 2006; and for Guatemala on July 1, 2006. The agreement was ratified in the Dominican Republic on March 1, 2007, leaving Costa Rica as the only member that still needed to ratify the agreement.[27]

FTAA

In June 1995, work was initiated at a meeting of 34 of the Western hemisphere's trade ministers (Cuba did not participate) to create a **Free Trade Area for the Americas (FTAA).** The purpose of this meeting was to take initial steps toward establishing a hemispheric free-trade agreement which would build upon the ongoing evolution of the region's many subregional trade agreements, such as NAFTA and MERCOSUR. Seven working groups (on market

---

[24]Joanna Klonsky, "Mercosur: South America's Fractious Trade Bloc," Council on Foreign Relations, obtained from www.cfr.org.

[25]U.S. Department of State: International Information Programs, "Central American Free Trade Agreement—Dominican Republic" updated April 4, 2007, obtained from http://usinfo.state.gov.

[26]Office of the U.S. Trade Representative, "CAFTA Policy Brief—February 2005," obtained from www.ustr.gov.

[27]Office of the U.S. Trade Representative, "Statement of U.S. Trade Representative Susan C. Schwab Regarding Entry Into Force of the CAFTA–DR for the Dominican Republic," March 1, 2007, obtained from www.ustr.gov.

access, customs procedures and rules of origin, investment, standards and technical barriers to trade, sanitary and phytosanitary measures, subsidies, and smaller economies) were established in the resulting Joint Declaration and Work Plan, and provisions were made for adding an additional four groups in the areas of government procurement, intellectual property rights, services, and competition policy. This is the most ambitious plan for hemispheric economic cooperation to date, and it undoubtedly will experience a number of serious obstacles that must be overcome prior to its implementation. (See USITC, *International Economic Review,* 1995, pp. 11–12.) The ministers of the 34 countries participating in the FTAA negotiations met in Quito, Ecuador, on November 1, 2002, to review progress in the establishment of guidelines for the next phase of negotiations. (See Free Trade Area of the Americas at www.ftaa-alca.org.) However, rising political tensions between Venezuela and the United States in 2006 and 2007 have impeded progress toward the completion of FTAA.

Chilean Trade Agreements

Beginning in the 1990s, successive Chilean governments have actively pursued trade-liberalizing agreements. Chile signed FTAs with Canada, Mexico, and Central America. Chile also concluded preferential trade agreements with Venezuela, Colombia, and Ecuador. An association agreement with MERCOSUR—Argentina, Brazil, Paraguay, Uruguay, and Venezuela—went into effect in October 1996. As part of an export-oriented development strategy, Chile completed landmark free-trade agreements in 2002 with the European Union and South Korea and agreement with the United States in 2004 that will lead to completely duty-free trade within 12 years. Chile, as a member of the Asia-Pacific Economic Cooperation (APEC) organization, is seeking to boost commercial ties to Asian markets. To that end, it has signed trade agreements in recent years with New Zealand, Singapore, Brunei, India, China, and, most recently, Japan. In 2007, Chile planned to begin negotiations with Thailand, Malaysia, and Australia. (See U.S. Department of State, Under Secretary for Public Diplomacy and Public Affairs, Background Notes: Chile, April 2007, www.state.gov)

While many of these agreements are having a positive impact on trade, Chile and Mexico may have the fastest-growing commercial relationship in Latin America. With the help of the free-trade agreement, trade between Chile and Mexico has expanded by nearly 2,000 percent since 1990.[28] In addition to free-trade agreements, Chile adopted a uniform 10 percent tariff rate on goods coming from countries with no special trading arrangements in 1999 and reduced that rate by 1 percent each year until it reached 6 percent in 2003. Further, Chile has indicated that it intends to continue to pursue additional bilateral free-trade agreements, which will of course result in an average tariff lower than 6 percent.[29]

APEC

The **Asia-Pacific Economic Cooperation (APEC)** forum was initiated in November 1989 at a ministerial meeting held in Canberra, Australia, with representatives from 12 countries participating. The association now has 21 members (Australia, Brunei, Canada, Chile, China, Hong Kong, Indonesia, Japan, the Republic of Korea, Malaysia, Mexico, New Zealand, Papua New Guinea, Peru, the Phillippines, Russia, Singapore, Taiwan, Thailand, the United States, and Vietnam), many of which participate in other subregional trade-liberalizing organizations. The trade liberalization efforts are focused on the development and adoption of concrete steps to achieve free trade and investment in the Asia-Pacific area by the year 2020. This work is fostered through annual forum ministerial meetings, with the annual meeting host being the organization's chair throughout the year. Inasmuch as the Asia-Pacific region is the world's largest and currently most dynamic region in terms of

---

[28]Diego Cevallos, "Chile-Mexico: Nothing Like Free Trade," *Inter Press Service News Agency*, April 7, 2007.

[29]Mary Anastasia O'Grady, "Chileans Opt for Free Trade While the U.S. Dawdles," *The Wall Street Journal,* October 8, 1999, p. A19.

combined GDP, APEC has the potential to become a major influence on the manner in which international trade and investment is conducted over the next 30 years.[30]

---

[30]The June/July/August 1996 issue of the USITC's *International Economic Review* provides an excellent overview of APEC. Our discussion drew from this source and from Central Intelligence Agency, *The World Factbook 1999* (Washington, DC: CIA, 1999), appendix C, obtained from www.odci.gov.

SUMMARY

This chapter examined the theory behind the formation of various types of economic integration projects. When a discriminatory trade policy regime of this sort is introduced, trade is created through displacement of high-cost domestic producers by lower-cost partner suppliers. This trade creation can enhance welfare. However, trade diversion through displacement of low-cost outside world sources of supply can also occur, and this may reduce welfare. Any conclusions on whether welfare will rise or fall must be based on an analysis of each particular coalition formation. When dynamic effects such as the realization of economies of scale and increased investment and technology flows are considered, the presumption is more likely that the partners will benefit from the union, and the outside world may also gain. The chapter also gave attention to the European Union—a single-market project that has caused excitement both within and outside Europe and has had important consequences for international trade. Another project, the CMEA, has disintegrated. However, this disintegration may bring enhanced welfare as market reforms and closer integration of Central and Eastern Europe and the former republics of the Soviet Union with other countries take place. Finally, important economic integration is occurring in the Western hemisphere with the implementation of the North American Free Trade Agreement (NAFTA), MERCOSUR, and the potential Free Trade Area for the Americas.

One note of caution should be made: There is considerable feeling among economists that economic coalitions among regional groupings of countries may not be as economically desirable as an alternative—*non*discriminatory decreases in trade barriers worldwide. In other words, the world may be moving toward blocs of countries and away from *global* integration. Political tensions and frictions can also result from the current discriminatory policy actions. A major question in this debate is whether the second-best route of discriminatory trade barrier reductions is more feasible than the first-best, nondiscriminatory reductions. The intense disagreement during the Uruguay Round of trade negotiations lends credence to this pessimistic view, although some success was indeed achieved in the Uruguay Round. More recently, the breakdown of the Doha Development Agenda further substantiates this view.

IN THE REAL WORLD:

ECONOMIC INTEGRATION IN AFRICA—TOO MUCH OF A GOOD THING?

Regional trading arrangements are generally perceived to be potentially beneficial in both the static and the dynamic sense. In the short run, member countries benefit as long as trade diversion does not outweigh trade creation effects. Long-run or dynamic gains occur through the well-known channels of increased efficiency through specialization, economies of scale, increased trade, and investments. A number of attempts at integration have been undertaken in Africa. Research focused on these arrangements has raised some interesting questions. On the static side, since these countries trade little with each other (less than 10 percent of African trade is intra-Africa trade), static losses through trade diversion are viewed as being negligible.

On the dynamic side, however, an IMF study by Robert Sharer has suggested that African integration initiatives are creating dynamic difficulties because of the overlapping and inconsistent nature of several of these regional undertakings. The complexity and overlapping nature of the many arrangements is demonstrated in Figure 4. The various organizations have overlapping memberships with internal inconsistencies, conflicting regulations and rules, and different strategies and objectives which work to impede the expansion of domestic markets and discourage both domestic and foreign investment. These integration issues may also tend to intensify political problems and issues in the area. Thus, as in many things, many simultaneous integration endeavors may well be too much of a "good thing."

IN THE REAL WORLD: *(continued)*

FIGURE 4   Overlapping Trading Arrangements in Eastern and Southern Africa

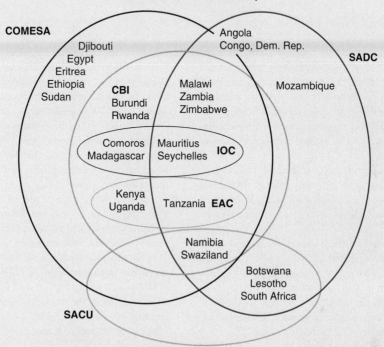

Regional trading arrangements in eastern and southern Africa overlap

Note:
CBI	Cross-Border Initiative
COMESA	Common Market for Eastern and Southern Africa
EAC	Commission for East African Cooperation
IOC	Indian Ocean Commission
SADC	Southern African Development Community
SACU	Southern African Customs Union

Many African countries belong to several regional groupings. In this figure, note that, of the 25 countries, only 6 (Djibouti, Egypt, Eritrea, Ethiopia, Mozambique, and Sudan) take part in only one trading arrangement. With multiple groupings, regulations can conflict, strategies can differ, and political difficulties can abound.

Source: Robert Sharer, "Trade: An Engine of Growth for Africa," *Finance and Development* 36, no. 4 (December 1999), pp. 26–29. Used with permission.

KEY TERMS

Asia-Pacific Economic Cooperation (APEC) forum
Canada–U.S. Free Trade Agreement
common external tariff
common market
customs union

dynamic effects of economic integration
EC92
economic union
European Community (EC)
European Union (EU)

"Eurosclerosis"
ex post income elasticity of import demand (YEM)
free-trade area (FTA)
Free Trade Area for the Americas (FTAA)

maquiladora program	second best	transition economies
MERCOSUR	Single European Act	transshipment
monetary union	static effects of economic	U.S.–Central America Free Trade
North American Free Trade	integration	Agreement–Dominican Republic
Agreement (NAFTA)	trade creation	(CAFTA–DR)
rules of origin	trade diversion	

QUESTIONS AND PROBLEMS

1. Suppose country A is considering forming a customs union with country B. Country A produces only manufactured goods and imports all its raw materials and agricultural products. Country B produces only raw materials and agricultural products and imports all its manufactured goods. Remembering the concepts of trade creation and trade diversion, is this union likely to be welfare enhancing? Why or why not?

2. It is often said that developing countries have little to gain from economic integration projects among themselves because they trade very little with each other. What is the reasoning behind this view? Do you agree with the conclusion? Explain.

3. When Portugal and Spain (which import agricultural goods from the United States) entered the EC in 1986, the United States threatened to place heavy duties on imports from the EC of wines, Scotch whisky, and other luxury-type goods unless the Community permitted greater access to other U.S. goods. What could have been the motivation behind the U.S. action, and would you have supported the action?

4. The terms *trade creation* and *trade diversion* are often applied in the context of assessing the impact of developed countries' tariff preferences for the products of developing

countries (the Generalized System of Preferences). How can these terms be useful in the GSP context?

5. What expected impacts of further integration in the EU could be detrimental to the United States? What expected impacts could be beneficial? In general, do you think the United States should be enthusiastic or worried about further integration in Europe? Why?

6. Why might it be argued that the development of APEC alongside integration efforts in the Western hemisphere increases the likelihood that regional agreements may be a step to freer world trade in general?

7. Why might the CMEA emphasis on "bilateral" balance within categories and between countries have been a detriment to attaining trade according to comparative advantage?

8. How would you explain reservations in the United States about the implementation of NAFTA? Do you think that NAFTA is a "good thing" or not? Explain.

9. "The countries of the world should follow the path of making nondiscriminatory reductions in trade barriers worldwide rather than the path of forming selective, discriminatory economic coalitions."

    (*a*) Build a case in favor of this statement.

    (*b*) Build a case against this statement.

INTERNATIONAL TRADE AND THE DEVELOPING COUNTRIES

LEARNING OBJECTIVES

- To become familiar with the various characteristics of developing countries.

- To learn how greater openness to trade can potentially contribute to more rapid economic growth.

- To understand the problems of export instability and terms-of-trade deterioration faced by developing countries.

- To comprehend the nature of and potential solutions to the external debt problems of developing countries.

INTRODUCTION

World Bank April 5, 2007   Ten years on from the 1997 East Asian Financial Crisis and the region is far wealthier, has fewer poor people, and a larger global role than ever before. People's incomes are well beyond where they were before the crisis and in some countries, like China, Vietnam, Cambodia, and Lao PDR, they're growing at exceptional rates. Over 100 million people across East Asia have left the ranks of the extreme poor since 2000 and poverty continues to fall.

Having grappled with the crisis and overcome many of the economic vulnerabilities that led to it, East Asia is fast becoming a middle income region. In fact, when Vietnam becomes a middle-rather than a low-income country—likely to be as early as 2010—more than 95 percent of East Asians will be living in middle income countries. At current growth rates, fewer than 25 million out of a total of about 2 billion East Asians will be living below the poverty line by 2020.[1]

How might the changing economic conditions described in this vignette be related to international trade and finance? The purpose of this chapter is to explore these relationships. We begin with a summary of various characteristics of developing countries.

AN OVERVIEW OF THE DEVELOPING COUNTRIES

In presenting the economic characteristics of developing countries, or the less developed countries (LDCs), it should be kept in mind that they are not a homogeneous group; there are many differences in levels of income, type of industrial structure, degree of participation in international trade, and types of problems faced in the world economy. Despite this caution regarding the diversity among LDCs, an examination of characteristics of these countries can be useful for emphasizing that the developing countries are very different from the developed or industrial countries (ICs). Table 1 provides data on selected economic and noneconomic characteristics grouped into a framework used by the World Bank in its *World Development Indicators 2006. Low-income* economies in this table are LDCs with annual per capita incomes of $875 or less in 2005, while *lower-middle-income* economies are LDCs with per capita incomes of $876 to $3,465. The category *upper-middle-income* economies embraces developing countries with per capita incomes of $3,466 to $10,725. Finally, a fourth category, *high-income* economies, covers economies with per capita incomes above $10,725. The data embrace 208 economies.

The table clearly indicates differences of the developing countries from each other. In general, however, the LDCs can be characterized as having low per capita incomes. Further, population growth rate, the share of agriculture in GDP, and infant mortality are higher and life expectancy is shorter than in the high-income countries. However, the growth of total GDP has recently been higher in low-income and lower-middle-income developing countries than in other countries. Exports as a percentage of GDP increased sharply for all developing country groups. Finally, the share of manufactured exports in total exports tends to be lower in developing countries than in high-income countries; this would be much more noticeable if China and India were excluded from the figure for low-income countries, but the precise figure is not available.

---

[1]"East Asia 10 Years After the Financial Crisis," World BankNews; obtained from www.worldbank.org.

TABLE 1   Economic and Noneconomic Characteristics of Developing Countries and High-Income Countries

	Low Income*	Lower-Middle Income[†]	Upper-Middle Income[‡]	High Income[§]
Population, 2005 (in millions)	2,353	2,474	599	1,011
GNI per capita, 2005 (in dollars)	580	1,918	5,625	35,131
Annual growth rate of GDP, 2005	7.5%	6.9%	5.5%	2.8%
Annual rate of population growth, 2005	1.8%	1.0%	0.4%	0.7%
Agricultural value added as percentage of GDP, 2005	21.6%	12.5%	6.5%	1.8%
Industry value added as percentage of GDP, 2005	28.1%	41.3%	31.8%	28.1%
Exports of goods and services as a percentage of GDPs				
1990	17%	17%	28%	19%
2004	24%	32.5%	37.6%	23.7%
Manufactured goods as percentage of total exports, 2002	58%	60%	60%	82%
High-technology exports as percentage of manufacturing exports, 2002	9%	17%	21%	23%
Infant mortality rate (per 1,000 live births), 2004	79.5	32.7	23.2	6.1
Years of life expectancy at birth, 2004	58.8	70.2	69.2	78.7

NA = not available or not applicable

Note: In occasional instances, a figure is for a different year than the year indicated.

*Low-income economies (54): Afghanistan, Bangladesh, Benin, Bhutan, Burkina Faso, Burundi, Cambodia, Central African Republic, Chad, Comoros, Democratic Republic of Congo, Côte d'Ivoire, Eritrea, Ethiopia, The Gambia, Ghana, Guinea, Guinea-Bissau, Haiti, India, Kenya, Democratic Republic of Korea, Kyrgyz Republic, Laos, Liberia, Madagascar, Malawi, Mali, Mauritania, Mongolia, Mozambique, Myanmar, Nepal, Niger, Nigeria, Pakistan, Papua New Guinea, Rwanda, São Tomé and Principe, Senegal, Sierra Leone, Solomon Islands, Somalia, Sudan, Tajikistan, Tanzania, Timor-Leste, Togo, Uganda, Uzbekistan, Vietnam, Yemen, Zambia, and Zimbabwe.

[†]Lower-middle-income economies (58): Albania, Algeria, Angola, Armenia, Azerbaijan, Belarus, Bolivia, Bosnia and Herzegovina, Brazil, Bulgaria, Cameroon, Cape Verde, China, Colombia, Republic of Congo, Cuba, Djibouti, Dominican Republic, Ecuador, Egypt, El Salvador, Fiji, Georgia, Guatemala, Guyana, Honduras, Indonesia, Iran, Iraq, Jamaica, Jordan, Kazakhstan, Kiribati, Lesotho, Former Yugoslav Republic of Macedonia, Maldives, Marshall Islands, Federated States of Micronesia, Moldova, Morocco, Namibia, Nicaragua, Paraguay, Peru, Philippines, Samoa, Serbia and Montenegro, Sri Lanka, Suriname, Swaziland, Syria, Thailand, Tonga, Tunisia, Turkmenistan, Ukraine, Vanuatu, West Bank and Gaza.

[‡]Upper-middle-income economies (40): American Samoa, Argentina, Barbados, Belize, Botswana, Chile, Costa Rica, Croatia, Czech Republic, Dominica, Equatorial Guinea, Estonia, Gabon, Grenada, Hungary, Latvia, Lebanon, Libya, Lithuania, Malaysia, Mauritius, Mayotte, Mexico, Northern Mariana Islands, Oman, Palau, Panama, Poland, Romania, Russian Federation, Seychelles, Slovak Republic, South Africa, St. Kitts and Nevis, St. Lucia, St. Vincent and the Grenadines, Trinidad and Tobago, Turkey, Uruguay, and Venezuela.

[§]High-income economies (56): Andorra, Antigua and Barbuda, Aruba, Australia, Austria, The Bahamas, Bahrain, Belgium, Bermuda, Brunei, Canada, Cayman Islands, Channel Islands, Cyprus, Denmark, Faeroe Islands, Finland, France, French Polynesia, Germany, Greece, Greenland, Guam, Hong Kong (China), Iceland, Ireland, Isle of Man, Israel, Italy, Japan, Republic of Korea, Kuwait, Liechtenstein, Luxembourg, Macao (China), Malta, Monaco, Netherlands, Netherlands Antilles, New Caledonia, New Zealand, Norway, Portugal, Puerto Rico, Qatar, San Marino, Saudi Arabia, Singapore, Slovenia, Spain, Sweden, Switzerland, United Arab Emirates, United Kingdom, United States, and Virgin Islands (U.S.).

Source: World Bank, *World Development Indicators 2006* (Washington, DC: World Bank, 2006), obtained from www.devdata.worldbank.org.

A Closer Look at the Least Developed Countries

The United Nations Conference on Trade and Development (UNCTAD) produced a report in 2002 on the status of the least developed countries in the world. This report focused on poverty in the 49 least developed of the world's 104 developing nations.[2] One chapter of the report focused on patterns of trade integration and poverty. In particular, the report challenged the conventional wisdom that persistent poverty in these countries is due to their low level of trade integration and insufficient trade liberalization.

[2]The 49 nations designated by UNCTAD as Least Developed Nations include Afghanistan, Angola, Bangladesh, Benin, Bhutan, Burkina Faso, Burundi, Cambodia, Cape Verde, Central African Republic, Chad, Comoros, Democratic Republic of the Congo, Djibouti, Equatorial Guinea, Eritrea, Ethiopia, The Gambia, Guinea, Guinea-Bissau, Haiti, Kiribati, Laos, Lesotho, Liberia, Madagascar, Malawi, Maldives, Mali, Mauritania, Mozambique, Myanmar, Nepal, Niger, Rwanda, Samoa, São Tomé and Principe, Senegal, Sierra Leone, Solomon Islands, Somalia, Sudan, Tanzania, Togo, Tuvalu, Uganda, Vanuatu, Yemen, and Zambia. See "Escaping the Poverty Trap," *The Least Developed Countries Report 2002,* United Nations Conference on Trade and Development, Geneva, pp. 103–117.

Kirchbach (2001) identified four accepted stylized facts about international trade relations of the least developed countries that do not necessarily reflect current realities:

1. Trade/GDP ratios are low in the least developed countries.
2. All least developed countries export primary commodities.
3. All least developed countries suffer from marginalization from global trade flows, and this tendency is inexorably increasing.
4. All least developed countries have closed trade regimes.[3]

Utilizing information for the 1980s and 1990s that is contained in the UNCTAD 2002 report can shed light on the validity of these stylized facts. (Comparable information for more recent years is not readily available.)

The Ratio of Trade to GDP

International trade is a critical component of GDP in the least developed economies. According to 1997–1998 data, exports and imports of goods and services constituted an average of 43 percent of their GDP. This average level of trade integration for the least developed countries was around the same as the world average and actually higher than that of high-income Organization for Economic Cooperation and Development (OECD) countries.

Measured at current prices, exports and imports of goods and services as a share of GDP for least developed countries as a group increased by 25 percent between 1987–1989 and 1997–1998. This increase was above the world average *but* less than that in other developing countries and much less than that of the "more globalized developing countries" (i.e., those with a higher ratio of trade to national income, such as Mexico and China). In addition, the export orientation of the least developed economies was generally lower than import dependence. Imports of goods and services were equivalent to 26 percent of GDP on average in least developed countries, while exports of goods and services constituted 17 percent of GDP (with 17 least developed countries having exports account for less than 10 percent of GDP). Trade integration is increasing for this group of countries but not at as rapid a rate as for low- and middle-income countries.

Primary Commodity Exports

For the least developed countries as a group, unprocessed primary commodities constituted 62 percent of total merchandise exports and processed primary commodities made up a further 8 percent of merchandise exports. This is a case where group averages mask the considerable differences among the least developed countries in the composition of exports. Of this group of 49 countries, 18 countries predominately exported either manufactures or services (or some combination of these) and 4 of the primary commodity exporters were oil exporters. Table 2 shows the extent of the shift for the least developed countries and the four subgroups.

An examination of the subgroups shows the increasing specialization that occurred as a result of more exposure to international trade between 1981–1983 and 1997–1999. The countries were moving more resources into the production of their comparative advantage goods, and the decomposition showed that different countries had comparative advantages in different areas. The long-standing belief that the least developed countries all had comparative advantages in unprocessed raw materials is not accurate for many of these nations. For the nonoil commodity exporters, unprocessed primary commodities grew from 65 percent of merchandise exports to more than 73 percent. Oil exporters showed an increase in

---

[3]F. von Kirchbach, "An Assessment of the Least Developed Countries Export Performance from a Business and Product Perspective," paper presented at the ITC Business Round Table, Third United Nations Conference on the Least Developed Countries, Brussels, May 16, 2001.

TABLE 2   Composition of Merchandise Exports of Subgroups of Least Developed Countries, 1981–1983, 1997–1999 (Percentage of Total Merchandise Exports)

	Nonoil Commodity Exporters		Oil Exporters		Manufactures and/ or Services Exporters		Manufactures Exporters	
	1981–1983	*1997–1999*	*1981–1983*	*1997–1999*	*1981–1983*	*1997–1999*	*1981–1983*	*1997–1999*
Primary Commodities								
Unprocessed	64.6%	73.6%	91.0%	96.0%	47.3%	23.5%	47.3%	20.3%
Processed	25.7	12.2	7.8	2.8	23.2	6.0	15.1	2.5
Total	90.3	85.8	98.8	98.8	70.5	29.6	62.4	22.8
Manufactures								
Low skill	8.6	11.2	0.7	0.7	25.5	65.6	33.8	74.6
High skill	1.1	3.0	0.5	0.5	4.0	4.9	3.8	2.6
Total	9.7	14.2	1.2	1.2	29.5	70.4	37.6	77.2
Grand Total	**100.0**	**100.0**	**100.0**	**100.0**	**100.0**	**100.0**	**100.0**	**100.0**

Source: UNCTAD secretariat estimates based on U.N. COMTRADE data.

unprocessed primary commodities from 91 percent to 96 percent. The manufactures exporters experienced an increase in the share of manufactures in merchandise exports from 38 percent to more than 77 percent. While dependence on exports of primary commodities does describe a substantial number of nations in the group, it is far from an accurate description of the least developed countries as a group.

Marginalization from Global Trade Flows

In spite of the importance of trade to the least developed countries, the size of the economies and their trade flows creates the impression that these economies are becoming insignificant (or marginalized) in global trade. The concept of marginalization is based on a fear that globalization results in a greater concentration of international trade and investment flows and that the benefits accrue to only a small number of countries. Merchandise exports of the least developed countries are only 0.5 percent of world merchandise exports. Over time, the share of these in world exports and imports has declined. This is a result of the exports and imports of the least developed countries growing less quickly than world exports and imports.

This apparent marginalism hides the changes occurring at a more individual level. The declines in the least developed countries' share of exports hit bottom in the early 1990s. After 1992, their share of global trade ceased to decline. The marginalization is most noticeable for nonfuel, primary commodity exporters. The least developed countries' share of oil exports rose in the 1980s, and their share of world manufactures exports rose significantly—doubling from 0.1 percent in 1988 to 0.2 percent in 1999. An examination of the disaggregated data indicates that the process of marginalization was limited to nonfuel, primary product exporters. Exporters of oil, manufactures, and services did not experience the same loss of market share. The positive trends in these areas were overshadowed by the extremely small portion of world trade accounted for by the least developed countries.

Closed Trade Regimes

The trade regimes in the least developed countries were much more open at the end of the 1990s than they were at the end of the 1980s. There is some evidence that suggests that least developed countries have gone further in dismantling trade barriers than other developing countries. While the designation of closed regimes may have been accurate in the 1980s, this generalization no longer applies to the majority of the least developed countries.

Trade Liberalization, Growth, and Poverty

The UNCTAD report provides a serious challenge to the common assumption that poverty in the least developed countries is due to their low level of integration. The lack of trade liberalization has also been called into question. First, many of the least developed countries have made substantial progress toward opening their economies without experiencing significant poverty reduction. In fact, the evidence suggests that, if countries are divided into four trade regimes (most closed, moderately closed, moderately open, and most open), economies that have adopted the most open and most closed trade regimes have actually experienced increases in poverty. The declines in poverty occurred in the countries that took a more moderate approach to liberalization. This evidence led to the position that the positive effects of trade liberalization on poverty are experienced in the long run and that short run gains depend on the implementation of "complementary measures" to offset some of the adjustment costs associated with opening an economy.

An examination of the potential role of international trade in the economic development process and some of the problems experienced is next. This is followed by a closer look at the empirical evidence of the effect of trade on economic growth in developing nations. The chapter concludes with an examination of trade policies that have been used in developing nations and of the developing countries' external debt position.

THE ROLE OF TRADE IN FOSTERING ECONOMIC DEVELOPMENT

Having looked at these general characteristics, we now examine some of the links between international trade and development and discuss several problems often associated with the international sector of the LDCs. We also consider particular strategies and policies that might be employed to overcome the problems and focus briefly on the manner in which international trade can influence changes in a developing economy. Because the links between growth and trade have already been discussed in Chapter 11, our concern here is not restricted to the changes in efficiency and capacity of the system but, rather, is with the broader set of effects that relate to the ability of the economy to meet its citizens' needs and wants over time. We are thus concerned here with both static and dynamic effects on the economic system that take place as a country exchanges goods and services with other countries, as well as the manner in which these trade-related effects can be influenced by economic policy.

The Static Effects of Trade on Economic Development

The static effects of trade have been thoroughly developed in earlier chapters. Put simply, if there is a difference between internal relative prices in autarky and those that can be obtained internationally, then a country can improve its well-being by specializing in and exporting the relatively less expensive domestic goods and importing goods that are relatively more expensive. From a development standpoint, the change in economic structure and factoral distribution of income that is assumed to accompany this adjustment is of clear concern. Because the economic systems of the developing countries tend to be somewhat unresponsive to changing price incentives, at least in the short run, factors of production may not move easily to the expanding low-cost sectors from the contracting higher-cost sectors. In this case the adjustment process takes on the characteristics of the specific-factors model (Chapter 8), and the gains from specialization are reduced in the short run. Remember from Chapter 6, however, that even if a country's production does not change at all, there are still gains from exchange. In addition, the characteristics of the import good— either in terms of quality for consumers or productivity in the case of capital and intermediate inputs—may improve the economy's ability to meet consumer desires. Imports may also help relieve short-run domestic bottlenecks and permit the economy to operate closer to its production-possibilities frontier—that is to say, more efficiently—on a consistent basis.

The static impact of trade on the production structure of the economy that occurs when specialization follows comparative advantage will result in a relative expansion of the sector(s) using relatively intensively the relatively abundant factor. For most developing countries, this results in incentives to expand labor-intensive production instead of more modern, capital-intensive production. This means expanding traditional agriculture, primary goods, and labor-intensive manufactures. International trade thus stimulates employment and puts upward pressure on wages, as suggested in the Heckscher-Ohlin explanation of the basis for trade. However, to the degree that developing countries are characterized by high degrees of unemployment, the impact of increased demand for labor on the wage level is often limited at best. Also, given the economic characteristics of many primary goods and labor-intensive manufactures, some observers question the desirability of a relative growth in the production of these traditional goods, particularly if this growth is at the expense of modern manufacturing. Because of the lower income and price elasticities of demand for these products and the instability of supply of agricultural and primary production due to factors such as weather conditions, greater specialization in these goods can result in a greater instability of income, even in the static sense. Income instability is also of concern in the dynamic sense and will be addressed again in the following section.

Further, to the extent that the developing country is a large country in terms of export goods, expansion of export supply may well lead to undesired terms-of-trade effects that will significantly reduce the expected static gains from trade and lead to a distribution of the gains from trade that favors the more developed trading partner. Finally, expanding production of basic labor-intensive products and relying on the industrialized countries for technology and skill-intensive manufactures and capital goods not only can lead to a critical economic dependency but also inextricably links the economic health of the developing country to that of the industrialized country.

In previous chapters we discussed the theoretical impact of trade on production assuming there was full employment. However, full employment is seldom the case in many developing countries. The situation suggests another potential gain from international trade that has been elaborated by Hla Myint (1958) and may help to explain the rapid growth of production and output of traditional agricultural and primary products in the developing countries in the nineteenth century.[4] Myint suggests that unemployment represents a potential production supply that exceeds domestic demand in the developing country. In this instance, international trade can provide a **vent for surplus,** that is, a larger market that will permit the country to increase its output and employment (conceptually, to move from well inside its production-possibilities frontier to a point nearer or perhaps on the PPF). Myint argues that vent for surplus is a more convincing explanation of *why* countries start to trade, while comparative advantage helps us to understand the *types* of commodities countries ultimately trade. From a development standpoint, the gains in income, employment, and needed or wanted import goods can influence the development process in a positive manner.

In sum, the static gains from trade for the developing country originate from the traditional gains from exchange and specialization as well as, perhaps, from a vent for surplus. However, because of the inflexibilities in the traditional economies and the nature of the traditional labor-intensive exports, the relative static gains from trade may be less than those for the more flexible industrial economy and also may be reduced by the undesirable effects of increased economic instability and terms-of-trade behavior.

---

[4]This idea is generally traced to Adam Smith's 1776 *The Wealth of Nations.*

The Dynamic Effects of Trade on Development

As in economic integration (Chapter 17), the biggest potential effect of trade on development likely rests with the dynamic effects. On the positive side, the expansion of output brought about by access to the larger international markets permits the LDC to take advantage of economies of scale that would not be possible with the limited domestic market. Thus, industries that are not internationally competitive in an isolated market may well be competitive by way of international trade if there are potential economies of scale. Further, because comparative advantages change over time and with economic development, international trade can foster the development of infant industries into internationally competitive ones by providing the market size and exposure to products and processes that would not happen in its absence. This, of course, is one of the reasons cited for using trade policy instruments (Chapter 15) to restrict imports or promote exports, although there are problems with using the policies in practice. Other dynamic influences of trade on economic development arise from the positive antitrust effects of trade, increased investment resulting from changes in the economic environment, the increased dissemination of technology into the developing country (e.g., the product cycle), exposure to new and different products, and changes in institutions that accompany the increased exposure to different countries, cultures, and products.

Few would disagree that trade can have positive effects on economic development. What is much less clear is the type of commodities a country should specialize in so that, over time, international trade in goods and services continues to foster growth and development, not hinder it. Because conditions in the developing countries differ so dramatically from the theoretical world of perfect competition and full employment utilized in many theoretical models, the static application of comparative advantage may not be very helpful in providing guidelines for trade and specialization in a dynamic LDC setting. It is often argued that participating in free trade based on the guidelines of simple comparative advantage may work against economic development in the developing country. It is important to examine briefly several of the more important disadvantages of unrestricted trade for the developing country, particularly because these concerns can have important implications for trade policy.

The possible negative effects of trade on development arise from economic factors that are ignored when focusing on static comparative advantage to delineate exports and imports. For example, market imperfections in developing countries generally result in private costs and benefits being different from social costs and benefits, particularly in the presence of externalities. Relying on private (market) prices in this environment can lead to a pattern of trade that is not consistent with either relative social costs or long-run development goals of the country (e.g., if an industry's growth causes extensive environmental damage). In a broader dynamic context, it must also be recognized that because the economywide production linkages vary between different commodities or sectors, the overall effect of growth in exports on the growth and development of the entire economy is likely to vary from commodity to commodity. Some commodities thus act like "growth poles" for the entire economy, while others such as primary production have little effect outside their own sector.[5] A further complication arises from the variation in the returns to scale characteristic among commodities. Thus, a country might not appear to have a relative cost advantage in a particular product at the level of production needed to fill the

---

[5]This is particularly true in a foreign enclave that produces a product or products essentially for export only and imports practically all intermediate inputs requiring capital and skilled labor. In this instance, the LDC experiences little more than a small increase in employment of production workers and increased sales of any primary inputs such as minerals or land used in the production process. The effect on the development of the economy in this case can be negligible.

home market, but there might well be a comparative advantage in that product at a higher level of production. In a similar fashion, a product that appears to have a current cost advantage but is characterized by decreasing returns to scale may find its export possibilities very limited. Finally, from an internal perspective, remember that the domestic supply and demand conditions that underlie both current and future comparative advantage have been and will continue to be influenced both by the imperfect nature of the markets and by government policy.

Another source of potential development problems that can arise with growth in international trade is the fact that the operation of markets and the characteristics of traded goods often differ between the developing countries and the industrialized countries. Many argue that these differences result in the greater share of trade-related benefits going to the industrialized countries and may even contribute to the furthering of underdevelopment in the LDCs. Two issues related to these differences, export instability and long-run changes in the terms of trade, have received considerable attention. We now look at these issues in more detail.

Export Instability

Export instability refers to the fact that the export earnings tend to fluctuate annually to a greater extent for developing countries than for industrialized countries (ICs). Often, the focus is not on export earnings (prices of exports times quantities of exports) but on export prices and their fluctuations. Whether the focus is on prices or on earnings, however, the variability is regarded as a problem because, with the relatively **high degree of openness** of many developing countries (i.e., a high ratio of foreign trade to gross domestic product, GDP), variability in the export sector is often associated with variability in GDP and the domestic price level. The internal instability is considered undesirable because of the uncertainties generated for producers and consumers. It can also put a strain on the rather ineffective macroeconomic policy instruments of the developing countries. In addition, planning for development is made more difficult. When export earnings are high in "good" years, development projects can be started that use imported equipment, but when export earnings subsequently decline, foreign exchange is not available to complete and to operate the projects, resulting in waste and a disrupted planning process.

Potential Causes of Export Instability

To account for price and earnings instability of the LDCs, economists usually list three main reasons. All three reasons are associated with the fact that many developing countries are relatively more engaged in the export of primary products than of manufactured goods. The first two reasons pertain to price variability, while the third reason focuses on total export earnings variation.

The first explanation for price instability in developing-country exports combines shifts in the demand curve for their exports with an inelastic supply curve of exports. The situation is illustrated in Figure 1, panel (a). Demand curve D_1 indicates the demand for the developing-country export good in time period 1, while curve D_2 indicates demand in time period 2. The supply curve S is assumed to apply to both periods. Note that the supply curve tends toward vertical, reflecting the supply inelasticity characterizing primary products. (For example, at the end of the harvesting period, a farmer has little choice but to sell most of the crop on the market, regardless of price.) When the demand curve shifts from D_1 to D_2, price rises from P_1 to P_2. If in a third period, demand then shifts back to position D_1, price will fall back to P_1. Obviously, there is considerable potential price instability in this scenario. A possible way to reduce the price instability would be for economic conditions in the buying countries (the ICs) to be stabilized. Hence, better macroeconomic measures in the industrialized or developed countries can reduce instability in the less developed countries.

FIGURE 1   Demand-Supply Shifts and Price Instability

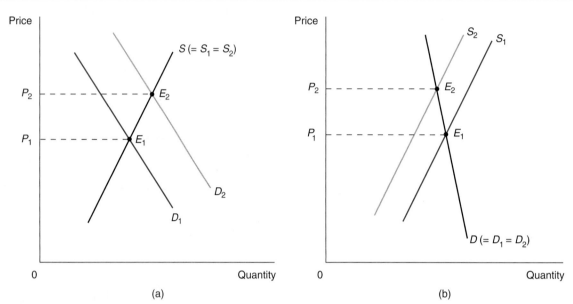

In panel (a), a shift of the export demand curve in period 1 (D_1) to the export demand curve in period 2 (D_2), in conjunction with a given inelastic supply curve in the two periods, yields a relatively large price increase. A shift back in demand to D_1 in a subsequent period would generate a substantial price decline. In panel (b), with an inelastic demand curve D for the primary product in the two periods, a shift in the supply curve in the first period (S_1) to supply curve S_2 in the second period likewise causes a relatively large price change. A shift back in supply to S_1 in the next period would generate substantial price instability for the two periods as a whole.

A second explanation for price instability [panel (b) of Figure 1] is the converse of the first one. Suppose that demand for the export good is inelastic; this is usually the case for primary products because either the demand is a derived demand for use in a final good or the product is a food product that characteristically faces low price elasticities. Shifts in the supply curve because of factors such as variable weather conditions in the producing countries can then cause substantial price instability. In panel (b), a constant demand curve is plotted against supply in the first period (S_1) and the second period (S_2). If weather conditions (such as a failure of the monsoons in India) in the second period reduce production, the price change is large, from P_1 to P_2. With a resumption of favorable conditions in the next period, S_2 shifts out again, and price again varies. In this case, the LDC may wish to search out alternative exports whose production is not so dependent on random factors.

A third explanation offered for instability is the high degree of **commodity concentration** in the export bundle, although this explanation is debated in the literature. (See Love 1986, 1990; Massell 1970, 1990.) In some LDCs, one or two goods constitute a majority of the total export earnings. This lack of diversification implies that dramatic price rises (or declines) in the one or two goods will cause total export earnings to rise (or fall) dramatically. If the bundle of goods were more diversified or less concentrated, then a price increase in some goods could be offset by price declines in other goods, making for greater stability in the total value of the export bundle. Examples of countries with relatively high degrees of commodity concentration are Saudi Arabia, where crude and refined petroleum account for more than 88 percent of total exports; Uganda, where coffee constitutes about 20 percent of exports; Zambia, where copper comprises 43 percent of exports; Côte d'Ivoire, where cocoa accounts for about 42 percent of exports; and Mauritius, where raw cane sugar accounts for 18 percent of exports.[6] Clearly there could potentially be some benefit to such developing countries from undertaking policies to increase the number of different types of goods exported, especially labor-intensive manufactured goods.

Long-Run Terms-of-Trade Deterioration	The problem of **long-run deterioration in the terms of trade** refers to the allegation that, over the span of several decades or so, there has been a persistent tendency for the commodity terms of trade (price of exports/price of imports) to fall for developing countries. If the world is viewed as consisting of two groups of countries—the LDCs and the ICs—then the implication is that the commodity terms of trade have been improving for ICs, because exports from LDCs (ICs) are imports into ICs (LDCs). In otherwords, the international economy is transferring real income from LDCs to ICs, an opposite transfer to that which many people think is desirable. At the extreme, the terms-of-trade behavior can generate immiserizing growth (see Chapter 11).

This hypothesis of secularly declining terms of trade (TOT) for LDCs is often referred to as the **Prebisch-Singer hypothesis** because of its popularization by two long-time United Nations economists, Raul Prebisch and Hans W. Singer. The hypothesis emerged in response to statistical studies showing that, particularly for Great Britain, the TOT had risen dramatically in the 50- to 100-year period ending with World War II. The inference was made that, because the ICs' TOT had improved, the LDCs' TOT must have deteriorated.

A number of economists pointed out that such an inference was invalid. (See Baldwin 1955; Ellsworth 1956; Meier 1968, chap. 3; Morgan 1959, 1963.) One reason concerns the way international trade data are recorded. Exports are usually recorded f.o.b. (free on board), which means that insurance and transportation costs are not included; however, imports are usually recorded c.i.f. (cost, insurance, and freight). Hence, $P_{exports}/P_{imports}$ for the ICs could have been rising because, as has been the case over the long run, transport costs had been falling (which would reduce the denominator of the TOT expression). Thus, the use of the reciprocal of the industrialized countries' TOT as an indication of the developing countries' TOT is invalid, because the recording procedure could be consistent with improving TOT for *both* LDCs and ICs due to the decline in transportation costs.

Another reason for objection to long-run studies of TOT behavior concerns quality changes in products. It is very difficult to incorporate quality changes into price indexes, and a rise in price for a product may not indicate a true price increase if the quality of the product purchased has also improved. Quality improvements have been greater in manufactured goods than in primary products in the long run. Thus, because the share of primary products (manufactured goods) in LDC exports is larger (smaller) than in LDC imports, even if $P_{exports}/P_{imports}$ is falling for the LDCs this may not be a true "deterioration" in the terms of trade. While the developing countries may be paying relatively more for their imports, they may also be receiving relatively better products.

Other economists used direct data for several developing countries to ascertain whether there had been a long-run deterioration in the terms of trade. (For a bibliography of such studies, see Diakosavvas and Scandizzo 1991.) As might be expected from economic research, both rising and falling trends in LDCs' TOT have been found. Many researchers have chosen not to examine the developing countries' TOT but the long-run behavior of primary product prices versus the prices of manufactured goods. Research has found a long-run relative decline in primary-product prices. (See Diakosavvas and Scandizzo

---

[6]United Nations, *2004 International Trade Statistics Yearbook,* Vol. I (New York: United Nations, 2006), pp. 299, 729, 980, 1168, and 1250–51.

TITANS OF INTERNATIONAL ECONOMICS:

RAUL PREBISCH (1901–1986) AND HANS WOLFGANG SINGER (1910–2006)

Raul Prebisch was born on April 17, 1901, in Tucaman, Argentina. When he graduated with an economics degree in 1923 from the University of Buenos Aires, he had already written nine professional journal articles, the first having appeared when he was 17. He was professor of political economy at his alma mater from 1925 to 1948, also serving simultaneously as director of economic research for the National Bank of Argentina (1927–1930) and undersecretary of finance for Argentina (1930–1932), among other posts. He then embarked upon a career with the United Nations, serving as executive secretary of the U.N.'s Economic Commission for Latin America (ECLA) from 1948 to 1962 and as secretary-general of the United Nations Conference on Trade and Development (UNCTAD, an organization based in Geneva) from 1964 to 1969. He subsequently became director-general of the U.N.'s Latin American Institute for Economic and Social Planning.

Dr. Prebisch wrote several influential studies, with particularly noteworthy ones being "Commercial Policy in the Underdeveloped Countries" (*American Economic Review*, May 1959), *The Economic Development of Latin America and Its Principal Problems* (1949), and *Towards a New Trade Policy for Development. Report of the Secretary-General of the United Nations Conference on Trade and Development* (1964). His thesis of the secular deterioration of the terms of trade of LDCs is his most widely cited contribution, but he was concerned with problems of industrialization of the LDCs throughout his career. He appears to have first crystallized the notion of a "center-periphery" in the world economy, whereby systematic forces emanating from the center (the DCs) cause great difficulties for the periphery (the LDCs). His ability to articulate his views at the international agency level has ensured that they have been and will be long-lasting.

Raul Prebisch was awarded several honorary degrees, including degrees from Columbia University and the Universidad de los Andes (Colombia). He also received the Jawaharlal Nehru Award for International Understanding in 1974, the Dag Hammarskjold Honorary Medal of the German U.N. Association in 1977, and the Third World Prize of the Third World Foundation in 1981.

Hans W. Singer was born in 1910 in Elberfeld (now Wuppertal), Rhineland, Germany. He earned his diploma in political science from Bonn University in 1931. He received his Ph.D. in economics from Cambridge University in 1936, doing his work during the formative years of Keynesian economics at Cambridge. He served as assistant lecturer in economics at Manchester University from 1938 to 1945, as economics research officer in the U.K. Ministry of Town and Country Planning in 1945–1946, and as lecturer in political economy at Glasgow University in 1946–1947. He then undertook a U.N. career, building and serving in the Economics Department of the U.N. Secretariat. He became professor of economics at the University of Sussex and its Institute of Development Studies in 1969 and remained on the institute's research team long after his "official" retirement.

Professor Singer's early concern was with unemployment, and he published *Unemployment and the Unemployed* in 1940. He then worked on problems of wartime planning. He subsequently turned to the area of economic development and made many contributions, including *Economic Development of Under-Developed Countries* (1950), *International Development, Growth and Change* (1964), and *Technologies for Basic Needs* (1977). Another work used in higher education was his text *Rich and Poor Countries* (with Javed A. Ansari, 4th ed., 1988). His most famous article is "The Distribution of Gains between Investing and Borrowing Countries" (*American Economic Review*, May 1950).

Professor Singer's work was of broad scope, extending beyond the terms-of-trade issue to the structure of the world economy, basic needs, food aid, and technology transfer. He took the lead in spreading knowledge of Third World problems worldwide. His ideas and efforts served as constant reminders that there is no "quick fix" to LDC problems and that development should be approached from the perspective of possible actions in DCs as well as in LDCs. In November 2004, Singer was awarded the first Lifetime Achievement Award from the Development Studies Association.

Sources: Mark Blaug, ed., *Who's Who in Economics: A Biographical Dictionary of Major Economists 1700–1986*, 2nd ed. (Cambridge, MA: MIT Press, 1986), pp. 696–97, 788–89; Luis E. Di Marco, ed., *International Economics and Development: Essays in Honor of Raul Prebisch* (New York: Academic Press, 1972), pp. xvii–xix; Gerald M. Meier and Dudley Seers, eds., *Pioneers in Development* (New York: Oxford University Press for the World Bank, 1984), pp. 173, 273–74; J. G. Palma, "Raul Prebisch," in John Eatwell, Murray Milgate, and Peter Newman, eds., *The New Palgrave: A Dictionary of Economics*, Vol. 3 (London: Macmillan, 1987), pp. 934–36; *Who's Who in the World*, 1st ed., 1971–1972 (Chicago: Marquis Who's Who, 1970), p. 746; *Who's Who in the World*, 10th ed., 1991–1992 (Wilmette, IL: Marquis Who's Who, 1990), p. 1004; www.ids.ac.uk/ids.

1991, and Spraos 1983, chap. 3.) As these authors note, however, this is not identical to secular deterioration in LDCs' terms of trade, since ICs also export primary products and LDCs also export manufactured goods. Some recent work has focused on a bilateral context. (See Appleyard 2006 for India–U.K. TOT behavior.)

Differing Income Elasticities of Demand

Several reasons have been offered for the alleged long-run TOT decline of developing countries. (See the various studies cited so far in this section and Singer 1987.) A compelling reason for believing in a long-run TOT decline centers on **differing income elasticities of demand for primary products and manufactured goods.** Empirical evidence indicates that the income elasticity of demand is higher for manufactured products than for primary products. It is usually greater than 1.0 for the former and less than 1.0 for the latter. Consequently, as LDCs and ICs both grow, they devote a larger (smaller) percentage of their incomes to the purchase of manufactured goods (primary products). Because many LDCs are net exporters of primary products and net importers of manufactures, the prices of their imports will rise more rapidly than the prices of their exports, other things equal.

Unequal Market Power

Another explanation for potential TOT deterioration is couched in terms of **unequal market power in product and factor markets** in ICs and LDCs. The general point is that primary products are sold in competitive world markets, while manufactured goods are often sold in an imperfectly competitive market setting where prices can be higher than would be the case with perfect competition. In addition, labor markets in ICs may contain imperfectly competitive elements if labor unions are strong and thus wages are relatively high, while labor in the primary-product sector in developing countries is not organized and cannot exert upward pressure on wages and prices. The result is that prices for primary products do not have the upward pressures put upon them that prices of manufactured goods do; therefore, the TOT of the LDCs suffer. There may also be an asymmetry in price behavior: primary-product prices may be slow to rise in the upswing of business cycles but fall in downswings, while manufactured goods prices rise in upswings and are slow to fall in downswings. Over the long run, developing countries' TOT decline.

Technical Change

A third explanation for a possible long-run decline in the developing countries' TOT is that the nature of technical change has worked to reduce the growth rate of demand for primary products. This reduction in the growth of demand has therefore, other things equal, resulted in less upward pressure on primary-product prices. A principal factor that has reduced relative demand growth (Singer 1987) is the growth of synthetic products, which have displaced natural products. Examples are synthetic rubber and fibers. It is also suggested that newer production processes in manufacturing industries in industrialized countries have economized on the use of raw materials. In the 1970s and 1980s, this process was demonstrated in the case of petroleum by the development of energy-saving technology and the search for alternative, economically feasible sources of energy such as solar power or safe nuclear power. Also, the recent attention in ICs to recycling and to conservation is expected to reduce further the growth of demand for primary products.

Multinational Corporations and Transfer Pricing

Finally, the behavior of multinational corporations (MNCs) through the mechanism of transfer pricing can worsen the LDCs' TOT. Suppose that a MNC operates a subsidiary in a developing country that is sending inputs to another subsidiary in an industrialized country, and at the same time the subsidiary in the IC is sending inputs to the LDC subsidiary. Because both subsidiaries are part of the same enterprise, such trade is called **intra-firm trade.** In intra-firm trade, prices are not necessarily true market prices because the goods do not pass through organized markets, and the recorded prices are merely bookkeeping entries for the firm. (See Chapter 12, page 238.)

In this context, suppose that the developing country has high profits taxes and severe restrictions on the **repatriation of earnings,** that is, on the transfer of profits back to the IC. On the other hand, there are lower profits taxes in the IC and there is no problem of repatriating profits. In such a situation, the MNC has an economic interest in enlarging profits recorded on the balance sheet of the industrialized country subsidiary and in reducing profits on the balance sheet of the LDC subsidiary. A strategy for doing so is to record the sales from the LDC subsidiary to the IC subsidiary at lower-than-market prices and to record the sales from the IC plant to the LDC plant at higher-than-market prices. If this strategy is followed, recorded profits will be lower in the high-tax, difficult-repatriation LDC and higher in the low-tax and easy-repatriation IC than would otherwise be the case. The MNC's total after-tax profits will rise because of this behavior.

From the standpoint of the LDCs' (ICs') terms of trade, this behavior means that $P_{exports}/P_{imports}$ will be lower (higher) than it would be if the goods had been traded through regular, organized markets. Hence, this institutional feature of MNCs can contribute to worsened TOT for the LDCs. However, it must be shown that this behavior has become increasingly more prevalent over time for the argument to explain a long-run *trend* in the TOT. Empirical work on the importance of MNC transfer pricing is difficult to conduct because of the privacy of individual firm data and because it is not known precisely what prices would have existed if trade had occurred through organized markets. The LDCs have been pressing for measures to regulate this type of intrafirm behavior, but they have achieved little success so far.

CONCEPT CHECK

1. What are three reasons the short-run or static gains from international trade may be less for the developing country than for an industrialized country?

2. How can international trade stimulate change in the economic system in the dynamic sense? What factors can inhibit trade from positively influencing the development process?

3. Why do developing countries have greater problems with export instability than industrialized countries?

4. What are two factors that contribute to possible downward pressure on the terms of trade for developing countries?

TRADE, ECONOMIC GROWTH, AND DEVELOPMENT: THE EMPIRICAL EVIDENCE

The previous section focused on the ways that international trade influences growth and development. The fact that there are some possible negative effects of trade on the growth and development process has stimulated numerous studies examining the possible link between exports, in particular, and economic growth.[7] Early studies linking various measures of export growth with growth in income suggested that they were significantly positively correlated and that exports did appear to be the "engine of growth" often referred to since the time of Smith and Ricardo. More recent studies, however, suggest a less clear conclusion and raise a number of questions about the effect of trade on economic growth. Econometric studies of individual countries over time (time-series analysis) and groups of countries at a point in time (cross-sectional analysis) have indicated statistically significant relationships between growth in both exports and imports and income growth. In a number of cases, particularly for middle-income countries, there appears to be a strong positive relationship between trade and growth through the direct effect of export earnings on GNP and the indirect effects (balance-of-payments effects) associated with the increased capacity to import needed capital and intermediate inputs. However, it is possible that increased

---

[7]A useful summary of these empirical analyses is contained in Edwards (1993).

income leads to greater imports and increased efficiency leads to greater exports; thus the causality may run from growth to trade rather than from trade to growth.

Another group of studies has suggested that growth in exports has a positive effect on growth and development because it stimulates increased saving and investment. These effects on aggregate saving result from either the higher propensity to save in the export sector or the effects on total saving of any changes in the distribution of income tied to the growth in the export sector. Again, however, the empirical results are not always conclusive.

In sum, while empirical analysis often supports the idea of a positive connection between the expansion of international trade and growth in income, a certain ambiguity remains. The manner and degree to which trade influences growth and development is complex and often country specific. The nature of the effect appears to vary with the degree of development, the nature of the economic system, and world market conditions outside the influence of the individual country. World business cycles in particular seem to play an important role, and the relationship between trade and growth increasingly appears to be more simultaneous than uniquely causal. While empirical analysis has not as yet provided a conclusive answer to the links between trade and growth, some of the models of growth through endogenous technological change that incorporate various effects of international trade might prove more successful.[8]

Another "fly in the ointment" that has recently emerged in the literature is the idea that institutions such as property rights, contracts, macroeconomic stabilization tools, and regulatory agencies for transport and finance are extremely important for growth. Indeed, some studies have found that, once the effect of institutions is allowed for, little or no additional explanatory power regarding growth is provided by a country's increased trade and integration with the world economy.[9] Thus, in general, while there is much analysis that stresses that trade is an engine of growth, there remains some doubt on the part of a number of observers.

TRADE POLICY AND THE DEVELOPING COUNTRIES

We now turn to a brief examination of the manner in which trade policy can be used to influence growth and development in developing countries. Our analysis is restricted to three areas: export instability, terms-of-trade behavior, and inward- versus outward-looking development strategies.

Policies to Stabilize Export Prices or Earnings

Several kinds of policies that conceptually can stabilize prices or export earnings have been used at various times. We consider a few general policies, but none of them has been judged very successful in practice.

International Buffer Stock Agreement

A policy that has continued to receive wide attention and is favored by many LDCs is an **international buffer stock agreement.** (The most well known of such agreements is the International Tin Agreement, which is currently inoperative.) Indeed proposals adopted at a special United Nations General Assembly session in 1974 called for an expansion in the number of such agreements as a means of generating greater benefits for LDCs in the world economy. In the international buffer stock agreement, producing nations (often joined by consuming nations) set up an international agency endowed with funds and a quantity of the commodity. If the world price of the good falls below the floor, the agency will buy it to bring the price up to the floor. On the other hand, if the world price rises above the ceiling, the agency will sell the good to bring the price down to the ceiling. If the

---

[8]For examples of these models, see especially Romer (1986) and Grossman and Helpman (1991).

[9]Dani Rodrik and Arvind Subramanian, "The Primacy of Institutions (and What This Does and Does Not Mean)," *Finance and Development* 40, no. 2 (June 2003), p. 32.

agency is successful, then producing (and consuming) countries have realized greater stability than would otherwise have been the case.

Another mechanism for introducing greater stability into LDC exports is an **international export quota agreement,** a type of agreement exemplified historically by the International Coffee Agreement and, less rigidly, by the Association of Coffee Producing Countries, which operated from 1993–2002. In an export quota agreement, producing countries choose a target price for the good (e.g., $2.50 per pound of coffee) and make a forecast of world demand for the coming year. Then they determine the quantity of supply that will, in conjunction with estimated world demand, yield the target price. Suppose that the estimated necessary supply is 400 million pounds of coffee. The agreement divides up the 400 million pounds among the supplying countries and stipulates that no country can export more than its designated share. If the forecast of demand is correct and supplying countries adhere to their quotas, then the price in the coming year will be at the target level.

The export quota agreement contains a mechanism for keeping prices stable. If the world price falls because of a decrease in demand, the export quotas of the supplying countries will be tightened and the price will return to $2.50. Analogously, if the world price rises, the quotas will be relaxed and the price will fall back to $2.50. Thus, greater stability is provided with the agreement in place than would otherwise have been the case.

Another mechanism for dealing with export instability focuses on alleviating the consequences of the instability for the developing countries. This mechanism is known as **compensatory financing.** An international agency is provided with funding and forecasts the growth trend of the export earnings of each participating LDC. (The International Monetary Fund has had a compensatory financing facility since 1963.) Suppose that export earnings in 2007 for the developing country fall below the forecast level. The agency responds by extending a short-term loan to the LDC, and the steady flow of foreign exchange to the LDC for the purchase of development imports is thus sustained. If, in 2010, the cycle turns around and the developing country's export earnings rise above trend, the loan can be repaid. Advocates of this approach emphasize that it is superior to international commodity agreements (ICAs) because compensatory financing does not interfere with the allocative function of prices.

Given the developing countries' interest in greater use of international commodity agreements, it is useful to indicate potential difficulties with such arrangements. From the standpoint of feasibility, the crucial features for success in a buffer stock agreement are the levels at which the ceiling price and the floor price are set. If the designated price range *does not contain the long-run free-market equilibrium world price,* then the agreement may not be sustainable. Suppose that the designated price range is from $3.75 to $4.00 per pound of tin but that the actual long-run free-market world price is $3.60 per pound. The result of the agreement will be that the agency will continually be purchasing the good and will exhaust its endowment of funds. It will also accumulate quantities of the good that can only be unloaded at a loss. Further, the price will not have been stabilized and the agency will have no funds with which to continue its operations. If, instead, the long-run equilibrium world price is $4.20 rather than $3.60, then the agency will exhaust its initial endowment of the good. While it will have accumulated funds with which to set up a new agreement at a higher price range, the buffer stock has not performed its stabilizing function. (See Johnson 1967, chap. V.)

There are also forecasting difficulties with export quota agreements. If long-run demand is weaker than estimated, then the supply on the world market from the producing countries will depress the price below what was desired. To raise the price, the countries must hold back exports and will be faced individually with the problem of an accumulation of stocks of the good. If long-run demand is stronger than estimated, individual country stocks will be depleted and countries can no longer stabilize the price. Despite the inability to stabilize, however, the latter situation benefits the LDCs because their export earnings will be higher than anticipated.

A more fundamental difficulty of the export quota arrangement is that, even if the demand and therefore price have been correctly estimated, the agreement must embody *all* exporters of the good or it will be undermined. If there are n exporting countries but only $n - 1$ of them participate, then the nth country will not be constrained in its exports. If it sells large quantities, the world price will fall below the target price. Further, the exporting countries in any export quota agreement must honor their quotas. If they secretly sell more than their allotted amounts, downward pressure on the good's price takes place. For example, although the Organization of Petroleum Exporting Countries (OPEC) is more a price-raising than a price-stabilizing organization, it at times has had difficulty in maintaining the target price of crude oil because individual members cut prices in order to sell larger-than-agreed-upon volumes.

Along the same line, consuming countries are often brought into export quota agreements, and therefore it is necessary that the entire set of consuming nations be included in the agreement. If this is not the case, the exporting countries will find outlets for additional sales in nonparticipating buying countries, and downward pressure will be put on the price. In sum, without full participation and adequate enforcement procedures, export quota agreements will not perform their stabilizing function.

Suggested Policies to Combat a Long-Run Deterioration in the Terms of Trade

Several general policy measures have been suggested for alleviating the alleged secular deterioration of the TOT of LDCs. We discuss these measures briefly beginning on page 437.

IN THE REAL WORLD:

THE LENGTH OF COMMODITY PRICE SHOCKS

An article by Paul Cashin and Hong Liang of the International Monetary Fund and C. John McDermott of the Reserve Bank of New Zealand (1999) sought to determine the likelihood of success of price stabilization schemes for primary commodities. As the history of such agreements suggests, there is reason for pessimism regarding their viability.

The approach of Cashin, Liang, and McDermott was first to note that about 25 percent of world merchandise trade is accounted for by primary products. In addition, on average, about one-half of export earnings of developing countries are derived from primary commodities. Indeed, a single product can often comprise a substantial portion of a country's export earnings. (See Table 3 as well as discussion earlier in this chapter.) Then Cashin, Liang, and McDermott pursued the question of how long would intervention by a price stabilization scheme have to occur in order to provide for stability over time in any given commodity's price, given that price "shocks" take place frequently.

Assembling monthly price data for 1957–1998 on 44 commodities, Cashin, Liang, and McDermott calculated the length of a typical deviation from trend of any given price shock or disturbance. More precisely, they calculated the length of time, after an initial disturbance in price (either up or down), that it took for the amount of the initial disturbance to be dissipated by one-half (that is, the half-life of the shock). The half-lives were quantified in months, and results are given in Table 4. Clearly, the length of time required for some prices to settle down is very long. Such long reaction periods mean that a stabilization scheme for any given product would not be likely to be successful without substantial funding to continue the program for several years. This can importantly account for the failure of the International Sugar Agreement in 1984, the International Tin Agreement in 1985, the International Cocoa Agreement in 1988, and the International Coffee Agreement in 1989. (Note that these four commodities all have long half-lives.) However, the alternative to price stabilization schemes, compensatory financing, might involve a very long commitment of funds in order to offset the shortfall in earnings for the duration of the effects from a downward price disturbance.

(continued)

IN THE REAL WORLD: *(continued)*

TABLE 3   Country Export Dependence on a Single Primary Commodity (Annual Average of Dollar Value of Exports, 1992–1997)

Commodity	50 Percent or More of Export Earnings	20–49 Percent of Export Earnings
Aluminum		Tajikistan
Bananas		Honduras, St. Vincent and the Grenadines
Cocoa	Saõ Tomé and Principe	Côte d'Ivoire, Ghana
Coffee	Burundi, Ethiopia, Uganda	Rwanda
Copper	Zambia	Chile, Mongolia
Copra and coconut oil	Kiribati	
Cotton		Benin, Chad, Mali, Pakistan, Sudan, Uzbekistan
Gold		Ghana, Papua New Guinea, South Africa
Iron ore	Mauritania	
Natural gas	Turkmenistan	Algeria
Petroleum	Angola, Bahrain, Republic of Congo, Gabon, Iran, Iraq, Kuwait, Libya, Nigeria, Oman, Qatar, Saudi Arabia, Venezuela, Yemen	Azerbaijan, Brunei, Cameroon, Ecuador, Equatorial Guinea, Norway, Papua New Guinea, Russia, Syria, Trinidad and Tobago, United Arab Emirates
Sugar		Guyana, Mauritius, St. Kitts and Nevis
Timber		Equatorial Guinea, Laos, Solomon Islands
Tobacco	Malawi	Zimbabwe

Source: Paul Cashin, Hong Liang, and C. John McDermott, "Do Commodity Price Shocks Last Too Long for Stabilization Schemes to Work?" *Finance and Development* 36, no. 3 (September 1999), p. 41.

TABLE 4   Duration of Commodity Price Shocks, January 1957–December 1998

Less than 1 Year	1 Year–4 Years	4 Years–8 Years	More than 8 Years
Bananas	Aluminum	Beef	Cocoa beans
Heating oil	Fishmeal	Coconut oil	Coffee (robusta)
Hides	Gasoline	Copper	Coffee (other milds)
Softwood (logs)	Iron ore	Groundnut oil	Cotton
Softwood (sawn wood)	Lamb	Lead	Gold
Sugar (European Union)	Rubber	Maize	Hardwood (logs)
Tea	Soybean meal	Palm oil	Hardwood (sawn wood)
	Soybeans	Phosphate rock	Natural gas
	Sugar (United States)	Soybean oil	Nickel
	Wheat	Wool (coarse)	Petroleum
		Wool (fine)	Rice
		Zinc	Sugar (free market)
			Tin
			Tobacco
			Triple superphosphate

Source: Paul Cashin, Hong Liang, and C. John McDermott, "Do Commodity Price Shocks Last Too Long for Stabilization Schemes to Work?" *Finance and Development* 36, no. 3 (September 1999), pp. 40–43.

Export Diversification

One strategy is increased **export diversification into manufactured goods** by the LDCs. If the export bundle increasingly contained relatively more manufactured goods, this would circumvent in part the difficulties experienced by the LDCs both with respect to the differing income elasticities of demand and the effects of technological change. The manufactured goods would presumably be labor-intensive goods in accordance with LDCs' abundant labor supplies and the Heckscher-Ohlin theorem. Such a strategy is easier to recommend than to implement, and long-term measures such as increased education may be necessary. Nevertheless, many developing countries have dramatically increased the share of manufactured goods in their exports in the last two to three decades.

Export Cartels

Another possible measure is the formation of an **export cartel** by developing countries. A significant feature of the success of OPEC in the 1970s was that, although the dramatic oil price increases caused difficulties for oil-importing LDCs, developing countries in general looked positively on OPEC's success because it demonstrated that at least some developing countries could organize to obtain a larger share of the gains from trade in the world economy. (See Bhagwati 1977, pp. 6–7.) However, it has become clear with OPEC that a redistribution via the export cartel route may not be a long-term solution to the difficulties of primary product exporters. To be successful, all exporting countries must be part of the process; there must not be strong substitution possibilities for the good in question; and members of the agreement must not cheat on the agreement. These conditions are most likely to be met where only a few countries dominate the world market and where demand is inelastic both in the short run and the long run. These conditions are not likely to be fulfilled for many primary products exported by developing countries.

Import and Export Restrictions

A third policy option is the use of developing-country import or export restrictions to improve the terms of trade. As discussed in Chapter 15, a country with the ability to influence world prices can gain welfare by imposing its optimum tariff (assuming no retaliation). However, economists are generally skeptical of the value to any particular developing country of adopting such trade restrictions. To influence the terms of trade, a country must be large in the economic sense in one or more of its export commodities, and this may not be the case for many LDCs. While industrialized countries' demand for primary products tends to be price inelastic—and hence there is scope for LDCs to improve their TOT by restrictions—the inelasticity applies to primary products as a whole and not to primary products from any one supplier. Demand curves facing any individual country are more elastic than those facing suppliers as a whole. Further, the difficulties of organizing many LDCs to act in concert were mentioned above. Finally, any reduction in the volume of trade by the use of restrictions will deprive LDCs of necessary development imports (e.g., machinery, transport equipment, parts) from the ICs and will introduce price distortions into the economy which can be disadvantageous for development.

Economic Integration Projects

A policy option receiving increased attention is the formation of economic integration projects among the developing countries themselves. These projects may be, for example, free-trade areas or common markets. The idea behind integration projects from the standpoint of the terms-of-trade problem is that the LDC member countries can avoid the potential TOT deterioration in their trade with industrialized countries by having increased trade among themselves. In addition, more market power in world markets may be possible by acting as a united front. Further, the enlarged market size within the region may stimulate investment, the emergence of manufactured goods production, and the diversification required to avoid export instability and TOT deterioration. However, as noted in Chapter 17, such unions run into difficulties regarding the sacrifice of national sovereignty and the distribution of benefits among the partner countries.

IN THE REAL WORLD:

COMECON FOREIGN TRADE PRICING STRATEGIES

The Council for Mutual Economic Assistance (CMEA or Comecon) began from a 1949 communique agreed upon by the Soviet Union, Bulgaria, Czechoslovakia, Hungary, Poland, and Romania. The stated purpose of the organization was to enable member states "to exchange economic experiences, extend technical aid to one another, and to render mutual assistance with respect to raw materials, foodstuffs, machines, equipment, etc." However, Joseph Stalin's desire to enforce Soviet domination of the small states of Eastern Europe and to mollify some states that had expressed interest in the Marshall Plan were also primary factors in its formation.

MEMBERSHIP

Albania joined the six original members in February 1949, and East Germany entered in 1950. Mongolia acceded to membership in 1962, and in the 1970s Comecon expanded its membership to include Cuba (1972) and Vietnam (1978). Political and ideological factors rather than geography united Comecon members. After 1978, Comecon consisted of 450 million people in 10 countries on three continents.

MARKET RELATIONS AND PRICING

It is not surprising, given the overwhelming size of the Soviet economy at the time, that intra-Comecon trade was dominated by exchanges between the Soviet Union and the other members. Exchanges of Soviet fuels and raw materials for capital goods and consumer manufactures characterized trade, particularly among the original members. Trade among the members was negotiated on an annual basis and in considerable detail at the governmental level. Early efforts to facilitate trade among members concentrated on uniform technical, legal, and statistical standards and on encouragement of long-term trade agreements.

In 1971, the Comprehensive Program for Socialist Economic Integration sought to increase quota-free trade. In addition, the comprehensive program called for improvement of administratively set prices used in intra-Comecon trade, which do not reflect costs or relative scarcities of inputs and outputs. In 1971, a price system developed governing exchanges among members under which prices agreed on through negotiation were fixed for five-year periods. The contract prices were based on adjusted world market prices averaged over the preceding five years. Under this system, intra-Comecon prices could and did depart substantially from relative prices on world markets. Relative to actual world prices, intra-Comecon prices in the early 1970s penalized raw materials exporters and benefited exporters of manufactures. After the oil price explosion of 1973, Comecon foreign trade prices swung still further away from world prices to the disadvantage of Comecon suppliers of raw materials, in particular the Soviet Union. By 1975, the gap between Comecon and world prices could no longer be ignored.

A substantial modification, known as the "Bucharest formula," was adopted in 1975. Under the modification, prices were fixed every year and were based on a moving average of world prices for the preceding five years. Under the new agreement, intra-Comecon prices were more closely linked to world prices. Throughout the 1970s, Comecon prices rose with world prices but with a lag. This system benefited non-Soviet members until the early 1980s because Soviet oil was considerably cheaper than OPEC oil. By 1983–1984, the system turned in the Soviet's favor because world oil prices began to fall, whereas the Soviet oil prices continued to rise based on the five-year lagged formula.

While this is an extreme case, Comecon is an example of an integration unit that was designed to increase trade among the members of the integration unit. Rather than focusing on comparative advantage and world market prices, Comecon depended on a system of administratively set prices to avoid major adjustments in terms of trade between members.

Source: Glenn E. Curtis, ed., *Czechoslovakia: A Country Study* (Washington, DC: Federal Research Division of the Library of Congress, 1992).

●

In recent years, there has been a resurgence of interest and participation in economic integration on the part of many developing countries. The ever-growing list of participants includes Mexico (NAFTA, APEC), the countries of MERCOSUR, Chile (in several FTAs), the Asian countries in APEC, the members of the Central American Common Market, members of the Andean Pact, and the participants in the Caribbean Common Market (CARICOM). (See Chapter 17 for a more in-depth discussion of groups involved in economic integration.) What is of particular note is that these various integration schemes increasingly involve groups of both developing and industrialized countries. These arrangements thus often facilitate the flow of new technologies and promote development in the developing countries that takes best advantage of their underlying comparative advantages. Given the experiences of a number of the developing and semi-industrialized countries, it is clear that integration arrangements will not automatically lock the developing country into specializing in the production of primary products.

CONCEPT CHECK

1. How can price instability in a product be related to the demand and supply elasticities of the product?

2. Why do economists tend to favor the use of compensatory financing rather than international commodity agreements to enhance efficient resource allocation in LDCs?

3. Why might diversification of LDC exports into manufactured goods help to alleviate any possible long-run deterioration in the LDCs' terms of trade?

4. Why does the mere existence of transfer pricing by multinational corporations in a manner unfavorable to LDCs not automatically imply that the transfer pricing has caused a long-run deterioration in the terms of trade of the LDCs?

Inward-Looking versus Outward-Looking Trade Strategies

In view of the preceding discussion, what is the appropriate trade strategy for LDCs? Economists and policymakers have debated two competing strategies regarding the trade sector. An **inward-looking strategy** is an attempt to withdraw, at least in the short run, from full participation in the world economy. This strategy emphasizes **import substitution,** that is, the production of goods at home that would otherwise be imported. This can economize on scarce foreign exchange and ultimately generate new manufactured exports without the export difficulties of primary products if economies of scale are important in the import-substitute industries and if the infant industry argument (see Chapter 15) applies. The strategy uses tariffs, import quotas, subsidies to import-substitute industries, and other measures of this type. In contrast, an **outward-looking strategy** emphasizes participation in international trade by encouraging the allocation of resources without price distortions. It does not use policy measures to shift production arbitrarily between serving the home market and foreign markets. In other words, it is an application of production according to comparative advantage; the current expression is that the LDCs should **get prices right.** Some analysts go further and focus particularly on **export promotion,** whereby policy steps such as export subsidies, encouragement of skill accumulation in the labor force and the use of more advanced technology, and tax breaks are used to generate more exports, particularly labor-intensive manufactured exports in accordance with the Heckscher-Ohlin theorem.

Trade Strategy and Economic Performance

Does the choice of which trade strategy to employ make a difference in the performance of the developing country economy? The World Bank's *World Development Report 1987* (chap. 5) examined experience for 41 LDCs in an attempt to answer this question. It classified countries according to four categories of trade strategy. A country was classified as a **strongly-outward-oriented economy** (SO) if it had few trade controls and if its currency was neither overvalued nor undervalued relative to other currencies and thus did not discriminate between exports and production for the home market in incentives provided. A country was classified as a **moderately-outward-oriented economy** (MO) if the incentives biased production slightly toward serving the home market rather than exports, effective rates of protection were relatively low, and the exchange rate was only slightly biased against exports (that is, home currency slightly overvalued).

A **moderately-inward-oriented economy** (MI) clearly favors production for the home market rather than for export through relatively high protection because of import controls, and exports are definitely discouraged by the exchange rate. Finally, a **strongly-inward-oriented economy** (SI) exhibits comprehensive incentives toward import substitution and away from exports through more severe measures than in MI.

The 41 countries were classified by their trade strategy for two periods, 1963–1973 and 1973–1985. Only three economies were classified as SO in each period: Hong Kong, South Korea, and Singapore. Ten countries were in the MO category in the first period and eight in the second; Brazil, Israel, Malaysia, and Thailand were so classified in both periods. The MI category contained 12 countries for 1963–1973 and 16 for 1973–1985. The countries appearing in this category in both periods were El Salvador, Honduras, Kenya, Mexico, Nicaragua, the Philippines, Senegal, and Yugoslavia. Finally, the SI category contained 16 economies in the first period and 14 in the second period, with Argentina, Bangladesh, Burundi, Dominican Republic, Ethiopia, Ghana, India, Peru, Sudan, Tanzania, and Zambia being so classified in both periods. Note the predominance of African and Latin American countries in the two inward-looking categories.

With respect to the comparative performance of countries operating under the different trade strategies, the World Bank staff's conclusions were strongly stated: "The figures suggest that the economic performance of the outward-oriented economies has been broadly superior to that of the inward-oriented economies in almost all respects" (World Bank 1987, p. 85). Various criteria of economic performance were examined to reach this conclusion. In terms of the average growth rates of real GDP, a ranking for 1963–1973 showed that, in terms of the four designations, SO > MO > MI > SI; for 1973–1985, the average growth rate of MI countries slightly exceeded that of MO countries, but the rest of the ranking remained intact. The same general pattern was true of growth rates of GNP per capita, with an average growth rate of 6.9 percent in the SO countries and 1.6 percent in the SI countries for 1963–1973. The average per capita GNP rates were 5.9 percent in the SO countries and *minus* 0.1 percent in the SI countries for 1973–1985. Further, saving as a percentage of GDP was greater for the two outward categories in the second period, although this was not true for the first period. The growth rates of manufactured exports among the outward countries substantially exceeded those of the inward countries in both periods. Finally, capital was used more efficiently (as expressed in lower quantities of capital required to get additional units of output) in the outward economies than in the inward economies.

A measure that did not show superior performance for the countries with outward orientation was the rate of inflation. These rates were close to each other in all four categories in 1963–1973, but the MO economies had the highest rates in 1973–1985, and the average rate for SO and MO countries exceeded that for MI and SI countries in those years. The World Bank explained this phenomenon by indicating that an outward strategy ties a country's inflation rate to that of the world economy to a greater extent than the inward strategy, and world inflation was high in the 1973–1985 period.

In addition to the general findings on the better economic performance under an outward-looking strategy, the World Bank suggests that outward orientation rather than inward orientation may lead to a more equal income distribution (World Bank 1987, p. 85). A reason for this result is that the expansion of labor-intensive exports generates employment opportunities, while import substitution policies often result in capital-intensive production processes that displace labor. Another benefit of the outward-looking strategy is that foreign-exchange shortages are less common. With import substitution, an initial saving of foreign exchange is often temporary because the replacement of imports of final goods by domestic production requires imports of raw materials, capital equipment, and components. The end result may be increased rather than decreased dependence on imports. (See Krueger 1983, pp. 7–8.)

The World Bank's findings (see also World Bank 1991) and those of advocates of comparative advantage have led to the recommendation that the LDCs adopt more outward-oriented policies. Indeed, the world economy in the late 1980s and the 1990s saw a strong emergence of support for the market—witness the economic reforms in Central and Eastern Europe and the former republics of the Soviet Union and also in many other LDCs. Moreover, the absence of an outward focus is evident in a number of slower-growing countries. For example, Africa's trade performance has lagged behind other countries. Its exports and imports have grown at three-fourths the world average rate since 1970, with the result that its share in world trade has fallen from 4 percent to around 2 percent today. In addition, Africa's trade-to-GDP ratio has grown more slowly than any other developing country region, and it appears to be the region least open to trade. Not surprisingly, its growth rate falls short of the 7 percent rate required for Africa to reach the Millennium Development Goal of halving poverty by 2015.[10]

Despite the seeming advantage of outward-looking policies, some economists and policymakers are reluctant to embrace the strategy wholeheartedly. First, expansion of manufactured exports, such as that attained by Hong Kong, South Korea, Singapore, Taiwan, and, recently, China, can run into protectionist barriers in the industrialized countries. Because the labor-intensive manufactured exports threaten long-existing industries in ICs (e.g., textiles and shoes), restrictions such as the Multi-Fiber Arrangement in textiles and apparel may have stifled this route to development for many LDCs. In addition, the export path may require skills in the labor force that are not yet fully developed and will require a large commitment of resources in order to do so (although import substitution runs into this same problem). Further, Paul Streeten (1982, pp. 165–66) has pointed out that there is a "fallacy of composition" in the outward-looking strategy because, while any one country may face high price elasticities of demand in manufactured goods exports, the demand facing all developing countries is less elastic than that facing any one country. Substantial price declines may occur if all LDCs follow the same path. In addition, some empirical studies dispute any positive relationship between exports and industrialization (see Chow 1987) or suggest that the positive link occurs only above some threshold income level (see Tyler 1981). Nevertheless, looking at the trade/growth experience of developing countries in recent decades and recent years, *The Economist* in 2001, after considering import substitution industrialization (ISI) and various objections to greater openness, concluded, "On the whole, ISI failed; almost everywhere, trade has been good for growth."[11]

It should be noted that some mix or sequence of the two strategies may be appropriate in some cases. For example, South Korea engaged in import substitution before embarking on its export-led growth path (see Singer and Ansari 1988, pp. 261–63). In cases of infant industries or where the Krugman-type protection arguments apply (see Chapter 15), this may be a good strategy. In addition, some have suggested (see Todaro and Smith 2003, chap. 13) that economic integration among developing countries may offer benefits because it is a combination of an outward-looking strategy (through freer trade with other LDC partners) and an inward-looking strategy in which the union as a whole is turning away from the rest of the world economy. In any event, the precise extent to which a country should turn outward or inward depends on the external and internal characteristics of that country. The policies to be recommended can be decided only on a case-by-case basis.

---

[10]Sanjeev Gupta and Yongzheng Yang, "Unblocking Trade," *Finance and Development* 43, no. 4 (December 2006), pp. 22–25.

[11]"Globalisation and Its Critics," *The Economist,* September 29, 2001, p. 12.

IN THE REAL WORLD:

TERRORISM AND ITS EFFECT ON DEVELOPING COUNTRIES

The increased risk and prevalence of global terrorism looms as a major threat to international trade and economic development. In a study of more than 200 countries from 1968 to 1979, Nitsch and Schumacher (2002) found that a doubling of the number of terrorist incidents decreased bilateral trade between targeted economies by about 6 percent. The fear of future terrorist acts creates uncertainty, which increases perceived risk. The uncertainty can affect investment and economic growth in a variety of ways.

Increased risk undermines investor confidence and reduces investors' willingness to commit to new projects. Over time, higher risk premiums increase required rates of return on investments and push investment away from riskier, potentially higher return investments toward lower risk, lower return, shorter term investments. Increased terrorism risks also tend to reduce consumers' willingness to spend, particularly on discretionary items and major consumer durables. Airline, travel, tourism, accommodation, restaurant, postal, and insurance services are particularly susceptible to terrorism risk. Currencies in economies perceived to carry terrorism risk may experience exchange rate volatility.

While terrorism costs affect all economies, the effect on developing economies may be disproportionately high. Many developing economies depend on trade for a relatively high percentage of their GDP. Any disruption in trade flows can have a severe impact on their economic growth. In addition, many developing economies rely on strong inflows of

foreign direct investment (FDI). Increases in terrorist activity can raise risk premiums and reduce FDI flows to economies considered at risk. Finally, insurance premiums may be higher on cargoes and vessels traveling to and from developing economies because of insurers' uncertainty about the adequacy of local security procedures.

Implementation of new security measures will require one-time investments in new infrastructure, but these costs should be viewed as an investment that will (by reducing the threat of terrorism) pay future dividends through reduced risk premiums and even increased trade efficiency. Standardized electronic manifest systems at ports save time and reduce costs through quicker processing of cargo. These systems are becoming necessary with rapidly expanding international trade, so expenditures on these new systems represent investments that increase efficiency and help counterterrorism. The threat of terrorism affects entire regions, so it makes sense to have coordinated regional efforts to counter such threats. Economies that fail to cooperate in multilateral counter-terrorism measures run the risk of marginalizing themselves from international transactions.

Sources: "The Costs of Terrorism and the Benefits of Cooperating to Combat Terrorism," paper presented by Dr. Geoff Raby, Deputy Secretary, Department of Foreign Affairs and Trade to APEC Senior Officials at Chiang Rai, Thailand, February 21, 2003; V. Nitsche and D. Schumacher, "Terrorism and Trade" paper presented at workshop, The Economic Consequences of Global Terrorism, DIW/German Institute for Economic Research, Berlin, June 2002. ●

Finally, an excellent overview of the history and more recent state of thinking on trade policy and economic development can be found in a paper by Anne O. Krueger (1997). After reviewing the theoretical, policy, and empirical work that had focused on this issue in the past 50 years, she points out several lessons that have been learned regarding the current state of knowledge in this area. Not surprisingly, the first lesson she cites is that empirical research that tests for the presence and relative importance of certain stylized facts is critical to the successful application of theory and policy selection. Nowhere is this more in evidence than in trade policy, where early policy decisions were based on facts that were often little more than a mixture of "touristic impressions, half truths and misapplied policy inferences" (Krueger 1997, p. 3). What has happened is a demonstration that developing countries can expand export earnings based on, among other things, increased exports of manufactures. In addition, there is also clear evidence that producers in these countries do indeed respond to economic incentives. The experience of the East Asian countries has been particularly effective in demonstrating the viability of trade policies that promoted industrialization through reliance on foreign markets (as opposed to domestic markets) and were based on sound ideas of comparative advantage that went beyond reliance on primary commodities. Krueger suggests that the East Asian experience demonstrated that the earlier export pessimism that underlay ideas of import substitution was perhaps more an indicator of inward-oriented trade and payments regimes than an outward focus based on dynamic comparative advantage. If nothing else, the East Asian experience put to rest the idea that developing countries with an outward focus would lock themselves permanently into a pattern of primary-product specialization.

In addition to the contribution of important analytical research and the development of better measurement techniques, Krueger also notes the critical importance of theory in demonstrating why simple interpretations of economic performance based on commonly held stylized facts were often in fact wrong. Thus, it is important that if theory results are to be useful to policymakers, the critical ideas must be able to be related to specific phenomena that are observable, hopefully quantifiable, and recognizable to the policymaker. While there is always the danger that theories will be misinterpreted or used incorrectly, they are crucial for analyzing problems, policies, and outcomes. However, she concludes, "No matter how careful economists are, special interests always will seize their research results in supporting their own objectives. And, no matter how sophisticated and careful research findings are, there always will be politicians formulating, and non-economists administering policies" (Krueger 1997, pp. 17–19). There is little doubt that a clear understanding of comparative advantage and the importance of fostering the presence of correct relative prices of products and factors is central to harnessing the potential role of international trade in promoting the development of the industrializing country. As nations decide to seek the advantages of increased involvement in the global economy, there are always new challenges to be met.

THE EXTERNAL DEBT PROBLEM OF THE DEVELOPING COUNTRIES

A final topic of concern with regard to the international sector and development is the external debt problem of the LDCs. This problem is intimately bound up with the matter of access to finance in the world economy. If industrialized country banks that have outstanding loans to the developing countries experience difficulties because of this debt, underpinning institutions in the world monetary system are placed in jeopardy. Table 5 provides an overview of the size of the external debt of LDCs, with data on the debt and its relationship to several key economic variables at the end of 2005.

TABLE 5   External Debt and Debt Ratios of Developing Countries, 2005

	External Debt ($ billions)	Debt as a Percentage of GDP	Debt as a Percentage of Exports of Goods and Services	Debt Service Ratio
Emerging Market and Developing Countries (145)	$3,012.3	28.9%	76.9%	15.3%
Africa (48)	289.4	35.9	92.4	10.9
Central and Eastern Europe (15)	604.7	49.6	110.0	22.1
Commonwealth of Independent States and Mongolia (13)	334.0	33.6	85.8	27.3
Developing Asia (23)	808.3	20.3	53.3	7.1
Middle East (13)	221.8	22.4	38.6	4.9
Western Hemisphere (33)	754.1	31.0	131.6	35.0

Note: The number of countries in the group are in parentheses.

Source: International Monetary Fund, *World Economic Outlook,* September 2006 (Washington, DC: IMF, 2006), obtained from www.imf.org.

Column (1) shows that Developing Asia, Latin America and the Caribbean countries (Western Hemisphere) and Central Eastern Europe have the largest dollar value of external debt. However, for a variety of reasons, including quicker adjustment policies to the debt problem and favorable export prospects, the Asian countries do not have as severe a debt problem as the Central and Eastern European countries, Latin American and Caribbean countries, and Africa. Column (2) is a measure of the LDCs' ability to carry the debt in relation to annual productive capacity, that is, the flow of annual output that conceptually could be available to repay the debt: The possible severity of the problem for all but Developing Asia and the Middle East is evident.

Column (3) emphasizes the point that even though a country may produce the goods and services with which to repay debt, it still must convert these resources into foreign exchange (i.e., hard, convertible currencies). Unless new external funds are forthcoming, this generation of foreign exchange has to occur through successful exporting. That is, in order to effectively transfer purchasing power back to the lenders as repayment, developing-country exports must be stimulated and imports reduced so that sufficient foreign exchange is available. This **transfer problem** of freeing up resources to accomplish repayment can be difficult indeed. The countries of the Western Hemisphere and Central and Eastern Europe have the highest debt/export ratios.

Finally, column (4) presents the debt service ratio, a measure that many economists judge is the best indicator of the debt problem facing LDCs. The **debt service ratio** is the percentage of annual export earnings that must be set aside for payment of interest on the debt and the scheduled repayment of the debt itself. When debt service ratios are of the order of the Western Hemisphere's 35.0 percent and the 27.3 percent in the transition economies of the former Soviet Union and Mongolia, the countries must devote large portions of their foreign exchange earnings to debt service. These large fractions of foreign exchange earnings are therefore not available for the purchase of needed imports, and imports must be reduced dramatically if the country is to avoid drawing down its stock of international reserves or incurring even more debt. (In the 1980s, many Latin American countries compressed imports to such an extent that living standards fell drastically.)

Causes of the Developing Countries' Debt Problem

Many factors have been suggested as having played a causal role in the LDC debt problem. However, the relative importance of the factors varies from country to country, and it is difficult to make generalizations.

1. A prominent element in discussions of the debt problem consists of the *oil price increases of 1973–1974 and 1979–1981.* The two "oil shocks" resulted in a huge increase in the oil import bills of many developing countries, and borrowing was necessary to finance the additional import expenditures. Much of the borrowing was from industrialized countries' commercial banks, which were recycling dollars deposited in them by members of OPEC (petrodollars).

2. Related to the oil price increases were the *recessions in the industrialized countries* in the 1970s and early to mid-1980s. The recessions resulted in large part from the oil shocks but also from anti-inflationary macroeconomic policies adopted in industrialized countries. From the standpoint of the LDCs, recessions in the ICs mean that purchases of LDC exports grow slowly or decline. With slower or negative export growth, LDCs must borrow more to continue a flow of imports.

3. *The behavior of real interest rates* was also important in generating and perpetuating the debt crisis. The real interest rate is equal to the nominal interest rate charged by lenders minus the expected rate of inflation. In the 1970s, this real rate was low and sometimes negative due to expectations of high inflation, and borrowers (the LDCs) were thus encouraged

to undertake new loans. However, the rapid fall in inflation in the 1980s in the United States in particular—associated with tight monetary policy—caused the real rate to rise. This meant that any additional LDC borrowing to finance repayment of existing debt imposed extra burdens on the developing countries.

4. In addition, *primary-product prices declined dramatically in the 1980s.* Because primary products constitute a large fraction of the exports of developing countries, this decline necessitated additional borrowing to finance needed imports for development. Many of these prices rose in the early 1990s but then fell again.

5. *Domestic policies within the developing countries* also played a role in generating the debt problem. If loans are used for consumption rather than for productive investment, or if the LDC inflates its price level rapidly by excessive monetary growth associated with government budget deficits, then repayment prospects are poor and new borrowing must be undertaken. Further, mismanagement of domestic financial institutions can exacerbate the problem. The ability to finance development without resorting to external borrowing is also hindered if domestic price controls inhibit an efficient allocation of resources or if the LDC's currency is pegged at an overvalued rate. Such overvaluation makes exports "too expensive" to foreign buyers and imports "too cheap" to domestic buyers, leading to a trade deficit.

6. Another factor associated with increasing indebtedness was *capital flight from the developing countries.* This phenomenon is harder to document precisely than previous reasons, but that the phenomenon exists is unquestionable. With very rapid inflations taking place in Latin American countries and low real interest returns, many domestic citizens sent funds to IC banks. With these funds not available for domestic use, the LDCs had to borrow more capital on international markets.

7. Finally, the hypothesis has emerged that a considerable portion of LDC indebtedness was due to "*loan-pushing*" by banks in the developed countries (Darity and Horn 1988). This view emphasizes that IC banks were awash in funds (importantly from the recycling of petrodollars) and, accompanied by the deregulation of financial institutions in the United States, were anxious to expand their loan portfolios. Hence, loans were often made that were not necessarily associated with sound economic analysis and did not adequately take risk factors into account. In many cases, the growing debt burden was effectively ignored by banks as LDC officials were aggressively talked into taking on more debt than their countries could absorb. Indeed, in the middle of 1982, "the nine largest U.S. banks had loans outstanding to developing countries and Eastern Europe amounting to 280 percent of their capital, and most had over 100 percent of capital in loans to just Brazil and Mexico."[12] This large and concentrated amount of outstanding loans also led to fears of collapse of the financial systems in industrialized countries if defaults occurred.

Possible Solutions to the Debt Problem

In seeking solutions to the developing-country debt problem, it is important to distinguish between the liquidity problem and the solvency problem. The *liquidity problem* in this context refers to the fact that although a debtor country will eventually be able to repay its debts, there is a short-run problem of financing debt service payments because the country's assets are not immediately convertible into a form acceptable to creditors. Hence, policies should provide for temporary finance until longer-run adjustments can take place. The *solvency problem* refers to the fact that the country is in such poor condition and has

---

[12]William R. Cline, "International Debt: From Crisis to Recovery," *American Economic Review* 75, no. 2 (May 1985), p. 185.

such dismal economic prospects that it will never be able to generate the resources to repay its debt. If the problem is insolvency, then some form of debt forgiveness must be instituted or the country will have to default on its obligations. Until 1982, the LDC debt problem was generally regarded as one of liquidity, but the announcement by Mexico (the second-largest LDC debtor, after Brazil) that it would not be able to meet debt service obligations due at that time set in motion a concern that the problem in many LDCs was really one of insolvency.

Changing Domestic Policies

In general, there are several broad categories of solutions that can be suggested for dealing with the debt problem. First, *LDCs can change their domestic policies so as to increase their ability to service the debt.* This strategy is a long-term one that regards the debt problem as a matter of temporary illiquidity. The emphasis of the International Monetary Fund and the World Bank on **structural adjustment policies** falls into this category. When the IMF negotiates with a debtor country concerning new loans, it will often approve the loans only if the LDC undertakes various measures to strengthen its long-term repayment prospects. The conditionality measures usually include reduction of government budget deficits and the money supply (to reduce inflation and the accompanying balance-of-payments deficits) and the adoption of a realistic exchange rate—meaning a devaluation of the domestic currency.[13] These steps are often called "austerity policies." Devaluation undertaken along with contractionary monetary and fiscal policies can improve the trade balance and put the debtor country in a better position for servicing debt with hard foreign currency. Other recommended policies usually include the elimination of government production and/or consumption subsidies and of distortionary price controls. These measures allow the market rather than government policy to allocate resources, which the IMF argues will improve efficiency. The attachment of such conditions to new lending by the IMF has generated considerable resentment among LDCs.

Debt Rescheduling

Another approach to the debt problem involves **debt rescheduling.** This approach also treats the debt problem as basically a liquidity rather than a solvency problem. In rescheduling operations, interest rates on the debt are often lowered, the time period of the loan is lengthened, or the grace period before repayments start is made longer. There have been a large number of reschedulings, particularly through the "Paris Club," a consortium of IC governments set up to deal with rescheduling of government (rather than commercial bank) loans. These reschedulings have been particularly relevant for Africa, where the debt is owed mostly to governments rather than to private banks. (Latin America's debt to banks is greater than to governments.)

Debt Relief

Recently, attention has been focused on **debt relief** or **debt reduction** rather than on rescheduling. A well-known earlier initiative along this line was the **Brady plan,** proposed by U.S. Secretary of the Treasury Nicholas Brady early in 1989. Details varied from country to country, but in this general strategy, a pool of money from the United States or from the World Bank and the IMF was used to guarantee new bonds issued by developing-country governments. These new bonds were offered to existing lenders in such a fashion that the amount of debt outstanding was reduced. For example, $10 billion of new debt might be issued to retire $20 billion of old debt. The advantage to the LDC is that its debt is decreased, as well as its interest payments. For the lending bank, $20 billion of claims on the developing country have

---

[13]One study of 24 LDCs indicated that failure to have an appropriate exchange rate had strongly negative implications for such performance characteristics as per capita income growth rate, export growth rate, and net investment rate. See Cottani, Cavallo, and Khan (1990).

been swapped for only $10 billion of claims, but the smaller amount is now guaranteed. An alternative procedure might involve no reduction in the principal of the debt but a lower interest rate on the new debt than on the old debt. It was also anticipated that the developing country would carry out market- and growth-oriented reforms such as relaxation of price controls, elimination of distortions, and policies to stimulate domestic savings and investment.

In 1996, the International Monetary Fund and the World Bank together designed a cooperative program with creditor countries to provide debt relief for developing countries that are having particular difficulties meeting debt service and repayment obligations. The **Heavily Indebted Poor Countries (HIPC) Initiative** is designed to assist countries that have what the IMF and World Bank regard as an "unsustainable debt burden."[14] Under the HIPC program, eligible countries adopt adjustment and reform programs that are regularly assessed by the IMF and the World Bank, and a defined procedure of review and financial assistance is laid out. The two multilateral institutions coordinate debt relief from individual country donors and flows of funds directly from the IMF and World Bank. An important aspect of the program is that, with debt burdens reduced, the HIPCs can spend more on development and quality-of-life items such as health and education. At the end of 2005, it was estimated that for the 40 countries identified as HIPCs, the cost of providing assistance to reduce debt to sustainable levels would be about $40 billion in net present value terms (i.e., taking account of the future flow of funds and debt obligations over time). About one-half of this amount was to be provided by individual donor countries and one-half by the two multilateral institutions. Substantial progress had been made and debt service had fallen dramatically (by about 2 percent of GDP) for the 30 countries that were operating under approved debt-relief packages. Because of this improvement, the countries were able to increase the share of their spending on social services because debt service was less onerous.

An interesting hypothesis that has emerged in the context of debt relief is that a reduction in debt might in fact *enhance* an LDC's likelihood of repaying debt and that such a forgiveness of debt by lending banks might actually help those banks. (See Krugman 1989 and Kenen 1990.) The first part of the hypothesis that a reduction in debt can increase the chance of repaying debt is straightforward. Suppose that a developing-country government has a large debt to foreign banks or governments, and therefore has incurred large future debt service obligations. In this situation, domestic investors in enterprises in the LDC may come to expect future tax increases by the LDC government so as to pay the future interest and amortization. This expectation of future higher taxes would dampen current growth-creating investment because the expected after-tax rate of return to investors is lower due to the anticipated increased taxes. Or suppose that it is general opinion that the LDC's current debt level is so high that it can never be repaid. In this case, default may be likely by the LDC, and this default would confirm to any foreign private investor considering entering the country that the country is in trouble and is not a good place to invest. Hence, there could be a halt to any inflow of potential growth-creating foreign investment for at least some time in the future. Through scenarios such as these, a high level of LDC debt per se can interfere with the developing country's current economic performance. The implication of the scenarios is that reductions in debt can stimulate domestic investment (because of anticipated *lower* future tax burdens) as well as foreign private investment (because of less likelihood of default and more optimistic assessments by foreign investors of the country's prospects).

This line of thinking on debt reduction as a means of stimulating LDC growth has led to a useful graphical construct, and this construct also enables us to see the second part of the debt reduction hypothesis—that it can be in the interest of foreign lending banks to "forgive"

---

[14]For further details, see "Debt Relief under the Heavily Indebted Poor Countries (HIPC) Initiative," Fact Sheet: obtained from www.imf.org.

FIGURE 2   The Debt-Relief Laffer Curve

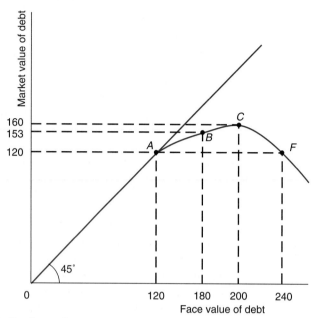

In the debt-relief Laffer diagram, in the range from the origin to point *A,* the outstanding debt of a less developed country is expected to be fully repaid. The value of the LDC's bonds in the secondary market is consequently equal to 100 percent of the face value of the bonds. From point *A* to point *C,* the market value of the debt increases with the face value but at a diminishing rate, being, for example, 85 percent at point *B* (=$153 million ÷ $180 million) and 80 percent at point *C* (=$160 million ÷ $200 million). Beyond point *C,* greater LDC debt is associated with a lower total market value. This reflects poorer growth and debt repayment prospects by the country as more debt is incurred since, for example, domestic firms may undertake less real investment because they expect taxes to be raised in order to service the very large debt.

some LDC debt. This graphical construct is the **debt-relief Laffer curve,** brought to prominence by Paul Krugman (1989).[15] To understand this construct, consider the concepts of the face value of debt and the market value of debt. The *face value of debt* is simply the nominal monetary value of the bonds or debt instruments, say, a $100 million bond held by an industrialized country bank representing $100 million that the bank has lent to the developing country. The face value of LDC debt is what is represented by the dollar figures in Table 5. The *market value of debt* refers to the actual trading prices of the bonds or debt instruments. LDC debt instruments (and of course most kinds of debt instruments) are sold (and bought) in a **secondary debt market** after the initial issuance if a holder wants to exchange the bonds for other assets (or someone else wants to exchange other assets for these bonds). Prices in these secondary markets are thought to reflect the "true" value of the claims, and for LDC debt, prices have sometimes gone below 20 percent of face value.

A debt-relief Laffer curve is shown in Figure 2.[16] The face value of debt is measured on the horizontal axis, and the market value of debt (the value in the secondary market) is plotted on the vertical axis. If lenders expect the debt to be fully repaid (including interest),

---

[15]The analogy is to the *Laffer curve* (named after Arthur B. Laffer) used in consideration of fiscal policy, whereby a reduction in the marginal tax rate can increase tax revenues.

[16]For an excellent exposition of the debt-relief Laffer curve, see "Sisters in the Wood: A Survey of the IMF and the World Bank," *The Economist,* October 12, 1991, pp. 24, 29–30, 33.

the market value is equal to the face value, and the relationship is represented by a 45-degree line from the origin. This is the case from the origin to point *A* (where $120 million of debt has a market value of $120 million). However, after point *A,* lenders do not expect the debt to be fully repaid, and the LDC bonds sell at a discount in the secondary market. Thus, at point *B,* $180 million of debt sells for $153 million, for the market value is only 85 percent of the face value ($153 million ÷ $180 million = 0.85), a discount of 15 percent. At point *C,* $200 million of debt would sell for $160 million in the secondary market, or at a 20 percent discount. Finally, after point *C,* we get the situation where additional debt beyond $200 million actually *reduces* the market value; for example, at point *F,* $240 million of debt has a market value of only $120 million. This downward-sloping range after point *C* represents the situation of our earlier discussion that the level of debt so reduces domestic and foreign investment that the country's growth and debt repayment prospects become very poor. In this range, a reduction of the developing country's debt from $240 million to $200 million would actually *increase* the market value of the debt from $120 million to $160 million. Hence, if the LDC is located beyond point *C,* there is a clear case for voluntary debt reduction or write-offs by the lending banks. Such action would increase the country's growth prospects and ability to repay debt, and it would also help the banks by raising the market value of their loan portfolios.

In the range between points *A* and *C,* the situation is somewhat different, but there is still some incentive for debt reduction by both the LDC and the lenders. Starting at point *C* and going to point *A,* lending banks could forgive $80 million of debt (=$200 million − $120 million), and the cost of writing off $80 million would be only $40 million (the reduction in the market value from $160 million to $120 million). Alternatively, if the developing country could obtain $40 million of resources from some other source such as the IMF or the World Bank or by its own efforts, it could "buy back" or cancel $80 million of its outstanding debt to the banks by giving the banks this $40 million. In either event or in some combination of buybacks and forgiveness, the LDC benefits from having less debt and lower future interest and amortization payments, and it has reduced its debt at a cost of 50 cents for each dollar of debt reduction. The banks will have reduced their holdings of risky LDC debt by $80 million but at a maximum cost of only $40 million. The banks have also increased the quality of the LDC debt that they continue to hold, as its market value ($120 million) is now 100 percent of its face value.

Given the debt-relief Laffer curve analysis, why have we not seen a greater amount of debt reduction in practice? The reason is that, for the forgiveness or buyback actions such as in the *A* to *C* range of the curve to be undertaken, negotiations must be successfully concluded by the developing country with *all* the bank lenders as a *group.* If this is not done, no *individual* lender has an incentive to do the debt reduction on its own. Suppose that there are only four lending banks—banks I, II, III, and IV—and that each of the four banks holds an equal face value of LDC debt of $50 million at point *C.* Suppose now that bank I forgives $20 million of the $50 million debt owed to it, reducing the LDC's total debt from $200 million to $180 million and moving the LDC from point *C* to point *B.* Given the shape of the debt-relief Laffer curve, this forgiveness by bank I has reduced the market value of the LDC's total debt from $160 million to $153 million. What has happened? Bank I formerly held $50 million face value LDC bonds with a market value of $40 million (because the market value at point *C* was 80 percent of the face value). It now holds $30 million of bonds (its original $50 million minus the $20 million forgiven) with a market value of $25.5 million. (The $25.5 million results because, at point *B,* market value is 85 percent of face value and $30 million × 0.85 = $25.5 million.) Hence, this bank has forgiven $20 million of debt, but it has done so at a cost of $14.5 million. (The original market value of bank I's holdings was $40 million, which has now been reduced to $25.5

million.) If all four banks each had simultaneously undertaken $20 million forgiveness, we would have moved from point *C* to point *A* on the curve, and the cost to bank I would have been only $10 million for its $20 million of debt reduction. Hence, the individual negotiation has cost bank I $4.5 million more (=$14.5 million − $10 million) than if all banks had negotiated reductions simultaneously. (Alternatively, in the case of a buyback by the LDC from bank I, the LDC would have had to pay bank I $14.5 million for the $20 million debt reduction in a single negotiation and only $10 million in the multiple negotiation.)

But matters are even worse for bank I when it alone forgives the $20 million debt. Because of its unilateral debt reduction, its competitor banks II, III, and IV have actually *gained*. With bank I's debt forgiveness to the LDC and the consequent movement from point *C* to point *B,* the ratio of market value to face value has risen from 80 percent ($160 million ÷ $200 million) to 85 percent ($153 million ÷ $180 million). The $50 million face-value bonds that each of these other banks still hold previously had a market value of $40 million (=$50 million × 0.80) but now have a market value of $42.5 million (=$50 million × 0.85). Bank I's action has benefited each other bank by $2.5 million (=$42.5 million − $40 million); each other bank is getting a "free ride" while bank I imposes a cost on itself of $14.5 million. Therefore, any one bank would not undertake the debt relief on its own. In this framework, then, without joint negotiations embracing all lenders, no action can be expected by any one bank to reduce developing country debt.

Debt-Equity Swaps   A final broad type of strategy for dealing with LDC debt involves **debt-equity swaps.** In this arrangement, a holder of a debt claim on a developing country exchanges the claim for local LDC currency, which is then used to acquire shares of stock in a productive enterprise in the LDC. Thus, the LDC reduces its debt and its interest obligations. In turn, the creditor no longer holds a bond whose repayment is uncertain, but instead holds equity in an ongoing company in the developing country. Whether this is advantageous to the creditor depends on the future performance of the company involved.

We do not explore other plans in this book, but a large number of such plans for reducing the burden of debt on LDCs exists. That the burden has been great is reflected in the fact that, for much of the 1980s, living standards fell in the debtor countries (particularly in Latin America) as they compressed imports and undertook austerity programs. Trade surpluses were generated through such measures, and there was in fact a large net *outflow* of capital from Latin America as repayments and interest exceeded new inflows. Indeed, a former chief economist for the World Bank, Stanley Fischer, in conjunction with Ishrat Husain wrote that the LDC adjustments "were made at a high price. Investment and output levels have fallen, domestic consumption and wages have been compressed. . . . As a result, most of the countries in Latin America and Africa now look back at almost a decade of lost growth" (Fischer and Husain 1990, p. 24).

In addition to the preceding specific measures, industrialized countries can undertake several general measures to lessen the severity of the developing-country debt problem. These measures can also be of benefit to the ICs as well. For example, a decrease in levels of tariff and nontariff protection against LDC export goods would increase the foreign exchange earnings of LDCs and hence their ability to repay debt, as well as improve welfare in the ICs via the standard arguments for freer trade. In addition, more rapid economic growth in the industrialized countries not only would increase well-being in the ICs but would stimulate LDC exports, foreign exchange earnings, and national income. Further, an increase in the amount of foreign aid given to the developing countries not only would be of use to them but, if such aid stimulates LDC growth, would also benefit the industrialized countries through increased exports sold to the LDCs. There is certainly scope for such an increase in aid as the United States, for example, in recent years has allocated two-tenths of

1 percent or less of its GDP to foreign aid. This aid can also be given indirectly if the IMF issues new Special Drawing Rights (SDRs)[17] and allocates proportionately more of them to developing countries. Such an allocation of SDRs could assist the LDCs in maintaining a flow of development imports, even when a large fraction of their current foreign exchange earnings is being used for debt service.

---

[17]The SDR is an international reserve asset created by the IMF in 1969 to supplement the existing official reserves of member countries. SDRs will be discussed in more detail in Chapter 29.

CONCEPT CHECK	1. Why do developing countries object to IMF conditionality?	3. Explain the usefulness of the concept of the debt service ratio.
	2. Explain the concept of the debt-relief Laffer curve.	

SUMMARY

The less developed countries in the world economy are characterized by relatively low levels of per capita income, a relatively high concentration of exports in primary products, and export instability; they may also face long-run forces that cause a deterioration in their commodity terms of trade. The trade problem of export instability and its potentially adverse implications for the LDCs is thought by many to be traceable to the primary product orientation of their export bundle, and they have focused on international commodity agreements as a means to alleviate this problem. These agreements can, however, reduce LDC export earnings and welfare under some circumstances. The alleged long-run deterioration in the terms of trade has various potential causes, several of which could be addressed by increased diversification of exports of LDCs. The countries face

a basic choice of the extent to which they wish to become active participants in the world economy through outward-looking policies or to turn inward through import-substitution policies. Some empirical evidence suggests that the outward-looking approach may enhance economic performance in comparison with the inward-looking approach, but the outward-looking strategy is not without its difficulties. In general, however, economists think that the outward-looking approach may help developing countries realize positive static and dynamic development effects of trade. Finally, along with trade problems, many developing countries face problems with servicing and repayment of external debt. Recent steps have begun to emphasize some elements of debt forgiveness to reduce the potential burden of debt upon the growth process.

KEY TERMS

Brady plan
commodity concentration
compensatory financing
debt-equity swaps
debt reduction
debt relief
debt-relief Laffer curve
debt rescheduling
debt service ratio
differing income elasticities of
    demand for primary products and
    manufactured goods
export cartel
export diversification into
    manufactured goods
export instability

export promotion
get prices right
Heavily Indebted Poor Countries
    (HIPC) Initiative
high degree of openness
import substitution
international buffer stock
    agreement
international export quota
    agreement
intra-firm trade
inward-looking strategy
long-run deterioration in the terms
    of trade
moderately-inward-oriented
    economy

moderately-outward-oriented
    economy
outward-looking strategy
Prebisch-Singer hypothesis
repatriation of earnings
secondary debt market
strongly-inward-oriented economy
strongly-outward-oriented
    economy
structural adjustment policies
transfer problem
unequal market power in product
    and factor markets
vent for surplus

QUESTIONS AND PROBLEMS

1. Why might the static gains from trade for the developing country differ from those experienced by industrialized countries?

2. How can international trade influence economic development positively over time?

3. The analysis in this book has heretofore indicated that all participating countries gain from international trade. If this is so, why do some observers argue that trade can actually contribute to underdevelopment in LDCs?

4. Why is export price instability judged to be a problem for the LDCs? Why might it seem more likely to occur for LDCs than for ICs?

5. Why should we be concerned about a long-run deterioration in the commodity terms of trade of the LDCs? How can such a deterioration be related to the concept of immiserizing growth discussed in Chapter 11?

6. This chapter has indicated that diversification of the LDCs' export bundles so that they contain relatively more manufactured goods could potentially alleviate both the instability problem and the possible terms-of-trade problem. Why so? In your view, would such diversification *necessarily* help developing countries? Explain.

7. In the context of external sector problems, what case can you build for the formation of common markets among LDCs? Considering Chapter 17 and this chapter together, would you recommend that such international coalitions be formed? Why or why not?

8. Build a case in favor of forgiveness of external debt of developing countries.

9. Build a case against forgiveness of external debt of developing countries.

part 5

FUNDAMENTALS OF INTERNATIONAL MONETARY ECONOMICS

So much of barbarism, however, still remains in the transactions of most civilized nations, that almost all independent countries choose to assert their nationality by having, to their own inconvenience and that of their neighbours, a peculiar currency of their own.

John Stuart Mill, 1848

The study of international economics encompasses not only micro issues related to the exchange of goods and services between countries but also macro issues regarding the interaction of international transactions with aggregate variables such as income, money, and prices. To assess the broader macro implications of international trade, it is necessary to understand the basic underpinnings of international monetary economics and the ways international trade and financial flows affect and are affected by the overall economy.

It is not uncommon for people to feel somewhat mystified by the entire process by which exchange rates are set, currencies move between countries, and the day-to-day activities of foreign exchange dealers and international bankers and investors take place. Even seasoned international travelers continue to be amazed that exchange rates are virtually the same in London, Paris, and New York and that it really is easy to buy, sell, travel, or invest internationally even though different countries and currencies are involved. In reality, many of the fundamental macro-money aspects are not that difficult to grasp and involve merely routine transactions, except that they are between countries. Nevertheless, these international transactions influence money, prices, and national income and can affect economic policy.

Part 5 introduces you to some of the basic principles of international monetary economics to provide a background for examining the policy dimensions of this activity. Chapter 19, "The Balance-of-Payments Accounts," will focus on how the international activity of a country is recorded and will explain how this information can be interpreted. Chapter 20, "The Foreign Exchange Market," provides an introduction to the foreign exchange markets and explains how they function on a daily basis to facilitate the exchange of goods, services, and investment. The foreign exchange market has been altered in recent years by the introduction of many new financial instruments. A sampling of this array of instruments is provided in Chapter 21, "International Financial Markets and Instruments: An Introduction." The analysis is extended into a more general framework in Chapter 22, "The Monetary and Portfolio Balance Approaches to External Balance," which covers those approaches to the determination of the balance of payments and exchange rates. The last two chapters in this part focus on how changes in exchange rates and the current account of the balance of payments lead to and are influenced by price and income adjustments in a country. ●

The study of the elasticities of supply and demand is, thus, the core of the theory of foreign exchange rates.

Fritz Machlup, 1939

THE BALANCE-OF-PAYMENTS ACCOUNTS

LEARNING OBJECTIVES

- To understand what is meant by a country's "balance-of-payments" statement and how it is constructed.

- To grasp the difference between alternative accounting balances within the balance of payments.

- To become aware of the recent balance-of-payments experience of the United States.

- To know what is meant by the international investment position of a country.

INTRODUCTION

China's Trade Surpluses and Deficits[1]

In the United States, virtually any consumer is aware of the huge volume of imports arriving from China. Indeed, there is so much concern about this "flood" of imports that there is continual talk about imposing new trade restrictions on China and about trying to persuade the Chinese to raise the value of their currency in order to make their goods more expensive to U.S. buyers. A consequence of the huge volume of imports is the fact that the United States has had a large merchandise trade deficit with China in recent years—$83 billion in 2001, $103 billion in 2002, $124 billion in 2003, $162 billion in 2004, and $201 billion in 2005. Dire statements and forecasts regarding the loss of American jobs and the dangers facing the U.S. manufacturing sector and economy have accompanied these trade deficits.

It is useful to point out, however, that the trade balance situation of China with the United States is not representative of China's entire trading relations. China's merchandise trade surplus with all of its trade partners was a more modest $34 billion in 2001, $44 billion in 2002, $45 billion in 2003, $59 billion in 2004, and $134 billion in 2005. These figures mean that, subtracting its U.S. trade, China had overall merchandise trade deficits with its other trading partners in these years because the surpluses with the United States were greater than the overall surpluses. As country examples, in 2005, China had merchandise trade deficits with South Korea ($41.8 billion), Japan ($16.4 billion), Malaysia ($9.5 billion), and the Philippines ($8.2 billion).

In addition, China has had a continual deficit in services, importing more services than it is exporting. Its balance of trade when combining goods and services together thus has been a surplus that is smaller than the goods (merchandise) surplus given earlier for each recent year. However, using another concept, China's official reserve transactions balance has shown surpluses in some years that are larger than the combined surpluses in goods and services. This concept and several other such balance-of-payment measures are explored in this chapter.

To carry out the many transactions involved in international trade, money is obviously necessary, but international transactions are also complicated by the fact that different countries use different currencies. A purely domestic transaction, such as the purchase of a chair made in North Carolina by a resident of South Carolina, involves no need to convert one currency into another. The buyer's "South Carolina dollar" is identical to the "North Carolina dollar" desired by the chair manufacturer—they are the same currency unit, the U.S. dollar. But the transaction is complicated when the North Carolina furniture maker sells the chair to a French citizen. The seller wishes to receive U.S. dollars, because that is the currency unit in which the firm's workers, suppliers, and shareholders are paid, while the French consumer wishes to complete the transaction with euros. Because each country participating in *international* trade generally possesses its own *national* currency unit, a foreign exchange market is needed to convert one currency into another. In a broad view, the foreign exchange market is thus the mechanism that brings together buyers and sellers of different currencies. The nature and operations of the foreign exchange market and the determination of the equilibrium exchange rate are dealt with in the following three chapters.

This chapter will focus on how foreign economic transactions are recorded for any specific country. The international transactions of a country encompass payments outward from the country for its imports, gifts, and investments abroad and payments inward for exports, gifts, and investments by foreigners. In recording these transactions,

---

[1]The data in this discussion of China come from International Monetary Fund (IMF), *Balance of Payments Statistics Yearbook 2006, Part 1: Country Tables* (Washington, DC: IMF, 2006), p. 199; IMF, *Direction of Trade Statistics Quarterly,* December 2006, pp. 96–97; Renee M. Sauers and Matthew J. Argersinger, "U.S. International Transactions: First Quarter 2006," U.S. Department of Commerce, *Survey of Current Business,* July 2006, p. 80.

a country is keeping its **balance-of-payments accounts.** These accounts attempt to maintain a systematic record of all economic transactions between the home country and the rest of the world for a specific time period, usually a year. You will learn the placement of various types of transactions in the accounts, how to interpret a country's balance-of-payments statement, and the meaning of different balances in the accounts such as the "balance of trade" and the "current account balance" that are frequently reported in the media. In addition, we will discuss the meaning of a related term, the *net international investment position* of a country. The stage will then have been set for understanding the foreign exchange market and the determination of exchange rates in later chapters. However, as a prelude, we first examine briefly the recent growth in international trade and payments activity.

RECENT GROWTH OF TRADE AND CAPITAL MOVEMENTS

The international transactions that are recorded in a country's balance-of-payments statement reflect summarily the size of that country's activity with the rest of the world taking place in any given year. An important part of that activity is trade in goods and services; extensive data on trade flows were provided in Chapter 1, but Table 1 gives an overall look at the rapid growth of trade in goods since 1973. (Services data are less reliable and available for this span of years.) This growth in value of world exports (which conceptually equal world imports) has in monetary terms been at an annual average rate of 9.5 percent during this 33-year period. There was a slowdown of trade between 1980 and 1985 because of world recession and because trade is measured in dollars (the large rise in the value of the dollar between 1980 and 1985 meant that greater trade measured in other currencies translated into fewer dollars), but the strong upward trend from 1973 to 2006 is clear.

However, international transactions have increasingly involved more than just trade in goods and services. Individuals, corporations, financial institutions, and governments now hold international assets to a considerably greater degree than previously. These assets range from bank deposits held overseas by domestic citizens and corporations to foreign bonds, stocks, and physical facilities (e.g., factory buildings in other countries).

TABLE 1   World Exports, Selected Years, 1973–2006

Year	Value of World Exports ($, billions)
1973	$ 582
1980	2,036
1985	1,947
1990	3,485
1995	4,890
2000	6,186
2006	11,762

Sources: 1973—General Agreement on Tariffs and Trade (GATT), *International Trade 88–89,* Vol. 2 (Geneva: GATT, 1989), table A3; 1980, 1985, 1990—GATT, *International Trade 90–91,* Vol. 2 (Geneva: GATT, 1992), p. 77; 1995—World Trade Organization (WTO), *Annual Report 1996,* Vol. II (Geneva: WTO, 1996), p. 1; 2000—WTO, *International Trade Statistics, 2001* (Geneva: WTO, 2001), p. 20; 2006—WTO, World Trade 2006, Prospects for 2007, Press Release 472, 12 April 2007, obtained from www.wto.org.

Table 2 provides some indicators of the increasing asset interdependence among countries in recent years. Row (1) portrays the increase in the stock of external assets held by banks reporting to the Bank for International Settlements (a multilateral "bankers' bank" in Switzerland that collects data from the world's commercial banks). These assets are claims by the banks on foreign individuals, corporations, banks, and governments. The 13.5 percent average annual rate of increase in these assets from a value of $602 billion in 1977 to $21.1 trillion in 2005 reflects how bank activities are rapidly becoming international in scope. Row (2) of Table 2 illustrates the general growth in the annual size of total stock and bond transactions across country lines (inflows and outflows) of several industrial countries, expressed as a percentage of gross domestic product (GDP). For example, the value of these transactions for the United States in 1975 was 4 percent in relation to GDP (or about $65 billion, since GDP was $1,638 billion), but it rose to 179 percent by 1999 (or about $16.6 trillion, since GDP was $9,268 billion, or $9.3 trillion). (The figure was even higher—223 percent—in 1998.) The annual average rate of increase in the dollar value of such transactions from 1975 to 1999 was about 26 percent. Row (3) of the table indicates another dimension of increasing financial stocks on an international basis—the amount of reserves held by central banks (primarily foreign currency) in order to be ready to deal with potential balance-of-payments problems. The size of these reserves increased from $228 billion in 1975 to almost $4.3 trillion in 2005, an annual average rate of increase of 10.3 percent. Finally, row (4) of Table 2 provides data on outflows of foreign direct investment (FDI) from countries. As noted in Chapter 12, FDI includes activities such as the purchase by

TABLE 2   Indicators of Increasing Financial Interdependence

	1975	*1980*	*1985*	*1990*	*1995*	*2000*	*2005*
(1) Total international bank lending (stocks at end of year) ($, billions)	$602 (1977)	$1,181	$2,580	$6,298	$8,073	$10,779	$21,125
(2) Cross-border transactions in stocks and bonds, as percentage of GDP							
Canada	3%	9%	27%	65%	187%	331% (1998)	NA
France	NA	5	21	54	187	415 (1998)	NA
Germany	5	7	33	57	167	334 (1999)	NA
Italy	1	1	4	27	253	640 (1998)	NA
Japan	2	8	62	119	65	85 (1999)	NA
United States	4	9	35	89	33	179 (1999)	NA
(3) International reserves of central banks, end of year ($, billions)	$ 228	$ 452	$ 481	$ 979	$1,521	$ 2,066	$ 4,288
(4) Total outflows of foreign direct investment (annual averages) ($, billions)	1976–1980	1981–1985	1986–1990	1991–1996	1994–1999	2000	2005
	$ 40	$ 43	$ 168	$ 281	$ 553	$ 1,245	$ 779

Notes: (a) NA = not available; (b) row (2) data are unavailable for years later than 1998 or 1999.

Sources: Bank for International Settlements (BIS), *69th Annual Report* (Basle: BIS, June 7, 1999), p. 118; BIS, *70th Annual Report* (Basle: BIS, June 5, 2000), p. 90; various issues of the *BIS Quarterly Review;* International Monetary Fund (IMF), *International Financial Statistics Yearbook 2002* (Washington, DC: IMF, 2002), pp. 6–7, 72–73; IMF, *International Financial Statistics Yearbook 2006* (Washington, DC: IMF, 2006), pp. 2, 42; IMF, *International Financial Statistics,* March 2007, pp. 2, 39; and United Nations Conference on Trade and Development (UNCTAD), *World Investment Report 1999* (Geneva: UNCTAD, 1999), p. 10, UNCTAD, *World Investment Report 2003* (Geneva: UNCTAD, 2003), p. 253; UNCTAD, *World Investment Report 2006* (Geneva: UNCTAD, 2006), p. 2, all obtained from www.unctad.org.

a domestic firm of a controlling interest in a foreign firm and the establishment of new plants abroad. This activity rose from an annual average of $40 billion in 1976 to 1980 to $1,245 billion in 2000, with particularly rapid increase in the 1990s. The 2000 figure was more than 30 times the average figure for 1976 to 1980. A drop in FDI then occurred after 2000 in response to world events and uncertainties.

In overview, the world economy has seen a very rapid growth in international transactions of both a real and a monetary sort over the last two to three decades. The remainder of this chapter will focus on how these transactions are recorded in the balance-of-payments accounts and in the international investment statement of a country.

CREDITS AND DEBITS IN BALANCE-OF-PAYMENTS ACCOUNTING

In keeping track of a year's international transactions for a country, the balance-of-payments accountant employs a variety of procedures. We do not need to worry about all the details because we are seeking only a working knowledge of the accounts for the purpose of interpreting and understanding broad economic trends, events, and policies. Nevertheless, it is essential to understand the classification system of credits and debits. As a general working rule, **credit items in the balance-of-payments accounts** reflect transactions that give rise to payments inward to the home country. The major items are exports, foreign investment inflows to the home country, and receipts of interest and dividends by the home country from earlier investments abroad. By convention, credit items (which give rise to a payments inflow) are recorded with a *plus* sign. **Debit items in the balance-of-payments accounts** reflect transactions that give rise to payments outward from the home country. The major items are imports, investments made in foreign countries by domestic nationals, and payments of interest and dividends by the home country on earlier investments made in it by foreign investors. By convention, debit items (which lead to a payments outflow) are recorded with a *minus* sign.

Our presentation of credit and debit items generally uses the analytic framework followed by the International Monetary Fund in its annual assemblage of balance-of-payments statistics for its 185 member countries and certain terminology employed by the U.S. Department of Commerce in its presentation of U.S. data. Items are grouped into the four major categories discussed below.[2]

Category I: Current account.   Credit items (+ sign) consist of exports of goods and services, income (such as interest and dividends) received from investments abroad as well as other factor income (e.g., wages) earned abroad, and a "unilateral transfer" item representing gifts received from abroad. Debit items (− sign) are imports of goods and services, income paid to other countries' residents from foreign investments and foreign factor services in the home country, and unilateral transfers representing gifts sent abroad.

Category II: Direct investment and other long-term financial flows.   This category and the next two constitute the *financial account* in a country's balance of payments.[3] Category II

---

[2]For a somewhat similar approach, see James C. Ingram, *International Economies,* 2nd ed. (New York: Wiley, 1986), chap. 3.

[3]The traditional term for the items in categories II, III, and IV has been *capital account.* However, the International Monetary Fund and the U.S. Department of Commerce now call the items the "capital and financial account," with the overwhelming majority of the transactions taking place in the financial account. The *capital account* term now refers to very limited and specific types of transactions, such as government international debt reduction or migrant capital transfers, that change asset positions but not in response to any normal profit-seeking or economic motivation. For simplicity and because the capital account transactions are relatively very unimportant, we will generally refer to the capital and financial account as the "financial account."

is concerned with changes in holdings of long-term real physical assets and financial assets, where *long-term* refers to assets with a maturity of one year or longer. If there is an increase in long-term assets in the home country held by foreign citizens, corporations, and governments (financial inflow to the home country), a credit entry (+ sign) is made; if a sale of these holdings by foreigners causes a decrease, a debit entry (− sign) is made (financial outflow from the home country). Alternatively, if domestic citizens, corporations, and governments increase their holdings of long-term assets abroad, a debit entry is made (financial outflow from the home country); if a sale of these assets decreases holdings abroad by the home country, a credit entry is made (financial inflow to the home country as the sale proceeds are brought home). An easy way to remember this treatment is to note that credits represent a *net increase in holdings of assets in the home country by the foreign country* and debits represent a *net increase in holdings of assets in foreign countries by the home country.*

Category III: Short-term nonofficial financial flows.   This category records transactions in short-term assets (maturity of less than one year). The transactions are basically private; that is, they are carried out by parties other than central banks or monetary authorities. As in category II, an increase in foreign holdings of these assets in the home country is a credit item and a decrease is a debit item. Alternatively, if the home country's private sector increases its holdings of these assets in foreign countries, the entry is a debit; a decrease is a credit.

Category IV: Changes in reserve assets of official monetary authorities (central banks).   If foreign central banks acquire assets (e.g., bank accounts) in the home country, this is a credit item; a decrease is a debit. On the other hand, if the home country's central bank acquires international reserve assets or assets of other countries (e.g., foreign bank deposits), this is treated as a debit item in balance-of-payments accounting; a sale of or decrease in such assets is a credit.

SAMPLE ENTRIES IN THE BALANCE-OF-PAYMENTS ACCOUNTS

To obtain a better grasp of balance-of-payments (BOP) accounting, it is helpful to use hypothetical transactions. In this example and in all discussions of the balance of payments, it is crucial to recognize that the principle of **double-entry bookkeeping** is employed. This means that any transaction involves two sides to the transaction, so the monetary amount is recorded *twice*—once as a debit and once as a credit. It follows that the *sum* of all the debits must be equal to the *sum* of all the credits; that is, the *total* BOP account statement must always be in balance. (Remember that the debits are recorded with a minus sign and the credits with a plus sign. The "equality" of the sums really means equality of the absolute values of the debits and the credits.)

Let us now turn to our hypothetical examples. We designate the home country as country A (for example, United States) and treat all foreign countries as one country—country B (for example, Britain). We will describe seven different transactions and indicate at each step the manner in which the transaction is recorded.

Transaction 1. Exporters of country A send $6,000 of goods to country B, receiving in exchange a short-term bank deposit (for example, checking account deposit) of $6,000 in country B.   In this transaction, the balance-of-payments accountant records the two sides of the transaction as follows:

Credit: Category I, Exports of goods, +$6,000

Debit: Category III, Increase in short-term private assets abroad, −$6,000

The credit entry is obvious. This particular debit entry occurs because country A's exporters now have checking account deposits in country B. These deposits are classified as short-term assets.

Transaction 2. Suppose that country A's consumers purchase $12,000 of goods from country B firms and that payment is made by citizens of country A by transferring $12,000 to the bank accounts of country B firms in country A (for example, in New York).   For this transaction, the entries made by the balance-of-payments accountant are

Debit: Category I, Imports of goods, −$12,000

Credit: Category III, Increase in foreign short-term private assets in country A, +$12,000

We list the debit entry first, using the practice in these examples of first recording the initial part of the transaction or the initiating entry, followed by the "financing" part of the transaction. Imports have gone up in this instance, but remember that imports constitute debit items; thus, a minus sign is affixed to the entry. In paying for the imports, home country citizens have increased the bank accounts of country B firms in country A; this entry for the financing of the imports has a positive sign because it is a net increase in foreign holdings of assets in country A.

Transaction 3. Residents of country A send $1,000 of goods to country B's citizens as a gift.   This is a special type of entry in the balance-of-payments accounts, and it differs from our previous entries because no purchase or sale is involved. Nevertheless, there has been economic interaction with foreigners, so it must be recorded somewhere. In this case, because goods have been sent from the home country, the credit entry is "exports." However, because double-entry bookkeeping is involved, a debit entry is mandated even though no "payment" has taken place. The balance-of-payments accountant "creates" a debit entry in this instance, much like a "goodwill" or "contributions" entry in an individual firm's balance sheet when there is no payment entry because a gift has been made. The entries for "transaction" 3 are

Credit: Category I, Exports of goods, +$1,000

Debit: Category I, Unilateral transfers made, −$1,000

Transaction 4. Country A firms provide $2,000 of shipping services to country B firms. Country B firms pay for these services by transferring some of their checking account deposits in country A banks to the accounts of country A shipping firms in country A banks. The transaction is recorded as:

Credit: Category I, Exports of services, +$2,000

Debit: Category III, Decrease in foreign short-term private assets in country A, −$2,000

The debit entry is explained by the fact that the foreign firms have reduced their bank accounts in home country banks and thus have fewer assets in country A.

Transaction 5. A country B firm sends $2,500 of dividends to its country A stockholders. Payment is made by the country B firm writing checks on its bank account in a country A bank.   This transaction is recorded as follows:

Credit: Category I, Investment (or factor) income receipts from abroad, +$2,500

Debit: Category III, Decrease in foreign short-term private assets in country A, −$2,500

The debit entry occurs because the foreign firm now has reduced assets in the home country.

Transaction 6. A citizen of country A purchases a $5,000 long-term corporate bond issued by a country B company. Payment is made by the A citizen by deducting this amount from his or her bank account in country A and transferring the funds to the country A bank account of the country B firm. This transaction is an exchange of assets, and no goods are involved. The bookkeeping entries recognize that a long-term financial asset (the bond) is acquired by the home country citizen in exchange for a short-term asset (the checking account deposit).

Debit: Category II, Increase in long-term assets abroad, $-\$5,000$

Credit: Category III, Increase in foreign short-term private assets in country A, $+\$5,000$

Transaction 7. This transaction previews the operation of a foreign exchange market when a country's central bank participates in the market. Suppose that commercial banks (which are regarded as "private citizens") in country B wish to decrease their A-currency balances (e.g., U.S. dollars) in country A banks by converting some of them into their own country's currency (e.g., British pounds). This desire to shift out of dollars may reflect, for example, the anticipation by the commercial banks of a lower future value of the dollar. One method of reducing dollar holdings is to sell them (for pounds) to the Bank of England, and the Bank of England is willing to buy dollars if it is committed, as in a system of fixed exchange rates, to keep the dollar from falling in value against other currencies. Transaction 7 consists of *the sale of $800 to country B's central bank by B's commercial banks. The foreign central bank's dollar accounts in country A banks are increased, and the foreign commercial banks have reduced their dollar balances in country A banks.* This exchange of dollar account holdings in country A banks can and does occur if country A is the United States, because foreign commercial banks as well as central banks maintain balances in New York banks. The balance-of-payments accountant for country A records this change in ownership of dollar assets in country A as follows:

Debit: Category III, Decrease in foreign short-term private assets in country A, $-\$800$

Credit: Category IV, Increase in foreign short-term official assets in country A, $+\$800$

There is no change in the total foreign holdings of dollar assets, but the distribution of such holdings has been altered between the foreign private and public sectors.

ASSEMBLING A BALANCE-OF-PAYMENTS SUMMARY STATEMENT

We can now turn to the construction of country A's balance-of-payments statement. In the real world, there are millions of transactions in any given year for a country such as the United States. But let us suppose that the seven transactions we worked through constitute the entire set of international transactions in a given year, and from these we build the BOP statement.

We first list in T-account form in Table 3 the debit and credit items enumerated in the previous section. The parenthetical numbers in the left-hand column indicate the transaction numbers. From these entries, we now assemble the BOP summary statement in Table 4 and work through this statement.

Looking first at exports and imports of goods, country A has imported $5,000 more of goods than it has exported ($7,000 of exports, $12,000 of imports). Adding the (+) exports of goods and the (−) imports of goods (or the subtraction of imports of goods from exports of goods) yields the **merchandise trade balance.** When this balance is positive, the result is referred to as a merchandise trade *surplus;* when negative, the result is a merchandise trade *deficit.* By convention, a surplus is often referred to as "favorable" and a deficit is

TABLE 3   International Transactions, Country A

Debits (−)		Credits (+)	
(1) Increase in short-term private assets abroad	−$ 6,000	Exports of goods	+$ 6,000
(2) Imports of goods	− 12,000	Increase in foreign short-term private assets in country A	+ 12,000
(3) Unilateral transfers made	− 1,000	Exports of goods	+ 1,000
(4) Decrease in foreign short-term private assets in country A	− 2,000	Exports of services	+ 2,000
(5) Decrease in foreign short-term private assets in country A	− 2,500	Investment income receipts from abroad	+ 2,500
(6) Increase in long-term assets abroad	− 5,000	Increase in foreign short-term private assets in country A	+ 5,000
(7) Decrease in foreign short-term private assets in country A	− 800	Increase in foreign short-term official assets in country A	+ 800
	−$29,300		+$29,300

TABLE 4   Balance-of-Payments Summary Statement, Country A

Category	
I. Exports of goods (+$6,000 + $1,000)	+$ 7,000
Imports of goods	− 12,000
Merchandise trade balance	−$ 5,000
Exports of services	+ 2,000
Imports of services	− 0
Balance on goods and services	−$ 3,000
Factor income receipts from abroad	+ 2,500
Factor income payments abroad	− 0
Balance on goods, services, and investment income	−$ 500
Unilateral transfers received	+ 0
Unilateral transfers made	− 1,000
Balance on current account (current account balance)	−$ 1,500
II. Net increase (+) in foreign long-term assets in country A	+ 0
Net increase (−) in long-term assets abroad	− 5,000
Balance on current account and long-term assets (basic balance)	−$ 6,500
III. Net increase (+) in foreign short-term private assets in country A (+$12,000 + $5,000 − $2,000 − $2,500 − $800)	+ 11,700
Net increase (−) in short-term private assets abroad	− 6,000
Official reserve transactions balance (overall balance)	−$ 800
IV. Net increase (+) in foreign short-term official assets in country A	+ 800
Net increase (−) in official reserve assets or official assets abroad	− 0
	$ 0

referred to as "unfavorable"—terms carried over from the period of Mercantilism (previously discussed in Chapter 2). The merchandise trade balance is usually quoted in newspapers and on the national television and radio news reports, and the figure is released on a monthly basis. However, you should note that it is a very incomplete measure of the balance of payments, since it omits many other items.

The merchandise trade balance is but one of several balances that can be identified in a balance-of-payments statement. To get to other balances and a broader picture of the international transactions of a country, we must add in other items from the transactions in Table 3. The next step is to add services to the merchandise trade balance. Because country A exported $2,000 of services and imported none, the services account has a surplus of $2,000 that is set against the balance-of-trade deficit of $5,000. The resulting **balance on goods and services** (often referred to in the press as "balance of trade") of −$3,000 gives the net flow of payments associated with goods *and* services transactions with other countries during the time period. Beginning in January 1994, this balance has been published monthly in the United States, although other balances below are available only on a quarterly basis.

Continuing with category I items, we now enter factor income receipts and payments (investment income, wages and salaries). When our investment income receipt of +$2,500 is entered (there were no factor income payments to foreign countries in our examples), we arrive at another balance—the **balance on goods, services, and factor income** (or just the **balance on goods, services, and income**) of −$500.

The next item to be included in our balance-of-payments summary consists of unilateral transfers. When transfers of −$1,000 are added to the balance on goods and services and investment income, we arrive at the **current account balance** or **balance on current account** of −$1,500.

The current account balance is important because it essentially reflects sources and uses of national income. Exports of goods and services generate income when they are produced, and gifts and factor income received from abroad are also a source of income in the current time period. On the other hand, the home country's citizens and government use current income to purchase imports of goods and services and to make gifts and factor income payments abroad.

Another way to view the current account balance is to relate it to aggregate income and expenditure. Remember the basic macroeconomic identity:

$$Y = C + I + G + (X - M) \qquad [1]$$

where

Y = aggregate income
C = consumption spending
I = investment spending on plant, equipment, and so forth
G = government spending on goods and services
X = exports
M = imports

In reality, X consists of all the credit items in the current account, not only exports, because they all generate income. Further, M consists of all current account debit items, which are uses of current income, not just imports. Now rearrange the identity:

$$Y - (C + I + G) = (X - M) \qquad [2]$$

This rearrangement indicates that the current account balance is simply the difference between income of the country and $(C + I + G)$, and $(C + I + G)$ constitutes spending by the country's residents during the time period. If a country has a current account deficit [$(X - M)$ is negative], it means that $(C + I + G)$ is greater than Y and the country is spending more than its income and living beyond its means. This has been the case in the United States since 1982.

Of course, if a country has a current account surplus [$(X - M)$ is positive], the country is spending less than its income; this has been the case with Japan since 1981.

This relationship of the current account balance to macroeconomics can be carried further. Besides expression [1], income can also be written as

$$Y = C + S + T \qquad [3]$$

meaning that income can be used only for the purposes of consumption (including imports and transfers abroad), saving, and paying taxes. If we then utilize expressions [1] and [3] by remembering that they both show equalities of variables with Y, we obtain

$$C + I + G + (X - M) = C + S + T$$

or

$$(X - M) = S + (T - G) - I \qquad [4]$$

If S is private saving and $(T - G)$ is government saving (which can be negative), then the current account balance is also the difference between a country's saving and the country's investment. Thus, a current account deficit [$(X - M)$ is negative] means that the country is *saving less than it invests* (that is, the country is not "saving enough"). This is another implication of the U.S. current account deficit since 1982. Of course, a current account surplus [$(X - M)$ is positive] indicates that the country is saving more than it invests.

We now turn to categories II, III, and IV in the BOP statement in Table 4. A main point to note is that, if the current account items have added up to −$1,500, the sum of these financial account items by themselves *must* be +$1,500. Why? Because the sum of the total credits (with a plus sign) and total debits (with a minus sign) of all the items in the balance of payments must be *zero* due to the nature of double-entry bookkeeping. Hence, when someone speaks of a "balance-of-payments deficit," that person cannot be speaking of *all* the items in the balance of payments because all of the items must sum to zero. The loosely used term "balance-of-payments deficit" therefore refers only to some *part* of the balance-of-payments statement, not to the entire statement. This part could be only the merchandise trade balance, or the balance on goods and services, or the current account balance, for example. The term "balance-of-payments deficit" is deficient because it lacks precision in indicating which items in the account are being discussed, and the term is clearly nonsensical if it refers to all of the items in the balance of payments.

Now return to our sample entries by adding category II, the long-term assets account. Since there was a long-term financial outflow of $5,000 and no long-term financial inflows, the value of category II by itself is −$5,000. When this is added to the current account figure of −$1,500, we have a new balance (of −$6,500), the **balance on current account and long-term assets.** This cumbersome term is sometimes shortened to the term **basic balance** to emphasize the point that the first two categories of the balance-of-payments statement reflect basic long-term forces in the economy of a country. The current account balance reflects such influences on the balance of payments as national income and its growth, spending habits, and international competitiveness; in addition, the long-term asset flows reflect the judgments of long-term investors on the relative profitability of investing overseas rather than in the home country. These decisions presumably embrace a long-term view on the economic future of particular industries and countries. Long-term relationships influencing the balance of payments must be distinguished from shorter-term forces such as sudden changes in interest rates or anticipated exchange rate movements. Shorter-term forces are most likely reflected by short-term financial capital movements in category III.

IN THE REAL WORLD:

CURRENT ACCOUNT DEFICITS*

As noted in the text, a current account deficit for a country means that the country is spending more than its income or, alternatively, is saving too little relative to its investment. However, it should not be assumed that a current account deficit (CAD) is necessarily a "bad thing" and that a country should focus its attention on adopting policies to obtain balance or a current account surplus. In actuality, there are times when a current account deficit can be viewed in a positive manner. For example, a CAD could reflect the positive development that the country is recovering from a recession more rapidly than are its trading partners. With the rapid recovery the higher incomes are leading to the purchase of more imports, while exports are not being boosted by any significant rise in incomes abroad. Or the home country may be an attractive source of foreign investment because of expected high returns due to favorable business conditions, technological change, or overall increases in productivity. The investment inflows produce a financial account surplus, which, as we will see must be associated with a current account deficit. Yet another source of a financial account surplus could be the liquidation of foreign production facilities and the subsequent transfer of financial capital to a domestic production site. Finally, net financial capital inflows associated with a CAD tend to put downward pressure on home country interest rates, stimulating investment, growth, and employment.

From a long-term perspective, developing countries may require a net investment inflow (and therefore a CAD) to assist them in their early efforts at industrialization. Even as their growth picks up and they become less reliant on foreign funds, the interest and/or dividend payments on the accumulated foreign capital stock can result in a current account deficit. Ultimately, however, if repayment is needed on some or all of the initial foreign investment, the developing country

will experience a current account surplus and a financial account deficit. This transition from a debtor (financial account inflow) nation to a creditor (financial account outflow) nation has been regarded by some economists as part of a natural sequence in the development process.

It goes without saying, however, that continual current account deficits cannot be ignored by policymakers (in both developing and developed countries). The concern here is not with the annual current account deficits per se, but with the potential growth in payments of factor service income to foreign investors that accompanies the increasing holdings of assets in the country by foreign entities. Rapid growth of payments of returns to foreign investment not only worsens the current account balance further but can quickly lead to the emergence of a "debt trap," where both the net debt position of the country and the current account deficit increase rapidly. In 2001, the U.S. current account deficit amounted to only 3.8 percent of GDP and the net foreign debt position to 19.0 percent of GDP. By 2003, the figures were, respectively, 4.8 percent of GDP and 19.4 percent of GDP; in 2005 they were 6.4 percent and 21.6 percent, respectively. The percentages have clearly been rising in recent years and are becoming sources of concern. If foreigners became less willing to acquire U.S. investments (that is, to finance the current account deficit), a "hard landing" for the economy could occur, with a slowdown in U.S. growth and increased unemployment as the economy adjusts to having to produce more than it is currently using in order to meet the necessary payments to foreign lenders.

*For useful discussion of many of these points, see "Schools Brief: In Defence of Deficits," *The Economist,* Dec. 16, 1995, pp. 68–69, and Wynne Godley, "Interim Report: Notes on the U.S. Trade and Balance of Payments Deficits," Jerome Levy Economics Institute of Bard College, Annandale-on-Hudson, NY, 2000.   ●

We now turn to category III, which covers flows of short-term private assets. This category has a high proportion of entries in the real world because the items in it reflect "financing" items for transactions in categories I and II and short-term financial capital transactions initiated on their own. There has been a net increase in foreign short-term private assets (credit item) in country A of $11,700 (= $12,000 + $5,000 − $2,000 − $2,500 − $800), and a debit item of an increase in short-term private assets abroad of −$6,000. Thus, category III by itself has a value of +$5,700 (= $11,700 − $6,000).

Finally, the cumulative balance after considering categories I to III (the current account, long-term asset flows, and short-term private asset flows) is −$800. This balance is the one that is generally meant when economists use the broad term *balance-of-payments deficit* (or *surplus*). A more precise phrasing is the "balance after considering goods, services, investment income, unilateral transfers, long-term asset flows, and short-term private asset flows." For simplicity, however, the balance is called the **official reserve transactions balance** or **overall balance,** which reflects the net effect of all transactions with other countries during the time period considered but excluding government short-term financial transactions ("official reserve transactions"). Because categories I to III have a sum of −$800, then category IV must by itself have a value of +$800; government activity was necessary to cover or "settle" the net balance of the previous transactions. (The balance has also been called the **official settlements balance.**) This $800 is essentially a measure of the amount of participation or intervention by the official monetary authorities in the foreign exchange market, the B central bank purchases of dollars in our example (see p. 462). In this context, economists sometimes use the phrases *autonomous items in the balance of payments* and *accommodating items in the balance of payments.* The term **autonomous items in the balance of payments** refers to international economic transactions that take place in the pursuit of ordinary economic goals such as profit maximization by firms and utility maximization by individuals. These transactions are undertaken independently of the state of the country's balance of payments and are reflected in categories I to III in the BOP statement. The term **accommodating items in the balance of payments** refers to transactions that occur because of other activity in the balance of payments, that is, the government items in category IV.

We have now used all the entries in the sample transactions in country A's balance of payments, and it should come as no surprise that the net result of all the entries is a balance of $0. Categories I to IV as a whole must sum to zero because each transaction in each category has been entered twice—once as a credit entry and once as a debit entry. Further, the current account balance (category I) *must* be equal but opposite in sign to the balance of the three financial accounts (categories II, III, IV) by themselves. This also is obviously a result of double-entry bookkeeping. Thus, our current account balance in the example (−$1,500) matches the sum of categories II to IV by themselves:

Category II	−$5,000
Category III	+5,700
Category IV	+800
Financial account balance	+$1,500

This **financial account balance** constitutes an additional measure of "balance" in the balance of payments that has received substantial attention in the United States.

In assembling the balance-of-payments statement, we have thus identified seven different measures of balance. These balances have different monetary values, and it is imperative when you hear or read about a country's "balance of payments" to understand which one is being discussed. The balances in our numerical example were:

Merchandise trade balance	−$5,000
Balance on goods and services	−3,000
Balance on goods, services, and factor income	−500
Current account balance (balance on current account)	−1,500
Balance on current account and long-term assets (basic balance)	−6,500
Official reserve transactions balance (overall balance)	−800
Financial account balance	+1,500

In practice, the decision of which balance to emphasize reflects the particular items that the analyst has in mind for reasons of policy or academic interest. There is no one true measure of a country's balance; the different balances reflect concentration on different items in the balance of payments. For example, the balance of trade may be the focus in studying international competitiveness in goods alone. The current account balance may be the focus in examining a country's national income-spending relationship. Further, the official reserve transactions balance may be the focus if interest centers on the amount of official government intervention in foreign exchange markets. Regardless of the focus, the assembling of the complete BOP statement is necessary if we are to analyze and interpret the international economic transactions of a country with the rest of the world during any particular time period.

CONCEPT CHECK

1. What does a balance-of-payments statement portray? Why is the BOP always in balance?
2. What is the difference between the current account balance and the balance of trade?
3. What rule do accountants follow in recording transactions in the balance of payments? In what manner would an export of wheat be recorded? A purchase of a foreign stock?

BALANCE-OF-PAYMENTS SUMMARY STATEMENT FOR THE UNITED STATES

Having worked extensively through the recording of sample transactions and the process of assembling a balance-of-payments summary statement for a hypothetical country, we now present the U.S. balance-of-payments statement for 2005 (Table 5).

TABLE 5   U.S. International Transactions, 2005 (billions of dollars)

Current account:	
Exports of goods	+$ 894.6
Imports of goods	− 1,677.4
Merchandise trade balance	−$ 782.7
Exports of services	+ 380.6
Imports of services	− 314.6
Balance on goods and services	−$ 716.7
Income receipts from abroad	+ 474.6
Income payments to foreigners	− 463.4
Balance on goods, services, and income	−$ 705.4
Unilateral transfers, net	− 86.1
(Government −$37.7)	
(Private −$48.4)	
Current account balance	−$ 791.5
Capital and financial account:	
Capital account transactions, net	−$ 4.4
U.S. official reserve assets, net (increase, −)	+$ 14.1
U.S. government assets abroad, other than official reserve assets, net (increase, −)	+$ 5.5
U.S. private assets abroad, net (increase, −)	−$ 446.4
Foreign official assets in the United States, net (increase, +)	+$ 199.5
Other foreign assets in the United States, net (increase, +)	+$1,012.8
Statistical discrepancy	+$ 10.4

Note: Components may not sum to totals due to rounding.

Source: Matthew J. Argersinger and Erin M. Whitaker, "U.S. International Transactions: Third Quarter 2006," U.S. Department of Commerce, *Survey of Current Business,* January 2007, p. 19.

The first point to note about this table is that it does not quite conform to the presentation discussed earlier. For approximately the last 30 years, the United States has not presented the financial account items in the category II (long-term assets account) and category III (short-term private assets account) format. Category IV (short-term official assets account) is also not listed per se but can be derived.[4] This change in presentation

---

[4]The reasons for this change in official presentation involve the movement from relatively fixed exchange rates to floating exchange rates in 1973 and need not concern us at this point.

IN THE REAL WORLD:

U.S. TRADE DEFICITS WITH JAPAN, CHINA, OPEC, AND CANADA

As noted in the text, the United States has had a merchandise trade deficit since 1971 (with the exceptions of 1973 and 1975). An important point to make with respect to this string of deficits is that they have been concentrated with relatively few countries. Figure 1 plots, for the period 1980–2005, the merchandise trade balances of the United States with Japan, China, the members of the Organization of Petroleum Exporting Countries (OPEC), and Canada.

The most sizable merchandise trade deficits have been with Japan. Japan is the third-largest buyer of U.S. exports (after Canada and Mexico) and the fourth-largest supplier of U.S. imports (after Canada, China, and Mexico). However, the trade is very unbalanced, as can be seen in the figure. For the 1980–2005 period as a whole, the *cumulative* deficit of the United States with Japan was $1,385 billion ($1.4 trillion), and this comprised about 23 percent of the total cumulative U.S. deficit of $6,003 billion ($6.0 trillion). The deficit with Japan averaged more than $53 billion annually during this 26-year period, with the highest deficit being $85 billion in 2005.

U.S. trade with China actually showed some small surpluses before 1986. However, since that time, there have been continuous deficits, with the deficits becoming larger than the U.S. deficits with Japan in the 2000–2005 period. China is the second-largest supplier of U.S. imports (many of which are, à la Heckscher-Ohlin, labor-intensive goods) and the fourth-largest buyer of U.S. exports. There has been a cumulative U.S. merchandise trade deficit with China over the 1980–2005 period of $1,110 billion, or $1.1 trillion (an average of $43 billion per year). This is about 18.5 percent of the cumulative U.S. total deficit from 1980–2005; thus, Japan and China together have accounted for more than 40 percent of the total cumulative U.S. deficit, and in one year (1991) the two countries accounted for 78 percent of the U.S. deficit.

U.S. trade with the Organization of Petroleum Exporting Countries (OPEC—the current members are Algeria, Angola, Indonesia, Iran, Iraq, Kuwait, Libya, Nigeria, Qatar, Saudi Arabia, United Arab Emirates, and Venezuela) has yielded smaller deficits than the trade with Japan and China. Nevertheless, over the 1980–2005 period, the cumulative deficit was $685 billion (more than 11 percent of the cumulative total deficit). The range for the annual figures has been from $9 billion to $93 billion with the $93 billion deficit occurring in 2005.

Another country with which the United States has had a continuous deficit in the 1980–2005 period was Canada. The cumulative deficit over those years was $634 billion, and the annual figure was more than $50 billion from 2000–2005. As indicated, Canada is the largest supplier of U.S. imports and the largest buyer of U.S. exports.

Finally, it should be noted that, although there have been very large deficits with Japan, China, the OPEC countries, and Canada, as well as smaller deficits with many other countries, there have been some countries with which the United States has had trade surpluses. For example, surpluses existed in 2005 with Singapore, Belgium-Luxembourg, the Netherlands, and Australia. For Belgium-Luxembourg and the Netherlands, there were continuous surpluses throughout the 1980–2005 period.

In overview, despite deficits and surpluses with particular countries, the most important figure from the policymaker's perspective is the total annual deficit and not the trade balances with individual countries. Nevertheless, when deficits are as large as those with Japan and China, they attract the public's attention, and officials may be pressured to tilt trade policy toward the situation with those countries.

Sources: Douglas B. Weinberg, "U.S. International Transactions, First Quarter 1994," U.S. Department of Commerce, *Survey of Current Business*, June 1994, p. 104; Renee M. Sauers and Matthew J. Argersinger, "U.S. International Transactions: First Quarter 2006," U.S. Department of Commerce, *Survey of Current Business*, July 2006, p. 80.

(continued)

IN THE REAL WORLD: *(continued)*

FIGURE 1   U.S. Trade Balance with Japan, China, OPEC, and Canada, 1980–2005

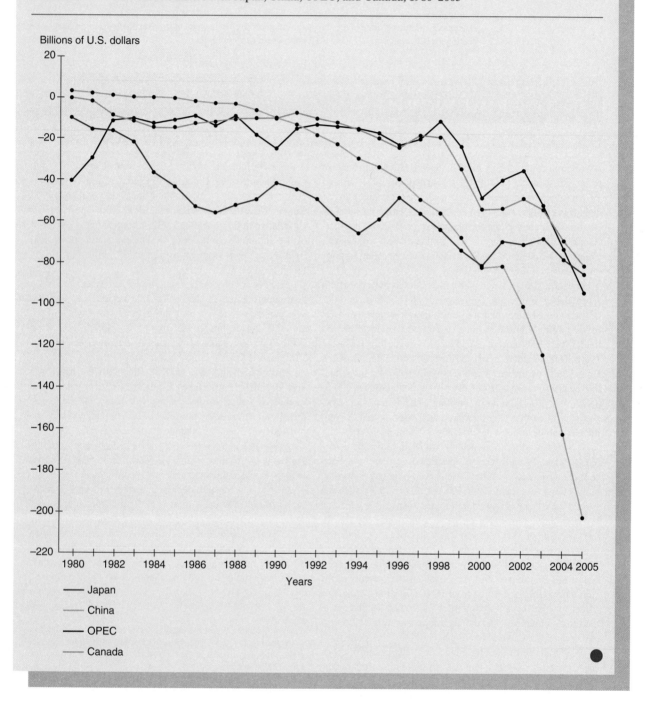

means that of the various balances above, only the merchandise trade balance; the balance on goods and services; the balance on goods, services, and investment income; and the current account balance are readily available in government publications. Prior to the change, official measures of the basic balance and the official reserve transactions balance were also given. (The financial account balance has never been officially listed.) The official reserve transactions balance and the financial account balance can still be derived from the figures, but the basic balance cannot. Despite the lack of conformity of official U.S. data to our conceptual presentation, we can still discuss them in reasonable concordance with that framework.

At the top of Table 5, you will notice that the United States had a large merchandise trade deficit of $894.6 billion in 2005. Except for 1973 and 1975, the United States has had a merchandise trade deficit every year since 1971, when the traditional U.S. merchandise surplus that had existed since the end of World War II ceased.

The merchandise trade deficit was somewhat offset by a surplus on services trade in 2005. The services surplus was $66 billion (exports of services of $380.6 billion minus imports of services of $314.6 billion). Important items in services are tourist expenditures and receipts, royalties and license fees, charges for telecommunications, banking, insurance, and so forth. Income receipts from abroad ($474.6 billion) and factor income payments (overwhelmingly investment income) to foreigners ($463.4 billion) resulted in a positive of $11.2 billion. The balance on goods and services (-716.7 billion) and the balance on goods, services, and income (-705.4 billion) both showed smaller deficits in 2005 than did the merchandise trade balance.

Moving next in Table 5 to unilateral transfers, the net result in 2005 was a debit (or net outflow) of $86.1 billion. When this deficit is coupled with the deficit on goods, services, and investment income, the result was a U.S. current account deficit of $791.5 billion, the largest in history.

How is it economically possible for the current account balance to be negative? The answer of course is that the balance-of-payments accounts must have an equal and offsetting capital and financial account surplus, that is, a net inflow of funds from abroad. Let us now look at the capital accounts for the United States in 2005 to examine this net financial capital inflow.

Although the U.S. official balance-of-payments accounts no longer list financial capital flow items systematically in the framework of our categories II, III, and IV, we can still glean useful financial information from the current U.S. presentation (which follows the IMF presentation). First, as referred to in footnote 3 of this chapter (page 459), a small capital account item (officially labeled "capital account transactions, net") now appears in the accounts. This item reflects special, one-time-type transactions such as government international debt operations or international transfers of assets by migrants and does not consist of typical financial transactions. The remaining financial account items represent our categories II, III, and IV, but items in categories II and III are combined and not listed separately. Consider the two headings "U.S. government assets abroad, other than official reserve assets" and "U.S. private assets abroad." The government asset transactions are those that do not involve the short-term, liquid assets of our category IV. The U.S. private assets category contains both long-term and short-term asset purchases and sales, including long-term direct investments, U.S. transactions in foreign securities of various maturities, and short-term claims on foreigners by U.S. banks and nonbanking firms. The two broad headings essentially represent the debit amount of "increase in U.S. assets abroad" (outflows), both long-term and short-term together, of the nonofficial type of categories II and III. The result in 2005 was a net debit amount of $+$5.5 - $446.4 = -$440.9$ billion.

Consider next "Other foreign assets in the United States," which indicates the change in assets in the United States held by foreigners, but it too is a consolidation of long-term as well as private short-term flows. There was a huge U.S. net credit amount of $1,012.8 billion in 2005.

Finally, look at the remaining two financial account items, "U.S. official reserve assets" and "Foreign official assets in the United States." These items correspond to our category IV (short-term official assets account). The "U.S. official reserve assets" entry has a *minus* sign if there is a net increase in reserve assets (since the increase is a debit item) and a *plus* sign if there is a net decrease. In 2005, there was a decrease of $14.1 billion. "Foreign official assets in the United States" indicates the change in holdings of assets in the United States by foreign central banks (+ if an increase, − if a decrease). The credit entry for 2005 indicates that foreign monetary authorities increased their holdings of U.S. assets by $199.5 billion, a large increase historically. When category IV as a whole is thus considered, we obtain a figure of +$213.6 billion = +$14.1 billion + $199.5 billion. Therefore, because of double-entry bookkeeping, *the sum of categories I through III for the United States must have been* −$213.6 *billion: Thus, the official reserve transactions balance for the United States in 2005 was a deficit of $213.6 billion.*[5]

Looking back over Table 5 as a whole, remember that the current account balance was −$791.5 billion (a current account deficit of $791.5 billion). Because double-entry bookkeeping means that the capital and financial accounts should add up to $791.5 billion, let's check this result. The financial account items and their net debit or credit values that we have identified are as follows:

Capital account transactions, net	−$4.4
U.S. government assets abroad, other than official reserve assets, net	+5.5
U.S. private assets abroad, net	−446.4
Other foreign assets in the United States, net	+1,012.8
U.S. official reserve assets, net	+14.1
Foreign official assets in the United States, net	+199.5
	+$781.1

What is wrong here? Why do the financial account items add up to +$781.1 billion rather than +$791.5 billion? The reason is that U.S. authorities use incomplete data in compiling the balance-of-payments statement. The accountants are unable to get enough information to make all the double entries in the double-entry bookkeeping framework. Data on trade are collected from customs information as goods enter and leave the United States, but data on the financing of trade and on financial flows are gathered independently from commercial banks and other institutions. Some transactions escape the recording and accounting framework altogether; this certainly applies to smuggling and money laundering, but it also applies to legal transactions. Further, the timing of the current account items and related flows in the financial account does not always exactly coincide with the same calendar year. Thus, the accountant creates a special category, **statistical discrepancy** or **net errors and omissions,** to deal with the fact that the sum of the debits and credits actually recorded is not zero in practice. In Table 5, you will note that the statistical discrepancy entry has a value of +$10.4 billion. (This item is often thought to consist primarily of unrecorded short-term financial capital flows, but unrecorded exports may also be involved—see Ott 1988.) When the +$10.4 billion is combined with the financial account figure of +$781.1 billion, we arrive at +$791.5 billion, a figure that matches the current account balance of −$791.5 billion.

---

[5]We are ignoring one small detailed procedure that makes the deficit very slightly smaller.

This completes our discussion of balance-of-payments accounting, perhaps in too detailed a fashion for your tastes(!). (For one of the authors, BOP accounting is his second favorite thing—the first is root canal work.) However, we think that a grasp of the fundamental concepts of the various balances and classifications is important for understanding international payments, the foreign exchange market, and macroeconomic policy decisions. While we have presented actual U.S. data for the BOP, the concepts and classifications apply to all countries.

INTERNATIONAL INVESTMENT POSITION OF THE UNITED STATES

We conclude this chapter by looking at another kind of statement that portrays the international economic relationships of a country, using the United States as our example. This statement indicates the **international investment position of a country,** or sometimes, if presented with the opposite sign, the **international indebtedness position of a country.**

A country's international investment position is related to the capital and financial accounts in its balance-of-payments statement, but it differs in an important way. The capital and financial accounts in a balance-of-payments statement shows the *flows* of financial capital during the year being examined. In the economist's terminology, the balance of payments is a *flow concept,* meaning that it portrays some type of economic activity during a particular time period. Flow concepts are the kind most frequently encountered in economic analysis, and familiar examples are national income during a year, investment expenditure by firms during a year, or sales of a good during a particular month. On the other hand, the international investment position is a stock concept rather than a flow concept. A *stock concept* examines the value of a particular economic variable at a point in time. Thus, the physical capital stock of a country at the end of a year, the number of automobiles in existence at the end of a given month, and the year-end size of the money supply are stock concepts. While the capital and financial accounts in the balance of payments show the size of flows during a year, the international investment position shows the *cumulative* size of a country's foreign assets and liabilities at a given point in time (usually defined as at the end of a particular year). The flows of funds during the year will change the size of the cumulative stock, and the end-of-the-year international investment position reflects this flow and all previous flows. The statement of the end-of-the-year international investment position allows the observer to compare the size of the country's foreign assets with the size of its foreign liabilities (that is, the total assets of foreign countries in this country). If the assets exceed the liabilities, the country is a **net creditor country;** if the liabilities exceed the assets, the country is said to be a **net debtor country.**

Given this background, Table 6 shows the statement of the U.S. international investment position at the end of 2005. Part A, "U.S.-owned Assets Abroad," indicates the claims of U.S. citizens and government on foreigners. (Some of the assets such as stock certificates may be physically held in the United States.) The first item, "U.S. official reserve assets," represents the stock of international reserve assets held by the U.S. government as contrasted with the flows of these assets during a given year which are indicated in a U.S. BOP statement. The second item, "U.S. government assets abroad other than official reserve assets," includes primarily U.S. government loans to other countries and funds paid by the United States as membership subscriptions to international organizations such as the International Monetary Fund and the World Bank. The category of "U.S. private assets abroad" embraces a variety of items, with the major items being U.S. direct investment abroad, U.S. holdings of foreign stocks, and U.S. claims reported by U.S. banks and nonbanks. (The bank claims item, for example, reflects deposits made in foreign financial institutions by U.S. banks and individual depositors.) The most rapidly growing item in the private assets category in recent decades in

TABLE 6   International Investment Position of the United States, December 31, 2005
(billions of dollars)

A. U.S.-owned Assets Abroad		
U.S. official reserve assets		$ 188.0
U.S. government assets abroad other than official reserve assets		77.5
U.S. private assets abroad		9,743.1
Direct investment abroad*	$2,453.9	
Foreign bonds	987.5	
Foreign corporate stocks	3,086.5	
U.S. claims on foreigners reported by U.S. banks and nonbanks, not reported elsewhere	3,215.2	
Total U.S. assets abroad		$10,008.7
B. Foreign-owned Assets in the United States		
Foreign official assets in the United States		$2,216.1
Other foreign assets in the United States		10,486.4
Foreign direct investment*	$1,874.3	
U.S. Treasury securities	704.9	
U.S. currency	352.2	
Corporate and other bonds	2,275.2	
Corporate stocks	2,115.5	
U.S. liabilities to foreigners reported by U.S. banks and nonbanks, not reported elsewhere	3,164.4	
Total foreign assets in the United States		$12,702.5
Net international investment position of the United States = total U.S.-owned assets abroad minus total foreign-owned assets in the United States = $10,008.7 minus $12,702.5		−$2,693.8

*Direct investment is valued at current cost.

Notes: (*a*) Data are preliminary. (*b*) Components may not sum to totals due to rounding.

Source: Elena L. Nguyen, "The International Investment Position of the United States at Yearend 2005," U.S. Department of Commerce, *Survey of Current Business,* July 2006, p. 17.

percentage terms has been U.S. private holdings of foreign corporate stocks (from $9.5 billion in 1976 to $3,086.5 billion in 2005, an annual average rate of increase of more than 22 percent.) The total value of foreign assets held by U.S. citizens and government at the end of 2005 was $10,008.7 billion, or $10.0 trillion.

Part B of Table 6 reflects foreign holdings of assets in the United States. The "foreign official assets in the United States" entry indicates the cumulative buildup of holdings by foreign central banks (importantly of China and Japan) of financial instruments such as U.S. Treasury securities and commercial bank deposits. There was a 2,023 percent total increase in these foreign official asset holdings in recent decades (from $104.4 billion in 1976 to $2,216.1 billion in 2005). There was also a huge increase in private holdings of U.S. assets reflected in the "other foreign assets in the United States" category. The figure for this category was $187.7 billion in 1976, and its increase to $10,486.4 billion by the end of 2005 represented a 5,487 percent total increase from 1976 to 2005 (!). As the United States has been running large current account deficits, the counterpart has been this inflow of foreign funds to finance these deficits. The cumulative amount of foreign direct investments (at current cost) in the United States, for example, stood at $47.5 billion in 1976 but increased to $1,874.3 billion by the end of 2005. Foreign private ownership of U.S. Treasury securities during the 1976–2005 period increased from $7.0 billion to $704.9 billion; private foreign holdings of U.S. corporate and other bonds increased from $12.0 billion to $2,275.2 billion; private foreign holdings of U.S. corporate stocks increased from $42.9 billion to $2,115.5 billion; and foreign holdings of U.S. currency rose from $11.8 billion to $352.2 billion. At the end of 2005, total foreign holdings (government plus private) of U.S. assets were $12,702.5 billion, or $12.7 trillion.

The commonly cited figure for a country's net international investment position is simply the difference between the country's assets abroad and the foreign assets in the country. This figure for the United States for 2005 is indicated at the bottom of Table 6, *minus* $2,693.8 billion. No country in the world has such a large negative net international investment position (that is, net international indebtedness position).

There are certainly disadvantages to such a position for the United States. For example, interest and dividends will have to be paid to overseas debt holders and stockholders in the future (as well as perhaps debt principal), which eventually involves a transfer of goods and real income abroad. (There is also worry that a "too large" amount of assets held by foreign individuals, firms, and governments can threaten a loss of national sovereignty.) However, the cumulative financial inflows, if productively used, will have generated the income with which to make these future payments. In addition, some economists think that the inflow of foreign funds may have kept U.S. interest rates lower than they would have been otherwise. Beyond consideration of the net debtor position itself, however, a very important point is that the huge $10.0 trillion of

IN THE REAL WORLD:

TRENDS IN THE U.S. INTERNATIONAL INVESTMENT POSITION

The international investment position of the United States has deteriorated markedly in recent years. From the 1980 level of +$360.8 billion, the figure turned negative by 1986 and then reached Table 6's −$2,693.8 billion at the end of 2005. The position over the 1976–2005 period is shown graphically in Figure 2. Remembering that the net international investment position shows the total stock of U.S. assets abroad minus the total stock of foreign assets in the United States, a decrease in the position reflects net financial flows inward to the United States (a financial account surplus/current account deficit). The dramatic decline in the U.S. position can be regarded as a reflection of the U.S. current account deficits. In turn, since the current account deficits reflected greater spending than income by the United States (or inadequate saving to finance investment), another way to view the deterioration in the U.S. international investment position is that foreign citizens, institutions, and governments have been financing the excess spending through a funds inflow to the United States.

A noteworthy departure from the pattern of the total net international investment position is the behavior of the net *direct* investment position. This category involves acquisition and startup of new factories and real production facilities. Throughout the 1976–2005 period, the stock of U.S.-owned

direct investment assets abroad has been greater than the stock of foreign-owned direct investment assets in the United States. The stock of foreign direct investments in the United States increased dramatically from 1976 to 2005 (rising from $47.5 billion to $1,874.3 billion), but U.S. direct investments abroad rose from $222.3 billion to $2,453.9 billion, thus maintaining the positive *net* position shown in Figure 2.

Finally, the net international investment position, when negative, implies that a country is a *net debtor* as referred to in the text. However, do not confuse the U.S. net debtor position with the popular term *national debt* (almost $9 trillion). That term is basically a misnomer because it refers to the debt of the U.S. federal government only, and most of these bonds (about 75 percent) are held by U.S. (not foreign) citizens, agencies, and institutions. When assessing relative claims of the United States versus claims of other nations on the United States, the net international investment position is a much more appropriate measure than the federal government's debt.

Source: Elena L. Nguyen, "The International Investment Position of the United States at Yearend 2005," U.S. Department of Commerce, *Survey of Current Business,* July 2006, pp. 18–19.

(continued)

IN THE REAL WORLD: *(continued)*

FIGURE 2   Net International and Direct Investment Positions of the United States, 1976–2005

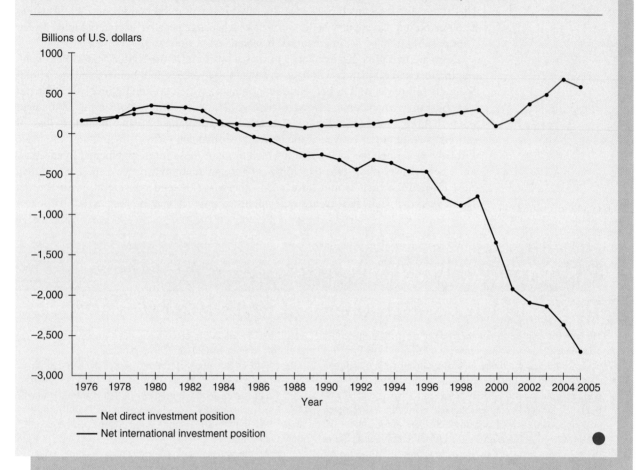

Billions of U.S. dollars

— Net direct investment position

— Net international investment position

U.S. assets abroad and the huge $12.7 trillion of foreign-held assets in the United States are a striking indication of the increased mobility of capital and the increased interdependence of countries in the modern world.

CONCEPT CHECK

1. How would you characterize the current U.S. balance-of-payments situation? How does it relate to the claim that the United States has been engaging in trade as though it had possession of an international credit card?

2. Why is the current account balance not exactly offset in practice by the financial account balance? What recording brings the BOP into balance?

3. What does it mean to say that the United States is a net debtor country? How long has this been the case?

SUMMARY

A balance-of-payments statement summarizes a country's economic transactions with all other countries during a particular time period, usually a year. In accordance with various accounting conventions, the statement indicates debits and credits in goods and services and investment income flows, unilateral transfers, long-term financial capital flows, short-term private financial capital flows, and short-term asset flows associated with activity by the country's monetary authorities. The statement is broadly divided into the current account and the financial account. A current account imbalance must be matched by an equal (but of opposite sign) financial account imbalance; for example, the large current account deficits of the United States

in recent years have been matched by large financial account surpluses. The most widely cited balances in a balance-of-payments statement are the merchandise trade balance and the current account balance. These and other balances (especially the official reserve transactions balance when central banks participate in the foreign exchange market) are useful for interpreting economic events and for guiding the decisions of policymakers. Finally, a country's statement of its net international investment position portrays the total assets of the country abroad and the total foreign assets in the home country. This statement indicates whether a country is a net debtor or a net creditor vis-à-vis foreign countries at a given point in time.

KEY TERMS

accommodating items in the
   balance of payments
autonomous items in the balance of
   payments
balance-of-payments accounts
balance on current account and long-
   term assets (or basic balance)
balance on goods and services
balance on goods, services, and
   factor income (or balance on
   goods, services, and income)

credit items in the balance-of-
   payments accounts
current account balance (or balance
   on current account)
debit items in the balance-of-
   payments accounts
double-entry bookkeeping
financial account balance
international investment position of a
   country (or international
   indebtedness position of a country)

merchandise trade balance
net creditor country
net debtor country
official reserve transactions balance
   (or overall balance or official
   settlements balance)
statistical discrepancy (or net errors
   and omissions)

QUESTIONS AND PROBLEMS

1. Explain how the following items would be entered into the U.S. balance of payments (the initiating entry):

   A disaster relief shipment of wheat to Bangladesh
   Imports of textile machinery
   Opening a $500 bank account in Zurich
   A $1,000,000 Japanese purchase of U.S. government bonds
   Hotel expenses in Geneva
   The purchase of a BMW automobile
   Interest earned on a bank account in London
   The Union Carbide purchase of a French chemical plant
   Sales of lumber to Japan
   The shipment of Fords to the United States from a Mexican production plant; and the profits from that same plant

2. What is the difference between the financial account and the current account?

3. What is meant by the "net international investment position" of the United States? What would happen to this net position if the United States experienced a current account surplus? Why?

4. Even though Japan has had very large trade surpluses in recent years, it has had official reserve transactions surpluses that are much smaller than the trade surpluses. (There was

even one official reserve transactions deficit.) What does this difference imply?

5. If the financial account balance must exactly offset the current account balance, why do government accountants bother to record the financial account?

6. Explain why a current account deficit indicates that a country is using more goods and services than it is producing.

7. "Direct foreign investment affects both the financial account and the current account over time." Agree? Disagree? Explain.

8. Suppose that two events occur simultaneously: (i) A firm in country A exports $1,000 of goods to country B and receives a $1,000 bank deposit in country B in exchange; and (ii) a country A immigrant gives $500 to a relative in country B in the form of a $500 buildup of the relative's bank account in country A.

   What is the impact of these two events on country A's (*a*) merchandise trade balance, (*b*) account balance, and (*c*) official reserve transactions balance?

9. Before the U.S. government began running its recent budget surplus, Japanese officials maintained that a key step for reducing the U.S. current account deficit was *not* that foreign markets should become more open to U.S. exports but, rather, that the U.S. government should reduce its budget deficit. Was there validity to this point? If so, why? If not, why not?

20

THE FOREIGN EXCHANGE MARKET

LEARNING OBJECTIVES

- ■ To grasp the fundamental underpinnings of the foreign exchange market.

- ■ To know the distinctions between various measures of the exchange rate.

- ■ To understand the roles of hedging, arbitrage, and speculation in foreign exchange markets.

- ■ To comprehend the links between the current spot rate and contracts to buy or sell foreign exchange in the future.

INTRODUCTION

The Case of the Wayward U.S. Dollar

The value of the euro declined steadily against the U.S. dollar from its introduction in 1999 at $1.16/€ through 2001, when it reached a low of $0.8952/€. At that point, numerous economists were claiming that the dollar was overvalued. Then, in the midst of more economically turbulent times, the trend reversed itself as the euro strengthened steadily, reaching nearly $1.30/€ in January 2004 before the dollar began to recover. By late March 2004 the price of the euro had fallen to $1.21, and it was also at that level in late August 2004. At the same time, the dollar also showed signs of renewed strength against the Japanese yen, the Swiss franc, and the British pound sterling. These recent movements in the value of the dollar have prompted considerable analysis and conjecture, both in terms of the effect of those changes on the U.S. trade balance as well as the forces underlying the strength of the dollar. Analysts are quick to point out that the continuing strength of the dollar is unusual in light of the recent stock market crash and the slow decline in the U.S. jobless rate. Criton M. Zoakos took note of the interesting fact that net portfolio capital inflows into the United States reached an all-time record in 2002 and continued through 2003 in spite of the currency movement and economic conditions in the United States.[1] Zoakos suggests that this is the result of the fact that Europe, Japan, and China are locked into export-driven macro policies dependent on the large U.S. market, and thus, they rely on relatively cheap currencies to promote exports and growth. The United States, on the other hand, is relying on entrepreneurial and high-tech-based growth, which generates higher rates of return than in the rest of the world and attracts foreign investment. At this point in time, relative interest rates and real returns to capital appear central to the strength of the dollar and the relative movements of other currencies. Many analysts thus suggest that the dollar will remain strong and maintain its position as the world's international reserve currency.

The movement of financial assets and goods and services shown in the balance of payments takes place between many different countries, each with its own domestic currency. Economic interaction can only occur in this instance if there is a specific link between currencies so that the value of a given transaction can be determined by both parties in their own respective currencies. This important link is the foreign exchange rate. This chapter examines how this link is established in the foreign exchange market and underlying economic factors that influence it, factors such as those mentioned in the preceding paragraph's typical news reports. The principal components of the market are analyzed and various measures of the exchange rate discussed. Finally, we discuss how the foreign exchange market and the financial markets are intertwined and of the formal relationship that exists between the foreign exchange rate and the interest rate.

THE FOREIGN EXCHANGE RATE AND THE MARKET FOR FOREIGN EXCHANGE

The **foreign exchange rate** is simply the price of one currency in terms of another (e.g., U.S.$/U.K.£ or, alternatively, U.K.£/U.S.$). This price can be viewed as the result of the interaction of the forces of supply and demand for the foreign currency in any particular

---

[1]Criton M. Zoakos, "Why the Dollar Is Different," *The International Economy,* Fall 2003, pp. 28–33. Also, see Jamie McGeever, "Dollar May Gain More Against Euro on ECB Outlook," *The Wall Street Journal,* March 29, 2004, p. C5; Timothy Aeppel, "Dollar's Decline is Mixed Blessing for Goods," *The Wall Street Journal,* December 19, 2003, p. A2; and "Will the Fallen U.S. Dollar Set the Stage for a Global Economic Boom a Year or Two From Now? (A Symposium of Views)," *The International Economy,* Summer 2003, pp. 30–44.

period of time. Although this price is fixed under some monetary system arrangements, if a country is to avoid continual BOP surpluses or deficits, the fixed exchange rate must be approximately that which would result from market determination of the exchange rate. We will therefore proceed to examine the foreign exchange rate assuming that it is the result of the normal market interaction of supply and demand. This market simultaneously determines hundreds of different exchange rates daily and facilitates the hundreds of thousands of international transactions that take place. The worldwide network of markets and institutions that handle the exchange of foreign currencies is known as the **foreign exchange market.** Within the foreign exchange market, current transactions for immediate delivery are carried out in the spot market and contracts to buy or sell currencies for future delivery are carried out in forward and futures markets. The nature of these specific markets and the manner in which they function will be discussed in greater detail later in the chapter.

Demand Side

Individuals participate in the foreign exchange market for a number of reasons. On the demand side, one of the principal reasons people desire foreign currency is to purchase goods and services from another country or to send a gift or investment income payments abroad. For example, the desire to purchase a foreign automobile or to travel abroad produces a demand for the currency of the country in which these goods or services are produced. A second important reason to acquire foreign currency is to purchase financial assets in a particular country. The desire to open a foreign bank account, purchase foreign stocks or bonds, or acquire direct ownership of real capital would all fall into this category. A third reason that individuals demand foreign exchange is to avoid losses or make profits that could arise through changes in the foreign exchange rate. Individuals who believe that the foreign currency is going to become more valuable in the future may wish to acquire that currency today at a low price in hopes of selling it tomorrow at a high price and thus make a quick profit. Such risk-taking activity is referred to as **speculation** in a foreign currency. Other individuals who have to pay for an imported item in the future may wish to acquire the needed foreign currency today, rather than risk the possibility that the foreign currency will become more valuable in the future and would increase the cost of the item in local currency. Activity undertaken to avoid the risk associated with changes in the exchange rate is referred to as **hedging.** The total demand for a foreign currency at any one point in time thus reflects these three underlying demands: the demand for foreign goods and services (and transfers and investment income payments abroad), the demand for foreign investment, and the demand based on risk-taking or risk-avoidance activity. It should be clear that the demands on the part of a country's citizens correspond to debit items in the balance-of-payments accounting framework covered in the previous chapter.

Supply Side

Participants on the supply side operate for similar reasons (reflecting credit items in the balance of payments). Foreign currency supply to the home country results firstly from foreigners purchasing home exports of goods and services or making unilateral transfers or investment income payments to the home country. For example, U.S. exports of wheat and soybeans are a source of supply of foreign exchange. A second source arises from foreign investment in the home country. Foreign purchases of U.S. government bonds, European purchases of U.S. stocks and placement of bank deposits in the United States, and Japanese joint ventures in U.S. automobile or electronics plants are all examples of financial activity that provide a supply of foreign exchange to the United States. Finally, foreign speculation and hedging activities can provide yet a third source of supply. The total supply of foreign exchange in any time period consists of these three sources.

The Market

Before moving on to more technical aspects of the foreign exchange market, let us take a moment to discuss in a general way how it operates (see Figure 1). The foreign exchange market here is presented from the U.S. perspective and, like any normal market, contains a downward-sloping demand curve and an upward-sloping supply curve. The price on the vertical axis is stated in terms of the domestic currency price of foreign currency, for example, $\$_{US}/franc_{Swiss}$, and the horizontal axis measures the units of Swiss francs supplied and demanded at various prices (exchange rates). The intersection of the supply and demand curves determines simultaneously the equilibrium exchange rate e_{eq} and the equilibrium quantity (Q_{eq}) of Swiss francs supplied and demanded during a given period of time. An increase in the demand for Swiss francs on the part of the United States will cause the demand curve to shift out to D'_{Sfr} and the exchange rate to increase to e'. Note that the increase in the exchange rate means that it is taking *more U.S. currency to buy each Swiss franc.* When this occurs, the U.S. dollar is said to be *depreciating* against the Swiss franc. In similar fashion, an increase in the supply of Swiss francs (to S'_{Sfr}) causes the supply curve to shift to the right and the exchange rate to fall to e''. In this case, the dollar cost of the Swiss franc is decreasing and the dollar is said to be *appreciating*. It is important to fix this terminology in your mind. **Home-currency depreciation** or **foreign-currency appreciation** takes place when there is an increase in the home currency price of the foreign currency (or, alternatively, a decrease in the foreign currency price of the home currency). The home currency is thus becoming relatively less valuable. **Home-currency appreciation** or **foreign-currency depreciation** takes place when there is a decrease in the home currency price of foreign currency (or an increase in the foreign currency price of home currency).

FIGURE 1   The Basic Foreign Exchange Market

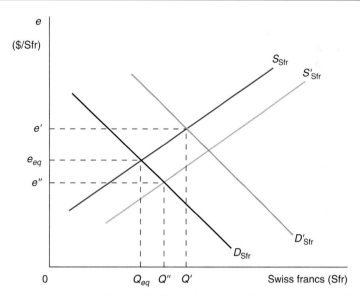

The equilibrium rate of exchange, e_{eq}, is determined by the interaction of the supply and demand for a particular foreign currency (in this case the Swiss franc). An increase in domestic demand for the foreign currency is represented by a rightward shift in the demand curve to D'_{Sfr}, which causes the equilibrium exchange rate to increase to e'. Because it now takes more units of domestic currency to buy a unit of foreign exchange, the domestic currency (the dollar) has depreciated. In a similar fashion, an increase in the supply of foreign exchange to S'_{Sfr} leads to an appreciation of the dollar, that is, to a lower equilibrium exchange rate e''.

In this instance, the home currency is becoming relatively more valuable. Changes in the exchange rate take place in response to changes in the supply and demand for foreign exchange at any given point in time.

The link between the balance of payments and the foreign exchange market can readily be shown using supply and demand. For purposes of this discussion, consider the supply and demand for foreign exchange as consisting of two components, one related to current account transactions and the other linked to the financial flows including the speculative and hedging activities (financial account transactions). In Figure 2, the demand and the supply of foreign exchange are each broken down in terms of these two components. Ignoring unilateral transfers, $D_{G\&S}$ and $S_{G\&S}$ portray the demand and supply of foreign exchange associated with the domestic and foreign demands for foreign and domestic goods and services, respectively. The demand and supply of foreign exchange associated with financial transactions are then added to each of the curves, creating a total demand and a total supply of foreign exchange. If the financial desire for foreign exchange is assumed to take place primarily for reasons such as expected profits, expected rates of return, and so forth (i.e., for reasons independent of the exchange rate), the total curves are drawn a fixed distance from the $D_{G\&S}$ and the $S_{G\&S}$ curves. If the exchange rate influences these financial flows, then the relationship between the goods and services curves and the total curves is more complex. For ease of discussion, however, we proceed with the curves as drawn in Figure 2.

FIGURE 2   The Foreign Exchange Market and the Balance of Payments

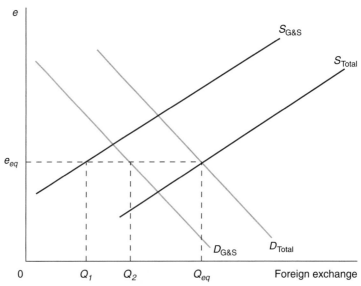

The demand and supply of foreign exchange are broken down into the transactions linked to the flows of goods and services (ignoring unilateral transfers), that is, the current account ($D_{G\&S}$,$S_{G\&S}$), and the transactions linked to financial transactions. Because the two must sum to D_{Total} and S_{Total}, desired financial transactions are the difference between the "Total" curves and the "G&S" curves. The equilibrium exchange rate e_{eq} will be determined by the interaction of D_{Total} and S_{Total}. In this case, e_{eq} is below that which would equate demand and supply in the current account, $D_{G\&S}$ and $S_{G\&S}$, leading to a current account deficit ($Q_2 - Q_1$). However, at e_{eq} the supply of foreign exchange resulting from financial transactions, ($Q_{eq} - Q_1$), is greater than the demand for financial transactions ($Q_{eq} - Q_2$) by the amount ($Q_2 - Q_1$). The surplus in the financial account thus exactly offsets the deficit in the current account at the equilibrium rate of exchange.

The equilibrium exchange rate is now seen to be determined by the intersection of the D_{Total} and the S_{Total} curves. This is not necessarily going to be the same exchange rate that would equilibrate $D_{\text{G\&S}}$ and $S_{\text{G\&S}}$. This would only be the case if the current account was exactly in balance at the equilibrium rate, e_{eq}. In Figure 2, the equilibrium rate is below that which would balance the current account. Consequently, at e_{eq} there is an excess demand $(Q_2 - Q_1)$ for foreign currency for trade in goods and services (the current account) and an offsetting excess supply $(Q_2 - Q_1)$ in foreign exchange in the financial account. The supply of foreign exchange arising from financial transactions $(Q_{eq} - Q_1)$ exceeds the demand for foreign exchange for financial transactions $(Q_{eq} - Q_2)$ by $(Q_2 - Q_1)$, the amount of the current account deficit. Thus, we again see that a deficit in the current account will be exactly offset by an equivalent surplus in the financial account at the market clearing exchange rate. Similarly, any surplus in the current account will be exactly offset by an equivalent deficit in the financial account at the equilibrium exchange rate.

THE SPOT MARKET

Having discussed the general nature of the foreign exchange market, we now turn to a more rigorous examination of this market. We begin by looking at the operation of the daily or current market, referred to as the **spot market,** and then examine the market for foreign exchange for future delivery (the forward market).

Principal Actors

As was indicated in the previous section, the motivations for demanding or selling foreign exchange are based in the transactions related to the current and financial accounts. These actions involve individuals and institutions of all kinds at the retail level and the banking system at the wholesale level. The major participants in the foreign exchange market are the large commercial banks, although multinational corporations whose day-to-day operations involve different currencies, large nonbank financial institutions such as insurance companies, and various government agencies including central banks such as the U.S. Federal Reserve and the European Central Bank also play important roles. Not surprisingly, the large commercial banks play the central role since the buying and selling of currencies most often involves the debiting and crediting of various bank accounts at home or abroad. In fact, most foreign currency transactions take place through the debiting and crediting of bank accounts with no physical transfer of currencies across country borders. Consequently, the bulk of currency transactions takes place in the wholesale market in which these banks trade with each other, the **interbank market.** In this market a large percentage of these interbank transactions is conducted by foreign exchange brokers who receive a small commission for arranging trades between sellers and buyers. The buying and selling of foreign exchange by the commercial banks in the interbank market that is not done through foreign exchange brokers, but directly with other banks, is called *interbank trading.* While bank currency transactions are done to meet their various retail customers' needs (corporations and individuals alike), banks also enter the foreign exchange market to alter their own portfolios of currency assets.

The Role of Arbitrage

As was indicated earlier, the foreign exchange market consists of many different markets and institutions. Yet, at any given point in time, all markets tend to generate the same exchange rate for a given currency regardless of geographical location. The uniqueness of the foreign exchange rate regardless of geographical location occurs because of **arbitrage.** As you recall, arbitrage refers to the process by which an individual purchases a product (in this case foreign exchange) in a low-priced market for resale in a high-priced market for the purpose of making a profit. In the process, the price is driven up in the low-priced market and down in the high-priced market. This activity will continue until the prices in the two markets are equalized, or until they differ only by the transaction costs involved. Because currency is being bought and sold simultaneously, there is no risk in this activity and hence there are always many potential arbitragers in the market. In addition, because of the speed of communications and the efficiency of transactions in foreign exchange, the spot market quotations for a given currency are remarkably similar worldwide, and any profit spread on a given currency is quickly arbitraged away.

In a world of many different currencies, there is also a possibility for arbitrage if exchange rates are not consistent between currencies. This point can be most easily seen in a three-currency example. Suppose the dollar/sterling rate is $1.40/£, and the dollar/Swiss franc rate is $0.70/Sfr. In this case, the franc/sterling rate must be 2 Sfr/£ for the three rates to be consistent and for there to be no basis for arbitrage [($1.40/£)/($0.70/Sfr) = 2 Sfr/£]. Suppose that the dollar/sterling rate increases to $1.60/£. This rate is inconsistent with the $0.70/Sfr and the 2 Sfr/£ rate, and there is a clear profit to be made by simultaneously buying and selling all three currencies. For example, one could take $1.40 and acquire 2 francs, use the 2 francs to buy 1 pound sterling, and immediately exchange the £1 for $1.60, thereby making a quick $0.20 profit. This is a situation of multicurrency arbitrage, in this case called **triangular arbitrage** since it involves an inconsistency between three different currencies. The triangular arbitrage produces **cross-rate equality,** meaning that all three exchange rates are internally consistent. Arbitragers are constantly watching the foreign exchange market for any inconsistencies, and they immediately buy and sell foreign exchange to take advantage of such a situation. In the preceding example, the arbitrage process should tend to drive up the dollar-franc price, drive up the franc-sterling price, and drive down the dollar-sterling price. These adjustments would take place until a new consistent equilibrium emerged—for example, $1.54/£, $0.74/Sfr, and 2.08 Sfr/£. (You should verify for yourself that there is no possibility for profitable arbitrage at these new prices.) The arbitrage process is thus relied upon not only to maintain a similar individual currency value in different foreign exchange markets but also to make certain that all the cross rates between currencies are consistent.

Different Measures of the Spot Rate

The discussion of the foreign exchange market to this point has focused on some of the more important conceptual factors underlying current or "on the spot" exchanges of currency between two countries. While this spot rate is certainly useful, it does not provide information about what the spot rate should be, given the nature and structure of the two countries; it does not provide any information on the change in overall strength of the domestic currency with respect to all of the home country's trading partners; and it does not give any indication of the real cost of acquiring foreign goods and services in a world of changing prices. To obtain information about the latter two factors, we must turn to alternative measures, measures which are often cited in the international sections of major news publications.

Let us look first at the problem of assessing the relative strength or weakness of a currency when a country has numerous trading partners, each with its own exchange rate. Because different exchange rates are similar to different commodities, we cannot simply add them together and take a mean. Just as in assessing economywide price changes, we therefore construct an index wherein each commodity (currency) can be appropriately weighted by its importance in a given country's international trade. To avoid the aggregation problem associated with adding up different currencies, each exchange rate is indexed to a given base year. The base year is assigned a value of 1, and all other observations for any given year are valued relative to it. For example, suppose we want to consider the average strength of the U.S. dollar in terms of other currencies. The dollar might, in the base

TABLE 1   Nominal Effective Exchange Rate Calculation (U.S. trade in billions of dollars)

	Exchange Rate			U.S. Trade, 2005	
Country	1999	2005	Index 2005	Exports and Imports	w_i
(1)	(2)	(3)	(4)	(5)	(6)
EMU	€1.0653/$	€0.8476/$	0.7957	504.3	0.262
Switzerland	SFr1.5045/$	SFr1.2452/$	0.8276	24.3	0.013
Sweden	Skr8.2740/$	Skr7.4731/$	0.9032	17.2	0.009
United Kingdom	£0.6172/$	£0.5493/$	0.8900	84.9	0.044
Canada	C$1.4852/$	C$1.2118/$	0.8159	503.3	0.261
Japan	¥113.700/$	¥110.220/$	0.9694	197.4	0.102
Mexico	Peso9.467/$	Peso10.8790/$	1.1491	292.5	0.152
China	Yuan8.281/$	Yuan8.1943/$	0.9895	301.6	0.157
Total				1,925.5	1.000

NEER = (0.796)(0.262) + (0.828)(.013) + (0.903)(0.009) + (0.890)(0.044) + (0.816)(0.261) + (0.969)(0.102)

    + (1.149)(0.152) + (0.990)(0.157)

  = 0.908

Sources: Data for exchange rates come from International Monetary Fund, *International Financial Statistics Yearbook 2006* (Washington, DC: IMF, 2006); information at the U.S. International Trade Commission website, www.usitc.gov.

year, be worth 0.6 British pound and 120 Japanese yen. Then, in some later year, the exchange rates or prices of the dollar might be 0.75 British pound and 90 Japanese yen. Clearly, in this example, the dollar has appreciated in terms of the pound (from 0.6 pound to 0.75 pound) and depreciated in terms of the yen (from 120 yen to 90 yen). The index for the value of the dollar in the later year would thus be 1.25 in terms of the pound (0.75/0.6 = 1.25) and 0.75 in terms of the yen (90/120 = 0.75). To find the change in the dollar's value on average from the base year to the later year, the procedure is then to weigh the value of the dollar in terms of a particular country's currency by the percentage of the country's trade that is done with that particular country. Thus, in the United Kingdom and Japan examples, if 20 percent of U.S. trade was with the United Kingdom, the weight accorded to the pound price of the dollar would be 0.2; if Japan accounted for 15 percent of U.S. trade, the yen price of the dollar would get a weight of 0.15. When this is done for all currencies involved in the sample or in a country's entire trade, the weights add up to 1.0. The end result of this process, a trade-weighted index of the average value of a country's currency, is called the **nominal effective exchange rate (NEER)** of the currency.[2]

To see how a NEER is calculated, consider the information in Table 1 for the United States and selected major trading partners for 1999 and 2005. The exchange rates are expressed in terms of units of foreign exchange per U.S. dollar. The levels of trade (exports plus imports) are indicated in column (5), the associated trade weights in column (6), the average exchange rates in columns (2) and (3), and the associated indexes of the price of the dollar for 2005 in column (4) (based on 1999 = 1.0). The NEER for 2005 can be calculated using the information [columns (4) and (6)] as shown in the table. The fact that the NEER has a value of 0.908 indicates that, on average over the 1999–2005 period with this set of trading partners, the dollar depreciated by 9.2 percent. This result occurs because, in

---

[2]Two nominal effective exchange rates appear daily in *The Wall Street Journal* in Section C, "Money and Investing."

recent years, the dollar depreciated against all of the currencies except the Mexican peso. This example illustrates the manner in which actual nominal effective exchange rates of a currency are calculated. [Note: To practice the technique using the given exchange rates, drop the EMU from the sample and recalculate the NEER. You should get a lower rate of depreciation for the dollar (5.2 percent), indicating how NEERs are sensitive to the choice of countries included in the sample.]

Another issue relates to the problem of interpreting changes in the exchange rate against any one currency when prices are not constant. When the prices of goods and services are changing in either the home country or the partner country (or both), we do not know the change in the *relative* price of foreign goods and services by simply looking at changes in the spot exchange rate and failing to take the new level of prices within both countries into account. For example, if the dollar appreciated against the yen by 10 percent, we would expect that, other things equal, U.S. goods would be 10 percent less competitive against Japanese goods in world markets than was previously the case. However, suppose that, at the same time that the dollar appreciated, U.S. goods prices rose more rapidly than Japanese goods prices. In this situation, the decline in U.S. competitiveness against Japanese goods would be more than 10 percent, and the nominal 10 percent exchange rate change would be misleading. For this reason, a **real exchange rate (RER)** is often calculated, where the RER embodies the changes in prices in the two countries in the calculation.

To illustrate, the average Japanese yen/dollar exchange rate in 1995 was ¥94.06/$1, and in 2005 this nominal exchange rate was ¥110.22/$1. This was a 17.2 percent appreciation of the dollar against the yen [(110.22 − 94.06)/94.06 = 0.172], leading one to expect substantially less competitiveness on the part of U.S. goods against Japanese goods. To calculate the real exchange rate, we must also look at prices, however. With 1995 = 100, U.S. consumer prices had risen to a level of 128.14 in 2005; with 1995 = 100, Japanese consumer prices had fallen to the 2005 level of 98.17. The real yen per dollar would then be calculated as follows:

$$\text{RER}_{2005} = e_{\text{¥/\$, 2005}} \times \left(\frac{\text{U.S. price index}_{2005}}{\text{Japanese price index}_{2005}} \right)$$

Thus, in our example,

$$\text{RER} = 110.22 \times \left(\frac{128.14}{98.17} \right) = 143.87$$

In this example, then, calculation of the real exchange rate indicates that, in terms of competitiveness in international markets, U.S. goods are at *more* of a disadvantage than the nominal rate had suggested. This result occurred because even though the dollar appreciated in nominal terms, U.S. prices rose *more* rapidly than Japanese prices (which actually fell). In real terms, the dollar appreciated not by 17.2 percent (as with the nominal rate) but by 53 percent [(143.87 − 94.06)/94.06 = 0.5296].

Another exchange rate concept, the **real effective exchange rate (REER),** calculates an effective or trade-weighted exchange rate based on real exchange rates instead of on nominal rates. In this case, the exchange rate indexes (such as those in Table 1) are calculated using real exchange rates rather than nominal exchange rates. The resulting indexes are then weighted, as usual, by the trade importance of the respective countries.

Another measure of the spot rate is concerned with identifying the true equilibrium rate that would lead to the current account (and hence the capital account) being in balance. An approach commonly used to estimate the underlying true equilibrium rate is the **purchasing**

power parity (PPP) approach and it exists in two versions, an absolute PPP version and a relative PPP version.

The PPP approach rests on the postulate that any given commodity tends to have the same price worldwide when measured in the same currency. This is sometimes referred to as the **law of one price,** which many believe operates if markets are working well both nationally and internationally. Under these conditions, arbitrage will quickly erase any price differences between different geographical locations. In the presence of transportation and handling costs, arbitrage will not cause prices to equalize between different geographical locations, but it is felt by proponents of the law of one price that this will not distort the general one-price concept. If goods and services do in fact seem to follow the law of one price, then, it is argued, the absolute level of the exchange rate should be that level that causes traded goods and services to have the same price in all countries when measured in the same currency. This is referred to as **absolute purchasing power parity.** For example, if a bushel of wheat costs $4.50 in the United States and £3 in the United Kingdom, then the exchange rate should be equal to $4.50 per bushel divided by £3 per bushel, or $1.50/£. If we generalize over many goods, the absolute PPP estimate of the equilibrium exchange rate would be

$$\text{PPP}_{\text{absolute}} = \text{price level}_{\text{US}}/\text{price level}_{\text{UK}}$$

when the price levels are expressed in dollars and pounds, respectively.

Not surprisingly, the absolute version of PPP does not seem to be borne out empirically. Factors such as transportation costs and trade barriers, which keep prices from equalizing across different markets, combined with the difference in the composition and relative importance of various goods, explain in part why the absolute version does not seem to hold. In short, every country's measure of the price level reflects a set of goods and services unique to that country and not directly comparable to the goods and services of other countries. For these reasons, a weaker version of PPP is often used that relates the *change* in the exchange rate to *changes* in price levels in the two countries. This is referred to as **relative purchasing power parity** $(\text{PPP}_{\text{rel}})$.

In the PPP_{rel} version, if prices in the home country are rising faster than prices in the partner country, the home currency will depreciate. If prices in the home country are rising slower than prices in the partner country, the home currency will appreciate. Given an initial base period exchange rate, the equilibrium rate (PPP_{rel} rate) at some later date will reflect the relative rates of price change in the two countries. More specifically, the PPP_{rel} rate (stated in terms of units of domestic currency per unit of foreign currency) should equal the initial period exchange rate multiplied by the ratio of the price index in the home country to the price index in the partner country. For instance as an example in the late 1990s, the PPPrel for a U.S.–U.K. situation for 1998, with 1995 as the base year, would be calculated as

$$1998 \, \text{PPP}_{\text{rel}}^{\$/£} = \left[e_{1995}^{\$/£} \right] \times \left[\text{PI}_{1998}^{\text{US}}/\text{PI}_{1998}^{\text{UK}} \right].$$

Hence, if $e_{1995}^{\$/£} = \$1.58/£$, $\text{PI}_{1998}^{\text{US}} = 107.0$, and $\text{PI}_{1998}^{\text{UK}} = 109.3$,

$$\text{PPP}_{\text{rel}}^{\$/£} = (\$1.58/£) \times (107.0/109.3)$$
$$= \$1.55/£$$

Because the actual exchange rate in 1998 was $1.66/£, PPP_{rel} suggests that the dollar was actually undervalued relative to the pound sterling in 1998 (the pound was overvalued relative to the dollar), based on the rates of price increase in the two countries over the period from 1995 to 1998. This conclusion, of course, rests on the assumptions that the exchange rate in 1995 was an equilibrium market rate and that the two price indexes used

IN THE REAL WORLD:

NOMINAL AND REAL EXCHANGE RATES OF THE U.S. DOLLAR

As examples of the nominal and real exchange rates of the dollar, consider Figures 3 and 4. Figure 3 illustrates the behavior of the nominal exchange rate (NER, or our usual *e*) of the U.S. dollar in terms of the Japanese yen over roughly the last two decades, as well as the movement of the real exchange rate (RER) of the dollar in terms of the yen over the same period. The graph shows that the nominal rate was above the real rate in every year prior to 1995 and below the real rate in the years after 1995. Technically, this pattern of difference in *levels* of the NER and RER reflects the fact that

1995 was the base year (when the consumer prices used in the construction of the RER were set equal to 100 in both countries) and the fact that Japan had less inflation throughout this period than did the United States. This technical difference in levels is not of major importance, however. What is important for interpretation from the graph is that, between 1985 and 1995, the NER fell to a greater extent than did the RER. This indicates that, although the dollar was falling considerably in nominal terms during this period, it was falling to a smaller degree in real terms than in nominal terms

FIGURE 3   Nominal and Real Yen/Dollar Exchange Rates, 1979–2005

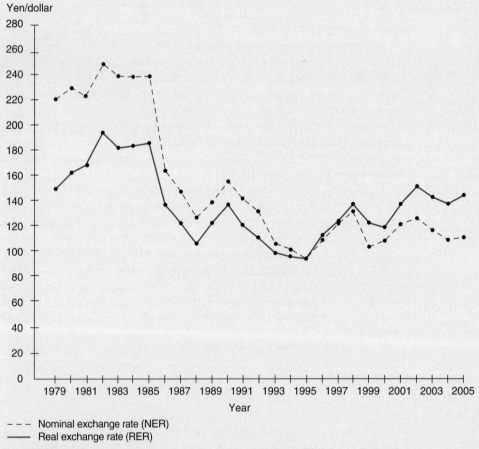

Note: Price indexes are 1995 = 100.

Sources: Calculated from data contained in International Monetary Fund. *International Financial Statistics Yearbook 1999* (Washington, DC: IMF, 1999); *International Financial Statistics Yearbook 2006* (Washington, DC: IMF, 2006).

(continued)

IN THE REAL WORLD: *(continued)*

FIGURE 4   U.S. Nominal Effective and Real Effective Rates, 1983–2006

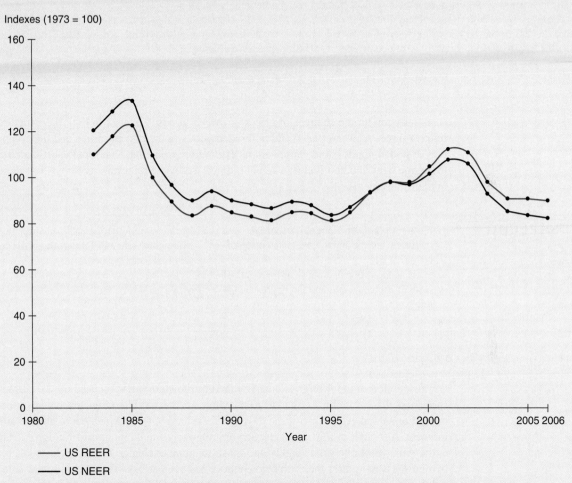

Source: Data contained in *Economic Report of the President,* February 2007 (Washington, DC: U.S. Government Printing Office, 2007), p. 356.

because U.S. prices were not as stable as Japan's. Hence, the depreciation of the dollar against the yen was a smaller percentage in real terms than in nominal terms, meaning that U.S. goods were not getting as much "boost" competitively as the nominal depreciation would suggest because greater inflation in the United States than in Japan was offsetting some of the dollar's nominal depreciation. After 1995, the real rate rose to a slightly greater extent than did the nominal rate, and this comparative behavior indicates that the dollar

was appreciating in real terms to a greater extent than in nominal terms. Again, the situation is that the relatively greater inflation in the United States than in Japan is hurting U.S. competitiveness more than the rise in the nominal rate would suggest.

Figure 4 portrays the behavior of the nominal effective exchange rate (NEER) of the U.S. dollar during 1983–2006 against the currencies of a broad group of U.S. trading partners (weighted by the relative importance of trade with the

(continued)

IN THE REAL WORLD: *(continued)*

United States). In these rates, the year 1973 is the base year, where both the NEER and the REER are equal to 100. The overall pattern in Figure 4 is rather similar to that in Figure 3. The nominal rate is above the real rate until the mid-1990s and then below it. Again, however, the relative changes are of most interest. Both rates declined from 1985 until 1995, but the fall in the NEER was greater than the fall in the REER. Hence, the improvement in competitiveness for U.S.

goods was not as great over this period as would be expected from looking at the nominal rate alone. After 1997, the real rate moved above the nominal rate, meaning that U.S. competitiveness was being hurt slightly more than the appreciation of the nominal rate would suggest. However, looking at Figure 4 as a whole, it should be emphasized that, unlike the situation in Figure 3, the NEER and the REER track each other fairly closely.   ●

accurately reflect the changes in prices of *traded* goods. Changes in both the structure of relative prices between traded and nontraded goods in the two countries and the composition of traded goods could cause serious estimation problems. Historically, estimated PPP exchange rates and nominal (the actual market) exchange rates have differed considerably in their movements.

CONCEPT CHECK	1. If the dollar/yen nominal exchange rate increases, has the dollar appreciated or depreciated? Why? 2. What is the difference between the nominal (actual) exchange rate and the real exchange rate?	3. If the euro/dollar actual exchange rate is below the relative PPP rate, why is the dollar said to be undervalued?

THE FORWARD MARKET

Our discussion of the foreign exchange market to this point has focused on the current or spot market for foreign exchange. Somewhere in the world foreign exchange is being bought or sold at every time of the day. Thus, exchange rates are subject to change at any moment. Although an individual can acquire relatively small amounts of foreign exchange at the going spot rate immediately, the most common exchange of currencies takes place two business days after the exchange contract has been struck. The two-day-later date, or **value date** when the transaction is completed, allows the bank accounts involved in the transaction sufficient time to clear. You can find daily quotations of the spot rate for the currencies of many countries in major news publications and can get current information by contacting many banks and financial exchange centers. Note that the quotations are for a specific time on the previous day and that they are the wholesale or interbank rates for transactions of $1 million or more. Retail customers pay a higher rate for foreign exchange; the difference between the two rates is the bank's charge for providing this service. Finally, commercial banks also make money in the foreign exchange markets by buying foreign exchange at a lower price than they sell it. For example, if you are traveling in England, you might pay $1.60/£ when you purchase pounds and receive only $1.58/£ when you sell back any unused pounds even though the exchange rate has not changed.

IN THE REAL WORLD:

THE BIG MAC INDEX

For well over a decade *The Economist* has annually evaluated the relative position of major currencies of the world by using its now well-known Big Mac Index (BMI—not to be confused with BMW!). The BMI is nothing more than an absolute PPP measure of the "true equilibrium value" of a particular currency based upon *one* commodity, a McDonald's Big Mac. The basic idea here is that a particular commodity should cost the same in a given currency wherever it is found in the world—if the prevailing exchange rate is the true underlying rate. Thus, the estimate of the PPP exchange rate (units of foreign currency/U.S. dollar) for a given currency is simply the value of the ratio of the Big Mac price in local currency divided by the U.S. dollar price. A currency is then determined to be undervalued or overvalued depending on whether the Big Mac price ratio is greater than the current spot rate (undervalued) or less than the current spot rate (overvalued). For example, the recent price of a Big Mac in Mexico was 29.0 pesos, while the U.S. price was \$3.22. The implied PPP exchange rate (pesos/\$) was thus 9.01 pesos/\$ (29.0 pesos/\$3.22). Because the actual spot exchange rate at that time was 10.9 pesos/\$, the BMI suggests that the Mexican peso was undervalued by 17 percent [=(9.0 − 10.9)/10.9]. Several examples from the most recent BMI are given in Table 2 for you to chew on.

TABLE 2   Big Mac Index Examples

| | The Hamburger Standard | | | |
	Big Mac Prices, Local Currency	Implied PPP	Actual Spot Rate, 1/31/07	Overvaluation (+) or Undervaluation (−) of Local Currency
United States	3.22	—	—	—
Brazil	6.4	1.99	2.13	−6%
China	11.0	3.42	7.77	−56
European Monetary Union	2.94	1.10	1.30	+19
Japan	280.0	87.0	121.0	−28
Mexico	29.0	9.01	10.9	−17
Switzerland	6.30	1.96	1.25	+57

The BMI has proved to be surprisingly consistent with other more sophisticated PPP measures over the years in spite of its many limitations. For example, the 1996 BMI turned out to be a useful predictor for the exchange rate movements of eight of twelve currencies of large industrial economies. In addition, the directions of movement of six of the seven currencies whose value changed by more than 10 percent were correctly indicated by the BMI. Further, the BMI implied that the euro was overvalued when introduced in 1999, and the euro did decline soon after its introduction. However, the euro recovered in late 2003 and early 2004 and continued to strengthen in recent years to where the BMI now indicates that it is overvalued. These successes came about in spite of the fact that the BMI assumes that there are no barriers to trade, including transportation costs. In addition, no provision is made for different tax structures, relative costs of nontraded inputs, or different market structures and profit margins.

Although it was originally developed for fun, the BMI has triggered not only annual interest and amusement but also several pieces of serious academic work. It now appears that many who initially turned up their noses at the BMI and asked "Where's the beef?" are now intrigued with the possibility that there might actually be something useful there to sink their teeth into.

Sources: "Big MacCurrencies," *The Economist*, April 12, 1997, p. 71; *The Economist*; "The Big Mac Index," February 1, 2007, obtained from Economist.com.

IN THE REAL WORLD:

SPOT AND PPP EXCHANGE RATES, 1973–2005/2006

Figure 5 illustrates the annual movements from 1973 to 1998 of the relative PPP rate (with 1995 = 100 for consumer prices) and the spot rate for dollars in terms of deutsche marks. Because the mark was replaced by the euro at the start of 1999, a relative PPP euro rate was constructed for the 1998–2006 period, using 1999 as the base year.

According to the PPP estimates in Figure 5, the dollar was overvalued in terms of the mark in almost all of the years. This was especially true in the 1982–1986 period. A possible explanation for this mid-1980s experience is that U.S. interest rates were very high at that time, and this attracted short-term funds from abroad and bid up the value of the

FIGURE 5   Spot and PPP Deutsche Mark/Dollar Rates, 1973–1998, and Spot and PPP Euro/Dollar Rates, 1999–2006

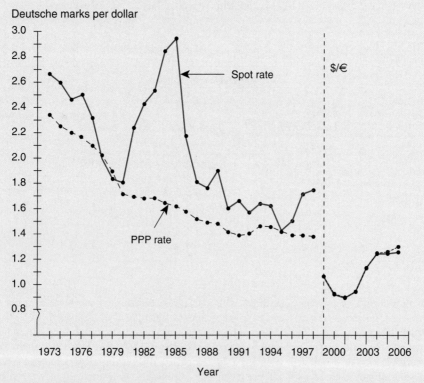

Sources: Data contained in International Monetary Fund, *International Financial Statistics Yearbook 1999* (Washington, DC: IMF, 1999); *International Financial Statistics Yearbook 2006* (Washington., DC: IMF, 2006).

The difference between the buying and selling price is the **retail spread** or the **retail trading margin.** These margins also exist at the wholesale level.

In many instances, however, transactions contracted at one point in time are not completed until a later date. For example, suppose that a U.S. automobile importer contracts to purchase 10 Rolls-Royce automobiles at a cost of £100,000 per automobile, which at the spot exchange rate of $1.50/£ would cost $150,000 per automobile, for a total contract cost of dollar substantially. This kind of influence on the exchange rate is not captured in PPP estimates. It is interesting to note that the nominal and PPP euro rates have remained remarkably close from 1999 to 2006.

In Figure 6, the pound is undervalued (dollar is overvalued) in some periods, especially in the mid-1980s, 2000, and 2001, and slightly overvalued in others. Note also that, in both graphs, there is a steady downward drift in the PPP rates (although the movement stabilized in the 2000–2002 period). These downward trends reflect the relatively greater inflation in the United States than in Germany/euro area and the relatively greater inflation in the United Kingdom than in the United States during this period. Recently both the PPP and nominal rates have drifted upward in similar fashion.

FIGURE 6   Spot and PPP Dollar/Pound Rates, 1973–2005

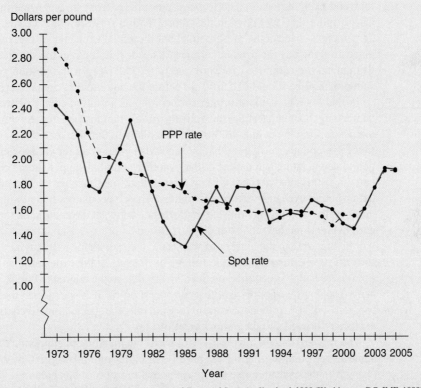

Sources: Data contained in International Monetary Fund, *International Financial Statistics Yearbook 1999* (Washington, DC: IMF, 1999); *International Financial Statistics Yearbook 2006* (Washington, DC: IMF, 2006).

$1,500,000. The delivery and payment date on the 10 automobiles is six months from the time the contract was signed. Because the contract is written in pounds sterling, the importer is faced with the possibility that the exchange rate may change within the six-month period. For example, the exchange rate might fall to $1.40/£, causing the dollar cost of the 10 cars to fall from $1.5 million to $1.4 million. On the other hand, the exchange rate could increase to, for example, $1.60/£. In either case, the cost of the autos changes by $100,000. The passage of time between when a contract is signed and the deal is finalized interjects an element of risk at the future point in time. If the contract above had been written in dollars instead of pounds sterling, the element of risk would have fallen on the U.K. exporter instead of the U.S. importer.

Because the contract in this case is written in pounds sterling, the risk falls on the importer. If the U.S. buyer does nothing and waits until the delivery day to purchase the £1 million, he or she is taking what is referred to as an **uncovered,** or **open, position.** Suppose that the importer was risk averse and wished to hedge against an unfavorable change in the exchange rate. What, if anything, can be done to reduce the risk of the pound appreciating against the dollar in the next six months? One alternative open to the importer is to acquire pounds sterling today at the rate of $1.50/£, invest them in England for the six-month interim period, then use the proceeds to meet the contract payment. This could of course involve transaction costs as well as the opportunity cost of any earnings differential if interest rates are higher in the United States than in the United Kingdom.

A second hedging option open to the importer is to contract today with a bank to acquire £1,000,000 on the delivery date for a specific number of dollars determined by the **forward exchange rate.** The forward rate differs from the spot rate in that the delivery date is more than two days in the future. With a forward contract, the foreign exchange agreement is made at the present time, but the actual exchange of currencies does not take place until the day the foreign currency is needed. In making this contract, the importer is guaranteed the contracted forward rate (e.g., $1.51/£) for the million pounds even if the spot pound price should rise to $1.60 before the automobiles are delivered.

In this case the bank or broker is operating as an intermediary between those who are demanding pounds sterling for delivery in six months and those who desire to supply pounds sterling in six months. Possible suppliers in this market are U.S. exporters who are to receive pounds sterling on that day and wish to contract forward to hedge the risk of the pound depreciating against the dollar. Another potential supply source consists of individuals or institutions who are willing to speculate (i.e., take an uncovered position) on the dollar-pound exchange rate in six months. These speculators hope to make an immediate profit on the delivery day due to the difference between the contracted forward rate and the current (spot) market rate on that day. If a speculator expects that the actual future spot rate will be higher than the current forward rate, the speculator will purchase foreign currency forward (take a **long position** in foreign exchange). If the expectation is realized, forward foreign exchange is acquired on the delivery date at the contracted price and then immediately resold at the spot price at that time for a profit. If it is expected that the actual future spot rate will be less than the current forward rate, the speculator will contract to sell foreign exchange forward, or take a **short position.**

The forward market thus consists of parties demanding or supplying a given currency at some future point in time for the purpose of either minimizing risk of loss due to adverse changes in the exchange rate (hedging) or making a profit (speculating). Obviously, expectations play an important role in this market, particularly on the part of those holding an uncovered position. The opportunity cost of hedging in this market consists of the difference between the contracted exchange rate and the rate that actually exists on the contracted delivery day. As a general rule, the more volatile the market in question, the greater the risk and hence the likely spread between the actual and the contracted rate. Compared with the first hedging option involving the acquisition of foreign currency at today's rate and short-term investment of the funds in the foreign country, however, hedging through the forward market is convenient and attractive to those unfamiliar with short-term investment opportunities in the foreign country in question. Information on the forward market is readily available to both hedgers and speculators. Daily quotations of forward rates on the previous day can also be found in major news publications (see Table 3).

TABLE 3   Spot and Forward Exchange Rates

Currencies   May 8, 2007

U.S.-dollar foreign-exchange rates in late New York trading

Country/Currency	Tues in US$	Tues per US$	US$ vs, YTD chg (%)	Country/Currency	Tues in US$	Tues per US$	US$ vs, YTD chg (%)
Americas				**Europe**			
Argentina peso*	.3248	3.0788	**0.6**	**Czech Rep.** koruna**	.04789	20.881	**0.2**
Brazil real	.4942	2.0235	**−5.3**	**Denmark** krone	.1817	5.5036	**−2.6**
Canada dollar	.9052	1.1047	**−5.3**	**Euro area** euro	1.3543	.7384	**−2.5**
1-mos forward	.9060	1.1038	**−5.3**	**Hungary** forint	.005499	181.85	**−4.5**
3-mos forward	.9076	1.1018	**−5.3**	**Malta** lira	3.1645	.3160	**−2.8**
6-mos forward	.9097	1.0993	**−5.2**	**Norway** krone	.1665	6.0060	**−3.7**
Chile peso	.001923	520.02	**−2.3**	**Poland** zloty	.3605	2.7739	**−4.5**
Colombia peso	.0004849	2062.28	**−7.9**	**Russia** ruble‡	.03876	25.800	**−2.0**
Ecuador US dollar	1	1	**unch**	**Slovak Rep.** koruna	.04036	24.777	**−5.1**
Mexico peso*	.0922	10.8460	**0.4**	**Sweden** krona	.1473	6.7889	**−0.8**
Peru new sol	.3159	3.166	**−0.9**	**Switzerland** franc	.8210	1.2180	**−0.1**
Uruguay peso†	.04190	23.87	**−2.1**	1-mos forward	.8232	1.2148	**−0.1**
Venezuela bolivar	.000466	2145.92	**unch**	3-mos forward	.8271	1.2090	**unch**
				6-mos forward	.8329	1.2006	**unch**
Asia-Pacific				**Turkey** lira**	.7485	1.3360	**−5.6**
Australian dollar	.8285	1.2070	**−4.7**	**UK pound**	1.9894	.5027	**−1.6**
China yuan	.1299	7.6960	**−1.4**	1-mos forward	1.9889	.5028	**−1.5**
Hong Kong dollar	.1279	7.8187	**0.5**	3-mos forward	1.9877	.5031	**−1.5**
India rupee	.02460	40.650	**−7.8**	6-mos forward	1.9849	.5038	**−1.4**
Indonesia rupiah	.0001125	8889	**−1.2**				
Japan yen	.008338	119.93	**0.8**	**Middle East/Africa**			
1-mos forward	.008372	119.45	**0.8**	**Bahrain** dollar	2.6524	.3770	**unch**
3-mos forward	.008437	118.53	**0.8**	**Egypt** pound*	.1757	5.6905	**−0.4**
6-mos forward	.008536	117.15	**0.8**	**Israel** shekel	.2513	3.9793	**−5.6**
Malaysia ringgit§	.2935	3.4072	**−3.5**	**Jordan** dinar	1.4104	.7090	**unch**
New Zealand dollar	.7372	1.3565	**−4.4**	**Kuwait** dinar	3.4583	.2892	**unch**
Pakistan rupee	.01645	60.790	**unch**	**Lebanon** pound	.0006616	1511.49	**unch**
Philippines peso	.0212	47.081	**−4.0**	**Saudi Arabia** riyal	.2666	3.7509	**unch**
Singapore dollar	.6591	1.5172	**−1.0**	**South Africa** rand	.1449	6.9013	**−1.3**
South Korea won	.0010835	922.93	**−0.8**	**UAE** dirham	.2723	3.6724	**unch**
Taiwan dollar	.03007	33.256	**2.1**				
Thailand baht	.03056	32.723	**−7.7**	**SDR††**	1.5212	.6574	**−1.1**

*Floating rate †Financial §Government rate ‡Russian Central Bank rate **Rebased as of January 1, 2005 ††Special Drawing Rights (SDR); from the International Monetary Fund; based on exchange rates for U.S., British and Japanese currencies.
Note: Based on trading among banks of $1 million and more, as quoted at 4 p.m. ET by Reuters.
Source: *The Wall Street Journal*, May 9, 2007, p. C14.

In addition to the forward market, there are two additional possibilities for buying and selling foreign exchange in the future. These two alternatives include buying or selling foreign exchange (major currencies only) in the foreign currency futures market or buying an option on the futures market. Basically, a **futures contract** is similar to a forward contract; it is an agreement to buy or sell a specified quantity of a foreign currency for delivery at a future point in time at a given exchange rate. More specifically, however, it generally refers to a futures contract entered into through the Chicago Mercantile Exchange (CME). Although they are remarkably similar, the futures contract differs from the forward contract in several ways. In the futures market, the contractor is represented by a foreign exchange broker who negotiates a contract for a standard amount of foreign exchange at the best rate possible. Once signed, the CME stands behind the futures contract and guarantees that the currency will be delivered and paid for on schedule. In addition, a margin deposit is required —generally a fixed percentage of the contract value. The futures contract is, however, resalable up until the time of maturity, whereas the forward contract is not. A final difference is the fact that a futures contract is available only for four specific maturity dates (the third Wednesday of March, June, September, and December); in contrast, forward transactions are private deals for any type of contract the two parties agree upon (usually one, three, or six months) from any beginning day. Although the futures market carries on activity similar to the forward market, it is argued that it is a useful element in the foreign exchange markets that adds an element of competition. In addition, because the futures market tends to be more highly centralized and standardized, it caters more to the smaller customer and the speculator than the forward market. The cost of using the futures market, however, appears to be higher than the cost of using the forward market.[3] For an example of currency futures quotations and how to interpret them, see Concept Box 1.

Another way to participate in the forward market is by participating in foreign currency options.[4] A **foreign currency option** is a contract that gives the holder the right to buy or sell a foreign currency at a specific exchange rate at some future point. Unlike the forward or futures contract, however, the holder is not obligated to exercise the option if he or she chooses not to. To participate in this market, one must either buy or sell an option contract.[5] The option buyer (holder) acquires the right to exchange foreign currency with the option seller (writer) for a fee or premium. This fee represents the maximum loss the buyer would experience should the option not be exercised. The completion of the option contract involves the actual exchange of the currencies.

There are basically two types of option contracts, puts and calls. The *call* option contract gives the holder the right to acquire foreign exchange for dollars at the contracted exchange rate, while the *put* option contract gives the holder the right to acquire dollars for foreign exchange at the contracted rate. Because options themselves are negotiable, there are four possible ways of participating in this market. We can buy a call option (acquiring the right to purchase foreign exchange), sell a call option (transferring the right to acquire foreign exchange), buy a put option (acquiring the right to purchase dollars), or sell a put option (transferring the right to purchase dollars). Each of these carries different risk and uncertainty. However, the most the option buyer can lose is the premium, while potential gains fluctuate with the spread between the contract exchange rate and the market rate.

---

[3]This paragraph has drawn heavily on Norman S. Fieleke, "The Rise of the Foreign Currency Futures Market," Federal Reserve Bank of Boston, *New England Economic Review,* March/April 1985, pp. 38–47. This article is an excellent evaluation of the role of the futures market. Of particular interest is the observation (p. 47) that standardization within the futures market is facilitated by the fact that the futures price and the spot price for a currency converge as the futures contract nears maturity, providing a link between the two prices that allows hedging to take place with relatively few maturity dates for futures contracts.

[4]This discussion is based on Brian Gendreau, "New Markets in Foreign Exchange," Federal Reserve Bank of Philadelphia, *Business Review,* July/August 1984, pp. 3–12.

[5]A "European option" is one that can be exercised only on the expiration date, while an "American option" is a contract that can be exercised anytime up to the expiration date.

CONCEPT BOX 1

CURRENCY FUTURES QUOTATIONS

Information on previous-day market activity on currency futures can be found in the financial section of major newspapers. The information in Table 4, from *The Wall Street Journal* of May 9, 2007, is typical of such presentations. The table describes market activity on Tuesday, May 8, 2007, and the terms and numbers have precise meanings. "CME" refers to the fact that these data originated in the Chicago Mercantile Exchange. To demonstrate the nature of the information found in these quotations, let's examine the data relating to the euro that describes contract activity on euro currency futures on the previous business day. As indicated in the first line, euro futures are traded in fixed lots of 125,000 euros. Focusing now on June delivery contracts of euros, the table indicates that the market opened at a price of $1.3620/€, the highest bid during the day was $1.3643/€, and the low bid was $1.3537/€. The market closed or "settled" at a price of $1.3565/€, and there were

231,170 outstanding contracts (open interest) at the end of the day for June delivery. This "settle" price represented an decrease of $0.0060/€ from the settle price of the previous business trading day, and, at the settle price, the contract value of one lot was $169,562.50 (= 125,000€ × $1.3565/€). The loss of $0.0060/€ on the day means that any party who has bought June futures on margin from a broker or seller (i.e., the buyer put up only a fraction—sometimes as low as 5 percent—of the value of the contract and borrowed the rest from the broker or seller) will pay a margin payment to the broker or seller reflecting the amount of the price decrease. In this case, a shift of $750 (= $0.006/€ × 125,000€) is made. This shift is referred to as *daily settlement* or *marking to market.*[*]

[*]See Robert W. Kolb, *Understanding Futures Markets,* 3rd ed. (Miami: Kolb Publishing, 1991), pp. 10–13.

TABLE 4   Currency Futures

	Open	High	Low	Settle	Change	Open Interest
Japanese Yen (CME)-¥12,500,000; $ per 100¥						
June	.8373	.8414	.8369	**.8381**	.0008	265,120
Sept	.8470	.8508	.8470	**.8479**	.0008	9,090
Canadian Dollar (CME)-CAD 100,000; $ per CAD						
June	.9084	.9097	.9053	**.9065**	−.0021	140,286
Sept	.9111	.9118	.9077	**.9087**	−.0021	2,781
British Pound (CME)-£62,500; $ per £						
June	1.9925	1.9959	1.9870	**1.9885**	−.0040	136,750
Sept	1.9897	1.9930	1.9856	**1.9865**	−.0040	707
Swiss Franc (CME)-CHF 125,000; $ per CHF						
June	.8281	.8291	.8226	**.8243**	−.0039	79,605
Sept	.8340	.8347	.8288	**.8301**	−.0039	313
Australian Dollar (CME)-AUD 100,000; $ per AUD						
June	.8240	.8301	.8234	**.8273**	.0030	111,264
Sept	.8230	.8277	.8230	**.8252**	.0030	899
Mexican Peso (CME)-MXN 500,000; $ per 10MXN						
May	...	...	...	**.92225**	...	0
June	.92275	.92550▲	.91850	**.92050**	...	93,600
Euro (CME)-€125,000; $ per €						
June	1.3620	1.3643	1.3537	**1.3565**	−.0060	231,170
Sept	1.3679	1.3682	1.3577	**1.3605**	−.0060	2,510

Source: *The Wall Street Journal,* May 9, 2007, p. C10.

Symmetrically, the most the seller can gain is the premium, while potential loss will fluctuate with the spread between the contract rate and the market rate at the time the option is exercised. The buyer is thus paying the seller to undertake the risk associated with exchange rate movements. The premium is the amount that is necessary for the seller of the option to assume the risk associated with the change in the exchange rate. Option contracts have been available since 1982. Foreign currency options provide an additional means of managing the risk of foreign exchange movements, and they are of particular value to those who wish to hedge against future transactions that may or may not occur. For an example of currency futures option quotations and how to interpret them, see Concept Box 2.

THE LINK BETWEEN THE FOREIGN EXCHANGE MARKETS AND THE FINANCIAL MARKETS

The foreign exchange market consists of the spot market, forward market, and futures/ options markets. Although our discussion treated these markets individually, in practice the exchange rates in these different markets are determined simultaneously in conjunction with the interest rates in various countries. To grasp why this is so, it is necessary to first examine the reasons why commercial banks, individuals, and companies might choose to buy or sell foreign assets, that is, assets denominated in currencies other than the home currency. While trade in merchandise and services for many years received the bulk of the attention in analyzing the foreign exchange market, the recent growth in the volume of transactions in foreign currency assets is such that these transactions clearly dominate the market today.

The Basis for International Financial Flows

International financial flows include a wide variety of transactions. The various categories include such items as bank lending of foreign currency, bank lending of domestic currency to foreigners, foreign bonds, domestic bonds, foreign and domestic equities, direct foreign investment, financial services such as banking and insurance, and various spot and forward currency transactions. These various transactions can be further subdivided on the basis of maturity into long-term or capital assets (a maturity one year or longer) and short-term or money market assets (maturity of less than one year). Money market assets include short-term government securities, certificates of deposit (CDs), and short-term corporate debt, to name just a few. They are traded in highly competitive markets, tend to involve a fixed rate of interest, and are highly liquid (easily convertible into cash). Capital markets, on the other hand, include not only long term CDs and bonds but also stocks, real investment, and other forms of equity for which a less certain rate of return exists. (See the next chapter for further discussion of international financial instruments.)

The decision to invest internationally rests on the expected rate of return on the international asset compared to domestic alternatives. If the expected rate of return is greater abroad than at home, one would expect domestic residents to invest abroad. If the expected rate of return on home assets is higher than that on foreign assets, foreigners would be expected to invest in the home country. If there are no barriers to investment flows, funds should move from areas of low return to areas of high return until the expected returns are similar. However, it is not quite that simple because there is a major difference between the domestic investment and the foreign alternative. The total return on the foreign asset to a potential home country investor includes not only the specific return on the asset in question but also any return associated with appreciation of the foreign currency against the home currency during the time of the investment (or loss if the foreign currency depreciates against the home currency). Thus, an investment in the United Kingdom made by a U.S. resident that earned 8 percent per year would actually yield a 10 percent return if the value of the English pound increased from $1.50 to $1.53 (a 2 percent appreciation of the pound) over the year between the initial investment date and the time of reconversion back into dollars. On the other hand, if the value of the pound

CONCEPT BOX 2

CURRENCY FUTURES OPTION QUOTATIONS

Just as in the case of currency futures, information on previous business-day market activity in currency futures options can be found in major newspapers. The information in Table 5, from *The Wall Street Journal* online on May 3, 2007, is typical of this type of information. The data summarize market behavior on the previous day, Wednesday May 2. Consider the various data provided for the euro (€). As with currency futures, "CME" in options refers to the fact that these data reflect market activity on the Chicago Mercantile Exchange. The table indicates that the futures options in euros are traded in lots of 125,000 euros. The various strike prices are stated in basis points (1 basis point equals 1/100 of a cent), so, for example, a price of 13300 reflects a price of $1.33/€ (or 0.752€/$1). If you wished to acquire option contracts to purchase 250,000 euros (two contracts) for June (a "call") at a price of 13600 ($1.36/€), one contract would cost you 107 basis points, or $0.0107/€, resulting in a cost per contract of $1,337.50 (=€125,000 × $0.0107/€) and a total cost $2,675 for the two contracts necessary to obtain the desired 250,000 euros. The value of each contract itself would be $170,000 (=€125,000 × $1.36/€), giving a $340,000 total for the two contracts.

If, instead, you wished to sell 250,000 euros in June, you would acquire a "put" that would cost you 85 basis points, or $0.0085/€. The cost of the two options would be $2,125(=€125,000 × $0.0085/€ × 2), and the value of the two contracts would again be $340,000. In contrast, a May-delivery put at a price of 13600 would cost $0.0023, or $575 for two contracts (= €125,000 ×$0.0023/€ × 2), and a September-delivery put contract at the price of 13600 would cost $0.015/€, or $3,750 for two contracts (= €125,000 ×$0.015/€ × 2).

Upon the delivery date, the holder of the contract has the option of whether to exercise the contract or buy (sell) on the open market. Returning to our first example of a June call option, if the market price in June was less than $1.36/€ and you wished to acquire euros, you would choose to buy euros on the open market and not exercise the option contract, thus losing only the initial cost of purchasing the contract. In this sense the option contract is an insurance policy that removes the risk of having to pay more than $1.36/€ on the delivery day in question. On the other hand, if you wished to sell euros on the June delivery date in question (own a put contract), you would exercise the option anytime the market price fell below $1.36/€. In this case the option contract removes the risk of receiving anything less than a price of $1.36/€ on the delivery date.

Finally, in the table, the trading volume on Wednesday, May 2, 2007 was 3,969 calls and 4,371 puts transacted, and 74,717 calls and 87,098 puts were left outstanding ("open int") at the end of the trading day.

TABLE 5   **Currency Futures—Option Prices**

Euro (CME)

125,000 Euros, cents per Euro

Strike Price	Calls			Puts		
	May	Jun	Sep	May	Jun	Sep
13200	4.220	4.260	4.920	0.010	0.060	0.360
13250	3.720	3.780	4.500	0.010	0.060	0.440
13300	3.220	3.320	4.110	0.005	0.110	0.540
13350	2.720	2.880	3.720	0.020	0.170	0.650
13400	2.220	2.450	3.360	0.005	0.240	0.780
13460	1.730	2.050	3.020	0.010	0.340	0.930
13600	1.240	1.690	2.690	0.020	0.480	1.100
13550	0.790	1.360	2.390	0.070	0.640	1.290
13600	0.450	1.070	2.110	0.230	0.850	1.500
13650	0.190	0.840	1.860	0.470	1.120	1.740
13700	0.080	0.650	1.630	0.860	1.430	2.000
13750	0.030	0.480	1.420	1.310	1.750	2.290
13800	0.015	0.360	1.230	1.790	2.130	—
Volume		**Calls**		3,969	**Puts**	4,371
Open interest		**Calls**		74,717	**Puts**	87,098

had fallen to $1.47, the U.S. investor would have realized only a 6 percent return on the U.K. investment. Depreciation of the currency in which the investment is denominated can thus offset, or more than offset, any apparent rate of return advantage of the foreign instrument.

The investor considers three elements when deciding whether to invest in the home country or in a foreign country: (1) the domestic interest rate or expected rate of return, (2) the foreign interest rate or expected rate of return, and (3) any expected changes in the exchange rate. In this situation, equilibrium in the financial markets does not necessarily lead to equality of interest rates or expected rates of asset yield between the two countries. To see why, let us examine the situation in which the investor would be indifferent between investing in the home country or in the foreign country, setting aside for the moment any consideration of differences in risk between the two investments. (We shall return to the issue of exchange rate risk and using the forward markets to insure oneself against it shortly.) Very simply, the investor would be indifferent between a domestic and a foreign investment whenever he or she expects to earn the same return on both after taking into account any expected change in the spot rate before the maturity date. Using the United States and the United Kingdom as an example, this parity condition for a 90-day or 3-month investment of $1 would be stated as follows:

$$\$1(1 + i_{NY}) = [(\$1)/(e)] \times (1 + i_{London})[E(e)] \qquad [1]$$
$$(1 + i_{NY})/(1 + i_{London}) = E(e)/e$$

where the interest rates are for 90 days, e is the spot rate in \$/£, and $E(e)$ is the **expected spot rate** in 90 days. Under this condition, a dollar invested in New York for 90 days will be worth the same amount as a dollar invested in London for 90 days (after converting the dollar to pounds sterling at the current spot rate and reconverting the principal plus interest back to dollars on the maturity date), given the interest rate in each of the two locations and the expectation regarding the 90-day spot rate. Thus, suppose that the annual interest rate in New York is 8 percent (= 90-day interest rate of 2 percent). Investing $1,000 in New York would produce an amount (principal plus interest) of $1,020 in 90 days. Suppose that the current spot rate is $1.60/£ and that the annual interest rate in London is 12 percent (= 90-day interest rate of 3 percent). Investing $1,000 in London would yield [$1,000/($1.60/£)] or £625 plus (£625)(0.03) or £643.75 in 90 days. An expected 90-day spot rate of $1.5845 would make the two investments equivalent [($1.5845/£) × £643.75 = $1,020].

Returning to equation [1], this equilibrium condition is often stated in a more general manner. The right-hand side of the equation, $E(e)/e$, is equal to (1 + **expected percentage appreciation of the foreign currency** over the 90-day period). This is because, for example, if $E(e) = \$1.76/£$ and $e = \$1.60/£$, then $E(e)/e = \$1.76/\$1.60 = 1.10$, or 1 plus the expected appreciation of the pound of 10 percent. Designating the expected percentage appreciation of the foreign currency as xa, $E(e)/e$ is equal to $(1 + xa)$ and equation [1] now becomes

$$(1 + i_{NY})/(1 + i_{London}) = (1 + xa), \text{ which equals}$$
$$(1 + i_{NY})/(1 + i_{London}) - 1 = xa \text{ which can be written as}$$
$$(1 + i_{NY})/(1 + i_{London}) - (1 + i_{London})/(1 + i_{London}) = xa$$
$$(i_{NY} - i_{London})/(1 + i_{London}) = xa \qquad [2]$$

This condition states that equilibrium in the international financial markets occurs whenever the expected appreciation (depreciation) of the foreign currency is roughly equal to the difference between the higher (lower) domestic return and the lower (higher) foreign return. Precise equilibrium condition [2] is usually approximated by

$$(i_{NY} - i_{London}) \cong xa \qquad [3]$$

because $(1 + i_{London})$ will not differ too much from 1. Because the investor is bearing all the risk of changes in the exchange rate, this equilibrium condition is referred to as **uncovered interest parity (UIP)**. Should this condition not hold, for example, $(i_{NY} - i_{London}) > xa$, investments in the United States are more attractive than those in the United Kingdom and investment funds would flow into the United States. If $(i_{NY} - i_{London}) < xa$, investment funds would be flowing to the United Kingdom.

It is important to note that a change in expectations about the future spot rate will lead to current investment flows, which force a change in the spot rate until the expected appreciation (depreciation) rate is again consistent with the difference in the two interest rates. Simply stated, the expected rate and the spot rate should move in tandem as long as the interest rate differential remains the same. Why does this take place? Assume that the financial markets are in equilibrium and that there is a sudden change in expectations regarding the dollar/pound exchange rate; for example, suppose the U.S. interest rate is 3 percent and the U.K. interest rate is 2 percent, and the expected appreciation of the pound then increases from 1 to 2 percent. This means that the expected return on U.K. investments is now higher (4 percent) than the expected return on equivalent U.S. domestic investments (3 percent) and investors would start investing in the United Kingdom. This activity increases the demand for pounds on the spot market, causing the price of pounds to increase (the dollar to depreciate against the pound). Investment in the United Kingdom, with the accompanying upward pressure on the dollar/pound spot exchange rate, continues until the expected rate of appreciation of the pound is again equal to the difference between the interest rates in the two countries. What has happened in the process is that the increase in the expected appreciation of the pound (or expected depreciation of the dollar), the rise in $E(e)$, has led to an appreciation of the pound in the spot market, a rise in e, until xa, which equals $[E(e)/e - 1]$, is again 1 percent. Expectations thus play an important role in exchange rate movements.

Of course, people do not have perfect foresight. Consequently, the actual return on the foreign investment in 90 days may not match what was expected when the investment decision was made. For example, foreign returns may be less certain because of unexpected changes in the exchange rate, possible limitations on the transfer of earnings back home, and so forth. The investor who is bearing the risk of changes in the foreign exchange rate and possible other factors may thus require an additional payment for undertaking the risk linked to these unanticipated developments. This additional financial factor is often called the **risk premium** (RP) and, expressed as a percentage, leads to a restatement of the previous equilibrium condition:

$$(i_{NY} - i_{London}) \cong xa - \text{RP} \qquad [4]$$

Thus, if the risk premium is 2 percent and i_{NY} is 6 percent, then $(i_{London} + xa)$ must equal at least 8 percent because of the additional 2 percent risk premium in order for the New York investor to place funds in London. If payments for undertaking foreign risk are an important factor, then not only changes in the expected exchange rate but also changes in the risk premium can contribute to sudden investment flows and to changes in the spot rate even when interest rates remain unchanged.

Covered Interest Parity and Financial Market Equilibrium

Up to now, our analysis has assumed that the risk of changes in the exchange rate is borne by the investor. Any risk associated with changes in the exchange rate can of course be hedged in the forward market if the investor does not want to go uncovered. Then the covered investment position includes the interest earned on the foreign investment plus the cost of the forward market hedge.

The link between the spot rate and the forward rate is often discussed in terms of premium and discount. When the exchange rate is stated in terms of domestic currency units per unit of foreign currency, the foreign currency is **at premium** whenever the forward rate is higher than the spot rate. If the forward rate is less than the spot rate, the foreign currency is **at discount.** It is common to define the link between the spot and forward rates in the following way:

$$p = [e_{fwd}/e] - 1$$

where e_{fwd} = the forward rate of the relevant period and where p, the percentage premium, is positive when the foreign currency is at premium and negative when the foreign currency is at discount. To illustrate, suppose that the actual pound price is \$1.608/£ in the 90-day forward market and \$1.600/£ in the spot market. The 90-day forward pound is then at a 0.5 percent premium $[(1.608/1.600) - 1 = 0.5$ percent].

The link between the foreign exchange market and the financial markets can readily be seen by examining two types of transactions that involve the spot rate, the forward rate, and interest rates. As you will recall, a several-month delay between the signing of an import–export contract for goods and services and the exercising of that contract interjects an element of risk into the transaction, because the exchange rate may change in the ensuing period of time. If the contract is written in the exporting country's currency, this risk falls on the importer, who has the choice of going uncovered (and absorbing the risk) or of hedging the risk. The risk may be hedged by buying the foreign currency in the spot market now and investing the proceeds abroad until the delivery date, or by using one of the forward markets. Presumably, the importer will choose the least expensive method. This will involve comparing the difference in the cost of the contract at the forward rate versus the current spot rate with the opportunity cost associated with acquiring foreign currency now and investing it abroad at an interest rate different from what the money is earning (costing) at home. Similarly, the forward rate will be considered by a short-term financial investor sending funds abroad to protect against a decline in the value of the foreign currency by the time the investment funds are returned home.

If the financial markets are working well, in equilibrium the risk-averse importer should be indifferent between hedging by using the short-term foreign investment and hedging by using the forward market, and the risk-averse short-term investor should be indifferent between the domestic and the foreign investments. The link between the spot market, forward markets, and the money markets that generates these equality conditions is achieved through **covered interest arbitrage.**

Consider now an investor determining whether to place funds at home (e.g., New York) or overseas (e.g., London). If the investor chooses to protect against the risk of spot rate fluctuations, that is, to cover, the forward market will be used. In this case the equilibrium condition is

$$\$1(1 + i_{NY}) = (\$1)(1/e)(1 + i_{London})(e_{fwd}) \quad [5]$$

$$(1 + i_{NY})/(1 + i_{London}) = (e_{fwd})/(e) = p + 1$$

$$[(1 + i_{NY})/(1 + i_{London})] - 1 = p$$

$$[(1 + i_{NY})/(1 + i_{London})] - [(1 + i_{London})/(1 + i_{London})] = p$$

$$(i_{NY} - i_{London})/(1 + i_{London}) = p \quad [6]$$

where e is the spot \$/£ rate, e_{fwd} is the \$/£ rate on 90-day forward currency, and p is the actual premium on 90-day forward pounds.

This condition can also be approximated, following the procedure with uncovered interest parity, by the following:

$$i_{NY} - i_{London} \cong p \quad [7]$$

In equilibrium, any difference in the interest rates between the two financial markets should be approximately offset by the foreign exchange premium. For example, if the $i_{NY-90} = 2.5$

percent and the $i_{\text{London}-90} = 2$ percent, the financial and exchange markets will be in equilibrium if the forward pound is contracted at a price which is 0.5 percent above the spot rate.[6] In this case the person who invests in London is receiving 2 percent on the short-term investment plus a 0.5 percent return due to the forward premium. The sum of these two returns is equal to 2.5 percent; that is, the return that would be received on a short-term investment in New York. It is clear that interest rates will not necessarily equalize between countries even if markets are functioning efficiently. In fact, one would not expect them to be equal as long as forward rates are different from spot rates.

Given the covered interest arbitrage condition, we can now predict the movement of financial investment between countries taking into account both the interest rates in the two countries and the foreign exchange markets. Whenever the interest rate differential ($i_{\text{home}} - i_{\text{foreign}}$) is greater than the premium (from the home-country perspective), funds would flow into the home country. Whenever the interest rate differential is less than the forward premium, investment funds would flow out of the home country. In equilibrium, we would expect no net short-term financial movements based on interest rate considerations.

The equilibrium condition is presented in Figure 7. The interest rate differential between New York and London is plotted on the vertical axis and the forward premium on the pound on the horizontal axis. With the axes scaled in a similar manner, the points of equilibrium between the interest rate differential and the premium are on the 45-degree line that passes through the origin. This line is referred to as the **covered interest parity (CIP)** line. The points located above the CIP line indicate conditions of disequilibrium that will produce inflows of foreign financial investments into New York, while those points lying below the line indicate conditions when funds should flow from New York to London.

The discussion to this point has proceeded assuming that there are no transaction costs involved in the interest arbitrage activity. In fact, such financial transactions are not without cost. Because these costs are incurred, we would not expect CIP to obtain. The equilibrium condition in this case needs to incorporate the transaction costs, so the approximate equilibrium condition becomes

$$i_{\text{NY}} - i_{\text{London}} \cong p \pm \text{transaction costs}$$

In Figure 7, the CIP line is bounded on either side by two dashed lines. These lines are drawn equidistant on either side of the CIP line at a rate of 0.25 percent, a commonly used rule of thumb for transaction costs. This is, at best, a general guideline, because costs vary considerably from transaction to transaction in response to many factors, including the size of the transaction. It is important to remember that transaction costs are incurred *both* in the financial transaction and in the acquisition and sale of foreign currency. Thus, it is not an inconsequential consideration. Robert Z. Aliber, a prominent international monetary specialist, has indicated that transaction costs are anywhere from 0.1 to 1 percent of the value of the transaction involved.[7]

It is also important to note that additional factors may contribute to the difference between interest rates in two countries. Capital market imperfections, differential costs in gathering information about alternative investments, and noncomparability of specific

---

[6]It is critical that the interest rate and the premium be calculated over the same period. In this case of a 90-day forward rate, for example, the appropriate rate of interest could be approximated by $i_{\text{annual}}/4$; in the case of a 180-day forward premium, $i_{\text{annual}}/2$; and so forth.

[7]Cited in Francisco Rivera-Batiz and Luis Rivera-Batiz (1994), p. 112. Frank McCormick (1979, p. 416), also cited in Rivera-Batiz and Rivera-Batiz, p. 112, estimated that 20 to 30 percent of the difference between the interest rate on Treasury bills in the United States and that in the United Kingdom could be explained by transaction costs.

FIGURE 7   The Covered Interest Parity Line

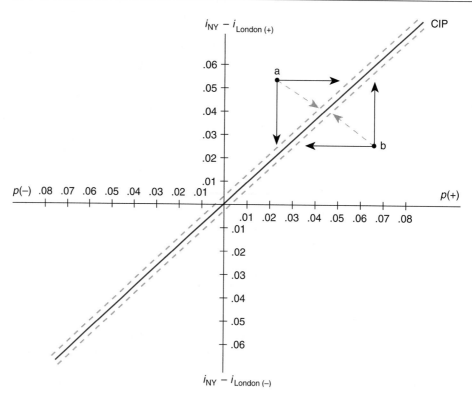

International financial markets are in equilibrium when any interest rate difference (for example, $i_{NY} - i_{London}$) between two countries is virtually equal to the foreign exchange premium p when financial transactions are costless. The possible equilibrium points are thus found on straight line CIP which passes through the origin and bisects the 90-degree angle (assuming that the scale on both the vertical and horizontal axis is the same). However, because financial transactions are not costless, the interest rate difference and the forward premium can differ in equilibrium by the amount of the transaction cost. Market equilibrium will thus lie in the neighborhood of the CIP line defined by the pair of dashed lines, whose distance from the CIP line reflects some average transaction cost.

assets all can contribute to the existence of interest rate differentials between countries beyond that explained by covered interest arbitrage. There is also the possibility that the political risk associated with investment in a foreign country will be a factor. Political risk, as noted earlier, reflects the fact that a foreign government can intervene in the financial markets and/or expropriate or freeze the capital assets of foreigners. The returns to assets can clearly be affected by the imposition of exchange controls and changes in government regulation.

Another point to make at this juncture is that a diagram very similar to Figure 7 can be employed to illustrate the concept of uncovered interest parity (discussed in the previous section). All that needs to be done is to relabel the horizontal axis from the premium on forward exchange, p, to expected appreciation of the foreign currency, $\{xa$ or $[E(e) - e]/e$ or $[E(e)/e] - 1\}$. The 45-degree CIP line then becomes a 45-degree UIP (uncovered interest parity) line. Then, if investors are located at a point such as point b in Figure 7, the expected appreciation of the foreign currency exceeds the interest rate differential. That is, $xa > i_{NY} - i_{London}$ or $i_{London} + xa > i_{NY}$. There is an incentive to send funds to London, which necessitates a spot purchase of pounds. The e increases and $[E(e)/e] - 1$ falls. In addition, with funds leaving New York, i_{NY} may rise and i_{London} may fall with the inflow into London. As you can see from the ($i_{London} + xa > i_{NY}$) expression, this means that the two sides of the inequality are converging. With complete UIP, the process would stop at the 45-degree line. In practice, however, the UIP line will not quite be reached because of transaction costs.[8]

In view of Figure 7 and its conceptual modification to embrace UIP, a very important point emerges. If CIP holds, this means that the premium on foreign currency is equal to the difference in interest rates between the two financial centers. However, if UIP holds, the expected rate of appreciation of the foreign currency is *also* equal to the difference in interest rates between the financial centers. Hence, if CIP and UIP both hold, the result is that the premium in the forward market *equals* the expected rate of appreciation of the foreign currency. This is a situation of an **efficient foreign exchange market** in that the forward rate is a measure of the expected exchange rate and that there are no further unexploited opportunities to make a profit. We will return to the concept of market efficiency in later chapters.

Simultaneous Adjustment of the Foreign Exchange Markets and the Financial Markets

Although we have shown the conditions under which financial flows will take place and the direction of their movement, little has been said about how the markets involved respond and whether the flows themselves generate a movement toward equilibrium in the sense used in this discussion. Let's return to covered interest arbitrage and analyze the adjustment process in our continuing U.S.–U.K. example, and examine four markets: (1) the London money market, (2) the New York money market, (3) the dollar/pound spot market, and (4) the dollar/pound forward market for time t. These four markets are presented in Figure 8. We begin by assuming that the interest rate differential is greater than the forward premium and that short-term investment thus has an incentive to flow to New York from London. As English investors withdraw funds from the London money market to invest in New York, the supply of loanable funds in London declines [shifts to the left in panel (a)], exerting upward pressure on i_{London}. These funds are then brought to the foreign exchange spot market to be exchanged for U.S. dollars, which shows up as a rightward shift in the supply curve of pounds sterling [panel (c)]. This influx of pounds has the effect of putting downward pressure on the dollar/pound spot exchange rate (appreciating the dollar). Because these investors are risk averse and wish to hedge against changes in the foreign exchange rate, they will at the same time purchase pounds sterling forward. This increases the demand for pounds (shifts the demand for pounds to the right) in the forward market [panel (d)] and puts upward pressure on the forward rate. Finally, as British investors make their desired investments in New York, there will be an increase in the supply of funds in the New York money market [a rightward shift of the supply curve in panel (b)] and a downward pressure on i_{NY}. Returning to our equilibrium condition, we note the nature of these adjustment pressures with arrows:

$$(i_{NY}{\downarrow} - i_{London}{\uparrow}){\downarrow} \quad \text{and} \quad (e_{fwd}{\uparrow}/e{\downarrow}){\uparrow} - 1 \rightarrow p{\uparrow}$$

Note that the movement of interest rates unambiguously makes the interest rate differential smaller. At the same time, the movement in the exchange rates unambiguously makes the forward premium larger.[9] Investment will continue to flow from London to New York until these movements of interest rates and exchange rates bring about a new equilibrium.

---

[8] Note that xa would also differ from the forward premium if there is a risk premium associated with uncovered arbitrage. With the risk premium (and no transactions costs). $i_{NY} - i_{London} \cong xa - \text{RP} = p$ in equilibrium and therefore $xa \cong p + \text{RP}$.

[9] Note also that, with an efficient foreign exchange market, a larger forward premium would also be matched by a larger xa or expected appreciation of the pound in the situation of uncovered interest arbitrage.

FIGURE 8   International Financial and Exchange Rate Adjustments

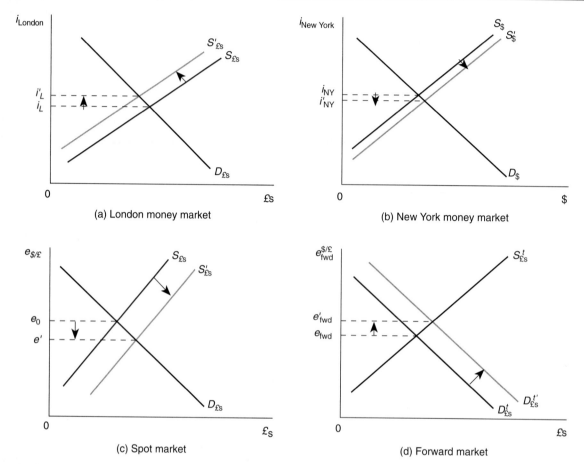

(a) London money market

(b) New York money market

(c) Spot market

(d) Forward market

Assuming that $i_{NY} - i_{London} > p\pm$ transaction costs, funds should move from London to New York. When this happens, the supply of loanable funds declines from $S_{£s}$ to $S'_{£s}$, putting upward pressure on the London interest rate (panel a). The conversion of pounds into dollars in the spot market (panel c) increases the supply of pounds, putting downward pressure on the spot rate (appreciating the dollar). Investors covering themselves against changes in the exchange rate then purchase pounds forward, increasing the demand in this market, putting upward pressure on the forward rate (panel d). Finally, when the funds are invested in New York, the supply of loanable funds increases there (panel b), placing downward pressure on i_{NY}. All of these price movements—the increase in i_{London}, the decrease in the spot rate, the increase in the forward rate, and the decline in i_{NY}—work to reduce the initial inequality. Market equilibrium attains in London and New York when the interest differential comes into line with the forward premium and transaction costs.

The nature of this adjustment process is shown back in Figure 7 by the arrows at point *a* and at point *b*. The adjustments from disequilibrium can take place through the foreign exchange markets (horizontal adjustments), the money markets (vertical adjustments), or some combination of the two. If interest rates are the adjustment mechanism, then movements in *equilibrium* interest rates should be highly correlated between the countries with major financial markets; in other words, increases (decreases) in interest rates in one country will be associated with increases (decreases) in interest rates in other countries. If exchange rates are doing the adjusting, then we would expect little or no correlation between interest rate changes in the leading industrial countries. A study by Kasman and Pigott (1988) indicated that for the United States, changes in the short-term interest rate are highly correlated with short-term interest rate changes in Canada but are poorly correlated with interest rate changes in other trading partners. Except for the Canadian result, these findings suggest that much of the equilibrium adjustment is taking place through the foreign exchange markets.

Before leaving this discussion, it is important to point out several additional factors that make it difficult to observe the adjustment process and that can cause the simple equilibrium condition not to be met. The existence of varying transaction costs mentioned earlier is one of these factors. A second factor that obfuscates the issue is the difficulty in choosing a representative interest rate in the two countries that is sufficiently comparable. Contributing to this problem is the fact that the variance of the distribution of returns on alternative investments within the countries may be different due to such things as different liquidities, different credit risks, and different tax treatments across what outwardly appear to be similar types of investments. Finally, the operation of the equilibrating process in the money and foreign exchange markets may be hampered by government policies and other institutional imperfections that slow or even impede altogether the adjustment process. If governments attempt to hold interest rates constant by monetary policy, then the short-run international financial market adjustment will necessarily fall even more heavily on the foreign exchange markets.

CONCEPT CHECK

1. What is the difference between the forward market, the futures market, and the options market?

2. Does it ever make sense to make a financial investment abroad at a lower interest rate than at home? If so, when? Why?

3. What is the covered interest parity line?

4. What is an uncovered interest parity line?

SUMMARY

This chapter focused on foreign exchange rates and the operation of the foreign exchange market. Attention was directed to the principal components of this market and how they influence the foreign exchange rate. The links between the spot market, the forward market, and interest rates were developed, and the market equilibrium condition between the money markets and the foreign exchange markets was established under uncovered and covered scenarios. Testing for the presence of uncovered parity is difficult in practice because of the problem of ascertaining expectations on exchange rates. Although the covered interest condition tends to hold empirically to some extent, it can be affected by such things as government policies in the participating countries, transaction costs, and the differing distribution of asset returns between countries. Some evidence seems to suggest that international financial adjustment takes place principally in the foreign exchange markets and not in the domestic money markets, adding further to exchange rate volatility under flexible exchange rates.

KEY TERMS

absolute purchasing power parity
arbitrage
at discount
at premium
covered interest arbitrage
covered interest parity (CIP)
cross-rate equality
efficient foreign exchange market
expected percentage appreciation of the foreign currency
expected spot rate
foreign currency option
foreign exchange market
foreign exchange rate

forward exchange rate
futures contract
hedging
home-currency appreciation (or foreign-currency depreciation)
home-currency depreciation (or foreign-currency appreciation)
interbank market
law of one price
long position
nominal effective exchange rate (NEER)
purchasing power parity (PPP)

real effective exchange rate (REER)
real exchange rate (RER)
relative purchasing power parity
retail spread (or retail trading margin)
risk premium
short position
speculation
spot market
triangular arbitrage
uncovered interest parity (UIP)
uncovered (or open) position
value date

QUESTIONS AND PROBLEMS

1. The United States presently has a current account deficit with Japan. What would happen to the dollar/yen spot exchange rate and the current account deficit if there were a decrease in Japanese investment in the United States? Incorporate the foreign exchange market into your answer.

2. Suppose that you observe the following exchange rates: $2/£; $0.0075/¥; and £0.005/¥. Is there cross-rate equality? If yes, why? If not, what would you expect to happen?

3. A dollar appreciation against the Swiss franc is no guarantee that the dollar will "go further" than it previously did in acquiring Swiss goods. Do you agree? Explain.

4. Explain the difference between the real exchange rate and the PPP exchange rate. What is the purpose of each?

5. Suppose the deutsche mark price of a dollar was 1.8175 DM/$ in 1980 and 1.7981 DM/$ in 1987. With 1980 = 100, if the price index for Germany was 121.11 in 1987 and that for the United States was 137.86 in 1987, was the dollar overvalued or undervalued in 1987 according to PPP? Explain.

6. Suppose that i_{NY} = 2 percent, i_{London} = 6 percent, xa (expected appreciation of the pound) = *minus* 1 percent (that is, the pound is expected to depreciate by 1 percent), and RP (risk premium for investing in London) is 2 percent. Assuming these numbers all apply to the same time period, explain why this is a disequilibrium situation and how uncovered interest parity is attained.

7. You observe that the U.K. annual interest rate is 2.5 percent, the U.S. annual interest rate is 3.8 percent, the 3-month forward rate is $1.8180/£, and the spot rate is $1.8034/£. Assuming that transaction costs are 0.2 percent, are the financial markets in equilibrium?

8. Using the information in Question 7, assume that the interest rate in the United Kingdom increases to 3.5 percent. What financial adjustments would you expect to see?

9. On May 8, 2007, *The Wall Street Journal* reported the following (for May 7):

   Prime interest rates: United States 8.25 percent; Switzerland 4.04 percent; Japan 1.875 percent

   Spot rates: $0.8257 = 1 Swiss franc; 120.06 Japanese yen = $1

   3-month forward rates: $0.8319 = 1 Swiss franc; 118.65 Japanese yen = $1

   (*a*) In terms of the dollar, was the Swiss franc at a forward discount or a forward premium? By what percent? Looking at the prime rates of the United States and Switzerland, is your calculated percentage discount/premium reasonably consistent with covered interest parity? Why or why not?

   (*b*) In terms of the Japanese yen, was the U.S. dollar at a forward discount or a forward premium? By what percent? Looking at the prime rates of Japan and the United States, is your calculated percentage discount/premium reasonably consistent with covered interest parity? Why or why not?

10. If you observe that the Swedish kroner in terms of the dollar is at a 1.2 percent 3-month forward premium, under what conditions could you therefore say that the kroner is expected to rise by 1.2 percent relative to the dollar in 3 months? Explain.

INTERNATIONAL FINANCIAL MARKETS AND INSTRUMENTS: AN INTRODUCTION

LEARNING OBJECTIVES

■ To become aware of the fundamental components of international financial markets.

■ To understand how global money markets, interest rates, and foreign exchange markets are interdependent.

■ To learn about the types and roles of international currency and monetary derivatives.

INTRODUCTION

Financial Globalization: A Recent Phenomenon?

In spite of the many different issues and disagreements surrounding globalization, the phenomenon is currently perceived as present in nearly all aspects of economic life and is often taken for granted. Further, it is generally viewed as a relatively recent phenomenon, particularly in the area of capital flows and international finance. In a recent article, Alan M. Taylor provides a historical look at the globalization of finance and points out some interesting facts.[1] Capital flows have indeed surged in volume in the past few decades in both the developing and developed world, often creating difficult challenges for policymakers. Surprisingly, a similar phenomenon took place in an earlier period of globalization between 1870 and 1914. The striking parallels between the two periods, roughly 100 years apart, have raised some interesting questions, particularly in light of the collapse of the earlier globalization phenomenon starting in 1914 and continuing through the 1940s and 1950s. While two world wars and a world depression certainly contributed to the striking changes in global finance, it seems prudent to step back and examine the current global capital phenomenon in terms of our earlier experiences.

While the global capital market did begin to grow in the 1960s, it did not reach the previous high levels of the earlier period until well into the 1980s. While the two growth periods are quite similar in terms of the changes in communications and transportation that accompanied the growth spurts, they do differ in terms of the type of foreign exchange regime in place and the challenges facing policymakers. The earlier period operated under a gold standard, while the current system contains of a variety of systems anchored by flexible exchange rate arrangements between the major world currencies. Taylor, does, however, point out an additional interesting difference between the two periods. In the earlier period, the volume of capital flows to developing regions was roughly equal to those flowing to the more wealthy countries. Today, relatively little capital is flowing to the developing countries, and the bulk of the capital flows are between wealthy countries and are intended to reduce risk through asset diversification and the fine-tuning of portfolios.

In today's rapidly globalizing world, where the value of foreign exchange transactions involving international assets far exceeds the value of foreign exchange transactions involving goods and services, it is important to examine more closely the nature of these modern transactions. The actors in the international financial system have developed a huge and bewildering variety of different types of traded assets, with each asset designed to satisfy particular liquidity, risk, and return demands of financial investors and asset holders. In this chapter we survey different general types of assets that are exchanged internationally, and we provide information on their size, characteristics, and markets. We begin by looking at international bank lending and then examine international bonds and stocks (equities). We then consider in some detail a number of specific financial instruments that belong to the broad category "financial derivatives." Our purpose here is to familiarize you in a general way with the range of financial instruments available for transferring wealth across country borders and to indicate the many possibilities that exist internationally for satisfying financial investors' particular preferences.

INTERNATIONAL BANK LENDING

In its coverage of money and banking, your introductory economics course made the implicit assumption when examining banks' balance sheets that loans and deposits of the banks were entirely domestic in nature. In other words, deposits (which are assets of the

---

[1] Alan M. Taylor, "Global Finance: Past and Present," *Finance and Development* (March 2004), pp. 28–31. The article was based on the book, *Global Capital Markets: Integration, Crisis, and Growth* (Cambridge, MA: Cambridge University Press, 2004), which Taylor coauthored with Maurice Obstfeld.

depositors and liabilities of the banks) placed into banks (and other depository institutions) were presumed to come from domestic citizens. These deposits provided checking accounts with which the depositors could carry out economic transactions, and savings and time deposit accounts from which the depositors could earn interest and thus provide for future consumption. The deposits provided funds from which the banks could, after satisfying bank legal reserve requirements, make domestic loans (which are assets of the banks and liabilities of the borrowers). However, this simple, straightforward textbook treatment has become less and less realistic over the past several decades, as depositors now seek international outlets for their savings and banks increasingly seek international borrowers for their funds. In addition, the domestic banks themselves now often have many branches located in foreign countries.

Table 1 shows why the exclusive domestic focus is no longer appropriate. The table presents data on **international bank lending.** Such lending or financing, which constitutes a loan across country borders, can occur for many reasons. For example, domestic banks may lend funds to private firms abroad that wish to undertake real investment projects and that find the domestic banks' lending terms to be more favorable than bank lending terms in the firms' own countries. Or domestic banks may purchase foreign financial instruments (such as certificates of deposit offered by foreign banks) with excess reserves in order to earn a higher return than is available domestically on comparable instruments. Or foreign banks may borrow funds from domestic banks to obtain domestic currency working balances to meet various needs of their (the foreign banks') customers.

The table gives a summary view of the cumulative stock of claims that has resulted from international bank lending as of September 2006. The first row gives the estimate by the Bank for International Settlements (BIS) of "total cross-border bank claims."[2] This figure refers to the claims of banks in a broad set of 40 countries, including all major countries. These claims are loans made by banks to borrowers in other countries, and they are obviously part of international lending. Row (2), "local claims in foreign currency," indicates loans by banks to domestic borrowers, but these loans have been made in *foreign* currency. Because the foreign currency was clearly obtained from foreign sources at some time in the past, it also reflects an international loan. The sum of these two items, row (3), represents the stock of **gross international bank lending**—$27,710.1 billion, or $27.7 *trillion,* in September 2006 (when valued in dollars using exchange rate conversions for the nondollar currency components).

TABLE 1   Gross and Net International Bank Lending, September 2006
            (billions of dollars)

Part A	
(1) Total cross-border bank claims	$24,545.0
(2) Local claims in foreign currency	3,165.1
(3) *Gross international bank lending*	27,710.1
(4) *Minus:* Interbank deposits	16,945.4
(5) *Net international bank lending*	10,764.7

Note: Components may not sum to totals because of rounding.

Source: Bank for International Settlements, *BIS Quarterly Review,* March 2007, p. A7.

---

[2]The BIS is an institution located in Geneva, Switzerland, that sponsors conferences of central bankers on international monetary cooperation, acts as a clearinghouse for central bank settlements, and deals with various other international banking matters.

However, an adjustment to this gross lending figure is necessary if we wish to determine the *net* stock of lending that has occurred over time. Simply put, if a U.S. bank lends $3 million to (i.e., deposits $3 million in) a German bank and a German bank lends the equivalent of $2 million to (i.e., deposits the equivalent of $2 million in) a U.S. bank, the net international flow of funds is only a $1 million outflow from the United States (whereas the gross flow is $5 million). Row(4) makes this type of adjustment by subtracting "interbank deposits." As is evident, this is a large figure—$16,945.4 billion. These interbank deposits occur, for example, because domestic (foreign) banks may maintain deposits in foreign (domestic) banks for the purposes of facilitating transactions with economic actors in the foreign (domestic) country, of earning favorable rates of return on particular certificates of deposit in the foreign (domestic) country, or of general portfolio diversification. In the case of portfolio diversification, risk is reduced by holding a wide variety of assets (by not "keeping all your eggs in one basket"), including foreign assets. When these interbank deposits are netted out, the stock of **net international bank lending** [row (5)] in September 2006 was $10,764.7 billion.

It is useful to examine gross international bank lending in more detail. This lending essentially consists of three components:

1. Domestic bank loans in domestic currency to nonresidents. This component would be exemplified by a bank in France lending euros to a U.S. firm for the firm's purchase of French exports.

2. Domestic bank loans in foreign currency to nonresidents. An example of this type of activity would be the lending of dollars by a bank in France to a U.S. firm so that the firm could undertake the purchase of oil supplies from a Saudi Arabian exporter who wishes to be paid in dollars (oil prices are in fact quoted in dollars).

3. Domestic bank loans in *foreign* currency to domestic residents. This situation would be represented by a bank in France lending dollars to a French citizen for the purchase of a U.S. Treasury bond.

In the literature, component 1 above (loans in domestic currency to nonresidents) is generally referred to as **traditional foreign bank lending.**[3] This type of activity has a long history: Banks are providing domestic currency to foreign citizens and firms for the financing of international trade. However, components 2 and 3 of the gross lending (loans in foreign currency to nonresidents and loans in foreign currency to domestic residents) became of large size beginning only in the 1960s. These two situations reflect the use of a currency outside the country that issues the currency, and they have been dubbed as representing activity in the **eurocurrency market.** Indeed, a *eurocurrency deposit* is defined as a deposit in a financial institution that is denominated in a currency other than the currency of the country in which the financial institution is located. Originally, this market was called the **eurodollar market** because the major deposits involved were dollar deposits located outside the United States, chiefly in Europe. With the rise in importance of other currencies in this market, "eurodollar" is often broadened to "eurocurrency" to include these other currencies. Of course, even the term *eurocurrency* is inadequate because such deposits are now also located in financial centers outside Europe (particularly Singapore and Hong Kong).

We now look in more detail at the origin and the implications of the eurodollar and eurocurrency markets. We focus in particular on eurodollars, because dollars constitute a

---

[3]See Johnston (1982, pp. 1–2). However, Johnston refers to international bank lending as comprising only components 1 and 3 rather than components 1, 2, and 3.

larger fraction of eurocurrency deposits than any other currency does and because the emergence of eurodollars was the catalyst for the later use of other currencies in these markets.

There are a number of ways in which a eurodollar or eurocurrency deposit can arise. A typical case[4] would be a situation where a U.S. exporter sells goods to a British buyer and receives dollar payment. (Assume that the foreign exchange market transaction to get the dollars has been carried out by the British importer.) However, the U.S. exporter may wish to leave the dollars abroad in a London bank (London is in fact the largest center for eurodollars in Europe) so that the dollars will be conveniently available for use, say, for foreign input purchases from British (or other European) firms. The London bank will keep this deposit as a *dollar* deposit, and it will be matched by a claim by the London bank on the U.S. bank in which the U.S. exporter has an account (and with which bank the London bank has a "correspondent" relationship). Like any bank deposit, this London deposit can now be loaned out by the British bank to customers who require dollars. Indeed, the amount of eurodollar deposits can grow in multiple fashion because the British bank can initiate the multiple-deposit expansion process associated with fractional reserve banking. Thus, if the original deposit by the U.S. exporter is $1 million and the bank wants to lend 90 percent of it, the loan of this $900,000 (say, to a London importing company for the purchase of goods from a French firm that wishes to have dollars) could be redeposited in Europe and would form the basis for another $810,000 loan (if 90 percent of the $900,000 is again lent out). As you may remember from discussing bank deposit expansion in your principles course, this series of loans (if 90 percent is always "re-lent") can lead to a cumulative total of $10 million in eurodollar deposits ($10 million = $1/0.10 \times$ the initial deposit of $1 million).[5] In this eurodollar expansion process, the loans involved are usually loans of six months or less, and the banks making the loans are referred to as **eurobanks,** even though the banks may be located outside Europe (such as in Singapore). In addition, the interest rate on the loans normally consists of a markup, the size of which depends on risk and market conditions, above the **London Interbank Offered Rate (LIBOR),** the rate at which Eurobanks lend among themselves.[6]

Historically, the eurodollar market began to be of significance in the 1950s. (See Kaufman 1992, pp. 317–18, and Gibson 1989, pp. 10–15.) At that time, due to Cold War considerations, the Soviet Union shifted dollar deposits out of the United States and placed them in London banks. In addition, dollar deposits in London were enhanced when Great Britain, worried about its balance-of-payments deficits and hence about its ability to maintain the value of the pound under the pegged exchange rates of the period, imposed some controls on the use of the pound for import and capital-outflow transactions. The consequence of this British government action was that British banks, desiring to continue financing these transactions, increasingly conducted them in dollars. Further, dollars were becoming considerably more abundant in Britain and Europe because of the large (for the time) official reserve transactions deficits in the U.S. balance of payments. Another factor at work, especially in the late 1960s, was the existence of legal ceilings (Regulation Q of the Federal Reserve) on the interest rates that could be paid by U.S. banks on their time and savings deposits. With higher interest rates available in Europe, U.S. depositors chose to

---

[4]For further discussion, see Kaufman (1992, pp. 311–25).

[5]However, it should be noted that, in the multiple expansion process, if a deposit of eurodollars is at any point borrowed by a *U.S.* bank, the process will stop because the deposit is no longer a eurodollar deposit (because the funds will be located in the United States). See Kvasnicka (1986, pp. 175–76).

[6]More precisely, LIBOR is the average of interbank rates offered for dollar deposits in London, based on the quotes of five major banks. These banks issue the quotes at 11 A.M. on each business day. LIBOR is listed every day in *The Wall Street Journal* and other financial publications.

place their dollars there, and the eurobanks were quite willing to receive them. An important reason for the ability of the eurobanks to offer higher rates was that eurodollars were not subject to any legal reserve requirements, unlike the situation with bank deposits in the United States. Thus, because eurobanks could lend a larger fraction of any given deposit than could U.S. banks, the eurobanks could earn higher returns from their deposits and could offer higher rates of interest to depositors in order to attract funds.

Two other factors that led to a rise in the eurodollar (eurocurrency) markets should be mentioned—one on the demand side and one on the supply side. On the demand side, there was a general monetary tightening in the United States toward the end of the 1960s because of inflationary pressures associated with the conduct of the Vietnam War. Due to this tightening, borrowers seeking dollars found them to be more expensive in New York and other American financial centers. This increasing difficulty in obtaining dollars from U.S. financial institutions particularly burdened foreign borrowers because two additional, restrictive policy steps had already been undertaken in the United States in the mid-1960s to reduce the worsening U.S. balance-of-payments problem by limiting capital outflows. These steps were the introduction by the Federal Reserve of voluntary foreign lending "guidelines" for banks (giving specific recommended percentage reductions for loans to particular geographic areas) and the imposition of the (nonvoluntary!) Interest Equalization Tax on loans taken out by foreigners from U.S. institutions and markets. This tax discouraged foreign borrowing because it amounted to an extra charge above the regular interest charge on the loans. Thus, due to these measures and the general monetary tightening, dollar loans from the United States were more difficult to obtain and pressure emerged for the buildup of dollar accounts abroad; rather than convert existing dollars abroad into their own currencies, foreign holders found it profitable to keep the deposits in dollar form overseas. In addition, some of the increased demand for eurodollars came from U.S. banks themselves. Because money was tight in the United States, U.S. banks sought to get dollar funds from their overseas branches and from foreign banks. This demand for eurodollars was facilitated by the fact that *lending* rates in Europe tended to be lower than those in the United States, even as *deposit* rates in Europe were higher. This rate structure existed because eurobanks were able to operate with lower margins between lending and deposit rates, in part because of the lack of reserve requirements on eurodollars, than were U.S. banks. Other factors that we examine later in this chapter were also involved.

On the supply side, new dollar deposits abroad grew for several reasons. A very important factor in their growth was the first "oil shock," in 1973–1974, when the Organization of Petroleum Exporting Countries (OPEC), after maintaining a partial export embargo, startled the world with a virtual quadrupling of oil prices. With oil prices being quoted and oil transactions being conducted in dollars, there was a vast inflow of dollars (known as "petrodollars") to the OPEC countries, and many of these dollars were deposited in banks in London and in other European cities. Indeed, despite the dramatic fall in oil prices during the 1980s, petrodollar deposits have continued at high levels ever since. For example, Herbert Kaufman (1992, p. 318) notes that, after the Iraqi invasion of Kuwait in 1990, the overthrown Kuwaiti government was still able to make a contribution to the financing of Operation Desert Storm because the Kuwaiti ruling family had perhaps $10 billion invested outside Kuwait, with a sizable amount in eurobanks.

With this background on the nature of the eurodollar and eurocurrency markets, we now briefly consider the significance of these markets. The major consequence of the rise of these markets is that the mobility of financial capital across country borders has been greatly increased. This means that interest rates (and general credit conditions) are increasingly linked across countries although, due to such factors as differing risk, transaction costs and other factors to be discussed later, interest rates are not equalized. Nevertheless, because the majority of deposits in the euromarkets are interbank deposits—deposits of one bank in another bank—and because banks are very sensitive to interest rate movements, the link is indeed strong despite the fact that interest rate equality is not achieved.

To elaborate, consider a hypothetical large U.S. bank. This bank is interested in attracting deposits and in earning interest from its subsequent loan of those deposits, and it is cognizant of conditions in both domestic and foreign money markets.[7] It compares the cost of obtaining an additional domestic deposit with the return from placing that deposit in the eurodollar market (either with a different bank or with an overseas branch of its own bank). The cost of acquiring the new deposit involves the interest rate to be paid to the depositor as well as the forgone opportunity cost incurred by holding any required reserves against the deposit.[8] However, in recent decades in the United States, the reserve requirement on nonpersonal (corporate) time deposits has been eliminated, so the cost on these deposits is basically only the interest cost. If this interest cost is less than the return in the eurodollar market *and* if the return in that market is greater than the return on comparable domestic assets, then placing the funds in the eurodollar market could be profitable. The outflow of funds from the United States would thereby perform an arbitrage function because the withdrawal of the funds from the U.S. money market would put upward pressure on U.S. interest rates and the inflow of funds to the eurodollar market would put downward pressure on eurodollar interest rates. The reverse pressures are set in operation when eurodollar rates are less than domestic rates, for then the U.S. bank would borrow funds from the euromarkets and lend them in the United States.

Thus the eurodollar and eurocurrency markets have been a force for moving interest rates across countries toward each other, and these markets have hence played a major role in enhancing financial integration across international borders. In addition, precisely because the markets have been a force for international integration, the consequence is that any country's monetary policy with respect to interest rates is less independent than would otherwise be the case. An attempt to raise interest rates in one country will lead to an inflow of funds, which will dampen the rise in the initial tight-money country and put upward pressure on interest rates in the other countries. Hence, it is no longer possible (at least in developed countries) to conduct a completely independent monetary policy. This increasing integration of financial markets could have been accomplished without the rise of the euromarkets per se, because the general relaxation of barriers to capital flows in recent decades would most likely have accomplished much the same result. Nevertheless, the rise of the eurodollar and eurocurrency markets hastened the process.

Finally, it is important to note that many observers worry that the surge in international bank lending in general and in euromarket activity in particular *has fostered potential economic instability.* Because a central bank of a country does not have jurisdiction over deposits abroad, there is no effective control of the amount of money in existence that is denominated in the country's currency. Eurodollars, for example, can be borrowed by U.S. banks for use *in the United States,* with the result that an attempt by the Federal Reserve to implement restrictive monetary policy can be made more difficult. Or a foreign subsidiary of a U.S. multinational firm can borrow dollars from German or U.K. banks and use these dollars to increase spending on U.S. goods at the same time that the Federal Reserve is trying to reduce U.S. bank loans as part of an anti-inflationary stance. Further, deposits denominated in dollars, say, in France, are also not under effective control

---

[7]See Kreicher (1982, pp. 11–13).

[8]Additional costs in the United States are (1) any premium that needs to be paid for the deposit insurance associated with the deposit and (2) any applicable state and local taxes. We neglect these items in our discussion for the moment.

of the French central bank. The uncontrolled growth associated with those deposits could potentially lead to undesirable consequences for *France,* too, if France wished to adopt an anti-inflationary policy.

---

1. What is a eurodollar deposit? Is the dollar deposit of a French company in a New York bank a eurodollar deposit? Why or why not?

2. What is the distinction between gross international bank lending and net international bank lending?

THE INTERNATIONAL BOND MARKET (DEBT SECURITIES)

Besides international bank lending, increasingly sizable activity has been taking place in the last several decades in the **international bond market.** The issuance of bonds by governments and corporations represents borrowing by the issuing entities, and the time period of the loan is generally longer than one year. Within the general bond category, a distinction is often made between *notes,* which have a maturity of less than 10 years, and *bonds,* which have a maturity of 10 years or longer. We will generally use the term *bonds* to refer to both of these types of debt instruments.

Bonds have a *face value* or *maturity value* (e.g., $1,000) which indicates the amount that will be paid back to the lender at the end of the life of the bond, and interest payments (or *coupon payments*) are usually made each year [e.g., $60 per year or a 6 percent ($=$$60/$1,000$) *coupon rate*].[9] In addition, the issuance of bonds often involves **bond underwriters,** which are banks and other financial institutions that conduct the sale of the bonds (for a fee) for the issuing entity. These underwriters purchase the bonds from the firms or governments, and the underwriters thus assume the risk that the bonds might not be sold. Further, in international bond markets, banks often join together to form a *loan syndicate* for marketing the bonds.

In considering the international bond market, a distinction is made between two situations (see Mendelson 1983, p. 5.1.3, and Magraw 1983, pp. 5.3.3–5.3.4):

1. The borrower in one country issues bonds in the market of another country (the host country) through a syndicate in the host country. The sale is mainly to residents of the host country, and the bonds are denominated in the currency of the host country. These transactions are said to be taking place in the **foreign bond markets.**

2. The borrower in one country issues bonds in the markets of many countries, with the help of a *multinational* loan syndicate, to residents of many countries. The bonds can be denominated in any of several different currencies (including the currency of the

---

[9]The market price of a bond does not have to equal the maturity value. In a simple, extreme example, suppose that an issuer of a bond is trying to sell the $1,000 face-value bond with the annual coupon payment of $60. If interest rates on competing assets are 10 percent, this issuer will not be able to sell the bond for $1,000 because the interest return to the buyer is only 6 percent. To induce a buyer to purchase the bond, the price would have to be lowered to $600. This is so because only at a $600 price will the actual interest rate or yield ($=$$60 coupon payment/$600 price) on this bond be equal to 10 percent, the yield that is obtainable on other assets in the market. Similarly, if market interest rates are 4 percent, the $1,000 face-value bond with a $60 coupon payment could be sold for $1,500 because then its yield would also be 4 percent ($=$$60/$1,500). The issuer would not be willing to sell it for any amount less than $1,500 as that would mean that the issuer would be paying a higher interest rate than is necessary for obtaining funds. Thus, an important feature of bond markets is that *interest rates and bond prices move inversely with each other.* In practice, the swings in bond prices when market interest rates change are not as wide as in this example for reasons that we need not go into, but the inverse relationship remains intact.

country of the issuer but also other currencies that are not necessarily of the countries in which the bonds are sold). These transactions are said to be taking place in the **eurobond markets.**

The two types of markets—the foreign bond markets and the eurobond markets—together constitute the aggregate international bond market. In actual practice, the distinction between foreign bonds and eurobonds is somewhat blurred (e.g., because one bank may underwrite an offering by itself and use neither a domestic syndicate nor a multinational syndicate). In either the foreign bond or the eurobond markets, the issued securities themselves can pay a fixed interest rate or a variable (floating) interest rate (usually tied to LIBOR). In addition, some bonds are sold at a substantial discount below face value and issued as "zero-coupon" bonds. In this instance, there are no regular interest payments, and the total interest is received when the bond matures at its face value.

Table 2 presents data on the size of the stock of international bonds (foreign bonds and eurobonds) and notes in existence at the end of 2006. In addition, some very short-term debt securities, called *money market instruments,* are listed. As can be seen from Part A of the table, the broad stock of international debt securities stood at $18.4 trillion at the end of

TABLE 2   Stock of International Debt Securities Issues, December 31, 2006 (billions of U.S. dollars)

Part A: Type of Instrument		
Money market instruments		$ 873.4
Bonds and notes		17,561.6
		$18,435.0
Part B: Location of Issuers of Instruments		
Developed countries		$15,827.0
United States	$4,040.5	
United Kingdom	2,500.2	
Germany	1,861.3	
Offshore centers		1,195.6
Other countries		825.0
International institutions		587.4
		$18,435.0
Part C: Currency Denomination of Instruments		
Euro		$ 8,658.1
U.S. dollar		6,686.7
British pound		1,595.5
Japanese yen		500.6
Other currencies		994.1
		$18,435.0
Part D: Type of Issuer of Instruments		
Commercial banks and other financial institutions		$14,334.5
Corporations		1,887.1
Governments		1,626.0
Other issuers		587.4
		$18,435.0

Source: Bank for International Settlements, *BIS Quarterly Review,* March 2007, pp. A85, A87–A91.

2006. The geographical locations of the issuers of the securities are listed in Part B—more than 82 percent are issued by borrowers located in developed countries. Bonds are also issued in *offshore centers,* such as the Cayman Islands, the Bahamas, and Netherlands Antilles. These centers are intermediary or "pass-through" locations for international funds:[10] because of tax or regulatory advantages, a branch of a U.S. bank in the Cayman Islands, for example, borrows from its parent bank in the United States in order to make loans to non-U.S. borrowers. The remaining issuers of the bonds in Table 2 are in developing countries or are multilateral institutions such as the World Bank and the International Monetary Fund. As is also evident from Table 2 (Part C), the euro, the U.S. dollar, the British pound, and the Japanese yen are the principal currencies of denomination of the debt securities, and other currencies are used for only about 5 percent of the securities. Finally, in Part D, we see the importance of commercial banks and other financial institutions in the underwriting and issuance of bonds. Significant in this item have been bank borrowing to finance mergers and acquisitions worldwide and, as globalization of asset markets proceeds, the relative shift of the composition of balance sheets toward international liabilities and away from domestic liabilities.

The growth of the international bond markets began in much the same way as did the eurodollar market. The imposition of the interest equalization tax, or IET (see the discussion earlier in this chapter on the origin of eurodollars), in mid-1963 is regarded as a main factor. (See Mendelsohn 1980, pp. 32–36.) This tax applied to the income from new and existing foreign securities (mainly European) held by U.S. citizens, and the consequence of its introduction was that the prices of such bonds fell in the United States in order to get Americans to purchase them. (Higher interest returns on the bonds were needed to cover the tax and to make the after-tax returns comparable with the returns on domestic bonds, and remember that higher interest rates on bonds mean lower prices on bonds.) When this tax restriction was followed in the mid-1960s by the "voluntary" lending restraints imposed on U.S. bank lending abroad and by suggested government guidelines for foreign direct investment by U.S. firms that aimed to reduce that investment, the consequence was that foreign borrowers moved away from the U.S. lending market and began issuing bonds in Europe. Foreign subsidiaries of U.S. firms abroad (which might previously have issued bonds in the United States) also issued bonds abroad. Hence, a stimulus was given to the growth of bond markets outside the United States. With the relaxation of capital controls in Europe that had been accomplished in the late 1950s and with the generally increasing economic integration taking place within the European Community, the new bond issues abroad were denominated in a variety of different currencies. By the mid-1970s, when the U.S. lending restraints and the IET were removed, the European markets had become sizable and the growth was irreversible.

The economic implications of the eurobond markets are much the same as those of the eurocurrency markets. Financial capital is increasingly able to flow across international borders and thus to intensify the tendency for interest rates on similar assets to equalize. From an economic perspective, the growth of these markets therefore results in a more efficient allocation of financial capital. However, as was also true for the eurocurrency markets, interest rates will not become exactly equal even on two identical assets (a domestic bond and a eurobond)—and not just because of transaction costs and other factors previously mentioned. An additional factor preventing equality is exchange rate risk. If a German

---

[10]See Eng and Lees (1983, p. 3.6.3).

holder of a U.S. dollar–denominated bond (which may in fact have been issued by a Swiss firm) judges that the dollar will fall during the life of the bond (or during the period when the holder possesses the bond, which may not be its entire life), the owner will need to be receiving a higher yield than would be received if the bond were denominated in euros and if there is any risk that cannot be covered or hedged. In a bond setting, there is likely to be more uncovered risk than in markets for shorter-term assets, because hedging instruments are not as available for the longer-term bond assets. Further, the availability and the frequency of use of hedging techniques decrease as the time period of bonds themselves lengthens, leading to the necessity of even greater compensation for risk.

Another implication of the international bond market is, of course, that foreign exchange markets themselves will be more active than would be the case if these markets did not exist. Bondholders may choose to purchase bonds of a particular currency denomination because they envision that interest rates differ more than is justified by exchange rate expectations, and an exchange market transaction may thus be necessary to obtain the particular currency in order to make the purchase. Similarly, at the bond's maturity date, an exchange market transaction may be mandated if the bond seller has no special need for the currency at that time. Further, the original bond issuer may also need to make an exchange market transaction to pay off the bond at maturity. Hence, the exchange markets will be subject to greater buffeting than would otherwise have been the case.

IN THE REAL WORLD:

INTEREST RATES ACROSS COUNTRIES

As suggested in the text, increased mobility of financial capital should set forces at work to narrow interest rate differentials across countries. In theory, and with other things equal, we would thus expect interest rates on similar assets to be nearly identical. However, as noted in the text and as will also be discussed at length later in the chapter, rates may not equalize in practice because of exchange rate premia, risk elements in the markets, and other reasons.

Nevertheless, with the increased integration of financial markets in recent years, we would not expect interest rates to diverge sharply from each other. In order to consider this conjecture with respect to bond markets, Table 3 gives data on government bond yields (average yields to maturity in annual percentage rates) for 13 developed countries and 11 developing countries in 2006. Column (1) lists nominal (market) interest rates for these assets; however, this column is not particularly meaningful because no allowance has been made for inflation rates. As you may recall, the *real interest rate* is more useful for making economic decisions. The approximate real interest rate can be found by subtracting the inflation rate from the nominal interest rate, and such an adjustment is necessary, for example, because an investor earning a 10 percent nominal return on a one-year

security is in fact earning only 2 percent in real, purchasing power terms if the inflation rate is 8 percent. Hence, column (2) of Table 3 indicates the 2006 inflation rate for the 24 countries, and column (3) lists the resulting real interest rates on bonds.

Column (3) suggests that, for the developed countries, there is considerable similarity in real interest rates, but they are obviously not identical. In addition to risk factors, the differences may also be partly explained by different maturities of bonds in the various markets. Further, because changes in price levels are used to convert the nominal yields into real yields, these price-level changes would necessarily have to move in accordance with relative purchasing power parity (PPP) to make real yields equal. Nevertheless, the real bond yields in Table 3 differ by 1 percentage point or less from the mean in all but one (Spain) of the developed countries.

Finally, the developing countries' real rates show greater dispersion than those of the developed countries, as the developing countries are not well integrated into the world financial system. Nevertheless, the differences do not seem as great as several years ago, suggesting that integration may be increasing.

(continued)

IN THE REAL WORLD: *(continued)*

TABLE 3　　Government Bond Yields in Developed and Developing Countries, 2006
(average yield to maturity in percent per annum)

	(1) Nominal Yield	*(2) 2006 Inflation Rate**	*(3) Real Yield*
Developed countries:			
Australia	5.62%	3.54%	2.08%
Belgium	3.84	1.79	2.05
Canada	4.30	2.01	2.29
Denmark	3.60	1.89	1.71
France	3.86	1.71	2.15
Germany	3.73	1.71	2.02
Italy	4.05	2.09	1.96
Japan	1.73	0.24	1.49
Netherlands	3.78	1.14	2.64
Spain	3.67	3.52	0.15
Switzerland	2.49	1.06	1.43
United Kingdom	4.27	3.19	1.08
United States	4.79	3.23	1.56
13-Developed-country mean	3.83%	2.09%	1.74%
Developing countries:			
Botswana	11.60%	11.56%	0.04%
Czech Republic	3.32	2.54	0.78
Ghana	16.42	10.92	5.50
Korea, Republic of	5.07	2.24	2.83
Malaysia	4.01	3.61	0.40
Mexico	8.39	3.63	4.76
Netherlands Antilles	6.75	3.07	3.68
Philippines	7.38	6.24	1.14
South Africa	7.94	4.64	3.30
Thailand	5.48	4.64	0.84
Venezuela	12.93	15.95	−3.02

*Inflation rates are percentage changes in consumer price indexes.

Source: International Monetary Fund, *International Financial Statistics,* April 2007, pp. 56, 59–61.

Finally, the existence of the international bond markets (as with the eurocurrency markets) can reduce the independence that exists for any given country's monetary authority. If the Bank of Canada wishes to drive down long-term interest rates to stimulate real investment, this attempt will be frustrated if Canadian bondholders switch to the purchase of foreign bonds where yields are now relatively higher (and bond prices are therefore relatively lower). This could result in a monetary outflow from Canada, possibly resulting in a worsened balance-of-payments position (under fixed exchange rates) and a depreciation of the Canadian dollar (under flexible exchange rates).

INTERNATIONAL STOCK MARKETS

Other assets that have become more widely traded across international borders in recent years are shares of common stocks (equities) of corporations. This type of asset differs from bonds in that the holding of stock by individuals and institutions (for example, insurance companies, pension funds) brings with it ownership of the company whose stock is held. Hence, in theory, there is an element of control involved with stocks that is absent from bonds. In practice, however, any one investor generally holds such a small relative amount of any given corporation's stock that effective control by that investor is precluded. Nevertheless, the financial features of stock differ in a way that makes the purchase decision more complicated than is the case with bonds and other debt instruments. An investor considering the acquisition of a company's stock is faced with making an uncertain projection of the company's future earnings, the variability of those earnings, the real factors lying behind demand for and supply of the company's product that may influence the firm's future courses of action, the ratio of the stock's price to the company's earnings per share, the dividend payout rate, and many other performance indicators. In the international context, expectations of the future exchange rate behavior of the foreign currency in which the stock is quoted relative to the home currency of the investor are also important, as well as the anticipated macroeconomic behavior of the country in which the stock is being sold. An individual investor in recent years has been increasingly able to shift the analysis of the selection of stock to mutual funds which bring together the financial resources of many buyers and which specialize in transactions in international stocks, but the fund managers themselves obviously still need to take account of all these influences.

Unfortunately, information on the size of stock purchases made across country borders is difficult to obtain. A general consensus among observers and participants in the market is that the volume of such equity transactions has been increasing with the spread of multinational companies, the increased mobility of capital in general, and the emergence and maturing of stock exchanges in many developing countries. Because stock transactions of the cross-border type have been increasing rapidly, it is possible that movements of stock prices across countries will tend to become increasingly similar to each other. This co-movement might arise because of the general result that occurs when markets become less separated or segmented and arbitrage occurs between them. However, stock markets can differ in this co-movement respect from usual markets because of the central role of expectations in stock markets and the resulting potential volatility that can emerge from sudden swings in those expectations. If the prices of stocks in market A soar while those in market B languish, investors may shift from B to A and drive prices further up in A and down in B because of expectations that A will continue to rise and B will continue to stagnate. On the other hand, the soaring prices in market A might yield the result that investors will expect them to fall and thus will shift the composition of their portfolios toward stocks in market B. In this case, the prices in the two markets might converge and, with regular such behavior, might never have diverged to a great extent in the first place—any rise in one market would cause a switch to the other market, causing a rise there.

In addition, a force that may generate a common trend movement of stock price indexes across countries is the phenomenon of **international portfolio diversification** to reduce risk in investors' portfolios. (See Mayo 1997, pp. 803–11.) If the price changes are not highly correlated with each other across countries, there is an advantage to holding stocks in several countries because a rise (fall) in one market will not be closely matched with a rise (fall) in other markets. Because many investors are risk averse, the purchase of stock in several markets will reduce the likelihood of wide swings in total portfolio value. Indeed, mutual funds with global scope are doing precisely this type of diversified investing. But if portfolios become diversified across international markets and if some balance between

IN THE REAL WORLD:

STOCK MARKET PERFORMANCE IN DEVELOPING/TRANSITION COUNTRIES

Stock markets in developing and transition countries have been increasing dramatically in recent years with respect to their size and participation by investors (including foreign investors). Much of this increased activity is associated with the general liberalization of the various economies that has featured, *inter alia,* reductions of tariff and nontariff barriers, relaxation of internal government controls on production and sale of goods, and privatization of former state enterprises. With this "freeing up" of the economies, however, market instability has increased, and turmoil has also emerged because of the removal of government provision of employment and income support. In addition, the prospects for increased income inequality have been enhanced with the arrival of the different and more risky environment.

Table 4 provides an indication of the potential gains and losses for financial investors in the face of the instability and yet the promise of the new, market-oriented regimes. The table lists the percentage changes in leading stock market price indexes roughly during calendar year 2006 in 25 "emerging market economies." (Stock price index information for these markets is available each week on the last page of *The Economist.*) Many of these countries' stock markets registered very impressive gains. This was especially true for China and Venezuela. Notice, however, that losses occurred in Saudi Arabia, Turkey, and Thailand.

TABLE 4 Performance of Stock Price Indexes, Developing Countries, December 30, 2005–January 10, 2007

| | Percentage Change | | | | Percentage Change | |
Country	In Local Currency	In Dollar Terms	Country		In Local Currency	In Dollar Terms
Argentina	32.4%	30.0%	Malaysia		23.7%	33.0%
Brazil	26.5	37.2	Mexico		45.4	40.3
Chile	34.3	26.8	Pakistan		8.6	6.4
China	143.4	151.7	Poland		38.4	50.2
Colombia	11.0	12.9	Russia		45.3	57.3
Czech Republic	6.3	22.3	Saudi Arabia		−54.8	−54.8
Egypt	10.9	11.7	Singapore		26.1	36.3
Hong Kong (China)	31.5	30.8	South Africa		35.6	17.3
Hungary	11.7	20.8	Taiwan		17.6	18.0
India	42.2	43.6	Thailand		−12.8	−0.8
Indonesia	47.1	59.4	Turkey		−7.9	−14.0
Israel	10.9	20.0	Venezuela		161.6	72.9
Korea, Republic of	−1.7	5.9				

Source: *The Economist,* January 13, 2007, p. 90.

the stocks across the various markets is maintained over time as portfolios grow, then the markets may well move in somewhat parallel fashion.

Before concluding this look at international equity markets, we take note of the emergence of a new investment vehicle for making such transactions across country borders. As indicated briefly earlier, **mutual funds** have become increasingly important for such purchases. (Mutual funds of this international type also have become prominent in bonds, but we concentrate here on stock funds.) These funds collect the savings of small individual investors as well as large institutional investors and place the pool of collected savings into portfolios of financial assets comprising equities of companies located in many different countries. From the standpoint of U.S. investors, there are four main types of such internationally focused mutual funds (Mayo 1997, pp. 810–11):

1. **Global funds** purchase packages of equities that contain stocks of corporations both in the United States and in other countries.
2. **International funds** do not hold U.S. securities but purchase exclusively the stocks of companies located in other countries.
3. **Emerging market funds** hold a portfolio of stocks of companies in developing countries—for example, in Argentina, the Czech Republic, Indonesia, and Malaysia.
4. **Regional funds** focus on securities of companies in particular geographic areas or countries—for example, in Asia, Latin America, China, Germany, and Japan.

To participate in these funds, and there are hundreds of such funds now, shares can be purchased in some cases on organized stock exchanges and in other cases (more prominent) directly from the mutual fund companies. Aside from the differing countries in which the various funds invest, there are other differing characteristics among them: *no-load* funds require no explicit charge for purchase or sale; *low-load* and *load* funds impose a charge for entering the portfolio; *redemption-charge* funds levy a fee upon exit; and *closed-end* funds are traded on regular stock exchanges and thus involve a broker's fee upon entry and exit. With mutual funds, the choice set for investors is indeed large.

Finally, with respect to stock markets, we close by emphasizing again that, as with international bonds and international bank lending, the increasing integration of these markets serves to facilitate the flow of capital toward its best use. As financial investors respond to perceived profit opportunities beyond their own borders, they are transferring capital to destinations where it can earn a higher return. As financial capital flows for the purchase of the stock of a foreign company that is productive and profitable, this raises the book value of the company and encourages its expansion because of its more favorable balance sheet.[11] Encouragement of profitable, productive firms and discouragement of poorly managed, unproductive companies of course serve to improve the allocation of world resources. In the broad context of international monetary economics, however, the use of international stock transactions to improve capital allocation potentially comes at a price. This price, especially if the stock transactions involve speculative behavior due to unfounded rumors and "bandwagon" effects, is the increased volatility in world financial markets (and particularly in foreign exchange markets) that can occur.

Thus far, we have focused in this chapter on international bank deposits and lending, international bond markets, and stock market activity in an international context. In overview, these various asset markets have been growing dramatically in size and scope in recent years. International investors now have open to them financial opportunities previously unavailable, and the activity in these increasingly integrated markets has meant that countries are becoming linked ever more tightly together economically. The effects of financial developments in one country spill over into other countries, and the new environment poses challenges as well as opportunities for economic actors.

---

[11]Because most stock purchases are of previously issued stock and not of newly issued stock, the funds flowing in for a stock purchase are generally not flowing to the company per se. However, the company's net worth or capital value on its balance sheet increases as its stock rises in price, and the company is thus in a better position to, among other things, obtain loans or issue new stock for the financing of expansion of the firm.

CONCEPT CHECK

1. Distinguish participation by an investor in foreign bond markets from participation by that investor in eurobond markets.

2. Why do bond prices and bond yields move inversely with each other?

3. Why would a financial investor wish to pursue international portfolio diversification?

FINANCIAL LINKAGES AND EUROCURRENCY DERIVATIVES

With this broad look at international banking, international bonds, and the international purchase of stocks as background, we now turn to a more detailed examination of particular financial instruments and financial strategies employed in the international asset and foreign exchange markets. As should be clear, the world of international finance is becoming increasingly complicated; at the same time, however, it is becoming increasingly fascinating.

Basic International Financial Linkages: A Review

In the previous chapter we discussed the formal links between the foreign exchange markets and the financial markets. It was seen that the decision to invest at home or abroad depends on the expected rate of return of the foreign and domestic alternatives under consideration. If the expected rate of return on domestic assets is higher, the individual will invest at home. Conversely, if the expected rate of return is higher on the foreign asset, the individual would be expected to invest abroad. If there are no barriers to financial investment flows, then funds should move from areas of low rates of return to areas of high rates of return until the expected returns are similar, differing only by the transaction costs involved in moving between the two markets.

It is critical, as noted earlier, to remember that rates of return on foreign investments result both from the return on the financial asset in question and from changes in the exchange rate over the period of the investment. Thus, the domestic investor must take into account (1) the expected rate of return on the domestic financial asset, (2) the expected rate of return on the foreign asset, and (3) any expected change in the exchange rate. The investor is thus indifferent between a foreign asset and a domestic asset only when he or she expects to earn the same return on each possibility after taking into account any gains or losses associated with expected changes in the exchange rate. This "parity" condition was stated more formally in the preceding chapter in the following manner:

$$(1 + i_{\text{home}})/(1 + i_{\text{foreign}}) = E(e)/e$$

where:
i_{home} = domestic rate of interest
i_{foreign} = foreign rate of interest
e = spot foreign exchange rate in units of domestic currency per unit of foreign currency
$E(e)$ = expected future exchange rate at the end of the investment period

This is more commonly expressed in terms of the expected percentage appreciation of the foreign currency. If xa is used to represent the expected percentage appreciation of the foreign currency, then $E(e)/e$ is equal to $(1 + xa)$ and the preceding equation simplifies to

$$(i_{\text{home}} - i_{\text{foreign}})/(1 + i_{\text{foreign}}) = xa$$

which is often approximated by

$$(i_{\text{home}} - i_{\text{foreign}}) \cong xa$$

This condition states that equilibrium occurs in the financial market whenever any difference in the interest rates in the two countries is approximately offset by the expected change in the exchange rate. (Ignore any transaction costs.) Because of the lack of perfect foresight, the actual return on the foreign investment may not equal that which was expected because of unanticipated changes in the exchange rate. Such unanticipated changes can lead to the attachment of a risk premium if actors are risk-averse, and if the premium is expressed as a percentage, RP, the preceding equilibrium condition is modified to become

$$(i_{\text{home}} - i_{\text{foreign}}) \cong xa - \text{RP}$$

From this basic exercise it is clear that the investment decision over time now involves two sources of risk. The first is the aforementioned risk associated with changes in the exchange rate, which affect the overall rate of return on the investment. The second source of risk is the *interest rate risk* that arises if the financial transaction is not to be undertaken and completed for a period of time.

As we discussed in the previous chapter, the foreign exchange risk can be removed (hedged) by using the forward market. In this case, the basic equilibrium condition in the financial market can be expressed in the following manner:

$$(i_{\text{home}} - i_{\text{foreign}}) \cong p$$

where p is the actual premium on the forward exchange rate, that is, $p = (e_{\text{fwd}}/e) - 1$. Thus, in equilibrium, any difference in the two interest rates must be approximately equal to the foreign exchange premium contracted in the forward market. These forward contracts can be purchased in the formal forward market, the futures market, or the options market. Therefore, as we pointed out in our discussion of the foreign exchange market, in the absence of capital controls or other market barriers, all credit markets (foreign and domestic) are linked to one another through arbitrage and currency expectations.

The financial activities of participants in the financial markets, including borrowing, lending, and the assignment of risk through hedging actions, ensure that the difference between interest rates in the two countries equals not only the forward premium (via forward contracts) but also the expected exchange rate change on the part of those who are bearing the risk of changes in the foreign exchange rate. As was demonstrated at the end of the previous chapter, if markets are efficient, the following should hold:

$$i_{\text{home}} - i_{\text{foreign}} \cong p = xa$$

However, to the extent that there is a risk associated with foreign exchange that cannot be avoided by combining foreign exchange holdings with other assets (i.e., a foreign exchange risk that cannot be diversified away), an additional risk premium, as noted earlier, would be required by those going uncovered; that is,

$$i_{\text{home}} - i_{\text{foreign}} \cong p = xa - \text{RP}$$

Whether or not such a risk premium exists is still a subject of considerable debate among financial researchers.

International Financial Linkages and the Eurodollar Market

How does the eurodollar market enter into these financial considerations? The presence of the eurodollar market in essence creates a second interest rate possibility in each currency. The financial investment now includes the following *six* financial variables, using the United States (home) and the United Kingdom (foreign) as the two country examples:

Interest rates:	U.S. interest rate
	U.K. interest rate
	euro*dollar* interest rate (foreign-held dollar funds)
	euro*sterling* interest rate (foreign-held British pounds)
Exchange rates:	spot rate (dollars/pound)
	forward exchange rate (dollars/pound)

Lenders and borrowers now have the alternatives of two different markets in which to operate, one at home and one abroad. The relationship between the rates in these markets would appear to be very straightforward. If all things were equal, eurobanks should pay no less than the deposit rate in the United States. If they paid less, why would depositors place their funds abroad instead of at home? Similarly, eurobanks cannot lend eurodollars at a higher lending rate than that in the United States; and further, why should a eurobank be willing to lend dollars at a rate lower than that in the United States? Thus, a priori, it appears as though the borrowing and lending rates in the United States should establish similar rates in the eurodollar market.

However, because of the different institutional settings, it can be argued that U.S. interest rates will likely bound the eurodollar rates, that is, the domestic lending rate lies above the eurocurrency lending rate and the domestic deposit rate lies below the eurocurrency deposit rate. This historically appears to have been the case, as was indicated earlier in this chapter. Available data on recent deposit rates are consistent with this observation. The relatively lower eurocurrency lending rate and relatively higher deposit rate can be explained from the stand- point of a foreign risk differential and an institutional cost differential. Turning first to the risk dimension, if potential lenders or borrowers perceive a relative difference in risk associated with the foreign deposit or loan, they will require a risk premium in the form of a lower lending rate or higher deposit rate. When U.S. borrowers or investors contract with a foreign bank, they become involved in a foreign jurisdiction. Thus the risk on the foreign deposits or loans is somewhat greater than the risk on similar transactions within the United States. The two dollar markets are thus separated by possible foreign government actions or restrictions that increase the risk of doing business abroad instead of at home. Legal restrictions or potential policy actions that might interfere with the movement of funds between, for example, a London bank and the United States can drive a wedge between U.S. domestic rates and eurodollar rates in the United Kingdom. Government policies can affect directly through restrictions on capital out- flows and foreign exchange controls that alter the nonresident convertibility of the dollar hold- ings abroad. In addition, there is always the slight possibility that the assets or liabilities of the eurobanks can be seized by the authorities where they operate. Further, differences in liquidity or institutional structure related to such things as the number and size of financial dealers and the accessibility of adequate financial information can also influence the risk environment.

From the cost perspective, banks face additional costs when utilizing domestic deposits compared with eurocurrency deposits. These additional costs arise whenever banks are not sub- ject to the reserve requirements or deposit insurance assessments on eurocurrency deposits that can be required on domestic deposits. It is obvious that the bank could earn more by being able to lend out a full deposit than by having to retain a certain percentage as a reserve requirement. In the presence of domestic reserve requirements, therefore, a U.S. domestic bank would pay a lower rate on domestic deposits than could be earned on eurodollar deposits abroad. Generaliz- ing, the deposit rates on eurocurrency should exceed domestic deposit rates of the same given currency by an amount equal to the relative cost of central bank regulation.[12]

---

[12]An estimate of the higher rate on Eurocurrency deposits taking into account any reserve requirement and any applicable deposit insurance fees charged on domestic deposits is therefore

Eurocurrency deposit rate = effective cost of domestic deposit

$$= (i_{\text{domestic deposit}} + \text{deposit insurance fees})/(1 - \text{reserve requirement})$$

Hence, if the reserve requirement is 5 percent, $i_{\text{domestic deposit}}$ is 8 percent, and the deposit insurance fee is 0.083 (=1/12) percent, then

Eurocurrency deposit rate = $(0.08 + 0.00083)/(1 - 0.05) = 0.08509$, or 8.51%

This ignores any differential tax treatment or any difference in bank regulatory practices regarding the two types of deposits.

IN THE REAL WORLD:

U.S. DOMESTIC AND EURODOLLAR DEPOSIT AND LENDING RATES, 1989–2005

Figure 1(a) illustrates the annual average bank deposit rate in the United States and the LIBOR one-year rate on dollar deposits as reported by the International Monetary Fund for the 1989–2005 period. Figure 1(b) does the same for the average lending rates. A simple estimate was made of the LIBOR one-year lending rate, because the IMF does not report that information. (The assumption was made that the percentage-point difference between the LIBOR deposit rate and the U.S. deposit rate also applied, in the reverse direction, to the LIBOR lending rate and the U.S. lending rate.) As can be seen from Figure 1(a), U.S. and eurodollar deposit rates tracked each other closely over the period, although eurodollar deposit rates were higher. Interestingly, the difference narrowed sharply in 1998. Assuming that eurodollar lending rates behaved in the manner described, they also would track U.S. lending rates but be below them, as shown in Figure 1(b).

FIGURE 1(a)   LIBOR and U.S. Deposit Rates

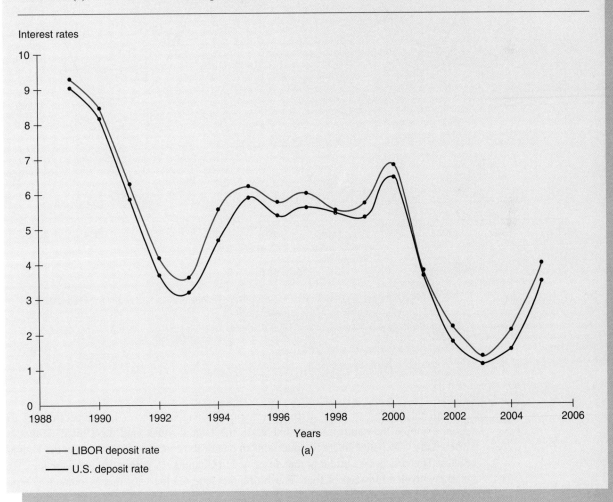

LIBOR deposit rate

U.S. deposit rate

(a)

(continued)

IN THE REAL WORLD: *(continued)*

FIGURE 1(b)   LIBOR and U.S. Lending Rates

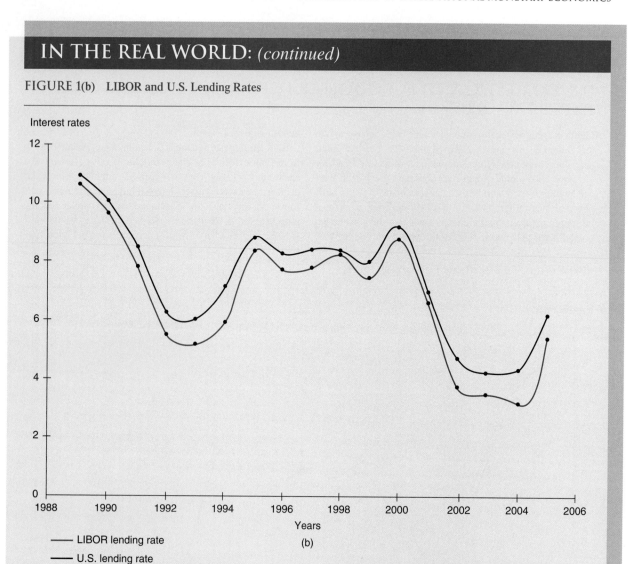

Interest rates

— LIBOR lending rate

— U.S. lending rate

(b)

The LIBOR deposit rate has historically been above the U.S. deposit rate, and the LIBOR lending rate has historically been below the U.S. lending rate. This pattern has greatly facilitated the development of the eurodollar market.

Sources: International Monetary Fund, *International Financial Statistics Yearbook 1999* (Washington, DC: IMF, 1999), pp. 106, 110, 112; *International Financial Statistics,* March 2000, pp. 44, 48, 50; *International Financial Statistics Yearbook 2003* (Washington, DC: IMF, 2003), pp. 66, 69, 73; *International Financial Statistics Yearbook 2006* (Washington, DC: IMF, 2006), pp. 65, 72.

With this expanded view of the international financial market in perspective, let us again examine the nature of adjustments in the United States and the United Kingdom when there is a change in credit conditions in one of the countries, for example, the United States. This process is similar to that described in Chapter 20, except that there are now six markets involved instead of four. The six markets are (1) the U.S. money market, (2) the U.K. money market, (3) the eurodollar market, (4) the eurosterling market, (5) the spot market, and (6) the forward market. Suppose that the markets start out in equilibrium and the following interest rate parity equilibrium rates prevail:

Lending i_{NY}	= 7%	Lending i_{London}	= 8%
Lending $i_{Eurodollar\ London}$	= 6.5%	Lending $i_{Eurosterling\ NY}$	= 7.5%
Deposit i_{NY}	= 5%	Deposit i_{London}	= 6%
Deposit $i_{Eurodollar\ London}$	= 5.5%	Deposit $i_{Eurosterling\ NY}$	= 6.5%
Spot $e_{\$/£}$	= \$1.6912/£	3-months forward $e_{\$/£}$	= \$1.6869/£

It can be easily demonstrated that the covered interest arbitrage parity condition holds across all pairs of rates, after dividing the annual interest rate difference by 4 so that it approximates the three-month forward period. For example,

$$i_{NY} - i_{London} \cong p$$
$$(0.07 - 0.08)/4 \cong (\$1.6869 - \$1.6912)/\$1.6912$$
$$-0.0025 \cong -0.0025$$

Suppose that the Federal Reserve moves to raise U.S. domestic interest rates by 1/2 percentage point. This will immediately make investments in New York more attractive to investors, and the markets will begin to adjust to a new equilibrium position taking into account the new interest rates in the United States. In all likelihood, the first adjustment to the rate changes in New York will take place in the eurodollar rate abroad. For London banks to maintain their dollar deposits, the eurodollar deposit rate will rise to 6 percent and the eurodollar lending rate will be bid up to 7 percent, thus maintaining the same spread difference as existed prior to the increase in the U.S. rates. At the same time, as U.K. investors attempt to take advantage of the higher U.S. rates, they will increase their demand for dollars (supply of British pounds) causing the spot dollar rate to appreciate. Simultaneously, investors who wish to insure themselves against unforeseen changes in the exchange rate will buy pounds forward (increase the supply of dollars forward), leading to a depreciation of the dollar in the forward market, just as was the case in the adjustment process discussed in the previous chapter. If U.K. interest rates remain unchanged, all adjustment to market equilibrium will take place in the foreign exchange market. However, upward pressure will come to bear on U.K. interest rates and the eurosterling rate. Increases in these rates will reduce the degree of change in the exchange rates to bring the markets into a new equilibrium position. With the new U.S. interest rates and U.K. rates/eurosterling rates remaining unchanged, market equilibrium would again take place if, for example, the three-month forward rate moved up (the dollar depreciated) to \$1.688/£ and the spot rate moved down (the dollar appreciated) to \$1.690/£. Of course, should interest rates in the United Kingdom (and the eurosterling rates) start to increase, we would expect to see the forward rates begin to decline and the spot rates begin to increase.

These financial adjustments are demonstrated in the six graphs in Figure 2. The tighter money market in the United States causes domestic interest rates to rise [graph (a)]. This immediately leads to an increase in demand for Eurodollars, which drives up Eurodollar rates until they again differ from U.S. domestic rates by the risk-cost differential [graph (b)]. The higher interest rates in the United States lead to an increase in the U.K. demand for dollars (supply of pounds) for financial investment in the United States because of the higher return [graph (c)]. At the same time, these investors will be selling dollars forward to return to pounds at the end of the investment period [graph (f)]. The other markets that might eventually be involved in the financial adjustment process are the U.K. money market [graph (e)] and the eurosterling market [graph (d)]. As funds move from the United Kingdom to the United States, upward pressure on U.K. domestic and eurosterling interest rates will be experienced. Should the Bank of England choose not to intervene to hold U.K. interest rates constant and consequently the U.K. rates rise, there will be further readjustments in all six markets until equilibrium again attains.

FIGURE 2   International Financial Adjustment in the Money Markets, Foreign Exchange Markets, and Eurocurrency Markets

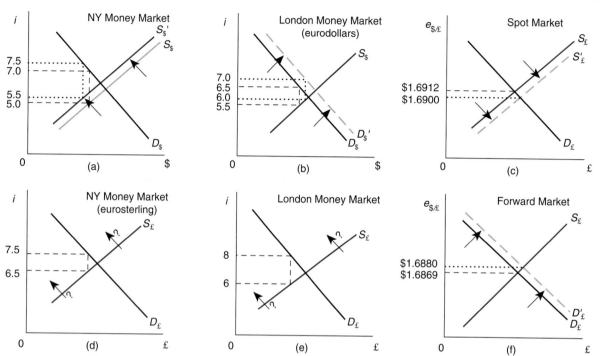

International financial adjustments in the presence of eurocurrency markets are demonstrated in these graphs. A tighter money market in the United States [leftward shift in the supply curve in graph (a)] causes domestic interest rates to rise. This leads to increased demand for eurodollars [rightward shift of the demand curve in (b)], which drives up eurodollar rates until they again differ from U.S. rates by the risk-cost differential. The higher U.S. interest rates lead to an increased U.K. supply of spot pounds [rightward shift of $S_£$ to $S'_£$ in (c)], which are hedged in the forward market [rightward shift of $D_£$ to $D'_£$ in (f)]. Further adjustments may occur in the U.K. money market and the eurosterling market that would lead to higher interest rates in these markets [graphs (d) and (e)], although the result is uncertain because the Bank of England may intervene to offset upward pressure on interest rates in the London money market. [Note: In graphs (a), (b), (d), and (e), the upper rates reflect lending rates and the lower rates indicate deposit rates. The lending and deposit rates form a bracket around what would be the common equilibrium rate if lending and borrowing rates were equal.]

Having observed how the foreign currency markets, the domestic financial markets, and the eurodollar markets interact, we now turn to a discussion of how interest rate risk can be reduced or eliminated in international financial markets.

Hedging Eurodollar Interest Rate Risk

A number of new international financial markets have emerged in recent years to provide alternative instruments for spreading risk related to both foreign exchange and future interest rates. Having discussed in the previous chapter how foreign exchange forward, futures, and options markets provide a means for reducing or avoiding foreign exchange risk, we now briefly introduce several of the more important instruments or tools that are available in the international financial markets to hedge interest rate risk. These financial instruments belong to a category of financial tools referred to as **derivatives.** Derivatives are simply financial contracts whose value is linked to or derived from an underlying asset. Examples of the underlying assets include stocks, bonds, commodities, loans, certificates of deposit (CDs), and foreign exchange. For many financial institutions, interest rate risk management is critical to their successful operation inasmuch as they often can anticipate future lending and future borrowing actions both at home and abroad and would prefer to reduce the risk of possible changes in the market interest rate prior to when the anticipated borrowing or lending occurs. Several of the more commonly used types of financial instruments or tools from which the manager can choose to hedge against unforeseen interest rate changes include (1) maturity mismatching, (2) future rate agreements, (3) eurodollar interest rate swaps, (4) eurodollar cross-currency interest rate swaps, (5) eurodollar interest rate futures, (6) eurodollar interest rate options, (7) options on swaps, and (8) equity financial derivatives. We will examine each one and then conclude with a short discussion of the current size and importance of these transactions in the international financial arena.[13]

Maturity Mismatching

Maturity mismatching is one of the easiest and simplest ways for financial institutions to remove the risk of changes in the interest rate between now and some future time. It is carried out by acquiring two or more financial contracts whose maturities overlap. For example, suppose that a fund manager knows that her company will receive $100,000 in three months and needs to hold those funds for dollar payment of a financial obligation six months from now. Being concerned that the interest rate may fall prior to the receipt of the funds, the fund manager looks for a way to lock in the current deposit rate for the three-month period during which the $100,000 cash surplus will be held. She accomplishes this by borrowing $100,000 for three months and investing it in a fixed-rate instrument for six months, which will mature just at the time it is needed for the future expected payment. When the $100,000 is received at the end of three months, it is then used to pay back the initial three-month loan when it comes due, while the invested funds continue to earn a known fixed amount of interest until they are needed six months from now. The cost of fixing the future interest rate now is the difference between the deposit rate and the loan rate for the first three months, that is, the three-month overlap. In similar fashion, if we wished to lock in a lending rate for six months, beginning two months from now, this could be accomplished by borrowing the needed funds today for an eight-month period, placing the funds in a short-term fixed-rate deposit for two months, and at the end of two months using the funds to pay the anticipated financial commitment. Again, by overlapping the maturities of two financial instruments, the future lending rate is secured at a known interest rate, and the cost of the hedge is the difference between the two-month deposit rate and the eight-month loan rate for the two-month overlap.

Future Rate Agreements

A **future rate agreement** (FRA) is essentially a contract between two parties to lock in a given interest rate starting at some given point in the future for a given time period. This instrument originated in the early 1970s and is often referred to as a *forward-forward*. (It is also sometimes referred to simply as a *forward rate contract*.) The procedure was modified in the mid-1980s through the development of a cash-compensation process whereby compensation is paid for deviations of the market interest rate from the contracted rate rather than through the actual borrowing or lending of funds between the two contract participants. The process works as follows: The two contracting parties agree on a particular lending or borrowing rate at some future date for a specific amount and loan period. For example, Ms. Jones may wish to secure the interest rate on a $10,000 loan in three months for a period of nine months. After negotiating through a broker over the future rate, a contract will be signed between Jones and the seller of the contract (Mr. Brown) whereby a loan rate of 7.5 percent is locked in for the time period under consideration. This contract guarantees the interest rate for both parties but does not

---

[13]For in-depth discussions of the eurodollar derivative instruments introduced here, see the excellent presentations in Bryan and Farrell (1996), Burghardt, Belton, Lane, Luce, and McVey (1991), and Dufey and Giddy (1994). The Burghardt et al. volume also provides very thorough coverage of the legal features of these instruments.

involve any commitments for the loan itself. In three months, when Ms. Jones needs the funds, she obtains a nine-month loan at the current market interest rate. If the market rate at the time of the loan is 7.8 percent, the other party in the FRA (Brown) pays her the difference between the market rate and the rate in the FRA, that is, 0.3 percent or 30 **basis points,**[14] for the specified $10,000 loan for nine months.[15] Should the market rate have fallen to 7.25 percent, Ms. Jones would reimburse Mr. Brown the difference, that is, 0.25 percent for the specified nine-month loan. Jones is thus hedged against any increase in the lending rate between now and the time of the actual undertaking of the loan. She is, however, locked out of receiving any benefits associated with a fall in the loan rate. Of course, if the market rate is the same as the contract rate, then no offsetting payments are made by either party and the contract terminates. In essence, Jones has contracted with Brown to exchange a floating or uncertain rate for a fixed rate over a specific time period. Indeed, an FRA is often defined as a *forward contract in which two parties agree to exchange a floating rate for a fixed rate for some future time period.* LIBOR is commonly used as the floating rate in these agreements.

Eurodollar Interest Rate Swaps

A **eurodollar interest rate swap** is similar to an FRA but involves several future periods. In this case parties agree to exchange interest rates of two different kinds for several periods in the future, each usually three or six months long. Again, one of the rates is generally the appropriate LIBOR rate, and the contract often involves the exchange of a fixed rate for a floating rate, as is the case in the one-period FRA. However, an interest rate swap can also involve an exchange of two floating interest rates where one is LIBOR and the second is another interest rate or an index of a package of rates, such as an index of eurocommercial paper rates. The case in which both sides are contracting a floating rate is referred to as a *basis swap* or a *floating-floating swap.* An interest rate swap works as follows: Suppose Ms. Smith has a three-year eurodollar-based loan at 8 percent and wishes that it were a variable-rate debt (perhaps because she expects interest rates to fall in the future) and Mr. Brown has a eurodollar loan on which he is paying six-month LIBOR plus 30 basis points (0.3 percent) and wishes to have a fixed-rate debt. Under the agreed-upon swap arrangement, Smith agrees to pay Brown the six-month LIBOR plus 0.3 percent every six months and Brown in turn agrees to pay Smith the 8 percent (perhaps plus some additional amount, for example, 50 basis points per annum). Smith has thus converted her fixed-rate commitment to a variable rate and Brown has converted his variable rate to a fixed rate. If interest rates decline, Smith will benefit by obtaining a cheaper loan. Brown feels relieved to have obtained a fixed rate more cheaply than obtaining a formal, new fixed-rate loan and refinancing, and he effectively has reduced his interest rate exposure. Should interest rates fall during the swap contract and threaten to rise again, Smith could phone a swaps trader and enter into a second swap arrangement to again fix the interest rate commitment but this time at the new, lower level.

Eurodollar Cross-Currency Interest Rate Swaps

The **eurodollar cross-currency interest rate swap** is a financial derivative that permits the holder of a floating interest rate investment or debt denominated in one currency to change it into a fixed-rate instrument in a second currency. It, of course, can also permit the holder of a

---

[14]A basis point is defined as one one-hundredth of a percent; that is, 1 percentage point contains 100 basis points.

[15]The actual amount paid by Brown (the seller) at the time of the loan is

$$\text{Cash} = (0.078 - 0.075)(270/360)(\$10,000)/[1 + (0.078)(270/360)]$$
$$= \$22.50/1.0585 = \$21.26$$

The interest rate differential (0.003) is adjusted to reflect the nine-month period (270/360) as opposed to one year. The entire amount is then discounted for the nine-month period because Brown will be meeting the contract payment at the beginning of the loan period and not at the end when the interest is due. The payment is thus reduced by the interest that the contract payment will earn over the nine-month period of the loan.

fixed-rate debt in one currency to convert it to a floating-rate debt in a second currency. It thus links several segments of international capital markets. It has all the characteristics of a normal interest rate swap except that it is a combination of an interest rate swap and a currency hedge.

CONCEPT CHECK

1. How can maturity mismatching remove the risk associated with a future interest rate change?
2. Why would a borrower want to use a future rate contract? What opportunity is being lost by doing so?
3. What is the risk being avoided by the use of an interest rate swap? What additional risk is avoided with a cross-currency interest rate swap?

Eurodollar Interest Rate Futures

Just as in the foreign exchange market, there are **eurodollar interest rate futures** in addition to interest rate forwards. Similar to currency futures, interest rate futures are contracts to deliver a certain amount of bank deposits at some future date at a specified interest rate or price. These may take the form of either eurodollar time deposits or eurodollar CDs of a major bank. They carry the locked-in interest rate that was agreed upon when the contract was signed, and the gain (loss) of the contract will depend on whether the interest rate on the day the contract comes due is less (more) than the contracted rate, multiplied by the amount of the contract.

These contracts differ from a forward market transaction in several ways. They are transacted or traded on organized exchanges such as the Chicago Mercantile Exchange. Three month futures interest contracts are sold in $1 million units and are traded in March, June, September, and December. Unlike the case in the forward market, where forward gains or losses are settled on the maturity date, gains and losses are settled on a daily basis in the futures market. Participants are required to maintain a "margin" account, and the daily gains or losses are added or subtracted from this account depending on whether the current daily rate is below or above the contract rate. Thus, for every 1 basis point decline (increase) in the current interest rate compared with the final settlement rate on the previous day, $25 is added to (subtracted from) the holder's margin account for each forward interest contract.[16] The daily cash settlements are based on the daily final settlement price of three-month LIBOR obtained from 12 reference banks randomly selected during the last 90 minutes of trading (Dufey and Giddy 1994, p. 189). For an example of interest rate futures and how to interpret them, see Concept Box 1, on page 534.

The futures market is thus useful for lenders/depositors who wish to lock into a specific future interest rate in eurocurrencies. If you know that you will have funds to invest in the future for a specific period of time, the futures market offers you the opportunity to avoid a fall in interest rates by fixing the interest rate now through buying a futures interest rate contract for eurodollar delivery at the expected future time. At the specific future date, the futures contract is completed and the contract margin adjustment funds plus the anticipated investment funds are invested at the current market rate of interest. If interest rates have fallen by the time the investment is made and the futures contract is due, the holder of the futures contract will settle the margin account payments due on the contract and invest them along with the new funds at the then-current interest rate. At the end of the investment period, she will earn approximately the same amount as the initial futures contract rate even though there was an actual decline in interest rates. The gain in the futures contract, which will be invested along with the newly acquired funds, will result in a rate of return similar to the initial rate in the futures contract even though the entire amount is earning a lower rate of market interest. This activity is referred to as a *long hedge*.

---

[16]This occurs because each of the contracts is for $1 million for three months. Each 1-basis-point change thus leads to a payment equal to ($1,000,000) (0.0001)/4 = $25. The minimum fluctuation in price is 1 basis point.

CONCEPT BOX 1

EURODOLLAR INTEREST RATE FUTURES MARKET QUOTATIONS

The quotations in Table 5 pertain to the Chicago Mercantile Exchange (CME), and the face value of each three-month contract is $1 million. Each basis-point (0.01 percent) change in the contract price is valued at $25 [=($1,000,000)(0.0001)/4]. The eurodollar futures "yield" is calculated on a 360-day basis. The price is equal to (100 − yield), or the yield is equal to (100 − the quoted price). Thus, with a "settle" price of 94.680 (row 3 in the table), the yield is 5.320 percent (=100 − 94.680). The prices listed are the various strike (contracting) prices for contracts expiring in the months indicated. On the actual expiration date, the third Wednesday of the expiration month, the futures yield converges to the cash market yield, that is, LIBOR. The "open" price is the initial contract price of the day, the "high" and the "low" indicate the ranges of price fluctuation during the day, and the "settle"

price or closing price is the reference price used to make the daily adjustment of margin accounts. In the case of the CME, the settle price is equal to (100 − spot LIBOR), obtained by taking two surveys of London banks (one at closing and one 90 minutes earlier). "Chg." refers to the change from the previous business day. In the case of July contracts (row 3 of the table), there was no change in price from the previous business day and hence no required margin payment. "Open interest" refers to the number of outstanding contracts. On the particular Monday in the table, futures contracts were sold for 11 years out (to December 2015), but the number of contracts declined as the length of time to the expiration date increased. The yield required by the seller increased steadily as the contract period moved further and further into the future.

TABLE 5   Quotes for Monday, May 7, 2007

	Open	High	Low	Settle	Chg.	Open Interest
Eurodollar (CME)—$1 million; points of 100%						
May	94.643	94.650	94.625	94.648	—	40,690
June	94.660	94.665	94.655	94.660	0.005	1,637,698
July	94.680	94.680	94.680	94.680	—	15,427
Sept	94.755	94.765	94.750	94.750	—	1,657,455
Mr08	95.110	95.110	95.080	95.085	0.005	1,492,034
Mr09	95.305	95.315	95.295	95.295	0.015	478,125
Mr11	95.030	95.035	95.010	95.010	0.010	94,665
Mr15	94.510	94.495	94.490	94.490	0.005	1,145
Dec15	94.420	94.405	94.405	94.405	0.010	685

Source: The Chicago Mercantile Exchange, www.data.tradingcharts.com/futures/quotes/ED.html.   ●

Similarly, potential borrowers in the future can guard against a rise in the borrowing rate by selling a futures contract for the period in the future during which they are going to be in need of borrowing funds (i.e., a contract to acquire funds at a specific loan rate). This activity is referred to as a *short hedge*. If interest rates rise by the time that the loan is needed, the seller receives the funds associated with the daily margin adjustment, which can be used to reduce the amount of the necessary loan. The result is that the borrower has the necessary funds over the period needed at approximately the contracted rate because the lower amount of the required borrowing offsets the higher market interest rate. More simply, the gain from the futures contract offsets the increased cash borrowing costs. In fact, the borrower actually ends up paying a slightly lower rate than would have been the case if the same hedge had been made using the forward market.[17] It should be pointed out that the eurodollar contract is unlikely to provide a perfect hedge there is unlikely to be a perfect match between the hedging instrument and the financial instrument being hedged. The lack of a perfect hedge is often referred to as *basis risk.*

When it is desired to hedge against changes in the interest rate for periods longer than three months, it is possible to do so by acquiring a series of successive futures contracts. For example, if someone wished to fix his return for a one-year period starting in September, he would simply purchase a December futures contract, a March futures contract, a June futures contract, and a September futures contract. As the December contract came to an end, it would be replaced by (rolled over into) the March contract, and that would be rolled over into the June contract and that into the September contract. He would thus be protected against shifts in the overall level of interest rates. This collection of multiple short-term three-month futures contracts to hedge changes in interest rates for a longer period is referred to as a **eurodollar strip.** Eurodollar futures can thus be used to hedge as much as seven years out (Dufey and Giddy 1994, p. 165). Another way to hedge a more distant future than is available directly in the futures markets is to acquire a shorter-term futures contract or strip and replace it with new contracts closer to the desired time period as each of the shorter contracts gains in liquidity. For example, you could acquire the strip just discussed, hold it for the first three-month period and roll it over into a new 12-month strip, and keep doing this until the desired period is attained, say, three years from now. Such hedging with a short-term futures contract that is subsequently replaced with other contracts is referred to as a *stack.*

Finally, it has become common to combine interest rate hedges with currency hedges to provide interest rate protection in a particular currency. For example, a eurobanker in France may be faced with needing to guarantee a French customer an interest rate for a future three-month loan in Swiss francs. To do so, the banker would lock in the future eurodollar interest rate with a eurodollar futures contract, and then couple that with both a forward contract to buy Swiss francs at the time the loan is made and a forward contract to sell Swiss francs three months later, when the loan is repaid.

Eurodollar Interest Rate Options

All of the hedging contracts discussed to this point essentially obligate the two parties to exchange something in the future. The **eurodollar interest rate option,** on the other hand, gives one party the right, but not an obligation, to buy or sell a financial asset under a set of prescribed conditions, including the relevant interest rate. As is the case with currency options, there are two types of transactions, *puts* and *calls.* The buyer of a **eurodollar call option** obtains the right to purchase a eurodollar time deposit bearing a certain interest rate (for example, 8 percent) on a specific date. This option will cost the buyer an up-front price called the *option premium.* If the market interest rate is above 8 percent, then the holder of the call option can choose not to exercise the option, place her funds in an account paying the higher rate of interest, and simply lose the up-front premium. Should the market rate be below 8 percent, then the buyer of the call will exercise the option and acquire the financial instrument bearing the higher interest rate. The buyer of the call is thus insured against a fall in the interest rate (without giving up the option of depositing at a higher rate later), and the up-front premium is the cost of the insurance policy. The higher the likelihood that interest rates will fall, the greater the likelihood that the option will be exercised and the higher the up-front premium.

---

[17]Intuitively, this takes place because the rate adjustment payments are made throughout the period prior to the completion of the contract with a futures contract, whereas the payment reflecting the interest rate adjustment in a forward contract is made at the end, when the contract is fulfilled. In this case, "time is money," and the relatively lower cost of the hedge with the futures contract reflects this fact.

CONCEPT BOX 2

EURODOLLAR INTEREST OPTION QUOTATIONS

The quotations in Table 6 reflect options on $1 million eurodollar deposits at the CME for Friday, May 4, 2007. The "strike price" is the exercise price and, as with futures, is quoted as (100 − yield). The strike prices (in basis points) are quoted in 0.25 percent intervals. Thus, if you were interested in investing $4 million in eurodollars in June (acquire eurodollar deposits) and were willing to pay to guarantee that you receive a $5^{1}/_{4}$ percent annual percentage rate, you would buy four April call option contracts at the strike price of 94.75 for which you would have to pay 50 basis points. Just as with futures, each basis point is worth $25, so the cost of the option contract would be 50 × $25, or $1,250 for each of the four contracts. You are now "long" by four call contracts, and the option writer is "short" by four option contracts. At expiration, if the market rate is above $5^{1}/_{4}$ percent, you will simply choose not to exercise the options, and you lose only the cost of the contracts. Similarly, if you wished to guarantee that you could borrow, say, 2 million eurodollars in June at $5^{1}/_{4}$ percent, you would purchase two June put option contracts that would cost you 50 basis points, or $1,250 for each contract. Again, should the market rate of interest be below $5^{1}/_{4}$ percent on the expiration date, you would choose not to exercise the option, would acquire a loan at the lower market rate of interest, and would lose only the $1,250 cost of each option contract. The estimated daily volume of puts and calls that were traded and the number of option contracts that were open at the end of the trading day (open interest) are given at the bottom of the table.

TABLE 6   Eurodollar Interest Futures Options, Friday, May 4, 2007

	Calls—Settle			Puts—Settle		
Strike Price	May	June	July	May	June	July
Eurodollar (CME) Contracts—$1 million; points of 100%						
9450	—	16.50	25.25	0.25	0.25	0.50
9475	4.00	4.00	13.50	0.25	0.50	1.25
9500	0.25	0.50	3.25	33.50	33.50	28.00
9525	0.25	0.50	1.25	—	58.50	50.75
9550	—	0.25	0.50	—	83.50	75.00
9575	—	0.25	—	—	108.50	—
				—no option offered		

Fri. vol. 230,150 calls; 130,050 puts

Open interest Fri—2,584,419 calls; 2,130,735 puts

Source: *The Wall Street Journal*, May 7, 2007, Market Data Center, WSJ.com.

The investor who purchases a **eurodollar put option** acquires the right to sell a eurodollar time deposit (acquire eurodollars) to the writer of the option contract for a specified interest rate at a future date. Again, should the spot rate on the date in question be above the contracted rate, the option will be exercised and the recipient of the eurodollar funds will have been protected against a rise in the cost of borrowing. On the other hand, if the lending rate is less than the contract rate on the contract date, the purchaser of the put contract will simply choose not to exercise the contract and will obtain the necessary funds at the lower market rate. The premium on the put option is thus the cost of insuring that the borrower does not end up paying a higher borrowing rate. For an example of interest option quotations and their interpretation, see Concept Box 2.

In both the case of a put and that of a call, eurodollar interest rate options contain an asymmetrical risk profile in that the purchaser can always choose not to exercise the option if it is not to his or her advantage. The writer of the option contract thus bears all the risk of an interest rate change and charges an option premium to compensate for that risk. In the forward, future, and swap arrangements discussed previously, both the writer and the buyer of the contract can potentially lose, depending on the nature of the interest rate change (symmetrical risk profile). The result of this risk difference implies that eurodollar interest rate options are most appropriate when expectations regarding interest rate changes on a given instrument are nonsymmetrical. For example, if an investor in floating-rate securities wants to ensure only against a likely fall in the market rate, purchasing a eurodollar call option effectively places a floor under the interest rate. Similarly, if the financial outlook suggests that interest rates may rise, the borrower wishing to protect herself against a rise in the lending rate can hedge by purchasing eurodollar put options. In like manner, a financial lender with a fixed-cap mortgage in place could protect himself against a rise in the market rate above the interest rate cap by purchasing put contracts in eurodollars. In similar fashion, lenders holding floating-rate notes guaranteeing never to pay less than some floor rate can protect themselves against falling rates by purchasing eurodollar interest rate call options.

Caps, floors, and collars.   The standard options interest rate derivatives just discussed are similar to futures in that they are traded in the same financial centers in standardized three month contracts in $1 million face-value units, with expiration dates in March, June, September, and December. Option contracts for longer periods of time can be constructed by combining several individual option contracts, as was done with futures contracts. The multiperiod hedge over several interest rate periods is essentially a strip of put or call options which provides a cap or a floor, that is, limits, on a floating interest rate. More specifically, a *cap* is a contract in which the seller agrees to compensate the buyer whenever the interest rate in question exceeds the contracted "ceiling rate" throughout a medium- or long-term financial transaction. As is the case with the futures contract, the buyer of the cap pays a premium (generally up front) to the seller for the insurance against having to pay more than the contracted rate throughout the loan period. If, on the other hand, interest rates fall below the contracted rate, nothing takes place, because this is another example of an asymmetric risk contract. Take, for example, the hypothetical case of Small and Company. Small has arranged to borrow $10 million for two and a half years at an assumed six-month LIBOR of 7 percent. To guarantee that the company will not have to pay more than 7 percent in each of the four subsequent six-month periods, the financial officer purchases a cap, contracted at a 7 percent ceiling rate for which he pays a premium of, say, 0.3 percent (30 basis points) of the $10 million being financed up front. Should LIBOR rise above 7 percent in any of the subsequent loan periods, the seller of the cap will pay Small and Company the difference between the cost of the six-month loan at current LIBOR and the 7 percent ceiling rate in the cap. Should the interest rate fall to 6.8 percent, nothing takes place between the contracting parties because this contract covers only where the interest rate rises above 7 percent. It is not uncommon to see an initial floating-rate loan contract carry an interest rate provision in which the contracting parties agree that the loan rate will never exceed a certain level, whatever happens to LIBOR. A floating-rate contract with a built-in interest ceiling is referred to as a *cap-floater.*

Similarly, like a strip of eurodollar call options, a *floor* is a contract that establishes an interest rate under which the financially contracted rate cannot fall for a series of future periods. For example, Ms. Jones has just contracted to lend $5 million to the Thompson Company for four years at six-month LIBOR, which at the time of the loan is at $7^1/_2$ percent. To protect herself from earning less than $7^1/_2$ percent should future LIBOR decline, Jones purchases a floor contract for a premium of 0.4 percent (40 basis points) of the initial loan amount, which fixes the floor at $7^1/_2$ percent. Should LIBOR fall below $7^1/_2$ percent in any of the seven future loan periods, the difference between market LIBOR and the contracted rate of $7^1/_2$ percent will be paid by the seller of the floor. Jones is thus protected against earning anything less than $7^1/_2$ percent. In both of these cases a floating-rate instrument has been modified into a fixed-rate instrument through use of the cap or floor contract. Finally, the simultaneous purchase of both a cap and a floor creates a *collar*. In this instance the borrower's rate cannot rise above a certain rate, but neither can it fall below a certain interest rate level. Caps, floors, and collars are similar to combinations of several short-term put and call options and can therefore be traded like other financial assets.

Options on Swaps

Following on the success of caps, it did not take financial markets long to develop the **options on swaps** derivative. These instruments offer an enormous amount of flexibility in corporate finance transactions. Just as you would expect, these financial contracts give the buyer the option to enter into a future swap or the right to cancel a future swap. In the first case (sometimes referred to as a "swaption"), purchasing a call option gives the buyer the right to receive a fixed rate in a swap and pay a floating rate. Purchasing a put option gives the buyer the right to pay a fixed rate in the swap and receive a floating rate. In contracting for the option to cancel a swap, buying a call option (a callable swap) gives the side paying a fixed and receiving a floating rate the right to cancel. In purchasing a put option to cancel a swap (a putable swap), the buyer paying the floating rate and receiving the fixed rate has the right to cancel.

Equity Financial Derivative

While commodity futures and options have existed for a long time and the derivative markets in currency and interest-bearing instruments have been exploding over the past two decades, international equity derivatives have started to be utilized relatively recently. In many countries such as the United States the equity option has existed domestically for many years, but it is only recently that international options and swaps have become widespread. With an *equity swap,* an investor can swap the returns on a currently owned equity to another investor for a price. As financial markets have globalized, it is increasingly common to find investors in one country contracting with market insiders or agents in another country to buy and hold equities and pass on to the foreign investor any gains and losses associated with the equity package for an agent's fee. This derivative allows the international investor to participate in a foreign equity market without having to pay local market execution fees or having to be concerned about the risk of being unfamiliar with local insider trading practices. It also protects the identity of the foreign investor. Thus, as in the other derivative markets, the equity derivatives serve to assist the global investor in the management of risk.

CONCEPT CHECK

1. Why would a potential borrower be interested in an interest rate futures contract? Would this person sell or buy a futures contract? Briefly explain.

2. Suppose the settle price of an interest rate futures contract on the Chicago Mercantile Exchange is 93.62. What is the yield on this contract?

3. Suppose that, in March, you hold a call option for May on a eurodollar time deposit at 6 percent. If the interest rate in May is 5 percent, would you exercise your option? Why or why not?

THE CURRENT GLOBAL DERIVATIVES MARKET

Futures have been traded on a wide variety of metals and agricultural commodities since the middle of the nineteenth century in the United States (and several centuries earlier in other parts of the world). However, in roughly the past 25 years, there has been monumental growth in the global use of foreign currency, interest rate, and equity derivatives. Why has this development taken place? Very simply, the participants in the international financial markets have found that the use of financial derivatives could increase their returns and/or lower their risk exposure. They can literally unbundle and alter their exposure to the foreign exchange risk, interest rate risk, and price risk embodied in assets and liabilities. International investors can now trade away the risks they are not comfortable with in exchange for a risk exposure more suitable to their personal tastes and finances. Inasmuch as different people are exposed to different types of risk, have different skills in assessing risk, have widely differing capacity to absorb risk, and have different risk preferences, the evolution of these derivatives has worked to make the global financial markets more efficient.

Table 7 and Figure 3 provide dramatic evidence of the rapid growth from 1987 to 2006 of a variety of derivative financial instruments available in world markets. The data originate from the BIS, and the dollar values refer to *notional values,* or reference amounts based on the gross values of contracts. Part A of Table 7, "Exchange-traded instruments," indicates that the stock of interest rate futures rose from $488 billion in 1987 to $24,473 billion in 2006, which works out to an annual average growth rate of 23.6 percent. Likewise, interest rate options grew rapidly, from $123 billion in 1987 to $38,170 billion in 2006, an annual average growth rate of 36.4 percent. The other components of Part A are smaller in size, but stock market index futures and options both had rapid annual average rates of growth (24.6 percent for stock market index futures and 60.8 percent for stock market index options). Note, however, that the notional value of currency options showed little change over the period. Part B of Table 7 provides data on *over-the-counter instruments,* meaning instruments whose contracts are negotiated through brokers and individual

TABLE 7   Values of Selected Global Derivative Instruments, Ends of Various Years, 1987–2006 (billions of dollars)

	1987	*1990*	*1994*	*1998*	*2002*	*2005*	*2006 (June)*
A. Exchange-traded instruments	$730	$2,291	$ 8,863	$13,932	$ 23,810	$ 57,816	$ 70,512
Interest rate futures	488	1,455	5,778	8,020	9,951	20,709	24,473
Interest rate options	123	600	2,624	4,624	11,760	31,588	38,170
Currency futures	15	17	40	32	47	108	178
Currency options	60	57	56	49	27	66	79
Stock market index futures	18	69	128	291	326	803	1,049
Stock market index options	28	94	238	917	1,700	4,543	6,563
B. Over-the-counter instruments	866	3,450	11,303	50,015	141,679	297,670	369,906
Interest rate swaps	683	2,312	8,816	36,362	79,120	169,106	207,323
Currency swaps	183	578	915	2,253	4,503	8,504	9,669
Interest rate options	0	561	1,573	7,997	13,746	28,596	36,856

Note: Components may not sum to totals because of rounding.

Sources: Bank for International Settlements, *69th Annual Report* (Basle, Switzerland: June 7, 1999), p. 132; International Monetary Fund, "International Capital Markets: Developments, Prospects, and Key Policy Issues," September 1999, tables 2.6 and 2.7; Bank for International Settlements, *BIS Quarterly Review,* March 2001, pp. 81, 83; *BIS Quarterly Review,* March 2004, pp. A99, A104; *BIS Quarterly Review,* March 2007, pp. A103, A108.

FIGURE 3   Values of Global Derivatives, 1987–2006

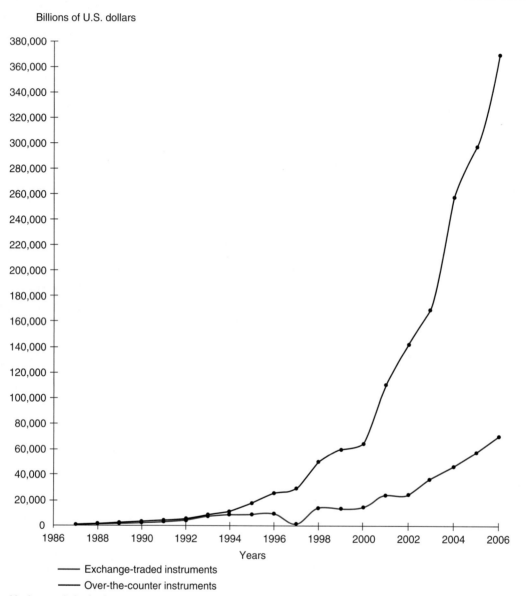

As discussed in the text, derivative instrument activity has been increasing very rapidly since the late 1980s. Such growth reflects the increasing interdependence of worldwide financial markets as well as the emergence of new financial instruments.

Sources: Bank for International Settlements, *69th Annual Report* (Basle, Switzerland: June 7, 1999), p. 132; International Monetary Fund, "International Capital Markets: Developments, Prospects, and Key Policy Issues," September 1999, tables 2.6 and 2.7; Bank for International Settlements, *BIS Quarterly Review,* March 2001, pp. 81, 83; *BIS Quarterly Review,* March 2004, pp. A99, A104; *BIS Quarterly Review,* March 2007, pp. A103, A108.

financial institutions rather than on organized exchanges. From the base of $866 billion in 1987, these instruments rose to a notional value of almost $370 *trillion* in 2006—this is an annual average growth rate of almost 39 percent. Figure 3 plots the annual figures from 1987 to 2006 for exchange-traded instruments and over-the-counter derivatives.

   Some of the recent growth in global finance can be attributed to new developments in the institutional aspects of lending. Individual bank lending to individual customers, which has been the banking norm for years, has been complemented recently by the development of the underwriting and syndication of financial credits and the subsequent trading of these credits in the financial markets, generally between banks. The syndication of the lending process occurs when a highly structured group of well-capitalized banks agree to provide a particular loan and then sell shares of the credits to a wider range of smaller and less well-informed banks. In the eurodollar markets the loan may thus originate in one country, while the ultimate lenders or holders of the loan credits reside in other countries. Administratively, it is typical for the syndicate to appoint a manager or agent who interacts with the borrower, thus retaining in part the banking principal–lending-agent relationship. The formal syndication loan agreement can take the form of a **direct loan syndicate** or a **loan participation syndicate.** In the first case, the direct loan syndicate, participant banks sign a common loan agreement that serves as the lending instrument. The participating banks essentially are co-lenders in this form of syndication. In the second case, that of a participation syndicate, a lead bank usually executes the loan instrument with the borrower and then syndicates the loan by entering into participation agreements with other banks. In this case, the participating banks are not formal co-lenders. Syndicated loan arrangements protect the borrower from the undue influence of any one bank and, at the same time, protect a single bank from being excessively exposed to the credit risk associated with a particular borrower. This latter characteristic is of particular value to international lenders who wish to diversify risk such as that associated with lending to sovereign borrowers. Perhaps even more importantly, in the rapidly expanding world of global finance, traditional financial links are becoming less and less important. Syndication permits the managing or agent bank to obtain funds for a particular borrower faster, in larger amounts, and likely at a lower cost than does the traditional single-bank approach. Indeed, syndication is the most prevalent way of lending in foreign markets whenever the borrowing amounts are large and the lending period exceeds 12 months (Dufey and Giddy 1994, p. 250). Growth in the international financial markets has thus been fostered not only by the development of new financial derivative instruments but also by changes in the forms of institutional lending that have increased the efficiency of international finance.

SUMMARY

This chapter provided a general profile of the markets and instruments that currently exist for facilitating financial capital flows among nations. International bank lending and international transactions in bonds and stocks are now of huge size and take place in financial centers worldwide. Within these markets, a wide variety of specific instruments, including many different kinds of derivatives, has emerged. These instruments enable international investors, particularly in eurocurrency markets, to unbundle the various aspects of risk associated with the instruments in order to better distribute and hedge the risks. A key aspect of modern lending technology is the ability to separate the currency of denomination of a particular financial instrument from its respective jurisdiction. Thus, the characteristics of a eurocurrency instrument can be separated or unbundled and repackaged in a manner that is more profitable and/or contains a risk profile that is more suitable to the individual investor. The wide array of instruments for dealing with the risk associated with exchange rates, interest rates, and equity prices clearly appears to be playing an important role in improving the efficiency of rapidly globalizing international financial markets.

KEY TERMS

basis points	eurobond markets	eurodollar interest rate option
bond underwriters	eurocurrency market	eurodollar interest rate swap
derivatives	eurodollar call option	eurodollar market
direct loan syndicate	eurodollar cross-currency interest	eurodollar put option
emerging market funds	rate swap	eurodollar strip
eurobanks	eurodollar interest rate futures	foreign bond markets

future rate agreement
global funds
gross international bank lending
international bank lending
international bond market
international funds

international portfolio
   diversification
loan participation syndicate
London Interbank Offered Rate
   (LIBOR)
maturity mismatching

mutual funds
net international bank lending
options on swaps
regional funds
traditional foreign bank lending

QUESTIONS AND PROBLEMS

1. What factors have been primarily responsible for the growth of the eurodollar market? Should growth in eurodollars be of concern to the U.S. Federal Reserve? Why or why not?

2. You notice in *The Wall Street Journal* that the interest rate in the U.S. money markets is $7^1/_2$ percent and the interest rate in London is 9 percent. Would you expect the pound to be at premium or discount? Why?

3. In addition to the interest rate information in Question 2, you also note that the deposit rate in the United States is $6^1/_2$ percent and the lending rate is $8^1/_2$ percent. Where would you expect the eurodollar deposit and lending rates to be? Why? What would you expect to happen to any difference between the above pairs of interest rates if U.S. local tax rates on international financial activity were reduced? Why?

4. What would you estimate the eurodollar deposit rate to be if the domestic U.S. dollar deposit rate is $6^1/_2$ percent, the reserve requirement on time deposits is 2 percent, and the combined cost of taxes and deposit insurance amounts to 10 basis points ($^1/_{10}$ percent)?

5. Explain in terms understandable to a noneconomist why, for example, when interest rates rise sharply, the subsequent headline in the newspaper may say "Bond Prices Plunge in Active Trading."

6. Why can a country's *nominal* interest rate never be negative? Why can a country's *real* interest rate indeed be negative? If a country has a negative real rate, do you think that this suggests that the country is not well integrated into world financial markets? Explain.

7. Because futures contracts are short-term, three-month contracts for fixed value, how can you use the futures market to hedge against longer-term risk for larger amounts of eurodollars?

8. Financial institutions have found themselves in short-run financial liquidity problems because of overexposure in the futures markets. Explain how this could happen if you took a "long position" in a foreign currency or a "long hedge" in a eurodollar deposit or CD.

9. Briefly explain the benefits that accrue to each of the contracting parties in a eurodollar interest rate swap. What is the difference between a normal swap and a basis swap? If a swap contract is signed and one of the parties wishes to return to his or her initial market position, for example, a floating rate, what, if anything, can be done?

10. Why are futures contracts defined as symmetrical contracts, while options, caps, and floors are described as asymmetrical contracts? How is the asymmetry dealt with in the latter type of contracts?

11. Explain how loan syndication has fostered international financial growth, particularly with regard to loans to governments (sovereign loans). What is the difference between a participation syndicate and a direct loan syndicate?

12. You wish to acquire a eurodollar interest rate option for $6 million in March and want to lock in a deposit interest rate of $7^1/_2$ percent. You look in the options market quotations under Mar and find the following information:

Strike Price	Calls—Settle	Puts—Settle
9200	0.50	0.05
9225	0.41	0.30
9250	0.54	0.15
9275	0.26	0.18

What will be the cost of using the options market to hedge the interest rate risk?

22

THE MONETARY AND PORTFOLIO BALANCE APPROACHES TO EXTERNAL BALANCE

LEARNING OBJECTIVES

- To know how the supply and demand for money can affect a country's balance of payments and exchange rate.

- To grasp how other financial assets besides money can influence exchange rates and international payments positions.

- To understand how a changing exchange rate can overshoot its new equilibrium value.

INTRODUCTION

The New Globalized Capital

For as long as multinational companies have existed—and some historians trace them back to banking under the Knights Templar in 1135—they have been derided by their critics as rapacious rich-world beasts. If there was ever any truth to that accusation, it is fast disappearing. While globalization has opened new markets to rich-world companies, it has also given birth to a pack of fast-moving, sharp-toothed new multinationals that is emerging from the poor world.

Indian and Chinese firms are now starting to give their rich-world rivals a run for their money. So far this year, Indian firms, led by Hindalco and Tata Steel, have bought some 34 foreign companies for a combined $10.7 billion. Indian IT-services companies such as Infosys, Tata Consultancy Services, and Wipro are putting the fear of God into the old guard, including Accenture and even mighty IBM. Big Blue sold its personal-computer business to a Chinese multinational, Lenovo, which is now starting to get its act together. PetroChina has become a force in Africa, including, controversially, Sudan. Brazilian and Russian multinationals are also starting to make their mark. The Russians have outdone the Indians this year, splashing $11.4 billion abroad, and are now in the running to buy Alitalia, Italy's state airline.[1]

Building on the previous exchange rate and international monetary material in Chapters 20 and 21, the next two chapters will introduce the reader to additional frameworks and terminology for understanding the determination of exchange rates. Increasingly important in that determination are the monetary and financial adjustments associated with the globalization of capital flows. These frameworks also provide the means for examining the effect of policy changes and other exogenous shifts on domestic and foreign financial markets. In this chapter, we examine two broad, aggregate approaches to the determination of a country's balance-of-payments (BOP) position and the exchange rate. These approaches emphasize the role of money and international asset exchanges as the primary forces at work in the foreign exchange markets, reflecting the much greater importance in recent years of financial transactions than trade flows in exchange market activity. More specifically, we study the monetary approach to the balance of payments and the exchange rate, which focuses on how a balance-of-payments deficit or surplus or a change in the spot exchange rate reflects an imbalance in a country's demand for and supply of money. The second approach, called the portfolio balance approach (or the asset market approach), moves beyond money alone and postulates that changes in a country's balance-of-payments position or exchange rate reflect changes in the relative demands and supplies of domestic and foreign financial assets. The chapter ends with a consideration of the phenomenon of "overshooting" in exchange markets and how this phenomenon contributes to exchange rate instability. In overview, an important result of looking at the monetary and portfolio balance approaches is that you can gain insights as to how asset movements influence exchange rates and why exchange rates can demonstrate considerable volatility in the real world. A brief discussion of empirical work pertaining to these two approaches is found in the appendix to this chapter.

THE MONETARY APPROACH TO THE BALANCE OF PAYMENTS

The **monetary approach to the balance of payments** emphasizes that a country's balance of payments, while reflecting real factors such as income, tastes, or factor productivity, is essentially a monetary phenomenon. This means that the balance of payments should be analyzed in terms of a country's supply of and demand for money. In the international

---

[1]"Globalization's Offspring: How the New Multinationals Are Remaking the Old," *The Economist,* April 7, 2007, p. 11.

payments context, attention is principally focused on category IV in the balance-of-payments accounting framework, the "official short-term capital account." If a country has a BOP deficit (i.e., an official reserve transactions deficit), then there is an outflow of international reserve assets. As we shall see, an outflow of international reserves implies that the country's supply of money exceeds its demand for money. Similarly, an official reserve transactions surplus implies that the country's money supply is less than its demand. If we are concerned about forces causing a BOP deficit or surplus, we must focus on the supply of and demand for money.

The Supply of Money   A country's supply of money can be viewed through the following basic expression:

$$M_s = a(BR + C) = a(DR + IR) \tag{1}$$

where: M_s = money supply
   BR = reserves of commercial banks (depository institutions) ⎤ central bank
   C = currency held by the nonbank public ⎦ liabilities
   a = the money multiplier
   DR = domestic reserves ⎤ central
   IR = international reserves ⎦ bank assets

The money supply has various definitions, but the monetary approach usually deals with either M1 or M2. *M1* is traditionally defined as currency held by the nonbank public (i.e., held outside financial institutions), traveler's checks, and all checkable deposits in financial institutions. *M2* includes the components of M1 but principally adds savings and time deposits (except for very large time deposits—of $100,000 or more in the United States) and a few other items. (This distinction between M1 and M2 per se is not important for our development of the basic monetary approach.) The amount of deposits in turn is a function of the amount of reserves of commercial banks (and other depository institutions such as savings and loan associations and credit unions) and the **money multiplier.**

The money multiplier reflects the process of multiple expansion of bank deposits, which is usually discussed in introductory courses. For example, if the required reserve ratio against deposits is 10 percent, an initial deposit of $1,000 in a bank creates $900 of excess reserves because only 10 percent (or $100) is required to be held by the commercial bank. The $900 of excess reserves can be lent out, which, after being spent by the loan recipient, will be redeposited in another (or the same) bank, which will generate 0.90 times $900 of new excess reserves (or $810) in the second bank. This $810 can then be lent, which keeps the process going. In the end, the original $1,000 gets "multiplied" by the money multiplier of $1/r$, where r is the required reserve ratio. In this example, with r of 10 percent, the original $1,000 deposit can lead to $1,000 \times (1/r) = $1,000 \times [1/0.10] = $10,000 of "money." The money multiplier in the example is thus $(1/r)$ or 10. However, this simple expression is unrealistic, as the money multiplier must be adjusted for such factors as leakages of deposits into currency, different required reserve ratios on savings and time deposits than on checkable deposits, and the holding of excess reserves by banks. (See any standard money and banking text for elaboration.) We are not interested in the mechanics, however, but in the fact that the a term in expression [1] reflects a general money multiplier process.

The sum of reserves held by banks plus currency outside banks ($BR + C$) is usually called the **monetary base.** This base originates on the liabilities side of the balance sheet of the central bank (the Federal Reserve in the United States). Currency is issued by the central bank, and part of the reserves of banks are held by the central bank (the other part is held as vault cash by the commercial banks). Thus, any increase in assets held by the central bank permits an increase in these liabilities and thereby permits an increase in the money supply. On the asset side of the central bank, the most important assets for our purposes are (1) loans and security holdings by the central bank, called domestic credit issued by the central bank or **domestic reserves,** and (2) **international reserves** held by the central bank, which consist of foreign exchange holdings and holdings of any other internationally acceptable asset.

It is important to understand the relationships between these assets (domestic and international reserves) and the money supply. Suppose that the central bank purchases government securities (increasing domestic assets or extending domestic credit) in open market operations. This will increase the reserves of commercial banks, lead to new loans, and thereby ultimately increase the money supply by a multiplied amount. In addition, suppose that the central bank purchases foreign exchange from an exporter; this acquisition of international reserves also increases the money supply because the exporter will deposit the central bank's check into a commercial bank or other depository institution and set in motion the multiple deposit expansion process. Thus, increases in central bank reserves permit a multiplied expansion of the money supply, and, analogously, decreases in these reserves will lead to a multiplied decrease in the money supply.

The Demand for Money

Consider now the demand for money. Remember that the term **demand for money** does not mean the demand for "income" or "wealth." Rather, it refers to the desire to hold wealth in the form of money balances (basically either currency or checking accounts, using the M1 definition of money) rather than in the form of stocks, bonds, and other financial instruments such as certificates of deposit. The demand for money (L) can be specified in the following general form:

$$L = f[Y, P, i, W, E(p), O] \tag{2}$$

where: Y = level of *real* income in the economy
P = price level
i = interest rate
W = level of real wealth
$E(p)$ = expected percentage change in the price level
O = all other variables that can influence the amount of money balances a country's citizens wish to hold

What are the predicted relationships between Y, P, i, W, and $E(p)$ (the independent variables) and L?

Real Income

We begin with the influence of the level of income. The relationship between Y and L is expected to be positive, reflecting the **transactions demand for money.** As your income rises, you will want to spend more on consumption. Thus, more money needs to be held to finance these additional transactions.

Price Level

A positive relationship is also expected between P and L, because a higher price level means that more money, that is, a larger cash balance, is required to purchase a given amount of goods and services.

Interest Rate

The influence of the interest rate on the demand for money is negative. If the interest rate rises, a smaller proportion of wealth is held in the form of money balances (currency and checking accounts in financial institutions) and more in the form of other assets, which are now more attractive. (Currency, of course, does not pay interest. Many checking accounts also do not pay interest; those that do pay interest pay lower rates than certificates of deposit or bonds.) Similarly, a fall in the interest rate will induce people to hold more of

IN THE REAL WORLD:

RELATIONSHIPS BETWEEN MONETARY CONCEPTS IN THE UNITED STATES

The various monetary concepts discussed in the text can be illustrated by an example. Looking first at bank reserves and deposits, the average reserves of all depository institutions in the United States in April 2007 were $40.9 billion.* The amount of currency held by the non-bank public was $774.1 billion. Hence, the monetary base obtained by summing these two components was $815.0 billion. Required reserve ratios against checkable deposits were 3 percent for the first $45.8 million of deposits in a bank and 10 percent for deposits above that level. The money supply (M1) was $1,368.3 billion. The money multiplier was thus $1,368.3 billion divided by the monetary base of $815.0 or 1.68.

Turning to the central bank, the Federal Reserve's balance sheet at the end of March 2007 is shown in summary form in Table 1. On the liabilities side of the balance sheet,

we see that banks and other depository institutions held $35.0 billion on deposit at the Federal Reserve. The item "Federal Reserve notes" represents currency issued by the Fed. With respect to assets, the loans and securities figure of $825.2 represents domestic credit issued by the Fed or domestic reserves. The gold and SDR accounts represent holdings of these international assets. (These assets are discussed in the last chapter in this book.) Finally, the other assets include foreign currency holdings, which are another component of international reserves held by the Fed. (Note: In the United States, not all international reserves are held by the Federal Reserve—some are held by the Exchange Stabilization Fund of the U.S. Treasury.)

*All figures in this case study are taken from Board of Governors of the Federal Reserve System, www.federalreserve.gov/releases, April 26, 2007.

TABLE 1   Balance Sheet, Federal Reserve Banks, April 25, 2007 (billions of dollars)

Assets		*Liabilities and Capital Accounts*	
Gold and SDR certificate accounts	$ 14.3	Federal Reserve notes	$805.5
Loans and securities	825.2	Deposits of depository institutions	35.0
Other assets (including assets denominated in foreign currencies)	44.8	Other deposits and liabilities	11.1
		Capital accounts	32.7
Total assets	$884.3	Total liabilities and capital accounts	$884.3

Sources: Board of Governors of the Federal Reserve System, *Federal Reserve Statistical Release* H 3, *Aggregate Reserves of Depository Institutions and the Monetary Base* and H 4.1, *Factors Affecting Reserve Balances,* April 26, 2007.

their wealth in the form of money, because the opportunity cost of holding money balances has fallen.[2] This relationship of the interest rate to the demand for money is often called the "asset" demand for money. It reflects not only the opportunity cost phenomenon discussed above but also the fact that, in order to undertake risk, wealth holders must be compensated. When the interest rate rises, people move out of money balances and into more risky assets because the compensation for doing so has increased.

An additional reason hypothesized by economists for the negative influence of the interest rate on money demand involves the relationship between interest rates and bond prices. (For elaboration, consult money and banking or intermediate macroeconomics texts such as Froyen 2005, chaps. 7 and 22.) As noted in the previous chapter, interest rates and bond

---

[2]When we speak of "the interest rate," we are referring to a general average level of interest rates in the economy.

prices are inversely related to each other. Briefly, because a bond usually pays a fixed money amount to the bondholder, say, $60 per year, the price of the bond in the bond markets determines the "yield" or interest rate that the holder of the bond is earning. This interest rate will be in line with other interest rates in the economy (because of asset market competition). To simplify, if the market price of the bond you hold is $600, then your receipt of $60 per year of interest is a 10 percent return (=$60/$600). However, if the bond price rises to $800, then your realized interest *rate* has fallen to 7.5 percent (=$60/$800). Similarly, if the price of the bond falls to $500, then the interest rate is 12 percent (=$60/$500).

In the context of the demand for money, suppose that financial investors have some conception of a "normal" interest rate and that the current interest rate is at that level. (Of course, different investors may have different views of what is the "normal" rate.) If the interest rate now rises above that level, investors will expect that it will fall back toward that level eventually. Because the rise in the interest rate means that there has been a fall in bond prices, individuals are thus expecting bond prices to rise when the interest rate falls back toward "normal." With the expected rise in bond prices, bonds are now an attractive asset to hold in comparison to money not only because of the higher interest rate but also because of the expected capital gain from the higher bond prices. Hence, smaller money balances will be desired. In the other direction, a fall in the interest rate below the normal level leads to an expectation that the interest rate will rise back toward normal. In other words, there is an expectation that bond prices will fall. In this situation, investors prefer money to bonds if the expected capital loss from the falling bond prices is larger than the interest return. Hence, the interest rate–bond price relationship gives us another reason for an inverse relationship between the amount of money demanded and the interest rate.

Real Wealth

The income level, price level, and the interest rate are thought to be the major influences upon the demand for money, but the remaining independent variables can also have an impact. With respect to W, real wealth, the influence on the demand for money is expected to be positive because, as a person's wealth rises, that person wants to hold more of all assets, including money.

Expected Inflation Rate

With respect to the expected inflation rate, $E(p)$, the hypothesized relationship is negative. If you expect prices to rise, you realize that this inflation will mean a decline in the real value of a constant *nominal* amount of money balances. In such a situation, there is an incentive to substitute away from holding money and toward holding nonmoney assets whose prices may rise with the inflation.

Other Variables

Finally, the O term is included to incorporate other influences on the demand for money. The O term reflects institutional features of the economy such as the frequency with which people receive paychecks. If you are paid weekly, your average money balances will be smaller than if you are paid on a monthly basis. Another institutional feature would be the importance of credit cards in the transactions network in the economy. The greater the relative importance of credit card transactions, the less money you need on hand on any given day. These institutional features are not thought to vary to any great extent, especially during relatively short time periods.

A frequently used and simple formulation of the demand for money hypothesizes that the general functional expression in [2] can be given the specific form of

$$L = kPY \tag{3}$$

where P and Y are defined as above and k is a constant term embodying all other variables. This simple formulation will sometimes be used later in our discussion.

Monetary Equilibrium and the Balance of Payments

The money market is in equilibrium when the amount of money in existence (the money supply) is equal to the amount of cash balances that the public desires to hold (money demand). In the most general case, this means that equilibrium is determined by using expression [1], the supply-of-money expression, and expression [2], the demand-for-money expression:

$$M_s = L \qquad [4]$$

or

$$\underbrace{a(DR + IR)}_{M_s} = \underbrace{a(BR + C) = f[Y, P, i, W, E(p), O]}_{L} \qquad [5]$$

Alternatively, we can write a simpler equation for monetary equilibrium by using expression [3] for money demand:

$$M_s = kPY \qquad [6]$$

This expression is often used and explicitly specifies that money demand depends primarily on the price level and the level of real income.

With this background, we now discuss the manner in which the monetary approach to the balance of payments uses the relationships between the supply of and demand for money in explaining BOP deficits and surpluses. *Suppose that the exchange rate is fixed.* Consider a situation where, from an initial equilibrium between money supply and money demand, the monetary authorities increase the supply of money by purchasing government securities on the open market (i.e., an increase in DR). Because the money market was originally in equilibrium, this **expansionary monetary policy** leads, because of the subsequent increase in BR and/or C, to an **excess supply of money.** (In the other direction, a decrease in the money supply would, other things equal, cause an **excess demand for money** and would be a **contractionary monetary policy.**) When M_s is greater than L, the cash balances people have on hand and in bank accounts exceed their desired cash balances. When this happens, people attempt to reduce their cash balances, an action that has several important effects on the BOP.

Current Account

First, the presence of excess cash balances means that individuals will spend more money on goods and services. This bids up the prices of goods and services (i.e., bids up P). Further, if the economy is not at full employment because of money wage rigidity or other rigidities, the level of real income (Y) rises. In addition, if part of any new real income is saved, the level of real wealth (W) in the economy increases. What is the consequence of these potential impacts, other things equal, on P, Y, and W on the current account in the balance of payments? A rise in P will lead to larger imports as home goods are now relatively more expensive compared to foreign goods; the rise in P will also make it more difficult to export to other countries. In addition, the increase in Y induces more spending, and some of this spending is on imports. Finally, increased wealth enables individuals to purchase more of all goods, some of which are imports and some of which are goods that might otherwise have been exported. Hence, the excess supply of money generates pressures leading to a current account deficit.

Private Capital Account

The presence of the excess cash balances also has an impact on the private capital account in the BOP. Because an alternative to holding cash balances is to hold other financial assets, some of the excess cash balances will be used to acquire such assets. This purchase of financial assets bids up their price and drives down the interest rate. At the same time, the purchase of financial assets will include the acquisition of some foreign financial assets since financial investors wish to hold a diversified portfolio. There will thus be a capital outflow to other countries, with the end result being a tendency for a deficit to occur in the private capital account.

Balance-of-Payments Deficit

Given these effects on the current account and the private capital account, it is obvious that a country with an excess supply of money has a tendency to incur a balance-of-payments deficit (official reserve transactions balance). The total effect on the current and private capital accounts combined is a net debit position, so the official short-term capital account (category IV) in the balance of payments must be in a net credit position to finance the official reserve transactions deficit (a decrease in *IR*). A way of summarizing these various reactions to the excess supply of money is to say that the excess supply causes individuals to switch to other assets than money, including physical assets (goods) as well as financial assets, and that some of these assets are foreign goods and financial assets. In turn, the acquisition of foreign goods and financial assets results in a balance-of-payments deficit. Clearly, a policy prescription for ending the BOP deficit emerges from this discussion: Eliminate the excess supply of money by halting the monetary expansion.

In the monetary approach to the balance of payments, however, a policy action may not be necessary to eliminate the excess supply of money. Consider the changes we have specified above: (1) *Y* is rising; (2) *P* is rising; (3) *i* is falling; and (4) *W* is rising. What do these four developments have in common? They all *increase the demand for money*. This point is important because it means that, even without policy action, the initial excess supply tends to be worked off because the demand for money will be rising. Further, the supply of money itself will be decreasing. This decrease occurs because the balance-of-payments deficit reduces the country's international reserves due to the excess demand for foreign exchange (to buy imports and foreign assets) at the fixed exchange rate. This reduction in reserves leads to a decrease in the money supply. The central bank might temporarily offset the decrease in the money supply (called "sterilization" of the money supply from the BOP deficit) by expansionary open-market operations, but this would set the whole process in motion again and the central bank would ultimately run out of international reserves. Thus, the conclusion of the monetary approach is that an excess supply of money will set forces in motion that will automatically eliminate that excess supply. When the excess supply has disappeared, the balance of payments is back in equilibrium.

Expected Inflation Rate

One complicating factor not addressed thus far in our discussion of the adjustment process to the excess money supply is the role of the expected inflation rate, $E(p)$. If the monetary expansion by the authorities generates expectations that prices will increase, this will *reduce* the demand for money. This reduction in money demand will, by itself, enlarge the excess supply of money, in contrast to the other four determinants of the demand for money. Hence, other things equal, the presence of the inflationary expectations will add to the BOP deficit and will mean that the job to be performed by *Y, P, i,* and *W* is greater. As these other determinants begin to work, however, the inflationary expectations should dampen unless the monetary authorities continue to pump new money into the economy.

Other Comments

We have focused to this point on a broad formulation of the demand for money, wherein we have specified five particular determinants of that demand. More traditional in textbook formulations of the monetary approach is the simple demand-for-money equation of expression [3]. In that simple context, if there is always full employment (and *Y* is therefore fixed), the introduction of new money by the monetary authorities has only one impact if *k* is assumed to be constant: The level of prices (*P*) will rise. (Economists call this simplified approach the "crude quantity theory of money.") The result is a BOP deficit because of inflation's effect on the current account, and the BOP deficit will continue until the excess supply of money is dissipated and prices have stabilized again. This basic model is instructive for emphasizing the link between the money supply, money demand, the price level, and the balance of payments, but it obviously leaves out other factors that influence the demand for money.

It should be evident that the general adjustment process to an excess supply of money in the monetary approach works in reverse when there is an excess demand for money. If, beginning from an equilibrium position, the monetary authorities contract the money supply, an initial excess demand for money occurs. Individuals hold smaller cash balances than they desire. They restore their cash balances by reducing spending on goods and services, which implies that the demand for imports falls. Income also falls because of the reduced spending, as does the price level (assuming that prices are somewhat flexible downward). When prices fall, exports increase and imports decrease. Thus, the current account moves into surplus. In addition, cash balances can be increased by selling off holdings of financial assets, including some sales to foreign citizens. These sales lead to a surplus in the private capital account in the balance of payments. With the official reserve transactions balance thus being in surplus, international reserves will be flowing into the country and expanding the money supply. The excess demand for money and the BOP surplus will eventually be eliminated.

In overview of the monetary approach to the balance of payments under fixed exchange rates, we see that it contains an automatic adjustment mechanism to any disturbances to monetary equilibrium. If the process is allowed to run its course, disequilibria in the money market and BOP deficits and surpluses will not exist *in the long run*. Any imbalances in the balance of payments reflect an imbalance between the supply of and demand for money, and these imbalances can be interpreted as part of an adjustment process to a discrepancy between the desired stock of money and the actual stock of money.

CONCEPT CHECK

1. What happens to the size of the money multiplier if the required reserve ratio increases? Why?

2. Why, other things equal, do increases in real income, real wealth, and the price level increase the demand for money, while increases in the interest rate and the expected inflation rate decrease the demand for money?

3. Explain why an excess supply of money in a fixed exchange rate regime will lead to a deficit in the balance of payments.

THE MONETARY APPROACH TO THE EXCHANGE RATE

To this point in the monetary approach, the analysis has assumed that the exchange rate is fixed. With that assumption, attention was drawn to the possibility of a deficit or surplus in the balance of payments. We now turn to the **monetary approach to the exchange rate** when the exchange rate is free to vary. With a flexible exchange rate, BOP deficits and surpluses will be eliminated by changes in the rate, but we need to examine the exchange rate changes in the context of money supply and demand.

Suppose that we begin from a position of equilibrium where M_s equals L. Now assume that the monetary authorities increase the supply of money and thereby create an excess supply of money. Remember that with an excess supply of money, the cash balances of individuals exceed the cash balances desired in connection with existing prices, real income, interest rates, wealth, and price expectations. The result of this money supply increase is that more spending by individuals occurs on goods and services and on financial assets in order to get rid of the excess money supply. With the increase in spending, there are increased imports, a possible decrease in exports as some such goods are now purchased by home country citizens, and an increase in purchases of financial assets from foreign citizens. With a flexible exchange rate, these factors are all working to cause a *depreciation of the home currency*. Hence, whereas a money supply increase under a fixed exchange rate leads to a BOP deficit, the money supply increase under a flexible rate leads to an **incipient BOP deficit** (i.e., there would be a BOP deficit if the exchange rate did not change) and therefore to a fall in the value of the home currency relative to other currencies. This depreciation is thus a signal that there is an excess supply of money in the economy.

As with a fixed exchange rate, the excess supply of money is only temporary if no further money supply increases by the authorities are introduced. This is because the depreciation itself causes Y (if the economy is below full employment) and P to rise (because foreign demand for exports and home demand for import-substitute goods is rising). The level of wealth will also rise when saving occurs out of any new real income. In addition, the interest rate will fall due to increased purchases of financial assets. These changes generate an increase in the demand for money, and, ultimately, the excess supply of money is absorbed by the growing money demand. (If we take a crude quantity-theory-of-money view, the only home variable that will be changing in the adjustment process will be P, but this change too will ultimately restore equilibrium between money supply and money demand.)

As in the fixed-rate analysis, a potentially disturbing factor is the existence of changing inflation expectations, $E(p)$. If the inflation resulting from the depreciation generates a rise in $E(p)$, this would decrease the demand for money and, other things equal, would *add* to the excess supply of money. Therefore, the increase in L generated by changes in $Y, P, W,$ and i needs to be greater than it would be if these increased inflation expectations were absent.

It should be clear that an excess demand for money will generate just the opposite reactions. With an excess demand (due to, say, a contraction of the money supply), individuals find that their cash balances fall short of those desired. Hence, spending is reduced on goods and services, and financial assets are sold to acquire larger cash balances. There is then an **incipient BOP surplus** (i.e., there would be a BOP surplus if the exchange rate did not change), and the result is an *appreciation of the home currency*. This appreciation also eventually comes to a halt because of the adjustment process. In overview, the monetary approach under a flexible rate parallels that of the fixed-rate case, except that the phrase *balance-of-payments deficit* is replaced by the phrase *depreciation of the home currency* and the phrase *balance-of-payments surplus* is replaced by the phrase *appreciation of the home currency*.

A Two-Country Framework

It is instructive to extend the monetary approach with a flexible exchange rate to a two country framework. A straightforward way to do this is to return to the simple money demand–money supply formulation in expression [6]. Assuming that the time period is long enough for full price adjustment and that absolute purchasing power parity holds (see Chapter 20), and defining the exchange rate e as the number of units of home currency per unit of foreign currency,

$$P_A = eP_B \text{ or } e = P_A/P_B \tag{7}$$

where P_A is the price level in country A (the home country), P_B is the price level in country B (the foreign country), and e is the exchange rate expressed in terms of number of units of A's currency per 1 unit of B's currency.

IN THE REAL WORLD:

MONEY GROWTH AND EXCHANGE RATES IN THE RUSSIAN TRANSITION

The transition from the extensive planning of the command system in Russia and the former republics of the Soviet Union, as well as in countries of Central and Eastern Europe, to a more market-oriented system was discussed in Chapters 17 and 18. The removal of price controls typically resulted in inflation. Workers pushed for higher wages to keep pace with rising prices, and the authorities often financed these increases with increases in the money supply.

The monetary approach to the exchange rate suggests the following outcomes. Increases in the supply of money create an excess supply of money. Individuals have excess cash and increase their spending on goods and services and financial assets. With a flexible exchange rate, these factors result in a depreciation in the home currency.

In the case of Russia, the growth rate of the money supply was over 100 percent annually from 1992–1995. The result was not only inflation rates over 100 percent but also significant depreciation in the value of the ruble relative to the U.S. dollar (see Table 2). It should be noted that in recent years a lower and more stable growth rate of the money supply has been accompanied by lower inflation rates than in the early 1990s and a much more stable exchange rate.

TABLE 2   Money Growth, Inflation, and Exchange Rates in Russia, 1992–1996

	1992	1993	1994	1995	1996
Money growth rate (annual percentage change)	779.9	317.6	200.7	102.8	33.6
Inflation rate (annual percentage change)	—	841.6	202.7	131.4	21.5
Exchange rate (rubles per U.S. dollar)	100	—	3,500	—	5,000

— = not available.
Sources: Money growth rates are from "Monetary and Financial Sector Policies in Transition Countries," *International Monetary Fund Reports 1997.*
Inflation rates are from "Inflation in Transition Economies: How Much? And Why?" IMF Working Paper, International Monetary Fund, 1997.
Exchange Rates are from www.gwu.edu/slavic/golosa/ruble.htm.

Now utilize expression [6]. For country A, we can write

$$M_{sA} = k_A P_A Y_A \qquad [8]$$

where: M_{sA} = money supply in country A
P_A = price level in country A
Y_A = real income in country A
k_A = a constant term embodying all other influences on money demand in country A besides P_A and Y_A

A similar expression can be written for country B, where all letters refer to the same items as in [8] but the subscript B is employed:

$$M_{sB} = k_B P_B Y_B \qquad [9]$$

Now divide each side of the equality in [8] by the corresponding side of the equality in [9]:

$$\frac{M_{sA}}{M_{sB}} = \frac{k_A P_A Y_A}{k_B P_B Y_B} \qquad [10]$$

Because $(P_A/P_B) = e$ by [7], we can obtain

$$\frac{M_{sA}}{M_{sB}} = \frac{k_A Y_A}{k_B Y_B} \times e \qquad [11]$$

A final rearrangement leads to

$$e = \frac{k_B Y_B M_{sA}}{k_A Y_A M_{sB}} \qquad [12]$$

This last expression is instructive because it shows the impact of changes in both economies on the exchange rate.[3] For example, if the money supply in country A (M_{sA}) increases and everything else is held constant, then e will rise by the same percentage as does the money supply. This is a strict monetary approach interpretation where, for example, a 10 percent rise in the home money supply will lead to a 10 percent depreciation of the home currency. (Remember that a rise in e is a fall in the relative value of the home currency.) We can also see from [12] that a rise in M_{sB} will lead to a proportional fall in e (an appreciation of the home currency). Thus, the monetary approach puts crucial importance on changes in relative money supplies as determinants of changes in the exchange rate. If a country is "printing money" faster than its trading partners are, its currency will depreciate; if a country is more restrictive with respect to its monetary growth than its trading partners, its currency will appreciate.

Expression [12] can also be used to indicate the effects of income changes in either economy. Suppose that national income in country A (Y_A) increases. What effect will this have on e? As should be clear, e will fall when Y_A rises (which increases A's demand for money), meaning that the home currency appreciates. Similarly, a rise in Y_B will cause a depreciation of A's currency. Hence, the implication in the monetary approach is that the faster-growing country will see its currency appreciate.

CONCEPT CHECK

1. Assuming a flexible exchange rate, explain the impact of an exogenous reduction in a country's money supply upon the value of the country's currency.

2. In the monetary approach, other things equal, what will happen to the exchange rate between the currencies of countries A and B if there is greater income growth in country B than in country A? Explain.

THE PORTFOLIO BALANCE APPROACH TO THE BALANCE OF PAYMENTS AND THE EXCHANGE RATE

The **portfolio balance** or **asset market approach** to the balance of payments and the exchange rate extends the monetary approach to include other financial assets besides money. This literature has primarily developed since the mid-1970s, and there is an extremely large number of asset approach models in existence. We will provide only a general discussion of these models, all of which emphasize a few overriding characteristics:

1. Financial markets across countries are extremely well integrated. Thus, individuals hold a variety of financial assets, both domestic and foreign.

---

[3]The relationships in [12] can also be examined through growth rates. Designating a percentage change by a dot (.) over a variable, expression [12] in terms of growth rates is

$$\dot{e} = (\dot{Y}_B - \dot{Y}_A) + (\dot{M}_{sA} - \dot{M}_{sB}) \qquad [12']$$

There are no k terms in [12'] because k_A and k_B are assumed to be constant.

2. Although holding both domestic and foreign financial assets, individuals regard these assets as *imperfect substitutes*. In particular, additional risk is generally thought to be associated with the holding of foreign financial assets. Hence, there is a positive risk premium attached to foreign assets. This premium was discussed in the preceding two chapters.[4]

3. Asset holders, with the objective of maximizing the return on their asset portfolio as a whole, stand ready to switch out of one type of asset and into another whenever events occur that alter the expected returns on various assets. These adjustments in portfolios have implications for the balance of payments (under some fixity in the exchange rate) and for the exchange rate (when the exchange rate has some variability).

4. In addition, this literature recognizes the importance of investor expectations regarding future asset prices (including the price of foreign exchange, which can be free to vary). The most common procedure hypothesized for the formation of expectations is that of **rational expectations,** whereby forward-looking, utility-maximizing investors utilize all available relevant information and a knowledge of how the economy and the exchange markets work in order to form forecasts.

Asset Demands

As with the monetary approach, the portfolio balance approach specifies the factors that influence the demand for money, but it also specifies the factors that influence the demand for other financial assets. The general framework of the approach is that there are two countries (a home country and a foreign country), two moneys or currencies (domestic money and foreign money), and two nonmoney securities, usually classified as bonds (a home bond and a foreign bond). The domestic bond yields an interest return i_d, while the foreign bond yields an interest return i_f. In this framework we consider below the demand functions for the various assets by home-country citizens. We designate demand for home money as L, demand for the home bond as B_d, and demand for the foreign bond as B_f. The typical home individual is assumed to be able to hold any of these three assets.[5]

Before proceeding with the demand functions, however, it is useful to discuss the relationship specified in portfolio balance models concerning interest rates in the two countries. Because the models assume mobile capital across countries, the uncovered interest parity relationship of the previous chapters is assumed to hold. With somewhat imperfect substitution between domestic and foreign assets, a risk premium term (RP) is also included. Therefore,

$$i_d = i_f + xa - \text{RP} \qquad [13]$$

where xa is the expected percentage change in value of the foreign currency. A positive xa is an expected appreciation of the foreign currency and a negative xa is an expected depreciation of the foreign currency. (Alternatively, a positive xa is an expected depreciation of the home currency, and a negative xa is an expected appreciation of the home currency.) The more formal specific definition of xa is

$$xa = \frac{E(e) - e}{e} = \frac{E(e)}{e} - 1 \qquad [14]$$

where $E(e)$ is the expected future spot exchange rate (expected future home-currency price of foreign currency). The risk premium RP, expressed as a positive percentage, is the extra

---

[4]It is possible that the risk premium could be negative if foreign assets are deemed to carry less risk than domestic assets. We ignore this possibility in our discussion.

[5]We follow the bulk of the literature in assuming that home country citizens do *not* hold foreign currency. This is a simplification but it makes the analysis more manageable than would otherwise be the case.

percentage compensation needed to induce the home investor to hold the foreign asset. With RP positive, $(i_f + xa)$ will be greater than i_d in equilibrium.

Let us now specify the demand functions of a typical home country individual for the three assets of home money, home bonds, and foreign bonds (a parallel set of demand functions exists for foreign individuals). Starting first with the home individual's demand for domestic money, consider the general functional form in expression [15]. (Note: The general framework described here is an adaptation of that presented in a useful article by William Branson and Dale Henderson 1985.)

$$L = f(\overset{-}{i_d}, \overset{-}{i_f}, \overset{-}{xa}, \overset{+}{Y_d}, \overset{+}{P_d}, \overset{+}{W_d}) \qquad [15]$$

where, in addition to the already-identified $i_d, i_f,$ and $xa,$

Y_d = home country real income
P_d = home country price level
W_d = home country real wealth

Note that RP is not included separately in [15] because, with $i_d = i_f + xa -$ RP from [13], RP is a residual and its influence is already embodied in the $i_d, i_f,$ and xa terms. In this expression, the plus or minus sign above each independent variable indicates the expected sign of the relationship between the independent variable and the demand for home money.

How do we explain the predicted signs of expression [15]? First, the negative sign for the i_d is clear from preceding discussions in this chapter. For similar reasons, a rise in i_f will induce the domestic citizen to stop holding as much domestic money and add to holdings of foreign bonds. The influence of xa works in the same manner as does $i_f,$ for a rise in xa indicates that the expected return from holding the foreign bond (which is denominated in foreign currency) has risen. The signs on real income, the domestic price level, and home wealth are as discussed earlier in the monetary approach.

Next consider the demand for domestic bonds or securities by the domestic individual (B_d). We write the demand for the asset as a function of the same independent variables:

$$B_d = h(\overset{+}{i_d}, \overset{-}{i_f}, \overset{-}{xa}, \overset{-}{Y_d}, \overset{-}{P_d}, \overset{+}{W_d}) \qquad [16]$$

These signs are consistent with the investor's motivations as discussed earlier. A rise in i_d will make domestic bonds more attractive because of their higher return. A rise in i_f causes the individual to desire to hold the now higher-yielding foreign bonds instead of domestic bonds, so i_f has a negative sign. A rise in xa acts in the same fashion. The wealth variable behaves as previously indicated for home money demand, but the signs on Y_d and P_d are *negative* in the case of home bond demand. Why so? The reason is rooted in the transactions demand for money. *Ceteris paribus,* a rise in income causes an increase in the transactions demand for money; if total wealth is assumed not to change because of the *ceteris paribus* assumption, then the investor will have to give up some holdings of domestic bonds in order to acquire money. Similar reasoning produces a negative sign for the domestic price level.

The demand function for the third and final asset, the foreign bond (B_f), is expressed in domestic currency by multiplying B_f by e and is given as

$$eB_f = j(\overset{-}{i_d}, \overset{+}{i_f}, \overset{+}{xa}, \overset{-}{Y_d}, \overset{-}{P_d}, \overset{+}{W_d}) \qquad [17]$$

In this demand function, the signs for $Y_d, P_d,$ and W_d can be explained in similar fashion as for the demand for domestic bonds. The signs on the interest rates are reversed from those in the domestic bond situation—a rise in i_d causes the investor to shift out of foreign bonds and into domestic bonds, and a rise in i_f (and in xa) causes bondholders to prefer the foreign bond to the domestic bond.

Once these various demand functions are specified in the portfolio balance model, a key feature of such models is evident: All three assets are substitutes for each other, and therefore any change in any variable will set in motion a whole host of adjustments on the part of investors. Further, it should be noted again that we have only discussed one-half of the demand functions, because foreign citizens are also going to have demand functions for the two bonds and for foreign money. Clearly, a complicated model can emerge.

Portfolio Balance

Given the various demands for assets as indicated earlier, the asset model then specifies supply functions for each asset. As a simplification, we consider the supply of money in each country to be under the control of each country's respective monetary authority. If so, then money supplies are exogenous to the model, meaning that they are determined by outside factors.[6] The supplies of the two bonds are usually treated as exogenous as well. If the bonds are government securities, then fiscal policy can clearly affect the volume of such securities in existence. If the bonds are private securities, decisions on their issuance may also be assumed to be outside the model per se. These bond supplies, together with the money supply (see MacDonald and Taylor 1992, p. 9), define the wealth of the domestic country (W_d) in terms of its own currency as

$$W_d = M_s + B_h + eB_o \qquad [18]$$

where M_s is the money supply of the home country, B_h is the stock of home bonds (government and private) actually held by domestic residents, and B_o is the stock of foreign bonds actually held by domestic residents. The stock of foreign bonds is multiplied by the exchange rate e in order to put the value of those assets into domestic currency terms.

When the asset demands are put together with the asset supplies, financial equilibrium is attained. It is important to note that equilibrium in the financial sector implies that *all* the individual asset markets are in equilibrium simultaneously. Thus, in portfolio balance equilibrium, the amount of each asset desired to be held is equal to the amount that is actually held—home money demand (L) equals the home money supply (M_s), home demand for domestic bonds (B_d) equals the home bonds actually held by domestic residents (B_h), and home demand for foreign bonds (eB_f) equals the stock of foreign bonds actually held by domestic residents (eB_o). The attainment of this equilibrium results in the determination of the equilibrium price of each bond, the equilibrium interest rate in each country, and the *equilibrium exchange rate.* The exchange rate emerges from the model because, in moving to equilibrium, any switches from (to) domestic bonds and money to (from) foreign bonds involve new demands for (supplies of) foreign exchange.

Portfolio Adjustments

Given that investors have reached equilibrium, we now consider several exogenous actions in the economy that will set into motion various adjustments in the financial sector. The overview of these adjustments is that an autonomous disturbance causes asset holders to rearrange their portfolios. The previous equilibrium portfolio for each investor is no longer an equilibrium portfolio; in response, the investors buy and sell the various assets in order to attain their new desired portfolio, whereupon the investors reach a new equilibrium position.

---

[6]However, more complex models allow for an endogenous money supply. This means that the model itself will generate changes in a country's money supply; for example, under fixed exchange rates, a balance-of-payments deficit results in a reduction in the deficit country's money supply as holdings of international reserves by its central bank decline.

1. Consider first the autonomous policy action of a *sale of government securities in the open market by the monetary authorities of the home country* (i.e., a contraction of the home money supply and an increase in the domestic bond supply). The immediate effect of this action is an increase in the home-country interest rate (i_d). How do asset holders react? One response is that the rise in i_d causes domestic citizens to reduce their demand for home money. (See expression [15].) In addition, the demand for foreign bonds will fall (see expression [17]) because of the negative relationship between i_d and eB_f. This decreased demand for foreign bonds occurs on the part not only of domestic asset holders but also of foreign country asset holders (whose demand functions were not shown earlier). Further, as indicated by expression [16], the quantity of domestic bonds demanded will rise because of their higher yield. Finally, foreign-country investors will also switch from holding their own currency to holding the home-country bond. (We did not show the demand function of foreigners for their own currency, but it would parallel [15].) Thus, adjustments take place in the markets for all four assets—the home and foreign currencies and the home and foreign bonds.

These adjustments continue until a new portfolio equilibrium is attained by all investors. Of interest are some of the implications of the adjustment process. For example, what is likely to happen to the foreign interest rate because of the rise in the domestic interest rate? It should be clear that i_f will rise. This will happen because the reduced demand for foreign bonds will drive down the price of foreign bonds and thus increase i_f.

In addition to the impact on i_f, of course, e will change if variability in the exchange rate is permitted. In terms of expression [14],

$$xa = \frac{E(e) - e}{e} = \frac{E(e)}{e} - 1$$

Hence, e will *fall* (the foreign-currency depreciates) because there are fewer purchases of foreign exchange in order to acquire foreign bonds and because there are greater purchases of home currency by foreign citizens in order to acquire domestic bonds.[7] Therefore, holding the expected future exchange rate $E(e)$ constant, *xa rises* because e has fallen. In sum, the previous uncovered interest parity (UIP) of $i_d = i_f + xa -$ RP has been disturbed by a rise in i_d due to the contraction of the domestic money supply. With i_d now greater than $(i_f + xa -$ RP), portfolio adjustments lead to a new equilibrium through a rise in i_f *and* a rise in *xa,* that is, through a rise in the foreign interest rate as well as a rise in the expected future appreciation of the foreign currency.[8]

We will carry this case of a monetary policy action no further, but note that other, "second-round" effects will ensue after the adjustments already discussed. (For example, the rise in i_d may reduce home-country real income.) Nevertheless, what we have said so far indicates the complexity and yet the potential usefulness of the comprehensive view of financial markets offered by the portfolio balance approach. The key point to be

---

[7]Note that, in the portfolio balance model, a rise in i_d causes an appreciation of the home currency. (If the exchange rate were fixed, the result would be a balance-of-payments surplus.) In the other direction, a fall in i_d would cause a depreciation of the home currency (and a BOP deficit with fixed rates). The effect of the interest rate on the exchange rate (or the BOP) is thus opposite to the effect in the monetary approach.

[8]We have also assumed that the risk premium (RP) remains unchanged. In addition, it should be noted that if the depreciation of the foreign currency (the fall in e) leads to a revision of the expected future exchange rate $E(e)$ itself toward a further depreciation of the foreign currency [a fall in $E(e)$], then, in expression [14], $E(e)$ and e will both be falling and the rise in *xa* will be less pronounced or could even be negative. In that case, the equilibrating job to be done for restoring uncovered interest parity by a rise in i_f in response to the rise in i_d will be even greater.

emphasized is that a contraction of the domestic money supply raises the home interest rate, the foreign interest rate, and the expected depreciation (perhaps) of the home currency, as well as causes an appreciation of the spot home currency.

2. As a second example of portfolio adjustments, consider a situation where, for whatever reason, home-country citizens decide that greater home inflation is likely in the future. In other words, individuals in the home country now have *greater inflationary expectations*. With a flexible exchange rate and with some notion of PPP that is often embodied in these models, the expectation of a future price rise at home implies that the home currency will be expected to depreciate. In terms of our demand functions, *xa* rises. What is the outcome from the standpoint of the portfolio adjustment process?

First consider the demand for home money. As expression [15] indicates, home money demand will decrease (the sign of *xa* is negative). In addition, expression [16] shows us that the demand for domestic bonds also decreases. Both of these demands are reduced because investors are demanding more foreign bonds (see expression [17]) in anticipation of the increased yield when converted into home currency at a later date. Thus, the adjustments in the portfolio generate a depreciation of the home currency because there is an excess supply of money at home and an outflow of funds to purchase foreign bonds. Clearly, the expectation of a depreciation can cause a depreciation. A variety of additional effects could be considered, but the important result is that greater inflationary expectations have generated a depreciation of the home currency. (Under a fixed exchange rate, the result would be a BOP deficit.)

3. Next, consider *an increase in real income in the home country*. By looking at the signs of the Y_d variable in [15], [16], and [17], we see the primary effect immediately. With an increase in home income, investors want to hold more domestic money because of an increased transactions demand for money. This point is familiar from the monetary approach. However, the portfolio balance approach enables us to see more explicitly the behavior involved. With increased income, individuals attempt to increase their money holdings by selling both domestic and foreign bonds. (Real income has a negative sign in [16] and [17].) Further, the sale of the foreign bond "improves" the balance of payments under a fixed exchange rate system and leads to an *appreciation of the home currency* under a flexible rate system. This is a result consistent with the monetary approach's view that an increase in income leads to a BOP surplus under fixed rates and to currency appreciation with flexible rates. In the portfolio adjustment model, however, the process is more evident.

4. Now consider an increase in home bond supply, for example, through issuance of new corporate bonds to finance the purchase of physical assets. This rise in domestic bonds/physical assets increases home-country wealth (W_d). What is the implication for the exchange rate? With portfolio diversification, expressions [15], [16], and [17] tell us that home investors will want to hold more domestic money, more domestic bonds, *and* more foreign bonds. If the domestic money supply is unchanged, the increased supply of domestic bonds will lead to a fall in home bond prices and a rise in i_d. Other things equal, the rise in i_d will induce a capital inflow into the home country, and with a flexible exchange rate the capital inflow will lead to an appreciation of the home currency. However, the increased demand for foreign bonds associated with the domestic wealth increase alone will, *ceteris paribus,* lead to a depreciation of the home currency. Hence, without more information on the relative strength of these opposing effects, the direction of impact on the exchange rate of the increase in home bond supply is indeterminate. Nevertheless, if domestic bonds and foreign bonds are good substitutes for each other, the capital inflow

from the relative rise in i_d is likely to yield a substantial increase in the purchase of domestic bonds relative to foreign bonds, offsetting any pure wealth effect on the demand for foreign bonds, and the home currency will on net appreciate. This result seems *prima facie* most likely in practice.

5.   Now consider another change: an increase in home-country wealth because of a home-country current account surplus. First, why does a current account surplus increase the wealth of the country with the surplus? Because, under balance-of-payments accounting, a country that has a current account surplus *must* have a capital account deficit; that is, with a current account surplus, the home country acquires foreign assets due to the net inflow of foreign exchange on current account. This increase in wealth (W_d) will increase the home country's demand for money (by expression [15]), its demand for domestic bonds (by expression [16]) and its demand for foreign bonds (by expression [17]). The increased demand for money will work to increase i_d, while the increased demand for domestic bonds will decrease i_d; hence, the net impact on i_d is indeterminate without more information. In the foreign country (the country with the current account deficit), there is a reduction in wealth and hence in that country's demand for money and its own bonds. The effect on i_f is thus also indeterminate. With uncertainty as to the effect on interest rates, therefore, no firm prediction can be made regarding the effect on the exchange rate. If bond market effects on interest rates dominate money market effects on interest rates, then i_d would fall relative to i_f and the wealth transfer would lead to a depreciation of the home currency relative to the foreign currency.

6.   Now consider one final change: an increase in the supply of foreign bonds because of a foreign government budget deficit (for elaboration, see Rivera-Batiz and Rivera-Batiz 1994, pp. 566–67). With an increase in the supply of already-risky foreign bonds, the risk premium in the UIP expression [13] will rise (and the right-hand side of the expression will thus fall). Other things equal, this would serve to *appreciate the home currency* (depreciate the foreign currency). In addition, if the foreign government budget deficit is associated with the expectation that foreign prices will rise, this too could cause a (purchasing power parity type of) depreciation of the foreign currency (appreciation of the home currency). Another useful way to think of the situation is that the increase in the supply of foreign currency–denominated bonds requires a reduction in their price to sell some of the new bonds to home-country investors. Such a price reduction to home investors can be accomplished by reducing e, since e multiplied by the foreign-currency price of the bonds gives the price to home-country investors of those bonds. No matter how the mechanism is viewed, the portfolio balance model suggests that a government budget deficit financed by issuing new bonds will depreciate the currency of the country with the government budget deficit.

Finally, it should be noted that, in the preceding six examples and in the portfolio balance model generally, the existence of a BOP surplus or deficit, or of a home-currency appreciation or depreciation, is only temporary. It occurs only while the adjustment process to the new equilibrium portfolios is taking place. Once the new desired portfolios have been attained, there is no longer any net flow out of or into foreign securities to or from domestic money or bonds, and the balance-of-payments imbalance or the exchange rate change ceases. A BOP deficit or surplus (and a depreciation or appreciation) will not exist once **asset stock equilibrium** (i.e., a simultaneous equilibrium of demands and supplies of all financial assets) has been achieved. Therefore, the presence of a continuing BOP imbalance or a continuing exchange rate change must mean that equilibrium in portfolio holdings has not been attained. The persistent disequilibrium occurs either from a slow adjustment process or from continuing exogenous changes.

EXCHANGE RATE OVERSHOOTING

Many different asset market models exist in the literature, and we have barely scratched the surface in discussing their characteristics. However, one additional feature of a large number of these models is that (within a flexible exchange rate framework) they often involve **exchange rate overshooting.** "Overshooting" occurs when, in moving from one equilibrium to another, the exchange rate goes beyond the new equilibrium but then returns to it. We present below two treatments of this phenomenon.

The first explanation of overshooting draws upon the work of Rudiger Dornbusch (1976). However, we adopt some simplifications to keep the discussion consistent with previous material in this chapter. These simplifications mean that it is not truly the Dornbusch model in some respects. Nevertheless, the general conclusions are those of Dornbusch, and these conclusions have been very influential in the literature and in interpretations of real-world events. As will be seen, Dornbusch focuses on two key phenomena—short-run asset market behavior and long-run PPP behavior.

Turning first to the asset market, Dornbusch assumes that the home country is a "small country," which in this context means that the country has no effect on world interest rates. In addition, perfect capital mobility is assumed, meaning that home and foreign financial assets are perfect substitutes (and that there is no risk premium). These assumptions mean that an equation similar to our earlier uncovered interest parity expression [13] (without the risk premium) applies. Hence:

$$i_d = i_f + xa \qquad\qquad [19]$$

where i_d and xa have the same meaning as in [13]. The term i_f in this expression refers to the given *world* interest rate. Dornbusch assumes that, because perfect capital mobility exists, there is extremely rapid adjustment in the asset market. Hence, the asset market equilibrium relationship in expression [19] quickly reestablishes itself if disturbed.

Let's begin by reviewing asset/money market equilibrium. Consider how goods prices and exchange rate behavior are reflected in equation [19] and how equilibrium is restored following a disturbance. Suppose the home price level rises. A higher price level will lead to an increase in the transactions demand for money and, with an assumed fixed money supply, i_d will rise. Thus, for the moment, i_d is greater than $(i_f + xa)$. Because i_f is fixed by outside world conditions, the entire asset market adjustment in [19] must come through xa. Now recall from our earlier discussions that an increase in the transactions demand for money will lead to an appreciation of the exchange rate. This appreciation plays a crucial role in restoring asset market equilibrium. The home currency must appreciate enough so that investors begin to *expect* it to *depreciate* toward its original level. More precisely, because of the inflation the home currency must appreciate until its expected rate of depreciation, $xa,$ is high enough to make the right-hand side of [19] equal to the now higher left-hand side. Thus, if i_d was originally 8 percent and i_f was also 8 percent, there was no expected depreciation of the home currency (or expected appreciation of the foreign currency). However, if the price rise and the resulting increased home demand for money raise i_d to 10 percent, xa must increase to 2 percent for equilibrium to be restored.

TITANS OF INTERNATIONAL ECONOMICS:

RUDIGER DORNBUSCH (1942–2002)

Rudiger Dornbusch was born on June 8, 1942, in Krefeld, Germany. He did undergraduate work in Geneva before coming to the United States in 1966, whereupon he entered the University of Chicago and received his Ph.D. in 1971. He was an assistant professor at Chicago in 1971 and at the University of Rochester in 1972–1973 and an associate professor at the Massachusetts Institute of Technology from 1975 to 1977. He was rapidly promoted to full professor at MIT in 1977, and later he was appointed Ford International Professor of Economics. He also held positions at Fundação Getúlio Vargas in Rio de Janeiro and at the Universidad del Pacífico in Lima, Peru.

Professor Dornbusch was an acknowledged expert on macroeconomics in an open economy context. His best-known work in that area is his "Expectations and Exchange Rate Dynamics" (*Journal of Political Economy,* December 1976). This paper is a classic pioneering piece on "overshooting" of exchange rates beyond their equilibrium level: it is cited on almost any occasion when overshooting is discussed, and it has been the source of a multitude of graduate examination questions. Also well known is his article "Devaluation, Money and Non-traded Goods" (*American Economic Review,* December 1973). This paper is a landmark for its incorporation of the nontraded sector into the analysis of exchange rate changes—a necessary incorporation since such changes affect all relative prices in the economy, not only the prices of traded goods. In addition, he wrote a widely respected intermediate level textbook, *Open Economy Macroeconomics.*

Professor Dornbusch also made his mark in other areas of economics, an achievement that is rare in this age of academic specialization. His paper (with Stanley Fischer and Paul A. Samuelson) "Comparative Advantage, Trade, and Payments in a Ricardian Model with a Continuum of Goods" (*American Economic Review,* December 1977) is regarded as the classic work on the extension of the Ricardian international trade model to a multicommodity world. More recently, Professor Dornbusch wrote on the external debt of developing countries and liberalization, which resulted in great demand for his consulting and advising services. In addition, in 1994 he coauthored a paper (with Alejandro Werner) that predicted the soon-to-occur Mexican peso crisis.

Besides his direct scholarly contributions and his policy advising, Professor Dornbusch served as co-editor of the *Journal of International Economics,* associate editor of the *Quarterly Journal of Economics* and the *Journal of Finance,* and advisor to the Institute for International Economics in Washington, DC. In addition, he was honored as a Guggenheim Fellow and as a Fellow of the American Academy of Arts and Sciences. He was also a vice president of the American Economic Association in 1990. He passed away on July 25, 2002.

Sources: Mark Blaug, ed., *Who's Who in Economics: A Biographical Dictionary of Major Economists 1700–1986,* 2nd ed. (Cambridge: MA: MIT Press, 1986), pp. 227–28; Rudiger Dornbusch, John H. Makin, and David Zlowe, eds., *Alternative Solutions to Developing-Country Debt Problems* (Washington, DC: American Enterprise Institute for Public Policy Research, 1989), p. xi; *Who's Who in America,* 47th ed., 1992–93, vol. 1 (New Providence, NJ: Marquis Who's Who, 1992), p. 896; Stanley Fischer, "Globalization and Its Challenges," *American Economic Review* 93, no. 2 (May 2003), pp. 1–30.

The equilibrium asset market schedule is shown in Figure 1 as line *AA.* The price level is represented on the vertical axis and the exchange rate on the horizontal axis. The previous paragraph has essentially explained the negative slope of this curve. Suppose that an initial equilibrium position is point *B,* with price level P_1 and exchange rate e_1. If there is a rise in the price level to P_2, a vertical movement to point *C* occurs. However, the higher prices and the accompanying increase in the demand for money set in motion an appreciation of the home currency (a decrease in *e*). This appreciation continues until point *F* is reached, with exchange rate e_2. Although Figure 1 does not show *xa* directly, the expected depreciation associated with e_2 is such that the asset market is again in equilibrium. The line *AA* thus shows all combinations of *P* and *e* that yield equilibrium in the asset market.

Let us now turn to the PPP feature of the Dornbusch model and consider how *P* and *e* are related to each other in the goods market. In the *short run* in the goods market, there is no

FIGURE 1   **Asset Market Equilibrium in the Dornbusch Model**

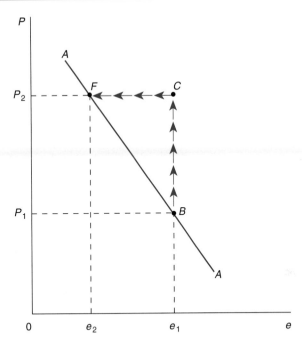

The AA schedule shows the various combinations of the price level P and the exchange rate e that satisfy the asset market equilibrium condition that $i_d = i_f + xa$. If, from an initial equilibrium position such as point B, the price level rises from P_1 to P_2, movement occurs to point C. This rise in prices increases the transactions demand for money, which, with a fixed money supply, increases domestic interest rate i_d. The increase in money demand causes the home currency to appreciate, indicated by the fall in e from e_1 to e_2. At new equilibrium point F, the equilibrium condition $i_d = i_f + xa$ is again satisfied. Because i_d has increased but the world interest rate i_f is fixed, equilibrium requires that xa increase by the amount by which i_d exceeds i_f. In other words, e must appreciate sufficiently to generate expectations of a future depreciation by the difference between the domestic interest rate and the world interest rate.

particular neatly specified relationship because goods prices are assumed to be "sticky"; that is, they adjust slowly to changing conditions. (In view of this price "stickiness," the Dornbusch model is often called a "fixed-price" monetary model as distinct from a "flexible-price" monetary model such as that used in the early part of this chapter.) This is in contrast to the asset market, where there is very quick adjustment from one equilibrium to another. However, in the *long run,* goods prices do adjust fully to the changed conditions in the economy. In the simple version of the Dornbusch model considered here, the economy is assumed to be at full employment and real income does not change. (A more complicated Dornbusch version drops this assumption.) In this situation, a depreciation of the home-country currency will, *when goods prices eventually adjust,* cause a proportional change in the home price level. This PPP relationship is depicted by the straight line from the origin, $0L$, in Figure 2. (Ignore the other features of the graph for the moment.) The line is upward sloping because depreciation of the home currency creates excess demand for home goods. The excess demand arises because exports are now cheaper to foreign buyers and because import substitutes produced at home are now relatively less expensive to home consumers. This excess demand will eventually bid prices up in proportional fashion.

Given these relationships between P and e in the asset and goods markets, let us now address the phenomenon of overshooting. In Figure 2 the asset market schedule AA from

FIGURE 2   **Adjustment to an Increase in the Money Supply in the Dornbusch Model**

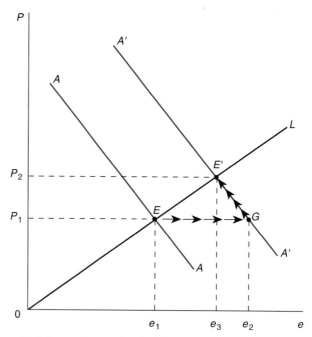

The ray $0L$ from the origin indicates the proportional relationship between changes in e and changes in P in the long run when goods prices adjust. The AA line is the asset market equilibrium schedule from Figure 1. Starting from long-run equilibrium point E, an increase in the money supply shifts AA to $A'A'$. With sticky goods prices, the exchange rate moves from e_1 to e_2. This depreciation of the home currency occurs until (the new, lower) i_d again equals $i_f + xa$ at point G. The term xa must become negative to restore equilibrium in the asset market, meaning that the home currency must depreciate until its expected appreciation matches the difference between the fixed i_f and i_d. As goods prices eventually begin to rise, movement occurs along $A'A'$ until the new long-run equilibrium position E' is reached. Exchange rate overshooting has occurred because the exchange rate change from e_1 to e_2 exceeds the long-run equilibrium rate change from e_1 to e_3.

Figure 1 and the goods market schedule $0L$ are put together. The initial equilibrium position is at E, where both markets are in equilibrium. The equilibrium exchange rate is e_1, and prices are in equilibrium at P_1. This is a long-run equilibrium position; therefore, e_1 is expected to persist. With e_1 expected to persist, $xa = 0$.

From this equilibrium position E, suppose that the monetary authorities now increase the money supply. The first effect of this action is a rightward shift in the AA schedule, to $A'A'$. This shift occurs because there is now an excess supply of money at the old equilibrium P and e. An elimination of this excess supply requires an increase in e and/or an increase in P, both of which increase the transactions demand for money and serve to absorb the excess supply. But, because goods prices are sticky and there is very rapid adjustment in the asset market, the adjustment occurs through the exchange rate and the next step is a horizontal movement from E to point G. This movement indicates a depreciation of the home currency (from e_1 to e_2). The depreciation occurs because the increased money supply has lowered domestic interest rates, and thus asset holders will shift their portfolios from home securities to foreign securities in order to earn a higher interest return. More importantly, asset holders expect a future depreciation of the home currency because of the money supply increase, and this will also cause home assets to be sold and foreign assets to be bought. The capital outflow resulting from these motivations will depreciate the home currency.

These adjustments take place quickly. The new equilibrium position *in the asset market* is found on the new asset equilibrium schedule $A'A'$ at point G. Because asset market equilibrium requires that $i_d = i_f + xa$, xa must be *negative* at point G because i_d has fallen while i_f is fixed. In other words, in the new asset equilibrium position, the home currency has depreciated so much that it is now *expected to appreciate*. (Remember that a negative xa is an expected depreciation of the foreign currency or an expected appreciation of the home currency.) This result occurs at e_2.

What happens after point G is attained? Recalling that the asset market maintains itself in equilibrium, upward movement takes place along the $A'A'$ schedule until E' is reached. This movement occurs because goods prices finally start to rise because of the excess demand for goods associated with the depreciated value of the home currency. As goods prices rise, the consequent increased transactions demand for money bids up the domestic interest rate, which results in an appreciation of the home currency until E' is attained. At long-run equilibrium position E', both the goods and asset markets are again in equilibrium. In comparison with original equilibrium E, expansionary monetary policy has raised prices (from P_1 to P_2) and has increased the exchange rate (depreciated the home currency) from e_1 to e_3.

There are two points to be emphasized. The most important one is that the exchange rate has indeed "overshot" its long-run equilibrium level. From e_1 it has risen to e_2 (depreciation of home currency) and then has fallen to e_3 (appreciation of home currency). Second, however, note that, in the adjustment from point G to point E', the home currency is appreciating at the same time that domestic prices are rising! This is hardly a result that conventional theory would lead us to expect. The Dornbusch model, in overview, has offered a mechanism that, in the opinion of many economists, has value in interpreting experiences in the post-1973 period, when most industrialized countries have had floating exchange rates.

Moving away from the Dornbusch model, with its incorporation of uncovered interest parity, overshooting can also occur in a framework that emphasizes covered interest parity and hence the forward market. (See Michael Melvin 2000, pp. 178–81.) To begin, recall from previous chapters that the covered interest parity condition between money markets is

$$i_d = i_f + (e_{fwd} - e)/e \tag{20}$$

where i_d is the domestic interest rate, i_f is the foreign interest rate (no longer necessarily a fixed world rate), e_{fwd} is the forward rate for foreign currency, and e is the spot rate for foreign currency. In other words, covered interest parity occurs when the domestic interest rate is equal to the foreign interest rate plus the forward premium on the foreign currency. If i_f is greater than i_d, then the foreign currency will be at a forward discount [that is, a negative forward premium because $(e_{fwd} - e)/e$ will be negative]. If i_d exceeds i_f, interest arbitrage will yield a positive forward premium.

How does [20] relate to [13] without the risk premium (or to expression [19])? The modern literature on exchange rates utilizes the concept of "efficiency" in the exchange markets. Efficiency in this context exists when the *current forward rate equals* the expected future spot rate. The key to this equality can be seen as follows: Suppose that the expected price of the Swiss franc in three months [the expected future spot rate, $E(e)$] is $0.75 per Swiss franc and the current forward rate on Swiss francs, e_{fwd}, is $0.73 per Swiss franc. In this situation, a speculator will buy Swiss francs on the forward market at $0.73 per Swiss franc at the present time because the speculator anticipates that, in three months, the Swiss francs can be sold for $0.75 per Swiss franc. Clearly this will put upward pressure on the current forward rate of the Swiss franc until an equilibrium is reached at which $E(e)$ equals e_{fwd} (ignoring transaction costs). Similarly, if the expected future spot rate is less than the current forward rate, speculators will sell the Swiss francs forward because they anticipate that Swiss francs can be bought in the future (to cover the forward sale obligation) at less than the forward price to be received. This sale of forward Swiss francs drives e_{fwd} down until it eventually is equal to $E(e)$. Speculative activity thus ensures that $E(e) = e_{fwd}$. If $E(e)$ is equal to e_{fwd} in practice—an extremely difficult hypothesis to test because of the empirical problem of ascertaining expectations—the exchange market is said to be an **efficient exchange market.** This term means that there are no unexploited profit opportunities.

The implications of this discussion for expression [20] are straightforward. That expression was

$$i_d = i_f + (e_{fwd} - e)/e$$

which can now be rewritten through substitution of $E(e)$ for e_{fwd} (because the two terms are equal to each other) as

$$i_d = i_f + [E(e) - e]/e$$

But $[E(e) - e]/e$ is simply the expected percentage change in the current e. Hence, $[E(e) - e]/e = xa$. Through further substitution we obtain

$$i_d = i_f + xa$$

which is expression [19] or expression [13] (without the risk premium), or uncovered interest parity. Thus, with an efficient market, covered and uncovered parity both hold, or, alternatively, the expected appreciation of the foreign currency is equal to the forward premium on the foreign currency. Hence, a currency with a forward price above its spot price is expected to increase in value, and a currency with a forward price below its spot price is expected to decline in value.

Let us return now to overshooting, using [20]. Suppose that beginning at the equilibrium position of [20], the domestic monetary authorities now increase the home money supply. Assuming little slack in the economy, the increase in the money supply causes individuals to expect that the home price level will rise. Because the higher prices will produce the expectation of an incipient BOP deficit, this means that market participants expect e to rise along with the price level. But the new expected spot rate, $E(e)$, will generate (as we have just seen) a new forward rate equal to it, because $E(e)$ must be the same as e_{fwd}. The result is that, in [20], the term $[e_{fwd} - e]/e$ will increase.

But wait a minute! In expression [20], i_d is equal to $i_f + (e_{fwd} - e)/e$, but we have just increased the right-hand side at the same time that we have *decreased* the left-hand side. The left-hand side (i_d) decreased because the increased home money supply has depressed the domestic interest rate. How is covered interest parity able to be maintained? The answer is that the two sides of the equation are made equal again by a rise in e, the current exchange rate. In fact, e must rise by *more* than e_{fwd} to maintain interest arbitrage equilibrium. If this adjustment in e did not occur, $i_f + (e_{fwd} - e)/e$ would be greater than i_d and interest arbitragers would have an incentive to send funds overseas by purchasing spot foreign exchange and simultaneously selling forward foreign exchange. Thus, after the increase in the money supply, interest arbitragers bid up e sufficiently so that the equilibrium in [20] is reestablished.

In this analysis, Melvin, like Dornbusch, hypothesizes that the prices of goods adjust slowly relative to the speed of adjustment in the exchange markets. When the price level finally does start to rise after the reestablishment of equilibrium in expression [20], there is an excess demand for money in the home country (due to the higher price level), and i_d therefore begins to rise. When i_d rises, there is an inflow of funds, so the home currency begins to appreciate. When prices have eventually adjusted to their new equilibrium level, the system settles down. The domestic currency has ultimately depreciated from its original level (i.e., e has risen) because of the increase in the money supply, but notice that the exchange rate adjustment (an overall depreciation) was accomplished by an initial larger depreciation that was then followed by an appreciation. Hence, the exchange rate overshot its new long-run equilibrium position, then returned to that position.

This concludes (thankfully?) our discussion of the phenomenon of overshooting. Many models have been developed to explain this phenomenon, and they have emerged in response to exchange rate behavior among the industrialized countries since 1973. As well as emphasizing stock equilibrium positions and adjustments, differential speeds of adjustment in different markets, and expectations, this literature has incorporated other influences such as "speculative bubbles," the role of surprising "news," and policy "reaction functions" on the part of the monetary authorities. While we do not go further in our development of overshooting, it should be clear that the complexity of the real world means that exchange rates do not always move smoothly and directly from one long-run equilibrium position to another.

CONCEPT CHECK

1. Why can the existence of a risk premium mean that $(i_f + xa)$ can exceed i_d in equilibrium?
2. In the portfolio balance model, why does a rise in domestic wealth lead to an appreciation of the home currency?
3. What will happen to the value of a country's currency in the foreign exchange markets if the country's citizens suddenly revise upward

their expectations of the home inflation rate? Why?

4. In the Dornbusch overshooting model, how is it possible that a country's currency can be appreciating at the same time that its price level is rising relative to the price level in other countries?

SUMMARY

The monetary approach to the balance of payments interprets a country's BOP deficits or surpluses (with fixed exchange rates) and currency depreciations or appreciations (with flexible exchange rates) as the results of a disequilibrium between the country's supply of and demand for money. If there is an excess supply of money, then a BOP deficit (or home-currency depreciation) will occur during the process of moving to equilibrium. Similarly, an excess demand for money generates a BOP surplus (or home-currency appreciation). The approach enables the analyst to make predictions concerning the effect on the external sector of changes in such economic variables as price levels, levels of real income, and interest rates.

The portfolio balance approach goes further than the monetary approach in that it incorporates expectations, other assets besides money, and a risk premium because home and foreign financial assets are imperfect substitutes. Investors hold an equilibrium portfolio of the various assets, and changes in economic

variables and conditions affect the composition and size of the desired portfolios. Recognizing that asset markets across industrialized countries are well (though not perfectly) integrated, the conclusion emerges that changes in absolute and relative demands and supplies of assets will have impacts on interest rates and exchange rates. A particular feature that has attracted widespread attention is the conclusion that exchange rate "overshooting" can occur.

In overview of the monetary and portfolio balance approaches, their objective is to explain the behavior of the external sector in an environment where countries are closely interrelated and where exchange rates change frequently and sizably (such as among major industrialized countries since 1973). They focus not on the current account but on the asset exchanges (financial/capital) that heavily influence exchange rates today (especially in the short run). With these approaches in mind, we turn next to other features of the exchange market, including considerations of the current account.

KEY TERMS

asset stock equilibrium
contractionary monetary policy
demand for money
domestic reserves
efficient exchange market
excess demand for money
excess supply of money
exchange rate overshooting

expansionary monetary policy
incipient BOP deficit
incipient BOP surplus
international reserves
monetary approach to the balance
   of payments
monetary approach to the exchange
   rate

monetary base
money multiplier
portfolio balance (asset market)
   approach
rational expectations
transactions demand for money

QUESTIONS AND PROBLEMS

1. Suppose that there is an increase in national income in a country. Under a fixed exchange rate system, according to the monetary approach, will the country's balance of payments (official reserve transactions balance) move toward surplus or toward deficit? Why? How would you modify your explanation (though not your conclusion) if you were using the portfolio balance approach in a fixed exchange rate context?

2. "A higher price level will increase the demand for money, but expectations of a rise in the price level will reduce the demand for money." Is this statement true or false according to the monetary approach? Why?

3. In the simple framework where $M_s = kPY$, suppose that k increases because of a change in the institutions of payment (e.g., people get paid larger amounts on a less frequent basis). What effect will this institutional change have on the country's exchange rate in a flexible exchange rate system? Explain.

4. Why is relative purchasing power parity (PPP) more likely to hold in a hyperinflationary period than in a more "normal" period of price behavior?

5. Do you think that the monetary approach is a satisfactory explanation of a country's exchange rate? Why or why not?

6. In the portfolio balance model, what effect, other things equal, will a foreign government's budget deficit financed by issuing bonds have on the home country's currency value and why? (Assume a flexible exchange rate.)

7. In the portfolio balance model, what effect will a rise in i_d have on the value of the domestic currency with a flexible exchange rate? Why? Why would this *not* be the result in the monetary approach?

8. "An increase in a country's money supply can result in a depreciation of the country's currency that 'overshoots' its long-run equilibrium level." Defend this statement.

9. What reasons can you suggest to support the standard assumption that asset markets adjust more rapidly to a disequilibrium situation than do goods markets?

10. Why is $i_f + xa$ equal to $i_f + (e_{fwd} - e)/e$ in an efficient exchange market (with no risk premium)?

11. In your view, what are the strengths of the portfolio balance or asset market approach as an explanation of exchange rate determination? What are the weaknesses of the approach?

 Appendix   A BRIEF LOOK AT EMPIRICAL WORK ON THE MONETARY AND PORTFOLIO BALANCE APPROACHES

EMPIRICAL TESTING ON THE MONETARY APPROACH

There has been a considerable amount of empirical testing of relationships in the monetary approach model. We present in this section a brief discussion of a few of these tests.

    We turn first to tests of the monetary approach under fixed exchange rates, focusing briefly on one early representative test. Junichi Ujiie (1978) did work on Japan for the fixed-rate period 1959–1972. His general testing equation was[9]

$$BOP = a + b\,\Delta D + c\,\Delta i^* + f\,\Delta Y \qquad [21]$$

---

[9]In the interest of simplicity, we are not listing all of Ujiie's independent variables.

The dependent variable is the balance-of-payments position.[10] If BOP is positive, there is an official reserve transactions surplus (or an inflow of international reserves) while a negative number constitutes a deficit (or an outflow of international reserves). On the right-hand side, a is a constant term, ΔD represents the change in domestic credit (which influences the monetary base), Δi^* indicates the change in *foreign* interest rates, and ΔY indicates the change in Japanese real income.[11] Ujiie hypothesized that an exogenous rise in domestic credit would worsen the BOP (a negative b), an exogenous rise in foreign interest rates would reduce the foreign demand for money and thus lead to a BOP surplus for Japan (positive c), and an exogenous increase in Japan's income would increase the demand for money, leading to a positive effect on the BOP (positive f).

After carrying out various tests, Ujiie's general conclusion was that the domestic credit variable clearly performed as expected (i.e., b was always negative in a statistically significant sense). On the other hand, he could not make any firm statements as to the signs of c and f. Hence, this test is robust with respect to the influence of changes in domestic credit and thereby the money supply, but uncertainty exists regarding the relationships of foreign interest rates and domestic income to the balance of payments. It seems fair to say that, considering Ujiie's and others' work with respect to a fixed-rate system, the money supply does seem to have its predicted relationship with the BOP position. However, there is disagreement as to the influence of other included variables.

We now turn to brief summaries of two empirical studies of the monetary approach under a flexible exchange rate regime. The first study was done by Jacob Frenkel (1978), former economic counselor of the International Monetary Fund and former governor of the Bank of Israel. The period examined is a favorite one chosen for studying the monetary approach—the German hyperinflation after World War I.[12] Frenkel employed natural logarithms of variables, an approach which results in the estimated coefficients of the independent variables being *elasticities*. Thus, a coefficient of 2.0 on an independent variable means that a 1 percent rise in the value of the independent variable would be associated with a 2 percent rise in the value of the dependent variable.

The Frenkel testing equation for the behavior of the German exchange rate from February 1921 through August 1923 was

$$\log e = a + b \log M_s + c \log E(\dot{p}) \qquad [22]$$

where: e = exchange rate (units of German marks per one U.S. dollar)
  a = a constant term
  M_s = German money supply
  $E(\dot{p})$ = a measure of inflationary expectations in Germany[13]

If the monetary approach has validity, b would be positive. Indeed, if the exchange rate moves proportionately with the money supply, we can make a stronger statement—that b should be 1.0. The term c is also expected to be positive, because greater expected price rises lead individuals to reduce their demand for money. This would generate an excess supply of money and a depreciation of the currency. The term a has no expected sign a priori and is inconsequential for our purposes.

For the German hyperinflation period, Frenkel found b to be highly significant statistically, with a value of +0.975. Thus, the exchange rate depreciated virtually proportionately with the money supply. In addition, the c term was a highly significant +0.591. This result is also consistent with the

---

[10]The *dependent* variable in a testing equation is the variable on the left-hand side, the variable being "explained." The *independent* variables, on the right-hand side of the equation, are variables thought to have a causal influence on the dependent variable. The terms such as b, c, and f show the extent of influence and are called the *coefficients* of the independent variables.

[11]In his tests, Ujiie actually employed the concept of "permanent income" rather than current income, but this is immaterial for our purposes.

[12]Hyperinflation is a situation where prices are rising extremely rapidly, such as more than 1,000 percent per year. In Germany during 1920–1923, the wholesale price index (1913 = 1.0) was 14.40 in December 1920 and 1,200,400,000,000 in December 1923. See Graham (1930, pp. 105–06).

[13]We will not go into details on the inflationary expectations measure. Economists have devised several such measures and have quarreled continuously over them.

monetary approach. The Frenkel test (among others) gives substantial support for the monetary approach to the exchange rate. In criticism, the point has often been raised that, in conditions of hyperinflation, prices dominate all other influences and the money supply dominates prices to the exclusion of all other factors. (Frenkel had also found a virtual identity of the movements of German price indexes with changes in the German money supply.) Thus, strong support for the monetary approach is almost inevitable. If more normal conditions rather than hyperinflation are selected, critics of the monetary approach doubt that such powerful results could be found.

A test for a nonhyperinflationary period was conducted by Rudiger Dornbusch (1980). Dornbusch considered the 1973–1979 period, during which there was sizable inflation by developed-country standards, but by no means was there an experience similar to that of Germany in the 1920s. In addition, there was substantial flexibility in the exchange rates of major industrialized countries.

Dornbusch estimated the following equation:

$$e = a + b(m_s - m_s^*) + c(y - y^*) + d(i - i^*)_s + f(i - i^*)_L \qquad [23]$$

This equation was estimated for five industrialized countries (Canada, France, Japan, the United Kingdom, the United States) as a group against West Germany, with the five countries being treated as the "home" country and West Germany as the "foreign" country. In this equation, e refers to the natural logarithm of the dollar-per-mark exchange rate.[14] The term a is again a constant term with no a priori expectation as to sign. The term m_s is the logarithm of the group's money supply, while m_s^* is the logarithm of the West German money supply. Similarly, y is the logarithm of real income in the group, while y^* is the logarithm of West German real income. The i and i^* terms refer to interest rates in the five countries and in West Germany, respectively. The subscript S refers to short-term interest rates and subscript L refers to long-term interest rates.

Consistent with the monetary approach, we expect b, d, and f to be positive. A faster rate of growth of money in the other countries relative to Germany [as reflected in an increase in the $(m_s - m_s^*)$ term] should result in an appreciation of the mark (i.e., e should rise). Similarly, an exogenous increase in interest rates in the other countries relative to Germany [as reflected in an increase in the $(i - i^*)$ terms] should cause an appreciation of the mark.[15] On the other hand, a faster increase in real income in the other countries than in Germany [an increase in $(y - y^*)$] should increase the relative demand for money in the other countries (according to the monetary approach). This will lead to an appreciation of the other currencies and a depreciation of the mark. Hence, c is expected to be negative.

Dornbusch's results were hardly encouraging for the applicability of the monetary approach for explaining exchange rate movements. Only the coefficients on the interest rates were of the expected sign and were also statistically significant. Dornbusch concluded that, at least from his testing, there is "little doubt that the monetary approach . . . is an unsatisfactory theory of exchange rate determination" (Dornbusch 1980, p. 151).

Given the sharply contrasting conclusions of Dornbusch and Frenkel with respect to the monetary approach to the exchange rate, there has been controversy over the validity of this approach. In a survey of relevant literature for the post-1973 period, when the exchange rates of major industrialized countries have been fluctuating, MacDonald and Taylor (1992, p. 11) offered the summary statement that the "monetary approach appears reasonably well supported for the period up to 1978" but that this is not true for studies using sample years after that time (into which they place the above Dornbusch study). In particular, Mark Taylor (1995, p. 29) noted that the later estimating equations for exchange rates often contained incorrect signs. For example, estimates for the dollar/mark exchange rate yielded results that implied that an increase in the German money supply would cause the mark to *appreciate*. There has been controversy over this relationship, as some economists think the unexpected sign is the result of mis-specifications in the equations, especially with respect to wealth effects. For instance, if wealth is increasing (perhaps due to an increase in the money supply itself),

---

[14]More precisely, it is the logarithm of the weighted-average value of the five countries' currencies expressed in terms of dollars per mark.

[15]Remember that in the monetary approach, a rise in the domestic interest rate reduces the demand for money, leading to an excess supply of money. The excess money supply generates depreciation. In this test, an increase in i will lead to depreciation of the five countries' currencies, that is, an appreciation of the mark.

individuals might wish to hold more mark-denominated assets. This could raise the value of the mark and more than offset the mark depreciation that would be expected under the monetary approach when the German money supply increased.

Two factors contributed to a revival in applied research on the economics of exchange rates. The application of new time-series methods (known as nonstationarity methods) to exchange rate analysis is the first. Frankel and Rose (1995) find that the monetary models received the most attention, but, in spite of new methods, they have not performed particularly well since the 1970s. Rogoff (1999) also maintains a pessimistic view of the monetary models. On the other hand, MacDonald and Taylor (1993, 1994), Chinn and Meese (1995), and MacDonald and Marsh (1997) have experienced success with the monetary model. These results led MacDonald (1999) to hold a more optimistic view of monetary models of exchange rates.

A second contributing factor has been the opportunity to examine exchange rate trends in the transition countries, particularly those slated for EU membership. Crespo-Cuaresma, Fidrmuc, and MacDonald (2005) used the monetary approach in their analysis of exchange rates in the Czech Republic, Hungary, Poland, Romania, Slovakia, and Slovenia. Their results indicate that the monetary model provides a relatively good explanation of the behavior of nominal exchange rates in a panel of six Central and Eastern European transition countries. By computing the equilibrium exchange rates based on monetary and real development in the nations, the results suggest that the nominal exchange rates against the euro may be overvalued particularly in the Czech Republic and Slovenia.

TESTING OF THE PORTFOLIO BALANCE MODEL

We briefly look now at empirical studies regarding the portfolio balance or asset market approach. Relatively little work has been done on testing the portfolio balance or asset market model because of difficulties encountered in relating the theoretical models to real-world data. In particular, as noted in Taylor (1995, p. 30), questions arise as to which nonmoney assets to include and how to obtain uniform data across countries. Further, uncertainty exists as to how to quantify the risk premium that reflects the imperfect substitutability of domestic and foreign assets.

The first test we examine is that of Jeffrey Frankel (1984). While all such studies face the problem that there are inadequate data on the composition of portfolios, Frankel employed various assumptions to obtain estimates for the 1973–1979 period and then tested hypothesized relationships. The dependent variable in his testing equations was the home currency/dollar exchange rate. (The "home country" in his analysis consists of five developed countries—Canada, France, West Germany, Japan, and the United Kingdom; the "foreign country" is the United States.) The independent variables were (1) wealth in the home country, W_h; (2) wealth in the foreign country (the United States), W_{US}; (3) the supply of home currency—denominated assets on the world market, B_h; and (4) the supply of foreign currency—(dollar-) denominated assets on the world market, B_{US}. (Note: The B terms have a slightly different meaning than they did in our earlier discussion because they apply to the entire world market, not only to holdings by domestic citizens.)

In terms of the portfolio balance model, W_h was expected to have a negative sign because increased wealth in the home country (e.g., West Germany) appreciates the home currency (see example 4 on page 559 in the chapter text and assume that the substitution effect between domestic and foreign bonds dominates the pure wealth effect), and thus the mark/dollar rate will fall. An increase in U.S. real wealth for analogous reasons causes the mark/dollar rate to rise and produces a positive sign for W_{US}. An increase in the supply of mark-denominated bonds B_h (such as through a German government budget deficit) would increase the mark/dollar exchange rate—generating a positive sign. (This follows from the discussion in example 6 on page 560.) Finally, for analogous reasons, a rise in the supply of foreign (U.S.) assets would generate a negative sign for B_{US}. More than half of the signs Frankel obtained for the 1973–1979 period were not as expected. While not all of these signs were statistically significant in his test, it is clear that the results are not very satisfactory from the standpoint of the portfolio balance model. The "wrong sign" occurred in two countries for W_h and B_h (Germany and the United Kingdom) and in three countries for B_{US} (France, Germany, and the United Kingdom); and only Canada had the correct sign for W_{US}.

Turning to other literature, attention has focused (despite the difficulties) on isolating the risk premium in the uncovered interest parity equilibrium equation $i_d = i_f + xa - RP$. A study by Kathryn Dominguez and Jeffrey Frankel (1993) attempted to measure the risk premium through survey data on exchange rate expectations. The risk premium was then tested as to its relationship to exchange rate variations (of the dollar/mark and dollar/Swiss franc rates) and to the composition of wealth between domestic and foreign assets. Of importance for this chapter, there did seem to be an association between relative size of domestic to foreign assets in portfolios and the risk premium that is consistent with the portfolio balance model's assumption that home and foreign assets are imperfect substitutes. (See also Taylor 1995, pp. 30–31.)

Among other studies, some interesting work was done by Richard Meese (1990) and by Meese and Kenneth Rogoff (1983). They attempted to ascertain whether standard asset market models can be of value in forecasting the exchange rate. The procedure first was to obtain, from several years data, an equation with the exchange rate as the dependent variable, using independent variables suggested by the monetary and portfolio balance models. Meese and Rogoff then used this equation to forecast the exchange rate for later periods and compared the forecast with the actual exchange rate that later did exist for those periods. The predictive success of the theoretical equation's forecast of the later spot rates was then compared with the success in predicting later spot rates (1) by using only the current period's forward rate for predicting next period's spot rate and (2) by predicting next period's spot rate as differing from this period's rate by only a random number (meaning the exchange rate is a "random walk").

Sadly for the theoretical equation, it performed less well (or more poorly) than did the random walk and the forward rate. This led Meese to conclude (1990, p. 132): "Economists do not yet understand the determinants of short- to medium-run movements in exchange rates." Other economists disagreed with this view, and the issue continues to generate theoretical and empirical investigation. Hence, although the portfolio balance (and monetary) models have suggested particular influences on the exchange rate, considerable work remains to be done to document these influences more convincingly. In view of the huge volume and rapid growth of international assets, as discussed in the previous chapter, this work is very important and necessary.

23

PRICE ADJUSTMENTS AND BALANCE-OF-PAYMENTS DISEQUILIBRIUM

LEARNING OBJECTIVES

- To understand how changes in exchange rates affect the movement of goods and services and the trade balances of countries.

- To grasp how price elasticity of demand relates to the stability of foreign exchange markets.

- To understand how the price adjustment mechanism functions under a system of fixed or pegged exchange rates.

INTRODUCTION

Price Adjustment: The Exchange Rate Question

In his semiannual Monetary Policy Report to the Congress on February 11, 2004, Federal Reserve Chairman Alan Greenspan made the following comments about the depreciation of the U.S. dollar:

> The recent performance of inflation has been especially notable in view of the substantial depreciation of the dollar in 2003. Against a broad basket of currencies of our trading partners, the foreign exchange value of the U.S. dollar has declined about 13 percent from its peak in early 2002. Ordinarily, currency depreciation is accompanied by a rise in dollar prices of imported goods and services, because foreign exporters endeavor to avoid experiencing price declines in their own currencies, which would otherwise result from the fall in the foreign exchange value of the dollar. Reflecting the swing from dollar appreciation to dollar depreciation, the dollar prices of goods and services imported into the United States have begun to rise after declining on balance for several years; but the turnaround to date has been mild. Apparently, foreign exporters have been willing to absorb some of the price decline measured in their own currencies and the consequent squeeze on profit margins it entails.[1]

This chapter examines how price adjustments—for example, the exchange rate changes referred to by Alan Greenspan—affect the external sector and the economy as a whole. Price changes in general, whether occurring in a system of flexible exchange rates or in a system of fixed exchange rates, have implications for policy, and the policies themselves will be examined in later chapters. In this chapter, we first analyze the nature of the response of traded goods and services to changes in the price of foreign exchange under a system of flexible exchange rates and the effect that these responses have on the current account balance. Particular attention will be paid to describing the market conditions that are necessary for current account imbalances to be corrected by changes in the exchange rate. In recent years, depreciation of a country's currency has not always been immediately accompanied by a reduction in its current account deficits, leaving the impression that the foreign exchange market may not behave as theory suggests. We therefore examine this issue from both a short-run and a longer-run perspective under flexible exchange rates. The discussion of flexible-rate adjustment is followed by an analysis of the price adjustment process when the exchange rate is fixed or not allowed to move outside certain limits.

This chapter should enable you to better grasp how changes in the foreign sector trigger short-run and medium-term price adjustments. It will help you to understand the difficulties of carrying out economic policy in the open economy when changes in the exchange rate and prices must be taken into account. Economic policy itself is the focus of later chapters.

THE PRICE ADJUSTMENT PROCESS AND THE CURRENT ACCOUNT UNDER A FLEXIBLE-RATE SYSTEM

In this section we examine the manner in which changes in the exchange rate affect the movement of goods and services between countries, that is, the nature of the current account. In Chapter 20, that market was presented in terms of components describing the current account and the financial/capital account. The demand for foreign exchange needed to purchase goods and services with respect to different exchange rates was graphed in a "normal" downward-sloping manner, and the supply of foreign exchange earned from exports of goods and services at various exchange rates reflected the positive relationship associated

---

[1]Testimony of Chairman Alan Greenspan before the Committee on Financial Services, U.S. House of Representatives, February 11, 2004, available at www.federalreserve.gov/boarddocs/hb/2004/february/testimony.htm.

with "normal" supply curves. In this normal market configuration, changes in the exchange rate triggered changes in expenditures between domestic and foreign goods consistent with well-known standard market adjustments. For example, assuming a current account deficit, an increase in the exchange rate (depreciation of the home currency) causes foreign goods to become more expensive, leading consumers to reduce consumption of imports and increase consumption of domestic alternatives. At the same time, home exports become relatively cheaper to foreign buyers, causing them to switch expenditures from their own products to the cheaper imports. The **expenditure switching** reflected in both of these responses contributes to a reduction in the current account deficit. Underlying this adjustment is the assumption that consumers and producers respond quickly to changes in the exchange rate and that supply prices of traded goods do not change with the changes in expenditures in either country (infinitely elastic supply). In addition, any possible effects on income, the interest rate, the expected profit rate, or other factors are also ignored. The adjustment to changes in relative prices brought about by changes in the exchange rate is called the **elasticities approach** to adjustment in the foreign exchange market, or the **price adjustment mechanism** that follows changes in the exchange rate. However, because current account adjustments do not always appear to take place in the manner described, it is important to take a closer look at this component of the foreign exchange market and its adjustments.

The Demand for Foreign Goods and Services and the Foreign Exchange Market

If we are to anticipate the effects of changes in the foreign exchange rate on the current account balance more accurately, it is critical that we understand the basic forces underlying this market. To do this, we turn to the sources of demand and supply for a currency within the current account and examine the factors that influence them. As you recall from Chapters 19 and 20, the current account-based demand for foreign currency results from the desire to purchase goods and services from another country and to make unilateral transfers. In a sense, the demand for foreign currency is a secondary or derived demand because the foreign currency is a means to acquiring something else.

Ignoring unilateral transfers, the demand for foreign currency in the current account is thus determined by the factors that drive the demand for real goods and services. The demand for real imports is influenced principally by the domestic price of any foreign good or service, the presence of any tariffs or subsidies, the price of domestic substitutes and/or complements, the level of domestic income, and tastes and preferences. The domestic price of the foreign good or service is of course the product of the price expressed in foreign currency times the appropriate exchange rate (e.g., $P_{US\$} = P_{UK£} \times e_{\$/£}$). Because the demand for foreign currency by the home country can also be viewed as the supply of home currency to the foreign country, if we know the demand for foreign exchange in each of two countries, the supply of foreign exchange to each country is also known.

To get a better feel for the nature of this unique relationship between a country's home demand for foreign currency (its consequent supply of domestic currency to the exchange market), consider the following hypothetical demands for foreign exchange in two countries, the United States and the United Kingdom (see Table 1). It is assumed that the demand for foreign exchange for acquiring goods and services responds to changes in the exchange rate because of its effect on the domestic price of foreign goods. The data in the table were constructed under the assumption that the supply prices of the traded goods are invariant with the quantity demanded [see column (3)]. In this example, the variation in the domestic price of the foreign good(s) is brought about by altering the exchange rate from \$1.50/£ to \$1.00/£ [column (1)]. When the U.K. pound becomes relatively cheaper (depreciates), the dollar price of the U.K. goods falls as shown in part (a) of Table 1. As this happens, the quantity demanded of the U.K. good rises due to normal income and substitution effects

TABLE 1   The Demand for Imported Goods and Services and the Foreign
Exchange Market

(1)	(2)	(3)	(4)	(5)	(6)	(7)
(a) United States						
$e_{\$/\pounds}$	$(e'_{\pounds/\$})$	P_{UK}	(P_{US})	Q_{D-US}	$Q_{D\pounds/-US}$	$Q_{\$\$/-US}$
\$1.50/£	(£0.67/\$)	£10	(\$15.00)	100 units	£1,000	1,500
\$1.25/£	(£0.80/\$)	£10	(\$12.50)	140 units	£1,400	1,750
\$1.00/£	(£1.00/\$)	£10	(\$10.00)	180 units	£1,800	1,800
(b) United Kingdom						
$(e'_{\$/\pounds})$	$e_{\pounds/\$}$	P_{US}	(P_{UK})	Q_{D-UK}	$Q_{D\$-UK}$	$Q_{S\pounds-UK}$
(\$1.50/£)	£0.67/\$	\$20	(£13.33)	100 units	\$2,000	£1,333
(\$1.25/£)	£0.80/\$	\$20	(£16.00)	80 units	\$1,600	£1,280
(\$1.00/£)	£1.00/\$	\$20	(£20.00)	60 units	\$1,200	£1,200

[column (5)]. Given the constant British price of the import good, the increase in U.S. quantity demanded of the U.K. good leads to an increase in the quantity demanded of pounds [column (6) of part (a)]. Hence, the quantity demanded of pounds varies inversely with the price of the pound, and a normal downward-sloping demand curve results. Changes in the exchange rate thus produce a movement along the demand curve for foreign exchange and a corresponding change in quantity demanded. The position of the demand curve, however, is determined by factors other than the exchange rate, and any change in these variables will cause the demand curve to shift. For example, an increase in income, an autonomous increase in domestic prices relative to foreign prices, and a shift in tastes and preferences toward the import good would all cause the demand curve for foreign exchange associated with goods and services to shift out.

Part (b) of Table 1 proceeds similarly with the U.K. demand for a U.S. good. The depreciation of the pound from \$1.50/£ to \$1.00/£ (that is, the appreciation of the dollar from £0.67/\$ to £1.00/\$) causes the United Kingdom to reduce its quantity demanded of the U.S. good [column (5)]. The smaller quantity demanded of the U.S. good at the lower \$/£ exchange rate results in a smaller quantity demanded of dollars [column (6)]. This demand for dollars is then converted into a supply of pounds in column (7) of part (b).

With this information, we can now proceed to graph the foreign exchange market for the U.S. dollar and the U.K. pound. This will be done both from the U.S. perspective [Figure 1(a)] and from the U.K. perspective [Figure 1(b)]. The demand curve for pounds in the United States is found by plotting the quantity of pounds demanded against the various exchange rates from part (a) of Table 1. The supply of pounds available to the United States from the United Kingdom at the various exchange rates is found by plotting the first and last columns of part (b) for U.S. goods. The intersection of the two curves indicates the exchange rate that leaves the current account in balance. In this case, the equilibrium rate lies somewhere between \$1.25 and \$1.50 per pound.

A similar procedure is followed in presenting the foreign exchange market from the perspective of the United Kingdom. The demand for dollars [column (6) of Table 1, part (b)] is plotted against the appropriate exchange rate [column (2) of part (b)] to generate the expected downward-sloping curve. It is important to note that the price on the vertical axis is the inverse of the exchange rate in the earlier case, that is, £/\$ rather than \$/£. For the

FIGURE 1   **The Demand and Supply of Foreign Exchange Resulting from Trade in Goods and Services**

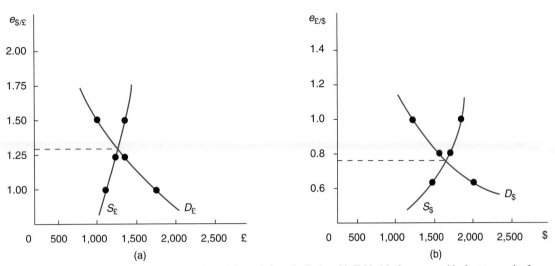

The market for foreign exchange that results from the demand for traded goods displayed in Table 1 is demonstrated in the two graphs. In panel (a), the market is presented from the vantage point of the United States. It shows the demand and supply of pounds that result from each country's demands for the other country's goods, at alternative dollar prices of the pound. In panel (b), the same demands are expressed in terms of the demand and the supply of dollars, at alternative pound prices of the dollar. The market equilibrium that results is the same, in that the $/£ price is the inverse of the £/$ exchange rate.

supply of dollars, we turn to the information on U.S. demand for U.K. products at different exchange rates. The quantity of dollars supplied from the United States [column (7) of Table 1, part (a)] at the various exchange rates is then plotted, and the intersection of the supply and demand curves again provides the equilibrium exchange rate. In this case, it lies somewhere between £0.67/$ and £0.80/$. (If we knew the equations for the demand curve and the supply curve, we could solve for the exact equilibrium price.) It is important to note here that the equilibrium exchange rate is the same in both cases because the figures show two ways of viewing the same market. One price is the reciprocal of the other. If, for example, the equilibrium exchange rate is $1.38/£ from the U.S. perspective, it would be 1/($1.38/£) or £0.72/$ from the U.K. perspective. Thus, it makes no difference whether the foreign exchange market is presented in pounds or dollars, since the same equilibrium exchange rate results.

The market shown in Figure 1 is stable with respect to deviations of the exchange rate from equilibrium. Comparative-statics analysis also suggests that shifts in demand and supply will lead to new equilibria appropriate to the changing market condition. For example, an increase in U.S. income would increase the demand for foreign goods and, hence, the demand for foreign exchange. This would cause the demand curve for foreign exchange to shift to the right, creating a current account deficit and requiring an increase in the price of pounds (a depreciation of the dollar) to balance the current account [see Figure 2(a)]. A similar effect would result from an increase in the U.S. price level relative to the U.K. price level. However, in this instance both of the curves will shift. U.S. demand for pounds will rise as consumers shift from the now higher-priced U.S. products to British goods and services. At the same time, British demand for U.S. goods and services (and hence the supply of pounds) will fall as British consumers shift from the now more expensive U.S.

FIGURE 2   Adjustment in the Foreign Exchange Market

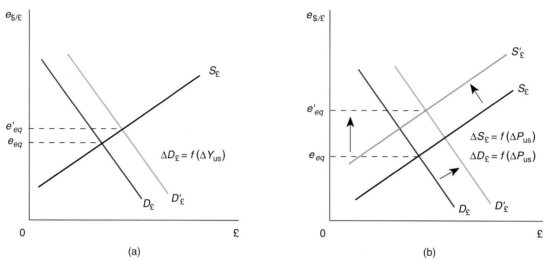

(a)   (b)

An increase in U.S. income increases the demand for U.K. goods and hence the demand for pounds as shown by the rightward shift in the demand curve in panel (a). This, of course, leads to a current account deficit at e_{eq}. Balance in the current account will be obtained only through depreciation of the dollar (that is, a higher exchange rate). An increase in U.S. prices, on the other hand, leads to a shift in both the demand and the supply curve of pounds, as U.S. consumers demand more of the now cheaper U.K. imports and U.K. consumers reduce their demand for U.S. goods and services. The combined result of the reduced supply of pounds and the increased demand for pounds is an even greater current account deficit and hence an even larger depreciation of the dollar to again reach a current account balance, as indicated in panel (b).

goods and services to the relatively cheaper domestic products. The result again is the increase in the dollar price of pounds [see Figure 2(b)] that is necessary to bring the current account into balance. Changes in expectations regarding future prices and exchange rates as well as changes in tastes and preferences would also shift the supply and demand curves for foreign exchange.

It is important to reiterate here that the current account can be brought into balance in this "normal" market example if the dollar depreciates when the demand for pounds exceeds the supply of pounds and if the dollar appreciates when pound supply exceeds pound demand.

Market Stability and the Price Adjustment Mechanism

Up to this point, we have assumed that the foreign exchange market is characterized by normal downward-sloping demand curves and upward-sloping supply curves. This condition was important because it generated a market equilibrium that can be characterized as being stable with respect to price (exchange rate). **Market stability** occurs when the characteristics of supply and demand are such that any price deviation away from equilibrium sets in motion forces that move the market back toward equilibrium. With downward-sloping demand and upward-sloping supply curves, a price that is too low creates an excess demand, causing consumers to bid up the price until supply again equals demand and the excess demand is removed. Similarly, a price that is set too high creates an excess supply, causing producers to begin lowering price until supply again equals demand. Thus, the market is stable with respect to deviations of price away from equilibrium. Stability thus ensures that price increases (currency depreciation) will remove an excess demand for foreign exchange (current account deficit) and price decreases (currency appreciation) will remove an excess supply of foreign exchange (current account surplus).

FIGURE 3   **Market Stability**

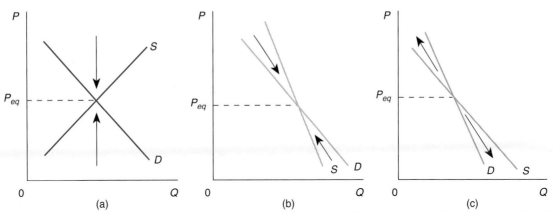

Panel (a) depicts a normal market with a downward-sloping demand curve and an upward-sloping supply curve. If price moves away from P_{eq}, forces of supply and demand are automatically set in motion to move price back to P_{eq}. Panel (b) demonstrates a market that is also stable with respect to price even though it has a downward-sloping supply curve. The fact that too low (high) a price still creates an excess demand (supply) means that market forces are automatically set in motion to return the market to equilibrium at P_{eq}. Panel (c), however, depicts an unstable market. If price is set too low (high), an excess supply (demand) occurs that leads to a further movement away from P_{eq}, not a movement back to equilibrium.

If the price adjustment mechanism is to work, it is necessary that the demand and supply curves have the appropriate configuration. In Figure 3, three different market configurations are shown (for any good or service, not just for foreign exchange). In panel (a), the supply and demand curves produce an excess demand when price is too low and an excess supply when price is too high. The market is thus stable in the manner discussed earlier. In panel (b), the demand curve has the usual negative slope, but the supply curve is backward sloping. However, the supply curve is steeper than the demand curve, with the result that there is still an excess demand when price is below the equilibrium price and an excess supply when price is above equilibrium. Thus, the market is also stable with respect to price. Finally, in panel (c) there is a third market configuration that is similar to (b) except that the backward-sloping supply curve is flatter than the demand curve. In this instance, a price below the equilibrium price leads to an excess supply, and a price above the equilibrium price leads to an excess demand. Because an excess demand leads to increases in price and an excess supply leads to decreases in price, any movement away from equilibrium sets in motion forces leading to further movements away from equilibrium, not movements back to equilibrium. Thus, this is an example of a market that is unstable with respect to price.

Returning to the foreign exchange market, can we expect that market to be "normal" as long as the demand for foreign goods and services is inversely related to price (that is, there is a downward-sloping demand curve)? To answer this question, consider the demand schedule in the United Kingdom for U.S. goods in Table 2. Note again that the price of U.K. imports rises [column (4)] to the British as the pound depreciates [columns (1) and (2)] and that U.K. consumers behave in a "normal" fashion by demanding a smaller quantity of U.S. goods and hence fewer dollars [column (6)]. However, even though quantity demanded falls, British consumers end up supplying *more* pounds sterling for the imports they would be willing to buy [column (7)]. If we now reconstruct this portion of the foreign exchange market from the U.S. perspective using this new example (see Figure 4), we find that we have a market characterized by a backward-sloping supply

TABLE 2   An Alternative U.K. Demand for U.S. Goods

UK′

(1)	(2)	(3)	(4)	(5)	(6)	(7)
$e'_{\$/£}$	$e_{£/\$}$	P_{US}	(P_{UK})	Q_{D-UK}	$Q_{D\$-UK}$	$Q_{S£-UK}$
(\$1.50/£)	£0.67/\$	\$20	(£13.33)	92 units	\$1,840	£1,227
(\$1.25/£)	£0.80/\$	\$20	(£16.00)	85 units	\$1,700	£1,360
(\$1.00/£)	£1.00/\$	\$20	(£20.00)	75 units	\$1,500	£1,500

FIGURE 4   The Foreign Exchange Market

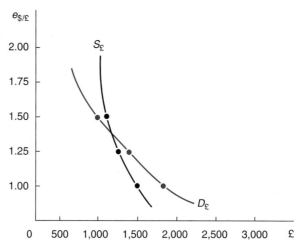

The alternative U.K. demand for imports of U.S. goods and services (see Table 2) produces a supply curve of pounds that is downward sloping (or backward sloping), not upward sloping. However, because the demand curve is still flatter than the supply curve, the equilibrium remains stable with respect to changes in price (foreign exchange rate).

curve of foreign exchange (pounds). However, because the supply curve is steeper than the demand curve, the market is still stable with respect to deviations in price. This example indicates that a backward-sloping supply curve of foreign exchange can occur even if foreign demand for imports is normal. Whether it produces a stable or an unstable market depends on the slopes of both the supply and the demand curves for foreign exchange. More about this later.

Explaining the Backward-Sloping Supply Curve of Foreign Exchange

Let us examine the circumstances that produced the backward-sloping supply curve of foreign exchange. If we return to the numerical examples in Tables 1 and 2 for the United Kingdom, note that the change in the exchange rate produced two effects. First, as the dollar became more expensive, more pounds sterling were required to buy each given unit of imports from the United States; at the same time, however, the number of units was falling because of the increase in price in terms of pounds. Whether the total quantity supplied of pounds increased or decreased with the change in the exchange rate depended on the relative size of these two effects.

The nature of this relationship can be measured by using the familiar concept of price elasticity of demand. This elasticity is simply the ratio of the percentage change in quantity demanded to the percentage change in price. Because we are examining rather large changes in both price and quantity and not small marginal changes in the neighborhood of a given price and quantity, it is appropriate to use an arc elasticity measure rather than a point elasticity estimate. This is done by using the means of the two quantity and price points over which the change in quantity and price is being examined. The arc elasticity is then defined as follows:

$$\eta_{arc} = \frac{\Delta Q/[(Q_1 + Q_2)/2]}{\Delta P/[(P_1 + P_2)/2]}$$

In the first numerical example in part (b) of Table 1, as the U.K. price increased from £13.33/unit to £16/unit [column (4)], the quantity demanded fell from 100 units to 80 units [column (5)]. The arc elasticity of demand for this change in price is equal to $(80 - 100)/[(100 + 80)/2]$ divided by $(16.00 - 13.33)/[(13.33 + 16.00)/2]$, which equals $(-)0.222/0.182 = (-)1.22$. Because the (absolute) value of the elasticity is greater than 1.0, demand is said to be elastic. If a similar calculation were carried out for the second change in the exchange rate in Table 1 (the increase in price from £16/unit to £20/unit), the arc elasticity is 1.29, which is also greater than 1.0 and hence elastic. The results confirm what we know about elastic demand. An increase in price leads to a decline in total expenditures because the percentage change in quantity demanded is greater than the percentage change in the price. Thus, whenever the partner country elasticity of demand for home-country products is elastic, the supply curve of foreign exchange will be upward sloping.

What happened in the case in Table 2 to make the supply curve of foreign exchange backward sloping? A quick calculation of the elasticity of demand for imports sheds some light on this question. As price rose from £13.33 to £16/unit, the quantity demanded fell from 92 units to 85 units. The arc elasticity over this range is equal to $(-)0.079/0.182$ or $(-)0.434$, which is less in absolute value than 1.0. Hence, demand for imports is inelastic in this range. After the price increase from £16 to £20/unit, quantity demanded fell from 85 units to 75 units. This indicates an elasticity of demand of $(-)0.125/0.222 = (-)0.563$, which again is less in absolute value than 1.0 and is inelastic. The inelastic demand means that at the higher import price in pounds, U.K. consumers are willing to supply more pounds (see the last column of Table 2). The mystery of the backward-sloping supply curve of foreign exchange is now solved. If foreign demand for home goods is inelastic, the supply curve of foreign exchange is backward sloping (that is, negatively sloped). If demand is elastic, the supply of foreign exchange will be upward sloping. For this relationship in the special case of a linear demand curve, see Concept Box 1.

Exchange Market Stability and the Marshall-Lerner Condition

Because a backward-sloping supply of foreign exchange will result whenever the partner demand for imports is inelastic, under what conditions will an unstable foreign exchange market result? In other words, will a depreciation of the home currency lead to a decrease in the excess demand for foreign exchange? If it does (does not), the exchange market is stable (unstable). Ignoring unilateral transfers and capital flows, the problem is to assess the change in the current account balance that results when there is a change in the exchange rate.[2] For a basic demonstration of the problem, consider the price and quantity

---

[2]Because instability occurs whenever the demand curve is steeper than the (backward-sloping) supply curve, the condition for stability must necessarily take the characteristics of both curves into account. For a simple derivation of the stability condition, see Dennis R. Appleyard and Alfred J. Field, Jr. (1986).

CONCEPT BOX 1

ELASTICITY OF IMPORT DEMAND AND THE SUPPLY CURVE OF FOREIGN EXCHANGE WHEN DEMAND IS LINEAR

Recall that with a linear demand curve, elasticity varies as we move from high prices to low prices. More specifically, at prices above the midpoint of the demand curve, demand is elastic; at prices below the midpoint, demand is inelastic; and at the midpoint, demand is unitary elastic. Because the U.S. price of the U.K. import good is being held constant, the change in price in our calculations is due entirely to changes in the exchange rate. In this case, the demand for dollars with respect to changes in the exchange rate has the same elasticity value as does the U.K. demand for imports with respect to U.K. domestic price of imports over the same range. Consider the U.K. demand curve for U.S. dollars in Figure 5(a). Corresponding to each range is a segment of the supply curve of pounds sterling to the United States [Figure 5(b)]. The elastic range of the U.K. demand curve for dollars corresponds to the upward-sloping portion of the supply curve of pounds. Because the price of foreign exchange from the U.S. perspective is the inverse of the price from the U.K. perspective ($/£ versus £/$), range *a* of high prices in the United Kingdom corresponds to low prices of foreign exchange in the United States. Consequently, as the foreign exchange rate falls in terms of £/$, it is rising in terms of $/£. Thus, as the exchange rate in £/$ is falling toward *b*, the point of unitary elasticity, it is rising toward *b* in $/£. At points below *b*, demand for dollars is inelastic and, hence, the supply of pounds sterling is backward sloping (range *c*). While these ranges hold specifically only for linear demand curves, the general relationship between import demand elasticity and the supply of foreign exchange holds. Inelastic import demand produces a backward-sloping supply curve of foreign exchange to the partner country, and elastic demand produces a normal, upward-sloping supply curve.

FIGURE 5   Import Demand and the Supply Curve of Foreign Exchange

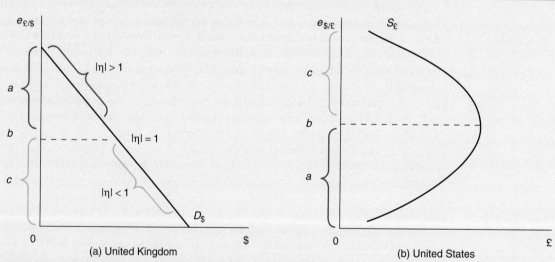

(a) United Kingdom

(b) United States

The elastic range of the foreign (U.K.) demand for home-country (U.S.) goods and services exports in panel (a) generates an upward-sloping supply curve of pounds in panel (b). In like fashion, the inelastic segment of the U.K. demand curve for imports of goods and services from the United States generates a backward-sloping supply curve of pounds to the United States. Thus, a country facing an inelastic foreign demand for its exports will experience a backward-sloping supply curve of foreign exchange. An overall elastic demand for exports will, on the other hand, produce the normal upward-sloping supply curve of foreign exchange.

FIGURE 6   Market Effects of a Change in the Foreign Exchange Rate

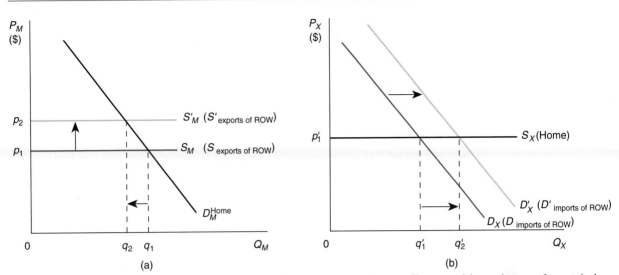

(a)   (b)

Assuming that the supply of exports is infinitely elastic in both countries (i.e., the supply curve of imports and the supply curve of exports in the home country are horizontal), a depreciation of the home currency leads to (1) an upward shift in the supply curve of imports from S_M to S'_M (due to the higher domestic price of imports in the home currency) and (2) a rightward shift in the demand for exports from D_X to D'_X (because the foreign currency price of home-country exports has fallen relatively). The effect of the depreciation on the value of imports depends on the elasticity of the demand for imports. Given that import outlays before the depreciation were p_1q_1 and after the depreciation are p_2q_2, the depreciation reduces import outlays only if import demand is elastic. If demand is inelastic, the value of import outlays in dollar terms actually rises. The value of export receipts increases unambiguously because a larger quantity q'_2 than the original q'_1 is purchased at a constant-dollar price. The ultimate impact of depreciation on the current account balance thus depends on the sum of these two effects and can be positive or negative depending on the elasticity of demand in each country for the other country's goods and services.

adjustments in Figure 6 (for expositional convenience, the demand curves are drawn as straight lines). Panel (a) shows the demand and supply schedules for the home country's imports, assuming that the price of the partner's [or rest of the world's (ROW's)] goods and services is constant. Panel (b) shows the demand and supply schedules for home-country exports (partner country's or ROW's imports) again assuming a constant price of the goods and services. The prices in both cases are expressed in home currency ($). The initial prices are p_1 and p'_1, with corresponding quantities q_1 and q'_1. Assume that there is a depreciation of the dollar (the home currency). When this happens, S_M (or the supply of exports to this country from the rest of the world) shifts vertically upward to S'_M in panel (a), and D_X shifts to D'_X (or the demand for imports from this country by the rest of the world) in panel (b). Because the domestic price of imports has gone up, the home country demands a smaller quantity. In the partner country, the *domestic* price of its imports has gone down even though the home-country export price has remained constant (because the partner country currency has appreciated), which causes its demand curve to shift to the right. This shift reflects the fact that foreigners are prepared to buy more home-country goods and services at each dollar price.

The ultimate effect on the current account balance depends on the changes in expenditures associated with the change in the exchange rate. If home-country demand is elastic, then the current account balance unambiguously improves with depreciation, because the increase in domestic price of imports leads to a reduction in total expenditures on imports and the reduced price of exports to foreigners leads to an increase in their expenditures on home-country exports. Similarly, the current account balance improves if home-country demand is unit elastic because total expenditures on imports will be unchanged and foreign expenditures on home-country exports will increase. If domestic demand is inelastic, however, the effect of depreciation is ambiguous. In this instance, the increase in the price of foreign goods and services leads to an increase in total expenditures for imports, which may or may not be offset by the increased expenditures by the partner country on exports. As long as the increase in foreign expenditures more than offsets the increased domestic expenditures on imports, the current account balance will improve with depreciation, and hence the foreign exchange market will be stable. If, however, the increase in domestic expenditures on imports is greater than the increase in expenditures on home-country exports, the current account balance will worsen with depreciation, and the foreign exchange market will be unstable.

As it turns out, the unstable result will not occur as long as the sum of the absolute values of the home-country price elasticity of demand for imports, η_{Dm}, and the price elasticity of demand for home-country exports (partner country imports), η_{Dx}, is greater than 1.0 in the case of initial balanced trade, that is, $|\eta_{Dm}| + |\eta_{Dx}| > 1$. In the case of unbalanced trade (expressed in units of home currency), the condition becomes

$$\frac{X}{M} |\eta_{Dx}| + |\eta_{Dm}| > 1$$

where X and M refer to total expenditures on exports and imports, respectively. This general condition for exchange market stability is referred to as the **Marshall-Lerner condition.**[3]

In the situation just discussed, the supply curves of imports and exports were horizontal, or "infinitely elastic." If we examine the effect of the exchange rate change on the current account balance when supply curves take their normal shape, the analysis is more complicated than in the previous case. In Figure 7, depreciation of the dollar shifts the supply curve S_M vertically upward by the percentage of the depreciation to S'_M. Thus, for example, the price p_3 associated with point F is 10 percent higher than price p_1 (associated with the point E) if the depreciation of the dollar is 10 percent. Such a 10 percent vertical shift occurs everywhere along S_M. Price p_3 would in fact have been the new equilibrium price if the S_M schedule had been horizontal, as in Figure 6(a). However, in Figure 7, the final price p_2 is lower than p_3. The final change in import outlays due to the depreciation thus involves looking at not only the elasticity of D_M but also the elasticity of S'_M. These elasticities in turn reflect the elasticities involved in the underlying conditions of consumption and production in both trading countries. We do not examine these underlying elasticities in this chapter, but clearly matters become more complex.

A similar analysis would apply to the export side. In a diagram for the export case (not shown), a depreciation of the home currency would shift D_X to the right along an *upward-sloping* S_X curve, and the export good's price would rise [whereas it does not in Figure 6(b)]. For market stability in cases of upward-sloping S_M and S_X curves, the Marshall-Lerner condition becomes more complicated. An extension for these cases is, however, beyond the scope of this text.[4]

---

[3]For a mathematical derivation of this result, see the appendix at the end of this chapter. We are discussing the balance in terms of the home currency because BOP accounts are kept in the home currency. The balanced-trade result is the same if examined in terms of foreign currency, but the unbalanced condition is then

$$|\eta_{Dx}| + \frac{M}{X} |\eta_{Dm}| > 1$$

[4]In the case of upward-sloping supply curves, it can be shown through more advanced treatments (and can also be reasoned out through graphs) that the simple Marshall-Lerner condition is a sufficient condition but no longer a necessary condition for depreciation to improve the current account balance. In other words, the absolute demand elasticities can sum to < 1 and the balance can still improve.

FIGURE 7   Import Market Response to Changes in the Foreign Exchange Rate When Foreign Supply Is Not Infinitely Elastic

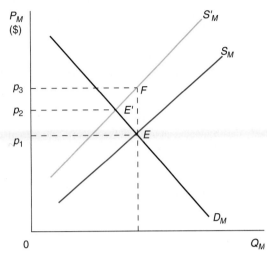

If foreign supply of traded goods is not infinitely elastic, the supply curve slopes upward to the right. Depreciation of the home currency will thus lead to an upward shift in the curve equal to the percentage change in the exchange rate. S'_M thus lies above S_M by a constant percentage of the price and not by a fixed amount (i.e., S'_M will diverge from S_M). The resulting change in the market price of imports will reflect both the elasticity of demand *and* the elasticity of supply of the traded goods and will be less than the percentage change in the exchange rate. This is demonstrated here, where the new equilibrium price p_2 reflects a smaller increase in domestic price (relative to p_1) compared with the effect of the depreciation of the currency EF.

Estimating the actual elasticities in international trade is a difficult job given the complex and changing nature of trade. Considerable controversy has existed over estimates of these elasticities, particularly with respect to the econometrics employed. Although some statistical results suggest that these elasticities are quite low, the general consensus from various studies appears to be that market responses to price changes are sufficiently large to generate a stable foreign exchange market. Because long-run elasticities are higher (in absolute value) than short-run elasticities, the time frame can be important. The short-run versus long-run nature of elasticities will be discussed in the next section.

CONCEPT CHECK

1. What is the difference between a stable market equilibrium and an unstable equilibrium? Will a downward-sloping supply curve always produce market instability? Why or why not?
2. What condition is required for stability in the foreign exchange market if both domestic and foreign supplies of traded goods are infinitely elastic?
3. How does the analysis of foreign exchange market stability relate to the impact of depreciation on the current account balance?

The Price Adjustment Process: Short Run vs. Long Run

In the last section, we established that depreciating the currency would reduce current account deficits and appreciating the currency would reduce current account surpluses as long as the sum of the absolute values of the foreign and domestic elasticities of demand for imports was greater than 1.0 (the Marshall-Lerner condition for market stability). In this situation, the changes in the exchange rate bring about appropriate switches in expenditures between domestic and foreign goods. Assuming a current account deficit, an increase in the exchange rate (depreciation of the home currency) causes foreign goods to become more expensive,

IN THE REAL WORLD:

ESTIMATES OF IMPORT AND EXPORT DEMAND ELASTICITIES

In a 1998 study by the Board of Governors of the Federal Reserve System, trade elasticities for the Group of Seven (G-7) countries were estimated. These estimates utilized quarterly data beginning in the mid-1950s or early 1960s and ending in late 1996 or early 1997 for Canada, Japan, the United Kingdom, and the United States. For Germany, France, and Italy the study utilized quarterly data beginning around 1970 and also ending in late 1996 or early 1997. Both short-run and long-run price elasticities for total imports and total exports were calculated. These estimates are listed in Table 3.

In the context of the Marshall-Lerner condition, the long-run estimates suggest that stability obtains as a general rule in all countries except France and Germany, where the sum of the absolute values of the two elasticities is less than 1.0. The estimated long-run elasticities, however, show much greater responsiveness than do the short-run elasticities. In all cases except the United States, the short-run estimates are very small (very inelastic) and are not close to meeting the Marshall-Lerner condition for market stability. This suggests that current account behavior may appear to be unstable in the immediate aftermath of a change in the exchange rate, for example, worsening in the presence of a currency depreciation.

TABLE 3   Estimated Price Elasticities of Demand for Imports and Exports

Country	Short-Run Import Price Elasticity	Short-Run Export Price Elasticity	Long-Run Import Price Elasticity	Long-Run Export Price Elasticity
Canada	−0.1	−0.5	−0.9	−0.9
France	−0.1	−0.1	−0.4	−0.2
Germany	−0.2	−0.1	−0.06	−0.3
Italy	0.0	−0.3	−0.4	−0.9
Japan	−0.1	−0.5	−0.3	−1.0
United Kingdom	0.0	−0.2	−0.6	−1.6
United States	−0.6	−0.5	−0.3	−1.5

Sources: Peter Hooper, Karen Johnson, and Jaime Marquez, "Trade Elasticities for G-7 Countries," Board of Governors of the Federal Reserve System, International Finance Discussion Papers no. 609, April 1998, pp. 5–8; *Trade Elasticities for the G-7 Countries,* Princeton Studies in International Economics no. 87 (August 2000), pp. 8–9.

leading consumers to reduce consumption of imports and increase consumption of domestic alternatives. At the same time, home exports become relatively cheaper to foreign buyers, causing them to switch expenditures from their own products to the cheaper imports. It was generally assumed in this analysis that consumers and producers responded quickly and that supply prices did not change with the switch in expenditures in either country (infinitely elastic supply). Any possible effects on income, the interest rate, the expected profit rate, or other variables were also ignored. In addition, it was assumed that a change in the exchange rate registered fully as a change in goods prices facing consumers in the buying country. Hence, for example, a 10 percent depreciation of the home currency results in a 10 percent reduction in the prices of the home country's goods to foreign consumers and a 10 percent rise in the prices of the foreign country's goods to home consumers. Such a situation is said to be one of **complete exchange rate pass-through.** Given these assumptions, the Marshall-Lerner condition is sufficient to bring about the desired change in expenditures.

As indicated earlier, short-run elasticities of supply and demand tend to be smaller (in absolute values) than long-run elasticities. On the demand side, consumers do not often

IN THE REAL WORLD:

EXCHANGE RATE PASS-THROUGH OF FOREIGN EXPORTS TO THE UNITED STATES

Jiawen Yang (1997) of George Washington University confirmed that complete pass-through of exchange rate changes does not generally occur in the case of foreign exports to the United States. Yang used a sample of imports in 87 U.S. manufacturing industries to calculate the **elasticity of exchange rate pass-through** during the December 1980–December 1991 period. This elasticity on an industry basis is the percentage change in the import price index for a good (in dollars) divided by the percentage change in the (nominal effective) exchange rate. If there is complete pass-through of an exchange rate change into import prices, the elasticity would be equal to 1.0, meaning that the exchange rate change is fully reflected in the dollar price of the good to U.S. consumers. If there is no pass-through, it would be equal to zero, indicating that, despite the exchange rate change, the dollar price to U.S. consumers does not change. If the elasticity is between 0 and 1, there is **partial exchange rate pass-through.** In his estimates of short-run pass-through ("short-run" meaning the impact of an exchange rate change during one quarter on the import price in the succeeding quarter), Yang's estimates were that, in 77 of the 87 industries, the elasticities of pass-through were positive but less than 1.0. This partial pass-through was reflected in an average elasticity of 0.3185, with elasticities in the 77 industries ranging from 0.025 in hardwood veneer and plywood to 0.757 in printing trades machinery. In general, he found that the nonelectric machinery and instruments industries had greater pass-through than did other industries. His estimates for long-run elasticities (using a slightly smaller sample) were higher, with some of the nonelectric machinery industries approaching a value close to 1.0.

Of particular interest in the Yang study was his attempt to investigate the determinants of the relative degree of pass-through across industries. First, for example, he postulated that the elasticity of pass-through would be higher with greater product differentiation in an industry, and his hypothesis was generally confirmed empirically. Second, Yang expected that pass-through would be smaller the greater the elasticity of marginal cost of production with respect to output in the supplying firms in the industry, and this result was also found in his empirical tests. Third, Yang specified that the degree of pass-through could be affected by the market share of foreign firms in the domestic market—his hypothesis was that the degree of pass-through would be inversely related to foreign firms' market share in the United States. However, Yang could find no significant relationship empirically between the degree of pass-through and the foreign firms' market share.

A later study by Giovanni Olivei (2002) of the Federal Reserve Bank of Boston also presented calculations of the elasticities of exchange rate pass-through for the United States. Olivei worked with data for 34 industries, imports of which accounted for about 75 percent of nonenergy merchandise imports into the United States. Using data from the 1981–1999 period, he obtained short-run elasticities of exchange rate pass-through on import prices as low as 0.06 (footwear), 0.07 (rubber manufactures, not elsewhere specified), and 0.09 (radio broadcast receivers). On the other hand, some of the long-run elasticities were as high as 0.92 (nonferrous metals), 0.89 (aluminum), and 0.87 (electrical circuitry equipment). To see if any changes had taken place over the period, he made separate estimates for the 1980s and the 1990s. For the 1980s, the industries' average long-run elasticity of pass-through was 0.50 (pass-through of 50 percent), but this fell to 0.22 in the 1990s (22 percent pass-through). Hence, a given exchange rate change had less than one-half the impact on import prices in the 1990s that it had in the 1980s. Olivei thus concluded that his study provided evidence that, consistent with Yang's hypothesis, market share of the foreign firms was inversely related to the extent of pass-through; that is, in the 1990s, the greater U.S. market penetration by products of foreign firms was causally related to the decline in the elasticity of exchange rate pass-through. ●

adjust immediately to changes in relative prices. Because it may take time for consumers to alter consumption plans or product commitments, they may be slow to react to changes in the exchange rate. In many cases, contracts may already have been signed that commit importers to a certain volume of imports at the previous exchange rate. Under certain scenarios, the volume of imports may even rise if importers view the initial change in the exchange rate as the first of several rises and purchase more now to avoid an even higher domestic price in the future. It is not surprising, then, to see the quantity of imports demanded and hence (other things equal) the amount of foreign exchange needed remain relatively constant in the short run even though the domestic currency is depreciating (i.e., the short-run demand for foreign exchange is vertical).With the passage of time, the demand curve for foreign exchange will more closely approximate the long-run demand curve as more normal quantity responses occur.

On the supply side of foreign exchange, the supply of exports may not increase immediately in response to depreciation simply due to the decision-making lags involved. These lags include (*a*) a recognition lag with respect to the change in the exchange rate, (*b*) a decision-making lag, (*c*) a production/inventory replacement lag, and (*d*) a delivery lag. The supply of exports also may not rise if producers choose to raise the domestic price in response to the increased foreign demand and to increase short-term profit margins at the expense of increased sales (that is, incomplete pass-through). In addition, contracts may already have been signed agreeing to provision of certain quantities at the old exchange rate. If the quantity of exports does not rise in the short run with depreciation of the currency, then the short-run supply curve of foreign exchange will be backward sloping as long as domestic prices remain constant or do not increase as fast as the exchange rate. However, with the passage of time, the supply curve will tend to take on the characteristics of the long-run response.

If the short-run responses of producers and consumers are similar to those described earlier, they can theoretically create certain problems with respect to the price adjustment

IN THE REAL WORLD:

JAPANESE EXPORT PRICING AND PASS-THROUGH IN THE 1990S

The concept of complete exchange rate pass-through, as noted earlier, involves a change in goods prices to foreign buyers by the same relative extent as the change in relative currency values. Thomas Klitgaard (1999) of the Federal Reserve Bank of New York sought to determine if this was the case with some particular Japanese exports to the United States in the 1990s. During that time, the yen strongly appreciated relative to the dollar from 1991 to 1995 and strongly depreciated from 1995 to 1998. He found that, for the particular goods and in both directions of movement of the yen, export prices from Japan did not move to the same degree as did the exchange rate. In other words, when the yen appreciated, for example, Japanese exporters reduced their profit margins to some extent to prevent the goods prices from rising as much as the price of the yen rose. (The analogous result occurred when the yen depreciated.) In general, Klitgaard concluded that a 10 percent change in the price of the yen would lead to roughly a 4 percent offsetting change in the profit margin (relative to the profit margin on goods sold in Japan). This finding suggests an offset of about 40 percent (4%/10% = 0.4) and therefore a pass-through of about 60 percent.

Utilizing exchange rate and price data, as well as other relevant information pertaining to costs and prices, Klitgaard constructed estimating equations for the behavior of prices in four prominent Japanese export industries—industrial machinery, transportation equipment, electrical machinery, and precision equipment. He was then able to use the estimating equations to simulate time paths of goods price changes that would follow upon a change in the value of the yen. These time paths are portrayed in Figure 8, panels (a) and (b). Although there are occasional irregularities, the export price changes for three of the aggregated products (industrial machinery, transportation equipment, and electrical machinery) converge within 18 months to about a 4 percent change, while the prices of precision equipment products converge within 18 months to about a 2 percent price change. Thus, pass-through is ultimately fairly substantial although not complete.

Source: Thomas Klitgaard, "Exchange Rates and Profit Margins: The Case of Japanese Exporters," Federal Reserve Bank of New York, *Economic Policy Review,* April 1999, pp. 41–54.

IN THE REAL WORLD: *(continued)*

FIGURE 8   Short-Run Response of Export Prices to a 10 Percent Yen Appreciation

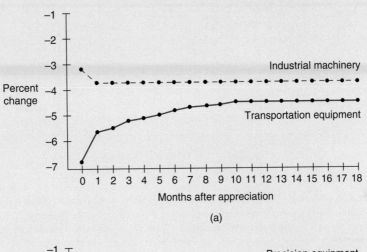

(a)

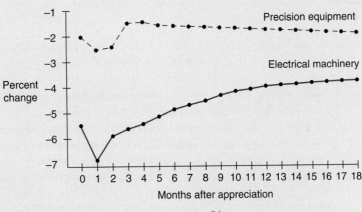

(b)

The simulated price patterns in the four industries portrayed suggest that Japanese export prices do fall to offset some of a simulated appreciation of the yen. The pass-through is about 60 percent for industrial machinery, transportation equipment, and electrical machinery and about 80 percent for precision equipment.

Source: Thomas Klitgaard, "Exchange Rates and Profit Margins: The Case of Japanese Exporters," Federal Reserve Bank of New York, *Economic Policy Review,* April 1999, p. 48. Used with permission.

mechanism. In Figure 9, panel (a), the normal long-run supply and demand for foreign exchange are shown with an equilibrium exchange rate that produces a current account deficit, although there is overall equilibrium in the balance of payments at rate e_{eq}. Suppose that there is now a reduction in the supply of foreign exchange, due, for example, to less foreign investment in the United States. This would immediately put upward pressure on the exchange rate, presumably leading to a reduction in the current account deficit.

However, suppose that short-run supply and demand curves for foreign exchange for goods and services have the shapes described earlier [as indicated by the dashed lines in Figure 9(b)].

FIGURE 9   Adjustment Time and the Foreign Exchange Market

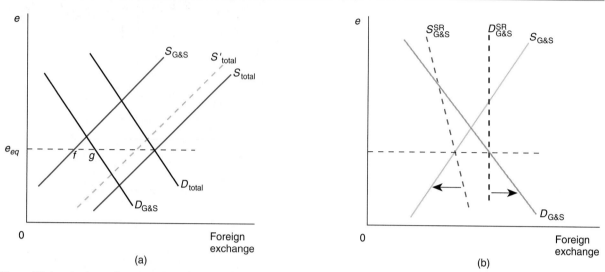

(a)   (b)

The equilibrium foreign exchange rate represented in panel (a) produces a deficit (fg) in the current account. A reduction in the supply of foreign exchange (to S'_{total}) would immediately depreciate the currency and reduce or possibly eliminate the current account deficit if the market responds in the short run in the manner depicted by supply and demand curves $S_{G\&S}$ and $D_{G\&S}$. However, in the short run, consumers and producers may be unable or unwilling to respond to the price signals given by the exchange rate change. The short run may thus be characterized by supply and demand curves of foreign exchange in the current account similar to those depicted by the dashed lines $S^{SR}_{G\&S}$ and $D^{SR}_{G\&S}$ in panel (b). In such an instance, depreciating the currency leads to a worsening of the current account deficit in the short run; that is, the gap between the two dashed curves gets wider with depreciation. Given enough time, consumers and producers respond in a manner consistent to that described by $S_{G\&S}$ and $D_{G\&S}$ in panel (a) and the depreciation leads, as expected, to a reduction in the current account deficit.

With a vertical demand curve for foreign exchange and a backward-sloping supply curve, an increase in the exchange rate will lead to a larger current account deficit, not a smaller one. In the short run, this will cause the dollar to depreciate even further as demand for foreign currency continues to exceed supply. The current account deficit will continue to worsen in this case until sufficient time has passed for quantities supplied and demanded to adjust to the change in relative prices and for the longer-run supply and demand configurations to come about. As this adjustment takes place, the current account deficit will begin to decline, and the market will seek a new long-run equilibrium consistent with the change in market conditions. This current account adjustment to changes in the exchange rate is often plotted against time, producing a graph like that shown in Figure 10. Due to the shape of the response curve, it is often referred to as the **J curve.** With the current account in deficit, a depreciation of the currency would presumably lead to a removal of the deficit. However, if consumers and producers are unresponsive in the short run, depreciation actually leads to a short-run worsening in the current account before it ultimately gets better. The longer both groups remain unresponsive to the change in the exchange rate, the deeper is the J curve response. Such an adjustment response is of concern to policymakers because it adds to the uncertainty already present in the market, although some evidence appears to suggest that there is a lag between exchange rate changes and trade adjustment. If short-run market conditions do not meet the Marshall-Lerner condition for stability, the exchange rate can overshoot the new long-run equilibrium rate and then adjust back down as the longer-run responses become evident.

Thus, considering the J curve, changing the exchange rate eventually leads to the predicted current account effects. In addition, other economywide indirect effects of an exchange rate change may have a bearing on the nature of the adjustment in the foreign sector. For example, depreciating the currency may stimulate income and employment as long as the export and

FIGURE 10   The J Curve

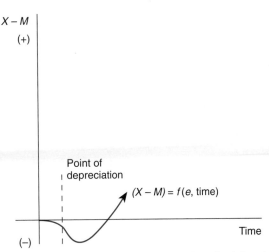

If consumers and producers do not respond immediately to changes in prices of traded goods and services resulting from shifts in the exchange rate, depreciation of the currency may actually lead to a worsening in the current account balance in the short run. If with the passage of time, however, the price effects do have an impact on both consumers and producers, the deficit will begin to narrow. The lagged adjustment response of the current account balance to depreciation of the currency traces out a locus that resembles the letter *J*. Hence, it is referred to as the J curve.

import-competing goods sectors and their intermediate good suppliers are at less than full employment. However, depreciation in an economy with little or no excess capacity may do nothing more than stimulate domestic price increases, which offset the initial effects of depreciation and lead to little or no change in the current account. Depreciation may also stimulate investment in export and import-competing industries and shift it away from other domestic uses. If such structural changes are not consistent with the long-run comparative advantages in the country, they can actually decrease growth of output, income, and employment. In a similar fashion, appreciation will stimulate contraction in export goods and import-competing goods. As such, it will tend to have a deflationary effect on the economy. To the extent the deflationary effect reduces income growth and hence imports, the indirect effects will again offset some of the direct effects of the appreciation. In cases where the indirect effects are further influenced by monetary or interest rate effects on investment, the short-run effect of changes in the exchange rate via the price adjustment mechanism becomes even less clear. In sum, while the price adjustment mechanism seems to function with certain regularity in long-run situations, the short-run effects are relatively more volatile and less certain.

THE PRICE ADJUSTMENT MECHANISM IN A FIXED EXCHANGE RATE SYSTEM

Gold Standard

Instead of letting the foreign exchange market determine the value of the exchange rate, countries often fix or peg the value of the domestic currency. In the case of a **gold standard** (as operated successfully in the world economy from 1880 to 1914), currencies are valued in gold, and all currencies that are pegged to gold are therefore automatically linked to each other. The price is maintained because the government stands ready to buy and sell gold to all customers at the pegged value. For example, if the dollar is fixed at $50 per ounce of gold and the pound sterling is fixed at £25 per ounce of gold, then the dollar/pound **mint par** exchange rate is $2/£. Should this rate or any of the related cross-rates get out of line, arbitrage will quickly bring them back in line.

Because the exchange rate is not allowed to change in this system, some other type of adjustment must be relied upon to make certain that the demand for foreign exchange is equal to the supply of foreign exchange. To ensure proper adjustment, the following **rules of the game** are assumed to hold under a gold standard:

1. There is no restraint on the buying and selling of gold within countries, and gold moves freely between countries.
2. The money supply is allowed to change in response to the change in gold holdings in a country.
3. Prices and wages are assumed to be flexible upward and downward.

IN THE REAL WORLD:

LAGGED RESPONSE OF NET EXPORTS TO EXCHANGE RATE CHANGES

An analysis by the Council of Economic Advisers of the changes in real net exports (exports minus imports) and the effective exchange rate in the United States suggests that the lag in producer and consumer response in the 1970s and 1980s was about six quarters (one and a half years). This analysis was extended by the authors beyond 1987 in Figure 11. (However, the exchange rate series used, which measured the dollar's value against 10 currencies, was discontinued after 1998 because of the introduction of the euro.) The figure indicates that if the movement of current net exports is compared with the movement in the effective exchange rate six quarters earlier, the movements are very similar in nature (highly correlated). For example, a rise of the exchange rate line (a depreciation of the dollar, given the arrangement of the left scale) is associated with a rise in real net exports (right scale), as we would expect. The two lines in terms of levels become more disparate after 1987, but the direction of change in each time period is still rather similar until after 1992. (Whether the post-1992 divergence represents a fundamental structural change cannot be easily ascertained.) This evidence generally supports the idea of time lags in the adjustment to changes in the exchange rate, and hence different short-run and long-run elasticities in the foreign exchange market.

FIGURE 11   U.S. Exchange Rate and Net Export Changes, 1969–1998

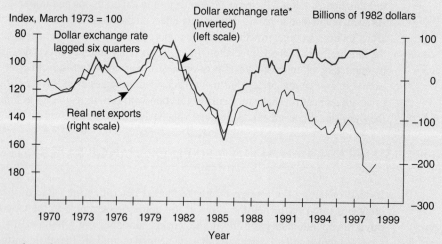

The figure indicates that real net export changes lagged six quarters track exchange rate changes rather well until about 1992.

*Nominal multilateral trade-weighted value of the dollar against the currencies of 10 industrialized countries.

Sources: *Economic Report of the President,* February 1988 (Washington, DC: U.S. Government Printing Office, 1988), p. 27; post-1987 data compiled by the authors from various years' *Economic Report of the President.*

The operation of a gold standard is straightforward. Consider the foreign exchange market in Figure 12(a) describing the dollar/pound exchange rate in a gold standard context. Assume that the market is initially in equilibrium at the pegged rate of $2/£. Now assume that the demand for pounds sterling rises due to an increase in income in the United States (shown by $D'_£$). With the increase in demand for pounds, there is now an excess demand at the pegged rate. The excess demand for pounds sterling will produce upward pressure on the exchange rate to remove the market disequilibrium. The fact that governments stand ready to buy and sell currency at the pegged rate means that there is automatically an upper and lower limit to the amount that the exchange rate can change. Buyers and sellers of foreign exchange know that they can always buy or sell the foreign currency at mint par by using gold as a medium of exchange. By buying gold domestically and then shipping it to the partner country, the mint par rate of exchange can be obtained. In fact, if the transaction costs and shipping costs associated with the movement of gold were zero, the exchange rates would never vary from the mint par value, because any difference in market value from the mint par value would quickly be arbitraged away. However, because the transaction/transport costs associated with the use of gold are not zero, the exchange rate can vary slightly as long as its movement away from mint par value does not exceed the amount of the costs associated with the exchange of gold.

To illustrate, assume that the cost of acquiring gold, shipping it to the partner country, and then exchanging it for the foreign currency is 2 percent of par value. In our example, this would mean that the cost would be $0.04 on either side of the mint par value of $2.00/£. As the exchange rate inches upward due to the increase in the demand for pounds, demanders will pay up to $2.04/£ but no more, because they can acquire all the pounds they wish at the rate of $2.04/£ by using gold as a medium of exchange. The supply of pounds sterling becomes perfectly elastic at this "break-even" price because it is assumed

FIGURE 12   The Foreign Exchange Market under a Gold Standard

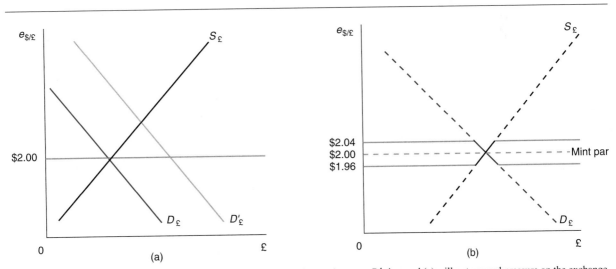

Under a fixed exchange rate system, an increase in the demand for foreign exchange to $D'_£$ in panel (a) will put upward pressure on the exchange rate and the home currency (the dollar) will begin to depreciate. However, assuming that the transaction/transport cost for acquiring and using gold to acquire pounds is 2 percent, a U.S. resident need never pay more than $2.04/£ [as indicated by the upper solid lines in panel (b)]. Hence when e approaches this point, gold will be purchased and used to acquire the needed foreign exchange; that is, gold exports from the United States will take place. Similarly, the British need never pay more than $1.96/£ [the lower solid lines in panel (b); $2.00 minus the 2 percent transaction/transport cost]. At that price, they can acquire all the dollars they wish by first buying gold and then exchanging the gold for dollars; that is, gold would flow into the United States. The unrestricted acquisition and use of gold as an intermediary between the two currencies will thus maintain the market exchange rate within the band around the mint par value determined by transaction/transport costs.

that an unlimited amount of pounds can be acquired at this price ($2.04/£) by buying and exporting gold to England and acquiring pounds at the pegged value. Similarly, a shift in the supply curve to the left, which would raise the exchange rate above $2.04/£, would cause domestic residents who desire pounds to use the gold mechanism to acquire them at $2.04/£ instead of using the more costly foreign exchange market. Thus, the demand curve for foreign exchange becomes horizontal at $2.04/£ as well. The upper break-even price at which the supply and demand for pounds become perfectly elastic is often referred to as the **gold export point.**

From the English perspective, a similar point exists at a price of $1.96/£. The English never need pay a higher price for dollars or receive a lower price for pounds than $1.96/£ (£0.51/$) because that is the cost associated with acquiring gold in England, shipping it to the United States, and exchanging it for dollars at the pegged rate. Thus, if the exchange rate starts edging downward from $2/£, it will never go beyond $1.96/£ because at that point gold will start moving into the United States to be exchanged for dollars. From the U.S. standpoint, the demand for pounds sterling also becomes perfectly elastic at this point because if the exchange rate fell below this level, it would immediately be profitable to acquire pounds sterling with dollars, purchase gold with the pounds sterling, ship it to the United States, convert it to dollars, and make a profit. This floor on the exchange rate set by transaction/transport costs is referred to as the **gold import point,** because any excess supply of pounds at that price will be converted into gold and shipped to the United States to be exchanged for U.S. dollars. Thus, the actual exchange rate in the foreign exchange market is automatically maintained within this narrow band by the unrestricted movement of gold between trading countries, relying on nothing more than free-market arbitrage and the government's commitment to stand behind its currency at the pegged value. The foreign exchange market under a gold standard thus takes on the configuration described in Figure 12(b), with the ceiling and floor to the rate set by the gold import and export points.

If the exchange rate remains fixed within these narrow bounds, does this mean that there is no price adjustment mechanism to correct any structural imbalance leading to gold flows? While relative price changes via exchange rate changes basically cannot occur, an aggregate price adjustment takes place as the money supply responds to the gold flow. Assuming a link between money and prices through a quantity theory of money relationship ($M_s = kPY$ from the preceding chapter), as gold leaves a country the money supply falls, leading to a fall in prices. Assuming in addition that the demand for tradeable goods is elastic, the fall in prices in the "deficit" country tends to reduce import outlays and increase export receipts. This effect is strengthened by the fact that the money supply and prices are increasing in the surplus country receiving the shipments of gold. Thus, the "price adjustment mechanism" that operates through the gold standard is an aggregate price effect operating through changes in the money supply resulting from the movement of gold. However, flexibility in wages and prices is obviously required for this mechanism to work. Price-wage rigidities in practice will thus be a hindrance to effective adjustment.

The change in the money supply can also lead to interest rate and income effects. Indeed, for many economists, the principal effect of changes in the money supply is on the level of interest rates and then indirectly on income and prices. From this perspective, a fall in the money supply will lead to an increase in interest rates, which will reduce investment, income, and hence aggregate demand in the economy. The fall in demand will lead to excess inventories and falling prices and wages. With the fall in prices comes an adjustment in the foreign exchange market similar to that discussed earlier. In addition, the increase in the interest rate will attract short-term capital from overseas (as appears to have been important in the actual gold standard period). An inflow of gold produces the opposite effects. Again, any price effect is an aggregate phenomenon, not a direct adjustment occurring only in the foreign sector.

Hence, the price adjustment mechanism in the gold standard works as a strong disciplinary force against inflation in a country because the inflation causes a "deficit" and sets the adjustment mechanism into motion. It should be noted, though, and as we develop further in Chapter 29, that countries with substantial inflation in the modern world are reluctant to undergo the discipline of the gold standard and have adopted various other exchange rate arrangements.

The Price Adjustment Mechanism and the Pegged Rate System

Exchange rates can, of course, be pegged without any direct reference to gold. Under a **pegged rate system,** governments fix the price of their currency and stand ready to support the fixed price in the foreign exchange market (government intervention). If an increase in the demand for foreign currency threatens to drive the exchange rate up beyond some stated limit, the government must stand ready to supply a sufficient amount of foreign exchange to hold the exchange rate within the limits or band it has agreed to. Similarly, any increase in supply of foreign exchange that will drive the exchange rate below the lower limit must be offset by sufficient government purchases of the foreign currency. The central bank thus stands ready to intervene by buying foreign currency when the domestic currency is strong and by selling foreign currency when the domestic currency is weak, in order to maintain the pegged value.

This type of system differs from a gold standard in that the initiative comes from central banks buying and selling foreign currencies in the intervention process rather than from individuals buying and selling gold. This requires that governments that peg their currencies must have a sufficient supply of foreign exchange reserves to defend the value of their currency. The adjustment effects under a pegged system are similar to those of the gold standard. Upward

IN THE REAL WORLD:

EXCHANGE RATE REGIMES IN TRANSITION ECONOMIES

The extremely high rates of inflation in the transition economies of Central/Eastern Europe, the former republics of the Soviet Union, and Mongolia have been discussed in earlier chapters (see Table 5 in Chapter 17). These countries chose a variety of different types of exchange rate regimes in their attempts to assist policymakers in their efforts to attain macroeconomic stability. After the initial turbulent transition years in the early to mid-1990s, most of these nations had, by 1997, selected an exchange rate regime and a focus for exchange rate policy. Of the 27 nations represented in Table 4, 8 selected a floating exchange rate, 7 selected a managed float, and the remaining 12 nations chose either a currency board or a targeted exchange rate with an explicit peg or narrow band. The closest approach to the gold standard discussed in this chapter consists of the currency board arrangement (discussed later in Chapter 28), where the money supply adjusts in response to

holdings of the specified foreign currency. Exchange rate policy thus does not fall into the "one size fits all" category for countries in transition. The types of exchange rate arrangements are discussed further in Chapter 29.

By 2006, however, a number of the countries had changed their exchange rate regime. The 4 nations that were using a currency board arrangement in 1997 were still using a currency board in 2006, but 2 of them had changed the nature of their boards because they had joined the European Union. The number of countries using a targeted exchange rate program with an explicit peg or a peg with a narrow band increased from 8 to 9. The largest growth occurred in the managed float category which increased from 7 countries to 12 countries. The biggest reduction came in the floating rate category, where there was a decline from 8 countries to 2.

(continued)

IN THE REAL WORLD: *(continued)*

TABLE 4   Exchange Rate Regimes in Transition Countries, 1997 and 2006

Exchange Rate Regimes	Regime in 1997	Regime in 2006
Currency board	Bosnia and Herzegovina	Bosnia and Herzegovina
	Bulgaria	Bulgaria
	Estonia	Estonia*
	Lithuania	Lithuania*
Targeted exchange rate	Croatia	Azerbaijan
	Hungary	Belarus
	Latvia	Hungary
	Macedonia	Latvia
	Poland	Macedonia
	Russia	Slovak Republic*
	Slovak Republic	Slovenia*
	Ukraine	Turkmenistan
		Ukraine
Managed floating rate	Belarus	Armenia
	Czech Republic	Croatia
	Georgia	Czech Republic
	Kyrgyz Republic	Georgia
	Slovenia	Kazakhstan
	Turkmenistan	Kyrgyz Republic
	Uzbekistan	Moldova
		Mongolia
		Romania
		Russia
		Tajikistan
		Uzbekistan
Floating rate	Albania	Albania
	Armenia	Poland
	Azerbaijan	
	Kazakhstan	
	Moldova	
	Mongolia	
	Romania	
	Tajikistan	

*Nature of arrangement has changed because the country joined the European Union.

Sources: "Monetary and Financial Sector Policies in Transition Countries," *International Monetary Fund Reports,* 1997; "De Facto Classification of Exchange Rate Regimes and Monetary Policy Framework," *International Monetary Fund Reports,* 2006, obtained from www.imf.org.

pressure on the exchange rate brought about by an increase in the demand for foreign exchange will cause the central bank to supply the market with foreign exchange (sell foreign exchange for domestic currency). The purchase of domestic currency by the central bank will lead to a reduction in the money supply and to macroeconomic adjustments in interest rates, income, and prices. Symmetrically, a market increase in the supply of foreign exchange will lead to the purchase of foreign currency by the central bank with domestic currency, which will increase the money supply and stimulate expansionary macro effects on interest rates, income, and prices.

If any of these automatic adjustment effects are to take place under a fixed-rate system, whether a formal gold standard or a pegged system, the central bank must allow the actions being taken in the foreign exchange market to exercise their influence on the domestic money supply. Thus, not only does the central bank lose control of the money supply as a policy tool for other purposes, but shocks in the foreign sector result in a direct macro adjustment through changes in interest rates, income, and prices. Structural disequilibria in the foreign sector can thus become the "tail that wags the dog" because the problem can be solved only by an economywide adjustment under a fixed-rate system. This will be discussed in greater detail in following chapters.

CONCEPT CHECK

1. Explain why producers and consumers respond differently to price (exchange rate) changes in the short run relative to the long run.
2. What effect can lagged consumer-producer response to exchange rate changes have on

the current account balance? On price adjustment in the foreign exchange markets?
3. How would a decrease in the demand for foreign exchange affect a country's supply of gold under a gold standard? Why?

SUMMARY

This chapter focused on issues related to price adjustments and balance-of-payments disequilibrium. The conditions underlying the demand and supply of foreign exchange were examined and the market stability conditions analyzed with respect to price adjustments. The link between the demand for traded goods and services and the elasticities that characterize the current account were developed, and the Marshall-Lerner condition for market stability was considered. Assuming market stability, the price adjustment mechanism under flexible exchange rates causes expenditure switching between foreign

and domestic goods and services as relative prices change with changes in the exchange rate. This expenditure-switching occurs to the extent that exchange rate changes influence goods prices (that is, to the extent that "pass-through" occurs). In the adjustment process under fixed-rate systems, any price adjustment takes place at the macro or aggregate level in response to changes in the money supply accompanying the gold or foreign exchange movements that are required to maintain the fixed rate. This macro adjustment process works best when "rules of the game" are followed.

KEY TERMS

complete exchange rate pass-through	gold export point	mint par
elasticities approach	gold import point	partial exchange rate pass-through
elasticity of exchange rate pass-through	gold standard	pegged rate system
	J curve	price adjustment mechanism
expenditure switching	market stability	rules of the game
	Marshall-Lerner condition	

QUESTIONS AND PROBLEMS

1. "The existence of a downward- (or backward-) sloping supply curve of foreign exchange is a *sufficient* condition for the generation of an unstable equilibrium position in the foreign exchange market." Assess the validity of this statement.
2. "The existence of a downward- (or backward-) sloping supply curve of foreign exchange is a *necessary* condition for

the generation of an unstable equilibrium position in the foreign exchange market." Assess the validity of this statement.
3. Suppose that both the supply curve of imports to country A and the supply curve of exports from country A are horizontal (as in Figure 6). Assume that at a predepreciation value of A's currency, country A sells 975 units of exports and purchases

810 units of imports. (You do not need to know the actual prices of imports and exports, but assume that trade is initially balanced.) Suppose now that there is a 10 percent depreciation of A's currency against foreign currencies and that because of the depreciation exports rise to 1,025 units and imports fall to 790 units. Would the simple Marshall-Lerner condition suggest that country A's current account balance has improved or deteriorated because of this depreciation of its currency? Explain carefully.

4. The U.S. dollar depreciated markedly against the yen in the early 1990s, and yet U.S. net imports from Japan continued to rise in the short run. How might this counterintuitive behavior be explained?

5. Do you as a consumer think that there is much of a time lag between when a price change of an imported good in your market basket occurs and when you react (if at all) to this price change? If so, why? If not, why not? If your reaction time is shared by all consumers of imports, what implication would there be for the impact of a change in currency values on the current account balance in the short run? Explain.

6. Sometimes the charge is made that a country (e.g., China) is arbitrarily enhancing its current account surplus by keeping its currency at "too low" a value, that is, that exchange market intervention by the central bank is keeping the country's currency depreciated below the free-market equilibrium value. How would such behavior influence the country's exports and imports? What assumption is being made regarding demand elasticities in making the charge of arbitrary enhancement of the surplus? Explain.

7. Suppose that under the gold standard the mint par of 1 ounce of gold is $40 in the United States, £20 in the United Kingdom, and 60 pesos in Mexico. Assume that the cost of transporting gold between any pair of countries is $1 (or equivalent in £ or pesos) per ounce.
   (a) Calculate (in $/£) the gold export point from the United States to the United Kingdom and the gold import point to the United States from the United Kingdom.
   (b) Calculate (in peso/£) the gold export point from Mexico to the United Kingdom and the gold import point to Mexico from the United Kingdom.
   (c) Calculate (in peso/$) the gold export point from Mexico to the United States and the gold import point to Mexico from the United States.

8. It has been argued that the appreciation of the yen against the dollar in the early 1990s did not have the anticipated effect on U.S. imports from Japan partly because the extent of pass-through was reduced by Japanese exporters during this period. Briefly explain what is meant by "pass-through" and how Japanese exporters would have been behaving if the allegation in the previous sentence were true.

 Appendix   DERIVATION OF THE MARSHALL-LERNER CONDITION

The requirements for stability in the foreign exchange market were discussed in the chapter, accompanied by a brief intuitive explanation. A more formal derivation of this important condition follows.
   Given the following definitions:

P_x, P_m = domestic prices of exports and imports, respectively

Q_x, Q_m = quantities of exports and imports, respectively

V_x, V_m = value of exports and imports, respectively

the domestic trade balance, B, is defined as

$$B = V_x - V_m = Q_x P_x - Q_m P_m \qquad [1]$$

and the change in the trade balance, dB, is defined as

$$dB = P_x dQ_x + Q_x dP_x - P_m dQ_m - Q_m dP_m \qquad [2]$$

Assuming that the supply prices of traded goods and services do not change, that is, the supply curves are perfectly elastic over the range of quantity change, then the change in the prices of traded goods and services is attributable only to changes in the exchange rate. Because we are viewing the trade balance in terms of domestic currency in this example, dP_x is therefore equal to 0, whereas P_m changes by the percentage increase in the exchange rate, k. Therefore, dP_m is equal to kP_m. [If the exchange rate increases (the domestic currency depreciates) by 10 percent, the domestic price of imports increases by 10 percent.] We utilize the following definitions of export and import demand elasticity:

$$\eta_x = (dQ_x/Q_x)/[d(P_x/e)/(P_x/e)] \qquad [3]$$

$$\eta_m = (dQ_m/Q_m)/(dP_m/P_m) \qquad [4]$$

where P_x/e is the price of domestic exports in foreign currency. Turning to equation [3], the elasticity definition is reworked to obtain an expression for dQ_x in terms of η_x:

$$\eta_x = (dQ_x/Q_x)/\{[(edP_x - P_xde)/e^2]/(P_x/e)\}$$
$$= [(dQ_x/Q_x)(P_x/e)]/[(edP_x - P_xde)/e^2]$$
$$= (dQ_x/Q_x)/[(dP_x/P_x) - de/e]$$

Because dP_x/P_x is assumed to be 0, then

$$\eta_x = (dQ_x/Q_x)/(-de/e)$$

thus,

$$\eta_x = (dQ_x/Q_x)/(-k)$$

and

$$\eta_x(-k)Q_x = dQ_x \qquad [5]$$

Using equation [4], we can rewrite dQ_m in terms of the import demand elasticity η_m, that is,

$$(\eta_mQ_mdP_m)/P_m = \eta_mQ_mk = dQ_m \qquad [6]$$

For a depreciation to improve the trade balance, the increase in the value of exports must exceed any increase in the value of imports. If demand for imports is elastic, that is no problem, because the value of total imports falls with the increase in price of foreign goods and services. If, however, demand for imports is inelastic, then depreciation of the currency leads to an increased expenditure for imports. We now return to equation [2] and rewrite it in terms of the two demand elasticities using [5] and [6], taking note that if depreciation is to improve the balance, $dB > 0$:

$$dB = P_x\eta_x(-k)Q_x - P_m\eta_mkQ_m - Q_mkP_m > 0$$

or

$$P_x\eta_xkQ_x + P_m\eta_mkQ_m + Q_mkP_m < 0$$

thus,

$$P_x\eta_xQ_x + P_m\eta_mQ_m < -Q_mP_m$$

and

$$\eta_x(P_xQ_x/P_mQ_m) + \eta_m < -1 \qquad [7]$$

or, stating the elasticities in absolute value terms,

$$|\eta_x|(P_xQ_x/P_mQ_m) + |\eta_m| > 1 \qquad [8]$$

The expressions in [7] and [8] constitute the Marshall-Lerner condition. In the case of balanced trade, $P_xQ_x/P_mQ_m = 1$, and thus the sum of the absolute values of the two elasticities must be greater than 1 if depreciation is to improve the balance. This is the basic Marshall-Lerner condition. When trade is not balanced, the condition is modified as indicated in [7] and [8] when the value of trade is measured in domestic currency.

24

NATIONAL INCOME AND THE CURRENT ACCOUNT

LEARNING OBJECTIVES

■ To understand how the incorporation of a foreign trade sector into a Keynesian income model alters the domestic saving/investment relationship and changes the multiplier.

■ To recognize that national income equilibrium may not be consistent with equilibrium in the current account.

■ To learn why income levels across countries are interdependent.

INTRODUCTION

**How Does GDP
Growth Cause Trade
Deficits?**

In March 2000, economist Catherine Mann of the Institute for International Economics, a think tank in Washington, DC, wrote the following:[1]

> The United States is enjoying an economic boom that is fueling the growth of its trade deficit. At current exchange rates, the strength of the U.S. economy, combined with slow growth in demand in many other parts of the world, will lead to further widening of the U.S. trade deficit . . . A change in the value of the dollar alone would narrow the trade gap for a while, but the deficit would soon begin to widen again. To put the U.S. current account and trade deficits back on a sustainable path will require structural reforms in the United States and its trading partners that encourage faster global growth, boost U.S. household savings rates, better prepare U.S. workers for technological changes in the global economy, and open up markets for U.S. exports.

This chapter is devoted to providing the analytical structure to interpret easily a statement such as this one by Catherine Mann. We examine the manner in which the macroeconomy influences and is influenced by changes in exports and imports. Thus, we move away from price relationships linking the external and internal sectors of the economy to the interrelationships between the two sectors that involve real national income. To accomplish this task, we develop the macroeconomics of an open economy—an economy with foreign trade—in the context of Keynesian income analysis. The basics of Keynesian income analysis, named after the British economist John Maynard Keynes, were likely presented in your principles course. The traditional single-country focus is supplemented here by examining the real income response to exogenous factors when countries are linked through international trade. The last section of the chapter is a synthesis of price and income effects.

THE CURRENT ACCOUNT AND NATIONAL INCOME

**The Keynesian
Income Model**

In a **Keynesian income model,** the focus is on aggregate spending in the entire economy. Aggregate spending consists of the desired expenditures on the economy's goods and services. An assumption is made that prices are constant, so the focus is on real income movements and not on price changes. In addition, monetary considerations such as the interest rate are assumed to be constant. It is also generally assumed that the economy is not at full employment, usually because of downward money wage rigidity. For example, because of institutional features such as unions or a desire by employers to keep the best workers from leaving due to wage decreases during slack times, the wage rate does not fall to clear the labor market during such periods.

In the simple open-economy Keynesian model, **desired aggregate expenditures** (E) during a time period consist of consumption spending by the economy's households on goods and services (C), investment spending by firms (I), government spending on goods and services (G), and export spending by foreign citizens on the country's products (X). In addition, because some of the domestic spending is on imports (M), these must be subtracted to obtain the demand for home goods and services. Hence, desired expenditures or aggregate demand can be written as

$$E = C + I + G + X - M \tag{1}$$

What determines the amount of C? Keynes hypothesized that the most important determinant of a country's current consumption spending is the amount of current income (Y) in

---

[1]Catherine L. Mann, "Is the U.S. Current Account Deficit Sustainable?" *Finance and Development* 37, no. 1 (March 2000), pp. 42–43.

TITANS OF INTERNATIONAL ECONOMICS:

JOHN MAYNARD KEYNES (1883–1946)

John Maynard Keynes was born in Cambridge, England, on June 5, 1883. The son of an economist (John Neville Keynes), he attended Eton and then King's College, Cambridge, where he received a degree in mathematics in 1905. He then studied under the neoclassical economist Alfred Marshall, who pleaded with him to become an economist. Keynes entered the British Civil Service in the India Office, and his first book, *Indian Currency and Finance* (1913), assessed the Indian currency system as an example of a gold/pegged exchange rate system. He attained widespread fame in 1919 when he wrote *The Economic Consequences of the Peace*. This book, as well as later famous journal articles, castigated the Treaty of Versailles for the heavy burdens it placed on Germany in connection with reparations payments after World War I. Keynes's view was that the price adjustments required for Germany to earn the foreign exchange to make the payments (i.e., the price changes needed to increase exports and decrease imports sufficiently that the current account surplus would match the required capital outflow associated with the payments) would be excessive. They would deteriorate Germany's terms of trade and welfare greatly, and the payments might never be accomplished because of their harshness.

Keynes then published the influential *A Treatise on Probability* in 1921. However, his most important academic contributions occurred in the 1930s—*A Treatise on Money* (1930) and, especially, *The General Theory of Employment, Interest and Money* (1936). *The General Theory* was a broadside attack on the apparatus of Classical economics with its view that the economy would settle automatically at the full-employment level of income. (The Classical view was very hard to sell to anyone during the Great Depression!) He emphasized the role of aggregate demand and the possibility of attaining national income equilibrium at less than full employment. The demand for money and its relationship to the interest rate also received revolutionary treatment and played a major role in his aggregate demand formulation. Keynesian analysis assigned a prominent role to fiscal policy in affecting national income and employment—which had

been denied in the Classical model. Keynes also met with Franklin D. Roosevelt, who was later to use public works expenditures as a measure for attempting to get out of the Depression. Although Keynes is reported not to have been impressed with FDR's economic knowledge, FDR wrote in a letter to Felix Frankfurter (later a long-time U.S. Supreme Court Justice), "I had a grand talk with K and liked him immensely" (quoted in Harrod 1951, p. 448).

Keynes's life was a whirlwind of activity. Aside from his roles as policy advisor to the British government and Cambridge don, he was a patron of the arts, a collector of rare books, editor of *The Economic Journal,* first bursar of King's College, and chairman of the board of the National Mutual Life Insurance Company. He also amassed a personal fortune through shrewd financial investments. In addition, Keynes was a member of the Bloomsbury circle, a group of artists, intellectuals, and writers that included Lytton Strachey and Virginia Woolf. Further, and most impressively to some, he married a premier Russian ballerina in 1925, giving rise to the ditty, "There ne'er was such union of beauty and brains, as when Lydia Lopokova wed John Maynard Keynes."

Keynes's final years were spent successfully negotiating a large war loan for Britain from the United States during World War II and hammering out the Bretton Woods agreement for the formation of the International Monetary Fund. With his usual persuasive powers, personal charm, and magnetism, he forcefully presented and fought for his proposals for the postwar international monetary system. In the end, the new Bretton Woods system (see the last chapter in this book) resembled more closely the American plan than the British plan, but he had been the dominant figure at the extended conference. John Maynard Keynes died on Easter Sunday, 1946.

Sources: R. F. Harrod, *The Life of John Maynard Keynes* (New York: Harcourt, Brace, 1951); Robert L. Heilbroner, *The Worldly Philosophers: The Lives, Times, and Ideas of the Great Economic Thinkers,* 3rd ed. (New York: Simon and Schuster, 1967), chap. 9; Don Patinkin, "John Maynard Keynes," in John Eatwell, Murray Milgate, and Peter Newman, eds., *The New Palgrave: A Dictionary of Economics,* vol. 3 (London: Macmillan, 1987), pp. 19–41.

the economy. In general terms, then, consumption depends on or is a function of disposable income of households; that is,

$$C = f(Y_d) \qquad [2]$$

where disposable income (Y_d) is income in the economy (Y) minus taxes (T); that is,

$$Y_d = Y - T \qquad [3]$$

The general expression [2] is usually written in a more precise way:

$$C = a + bY_d \qquad\qquad [4]$$

This equation is a standard Keynesian **consumption function.** To put numerical content to it, suppose we specify

$$C = 100 + 0.80Y_d$$

This equation indicates that if disposable income is $600 (in billions, e.g.), then consumption spending is equal to $100 plus (0.80 × $600), or $100 plus $480, or $580. If disposable income rises to $700, then consumption spending is equal to $100 plus (0.80 × $700) = $100 + $560 = $660.

In this consumption function, the a term (or $100 in the example) is designated as **autonomous consumption spending,** meaning that this amount of consumption spending is determined by *other things besides income.* These "other things" can consist of the level of interest rates, the size of the population, attitudes toward thrift, the level of accumulated wealth, expectations of future income, and so forth. The part of consumption that does depend on current income is labeled bY_d, or $0.80Y_d$, and is known as **induced consumption spending.** Within the induced consumption component bY_d, a key feature is the term b, or 0.80 in our example. The b is known as the **marginal propensity to consume,** or **MPC.** The MPC is defined as the change in consumption divided by the change in disposable income, that is, the fraction of additional Y_d spent on consumption goods. Therefore, designating "change in" by Δ,

$$MPC = \Delta C / \Delta Y_d \qquad\qquad [5]$$

In addition to this consumption propensity, the **marginal propensity to save,** or **MPS,** is defined as the change in saving (S) divided by the change in disposable income, that is, the fraction of any additional Y_d allocated to saving:

$$MPS = \Delta S / \Delta Y_d \qquad\qquad [6]$$

Because any change in income can be allocated only to consumption and saving, it follows that

$$MPC + MPS = 1.0 \qquad\qquad [7]$$

In our sample consumption function, where MPC = 0.80, the MPS must equal 0.20.

Finally, the consumption function $C = a + bY_d$ immediately tells us the nature of the **saving function** for households in the economy. Remembering that by definition disposable income can be allocated only to consumption and saving, the saving function can be easily obtained:

$$
\begin{aligned}
Y_d &= C + S \\
&= a + bY_d + S \\
S &= Y_d - (a + bY_d) \\
&= -a + (1 - b)Y_d
\end{aligned}
$$

or

$$S = -a + sY_d \qquad\qquad [8]$$

where $s(=1 - b)$ is the marginal propensity to save.

The consumption and saving functions are illustrated in Figure 1. Panel (a) portrays the consumption function for $C = 100 + 0.80Y_d$ and panel (b) shows the associated saving function $S = -100 + 0.20Y_d$. Relating Figure 1(a) to the consumption function equation, the a term (or 100) is the height of the intercept on the vertical axis, while the

FIGURE 1   **Consumption and Saving Functions**

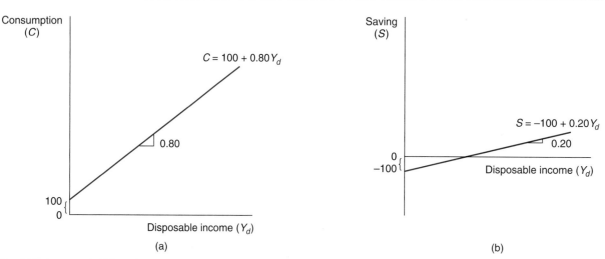

Panel (a) shows a typical Keynesian consumption function. The autonomous component (100) is consumption that is independent of disposable income. The induced component of consumption is 0.80 times the disposable income level, with 0.80 being the marginal propensity to consume (MPC). Because the MPC is constant in this example at 0.80, the consumption function is a straight line. Panel (b) shows the associated saving function by households. Because $Y_d = C + S$, therefore $S = Y_d - C = Y_d - (100 + 0.80Y_d) = -100 + 0.20Y_d$. This function is a straight line with a slope of 0.20, which is the marginal propensity to save (MPS).

slope of the consumption schedule is b, that is, the MPC (or 0.80). Because the MPC is constant, the slope is constant, meaning that the consumption function is a straight line. Similarly, the intercept in Figure 1(b) is *minus a* (or $-$ 100), and the slope is s, the MPS (or 0.20).

We now turn to investment spending. Remember that investment decisions (in the sense of *real* investment spending on plant and equipment, residential construction, and changes in inventories, not in the sense of financial investment in stocks, bonds, etc.) are made by business firms and not by households. Thus there is no necessary direct link between consumption spending and investment spending. In this simple income model, investment is usually assumed to be entirely autonomous or independent of current national income in the economy, meaning that investment spending is determined by factors other than income (for example, interest rates, wage rates, and the expectations of firms concerning the future). When investment is assumed to be independent of current income, the investment equation is written as

$$I = \bar{I} \qquad\qquad [9]$$

where the bar means that investment is fixed at a given amount for all levels of income. Thus, the equation $I = 180$ would indicate that investment spending by firms is $180 no matter what the level of income in the economy. The assumption that I is independent of income is clearly unrealistic in a strict sense. However, it may well be the case that interest rates, wage rates, technological change, and so forth, are more important for the investment decision than is the current level of national income. The graphical depiction of the autonomous investment function is given as the line $I = 180$ in Figure 2.

Government spending on goods and services in the simple Keynesian open-economy model (G) is also assumed to be independent of current income. This means that G is treated as being dependent on government priorities with respect to items such as national

FIGURE 2   Autonomous Investment, Government Spending, Tax, and Export Schedules

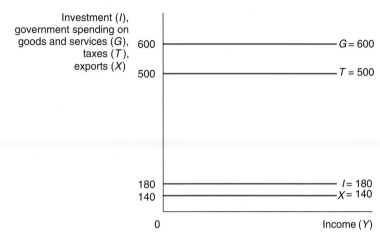

Investment, government spending on goods and services, taxes, and exports are all assumed to be autonomous or independent of current income in the simple Keynesian model (i.e., they depend on factors other than income). Thus, in our numerical example, $I = 180$, $G = 600$, $T = 500$, and $X = 140$ no matter what the level of national income.

defense, highways, and education and on policy measures, and not on the level of national income. This is also a simplification:

$$G = \overline{G} \qquad\qquad [10]$$

In terms of our numerical example, assume that $G = 600$. This autonomous government spending on goods and services is represented by the $G = 600$ line in Figure 2.

Along with government spending, of course, we must also introduce taxes. In the simplest tax case, we assume that taxes are independent of income; that is,

$$T = \overline{T} \qquad\qquad [11]$$

In this formulation, taxes are autonomous and are, for example, levied on something other than current income such as wealth or property. Clearly, it is unrealistic to assume that taxes are not a function of income in the economy. However, in the body of this chapter, we will utilize that assumption both because it makes the analysis simpler and because the focus of the chapter is on the foreign sector's interactions with national income and not on the government sector's interactions with national income. (A Keynesian model where taxes depend on income is presented in Appendix A.) For our continuing numerical example, we hence assume $T = 500$, and this fixed amount of taxes is indicated in Figure 2. (Note in the figure that government spending does not have to equal taxes in any given year, and this is obviously realistic!)

Finally, turning to the external sector of the Keynesian open-economy income model, exports are also specified as being autonomous or independent of the country's current level of national income. The export equation is thus

$$X = \overline{X} \qquad\qquad [12]$$

where $\overline{X}$ indicates the autonomous exports. To continue our numerical example, let us say that

$$X = 140$$

Exports are constant at $140. This is also represented graphically in Figure 2. Home-country exports are more likely to depend on other countries' incomes than upon home income, because domestic exports are dependent on the buying power of other countries as determined by their incomes. In addition, home exports depend on nonincome factors such as relative prices of domestic goods compared with foreign goods, the exchange rate (assumed to be fixed in the Keynesian model), innovation in home export industries, and foreign tastes and preferences. If any of these factors change so that more domestic exports are demanded, then the export function will shift vertically upward in parallel fashion; if other countries decreased their demand for the home country's goods, the export line would shift vertically downward in a parallel manner.

In the simple Keynesian macro model, imports (M) are generally made to depend on only one variable—the level of home-country income. The relationship between imports and national income is expressed by the **import function.** Its general form is

$$M = f(Y) \qquad [13]$$

A specific form is

$$M = \overline{M} + mY \qquad [14]$$

Here, $\overline{M}$ represents **autonomous imports,** the amount of spending on imports that is independent of income. This spending on imports depends on factors such as tastes and preferences for foreign goods as opposed to home goods, and relative prices of foreign goods compared with home goods. The term mY refers to **induced imports,** the spending on foreign goods that is dependent on the level of income. As the income of a country rises, more spending occurs on goods and services, and some of this additional spending is on imported goods and services. If imports consisted only of consumption goods and services, disposable income (Y_d) would appear in expression [14] rather than national income (Y). However, we assume here (and it is true in practice) that imports contain not only consumption goods and services but also inputs into the domestic production process (which depend on total income). Hence we use Y in the import equation rather than Y_d. Continuing with our numerical example, suppose

$$M = 20 + 0.10Y$$

This equation states the value of autonomous imports as $20 and the value of induced imports as 0.10 times the income level. The figure 0.10 (or the letter m in expression [14]) is the **marginal propensity to import,** or **MPM.** This concept is defined as the change in imports divided by the change in income:

$$MPM = \Delta M / \Delta Y \qquad [15]$$

If income rises by $100 and the MPM is 0.10, an additional $10 will be spent on imports. The MPM is to be distinguished from the **average propensity to import,** or **APM,** which is the total spending on imports divided by total income:

$$APM = M / Y \qquad [16]$$

Another term emerges from this analysis: the **income elasticity of demand for imports or YEM,** which is the percentage change in the demand for imports divided by the percentage change in income and was also noted in Chapter 11. The term has useful applications because it indicates the percentage growth in imports that will occur as a country's national income grows over time. It can be shown that the YEM is related in simple fashion to the APM and the MPM:

FIGURE 3   A Keynesian Import Function

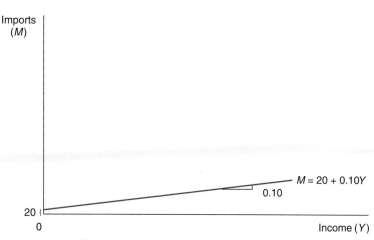

The autonomous component of imports (20) reflects imports purchased independently of income. The induced component of imports is 0.10 times the income level, with 0.10 indicating the marginal propensity to import (MPM). With a constant MPM, the import function is a straight line.

$$\text{YEM} = (\%\,\Delta M)/(\%\,\Delta Y) \qquad [17]$$
$$= (\Delta M/M)/(\Delta Y/Y)$$
$$= (\Delta M/\Delta Y)/(M/Y)$$
$$= \text{MPM}/\text{APM}$$

Thus, if a country's MPM exceeds its APM, imports relative to income will rise as the country's income grows (YEM is elastic). If MPM is less than APM, the YEM is inelastic and imports will fall as a fraction of income as income rises. Finally, if MPM equals APM, the YEM is unit elastic and imports as a fraction of national income stay the same as income rises. In the past several decades, trade as a fraction of national income in the United States has been rising, indicating the MPM of the United States is larger than the APM.

The import function is shown in Figure 3, plotting the specific function given earlier, namely, $M = 20 + 0.10Y$. The intercept of the import function is located at the value of autonomous imports, $\overline{M}$. The slope of the (straight-line) import function is the MPM, or 0.10 in our example.

Determining the Equilibrium Level of National Income

The next step in the analysis involves the actual determination of the **equilibrium level of national income** in this type of model. The equilibrium income level is the level at which there is no tendency for the income level to rise or to fall (i.e., the economy is "at rest"). This level of income occurs when desired spending exactly matches the production level of the economy. If such is the case, then there is no net tendency for economic activity to change. However, if spending exceeds production (which equals income), then firms have not produced enough output to meet demand and their inventories of goods will fall. Output will consequently rise in order to prevent this unintended depletion of inventories. On the other hand, if production exceeds spending, there will be unintended inventory accumulation. This accumulation will be a signal to producers to reduce their output, and production will decline until it equals the level of demand. Thus, at income levels both above and below the equilibrium level, forces are at work to return the economy to the equilibrium income level.

FIGURE 4   The Equilibrium Level of Income

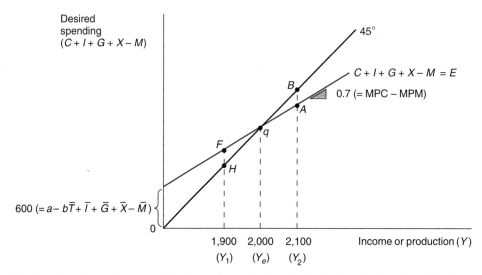

Total desired spending on domestic goods in relation to income is indicated by the $C + I + G + X - M$ line, with a slope of [MPC − MPM]. Equilibrium income level $0Y_e$ (or 2,000 in our example) occurs where desired spending equals production. At lower income level $0Y_1$ (or 1,900), spending ($=Y_1F$) is greater than production ($=0Y_1 = Y_1H$), so inventories are being depleted and production expands to $0Y_e$. At income level $0Y_2$ (or 2,100) above $0Y_e$, spending ($=Y_2A$) is less than production ($=0Y_2 = Y_2B$), so inventories are accumulating and production contracts to $0Y_e$ (2,000).

The determination of the equilibrium level of income is shown graphically in Figure 4, utilizing our numerical example. Remembering that, in our example,

$$
\begin{aligned}
C &= 100 + 0.8Y_d &\qquad G &= 600 \\
Y_d &= Y - T &\qquad X &= 140 \\
T &= 500 &\qquad M &= 20 + 0.1Y \\
I &= 180
\end{aligned}
$$

AVERAGE PROPENSITIES TO IMPORT, SELECTED COUNTRIES

Table 1 presents the average propensities to import for five major industrialized countries from 1973 through 2006. As can be seen, there has been a major increase in openness for the United States. In addition, there appears to have been some increase in the APM for Canada (especially in recent years) and some increase for France. For the United Kingdom, inspection of the data suggests little change for most of the period. Japan's average propensity to import declined and then rose, with little overall change. It likely followed the price of imported oil (very important for the Japanese economy) in a general way. The results for Canada, Japan, and the United States are in a general way broadly consistent with careful estimates of long-run income elasticities of demand made by Peter Hooper, Karen Johnson, and Jaime

Marquez,* who estimated the YEM to be 1.4 for Canada, 0.9 for Japan, and 1.8 for the United States. However, these economists estimated the YEM to be 1.6 for France, which is somewhat larger than might be inferred from looking at Table 1, and the YEM for the United Kingdom to be 2.2, which is not suggested by the relative stability of the United Kingdom's APM data in Table 1. Clearly, examination of APMs such as in Table 1 can offer tentative suggestions, but more detailed work is necessary for precise conclusions regarding the trend in the openness of a country.

*Peter Hooper, Karen Johnson, and Jaime Marquez, *Trade Elasticities for the G-7 Countries*, Princeton Studies in International Economics no. 87, August 2000, p. 8.

IN THE REAL WORLD: *(continued)*

TABLE 1   Average Propensities to Import, Selected Countries, 1973–2006

Year	Canada	France	Japan	United Kingdom	United States
1973	.220	.167	.100	.254	.066
1974	.246	.217	.143	.322	.085
1975	.241	.179	.128	.271	.075
1976	.229	.203	.128	.291	.083
1977	.235	.204	.115	.290	.090
1978	.249	.191	.094	.269	.092
1979	.265	.206	.125	.274	.098
1980	.264	.228	.144	.249	.105
1981	.261	.238	.138	.238	.101
1982	.221	.240	.136	.244	.093
1983	.221	.228	.120	.256	.093
1984	.249	.239	.121	.286	.103
1985	.258	.239	.108	.278	.099
1986	.264	.206	.073	.265	.102
1987	.255	.207	.072	.266	.107
1988	.258	.212	.077	.266	.108
1989	.255	.226	.088	.278	.107
1990	.256	.223	.094	.266	.108
1991	.256	.219	.083	.242	.104
1992	.274	.209	.077	.248	.105
1993	.301	.192	.069	.265	.108
1994	.328	.210	.071	.272	.115
1995	.341	.216	.078	.288	.122
1996	.344	.217	.094	.298	.123
1997	.375	.228	.098	.286	.127
1998	.394	.237	.091	.278	.128
1999	.393	.241	.087	.282	.135
2000	.399	.277	.096	.301	.150
2001	.378	.270	.099	.301	.138
2002	.367	.254	.101	.293	.137
2003	.338	.246	.104	.284	.141
2004	.340	.255	.114	.284	.153
2005	.339	.271	.129	.301	.162
2006	.339	.289	NA	.328	.168
Average for period	.293	.226	.103	.277	.113

NA = not available.
Note: Figures are imports of goods and services in the GDP accounts divided by GDP.
Sources: Calculated from data in International Monetary Fund (IMF), *International Financial Statistics Yearbook 2002* (Washington, DC: IMF, 2002), pp. 334–35, 482–83, 608–09, 1032–33, 1040–41; IMF, *International Financial Statistics Yearbook 2006* (Washington, DC: IMF, 2006), pp. 211, 301, 368, 607, 611; IMF, *International Financial Statistics,* April 2007, pp. 248, 420, 552, 1028, 1036.

Then the E (desired expenditures or spending line) is

$$E = C + I + G + X - M$$
$$= 100 + 0.8Y_d + 180 + 600 + 140 - (20 + 0.1Y)$$
$$= 100 + 0.8(Y - 500) + 180 + 600 + 140 - (20 + 0.1Y)$$
$$= 1,000 + 0.8Y - 400 - 0.1Y$$
$$= 600 + 0.7Y$$

This equation indicates that the intercept of the expenditures or spending line in Figure 4 is 600 [=the sum of all autonomous $= (a - b\overline{T} + \overline{I} + \overline{G} + \overline{X} - \overline{M})$] and the slope is 0.7 [=the marginal propensity to consume minus the marginal propensity to import $= (0.8 - 0.1) = 0.7 = (b - m)$]. Another important line in the diagram is the 45-degree line. Because a 45-degree line has the property that each point on it is equidistant from the vertical axis (spending) and the horizontal axis (production), it is clear that, for the economy to be in equilibrium, the economy must be located somewhere on this line. The equilibrium point q occurs where the $C + I + G + X - M$, or spending, line intersects the 45-degree line, and the equilibrium level of income associated with point q is income level $0Y_e$. Because $C + I + G + X - M$ shows desired spending and the 45-degree line illustrates points that are equidistant from both axes, the intersection of the E line with the 45-degree line gives us the single point where production equals spending.

In terms of our numerical example, the equilibrium where $E = Y$ or spending = production is found in straightforward fashion. We have established earlier that $E = 600 + 0.7Y$, so, for equilibrium,

$$E = Y$$
$$600 + 0.7Y = Y$$
$$600 = Y - 0.7Y$$
$$600 = 0.3Y$$
$$Y = 600/0.3 = 2,000$$

To see that 2,000 is indeed the equilibrium level, let us check the sum of the spending items to determine if they add up to 2,000. First, look at consumption. With an income level of 2,000 and taxes of 500, this means that disposable income is 1,500 (= 2,000 − 500). Because the consumption function is $C = 100 + 0.8Y_d$, this means that consumption is $100 + (0.8)(1,500) = 100 + 1,200 = 1,300$. Investment is constant at 180, government spending is constant at 600, and exports are constant at 140. Finally, imports, which must be subtracted, are equal to $20 + 0.1Y = 20 + (0.1)(2,000) = 20 + 200 = 220$. Thus, at the national income level of 2,000, spending $= C + I + G + X - M = 1,300 + 180 + 600 + 140 - 220 = 2,000$. Thus, at the equilibrium level of income, desired spending equals production and there is no unintended change in inventories of firms.

Let us consider briefly what happens if national income is not at the equilibrium level $0Y_e$ or 2,000. In Figure 4, consider the lower income level $0Y_1$ or 1,900. At $0Y_1$, spending is indicated by the height of the E line (distance Y_1F) and production is $0Y_1$, which because of the nature of the 45-degree line, is equal to distance Y_1H. In numbers, spending (E or distance Y_1F) is $600 + (0.7)(1,900) = 600 + 1,330 = 1,930$ and production (Y or Y_1H) is 1,900. Because spending of 1,930 is thus greater than production of 1,900 at income level $0Y_1$ by 30 (or distance HF), inventories of firms will decline; as firms then step up their production to eliminate this inventory depletion, income in the economy will rise until $0Y_e$ is reached and spending equals production. A similar analysis applies to income level $0Y_2$ (or 2,100), which is above the equilibrium level of income. At $0Y_2$, households and firms want to spend the amount Y_2A, which in numbers is equal to $600 + (0.7)(2,100) = 600 + 1,470 = 2,070$. However, production equals distance Y_2B (= $0Y_2$ by the construction of the 45-degree line) or 2,100. Hence, production exceeds spending (by AB or 30), and unintended inventory accumulation will lead to cutbacks in production. The cutbacks will continue until the income level reaches $0Y_e$ or 2,000.

Leakages and Injections

An alternative method of determining the equilibrium level of income is to represent the equilibrium income level as that level that equates desired or planned saving, imports, and taxes with desired investment, government spending, and exports. In this approach, saving,

FIGURE 5   **Alternative Representations of the Equilibrium Level of Income**

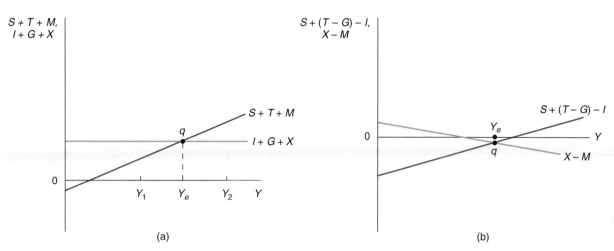

In panel (a), the equilibrium level of income $0Y_e$ occurs where the leakages from the domestic spending stream ($S + T + M$) are equal to the injections into the spending stream ($I + G + X$). At income levels below (above) $0Y_e$, injections are greater (less) than leakages, so there is pressure to expand (contract) income. Panel (b) shows an alternative representation using the relationship that, since $S + T + M = I + G + X$, then $S + (T - G) - I = X - M$. In this graph, equilibrium income level $0Y_e$ occurs simultaneously with a current account deficit (that is, $X - M < 0$).

imports, and taxes are thought of as **leakages** from the spending stream, in that they represent actions that reduce spending on domestic products. Investment, government spending, and exports are **injections** into the spending stream and therefore lead to home production. If the leakages exceed the injections, then there is downward pressure on spending and hence on income. If the injections exceed the leakages, there is pressure for expansion in the economy.

This approach is illustrated in Figure 5, panel (a), which shows the saving, tax, and import functions combined into an $S + T + M$ function and the autonomous investment, government spending, and export schedules combined into an $I + G + X$ schedule. The equilibrium level of income is situated immediately below point q where the two schedules intersect, at income level $0Y_e$. This $0Y_e$ is the same $0Y_e$ as in Figure 4 because the two figures employ the same basic information but in a different form.[2] If the economy is at an income level below $0Y_e$, such as $0Y_1$, ($I + G + X$) exceeds ($S + T + M$). That the equilibrium level is the same as previously in terms of our numerical example can be shown by calculating the leakages at the income level 2,000 and then comparing their sum with the injections. Because consumption in our example was $100 + 0.8Y_d$, and because saving = disposable income minus consumption, saving

---

[2]In the equilibrium expression $Y = C + I + G + X - M$, the right-hand side consists of expenditures that generate income, or it can be thought of as sources of income. Now consider the expression $Y = C + S + T$. The right-hand side of this equation indicates the uses of the income generated in the economy (for consumption, for saving, and for taxes). Because uses of income must equal sources of income,

$$C + S + T = C + I + G + X - M$$
$$S + T = I + G + X - M$$
$$S + T + M = I + G + X \qquad \qquad [18]$$

Expression [18] is another way of writing the equilibrium condition, and the intersection of the two schedules in panel (a) of Figure 5 thus also yields the equilibrium level of income.

equals $= Y_d - (100 + 0.8Y_d) = -100 + (1 - 0.8)Y_d = -100 + 0.2Y_d$. With income of 2,000 and taxes of 500, $Y_d = 1,500$ and saving $= -100 + (0.2)(1,500) = -100 + 300 = 200$. The import leakage is $M = 20 + 0.1Y = 20 + (0.1)(2,000) = 20 + 200 = 220$. Hence, with $S = 200, T = 500$, and $M = 220$, total leakages are $200 + 500 + 220 = 920$. Injections in our example were $I = 180$, $G = 600$, and $X = 140$, for total injections of $180 + 600 + 140 = 920$. Clearly, at the income level of 2,000, leakages equal injections.

Again, if the economy is at an income level below $0Y_e$ or 2,000, the economy will expand because injections into the spending stream exceed leakages or withdrawals from that stream. For example, if $0Y_1$ in Figure 5(a) is 1,900, with $T = 500$, then $S = -100 + (0.2)(1,900 - 500) = -100 + (0.2)(1,400) = -100 + 280 = 180$. At the income level of 1,900, $M = 20 + (0.1)(1,900) = 20 + 190 = 210$. Hence, while injections have remained at 920, total leakages are now $180 + 500 + 210 = 890$ and are 30 short of the injections. Inventories decline by 30 and income rises toward the equilibrium level of 2,000 or $0Y_e$. At income level $0Y_2$ (say, 2,100), the opposite is the case. Leakages will exceed injections (by 30 in our example), inventories will accumulate (by 30), and production will be cut back (to 2,000).

Income Equilibrium and the Current Account Balance

A second alternative representation of equilibrium focuses on the current account balance for the economy. (In our model, $X - M$ embraces exports and imports of all goods and services; since we have no unilateral transfers in the model, $X - M$ is thus the current account balance.) In this approach, we take the equilibrium condition of

$$S + T + M = I + G + X$$

and rearrange it to obtain

$$S + (T - G) - I = X - M \qquad [19]$$

In expression [19], S is private saving and $(T - G)$ is government saving (which can be negative). Thus, the expression makes the important point that, in an open economy, the difference between a country's total saving (private + government) and the country's investment equals the current account balance. If $X < M$, the country is saving domestically less in total than it is investing; the shortfall is being made up by a net inflow of foreign saving. This has been the case for the United States for most of the past 25 years. If $X > M$, the country is saving more than it is investing domestically (and hence it is investing abroad via a capital outflow, with the capital/financial account outflow being equal to the current account surplus). The expression also helps us understand Catherine Mann's point at the start of this chapter that an increase in U.S. household saving rates could reduce the U.S. trade and current account deficits.

Utilizing expression [19], we can then plot two new schedules as in Figure 5, panel (b). The upward-sloping $S + (T - G) - I$ line subtracts the *fixed* autonomous amount of investment and the *fixed* autonomous amount of government spending from private saving and taxes. Because S depends positively on Y, the line is clearly upward sloping. The $X - M$ line slopes downward because, at higher levels of Y, rising amounts of imports are being subtracted from a *fixed* amount of autonomous exports. As should be evident, the intersection of these two lines (at q) will also yield the equilibrium level of income $0Y_e$.

The virtue of this approach is that the state of the current account balance that exists at the equilibrium level of income can be observed. (In our numerical example, $X = 140$ and $M = 220$ at equilibrium, so the current account is in deficit by 80.) Further, an important point that emerges from this discussion is that, even though the economy is in income equilibrium, it is not necessary that the current account balance be zero. In Figure 5(b), the existence of the current account deficit when the economy is at its equilibrium income is reflected in the fact that the equilibrium position q is below the horizontal axis. If q occurs at a point above the horizontal axis, there would be a current account surplus; if q lies on the horizontal axis, $X = M$, which indicates balance in the current account.

CONCEPT CHECK

1. Explain why an income level below the equilibrium level of income cannot persist.
2. Suppose that imports are entirely induced, that is, that the import function is $M = mY$ (with m being the marginal propensity to import). What is the APM in this case? What is the value of the YEM?
3. If the economy is at its equilibrium level of income and has a current account deficit, what must be true of the total amount of saving (private plus government) in the economy relative to the amount of investment? How is the excess of investment over saving being financed?

The Autonomous Spending Multiplier

A familiar concept contained in Keynesian income models is the **autonomous spending multiplier.** The autonomous spending multiplier is used to answer the following question: If autonomous spending on $C, I, G,$ or X is changed, by how much will equilibrium income be changed? Graphically, as in Figure 4 earlier, this question is simply, if $(C + I + G + X - M)$ shifts in parallel fashion, what will be the ΔY as the economy responds to the change in autonomous spending?

Changes in Autonomous Consumption, Investment, Government Spending, and Exports

To answer this question, suppose that autonomous investment in our numerical example rises to 210 from its original level of 180. (This could be to $210 billion from $180 billion for example.) The best way to think of the multiplier concept is in terms of **rounds of spending in the multiplier process.** The autonomous increase of 30 in investment (assumed to be spent on domestic goods) generates production (and income) of 30 as firms produce the new machinery, for example, that is now in demand. The workers and owners of the firms producing the machinery receive 30 in income. Because taxes do not depend on income in this simplified model with which we are working, the 30 of new income will translate into 30 of new disposable income.[3] But what happens to this 30 of new disposable income? *Some* of it will be spent as indicated by the MPC. So a second round of spending will occur; in our example with MPC = 0.8, 24 will be spent [= (0.8)(30)]. However, some of this new spending will be on imports and will not lead to increased domestic production. In addition, remember that in our model, imports are a function of total income and not just disposable income because, besides consumption goods, some imports are also inputs for the new production being generated in this round. With our MPM of 0.1, imports go up by the MPM times the change in total income, or 3 [= (0.1)(30)]. This 3 amount must be subtracted from the 24 of second-round spending because the 3 does not generate domestic production and income, resulting in a net effect of 21 (= 24 − 3) in this second round of the multiplier process. In sum, the 30 of production in the first round has led to 21 of new domestic spending and income in the second round; 70 percent gets "re-spent."

The process continues into a third round. The 21 of spending from the second round leads to 21 of new income for the workers and firms producing the goods purchased in that second round. Of the 21 of new income (and new disposable income) thus generated, with the MPC of 0.8, 16.8 [= (0.8)(21)] will be spent. However, spending on imports will increase by the MPM times the 21 change in total income, and this 2.1 of imports [= (0.1)(21)], when subtracted from the 16.8 of spending, leaves a net increase in spending

---

[3]For a model that has taxes that depend on income, see Appendix A of this chapter.

on domestic goods in the third round of 14.7. Thus, 70 percent of the second-round amount of 21 has been re-spent in the third round. This 14.7 of spending leads to new income, and a fourth round is started. Theoretically, this process goes on through an infinite number of rounds, although the amount of new income generated in each cycle rapidly gets smaller.

What is the ultimate change in income occurring because of the original 30 of new investment? The total change in income after all the rounds have been completed equals the sum of the following geometric series:

$$\Delta Y = 30 + 21 + 14.7 + \cdots$$
$$= 30 + (0.7)(30) + (0.7)^2(30) + \cdots$$

which, mathematically, can be shown to be

$$\Delta Y = [1/(1 - \text{fraction re-spent in each round})](\text{initial } \Delta I)$$
$$= [1/(1 - 0.7)](30)$$
$$= (1/0.3)(30) = (3\ 1/3)(30) = 100$$

The 0.7 in the $(1 - 0.7)$ denominator term derives from the 70 percent re-spent in each round; in symbols, this 70 percent is [MPC − MPM] or $(0.8 - 0.1) = 0.7$. Thus, the initial increase in autonomous investment spending of 30 has led to a total change in income of 100. An initial change in autonomous consumption spending[4] or in autonomous government or export spending of 30 would have had the same 100 impact on income as the 30 change in autonomous investment. The "multiplier" is simply the total change in income divided by the initial change in autonomous spending, or \$100/\$30 = 3⅓. The formula for calculating the autonomous spending multiplier in the open economy (k_o) is

$$k_o = \frac{1}{1 - (\text{MPC} - \text{MPM})}$$

or

$$k_o = \frac{1}{1 - (\text{MPC} - \text{MPM})} = \frac{1}{\text{MPS} + \text{MPM}} \qquad [20]$$

or, in our example,

$$k_o = \frac{1}{1 - 0.8 + 0.1} = \frac{1}{0.2 + 0.1} = 3\tfrac{1}{3}$$

Expression [20] is the basic **open-economy multiplier.** If the economy were a closed economy, there would be no imports (or exports). Hence, the MPM would be zero and the closed economy multiplier would be $1/(1 - \text{MPC})$. This multiplier would be larger than the open economy multiplier (for any given MPC) because there is no leakage of spending out of the domestic economy into imports.

Changes in Autonomous Imports

A further multiplier exists in the open economy. We have dealt previously with autonomous increases in consumption, investment, government spending on goods and services, and exports. But autonomous imports $\overline{M}$ constitute another type of autonomous spending in the open economy. What happens if $\overline{M}$ increases? This one is tricky. If the demand for imports increases autonomously, this is equivalent to an autonomous *decrease* in the demand for domestic goods. Therefore, in national income models, an autonomous increase in imports

---

[4]It is assumed in all cases that the first round of spending is entirely on domestic goods.

IN THE REAL WORLD:

MULTIPLIER ESTIMATES FOR INDIA

There have been many, many estimates of open-economy multipliers for different countries over different time periods, usually for high-income or developed countries. However, attempts have also been made to estimate the multiplier for some developing countries, especially as comprehensive and more reliable data have become available. For example, in 1994, D. P. Bhatia published calculations of various multipliers for the Indian economy.* He approached the estimations from two perspectives—at the aggregate level directly (such as we have done in this chapter) and at the sectoral level, whereby multipliers were estimated for each sector of the economy and then aggregated to get an economywide figure. The direct aggregate-level estimates are most relevant for this chapter, and he obtained the following results with this procedure (given on his p. 46):[†]

1973–1974: marginal propensity to save = 0.30967
marginal propensity to import = 0.05449
multiplier = 1/(0.30967 + 0.05449) = 1/(0.36416)
= 2.74605

1978–1979: marginal propensity to save = 0.42487
marginal propensity to import = 0.06206
multiplier = 1/(0.42487 + 0.06206) = 1/(0.48693)
= 2.05368

1983–1984: marginal propensity to save = 0.18092
marginal propensity to import = 0.14323
multiplier = 1/(0.18092 + 0.14323) = 1/(0.32415)
= 3.08499

Hence, during the period from 1973–1974 through 1983–1984, the multiplier fell and then rose. Bhatia notes

(and this is evident from the numbers given) that the marginal propensity to save (MPS) and the marginal propensity to import (MPM) both increased between 1973–1974 and 1978–1979. Clearly these increases would cause a drop in the value of the multiplier as the leakages from the spending stream increased, and the multiplier decreased from its 1973–1974 value of 2.75 to a value of 2.05 in 1978–1979. Between 1978–1979 and 1983–1984, the MPS fell dramatically, which would increase the size of the multiplier, and the MPM rose sharply (partly reflecting greater spending on imports due to increases in oil prices), which would decrease the multiplier. On balance, the multiplier rose to 3.08 in 1983–1984.

With any estimates of this sort, though, it is useful to keep in mind that data problems do exist and that there are numerous different estimating techniques. (Bhatia's estimates from his sectoral procedure yielded higher multipliers than those given here, although the pattern of a decrease from 1973–1974 to 1978–1979 and then an increase to 1983–1984 remained intact.) In addition, we must always ask ourselves whether there are economic explanations that are consistent with the statistical results (such as the large increase in the Indian MPS from 1973–1974 to 1978–1979). Bhatia's paper does not pursue such explanations.

* D. P. Bhatia, "Estimates of Income Multipliers in the Indian Economy," *Indian Economic Journal* 42, no. 1 (July–September 1994), pp. 39–56.
† The Indian fiscal year ends in March; hence, 1973–1974, for example, runs from April 1973 through March 1974.   ●

will lead to a *decrease* in the level of income. The autonomous increase in imports reflects a decrease in spending on domestic goods, which leads to lower income. Because the multiplier process for an autonomous increase in imports operates in a *downward* direction, the multiplier for a change in autonomous imports is equal to *minus k_o*; that is,

$$\Delta Y/\Delta M = -k_o$$
$$= -\frac{1}{1 - MPC + MPM} \tag{21}$$

There is no conflict between this negative effect of an increase in imports in macro models and the positive effect of imports on national well-being in international trade theory. Trade theory assumes that the country is always at full employment and on its production-possibilities frontier both before and after the change in imports. In the macro models, we are making no such assumption that the economy is always at its maximum output.

With this import multiplier in mind, what will happen if exports and imports both increase autonomously by the same amount? The net effect of an autonomous balanced change in the size of the foreign trade sector (i.e., an equal autonomous change in exports and imports) is *zero*. This occurs because the export change has a multiplier of k_o while the autonomous import change has a multiplier of minus k_o. The two changes cancel each other out with respect to their impact on national income.

The Current Account and the Multiplier

Having examined the multiplier in the Keynesian income model, let us now look at relationships between national income, the current account balance, and the multiplier. First, recall the earlier point that national income equilibrium can coexist with a deficit in the current account. Suppose that, as a policy objective, we wish to eliminate the current account deficit by reducing imports, with the reduction in imports to be accomplished by reducing national income (through contractionary macroeconomic policy). *By how much would national income have to be reduced to eliminate the current account deficit?* The answer is easy to obtain. For instance, in our earlier numerical example, there was a deficit of 80 (X was 140, M was 220); we must contract income enough so that imports fall by 80. Remembering the MPM, this means that income must fall enough so that the change in income multiplied by the MPM equals -80. Thus, if the ΔM target is -80,

$$\Delta M = \text{MPM} \times \Delta Y$$
$$-80 = 0.10 \times \Delta Y$$
$$\Delta Y = -800$$

The level of income must fall by 800 to reduce imports by an amount that will restore balance in the current account. If the economy is at less than full employment, this might be a large contraction in income that would not be welcomed. There is a conflict between an "internal" target for the economy, such as full employment, and an "external" target, such as balance in the current account.

Second, suppose that we want to take policy measures to expand *exports* (e.g., by depreciating the value of our currency relative to other currencies and assuming that the Marshall-Lerner condition holds) as a way of eliminating the current account deficit. If exports increase by 80, will this eliminate the current account deficit? The answer is no. If exports increase by 80, then the open-economy multiplier of $3\frac{1}{3}$ is applied to this autonomous increase in exports. The level of Y will rise by $(80)(3\frac{1}{3})$, or 266.67, to 2,266.67 from the original 2,000. But because Y has risen by 266.67, there will be induced imports of the MPM ($= 0.10$) times 266.67, or 26.67. The expansion of exports (by 80) has cut the deficit by 53.33 ($= 80 - 26.67$) but has not eliminated it. It can also be noted that this analytical result of the export increase leading to a reduction in the deficit is what lies behind Catherine Mann's indication in the statement at the beginning of this chapter that faster global growth would reduce the U.S. trade and current account deficits. The reductions would occur because faster income growth in other countries would lead to increased exports from the United States since other countries have a positive marginal propensity to import from the United States.

This relationship between an increase in exports and the resulting increase in imports, though a smaller import increase than the initial increase in exports, is an important one. It is important because it shows that, given a disturbance in the foreign sector of the economy such as a rise in exports (it could also be a fall in exports or an autonomous rise or fall in imports), forces are set in motion to dampen the effect of that disturbance on the current account balance. Thus, in our example, when exports increased by 80, the current account balance didn't improve by the full 80 because imports increased by 26.67. The current account balance *did* improve, but by less than the initial disturbance. Because the initial export increase was partly offset by induced imports, there was at least *some* adjustment to the initial disturbance, but there was not full adjustment because imports did not rise by 80 and eliminate the effect of the export increase on the current account balance. This phenomenon of a current-account disturbance not leading to a full offset of the disturbance is called **partial current account adjustment** to any initial disturbance.

Foreign Repercussions and the Multiplier Process

A final matter to consider in our treatment of Keynesian income models is **foreign repercussions.** In the real world, when spending and income change in a home country, changes are transmitted to other countries through changes in imports of the home country. As reactions to the changes in trade occur in the other countries, there will be feedback upon the original home country. While full-scale econometric models of the world economy with hundreds of equations have been used to trace through foreign repercussions, we are less ambitious in this chapter. We give one limited example of how such repercussions can be taken account of in relatively simple macroeconomic models. This example concerns the multiplier process.

In the traditional (no-repercussions) open-economy multiplier process, an autonomous investment increase in the United States, for example, will cause a rise in U.S. income by the change in investment times the standard open-economy multiplier. This multiplied change in income will generate an induced rise in imports (by the MPM times the change in income). Thus, in the following schematic diagram:

$$\uparrow I_{US} \longrightarrow \uparrow Y_{US} \longrightarrow \uparrow M_{US}$$

The process stops here in the model we have been using so far. However, when foreign repercussions are permitted in the model, the process continues. The rise in imports into the United States constitutes a rise in exports of the rest of the world (ROW). When exports in ROW increase, this initiates a multiplier process in ROW and a rise in ROW income. This rise in income causes ROW to import more goods based on its marginal propensity to import. Finally, at least some of the increased imports into ROW will be exports of the United States! These increased exports will then set in motion additional spending and income generation in the United States. Further, this additional U.S. income will cause more U.S. imports, and so on. The process continues in ever-diminishing amounts. The multiplier mechanism when foreign repercussions exist can be represented by the following flow diagram:

$$\uparrow I_{US} \rightarrow \uparrow Y_{US} \rightarrow \uparrow M_{US} = \uparrow X_{ROW} \rightarrow \uparrow Y_{ROW} \rightarrow \uparrow M_{ROW} \rightarrow \uparrow X_{US}$$
$$\uparrow \qquad\qquad\qquad\qquad\qquad\qquad\qquad\qquad\qquad\qquad \downarrow$$
$$\leftarrow \leftarrow \leftarrow \leftarrow \leftarrow \leftarrow \leftarrow \leftarrow \leftarrow \leftarrow \leftarrow \leftarrow \leftarrow \leftarrow \leftarrow$$

As you can see, we continue going through the loop until the marginal changes in income approach zero.

When all of these repercussions have occurred, the total change in income in the United States that results from the initial increase in investment will be *larger* than was the case when repercussions were not considered because of the additional feedback on U.S. income from the rest of the world. The expression for this repercussions multiplier, the **open-economy multiplier with foreign repercussions,** is complicated and is explored further in Appendix B of this chapter.

The "foreign repercussions process" emphasizes that countries of the world are interdependent with respect to macroeconomic activity. When a boom (or recession) occurs in one country, it will be transmitted to other countries and will then feed back upon the originating country. We can therefore graph one country's income level as being positively related to other countries' income levels, and likewise can graph other countries' income

FIGURE 6   Income Interdependence between Countries

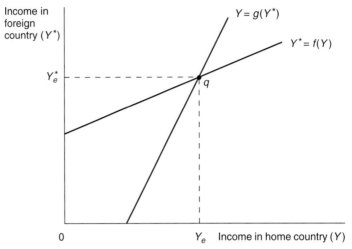

Because imports of one country are exports of the other country, a rise in income in one country will stimulate exports and therefore income in the other country. Thus, income in the foreign country (Y^*) is dependent on income in the home country (Y), and vice versa. There is simultaneous national income equilibrium in the two countries where the two lines intersect (that is, at Y_e and Y^*_e).

levels as being positively related to the first country's income level, as in Figure 6. This graph demonstrates the simultaneous determination of equilibrium income in the two countries. Consequently, both levels of income are altered whenever autonomous spending in any one country changes (which would be a shift in one of the income lines) and macroeconomic variables can move together across countries.

CONCEPT CHECK

1. What happens to the size of the open-economy multiplier (without foreign repercussions) if, other things being equal, the marginal propensity to import increases? Explain in economic terms, not just in algebraic terms.

2. Explain why an autonomous increase in investment spending in a country will lead to a greater increase in national income in that country if foreign repercussions are important than it would if foreign repercussions are unimportant.

AN OVERVIEW OF PRICE AND INCOME ADJUSTMENTS AND SIMULTANEOUS EXTERNAL AND INTERNAL BALANCE

This and the preceding chapter have been concerned with how the exchange rate and the state of the balance of payments lead to effects on the current account and the internal sector of the economy. In the previous chapter, we examined the manner by which a change in the exchange rate affects export receipts and import outlays and the current account balance through altering the relative prices of home and foreign goods. In a context of fixed exchange rates, we discussed how a disequilibrium in the balance of payments (a deficit or surplus) sets into motion money supply changes and internal price changes so as to improve (deteriorate) the current account in the case of a BOP deficit (surplus). In this chapter, we noted that a disturbance in the current account (such as an autonomous increase in exports) leads to national income changes, which in turn partly (but not completely) offset the initial current account disturbance through induced changes in imports.

IN THE REAL WORLD:

CORRELATIONS OF MACROECONOMIC VARIABLES ACROSS COUNTRIES

As is evident from the discussion of foreign repercussions in the text, macroeconomic activity in one country "spills over" into other countries through the multiplier process. Hence, upward (downward) movement in one economy can lead to upward (downward) movement in another economy. Of course, each country in the world is also subject to its own independent shocks and economic idiosyncrasies, so countries' economies will not keep perfectly in line with each other. Nevertheless, macroeconomic theory leads us to expect that there should be some positive relationship across countries with respect to aggregate economic variables.

Table 2 presents information (obtained from a sample running from 1970 to 1990) on the correlation or co-movement of various macroeconomic variables in nine industrial countries with comparable variables in the United States. To interpret the table, consider the correlation coefficient in the upper-left-hand corner of the table. The 0.60 coefficient for Australian output (real GDP) with U.S. output indicates a fairly strong relationship of the two outputs over time. (Two variables that are perfectly correlated with each other,

meaning that their movements are identical, would have a correlation coefficient of 1.0; if there is absolutely no relationship between the variables, the correlation coefficient would be 0.0; and if the variables are perfectly oppositely correlated, the coefficient would be -1.0.) In the table, real GDP movements in all nine countries are fairly well correlated with the movement of U.S. real GDP, with the strongest relations being between Germany and the United States (0.85) and between Canada and the United States (0.81). Movements in consumption are also reasonably strongly correlated (except for Australia and Italy) with U.S. consumption movements, as are movements in employment (again, except for Australia and Italy). Aggregate investment movements are not particularly linked for Australia and France and not at all for Canada. The negative correlations for net exports reflect the fact that U.S. negative net exports imply positive net exports for trading partners of the United States. All in all, macro aggregates of these other industrial countries do tend to move with the U.S. aggregates, indicating that economic activity does get transmitted across country borders.

TABLE 2   Correlations of Macroeconomic Variables in Several Industrial Countries with U.S. Variables

	Output (real GDP)	*Consumption*	*Investment*	*Employment*	*Net Exports*
Australia	0.60	-0.13	0.21	-0.17	0.03
Austria	0.54	0.45	0.57	0.58	0.29
Canada	0.81	0.46	0.00	0.50	-0.10
France	0.46	0.42	0.22	0.36	-0.25
Germany	0.85	0.64	0.66	0.60	-0.23
Italy	0.49	0.04	0.39	0.11	-0.28
Japan	0.66	0.49	0.59	0.48	-0.59
Switzerland	0.48	0.48	0.38	0.43	-0.10
United Kingdom	0.64	0.42	0.46	0.68	-0.11

Source: Marianne Baxter, "International Trade and Business Cycles," in Gene M. Grossman and Kenneth Rogoff, eds., *Handbook of International Economics,* vol. III (Amsterdam: Elsevier-Science, 1995), p. 1806.

An important feature of the interrelationships between the current account and the internal economy, and one that will be examined in more detail in subsequent chapters, is the possible conflict between the macroeconomic goals of "external balance" and "internal balance." **External balance** in this context refers to balance in the current account ($X = M$), while **internal balance** refers to the desirable state of the economy where there is a low level of unemployment together with reasonable price stability. There are clearly four possible combinations of departures from external and internal balance:

> *Case I:*   Deficit in the current account; unacceptably high unemployment.
>
> *Case II:*   Deficit in the current account; unacceptably rapid inflation.
>
> *Case III:*   Surplus in the current account; unacceptably rapid inflation.
>
> *Case IV:*   Surplus in the current account; unacceptably high unemployment.[5]

If policymakers are confronted with any one of these four combinations in a situation of fixed exchange rates, what should the macroeconomic policy stance be? We first discuss the straightforward Cases II and IV and then turn to the more complicated Cases I and III.

Case II: Current Account Deficit and Inflation

In this case restrictive or contractionary aggregate demand–oriented monetary and fiscal policy (i.e., a reduction in the money supply, a decrease in government spending, an increase in taxes) is in order. With the adoption of such policies, the price level and the level of national income will fall. The falling prices—or at least prices that are rising less rapidly than prices in other countries—will expand exports and reduce imports, and the fall in income will also reduce imports via the MPM. Thus the restrictive policies will improve the current account and move the economy toward external balance, as well as dampen the inflation and move the economy toward internal balance. However, the degree of restriction needed to attain external balance may differ from the degree of restriction needed to attain internal balance, and thus policymakers may not be able to attain both targets simultaneously. Nevertheless, the direction of policy will be correct.

Case IV: Current Account Surplus and Unemployment

In this case, of course, policy is moving in the opposite direction from case II. Expansionary monetary and fiscal policy—an increase in the money supply, an increase in government spending, a reduction in taxes—will stimulate national income and also induce more imports. In addition, any price pressures generated by the expansion will reduce exports and increase imports. Thus, the direction of policy works to reduce the current account surplus and to reduce the amount of unemployment, although of course the degree of necessary expansion may differ with respect to attainment of each particular goal.

Case I: Current Account Deficit and Unemployment

In this case, even the *direction* of the appropriate policy stance is unclear. Expansionary monetary and fiscal policy to decrease unemployment will worsen the current account through induced imports by the MPM times the rise in income. In addition, if the price level rises due to the expansionary policy, exports will fall and imports will rise, thus worsening the already existing current account deficit. On the other hand, contractionary policy to reduce the current account deficit will drive national income downward and worsen the unemployment situation.

Case III: Current Account Surplus and Inflation

In this case, expansionary policy will reduce the current account surplus but worsen the inflation. However, contractionary policy to alleviate the inflation will enlarge the current account surplus.

---

[5]Of course, as the experience of the 1970s particularly indicated, it is also possible to have unacceptably high unemployment and unacceptably rapid inflation at the same time. We deal here only with the traditional macroeconomic analysis that treats the economy as having one of these internal problems but not the other simultaneously. The "stagflation" situation of high unemployment and rapid inflation at the same time is discussed more thoroughly in Chapter 27.

Hence, the attainment of one "balance" in either of these last two cases will worsen the situation with respect to the other "balance." There is thus a conflict between the attainment of external balance and internal balance in these two cases. The policymakers may have to decide which goal is more important.

In the conflict cases, however, as well as in cases II and IV, where the degree of needed policy restriction or expansion was in doubt, it *is* possible to have the relative price effects and the income effects work together to attain both goals simultaneously. This can be accomplished by using a *change in the exchange rate* as an instrument of policy. This change in the exchange rate can be interpreted as a change in the official parity rate in a fixed-but-adjustable-rate system (for example, the Bretton Woods system from 1947 to 1971, discussed in the last chapter of the book) or as government intervention to influence the exchange rate in a more flexible exchange rate system, such as currently exists for many countries. Hence, in a model such as that of Swan (1963), a country with unemployment and a current account deficit could devalue (depreciate) its currency in order to alleviate the current account problem as well as to provide economic stimulus from enhanced exports and reduced imports. In the other previous conflict situation of inflation and a current account surplus, an upward revaluation (appreciation) of the country's currency would work, through a decrease in exports and an increase in imports, to remove the surplus as well as to dampen the inflation.

SUMMARY

This chapter considered the interrelationships between the current account and national income in the context of an open-economy Keynesian model. The equilibrium level of income occurs when desired aggregate expenditures equal production or, alternatively, when desired $S + T + M$ equals desired $I + G + X$ or $S + (T - G) - I$ equals the current account balance. In this model, increases in autonomous spending on consumption, investment, government spending, or exports lead to multiplied increases in national income through the multiplier of $1/(1 - \text{MPC} - \text{MPM})$ or $1/(\text{MPS} + \text{MPM})$. The presence of "foreign repercussions" introduces additional features into the multiplier process, with these repercussions embodying the role of interdependence among economies in national income determination. In Keynesian income models in general, if the current account is in equilibrium, a disturbance to that equilibrium will set forces in motion to restore current account balance. However, only partial adjustment rather than a full restoration of current account balance will occur.

An important point emerging from the Keynesian income model is that, with a fixed exchange rate, equilibrium in national income need not occur with simultaneous equilibrium in the current account. Policymakers confront targets of both external and internal balance, and it may be difficult to attain both targets even if explicit changes in the exchange rate are permitted. Further policy considerations are explored in the next three chapters.

KEY TERMS

autonomous consumption spending
autonomous imports
autonomous spending multiplier
average propensity to import (APM)
consumption function
desired aggregate expenditures
equilibrium level of national income
external balance
foreign repercussions

import function
income elasticity of demand for imports (YEM)
induced consumption spending
induced imports
injections
internal balance
Keynesian income model
leakages
marginal propensity to consume (MPC)

marginal propensity to import (MPM)
marginal propensity to save (MPS)
open-economy multiplier
open-economy multiplier with foreign repercussions
partial current account adjustment
rounds of spending in the multiplier process
saving function

QUESTIONS AND PROBLEMS

1. Using the Keynesian model, explain the effect on national income of an autonomous increase in saving.
2. Given the following simple Keynesian model:

$$E = C + I + G + X - M \qquad I = 150$$
$$C = 50 + 0.85Y_d \qquad G = 300$$
$$Y_d = Y - T \qquad X = 80$$
$$T = 400 \qquad M = 10 + 0.05Y$$
$$Y = E \text{ in equilibrium}$$

   (a) Determine the equilibrium level of income.
   (b) When the equilibrium income level is attained, is there a surplus or a deficit in the current account? Of how much?
   (c) What is the size of the autonomous spending multiplier?
3. In the model of Question 2, by how much would income have to change in order to make $X = M$ (with no change in X)? How much change in autonomous investment would be necessary to generate this change in income?
4. Explain why a country with a current account surplus (such as China) can be said to be saving more than it invests.
5. Germany has consistently pursued an anti-inflationary domestic policy that has resulted in sizable unemployment and a lower rate of economic growth than would otherwise have been the case. Why might Germany's trading partners have reacted adversely to such a German policy stance?
6. In trade negotiations with the Japanese over the large U.S. trade deficit with Japan, the Clinton administration urged the Japanese government to undertake a more expansionary fiscal policy. If the Japanese government did so, how might the U.S. trade deficit with Japan be reduced? Could U.S. imports from Japan rise because of the expansionary policy? Explain.
7. You are given the following four-sector Keynesian income model:

$$E = C + I + G + (X - M) \qquad I = 230$$
$$C = 120 + 0.75Y_d \qquad G = 560$$
$$Y_d = Y - T \qquad X = 350$$
$$T = 40 + 0.20Y \qquad M = 30 + 0.10Y$$
$$Y = E \text{ in equilibrium}$$

   (a) Calculate the equilibrium income level (Y_e).
   (b) Calculate the amount of taxes collected when the economy is at Y_e. Then indicate whether the government has a surplus or deficit at Y_e and calculate the value of the surplus or deficit.
   (c) Calculate the value of net exports when the economy is at Y_e.
   (Note: To answer this question, you need to read Appendix A of this chapter.)
8. Suppose that there are two countries in the world economy, countries I and II. The countries possess the following marginal propensities: $\text{MPC}_I = 0.7$; $\text{MPM}_I = 0.1$; $\text{MPC}_{II} = 0.8$; $\text{MPM}_{II} = 0.2$. There is no government sector. Using the formula for the open-economy multiplier with foreign repercussions, calculate the effect on country I's income of a rise in autonomous investment in country I of $35 billion. (Note: To answer this question, you need to read Appendix B of this chapter.)

 Appendix A   THE MULTIPLIER WHEN TAXES DEPEND ON INCOME

The open-economy multiplier when taxes depend on income is smaller than the open-economy multiplier when taxes are entirely autonomous or lump sum in nature (as was the case in the body of this chapter). To illustrate, building on the numerical example in the chapter, suppose that, as before,

$$C = 100 + 0.8Y_d \qquad G = 600$$
$$Y_d = Y - T \qquad X = 140$$
$$I = 180 \qquad M = 20 + 0.1Y$$

However, suppose that the tax function, instead of $T = 500$, is now

$$T = 40 + 0.25Y$$

This expression indicates that, besides an autonomous or lump-sum component of taxes (40), there is also a component that depends on income (0.25Y). The 0.25 in this example is the *marginal tax rate,* or t in general form. The marginal tax rate is the fraction of an additional unit (dollar) of income that must be paid in taxes—25 percent in this example. With this tax function, the equation for disposable income becomes

$$Y_d = Y - (40 + 0.25Y)$$
$$= -40 + 0.75Y$$

To examine the effect of this change in the tax structure on the multiplier and the rounds of spending in the multiplier process, let us now suppose that, as in the body of the chapter, investment increases by 30. In the first round of the multiplier process, producers of the new capital goods increase their output by 30. (We again assume that the first round of spending is entirely on domestic goods.) This output increase of 30 increases income of the workers in the capital goods industries by 30. How much spending will take place in the second round of the multiplier process? The second-round spending will be less than the MPC (0.8) times the change in income (30) because taxes now have to be paid before any more spending takes place. With the marginal tax rate of 25 percent, the recipients of the 30 in income must pay $(0.25)(30) = 7.5$ in taxes. Hence, although income increased by 30, *disposable* income increased by only 22.5 ($= 30 - 7.5$). Applying the MPC of 0.8 to the 22.5 increase in disposable income, households in the second round thus spend 18 $[= (0.8)(22.5)]$ more on goods and services. However, remember that some of the new spending in the economy is on imports and, in our example, this is 0.1 of the new *total* income (not the new disposable income). Hence, with the total income increase of 30, imports will increase by 3 $[= (0.1)(30)]$. Thus, in the second round, the amount of spending on domestic goods is 15 ($= 18 - 3$). This "second-round" result is 50 percent of the first round spending (unlike in our earlier example where it had been 70 percent of first-round spending).

Let us trace this multiplier process through one more round. Of the new domestic production and income of 15 generated in the second round, 25 percent must be paid in taxes—an amount of $(0.25)(15) = 3.75$. Thus, disposable income rises in the third round by 11.25 ($= 15 - 3.75$). To the 11.25, the MPC of 0.8 applies, and consumption increases by 9 $[= (0.8)(11.25)]$. With imports increasing by 1.5 ($= 10$ percent of the 15 total new income coming from the second round), spending on domestic goods hence rises by 7.5 ($= 9 - 1.5$) or 50 percent of the second-round figure of 15.

To cut to the chase, the many rounds of spending yield a series of income changes

$$\Delta Y = 30 + 15 + 7.5 + \cdots$$

As noted earlier in the chapter, such a series sums to

$$\Delta Y = [1/(1 - \text{fraction re-spent in each round})](\text{initial } \Delta I)$$

or, in this case because 50 percent is re-spent in each round,

$$\Delta Y = [1/(1 - 0.5)](30)$$
$$= (1/0.5)(30) = 60$$

The multiplier is thus 2.0 ($= 60/30$ or $1/0.5$). It has been reduced from the $3\frac{1}{3}$ of the earlier example in the chapter because taxes are now an additional leakage in each round of the spending process after the first round.

In conceptual terms, the open-economy multiplier when taxes depend on income (k^*_o) is given by the expression

$$k^*_o = \frac{1}{1 - \text{MPC}(1 - t) + \text{MPM}} \qquad [22]$$

or, alternatively,

$$= \frac{1}{1 - \text{MPC} + \text{MPC} \times t + \text{MPM}} \qquad [22']$$

If $t = 0$, we are back at the original multiplier. With the current numbers in this appendix, you can plug in MPC $= 0.8$, $t = 0.25$, and MPM $= 0.1$ to verify that the multiplier $= 2.0$.

One final note: If, unlike in our analysis in this chapter and this appendix, imports are made to depend on *disposable* income rather than on total income, the open-economy multiplier becomes

$$k^{**}_o = \frac{1}{1 - \text{MPC}(1 - t) + \text{MPM}(1 - t)} \qquad [23]$$

which is slightly smaller than the multiplier in expressions [22] and [22'].

Appendix B   DERIVATION OF THE MULTIPLIER WITH FOREIGN REPERCUSSIONS

This appendix derives the autonomous spending multiplier when foreign repercussions are taken into account. To simplify to some extent the complicated algebra, we assume that there is no government sector (in either country), and hence $G = 0$ and $t = 0$. Note that the standard open-economy multiplier in this case is $1/(1 - \text{MPC} + \text{MPM})$ or $1/(\text{MPS} + \text{MPM})$.

In the derivation, we designate foreign country variables with a *; unstarred variables refer to the home country. Consumption contains the usual autonomous component and induced component in both countries, as does the import function. Investment and exports are autonomous. The equations for the two economies are thus

$$E = C + I + X - M \qquad\qquad E^* = C^* + I^* + X^* - M^*$$

$$C = a + bY \qquad\qquad C^* = a^* + b^*Y^*$$

$$I = \overline{I} \qquad\qquad I^* = \overline{I}^*$$

$$X = \overline{X} \qquad\qquad X^* = \overline{X}^*$$

$$M = \overline{M} + mY \qquad\qquad M^* = \overline{M}^* + m^*Y^*$$

$$Y = E \text{ and } Y^* = E^* \text{ in equilibrium}$$

The equilibrium level of income for the home country is found by substitution into the $Y = C + I + X - M$ equilibrium expression:

$$Y = a + bY + \overline{I} + \overline{X} - (\overline{M} + mY)$$

$$Y - bY + mY = a + \overline{I} + \overline{X} - \overline{M}$$

$$Y = \frac{a + \overline{I} + \overline{X} - \overline{M}}{(1 - b + m)} \qquad\qquad [24]$$

However, in this two-country model, the exports of the home country are equal to the imports of the foreign country, so [24] can be written

$$Y = \frac{a + \overline{I} + \overline{M}^* + m^*Y^* - \overline{M}}{(1 - b + m)}$$

For simplification, we substitute s (the marginal propensity to save in the home country) for $(1 - b)$, because b is the home country's marginal propensity to consume:

$$Y = \frac{a + \overline{I} + \overline{M}^* + m^*Y^* - \overline{M}}{s + m} \qquad\qquad [25]$$

A similar procedure for obtaining equilibrium income in the foreign country yields the equation for Y^* as

$$Y^* = \frac{a^* + \overline{I}^* + \overline{M} + mY - \overline{M}^*}{s^* + m^*} \qquad\qquad [26]$$

where s^* is the foreign country's marginal propensity to save.

To obtain multipliers for the home country, expression [26] is substituted into expression [25]:

$$Y = \frac{a + \overline{I} + \overline{M}^* - \overline{M} + m^*\left(\dfrac{a^* + \overline{I}^* + \overline{M} + mY - \overline{M}^*}{s^* + m^*}\right)}{s + m}$$

$$Y = \frac{(s^* + m^*)(a + \overline{I} + \overline{M}^* - \overline{M}) + m^*(a^* + \overline{I}^* + \overline{M} + mY - \overline{M}^*)}{(s^* + m^*)(s + m)}$$

$$(s + m)Y = \left(\frac{(s^* + m^*)(a + \overline{I} + \overline{M}^* - \overline{M}) + m^*(a^* + \overline{I}^* + \overline{M} - \overline{M}^*)}{s^* + m^*}\right) + \frac{m^*mY}{s^* + m^*}$$

$$(s^* + m^*)(s + m)Y - m^*mY = (s^* + m^*)(a + \overline{I} + \overline{M}^* - \overline{M}) +$$
$$m^*(a^* + \overline{I}^* + \overline{M} - \overline{M}^*)$$

Therefore equilibrium income Y can be expressed as

$$Y = \left(\frac{s^* + m^*}{ss^* + ms^* + sm^*}\right)(a + \overline{I} + \overline{M}^* - \overline{M}) +$$

$$\left(\frac{m^*}{ss^* + ms^* + sm^*}\right)(a^* + \overline{I}^* + \overline{M} - \overline{M}^*) \qquad [27]$$

Expression [27] can be used to obtain a variety of multipliers. The autonomous investment multiplier in the home country simply involves looking at the ΔY associated with a ΔI:

$$\frac{\Delta Y}{\Delta I} = \frac{s^* + m^*}{ss^* + ms^* + sm^*}$$

or

$$= \frac{1 + \dfrac{m^*}{s^*}}{s + m + m^*(s/s^*)} \qquad [28]$$

Inspection of this multiplier indicates that it is larger than it would be if there were no foreign repercussions. The standard no-repercussions open-economy multiplier (i.e., expression [20] in the chapter) is

$$\frac{1}{1 - \text{MPC} + \text{MPM}} = \frac{1}{\text{MPS} + \text{MPM}}$$

or, in the symbols of this appendix, $1/(s + m)$. Expression [28] is larger than this multiplier because the percentage increase in the numerator in [28] from that in [20] is larger than the percentage increase in the denominator.

The investment multiplier in [28] applies also to a change in autonomous consumption (i.e., to a change in "a"). However, note that, unlike the case where foreign repercussions are absent, the foreign repercussions multiplier for an autonomous change in *exports* of the home country will differ from the foreign repercussions multiplier for a change in autonomous investment (or consumption). Looking at expression [27], an autonomous change in exports for the home country is a change in autonomous *imports* $(\overline{M}^*)$ for the foreign country. Thus,

$$\frac{\Delta Y}{\Delta X} = \frac{\Delta Y}{\Delta M^*} = \frac{s^* + m^*}{ss^* + ms^* + sm^*} - \frac{m^*}{ss^* + ms^* + sm^*}$$

$$= \frac{s^*}{ss^* + ms^* + sm^*}$$

$$= \frac{1}{s + m + m^*(s/s^*)} \qquad [29]$$

The multiplier in [29] is smaller than the multiplier in [28] because of the absence of the m^*/s^* term in the numerator of [29]. Expression [29] is also *smaller than* the $[1/(s + m)]$ multiplier *when there are no foreign repercussions*. The economic reason is that an autonomous increase in home exports, while it stimulates home production and generates an expansion in home income, is also an autonomous increase in foreign country imports. The increase in autonomous foreign imports is at the expense of foreign consumption of goods produced in the foreign country, and it thus initiates a downward movement of income abroad. The decrease in foreign income in turn induces a decrease in purchases of home-country exports through the operation of the marginal propensity to import in the foreign country, and it generates a downward movement in *home-country* income that partly offsets the upward income effects of the original autonomous export increase in the home country.

Another multiplier of interest is the effect of a change in autonomous investment in the *foreign country* upon *home-country* income. If I^* is changed in expression [27], the effect upon Y is

$$\frac{\Delta Y}{\Delta I^*} = \frac{m^*}{ss^* + ms^* + sm^*}$$

$$= \frac{\dfrac{m^*}{s^*}}{s + m + m^*(s/s^*)} \qquad [30]$$

Obviously, the introduction of foreign repercussions makes multiplier analysis more complex!

part 6

MACROECONOMIC POLICY IN THE OPEN ECONOMY

The ultimate objectives of monetary and fiscal policy are economic growth and rising standards, *not* exchange-rate stability or current account balance per se. Nonetheless, reasonably stable exchange rates and sustainable external balances are important aspects of a healthy economy. Particularly when these variables get far out of line, they should be of concern to policymakers.

Council of Economic Advisers, 1990

In the previous part, we examined how international transactions affect the overall economy and how the foreign exchange market functioned. In addition, we discussed how the effect of international transactions could be incorporated into macroeconomic theory for the purpose of policy analysis. It is obvious that the pursuit of domestic targets such as price stability, high employment, and economic growth through the use of monetary and fiscal policy is more complex in the open economy than in the closed economy. This is due in part to the fact that, as noted briefly in the previous chapter, macro policy now has to concern itself with external objectives as well as internal objectives. In addition, the fact that international transactions not only affect the impact of macro policy but are in turn affected by those policy actions means that the effects of policy go beyond a country's borders, thus complicating the problem.

In this part, we expand our analysis of the problems associated with pursuing internal and external targets using monetary and fiscal policy in the open economy. The nature of the policy problem varies with the type of exchange rate arrangement in place and also with the ease with which financial capital moves between countries. Hence, we approach the problem by examining in detail the effects of policy under different institutional settings. Chapter 25 analyzes the effects of macro policy in the situation where a fixed exchange rate system is being used, taking note of how the degree to which capital moves between countries influences the results. This discussion is followed in Chapter 26 by an analysis of policy effects under a flexible exchange rate system, again focusing largely on the influence of different degrees of capital mobility. Chapter 27 then examines the effects of macroeconomic policy in the open economy when prices are allowed to change and looks as well at the effects of international shocks. ●

In some cases, by not putting policy issues in an international perspective, we provide students with the "wrong" answers.

Joseph E. Stiglitz, 1993

25

ECONOMIC POLICY IN THE OPEN ECONOMY UNDER FIXED EXCHANGE RATES

LEARNING OBJECTIVES

- To understand general equilibrium in the macroeconomy using the *IS/LM/BP* model.

- To grasp the impact of changes in fiscal policy on income, trade, and interest rates under fixed exchange rates.

- To grasp the impact of changes in monetary policy on income, trade, and interest rates under fixed exchange rates.

- To perceive how varying degrees of capital mobility alter the effectiveness of fiscal and monetary policy under a system of fixed exchange rates.

INTRODUCTION

**The Case of the
Chinese Renminbi
Yuan**

The yuan (RMB) has essentially been fixed to the U.S. dollar since 1994. As China's trade surpluses both with the United States and overall have grown, many have argued that its export success has been the result of an undervalued yuan. At the same time, there has been an ever-increasing flow of foreign investment into China, adding to the tremendous productive capacity of the country. Many fear that this increased productive capacity will be deflationary at the world level, seriously disrupting the worldwide economic system. In an article in *The International Economy*,[1] 30 international experts from different professional backgrounds expressed their opinions about the degree to which the yuan is undervalued and the effect, if any, the undervaluation has had on world trade and finance. Not surprisingly, there was a wide variety of views ranging from "China should float the renminbi and permit it to appreciate in the currency markets" to "there is no clear evidence that the currency is undervalued."

How do we go about evaluating such different positions? What does the nature of the exchange rate system have to do with the issues of foreign investment, currency accumulation, and the effect on the domestic money supply? How do we take into account the many aspects of this difficult domestic and international issue? In this chapter we develop a framework for analysis of macroeconomic issues and policy that will provide a basis for analyzing these important questions. More specifically, we focus on the situation wherever a country has chosen to fix the exchange rate and not let it float on a regular basis. Of particular interest is the manner in which discretionary economic policy influences the macroeconomy under fixed exchange rates. Because the effects of discretionary policy are different under a flexible exchange rate system compared with a fixed-rate system, we then consider economic policy under flexible exchange rates in the following chapter. Although the major industrial countries tend to have flexible rate systems today, many countries still peg their currencies and thus have to contend with the effects of fixed rates when carrying out macroeconomic policy. This is true to an extreme for the 13 European countries that have adopted a common currency, the euro, although the euro is flexible against most other currencies of the world.

Prior to current monetary arrangements (discussed in detail in the last chapter in the book), the international monetary system was characterized by fixed exchange rates, and there is continual pressure on the part of many individuals to return to some sort of fixed standard. In our consideration of economic policy under fixed rates, we first examine a fixed-rate model that separates monetary policy from fiscal policy and that provides some guidance in the selection of appropriate policy instruments. We then introduce a macroeconomic framework that specifically incorporates the money markets, the real sector, and the foreign sector (the *IS/LM/BP* model), which we use to examine the effects of alternative policy actions under fixed exchange rates (in this chapter) and under flexible exchange rates (in the next chapter). Command of this material should help you understand both the impact of various policy actions within a broad and rigorous macroeconomic framework and the effects of the exchange rate system on macroeconomic policy actions. Consideration of possible price effects accompanying these policy actions will be discussed in Chapter 27.

TARGETS, INSTRUMENTS, AND ECONOMIC POLICY IN A TWO-INSTRUMENT, TWO-TARGET MODEL

As an introduction to policy analysis in the open economy, we begin by developing a very basic framework that will allow us to examine the interaction between policies aimed at attaining external balance and those aimed at other domestic targets such as full employment and price

---

[1]"Is the Chinese Currency, the Renminbi, Dangerously Undervalued and a Threat to the Global Economy? (A Symposium of Views)," *The International Economy* 17, no. 2 (Spring 2003), pp. 25–39.

IN THE REAL WORLD:

EXCHANGE RATE ARRANGEMENTS

It is commonly believed that most countries of the world have adopted flexible exchange rates. Interestingly, the majority of the countries of the world do not let their currency float freely and have adopted some type of a nonflexible exchange rate system. In fact, less than 15 percent of the members of the International Monetary Fund (IMF) freely float their currencies. Table 1 contains an overview of the various types of arrangements being used in the world. The number of countries utilizing the various systems as of July 31, 2006 (the latest data available), and the relative importance of each system are indicated. The particular countries in each category are given in Chapter 29.

TABLE 1   Current Exchange Rate Regimes in the World[*]

Exchange Rate Regimes	Number	Percentage
1. *Exchange arrangements with no separate legal tender:* The currency of another country circulates as the sole legal tender or the member belongs to a monetary or currency union in which the same legal tender is shared by the members of the union.	41	21.9%
2. *Currency board arrangements:* A monetary regime based on an explicit legislative commitment to exchange domestic currency for a specified foreign currency at a fixed exchange rate, combined with restrictions on the issuing authority to ensure the fulfillment of its legal obligations.	7	3.7
3. *Other conventional fixed peg arrangements:* The country pegs its currency (formally or de facto) at a fixed rate to a major currency or a basket of currencies where the exchange rate fluctuates within a narrow margin of less than ±1 percent around a central rate.	52	27.8
4. *Pegged exchange rates within horizontal bands:* The value of the currency is maintained within margins of fluctuation around a formal or de facto fixed peg that are wider than at least ±1 percent around a central rate.	6	3.2
5. *Crawling pegs:* The currency is adjusted periodically in small amounts at a fixed, preannounced rate or in response to changes in selective quantitative indicators.	5	2.7
6. *Managed floating with no preannounced path for the exchange rate:* The monetary authority influences the movements of the exchange rate through active intervention in the foreign exchange market without specifying, or precommitting to, a preannounced path for the exchange rate.	51	27.3
7. *Independent floating:* The exchange rate is market determined, with any foreign exchange intervention aimed at moderating the rate of change and preventing undue fluctuations in the exchange rate, rather than at establishing a level for it.	25	13.4
	187	100.0%

[*]As of July 31, 2006.

Source: International Monetary Fund, *De Facto Classification of Exchange Rate Regimes and Monetary Policy Framework, July 31, 2006* (Washington, DC: IMF, 2006), pp. 4–7, obtained from www.imf.org.

stability. One of the early models that differentiated the effects of monetary and fiscal policy on the open economy was developed by Robert Mundell (1962). The separation of monetary and fiscal policy was accomplished by extending the current account analysis of that time to include capital flows as well. "External balance," or "balance-of-payments equilibrium," was thus defined by Mundell to mean a zero balance in the official reserve transactions balance.[2] The

---

[2]Note that this definition of *external balance* differs from the definition given at the end of the preceding chapter, where the term referred to balance in the current account.

TITANS OF INTERNATIONAL ECONOMICS:

ROBERT A. MUNDELL (BORN 1932)

Robert A. Mundell was born on October 24, 1932, in Kingston, Ontario, Canada. He received his B.A. from the University of British Columbia in 1953, did postgraduate work at the University of Washington and the London School of Economics and Political Science, and earned his Ph.D. (very rapidly!) from the Massachusetts Institute of Technology in 1956. He has taught at the University of British Columbia, Stanford University, the Johns Hopkins University Center in Bologna, Italy, McGill University, the University of Waterloo, and the University of Chicago. He is currently a professor at Columbia University. He has also been very active as a consultant and adviser, having worked with the U.S. Department of the Treasury, the Inter-American Development Bank, the World Bank, and the European Economic Community. He also is greatly envied because, despite his professional commitments, he finds time to be with his family in their palazzo near Siena, Italy.

Professor Mundell's work has been diverse and extremely influential. He has published articles in many economics journals, as well as important books such as *The International Monetary System—Conflict and Reform* (1965), *International Economics* (1968), and *Monetary Theory—Interest, Inflation, and Growth in the World Economy* (1971). He made a seminal contribution to the theory of optimum currency areas (discussed in Chapter 28). His work on monetary and fiscal policy under fixed and flexible exchange rates (discussed in this and the succeeding chapter) has been widely used, and it has had influence on actual policy. In addition, he did creative work on factor mobility in the context of international trade theory (discussed in Chapter 8), and he demonstrated how movements of factors of production can be substitutes for movements of goods in terms of impacts on relative factor prices. Further, he is regarded as a founder of the monetary approach to the balance of payments (discussed in Chapter 22) and as a father (if not *the* father) of supply-side economics. Indeed, Mundell's work in supply-side economics was of such import that fellow supply-sider Arthur Laffer has written (1999, p. A16) that "Mr. Mundell has been as influential as John Maynard Keynes, the difference being that Mr. Mundell was right." While not all economists would share that view, the consensus is that this brilliant man has made enduring contributions to the subject of economics.

Professor Mundell has played a major role in stimulating macroeconomists in particular to "think internationally," and international economics would be much different if Mundell had not devoted his energies to the area. The culmination of his career (at least to date!) was the awarding to him of the Nobel Prize in economic science in 1999.

Sources: Arthur B. Laffer, "Economist of the Century," *The Wall Street Journal,* October 15, 1999, p. A16; "Man of the Hour," *The Economist,* October 16, 1999, p. 82; David Warsh, *Economic Principals: Masters and Mavericks of Modern Economics* (New York: The Free Press, 1993), pp. 192–96; *Who's Who in the World: 2000 Millennium Edition* (New Providence, NJ: Marquis Who's Who, 1999), p. 1514.

attainment of the external balance target is influenced by both monetary policy and fiscal policy. For example, an increase in the money supply will reduce interest rates, leading to a reduction in short-term financial capital inflows or an increase in short-term financial capital outflows and to a BOP deficit. Expanding government spending will lead to increased income and an increase in imports and also to a BOP deficit.[3] Because expansionary monetary policy and fiscal policy are assumed to affect the balance of payments in a similar fashion, we can conclude that maintaining balance-of-payments equilibrium for a given exchange rate requires an opposite use of monetary and fiscal policy in this model; that is, expansionary fiscal policy must be accompanied by contractionary monetary policy and vice versa.

There is a similar policy relationship with respect to the internal balance target. Increases in the money supply tend to lower the interest rate and thus to stimulate real investment. If this is not to be expansionary and/or inflationary, the increase in investment

---

[3]In this Mundell model, it is assumed that expansionary fiscal policy worsens the balance of payments. As we see later, expansionary fiscal policy can improve the balance of payments under certain circumstances.

must be offset by a decrease in government spending or by an increase in taxes that will reduce consumption spending. Similarly, maintenance of a given domestic internal balance target indicates that any increase in government spending (or any increase in consumption spending via a decrease in taxes) must be offset by some decrease in domestic investment through monetary policy actions if inflationary pressures are not to ensue.

The policy problem in this instance is demonstrated graphically in Figure 1 using a **Mundell-Fleming diagram.** The effects of monetary policy are captured through the use of different rates of interest on the vertical axis. Fiscal policy is represented through the levels of net government spending $(G - T)$ plotted on the horizontal axis. The inverse relationship between the two policy instruments is shown by upward-sloping curves, because higher interest rates reflect, *ceteris paribus,* a smaller money supply. Internal balance is represented by the *IB* curve and external balance by the *EB* curve. In this case, each curve shows combinations of monetary and fiscal policy [i and $(G - T)$] that bring about internal and external balance, respectively.

Although both curves slope upward for the reasons given earlier, the *EB* curve is drawn flatter than the *IB* curve because changes in the money supply (and hence the interest rate) are assumed to have a greater relative effect on external balance than on internal balance. This is generally thought to be the case because changes in the interest rate affect the balance of payments through both the capital and the current accounts. A rise in the interest rate causes not only an increase in net short-term capital inflows but also reduced domestic real investment and income, which acts to reduce imports. Changes in the interest rate thus exert both a direct and an indirect effect on the balance of payments, whereas they affect

FIGURE 1   Internal Balance, External Balance, and Policy Instrument Classification in a Mundell-Fleming Diagram

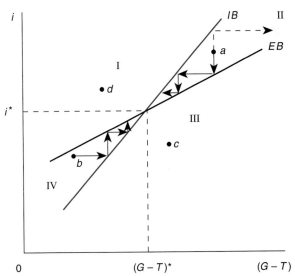

The *IB* curve reflects all combinations of interest rates i (monetary policy) and net government spending $(G - T)$ that lead to the attainment of domestic targets, that is, internal balance. Similarly, the flatter *EB* curve reflects all combinations of i and $(G - T)$ that generate equilibrium in the balance of payments for a given exchange rate. Points above the *IB* curve reflect unacceptably high unemployment, and points below reflect unacceptably rapid inflation. Similarly, points above the *EB* curve represent a surplus in the balance of payments, and points below represent a deficit. It is clear that internal balance and external balance are obtained simultaneously only at i^* and $(G - T)^*$. Finally, if the economy is not at i^* and $(G - T)^*$, monetary policy should be pursued to reach external balance and fiscal policy to reach internal balance.

the internal balance target only through the direct effect on real investment. This assumption allows us to reach a conclusion about the appropriate assignment of policy instruments to the *IB* and *EB* targets (that is, effective policy classification).

In Figure 1 it is clear that only one combination of monetary policy and fiscal policy will allow the simultaneous attainment of both targets, that of i^* and $(G - T)^*$. Any other combination will lead to one or both of the targets not being met. All points to the left of or above the *IB* curve reflect combinations of the two instruments where the interest rate is too high given the fiscal policy stance, resulting in low investment, low income, and unemployment. Similarly, all points to the right of or below the *IB* curve lead to real investment levels that are too high, contributing to inflation. Points to the left of or above the *EB* curve reflect interest rates that are higher than necessary to bring the balance of payments into equilibrium at the given exchange rate, and hence generate a surplus in the balance of payments due to capital inflows. Points to the right of or below the *EB* curve reflect a balance-of-payments deficit because the low interest rate leads to financial capital outflows. The graph can thus be divided into four quadrants, each reflecting a different combination of missed targets:

    I. Unacceptably high unemployment; balance-of-payments surplus

    II. Unacceptably rapid inflation; balance-of-payments surplus

    III. Unacceptably rapid inflation; balance-of-payments deficit

    IV. Unacceptably high unemployment; balance-of-payments deficit

Again we see that the simultaneous attainment of the two targets can take place only by careful choice of the two instruments involved. For example, if the economy is at point *a*, altering one instrument will permit the attainment of one target but not both. To reach equilibrium, both instruments must be utilized.

A further important point needs to be made relating to the assignment of instruments to targets. Given the nature of the *IB* and *EB* functions, it will be more efficient to assign the monetary policy instrument to pursue *EB* and fiscal policy instruments to pursue *IB* targets. This becomes obvious when we consider the possible sequence of policy decisions that could take place at point *a*. If monetary policy is directed toward the *IB* target, a decrease in the money supply (an increase in the interest rate) is required. If the fiscal policy instrument is then directed toward the *EB* target, expansionary fiscal action is required. These steps (shown by the dashed arrow in region II of Figure 1) would move the economy even farther away from i^* and $(G - T)^*$, not closer. On the other hand, devoting monetary policy to the *EB* target and fiscal policy to the *IB* target[4] leads to a sequence of policy steps that drives the economy closer to the desired levels of i^* and $(G - T)^*$ (indicated by the solid arrows in region II). A similar conclusion would be reached for points *b, c,* or *d*. This model thus suggests that effective policy classification of policy instruments and targets is an important element in the successful administration of economic policy in the open economy under fixed exchange rates.

CONCEPT CHECK

1. What is the difference between internal balance and external balance?

2. If the economy is operating at *c* in Figure 1, what policy actions should be carried out to reach the internal balance target? Why?

3. Which policy tool should be used to attain external balance in the Mundell-Fleming model? Why?

---

[4]The reader may recall from other courses that fiscal policy has an effect on interest rates, because an expansionary policy, for example, will raise income, raise money demand, and therefore raise interest rates (given a fixed money supply). In the Mundell model, the monetary authorities are assumed to recognize this effect when implementing policy to meet any interest rate target.

GENERAL EQUILIBRIUM IN THE OPEN ECONOMY: THE *IS/LM/BP* MODEL

Building on the introduction to policymaking in the open economy provided by the Mundell-Fleming model, we now turn to a broader general equilibrium construct that specifically incorporates the money market relationships developed in Chapter 22 and the real sector or income effects discussed in Chapter 24. In addition, the model specifically incorporates the effects of international trade and international capital flows on equilibrium in the open-economy model.

General Equilibrium in the Money Market: The *LM* Curve

Equilibrium in the money market occurs when the supply of money is equal to the demand for money. In Chapter 22 we covered both the supply of and the demand for money in considerable detail, and we presented the concept of money market equilibrium conceptually and algebraically in the following general manner:[5]

$$M_s = L$$

or

$$a(DR + IR) = a(BR + C) = f[\overset{+}{Y}, \overset{-}{i}, \overset{+}{P}, \overset{+}{W}, \overset{-}{E(p)}, \overset{?}{O}]$$

where: M_s = money supply
  L = money demand
  a = money multiplier
  DR = domestic reserves held by the central bank
  IR = international reserves held by the central bank
  BR = reserves of commercial banks and other depository institutions
  C = currency held by the nonbank public
  Y = level of real income in the economy
  i = domestic interest rate
  P = price level
  W = level of real wealth
  $E(p)$ = expected percentage change in the price level
  O = all other variables that can influence the amount of money balances the country's citizens wish to hold (for example, the foreign interest rate, expected changes in the exchange rate if the exchange rate is not fixed, risk premium for holding foreign assets)

The nature of the effect of changes in the principal independent variables on money demand is indicated above each demand variable in equation [1]. Because the income level and the interest rate are thought to be the two major influences on the demand for money, we focus our attention on these two variables with regard to money market equilibrium. Holding the variables other than Y and i constant, there will be a transactions demand for money fixed by a given level of income and an asset demand for money determined by the domestic interest rate (given the foreign interest rate, the foreign risk premium, and other financial considerations). Further, for any given income level, a graph of the demand for money can be portrayed as the downward-sloping L curve in Figure 2. This graph enables us to focus on the inverse relationship between the interest rate and the demand for money, holding other things constant. You will recall the various explanations for the inverse relationship; for example, a higher interest rate means an increase in the opportunity cost of

---

[5]See expressions [1], [2], and [5] in that chapter.

FIGURE 2   **Equilibrium in the Money Market**

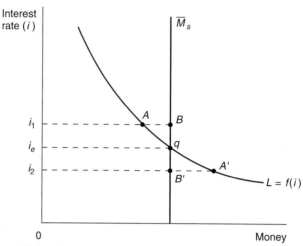

The fixed money supply is indicated by the vertical line M_s. The demand for money is represented by the L curve, and the equilibrium interest rate is i_e. Above i_e at interest rate i_1, the demand for money is equal to horizontal distance i_1A, which is less than the supply of money i_1B. With an excess supply of money, people purchase bonds, which drives up bond prices and reduces the interest rate—a process that continues until i_e is reached. Below i_e, there is an excess demand for money. People sell bonds to obtain money, bond prices fall, and the interest rate rises until i_e is attained.

holding non-interest-bearing money assets and reduces the amount of money that people wish to hold. If any of the "other things" besides the interest rate change, the L curve will shift (e.g., a rise in income shifts the L curve to the right because greater transactions demand for money would exist at each interest rate).

Having looked at the demand for money, let us comment briefly on the supply of money. For the time being, we assume that the supply of money at any given point in time is *fixed*. The money supply is presumed to be under the control of the monetary authorities (such as the Board of Governors of the Federal Reserve System in the United States). The specification of a fixed money supply (call it amount $\overline{M}_s$) is represented by the vertical line in Figure 2. Increases (decreases) in the supply of money shift this line to the right (left). The demand and supply of money jointly determine the **equilibrium interest rate,** at rate i_e.

Interest rate i_e is the equilibrium rate because, at any other rate, there is either an excess supply of or an excess demand for money. For example, at interest rate i_1, the amount of money demanded (represented by the horizontal distance i_1A) is less than the money supply (represented by the distance i_1B). The excess supply of money AB indicates that people hold more of their wealth in the form of money (distance i_1B) than they wish to hold (distance i_1A) at this relatively high interest rate. In response, the money holders will purchase other assets such as bonds with their excess cash balances. These asset purchases drive up the price of bonds and drive down the interest rate. (Remember the inverse relationship between bond prices and interest rates.) This process continues until the interest rate falls to the level at which the existing money supply is willingly held (at interest rate i_e). In the opposite situation, at low interest rate i_2, there is an excess demand for money of $B'A'$. People sell bonds and other assets to build up their money balances, and this action drives down the price of bonds and other assets and drives up the interest rate until the equilibrium rate is reached.

In light of Figure 2, consider what will happen when there are changes in the demand and supply of money. If the monetary authorities increase the supply of money, then line $\overline{M}_s$ shifts to the right (not shown). The resulting excess supply of money at old equilibrium interest rate i_e causes the interest rate to fall to the level corresponding to the intersection of demand curve L with the new money supply line. Going in the other direction from $\overline{M}_s$, a decrease in the supply of money shifts $\overline{M}_s$ to the left. Excess demand for money at old interest rate i_e causes the interest rate to rise to a new equilibrium level. Considering shifts in the demand curve, an increase (decrease) in the demand for money would shift the L curve to the right (left) and generate an excess demand for (supply of) money, given the money supply $\overline{M}_s$; the interest rate will rise (fall).

To this point, we have focused on the interest rate and equilibrium between the demand for and supply of money. But this is only a partial analysis because it has neglected the other main determinant of the demand for money—the level of income in the economy. We now introduce the role of income in money market equilibrium.

When we obtained the equilibrium interest rate in Figure 2, the interest rate was the only explicit determinant of the demand for money. Suppose that this is not so and that the level of Y in the economy goes up. Remembering expression [1], the level of income is positively associated with the demand for money. Consider Figure 3, panel (a). The L curve is the one we have been using, and we indicate by the parenthetical expression that this L curve is associated with income level Y_0. If income rises to Y_1, then we *generate a new L curve* indicated by L' and by the Y_1 in parentheses. More money is demanded at this higher income level, and the equilibrium interest rate rises from i_0 to i_1. Similarly, a fall in income from Y_0 to Y_2 leads to a fall in the demand for money curve to L'', with the lower level of income Y_2 indicated in parentheses. The decrease in the income level has thus led to a lower equilibrium interest rate (i_2).

FIGURE 3   Income and the Interest Rate: The *LM* Curve

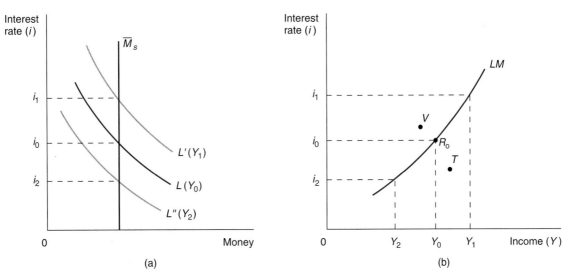

In panel (a), an increase in income from Y_0 to Y_1 increases the demand for money from L to L' and results in a rise in the interest rate from i_0 to i_1. A decrease in income from Y_0 to Y_2 decreases the demand for money from L to L'' and leads to a fall in the interest rate from i_0 to i_2. This positive relationship between Y and i is portrayed by the *LM* curve in panel (b), which shows the various combinations of income and the interest rate that yield equilibrium in the money market. To the right of the *LM* curve, such as at point T, there is an excess demand for money; to the left of the *LM* curve, such as at point V, there is an excess supply of money. In either case, movement will take place to the *LM* curve.

This discussion of the relationship between the income level, the interest rate, and money market equilibrium leads us to a graphical construct, the *LM* curve. The **LM curve** *shows the various combinations of income and the interest rate that produce equilibrium in the money market.*[6] Such a curve is illustrated in Figure 3, panel (b). At each point on this curve, for the particular income level on the horizontal axis, the associated interest rate on the vertical axis is the interest rate that makes the demand for money equal to the *fixed* supply of money. Thus, at point R_0, the income level Y_0 and the interest rate i_0 together give equilibrium in the money market when the money supply is $\overline{M}_s$.

Why does the *LM* curve slope upward? Suppose that the level of income rises from Y_0 to Y_1. As indicated, the increase in income will generate an increase in the demand for money as L in Figure 3(a) shifts to L'; the interest rate thus rises from i_0 to i_1. Once the interest rate has risen to i_1, the excess demand for money has been eliminated and the money market is again in equilibrium. Similarly, if income falls from Y_0 to Y_2, the decrease in the demand for money to L'' lowers the equilibrium interest rate to i_2. From this discussion, we can see that any point to the right of the *LM* curve, such as point *T*, is associated with an excess demand for money. At point *T*, the interest rate is too low for the income level; equilibrium in the money market requires a higher *i*. (Alternatively, the income level is too high for the given interest rate; equilibrium requires a lower income and thus a lower demand for money in order to be at the interest rate associated with *T*.) Similarly, any point to the left of the *LM* curve, such as point *V*, involves an excess supply of money. For the income level associated with *V*, the interest rate needs to be lower in order to have equilibrium in the money market (or the income level needs to be higher for the interest rate associated with *V*).

A final point to make at this juncture is that increases in the demand for money (due to other things besides a rise in income) or decreases in the supply of money will shift the *LM* curve to the *left*. In either situation, the interest rate rises for any given income level, which is analogous to saying that the income level must fall to maintain the same interest rate. Thus, each interest rate is plotted against a lower income level than before the increase in the demand for money or the decrease in the supply of money. By reverse reasoning, decreases in the demand for money (due to other things besides a fall in income) and increases in the supply of money will shift the *LM* curve to the *right*. With either a decrease in the demand for money or an increase in the supply of money, the interest rate is lower for each given income level or, expressed differently, a lower income level is associated with each given interest rate.

CONCEPT CHECK

1. What effect will an increase in income have on the demand for money? The *LM* curve? Why?

2. Explain why the *LM* curve slopes upward.

3. If bank reserves increase, what happens to the supply of money? The *LM* curve? Why?

General Equilibrium in the Real Sector: The *IS* Curve

In the preceding chapter we examined the goods and services markets, or the real sector of the economy. We indicated that, in income equilibrium, the "leakages" of saving, imports, and taxes were equal to the "injections" of investment, exports, and government spending on goods and services. However, a key feature was that the monetary sector was neglected in that real-sector

---

[6]Note that all variables (and especially the price level) influencing the demand for money other than the interest rate and income are being held constant along any given *LM* curve. The relationship of the price level to the *LM* curve is developed in detail in Chapter 27.

FIGURE 4   Income and the Interest Rate: The *IS* Curve

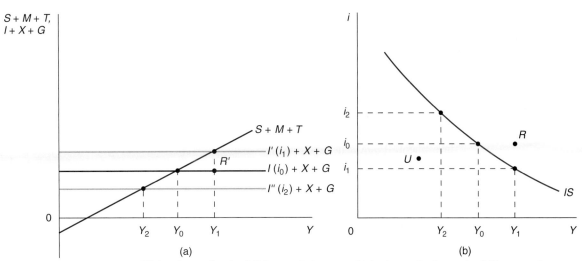

In panel (a), with interest rate i_0, equilibrium income is at level Y_0 because leakages equal injections at that income level. However, a lower interest rate i_1 will increase investment spending and shift $I(i_0) + X + G$ to $I'(i_1) + X + G$; income will rise from Y_0 to Y_1. Similarly, a higher interest rate i_2 will cause $I(i_0) + X + G$ to shift downward to $I''(i_2) + X + G$, resulting in a lower income level Y_2. The inverse relationship between the interest rate and income is plotted on the *IS* curve in panel (b), which shows the various combinations of i and Y that produce equilibrium in the real sector. To the right of the *IS* curve, such as at point R, $(S + M + T) > (I + X + G)$, and there is downward pressure on the income level. To the left of the *IS* curve, such as at point U, $(I + X + G) > (S + M + T)$, and there is upward pressure on the income level. Points off the *IS* curve thus generate movement to the *IS* curve.

analysis, meaning that we were assuming that the *interest rate was constant.* It is now time to relax that assumption! In Figure 4(a), the i_0 in parentheses indicates that the interest rate is held constant at some interest rate i_0 when we consider the $I(i_0) + X + G$ line. With this interest rate, the equilibrium level of income is Y_0. What if we reduce the interest rate from i_0 to i_1? Investors will want to undertake greater amounts of investment because borrowing costs have been lowered, and some investment projects that were previously unprofitable because their return was less than the borrowing costs are now profitable. (Remember that *investment* in the real sector refers to plant and equipment spending by firms, residential construction, and changes in inventories, *not* to the purchase of financial assets.) Empirical studies have indeed shown that residential construction spending is particularly sensitive to the rate of interest, but plant and equipment also responds to the interest rate (albeit to a smaller degree).[7]

Because of the responsiveness of investment to the interest rate, the lower interest rate i_1 is associated with an investment line (and therefore $I + X + G$ line) that is higher. The line $I(i_0) + X + G$ shifts upward to $I'(i_1) + X + G$, and the result is an intersection with the $S + M + T$ line at a *higher* equilibrium level of income Y_1. Similarly, a rise in the interest rate from i_0 to i_2 causes the $I(i_0) + X + G$ line to shift vertically downward to $I''(i_2) + X + G$. Thus, i_2 is associated with a lower level of income Y_2.

This relationship between the interest rate (reflecting the importance of monetary variables), investment, and the resulting equilibrium level of income gives us the information needed to generate the *IS* curve. The **IS curve** *shows the various combinations of income and the interest rate that produce equilibrium in the real sector of the economy.* In our model, this is equivalent

---

[7]It is also possible that exports may increase with a lower interest rate if financing is thus easier.

to saying that the *IS* curve shows the combinations of income and the interest rate that make investment plus exports plus government spending equal to saving plus imports plus taxes. Thus, in Figure 4, panel (b), interest rate i_0 is plotted against income level Y_0, because this is one combination of the interest rate and income that generates equality between $(S + M + T)$ and $(I + X + G)$. The lower interest rate i_1 is plotted against the higher income level Y_1; in the opposite direction, the higher interest rate i_2 is associated with the lower income level Y_2.

If the economy is situated to the right of the *IS* curve, such as at point R in panel (b), then disequilibrium exists because saving plus imports plus taxes exceeds investment plus exports plus government spending. The income level is "too high" for the associated interest rate, and the high income level gives "too much" saving, taxes, and imports. Alternatively, for the income level at R, the interest rate is "too high" and is thus choking off investment. [Point R in Figure 4(b) is analogous to point R' in Figure 4(a).] Income falls until the *IS* curve is reached through cutbacks of production because of unintended inventory accumulation at the higher levels of income. To the left of the *IS* curve, investment plus exports plus government spending exceeds saving plus imports plus taxes, and there is expansionary pressure due to unintended inventory depletion. For the given interest rate at point U, income is too low to generate enough saving, taxes, and imports to match investment, exports, and government spending. [Alternatively, for a given income level, the "too low" interest rate makes desired $(I + X + G)$ exceed desired $(S + M + T)$.]

What causes shifts in the *IS* curve? Clearly any change in autonomous investment, exports, government spending, saving, taxes, or imports will do so. An increase in autonomous investment (due to something other than a fall in the interest rate), autonomous exports, and government spending or an autonomous *decrease* in saving, taxes, and imports will shift the *IS* curve to the right. Hence, for example, an autonomous decrease in saving in Figure 4(a) could shift the $(S + M + T)$ line to the right and through point R', and this would shift the *IS* curve in Figure 4(b) to the right and through point R. On the other hand, an autonomous decrease in I, X, or G or an autonomous increase in S, M, and T will shift the *IS* curve to the left.

Simultaneous Equilibrium in the Monetary and Real Sectors

The simultaneous determination of income and the interest rate when both sectors of the economy are considered involves plotting the *IS* curve and the *LM* curve on the same diagram, as in Figure 5. Equilibrium occurs where the two curves intersect at point q, giving the income level Y_e and the interest rate i_e. This is the only combination of income and the interest rate that simultaneously gives equilibrium in both sectors of the economy.

If the economy has not settled at Y_e and i_e, forces are set in motion to move to this equilibrium position. For example, suppose that the economy is at point F. Because we are to the right of the *IS* curve, then $(S + M + T)$ is greater than $(I + X + G)$, so there is contractionary pressure on the level of income. But, because we are also to the right of the *LM* curve, the demand for money exceeds the supply of money and therefore the interest rate rises. These forces eventually move the economy to point q. However, various *paths* of adjustment might actually be taken, depending on the speed of adjustment in each sector. For example, from point F, the economy might first move vertically to a position on the *LM* curve; the monetary sector would then be in equilibrium but the real sector would not. We could then move horizontally to the *IS* curve where real sector equilibrium is attained, but then the economy would be to the left of the *LM* curve and would have an excess supply of money. This would drive interest rates downward and move us vertically to the *LM* curve. However, we would now be below the *IS* curve. The process of adjustment would continue.

Equilibrium in the Balance of Payments: The *BP* Curve

We need to introduce a further construct to describe the balance of payments in an open economy. This analytical device, the ***BP* curve,** *shows the various combinations of income and the interest rate that produce equilibrium in the balance of payments.* In this context,

FIGURE 5   Simultaneous Equilibrium in the Real and Monetary Sectors

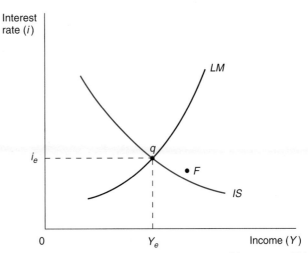

Only at point q is there equilibrium in both the real and monetary sectors of the economy. If the economy is situated away from q at point F, saving plus imports plus taxes exceeds investment plus exports plus government spending; in addition, there is an excess demand for money. Movement occurs (by any of a number of different paths) to point q. Any other point away from point q also sets forces in motion to move the economy to point q.

we are including both the current account and international financial capital flows in the balance of payments. In terms of the balance-of-payments accounting categories, not only category I (the current account) but also category II (long-term capital flows) and category III (short-term private capital flows) are considered (see Chapter 19). We are *not* dealing with category IV (official reserve short-term capital flows). The focus is on all items in the balance of payments besides government official reserve asset and liability changes. Balance-of-payments equilibrium in this sense means a zero balance in the official reserve transactions balance.

For the purpose of obtaining the *BP* curve, we consider how the income level and the interest rate affect a country's balance of payments. It is important to note that a given *BP* curve is constructed under the assumption of a *fixed* exchange rate. In addition, a number of other variables such as the foreign interest rate, foreign price level, expected exchange rate, and foreign wealth are assumed to be constant. Income in this analysis is presumed primarily to influence the current account through the effect of income on imports. Other things being equal, a rise in income induces more imports (by the marginal propensity to import times the change in income). With exports independent of income, this rise in imports means that the current account tends to deteriorate (move toward deficit) by the amount of the rise in imports. These changes would be reversed for a decline in income. On the other hand, the interest rate is assumed to have its primary influence on the capital account, and particularly on category III (short-term private financial capital flows). If the interest rate rises, liquid short-term financial capital from abroad comes into the home country to earn the higher interest rate, and some domestic short-term capital will "stay home" rather than be sent abroad. The inflow of foreign short-term capital and the reduced outflow of home capital move the capital account toward a surplus. If the interest rate declines, these responses are in the opposite direction.

With this background, examine the *BP* curve in Figure 6. Because the curve shows the various combinations of income and the interest rate that produce balance-of-payments (BOP)

FIGURE 6   Income and the Interest Rate: The *BP* Curve

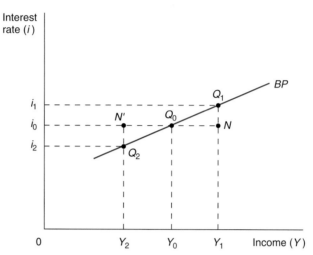

The *BP* curve shows the various combinations of income and the interest rate that yield equilibrium in the balance of payments. The curve slopes upward because a higher income level induces more imports and worsens the current account; a rise in the interest rate is then necessary to increase short-term capital inflows (and to reduce short-term capital outflows), which in turn improve the capital account and offset the worsening of the current account. A movement from point Q_0 to point N worsens the current account and must be offset by a rise in the interest rate from i_0 to i_1 to improve the capital account sufficiently to move the economy back to BOP equilibrium. Points to the right of the *BP* curve are associated with a BOP deficit; points to the left of the curve are associated with a BOP surplus.

equilibrium, point Q_0 is one such point. The income level associated with this point is Y_0 and the interest rate is i_0. Why does the *BP* curve slope upward? Consider a starting point of Q_0 and introduce a rise in income. This rise in income (with no change in the interest rate) will move us horizontally to the right of Q_0, say, to point N. The balance of payments will move into deficit because the higher income level will have generated more imports. If the interest rate is then increased from i_0 to i_1, this will eliminate the BOP deficit. Why? Because the rise in the interest rate will generate net short-term capital inflows that will have a positive effect on the BOP and will completely offset the negative effect in the current account when we reach point Q_1. The current account deterioration is offset by the (private) capital account improvement, because Q_1 has a zero BOP deficit or surplus by definition. Thus, point Q_1 illustrates that income level Y_1 and interest rate i_1 also combine to produce BOP equilibrium.

It is clear that point Q_2 with an income level (Y_2) lower than Y_0 and an interest rate i_2 lower than i_0 shows another combination of Y and i that yields BOP equilibrium. If income falls from Y_0 to Y_2, this means reduced imports, a movement to point N', an improvement in the current account, and a BOP surplus. However, a reduction in the interest rate from i_0 to i_2 will cause the short-term private capital account to deteriorate by enough to offset the improvement in the current account. The capital account deteriorates because short-term funds seeking a higher rate of interest now leave the country and fewer foreign funds come into the country. With this reduction in the interest rate, movement takes place from point N' to point Q_2, another point on the BP schedule.

If the economy is located to the right of the *BP* curve, then there is a BOP *deficit* because, for any given interest rate, the income level is leading to an "excessive" amount of imports, and the interest rate is "too low" to attract a capital inflow sufficient to match the current account's movement toward deficit. The result is that the balance of payments as a whole (official reserve transactions balance) is in deficit. For the reverse reasons, if the economy is located to the left of the *BP* curve, there is a BOP *surplus*. Later in the chapter we discuss the process by which an economy that is not located on its *BP* curve adjusts in order to attain balance-of-payments equilibrium.

An additional point about the *BP* schedule is that the precise value of the upward slope of the *BP* curve importantly depends on the degree of responsiveness of the short-term private capital account to changes in the interest rate. To demonstrate this point, consider the horizontal movement from point Q_0 to point N in Figure 6. This movement generated a movement toward current account deficit, and a return to BOP equilibrium required a rise in the interest rate. Other things being equal, if short-term capital flows are very responsive to changes in *i*, then a small rise from i_0 to i_1 will generate the requisite capital inflow. However, if capital flows are *not* very responsive to changes in the interest rate, a much larger rise in i_0 will be needed to return the economy to BOP equilibrium. The conclusion is that the less (more) responsive short-term capital flows are to the interest rate, the *steeper* (flatter) the *BP* curve will be.[8]

Although up to now it has been assumed that equilibrium in the foreign sector is described by an upward-sloping *BP* curve, this is not always the case. The upward-sloping relationship between *i* and *Y* in the open economy results whenever there are some impediments to the flow of short-term capital between countries (or the country is financially a "large country," able to influence the international level of interest rates; that is, the country is not a price taker with respect to the interest rate). Thus, the case where the *BP* curve slopes upward is referred to as the case of **imperfect capital mobility.** It is assumed that short-term capital is not completely restricted from moving between countries in response to changes in the interest rate but that the movement of short-term capital is not so complete as to remove all differences between the domestic interest rate and the international interest rate [see Figure 7, panel (a)].

FIGURE 7   The *BP* Curve under Different Capital Mobility Assumptions

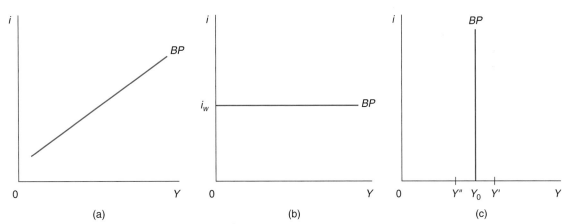

In panel (a), the upward-sloping *BP* curve indicates that capital is imperfectly mobile. In this case, capital moves between countries in response to changes in relative interest rates, but not so easily that domestic interest rates become identical to world interest rates. In panel (b), the horizontal *BP* curve reflects perfect capital mobility, and the domestic interest rate is always equal to the world interest rate. Any slight changes in the domestic interest rate will lead to sufficiently large movements of short-term capital so that the domestic rate will become equal again to the world rate. In panel (c), the *BP* curve is vertical, indicating that the barriers to capital movements are such that there is no short-term capital response to changes in the domestic interest rate; that is, there is perfect capital immobility. In this case, there is only one level of income (and imports) consistent with the level of exports and the controlled net capital inflows.

---

[8]The slope of the *BP* curve also depends on the extent to which changes in the interest rate affect real investment (plant and equipment, residential construction, changes in inventories) and, in turn, by the extent to which such real investment responses affect income and imports. However, the international short-term capital-flow responses are the most crucial in practice.

This result also occurs in the context of a portfolio balance model, even with uncovered interest parity. As you will recall, the imperfect substitutability between foreign and domestic assets means that there is a risk premium associated with holding assets other than those of an investor's own country. Thus, in this case, the domestic interest rate will be above the foreign interest rate because the net capital inflow means that foreign investors' risk premium has increased since they are now holding relatively more home country assets.

The upward-sloping BP curve can be contrasted with the case of **perfect capital mobility,** where the BP curve is fixed horizontally at the level of the world interest rate, i_w [panel (b) of Figure 7]. In this case, any slight deviation of the domestic interest rate away from the international rate leads to a movement of short-term capital sufficient to return the domestic rate to the level of the international rate. For example, suppose that an increase in the domestic money supply leads to a reduction in the domestic interest rate. This action causes financial investors to immediately move their short-term capital out of the country as they adjust their portfolios to include more foreign assets. This outward capital flight and resultant BOP deficit will reduce the holdings of international reserves (as such reserves are used to purchase domestic currency to maintain the fixed exchange rate) and hence the money supply, and it will continue until the domestic interest rate is once again at the international level. An increase in the domestic interest rate above the international level would trigger an inflow of short-term capital and a BOP surplus, which would increase the international reserves of the country and the money supply. This would take place until the domestic rate was once again at the level of the international rate. In this situation, there is perfect substitutability between foreign and domestic financial assets, and any interest rate differences are instantaneously removed by international capital flows.

Because the interest rate does not change with perfect capital mobility, what effect do changes in other economic variables have on the foreign sector? Remember that the BOP is influenced by variables such as the exchange rate, relative prices of traded goods, expected prices, and the expected profit rate in both countries as well as the level of Y and i. Suppose that there is an increase in the expected domestic profit rate that stimulates an inflow of long-term real investment (improvement in the capital account), which in turn stimulates income. To maintain the pegged exchange rate $e,$ the central bank will purchase foreign exchange with domestic currency, thereby increasing the domestic money supply and facilitating the expansion of income. The increase in domestic income will stimulate an increase in imports, causing a deterioration in the current account that exactly offsets the improvement in the capital account.

Changes in exogenous economic factors thus ultimately stimulate changes in the domestic money supply until the economy is once again in equilibrium. As this adjustment takes place, it can lead to a different composition in the balance of payments. More specifically, holding everything but domestic income constant, movements from left to right along the BP curve reflect a transition in the composition of the balance of payments from one of surplus in the current account (on the left) to one of deficit in the current account (on the right). In similar fashion, the capital account is changing from that of deficit (on the left) to a position of surplus (on the right) over the same income range. It must be emphasized that when there is perfect mobility in the capital markets in the open economy, the horizontal BP curve remains fixed at the level of the international interest rate. Changes in exogenous factors simply bring about movement in the domestic equilibrium along the BP curve concomitant with appropriate changes in the composition of the balance of payments. The country wishing to attain *current account* balance is thus forced to accept the level of income that is consistent with that particular composition in the balance of payments.

It is not uncommon to find countries with a pegged exchange rate strictly controlling the foreign sector both in the commodity markets and in the capital markets. This is not

IN THE REAL WORLD:

THE PRESENCE OF EXCHANGE CONTROLS IN THE CURRENT FINANCIAL SYSTEM

Although few countries exercise complete exchange control, a surprising number of restrictions are in place around the world on access to foreign exchange and the uses to which it can be applied. Table 2 summarizes the degree to which various foreign exchange controls are in place within the membership of the International Monetary Fund. A cursory examination seems to suggest that capital is indeed somewhat, if not perfectly, immobile for many countries of the world. Relatively mobile capital conditions probably exist only for the major trading countries of the world whose financial markets have become increasingly integrated in recent years. Even in those cases, however, many different circumstances cause capital not to be perfectly mobile.

TABLE 2   Foreign Exchange Restrictions in 187 IMF Countries, 2005[*]

Type of Restriction	Number of Countries	Percentage of Countries
Exchange rate structure:		
Dual exchange rates	6	3.2%
Multiple exchange rates	5	2.7
Control on payments for invisible transactions and current transfers	89	47.6
Proceeds from exports and/or invisible transactions		
Repatriation requirements	92	49.2
Surrender requirements	69	36.9
Capital transactions:		
Controls on:		
Capital market securities	135	72.2
Money market instruments	116	62.0
Collective investment securities	112	59.9
Derivatives and other instruments	95	50.8
Commercial credits	101	54.0
Financial credits	121	64.7
Guarantees, sureties, and financial backup facilities	87	46.5
Direct investment	150	80.2
Liquidation of direct investment	50	26.7
Real estate transactions	142	75.9
Personal capital transactions	96	51.3
Provisions specific to:		
Commercial banks and other credit institutions	161	86.1
Institutional investors	104	55.6

*Restrictions in place generally as of December 31, 2005.

Note: There are 184 IMF member countries, but Aruba, Hong Kong, and the Netherlands Antilles (not separate countries) have their own particular arrangements and are listed separately by the IMF. They are included in this listing.

Source: International Monetary Fund, *Annual Report on Exchange Arrangements and Exchange Restrictions 2006* (Washington, DC: IMF, 2006), pp. 32, 38.

uncommon in developing countries and can be the result of having an overvalued exchange rate, which the governments ultimately maintain by strict foreign exchange control. In this case, the *BP* relationship is characterized by **perfect capital immobility** [Figure 7(c) on page 643]. When short-term capital flows are strictly controlled and not permitted to respond to changes in the interest rate, the *BP* curve is *vertical* at the level of income that is consistent with the controlled use of foreign exchange pursued by government policymakers. Given the control on the capital accounts, only one level of income (and hence imports) is consistent with the given exchange rate. Should income rise, for example, from Y_0 to Y', the level of imports induced by the higher income would be too high and there would be a BOP deficit, putting upward pressure on the exchange rate (pressure toward depreciation of the domestic currency). To maintain the value of the domestic currency, the government would have to purchase it in the exchange market with foreign exchange reserves. In so doing, the domestic money supply would decline, raising domestic interest rates and reducing domestic investment and income until the domestic economy was once again back in equilibrium on the *BP* curve. Similarly, a fall in income from Y_0 to Y'' would lead to reduced demand for foreign exchange, government purchases of foreign exchange to maintain the exchange rate, and hence an expansion of the money supply until the economy was once again in equilibrium on the *BP* curve. The requisite changes in the money supply will thus automatically keep the economy on the *BP* curve.

In sum, the slope of the *BP* curve reflects the nature of capital mobility in the country under analysis. The more capital flows are restricted and short-term capital movements are not permitted to respond to changes in the domestic interest rate, the steeper the slope of the *BP* curve. Similarly, the less restricted are movements of capital and the more the country in question is financially a small country, the flatter the *BP* curve will be.

Finally, remember that the *BP* curve is drawn for a *specific exchange rate*. If the home country is the United States, for example, and if the exchange rate between the dollar and other currencies changes, then a different *BP* curve emerges. The simple rule is this: A depreciation of the home currency against foreign currencies shifts the *BP* curve to the right, and an appreciation of the home currency against foreign currencies shifts the *BP* curve to the left. To grasp this rule, consider an existing *BP* curve such as that shown in Figure 6. If the home currency depreciates, then the home country's current account balance will improve, assuming that the Marshall-Lerner condition is met. For any given interest rate on the "old" *BP* curve, there is now a surplus in the balance of payments. Hence, a larger level of *Y* is needed for each *i* to have BOP equilibrium, because the larger *Y* will induce more imports and eliminate the BOP surplus. Each interest rate must now be plotted against a higher level of income to show the combinations of the interest rate and the income level that produce BOP equilibrium. This means that the "new" *BP* curve (not shown) will be to the right of the "old" *BP* curve.[9]

In addition, changes in a number of other variables will also shift the *BP* curve. Because changes in these factors can influence equilibrium in the open economy, it is useful to mention several of them before proceeding further. For example, an autonomous increase in exports will cause the *BP* curve to shift to the right or downward because a lower rate of interest will now be sufficient to maintain BOP equilibrium with the stronger balance on current account. This would also be the case with an autonomous decrease in home-country imports. Such a downward shift could also result from changes in monetary variables such as a fall in the foreign interest rate. Also, changes in expectations can influence equilibrium in the foreign sector and hence the *BP* curve. Further discussion of these and other factors and their effect on the *BP* curve is presented in the next chapter.

---

[9]In the case of perfect capital mobility, changes in the exchange rate simply lead to movements along the *BP* curve, because the height of the horizontal *BP* curve is determined by the international rate of interest.

FIGURE 8   Simultaneous Equilibrium in the Real and Monetary Sectors and in the Balance of Payments

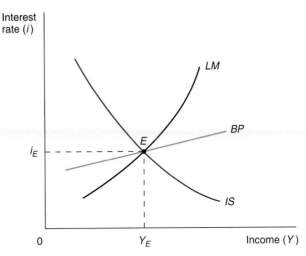

Only at point E is there equilibrium between saving plus imports plus taxes and investment plus exports plus government spending, between the demand and supply of money, and in the balance of payments. With the schedules as drawn, Y_E and i_E are thus the economywide equilibrium levels of income and the interest rate. Any other combination of Y and i is associated with disequilibrium in at least one part of the economy.

Equilibrium in the Open Economy: The Simultaneous Use of the *LM*, *IS*, and *BP* Curves

As a final step for preparing for the discussion of economic policy in the open economy, we bring together the *LM, IS,* and *BP* curves in Figure 8. There is simultaneous equilibrium in the money market, the real sector, and the balance of payments at point E, where all three schedules intersect. The income level associated with this three-way equilibrium is Y_E and the interest rate is i_E. However, this equilibrium position may not be optimal in terms of a country's economic objectives. In such cases, there is a role for macroeconomic policy in order to attain the objectives.

Having established general equilibrium in the *IS/LM/BP* framework, we now turn to a discussion of the nature of this equilibrium and the adjustment processes that move the system to that point.[10] To begin our analysis, we first examine the automatic BOP adjustment mechanism under a fixed-rate system. To do this, we begin with the economy in equilibrium at point E (Y^*, i^*) in Figure 9 and examine what happens when a shock to the system takes place. For example, suppose that there is an increase in foreign income, which increases the level of exports in the home economy. This exogenous change in exports shifts the *BP* curve to the right to *BP′* because any given level of the interest rate can now be associated with a higher income level and still have BOP equilibrium. An official reserve transactions surplus will now occur as long as the domestic economy remains at the initial equilibrium at point E.[11] However,

---

[10]Remember that the basic *IS/LM/BP* framework assumes that the price level remains fixed. This assumption will be dropped in Chapter 27.

[11]It is common to refer to the official reserve transactions surplus as a balance-of-payments surplus and to an official reserve transactions deficit as a balance-of-payments deficit. Remember from Chapter 19, though, that balance-of-payments surplus and balance-of-payments deficit are not strictly correct terms because, if all items in the BOP accounts are included, the "balance" is zero. The concept of concern in this and succeeding chapters, unless otherwise indicated, is the net result of all transactions other than official government intervention in the foreign exchange market—this is the official reserve transactions balance (sometimes called the overall balance).

FIGURE 9   Automatic Adjustment under Fixed Exchange Rates

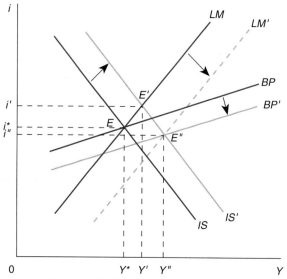

Starting with the economy in equilibrium at i^* and Y^*, an increase in foreign income leads to an autonomous increase in exports, causing the *IS* curve to shift to the right and the *BP* curve to shift to the right. An inflow of foreign reserves now occurs due to both the increase in exports (which improves the current account) and the higher domestic interest rate i' (which improves the capital account). Assuming that the government does not intervene to sterilize the effects on the money supply, this ORT surplus leads to an expansion in the money supply, causing the *LM* curve to shift to the right. The surplus and the expansion of the money supply continue (the *LM* curve continues to shift to the right) until a new equilibrium is reached at Y'' and i''.

the domestic equilibrium will no longer remain at Y^* and i^* because the expansion of exports causes the *IS* curve to shift outward to *IS'*, raising the level of income and the interest rate to $E'(Y', i')$.

Given the *official reserve transactions* or ORT surplus that will occur at E', the economy will not remain at this point. Because the country is operating under a fixed-rate system, it has committed itself to keep constant the value of its currency. Under such a system, the central bank must stand ready to purchase the surplus foreign currency in the exchange market to prevent the appreciation of the domestic currency. Because the foreign exchange is purchased by the central bank with domestic currency, there is expansion of the domestic money supply. In our *IS/LM/BP* analysis, this has the effect of shifting the *LM* curve to the right. This **automatic monetary adjustment** will continue until there is no longer an inflow of foreign exchange reserves. This will occur when the *IS, LM,* and *BP* curves again intersect at a common point $E''(Y'', i'')$ consistent with the new higher level of exports.

An official reserve transactions deficit would produce automatic reactions opposite to these just described for a surplus. The deficit would cause the domestic central bank to sell foreign exchange in return for domestic currency so as to keep foreign currencies from appreciating (i.e., buy home currency with foreign exchange so as to keep the home currency from depreciating), which would reduce the home money supply in private hands. This would shift the *LM* curve to the left. In this deficit case, the reverse of Figure 9's surplus case, the deficit means that the *IS* and *BP* curves would be intersecting to the left of the *LM* curve. The reduction in the money supply and the leftward shift of the *LM* curve would continue to take place until the *LM* curve moved far enough to the left to yield again a threeway equilibrium intersection of the *IS, LM,* and *BP* curves.

Under a fixed exchange rate, the automatic adjustment mechanism is the change in the domestic supply of money brought about by an underlying surplus or deficit in the balance of payments at the pegged exchange rate. Because the exchange rate cannot be changed under a pegged rate system, equilibrium combinations of *i* and *Y* (where *IS* and *LM* intersect) must necessarily lie on the *BP* curve dictated by underlying international economic considerations. As long as the exchange rate remains fixed, domestic policymakers may be faced with choosing between hitting a target interest rate (e.g., to reach a particular growth target) and a target level of income (and hence employment). It should be emphasized, however, that the economy will automatically adjust to the new equilibrium levels as long as the central bank does nothing to interfere with the adjustment process by **sterilization,** or the offsetting of the effects of maintaining the fixed value of the currency in the foreign exchange market. Sterilization would be accomplished in Figure 9 by the central bank selling government securities in the open market, causing a shift from *LM′* back to *LM.* Such sterilization, however, will perpetuate the balance-of-payments disequilibrium. Further, given the huge volume of capital flows across country borders in today's world, the question arises as to whether foreign central banks have enough international reserves to permit the continual acquisition of them by the domestic central bank for any length of time and in sufficient size to offset the intense exchange rate pressure.

Finally, it should be noted that nothing yet has been said about changes in prices. The above automatic adjustment process relies solely on monetary and income effects. The incorporation of price effects that might accompany this kind of adjustment is presented in Chapter 27.

CONCEPT CHECK

1. Ignoring the *LM* curve, suppose that the economy is located at a point to the left (right) of the *IS* curve. Why is there pressure for the economy to expand (contract)?
2. In Figure 5, suppose that the economy is located to the left of the *IS* curve and also to the left of the *LM* curve. Is $(S + M + T)$ greater or less than $(I + X + G)$? Is there an

excess demand or excess supply of money? What will happen to income and why?
3. Explain the rationale for an upward-sloping *BP* curve.
4. Explain how the degree of capital mobility affects the degree of slope of the *BP* curve.

THE EFFECTS OF FISCAL POLICY UNDER FIXED EXCHANGE RATES

The effect of expansionary fiscal policy under various international capital mobility assumptions is presented in Figure 10. First, consider the effect of fiscal policy under conditions of perfect capital immobility, as shown in panel (a). Beginning at Y_0 and i_0 an increase in government spending or a decrease in taxes shifts the *IS* curve to the right, putting upward pressure on domestic income and interest rates. As the economy begins to expand, there is an increase in desired imports and an increase in demand for foreign exchange. To maintain the exchange rate, the central bank sells foreign exchange for home currency, thus reducing the money supply. This leads to a leftward shift in the *LM* curve, which continues until the domestic interest rate has risen sufficiently to bring about a decrease in domestic investment, exactly offsetting the increase in government spending. The only effect of increased government spending under conditions of perfectly immobile capital is a **crowding out** of an equivalent amount of domestic investment; that is, the

FIGURE 10   Fiscal Policy with Fixed Rates under Different Capital Mobility Assumptions

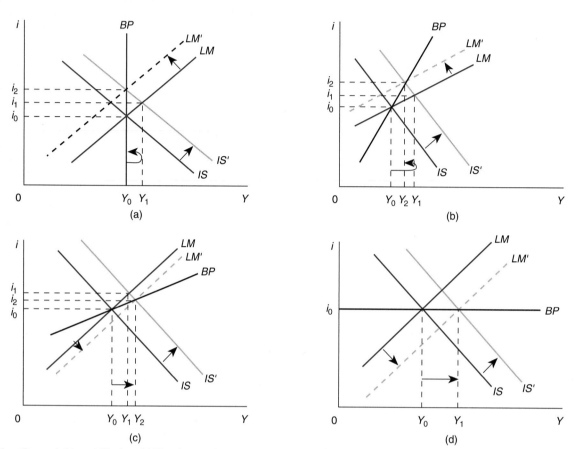

With perfect capital immobility [panel (a)], an increase in government spending (or a decrease in autonomous taxes) shifts the *IS* curve right, leading to increased income and imports. Because there is no short-term capital movement, an official reserve transactions deficit occurs. This leads to a fall in the domestic money supply, shifting the *LM* curve left and increasing *i* until there is once again equilibrium at Y_0. The increase in *G* has led to an equivalent crowding out of domestic investment. A similar result takes place in panel (b), with relative capital immobility, although the presence of some responsiveness of short-term capital to changes in the interest rate means that the crowding out of investment is not complete and there is a slight expansion of income. With relative capital mobility [panel (c)], the expansionary fiscal policy and the accompanying increase in domestic interest rates lead to a surplus and an expansion of the money supply, causing income to increase even more to Y_2 because the crowding out of domestic investment is considerably reduced. Finally, with perfectly mobile capital there is no change in the interest rate with the expansionary policy, because there is a sufficient inflow of short-term capital (and increase in the domestic money supply) to finance the increase in net *G* without reducing domestic investment.

increased *G* has raised *i* and has decreased *I* by the same amount that *G* increased. Income and employment remain at their initial equilibrium levels. Fiscal policy is thus ineffective in stimulating income and employment in the case of perfectly immobile capital.

Figure 10, panel (b), reflects a situation with some degree of capital mobility, but where international capital flows are fairly unresponsive to changes in the interest rate so that the *BP* curve is steeper than the *LM* curve. We designate this situation as one of **relative capital immobility.** Starting from Y_0 and i_0, an increase in net government spending leads to a new domestic equilibrium at Y_1 and i_1. However, because this new equilibrium is below the *BP* curve, there is an official reserve transactions deficit. With the exchange rate fixed, the government must provide the necessary foreign exchange to meet the deficit and to maintain the value of the domestic currency. When this happens, the money supply declines and the LM curve shifts to the left until levels of income and the interest rate are reached that are consistent with BOP equilibrium. This new equilibrium is represented by Y_2 and i_2. We see that fiscal policy is somewhat effective in expanding income and employment in this case, although some of the expansionary effect has been offset by crowding out of domestic investment because of the new, higher equilibrium interest rate. Clearly, the less mobile capital is (and hence the steeper the BP curve), the less effective fiscal policy is in altering the level of income.

Figure 10, panel (c), demonstrates a case in which capital shows some degree of immobility because the BP curve is upward sloping, but where the balance of payments is more responsive to changes in the interest rate than is the domestic money market (the LM curve). This is a situation of **relative capital mobility.** From Y_0 and i_0, an expansionary fiscal policy causes the domestic economy to seek a new equilibrium at Y_1 and i_1, which produces a surplus in the balance of payments. This comes about because the increase in the inflow of short-term capital more than offsets the increase in imports at the higher levels of Y and i. With a BOP surplus, the central bank is forced to purchase the surplus foreign exchange to maintain the exchange rate, which causes the money supply to expand and the LM curve to shift to the right. The expanding money supply causes a further expansion of the economy to Y_2 and i_2.[12] In this case, fiscal policy is complemented by the monetary effects associated with the automatic adjustments under a fixed exchange rate system.

We now turn to the final case, that of perfectly mobile capital, which is illustrated in Figure 10, panel (d). This case is similar to the previous case except for the fact that there is no crowding out of domestic investment because the interest rate remains fixed at the international level. This results from the fact that short-term capital movements instantaneously respond in large-scale fashion to the slightest movement of the interest rate on either side of the international rate because domestic and foreign financial assets are perfect substitutes. With an increase in net government spending, there is immediate upward pressure on the domestic interest rate, which stimulates an inflow of short-term capital and a surplus on all transactions other than governmental intervention. To keep the domestic currency at the pegged rate, the central bank purchases the surplus foreign currency in exchange for domestic currency. This expands the money supply, and this expansion continues until the interest rate effects due to the increase in government spending have been exactly offset by the inflow of short-term capital and the concomitant increase in the domestic money supply. This adjustment is shown by the rightward shift in the LM curve until it intersects the new IS' at a point on the horizontal BP curve. Expansionary fiscal policy is thus totally effective in the case of perfectly mobile capital, in that the economy suffers no offsetting crowding-out effects through increases in the interest rate. With perfectly mobile capital, the full expansion of income is facilitated by the inflow of short-term capital.

This analysis of fiscal policy under fixed rates leads to the conclusion that, to varying degrees, fiscal policy is effective in influencing income under fixed exchange rates except when capital is perfectly immobile. The greater the mobility of capital, the greater the effectiveness of fiscal policy. Although our discussion focused only on expansionary policy, the arguments are symmetric in nature; thus, a reduction in government spending or an increase in taxes will move the IS curve to the left and will generate the opposite effects in terms of ultimate changes of the money supply in response to capital flows resulting from the pressures on the interest rate.

---

[12]Portfolio balance considerations would suggest that this may not be the final equilibrium. If the capital inflow was part of a portfolio stock adjustment shift, the capital flows would fall off after completion of the stock adjustment. This would shift the BP curve to the left, setting off further changes. See Willett and Forte (1969, pp. 242–62).

THE EFFECTS OF MONETARY POLICY UNDER FIXED EXCHANGE RATES

The effects of expansionary monetary policy under the different assumptions of capital mobility are demonstrated in Figure 11. Beginning with the system in equilibrium at Y_0 and i_0, we examine the effects of rightward shifts in the LM curve brought about by increases in the money supply. Figure 11, panel (a), describes the situation with perfect capital immobility, with each successive graph demonstrating cases of greater and greater international capital mobility.

An increase in the money supply shifts the LM curve to the right. In every instance, there is a new intersection of the IS and LM curves at a combination of i and Y that lies

FIGURE 11   Monetary Policy with Fixed Rates under Different Capital Mobility Assumptions

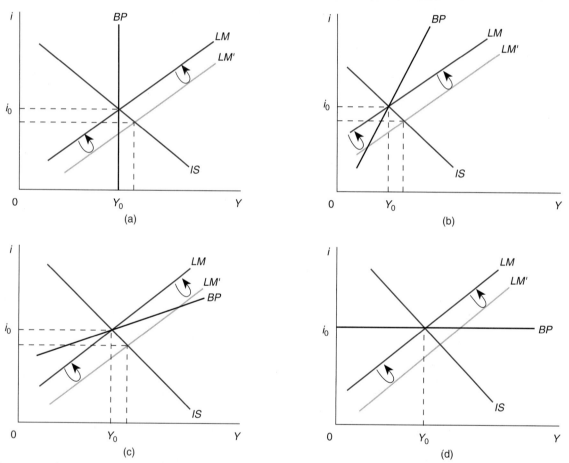

Starting with the economy in equilibrium at Y_0 and i_0, expansionary monetary policy leads to a rightward shift in the LM curve, lowering domestic interest rates and stimulating income. When capital is perfectly immobile [panel (a)], the increase in income stimulates imports and creates an official reserve transactions deficit. As the central bank sells foreign exchange to maintain the pegged rate, the money supply declines, causing the LM curve to shift leftward until the initial equilibrium point is again attained. When capital is imperfectly mobile [panels (b) and (c)], the increase in the money supply leads to a deficit as imports increase *and* net short-term capital inflows decline or become negative. As before, attempts by the central bank to maintain the fixed exchange rate lead to a decline in the money supply, bringing the economy again to Y_0 and i_0. Finally, in the case of perfectly mobile capital [panel (d)], the slightest drop in domestic interest rate i instantaneously leads to a large-scale outflow of short-term capital. Again, the central bank must provide the desired foreign exchange to support the exchange rate, and the money supply declines. This continues until there is no further downward pressure on i, that is, at Y_0.

below or to the right of the *BP* curve and thus is associated with a deficit and downward pressure on the value of home currency or potential appreciation of foreign currency. The result is, of course, a loss of international reserves, as the central bank intervenes to provide the needed foreign currency to prevent the foreign exchange appreciation. In the process of selling the desired foreign exchange, home currency is acquired by the central bank and the money supply falls. The effect is exactly analogous to that of selling short-term government bonds under open-market operations. The reduction in the money supply has the effect of shifting the *LM* curve back to the left. Because this will continue until *IS* and *LM* again intersect on the *BP* curve, we can immediately see that monetary policy is completely ineffective for influencing income under a system of fixed exchange rates, regardless of the degree of capital mobility. This is demonstrated in Figure 11 by the pair of arrows in each figure, which indicate that the *LM* curve first shifts to the right and then shifts back to the original position due to the automatic adjustment mechanism under fixed rates. It should be noted that the shift back to the original position can be delayed if the monetary authorities undertake open-market purchases of domestic securities, that is, sterilization operations to maintain the domestic money supply. This postponement cannot be sustained indefinitely, however, because the country may soon decrease its stock of foreign exchange reserves below a target level. Thus, in the end under a fixed-rate system, a country loses the use of discretionary monetary policy to pursue economic targets. Alternatively, the country may weaken its commitment to the fixed-rate system.

THE EFFECTS OF OFFICIAL CHANGES IN THE EXCHANGE RATE

Although changing the exchange rate cannot be an active tool of discretionary policy under a fixed-rate system, it is useful to examine briefly the macroeconomic effects of an official decision to change the pegged value of the home currency under the various capital mobility scenarios above. Because structural changes may at times require the devaluation/upward revaluation of a currency, it is important to understand how such changes would affect the economy. We proceed in the same manner as above. The four different market conditions are described in Figure 12.

Changes in the exchange rate lead to expenditure switching between foreign and domestic goods and hence will affect both the *IS* curve and the *BP* curve. For example, as the currency is devalued or depreciates,[13] imports become more expensive to domestic residents and exports become cheaper to trading partners. Consequently, depreciation will generate an expansion of exports and a contraction of imports, leading to a rightward shift in the *IS* curve.[14] An appreciation of the currency would do the opposite. The effect of changing the exchange rate on the *BP* curve will depend on the nature of international capital mobility.

Consider first the case of perfectly immobile capital in panel (a) of Figure 12. Beginning at Y_0 and i_0, depreciation of the currency shifts the *BP* curve to the right (*BP'*). Exports increase and imports decrease because of the depreciation, causing the *IS* curve to shift to the right (*IS'*). Once the real expenditure changes have taken effect, any additional adjustment required will take place through automatic changes in the money supply (in the absence of sterilization). For example, if the *IS* shift moves the domestic economy to Y_1 and i_1, domestic

---

[13]Changes in an official pegged exchange rate are usually called *devaluations* (for a rise in *e*) or *upward revaluations* (for a fall in *e*). The terms *depreciation* or *appreciation* represent the actual market rate movements of the currency's value.

[14]Again we are assuming that the Marshall-Lerner condition is satisfied.

FIGURE 12   Expenditure Switching with a Pegged-Rate Change under Different Capital Mobility Assumptions

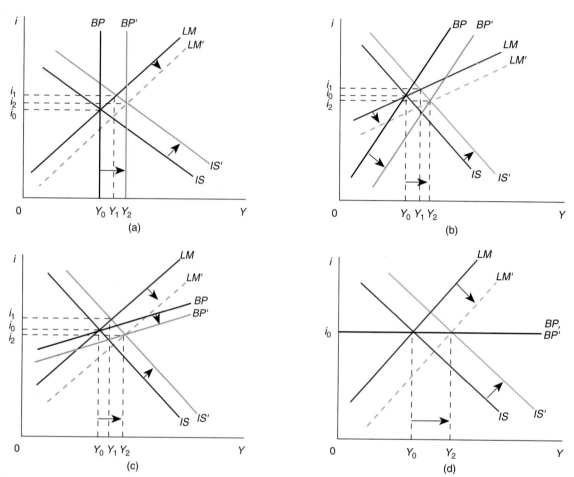

Starting at equilibrium at Y_0 and i_0, a depreciation of the currency leads to increased exports and decreased imports, shifting both the *IS* and the *BP* curves to the right and raising the level of income and the interest rate. With imperfect capital mobility [panels (b) and (c)], the improvement in the current account balance coupled with the higher relative domestic interest rate produces a surplus in the balance of payments. There is then an expansion in the money supply (rightward shift of the *LM* curve) as the central bank buys foreign exchange to maintain the pegged exchange rate, and a further increase in income to Y_2. A similar but less strong expansion in income occurs in panel (a) when capital is perfectly immobile, because there are no short-term capital movements taking place as the domestic interest rate rises. However, under perfect capital mobility [panel (d)], the upward pressure on the interest rate generates very large inflows of short-term capital. As the central bank purchases foreign exchange to maintain the new exchange rate, the money supply expands until there is no longer any upward pressure on the interest rate (at Y_2).

equilibrium (the intersection of *LM* and *IS'*) is to the left of the *BP'* curve, indicating an ORT surplus. This surplus will cause the central bank to purchase the foreign exchange necessary to hold the new value of the currency, and, in the process, increase the money supply. The increase in the money supply will show up as a rightward shift in the *LM* curve and continue until the *LM'* and *IS'* curves intersect at a point on the new *BP'* curve at Y_2. Under perfect capital immobility, expenditure switching does have an effect on income (and prices).

Under imperfect capital mobility [panels (b) and (c)], depreciation again leads to a rightward shift in both the *BP* and the *IS* curves. The expansionary effects associated with expenditure switching lead to higher levels of income and the interest rate and again to a

BOP surplus. Central bank intervention to peg the new value of the currency leads to an expansion of central bank holdings of international reserves and, consequently, an expansion of the money supply. The increase in the money supply leads to a rightward shift in the LM curve, which continues until the economy is again in equilibrium at the level of Y_2 and i_2 where the three new curves intersect. Devaluation has altered the locus of points that produce equilibrium in the balance of payments, and the economy has found levels of income and the interest rate compatible with the new exchange rate. From a policy perspective, we again see that devaluation has had an expansionary effect on the economy. An upward revaluation of the domestic currency would have the opposite effect because it would stimulate imports and reduce exports, leading to a lower level of income.

The final case [panel (d)], that of perfect capital mobility, is slightly different in that altering the value of the currency does not change the position of the BP curve. With perfectly mobile capital, BP remains fixed at the level of the international interest rate. What does take place, as indicated earlier in this chapter, is that altering the value of the currency leads to a movement along the BP curve. For example, a devaluation (depreciation) of the currency again leads to a rightward shift in the IS curve due to the expansion of exports and the contraction of imports

IN THE REAL WORLD:

THE RISE AND FALL OF A CURRENCY BOARD— THE CASE OF ARGENTINA

As noted in the text, a country's monetary policy loses effectiveness in influencing national income under a system of fixed exchange rates. An example of fixed exchange rates in practice that is currently used by seven countries is the concept of a **currency board.** In this arrangement, a fixed rate is established between a home country's currency and some internationally accepted, stable major currency. Further, the money supply of the home country is tied to the country's holdings of the internationally accepted currency. Thus, the money supply can increase only if there is an inflow of the international currency (say, the dollar) because of an official reserve transactions surplus, which in turn is due to an export surplus, a private capital inflow, or both. Analogously, with an official reserve transactions deficit, the country's reserves of the dollar flow out and the money supply is contracted. Hence, if there is rapid inflation, for example, the automatic adjustment mechanism characteristic of fixed exchange rate regimes is activated and the inflation is severely weakened because of the currency board's tie of the home currency's value to the international asset.

Argentina is a prominent example of a country that enacted a fixed-rate tie through a currency board. In the 1980s, the country had substantial inflation. For example, the June 1989 consumer price index (CPI) was 1,471 percent above the CPI level of a year earlier. Further, by March 1990, the CPI had risen *20,266 percent* above that of March 1989. Real GDP fell by 23 percent over the 1980s decade as a whole.

Given this disastrous economic performance, Argentina instituted a variety of reforms, including trade liberalization, more restrictive fiscal policy, and privatization. However, most important was the 1991 Convertibility Law, which aimed to divorce money creation from the political arena by fixing a one-for-one exchange rate between the Argentine peso and the U.S. dollar. Subsequently, by 1998 the inflation rate had fallen to 1 percent, and real output per person grew at an annual average rate of 4.6 percent from 1992 to 1998. This economic success did come at the cost of forgoing an independent role for monetary policy, but clearly this may not have been a bad thing. However, a currency board arrangement in general does mean that, should an unexpected shock such as an export shortfall occur, the economy would shrink because the money supply would contract and there is no possibility of offsetting the contraction within a currency board framework. Further, the currency board arrangement may not be completely insulated from speculative attacks on the currency if doubts exist about the permanent viability of the arrangement. In fact, Argentina at times experienced interest rates above dollar interest rates as investors demanded a risk premium to keep capital from leaving the country.

(continued)

IN THE REAL WORLD: *(continued)*

Unfortunately for Argentina, several of the aforementioned problems did arise, spelling doom for the currency board arrangement. Problems began to arise in 1998, when the government had to reduce its budget deficit because of the increase in the debt load from 29 percent of GDP in 1993 to 41 percent in 1998. A concomitant financial crisis in Brazil and accompanying currency devaluation further contributed to Argentine problems, and a recession subsequently ensued in late 1998 and 1999 that resulted in falling tax revenues and a further widening of the government deficit. This raised further concern about the ability of the government to service its debts, which depressed the financial markets and further deepened the recession. A series of tax hikes ensued in 2000, which were expected to reduce the deficit, lower interest rates, and pull the country out of recession. However, things only got worse as rising criticism of the tie to the dollar and its role in bringing about the recession stimulated concern that a devaluation of the peso was in the offing. Various attempts were made to obtain an infusion of dollars into the country, ranging from seeking more international bank lending to new IMF loans to a debt swap arrangement proposed by Finance Minister Cavallo. When these arrangements failed in late 2001, economic meltdown ensued, as increases in bank account withdrawals triggered fears of a potential bank run, leading to a freeze on bank deposits that was followed soon after by a default on foreign debt. During this turbulent period there was great political instability as President Saa, Economic Minister Cavallo, and all the ministers eventually resigned. On December 30, 2001, the legislative assembly chose Eduardo Duhalde as the new president, and on January 2, 2002, he assumed power and officially ended the currency board and floated the peso.

Economists point out several key lessons to be learned about the adoption of a hard currency peg and the use of currency boards. First, Argentina failed to meet many of the key requirements for success—it is subject to very different shocks than the United States, resource and product markets are not very flexible, its structure of foreign trade is very different from the United States, and it is relatively closed. Thus, as the U.S. dollar strengthened in the 1990s, Argentine goods faced increasing price pressure in the world, and a resulting weaker current account added to recession forces. Thus, in retrospect, it appears that increased flexibility in domestic markets coupled with a greater opening to trade would have been useful. It is also suggested that the Argentine crisis points out the need for prudent regulations of the banking system and control of loans to both households and firms. As a result it is argued that much of the crisis could possibly have been avoided by either using the dollar as a circulating currency (dollarization) or by floating the peso in 1999. However, currency board arrangements often tend to lack clear transition or exit rules as warranted by changes in the economic environment. Also, such moves are often not feasible politically.

Sources: David E. Altig and Owen F. Humpage, "Dollarization and Monetary Sovereignty: The Case of Argentina," Federal Reserve Bank of Cleveland *Economic Commentary,* September 15, 1999; Andrew Berg and Eduardo Borensztein, "The Dollarization Debate," *Finance and Development,* March 2000, pp. 38–41; Steve H. Hanke, "How to Make the Dollar Argentina's Currency," *The Wall Street Journal,* February 19, 1999, p. A19; "No More Peso?" *The Economist,* January 23, 1999, p. 69; Augosto de la Torre, Eduardo Levy Yeyati, and Sergio L. Schmukler, *Living and Dying with Hard Pegs: The Rise and Fall of Argentina's Currency Board,* World Bank, March 2003; Guillermo Perry and Luis Serven, *The Anatomy of a Multiple Crisis: Why Was Argentina Special and What Can We Learn from It?* World Bank, June 2003; Paul Blustein, "Argentina Didn't Fall on Its Own," *The Washington Post,* August 3, 2003, p. A01; Mary Anastasia O'Grady, "Take Argentina Off Life Support," *The Wall Street Journal,* August 15, 2003, p. A9.

that will accompany it. As the economy expands in response to the increase in demand for domestic goods, the rise in the domestic interest rate will precipitate an inflow of short-term capital, putting upward pressure on the home currency. As the central bank purchases the excess foreign exchange (at the new pegged rate) the money supply increases, shifting *LM* to the right. The net short-term capital position will continue to improve (and the money supply to expand) until the *IS* and the *LM* curves again intersect on the *BP* line. This new equilibrium will necessarily be at a higher level of income.[15] Thus, we conclude that changing the exchange rate under a fixed-rate regime will influence the level of economic activity, regardless of the

---

[15]Remember that prices are held constant in this analysis and that income is not necessarily at the full employment level. We also assume that the foreign countries do not match the initial devaluation with devaluation of their own currencies.

mobility of capital. As with fiscal policy, the effect will be the greatest under conditions of perfect capital mobility where there are no crowding-out effects to offset the expansion in demand for domestic goods and services brought about by the change in value of the currency.

CONCEPT CHECK	1. What will be the situation in the balance of payments if the *IS-LM* intersection is below the *BP* curve? What then takes place in the economy under fixed exchange rates? Why?	2. Is monetary or fiscal policy more effective under fixed rates? Why?

SUMMARY

This chapter examined macroeconomic policy under a system of fixed exchange rates. With prices and exchange rates fixed, it became evident very early that there was no guarantee that internal balance targets and external balance targets would necessarily be reached simultaneously. We then introduced a model incorporating the monetary sector, real sector, and the balance of payments (the *IS/LM/BP* model). The effectiveness of domestic monetary and fiscal policy under fixed exchange rates was then analyzed under different international capital mobility assumptions. Monetary policy was generally ineffective in influencing income, whereas fiscal policy had varying degrees of effectiveness depending on the degree of capital mobility. Only when capital was perfectly immobile was fiscal policy totally ineffective in stimulating output and employment. Official changes in the exchange rate (to the extent permitted) were also effective in stimulating economic activity. However, because changing the exchange rate is often difficult under a pegged-rate system, countries may find themselves with an incorrectly valued exchange rate and therefore unable to meet their internal and external balance targets.

KEY TERMS

automatic monetary adjustment	imperfect capital mobility	perfect capital mobility
BP curve	*IS* curve	relative capital immobility
crowding out	*LM* curve	relative capital mobility
currency board	Mundell-Fleming diagram	sterilization
equilibrium interest rate	perfect capital immobility	

QUESTIONS AND PROBLEMS

1. Explain carefully why a country settles in equilibrium at the intersection of the *IS, LM,* and *BP* curves.
2. Why is domestic monetary policy ineffective in an open economy under a fixed exchange rate regime?
3. What will happen to the relative holdings of foreign and domestic assets by the home country if there is an increase in the money supply and capital is perfectly mobile? Why?
4. Explain why a developing country with a fixed exchange rate and foreign exchange controls in place (perfectly immobile capital) may find itself dependent on growth in exports, foreign investment, or foreign aid to attain economic growth.
5. Under what capital flow conditions is fiscal policy least effective in a fixed-rate regime? Most effective? Why?
6. Why does devaluing the domestic currency have an expansionary effect on the economy? Does this expansionary effect take place if capital is perfectly immobile? Why or why not?
7. Suppose you were instructed to construct a *BP* curve of one state in the United States with another, such as New York's *BP* curve with Illinois. What general slope would you expect for this curve and why?

8. Why must countries, especially those prone to official reserve transactions deficits, maintain relatively large holdings of foreign exchange reserves in a fixed exchange rate system?
9. Japan has been running huge current account surpluses in the last decade. Because of concern over this surplus (and over the associated U.S. current account deficit with Japan), U.S. government officials for several years urged the Japanese government to adopt a more expansionary fiscal policy stance. Using an *IS/LM/BP* diagram (assuming that the *BP* curve is flatter than the *LM* curve) and starting from a position of equilibrium, explain how the adoption of such a policy stance would affect Japan's national income, current account, capital account, and money supply. Would your conclusions be different if the *BP* curve were steeper than the *LM* curve? Why or why not? (Note: Assume throughout your answer that Japan does not allow the value of the yen to change.)
10. If financial capital is relatively mobile between countries, what difficulties emerge if the various countries have different interest rate targets for attaining domestic inflation and/or growth objectives? (Assume fixed exchange rates.)

26

ECONOMIC POLICY IN THE OPEN ECONOMY UNDER FLEXIBLE EXCHANGE RATES

LEARNING OBJECTIVES

■ To grasp the impact of fiscal policy on income, trade, and exchange rates under flexible exchange rates.

■ To grasp the impact of monetary policy on income, trade, and exchange rates under flexible exchange rates.

■ To understand how external economic shocks affect the domestic economy under flexible exchange rates.

INTRODUCTION

Is There a Case for Flexible Rates?

In recent years, many of the developing economies throughout the world—from Latin America to Southeast Asia to North Africa—that had fixed exchange rates experienced financial crises. They are being increasingly advised to move away from pegged exchange rates or intermediate, less rigid, fixed rates and to adopt flexible exchange rates. Generally the advice urges them to adopt a flexible-rate regime and devote their monetary policy to other domestic targets such as inflation. Over the past 10 years, a number of Latin American countries have moved away from a variety of fixed-rate regimes and adopted either flexible rates or a hard peg via currency boards or dollarization. Chile, Brazil, Mexico, and Venezuela are examples of those who moved to flexible rates, while Argentina chose to use a currency board and Ecuador and El Salvador adopted the U.S. dollar as legal tender (dollarized). As noted in the previous chapter, Argentina recently was forced to abandon the currency board and move to a more flexible arrangement. The proponents of flexible exchange rate regimes argue that flexible exchange rates would help the developing economies deal with external shocks better, improve financial stability, and reduce the risk of a resulting banking crisis. What is the basis for this viewpoint? What are the benefits and the costs of adopting a flexible exchange rate system? Is it likely to enhance the ability of countries who are globally integrating both economically and financially to reap the benefits of increased economic integration, or does it make them even more vulnerable to the destructive winds of global economic fluctuations and the policies of the more industrialized world?

If the exchange rate continuously adjusts to maintain equilibrium in the foreign exchange market, there is no longer a need for central banks to intervene to remove any excess supplies or demands for foreign exchange. Consequently, the monetary authorities have control over the money supply and can use it to pursue domestic targets. A system of flexible rates thus significantly affects the policy environment and the effects of policy actions. In this chapter we examine the effects of monetary policy and fiscal policy under a flexible-rate regime, comparing and contrasting the effects of policy actions under different capital mobility assumptions. We also evaluate the way a flexible-rate regime responds to external economic shocks. By the end of the chapter, you will have learned why monetary policy and fiscal policy differ markedly in their ability to influence national income under flexible exchange rates and why the effects of each are different when compared to a fixed-rate system.

THE EFFECTS OF FISCAL AND MONETARY POLICY UNDER FLEXIBLE EXCHANGE RATES WITH DIFFERENT CAPITAL MOBILITY ASSUMPTIONS

In this section, we examine the effects of economic policy under flexible rates using the *IS/LM/BP* model employed in the last chapter. The distinct feature of the analysis in this chapter is that domestic responses to combinations of income and interest rates that lie off the *BP* curve will produce disequilibrium situations in the foreign exchange market, which will lead to an adjustment in the exchange rate that brings the foreign exchange market back into equilibrium. As this happens, the *BP* curve will shift, reflecting the new equilibrium exchange rate. Consider, for example, the *BP* curves in Figure 1. Because the exchange rate is now subject to change, we denote a specific *BP* equilibrium by an exchange rate subscript, for example, BP_0 for initial exchange rate e_0. Suppose that the domestic economy moves to a point below the BP_0 curve. At this point, the domestic interest rate is too low to attain equilibrium in the balance of payments for any level of income in question, and the economy begins experiencing a balance-of-payments deficit (official reserve transactions deficit) under the exchange rate e_0. However, because we have a flexible-rate system, as the economy begins to experience the deficit pressure, the home currency depreciates. Consequently, the country never experiences the deficit but, rather, observes a depreciation of the currency instead.

The initial disequilibrium in the foreign sector at point *a,* brought about by the new level of income and interest rate, is often referred to as an **incipient BOP deficit,** because it is not observed as a deficit per se but triggers a depreciation of the currency and a shift in the *BP*

FIGURE 1   The Effects of Changes in the Exchange Rate on the *BP* Curve

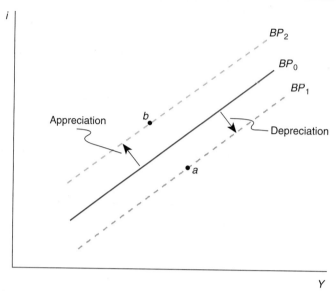

Initial balance-of-payments equilibrium at the exchange rate e_0 is depicted by the BP_0 curve. A depreciation of the currency leads to an expansion of exports and a contraction of imports. Thus, for any given level of income, a larger amount of net capital outflows, and thus a lower rate of interest, is required to balance the balance of payments. The *BP* curve thus shifts down (to the right) with currency depreciation to BP_1. In analogous fashion, an appreciation of the currency leads to greater imports and fewer exports, thus requiring a smaller amount of net capital outflows (or larger net capital inflows) to obtain external balance. A higher interest rate is therefore required at all levels of income, causing the *BP* curve to shift up (or leftward) to BP_2.

curve to BP_1. The lower *BP* curve reflects the fact that at the new, depreciated value of the home currency, any given income level (with its now more favorable current account position due to the enhanced exports and reduced imports caused by the depreciation) is associated with a lower interest rate (which worsens the capital/financial account through additional net capital outflows that exactly offset the more favorable current account). Alternatively, any given interest rate is, in BOP equilibrium with the now-depreciated home currency, consistent with a higher level of income on BP_1 than on the original BP_0. Analogously, a combination of domestic income and the interest rate at point *b,* which lies above the initial *BP* curve, will trigger an **incipient BOP surplus** that causes the exchange rate to appreciate and shifts the *BP* curve to BP_2. It is important to emphasize the difference between the adjustment mechanisms under flexible and fixed rates. Under flexible rates, any disequilibrium leads to a change in the exchange rate and a shift in the *BP* curve. Under fixed rates, a disequilibrium in the foreign sector leads to a change in the money supply and a shift in the *LM* curve.

Finally, it must be noted that a number of different factors influence the position of the *BP* curve in addition to the exchange rate. These factors are assumed to be unchanged in our analysis, but they can, and often do, change. Changes in any one of these factors can cause the *BP* curve to shift, triggering a macroeconomic response. For a brief overview of several of the more important factors and the manner in which they affect the *BP* curve, see Concept Box 1.

The Effects of Fiscal Policy under Different Capital Mobility Assumptions

Now we can turn to consideration of the effects of fiscal policy under the various international financial capital mobility assumptions. Expansionary fiscal policy is represented by a rightward shift in the *IS* curve, and its impacts are shown in Figure 2 (page 662). Each of the four diagrams again reflects a different assumption about capital mobility. In each case, we begin with

CONCEPT BOX 1

REAL AND FINANCIAL FACTORS THAT INFLUENCE THE BP CURVE

A number of different factors influence the nature of the current account and the capital/financial account in the balance of payments in addition to the domestic level of income, the domestic interest rate, and the current (spot) exchange rate. The level of exports is influenced by domestic and foreign price levels, the level of income in the rest of the world, and foreign tastes and preferences. Home-country imports are also influenced by the level of foreign and domestic prices as well as by tastes and preferences. Capital flows depend on foreign interest rates, expected profit rates in both the home and foreign countries, expected future exchange rates, and the perceived risk associated with the investment alternatives.

All of these additional considerations are being held constant for a specific external balance (*BP*) curve. Should any of the factors change, the *BP* curve will shift to offset the effects of the changing condition and thus continue to reflect external balance. For example, an increase in foreign income will increase home-country exports, thus permitting a higher level of domestic income to obtain balance-of-payments equilibrium for every interest rate. The *BP* curve will therefore shift to the right. A decrease in the foreign price level would have the opposite effect, leading to an increase in home country imports, a higher necessary rate of interest to balance the balance of payments, and hence a leftward shift in the *BP* curve.

Changes in financial variables will also shift the *BP* curve. For example, an increase in the foreign interest rate will stimulate an increase in short-term financial capital outflows from the home country. A higher domestic interest rate will therefore be required to balance the balance of payments for every given level of income, and the *BP* curve shifts to the left. A similar adjustment would take place for an increase in the expected profit rate abroad or a decrease in the expected profit rate at home. Finally, if investors' expectations regarding the future value of the exchange rate change—for example, there is an increase in the expected appreciation of the home currency—this would lead to a shift in the *BP* curve. An increase in the expected appreciation of the home currency leads to an inflow of short-term capital and hence to a rightward shift in the *BP* curve, because it now takes a lower rate of interest for each level of income to maintain external balance. These effects are summarized in Table 1.

TABLE 1   Exogenous Factors and Shifts in the *BP* Curve

Increase in foreign income	*BP* curve shifts right (down)
Increase in foreign prices	*BP* curve shifts right
Increase in domestic prices	*BP* curve shifts left (up)
Increase in the expected profit rate:	
Foreign	*BP* curve shifts left
Domestic	*BP* curve shifts right
Increase in the foreign interest rate	*BP* curve shifts left
Increase in expected home currency appreciation	*BP* curve shifts right
(depreciation)	(left)

the economy in equilibrium at Y_0 and i_0 and then examine the effect of an increase in government spending (or a decrease in taxes), which is captured by a shift in the *IS* curve to *IS'*.

Beginning with panel (a), an increase in government spending increases domestic demand for goods and services (*IS'*), leading to higher equilibrium income and a higher interest rate. Because capital is perfectly immobile, the increase in income creates an incipient deficit and causes the currency to depreciate. With depreciation of the currency, BP_0 shifts to the right to BP_1. At the same time, the depreciation of the currency causes exports to increase and imports to decrease, resulting in a further rightward shift of the *IS* curve to *IS''*. These adjustments stop when the *IS, LM,* and *BP* curves again intersect at a common

FIGURE 2   Fiscal Policy in the Open Economy with Flexible Exchange Rates under Alternative Capital Mobility Assumptions

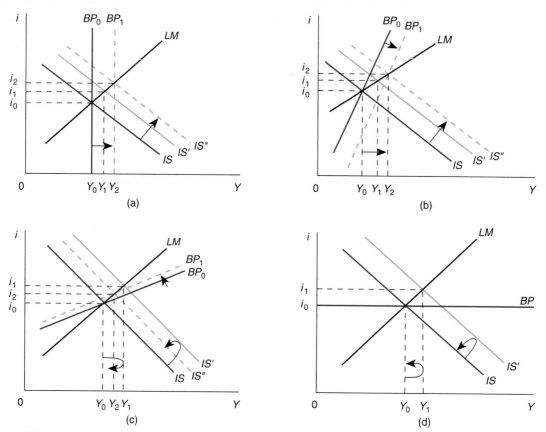

Starting at equilibrium Y_0 and i_0, an expansionary fiscal policy shifts the IS curve right (IS'). This causes income and imports to rise, leading to an incipient deficit when capital is perfectly immobile [panel (a)] or relatively immobile [panel (b)], and a depreciation of the home currency. Currency depreciation shifts the BP curve right (BP_1), and increases exports and decreases imports, which generates an additional shift in the IS curve (IS''). A new, higher equilibrium, Y_2 and i_2, results. However, when capital is relatively mobile [panel (c)], the effectiveness of fiscal policy is reduced. In this case, expansionary fiscal policy (IS') produces an incipient surplus and currency appreciation. The BP curve thus shifts up and the IS curve shifts left as imports increase and exports decrease. The trade adjustment offsets some of the expansionary effect of the fiscal policy, and the expansionary effect on income is reduced, not enhanced as it was when capital was immobile or relatively immobile. Finally, note that with perfectly mobile capital [panel (d)], fiscal expansion sets in motion a currency appreciation that continues until the current account effect ($-\Delta X, +\Delta M$) completely offsets the initial fiscal policy, leaving income at Y_0.

point (Y_2, i_2). In the case of perfectly immobile capital, the adjustment in the foreign sector produces a secondary expansionary impulse through the increase in net exports. Note that because the adjustment in the foreign sector is taking place through the exchange rate, there is no change in the money supply and hence no change in the LM curve.

Figure 2, panel (b), illustrates the situation of relative capital immobility, where international short-term capital movements are less responsive to changes in the interest rate than are the domestic financial markets. In this case, the BP curve is steeper than the LM curve. Increases in government spending again have an expansionary effect on the economy, leading to an incipient deficit in the balance of payments. The deficit pressure is less than it was when capital was perfectly immobile, because there is some degree of short-term capital response to changes in the domestic interest rate. An incipient deficit arises because induced imports from the higher Y outweigh the increased net capital inflow, and the resulting depreciation of the currency leads to a rightward shift of the BP curve to BP_1. An additional rightward shift of the *IS* curve to *IS″* occurs as net exports increase with the depreciating currency. While the effects are smaller than those under perfect capital immobility, fiscal policy is still effective in expanding national income, and the adjustment of the foreign sector supplements the initial effect of the increase in government spending.

In panel (c), we have the case of relative mobility of international short-term financial capital, where the *BP* curve is flatter than the *LM* curve. While there is still imperfect mobility of capital in this instance, the foreign sector is seen to be more responsive to changes in the interest rate than the domestic money markets. An increase in government spending leads to an incipient *surplus* in the balance of payments due to net capital inflows more than offsetting the current account deficit and, hence, appreciation of the currency. With the currency appreciation, the *BP* curve moves to the left. The deterioration in the current account has an impact on aggregate demand as well, shifting the *IS* curve to the left. Consequently, the system comes to rest at a level of income Y_2 instead of Y_1. This takes place because part of the expansionary effect of the increase in government spending is offset by the deterioration in the current account that accompanies the appreciation of the currency. In this case, the foreign sector adjustment *dampens* the initial expansionary effect of the increase in government spending.

In the final scenario in panel (d), that of perfect capital mobility, we see that the shift in the *IS* curve to *IS′* due to the increase in government spending again causes an incipient surplus in the balance of payments (Y_1, i_1). This triggers an appreciation of the home currency (due to large-scale capital inflows), which continues until the current account balance deteriorates sufficiently to offset exactly the initial increase in government spending. The *IS* curve will settle in the same position as before the increase in *G*. Thus, the principal real result of the increase in *G* is that it leads to a reduction in exports and an increase in imports, that is, to a change in the composition of GDP and the balance of payments. Because income has not expanded, the increase in government spending has essentially been facilitated by an increase in imports and a decrease in exports. Thus, exports have been "crowded out" and the imported goods have been "crowded in" by increased government spending. Note, however, that there has been no crowding out of real investment because, with perfectly mobile capital, the interest rate remains fixed at the international rate.

As you will have noted, in the circumstance where capital is neither perfectly mobile nor perfectly immobile, the effect of expansionary fiscal policy on the exchange rate is indeterminate without knowledge of the relative slopes of the *BP* and *LM* curves. If the *BP* curve is steeper than the *LM* curve (relative capital immobility), the home currency depreciates; if *BP* is flatter than *LM* (relative capital mobility), the home currency appreciates. Likewise, from a portfolio balance perspective, there is indeterminacy regarding the effect of the expansionary fiscal policy on the exchange rate. For example, if the expansionary policy involves a government budget deficit and the consequent issuance of new government bonds, then home-country bonds may become more risky to foreign portfolio owners because there is now a greater supply of the home bonds. A depreciation of the domestic currency would then occur to induce foreign bondholders to buy the new bonds. This increase in riskiness is tantamount to making the *BP* curve steeper, approaching or becoming steeper than the *LM* curve (i.e., becoming the relative capital immobility case). On the other hand, if the expansionary fiscal policy did not involve issuing new bonds (i.e., there is no government budget deficit), the home currency would appreciate because of the short-term capital inflow response to the higher domestic interest rate. Finally, if deficit spending occurred but the deficit was financed by printing money rather than by issuing government bonds, the money supply increase would cause the home currency to depreciate. (As we see in the next section, increasing the money supply leads to depreciation.) Hence, portfolio balance considerations also yield uncertainty regarding the impact of the expansionary fiscal policy on the exchange rate.

An overview of the effects of fiscal policy under flexible rates thus indicates that the effectiveness of fiscal policy depends strongly on the degree of international mobility of capital. When capital is completely or relatively immobile, fiscal policy is effective in moving the economy to income and employment targets, and more so than under fixed exchange rates because of the extra income stimulus provided by the currency depreciation. On the other hand, as capital becomes more and more mobile, fiscal policy becomes less and less effective. In the case where capital is relatively mobile (*LM* steeper than *BP*), fiscal policy is less effective under flexible rates than under fixed rates because of the income-depressing effect of the currency appreciation. For the extreme case of perfect capital mobility, fiscal policy is totally ineffective. As financial capital becomes more and more mobile in our shrinking world, fiscal policy will become less and less effective for influencing the level of income and employment. While a flexible-rate system thus severely weakens the fiscal instrument in a world of mobile capital (because the adjustments in the foreign exchange markets can severely offset the effects of discretionary fiscal policy), it does free up the monetary policy instrument, as will be seen in the following section.

The Effects of Monetary Policy under Different Capital Mobility Assumptions

The economic response to increases in the money supply is straightforward and consistent across the different capital mobility scenarios (see Figure 3). Increases in the money supply shift the *LM* curve to the right and in all four cases expand domestic income from the initial Y_0, put downward pressure on the domestic interest rate from the initial i_0, and produce an incipient deficit in the balance of payments. Under a system of flexible rates, expansionary monetary policy leads to a depreciation of the domestic currency, accompanied by an increase in exports and a decrease in imports. With the depreciation, both the *BP* curve and the *IS* curve shift to the right. The end result is an increase in equilibrium income and a strengthening of the trade balance.

Looking more closely at each case, in the situation of perfectly immobile capital [panel (a)], the incipient deficit is caused by the increase in imports that accompanies the higher level of domestic income. Because capital flows are completely insensitive to changes in the interest rate, there is no capital-flow response to the monetary policy action. Consequently, the currency needs to depreciate only enough to offset the income effect on imports. As the currency depreciates, the *BP* curve shifts to the right from BP_0 to BP_1 and the increase in net exports also shifts the *IS* curve to the right to IS'. The system will eventually come to rest at a new equilibrium with a higher level of income Y_2, a depreciated currency, and a lower interest rate.[1] Note that the expenditure effects associated with the depreciation further enhance the initial effects of the monetary expansion.

---

[1]The interest rate falls unambiguously because the *BP* curve shifts to the right to a greater extent than does the *IS* curve at any given interest rate. Remembering the autonomous spending multiplier from Chapter 24, the change in income at each interest rate is the depreciation-induced improvement in the trade balance (the net addition to spending in the economy at each interest rate) times the multiplier. This income change equals the size of the horizontal shift in the *IS* curve; that is,

$$\Delta Y_{IS} = \Delta (X - M) \times (1/[1 - \text{MPC} (1 - t) + \text{MPM}]) \tag{1}$$

On the other hand, the *BP* curve shifts to the right at any given interest rate by the amount of increase in income needed to generate sufficient imports to restore balanced trade after the currency depreciation. In other words, imports must rise by the amount necessary to match the initial improvement in the trade balance; that is, imports must change by MPM × ΔY. Hence,

$$\Delta M = \text{MPM} \times \Delta Y \tag{2}$$

or the necessary rightward shift in the *BP* curve at each given interest rate is

$$\Delta Y_{BP} = \Delta M/\text{MPM} \tag{3}$$

Because trade balance is restored after the *BP* shift, this means that ΔM associated with the *BP* shift is equal to $\Delta(X - M)$ associated with the *IS* shift. Letting $\Delta M = \Delta(X - M) = a$ in expressions [3] and [1], we see that $\Delta Y_{BP} = a/\text{MPM}$ and $\Delta Y_{IS} = a/[1 - \text{MPC}(1 - t) + \text{MPM}]$. Because $[1 - \text{MPC}(1 - t)]$ is a positive number, the denominator in the ΔY_{IS} expression is larger than the denominator in the ΔY_{BP} expression, and hence with an identical numerator, ΔY_{BP} is greater than ΔY_{IS}. In other words, the *BP* curve shifts farther to the right than does the *IS* curve at any given interest rate.

FIGURE 3   Monetary Policy in the Open Economy with Flexible Exchange Rates
under Alternative Capital Mobility Assumptions

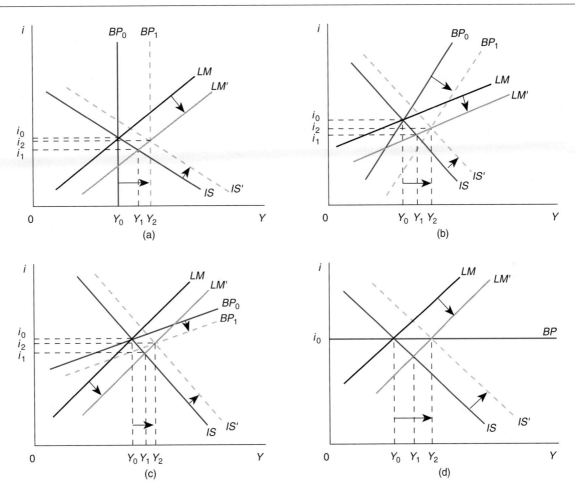

Starting at equilibrium at Y_0 and i_0, expansionary monetary policy shifts the LM curve to the right (LM'), lowering the interest rate and increasing income (Y_1, i_1). The lower interest rate reduces a net capital inflow or worsens a net capital outflow [except in case (a)], and the higher income level increases imports. Consequently, there is an incipient deficit in the balance of payments, resulting in a depreciation of the home currency and a rightward shift in the BP curve (BP_1). However, depreciation increases exports and decreases imports, causing a rightward shift of the IS curve (IS'). Depreciation (rightward shift of the BP curve) and improvements in the trade balance (rightward shift of the IS curve) continue until all three curves again intersect at a common point and equilibrium is obtained (Y_2 and i_2). In the case of perfect capital mobility [panel (d)], all the adjustments take place along the BP curve, because it remains horizontal at the world rate of interest. With flexible exchange rates, expansionary monetary policy is effective in influencing income regardless of the degree of capital mobility, and the current account effects complement the monetary policy in all cases.

The expansion of the money supply under imperfect capital mobility [panels (b) and (c)] leads to a fall in the domestic interest rate and in turn stimulates a short-term capital outflow, worsening the short-term capital account. Thus, both short-term capital movements and the increase in domestic income put downward pressure on the value of the home currency. The more responsive international capital flows are to changes in the domestic interest rate (the flatter the BP curve), the greater the additional pressure will be. Consequently, the more interest-elastic the BP curve is, the greater the depreciation that will take place to maintain equilibrium in the balance of payments. Because the expansion in net exports is greater with a greater depreciation, the overall expansionary effects of monetary policy are larger the more mobile international capital is. This is verified in the last case, panel (d), where capital is perfectly mobile and the *BP* curve is horizontal. Because capital is very responsive to the slightest change in the domestic interest rate, expansion of the money supply generates a very large capital outflow and a depreciation of the home currency. This depreciation leads to a large expansion of net exports (exactly offsetting the capital outflow), which in turn stimulates national income.

The more mobile international capital is, the more effective monetary policy is. However, the more mobile international capital is, the greater the degree to which expansionary monetary policy depends on the adjustment in the foreign trade sector to bring about the increase in income and employment. If the interest rate does not initially change, or changes very little with respect to changes in the money supply, then investment may not respond and the income expansion must come about through shifts in the *IS* function via changes in exports and imports. With all mobility assumptions, however, the subsequent adjustments in the foreign trade sector strengthen the initial impact of the growth in the money supply. It can be concluded, therefore, that, in general, monetary policy is more effective under flexible exchange rates than under fixed exchange rates.

Policy Coordination under Flexible Exchange Rates

A general conclusion reached in the preceding analysis of fiscal and monetary policy is that monetary policy is consistently effective in influencing national income under flexible rates and that it is stronger the more mobile is international short-term capital. Fiscal policy is less effective under flexible rates than under fixed rates when capital is relatively or perfectly mobile. This results from the fact that the expenditure-switching effects can work against fiscal policy, whereas they complement monetary policy. It is not surprising, then, that policymakers may find it desirable to use both instruments in a coordinated fashion to achieve domestic targets. **Monetary policy–fiscal policy coordination** will permit policymakers to strive for other targets besides income, such as an interest rate target, stability of the foreign exchange rate, or a desired combination of government spending, export production/employment, and output/employment in the import-competing sector. Joint use of monetary and fiscal policies will allow the policymaker some control over the nature of the structural adjustment and over the distribution of the economic effects of the policies adopted.

This point can be seen in Figure 4. Let us start with the economy initially in equilibrium at Y_0 and i_0. Suppose that a target of Y^* and i^* is set, which would permit the expansion of the economy without affecting the exchange rate and hence relative prices. Turning first to panel (b), let us examine how attempts to reach that point using monetary policy alone will fare. Expanding the money supply alone (LM') leads to depreciation of the domestic currency (a rightward shift of BP) and an expansion of net trade in the foreign sector (a rightward shift of *IS*). Because the new equilibrium must lie on LM' with a depreciated currency (a lower BP), the equilibrium rate of interest will be less than i^*. Such an equilibrium interest rate is illustrated by i', occurring at the intersection of IS', LM' and BP_1. In this instance, both targets would be missed because Y' is less than Y^* and i' is less than i^*. In addition, exporters and import competitors would be rewarded and the nontraded sector would be harmed by the change in relative prices brought about by the change in the exchange rate.

If, on the other hand, government officials attempted to attain Y^* using only fiscal policy and they were successful, interest rates would be driven up to i_{y*}, as demonstrated in panel (a), clearly missing the target i^*. In all likelihood, it would prove difficult to attain Y^* with only fiscal policy, because expansionary fiscal policy (i.e., a rightward shift in the *IS* curve to IS_{FP}) will create an incipient surplus, causing the currency to appreciate (a leftward shift of the *BP* curve). With the currency appreciating, exports decrease and imports

FIGURE 4   Monetary–Fiscal Policy Coordination under Flexible Exchange Rates

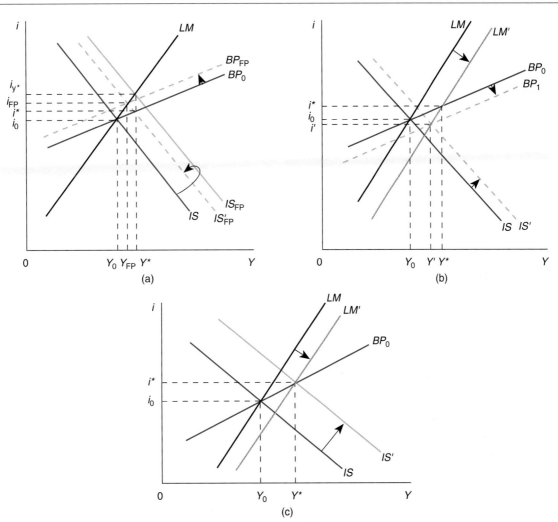

With the economy in equilibrium at Y_0 and i_0, policymakers decide that it would be desirable to be at Y^* and i^*. However, it is possible to reach this combination only by the coordinated use of monetary and fiscal policies as shown in panel (c). Turning to panel (a), attempts to use only fiscal policy (a rightward shift in the IS curve to IS_{FP}) will lead to an incipient surplus and appreciation of the home currency. Consequently, the BP curve starts shifting left, and at the same time exports decrease and imports increase, causing the IS curve to shift left. The new equilibrium that must be on the LM curve will either miss the interest rate target at Y^* (i.e., i_{y*} will exist instead of i^*) or miss both targets such as at Y_{FP} and i_{FP} (IS'_{FP}, BP_{FP}, LM). Attempts to use only monetary policy (a rightward shift in the LM curve to LM'), as demonstrated in panel (b), will lead to an incipient deficit and depreciation of the currency. Consequently, the BP curve will start shifting right (toward BP_1) and, as exports increase and imports decrease, the IS curve will also start shifting to the right. The new equilibrium will occur on LM', but with a depreciated currency and hence with the IS' and BP_1 curves. Consequently, attempts to attain Y^* will lead to an interest rate less than i^*, or to a new equilibrium at i' and Y', which misses both targets. Hence, as shown in panel (c), the only way to attain the two targets simultaneously is with coordinated use of the two instruments.

increase, and the IS curve shifts back leftward to IS'_{FP}. The system thus moves to a new equilibrium on the LM curve, for example, the intersection of IS'_{FP} and BP_{FP}, which misses both targets. The use of fiscal policy alone will lead to an interest rate that is too high and in all likelihood a level of income below Y^*. Attempts to reach Y^* by additional government spending will simply drive the interest rate higher. Further, in this process, exporters and producers of import substitutes would be hurt and the nontraded sector would gain.

The only way to obtain the two targets in question without causing exchange rate changes and affecting relative prices—and therefore, the structure of the economy—is to rely on both of the instruments. In Figure 4(c), Y^* and i^* are obtained by the joint use of monetary and fiscal policies (IS' and LM'), which allows the economy to expand to Y^* without stimulating any expenditure-switching effects. For similar reasons, policymakers will likely find it effective to use both policy instruments to respond to exogenous shocks should they feel that a policy response is appropriate.

CONCEPT CHECK

1. Under what capital mobility conditions is fiscal policy effective in pursuing an income target in a flexible exchange rate system? When is it totally ineffective? Why?

2. Why is it said that the effectiveness of monetary policy in altering income is enhanced by induced changes in the foreign sector in a flexible exchange rate system?

THE EFFECTS OF EXOGENOUS SHOCKS IN THE IS/LM/BP MODEL WITH IMPERFECT MOBILITY OF CAPITAL

The analysis to this point has focused on the effects of monetary and fiscal policy, holding a number of important variables constant. These include such variables as the level of prices at home, the level of prices abroad, and the interest rate abroad, as well as the expected profit rates at home and abroad, the expected exchange rates, and the trade policies and economic institutions at home and abroad. Because these variables can, and often do, change abruptly or unexpectedly, it is useful to examine briefly the effects of changes in selected variables through comparative statics to get some idea of how economic "shocks" are transmitted in an interdependent world under flexible exchange rates.

Suppose that there is a sudden increase in the level of foreign prices, that is, a **foreign price shock** (see Figure 5).[2] There will be an expansionary effect (a shift of the IS curve to the right) on the home economy as exports increase and imports decrease in response to the price change in question. In addition, there will be a rightward shift in the BP curve (from BP_0 to BP'_0) because the expenditure-switching effect of the increase in foreign prices means that a higher level of domestic income is consistent with BOP equilibrium for each given home interest rate. With the increased spending (IS') on the country's products, income and the interest rate begin to rise. The rise in the domestic interest rate generates upward pressure on the value of the home currency (appreciation) because of short-term capital inflows, as has the improvement in the current account, and the BP curve will begin to shift back up. As the currency continues to appreciate, exports fall and imports rise, shifting the IS curve back toward its initial position. The final result is a return to the original Y_0, i_0 equilibrium position. Thus, we see that under (completely) flexible rates the economy is insulated from price shocks originating outside the country. This case is relevant to the period since 1972, when considerable price variability occurred in major commodity groups.

Suppose on the other hand that there is a sudden increase in domestic prices, that is, a **domestic price shock** (see Figure 7 on page 671). In this case, equilibrium in all three sectors will be affected. An increase in domestic prices will reduce the real money supply, shifting the LM curve to the left. At the same time, increased domestic prices will reduce the competitiveness of home exports and make imports more attractive to domestic consumers. Consequently,

[2]For simplicity, we are ignoring any effect on domestic prices of the foreign price change. Such effects would not change the central conclusion of the analysis.

FIGURE 5   Foreign Price Shocks and Macroeconomic Adjustment in the Open Economy

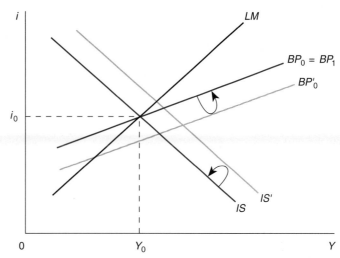

An increase in foreign prices causes the BP curve to shift out to BP'_0 and exports to rise and imports to fall. The improved current account shifts IS right to IS', putting upward pressure on income and the interest rate. The improved current account and the higher domestic rate of interest produce an incipient balance-of-payments surplus, and the home currency begins to appreciate. With currency appreciation, the BP curve moves upward and the IS curve moves leftward. Equilibrium is again reached at Y_0 and i_0 as the appreciating currency offsets the foreign price shock.

IN THE REAL WORLD:

COMMODITY PRICES AND U.S. REAL GDP, 1972–2006

Price shocks can originate in a number of ways, for example, increases in the money supply, fiscal expansion, simultaneous expansion of several key industrial countries, sudden increases in wages, and changes in real commodity prices. Figure 6 focuses on commodity price changes and portrays the movement of world wholesale prices of food, agricultural raw materials, metals, and petroleum over the period 1972–2006. Oil prices almost quadrupled from 1973 to 1974 and then almost tripled from 1978 to 1980, before falling about 60 percent from 1980 to 1986. However, petroleum prices have spiked upwards in recent years, reaching the $75–$80/bbl range in July 2007 (not shown on graph). There was clearly considerable price variability during this period in the other, broader commodity categories as well. Interestingly, all these commodity prices have also risen in recent years, particularly in metals.

However, despite these major price shocks, real GDP in the United States demonstrated relatively steady growth over these years. Because major countries' exchange rates became more flexible in 1973, this relative stability of GDP is consistent with the notion that flexible rates tend to insulate an economy from external price shocks. Nevertheless, we do not wish to minimize the impact of the shocks, because unemployment and inflation in industrial countries were affected in particular by the OPEC price hikes in 1973–1974. The insulation from exogenous forces that was expected to accompany flexible exchange rates has not been complete (although exchange rates were and still are not completely flexible).

Sources: International Monetary Fund (IMF), *International Financial Statistics Yearbook 2002* (Washington, DC: IMF, 2002), pp. 186–89; IMF, *International Financial Statistics Yearbook 2006* (Washington, DC: IMF, 2006), pp. 122–23, IMF, *International Financial Statistics,* May 2007, pp. 72–73; U.S. Department of Commerce, *Survey of Current Business,* May 2007, p. D-47.

(continued)

IN THE REAL WORLD: *(continued)*

FIGURE 6   Commodity Prices and U.S. Real GDP, 1972–2006

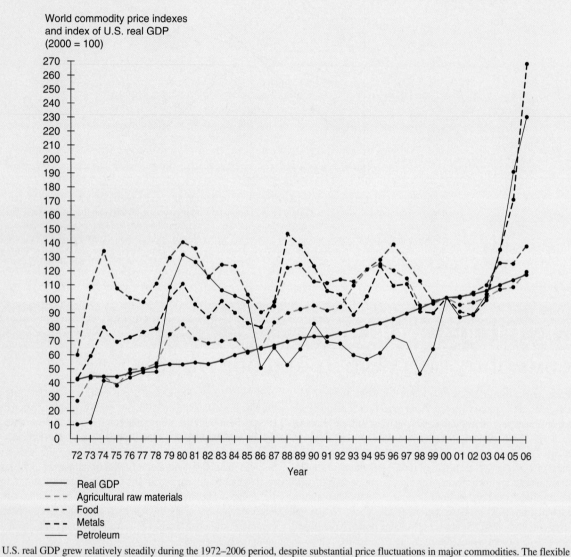

U.S. real GDP grew relatively steadily during the 1972–2006 period, despite substantial price fluctuations in major commodities. The flexible exchange rate of the dollar during this period appears to have provided some insulation of the economy from the external shocks.

the *IS* curve will shift to the left. Finally, these same trade effects will lead to an upward shift of the *BP* curve, because it will now take a higher interest rate to attract sufficient short-term capital to bring the balance of payments into balance at every level of income. These adjustments are shown in Figure 7 by LM', IS', and BP_1. The new equilibrium will lie along LM' at a higher interest rate (i_1) and a lower level of income (Y_1) than the initial equilibrium (i_0, Y_0),

FIGURE 7   Open-Economy Adjustment to Domestic Price Shocks in a Flexible-Rate Regime

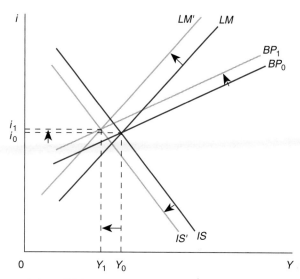

Assume that the economy is in equilibrium at Y_0 and i_0. An increase in the domestic price level will affect equilibrium in all three sectors. The *LM* curve will shift to the left to *LM'* as the real supply of money falls. The *IS* curve will shift to the left as exports fall and imports rise. Finally, the *BP* curve will shift upward as the deteriorating trade balance requires a higher rate of interest for every level of income to balance the balance of payments. Equilibrium will occur on *LM'* at a lower level of income (Y_1) and a new rate of interest (i_1).

although i_1 could be less than i_0. Should the initial shifts in the *IS* and *BP* curves not lead to a simultaneous equilibrium point with *LM'*, a change in the exchange rate will occur, because an *IS/LM* equilibrium point that does not lie on the *BP* curve will bring about the requisite exchange rate adjustment.

Next, from an initial i_0, Y_0, suppose that there is an increase in the foreign interest rate, that is, a **foreign interest rate shock** (see Figure 8). Because this will make foreign short-term investments more attractive and cause portfolio adjustments, we would expect an increased outflow (or decreased inflow) of short-term capital. With the new, higher interest rate abroad and the same exchange rate, a higher domestic interest rate is now required to balance the balance of payments at all income levels. Consequently, there is an upward shift in the *BP* curve from BP_0, i_{f0} to BP_0, i_{f1}. With the new *BP* curve, the previous equilibrium level of interest (i_0) is too low for attaining domestic balance-of-payments equilibrium, and an incipient deficit appears. The domestic currency depreciates (shifting BP_0, i_{f1} to BP_1, i_{f1}), and this depreciation stimulates exports and decreases imports. This current account effect (driven by the capital/financial account developments) leads to a rightward shift in the *IS* curve to *IS'*. Eventually, a new equilibrium is reached on the *LM* curve with the new *BP* and *IS* curves. Both the interest rate (i_1) and the income level (Y_1) have increased. Thus, the initial rise in the foreign interest rate has led to an increase in the domestic interest rate as well as to a depreciation of the home currency.

An additional consideration relates to portfolio adjustments. Because the foreign interest rate has risen, home-country asset holders will also reduce their demand for domestic *money* as they rearrange their portfolios to take advantage of the higher foreign interest rate. With a decrease in home money demand, the *LM* curve of Figure 8 will shift to the right. The initial incipient BOP deficit will be even larger than discussed in the previous

FIGURE 8   Foreign Interest Rate Shocks and Macroeconomic Adjustment
in a Flexible-Rate Regime

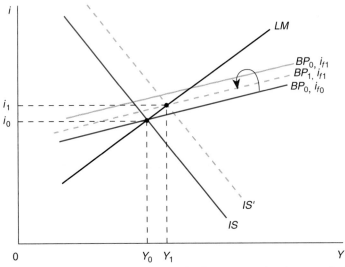

From the starting point of Y_0 and i_0, the increase in the foreign interest rate makes short-term foreign investments more attractive. It therefore takes a higher domestic rate of interest to maintain external balance for all levels of income, and the *BP* curve shifts up to BP_0, i_{f1}. As domestic investors increase their short-term financial investments abroad, there is an incipient deficit and the home currency depreciates (the *BP* curve moves downward). Depreciation stimulates exports and discourages imports, causing the *IS* curve to shift to the right. A new equilibrium results at a higher level of income (Y_1) and interest rate (i_1) at the intersection of *LM*, *IS'*, and BP_1, i_{f1}. In addition, if the higher foreign interest rate reduces the home demand for money, *LM* will shift farther to the right and income will rise even further.

paragraph, and the depreciation of the home currency will be even greater. The simultaneous intersection of the final *BP, LM,* and *IS* curves will, as before, be at a higher income level than Y_1. While there is no a priori way to discern whether the domestic adjustment to foreign interest rate shocks occurs relatively more via the exchange rate rather than via the domestic interest rate, some empirical evidence suggests that the exchange rate in practice carries the bulk of the adjustment between the United States and its major trading partners, with the possible exception of Canada (see page 506 in Chapter 20).

As a last example of a shock, consider the case of a **shock to the expected exchange rate.** Suppose that because of some exogenous event (such as the election of a foreign government that is expected to stabilize its country economically), there is now an expected greater appreciation of the foreign currency (or, alternatively, an expected greater depreciation of the home currency). Recall the uncovered interest parity (UIP) expression from earlier chapters (and ignore any risk premium):

$$i_d = i_f + xa$$

where i_d = the domestic interest rate, i_f = the foreign interest rate, and xa = the expected percentage appreciation of the foreign currency. From an initial UIP equilibrium, the rise in xa will now make the term ($i_f + xa$) greater than i_d and there will thus be a short-term capital outflow from the home country to the foreign country. This change in the expected exchange rate has the same effects in the *IS/LM/BP* diagram as did the foreign interest rate shock considered earlier, and Figure 8 can also be used to interpret this case. In terms of the figure, the rise in xa shifts the BP curve upward (to the left) because a higher domestic interest rate is now needed for home-country BOP equilibrium at each income level. There is an incipient deficit at the old equilibrium income level Y_0, and depreciation of the domestic currency thus takes place, moving the IS curve to the right and also causing the BP curve to move back to the right. The end result (as at Y_1 and i_1) is a higher income level and, as the UIP expression also suggests, a higher domestic interest rate.

In overview of external shocks, it is important to note that the greater the economic interdependence among countries, the greater the general likelihood that foreign shocks (other things equal) will have an effect on domestic interest rates and/or the exchange rate. Domestic policymakers are forced to make decisions that take into account both domestic variables and foreign economic variables, so policymaking becomes more difficult.

For example, in the foreign interest rate shock case, a rise in the foreign rate led to an increase in the domestic interest rate. However, the domestic economy may be in such a state that domestic authorities do not wish to have a higher domestic interest rate. To offset the rise in the domestic rate, suppose the monetary authorities increase the money supply (to sterilize the interest rate effects). From i_1, Y_1 in Figure 8, this shifts LM to the right (not shown) and generates an incipient deficit. The BP curve shifts to the right, as will the IS curve due to the currency depreciation. The income level rises above Y_1 and the interest

IN THE REAL WORLD:

POLICY FRICTIONS IN AN INTERDEPENDENT WORLD

The effect of international economic interdependence on policy decisions is clearly in evidence as the United States, Europe, and Japan in recent years have been faced with widely different economic problems and circumstances. After the European Union adopted a new currency, the euro (discussed in Chapter 29), its value declined by 25 percent in the first 16 months after its launch in January 1999. With relatively high unemployment and low inflation in Europe, the European Central Bank and national central banks hesitated to raise interest rates to halt the downward spiral of the euro. At the same time, the United States faced inflationary pressures that the Federal Reserve attempted to keep under wraps by a succession of interest rate increases, coupled with increasing current account deficits. The higher U.S. interest rates put further pressure on the euro, as short-term financial capital was attracted to the United States. Meanwhile, Japan found itself in economic recession, along with a growing current account surplus. Japan thus had little incentive to raise domestic interest rates. As the U.S. interest rates increased, interest rate differentials with Japan and Europe became larger, leading to continued financial investment flows to the United States and further pressure on the euro, the yen, and interest rates outside the United States. The strong dollar also contributed to continued and expanding U.S. current account deficits. However, the situation

began to change in 2001 as the United States began to slide into recession. This led to a succession of interest rate reductions by the Federal Reserve, which, by 2003, resulted in the lowest interest rates in many years. Not surprisingly, the dollar began to depreciate in late 2002 and 2003, especially against the euro. From 2003 onward, the euro continued to strengthen against the U.S. dollar and reached a value over $1.37 in July 2007. This rise occurred as European growth rates increased and as doubts arose concerning the huge U.S. federal government and current account deficits. The large and growing U.S. trade deficit with China, thought by many to be the result of the deliberately undervalued Renminbi yuan, generated congressional concern and led to political tensions between the two countries. At the time of this writing, the tensions surrounding the exchange rate controversy were creating uncertainties about the future direction of U.S. trade policy.*

*For discussion of the need for coordination of policy among the United States, Europe, and Japan in the context of a plea for greater exchange rate stability, see George Melloan, "U.S. Inflation Will Complicate the Euro-Quandary," *The Wall Street Journal*, May 2, 2000, p. A27; "Will the Fallen Dollar Set the Stage for a Global Economic Boom a Year or Two from Now?" *The International Economy*, Summer 2003, pp. 30–44. ●

rate falls below i_1, perhaps all the way to i_0. The country has thus negated to at least some extent the original effects of the foreign interest rate increase, but it has also generated depreciation of the home currency. The foreign country in turn has now experienced an appreciation of its currency to a greater extent than it originally expected. Consequently, its income level may fall, and it may consider taking appropriate policy actions to counter these effects. Note, of course, that changes in the exchange rate are important actors in this scenario.

To reduce the degree of instability in exchange rates and domestic variables caused by this kind of sequence of policy reactions, a case can be made that there should be greater **international macroeconomic policy coordination** in a regime of flexible exchange rates. Such coordination of macro policy is currently being fostered. The most obvious examples of such joint consultations in practice consist of the annual economic summits held each summer by leaders of the Group of Seven or **G-7 countries** (Canada, France, Germany, Italy, Japan, the United Kingdom, and the United States).

CONCEPT CHECK

1. Explain the effect that a decrease in foreign prices has on the open economy under a flexible exchange rate system.

2. Using the *IS/LM/BP* framework, explain how an increase in the foreign interest rate influences the home-country interest rate in the open economy under flexible exchange rates.

IN THE REAL WORLD:

MACROECONOMIC POLICY COORDINATION, THE IMF, AND THE G-7

According to a 1991 IMF task force report, "Improving international coordination of national economic policies should be a major objective of industrial countries."[a] The director of the task force, Robert Solomon, pointed out that, because the world had become increasingly integrated both with respect to trade and capital mobility, policymakers must take into account that their policy actions have spillover effects in other countries:

The failure to coordinate policies can be "dramatic," Solomon argued. He suggested that economic policy coordination among the major industrial countries could have averted at least some of the very sharp run up in inflation that followed the adoption of expansionary fiscal and monetary policies in 1972–73. Similarly, he observed, the 1981–82 downturn might have been less severe.

Policy coordination among industrial countries, Solomon contended, should aim to harmonize targets. Industrial countries should also seek to maintain consistency in the goals and targets that they pursue and in the instruments that they utilize. The Group of 7 generally aims for high levels of employment and growth and for relative price stability. Its instruments are primarily monetary and fiscal policy.[b]

Because of the increased interdependency, the task force urged that governments become more flexible in their fiscal policy and that fiscal policy be focused more on medium term targets instead of on short-term fine-tuning exercises.

In keeping with the greater focus on international coordination, the G-7 countries issued the following typical statement after their January meeting in New York in 1991:

The finance ministers and central bank governors of Canada, France, Germany, Italy, Japan, the United Kingdom, and the United States met on January 20 and 21, 1991, in New York City for an exchange of views on current international economic and financial issues. The Managing Director of the IMF [Michel Camdessus] participated in the multilateral surveillance discussions.

The ministers and governors reviewed their economic policies and prospects and reaffirmed their support for economic policy coordination at this critical time. . . .

Implementation of sound fiscal policies, combined with stability-oriented monetary policies, should create conditions favorable to lower global interest rates and a stronger world economy. They also stressed the importance of a timely and successful conclusion of the Uruguay Round.

IN THE REAL WORLD: *(continued)*

. . . They agreed to strengthen cooperation and to monitor developments in exchange markets.

The ministers and governors are prepared to respond as appropriate to maintain stability in international financial markets.[c]

This emphasis on policy coordination has become a permanent feature of the world policymaking environment. For example, in July 1992, the G-7 leaders pledged to continue to promote monetary and fiscal policies that would support economic recovery without reigniting inflation and that would permit lower interest rates by reducing members' budget deficits and government spending.[d] In July 1993, the G-7 also demonstrated interest in specific country policies by encouraging Japan to implement macroeconomic policies that would reduce Japan's trade surplus and by praising President Bill Clinton for his efforts toward reducing the U.S. federal government budget deficit. Increasingly, other economic actions have also been agreed to by the G-7, such as the 1993 commitment of $3 billion of financial aid to Russia for assistance in the privatization of government enterprises.[e] Further, in June 1995, the G-7 countries introduced measures to reduce the likelihood of future crises similar to that of Mexico in late 1994 and early 1995,[f] when huge amounts of foreign capital exited the country and the value of the peso dropped precipitously in currency markets. In May 1998, the leaders (whose countries are now increasingly known as the G-8

since Russia began participating at that time) took a more worldwide view and issued a general statement that multilateral cooperation was needed to ensure that all countries, especially low-income countries, benefited from growing globalization.[g]

In more recent years the G-8 has, for example, agreed on policy steps regarding forgiveness of part of the external debt of developing countries. A recent useful overview of the G-7's evolution was provided by Japan's former vice finance minister, Tomomitsu Oba.[h] He noted that the character of the group has changed significantly as Russia and recently China have been invited to the meetings. Further, Brazil, India, South Africa, and Mexico also attended the February 2007 meeting.

[a]"Task Force Backs Macroeconomic Policy Coordination," *IMF Survey,* February 4, 1991, p. 33.

[b]Ibid., p. 41.

[c]Ibid.

[d]"G-7 Leaders Urge Strong IMF-Supported Policies in States of Former U.S.S.R.," *IMF Survey,* July 20, 1992, p. 226.

[e]David Wessel and Jeffrey Birnbaum, "U.S. Lines Up Aid for Russia at G-7 Meeting," *The Wall Street Journal,* July 9, 1993, pp. A3–A4.

[f]See "G-7 Offers Proposals to Strengthen Bretton Woods Institutions," *IMF Survey,* July 3, 1995, pp. 201–05.

[g]"Group of Eight Leaders Focus on Asian Crisis, Monetary Cooperation, Debt Relief Issues," *IMF Survey,* May 25, 1998, pp. 157–58.

[h]Tomomitsu Oba, "G7 Reflections," *The International Economy,* Spring 2007, p. 62.

SUMMARY

This chapter examined the automatic adjustment process under flexible exchange rates and the effects of discretionary economic policy under different capital mobility assumptions. It was found that monetary policy is effective in influencing income under flexible exchange rates, whereas it was ineffective under fixed rates. Further, the degree of effectiveness under flexible rates increases with the degree of capital mobility. Fiscal policy, on the other hand, was found to be much less effective under flexible rates than under fixed rates as capital becomes very mobile internationally, since expenditure-switching effects dampen the initial effects. The effects of fiscal policy

on national income are the strongest when capital is immobile. The flexible-rate system does, however, give the country more policy options than a fixed-rate system because the external sector is always in balance. If a country wishes to attain several domestic targets, the coordinated use of monetary and fiscal policies can be helpful. The chapter concluded with a discussion of automatic adjustment to exogenous shocks under a flexible-rate system. The realization that a number of these shocks are often taking place simultaneously makes one keenly aware of the difficulties surrounding effective policymaking in a system of flexible rates.

KEY TERMS

domestic price shock
foreign interest rate shock
foreign price shock
G-7 countries

incipient BOP deficit
incipient BOP surplus
international macroeconomic
    policy coordination

monetary policy–fiscal policy
    coordination
shock to the expected exchange rate

QUESTIONS AND PROBLEMS

1. What will happen under flexible rates if the intersection of the *IS* and *LM* curves is below (or to the right) of the *BP* curve? Why?

2. What exogenous real and financial factors influence the position of the *BP* curve?

3. Under what capital mobility conditions is fiscal policy totally ineffective in influencing income? Explain why this result occurs.

4. One strong argument for a flexible exchange rate system is that it frees up monetary policy for use in pursuing domestic targets. Explain why this is so.

5. Why does monetary policy get a boost from the external sector under a flexible-rate system?

6. Suppose that policymakers decide to expand the economy by increasing the money supply. Based on the trade effects, who do you expect to favor such a policy? Who is likely to be against this policy? Why?

7. If short-term capital is neither perfectly immobile nor perfectly mobile internationally, why is the predicted impact of expansionary fiscal policy on the exchange rate ambiguous?

8. Explain, using the *IS/LM/BP* model, how a rise in the expected appreciation of the foreign currency can lead to an increase in domestic interest rates.

9. Why might it be argued that recent changes in international prices of food and energy have had a smaller impact on the U.S. economy than would have been the case under the pre-1973 pegged-rate system?

10. "A sudden increase in interest rates in the European Union would likely lead to both depreciation of the U.S. dollar and upward pressure on U.S. interest rates." Agree? Disagree? Why?

27

PRICES AND OUTPUT IN THE OPEN ECONOMY

Aggregate Supply and Demand

LEARNING OBJECTIVES

■ To understand the fundamental links between international transactions and aggregate demand and aggregate supply.

■ To grasp how economic shocks and policies affect prices and output.

■ To comprehend the differences between macroeconomic adjustment under fixed exchange rates and under flexible exchange rates.

■ To appreciate the difference between short-run and long-run effects of macro policies on output and prices.

INTRODUCTION

Crisis in Argentina

The Argentine economy suffered a severe economic crisis during 2001 and 2002. Research by Murphy, Artana, and Navajas[1] indicates that poverty stretched to one in every three homesteads in the suburbs of Buenos Aires. In addition, the combination of a traumatic departure from convertibility of the peso into dollars, a financial crisis, and public debt default undermined local and foreign investor confidence. Murphy, Artana, and Navajas believe that the crisis owed its existence to four main causes:

1. Inappropriate fiscal policy.

2. Wage and price rigidities inconsistent with a fixed exchange rate.

3. A considerable, adverse external shock.

4. Political turmoil.

This chapter focuses on the framework necessary to examine the effect of policy actions and external shocks (like those in Argentina) on prices and output in both fixed and flexible exchange rate systems. The analysis of the open economy up to this point has proceeded under the assumption that expansion and contraction of the macroeconomy would take place without affecting the level of prices. Although the comparative statics of a change in prices were examined in terms of the macroeconomic adjustment that would accompany such an exogenous shock in the previous chapter, no attempt was made to incorporate price changes endogenously into the analysis. Because changes in prices are a very important aspect of economic activity in the open economy, it is imperative to consider the interaction between the foreign sector and the domestic price level in the open macroeconomy. We will pursue this line of analysis using an aggregate demand and supply framework that incorporates the effects of trade and financial flows. The presentation begins by reviewing the concepts of aggregate demand and supply in the closed economy, taking into account differences between short-run and long-run effects. We then open the economy and examine the effects of international transactions on the aggregate demand and supply curves under fixed exchange rates and flexible exchange rates. The chapter concludes with a discussion of monetary and fiscal policy in the open-economy demand and supply framework and of the responsiveness of the economy to various shocks. Consideration of the price level complicates policy problems and, consequently, the design of effective macroeconomic policy. In the long run, measures that increase aggregate supply are paramount for increasing national income.

AGGREGATE DEMAND AND SUPPLY IN THE CLOSED ECONOMY

Aggregate Demand in the Closed Economy

We begin by reviewing the link between aggregate demand and prices in the closed macroeconomy. In Chapter 25 income and interest rate equilibrium was described using the *IS* and *LM* curves to portray equilibrium in the real sector and the money market, assuming that prices were constant. From the demand perspective, macroeconomic equilibrium takes place at the level of income and the interest rate determined by the intersection of the *IS* and *LM* curves. What happens to equilibrium in this model when prices change? Because equilibrium in the goods sector is measured in real terms, price changes

---

[1]This discussion is drawn from Ricardo Lopez Murphy, Daniel Artana, and Fernando Navajas, "The Argentine Economic Crisis," *Cato Journal* 23, no. 1 (Spring/Summer 2003), pp. 23–28.

FIGURE 1   Derivation of the Aggregate Demand Curve in the Closed Economy

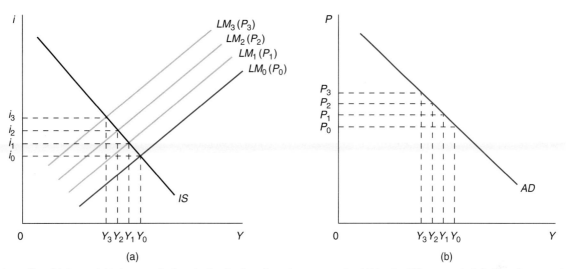

Starting at Y_0 and i_0 in panel (a), increases in the price level reduce the real money supply, shifting the LM curve to the left. Therefore, a particular LM curve is associated with each higher price level (e.g., LM_1 for P_1, LM_2 for P_2). With each new, higher price level, P_i, there is a new, lower equilibrium level of income Y_i determined by the intersection of the LM_i and the IS curve (e.g., for P_0, Y_0; for P_2, Y_2; etc.). These pairs of price levels and equilibrium income levels are now plotted on a different graph in panel (b), with price levels measured on the vertical axis and real income levels represented on the horizontal axis. Because successively lower equilibrium levels of income are associated with successively higher price levels, a normal downward-sloping aggregate demand curve results.

do not directly affect the IS curve. Changes in price do, however, affect the size of the real money supply, M_s/P. As the price level rises, the real money supply declines; a decline in the real money supply will have the effect of shifting the LM curve to the left. Such a shift is shown in Figure 1(a) by four LM curves (LM_0, LM_1, LM_2, LM_3) associated with four different price levels, where $P_0 < P_1 < P_2 < P_3$. Associated with each price level is an equilibrium level of income, Y_0, Y_1, Y_2, and Y_3. The higher the price level, the lower the equilibrium level of income.

The level of prices and the corresponding equilibrium level of income can be used to generate an aggregate demand curve in panel (b). Note that the vertical axis measures the price level and not the interest rate, while the level of real income is still measured on the horizontal axis. When the price level–equilibrium income coordinates are plotted, they produce a normal downward-sloping **aggregate demand curve** (*AD*), which shows the level of real output demanded at each price level. The slope of the *AD* curve is determined jointly by the slopes of the *IS* and the *LM* curves. The more elastic these curves are, the more elastic the *AD* curve is. Any change in the slope of either the *IS* or the *LM* curve will lead to a similar change in slope of the *AD* curve.

Similarly, the position of the *AD* curve is determined by the positions of the *IS* and *LM* curves. If the *IS* curve shifts to the right, it will lead to higher equilibrium levels of income for each respective price level. Consequently, a rightward (leftward) shift in the *IS* curve will lead to a rightward (leftward) shift in the *AD* curve. For example, an increase in government spending or domestic investment will lead to a rightward shift in the *IS* curve and hence in the *AD* curve. An increase in the tax *rate* would make the *IS* curve steeper and hence the *AD* curve steeper. Because it is changes in the nominal money supply (for given price levels) that shift the *LM* curve, an increase in the money

TABLE 1   Factors Affecting Aggregate Demand

Condition	Outcome	Possible Cause
Slope of Aggregate Demand:		
Flatter *IS* or *LM*	More elastic *AD*	Decrease in tax rate, increase in elasticity of demand for money
Steeper *IS* or *LM*	Less elastic *AD*	Decrease in responsiveness of investment to the interest rate
Position of Aggregate Demand:		
IS shifts right	Rightward shift in *AD*	Increase in government spending
IS shifts left	Leftward shift in *AD*	Decrease in autonomous investment
LM shifts right	Rightward shift in *AD*	Expansionary monetary policy
LM shifts left	Leftward shift in *AD*	Contractionary monetary policy

supply shifts the *LM* curve to the right and, *ceteris paribus,* leads to higher equilibrium income and hence a rightward shift in the *AD* curve. Contractionary monetary policy would, on the other hand, lead to a leftward shift in the *AD* curve. These results are summarized in Table 1. Finally, any change in the transactions demand for money or in the asset demand for money would lead to a change in slope and/or position of the *LM* curve and therefore a change in slope and/or position of the *AD* curve, the details of which are not critical for this chapter.

Aggregate Supply in the Closed Economy

Aggregate domestic supply is determined by the level of technology, the relative quantity of available resources, the level of employment of those resources, and the efficiency with which they are used. In the short run, factors such as the level of capital, natural resources, and technology are assumed to be fixed. This leaves labor as the principal variable input that firms hire to maximize expected profits. In this situation, the representative firm will maximize profits where marginal cost equals marginal revenue. In the case of labor, this means hiring labor up to the point where the marginal factor cost (which equals the nominal wage rate with competitive labor markets) is equal (with competitive product markets) to the marginal product of labor times the price of the output (marginal revenue product). The nominal value of the additional worker is thus determined by the productivity of labor and the price level.

The relationship between labor and output can be represented by an **aggregate production function** such as that in panel (a) of Figure 2. Real output is shown to vary positively with labor employed, given the level of technology and the fixed availability of other inputs such as level of capital stock. The shape of the curve indicates that the marginal productivity of labor declines with additional employment of the labor input, because each successive unit of labor contributes less to output than the unit preceding it. The slope of the production function is the marginal physical productivity of labor (MPP_N), which is plotted in panel (b). The decreasing productivity of labor causes the MPP_N schedule to have a downward slope. Multiplying MPP_N by different levels of prices produces different marginal revenue product curves of labor (MRP_{N0}, MRP_{N1}, MRP_{N2}). Inasmuch as these MRP_N curves show the value of labor to producers at different levels of employment and prices, they can each be viewed as an **aggregate demand curve for labor.**

Given a particular wage rate, one can immediately see the level of employment that will lead to a maximization of profits, *ceteris paribus.* For example, if the wage rate is W_0 and the price level is P_0, the desired level of employment is N_0. It is also apparent that if the

FIGURE 2   Aggregate Production and the Demand for Labor

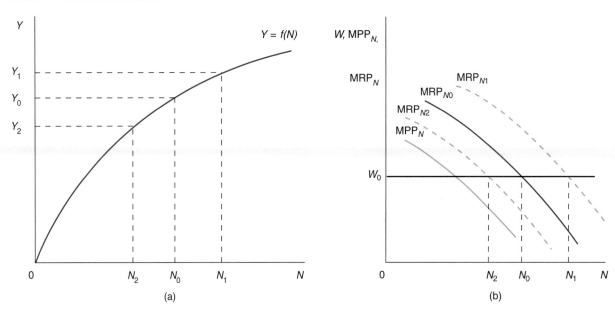

The aggregate production function is represented in panel (a). Given the level of technology and a fixed amount of other inputs, aggregate output is determined by the level of employment of labor, N. The decreasing slope of the production function indicates that the marginal product of each successive worker is getting smaller. The marginal physical product of labor (MPP_N) is then plotted against level of employment N in panel (b). If the MPP_N is multiplied by the price level P, the resulting marginal revenue product (MRP_N) indicates the value of using that particular unit of labor in production and is, therefore, the derived demand curve for labor. To maximize profits, producers should employ labor up to N_0, where the wage rate W_0 is equal to the MRP_{N0} when prices are P_0, N_1 when prices are P_1, etc. Note that an increase in the price level to P_1 (decrease to P_2) leads to a higher (lower) MRP of labor and hence to greater (less) employment and output.

price level changes, the MRP_N curve will change. An increase in prices will cause the MRP_N to shift to the right, and a decrease in prices will cause it to shift to the left. Thus, for a fixed wage rate, W_0, an increase in the price level leads to a rightward shift in the MRP_N curve and hence to a higher level of employment and output. A reduction in the price level leads to a leftward shift in the MRP_N curve and to a reduction in the optimal level of employment and output. If we now plot these combinations of different price levels and equilibrium output at the wage W_0, we obtain the upward-sloping **short-run aggregate supply curve** (see Figure 3). It needs to be noted that the marginal revenue product can also be altered by changes in the factors normally held constant, for example, changes in technology, changes in the level of capital stock, or changes in managerial efficiency. These changes are commonly viewed as long-run changes, as opposed to the short-run change brought about by the change in price level.

The aggregate supply curve in Figure 3 was derived assuming that firms could hire all the labor they wished, up to full employment, at the fixed wage W_0. However, microeconomic theory and practical experience indicate that while that assumption may hold in labor surplus economies, in industrialized economies with relatively high levels of employment, an increase in the quantity of labor supplied can be obtained in the short run only by increasing the wage rate. This line of thinking sees the labor supply curve as an upward-sloping curve, and not as a horizontal line as at W_0 in Figure 2(b). Its slope and position are influenced by such factors as the value of leisure, institutional factors, the characteristics of the labor force, and expectations regarding prices.

FIGURE 3   The Aggregate Supply Curve with a Fixed Wage

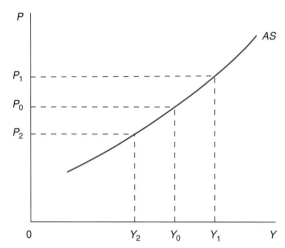

In panel (b) of Figure 2, higher price levels lead to increased demand for labor as producers hire labor so as to maximize profits for a given wage rate W_0. Higher levels of employment, such as N_1, lead to a higher level of output Y_1 [in Figure 2(a)]. If we now plot the level of prices against the resulting level of income at the level of employment that maximizes profits (for example, Y_1, P_1; Y_0, P_0), an upward-sloping aggregate supply curve results.

Labor market equilibrium with an upward-sloping aggregate supply curve of labor is shown in Figure 4(a), with an initial equilibrium at W_0 and N_0. If we again increase the price level, output increases, but not as greatly as it did when the labor supply curve was horizontal. Thus, we again get an upward-sloping aggregate supply curve of output [panel (b)], but it is now steeper than it was with the horizontal labor supply curve. In general, the greater the increase in wages necessary to attract the additional labor, the steeper the short-run aggregate supply curve of labor in Figure 4(a) will be.

It is generally accepted in the macroeconomics and labor economics literature that the quantity of labor supplied depends ultimately on the real wage received, and not on the money wage. Because the aggregate supply curve of labor is drawn under a given level of price expectations, changes in the price level that affect price expectations will cause the labor supply curve to shift—once workers *realize* that prices have changed. The realization that prices are higher than expected will lead labor to demand a higher nominal wage so that the same amount of labor is being provided at the same *real* wage. In other words, nominal wage increases eventually offset the increase in prices as workers adjust their wages to the new level of expected prices.

The worker adjustment to higher prices is shown in Figure 5. An increase in price leads to a new MRP'_N and a higher level of employment and income. However, once workers realize that prices are higher than expected, they increase their wage demands, shifting the short-run supply curve of labor to the left (S'_N) until it intersects MRP'_N at the original equilibrium level of employment. Thus, if labor is given sufficient time to respond, an increase in the price level simply leads to an offsetting increase in nominal wages and no real effect on employment and output. The longer labor takes to adjust its wage demands (the stickier wage movements are), the greater the short-run effect of price changes on output and employment. However, if wage demands change as quickly as prices (which takes place under the rational expectations assumption, where price changes are fully anticipated), then a price increase produces no change in real output or employment. The employment of labor is constant, and the aggregate

FIGURE 4   Variable Wages and the Aggregate Supply Curve

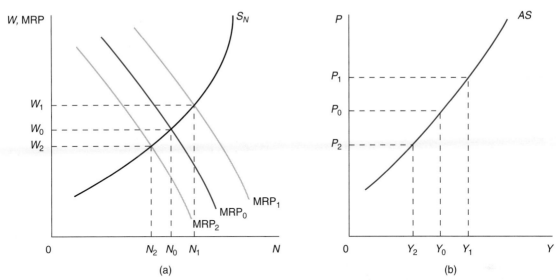

(a)   (b)

In panel (a), the labor market is characterized by a more typical upward-sloping supply curve of labor, instead of the infinitely elastic supply curve used in Figure 2(b). As a result, the increases in the MRP_N brought about by the increases in the price level lead to smaller increases in output compared with the previous case. Hence, the aggregate supply curve presented in panel (b) above will be steeper than the AS curve in Figure 3. The greater the wage increase required to increase the quantity supplied of labor, the steeper the AS curve.

FIGURE 5   Labor Market Adjustment to Higher Prices

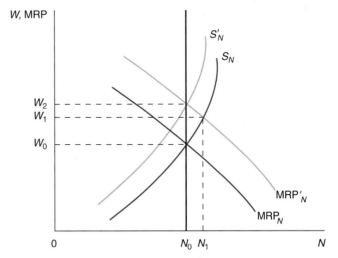

An initial increase in prices increases the MRP of labor to MRP'_N, stimulating a short-run increase in employment (from N_0 to N_1), income, and wages (from W_0 to W_1). However, because the labor supply is determined by the real wage and not the money wage, once workers realize that prices have risen, they alter their wage demands (shift the labor supply curve vertically upward) until they again are offering the same amount of labor at the same real wage as previously, that is, N_0 at W_2 given the new price level. After sufficient time has passed for labor to adjust to the new price level, the labor market is again in equilibrium at the initial level of employment N_0.

FIGURE 6   Equilibrium in the Closed Economy

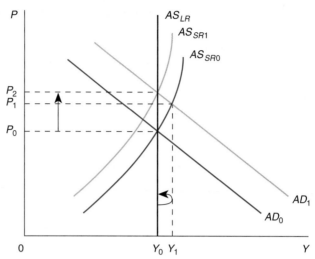

The initial equilibrium occurs at the point where AD_0, AS_{LR}, and AS_{SR0} intersect at Y_0,P_0. Expansionary forces in the economy shift the AD curve rightward to AD_1, increasing prices to P_1 and income to Y_1 (assuming that wage increases lag behind price increases). When workers realize that the price level has risen, altering their price expectations, wages begin to rise as the short-run aggregate supply curve shifts up. This will continue until the actual price level again equals the expected price level, which now occurs at P_2, Y_0 (the intersection between AS_{LR}, AS_{SR1}, and AD_1). The only way to increase income in the long run is to shift AS_{LR} to the right through accumulation of capital, changes in technology, and so on.

supply curve is vertical both in the short run and in the long run at the initial equilibrium level—sometimes referred to as the **natural level of employment** (i.e., the level of employment at which the actual price level equals the expected price level by workers). Note that the natural level of employment need not correspond with some society-defined level of full employment (e.g., 95 percent employment or 5 percent unemployment). The equilibrium level of income associated with the natural level of employment is designated the **natural level of income.**

There is considerable debate among macroeconomic theorists about whether wages are in fact sticky and about the length of the possible adjustment lag in the labor markets. Keynesians postulate a longer adjustment period due to various rigidities and market imperfections than do the Monetarists, and therefore a greater role for discretionary policy. The New Classical writers, a school of writers that emerged in the 1970s, generally adopt a rational expectations assumption, which leads to nominal wages rising as fast as prices. In this framework, workers immediately perceive the impact on real wages of any event that was anticipated and immediately act to maintain the same real wage. Consequently, a vertical short-run–long-run aggregate supply curve results. Hence, while most concur that the **long-run aggregate supply curve** of output is vertical at the natural level of income, there is a difference of opinion about the existence of a nonvertical short-run aggregate supply curve and the extent to which there is a short-run response of output to prices. Finally, increases in the natural level of employment and output are stimulated by changes in technology, increased quantities of capital, more efficient management, and growth in the supply and quality of the labor force.

Equilibrium in the Closed Economy

Given the aggregate demand and the short-run and long-run aggregate supply curves, we can now examine equilibrium in the closed economy. **Aggregate supply–aggregate demand equilibrium** occurs where all three curves (AS_{LR}, AS_{SR0}, AD_0) intersect, for example, P_0 and Y_0 in Figure 6. Suppose that from this position there is an increase in aggregate demand due

IN THE REAL WORLD:

U.S. ACTUAL AND NATURAL INCOME AND UNEMPLOYMENT

Table 2 contains 1965–2004 figures for U.S. actual real GDP, estimates of the natural levels of GDP, and the actual and natural unemployment rates. The actual levels of income were above the natural levels in the late 1960s. However, the actual levels tended to be below the natural levels from 1970 until the late 1980s and then rose above the natural levels in 1987–1990 and from 1997–2001. The actual levels then fell below the natural levels from 2002–2004. An examination of actual and natural unemployment rates demonstrates more volatility. Actual unemployment rates are below the natural rates from 1965–1974. Actual rates exceed natural rates from

1975 to 1977 and from 1980 to 1986, with a brief period in 1978–1979 where the actual dropped below the natural rate. When the actual GDP rose above the natural rate from 1987 to 1990, it pulled the actual unemployment rate below the natural rate. When actual GDP fell below natural GDP from 1991 to 1995, the actual unemployment rate rose above the natural rate. The strength of the expansion in the late 1990s pulled actual unemployment rates back below the natural rate from 1997 to 2001. Actual unemployment then rose above the natural level from 2002–2004, following the recession that began in 2001.

TABLE 2   Actual and Natural Income and Unemployment in the United States, 1965–2004

Year	Real GDP* Actual	Real GDP* Natural	Unemployment Rates Actual	Unemployment Rates Natural	Year	Real GDP* Actual	Real GDP* Natural	Unemployment Rates Actual	Unemployment Rates Natural
1965	3,190.3	3,105.6	4.5	6.0	1985	6,037.4	6,092.4	7.2	6.4
1966	3,400.8	3,236.8	3.8	6.2	1986	6,260.5	6,286.7	7.0	6.4
1967	3,484.2	3,368.2	3.9	6.3	1987	6,476.4	6,469.7	6.2	6.4
1968	3,650.8	3,504.3	3.6	6.4	1988	6,745.3	6,651.8	5.5	6.3
1969	3,763.7	3,645.0	3.5	6.3	1989	6,979.2	6,835.5	5.3	6.3
1970	3,772.4	3,787.9	5.0	6.3	1990	7,104.4	7,027.1	5.6	6.2
1971	3,898.1	3,932.5	6.0	6.2	1991	7,079.1	7,229.5	6.9	6.1
1972	4,110.2	4,076.8	5.6	6.2	1992	7,317.0	7,451.7	7.5	5.9
1973	4,341.9	4,203.1	4.9	6.2	1993	7,531.3	7,678.9	6.9	5.7
1974	4,315.8	4,349.2	5.6	6.2	1994	7,836.8	7,892.5	6.1	5.6
1975	4,304.2	4,504.1	8.5	6.1	1995	8,044.6	8,113.6	5.6	5.4
1976	4,551.1	4,666.8	7.7	6.2	1996	8,318.5	8,383.9	5.4	5.4
1977	4,751.6	4,810.6	7.1	6.2	1997	8,698.1	8,683.7	5.0	5.3
1978	5,012.5	4,963.3	6.1	6.3	1998	9,076.2	8,970.6	4.5	5.2
1979	5,174.6	5,092.2	5.8	6.3	1999	9,437.3	9,260.3	4.2	5.1
1980	5,161.6	5,229.8	7.2	6.3	2000	9,863.3	9,607.7	4.0	5.0
1981	5,288.2	5,391.6	7.6	6.2	2001	9,933.9	9,931.9	4.7	5.0
1982	5,184.5	5,561.7	9.7	6.3	2002	10,074.8	10,270.3	5.8	5.0
1983	5,414.0	5,737.3	9.6	6.3	2003	10,381.3	10,690.7	6.0	5.0
1984	5,817.9	5,923.1	7.5	6.3	2004	10,841.9	11,064.8	5.5	5.0

*Billions of 2000 chained dollars.

Source: Robert J. Gordon, *Macroeconomics,* 10th ed. (Boston, MA: Pearson Addison Wesley, 2006), pp. A2, A3.

to an increase in government spending or an increase in the money supply. This will cause the aggregate demand curve to shift to the right. As this takes place, there will be an increase in the level of prices and a short-run increase in income as the economy moves to the new short-run equilibrium P_1, Y_1. This, of course, assumes that labor does not demand an instant adjustment in the nominal wage. Once labor alters its expectation about the level of prices, wages begin to rise as the short-run supply curve shifts vertically upward. This will continue until the new aggregate demand curve (AD_1), the long-run supply curve (AS_{LR}), and the new short-run supply curve (AS_{SR1}) all intersect at a common point (P_2, Y_0). At that price level, actual prices are equal to the expected prices on which the short-run supply curve is based. Although this new aggregate supply–aggregate demand equilibrium will be at the same natural level of output Y_0 (and employment), the increase in demand will have generated a higher level of prices P_2 and will have had only a temporary effect on aggregate output. The adjustment of output from Y_0 to Y_1 and back to Y_0 is indicated by an arrow in Figure 6. The only way that a permanent change in the natural rate of output and employment can occur is if there is a change in basic underlying variables such as technology or the level of capital stock. For expansionary economic policy to have any permanent effect on income and output rather than only to increase prices, it must change one or more of these underlying variables.

CONCEPT CHECK

1. Why does an increase in the price level lead to a lower equilibrium income in the *IS-LM* framework? What determines the slope of the resulting aggregate demand curve?

2. Why does an increase in the price level lead to both an increase in the demand for labor and a decrease (vertically upward shift) in the supply curve of labor? Do these shifts take place simultaneously?

3. What is meant by the natural level of income and employment?

AGGREGATE DEMAND AND SUPPLY IN THE OPEN ECONOMY

Opening the economy clearly affects the aggregate demand curve. Although there are possible long-run supply effects through international investment flows, technological innovations, and improved management techniques, from a policy standpoint the opening of the economy has considerably greater implications for short-term and medium-term aggregate demand. Consequently, we will focus on the nature of aggregate demand in the open economy under fixed and flexible exchange rates.[2] In this exercise, it will be assumed that capital is relatively mobile internationally (but not perfectly mobile) for the country in question; that is, the *BP* curve is upward sloping and flatter than the *LM* curve.

Aggregate Demand in the Open Economy under Fixed Rates

When the economy is opened, the discussion of aggregate demand must consider not only domestic equilibrium in the goods market (the *IS* curve) and the money market (the *LM* curve) but also equilibrium in the foreign sector (the *BP* curve). Such an initial equilibrium (i_0, Y_0) is shown in Figure 7(a). To obtain the domestic aggregate demand curve under fixed exchange rates [panel (b)], suppose prices increase. The increase reduces the real money supply and causes the *LM* curve to shift to the left. In addition, however, the increase in the domestic price level alters relative prices with trading partners as exports become more expensive and imports become relatively cheaper. The increase in the domestic price level

---

[2]When a country imports intermediate inputs, the aggregate supply curve in the open economy also depends on the exchange rate. A depreciation of the home currency would shift aggregate supply curves leftward due to the higher domestic prices of imported intermediate inputs, and an appreciation would shift them to the right for the opposite reason.

FIGURE 7   Aggregate Demand in the Open Economy under Fixed Rates

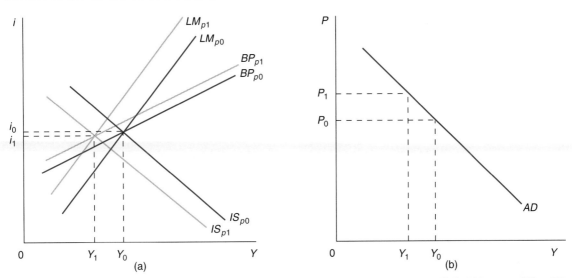

With the initial price level P_0, equilibrium occurs at i_0 and Y_0. An increase in the price level to P_1 causes (1) the *LM* curve to shift to LM_{p1} due to the decline in the real money supply; (2) the *BP* curve to shift up to BP_{p1}, as foreign goods become relatively cheaper and domestic exports become relatively more costly; and (3) the *IS* curve to shift left to IS_{p1}, as the current account deteriorates. The new equilibrium will occur at the intersection of IS_{p1}, LM_{p1}, and BP_{p1} at Y_1 and i_1. Should the intersection of IS_{p1} and LM_{p1} initially be above or below BP_{p1}, the balance of payments will not be in balance and pressure on the exchange rate occurs. As the central bank acts to maintain the exchange rate, the domestic money supply changes, shifting the *LM* curve into equilibrium at i_1 and Y_1. When the two price levels P_0 and P_1 are plotted against the two equilibrium levels of income Y_0 and Y_1 in panel (b), a downward-sloping aggregate demand curve *AD* results.

thus leads to an expansion of imports and a contraction of exports. The change in relative prices causes the *BP* curve to shift to the left, because it now will take a higher level of the interest rate to generate the needed net short-term capital inflow to offset the deteriorating trade balance. The deterioration in the trade balance—that is, the expansion of imports and the contraction of exports—will also cause the *IS* curve to shift to the left. In sum, increasing the level of prices causes the *LM* curve to shift left (LM_{p1}), the *BP* curve to shift left (BP_{p1}), and the *IS* curve to shift left (IS_{p1}). Price increases thus lead not only to a decrease in the real money supply but also to changes in relative prices and hence in the demand for real domestic output.

With all three markets adjusting to the change in the level of prices, what will guarantee that a new equilibrium will result? How can we be certain that the three curves will again intersect at a common point? The change in relative prices will lead to new *IS* and *BP* curves, consistent with the new price level. If the intersection between the IS_{p1} and the LM_{p1} is not on the BP_{p1} curve, then there will be disequilibrium in the balance of payments (official reserve transactions balance). If they intersect above the BP_{p1} curve, then a balance-of-payments surplus will result. Under fixed rates, a surplus will lead to an expansion in the money supply (assuming no sterilization) as the central bank purchases foreign exchange with domestic currency to maintain the pegged exchange rate. Consequently, the *LM* curve will shift right until there is no longer a surplus in the balance of payments and the economy is once again in equilibrium. Similarly, should IS_{p1} and LM_{p1} intersect at a point below the BP_{p1} curve, a balance-of-payments deficit will occur. As the central bank seeks to maintain the pegged value of the currency by selling foreign exchange for domestic currency, the money supply declines (with no sterilization), shifting the *LM* curve even further to the left.

This continues until IS_{p1}, LM_{p1}, and BP_{p1} intersect at a common point. Central bank intervention to maintain the value of the currency thus will automatically cause the LM curve to move to the new equilibrium point, which must lie on BP_{p1}.

Aggregate Demand in the Open Economy under Flexible Rates

The aggregate demand curve in the open economy under a flexible-rate system is obtained in the same manner. Increases in the domestic price level lead to leftward shifts in the LM, IS, and BP curves, just as in the case of fixed exchange rates.[3] The principal difference between fixed and flexible rates lies in the adjustment process once the change in domestic prices has affected the three markets. If the leftward shifts in the three curves do not initially produce a new equilibrium—that is, the intersection of IS_{p1} and LM_{p1} is not on the BP_{p1} curve—the balance of payments will not be in equilibrium. If this occurs, there will either be an **incipient surplus** (if the new IS-LM equilibrium is above the new BP curve) or an **incipient deficit** (if the IS-LM equilibrium is below the new BP curve). In the case of an incipient surplus, the exchange rate will appreciate, shifting both the BP curve and the IS curve even further left. This adjustment will continue until simultaneous equilibrium is once again attained in all three markets. This adjustment process and the resulting new equilibrium are shown in Figure 8(a). Note that under flexible rates, any needed adjustment to the LM shift takes place in the foreign sector and the goods markets. If the price increase had produced an incipient deficit instead, then the currency would have depreciated, leading to rightward shifts in the IS and BP curves until equilibrium is once again attained.

Regardless of the adjustment process, an increase in prices leads to a decline in equilibrium income, producing the normal downward-sloping aggregate demand curve [panel (b) of Figure 8]. Because of the nature of the further BP shift and its repercussions on IS after the initial shifts in these curves under flexible exchange rates (in contrast to the LM shifts under fixed rates), the aggregate demand curve in the open economy under flexible exchange rates might well have a different degree of negative slope than under a fixed-rate system.

THE NATURE OF ECONOMIC ADJUSTMENT AND MACROECONOMIC POLICY IN THE OPEN-ECONOMY AGGREGATE SUPPLY AND DEMAND FRAMEWORK

The Effect of Exogenous Shocks on the Aggregate Demand Curve under Fixed and Flexible Rates

In the open economy, any factor that affects the IS curve, the LM curve, or the BP curve can potentially influence the aggregate demand curve. The way it influences the AD curve depends, however, on whether there are fixed or flexible rates. For example, an increase in the foreign price level will stimulate domestic exports and reduce domestic imports. This has the effect of stimulating income as the BP curve and the IS curve both shift to the right due to the improvement in the current account. Under a fixed-rate system, this would produce a balance-of-payments surplus, which will lead to an expansion of the money supply and a further expansion in the economy. The end result, then, would be a rightward shift of the AD curve. Under flexible rates, however, the incipient surplus that accompanies the improvement in relative prices will lead to an appreciation of the home currency. This change in the exchange rate neutralizes the initial increase in foreign prices. As the appreciation takes place, the BP and IS curves shift back to the initial equilibrium. There is thus no lasting effect of the initial change in relative prices under a flexible-rate system and no permanent change in the AD curve. We can generalize from this example and see that any

---

[3]The determination of the precise effect of price-level changes on the LM curve is considerably more complicated with flexible rates than with fixed rates. The reason is that, as the exchange rate changes, this will alter the domestic prices of imported goods, and these prices are part of the domestic price level. Thus changes in the exchange rate itself can affect the position of the LM curve. However, this factor does not alter the normal direction of shift of LM in response to price-level changes.

FIGURE 8   Aggregate Demand in the Open Economy under Flexible Rates

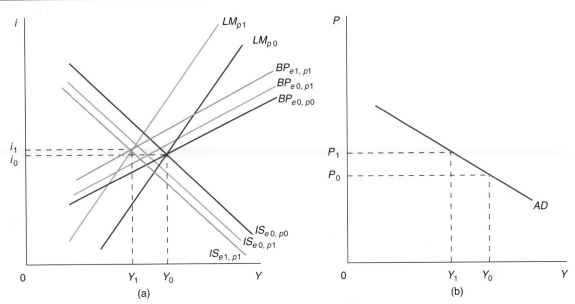

Starting from equilibrium at Y_0 and i_0 in panel (a), an increase in the price level from P_0 to P_1 reduces the real money supply, shifting the LM curve to LM_{p1}. It also raises the relative price of domestic products, leading to an upward shift in the $BP_{e0,p0}$ curve to $BP_{e0,p1}$ and a leftward shift in the $IS_{e0,p0}$ curve to $IS_{e0,p1}$ as the current account deteriorates. Should the new IS and LM curves not intersect on $BP_{e0,p1}$, there will be either an incipient surplus or an incipient deficit and the exchange rate will adjust (causing the IS and the BP curves to further adjust) until the system is in equilibrium at Y_1 and i_1 (in the case of $IS_{e1,p1}$, LM_{p1}, and $BP_{e1,p1}$). When the old and the new levels of equilibrium income corresponding to the two price levels are plotted [panel (b)] against the two price levels, the downward-sloping aggregate demand curve AD is obtained.

shock originating in the foreign trade sector or current account will have an effect on the AD curve under fixed rates but not under completely flexible rates.

A shock originating in the foreign financial sector or capital account has a different effect in this model. Suppose there is an increase in the foreign interest rate. This will stimulate an outflow of short-term capital from the home country, producing either a deficit under fixed rates or an incipient deficit under flexible rates. In the fixed-rate case, the financial shock will cause the BP curve to shift to the left and the LM curve to shift to the left as the central bank responds to the new deficit pressure. Hence the AD curve will shift to the left. In the case of flexible rates, the shift in the BP curve will produce an incipient deficit, which will cause the home currency to depreciate. As the depreciation takes place, it will stimulate exports and reduce imports, leading to a rightward shift in both the IS function and the BP curve along the fixed LM curve. As a result, the AD curve will shift to the right. The AD curve shifts under either system, but in opposite directions due to the different nature of the adjustment in each case. Of course, remembering portfolio balance considerations, the increase in the foreign interest rate would also reduce the domestic demand for money, causing the LM curve to shift to the right. This would lead to an even greater rightward shift of the AD curve under flexible rates and an even greater leftward shift of the AD curve under fixed rates (as the BOP deficit to be adjusted to would be even greater).

Now consider the effect of domestic shocks originating in the real sector. A change in a variable that affects the real sector and the current account will cause a change in aggregate demand under fixed rates but will have little effect under flexible rates. For example, suppose that there is a shift in tastes and preferences away from foreign automobiles toward domestically produced automobiles. This change in the "state of nature" would cause the *IS* curve to shift out (due to the decline in autonomous imports) and cause the *BP* curve to shift to the right as well. Under fixed rates, this will create a surplus in the balance of payments, leading to an expansion in the money supply and a rightward shift in the *LM* curve. This adjustment will take place until all three sectors are again in equilibrium at a higher level of income and will result in a rightward shift in the *AD* curve. Under flexible rates, however, the incipient surplus resulting from the change in tastes and preferences will lead to appreciation of the home currency. As the currency appreciates, the *BP* curve and the *IS* curve will both shift back to the left as the appreciation of the currency adjusts for the change in tastes and preferences. Consequently, there will be less overall change in aggregate demand once the expenditure-switching adjustment has taken place under flexible rates relative to fixed rates.

Changes in a domestic financial variable also generate different effects under the two systems. Suppose there is an exogenous shift of preferences in desired portfolio composition by domestic citizens toward domestic short-term investments and away from foreign short-term investments. The immediate effect of this change will be a rightward shift in the *BP* curve, due to the reduced outflow of short-term capital, creating a surplus in the balance of payments under fixed rates and an incipient surplus under flexible rates. This will prove to be expansionary under fixed rates, because the *LM* curve shifts out as the central bank responds to the surplus in the balance of payments. Under flexible rates, however, an appreciation of the currency results, leading to a worsening of the current account and a leftward shift in the *IS* curve and the new *BP* curve. The end result is a fall in income and hence in aggregate demand.

The Effect of Monetary and Fiscal Policy on the Aggregate Demand Curve under Fixed and Flexible Rates

As we learned in the preceding chapters, monetary policy and fiscal policy have different effects under the two different exchange rate regimes. Turning first to the case of fixed exchange rates, it was observed that monetary policy is ineffective for influencing income in a fixed exchange rate system under the various mobility assumptions. On the other hand, fiscal policy was found to be effective in all cases except when capital was perfectly immobile internationally. If we continue to restrict our analysis to the case of relatively mobile capital (*BP* curve flatter than *LM* curve) for ease of discussion, we can generalize and say that expansionary fiscal policy will shift the *AD* curve to the right and contractionary fiscal policy will shift it to the left. In contrast, altering the money supply will have no effect on the *AD* curve in a fixed-rate system unless the central bank continually sterilizes the balance-of-payments effect on the money supply (i.e., replaces the change in foreign exchange reserves by open market purchases or sales of domestic bonds).

Under a flexible-rate system, monetary policy was always shown to be effective regardless of the mobility assumption. The greater the mobility of capital, the more effective is discretionary monetary policy in influencing income. Fiscal policy, however, was less effective under flexible rates than under fixed rates when the *BP* curve was flatter than the *LM* curve, and more effective when the *BP* curve was steeper than the *LM* curve. The more mobile is capital, the less effective is fiscal policy, as short-term capital flows offset much of the effect of the discretionary policy. In the extreme case, when capital is perfectly mobile, fiscal policy is totally ineffective. Consequently, fiscal policy will have a weak effect on the *AD* curve under the relatively mobile capital assumption we have adopted for this discussion. Thus, fiscal policy under flexible rates will generally be relatively ineffective in shifting the *AD* curve compared with fixed rates, whereas expansionary (contractionary) monetary policy will shift the *AD* curve to the right (left) under a system of flexible exchange rates and monetary policy has no effect on *AD* under fixed rates (without sterilization).

TABLE 3   Influences on Aggregate Demand under Fixed and Flexible Exchange Rates

	Fixed Rates	*Flexible Rates*
Change in partner-country variable that increases home-country exports	Shifts *AD* right	No effect on *AD*
Change in partner-country variable that alters short-term capital flows in partner-country favor	Shifts *AD* left	Shifts *AD* right
Change in home-country variable that reduces home-country exports	Shifts *AD* left	No effect on *AD*
Change in home-country variable that stimulates short-term capital inflow	Shifts *AD* right	Shifts *AD* left
Expansionary monetary policy	No effect on *AD* (without sterilization)	Shifts *AD* right
Expansionary fiscal policy	Shifts *AD* right	Little effect on *AD* (slight rightward shift)

Summary

Before moving on to an examination of how domestic and foreign policies and other selected economic variables affect prices and output in the open economy, let us take a moment to summarize how the *AD* curve is affected by changes in variables under fixed and flexible rates. We continue to assume that the mobility of capital is such that the *BP* curve is upward sloping and flatter than the *LM* curve. These results are summarized in Table 3. Because the effects on the *AD* curve of changes in these variables are symmetrical, the results in Table 3 have been limited to one example per type of influence. Test your understanding of the adjustment process under fixed and flexible rates by examining both positive and negative changes in an important economic variable to verify the symmetry of the *AD* adjustment.

MONETARY AND FISCAL POLICY IN THE OPEN ECONOMY WITH FLEXIBLE PRICES

Having looked at the nature of aggregate supply and aggregate demand and the factors that influence them, we are now ready to examine the effect of discretionary economic policy in the open economy when prices are not fixed. Because the short-run–long-run distinction is important with regard to supply response, we pay close attention to the time frame under consideration when discussing the likely economic effects of a policy action.

Monetary Policy

As you are now well aware, the effect of monetary policy on the domestic economy depends on the type of exchange system under consideration. Because monetary policy has a limited effect on aggregate demand under a fixed exchange rate system, we can ignore that case. However, we found that monetary policy was an effective policy instrument under flexible rates. In that case, expansionary monetary policy had the effect of shifting the *AD* curve to the right. The economic implications of that policy are examined in Figure 9. We begin with the economy in equilibrium at Y_0 and P_0 (point E), the intersection of the long-run supply curve (AS_{LR}), the short-run supply curve (AS_{SR0}), and the aggregate demand curve (AD_{M0}). *Remember, at that point, actual prices equal expected prices.* The expansion of the money supply leads to a rightward shift in the *AD* curve to AD_{M1}, creating a disequilibrium condition. Assuming that there is a lag between the change in the price level and workers' demands for higher wages, the economy will respond to the increase in demand. As output increases, prices begin to increase and the economy moves to a new short-run equilibrium at F.

FIGURE 9   The Effect of Monetary Policy in the Aggregate Supply-Demand Framework under Flexible Rates

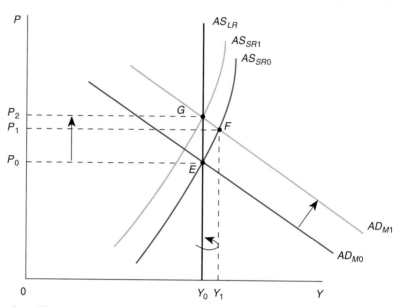

Beginning in equilibrium at point E, expanding the money supply causes the AD curve to shift right to AD_{M1}, putting upward pressure on income and prices in the short run. A new short-run equilibrium is established at F on the short-run supply curve AS_{SR0} at (Y_1, P_1). However, once workers realize that prices have risen and that their real wages have fallen, they will demand higher wages so that the same labor will be supplied at the same real wage as initially. The increase in nominal wages causes the short-run supply curve to shift upward along AD_{M1}, leading to a further increase in prices. A new equilibrium is reached at G, where AS_{LR}, AS_{SR1}, and AD_{M1} intersect. At this point, the actual price level P_2 equals the expected price level and the economy is again in equilibrium. The short-run expansionary effect on income is offset by the ultimate increase in the wage rate, leaving the economy again at Y_0 but at the higher price level P_2.

However, once labor realizes that the actual price level is higher than the expected price level and has time to respond, workers will raise their wage demands commensurate with the increase in prices so that the same amount of labor is being supplied at the same real wage. This will cause the short-run aggregate supply curve to shift left until the expected price level is again equal to the actual price level, given the new larger supply of money. This equilibrium is point G, where AS_{SR1}, AS_{LR}, and AD_{M1} intersect at (Y_0, P_2). After all adjustments have taken place, the economy is again at the natural level of income Y_0 but at a higher price level P_2. Expansionary monetary policy can produce a short-run increase in income and employment, but it will last only until workers adjust their wage demands to the new higher level of prices.[4]

Given the change in the price level or rate of inflation as a result of the expansion in the money supply, what if anything can be said about the accompanying changes in the other key monetary variables, specifically the nominal rate of interest and the exchange rate? If we adopt the monetary approach perspective developed in Chapter 22, several clear conclusions can be reached. Following the relative purchasing power parity view, in the long

---

[4]Another factor involved is that, to the extent that there are intermediate goods imports, the depreciation of the home currency from the expansionary monetary policy will raise the costs of production of domestic firms. This also will shift the short-run aggregate supply curve (as well as the long-run aggregate supply curve) to the left. We generally ignore this repercussion but refer to it in occasional cases later in this chapter.

run the exchange rate will rise (the home currency will depreciate) proportionally with the rise in the price level in the home country relative to that in the trading partner.

In addition, it is generally agreed that the real rate of interest is what concerns investors (i.e., the rate at which purchasing power is increased over the investment period because of the sacrifice of current consumption). From this perspective, the nominal interest rate (what we have been calling the "interest rate" under the earlier fixed-price assumption) consists of two components: the real interest rate or rate of time preference, and a payment for expected inflation. Therefore, $i = i_r + E(\dot{p})$, [or $i_r = i - E(\dot{p})$], where i is the nominal rate of interest, i_r is the real interest rate, and $E(\dot{p})$ is the expected inflation rate. If real rates of interest are equalized (or differ by a more or less constant amount due to imperfect capital mobility) between any two countries through interest arbitrage, it follows that any difference in the nominal rates of interest must be attributable to differences in the expected inflation rate in the two countries.[5] Therefore, an increase in the domestic inflation rate (with the expectation that it would continue), *ceteris paribus,* should lead to a comparable relative increase in the domestic nominal interest rate. For example, if the U.S. rate of inflation were to rise from 4 to 6 percent and the U.K. inflation rate and rate of interest remain constant, nominal interest rates in the United States should rise by 2 percentage points. Finally, because the change in relative prices is driving both a change in the nominal exchange rate and a change in the nominal interest rate, the percentage change in the relative nominal interest rates between two countries should equal the expected percentage change in the exchange rate. This is, of course, another way of stating the uncovered interest parity condition discussed in previous chapters.[6] Basically, this can be thought of as extending the application of the law of one price to the financial markets (investors are receiving the same expected real rate of return in both countries when those rates are expressed in a single currency). In sum, after the long-run adjustments to the increased domestic money supply have been completed, there will be, in the domestic country, no change in income, an increase in the price level, an increase in the nominal interest rate, and an increase in the exchange rate (depreciation of the home currency).

Next, however, suppose that we begin with the economy in disequilibrium at a level of income Y_0 that is less than the natural level of income, Y_N (i.e., point H in Figure 10). Is there perhaps a stronger rationale for using expansionary monetary policy in this instance? Expanding the money supply will cause the AD curve to shift up to a new long-run equilibrium, at P_1 and Y_N (point K). Domestic income will have increased, but again at the expense of an increase in the price level. On the other hand, because P_1 is consistent with the expected level of prices on AS_{SR0}, there will be no pressure on the part of labor to increase wages (and hence prices) further.

Suppose instead that there had been no policy reaction to the recession reflected by Y_0 and P_0. If wages and prices are flexible downward, once it is recognized that the actual

---

[5]In a U.S.–U.K. example, $i_{US} - i_{UK} = E(\dot{p})_{US} - E(\dot{p})_{UK}$, where i refers to the nominal interest rate and $E(\dot{p})$ to the expected inflation rate in each country as indicated by the subscript. This general relationship between relative nominal interest rates and relative inflation rates is referred to as the *Fisher effect* (after the early-20th-century American economist Irving Fisher).

[6]Recall that the uncovered interest parity condition was, in an example case of the United States and the United Kingdom,

$$i_{US} = i_{UK} + xa \quad \text{or} \quad i_{US} - i_{UK} = xa$$

where xa was the expected rate of appreciation of the pound against the dollar, ignoring any risk premium. The term xa in turn is equal to $[E(e) - e]/\, e$, where $E(e)$ is the expected future exchange rate and e is the current spot rate (both in $/£).

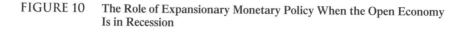

FIGURE 10   The Role of Expansionary Monetary Policy When the Open Economy
Is in Recession

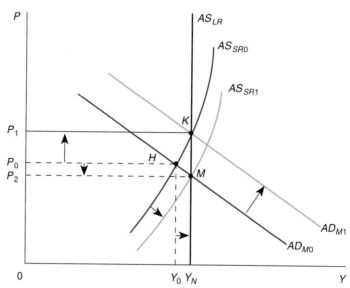

With the economy in equilibrium below Y_N at H, expanding the money supply causes the aggregate demand
curve to shift right to AD_{M1}, and it then intersects AS_{LR} and AS_{SR0} at K. At that point, expected prices equal
actual prices and aggregate demand equals both long- and short-run aggregate supply, so there will be no further
adjustment. The economy is now at the natural level of income, but at a higher price level, P_1. If policymakers
do nothing at H, and wages and prices are flexible downward, labor will eventually realize that the actual level
of prices, P_0, is less than the expected level, P_1, and the wage rate will fall to increase the level of employment.
This will cause the short-run aggregate supply curve to begin to drift down (along with prices) until long-run
and short-run aggregate supply and aggregate demand are in equilibrium at M and the actual level of prices
equals the expected level of prices, P_2.

level of prices, P_0, is less than the expected level of prices, P_1, the recession and unemployment should produce a fall in expected prices and consequently in the nominal wage
rate. As expected prices decline, the short-run aggregate supply curve begins to shift downward to AS_{SR1} from AS_{SR0}. As actual prices begin to fall, movement occurs along AD_{M0},
exports increase, and imports decrease. These adjustments continue until the economy is
once again in equilibrium at Y_N, but now at price level P_2 (point M).

In the situation where Y_0 is less than Y_N, there are thus two adjustment processes leading to long-run equilibrium at Y_N. One process relies on discretionary monetary policy and
the other on the natural market mechanism, assuming that wages and prices are flexible in
both the upward and downward direction. Critics of the policy action point to the inflationary pressures stimulated by the expanding money supply, arguing that these pressures
will contribute to further expectations regarding discretionary government policy and further price increases. Economists in favor of policy argue that, in reality, wages are not very
flexible in the downward direction and that market adjustments take a long time to work
themselves out. Thus, in this view, while the automatic adjustment may work to some
degree, the adjustment cost of the recession in terms of lost output, unemployment, and
social programs is far too high to leave to uncertain market forces.

In sum, monetary policy under flexible rates can cause short-run increases in income
above the natural level of income as long as wage adjustments lag behind price increases.
Eventually, however, the income gains will be lost as labor adjusts its wage demands to the

new, higher level of prices. The increase in output and employment is thus temporary and ultimately leads only to higher prices and wages. Monetary policy can be effective in stimulating the economy when the economy is below the natural rate of employment, but again at the expense of higher prices. However, relying on the market mechanism and not on monetary policy may entail a long adjustment period and may be ineffective if wages are rigid downward.

Currency Adjustments under Fixed Rates

Aided by Figures 9 and 10, we can also briefly discuss another policy that is in the purview of the monetary authorities. Suppose that an economy is operating under a *pegged* exchange rate but that it now undertakes an official devaluation of its currency. In the context of an *IS/LM/BP* diagram, such a policy shifts *BP* to the right and also shifts *IS* to the right through the net export stimulus. There will be a BOP surplus and expansion of the money supply as the new exchange rate is pegged. The result is a shift of *AD* to the right as in Figure 9 (but for the reason that *BP, IS,* and *LM* have all shifted to the right). There is a temporary expansion of income as in Figure 9 until workers adjust their nominal wage, but the end result is then only inflation. Even worse, however, if intermediate imports are important as in many developing countries, AS_{SR1} and AS_{LR} will shift to the left because of the devaluation, leading to what has been called **contractionary devaluation** because output has fallen. This issue has been debated for developing countries, but for those countries it is possible that point *H* in Figure 10 is a more likely starting point and AS_{SR0} also may be flatter. In that case, no contraction of output (and some expansion) and only mild inflation may follow the devaluation.

Fiscal Policy

As noted in the previous chapter, fiscal policy is relatively ineffective in increasing the level of national income under flexible rates if short-term capital is relatively mobile (*BP* curve flatter than *LM*) or perfectly mobile (horizontal *BP* curve). To the extent that there is any effect on *AD,* the price and output effects are qualitatively similar to monetary policy, except that the home currency will *appreciate* due to the relatively higher domestic interest rate.[7] If capital is relatively immobile (*BP* curve steeper than the *LM* curve) or perfectly immobile (vertical *BP* curve), the price and output effects are larger as the *AD* curve shifts to a greater extent. In these situations, the home currency depreciates. In the fixed-rate case, expansionary fiscal policy will shift *AD* to the right, just as expansionary monetary policy did under flexible rates (see Figure 11). Assuming there is a lag between price increases and wage adjustments, the economy will expand in the short run from Y_0 and P_0 (point *E*) to Y_1 and P_1 (point *F*). At that point, the actual level of prices (P_1) will be higher than the initial expected level (P_0). Once the nominal wage of labor begins adjusting to the rising price level, the short-run supply curve will shift upward. This will continue until AS_{SR1}, AS_{LR}, and AD_{G1} intersect at a common point (Y_0, P_2). Expansionary fiscal policy can thus stimulate income and employment in the short run under fixed rates, but only temporarily. Once labor adjusts its wage demands, the economy returns to the natural level of income and employment. Should this happen very quickly, fiscal policy will only generate inflation, even in the short run.

The implications of the recession situation for fiscal policy under fixed rates are analogous to those of monetary policy under flexible rates. Recall that with the economy in recession as in Figure 10, there is greater unemployment than is the case when the natural rate is attained. The movement back to the natural level of income can take place through fiscal stimulus or through reliance on the market adjustment of wages and prices. Use of the fiscal

---

[7]If intermediate goods imports are significant, the short-run and long-run aggregate supply curves will also shift to the right because of the appreciation.

FIGURE 11   The Effect of Fiscal Policy in the Aggregate Demand-Supply Framework under Fixed Exchange Rates

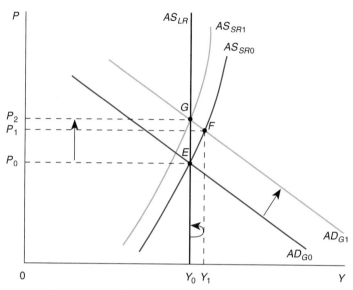

With the economy in equilibrium at Y_0 and P_0, expansionary fiscal policy shifts the aggregate demand curve rightward from AD_{G0} to AD_{G1}. The expansion in demand causes the price level to rise to P_1 and output to expand to Y_1, assuming that there is a lag in the wage adjustment to the increase in prices. Once workers realize that the actual price level is now above the expected price level P_0, they demand higher wages, shifting the short-run aggregate supply curve to the left. This results in a decline in employment and income that will continue until the economy is back in equilibrium, that is, where AS_{SR1}, AS_{LR}, and AD_{G1} intersect at a common point. This occurs at P_2 and Y_0. Because supply now equals demand and actual prices P_2 equal expected prices P_2, no further adjustments will take place.

instrument will lead to an increase in the price level, whereas the market adjustment will lead to lower wages and prices. The issues that once again emerge are the degree to which prices and wages are downwardly flexible and the length of time of the market adjustment process. Keynesian theorists tend to lean toward more policy intervention, whereas the Monetarists and the New Classical theorists place primary emphasis on the market solution.

Economic Policy and Supply Considerations

The analysis up to now has focused entirely on the effect of monetary and fiscal policy on aggregate demand. At this point, it is important to indicate that economic policy can also have an effect on aggregate supply. If discretionary economic policy is to have any lasting effect other than to increase prices, it must contribute to a growing production capacity, that is, a rightward shift in the long-run aggregate supply curve. Monetary and fiscal policies that encourage improvements in technology (either directly or indirectly through programs such as a space program), improve the quality and mobility of the labor force, stimulate private accumulation of capital, or provide needed social infrastructure can have a lasting effect on income and employment. The effect of such policies is demonstrated in Figure 12. Expansionary discretionary policy (e.g., a tax cut) again causes the AD curve to shift to the right to AD', producing some income and employment gains in the short run along with the increase in prices. Suppose, however, it also leads to a rightward shift in the long-run supply curve to AS'_{LR}. (This shift could occur if the tax cut encouraged increased saving, investment, and/or work effort, as would be stressed by supply-side economists.) After all the adjustments have taken place, the economy now finds itself at a higher natural level of employment and income

FIGURE 12   Economic Policy and Shifts in the Long-Run Aggregate Supply Curve

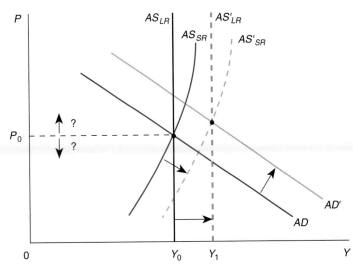

Starting with the economy in equilibrium at Y_0 and P_0, suppose that discretionary monetary and/or fiscal policy is undertaken that has an effect on domestic long-run supply conditions. The expansionary effect increases income and prices in the short run but eventually shifts the long-run and short-run supply curves to the right. A new equilibrium will result at Y_1, where AS'_{LR}, AS'_{SR}, and AD' intersect. Because the new price level will depend on the relative movements of the curves, the exact position of the new equilibrium is uncertain.

(Y_1), and economic growth has occurred. The new price level could be higher, lower, or about the same as the equilibrium price level prior to the policy undertaking, depending on the relative shifts in all three curves. If tax policy stimulates a large supply response and little AD response under flexible rates, the end result can be higher income and employment, a lower price level, and an appreciated currency. What is critical here is that the ultimate effect on the level of income and employment depends on the degree to which there is a demand response and a long-run supply response. To be effective, government policy must be aware of the implications of its policy actions on long-run supply conditions.

This effect on income and employment is particularly important if we recall from earlier in the chapter that some unemployment (the natural level) exists at the natural level of income Y_0. The implication of the preceding paragraph is that policy actions that shift AD to the right, as well as shift AS_{LR} to the right, are considerably more likely to result in a reduction of unemployment than are actions that affect AD only.

CONCEPT CHECK

1. Why could the AD curve in the open economy have a different degree of downward slope than the AD curve in the closed economy?

2. Under what conditions will expansionary policy increase income in the short run? In the long run?

3. What effect will an increase in exports have on the economy under flexible rates? Under fixed rates?

EXTERNAL SHOCKS AND THE OPEN ECONOMY

To conclude this chapter on the open economy with flexible prices, let us concentrate more specifically on the effects of some external shocks to the economy. Suppose that there is an increase in the world price of a critical imported intermediate input for which

IN THE REAL WORLD:

ECONOMIC PROGRESS IN SUB-SAHARAN AFRICA

A set of countries in which growth is finally beginning to emerge and in which supply-type policy factors seem to be playing a role consists of nations in Sub-Saharan Africa. Many of these countries, after stagnation for decades, have instituted, at the behest of and with assistance from the World Bank and the International Monetary Fund, structural reforms. These reforms embody measures such as removal of price controls, liberalization of imports, improved agricultural marketing systems, privatization of public enterprises, and more efficient tax systems. The reforms can be thought of as having increased productive capabilities by changing institutions, and they shift aggregate supply curves to the right. At the same time, measures such as the introduction of new monetary policy instruments and the reduction in government budget deficits as a percentage of GDP have led to slower increases in aggregate demand (smaller rightward shifts in the AD curve). Overall, the result has been an improvement in the rate of growth of real GDP as well as a decrease in inflation rates at the end of the 1990s and in the 2000s. The experience is captured in Table 4. The first row for each indicator includes Nigeria and South Africa, which together account for about 50 percent of the region's activity; the second row excludes them because

their experience differs slightly from the rest of the countries (e.g., Botswana, Congo, Namibia, Sudan, and Tanzania), especially with respect to inflation. Nigeria and South Africa have had less inflation than the other countries.

The World Bank and IMF policies have been severely criticized because they can lead to a more unequal distribution of income and to increased dislocation of unskilled labor. Further, poverty is still stark and sweeping in sub-Saharan Africa. The 1998 per capita GNP for the region was only $510 ($1,440 in purchasing-power-parity terms) and by 2005 this had risen to $746 ($2,004 in purchasing-power-parity terms). The recent progress is encouraging in that aggregate supply is increasing while the inflationary consequences of aggregate demand shifts are being reduced.

Sources: Alassane D. Outtara, "Africa: An Agenda for the 21st Century," *Finance and Development,* March 1999, pp. 2–5; Evangelos A. Calamitsis, "Adjustment and Growth in Sub-Saharan Africa: The Unfinished Agenda," *Finance and Development,* March 1999, pp. 6–9; Ernesto Hernández-Catá, "Sub-Saharan Africa: Economic Policy and Outlook for Growth," *Finance and Development,* March 1999, pp. 10–12; World Bank, *World Development Indicators 2000* (Washington, DC: World Bank, 2000), p. 12; *World Development Indicators 2007* (Washington, DC: World Bank, 2007), p. 16.

TABLE 4   Inflation and Real GDP Growth in Sub-Saharan Africa, 1989–2006

	1989–1998	1999	2000	2001	2002	2003	2004	2005	2006
Growth in real GDP	2.1%	2.7%	3.4%	4.5%	3.7%	4.2%	6.0%	6.0%	5.7%
Excluding Nigeria and South Africa	2.3	3.2	2.4	5.9	4.0	3.7	6.7	6.5	6.3
Percentage change in consumer price index	33.5	14.9	17.4	15.5	12.0	13.2	9.5	10.5	11.5
Excluding Nigeria and South Africa	52.9	23.7	28.8	22.2	13.7	18.4	14.1	14.0	16.8

Source: International Monetary Fund, *World Economic Outlook,* April 2007 (Washington, DC: IMF, 2007), pp. 217, 225, obtained from www.imf.org.

domestic demand is relatively inelastic. With a flexible-rate system, this causes depreciation of the home currency and an expansion of domestic aggregate demand in response to the expenditure-switching effects of the depreciation. At the same time, the higher world price of the critical intermediate good leads in Figure 13 to a leftward shift in both the short-run supply curve (from AS_{SR0} to AS_{SR1}) and the long-run supply curve (from AS_{LR0} to AS_{LR1}).

FIGURE 13   The Effect of a Price Shock of an Imported Input in the Open Economy

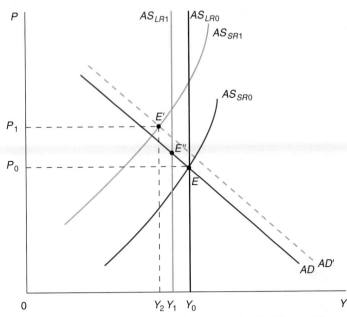

With the economy in equilibrium at *E,* a sudden increase in the price of a critical imported intermediate good for which demand is inelastic leads to depreciation of the currency and to a rightward shift in the aggregate demand curve to *AD'*. At the same time, it causes both the short-run and the long-run aggregate supply curves to shift left as production costs rise. The economy contracts to *E'*, with a higher price level P_1 and a new short-run equilibrium income Y_2 (that is, the economy is experiencing stagflation). Attempts on the part of labor to increase nominal wages would lead to more inflation and unemployment (not shown). Attempts to use expansionary monetary policy to increase income in this instance also would lead to further price increases (not shown). If wages were flexible downward, a fall in the nominal wage could move the economy into equilibrium at *E''* and Y_1 (but not Y_0).

As you can see in the figure, both effects put upward pressure on the price level. If the price shock is sufficiently large, it could alter domestic supply conditions so much that the new equilibrium income is at Y_2 (i.e., less than Y_1). Declining income coupled with rising inflation is often referred to as **stagflation.** The United States has, in fact, experienced two periods of stagflation in recent decades, both associated with sharp increases in petroleum prices. Attempts in the short run to ease the stagflation at point *E'* by expansionary monetary policy will lead to even higher prices. Attempts by labor to raise the nominal wage to offset the initial price shock would shift the short-run aggregate supply curve even further to the left, making the stagflation even worse. However, if wages were flexible downward at *E'*, a fall in the nominal wage rate would shift the short-run aggregate supply curve to the right, increasing income and employment until it reached *E''* and Y_1 (not, however, *E* and Y_0). Thus, external shocks that affect both supply and demand conditions create special problems for macro policy, for there may be little that can be done in the short run (absent effective and quick supply-side tax policies) to facilitate the needed structural adjustment without generating further inflation.

Consider as a second external shock a foreign financial shock that triggers an inflow of short-term capital into the home country. Under flexible rates this will cause the *AD* curve to shift to the left as the home currency appreciates in value. As indicated in Figure 15 on page 701, this will lead to lower income and prices in the short run as the expenditure-switching

IN THE REAL WORLD:

INFLATION AND UNEMPLOYMENT IN THE UNITED STATES, 1970–2005

Figure 14 indicates inflation (GDP deflator) and unemployment rates in the United States in recent decades. The two time-series seem to move together rather consistently over most of the time period. However, two periods clearly stand out. During both the 1973–1975 period and the 1979–1981 period, the economy was experiencing high and increasing inflation rates and rising unemployment rates. Both of these periods followed upon sizable increases in petroleum prices. The increases in petroleum prices shifted the aggregate supply curves leftward, raising the actual unemployment rate.

In contrast, oil price increases due to the 1990 Iraqi invasion of Kuwait and the subsequent embargo on trade with Iraq do not appear to be associated with a rise in the U.S. inflation rate. Further, the more typical movement of inflation and unemployment associated with the business cycle appears in the 1986–1989 period, the 1990–1992 period, and from 2003–2005. Finally, in the early to mid-1980s and from 1993 to 1998, unemployment and inflation rates simultaneously fell. This suggests that there was important movement of the aggregate supply curves to the right in those years.

FIGURE 14   U.S. Inflation and Unemployment Rates, 1970–2005

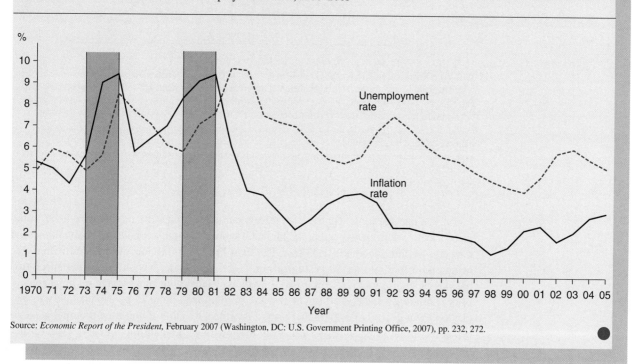

Source: *Economic Report of the President*, February 2007 (Washington, DC: U.S. Government Printing Office, 2007), pp. 232, 272.

effects come into play (a movement from E to E'). In this case, expansionary monetary policy could be used to offset the initial short-term capital inflow, moving the economy back to the natural level of income and to the initial prices. This would, of course, then lead to a decline in the value of the home currency in the short run as the interest rate fell in response to the monetary action. The movement back to macro equilibrium could also take place through a downward or rightward shift in the short-run supply curve (not shown), once labor adjusts its price expectations to the new, lower price level. In either case, the adjustment process is not complicated by an initial supply effect as it was in the previous

FIGURE 15   A Foreign Financial Shock and Adjustment in the Open Economy

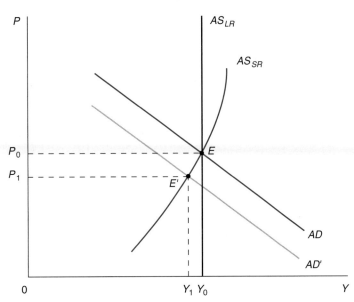

In this case, a foreign financial shock triggers an inflow of short-term capital into the home country, appreciating the currency and reducing aggregate demand to AD'. As a result, the economy will move to E', experiencing a lower level of income, employment, and prices in the short run. In this instance, expansionary monetary policy could increase aggregate demand and move the economy back to Y_0. The movement to Y_0 could also take place through a reduction in the nominal wage as labor realizes that the actual price level is below the expected price level P_0. This would cause AS_{SR} to shift to the right until equilibrium (not shown) is once again attained at Y_0.

example. The adjustments following this shock would also occur if the initial event were a change in expectations regarding the exchange rate such that the home currency was expected to rise in value.

As a final example (can you put up with one more example?!), let us examine the effect of an improvement in aggregate productivity, as seems to have been occurring in recent years with the new information technology. To see how productivity growth affects the open economy, consider an improvement in technology that shifts the supply curves AS_{LR0} and AS_{SR0} to the right (see Figure 16). If aggregate demand does not change from AD_{M0}, the new equilibrium level of income will lie to the left (at point E_1) of the new long-run supply curve (AS_{LR1}). For the economy to take further advantage of the new productivity gains, there must either be an increase in aggregate demand or a further downward shift in the short-run supply curve (by the labor market adjustment process). Proper growth in the money supply would lead to growth in aggregate demand that causes the economy to move to the new, higher level of income made possible by the productivity change without any major impact on prices from the original price level (point E_2).

On the other hand, the lower level of prices in place at Y_1 could eventually stimulate a fall in the expected level of prices on the part of labor, a consequent fall in wages from W_0 to W_1, and a rightward shift in the short-run supply curve. This adjustment continues to take place until the three curves intersect at the new level of income that reflects the new, higher level of technology (point E_3).

FIGURE 16   Technological Change and Adjustment in the Open Economy

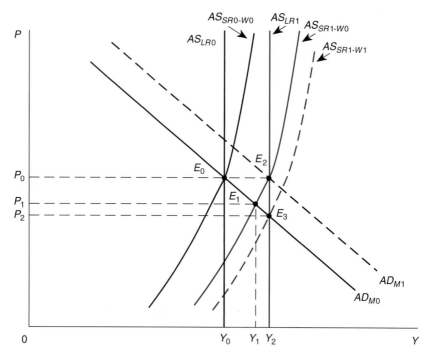

The improvement in technology shifts the aggregate supply curves to the right from AS_{LR0} to AS_{LR1}, and $AS_{SR0\text{-}W0}$ to $AS_{SR1\text{-}W0}$. With no change in aggregate demand, equilibrium moves to E_1 at a higher level of income Y_1 and a lower level of prices P_1. Because $Y_1 < Y_2$, the economy is operating below the natural level of income and employment. In this instance, the economy can move to Y_2 (the natural level) through the use of expansionary monetary policy, which would shift the aggregate demand curve to the right (AD_{M1} at E_2), or wait for a fall in nominal wages, which would shift the short-run aggregate supply curve to the right until it reached Y_2 at E_3. Expansionary policy would cause the price level to drift back up from P_1, whereas the reduction in the nominal wage would lead to further deflation to P_2.

This latter wage adjustment process relies on the assumption that prices and wages are downwardly flexible. On the other hand, the first situation of reliance on monetary policy requires that the monetary authorities correctly gauge the increase in the money supply necessary to move to the new natural level of income, and not beyond. Overestimating the growth in income capacity of course would lead to an overexpansion of the money supply and thus of aggregate demand, a response that would trigger an increase in the price level and expected prices and lead to continued inflation.

Finally, with the productivity increase, if the price level does fall to a value such as P_2 in Figure 16, this can have an effect on the nominal interest rate and the expected exchange rate. If the lower price level reduces inflationary expectations, then the nominal interest rate in the country will fall. With the reduced inflationary expectations, there may also occur a lower expected percentage depreciation (or an expected appreciation) of the home currency.

SUMMARY

This chapter focused on the open economy when prices are flexible. This was accomplished by deriving an aggregate demand curve for the open economy and combining it with aggregate supply curves. Both a short-run aggregate supply curve and a long-run aggregate supply curve were employed in the analysis. The aggregate demand–aggregate supply framework was then used to examine the effects of changes in policy variables and in exogenous variables. This was done for both a flexible-rate system and a fixed-rate system. The analysis demonstrated the automatic adjustment mechanism present when prices and wages are flexible. In addition, it pointed out the difference in the adjustment mechanism under fixed rates compared with that under flexible rates. Attempts to increase income and employment beyond the natural level by increasing aggregate demand ultimately lead only to increases in prices under either exchange rate regime. In the case when the economy was operating at a level below the natural level of employment, discretionary policy was seen to be effective in moving the economy back to the natural level, but only by increasing prices. Given sufficient time with actual employment below the natural level, the economy automatically would move back to the natural level through a fall in prices. The uncertainty surrounding the downward flexibility in prices and wages and the time required for such an adjustment underlie the view by many that the preferable adjustment mechanism is discretionary monetary policy under flexible-rate regimes and discretionary fiscal policy under fixed-rate regimes. The chapter concluded with a discussion of the effect of several exogenous shocks to the open economy operating under a flexible-rate system.

KEY TERMS

aggregate demand curve
aggregate demand curve for labor
aggregate production function
aggregate supply–aggregate
   demand equilibrium

contractionary devaluation
incipient deficit
incipient surplus
long-run aggregate supply curve

natural level of employment
natural level of income
short-run aggregate supply curve
stagflation

QUESTIONS AND PROBLEMS

1. What is meant by the natural level of income and employment? Why is the long-run aggregate supply curve vertical at the natural level?
2. What is the difference between the short-run aggregate supply curve and the long-run aggregate supply curve? Are they ever the same?
3. Is it possible that increased international economic transactions could affect the aggregate supply curves? Why or why not?
4. In the 1990s Germany attempted to control inflation through a restrictive monetary policy and high interest rates. Explain how this might have influenced income and prices in the United States.
5. Explain how appreciation of a country's currency could affect its aggregate supply curves when imported intermediate inputs are sizable.

6. If discretionary economic policy is to have more than a short-run effect on income and employment, what needs to take place?
7. If a country finds itself experiencing stagflation under a flexible-rate system, why is expansionary monetary policy unlikely to cure the problem? Why are technological improvements or general productivity improvements so critical in this situation?
8. Suppose that a home country's currency is expected to depreciate in a flexible-rate system. Trace through the effects on home country *AD, AS,* prices, and income (output).
9. Suppose the economy is operating below its natural level of income (e.g., at point *H* in Figure 10). Would you recommend the use of expansionary policy in this instance? Why or why not?

part 7

ISSUES IN WORLD MONETARY ARRANGEMENTS

Flexible exchange rates are a means of combining interdependence among countries through trade with a maximum of internal monetary independence; they are a means of permitting each country to seek for monetary stability according to its own lights, without either imposing its mistakes on its neighbors or having their mistakes imposed on it.

Milton Friedman, 1953

Under floating exchange rates, the U.S. economy has suffered unprecedented financial instability for nearly 20 years.

Lewis E. Lehrman, 1990

In the past 40 years, the world has experienced considerable change in economic activity and in the nature of the world economy. Nations are becoming more closely linked through international trade and finance. The international monetary system has changed; a former large creditor country, the United States, has emerged as the world's largest debtor nation; and many of the developing countries find themselves with continuing development problems and relatively large amounts of foreign debt. In addition, the relatively fixed exchange rate system established at the end of World War II collapsed in the early 1970s. Since that time, individual countries and groups of countries have adopted a variety of different exchange rate arrangements, and greater variability in exchange rates has been a prominent feature of the international economy. Indeed, some observers think that the degree of exchange rate flexibility has been excessive, and they long for a more stable system of rates that might provide for greater economic stability worldwide.

This part of the book is concerned with debates regarding the desirable nature of international monetary arrangements. Chapter 28 examines issues in the choice of floating versus fixed exchange rates, as well as exchange rate arrangements that feature compromises between completely flexible and completely fixed rates. Chapter 29 focuses on the current international monetary system, tracing its recent origins and evaluating its effectiveness. It concludes with a discussion of possible alternatives to the current system. ●

Some have concluded that the foreign-exchange market is not working well. The conclusion is fed by recent developments in international financial markets, on the one hand, and by a number of academic findings on the other. . . .

. . . Having looked over the various proposals for radical reform, one is left wondering whether their drawbacks are not greater than those of the present system of (managed) floating, imperfect as it is.

Jeffrey A. Frankel, 1996

FIXED OR FLEXIBLE EXCHANGE RATES?

LEARNING OBJECTIVES

- To learn the differing impacts of fixed and flexible exchange rates on international trade, international investment, and resource allocation.

- To grasp how the macroeconomic responses to foreign and domestic shocks are influenced by the exchange rate system in place.

- To recognize the advantages and disadvantages of a currency board.

- To understand the strengths and weaknesses of exchange rate systems that combine elements of both fixed and flexible exchange rates.

INTRODUCTION

Slovenia's Changeover to the Euro—A Clear Success

The changeover to the euro in Slovenia went smoothly and, although the prices, of some goods and services increased, overall inflation remained broadly stable. For the other countries waiting to adopt the euro, the experience shows that the "Big Bang" approach—that is, irrevocably locking the exchange rate and simultaneously introducing the euro banknotes and coins—works, and that a two-week dual circulation period is sufficient provided that the changeover is timely and well prepared. In some aspects, for example, return of legacy cash, Slovenia even performed better than when the euro cash was introduced in 2002, thereby minimizing costs and burdens on business.

"Slovenia's adoption of the euro was a swift and smooth affair. This once more underlines the importance of early and careful preparations and of timely information and communication on the euro," said European Economics and Monetary Affairs Commissioner Joaquin Alumnia. Slovenia became the 13th member of the euro area when it adopted the euro on January 1, 2007. Contrary to the first group of countries that started fixing irrevocably the conversion rate of their currency into the euro in 1999 (2001 for Greece) and got the euro cash only three years later (one year for Greece), Slovenia selected a Big Bang scenario, where the two steps took place simultaneously. All EU countries that have yet to adopt the euro and have drawn up a so-called National Changeover Plan also plan for a Big Bang scenario. This makes sense because the euro has been in circulation for five years.[1]

Slovenia's transition was in contrast to the exchange rate approach taken by Slovakia (Slovak Republic). Slovakia first fixed its own currency's value to the euro. It then proceeded to adopt a new currency altogether, one that floats.

A prominent issue in any consideration of the effective use of economic policy in the open economy, as well as in discussions of the desirable nature of the international monetary system, is the degree of exchange rate flexibility that should be permitted. We have dealt with this issue in preceding chapters, and in the next chapter we deal with it again in the recent historical context. However, it is useful at this point to bring together a variety of relevant arguments. The first section of this chapter does so by examining the arguments for fixed or flexible rates in the context of major substantive issues. In this discussion the term *fixed exchange rates* refers to a system that permits only very small, if any, deviations from officially declared currency values. By *flexible exchange rates* we mean rates that are *completely* free to vary or float; that is, the foreign exchange market is cleared at all times by changes in the exchange rate and not by any buying and selling of currencies by the monetary authorities. We then examine the controversy in the broader context of the theory of optimum currency areas. Finally, we look at cases of exchange rate flexibility located between the two extremes. The overall intent of the chapter is to acquaint you with the various economic implications of the choice regarding the exchange rate regime that a country should select. The choice is not an easy one, and "middle-ground" solutions are possible as well as the two extremes of fixed rates and completely flexible rates.

CENTRAL ISSUES IN THE FIXED-FLEXIBLE EXCHANGE RATE DEBATE

Do Fixed or Flexible Exchange Rates Provide for Greater "Discipline" on the Part of Policymakers?

A point made in favor of fixed exchange rates is that such a system provides for the "discipline" needed in economic policy to prevent continuing inflation. That is, in a fixed-rate system, there should be no tendency for greater inflation to occur in one country than in the world as a whole. Consider a country with a balance-of-payments (BOP) deficit. If the cause of the deficit is a more rapid inflation than that in trading partners, then the country's authorities will need to apply anti-inflationary policy to protect the country's international

---

[1]European Commission, "Slovenia's Changeover to the Euro—A Clear Success," press release, May 10, 2007.

reserve position. The fixed-rate system virtually forces this type of policy action, because failure to do so will lead to an eventual elimination of the country's international reserves if the automatic adjustment mechanism takes considerable time.

What about the situation in a BOP surplus country? Given the objective of a fixed exchange rate, the forces working in the opposite direction from that for a deficit country are set into motion. Accumulation of foreign exchange reserves (which may be difficult to sterilize) will expand the money supply. This enhancement of the money supply will drive the interest rate downward, increase aggregate demand and prices, increase private purchases of goods and foreign financial assets, and thus eliminate the surplus.

Note that the result in the preceding discussion is a tendency for *deflation* in the deficit country and *inflation* in the surplus country. Therefore, if prices are flexible in both directions, it is likely that prices will be relatively stable in the world as a whole. In practice, the world could have some inflation if prices are less flexible downward than upward. However, the inflation will probably not be as rapid as it would be if the discipline of the fixed rates did not exist.

In addition to this emphasis on the discipline of fixed exchange rates, proponents of such a system stress that *flexible* rates could actually aggravate inflationary tendencies in a country. The point is made that, under flexible rates, inflation in a country becomes self-perpetuating; this argument is sometimes called the **vicious circle hypothesis.** Suppose that a country is undergoing rapid inflation because of an excess supply of money and excess demand in the economy. The inflation will cause the country's currency to depreciate in the exchange markets, which will add to aggregate demand in the economy and generate further inflationary pressure. In addition, the rise in prices will lead to correspondingly higher money wages, which also induces more inflation (see the preceding chapter). Thus, inflation will cause depreciation, but the depreciation itself will cause further inflation. This sequence of events continues until the monetary authorities put a stop to the monetary expansion.

Two major replies can be made to these points. First, with respect to the vicious circle hypothesis, flexible-rate advocates think that the depreciation that was a response to the inflation and that is alleged to cause further inflation can actually be a clear signal to the authorities that monetary restraint is needed. This signal can therefore lead to the quick instigation of anti-inflationary policies. Thus, in this view, the danger of inflation is no greater under flexible than under fixed rates.

In response to the alleged discipline provided by the fixed-rate system, it can be questioned whether such discipline is necessarily always desirable. Countries also have other domestic goals besides maintenance of the fixed exchange rate and price stability, such as the generation of high levels of employment and of reasonably rapid economic growth. A BOP deficit implies that whether the adjustment is accomplished through the automatic reduction of the money supply or through contractionary discretionary macroeconomic policies, the attainment of these other domestic goals may have to be sacrificed or at least pursued in a less determined fashion. If the deficit country is already in a state of high unemployment and slow economic growth, the contractionary tendencies will serve to worsen the internal situation. The United States faced this dilemma in a number of years in the 1960s.

On the other hand, if a country has a BOP surplus, there is upward pressure on the price level because of the expanding money supply. While this could potentially be helpful from the standpoint of employment and growth, it will aggravate internal performance with respect to the goal of price stability. For example, Germany has often had a BOP surplus but at the same time did not want its inflation rate to rise. Thus, whether a country is in BOP deficit or surplus, the attainment of some internal goal will be frustrated because of the fixed-rate system.

The resolution of the question of whether discipline and hence price stability is more prevalent with fixed rates than with flexible rates requires extensive empirical research. It can be noted that world inflation was more rapid in the floating-rate period of the 1970s than in the pegged rate period of the 1960s, but events occurring independently of the exchange rate system—such as the behavior of OPEC—undoubtedly played a role in generating this difference in world inflation.

Would Fixed or Flexible Exchange Rates Provide for Greater Growth in International Trade and Investment?

A long-standing point made by proponents of fixed rates is that flexible rates are less conducive to the expansion of world trade and foreign direct investment than are fixed rates. In particular, a flexible exchange rate system is judged to bring with it a considerable amount of risk and uncertainty. Suppose that a U.S. exporter is considering a sale of goods to an Estonian buyer for future delivery in 30 days and that the exporter requires a price of $1,000 per unit to be willing to make the sale. If the Estonian buyer is willing to pay 6,000 krooni per unit *and* if the expected exchange rate in 30 days is 6 krooni = $1, then there is a basis for a contract and the sale will be made. However, if the exchange rate changes to 6.5 krooni = $1 by the end of the 30 days, then the U.S. firm will have made an unwise decision, because only $923.08 (=6,000 krooni ÷ 6.5 krooni/$) rather than $1,000 will be received.

In the context of this example, the case for fixed rates is that current decisions can be more certain as to their prospective future outcomes because the risk of a change in the value of the foreign currency (a depreciation in this case) is relatively small. With a flexible rate instead of a fixed rate and with the natural characteristic of risk aversion of most firms and individuals, the exporting firm will require some insurance against the exchange rate change. This insurance can take the form of holding out for a slightly higher expected price than $1,000 or of hedging in the forward market (which incurs the transaction cost of hedging), although active forward markets exist only for major currencies. Further, it should be noted that the rapid increase in international financial derivatives (discussed in Chapter 21) now provides a wide variety of instruments for hedging the risks associated with international financial transactions. In any event, there is a cost, which means that, other things equal, a smaller volume of trade will occur under flexible rates than under fixed rates. With a reduced volume of international trade, there is less international specialization and lower world welfare.

Aside from focusing on the potential reduction in the volume of trade, proponents of fixed rates also judge that the amount of long-term foreign direct investment will be less under flexible rates than under fixed rates. Any firm contemplating the building of a plant overseas, for example, will be concerned about the size of the return flow of repatriated profits in the future. If the exchange rate varies, then the real value of the return flow when converted into home currency may be less than anticipated when the original investment was made (if prices in the two countries have not moved proportionately with the exchange rate). In view of this prospect, firms will be more timid about investing overseas, and consequently capital may not flow to areas where the "true" rate of return is greatest. World resource allocation will hence be less efficient under flexible rates, and a fixed-rate system can prevent this reduced efficiency. The risk and uncertainty argument is thought to be stronger in the case of long-term investment than in the case of international trade because long-term forward currency contracts and other instruments for hedging are more difficult to acquire and more costly than short-term contracts to cover trade risk.

However, with respect to this alleged adverse effect of flexible rates on foreign investment, a directly opposite case can also be made. (See McCulloch 1983, pp. 9–10.) Given overseas profit and price volatility in terms of domestic currency due to a floating exchange rate, firms may decide to reduce risk and uncertainty by producing in the foreign country itself. The foreign market will then be supplied from the foreign plant. In this interpretation, the existence of floating rates in recent decades might actually have *increased* the amount of foreign direct investment. Indeed, foreign direct investment, especially into the United States, has grown during the floating-rate period, but of course we do not know what that investment would have been under fixed rates.

In further reply to the arguments concerning the volume of trade and investment, proponents of flexible rates note that governments under *fixed* rates have often been unwilling to undergo the internal macroeconomic adjustments necessary for dealing with BOP deficits. The deficit situation eventually requires contraction of national income, yet a country with unemployment and slow economic growth may seek to postpone such income adjustment by using expansionary policy to sterilize the effect of the BOP deficit on the domestic money supply. However, as reserves continue to decline, countries have resorted to import restrictions and controls on capital outflows as devices for reducing BOP deficits. It is debatable whether such trade and investment restrictions have been successful in accomplishing their BOP objective, but they clearly interfere with efficient resource allocation and reduce welfare.

In view of this behavior under fixed exchange rates, the argument is made that restrictions on trade and capital movements for BOP purposes are unnecessary in a flexible-rate system. Movements in the exchange rate will eliminate the BOP deficit, thus undermining the rationale for the restrictions. Trade can then take place in accordance with comparative advantage and capital can flow to locations where its marginal productivity is highest. Nevertheless, if the rationale for the restrictions under fixed rates is protectionism and the BOP objective is only being used as a cover for this rationale, the adoption of floating rates may not lead to a removal of the restrictions.

The question of whether or not flexible rates reduce the volume of international trade and investment in comparison with a fixed-rate system is difficult to answer, because the economist cannot take a country into a laboratory and conduct a test with all other conditions held constant. Nevertheless, the literature has tried to evaluate the argument, especially with respect to the volume of trade.

IN THE REAL WORLD:

EXCHANGE RISK AND INTERNATIONAL TRADE

Economists disagree over whether fluctuations in exchange rates and their associated risks reduce the amount of international trade below what it would otherwise be. Peter Hooper and Steven Kohlhagen's frequently cited article (1978) indicated that exchange rate variability had no significant effects on trade. More recent work in the late 1980s disputed this conclusion.

A paper by Jerry Thursby and Marie Thursby (1987) suggested that trade is inhibited by exchange rate volatility. This paper is of broad scope, focusing on the determinants of trade, including the role of exchange rate risk, of 17 industrialized countries over the period 1974–1982. The model tested was one of bilateral trade, where equations were developed for each country's trade with each of the other 16 countries. Income (total and per capita), distance between the trading partners, import and export prices, and home consumer prices were among the independent variables included. For consideration of exchange risk, the variability of the spot rate around a predicted trend was the independent variable, and variability in both the nominal and the real exchange rate was examined.

Of interest for this chapter, the Thursbys found that 15 of the 17 countries had negative relationships between size of trade and nominal rate variability, with the results for 10 of the 15 countries being statistically significant. The results using the real exchange rate were virtually identical to those using the nominal rate. Thursby and Thursby concluded that there was "strong support for the hypothesis that exchange risk affects the value of bilateral trade" (p. 494).

Another test of the effect of exchange risk on trade was conducted by David Cushman (1988). He examined U.S. bilateral exports and imports with six trading partners

(continued)

IN THE REAL WORLD: *(continued)*

(Canada, France, Federal Republic of Germany, Japan, the Netherlands, the United Kingdom) from 1974 to 1983. Five different measures of risk involving the real exchange rate were used, with each measure incorporating different assumptions about expectations patterns of traders (for example, expectations based on recent spot rate variability, forward rate behavior in relation to the spot rate) and time horizons. Allowance for the influence on trade of other factors such as real income, capacity utilization, and unit labor costs was made. Of the 12 U.S. bilateral flows, 10 showed negative effects of exchange rate risk on trade, with 7 of the 10 having statistical significance. Cushman concluded (p. 328) that "in the absence of risk, U.S. imports would have been about 9% higher, and U.S. exports about 3% higher on average during the period."

Nevertheless, debate has continued. For example, Joseph Gagnon (1993) argued from a theoretical model with numerical analysis that the variability in exchange rates of industrial countries could have had no significant effect on the volume of trade. However, a 1996 IMF study (Ito, Isard, Symanski, and Bayoumi 1996) examined exchange rate variability and trade among the then-18 member countries of the Asia-Pacific Economic Cooperation Forum (APEC) and concluded that there was very strong evidence that medium-term exchange rate volatility does affect trade and can definitely cause complications for the economies of the countries. In addition, the volatility can affect the pattern of foreign direct investment by causing firms to diversify such investment on a geographic basis so as to reduce their exposure to risk.

Not convinced, however, Udo Broll and Bernhard Eckwert (1999) built a theoretical case that greater exchange rate volatility, under some circumstances, can actually *increase* the volume of trade. Their analysis considers a domestic firm that can sell in competitive home and/or world markets. When the home currency depreciates, this increases the domestic

currency price of the export good and the firm enjoys larger profit margins from export sales than it did prior to the depreciation. The firm responds by selling larger quantities in the export markets. When the home currency later appreciates, in analogous fashion, profit margins from exporting will fall. However, the firm can avoid the falling export profit margins by selling its product on the home market—exporting is only an option, not a requirement. If the exchange rate varies sizably, the profit from exporting in the favorable situation will be larger than it would be with subdued exchange rate volatility, since there is a chance for a bigger payoff from home currency depreciation. In the meantime, losses from appreciation can be avoided by selling at home instead. Overall, the firm in general can be more profitable with greater rather than less exchange rate volatility, and Broll and Eckwert demonstrate that the average amount of exporting by the firm can also be larger with the greater volatility (although the result does depend on certain assumptions regarding aversion to risk).

Clearly the issue has become an empirical question. While the conventional expectation that exchange rate uncertainty will dampen trade due to risk aversion still exists, the empirical literature has not produced a clear answer. Wang and Barrett (2002) suggest that a portion of the controversy is related to data that is too aggregated and point to a need to correct for a variety of econometric issues that plague this literature. Using sector- and market-specific monthly data on trade between Taiwan and the United States (1989–1998), Wang and Barrett examine the impact of expected exchange rate risk on Taiwanese exports. In seven of eight sectors examined, exchange rate volatility proves to be statistically insignificant. The only exception is agriculture, which appears to respond negatively and significantly to expected exchange rate volatility. Their results show that failure to address issues of non-normality in the regression residuals result in a substantial overstatement of the negative effect of exchange rate risk on trade flows. ●

Would Fixed or Flexible Exchange Rates Provide for Greater Efficiency in Resource Allocation?

Another argument put forward for fixed exchange rates is that the wasteful resource movements associated with flexible exchange rates are avoided. This argument states that, with a system where exchange rates can vary substantially, there can be constantly changing incentives for the tradeable goods sectors. If the country's currency depreciates in the exchange markets, then factors of production will be induced to move into the tradeable goods sectors and out of the nontradeable goods sectors because the production of exports and import substitutes is now more profitable. However, if the currency then appreciates, the incentives reverse themselves and resources move out of tradeables and into nontradeables. Therefore, if fluctuations in the exchange rate occur, there will be constant movement of factors between the sectors and this movement involves economic waste because factors are temporarily displaced, labor may need to be retrained, and so forth. Further, if resources are unwilling to undergo continuous movement, there is a more permanent misallocation and inefficiency. These various reductions in efficiency and welfare could be avoided if the exchange rate were not allowed to change in the first place.

However, in response, proponents of flexible rates attack a fixed-rate system because of its key characteristic that it fixes the most important price in any economy, the exchange rate. The main point is that, from microeconomic theory, the fixing of any price interferes with efficient resource allocation because optimum resource use is attained when prices are free to reflect true scarcity values. The absence of a flexible price for foreign exchange in a fixed-rate system generates widespread price distortions and gives misleading signals and therefore inhibits efficient resource allocation. (Such a situation is common in developing countries, where fixed exchange rates have often been chosen over flexible rates.) The interference with efficiency can be best seen in the situation where a country's currency is overvalued but the fixed-rate system does not permit a devaluation. In this instance, export industries are penalized because of the arbitrary level of the exchange rate, and yet comparative advantage theory tells us that the export sector contains the relatively most efficient industries in the economy. This argument is given further strength by noting that comparative advantage is not a static phenomenon. Rather, any country's comparative advantage industries are changing over time as new resources, new technology, and new skills emerge. Such dynamic changes lead to and are caused by variations in relative prices. If the exchange rate is fixed, then the resource-allocating role of changing relative prices is prevented from generating its maximum benefits.

In addition, a second efficiency objection to a fixed-rate system is that resources need to be tied up in the form of international reserves. The successful operation of a fixed exchange rate system requires that countries maintain working balances of reserves to finance deficits in the balance of payments. Even if a deficit is temporary (perhaps because of seasonal factors in the trade pattern) and will reverse itself, reserve assets are needed to meet the temporary excess demand for foreign exchange so as to maintain the pegged exchange rate. In addition to these working balances, which reflect the **transactions demand for international reserves,** countries may also wish to hold extra reserves to guard against any unexpected negative developments in the balance of payments. Hence, there is also a **precautionary demand for international reserves.**

In this context, economic behavior by governments dictates that calculations be made of the costs versus benefits of holding reserves (the benefits being that macroeconomic adjustments such as a reduction in national income do not have to take place because temporary sterilization can be accomplished). The costs are the *opportunity costs* of holding part of the country's wealth in the form of reserves rather than in the form of productive capital stock. The forgone capital stock would have earned the marginal productivity of capital in the country, and this lost output is a measure of the cost of holding international reserves to defend a pegged exchange rate. Quantitative assessments can be made of these benefits and costs, and the country will be holding its **optimal size of international reserves** when the marginal benefit is equal to the marginal cost. The marginal cost will not be zero, however, so the fixed-rate system implies a burden in terms of forgone output.

In this framework, the argument in favor of flexible rates is that such a system eliminates the need for central banks to hold international reserves. If the exchange rate clears the market, resources are therefore freed to be used more productively elsewhere in the economy. Hence, the forgone capital stock and the forgone output which that capital would have produced do not have to be sacrificed.

Is Macroeconomic Policy More Effective in Influencing National Income under Fixed or Flexible Exchange Rates?

Another argument made in favor of fixed rates is that fiscal policy is more effective in influencing the level of national income under fixed rates than under flexible rates. The basic point is that expansionary fiscal policy, for example, shifts the *IS* curve to the right in the *IS/LM/BP* diagram. With relatively mobile capital internationally (*BP* curve flatter than the *LM* curve), the policy generates a BOP surplus under fixed rates because of the rise in the interest rate and the subsequent net inflow of short-term capital, which expands the money supply and aids in the effort to expand national income. With a flexible exchange rate, the appreciation caused by the capital flow would work to return national income toward its original level. If international capital is relatively immobile, a BOP deficit occurs under fixed rates, weakening the income effect of the expansionary fiscal policy; with flexible rates, a depreciation of the home currency adds stimulus to income. Ultimately, of course, the outcome depends on the degree of mobility of short-term capital. At least among the industrialized countries, such capital is very mobile, and so the superior effectiveness of fiscal policy under fixed rates seems to be a valid argument.

However, whatever the degree of international capital mobility, monetary policy is more effective for influencing the level of national income in a flexible-rate system than in a fixed-rate system. This point was examined extensively in the previous two chapters. An expansion of the money supply to increase national income generates a depreciation of the home currency, and this will act to reinforce the income-increasing impact of the monetary expansion. A similar reinforcement mechanism applies in the case of contractionary monetary policy.

Hence, to an important extent, the comparative effectiveness of macro policy is a debatable issue only if fiscal policy is preferred to monetary policy as the instrument of choice. This decision on fiscal policy vis-à-vis monetary policy involves various other considerations with respect to direct versus indirect government influence on the economy and the proper role of government. The preference will vary from country to country.

Another argument that has been made for flexible rates is that such a system permits monetary and fiscal policies to be directed solely toward the attainment of internal economic goals. The point was made earlier that under fixed rates, policy authorities might have to sacrifice the attainment of internal objectives (e.g., full employment) to satisfy the external objective of BOP equilibrium. On the other hand, if the exchange rate is flexible, the exchange rate itself will take care of any balance-of-payments problems: A deficit (surplus) situation will promptly set a depreciation (appreciation) of the home currency into operation, and this depreciation (appreciation) will remove the deficit (surplus). Hence, there is no need to use monetary and fiscal policies to deal with imbalances in the BOP, and these instruments can be directly used to deal with internal problems (that is, the "balance-of-payments constraint" on policy has been removed).

Proponents of this argument point to the fact that effective policymaking requires that the number of instruments match the number of targets (see Chapter 25). The virtue of the floating-rate system is that an additional (automatic) instrument—the exchange rate—has been added. Thus, if the three targets are BOP equilibrium, full employment, and price stability, the three instruments are the exchange rate, fiscal policy, and monetary policy. Because the exchange rate is now handling BOP problems, fiscal policy can be directed toward raising the level of employment and monetary policy can be directed toward achieving price stability. Hence, the arsenal of instruments is enhanced under a floating-rate system.

In assessing this argument, note that a conflict will not necessarily arise between the policies needed for attaining BOP equilibrium and those needed for reaching internal targets. For example, a country with a BOP deficit *and* rapid inflation will require a contractionary policy stance for reaching both the external target and the internal target of price stability, although the degree of contraction necessary for reaching each respective target may differ. Similarly, a country with a BOP surplus and excessive unemployment will find that expansionary policies will work to remove the surplus as well as the unemployment, although again the extent of policy action may differ for each respective target. In the other cases—BOP deficit together with unemployment and BOP surplus together with inflation—the fixed-rate system imposes a constraint on the conduct of policy for the attainment of the internal target. Imaginative devices such as the use of monetary policy to attain the external target and of fiscal policy to attain the internal target (the Mundell prescription in Chapter 25) may be tried in these conflict situations, but they may also not be very successful.

CONCEPT CHECK

1. What is meant by "discipline" in the world economy, and how might fixed exchange rates work to promote such discipline?
2. Why might a fixed-rate system potentially enhance the growth of foreign trade and investment in the world economy?
3. How can the existence of the transactions and precautionary demands for international reserves reduce world output over what would otherwise be the case?
4. Explain why it can be uncertain whether fiscal policy is more effective for influencing national income under fixed exchange rates than under flexible exchange rates.

Will Destabilizing Speculation in Exchange Markets Be Greater under Fixed or Flexible Exchange Rates?

A major concern expressed by some economists is that a system of flexible exchange rates will be characterized by **destabilizing speculation.** This argument stresses that the normal fluctuations that occur with flexible rates are augmented by the behavior of speculators attempting to make profits on the basis of their anticipations of future exchange rates. If a currency depreciates (appreciates), speculators will project forward the depreciation (appreciation) and will conclude that their optimal strategy is to sell (buy) the currency. These sales (purchases) will worsen the depreciation (appreciation). The result of this

---

IN THE REAL WORLD:

RESERVE HOLDINGS UNDER FIXED AND FLEXIBLE EXCHANGE RATES

As noted in the text, the elimination of the need to hold international reserves and therefore of the opportunity costs of holding reserves is an advantage of a flexible-rate system over a fixed-rate system. It is therefore instructive to examine the comparative size of international reserves in a regime of fixed exchange rates and in a regime where exchange rates can vary considerably. Table 1, column (2), lists international reserves held by central banks during the 1960–1972 years of the Bretton Woods pegged exchange rate system in the world economy (see the next chapter) and since 1973, when currencies began floating subsequent to the breakdown of Bretton Woods. For relative comparison purposes, total world merchandise imports are also given in column (3), as is the ratio of reserves to imports in column (4). This reserves/imports ratio is often used as a rough indicator of the ability of countries to finance BOP deficits under a fixed-rate system.

With the advent of flexible rates in 1973, you would expect that the reserve ratios would have declined dramatically, because a flexible-rate system in theory requires no reserves. However, the table indicates that, in absolute size, reserves increased dramatically in the 1973–2006 period, rising from $184.2 billion at the end of 1973 to $5,134.3 billion at the end of 2006. Nevertheless, reserve holdings relative to imports have been somewhat lower in the floating-rate period (33.3 percent for the period as a whole) than in the 1960–1972 fixed-rate period (37.6 percent). The fall in the reserve/imports ratio suggests that at least the *relative* opportunity cost of holding reserves has declined. Of course, since countries still do intervene to influence exchange rates (that is, the system is not a complete flexible-rate system, especially with respect to developing countries), it would not be expected that reserve holdings would disappear.

(continued)

IN THE REAL WORLD: *(continued)*

TABLE 1   Absolute and Relative Reserves of Central Banks, 1960–2006

(1) Year	*(2)* World Reserves*	*(3)* World Imports†	*(4)* Ratio	*(1)* Year	*(2)* World Reserves*	*(3)* World Imports†	*(4)* Ratio
1960	$ 60.0	$ 125.9	47.7%	1973	$ 184.2	$ 562.9	32.7%
1961	62.0	130.6	47.5	1974	220.1	827.7	26.6
1962	62.9	137.4	45.8	1975	227.6	875.2	26.0
1963	66.8	149.4	44.7	1976	258.1	981.9	26.3
1964	69.1	167.0	41.4	1977	321.3	1,124.3	28.6
1965	71.2	181.7	39.2	1978	367.2	1,297.0	28.3
1966	72.8	203.8	35.7	1979	403.1	1,638.3	24.6
1967	74.6	213.1	35.0	1980	452.4	2,014.7	22.5
1968	77.8	236.3	32.9	1981	422.6	1,996.2	21.2
1969	78.7	268.6	29.3	1982	398.4	1,878.9	21.2
1970	93.2	313.5	29.7	1983	414.2	1,817.1	22.8
1971	134.2	344.8	38.9	1984	431.6	1,937.9	22.3
1972	159.2	407.9	39.0	1985	481.3	1,964.6	24.5
				1986	552.8	2,143.5	25.8
				1987	767.1	2,512.3	30.5
				1988	775.1	2,877.4	26.9
				1989	820.1	3,113.9	26.3
				1990	979.2	3,530.7	27.7
				1991	1,038.5	3,651.0	28.4
				1992	1,036.1	3,880.2	26.7
				1993	1,141.6	3,830.6	29.8
				1994	1,302.7	4,228.1	30.8
				1995	1,520.8	5,046.5	30.1
				1996	1,693.0	5,299.2	31.9
				1997	1,749.3	5,644.7	31.0
				1998	1,805.6	5,575.9	32.4
				1999	1,928.3	5,797.2	33.3
				2000	2,065.5	6,573.3	31.4
				2001	2,186.4	6,332.7	34.5
				2002	2,567.3	6,570.7	39.1
				2003	3,201.4	7,671.6	41.7
				2004	3,915.5	9,370.1	41.8
				2005	4,288.1	10,631.2	40.3
				2006	5,134.3	12,223.3	42.0
Average, 1960–1972	$ 83.3	$ 221.5	37.6%	Average, 1973–2006	$ 1,325.0	$ 3,983.0	33.3%

*In billions of dollars. Reserves consist of gold, foreign exchange holdings, reserve position in the International Monetary Fund (IMF), and holdings of special drawing rights (SDRs). The valuation of reserves is at the end of each year in SDRs, converted to dollars at the prevailing $/SDR rate. Gold is valued at 35 SDRs = 1 ounce of gold. The reserve components are explained in more detail in the next chapter.

†In billions of dollars, valued c.i.f.

Sources: International Monetary Fund publications: *International Financial Statistics Yearbook 1988* (Washington, DC: IMF, 1988), pp. 68, 124, 716–17; *International Financial Statistics Yearbook 2002* (Washington, DC: IMF, 2002), pp. 72–73, 132–33, 1034–35; *International Financial Statistics Yearbook 2006* (Washington, DC: IMF, 2006), pp. 2, 42, 83; *International Financial Statistics,* May 2007, pp. 2, 39, 65.

speculative behavior is that cyclical fluctuations in exchange rates will have greater amplitude than otherwise would be the case.

This argument is illustrated in Figure 1. Line R shows regular (nonspeculative) fluctuations around the long-run equilibrium value of the exchange rate $\bar{e}$. Suppose that, from initial point A, the home currency begins to depreciate toward point B. With destabilizing speculation, speculators judge that, at a point like B, the currency will continue to depreciate. They sell the currency in anticipation of buying it back later at a lower price, driving e beyond the normal peak (point C). After the currency turns around and begins to appreciate, at point F the speculators will expect continued appreciation and will buy the home currency in anticipation of a future sale at a higher home-currency price. This action will carry the exchange rate below the normal trough of e at point G. The cycle with destabilizing speculation is represented by R' (which need not have peaks and troughs at the same time as R or the same cycle lengths). Such behavior of the exchange rate, even without destabilizing speculation, is also characteristic of the overshooting phenomenon, discussed in Chapter 22.

However, a contrary case can also be made for **stabilizing speculation.** Suppose that, after the movement from A to B, speculators think that the currency has "depreciated enough" in view of the fundamentals of the economy and that it is now time to *buy* the currency. Speculative purchases of the home currency at B will cause the upswing of the cyclical movement to be diminished rather than enhanced. The sale of the currency on the downswing of the cyclical movement at point F will also dampen the cycle in that direction.

FIGURE 1   Destabilizing and Stabilizing Speculation

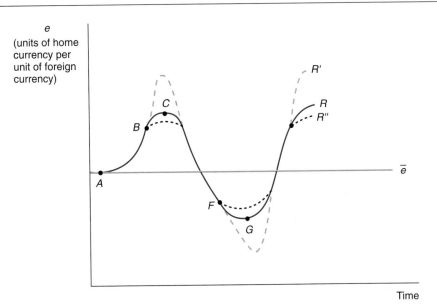

Normal fluctuations in the exchange rate around its equilibrium value $\bar{e}$ are pictured by line R. With destabilizing speculation, when a depreciation of the home currency occurs between point A and point B, speculators project a further depreciation and sell the home currency. This causes the home currency to depreciate to a level beyond that associated with its "normal" low value at point C. In the downswing of e, speculators project forward the appreciation of the home currency and purchase it at F. These purchases lead to a home currency value greater than its "normal" high value at point G. The resulting line R' has greater amplitude than R. If speculation were stabilizing, speculators would purchase the home currency at B and sell it at F, generating line R'' with a smaller amplitude than R.

With stabilizing speculation, the entire cycle is represented by dotted line R'', and greater stability exists than with the normal cycle R.

Debate on the nature of speculation has gone on for a number of years, and there is no unanimity of views. Milton Friedman, a longtime proponent of flexible rates, maintained that destabilizing speculation cannot persist indefinitely. Such speculation would imply that speculators are selling the home currency when its price is low (at point B in Figure 1) and buying the home currency when its price is high (at point F). Surely this is not the way to make a profit! Stabilizing speculation, on the other hand, involves the profitable activity of buying the currency at a low price and selling it at a high price. Thus, because speculation continues to exist in the real world, it must be profitable and therefore stabilizing. This conclusion on the profitability of speculation and its implication regarding stability have been disputed in more complex analyses. At issue is the nature of expectations. If a change in a variable leads to the expectation that the variable will return to (depart farther from) some "normal" level, the speculation will be of the stabilizing (destabilizing) sort. We do not know what circumstances will generate one or the other type of expectation.

Recent studies have explored the question of expectations in relation to policy actions. If speculators can figure out how the monetary authorities will react to an exchange rate change, then this knowledge can be profitable. For example, if a depreciation of the dollar causes the Federal Reserve to buy dollars and if speculators anticipate that action, the speculators will buy dollars ahead of the Federal Reserve to profit from the forthcoming rise in the dollar's price. The result is consistent with "stability." Other matters, such as the degree of confidence speculators place in the Federal Reserve, are also involved. Finally, much work has been done on how expectations are formed. Are expectations "adaptive" (based on recent past behavior) or are they "rational" and forward-looking (based on all available information on how the economy works and how policy authorities react)?

Because speculation may be destabilizing in a flexible-rate system, do we therefore conclude that it is stabilizing in a fixed-rate system? Some economists think that fixed rates do indeed invite stabilizing speculation, because the floor and ceiling for a rate suggest that the rate will never go outside those limits. Hence, when a currency falls to its floor value, speculators know that it will go no lower and could turn around, so they will likely buy it. This will turn the currency's value upward. This scenario in reverse would occur at the ceiling.

However, this argument rests on the assumption that central banks can indeed enforce the floor and ceiling limits. But this may not be the case. Suppose that, as in the Bretton Woods system, currencies are permitted to vary ± 1 percent from their parity values. If the parity value of the British pound is \$2.00 = £1, then the floor price of the pound is \$1.98 and the ceiling is \$2.02. In addition, suppose that because of greater inflation in Britain than in the United States, the pound starts to fall in value from parity toward the floor and that it eventually hits the floor. At this point, the British authorities will be using some of their international reserves to buy pounds to keep the pound from falling further. However, if Britain does nothing to slow down its inflation rate, speculators will sell large volumes of pounds on the exchange markets because the speculators essentially have a *one-way bet*. The massive sales of pounds by speculators then will ensure that the prediction of a fall in the value of the pound is a self-fulfilling prophecy, because the continued sales will exhaust British reserves as the Bank of England futilely tries to purchase sufficient pounds. The speculators will have sold pounds at \$1.98 and will later be able to buy them back at a lower price.

This speculative behavior against weak currencies thus makes it very difficult to keep the fixed exchange rates intact. And the Bretton Woods system did indeed have a number of

TITANS OF INTERNATIONAL ECONOMICS:

MILTON FRIEDMAN (1912–2006)

Milton Friedman was born in Brooklyn, New York, on July 31, 1912, the son of a poor immigrant family. He earned his A.B. at Rutgers in 1932, his master's degree at the University of Chicago in 1933, and his Ph.D. at Columbia in 1946. During the time between his master's and his Ph.D., he worked for the National Resources Committee in Washington, the National Bureau of Economic Research in New York, the U.S. Treasury Department, and the War Research division of Columbia University, as well as performing short-term teaching stints at the universities of Wisconsin and Minnesota. After finishing his Ph.D., he taught at the University of Chicago from 1948 to 1982 and was the Paul Russell Snowden Distinguished Service Professor of Economics from 1962 to 1982. He became a Senior Research Fellow at the Hoover Institution at Stanford University in 1977 and remained an active scholar until his death on November 16, 2006.

Milton Friedman's contributions to economics are legendary and of extremely wide scope. His early work concentrated on statistical methods, but he then ventured into other areas. Still widely discussed is his 1953 book, *A Theory of the Consumption Function,* in which he developed the hypothesis that consumption spending by households depended not on current income but on the longer-term notion of permanent income, an expectation of income flows over many years. In this light, short-term transitory changes in current income would have virtually no impact on current consumption. Even more well known is Friedman's work on money and economic activity, and he is hailed as having been the driving force behind monetarism and its emphasis on monetary policy rather than on fiscal policy for influencing the macroeconomy. His work was both historical [e.g., Friedman and Anna J. Schwartz, *A Monetary History of the United States, 1867–1960* (1963)] and theoretical (e.g., "The Role of Monetary Policy," *American Economic Review,* March 1968). It led to such familiar doctrines as the modern quantity theory of money and the automatic "rule" for monetary growth. Friedman is also widely regarded as the father of the concept of the "natural" rate of unemployment, an attack on the notion of a downward-sloping Phillips curve reflecting a trade-off between inflation and unemployment. In addition, he was the leading proponent of flexible exchange rates.

Throughout Professor Friedman's career, he was vitally concerned that economics be "practical." His widely cited view was that theory should not be judged by its assumptions but by whether it can satisfactorily predict economic behavior in the real world. In addition, he stressed continually the role of individuals, the market, and laissez-faire, even suggesting in his popular 1962 book, *Capitalism and Freedom,* that licensing of medical practitioners should be abolished because it is a barrier to entry and thus to efficient resource allocation. He was constantly suspicious of government intervention and regulation, and his public television series, *Free to Choose,* made his views known to millions worldwide. He is also known for the absolute clarity of expression that helped to popularize his ideas. In the context of this chapter, for example, he made the case that the adoption of flexible exchange rates is analogous to the adoption of daylight saving time. Instead of going through the confusion and inefficiency of having everyone move all their activities one hour earlier every summer, why not just change the clock?

For his many contributions, Milton Friedman was elected president of the American Economic Association for 1967 and was awarded the Nobel Prize in economics in 1976. In addition, he received honorary doctorates from many colleges and universities. His awards were innumerable, and some of them are seldom given to ordinary academics—we note in particular such honors as "Chicagoan of the Year" and "Statesman of the Year." In a press release upon Friedman's death, John L. Hennessy, the president of Stanford University said, "Today Stanford lost a great scholar and our country has lost one of its leading economists. Dr. Friedman's ability to explain complicated economic theories has had a profound impact beyond the university. We will miss his candor and intelligence, but we are quite certain that his insights will live for generations."

Sources: Mark Blaug, ed., *Who's Who in Economics: A Biographical Dictionary of Major Economists 1700–1986,* 2nd ed. (Cambridge: MIT Press, 1986), pp. 291–93; John Burton, "Positively Milton Friedman," in J. R. Shackleton and Gareth Locksley, eds., *Twelve Contemporary Economists* (London: Macmillan, 1981), pp. 53–71; Alan Walters, "Milton Friedman," in John Eatwell, Murray Milgate, and Peter Newman, eds., *The New Palgrave: A Dictionary of Economics,* vol. 2 (London: Macmillan, 1987), pp. 422–27; *Who's Who in America,* 46th edition 1990–1991, vol. 1 (Wilmette, IL: Marquis Who's Who, 1990), p. 1119; *Who's Who 1997* (New York: St. Martin's Press, 1997), p. 692; Hoover Institution, "Milton Friedman, Noted Economist, Nobel Laureate, and Hoover Senior Research Fellow, Dies at 94," press release, November 16, 2006.

instances of speculative attacks on currencies and changes in parity values. Further, speculation clearly played a role in upsetting the pegged rates among some members of the European Community in 1993. In practice, the applicability of this argument against the *viability* of a fixed rate system depends in large part on the degree of confidence speculators place in governments. If government policymakers are able to implement effective measures for dealing with imbalances in the balance of payments, then speculators might behave in a stabilizing manner. Finally, the force of the argument also depends on the size of the speculative capital flows in relation to the size of the countries' international reserves. Most observers feel that the volume of potential speculative capital is currently large enough to cause difficulty for any central bank.

However, if the destabilizing speculation under fixed rates is an important phenomenon, it in a sense makes all previous points in the fixed-flexible debate rather moot, because the fixed-rate system may in fact not be viable with the existence of today's potentially huge volume of speculative capital. Indeed, many economists think that the structural and policy differences among countries make it highly unlikely that a fixed-rate system can operate successfully. An emphasis in this line of reasoning is that unemployment-inflation combinations differ across countries. In some countries (e.g., Sweden), the policy authorities aim for low levels of unemployment rather than toward the avoidance of inflation. In other countries (e.g., Germany), the preferences may be reversed. A physically small economy with a mobile labor force (e.g., Switzerland) may be able to attain a lower unemployment rate without incurring rapid inflation than can a physically large country with substantial structural unemployment (e.g., the United States). For these reasons and others (such as an ineffective tax collection system characteristic of many developing countries), some countries tend to have chronic higher inflation rates than other countries. The more rapidly inflating countries will find themselves with frequent BOP deficits, and countries with greater price stability will be running BOP surpluses. With limited international reserves, slow adjustment, and destabilizing speculation, deficit countries will ultimately have to devalue and the fixed-rate system will break down.

Will Countries Be Better Protected from External Shocks under a Fixed or a Flexible Exchange Rate System?

An important argument against a fixed exchange rate system is that, in such a system, business cycles will be transmitted from one country to other countries, meaning that no country is able to insulate itself from external real shocks. If a foreign country goes into a recession, it will buy less of the home country's exports. As a result, national income will fall in the home country. If foreign repercussions are important, the fall in income in the home country will then reduce the home country's purchases from the foreign country, which will in turn worsen the recession overseas and eventually feed back again upon the home country. The same scenario in an upward direction also occurs, resulting in the transmission of inflation from one country to another.

The fixed-rate system contributes to this transmission of business cycles because the exchange rate is a passive part of the process. In a *flexible*-rate situation, the exchange rate would take an active part in mitigating the transmission. For example, in the recession case above, the initial decline in the home country's exports (a leftward shift of its *IS* and *BP* curves) would cause a depreciation of the home currency and would stimulate the home country's production of exports and import substitutes. This would offset the downward thrust on income as the curves shifted back to their original positions. A similar offset would occur if an overseas boom had started the process. Thus, the flexible exchange rate serves to insulate the economy from external real sector shocks.

Note, however, that we have only discussed external *real* sector shocks so far in this section. Suppose instead that the external sector shock is a financial sector shock, such as a rise in interest rates abroad. As noted in Chapter 26, this causes the home country's *BP* curve to shift to the left, leading to an incipient deficit in the balance of payments as home country short-term funds move overseas. The home currency will then depreciate, shifting the *IS* curve to the right and shifting the *BP* curve rightward toward its original position. With the

LM curve unchanged, the result is a higher level of home income. On the other hand, if the exchange rate had been fixed, the initial leftward shift in the *BP* curve and the resulting BOP deficit would have resulted in monetary contraction and a fall in home income. Thus, there is "insulation" in neither exchange rate system, but home national income moves in opposite directions depending on the system being used. Which result is more desirable will depend on the state of the domestic economy at the time of the foreign financial shock.

Finally, although this section has been concerned with external shocks, it can be noted that, under flexible rates, *internal* shocks to the economy can be more *destabilizing* to national income than under fixed rates. A domestic monetary or financial shock (a shift in the *LM* curve) produces a greater income response under flexible rates than under fixed rates. The same conclusion on income response applies for an internal real sector shock if the *BP* curve is steeper than the *LM* curve (relative capital immobility). However, the real sector shock yields less income response under flexible rates than under fixed rates if the *BP* curve is flatter than the *LM* curve (relative capital mobility). Hence, to determine whether flexible or fixed rates make for greater instability with respect to internal real sector shocks in practice, some determination must be made of the international responsiveness of short-term capital to changes in interest rates.

This concludes our discussion in this chapter of major issues in the fixed versus flexible exchange rate debate. In practice, the world has moved from a system of relatively fixed rates in the 1950s and 1960s to a system of considerably greater flexibility in exchange rates since 1973. As we shall see in the last section of this chapter, however, it is unnecessary to think only in terms of fixed rates versus completely flexible exchange rates. Some hybrid systems are possible, and these hybrids have also been important in practice in recent years.

IN THE REAL WORLD:

"INSULATION" WITH FLEXIBLE RATES—THE CASE OF JAPAN

A study to determine whether an economy is more insulated from outside shocks under flexible than under fixed exchange rates was carried out by Michael Hutchison and Carl E. Walsh (1992). Reacting to some 1980s literature that questioned whether flexible rates really "insulated" an economy (e.g., Dornbusch 1983, Baxter and Stockman 1989), Hutchison and Walsh focused specifically on Japan. For the fixed-rate regime, they examined the period from the fourth quarter of 1957 through the fourth quarter of 1972; for the flexible-rate regime, they looked at the period from the fourth quarter of 1974 through the fourth quarter of 1986. While their work indicated that the proportion of variation in Japanese real GNP due to foreign shocks was considerably larger in the flexible-rate period than in the fixed rate period, this variation could have occurred because there were more severe external shocks in the flexible-rate period (such as the oil shocks and the recessions in the industrialized countries in the 1970s and early 1980s). Thus, Hutchison and Walsh concerned themselves with the effects of shocks after controlling for the size of the shocks. Their statistical work estimated the impacts on

Japan over time of a one-unit shock in oil prices (in real terms), a one-unit shock in U.S. real GNP, and a one-unit shock in the U.S. nominal money supply (M1).

What conclusions were reached? First, Hutchison and Walsh indicated that, after several quarters, a real oil price increase (by itself) caused a marked decline in the level of Japanese real GNP. However, the decline under fixed rates was significantly greater than under flexible rates. Similarly, a one-unit change in U.S. GNP was long lasting in its effect on Japan in both exchange rate systems, but the effect was greater under fixed rates. In the case of a U.S. money supply shock, the effect on Japan was the same for both exchange rate systems.

Thus, the overall conclusion of Hutchison and Walsh was that, in the case of Japan, flexible rates generally provided more "insulation" from external shocks than did fixed rates. Another interesting result from their model was that an initial one-unit Japanese real GNP shock (an *internal* shock) also had less total effect on Japan itself under flexible rates than under fixed rates. This result logically follows if the *BP* curve for Japan is flatter than the *LM* curve.   ●

CURRENCY BOARDS

In decisions regarding the type of exchange-rate system to employ, a relatively new arrangement that is of a fixed exchange rate nature has been chosen by several countries. This arrangement is a currency board. A **currency board** is a monetary authority with a mandate to issue domestic currency that can be exchanged for a foreign (reserve or anchor) currency at a fixed exchange rate. By following strict money supply rules, the currency board severely restricts the government's monetary policy authority. The board cannot conduct monetary policy by changing the monetary base (bank reserves plus currency in circulation) with the traditional tools of monetary policy such as open market operations. The monetary base increases only when the private sector sells foreign exchange to the board at a fixed rate to meet the private sector's demand for national currency. Buying foreign currency from the currency board to finance a balance-of-payments deficit reduces the monetary base. Under a currency board system, the government cannot monetize budget deficits.[2]

In a currency board arrangement, the commitment to exchange the local currency for the reserve (or anchor) currency at a fixed exchange rate normally does not include any quantitative limit. This commitment means that the monetary authority must have sufficient foreign exchange reserves to meet demand. Countries adopting currency boards have sought to maintain at least 100 percent backing of the monetary base. The 100 percent backing of the monetary base with foreign currency means that the money supply is almost completely beyond the influence of decisions by government officials and the monetary authorities.[3]

A currency board combines three elements. The first is a fixed exchange rate between the country's currency and the "anchor" currency. The second is automatic convertibility of the currency. The third is a long-term commitment to the system, in many cases made explicit by the central bank law. The main reason a country adopts a currency board is to demonstrate that it is pursuing an anti-inflationary policy.[4]

Advantages of a Currency Board

Four major advantages are usually cited when comparing a currency board arrangement with a central bank with discretionary control of the money supply.

1. A currency board *ensures convertibility*. The maintenance of a 100 percent reserve system makes it certain that assets are available to cover any demand for conversion into foreign currency.

2. A currency board *instills macroeconomic discipline*. Because the currency board is prohibited from buying domestic assets, it cannot finance a fiscal deficit. The government is forced to borrow from the public at home or abroad or maintain a balanced budget. In other words, the government cannot simply "print money" to finance a government budget deficit because the money supply is strictly tied to the quantity of foreign exchange held by the currency board. It is hence also argued that a currency board will secure discipline over inflation. The process of tying the local currency to a reserve (and presumably low inflation) currency at a fixed exchange rate enhances price stability.

3. *A guaranteed payment adjustment mechanism is provided*. The payment adjustment mechanism is simply the gold-standard adjustment mechanism that is actually a version of

---

[2]N. B. Gultekin and K. Yilmaz, http://home.ku.edu.tr/ kyilmaz/papers/parakurf.pdf.

[3]Iikka Korhonen, "Currency Boards in the Baltic Countries: What Have We Learned?" Bank of Finland Institute for Economies in Transition Discussion Papers No. 6 (1999).

[4]Anne-Marie Gulde (1999), p. 37.

IN THE REAL WORLD:

CURRENCY BOARDS IN ESTONIA AND LITHUANIA

Estonia was the first Baltic country to adopt its own currency (the kroon) after the breakup of the Soviet Union and the first to adopt a currency board system. The currency board was seen as a quick way to foster confidence in the currency. This was a key point in a newly independent country with a fragile economic and political situation.

The Estonian currency board was defined and its operating procedures set up in May 1992. The Estonian parliament passed the currency law, the law on backing of the Estonian kroon, and the foreign exchange law. The Estonian currency board was not the strictest possible version. The Bank of Estonia kept some authority over how much capital inflows are allowed to boost the monetary base, and a minimal reserve requirement was maintained for commercial banks. In any case, the currency board was required to keep sufficient foreign currency reserves to cover money in circulation (110 percent reserves in practice), and exporters must surrender their export earnings in exchange for domestic currency within two months. The Estonian kroon was pegged to the German mark at a rate of 1 mark = 8 krooni at its rollout in June 1992.

The exchange rate agreement was successful in bringing inflation rates down, especially compared with other former Soviet states. Additional evidence of the success of the currency board system is found in capital movement data. In the last half of 1992, the foreign assets of the Bank of Estonia increased by $135 million. A substantial portion of this increase was the restoration of Estonia's prewar gold reserves and cannot be directly attributed to the currency board. In 1993, foreign assets of the Bank of Estonia increased by another $133 million (6 percent of GDP). Much of this inflow was related to the sale of many companies formerly owned by the government to foreign investors, but macroeconomic stability was a critical factor in their investment decisions.

The early Estonian experience suggests that inflation can indeed be brought under control in such a system. The inflation rate dropped to "only" 90 percent in 1993, and it fell to 48 percent in 1994, 29 percent in 1995, 23 percent in 1996, and 11 percent in 1997. The inflation rates remained under control with inflation at 4.0 percent in 2000 and 1.3 percent in 2003. Inflation stood at 4.4 percent in 2006. All the economic news was not positive, as Estonia followed the other transition economies and experienced a substantial drop in real GDP in the early 1990s. Real GDP fell by 26 percent in 1992, by 8.5 percent in 1993, and by 2.7 percent in 1994. In 1995, real GDP growth became positive at 2.9 percent and has continued with average annual increases of 5.3 percent

from 1996–2000 and 8.7 percent from 2000–2005. The impressive growth rate in 2006 was 11.4 percent.

Estonia has continued to utilize a currency board to ensure price stability and thereby allow the smooth adjustment of the price level and structure with that of the other EU members. The Estonian kroon is now fixed against the euro at 1 EUR = 15.6466 EEK rather than against the German mark. In addition, Estonia has begun the process of becoming a full member of the European Monetary Union through participation in the Exchange Rate Mechanism (ERM) II. The exchange rate against the euro remains unchanged as part of the ERM II, so Estonia is maintaining the currency board arrangement until the adoption of the euro.

Lithuania took a more gradual approach to currency reform. Political disagreements prevented the introduction of a new currency until June 1993. Prior to this introduction, Lithuania had a dual exchange rate system with Russian rubles remaining in circulation alongside an interim currency called talonas (coupons). The rubles began to be withdrawn from circulation, and beginning in October 1992, the use of the ruble was forbidden. Talonas were used until June 1993, when authorities announced the introduction of the new currency, the Lithuanian lita. After July 1993, the use of talonas and foreign currency was banned.

These two years of monetary uncertainty also resulted in rather lax monetary policy. In the first quarter of 1994, the money supply (M_1) rose by 134 percent, and inflation in Lithuania was considerably higher than in Estonia. The high inflation was naturally reflected in the external value of the Lithuanian currency: The talonas depreciated markedly against the dollar. The volatility of the exchange rate and low credibility of monetary policy led to a debate about the appropriate exchange rate regime. In March 1994, Lithuania followed Estonia and adopted a currency board. The new arrangement became effective in April 1994 and pegged the litas to the U.S. dollar at a rate of $1 = 4 litas.

Even after the establishment of the currency board, Lithuania continued to experience higher inflation than Estonia until 1996. In 2000, the inflation rate was down to 1.1 percent and in 2003, prices actually fell. In 2006, however, the inflation rate was 3.8 percent. The inflow of capital into Lithuania after the introduction of the currency board was as high as Estonia's. Foreign assets of the Bank of Lithuania increased by $180 million in 1994, which was almost 7 percent of GDP. Capital inflows are positively correlated with investor confidence in the economic policies of a particular country, and the new currency

(continued)

IN THE REAL WORLD: *(continued)*

board arrangement in Lithuania seems to be associated with the increased confidence. Lithuania's real GDP experience is also similar to Estonia's. After falling in the early 1990s, real GDP grew by 7.0 percent in 1997 and has continued with growth of 6.6 percent in 2001, 10.3 percent in 2003, and 7.5 percent in 2006.

On February 2, 2002, the Lithuanian lita was repegged to the euro and in April 2004 the currency board system celebrated its 10th anniversary. In 2005, the focus turned to the development of a National Changeover Plan for euro adoption. The first version of the changeover plan was approved in September 2005 and a renewed National Changeover Plan was adopted in April 2006, along with the Public Information on the Euro Adoption and Communication Strategy of Lithuania. According to current estimates, the most favorable target for Lithuania to join the euro zone is in 2010.

Overall, the economic performance in Lithuania and Estonia seem to have been positively affected by the establishment of currency boards. The currency boards have been associated with price stabilization in both countries. In addition, the prohibition of central bank financing of public debt can probably be credited with the relatively low deficits in both Lithuania and Estonia. While both economies experienced serious drops in output during the initial stages of transition, these two economies were among the first members of

the former Soviet Union to experience GDP growth. The positive output growth was not enough to prevent increases in unemployment in both nations. It is obvious that these Baltic nations have managed their economic transitions more successfully than other former Soviet republics. While the implementation of currency boards are only part of the macroeconomic stabilization process, in these cases they contributed to gaining credibility for new currencies. The boards have helped both countries become members of the European Union and have facilitated their future entry into the euro zone.

Sources: Iikka Korhonen, "Currency Boards in the Baltic Countries: What Have We Learned?" Bank of Finland Institute for Economies in Transition Discussion Papers No. 6 (1999); International Monetary Fund, *World Economic Outlook,* September 2004, pp. 213, 215; Eesti Pank, Bank of Estonia, "Estonian Monetary System," http://www.eestipank.info/pub/en, 2006; Lithuanian Free Market Institute, "The Currency Board—Lithuania's Weightiest Reform—Marks the 10th Anniversary," http://www.freema.org/index.php/menu/newsroom/press_release, August 4, 2004; Bank of Lithuania, "The New National Changeover Plan and the Public Information on the Euro Adoption and Communication Strategy of Lithuania Have Been Approved," http://www.euro.lt/en/news/introduction-of-the-euro-in-lithuania, April 27, 2007; International Monetary Fund IMF, *World Economic Outlook,* September 2006, pp. 197, 205; IMF, *World Economic Outlook,* April 2007, pp. 219, 227, obtained from www.imf.org.

David Hume's price-specie-flow mechanism (discussed in Chapter 2). These three advantages combine to create greater confidence in the system.

4. The increased confidence leads to *the promotion of higher rates of trade, investment, and growth.*

Disadvantages of a Currency Board

When comparing a currency board with a central bank, eight potential disadvantages are cited:

1. *The seigniorage problem.* Given that the currency board earns interest on its foreign currency reserves, the cost of the currency board arrangement is the difference between the interest earned on the foreign currency and the yield on the additional investments that could have been made at home if domestic assets were to replace foreign assets in the portfolio of the monetary authority. Given the limited investment options available to central banks in many countries, the difference in yield may be small or nonexistent.

2. *The startup problem.* This refers to the difficulty associated with gathering enough reserve currency to provide the 100 percent reserves necessary to back the monetary base. The financial feasibility of beginning a currency board must be examined on a case-by-case basis.

3. *The transition problem.* This refers to the danger that at the established fixed exchange rate, the local currency may quickly become overvalued when instituted in a high-inflation economy. There is little doubt that the fixed exchange rate, when adhered to

long enough, will bring inflation under control. The question is how large the initial overvaluation will be and how long the transition period will last.

4. *The adjustment problem.* This refers to the increased cost of securing balance-of-payments adjustment when the exchange rate cannot be changed. The existence of a currency board precludes the use of the exchange rate to help correct an overvaluation.

5. *The management problem.* This is the inability to use the normal tools of monetary policy such as open market operations to conduct active monetary policy. This fifth problem may not actually be a problem in countries that have a history of abusing monetary policy. Taking the ability to increase the money supply out of the hands of the monetary authorities may be the main reason for turning to a currency board.

6. *The crisis problem.* The currency board can only issue domestic currency in exchange for foreign currency. The inability to issue domestic currency against domestic assets prevents the currency board from serving as a lender of last resort. This creates a problem if a bank is solvent but illiquid because the monetary authority cannot provide the necessary liquidity to prevent a crisis. On the other hand, this may actually force the financial system to be more prudent.

7. *The political problem.* The final two disadvantages are political in nature. The political problem is related to the question of whether fiscal policy will actually be disciplined by the establishment of a currency board. If the country has not made the commitment to a balanced budget, the currency board does not prevent the financing of a deficit by borrowing at home or even abroad. The currency board seems to be a good device to reinforce a commitment to fiscal discipline, but cannot impose that discipline where is does not exist.

8. *The monetary sovereignty problem.* The rules of a currency board take the control of the money supply out of the hands of the domestic monetary authority and increase the influence of the "anchor" economy.[5]

OPTIMUM CURRENCY AREAS

A concept that lies under the surface in the previous discussion concerning fixed versus flexible exchange rates is that of the **optimum currency area.** An optimum currency area is an area that, for optimal balance-of-payments adjustment reasons as well as for reasons of effectiveness of domestic macroeconomic policy, has fixed exchange rates with countries in the area but flexible exchange rates with trading partners outside the area. In other words, it may be best for the 50 states of the United States to have fixed rates among themselves (which they do to the extreme since a common currency is employed) but flexible rates vis-à-vis other countries. Similarly, 11 members of the European Union had completely fixed exchange rates among their own currencies when they adopted the new currency unit, the **euro,** on January 1, 1999. What determines the domain (or size) of an optimum currency area? An answer to this question may be helpful in resolving the fixed rate–flexible rate debate.

There have been two main analyses of the necessary characteristics of an optimum currency area. Robert Mundell (1961) focused on the degree of factor mobility between countries and on economic structure. Suppose that the only two countries in the world are the United States and Canada, that a flexible exchange rate exists between them, and that variations in the

---

[5]John Williamson, "What Role for Currency Boards?" Institute for International Economics, *Policy Analyses in International Economics* 40 (September 1995).

exchange rate smoothly handle any BOP problems. Suppose also, however, that the eastern part of each country specializes in manufactured goods (e.g., automobiles) while the western part of each country specializes in natural resource products (e.g., lumber products). In addition, assume that factors of production do not move easily between east and west in each country and between the two types of industries. Suppose now that there is a shift in the composition of demand by consumers from automobiles to lumber products. The effect of this demand shift can be to generate inflationary pressures in the western portion of each country and to cause unemployment in the eastern part. In this situation, the Federal Reserve could expand the U.S. money supply to alleviate the eastern U.S. unemployment, but this would aggravate the inflation in the western United States. Or the Federal Reserve could contract the money supply to alleviate the inflation in the west, but this would aggravate the unemployment in the east. The same dilemma would exist for the Bank of Canada with respect to the Canadian east and west. In this context, a smooth adjustment mechanism (the flexible exchange rate) exists between the *countries* but not between the *regions* in each country.

What is the way out of the dilemma? In Mundell's view, the problem is that the flexible exchange rate pertains to the national *political* units (the United States and Canada) while fixed rates exist (within the countries) between regions that are economically dissimilar and have little factor mobility between them. The situation would be much improved if the *economic* units of the eastern United States and eastern Canada adopted a fixed exchange rate between them, as should the western United States and western Canada. Further, the exchange rate between the East (comprising the eastern parts of both countries) and the West (comprising the western parts of both countries) should be flexible. Then, with the preceding shift of demand from automobiles to lumber products, the currency of the West would appreciate relative to the currency of the East. In addition, the monetary authorities in both countries could use contractionary policy in the West and expansionary policy in the East. The unemployment and inflation problems could both then be avoided.

The point of this discussion is that there is a role to play for both fixed and flexible rates. Countries that are similar in economic structure and have factor mobility between them should have fixed exchange rates among themselves, for they comprise an optimum currency area. They should also adopt flexible exchange rates relative to the rest of the world. Needless to say, an optimum currency area within which rates are fixed is not necessarily an individual country.

In later work extending his ideas on optimum currency areas, Mundell (1997) distinguished between a "true" currency area and a "pseudo" currency area. In the former, the currency area adopts a monetary system such as a gold standard that contains an automatic adjustment mechanism. This mechanism, coupled with a commitment to stability, is "in times of peace" virtually absolute. A pseudo currency area, on the other hand, does not allow an automatic adjustment mechanism to function and a certain degree of country autonomy exists with regard to changes in parities. Consequently, interest rates can diverge in response to expected changes in exchange rates, and destabilizing speculation can occur. Because Mundell judges that modern currency areas tend to be pseudo in nature, he thinks that successful functioning of these agreements requires that the countries involved have sufficiently similar political and/or economic interests and a willingness to adapt when the situation demands it. In the absence of such political commitment, in Mundell's view, the member countries are unlikely to achieve the anticipated benefits of membership in the currency area.

Another noteworthy contribution regarding the characteristics of an optimum currency area is that of Ronald McKinnon (1963). McKinnon was concerned with the choice of a flexible exchange rate versus a fixed exchange rate in the contexts of BOP adjustment and of maintaining price-level stability. His analysis involved the distinction between a relatively open economy and a relatively closed economy. A relatively open (closed) economy is one that has a high (low) ratio of production of tradeable goods to production of nontradeable goods. Consider the open economy. If it has a flexible exchange rate, then a depreciation of its currency will raise the domestic price of imports and subsequently the price of domestic import-competing goods. Similarly, the depreciation increases the domestic price of exportable goods, because foreign demand for home exports increases with the depreciation. Because the prices of these tradeable goods are increasing, and because the tradeables comprise most of the country's production, the depreciation results in domestic inflation, which is roughly of the same percentage as the percentage by which the currency has depreciated. For the open economy, therefore, depreciation associated with the flexible exchange rate will do little to improve a BOP deficit and do much toward contributing to domestic inflation. This country might better be advised to maintain a fixed exchange rate.

In contrast, the relatively closed economy will find that a depreciation associated with a flexible exchange rate will have less effect on the domestic price level. Although the depreciation causes a rise in the price of tradeable goods, the price of these tradeables is not a very important component of the country's entire price level. But the rise in the price of tradeables relative to nontradeables will induce more production of tradeables, and the balance of payments will be easily improved by depreciation. Hence, for relatively closed economies, a flexible exchange rate can be very useful because it facilitates BOP adjustment without adding substantially to domestic inflation.

In the context of the fixed rate–flexible rate debate, McKinnon's analysis suggests that relatively open countries should consider fixed rates, while relatively closed economies should adopt floating rates with the outside world. This set of ideas can be married to Mundell's analysis by suggesting that open economies with factor mobility between them can, given sufficient political commitment, join together to form a currency area, while relatively closed countries can "go it on their own." In any event, these various considerations indicate that the optimum currency area is *not* the world as a whole. Obvious implications for the debate concerning fixed rates versus flexible rates are (*a*) to form blocs of similar countries, with fixed rates among the members of each bloc (such as perhaps within the European Union or within much of East Asia) and (*b*) to have exchange rate flexibility between the several blocs.

CONCEPT CHECK

1. Is the adoption of a fixed exchange rate system a guarantee that destabilizing speculation will not occur? Why or why not?
2. Explain how a sudden rise in the price level in foreign countries can be less inflationary for the home country in a system of flexible exchange rates than in a system of fixed exchange rates.
3. Explain Mundell's point that a country may not be an optimum currency area.

HYBRID SYSTEMS COMBINING FIXED AND FLEXIBLE EXCHANGE RATES

Amid the continuing debate between proponents of fixed rates and proponents of flexible rates, several compromise or hybrid proposals have emerged. These proposals attempt to incorporate the attractive features while minimizing the unattractive features of each extreme system. We consider three such systems in this chapter; further discussion in the context of the current international monetary system is provided in the next chapter.

Wider Bands

This proposal takes as a point of comparison the Bretton Woods system, where exchange rates were permitted to vary by 1 percent on either side of parity values. The proposal for **wider bands** states that the permissible variations around parity should be set at some larger value, such as 10 percent around parity. Because a substantial amount of variation is permitted with this wider band, the exchange rate is able to carry out a balance-of-payments adjustment. For example, if a country has a BOP deficit, the home currency could depreciate by up to 10 percent from its parity value, and this larger depreciation could be successful in altering exports and imports in the desired direction. Because the exchange rate is handling much of the BOP adjustment, there is less need for monetary and fiscal policies to be diverted from seeking the attainment of internal economic goals. In addition, because the variation from parity is limited to 10 percent, the wider band system still preserves some of the discipline of the fixed-rate system and also means that the problem of risk interfering with trade and investment is constrained, as is the problem of wasteful resource movements due to large and reversible movements in the exchange rate.

Nevertheless, because the proposal for wider bands maintains some limitations on exchange rate variability, it does not deal with some of the objections to fixed rates. For example, if countries consistently have different inflation rates, this system may break down, just as would a fixed-rate system. If Sweden inflates more rapidly than does Switzerland because of a different unemployment-inflation preference, then sooner or later the Swedish krona/Swiss franc rate will hit the ceiling. If no corrective steps or alterations in relative preferences by policymakers occur, a change in the krona/Swiss franc parity value will be required because Sweden will deplete its international reserves. Further, when the rate first hits the ceiling, speculators will have a one-way bet against the krona, and thus speculative pressure against the krona is apt to ensure that a devaluation of the krona will occur.

Finally, other objections to the wider bands proposal can be raised. Because a total change in a currency's value of 20 percent is permitted (10 percent on either side of parity), there are still some additional risks introduced for international trade and investment, as well as some possibility of wasteful resource movements because of the rate changes. In addition, international reserves—with their associated opportunity costs—still need to be held, and business cycles will still be transmitted across country borders. A sophisticated extension of the wider bands proposal, known as the *target zone proposal,* meets some of the objections to wider bands and is discussed in the next chapter.

Crawling Pegs

In the system known as the **crawling peg,** a country specifies a parity value for its currency and permits a small variation around that parity (such as ± 1 percent from parity). However, the parity rate is adjusted regularly by small amounts as dictated by the behavior of such variables as the country's international reserve position and recent changes in the money supply or prices. (The adjustment can be accomplished by following a strict formula or by use of judgment by the policymakers.) When these variables indicate potential pressures for the country (such as when international reserves decline markedly), the currency's parity value is officially devalued by a small percentage. Of course, when the parity value is thus changed, the 1 percent band now applies to the *new* parity.

A stylized example of a crawling peg system is given in Figure 2. The solid lines indicate the ceiling and the floor associated with the peg, while the dotted line indicates the path of the actual exchange rate. Note that the actual rate is between the ceiling and floor until point A is reached. This ceiling rate after A can be maintained only by using up some international reserves; but continued use of the reserves eventually will trigger a change of the parity value, as reflected in the higher band (reflecting devaluation of the home currency) after point B. (For simplicity, we do not show a parity value line.) A continuation of this process occurs at points C and D. Then, if the currency reverses itself and hits the floor at point F, a buildup of reserves eventually will set off an increase in the parity value at point G, so the range shifts downward.

FIGURE 2   A Crawling Peg

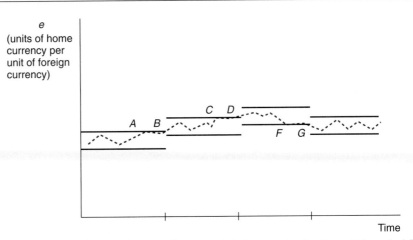

In this crawling peg example, the exchange rate fluctuates within its narrow band until point *A* is reached. The loss of reserves from *A* to *B* and any other indicators of currency weakness trigger a small devaluation of the parity value. When difficulties again occur from point *C* to point *D,* another small official devaluation takes place. This new parity value continues until a reserve buildup occurs from point *F* to point *G*, whereupon the parity value of the home currency is raised.

Advocates of the crawling peg concept point out that, at least in theory, the existence of the ceiling and floor can provide for some discipline on the part of the monetary authorities. In addition, the fact that the rate is periodically changed means that a role for the exchange rate in BOP adjustment is maintained. Finally, because each change is a small one, there is less danger of large-scale speculation against the currency.

An argument against the crawling peg is that a major change in the country's balance-of-payments position because of an internal or external shock may require a sizable change in the exchange rate to restore BOP equilibrium. If adherence to a strict crawling peg occurs, then a sacrifice of the pursuit of internal goals may be required if a large exchange rate change is not possible. Further, if the small parity changes are frequent (and unpredictable), there may still be some additional risks associated with international trade and investment. Finally, if experience is any guide, crawling pegs conducted in a context of unstable internal economic conditions (such as extremely rapid inflation) may amount virtually to a flexible exchange rate system. At the time of this writing, Bolivia, Botswana, Costa Rica, Iran, and Nicaragua have crawling peg exchange rate arrangements.

Managed Floating   The final hybrid arrangement of fixed and flexible exchange rates that we consider in this chapter is designated by the broad term **managed floating,** the term that is generally applied to the current international monetary system (see the next chapter). In general, a managed floating regime is characterized by *some* interference with exchange rate movements, but the intervention is discretionary on the part of the monetary authorities. In other words, there are no announced guidelines or rules for intervention, no parity exchange rates or announced target rates, and no announced limits for exchange rate variations. Rather, a country may intervene when it judges that it would be well served by doing so. For example, intervention to appreciate the home currency (or to keep it from depreciating so fast) might be desirable to fight domestic inflationary pressures, or intervention to prevent an appreciation might be desirable for assisting in reaching an employment target. Sometimes the intervention by a

IN THE REAL WORLD:

A CRAWLING PEG IN COLOMBIA

A country that employed a crawling peg system for a number of years is Colombia. In the Colombian case, the authorities followed "a policy of adjusting the peso in small amounts at relatively short intervals, taking into account (1) the movements of prices in Colombia relative to those in its major trading partners; (2) the level of Colombia's foreign exchange reserves; and (3) Colombia's overall balance of payments performance."* Despite small adjustments in each instance in a crawling peg system, however, the cumulative change in currency value can be rather large over a period of a few years. Table 2 presents relevant information for Colombia for the period 1980–1990. Following this experience, in mid-1991 Columbia instituted a more directly market-oriented exchange vote system. (It is noteworthy that other countries that previously had crawling pegs have also abandoned them.)

As can be seen from column (2) of the table, Colombia's peso/dollar exchange rate of 47.28 in 1980 rose to 502.26 in 1990. This was a 962 percent increase in the price of the dollar

in terms of pesos or, when the exchange rate is expressed as dollars per peso [and put into indexes as in column (3)], a decline in the peso of more than 90 percent. A prime reason for this depreciation of the peso was the 736 percent rise in Colombia's CPI from 1980 to 1990 (not shown in the table). However, the fall in the peso relative to the dollar was unrepresentative of the size of the overall decline in its value. The nominal effective exchange rate [column (4)] of the peso against the trade-weighted average of all trading partners fell "only" from 148.7 to 52.0 from 1980 through 1990—a 65 percent decline. When adjusted for relative internal prices via the real effective exchange rate in column (5), the peso fell from an index of 107.0 to 54.5—a fall of "only" 49 percent. Nevertheless, Colombia's experience suggests that a crawling peg may indeed crawl rapidly!

*International Monetary Fund, *Exchange Arrangements and Exchange Restrictions: Annual Report 1990* (Washington, DC: IMF, 1990), p. 105.

TABLE 2   Exchange Rate Behavior in Colombia, 1980–1990

(1)	(2)	(3)	(4)	(5)
		Indexes of Value of Peso (1985=100)		
Year	Pesos per U.S. $	Versus $	Nominal Effective Rate	Real Effective Rate
1980	47.28	300.9	148.7	107.0
1981	54.49	261.0	145.8	118.1
1982	64.08	222.0	141.6	125.9
1983	78.85	180.4	134.2	125.3
1984	100.82	141.1	122.8	114.7
1985	142.31	100.0	100.0	100.0
1986	194.26	73.3	70.2	74.5
1987	242.61	58.6	58.2	66.4
1988	299.17	47.5	54.0	64.1
1989	382.57	37.1	53.8	61.7
1990	502.26	28.3	52.0	54.5

Source: International Monetary Fund, *International Financial Statistics Yearbook 1993* (Washington, DC: IMF, 1993), pp. 282–83. Column (3) calculated by the authors.

particular country takes the form of **coordinated intervention** with other countries, such as when several industrialized nations (the G-7 industrialized countries) agreed to drive the U.S. dollar down in value in 1985 and then agreed in 1987 that the dollar had fallen far enough. In general, a country tends to intervene to slow down a movement in the exchange rate in a particular direction, a type of intervention called **leaning against the wind.** If the intervention is designed to intensify the movement of the currency in the direction in which it is already moving, the intervention is called **leaning with the wind.**

An advantage cited for managed floating is that the country is not locked into some pre-arranged course of action by formal rules and announcements. This greater freedom to tailor policy to existing circumstances is thought to be superior to sticking to a set of rules devised in some prior period that is no longer relevant. In addition, in contrast to a fixed-rate system, the exchange rate under managed floating is allowed to play some role in external sector adjustment. Further, internal policy is not constrained to the extent that it is under a fixed-rate system. In comparison with a purely flexible-rate system, the country is able to moderate wide swings in the exchange rate that can have adverse price level risk and resource movement implications. Speculation is also more difficult because speculators do not know the timing of the intervention, the potential size of the intervention, or even necessarily the direction of the intervention.

Working against the concept of managed floating is the possibility that, without a set of rules and guidelines for each country, various nations may be working at cross-purposes. For example, Japan may want to moderate a rise in the value of the yen in terms of dollars at the same time that the United States wants to drive the dollar down in terms of the yen. A form of economic warfare can then ensue. In addition, because exchange rates can vary substantially with a managed float, there is still a possibility that traders may be wary of full participation in international trade because of the risks of exchange rate variation.

There is a danger of abuse to the free market allocation of resources according to comparative advantage if countries use intervention to engage in what is called **exchange rate protection.** A contrived comparative advantage can be gained from such protection, and world resources may not be used in their most efficient manner. For example, many observers thought that Japan was intervening in the early 1980s to keep the value of the yen down in exchange markets. The advantage to Japan of this undervaluation of the yen would be that Japan's enhanced exports and depressed imports would provide a boost to Japanese GNP. When countries tend to manipulate their managed floats in this fashion to pursue particular goals at the expense of other countries, the behavior is referred to as **dirty floating.**

Finally, some economists have questioned the ability of a single country to meaningfully influence its exchange rate in any event. (See Taylor 1995, pp. 34–37.) The size of any country's foreign exchange reserves is very small relative to the size of total foreign exchange market activity. The ability to convince foreign exchange market participants that the government is both willing and able to influence the exchange rate is critical for successful intervention.

CONCEPT CHECK

1. What alleged disadvantages of a fixed-rate system are still present in the proposal for wider bands around parity?

2. Why is destabilizing speculation considered conceptually rather unlikely in a crawling peg system?

SUMMARY

This chapter surveyed issues in the debate over fixed versus flexible exchange rates. Those who prefer fixed rates to flexible rates stress the monetary discipline provided by the fixed-rate system and the conducive environment supplied for growth in international trade and investment—features alleged to be absent in a flexible-rate system. In addition, flexible rates are thought to generate various resource allocation inefficiencies and destabilizing speculation. Flexible rates may also aggravate the impacts of internal shocks on the economy. On the other hand, proponents of flexible rates point to the constraint on the attainment of internal goals inherent in a fixed-rate system, to the beneficial role of a free market in foreign exchange, and to the enhanced effectiveness of monetary policy for influencing national income. Further, countries with flexible exchange rates are thought to be insulated from external shocks.

We examined compromise or hybrid systems, specifically the proposal for wider bands of permissible exchange rate variations, the crawling peg, and managed floating. These proposals satisfy to some extent the proponents of both fixed and flexible rates, but they also dissatisfy both sides in the debate because of other implications.

Given this background to exchange rate arrangements, we turn in the next chapter to a discussion of exchange rate arrangements and developments in the international monetary system since the end of World War II. In addition, proposals for "reform" of the system will be examined.

KEY TERMS

coordinated intervention	leaning against the wind	stabilizing speculation
crawling peg	leaning with the wind	transactions demand for
currency board	managed floating	international reserves
destabilizing speculation	optimal size of international reserves	vicious circle hypothesis
dirty floating	optimum currency area	wider bands
euro	precautionary demand for	
exchange rate protection	international reserves	

QUESTIONS AND PROBLEMS

1. Why does the presence of different country preferences on possible inflation-unemployment trade-offs pose a problem for a system of fixed exchange rates?

2. What case can be made that flexible exchange rates reduce the flow of long-term foreign direct investment? What case can be made that flexible rates might actually lead to *more* foreign direct investment?

3. In what way might the relative susceptibility of a country to external shocks rather than internal shocks condition the choice between a fixed or flexible exchange rate for that country? Explain.

4. "If you believe that free markets maximize welfare, then you should also believe that a free exchange rate is an integral part of welfare maximization." Discuss.

5. Must the adoption of a flexible exchange rate mean that the rate will actually vary considerably over time? Why or why not?

6. Much discussion concerning floating rates stresses the risks to trade and investment involved with such a system. Is risk necessarily a bad thing? Why or why not?

7. Does a currency board seem to be a useful, practical arrangement for a country? What factors seem critical for a currency board's success?

8. Under what conditions would the world as a whole be an optimum currency area? Do you think that the industrialized countries should be one optimum currency area and the developing countries another? Explain.

9. "The hybrid systems combining fixed and flexible exchange rates are merely ways of avoiding having to make a choice between a fixed rate and a flexible rate. These systems invariably involve the 'worst of both worlds.'" Discuss.

10. In the early 1990s, the foreign exchange reserves of Chile increased dramatically as foreign investment flows into the country increased substantially because of the favorable investment climate and impressive economic growth. At the same time, Chile began intervening in foreign exchange markets to stabilize the exchange value of its peso. How might these two events be related to each other?

11. Explain Mundell's distinction between a "true" currency area and a "pseudo" currency area. Why is this distinction important?

29

THE INTERNATIONAL MONETARY SYSTEM

Past, Present, and Future

LEARNING OBJECTIVES

- ■ To become familiar with the key characteristics of an effective international monetary system.

- ■ To appreciate the historical evolution of the international monetary system from Bretton Woods to the present time.

- ■ To grasp the purpose of the IMF and understand its strengths and weaknesses.

- ■ To gain familiarity with existing alternative monetary arrangements.

- ■ To become aware of several proposals for reform of the current international monetary system.

INTRODUCTION

**The IMF Seeks
Stability**

Financial problems in one nation often spill over and contaminate others. Problems in a country's financial system can reduce the effectiveness of monetary policy, create the need to rescue financial institutions in crisis, deepen recessions, and lead to capital flight. The IMF is now actively involved in promoting the financial system soundness in its member countries.

Economic stability means avoiding large swings in economic activity, high inflation, and excessive volatility in exchange rates and financial markets. The IMF is taking a greater role in promoting global economic stability with a combination of surveillance, technical assistance, and lending. All IMF members agree to subject their economic and financial policies to the scrutiny of the international community. This scrutiny includes annual consultations with IMF staff. In addition, the IMF and World Bank collaborate to conduct in-depth assessments of countries' financial sectors under the financial sector assessment program (FSAP).

The IMF has worked to assess countries' vulnerabilities to crisis and provide technical assistance to design and implement sound economic policies. Even the best policies cannot remove all instability, so the IMF also has a program to provide financial assistance. The lending programs are designed to limit disruptions to domestic and global economies and help restore confidence, stability, and growth.[1]

As these comments from the International Monetary Fund imply, for countries to participate effectively in the exchange of goods, services, and assets, an international monetary system is needed to facilitate economic transactions. If the ability to import goods is limited because of a scarcity of foreign exchange reserves, for example, then countries will be tempted to impose tariffs, quotas, and other trade-restricting devices to conserve on their foreign exchange. In addition, controls on the outward movement of private funds from a reserve-scarce country may be imposed, or limitations on the ability of the country's citizens to travel overseas may be instituted.

To be effective in facilitating movement in goods, services, and assets, a monetary system most importantly requires an efficient **balance-of-payments adjustment mechanism** so that deficits and surpluses are not prolonged but are eliminated with relative ease in a reasonably short time period. Further, unless the system is characterized by completely flexible exchange rates, (*a*) there must be an adequate supply of **international liquidity,** that is, the system must provide adequate reserves so that payment can be made by BOP deficit countries to surplus countries, and (*b*) the supply of international liquidity must consist of **internationally acceptable reserve assets** that are expected to maintain their values.

Historically, international monetary systems have contained widely differing characteristics. Among those characteristics have been differences in the degree of exchange rate flexibility. About a hundred years ago, the prevailing international monetary system was the international gold standard (1880–1914). In this system (see Chapter 23), gold constituted the international reserve asset and gold's value was fixed by the declared par values that countries specified. This willingness to back currencies with an internationally acceptable reserve asset (gold) helped contribute to relatively free trade and payments. At the same time, balance-of-payments adjustment has been judged to have been relatively smooth during the 1880–1914 period. Little gold actually appears to have flowed from one country to another because central banks were willing to alter interest rates (raise them in the case of a deficit country, lower them in the case of a surplus country) in response to the

---

[1]These paragraphs are based on "How the IMF Promotes Global Economic Stability: A Factsheet," IMF External Relations Department (April 2004).

external payments position. These changes in money market conditions meant that adjustments to balance-of-payments positions were greatly facilitated by the international flows of short-term capital. (For elaboration, see Bloomfield 1959, 1963, and Triffin 1964.)

The international gold standard broke down with the advent of World War I. In the 1920s, countries permitted a great deal of exchange rate flexibility, and there has been controversy over the extent to which this international monetary system was, in fact, efficient. Nevertheless, the extensive fluctuations in exchange rates did maintain a reasonably close relationship with purchasing power parity predictions. In the middle of the decade, however, Britain (then the financial center of the world) attempted to restore the gold standard, adopting the old prewar par value of the pound. That par value greatly overvalued the pound and caused payments difficulties for Britain. With the tremendous decline in economic activity in the 1930s, payments difficulties emerged for many countries. Extensive attempts to restore some fixity in countries' exchange rates soon gave way to a series of competitive depreciations of currencies. Although single-country depreciation alone can stimulate employment and output in that country, when many countries depreciate their

IN THE REAL WORLD:

FLEXIBLE EXCHANGE RATES IN POST–WORLD WAR I EUROPE: THE UNITED KINGDOM, FRANCE, AND NORWAY

One strong argument against a flexible exchange rate system is that it results in considerable instability of the exchange rate and the rate consequently deviates significantly from the equilibrium rate as measured, for example, by purchasing power parity (PPP). In an interesting study in the late 1950s, S. C. Tsiang (1959) examined the flexible exchange rate experience of the United Kingdom, France, and Norway during the period following World War I. All three countries moved to flexible rates in 1919 and were floating their currencies through the mid- to late 1920s. The movements of each country's dollar exchange rate, the relative PPP rate, and wholesale price levels are indicated in Figure 1.

All three graphs indicate that there was considerable volatility of the exchange rates during the initial phase of the system from 1919 to 1921. This, however, is not surprising, given the turbulent nature of the immediate postwar years, during which there were periods of scarcity, inflation, and recession. However, with the return of relative world stability in 1921, the floating exchange rates of the three countries appear to have followed PPP exchange rates very closely. What is critical here is not that there was divergence between actual exchange rates and PPP rates but that the degree of divergence did not become increasingly large or sporadic.

The intriguing feature of this period is that the spot rates tended to move in a correlated fashion with PPP rates in all

three countries even though monetary policy and domestic price experiences were different. The United Kingdom deliberately undertook contractionary monetary policy to reduce relative prices and increase the value of its currency, whereas Norway initially adopted a more expansionary policy, which increased relative prices, and then moved to a contractionary period with falling prices. France, on the other hand, chose a relatively easy money policy with greater increases in prices through the mid-1920s.

Tsiang's research suggests that the policy-induced inflationary environment in France contributed to greater divergences between the spot and PPP rates compared with those in the United Kingdom and Norway. It also increased the speculative pressures on the exchange rate, adding increasingly to its volatility. However, there is no evidence that the franc fell into a vicious cycle of appreciation and depreciation inhibiting economic activity and seriously affecting France's foreign exchange reserves. The results in general suggest that foreign exchange instability in this period seems to have resulted from external factors and domestic policy actions, not the inherent instability of flexible rates. Such a conclusion is not inconsistent with experiences in the 1970s and 1980s, when external factors such as the oil-price shocks and the uncoordinated nature of monetary and fiscal policy in the world certainly contributed to the instability of the dollar.

(continued)

IN THE REAL WORLD: *(continued)*

FIGURE 1   Wholesale Prices, Exchange Rate Movements, and PPP in the United Kingdom, France, and Norway in the 1920s

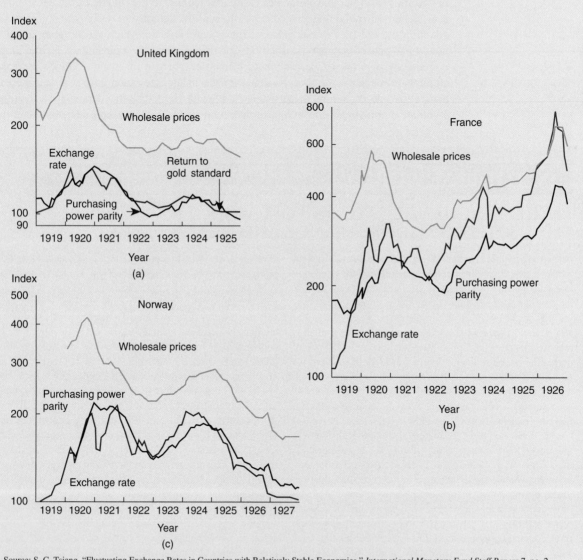

Source: S. C. Tsiang, "Fluctuating Exchange Rates in Countries with Relatively Stable Economies," *International Monetary Fund Staff Papers* 7, no. 2 (October 1959), pp. 250, 257, 260. Note that a logarithmic scale is used on each vertical axis.

currencies in retaliatory fashion, the expected beneficial results are short-lived or do not occur at all. Restrictive trade policies such as the infamous Tariff Act of 1930 (Smoot-Hawley) in the United States had also been instituted. These various actions led to great reductions in the volume and value of international trade. The measures also worsened the

Great Depression, and the low level of economic activity continued throughout most of the 1930s. Economic activity spurted upward with the advent of World War II, but involvement in the war prevented comprehensive consideration and adoption of a new system of international payments.

In this chapter, we begin at the end of World War II and describe the international monetary system set up at that time. We then discuss changes that occurred, and examine the current system and issues concerning the type of system needed for the evolving world economy. With the material of this chapter in hand, you will be in a better position to evaluate policy issues pertaining to international monetary affairs.

THE BRETTON WOODS SYSTEM

As World War II was drawing to a close, the historic United Nations Monetary and Financial Conference was held in Bretton Woods, New Hampshire, in 1944. From this conference emerged two international institutions that are still extremely prominent in the world economy—the International Monetary Fund and the International Bank for Reconstruction and Development (IBRD), now a somewhat broader institution commonly known as the World Bank. The initial focus of the World Bank was to provide long-term loans for the rebuilding of Europe from the devastation of World War II, but since the 1950s it has been concerned with providing long-term loans for projects and programs in developing countries. This institution is more properly considered in courses on economic development, so we focus on the IMF in our discussion below.

The Goals of the IMF

The **International Monetary Fund (IMF)** was the key institution in the functioning of the post–World War II international monetary system known as the **Bretton Woods system.** In this context, the IMF had several objectives.

In broad terms one important goal of the IMF was to *seek stability in exchange rates.* When the institution was first set up and for three decades thereafter, the IMF charter called for a system of **pegged but adjustable exchange rates.** As the "linchpin" of the Bretton Woods system, the dollar was defined by the United States as having a value of $\frac{1}{35}$ of an ounce of gold. Other countries then defined their currency values in terms of the dollar. Thus, parity values were established by agreement, but variations of 1 percent above and below parity were permitted. These limits were to be maintained by central banks, which would buy dollars if the price of the dollar fell to the -1 percent floor or would sell dollars if the price of the dollar rose to the $+1$ percent ceiling. The word *adjustable* in the phrase "pegged but adjustable" refers to the fact that, if a country experienced prolonged BOP deficits or surpluses at the pegged exchange rate, an IMF-approved devaluation or upward revaluation of the currency's parity value could be undertaken. In fact, as the IMF evolved, there were few changes in parity values. The desire for stable and relatively fixed rates was a reaction to the wide fluctuations, the competitive depreciations, the shrinkage in trade, and the instability of the world economy in the interwar period of the 1920s and 1930s.

Another objective of the IMF was (and continues to be) the *reconciliation of country adjustments to payments imbalances with national autonomy in macroeconomic policy.* As you may remember, the conceptual gold standard adjustment mechanism involved, for deficit countries, a fall in wages and prices as gold flowed out. This mechanism, or the alternative mechanism of an increase in interest rates to attract foreign short-term capital, posed the difficulty that the resulting contraction of economic activity could cause a rise in unemployment and a fall in real income. In contrast, a surplus country experienced upward pressure on its wages and prices, downward adjustments in its interest rates, and the resulting threat of inflation. But, if the rules of the game were being followed, internal objectives were to be sacrificed to the objective of attaining balance-of-payments equilibrium. After the Great Depression of the 1930s, governments were unwilling to use their monetary and fiscal policy instruments solely for external balance. Conflicts arose between the external target and the internal targets of macroeconomic policy. The IMF sought to reduce this conflict.

Attempts were made to alleviate the conflict through the use of loans by the IMF to deficit countries. The rationale behind these short-term loans (three to five years) was that a country's BOP deficit might be temporary because of the stage of the business cycle in which the country was located. If a loan could provide finance to the borrower until the payments imbalance reversed itself, then there would be no need for alteration of the deficit nation's macro policies in the direction of sacrificing internal goals. In addition, an IMF loan might reduce the likelihood that the deficit country would impose tariffs and other restrictive instruments on imports to conserve its foreign exchange reserves. Along the same line, fewer exchange controls on capital movements might be introduced. Hence, the availability of IMF loans not only could serve the purpose of giving more autonomy to domestic macro policy instruments but also contributed to a third objective of the IMF: *to help preserve relatively free trade and payments in the world economy.*

What were the sources of the funds for the BOP loans? When a country joins the IMF (there are now 185 IMF member nations, an increase of 1 in 2007 when the country of Serbia and Montenegro became two separate countries), it is assigned an **IMF quota.** This country quota is a sum of money to be paid to the IMF based on such factors as the national income of the country and the size of its foreign trade sector. Thus, for example, Kenya has a quota of $413.7 million, while the United States has a quota of $56.6 billion. (See Table 1 for the

TABLE 1   Selected IMF Country Quotas, April 30, 2007

	SDRs* (millions)	U.S. Dollars (millions) (1.524180/SDR)	Percent
All countries	**216,747.8**	**330,362.7**	**100.00**
Industrial Countries	**130,566.6**	**199,007.0**	**60.24**
Australia	3,236.4	4,932.9	1.49
Canada	6,369.2	9,707.8	2.94
France	10,738.5	16,367.4	4.95
Germany	13,008.2	19,826.8	6.00
Italy	7,055.5	10,753.9	3.26
Japan	13,312.8	20,291.1	6.14
Sweden	2,395.5	3,651.2	1.11
United Kingdom	10,738.5	16,367.4	4.95
United States	37,149.3	56,622.2	17.14
Developing Countries	**86,181.2**	**131,355.7**	**39.76**
Africa	**11,498.1**	**17,525.2**	**5.30**
Algeria	1,254.7	1,912.4	0.58
Côte d'Ivoire	325.2	495.7	0.15
Kenya	271.4	413.7	0.13
Nigeria	1,753.2	2,672.2	0.81
South Africa	1,868.5	2,847.9	0.86
Zambia	489.1	745.5	0.23
Asia	**25,061.4**	**38,198.1**	**11.56**
China	8,090.1	12,330.8	3.73
Fiji	70.3	107.1	0.03

TABLE 1   Selected IMF Country Quotas, April 30, 2007 (*continued*)

India	4,158.2	6,337.8	1.92
Indonesia	2,079.3	3,169.2	0.96
Pakistan	1,033.7	1,575.5	0.48
Philippines	879.9	1,341.1	0.41
Singapore	862.5	1,314.6	0.40
Thailand	1,081.9	1,649.0	0.50
Europe	**17,524.9**	**26,711.1**	**8.09**
Bulgaria	640.2	975.8	0.30
Croatia	365.1	556.5	0.17
Kazakhstan	365.7	557.4	0.17
Poland	1,369.0	2,086.6	0.63
Russian Federation	5,945.4	9,061.9	2.74
Turkey	1,191.3	1,815.8	0.55
Ukraine	1,372.0	2,091.2	0.63
Middle East	**16,162.9**	**24,635.2**	**7.46**
Egypt	943.7	1,438.4	0.44
Iran	1,497.2	2,282.0	0.69
Iraq	1,188.4	1,811.3	0.55
Israel	928.2	1,414.7	0.43
Kuwait	1,381.1	2,105.0	0.64
Saudi Arabia	6,985.5	10,647.2	3.22
Western Hemisphere	**15,933.9**	**24,286.1**	**7.34**
Argentina	2,117.1	3,226.8	0.98
Brazil	3,036.1	4,627.6	1.40
Chile	856.1	1,304.9	0.39
Colombia	774.0	1,179.7	0.36
Dominica	8.2	12.5	0.00
Mexico	2,585.8	3,941.2	1.19
Peru	638.4	973.0	0.29
Venezuela	2,659.1	4,052.9	1.23

*SDRs (special drawing rights) are an international reserve asset introduced in 1970 and discussed later in this chapter, and the IMF uses the SDR as its unit of account.
Source: International Monetary Fund, *International Financial Statistics,* April 2007, obtained from www.imf.org.

size of current IMF quotas for selected countries.) Under the original rules of the IMF, each country's quota was to be paid 25 percent in gold and 75 percent in the country's own currency.[2] When all countries subscribed their quotas, the IMF became a holder of gold and of a pool of member country currencies.

How do these quotas link up with balance-of-payments loans to member countries? Suppose that Kenya has a BOP deficit and that it needs, because of a foreign exchange shortage, to obtain British pounds to pay for some of its imports. Kenya can "borrow" or "draw" pounds from the IMF because the IMF has a quantity of pounds on hand from the United Kingdom quota. According to IMF rules, a country can potentially obtain loans of up to 125 percent of its quota. This figure of 125 percent is divided into five segments (or *tranches,* as they are officially called), with the first 25 percent called the **gold tranche** or

---

[2]The 25 percent is now paid in internationally acceptable "hard" currencies rather than in gold.

reserve tranche, the next 25 percent called the first **credit tranche,** the next 25 percent the second credit tranche, and so on. The application for the first 25 percent is automatically approved by the IMF, but, as a country gets further and further into the credit tranches, the IMF will attach increasingly stringent conditions before approving the additional loans. These conditions are designed to ensure that the borrowing country is taking action to reduce its BOP deficit. For example, the IMF may prescribe that the country adopt certain monetary and fiscal policies or may even recommend a change in the value of the borrowing country's currency. These potential interferences by an international agency with the national policies of members have generated considerable ill will, because they are regarded by would-be borrowers as intrusions upon national sovereignty. Incidentally, the IMF levies a small service charge on these BOP loans; there is no interest charge on reserve tranche loans, but interest is assessed on credit tranche loans.

The Bretton Woods System in Retrospect

Most economists judge the Bretton Woods system to have performed well from its implementation at the end of World War II until the mid-1960s. World trade grew relatively rapidly during this period, and the major European countries removed most of their postwar exchange restrictions. In addition, Europe and Japan recovered from the World War II devastation, and growth in the world economy occurred with no major setbacks or recessions.

Despite this seeming success, some important problems emerged in the Bretton Woods system. Economists see these problems as falling broadly into three principal areas, and these areas correspond to the important functions of an international monetary system with which we began this chapter.[3]

The Bretton Woods international monetary system was thought to be facing an **adequacy of reserves problem** or **liquidity problem.** In general terms, this problem can be stated as follows: When world trade is growing rapidly, it is likely that the size of payments imbalances will grow in absolute terms. Hence, there is an increased need for reserves to finance BOP deficits. The framers of the Bretton Woods agreement envisioned that gold would be the primary international reserve asset, but the supply of gold in the world economy was growing at a rate of only 1 to 1.5 percent per year while trade in the 1960s was growing at a rate of close to 7 percent per year. Hence, the fear was that reserves in the form of gold were not increasing rapidly enough to deal with larger BOP deficits. If reserves do not grow roughly apace with BOP deficits, the danger exists that countries will use trade and payments restrictions to reduce their deficits, and these policies could reduce the gains from trade and the rate of world economic growth.

The second problem, the **confidence problem,** was related to the liquidity problem. Because the supply of gold held by central banks was growing relatively slowly, the growing international reserves consisted mostly of national currencies that were internationally acceptable and were thus being held by the central banks. The two national currencies held in largest volume were the U.S. dollar and the British pound. But, particularly with the dollar, this fact posed a danger to central banks. The dollar was the linchpin of the system because of the gold guarantee that the United States stood ready to buy and sell gold at $35 per ounce. However, the dollars held by non-U.S. central banks began to exceed by a substantial margin the size of the U.S. official gold stock. This gold stock itself was also being depleted by U.S. BOP deficits. If all foreign central banks attempted to convert their dollars into gold, the United States did not have enough gold to meet all demands. In addition, there were even larger amounts of dollar deposits located outside the United States in

---

[3]See, for more complete discussion, Fritz Machlup (1964); Machlup and Burton G. Malkiel (1964); Robert Triffin (1960).

foreign private hands (eurodollar deposits). These dollars could also be a claim on the U.S. gold stock. There was thus a loss of confidence in the dollar, that is, loss of confidence in what had become the principal reserve asset of the monetary system. Further, if the United States attempted to increase its ability to meet the conversion of dollars into gold by devaluing the dollar relative to gold (for example, by changing the price from $35 to $70 per ounce), then central banks that held dollars would suffer a reduction in the value of their reserves in terms of gold. Such a devaluation would surely have started a massive "run" on gold and would have brought the Bretton Woods system to a quick termination.

The third perceived problem of the Bretton Woods system was the **adjustment problem.** This refers to the fact that in the actual operation of the Bretton Woods system, individual countries had prolonged BOP deficits or surpluses. This was particularly true for the United States (deficits) and West Germany (surpluses). There did not seem to be an effective adjustment mechanism, because automatic forces were not removing the imbalances. Countries directed monetary and fiscal policies toward internal targets rather than external targets, and thus the contraction (expansion) in the money supply expected of a deficit (surplus) country did not occur (i.e., sterilization was taking place). This was especially true with respect to the U.S. BOP deficit because of U.S. concern about slow economic growth and high unemployment. (In fact, the United States could sterilize without worrying excessively about a loss of reserves, since its own currency was being used as reserves.) In a similar vein, Germany's concern about inflation prevented it from adjusting to a BOP surplus by expanding its money supply.

GRADUAL EVOLUTION OF A NEW INTERNATIONAL MONETARY SYSTEM

Any attempt to recount the events associated with the gradual disintegration of the Bretton Woods system is bound to be arbitrary in its selection of events. With this caveat in mind, we summarize below the developments we regard as significant for the evolution of the current international monetary system.

Early Disruptions

In 1967, the British pound was officially devalued from its parity exchange rate of $2.80/£1 to $2.40/£1 (a 14 percent devaluation). This devaluation was a consequence of declining U.K. foreign exchange reserves in large part due to speculative short-term capital flows. The devaluation was significant because the pound and the dollar were **key currencies,** that is, the two national currencies most prominently held by central banks as official international reserves. The fact that the value of an international reserve asset had been changed suggested that the exchange rate pegs of Bretton Woods might not be sustainable.

A second important event was the decision by major central banks in 1968 that they would no longer engage in gold transactions with private individuals and firms. This decision meant that, henceforth, the central banks would no longer buy and sell gold in the private market but would continue to do so with each other. Transactions in gold between central banks would be made at the official gold price of $35 per ounce, but private individuals would buy and sell among themselves at whatever price cleared the private market (which at one time thereafter exceeded $800 per ounce). This new structure for gold was called the "two-tier gold market."

Some background is necessary to understand the significance of this event. Prior to 1968, because central banks had been willing to buy and sell gold with private individuals (although the U.S. government had not been willing to do so with its own citizens), there was only one price for gold. Central banks bought and sold at the $35 price, and, if the price in private markets tended to rise above (fall below) $35, dissatisfied buyers (sellers) could obtain (sell) gold from (to) the central banks at the $35 price. However, because of the uncertainties associated with the confidence problem in the 1960s, private speculators anticipated that the dollar might be devalued in terms of gold. They therefore were eager to buy gold at $35 per ounce for resale later at the expected higher price. This private demand for gold put upward pressure on its price, pressure which could be relieved only by sales of gold by central banks, reducing official reserves. To stem this outflow of gold to private buyers, the two-tier market was instituted.

The refusal of central banks to deal in gold with private individuals and firms was judged to be important symbolically because it represented a first step toward reducing the relative importance of gold in the international monetary system. Because the central banks were no longer dealing in gold with private citizens, gold holdings were frozen in size in the central banks' overall international reserve portfolios. As international reserves later grew through accumulation of more dollars in particular, gold constituted a declining fraction of total reserves.

Special Drawing Rights (SDRs)

A major development in the international monetary system occurred in 1970 when a new international asset appeared. This development was the introduction of **special drawing rights (SDRs)** by the IMF.[4] Unlike gold and other international reserve assets, the SDR is a paper asset (sometimes called "paper gold") created "out of thin air" by the IMF. On January 1, 1970, the IMF simply entered on the books of all participating members a total of $3.5 billion worth of SDRs. The SDR itself was defined as equal in value to $\frac{1}{35}$ of an ounce of gold and thus as equal in value to one U.S. dollar. The total of $3.5 billion was divided among member countries in proportion to the share of total IMF quotas of each member country. Additional SDRs have been created on several occasions since 1970.

The SDRs that a member country receives in an allocation add to international reserves and can be used to settle a BOP deficit in a fashion similar to any other type of international reserve asset. For example, if India needs to obtain Japanese yen to finance a deficit, it can do so by swapping SDRs for yen held by some other country (e.g., France) that the IMF designates. Thus, the SDR could help to alleviate the liquidity problem discussed earlier. Further, because the SDR is not a national currency, and because it might eventually replace national currencies such as the dollar in reserve portfolios, the new instrument could potentially alleviate the confidence problem.

In the preceding India example, where SDRs were exchanged for yen, a skeptic might question why France would be willing to part with some of its yen in exchange for a bookkeeping-entry paper asset. This question goes to the heart of a more basic question: "Why do some assets serve as money, while others do not?" The answer to this more basic question is that an asset serves as money if it is *generally acceptable in exchange;* one party to a transaction will accept the asset if that party knows that it too can use the asset to acquire other assets. SDRs have become "international money" because the recipient of the SDRs knows that it can use them to acquire other currencies from other countries later. Further, in the SDR scheme, each participant agreed to stand ready to accept SDRs to the extent of twice its accumulated SDR allocations.

Another feature of SDRs is that if a country is a net recipient of SDRs, meaning that it holds more than it has been allocated by the IMF, it receives interest on its excess holdings. Similarly, if a country holds less than its allocation of SDRs, that country pays interest on its shortfall. These rules help to encourage caution in the use of SDRs.

---

[4]For extensive discussion of the SDR concept and agreement, see Machlup (1968).

A final aspect of the SDR concerns its valuation. In the initial allocation of this new asset, the SDR equaled one U.S. dollar. With the later devaluations of the dollar (discussed next) and the advent of greater flexibility in exchange rates during the 1970s, the equality of the SDR and the dollar was discarded. The SDR is now valued as a weighted average of the values of four currencies: 44 percent for the U.S. dollar; 34 percent for the euro, 11 percent for the Japanese yen, and 11 percent for the British pound. The latest revision of the weights became effective January 1, 2006.

The Breaking of the Gold-Dollar Link and the Smithsonian Agreement

Chronologically, the next event of major significance occurred on August 15, 1971. At that time, because of continuing U.S. BOP deficits, escalating inflation, and lagging economic growth, the Nixon administration undertook several drastic steps. Most importantly, *the United States announced that it would no longer buy and sell gold with foreign central banks.* This action amounted to an abandonment of the Bretton Woods system, because the willingness of the United States to buy and sell gold at $35 per ounce had been the linchpin of that system. In addition, the administration temporarily froze wages and prices (to help in the anti-inflation effort), imposed a temporary 10 percent tariff surcharge on all imports (to help in reducing the BOP deficit), and instituted a tax credit for new productive investment (to stimulate economic growth), among other actions. From the standpoint of the exchange rate system, the cessation of the willingness to buy and sell gold was the key policy change because it altered the nature of the existing system. Without the "gold guarantee," there was no anchor to the value of the dollar. Foreign central banks were faced with the decision of whether or not to continue buying and selling dollars at the previously established parity values.

After this action, there was considerable turbulence in the international monetary system. To stem the speculation and uncertainty, the chief monetary officials of the leading industrial nations convened in Washington at the Smithsonian Institution in December 1971 to work out a new set of exchange rate arrangements. This meeting led to the **Smithsonian Agreement,** which established a new set of par values (called *central rates*). The deutsche mark and the Japanese yen were revalued upward by 13 percent and 17 percent, respectively. In addition, countries agreed to permit variations of 2.25 percent on either side of the central rates, thus introducing greater exchange rate flexibility than had been allowed under the ±1 percent variations of the Bretton Woods arrangements. Further, the United States changed the official price of gold from $35 to $38 per ounce. This devaluation of the dollar against gold was important symbolically rather than practically, because the United States was no longer buying and selling gold. The symbolism was that the United States, by devaluing its currency, was politically admitting that it was at least partly responsible for the troubles of the international monetary system (through the continual U.S. BOP deficits). The Smithsonian Agreement generated optimism for the future among participating governments, and President Nixon called it "the most significant monetary agreement in the history of the world" (quoted in Ellsworth and Leith 1984, pp. 508–09).

This judgment regarding the Smithsonian Agreement was premature, as continued speculation against the dollar resulted in further changes. Britain began floating the pound in June 1972. Early in 1972, the six countries of the European Community also began a joint float of their currencies, which meant that these countries (Belgium, France, Italy, Luxembourg, the Netherlands, West Germany) kept their own currencies tied closely together (±2.25 percent from specified values) but the currencies could vary by larger amounts against other currencies (although the 2.25 percent variation was also maintained against the dollar). In February 1973, the U.S. dollar was again devalued against gold (to $42.22 per ounce). Other currencies began floating either freely or in controlled fashion in 1973.

The Jamaica Accords

The next significant development occurred with the **Jamaica Accords** of January 1976. After consultation with officials of leading countries, the IMF made a series of changes that were incorporated into the IMF's Articles of Agreement.[5] The most important of these changes were the following:

1. Each member country was free to adopt its own preferred exchange rate arrangements. Thus, for example, a country might tie its currency's value to some particular currency, or it might let its currency float freely against all currencies, or it might peg its currency's value to some "basket" of currencies of countries with which it was most heavily involved in trade.

2. The role of gold was downgraded in the international monetary system. To this end, the official price of gold was eventually abolished and the IMF itself sold one-third of its gold holdings. Some of the proceeds were used to benefit developing countries.

3. The role of the SDR was to be enhanced. It was anticipated that SDRs would become very important in the reserve asset portfolios of central banks, although this objective has not been achieved.

4. The IMF was to maintain **surveillance** of exchange rate behavior. In general terms, this meant that the IMF intended that its members would seek to "avoid manipulating exchange rates . . . to prevent effective balance of payments adjustment" and would foster "orderly economic and financial conditions and a monetary system that does not tend to produce erratic disruptions."[6] These broad objectives essentially mean that the IMF advises its members, through regular consultations, on their exchange rate actions so that the international monetary system does not become subject to considerable uncertainty and instability.

The European Monetary System

A significant development in international monetary arrangements began in March 1979 with the inauguration of the **European monetary system (EMS).**[7] This system was an outgrowth of the joint float (sometimes called the "European Snake" because of the wave-like movements of the six currencies as a unit against other currencies) that had begun in 1972. The first key feature of the EMS of the European Community members was the creation of a new monetary unit, the **European currency unit** or **ecu,** in terms of which central rates for the countries' currencies were defined. The value of the ecu was a weighted average of EMS member currencies and the ecu was used as the unit of account for recording transactions among EMS central banks.

A second key feature of the original EMS was that each currency was generally to be kept within 2.25 percent of the central rates against the other participating currencies, and a mechanism was put in place requiring central bank action as exchange rates approached the limits of divergence permitted from the central rates. There were also provisions for periodic realignments of the central rates. Third, the EMS participating currencies were to move as a unit in floating fashion against other currencies, including the U.S. dollar. This set of exchange rate rules was known as the **exchange rate mechanism (ERM)** of the EMS. Finally, the **European Monetary Cooperation Fund (EMCF),** a "banker's bank" similar to the IMF, was established for receiving deposits of reserves from the EMS members and making loans to members with BOP difficulties.

---

[5]The changes officially went into effect on April 1, 1978. See *IMF Survey,* April 3, 1978, pp. 97–107.

[6]*IMF Survey,* April 3, 1978, p. 98.

[7]For more complete discussion, see Commission of the European Communities (1986) and *The ECU* (1987).

The European monetary system was conceived as a means of promoting greater exchange rate stability within Europe and, because of this stability and certainty, for generating more stable and soundly based economic growth. Because greater stability in exchange rates requires some degree of harmonization in macroeconomic policies, the EMS also promoted convergence of policies and inflation rates.

The Maastricht Treaty   In December 1991, the members of the European Community (EC) extended the EMS and took a dramatic step toward future monetary union. The **Maastricht Treaty** laid out a plan for the establishment of a common currency and a European central bank by, at the latest, January 1, 1999. Along with the implementation of various other changes to bring about closer trade and capital market integration, the participating European countries would have at that time a full **Economic and Monetary Union (EMU).** The transition to EMU was to take place in stages.[8] In stage I, countries not yet participating in the ERM would begin to do so. Members of the EC were also to take steps toward convergence in their economic performance, as measured by inflation differentials, exchange rate stability, differences in interest rates, and fiscal deficits and government debt. In stage II (which began on January 1, 1994), the EC was to intensify its examination of whether the various criteria for convergence of economic performance were being met, and countries were expected to remove virtually all remaining restrictions on the flow of capital between them. In addition, the EMCF would be replaced by the European Monetary Institute (EMI), consisting of the national central bank governors and a president, which would strengthen monetary cooperation. Finally, when stage III began, members were to irrevocably fix their exchange rates and form the monetary union with a common currency, the **euro.** The EMI was then to be replaced by the **European System of Central Banks (ESCB),** a communitywide institution consisting of the national central banks themselves working with a multinational component known as the **European Central Bank (ECB).** The ESCB would be the *supranational monetary authority, with control over monetary policy and exchange rate policy for the entire European Community.*[9]

To the surprise of doubters, the EMU did indeed begin operations on January 1, 1999. Of the 15 European Union countries, 11—Austria, Belgium, Finland, France, Germany, Ireland, Italy, Luxembourg, the Netherlands, Portugal, and Spain—fixed their exchange rates by irrevocably defining their currencies in terms of the euro, which thereby defined the currencies irrevocably in terms of each other. For example, with 6.55957 French francs defined as equal to 1 euro and 1.95583 German marks equal to 1 euro, the result is that 3.35385 French francs equal 1 German mark (6.55957/1.95583 = 3.35385). The euro in turn floated against other non-EMU currencies, and it had a value of approximately $1.16 at the time of its introduction. Bank accounts in the Euro Area or "Euroland" (the 11 members of EMU) and many financial transactions immediately began to be denominated in euros. The individual countries' currencies remained in circulation until early 2002, when they ceased to be legal tender and were taken out of circulation. Euro notes and coins first appeared on January 1, 2002.

The establishment of the EMU was a milestone in world monetary history. It is particularly important to note that no one simply announces fixed exchange rates and a new currency and then assumes that all will be well for the foreseeable future. Macro policies to bring economic variables into consistency across countries are necessary for a monetary union and fixed rates to survive. To this end, the Maastricht Treaty had specified

---

[8]See *A Single Currency for Europe: Monetary and Real Impacts* (1992), pp. xi, 3.

[9]"European Leaders Agree to Treaty on Monetary Union," *IMF Survey,* January 6, 1992, pp. 2–3.

convergence criteria. For a country to be permitted to join the EMU, (1) the country's inflation rate of consumer prices could not be greater than 1.5 percentage points above the average of the three lowest-inflation EU countries; (2) the country's long-term government bond interest rate could not be more than 2 percentage points above that interest rate average in the three lowest-inflation countries; (3) the government budget deficit of the entering country could not exceed 3 percent of GDP; and (4) the ratio of total government debt to GDP of the country must be 60 percent or lower.[10]

Why are such criteria necessary? First, with regard to the inflation rate criterion, if a country inflates more rapidly than its major trading partners, it is likely to incur a trade deficit as exports fall off (because they are now less competitive) and imports rise (because they are now relatively cheaper compared to home goods). This deficit situation would put pressure on the country's currency, moving it toward depreciation. Second, if a country's interest rates are higher than those in other countries, there would be upward pressure on the country's currency. This pressure could come from two sources: (1) the higher interest rates attract mobile capital from other countries and (2) the higher interest rates slow down economic activity in the country and lead to a reduction in imports. Both of these developments would tend to generate an incipient surplus in the balance of payments and potential appreciation of the home currency.

Turning to the fiscal criteria, an excessive deficit/GDP ratio could imply currency trouble because such expansionary policy could put upward pressure on the country's currency if government borrowing bids up interest rates and attracts short-term portfolio capital. (Note: In the terminology of Chapter 24, this implies that the *BP* curve is flatter than the *LM* curve, which is surely the case in the EMU countries.) Finally, if the ratio of total government debt to GDP exceeds 60 percent, the implication is that the high level of debt (and 60 percent per se is clearly an arbitrary number) might pose problems for the country. In particular, investors might lose confidence in the government's ability to service and carry the debt, and this means that holdings of government bonds might be sold off. This movement away from the bonds, if done by foreign investors, would put downward pressure on the value of the country's currency.

When the Maastricht Treaty was originally signed, there were substantial divergences among countries with respect to interest rates, inflation rates, and the fiscal variables. However, concerted efforts (and sometimes creative bookkeeping, such as when the French government recorded a privatization sale as a regular receipts inflow for the purpose of reducing its deficit/GDP ratio) brought about remarkable convergence in the previously mentioned indicators. In the end, Greece was the only European Union member seeking admission to EMU that was denied, as it failed to meet all four criteria. Greece was granted entry after a delay. The government debt/GDP ratios of Belgium and Italy were about twice the 60 percent criterion, but these divergences were ignored. Three EU member countries—Denmark, Sweden, and the United Kingdom—chose not to join the EMU.

An important reason a country might not want to join the EMU is that, as has been mentioned in earlier chapters, monetary policy independence for a country's central bank is completely lost with absolutely fixed exchange rates and, of course, with a common currency. Monetary authority in the case of the EMU is, as noted earlier, lodged with the European System of Central Banks, composed of the supranational European Central Bank and the national central banks. The executive board of the ECB actually conducts

---

[10]Another specified criterion was that, for the two years prior to entry, the country's currency value must not have been changed within the European Monetary System. In fact, some currency values fluctuated considerably in the period leading up to the EMU, and the other four criteria listed in the text were the main ones considered.

monetary policy in accordance with general instructions from the governing council, which contains representatives from all Euro Area countries.[11] The ESCB established early on what its major priority would be: "The primary objective of the ESCB shall be to maintain price stability" (Article 2 of the ESCB Statute, quoted in Issing 1999, p. 19). This objective (often thought to mean no more than 2 percent inflation) is consistent with the notion that the tight-money policies of the German Bundesbank, which was very anti-inflationary, have been carried over into the EMU. The objective may also mean, if in fact there is a trade-off between inflation and unemployment and if the ESCB sticks firmly to this objective, that the double-digit unemployment rates in several EU countries in the 1990s may persist for a sustained period.

With monetary policy being conducted at the EMU level rather than at the individual country level, the only macro policy available for country governments is fiscal policy. With adherence to the relevant convergence criteria as well as with the signing of the Stability and Growth Pact of 1997, members of EMU committed themselves to keep government budgets close to balance.[12] Nevertheless, because the deficit can go up to 3 percent of GDP, there is room for fiscal stimulus if the tight-money policies of the ESCB are deemed too restrictive. A country could, for example, set its "structural deficit," the deficit that would exist even if the country had a high level of employment (the "natural rate" from Chapter 27), at 1 to 1½ percent of GDP to provide some net stimulus to the economy from the excess of government spending over tax revenues. Even if recession occurred and tax revenues fell, the government could still be providing stimulus and staying within the 3 percent of GDP limit. Thus, there is some possible role for fiscal policy at the individual country level, but the Growth and Stability Pact did specify financial sanctions that can be applied to a country if the 3 percent deficit/GDP ratio is exceeded.

While it is still too early to come to a definitive conclusion about the performance of the EMU and the euro, there are some positive signs. Vice President Noyer of the European Central Bank (ECB) discussed the following success factors in a February 2002 speech:

1. The changeover from individual currencies to the euro progressed smoothly and was met with enthusiasm from European citizens.

2. The elimination of exchange rate risks and the lower transaction costs within the euro area has created new opportunities for business and promoted efficiency and competitiveness.

3. The euro has been a catalyst in the process of financial integration.

4. The euro has become the second most widely used currency and plays a role in the exchange rate regimes of more than 50 countries outside the euro area.[13]

The two years following ECB Vice President Noyer's speech witnessed a steady rise in the value of the euro relative to the U.S. dollar. From an initial value of $1.16 the euro had fallen to a level consistently below $0.90. In May 2002, the euro value rose above $0.90 and continued to appreciate and reached $1.28 in February 2004. By July 2007, the euro had risen above $1.37.

---

[11]For extensive discussion of monetary policy procedures in the EMU, see Otmar Issing, "The Monetary Policy of the Eurosystem," *Finance and Development,* March 1999, pp. 18–21.

[12]For extensive discussion of policy in the EMU, including considerable attention to fiscal policy, see International Monetary Fund, *World Economic Outlook,* October 1998 (Washington, DC: IMF, 1998), chap. 5.

[13]"Success Factors of the Euro and the ECB," speech by Christian Noyer, vice president of the European Central Bank, at the symposium *World Economic Climate after the Introduction of the Euro,* organized by Japan Center for International Finance and Sumitomo-Life Research Institute, Tokyo (February 13, 2002).

The enlargement of the EU in 2004 and 2007 included provisions (the Maastricht Treaty) by which all new members are eligible to join the single European currency, the euro. The differences in economic performance are leading to very different changeover plans in these countries. In preparation for euro adoption, the countries are required to meet the established entry conditions related to inflation, budget deficits, exchange rate stability, and legal compatibility. In addition, as war the case with the original members of the euro zone, the countries must also fix the exchange rate between their local currency and the euro to support the continuous integration with the European Economic Area as part of the exchange rate mechanism known as ERM II.[14]

The first of the new entrants to adopt the euro was Slovenia. The move to the euro took place on January 1, 2007. Slovenia followed the Big Bang approach in which the irrevocable locking of the exchange rate and introduction of the euro banknotes and coins occurred simultaneously. The dual circulation period only lasted for two weeks. The Slovenian changeover was a swift and smooth affair that appears to be the model for future adoptions.[15]

Exchange Rate Variations

We conclude this survey of the evolution of the international monetary system by noting that, in general, exchange rate variations among major currencies have been very large since the breakdown of Bretton Woods. Fluctuations in nominal exchange rates have also been accompanied by large changes in *real* exchange rates. Hence, there have been substantial variations in international competitiveness as well as dislocations in the export and import-competing sectors of countries. In addition, the most important variations in relative currency values have occurred with respect to the U.S. dollar, which rose dramatically from 1980 to 1985 and then fell dramatically after 1985 (especially from 1985 to 1987). As a consequence, in September 1985 the Plaza Agreement was reached in New York by central bankers from France, Japan, the United States, the United Kingdom, and West Germany. In this agreement, the five countries stated that the dollar needed to be lowered in value and that their central banks stood ready to intervene to accomplish this objective. The dollar did indeed fall in subsequent months, and the Louvre Accord was then announced in February 1987. In this accord, the G-7 countries declared that the dollar had fallen far enough (40 percent since 1985). The dollar was henceforth to be stabilized in a relatively narrow range (but unspecified as to the exact range) by cooperative central bank action.

Short-Run Fluctuations in the 1990s

Changes in the value of the dollar (as well as in the value of other currencies) continued through the 1990s. For example, from September 1992 to September 1993, the dollar rose by 14 percent in terms of the German deutsche mark, 18 percent in terms of the British pound, 31 percent in terms of the Spanish peseta, and 50 percent in terms of the Swedish krona. Greater changes occurred against the currencies of some developing countries—for example, a 95 percent rise in terms of the Brazilian cruzeiro reàl. However, while rising against most currencies, the dollar *fell* in terms of the Japanese yen by 12.5 percent. (Indeed, the trade-weighted nominal value of the yen—the effective exchange rate—rose by 25 percent over that period.)[16] Further, in 1994 the dollar fell by more than 10 percent against both the deutsche mark and the yen, and in early 1995 it dropped to post–Bretton

---

[14]"Enlargement and the Euro," EurActiv.com, January 29, 2007, obtained from www.euractiv.com/en/enlargement/enlargement-euro/.

[15]The European Commission, "Slovenia's Changeover to the Euro—A Clear Success," press release, May 10, 2007.

[16]*The Economist,* October 2, 1993, p. 112.

IN THE REAL WORLD:

ADOPTING THE EURO IN THE NEW MEMBER STATES

The expansion of the European Union in 2004 and 2007 included an expectation that the new members would adopt the common currency. Prior to adoption, a country must meet the Maastricht criteria and be a member of the ERM II for at least two years. Seven of the 10 new member states have already joined ERM II (Cyprus, Estonia, Latvia, Lithuania, Malta, Slovakia, and Slovenia). Compliance with the Maastricht criteria is assessed by the Council of the EU finance ministers based on reports by the Commission and the European Central Bank.

A summary of the progress of the new member states appeared in the EU News and Policy Position Forum, EurActive.com. The main elements of that summary are presented here to provide a guide to the progress of individual countries. Relevant data regarding each country's performance toward meeting the Maastricht criteria are provided in Table 2.

According to the assessment of European Commissioner for Financial and Monetary Affairs Joaquin Almunia, the new member states are a "very heterogeneous group," and yet "some common features and policy challenges can be identified":

- While income levels vary widely among the new member states, their aggregate per-capita GDP is still only about half the euro area average. The gap is gradually closing as actual and potential growth rates are generally higher than in the euro area, but fostering real convergence will remain a key policy theme for many years to come.

- Most of the new member states have also undergone a momentous transition from planned to market economies over the past 15 years. While the transition process has found its "official" completion with EU accession, some post-transition features still shape the policy environment in some countries. These include the need to complete the price liberalization process and the need to upgrade an outdated capital stock. Structural change, for example in the financial sector, is still rapid and ongoing and needs to be managed effectively.

- As they seek to increase their scarce productive capital through high public and private investment, most new member states also run sizable current account deficits as the process is not fully matched by domestic savings.

- Current account sustainability is not a major concern given the generally high degree of macroeconomic stability, the significant share of FDI in current account financing, and the ongoing integration into the EU economy. Still, vigilance is needed to ensure that these imbalances do not become unsustainable or make the economies vulnerable to shocks.

- A major achievement of the new member states has been the successful pursuit of disinflation. Monetary policy frameworks have been strengthened, and central banks are overall credible in their mandates to pursue price stability.

Estonia, Lithuania, and *Slovenia* joined the Exchange Rate Mechanism (ERM II) in June 2004. Central exchange rates for the three currencies (the Estonian kroon, the Lithuanian lita, and the Slovenian tolar) against the euro and fluctuation bands within ERM II were established on June 27, 2004. The rates were fixed at 1 euro against 15.6466 Estonian krooni, 3.45280 Lithuanian litas, and 239.640 Slovenian tolar. Under ERM II, the three countries' currencies must not deviate by more than 15 percent up or down against the euro from the agreed rates. Slovenia started using euro notes and coins on January 1, 2007. Estonia and Lithuania have adopted changeover plans targeting 2009.

A high deficit figure and public debt exceeding the Stability and Growth Pact criteria forced *Cyprus* to postpone its application for ERM II membership in the summer of 2004. Finally, Cyprus entered ERM II in April 2005. The country's target date for eurozone membership is January 1, 2008.

In *Poland,* the government has to date refused to make binding decisions on the euro's adoption. Consequently, no target date has been set.

Malta is also a new member state with an excessive budget deficit. The country has agreed to meet Stability Pact's criteria. It joined ERM II on May 2, 2005. The earliest possible date for the euro's introduction is January 1, 2008.

Latvia joined ERM II in May 2005. The likely date for the euro's introduction is 2008 in light of high inflation and a heavy government current transactions deficit.

Slovakia joined ERM II in late November 2005. The country expects to adopt the euro in January 2009.

Hungary has overshot the fiscal deficit targets and has not yet joined ERM II. Due to the slow pace of deficit

(continued)

IN THE REAL WORLD: *(continued)*

reduction, the country's original 2010 target date for the euro's adoption is likely to be shifted to some time in or after 2012.

The government of the *Czech Republic* has declared its commitment to adopting the euro by 2010. However, high national debt may delay eurozone membership.

TABLE 2   Progress toward Maastricht Criteria by New EU Member States (2004/2005 data)

Country	Inflation Rate (June 2004– June 2005)	Government Deficit (% of GDP)	Government Debt (% of GDP)	Maastricht Criteria Met
Maastricht reference value	**2.3**	**−3.0**	**60.0**	
Cyprus	2.5	−4.1	71.9	0
Czech Republic	2.1	−3.0	37.4	4
Estonia	4.1	+1.8	4.9	3
Hungary	5.0	−5.4	60.4	0
Latvia	7.0	−0.7	14.3	3
Lithuania	2.7	−2.5	19.7	3
Malta	2.4	−5.2	75.0	1
Poland	3.8	−6.8	47.7	1
Slovakia	4.5	−3.3	43.6	2
Slovenia	3.0	−1.9	29.4	3

Sources: "The Euro and the New Member States," a speech by European Commissioner for Financial and Monetary Affairs Joaquin Almunia for the Kangaroo Group Lunch Debate, September 13, 2005; "Adopting the Euro in the New Member States," EurActiv.com, February 3, 2006, obtained from www.euractiv.com/en/enlargement/.

Woods lows against those two currencies. To put these changes in perspective, in 1973, at the beginning of the floating-rate period, 2.70 deutsche marks exchanged for 1 dollar; by March 1995 the figure was 1.38 marks per dollar. For Japan, the exchange rate was 280 yen per dollar in 1973, and it had fallen to 85 yen per dollar by June 1995. However, the dollar rebounded steadily against most currencies in 1996 and gained even faster momentum in early 1997, showing especially strong gains against the mark and the yen. The strengthening of the dollar against the yen took place as a lower Japanese discount rate and increased confidence in the U.S. economy revived Japanese capital flows to the United States. By June 1998, the dollar was more than 40 percent above its value at the end of 1994 in terms of yen. With respect to other currencies, the real trade-weighted value of the British pound rose by 30 percent from 1995 to 1999, while the real trade-weighted value of the yen fell by over 25 percent from 1995 to 1998 and then rose back almost to the 1995 level by the end of 1999. In considering such volatility of real exchange rates, Taylor and Sarno (1998) concluded in a test of movements of the yen, the mark, the French franc, the pound, and the U.S. dollar, that over the long run exchange rates seek purchasing-power-parity levels; however, there is little evidence of movement toward PPP in the short run. In the new century, exchange rate movements (sometimes sizable) have continued. For example, from January 2003 to January 2005, the trade-weighted value of the U.S. dollar fell by

12.8 percent. During the period from January 2005 to January 2006, the value of the dollar rose by 0.9 percent, but then fell by 1.8 percent by January 2007. The dollar is not alone in the exchange rate fluctuations. The trade-weighted value of the Japanese yen fell by 32 percent between 2000 and 2007 and hit its lowest point since 1970 in January 2007.[17] From May 2006 to May 2007, the dollar appreciated 10 percent against the yen but declined 5.1 percent against the euro.

CONCEPT CHECK

1. What were the key elements of the international monetary system devised at Bretton Woods?

2. What led to the breakdown of the Bretton Woods system?

3. What are the convergence criteria for EMU? Why are they necessary?

CURRENT EXCHANGE RATE ARRANGEMENTS

Since the breakdown of the Bretton Woods pegged-rate system, and pursuant to the amended IMF Articles of Agreement of 1978, countries have chosen a variety of exchange rate arrangements. There is no longer a uniform system, and the current arrangements are often called a "nonsystem." The IMF classifies the arrangements chosen by its individual members into eight categories, as shown in Table 3.

The first category pertaining to exchange rate arrangements is obviously one of complete absence of rate flexibility. In fact, in the category of "exchange arrangements with no separate legal tender," the countries generally have no independent currency of their own. Thus, for example, the Marshall Islands, Micronesia, and Panama use the U.S. dollar as their currencies, although Panama also has its own currency, the balboa, in circulation at an exchange rate of $1.00 = 1$ balboa.[18]

The second category, "currency board arrangements," also involves no ability to change the exchange rate. Currency boards are starting to become fashionable, and we may well see more of them in coming years. As noted in Chapter 28, under this arrangement, a country's currency is fixed in value in terms of some particular hard currency, and the amount of the domestic currency can change only when reserves of the hard currency change. Thus, if reserves increase, the domestic money supply can be expanded; if reserves decrease, the domestic monetary authority must decrease the domestic money supply, thereby reducing the balance-of-payments deficit and hence the reserve outflow.

Categories 3 and 4 in Table 3 indicate situations where very minimal exchange rate variations are permitted. In these categories, the largest variation allowed is ± 1 percent around a specified parity value. In category 3, the peg is to a single currency, for example, the Bahamian dollar to the U.S. dollar or the Nepali rupee to the Indian rupee. In category 4, the peg is to a "basket" or "composite" of currencies of the major trading partners of the country in question or to the SDR.

Categories 1 through 4 comprise 98 IMF members, 52 percent of the total number, and thus it is far wide of the mark to say that the world has fully embraced floating exchange

---

[17]"Carry On Living Dangerously," *The Economist,* February 8, 2007, and Board of Governors of the Federal Reserve System.

[18]For discussion of the pros and cons of the use of the dollar as circulating currency by countries, see Thomas Jennings, "Dollarization: A Primer," USITC *International Economic Review,* April/May 2000, pp. 8–10. Interestingly, Jennings notes that there may be $300 billion in U.S. currency held by foreigners.

TABLE 3   Exchange Rate Arrangements as of April 30, 2007

Category	*Countries*	*Number of Countries*
1. Exchange arrangements with no separate legal tender	*Another currency as legal tender:* Ecuador, El Salvador, Kiribati, Marshall Islands, Federated States of Micronesia, Palau, Panama, San Marino, Timor-Leste	42
	Eastern Caribbean Currency Union (ECCU): Antigua and Barbuda, Dominica, Grenada, St. Kitts and Nevis, St. Lucia, St. Vincent and the Grenadines	
	West African Economic and Monetary Union (WAEMU): Benin, Burkina Faso, Côte d'Ivoire, Guinea-Bissau, Mali, Niger, Senegal, Togo	
	Central African Economic and Monetary Community (CEMAC): Cameroon, Central African Republic, Chad, Republic of Congo, Equatorial Guinea, Gabon	
	Euro Area: Austria, Belgium, Finland, France, Germany, Greece, Ireland, Italy, Luxembourg, Netherlands, Portugal, Slovenia, Spain	
2. Currency board arrangements	Bosnia and Herzegovina, Brunei, Bulgaria, Djibouti, Estonia, Hong Kong (China), Lithuania	7
3. Fixed peg against a single currency	Aruba, Azerbaijan, The Bahamas, Bahrain, Barbados, Belarus, Belize, Bhutan, Cape Verde, China, Comoros, Egypt, Eritrea, Guyana, Honduras, Iraq, Jordan, Kuwait, Latvia, Lebanon, Lesotho, Macedonia, Maldives, Malta, Mauritania, Namibia, Nepal, Netherlands Antilles, Oman, Pakistan, Qatar, Saudi Arabia, Seychelles, Solomon Islands, Suriname, Swaziland, Syria, Trinidad and Tobago, Turkmenistan, Ukraine, United Arab Emirates, Venezuela, Vietnam, Zimbabwe	44
4. Fixed peg against a composite ("basket")	Fiji, Libya, Morocco, Samoa, Vanuatu	5
5. Pegged exchange rates within horizontal bands	Cyprus, Denmark, Hungary, Slovak Republic, Tonga	5
6. Crawling pegs	Bolivia, Botswana, Costa Rica, Iran, Nicaragua	5
7. Managed floating with no predetermined path for the exchange rate	Afghanistan, Algeria, Angola, Argentina, Bangladesh, Burundi, Cambodia, Colombia, Croatia, Czech Republic, Dominican Republic, Ethiopia, The Gambia, Georgia, Ghana, Guatemala, Guinea, Haiti, India, Indonesia, Jamaica, Kazakhstan, Kenya, Kyrgyz Republic, Laos, Liberia, Madagascar, Malawi, Malaysia, Mauritius, Moldova, Mongolia, Mozambique, Myanmar, Nigeria, Papua New Guinea, Paraguay, Peru, Romania, Russia, Rwanda, São Tomé and Principe, Serbia and Montenegro, Singapore, Sri Lanka, Sudan, Tajikistan, Thailand, Tunisia, Uruguay, Uzbekistan, Yemen, Zambia	53
8. Independently floating	Albania, Armenia, Australia, Brazil, Canada, Chile, Democratic Republic of the Congo, Iceland, Israel, Japan, Republic of Korea, Mexico, New Zealand, Norway, Philippines, Poland, Sierra Leone, Somalia, South Africa, Sweden, Switzerland, Tanzania, Turkey, Uganda, United Kingdom, United States	26

Source: International Monetary Fund, *Annual Report of the Executive Board for the Financial Year Ended April 30, 2007* (Washington, DC: IMF, 2007), obtained from www.imf.org.

rates. Note that many of the countries involved in this near or complete fixity of the exchange rate are small, developing countries. In these countries, it is advantageous to tie to or adopt the currency of the major trading partner; a floating or flexible rate with the leading trading partner could generate instability in the developing country's trade, payments, and GDP. In addition, if the small country has a debt denominated in U.S. dollars (as many countries do), it is worthwhile to peg to the U.S. dollar. Otherwise, for example, if the Bahamian dollar depreciated against the U.S. dollar, payment of interest and repayment of principal would require a greater generation of Bahamian dollar resources and a greater resource burden on The Bahamas than would otherwise be the case.

Categories 5 and 6 in Table 3 include countries that permit greater change in exchange rates than do those in the first four categories, but the arrangements are by no means floating ones. Category 5, "pegged exchange rates within horizontal bands," refers to a situation where the permitted variation is greater than ±1 percent around parity. Category 6, the "crawling peg" arrangement (see Chapter 28), is a situation where the value of the currency is changed periodically to a small extent either in a preannounced fashion or in response to a set of indicators (e.g., changes in the international reserve position of the country). Bolivia, Botswana, Costa Rica, Iran, and Nicaragua currently have this arrangement in place, and Colombia and other countries have utilized it in the past. All in all, when categories 1 through 6 are accounted for, 108 of the countries (58 percent) fall into these fixed or relatively fixed categories.

Categories 7 and 8 combine to make up the other 42 percent of exchange rate arrangements. Category 7, "managed floating" means that central bank intervention occurs to influence the exchange rate but the intervention is made irregularly and without preannouncement even as to direction. Finally, in "independent floating," the rate is basically market-determined. Intervention occasionally occurs but relatively rarely, and the intervention is usually undertaken to moderate (but not reverse) a swing. This situation, as indicated in Chapter 28, is known as leaning against the wind.

The advantages and disadvantages of fixed versus floating rates were examined in the preceding chapter. It is clear that there are many forces at work and many variables to be considered by a country's authorities when selecting the degree of exchange rate flexibility to be permitted. The type of exchange rate arrangement that is best for one country may not be the best for another country with differing features and institutions, and the best arrangement for a country at one point in time may not be the best at another point. For example, the liberalization in many developing countries in the 1990s led to *relatively* greater adoption of more flexible exchange rate arrangements than was previously the case.

EXPERIENCE UNDER THE CURRENT INTERNATIONAL MONETARY SYSTEM

The historical record of the post–Bretton Woods international monetary system has been widely discussed and widely debated. A general consensus of economists regarding the operation of that system, often characterized by the general term *managed float* (especially for industrialized countries), is presented in this section. However, because the experience is relatively recent and because the system is still evolving, it is not certain that the views expressed will stand the test of time.

1. The post–Bretton Woods international monetary system has been characterized by substantial variability in exchange rates of the major industrial countries. This statement applies to nominal exchange rates and real exchange rates, and it is contrary to the expectations of many proponents of floating rates that the rates would move to an equilibrium level and then would show reasonable stability at that level. Even for countries with fixed nominal rates, there have been periodic official devaluations, and real exchange rates have varied in the presence of the fixed nominal rates.

2. Another feature of the international monetary system associated with this variability in exchange rates is that overshooting of exchange rates has occurred. Overshooting was discussed in Chapter 22.

3. A third characteristic of the post–Bretton Woods monetary system is that the variability in exchange rates has had *real economic effects*. This characteristic has occurred because the variations in nominal exchange rates have not perfectly matched the variations in purchasing power parity (PPP) exchange rates, and thus real exchange rates have varied. If a country's currency undergoes a real depreciation, then the tradeable goods sectors of that country will attract resources because those sectors are now relatively more profitable than the nontradeable goods sectors. If the exchange rate then appreciates, the incentives will be shifted in the opposite direction, and resources will move out of the tradeable goods sectors and into the nontradeable goods sectors. However, such resource movements are not costless. Factors of production may have to move physically, retraining of workers may be needed, and unemployment occurs during the transition period. In addition, exchange rate variability can operate as a disincentive for direct investment flows between countries because it can generate arbitrary losses. For example, a firm making an investment in a foreign country at one exchange rate may want to repatriate profits at a later date but may find that the foreign currency has greatly depreciated and thus fewer units of home currency are being realized than was originally expected. The firm might therefore be less inclined to make such investments in the future. Thus, by various mechanisms, exchange rate movements may well lead to reduced output in the world economy.

4. Another widely noted feature of the current international monetary system is that the system does not seem to have insulated countries from outside economic disturbances to the extent expected. Remember from earlier chapters that one of the alleged advantages of a floating-rate system is that insulation would occur, and hence that there would be little transmission of business cycles from one country to another. However, the conclusion of most observers is that business cycles have been transmitted across country lines in the floating-rate period for industrialized countries and that these countries have indeed had to worry about real external shocks.

Why do observers judge that the current system does not provide insulation? The most important reason is that central banks of the major industrial countries have been unwilling to allow complete flexibility in their exchange rates. The consequent official intervention in the exchange markets reflects the fact that the central banks may well have exchange rate targets in mind, as well as targets for national income. For example, authorities may wish to avoid a depreciation because it causes dislocations in the nontradeable goods sectors and worsens home inflation. In addition, they may also wish to limit the degree of appreciation, because appreciation can cause problems for the tradeable goods sectors and run into political opposition. The end result is that exchange rates have not been as flexible as in floating-rate theory, and therefore insulation from real external shocks has not occurred to the extent expected by proponents of flexible exchange rates.

5. Because exchange rates have not been fully flexible, another expectation of the proponents of flexible exchange rates has not been met: It was anticipated that, with floating rates, countries would not need to hold as large a volume of international reserves as under fixed rates, because reserve movements would not be needed in a major way to finance BOP deficits. However, in the post–BrettonWoods years, countries have added to their international reserves. Thus, the demand for international reserves has not decreased absolutely with floating rates, although reserves relative to imports have fallen.

We have at least a partial explanation for the central banks' behavior from item 4, where we noted that intervention continues to take place. Because the United States had BOP deficits over much of the period, more dollars were supplied to the exchange markets than would otherwise have been the case. When foreign central banks purchased these dollars to mitigate the fall in the value of the dollar, the dollars were added to the international

TABLE 4   Central Bank International Reserves as of April 30, 2007*

Reserve Asset†	*Value ($, billions)*	*Percent of Total Reserves*
1. Gold	$ 45.9	0.89%
2. SDRS	51.0	0.98
3. Reserve positions in the IMF	26.4	0.51
4. Foreign exchange	5,055.5	97.62
Total reserves	$5,178.8	100%

*The figures pertain only to IMF members.

†Gold valued at a fixed 35 SDR per 1 ounce of gold, SDR values have been converted to dollars at a prevailing rate: 1 SDR = $1.51.

Source: International Monetary Fund, *International Financial Statistics,* April 2007, obtained from www.imf.org.

reserves of the foreign central banks. At the same time, because dollars are not counted as part of the reserves of the United States, there was no decline in the value of U.S. reserves. The result has been an increase in total world reserves.

To explore the increase in international reserves further, Table 4 presents recent information. As can be seen, the reserves of central banks are composed of four items:

Gold. The gold holdings of central banks constitute 0.9 percent of international reserves of central banks. However, the IMF values gold at the previous official price of 35 SDRs = 1 ounce of gold. At the time of the information in this table, the SDR was equal to $1.51, so this gold valuation is at a price of almost $53 per ounce. This is hardly a realistic price, because private market gold has been selling at around $300 per ounce for a number of years. If official gold holdings were valued at the market price, international reserves would be much larger, as would the share of gold in these reserves.

SDRs. Because SDRs make up only 1 percent of international reserves, it is clear that the IMF's objective of developing the SDR into a major international asset has not yet been achieved.

Reserve positions in the IMF. This element of international reserves roughly refers to the first 25 percent of countries' IMF quotas. A country can automatically obtain a loan of this size from the IMF when in BOP difficulties. This item is also a small fraction of world reserves (0.5 percent).

Foreign exchange. This currently accounts for 97.6 percent of central bank reserves and is clearly the major international reserve asset central banks have at their disposal for settling BOP deficits. The U.S. dollar constitutes the major component of these foreign exchange holdings, but euros and Japanese yen are becoming increasingly important.

The point of this discussion of international reserves is that central banks continue to hold a sizable volume of reserves. (Indeed, reserves increased from $159.2 billion at the end of 1972—just prior to the advent of floating—to the April 2007 figure of $5,178.8 billion.) Such large reserves would not be needed in a truly flexible exchange rate system.

6. A further conclusion regarding the current international monetary system that commands fairly wide agreement is that there has not been an increase in inflation in the world economy because of the presence of greater floating of exchange rates. Recall that a fear concerning the adoption of flexible rates was that a "vicious circle" of inflation would develop. While the period from 1973–1974 until the early 1980s was indeed characterized by historically high inflation rates, it is not generally thought that this inflation was directly

attributable to flexible exchange rates. Rather, the behavior of the Organization of Petroleum Exporting Countries (OPEC), of macroeconomic policymakers, and of price expectations played more crucial roles. Indeed, some observers doubt that the BrettonWoods system itself could have survived this inflationary episode. The floating-rate system permitted easier adjustment to the disturbances of this period than fixed rates would have done. It is interesting to note that, recently, there has been some concern about possible *deflation* in the world economy, although the concern is not particularly associated with floating rates per se.

7. Many observers also think the fear that the volume of world trade would shrink in the face of the risk associated with flexible rates has not been borne out. World trade grew more rapidly than world production during the 1970s. In the early 1980s, trade growth dropped off sharply with stagflation from the second oil crisis and U.S. tight monetary policy, but trade continued to grow more rapidly than world production. Since that time, trade and production growth rates rose in the late 1980s, fell off with the recession of 1990–1991, and then recovered. In the 1990s and through 2005, trade continued to grow more rapidly than world output (with the exception of 2001, when they both fell slightly), although this might also have occurred under fixed rates.

Finally, a series of events took place in 1997–1998 that caused many observers to consider a revamping of the entire "international financial architecture." This set of events is considered in the next subsection.

The Asian Crisis: The Miracle Unravels[19]

Throughout the 1980s and early 1990s the miracle economies of Southeast Asia were touted as shining examples of successful growth and development based on "outward-looking" strategies. Rather than pursuing more traditional closed-economy policies in the presence of continued domestic price distortions, these countries embraced export-oriented strategies which involved the freeing up of financial and commodity markets and an openness to trade and foreign investment. The effects were extremely positive, with the result that through the early 1990s countries such as South Korea, Thailand, and Indonesia continued to demonstrate strong growth in the presence of fiscal surpluses, reasonably low current account deficits, and moderate rates of inflation. Only Thailand suggested any financial strain, as its current account deficit remained in the area of 5 percent of GDP, a common early sign of potential financial problems. Nonetheless, they all continued to receive strong credit ratings by both public and private organizations.

However, the seeds of the forthcoming financial crisis were being sown in several ways. The positive economic environment resulted in substantial real investment by both foreign and domestic investors, which led to overinvestment in several sectors and a consequent eroding of the rates of return on the new capital such as, for example, in the electronics industry. A speculative bubble of sorts emerged, abetted by bad (nonperforming) loans of financial institutions that reflected weak management, little risk control, the lack of enforcement of prudent rules, inadequate supervision, and the continuation of government-directed lending practices. These activities led to a financial overheating that spread into

---

[19]Much of this section draws on the following sources: International Monetary Fund (IMF), *International Financial Statistics,* March 2000, pp. 396, 448, 754; IMF, *World Economic Outlook,* May 1998 (Washington, DC: IMF, 1998), chap. 1; IMF, *World Economic Outlook,* May 1999 (Washington, DC: IMF, 1999), chap. 1; IMF, *World Economic Outlook,* October 1999 (Washington, DC: IMF, 1999), chap. 1; Bank for International Settlements, *68th Annual Report* (Basle: BIS, June 8, 1998), chap. 7; Joseph P. Joyce, "The Lessons of Asia: IMF Policies and Financial Crises," Working Paper 99-02, Department of Economics, Wellesley College, May 1999.

inflated property and stock market prices. An additional major complication in dealing with the situation when it began to self-correct was the increasing difficulty of maintaining exchange rate policies that rested on a close peg to the U.S. dollar. The fixed exchange rates not only fostered foreign borrowing and/or foreign investment but also complicated the response of the monetary authorities when the initial waves of the crisis began. Finally, the situation was further hampered by political uncertainties which increasingly ate away at investor confidence and increased the reluctance of foreign creditors to roll over short-term debt once the crisis began.

The Asian crisis is interesting in that it was fueled by rapidly growing deficits in the capital accounts rather than deficits in the current accounts, which had been the previous pattern in many developing countries. The first sign of a problem appeared early in 1997 when Thailand's capital account turned from a positive $2.4 billion surplus in the first quarter to a $3.9 billion deficit in the second quarter because of capital flight and loss of confidence. The Thai central bank intervened heavily to support the baht and then floated the currency on July 2, 1997. In spite of the floating of the currency, a massive outflow of funds still took place and the baht depreciated by more than 50 percent by January 1998. With the floating of the Thai baht, the contagion began to spread to other countries in the region. In an attempt to slowdown the spread, on July 11 both Indonesia and the Philippines widened the bands around their currencies, and on August 14 the Indonesian rupiah was floated. During July the Malaysian ringgit fell by 4.8 percent, and equity prices in Hong Kong and Taiwan peaked in August. The effects continued to spread into the fall as pressure mounted against the Hong Kong dollar and the Taiwan dollar, and the pressure on equity markets also intensified. By the end of October, the effects were being felt in both Russian and Latin American equity markets. By early November South Korea was forced to widen its exchange rate bands; on December 16, it elected to float the won. As the crisis in Asia deepened, the economies suffered. For example, from 1997 to 1998, real GDP *fell* by 6 percent in South Korea, 11 percent in Thailand, and 13½ percent in Indonesia. A genuine fear was that the real and monetary effects would be passed on to other countries through appreciation of key currencies such as the dollar and through increased current account deficits (or reduced surpluses) in the industrialized countries. In other words, depreciation of the Asian currencies reduced the exports and increased the imports of other countries, hence posing the threat of spreading the recession worldwide. Collapse of the Russian ruble and Russian default on some debt in the autumn of 1998 was attributed to the contagion from Asia, as were threats to the stability of the Brazilian currency. While some observers thought that the United States might be hit hard, this result did not occur.

In retrospect, it is clear that the crisis was fueled by a combination of factors related to speculative overinvestment, inadequate institutional development and oversight, and the ease of moving short-term capital quickly from one country to another amid the prospect of worsening economic conditions. In this respect, the Asian crisis was different from financially generated crises such as occurred in Mexico in 1994 both in terms of its size and its speed. However, investor confidence turned positive in 1998 and was a critical factor in turning the situation around, as recovery subsequently began earlier and has moved faster than many imagined possible. As the IMF finally moved away from recommending the traditional policies of monetary and fiscal restraint (which indeed did not necessarily seem warranted) and toward institutional reform, financial stabilization, strengthened exchange rates, and relaxed monetary policies, the Asian countries began to rebound. For the region as a whole, commodity prices began to recover, capital inflows returned, an upturn began in the electronics industry, and inflation declined. There was clearly a need for continued structural and institutional reforms, however, and there was fear that too rapid a recovery would slow down these needed changes in the corporate, financial, and public sectors. All in all, there were positive signs of recovery in Korea, Malaysia, Thailand, Indonesia, the Philippines, Hong Kong, Singapore, and China. All these countries, with the exception of Singapore, returned to positive output growth by the first year of the new century.

The globalization of world finance and the opening up of financial markets is creating a new world environment which both increases the efficiency of world financial capital and generates a need for institutional change, for different IMF policies, and perhaps for new lending facilities and institutions. Numerous proposals have come forward for new institutional arrangements that might be better equipped to deal with incipient financial crises. Clearly "flights from risk" remain a real possibility throughout the world, whether it be in Eastern Europe, Russia, Latin America, Africa, or Asia.

CONCEPT CHECK	1. How would you describe the current international monetary system in terms of the nature of the exchange rate arrangements? 2. Why might countries with one main trading partner tend to opt for a fixed exchange rate with that partner rather than a flexible rate?	3. What are two of the more serious problems that have surfaced with the current system?

SUGGESTIONS FOR REFORM OF THE INTERNATIONAL MONETARY SYSTEM

In view of the various performance characteristics of the current international monetary system, many observers have proposed changes in the system in order to make it work better. The principal objection to the present arrangements concerns the considerable exchange rate volatility in the currencies of the major industrialized countries (especially the United States, the EU, and Japan) and its potential adverse effects. Because these countries are so important in the world economy and because much of world trade and payments is denominated in their currencies, it is thought that some means must be found for reducing exchange rate variability. In this section we briefly review proposals that have been discussed.

A Return to the Gold Standard

Proponents of returning to a gold standard emphasize the need for an anchor for price levels within countries. The argument for a gold standard is that if currencies are defined in terms of gold *and national money supplies are tied to the size of countries' gold stocks,* then long-running BOP deficits and surpluses would not exist because of automatic adjustment, and the world would have less inflation because money supplies could not grow faster than the world's gold stock. There could also be reduced risks associated with holding currencies as international reserves because exchange rates would be fixed. Further, because gold would be the principal reserve asset in official reserve portfolios, stability would be introduced because foreign currencies would constitute a small portion of international reserves. Finally, if countries do indeed stick to their gold parities, the system eliminates the substantial volatility in exchange rates that has been of so much recent concern.

The principal disadvantage of this proposal is that it places the goal of external balance (i.e., BOP equilibrium) above the internal goals of full employment and economic growth. Suppose that a country is running a BOP deficit; it is then expected to undergo a reduction of its gold stock and a contraction of its money supply. However, if the BOP deficit coincides with recession and slow growth internally, then contraction of the money supply will reduce economic activity even further. Because prices and wages in the modern economy tend to be inflexible in the downward direction, the result of monetary contraction will be a reduction of output and a rise in unemployment. The rise in interest rates expected of a deficit country would also deter long-term investment, which is necessary for sustained economic growth. This sacrifice of internal goals in the interests of BOP equilibrium is not a sacrifice many countries are politically prepared to make. Also, a surplus country will find inflationary pressures put upon it from the inflow of gold and international reserves, and a surplus country with a strong aversion to inflation (e.g., Germany, historically) will be unlikely to sacrifice its internal goal of price stability. Another disadvantage of the gold standard is that exchange rate changes are not available for reallocating resources as comparative advantage changes, and sticky internal prices could not accomplish the reallocation easily.

A proposal that has some similarities to the gold standard was put forward by Ronald McKinnon (1984, 1988); indeed, it has been dubbed the "gold standard without gold." McKinnon would have the central banks of the United States, Japan, and Germany (which would now be the banks of the European Union) jointly announce fixed nominal exchange rate targets among their currencies (with small actual deviations permitted). The rates would be set according to PPP at the time of announcement, and a constant price level for traded goods would be sought. Monetary policy would be directed toward preserving these rates and the constant price level. With exchange rates and policies thus "anchored," destabilizing short-term capital flows would become stabilizing. Again, however, sacrifice of national autonomy and unavailability of exchange rate changes to perform resource reallocations are present in this system, and unsterilized intervention would be used when necessary.

A World Central Bank

This proposal has been made in many different forms over several decades [e.g., by John Maynard Keynes in the early 1940s, Robert Triffin (1960), Richard Cooper (1986), and most recently by Robert Mundell (2000)]. The plans propose different degrees of control to be exercised by a new, centralized monetary institution, but all have some common elements. To set up the institution, at least part of the international reserves of the participating countries would be deposited in the new institution. This new bank would then have at its command billions of dollars of assets with which it could manage the world money supply. If faster (or slower) monetary growth were needed, the authority could vary its purchase of government bonds in world financial markets (much as the Federal Reserve in the United States conducts its open-market operations) to accomplish its objective. It could also make loans to countries in BOP difficulties, and variations in the authority's lending rate would influence the amount of borrowing (as the Federal Reserve in the United States does with its discount rate), which would in turn affect the size of the world money supply.

In an extreme form of the proposal, the new world central bank would issue a world currency as the means of controlling the world money supply. In this version, as well as in less extreme versions such as that of Mundell, countries have absolutely fixed exchange rates. (See Concept Box 1.) If currencies are tied together permanently at fixed rates, then a next step toward a common currency is facilitated, such as has been done on a regional basis with the euro. The end result is a movement toward a worldwide currency area, and the instability associated with fluctuating exchange rates is eliminated.

The principal impetus behind a controlled world money supply is the view that today's fluctuations in exchange rates are due to the differing and uncoordinated macroeconomic policies (especially monetary policies) of the major industrialized countries. In the current system, if country A expands its money supply relative to that of country B, then the relatively

CONCEPT BOX 1

A WORLD CENTRAL BANK WITHIN A THREE-CURRENCY MONETARY UNION

Nobel laureate Robert Mundell has reintroduced the idea of a world optimal currency area with a world central bank in an interesting and novel way. Citing the existence of wide swings in exchange rates that are not based on underlying economic fundamentals as the biggest threat to world prosperity, he argues that central banks must commit themselves to active and consistent intervention in the foreign exchange markets to reduce exchange rate volatility to maintain prosperity and stimulate growth and development worldwide. Because recent events have led to a notable convergence of inflation rates in Japan, Europe, and the United States, he states that this is a logical time to focus on a coordinated effort to stabilize exchange rates. However, to accomplish this, the "Big Three" (the European Union, the United States, and Japan) must all agree to participate in such intervention, to refrain from sterilizing the effects of such intervention, and to intervene in both the spot and the forward markets. Finally, the public must believe that the governments will actively support such exchange rate intervention with appropriate monetary policy.

This approach to exchange rate stability would logically take place in a single-currency world monetary union. However, Mundell acknowledges that such a monetary union is not politically feasible at this point. The three geographic areas are sufficiently large to provide a basis for world monetary integration—the United States represents approximately 30 percent of world output, "Euroland" approximately 20 percent, and Japan 15 percent. As mentioned in Chapter 26, increased globalization has made coordination of policies a necessary condition for realization of domestic goals among these important trading groups, and exchange rate volatility is clearly counterproductive to all concerned. In these complicated circumstances, Mundell argues that a reasonable compromise would be to create a world central bank producing its own international asset, which would be backed by reserves of dollars, yen, euros, and gold. It would have the advantage of involving power sharing and a broader set of options to which smaller countries could tie their currencies. In many ways it is similar to the idea proposed at Bretton Woods by John Maynard Keynes but perhaps more politically palatable and at a more logical time in history. Is it possible that the time has arrived for a world central bank and an international currency built on the strength of these three strong regional currencies which would be the property of all nations of the world?

Source: Robert Mundell, "Threat to Prosperity," *The Wall Street Journal*, March 30, 2000, p. A30.

●

lower interest rates in country A will cause an outflow of mobile short-term capital from A to B. This outflow will depress the country A currency value relative to that of B. Further, the depreciation of the A currency and the appreciation of the B currency will generate greater inflation in A relative to B, which can set in motion a further depreciation of A's currency. At the heart of the problem of the exchange rate changes is the differing monetary stance, which in turn can reflect differences in the desired inflation-unemployment trade-off in the two countries. By centralizing monetary policy in a new world institution, these destabilizing differences in monetary growth among countries can be avoided.

This plan in general could indeed work to reduce the amount of exchange rate instability and the effects of divergent monetary policies in the major industrialized countries. But the main criticism of proposals for a world central bank is that it is unrealistic to think that all countries would ever completely give up autonomy over their individual monetary policies. National sovereignty over economic policy is a cherished and firmly ingrained tradition. Proponents of such plans would argue that such autonomy is largely lost already in the current system because of the extremely high mobility of short-term capital across country borders. However, the lost autonomy is not as true for large countries as for small ones, and country officials *think* that they have considerable monetary control and thus will oppose such a plan.

The Target Zone Proposal

The leading proponent of the **target zone proposal** is John Williamson (1985, 1987, 1988). This plan attempts to reduce the element of conflict between internal goals and the external goal of BOP equilibrium. The major industrialized countries would first negotiate a set of mutually consistent targets for their *real effective* exchange rates. Absolute fixity of these rates is not envisaged, but rather each country would permit its real effective exchange rate to vary in, for example, a zone of 10 percent in either direction from the target rate. The target rate itself for each country would be chosen as the exchange rate that would be estimated to reconcile external and internal balance over a *medium-run* time period. If the exchange rate moved close to the ceiling or floor of the zone, this would be an indication that policy steps should be taken to moderate or reverse the movement, but there is no absolute requirement that the rates be kept between the ceiling and the floor. Rather the limits of the zone can be thought of as soft margins instead of hard boundaries.

Policy Actions in the Target Zone System

What would be the policy actions necessary in the target zone system? The most important policy tool would be monetary policy rather than fiscal policy. Fiscal policy would play a key role in attaining the internal target (e.g., reasonably full employment with reasonable price stability), but monetary policy is crucial because it can work to attain the internal goal as well as the external goal. In Williamson's framework, the immediate external goal is not balance-of-payments equilibrium per se but, rather, the existence of reasonable stability in the real effective exchange rate around the target rate. If the real effective exchange rate begins to move toward the ceiling price for foreign exchange (a real depreciation of the home currency), this would indicate that inflation is too high relative to that in foreign trading partners. A rise in interest rates would work to moderate the inflation but also would induce an inflow of short-term capital and thus moderate the home currency depreciation. Similarly, a downward movement of the real effective exchange rate (a real appreciation of the home currency) would indicate that the country's macroeconomic policy is too restrictive relative to that of other countries, so an easing of monetary policy is called for with respect to attaining both the internal and external targets. Monetary policy is supposed to be mainly directed toward internal goals, but because of capital mobility, it has the side benefit of assisting in stabilizing the exchange rate. However, it is clear that the success of such a plan would be dependent upon both the use of coordinated intervention in exchange markets by key central banks and a transparent mechanism for making gradual changes in the zones if it is clear that fundamental changes in the participating economies are making the previously established zones inconsistent or obsolete.

Williamson's target zone proposal has desirable features in that it keeps internal goals at the forefront while also addressing exchange rate instability. In addition, the plan's focus is on real exchange rates rather than on nominal exchange rates, and the former are more influential for economic activity than the latter. However, real exchange rates are more difficult to manage than are nominal exchange rates, and it is also crucial that the target rate be chosen reasonably accurately. If the estimate of the target rate is incorrect, the operation of the proposal perpetuates a misalignment of exchange rates, which can interfere with efficient resource allocation in the world economy. Also, if a situation of "stagflation" occurs, in which unemployment and inflation may both be rising at the same time, it is not clear that the target zone plan would be useful without supplementation by additional policy instruments.

The Krugman Version of the Target Zone

Another version of the target zone proposal was put forward by Paul Krugman (1991). (See also Svensson 1992, pp. 121–25.) Unlike Williamson, Krugman would set upper and lower limits to the *nominal* effective exchange rate rather than to the real rate, and the limits would be *permanent* rather than "soft" limits. To build the case for the zone, Krugman develops a simple monetary/asset market model for the determination of the exchange rate. The exchange rate e (home-currency price of one unit of spot foreign exchange) depends only on the home money supply, changes or shocks in the velocity of money, and the expected rate of depreciation of the home currency. In his equation, an increase in the home money supply will depreciate the home currency and its coefficient is therefore positive. An increase in the velocity of money (rate of usage or turnover of money) acts like an increase in the money supply and thus would also depreciate the currency. (Krugman postulates that changes in velocity are random.) Finally, Krugman employs uncovered interest parity (UIP) in asset markets, so that an increase in the expected rate of depreciation of the home currency (an increase in xa in the terminology of previous chapters) depreciates the home currency (a positive coefficient).

In the Krugman target zone model, the monetary authorities stand ready to decrease the money supply if e reaches the specified upper limit (i.e., a depreciation of the home currency to its lower limit). Similarly, the authorities will increase the money supply if e falls to the floor (an appreciation of the home currency to its upper limit). A difference in the Krugman proposal from the Williamson proposal in this respect is that the monetary authorities basically act only *if* the exchange rate hits the limits—there is no change of behavior as the rate merely approaches the limits. In addition, Krugman postulates that the ceiling and floor may well never be reached, so the monetary authorities may not have to act at all. This result would occur if market participants had full confidence in the monetary authorities' ability to maintain the limits.

The Krugman target zone proposal thus results in stability of exchange rates and offers a means of reducing the volatility of exchange rates in today's increasingly integrated financial world. Major criticisms of the plan concern the assumption of perfect credibility of the specified limits and the postulated confidence in and effectiveness of the monetary authorities. In addition, empirical tests of the relationship between the expected rate of change in the exchange rate and the exchange rate itself have not always yielded the Krugman relationship, and the actual existence of UIP has also been questioned. Further, other things influence the exchange rate besides the money supply, velocity, and the expected change in the exchange rate.[20] Little is also said about "internal balance" objectives. Nevertheless, given the desire of many observers to see more stability in exchange rates, this proposal as well as the Williamson proposal will continue to be debated, and they may suggest forthcoming modifications in the international monetary system.

Controls on Capital Flows

This approach to the problem of exchange rate instability in the currencies of major countries states that the obvious major cause of the instability is the fact that short-term capital moves so freely between countries, a view enhanced by the 1997–1998 Asian crisis. Many of these flows of capital have nothing to do with "economic fundamentals" such as inflation rates, resource productivity, and general economic conditions. Rather, they reflect reactions to rumors, political events, and "bandwagon effects" and "herd instincts," where speculation against a currency in and of itself generates further speculation against that currency. Such volatile short-term capital flows cause considerable instability in exchange rates, and this instability is exacerbated by overshooting. Hence, so this approach specifies, a remedy is to impose limitations on the inflow and outflow of funds from major countries that are responding to such "uneconomic" motivations.

---

[20]Svensson (1992, pp. 125–39) discussed these and other objections to the Krugman proposal, as well as cases of imperfect credibility. Krugman regards the target zone proposal as less stabilizing when there is imperfect credibility, but it is still stabilizing (see Krugman 1991, p. 680).

Capital flows among countries could be restricted in a number of ways. A major proposal that has attracted attention for some time is that of James Tobin (1978), who suggested imposing an international tax on all spot transactions involving the conversion of one currency into another in securities markets. Such a tax would presumably discourage speculation by making currency trading more expensive, thereby reducing the volume of destabilizing short-term capital flows. [Tobin (1995) also hypothesized that, by generating greater interest rate differentials across countries, the tax—say, of 0.5 percent of transaction value—would create room for individual country monetary policies to be more effective in macroeconomic stabilization.] While the tax has the potential advantages of reducing some of the marginally based speculative transactions or market "noise" and of fostering international cooperation on tax policy, there are a number of problems with a transactions tax of this type.

Spahn (1996, p. 24) pointed out that there are four main problems with a Tobin tax that would inhibit its effectiveness. First, to limit the market distortions resulting from such a tax, the tax base would have to be as broad as possible and would have to exclude no category of market participants. However, a strong argument can be made that financial intermediaries or "market makers" who increase market liquidity should not be taxed. Unfortunately, the Tobin tax cannot distinguish between normal institutional trading that ensures market liquidity and efficiency and destabilizing financial activity. Second, there is the question of what type of transaction to tax. If the tax is applied only to spot transactions, it can easily be avoided by going into the derivatives market. Taxing the initial contractional value (or notional value) of derivatives, however, would likely severely injure the derivatives market. Applying a different tax rate to derivatives than to other instruments is a possibility, but a selective tax system would be arbitrary and extremely difficult to administer. Third, it can be argued that the tax should be applied only when markets are clearly in disequilibrium. Thus, the tax rate would be zero during conditions of stability and equilibrium and increase in accordance with the deviation from equilibrium. This, however, would again contradict Tobin's idea of a one-tax system and would also be incredibly complex to administer. Finally, there is the question of the distribution of revenues. Distribution of tax revenues is a controversial political question within countries, to say nothing of between countries. Significant costs could be incurred in simply trying to arrive at international consensus on this issue.

In response to these problems, Spahn (pp. 26–27) suggested a two-tiered Tobin tax that would consist of a minimal-rate transactions tax and an exchange rate surcharge that would be applied only during periods of great exchange market turbulence. Although it certainly would not deter sudden speculation based on fear of an event such as a payment default, the two-tier tax would be useful as a short-term monetary stabilization tool that could smooth market adjustment. It should not, however, be viewed as a means of dealing with underlying structural problems. In response to this idea, Stotsky (1996) argued strongly against employing such a tax. Like the Tobin tax, it may not work simply because there is little evidence that market volatility is reduced by these kinds of taxes. (For a different view, see Frankel 1996, p. 156.) Further, the increased transaction costs hinder market operations and efficiency. In addition, the use of variable tax rates can create uncertainty with respect to market prices and can be burdensome administratively. Finally, Stotsky questioned the desirability of mixing monetary policy and tax policy, given the political and administrative differences in the way they are enacted. Thus, while discussion continues regarding the viability and/or desirability of using a Tobin-type tax to reduce exchange rate instability, the lack of any consensus on its overall effects suggests that it is unlikely that it will be adopted in the near future.

Another approach to controlling capital flows which has been utilized by a number of countries involves adopting a system of **dual exchange rates** or **multiple exchange rates.** In this situation, a different exchange rate is employed depending on the nature of the foreign transaction. If British pounds are being purchased for normal trade transactions or for long-term overseas investment, the exchange rate might be specified as $1.80/£1; however, if the transaction involved a short-term capital flow, an exchange rate of $2.70/£1 might be used. The 50 percent higher price for the short-term capital transaction would presumably discourage such transactions. Or the central bank of the country could also restrict capital flows by exercising moral suasion or "jawboning" against capital outflows, as the United States did in the late 1960s through its "voluntary" restrictions on bank lending overseas. ("Guidelines" were published by the Federal Reserve.) Stronger measures such as outright prohibitions might also be adopted.

Capital movements between countries that are in the interests of economic efficiency are eminently desirable. If capital moves from a country where the marginal product of capital is low to a country where the marginal product of capital is high, there is an increase in world output and greater efficiency in resource allocation from the capital flow. However, proponents of capital controls contend that a large fraction of the capital flows in the floating-rate period has not been of this type. Rather, the daily movements of speculative funds in and out of leading countries' financial markets may be hindering efficient resource allocation because traders and long-term investors are receiving misleading and uncertain signals. In addition, the fluctuations in real exchange rates that can result from these flows may be causing wasteful resource movements.

In general, economists dislike capital controls. The danger is that the controls will prevent the flow of capital that is moving in response to true marginal productivity differences. Further, there is no effective way to sort out which capital movements are "good" and which are "bad," and capital controls are easy to evade. For example, with dual exchange rates, a firm buying components from a foreign subsidiary could evade the capital controls by simply overstating the price of imported goods. Thus, capital is being moved out of the country to the foreign subsidiary. Nevertheless, there appears to be no time in the postwar period when at least some countries did not have capital controls (industrialized as well as developing countries). It is possible that such controls could become more widespread in the future if countries find no other solutions to the current problems with exchange rate instability.

Finally, in the aftermath of the Asian crisis resulting from sudden capital outflows, numerous plans have been suggested for altering the architecture of the international monetary system and institutions. Proposals for reform have been proffered by Canada, France, the United Kingdom, and the United States, as well as the IMF and the Group of Seven. In addition, proposals have come forward from various private individuals including investors George Soros and Henry Kaufman and well-known economists Allan Meltzer, Robert Litan, Sebastian Edwards, C. Fred Bergsten, and Willem Buiter and Anne Sibert. Much of the discussion is focused on the role and nature of the IMF and its ability to work effectively in crisis situations revolving around short-term capital flows; suggestions are made for such changes as introduction of additional supervisory committees, public insurance facilities, contingency finance mechanisms, and bankruptcy courts. To the extent that the world economic environment has changed and the mission and architecture of the IMF needs to be altered, a rigorous discussion of these issues, alternative plans, and operating procedures is healthy (and also beyond the scope of this book!). Not surprisingly, however, many of the ideas put forth tend to be politically infeasible, to be technically inoperable, or to stand little chance of making any significant overall improvement in the current monetary system.

There is, however, little doubt that elements of some of these proposals will find their way into serious consideration as the architecture of the system is altered during the upcoming years.[21]

Greater Stability and Coordination of Macroeconomic Policies across Countries

The proponents of this proposal attribute exchange rate instability among major industrialized countries primarily to two factors: (*a*) the macro policies of any given country tend to be unstable; and (*b*) macro policies across countries are often working in opposite directions. With respect to (*a*), evidence is provided by the proponents of stability and coordination that easy monetary policy, for example, is soon followed by an abrupt change to tight monetary policy. In this environment, short-term capital may leave the country because of low interest rates in the first period but then return in the next period when interest rates are higher. There will also be continuing reevaluation of expectations regarding the future stance of the monetary authorities, and these changes in expectations in and of themselves can induce capital flows. With respect to (*b*), if one country is pursuing an expansionary monetary policy while another is pursuing contractionary policy, then capital will flow toward the contractionary policy country; when both countries reverse their policies due to changing internal circumstances, capital will flow in the other direction. The result of these swings in the flow of short-term funds is a considerable amount of exchange rate variability.

A general view among economists is that floating exchange rates would be more stable if the private sector had firmer and less volatile expectations concerning future exchange rates. If countries adopted more stable macro policies, these policies not only would contribute to the attainment of domestic economic goals but would also stabilize expectations about exchange rates. If confident predictions can be made because of coordinated and stable policies, then minor shocks and rumors will not have sizable impacts upon exchange rates, and the rates will by and large be stable. Thus, the basic thrust of the policy coordination proposal is for greater stability and uniformity in macro policy, to be achieved by periodic conferences and constant communication among the policy authorities in the major industrialized countries. For example, the semiannual joint meetings of the members of the IMF and the World Bank have stressed policy coordination for achievement of various goals.

A major existing forum for discussing policy coordination, and one that receives wide coverage in the press, consists of the annual summit meetings held by leaders of the Group of Seven (see discussion on pages 674–75 of Chapter 26.). However, the actual effectiveness of the G-7 (or G-8, if Russia is included) in coordinating and leading world response to international problems has been the subject of discussion as of late. Bergsten and Henning (1996) regard the G-7 as having attained some notable successes in the late 1970s and in the 1980s. However, they argue that the leadership and the effectiveness of the group declined in the 1990s and that there has been a loss of confidence in the group's ability to undertake successful collective strategies, even when it may wish to do so, due to major changes in global economic conditions. More specifically, the current huge volume of international flows of private capital almost certainly precludes the G-7 from effectively being able to influence the currency markets. In addition, the presence of government budget deficits interferes with the scope and flexibility of

---

[21]For an excellent overview and evaluation of many of these plans, see Barry Eichengreen, *Toward a New International Financial Architecture* (Washington, DC: Institute for International Economics, 1999). For a description of the Buiter–Sibert plan, see "Calming the Waters," *The Economist,* May 1, 1999, p. 74.

fiscal policy. Finally, with the primacy of monetary policy in the current international financial system, the major central banks that have become more important players in the world economy strongly defend their institutional independence from other governmental authorities in key countries such as the United States and the nations of the European Union.

Bergsten and Henning offered a set of recommendations regarding the G-7. They argue for supporting and modifying ongoing initiatives to create an early warning system to head off financial crises and to have available the necessary resources to deal with such crises when they do erupt. In addition, the G-7 should focus on the management of flexible rates, perhaps within a broad target zone system of rates, and not be concerned with coordination of G-7 members' own domestic macroeconomic policies directly. The G-7 should also undertake institutional reforms involving a greater participatory role for the central banks consistent with the management of exchange rates and stability of the rapidly expanding international financial markets. Finally, the G-7 should contemplate changes in its own membership, perhaps eventually including emerging economic powers to both enhance its own legitimacy and revitalize G-7 leadership. (As noted in Chapter 26, Russia, Brazil, China, India, Mexico, and South Africa attended the February 2007 meeting.)

Operationalizing any plan for greater stability and coordination in policies faces many difficulties. In addition to the institutional difficulties such as those of the G-7, the implementation of coordinated macro policies encounters variable and sometimes lengthy time lags in recognizing the current situation, devising and implementing the appropriate policy responses, and waiting for the policies to take effect. In addition, external shocks such as the oil crises and changes in expectations make accurate forecasting difficult. A major problem of policy coordination is also its feasibility. If business cycles do not hit all major countries at the same time (i.e. the countries are "out of phase" with each other), it will be difficult to get the policy authorities to agree on the proper macroeconomic stance. Finally, coordinated policymaking involves some sacrifice of national autonomy, and countries tend to resist such an infringement on their sovereignty.

CONCEPT CHECK

1. What obstacles does the G-7 face in implementing coordination of macro policy?
2. How does a target zone system differ from a world central bank system?
3. Why do economists in general not like the extensive use of capital controls?
4. How might the Tobin tax reduce exchange rate volatility?

THE INTERNATIONAL MONETARY SYSTEM AND THE DEVELOPING COUNTRIES

An additional broad topic regarding the international monetary system concerns the type of international monetary arrangements that seem most suitable for the developing countries, also called the less developed countries (LDCs). We have earlier discussed reasons as to why many developing countries prefer fixed exchange rates to flexible rates, and developing countries in general want to avoid the volatility in exchange rates that has occurred in recent years. However, a relatively fixed-rate framework also implies that participating countries must maintain adequate holdings of international reserve assets. But the developing countries have not been able to build up or even maintain their reserve stocks because of their needs for capital goods imports as well the capital flight from LDCs toward industrialized countries (ICs), where the real rate of return on capital may be higher and more stable. Hence, LDCs conclude that any reform of the international monetary system should include adequate provision for creation of new international reserves and liquidity.

Another issue of concern to LDCs with respect to the current international monetary system is the issue of **IMF conditionality.**[22] This term refers to the fact that when a developing country draws resources or borrows from the IMF, the increasing use of the credit tranches and/or other funding facilities can have "strings" attached. The strings can include such items as IMF insistence that steps be taken to halt inflation, alter fiscal policies, remove price controls, adopt more market-oriented policies, allow the currency to float for a while, and so forth.[23] However, the LDCs may not judge such policy steps as necessary parts of their development strategy. Hence, the IMF is regarded as imposing a specific strategy for development upon the developing country and as interfering with national sovereignty. The IMF position is that, as with any bank, its loans must be repaid and any lender can impose conditions that it thinks will help to ensure repayment. Although conditionality is a feature of virtually all IMF loans, the kind and size of loans available from the IMF now are much larger than the original balance-of-payments loans through the reserve tranche and the standard credit tranches that could provide up to 125 percent of a country's quota. A variety of "facilities" are now in existence beyond the original loan mechanism, such as an extended fund facility (for longer-term loans), a compensatory financing facility (to cover LDC export shortfalls, excessive spending on cereal imports, and other special occurrences), a poverty reduction and growth facility (also longer-term loans), a supplemental reserve facility (to provide assistance in the event of capital account pressure due to a loss of confidence in the country's currency), and contingent credit lines (to protect countries from the spread of financial crises). In total, a country can conceivably borrow more than 500 percent of its quota. Therefore, though conditionality imposes unwanted restrictions on the developing countries and discussions ought to pursue the issue, the pool of resources available from the IMF is potentially quite sizable. Nevertheless, conditionality is a very heated issue, and the topic extends beyond economics with its implications for national sovereignty and political power.

There is also a developing-country view that the international monetary system ought to generate more stability in the world economy. If business cycles occur frequently in the industrialized countries, these variations in economic activity will spill over to the LDCs because the purchases of their exports by the ICs will be unstable. Hence, economic fluctuations in the industrialized countries will be transmitted to the LDCs. From this point of view, the attainment of more stability and coordination of macro policies in the industrialized countries would be very desirable. Besides reducing the instability in developed-country exchange rates, it might provide greater macro stability for the LDCs if it succeeded in stabilizing conditions in the industrialized countries. The same kind of enhanced stability could also come from the adoption of an effective target zone system. However, these stability benefits would probably not come from a return to the gold standard. Economic activity within the ICs could become more variable under the BOP adjustment requirements of that system (even though exchange rates would be fixed).

Finally, the developing countries have argued for increasing the openness and transparency of decision making in key international organizations such as the IMF and the World Bank and for a greater voice in the overall process. Without a stronger voice, the developing countries feel that the current decision-making machinery may tend to benefit the rich at the expense of the poor.

---

[22]For elaboration, see Peera (1988, pp. 303–11).

[23]The conditionality issue also concerns loans from the World Bank.

SUMMARY

The choice of an international monetary system involves consideration of the adequacy of the volume of international reserve assets, the confidence countries place in those assets, the extent to which effective balance-of-payments adjustment occurs, the amount of national autonomy in economic policy that is desirable, and the degree to which variations in exchange rates cause instability in macroeconomic performance. The Bretton Woods system involved pegged but adjustable exchange rates built around parity rates defined in terms of the U.S. dollar, which in turn was defined in terms of gold. This system permitted substantial growth of trade and investment during its operation, but it broke down in the early 1970s under the strain of growing trade and the uncertainty regarding the value of the dollar. Since the breakdown, countries have adopted a wide variety of exchange rate arrangements, and the current international monetary system is often called a "nonsystem." Recent experience has been characterized by considerable volatility in nominal and real exchange rates of leading industrial countries and by continued transmission of economic fluctuations from country to country, although the volume of trade and payments has grown substantially. In particular, with increased financial interdependence around the globe, sudden capital withdrawal, such as from Asian countries in 1997, can trigger potential worldwide disruption.

A number of proposals have been made for change in the current arrangements, including a return to a gold standard, the establishment of a world central bank, and the implementation of target zones for exchange rates. To reduce instability in exchange rates and in the world economy, the leading industrialized countries have attempted greater coordination of their macroeconomic policies, but other possibilities include the levying of a tax on exchange market transactions and the adoption of additional restrictions on and supervision of short-term capital flows. Finally, the developing countries prefer an international monetary system with greater stability of exchange rates and one in which they have a greater participatory voice.

KEY TERMS

adequacy of reserves problem (or liquidity problem)

adjustment problem

balance-of-payments adjustment mechanism

Bretton Woods system

confidence problem

convergence criteria

credit tranche

dual exchange rates (or multiple exchange rates)

Economic and Monetary Union (EMU)

euro

European Central Bank (ECB)

European currency unit (ecu)

European Monetary Cooperation Fund (EMCF)

European monetary system (EMS)

European System of Central Banks (ESCB)

exchange rate mechanism (ERM)

gold tranche (or reserve tranche)

IMF conditionality

IMF quota

international liquidity

International Monetary Fund (IMF)

internationally acceptable reserve assets

Jamaica Accords

key currencies

Maastricht Treaty

pegged but adjustable exchange rates

Smithsonian Agreement

special drawing rights (SDRs)

surveillance

target zone proposal

QUESTIONS AND PROBLEMS

1. What are the key characteristics of an effective international monetary system? Does the current system meet these requirements?

2. What were the main problems in the Bretton Woods system? Are such problems present in the current system?

3. Why are SDRs often referred to as "paper gold"? What role do they play in the current system?

4. What is the similarity, if any, between a gold standard and a world central bank? What is the difference?

5. What were the original purposes of the IMF? Have they changed since Bretton Woods? What is the justification for IMF surveillance?

6. Why might it be said that a target zone system contains both the best and the worst of flexible and fixed exchange rate systems?

7. "A target zone system will work only if there is coordination of economic policies among country participants. On the other hand, if this effective coordination of monetary and fiscal policy exists among the members, there is no need for a target zone system!" What is the logic behind this statement?

8. From the standpoint of any given EU member country, what are the potential advantages of joining EMU? What are the potential disadvantages?

REFERENCES FOR FURTHER READING

CHAPTER 2

Coats, A. W. "Adam Smith and the Mercantile System." In *Essays on Adam Smith.* Edited by Andrew S. Skinner and Thomas Wilson. Oxford: Clarendon Press, 1975, pp. 218–36.

Ellsworth, Paul T. *The International Economy.* 4th ed. London: Macmillan, 1969. Chapters 2–3.

Heckscher, Eli F. *Mercantilism.* Vols. I and II. London: Allen & Unwin, 1935.

Hume, David, "Of the Balance of Trade." In *David Hume: Writings on Economics.* Edited by Eugene Rotwein. Madison: University of Wisconsin Press, 1955, pp. 60–77.

Smith, Adam. *An Inquiry into the Nature and Causes of the Wealth of Nations.* 1776. Reprint. London: J. M. Dent and Sons, 1977. Book IV.

Viner, Jacob. *Studies in the Theory of International Trade.* New York: Harper and Brothers, 1937. Chapters I–IV.

CHAPTER 3

Allen, William R. (ed.). *International Trade Theory: Hume to Ohlin.* New York: Random House, 1965. Chapter 3.

Chacholiades, Miltiades. *International Trade Theory and Policy.* New York: McGraw-Hill, 1978. Chapters 2–3.

Chipman, John S. "A Survey of the Theory of International Trade, Part 1: The Classical Theory." *Econometrica* 33, no. 3 (July 1965), pp. 477–519.

Haberler, Gottfried. *The Theory of International Trade.* London: William Hodge, 1936. Chapters X–XI.

Irwin, Douglas A. *Against the Tide: An Intellectual History of Free Trade.* Princeton, NJ: Princeton University Press, 1996. Chapter 6.

Mill, John Stuart. *Principles of Political Economy.* 1848. Reprint. London: Longmans, Green, 1920. Book III, Chapters XVII–XVIII.

Ricardo, David. *The Principles of Political Economy and Taxation.* 1817. Reprint. London: J. M. Dent and Sons, 1948. Chapters I, VII, XXII.

Samuelson, Paul A. "Where Ricardo and Mill Rebut and Confirm Arguments of Mainstream Economists Supporting Globalization." *Journal of Economic Perspectives* 18, no. 3 (Summer 2004), pp. 135–46.

Viner, Jacob. *Studies in the Theory of International Trade.* New York: Harper and Brothers, 1937. Chapters VIII–IX.

CHAPTER 4

Appleyard, D. R.; P. J. Conway; and A. J. Field, Jr. "The Effects of Customs Unions on the Pattern and Terms of Trade in a Ricardian Model with a Continuum of Goods." *Journal of International Economics* 27, no. 1/2 (August 1989), pp. 147–64.

Balassa, Bela. "An Empirical Demonstration of Classical Comparative Cost Theory." *Review of Economics and Statistics* 45, no. 3 (August 1963), pp. 231–38.

Carlin, Wendy; Andrew Glyn; and John Van Reenen. "Export Market Performance of OECD Countries: An Empirical Examination of the Role of Cost Competitiveness." *Economic Journal* 111, no. 468 (January 2001), pp. 128–62.

Dornbusch, Rudiger; Stanley Fischer; and Paul A. Samuelson. "Comparative Advantage, Trade, and Payments in a Ricardian Model with a Continuum of Goods." *American Economic Review* 67, no. 5 (December 1977), pp. 823–39.

Golub, Stephen S. "America-Firsters Have It Backward." *The Wall Street Journal,* Jan. 16, 1996, p. A14.

Haberler, Gottfried. *The Theory of International Trade.* London: William Hodge, 1936. Chapters X–XI.

MacDougall, G. D. A. "British and American Exports: A Study Suggested by the Theory of Comparative Costs, Part I." *Economic Journal* 61, no. 244 (December 1951), pp. 697–724.

Mill, John Stuart. *Principles of Political Economy.* 1848. Reprint. London: Longmans, Green, 1920. Book III, Chapters XVII–XXII, XXV.

"Not So Absolutely Fabulous." *The Economist,* Nov. 4, 1995, p. 86.

Stern, Robert M. "British and American Productivity and Comparative Costs in International Trade." *Oxford Economic Papers* 14, no. 3 (October 1962), pp. 275–96.

CHAPTER 5

Haberler, Gottfried. *The Theory of International Trade.* London: William Hodge, 1936. Chapter XII.

Heller, H. Robert. *International Trade: Theory and Empirical Evidence.* 2nd ed. Englewood Cliffs, NJ: Prentice-Hall, 1973. Chapter 5 and Appendix.

Katz, Michael L., and Harvey S. Rosen. *Microeconomics.* 3rd ed. Boston: Irwin/McGraw-Hill, 1998. Chapters 2, 8–9, 12.

Samuelson, Paul A. "International Factor-Price Equalisation Once Again." *Economic Journal* 59, no. 234 (June 1949), pp. 181–97.

Savosnik, K. M. "The Box Diagram and the Production Possibility Curve." *Economisk Tidskrift* 60, no. 3 (September 1958), pp. 183–97.

Scitovsky, T. de. "A Reconsideration of the Theory of Tariffs." *Review of Economic Studies* 9, no. 2 (Summer 1942), pp. 89–110.

CHAPTER 6

Bhagwati, Jagdish N.; Arvind Panagariya; and T. N. Srinivasan. *Lectures on International Trade.* 2nd ed. Cambridge, MA: MIT Press, 1998. Chapter 19.

Chacholiades, Miltiades. *International Trade Theory and Policy.* New York: McGraw-Hill, 1978. Chapters 5 and 16.

Haberler, Gottfried. "Some Problems in the Pure Theory of International Trade." *Economic Journal* 60, no. 238 (June 1950), pp. 223–40.

Heller, H. Robert. *International Trade: Theory and Empirical Evidence.* 2nd ed. Englewood Cliffs, NJ: Prentice-Hall, 1973. Chapter 5.

Hickok, Susan. "The Consumer Cost of U.S. Trade Restraints." Federal Reserve Bank of New York *Quarterly Review* 10, no. 2 (Summer 1985), pp. 1–12.

Leontief, Wassily W. "The Use of Indifference Curves in the Analysis of Foreign Trade." *Quarterly Journal of Economics* 47, no. 3 (May 1933), pp. 493–503.

Poole, William. "Free Trade: Why Are Economists and Noneconomists So Far Apart?" Federal Reserve Bank of St. Louis *Review,* September/October 2004, pp. 1–6.

Samuelson, Paul A. "The Gains from International Trade Once Again." *Economic Journal* 72, no. 288 (December 1962), pp. 820–29.

Spilimbergo, Antonio; Juan Luis Londoño; and Miguel Székely. "Income Distribution, Factor Endowments, and Trade Openness." *Journal of Development Economics* 59, no. 1 (June 1999), pp. 77–101.

Tower, Edward. "The Geometry of Community Indifference Curves." *Weltwirtschaftliches Archiv* 115, no. 4 (1979), pp. 680–99.

Wall, Howard J. "Using the Gravity Model to Estimate the Costs of Protection." Federal Reserve Bank of St. Louis *Review* 81, no. 1 (January/February 1999), pp. 33–40.

CHAPTER 7

Bhagwati, Jagdish N.; Arvind Panagariya; and T. N. Srinivasan. *Lectures on International Trade.* 2nd ed. Cambridge, MA: MIT Press, 1998, pp. 20–26, 72–76, and Appendixes A and C.

Cashion, Paul, and Catherine Pattillo. "The Duration of Terms of Trade Shocks in Sub-Saharan Africa." *Finance and Development* 37, no. 2 (June 2000), pp. 26–29.

Chacholiades, Miltiades. *International Trade Theory and Policy.* New York: McGraw-Hill, 1978. Chapter 6.

Haberler, Gottfried. *The Theory of International Trade.* London: William Hodge, 1936. Chapter XI.

Marshall, Alfred. *Money, Credit and Commerce.* London: Macmillan, 1929. Book III, Chapters 6–8 and Appendix J.

Meade, James E. *A Geometry of International Trade.* London: George Allen and Unwin, 1952. Chapters II–III.

Meier, Gerald M. *The International Economics of Development: Theory and Policy.* New York: Harper and Row, 1968. Chapters 2–3.

Mill, John Stuart. *Principles of Political Economy.* 1848. Reprint. London: Longmans, Green, 1920. Book III, Chapters XVII–XVIII.

CHAPTER 8

Bhagwati, Jagdish N.; Arvind Panagariya; and T. N. Srinivasan. *Lectures on International Trade.* 2nd ed. Cambridge, MA: MIT Press, 1998. Chapters 5–7.

Busse, Matthias. "Do Labor Standards Affect Comparative Advantage in Developing Countries?" *World Development* 30, no. 11 (November 2002), pp. 1921–32.

Chacholiades, Miltiades. *International Trade Theory and Policy.* New York: McGraw-Hill, 1978. Chapters 8–10.

Heckscher, Eli F. "The Effect of Foreign Trade on the Distribution of Income." In American Economic Association, *Readings in the Theory of International Trade.* Edited by Howard S. Ellis and Lloyd A. Metzler. Philadelphia: Blakiston, 1950. Chapter 13.

Jones, Ronald W. "A Three-Factor Model in Theory, Trade and History." In *Trade, Balance of Payments and Growth: Essays in Honor of C. P. Kindleberger.* Edited by J. N. Bhagwati et al. Amsterdam: North-Holland, 1971, pp. 3–20.

Jones, Ronald W., and J. Peter Neary. "The Positive Theory of International Trade." In *Handbook of International Economics.* Vol. I. Edited by Ronald W. Jones and Peter B. Kenen. Amsterdam: North-Holland, 1984. Chapter 1.

Mundell, Robert A. "International Trade and Factor Mobility." *American Economic Review* 47, no. 3 (June 1957), pp. 321–35.

Neary, J. Peter. "Short-Run Capital Specificity and the Pure Theory of International Trade." *Economic Journal* 88 (September 1978), pp. 488–510.

Ohlin, Bertil. *Interregional and International Trade.* Cambridge, MA: Harvard University Press, 1933.

Samuelson, Paul A. "International Factor-Price Equalisation Once Again." *Economic Journal* 59, no. 234 (June 1949), pp. 181–97.

Stolper, Wolfgang F., and Paul A. Samuelson. "Protection and Real Wages." *Review of Economic Studies* 9 (November 1941), pp. 58–73.

CHAPTER 9

Baldwin, Robert E. "Determinants of the Commodity Structure of U.S. Trade." *American Economic Review* 61, no. 1 (March 1971), pp. 126–46.

Baldwin, Robert E., and Glen G. Cain. "Shifts in Relative U.S. Wages: The Role of Trade, Technology, and Factor Endowments." *Review of Economics and Statistics* 82, no. 4 (November 2000), pp. 580–95.

Ball, David S. "Factor-Intensity Reversals in International Comparison of Factor Costs and Factor Use." *Journal of Political Economy* 74, no. 1 (February 1966), pp. 77–80.

Bhagwati, Jagdish N. "The Pure Theory of International Trade: A Survey." *Economic Journal* 74, no. 293 (March 1964), pp. 1–78. (See especially pp. 21–26.)

Bharadwaj, R. "Factor Proportions and the Structure of Indo-U.S. Trade." *Indian Economic Journal* 10 (October 1962), pp. 105–16.

Borjas, George J.; Richard B. Freeman; and Lawrence F. Katz. "On the Labor Market Effects of Immigration and Trade." *In Immigration and the Work Force: Economic Consequences for the United States and Source Areas.* Edited by George J. Borjas and Richard B. Freeman. Chicago: University of Chicago Press, 1992, pp. 213–44.

Bowen, Harry P.; Edward E. Leamer; and Leo Sveikauskas. "Multicountry, Multifactor Tests of the Factor Abundance Theory." *American Economic Review* 77, no. 5 (December 1987), pp. 791–809.

Burtless, Gary. "International Trade and the Rise in Earnings Inequality." *Journal of Economic Literature* 33, no. 2 (June 1995), pp. 800–16.

Conway, Patrick J. "The Case of the Missing Trade and Other Mysteries: Comment." *American Economic Review* 92, no. 1 (March 2002), pp. 394–404.

Davis, Donald R., and David E. Weinstein. "Empirical Tests of the Factor Abundance Theory: What Do They Tell Us?" *Eastern Economic Review* 22, no. 4 (Fall 1996), pp. 433–40.

Davis, Donald R.; David E. Weinstein; Scott C. Bradford; and Kazushige Shimpo. "Using International and Japanese Regional Data to Determine When the Factor Abundance Theory of Trade Works." *American Economic Review* 87, no. 3 (June 1997), pp. 421–46.

Deardorff, Alan V. "Testing Trade Theories and Predicting Trade Flows." In *Handbook of International Economics.* Vol. I. Edited by Ronald W. Jones and Peter B. Kenen. Amsterdam: North-Holland, 1984. Chapter 10. (See especially pp. 478–93.)

Federal Reserve Bank of New York. *Economic Policy Review* 1, no. 1 (January 1995). Entire issue is devoted to papers and discussion of the U.S. increased wage inequality.

Feenstra, Robert C. "Integration of Trade and Disintegration of Production in the Global Economy." *Journal of Economic Perspectives* 12, no. 4 (Fall 1998), pp. 31–50.

Feenstra, Robert C., and Gordon H. Hanson. "Aggregation Bias in the Factor Content of Trade: Evidence from U.S. Manufacturing." *American Economic Review* 90, no. 2 (May 2000), pp. 155–60.

———. "Globalization, Outsourcing, and Wage Inequality." *American Economic Review* 86, no. 2 (May 1996), pp. 240–45.

———. "Global Production Sharing and Rising Inequality: A Survey of Trade and Wages." In *Handbook of International Trade.* Edited by E. Kwan Choi and James Harrigan. Malden, MA: Blackwell Publishers, 2003, pp. 146–87.

Fortin, Nicole M., and Thomas Lemieux. "Institutional Change and Rising Wage Inequality: Is There a Linkage?" *Journal of Economic Perspectives* 11, no. 2 (Spring 1997), pp. 75–96.

Freeman, Richard B. "Are Your Wages Set in Beijing?" *Journal of Economic Perspectives* 9, no. 3 (Summer 1995), pp. 15–32.

Gottschalk, Peter. "Inequality, Income Growth, and Mobility: The Basic Facts." *Journal of Economic Perspectives* 11, no. 2 (Spring 1997), pp. 21–40.

Harkness, Jon, and John F. Kyle. "Factors Influencing United States Comparative Advantage." *Journal of International Economics* 5, no. 2 (May 1975), pp. 153–65.

Hartigan, James C. "The U.S. Tariff and Comparative Advantage: A Survey of Method." *Weltwirtschaftliches Archiv* 117, no. 1 (1981), pp. 61–109.

Helpman, Elhanan. "The Structure of Foreign Trade." *Journal of Economic Perspectives* 13, no. 2 (Spring 1999), pp. 121–44.

Hufbauer, G. C. *Synthetic Materials and the Theory of International Trade.* Cambridge, MA: Harvard University Press, 1966. Appendix B.

Hummels, David; Dana Rapoport; and Kei-Mu Yi. "Vertical Specialization and the Changing Nature of World Trade." Federal Reserve Bank of New York *Economic Policy Review* 4, no. 2 (June 1998), pp. 79–99.

Johnson, George E. "Changes in Earnings Inequality: The Role of Demand Shifts." *Journal of Economic Perspectives* 11, no. 2 (Spring 1997), pp. 41–54.

Keesing, Donald B. "Labor Skills and Comparative Advantage." *American Economic Review* 56, no. 2 (May 1966), pp. 249–58.

Leamer, Edward E., and James Levinsohn. "International Trade Theory: The Evidence." In *Handbook of International Economics,* Vol. III. Edited by Gene M. Grossman and Kenneth Rogoff. Amsterdam: Elsevier, 1995. Chapter 26.

Lemieux, Thomas. "Increasing Residual Wage Inequality: Composition Effects, Noisy Data, or Rising Demand for Skill?" *American Economic Review* 96, no. 3 (June 2006), pp. 461–98.

Leontief, Wassily W. "Domestic Production and Foreign Trade: The American Capital Position Re-Examined." In *International Trade: Selected Readings.* Edited by Jagdish Bhagwati. Middlesex, England: Penguin Books, 1969, pp. 93–139. Original in *Proceedings of the American Philosophical Society* 97 (September 1953), pp. 332–49.

———. "Factor Proportions and the Structure of American Trade: Further Theoretical and Empirical Analysis." *Review of Economics and Statistics* 38, no. 4 (November 1956), pp. 386–407.

Maskus, Keith E. "A Test of the Heckscher-Ohlin-Vanek Theorem: The Leontief Commonplace." *Journal of International Economics* 19, no. 3/4 (November 1985), pp. 201–12.

Minhas, B. S. "The Homohypallagic Production Function, Factor-Intensity Reversals and the Heckscher-Ohlin Theorem." *Journal of Political Economy* 70, no. 2 (April 1962), pp. 138–56.

Mishel, Lawrence; Jared Bernstein; and Sylvia Allegretto. *The State of Working America 2006/2007.* Ithaca, NY: Economic Policy Institute and Cornell University Press, 2007.

Reeve, T. A. *Essays in International Trade.* Ph. D. dissertation. Harvard University, 1998.

Richardson, J. David. "Income Inequality and Trade: How to Think, What to Conclude." *Journal of Economic Perspectives* 9, no. 3 (Summer 1995), pp. 33–55.

Rosefielde, Steven. "Factor Proportions and Economic Rationality in Soviet International Trade 1955–1968." *American Economic Review* 64, no. 4 (September 1974), pp. 670–81.

Sachs, Jeffrey D., and Howard J. Shatz. "U.S. Trade with Developing Countries and Wage Inequality." *American Economic Review* 86, no. 2 (May 1996), pp. 234–39.

Schott, Peter K. "One Size Fits All? Heckscher-Ohlin Specialization in Global Production." *American Economic Review* 93, no. 3 (June 2003), pp. 686–708.

Slaughter, Matthew S. "Globalisation and Wages: A Tale of Two Perspectives." *The World Economy* 22, no. 5 (June 1999), pp. 609–29.

Staiger, Robert W.; Alan Deardorff; and Robert M. Stern. "The Effects of Protection on the Factor Content of Japanese and American Foreign Trade." *Review of Economics and Statistics* 70, no. 3 (August 1988), pp. 475–83.

Stern, Robert M., and Keith E. Maskus. "Determinants of the Structure of U.S. Foreign Trade, 1958–1976." *Journal of International Economics* 11, no. 2 (May 1981), pp. 207–24.

Stolper, Wolfgang F., and Karl W. Roskamp. "Input-Output Table for East Germany with Applications to Foreign Trade." *Bulletin of the Oxford University Institute of Statistics* 23 (November 1961), pp. 379–92.

Svaleryd, Helena, and Jonas Vlachos. "Financial Markets, the Pattern of Industrial Specialization and Comparative Advantage: Evidence from OECD Countries." *European Economic Review* 49, no. 1 (January 2005), pp. 133–44.

Tatemoto, Masahiro, and Shinichi Ichimura. "Factor Proportions and Foreign Trade: The Case of Japan." *Review of Economics and Statistics* 41, no. 4 (November 1959), pp. 442–46.

Topel, Robert H. "Factor Proportions and Relative Wages: The Supply-Side Determinants of Wage Inequality." *Journal of Economic Perspectives* 11, no. 2 (Spring 1997), pp. 55–74.

Trefler, Daniel. "The Case of the Missing Trade and Other Mysteries." *American Economic Review* 85, no. 5 (December 1995), pp. 1029–46.

Trefler, Daniel, and Susan Chun Zhu. "Beyond the Algebra of Explanation: HOV for the Technology Age." *American Economic Review* 90, no. 2 (May 2000), pp. 145–49.

Vanek, Jaroslav. *The Natural Resource Content of United States Foreign Trade 1870–1955.* Cambridge, MA: MIT Press, 1963.

Wahl, Donald F. "Capital and Labour Requirements for Canada's Foreign Trade." *Canadian Journal of Economics and Political Science* 27 (August 1961), pp. 349–58.

Wood, Adrian. "The Factor Content of North-South Trade in Manufactures Reconsidered." *Weltwirtschaftliches Archiv* 127, no. 4 (1991), pp. 719–43.

———. *North-South Trade, Employment, and Inequality: Changing Fortunes in a Skill-Driven World.* Oxford: Clarendon Press, 1994.

———. "How Trade Hurt Unskilled Workers." *Journal of Economic Perspectives* 9, no. 3 (Summer 1995), pp. 57–80.

CHAPTER 10

Balassa, Bela. "Intra-Industry Specialization: A Cross-Country Analysis." *European Economic Review* 30, no. 1 (February 1986), pp. 27–42.

Bergstrand, Jeffrey H. "The Heckscher-Ohlin-Samuelson Model, the Linder Hypothesis and the Determinants of Bilateral Intra-industry Trade." *Economic Journal* 100, no. 403 (December 1990), pp. 1216–29.

Bhagwati, Jagdish N.; Arvind Panagariya; and T. N. Srinivasan. *Lectures on International Trade.* 2nd ed. Cambridge, MA: MIT Press, 1998. Chapter 11.

Bhagwati, Jagdish, and T. N. Srinivasan. *Lectures on International Trade.* Cambridge, MA: MIT Press, 1983. Chapters 8 and 26.

Brander, James A. "Intra-Industry Trade in Identical Commodities." *Journal of International Economics* 11, no. 1 (February 1981), pp. 1–14.

Brander, James, and Paul Krugman. "A 'Reciprocal Dumping' Model of International Trade." *Journal of International Economics* 15, no. 3/4 (November 1983), pp. 313–21.

Broda, Christian, and David E. Weinstein. "Variety Growth and World Welfare." *American Economic Review* 94, no. 2 (May 2004), pp. 139–44.

Deardorff, Alan V. "Testing Trade Theories and Predicting Trade Flows." In *Handbook of International Economics.* Vol. I. Edited by Ronald W. Jones and Peter B. Kenen. Amsterdam: North-Holland, 1984. Chapter 10. (See especially pp. 493–513.)

Dinopoulos, Elias; James F. Oehmke; and Paul S. Segerstrom. "High-Technology-Industry Trade and Investment: The Role of Factor Endowments." *Journal of International Economics* 34, no. 1/2 (February 1993), pp. 49–71.

Dollar, David. "Technological Innovation, Capital Mobility, and the Product Cycle in North-South Trade." *American Economic Review* 76, no. 1 (March 1986), pp. 177–90.

Falvey, Rodney E. "Commercial Policy and Intra-Industry Trade." *Journal of International Economics* 11, no. 4 (November 1981), pp. 495–511.

Falvey, Rodney E., and Henryk Kierzkowski. "Product Quality, Intra-Industry Trade and (Im)perfect Competition." In *Protection and Competition in International Trade: Essays in Honor of W. M. Corden.* Edited by Henryk Kierzkowski. Oxford: Basil Blackwell, 1987, pp. 143–61.

Feenstra, Robert C.; James R. Markusen; and Andrew K. Rose. "Using the Gravity Equation to Differentiate among Alternative Theories of Trade." *Canadian Journal of Economics* 34, no. 2 (May 2001), pp. 430–47.

Flam, Harry, and Elhanan Helpman. "Vertical Product Differentiation and North-South Trade." *American Economic Review* 77, no. 5 (December 1987), pp. 810–22.

Greytak, David, and Richard McHugh. "Linder's Trade Thesis: An Empirical Examination." *Southern Economic Journal* 43, no. 3 (January 1977), pp. 1386–89.

Greytak, David, and Ukrist Tuchinda. "The Composition of Consumption and Trade Intensities: An Alternative Test of the Linder Hypothesis." *Weltwirtschaftliches Archiv* 126, no. 1 (1990), pp. 50–58.

Grubel, Herbert G. "The Theory of Intra-Industry Trade." In *Studies in International Economics.* Edited by I. A. McDougall and R. H. Snape. Amsterdam: North-Holland, 1970, pp. 35–51.

Grubel, Herbert G., and P. J. Lloyd. *Intra-Industry Trade: The Theory and Measurement of International Trade in Differentiated Products.* New York: John Wiley and Sons, 1975.

Gruber, William; Dileep Mehta; and Raymond Vernon. "The R&D Factor in International Trade and Investment of United States Industries." *Journal of Political Economy* 75, no. 1 (February 1967), pp. 20–37.

Hanink, Dean M. "An Extended Linder Model of International Trade." *Economic Geography* 64, no. 4 (October 1988), pp. 322–34.

———. "Linder, Again." *Weltwirtschaftliches Archiv* 126, no. 2 (1990), pp. 257–67.

Helpman, Elhanan. "The Structure of Foreign Trade." *Journal of Economic Perspectives* 13, no. 2 (Spring 1999), pp. 121–44.

Hoftyzer, John. "Empirical Verification of Linder's Trade Thesis: Comment." *Southern Economic Journal* 41, no. 4 (April 1975), pp. 694–98.

———. "A Further Analysis of the Linder Trade Thesis." *Quarterly Review of Economics and Business* 24, no. 2 (Summer 1984), pp. 57–70.

Hufbauer, G. C. *Synthetic Materials and the Theory of International Trade.* Cambridge, MA: Harvard University Press, 1966.

Hummels, David; Dana Rapoport; and Kei-Mu Yi. "Vertical Specialization and the Changing Nature of World Trade." Federal Reserve Bank of New York *Economic Policy Review* 4, no. 2 (June 1998), pp. 79–99.

Jones, Ronald W.; Hamid Beladi; and Sugata Marjit. "The Three Faces of Factor Intensities." *Journal of International Economics* 48, no. 2 (August 1999), pp. 413–20.

Jones, Ronald W., and J. Peter Neary. "The Positive Theory of International Trade." In *Handbook of International Economics.* Vol. I. Edited by Ronald W. Jones and Peter B. Kenen. Amsterdam: North-Holland, 1984. Chapter 1.

Keesing, Donald B. "The Impact of Research and Development on United States Trade." *Journal of Political Economy* 75, no. 1 (February 1967), pp. 38–48.

Kemp, Murray C. *The Pure Theory of International Trade.* Englewood Cliffs, NJ: Prentice-Hall, 1964. Chapter 8.

Kennedy, Thomas E., and Richard McHugh. "An Intertemporal Test and Rejection of the Linder Hypothesis." *Southern Economic Journal* 46, no. 3 (January 1980), pp. 898–903.

———. "Taste Similarity and Trade Intensity: A Test of the Linder Hypothesis for United States Exports." *Weltwirtschaftliches Archiv* 119, no. 1 (1983), pp. 84–96.

Kravis, Irving B., and Robert E. Lipsey. "Sources of Competitiveness of the United States and of its Multinational Firms." *Review of Economics and Statistics* 74, no. 2 (May 1992), pp. 193–201.

Krugman, Paul R. *Geography and Trade.* Leuven, Belgium: Leuven University Press, and Cambridge, MA: MIT Press, 1991.

———. "Increasing Returns, Imperfect Competition and the Positive Theory of International Trade." In *Handbook of International Economics.* Vol. III. Edited by Gene M. Grossman and Kenneth Rogoff. Amsterdam: Elsevier, 1995. Chapter 24.

———. "Increasing Returns, Monopolistic Competition, and International Trade." *Journal of International Economics* 9, no. 4 (November 1979), pp. 469–79.

———. "A Model of Innovation, Technology Transfer, and the World Distribution of Income." *Journal of Political Economy* 87, no. 2 (April 1979), pp. 253–66.

———. "New Theories of Trade among Industrial Countries." *American Economic Review* 73, no. 2 (May 1983), pp. 343–47.

Krugman, Paul, and Raul Livas Elizondo. "Trade Policy and the Third World Metropolis." *Journal of Development Economics* 49, no. 1 (April 1996), pp. 137–50.

Leamer, Edward E., and James Levinsohn. "International Trade Theory: The Evidence." In *Handbook of International Economics.* Vol. III. Edited by Gene M. Grossman and Kenneth Rogoff. Amsterdam: Elsevier, 1995. Chapter 26.

Linder, Staffan Burenstam. *An Essay on Trade and Transformation.* New York: John Wiley and Sons, 1961.

Linnemann, Hans. *An Econometric Study of International Trade Flows.* Amsterdam: North-Holland, 1966.

Markusen, James R.; James R. Melvin; William H. Kaempfer; and Keith E. Maskus. *International Trade: Theory and Evidence.* New York: McGraw-Hill, 1995. Chapters 11–13.

McPherson, M. A.; M. R. Redfearn; and M. A. Tieslau. "A Re-examination of the Linder Hypothesis: A Random-Effects Tobit Approach." *International Economic Journal* 14, no. 3 (Autumn 2000), pp. 123–36.

Morrall, John F., III. *Human Capital, Technology, and the Role of the United States in International Trade.* University of Florida Social Sciences Monograph No. 46. Gainesville: University of Florida Press, 1972.

Pöyhönen, Pentti. "A Tentative Model for the Volume of Trade between Countries." *Weltwirtschaftliches Archiv* 90, no. 1 (1963), pp. 93–99.

Posner, Michael V. "International Trade and Technical Change." *Oxford Economic Papers,* New Series 13, no. 3 (October 1961), pp. 323–41.

Qureshi, Usman A.; Gary L. French; and Joel W. Sailors. "Linder's Trade Thesis: A Further Examination." *Southern Economic Journal* 46, no. 3 (January 1980), pp. 933–36.

Ruffin, Roy J. "The Nature and Significance of Intra-industry Trade." Federal Reserve Bank of Dallas *Economic and Financial Review,* Fourth Quarter 1999, pp. 2–9.

Sailors, Joel W.; Usman A. Qureshi; and Edward M. Cross. "Empirical Verification of Linder's Trade Thesis." *Southern Economic Journal* 40, no. 2 (October 1973), pp. 262–68.

Thursby, Jerry G., and Marie C. Thursby. "Bilateral Trade Flows, the Linder Hypothesis, and Exchange Risk." *Review of Economics and Statistics* 69, no. 3 (August 1987), pp. 488–95.

Tinbergen, Jan. *Shaping the World Economy: Suggestions for an International Economic Policy.* New York: The Twentieth Century Fund, 1962. Appendix VI.

Vernon, Raymond. "International Investment and International Trade in the Product Cycle." *Quarterly Journal of Economics* 80, no. 2 (May 1966), pp. 190–207.

———. "The Product Cycle Hypothesis in a New International Environment." *Oxford Bulletin of Economics and Statistics* 41, no. 4 (November 1979), pp. 255–67.

Wells, Louis T., Jr. "Test of a Product Cycle Model of International Trade: U.S. Exports of Consumer Durables." *Quarterly Journal of Economics* 83, no. 1 (February 1969), pp. 152–62.

CHAPTER 11

Arora, Vivek, and Athanasios Vamvakidis. "Economic Spillovers." *Finance and Development* 42, no. 3 (September 2005), pp. 48–50.

Bhagwati, Jagdish N. "Immiserizing Growth: A Geometrical Note." *Review of Economic Studies* 25 (June 1958), pp. 201–5.

Grossman, Gene M., and Elhanan Helpman. *Innovation and Growth in the Global Economy.* Cambridge, MA: MIT Press, 1991.

———. "Endogenous Innovation in the Theory of Growth." *Journal of Economic Perspectives* 8, no. 1 (Winter 1994), pp. 23–44.

Hicks, John R. *Essays in World Economics.* Oxford: Clarendon Press, 1959. Chapter 4.

Johnson, Harry G. "Economic Development and International Trade." In Harry G. Johnson, *Money, Trade and Economic Growth.* Cambridge, MA: Harvard University Press, 1962. Chapter 4.

Kuznets, Simon. *Modern Economic Growth: Rate, Structure, and Spread.* New Haven: Yale University Press, 1966. Chapter 6.

Meier, Gerald M. *The International Economics of Development.* New York: Harper and Row, 1968. Chapters 2–3.

Myrdal, Gunnar. *An International Economy.* New York: Harper and Row, 1956.

Pack, Howard. "Endogenous Growth Theory: Intellectual Appeal and Empirical Shortcomings." *Journal of Economic Perspectives* 8, no. 1 (Winter 1994), pp. 55–72.

Prebisch, Raul. "Commercial Policy in the Underdeveloped Countries." *American Economic Review* 49, no. 2 (May 1959), pp. 251–73.

Romer, Paul M. "Capital Accumulation in the Theory of Long-Run Growth." In *Modern Business Cycle Theory.* Edited by Robert J. Barro. Cambridge, MA: Harvard University Press, 1989, pp. 51–127.

———. "The Origins of Endogenous Growth." *Journal of Economic Perspectives* 8, no. 1 (Winter 1994), pp. 3–22.

Rybczynski, T. M. "Factor Endowment and Relative Commodity Prices." *Economica* 22, no. 84 (November 1955), pp. 336–41.

Singer, Hans W. "The Distribution of Gains between Investing and Borrowing Countries." *American Economic Review* 40, no. 2 (May 1950), pp. 473–85.

Solow, Robert M. "Perspectives on Growth Theory." *Journal of Economic Perspectives* 8, no. 1 (Winter 1994), pp. 45–54.

CHAPTER 12

Barrell, Ray, and Nigel Pain. "An Econometric Analysis of U.S. Foreign Direct Investment." *Review of Economics and Statistics* 78, no. 2 (May 1996), pp. 200–07.

Biswas, Romita. "Determinants of Foreign Direct Investment." *Review of Development Economics* 6, no. 3 (October 2002), pp. 492–504.

Borjas, George J. "The Economics of Immigration." *Journal of Economic Literature* 32, no. 4 (December 1994), pp. 1667–718.

———. *Heaven's Door.* Princeton, NJ: Princeton University Press. 1999.

———. "The Intergenerational Mobility of Immigrants." *Journal of Labor Economics* 11, no. 1 (January 1993), pp. 113–35.

———. "National Origin and the Skills of Immigrants in the Postwar Period." In *Immigration and the Workforce: Economic Consequences for the United States and Source Areas.* Edited by George J. Borjas and Richard B. Freeman. Chicago: University of Chicago Press, 1992, pp. 17–47.

Borjas, George J.; Richard B. Freeman; and Lawrence F. Katz. "On the Labor Market Effects of Immigration and Trade." In *Immigration and the Workforce: Economic Consequences for the United States and Source Areas.* Edited by George J. Borjas and Richard B. Freeman. Chicago: University of Chicago Press, 1992, pp. 213–44.

Branstetter, Lee G., and Robert C. Feenstra. "Trade and Foreign Direct Investment in China: A Political Economy Approach." *Journal of International Economics* 58, no. 2 (December 2002), pp. 335–58.

Carrington, William J., and Enrica Detragiache. "How Extensive Is the Brain Drain?" *Finance and Development* 36, no. 2 (June 1999), pp. 46–49.

di Giovanni, Julian. "What Drives Capital Flows? The Case of Cross-Border M&A Activity and Financial Deepening." *Journal of International Economics* 65, no. 1 (January 2005), pp. 127–49.

Freeman, Richard B. "People Flows in Globalization." *Journal of Economic Perspectives* 20, no. 2 (Spring 2006), pp. 145–70.

"Globalisation with a Third-World Face." *The Economist,* April 9, 2005, p. 66.

Glytsos, Nicholas P. "Measuring the Income Effects of Migrant Remittances: A Methodological Approach Applied to Greece." *Economic Development and Cultural Change* 42, no. 1 (October 1993), pp. 131–68.

Graham, Edward M., and Paul R. Krugman. *Foreign Direct Investment in the United States.* 3rd ed. Washington, DC: Institute for International Economics, 1995.

Greenwood, Michael J., and John M. McDowell. "Differential Economic Opportunity, Transferability of Skills, and Immigration to the United States and Canada." *Review of Economics and Statistics* 73, no. 4 (November 1991), pp. 612–23.

Hanson, Gordon H. "Illegal Migration from Mexico to the United States." *Journal of Economic Literature* 44, no. 4 (December 2006), pp. 869–924.

Hymer, Stephen. "The Multinational Corporation and the Law of Uneven Development." In *Economics and the World Order: From the 1970's to the 1990's.* Edited by Jagdish N. Bhagwati. New York: Free Press, 1972, pp. 113–40.

"The Longest Journey: A Survey of Migration." *The Economist,* November 2, 2002 (following p. 50).

MacDougall, G. D. A. "The Benefits and Costs of Private Investment from Abroad: A Theoretical Approach." *Economic Record* 36 (March 1960), pp. 13–35.

Mallampally, Padma, and Karl P. Sauvant. "Foreign Direct Investment in Developing Countries." *Finance and Development* 36, no. 1 (March 1999), pp. 34–37.

Markusen, James R. "The Boundaries of Multinational Enterprises and the Theory of International Trade." *Journal of Economic Perspectives* 9, no. 2 (Spring 1995), pp. 181–96.

Meier, Gerald M. "Benefits and Costs of Private Foreign Investment—Note." In Gerald M. Meier, *Leading Issues in Economic Development.* 6th ed. New York: Oxford University Press, 1995, pp. 247–55.

———. *The International Economics of Development.* New York: Harper and Row, 1968. Chapter 6.

Ratha, Dilip. "Remittances: A Lifeline for Development." *Finance and Development* 42, no. 4 (December 2005), pp. 42–43.

Root, Franklin R., and Ahmed A. Ahmed. "Empirical Determinants of Manufacturing Direct Foreign Investment in Developing Countries." *Economic Development and Cultural Change* 27, no. 4 (July 1979), pp. 751–67.

———. "Sending Money Home: Trends in Migrant Remittances." *Finance and Development* 42, no. 4 (December 2005), pp. 44–45.

Simon, Julian L. *The Economic Consequences of Immigration.* Oxford and Cambridge, MA: Blackwell in association with the Cato Institute, 1989.

U.N. Conference on Trade and Development. *World Investment Report 1998: Trends and Determinants (Overview).* New York and Geneva: United Nations, 1998.

Veugelers, Reinhilde. "Locational Determinants and Ranking of Host Countries: An Empirical Assessment." *Kyklos* 44, no. 3 (1991), pp. 363–82.

Wright, Robert E., and Paul S. Maxim. "Immigration Policy and Immigrant Quality: Empirical Evidence from Canada." *Journal of Population Economics* 6, no. 4 (November 1993), pp. 337–52.

CHAPTER 13

Alexandraki, Katerina. "Preference Erosion: Cause for Alarm?" *Finance and Development* 42, no. 1 (March 2005), pp. 26–29.

Appleyard, Dennis R., and Alfred J. Field, Jr. "The Effects of Offshore Assembly Provisions on the U.S. Tariff Structure." *Journal of Economic Studies* 9, no. 1 (1982), pp. 3–18.

Balassa, Bela. "Tariff Protection in Industrial Countries: An Evaluation." *Journal of Political Economy* 73, no. 6 (December 1965), pp. 573–94.

————. *Trade Liberalization among Industrial Countries: Objectives and Alternatives.* New York: McGraw-Hill, 1967. Chapter 3.

Bradford, Scott. "Paying the Price: Final Goods Protection in OECD Countries." *Review of Economics and Statistics* 85, no. 1 (February 2003), pp. 24–37.

Cooper, Richard N. *The Economics of Interdependence: Economic Policy in the Atlantic Community.* New York: Columbia University Press, 1968. Chapters 7 and 9.

Corden, W. Max. "The Structure of a Tariff System and the Effective Protective Rate." *Journal of Political Economy* 74, no. 3 (June 1966), pp. 221–37.

Deardorff, Alan V., and Robert M. Stern. *The Michigan Model of World Production and Trade: Theory and Applications.* Cambridge, MA: MIT Press, 1986.

Finger, J. Michael. "Trade and Domestic Effects of the Offshore Assembly Provision in the U.S. Tariff." *American Economic Review* 66, no. 4 (September 1976), pp. 598–611.

Finger, J. Michael, and Andrzej Olechowski (eds.). *The Uruguay Round: A Handbook on the Multilateral Trade Negotiations.* Washington, DC: World Bank, 1987.

Greenaway, David, and Chris Milner. "Effective Protection, Policy Appraisal and Trade Policy Reform." *The World Economy* 26, no. 4 (April 2003), pp. 441–56.

Grossman, Gene M., and Alan O. Sykes. "A Preference for Development: The Law and Economics of GSP." *World Trade Review* 4, no. 1 (March 2005), pp. 41–67.

Haberler, Gottfried. *The Theory of International Trade,* London. William Hodge, 1936. Chapters XV, XIX, XX.

Irwin, Douglas A. "Changes in U.S. Tariffs: The Role of Import Prices and Commercial Policies." *American Economic Review* 88, no. 4 (September 1998), pp. 1015–26.

Johnson, Leland. "Problems of Import Substitution: The Chilean Automobile Industry." *Economic Development and Cultural Change* 15, no. 2, part 1 (January 1967), pp. 202–16.

CHAPTER 14

Baldwin, Robert E. "Trade Policies in Developed Countries." In *Handbook of International Economics.* Vol. I. Edited by Ronald W. Jones and Peter B. Kenen. Amsterdam: North-Holland, 1984. Chapter 12.

Beghin, John C.; Barbara El Osta; Jay R. Cherlow; and Samarendu Mohanty. "The Cost of the U.S. Sugar Program Revisited." *Contemporary Economic Policy* 21, no. 1 (January 2003), pp. 106–16.

Cline, William R. *The Future of World Trade in Textiles and Apparel.* Rev. ed. Washington, DC: Institute for International Economics, 1990.

Feenstra, Robert C. "How Costly Is Protectionism?" *Journal of Economic Perspectives* 6, no. 3 (Summer 1992), pp. 159–78.

Field, Alfred J., and Umaporn Wongwatanasian. "Tax Policies' Impact on Output, Trade and Income in Thailand," *Journal of Policy Modeling* 29, no. 3 (May/June 2007), pp. 361–80.

Gardner, Bruce L. "The Political Economy of the Export Enhancement Program for Wheat." In *The Political Economy of Trade Protection.* Edited by Anne O. Krueger. Chicago and London: University of Chicago Press, 1996, pp. 61–70.

Hickok, Susan. "The Consumer Cost of U.S. Trade Restraints." Federal Reserve Bank of New York *Quarterly Review* 10, no. 2 (Summer 1985), pp. 1–12.

Hufbauer, Gary Clyde, and Kimberly Ann Elliott. *Measuring the Costs of Protection in the United States.* Washington, DC: Institute for International Economics, 1994.

Leff, Nathaniel H. "The 'Exportable Surplus' Approach to Foreign Trade in Underdeveloped Countries." *Economic Development and Cultural Change* 17, no. 3 (April 1969), pp. 346–55.

Meyers, William H., et al. "The Impact of EEP Removal on U.S. Wheat." Food and Agricultural Research Institute paper, March 1997. Obtained from www.card.iastate.edu.

Tsakok, Isabelle. *Agricultural Price Policy: A Practitioner's Guide to Partial-Equilibrium Analysis.* Ithaca, NY: Cornell University Press, 1990.

U.S. International Trade Commission. *The Economic Effects of Significant U.S. Import Restraints, Phase I: Manufacturing.* USITC Publication 2222. Washington, DC: USITC, October 1989.

————. *The Economic Effects of Significant U.S. Import Restraints: Fifth Update 2007.* USITC Publication 3906. Washington, DC: February 2007.

Wall, Howard J. "Using the Gravity Model to Estimate the Costs of Protection." Federal Reserve Bank of St. Louis *Review* 81, no. 1 (January/February 1999), pp. 33–40.

CHAPTER 15

Baldwin, Robert E. "The Case against Infant Industry Protection." *Journal of Political Economy* 77, no. 3 (May/June 1969), pp. 295–305.

Bell, Martin; Bruce Ross-Larson; and Larry E. Westphal. "Assessing the Performance of Infant Industries." *Journal of Development Economics* 16, no. 1–2 (September–October 1984), pp. 101–28.

Bhagwati, Jagdish N.; Arvind Panagariya; and T. N. Srinivasan. *Lectures on International Trade.* 2nd ed. Cambridge, MA MIT Press, 1998. Chapters 16–24, 30.

Brander, James A., and Barbara J. Spencer. "Tariff Protection and Imperfect Competition." In *Monopolistic Competition in International Trade.* Edited by Henryk Kierzkowski. Oxford: Oxford University Press, 1984. pp. 194–206.

————. "Tariffs and the Extraction of Foreign Monopoly Rents under Potential Entry." *Canadian Journal of Economics* 14, no. 3 (August 1981), pp. 371–89.

Coleman, Brian. "Airbus Subsidies Are Invisible to Radar." *The Wall Street Journal,* Mar. 4, 1993, p. A10.

Collie, David. "Export Subsidies and Countervailing Tariffs." *Journal of International Economics* 31, no. 3/4 (November 1991), pp. 309–24.

Corden, W. M. "The Normative Theory of International Trade." In *Handbook of International Economics.* Vol. I. Edited by Ronald W. Jones and Peter B. Kenen. Amsterdam: North-Holland, 1984. Chapter 2.

Eaton, Jonathan, and Gene M. Grossman. "Optimal Trade and Industrial Policy under Oligopoly." *Quarterly Journal of Economics* 101, no. 2 (May 1986), pp. 383–406.

George, Henry. *Protection or Free Trade: An Examination of the Tariff Question, with Especial Regard to the Interests of Labor.* 1886. Reprint. Garden City, NY: Doubleday Page, 1911. Some of George's admirable pronouncements are provided in C. Lowell Harriss, "Guidance from an Economics Classic: The Centennial of Henry George's 'Protection or Free Trade,' " *American Journal of Economics and Sociology* 48, no. 3 (July 1989), pp. 351–56, and "A Banana into a Cage of Monkeys," *The Wall Street Journal,* Sept. 5, 1989, p. A18.

Grossman, Gene M. (ed.). *Imperfect Competition and International Trade.* Cambridge, MA: MIT Press, 1992.

Grossman, Gene M., and J. David Richardson. *Strategic Trade Policy: A Survey of Issues and Early Analysis.* Special Papers in International Economics No. 15. Princeton, NJ: International Finance Section, Princeton University, April 1985. Reprinted in shortened form in *International Trade and Finance: Readings.* 3rd ed. Edited by Robert E. Baldwin and J. David Richardson. Boston: Little, Brown, 1986, pp. 95–114.

Helpman, Elhanan, and Paul R. Krugman. *Trade Policy and Market Structure.* Cambridge, MA: MIT Press, 1989.

Hufbauer, Gary Clyde; Diane T. Berliner; and Kimberly Ann Elliott. *Trade Protection in the United States: 31 Case Studies.* Washington, DC: Institute for International Economics, 1986.

Hufbauer, Gary Clyde, and Kimberly Ann Elliott. *Measuring the Costs of Protection in the United States.* Washington, DC: Institute for International Economics, 1994.

Ingram, James C. *International Economics.* 2nd ed. New York: John Wiley, 1986. Chapter 16.

Ingram, James C., and Robert M. Dunn, Jr. *International Economics.* 3rd ed. New York: John Wiley, 1993. Chapter 7.

Irwin, Douglas A., and Nina Pavcnik. "Airbus versus Boeing Revisited: International Competition in the Aircraft Market." *Journal of International Economics* 64, no. 2 (December 2004), pp. 223–45.

Johnson, Harry G. "Optimum Tariffs and Retaliation." *Review of Economic Studies* 21 (1953–54), pp. 142–53.

Krueger, Anne O., and Baran Tuncer. "An Empirical Test of the Infant Industry Argument." *American Economic Review* 72, no. 5 (December 1982), pp. 1142–52.

Krugman, Paul R. "Import Protection as Export Promotion: International Competition in the Presence of Oligopoly and Economies of Scale." In *Monopolistic Competition in International Trade.* Edited by Henryk Kierzkowski. Oxford: Oxford University Press, 1984, pp. 180–93.

———. "Is Free Trade Passé?" *Journal of Economic Perspectives* 1, no. 2 (Fall 1987), pp. 131–44.

———. *Pop Internationalism.* Cambridge, MA: MIT Press, 1996.

———. "What Do Undergrads Need to Know about Trade?" *American Economic Review* 83, no. 2 (May 1993), pp. 23–26.

Meier, Gerald M. "Infant Industry." In *The New Palgrave: A Dictionary of Economics.* Vol. 2. Edited by John Eatwell, Murray Milgate, and Peter Newman. London: Macmillan, 1987, pp. 828–30.

Palmeter, David. "A Note on the Ethics of Free Trade." *World Trade Review* 4, no. 3 (November 2005), pp. 449–67.

Petri, Peter A. *Modeling Japanese-American Trade: A Study of Asymmetric Interdependence.* Cambridge, MA: Harvard University Press, 1984.

Robinson, Joan. "Beggar-My-Neighbour Remedies for Unemployment." In Joan Robinson, *Essays on the Theory of Employment.* 2nd ed. Oxford: Basil Blackwell, 1947. Part III, Chapter 2.

Slotkin, Michael H. *Essays in Strategic Trade Policy.* Ph.D. dissertation. University of North Carolina at Chapel Hill, 1995.

Spencer, Barbara J., and James A. Brander. "International R&D Rivalry and Industrial Strategy." *Review of Economic Studies* 50, no. 163 (October 1983), pp. 707–22.

"A Survey of World Trade." *The Economist,* Sept. 22, 1990 (following p. 60).

Westphal, Larry E. "Empirical Justification for Infant Industry Protection." World Bank Staff Working Paper No. 445, March 1981, Washington, DC.

CHAPTER 16

Allen, Mark. "Complex Conclusions of Tokyo Round Add Up to Framework for Future Trade." *IMF Survey,* May 7, 1979, pp. 133–37.

Amiti, Mary, and Shang-Jin Wei. "Demystifying Outsourcing." *Finance and Development* 41, no. 4 (December 2004), pp. 36–39.

Anderson, James E. "The Uruguay Round and Welfare in Some Distorted Agricultural Economies." *Journal of Development Economics* 56, no. 2 (August 1998), pp. 393–410.

Baicker, Katherine, and M. Marit Rehavi. "Policy Watch: Trade Adjustment Assistance." *Journal of Economic Perspectives* 18, no. 2 (Spring 2004), pp. 239–55.

Baldwin, Robert E. "An Economic Evaluation of the Uruguay Round Agreement." *The World Economy,* 1995 Supplement on Global Trade Policy, pp. 153–72.

———. "The Political Economy of Postwar United States Trade Policy." In *International Trade and Finance: Readings.* 2nd ed. Edited by Robert E. Baldwin and J. David Richardson. Boston: Little, Brown, 1981, pp. 64–77.

———. "The Political Economy of Trade Policy." *Journal of Economic Perspectives* 3, no. 4 (Fall 1989), pp. 119–37.

———. "The Political Economy of Trade Policy: Integrating the Perspectives of Economists and Political Scientists." In *The Political Economy of Trade Policy: Papers in Honor of Jagdish Bhagwati.* Edited by Robert C. Feenstra, Gene M. Grossman, and Douglas A. Irwin. Cambridge, MA, and London: MIT Press, 1996, pp. 147–73.

———. "Trade Policies in Developed Countries." In *Handbook of International Economics.* Vol. I. Edited by Ronald W. Jones and Peter B. Kenen. Amsterdam: North-Holland, 1984. Chapter 12.

Bhagwati, Jagdish. *In Defense of Globalization.* New York: Oxford University Press, 2004.

Blonigen, Bruce A., and David N. Figlio. "Voting for Protection: Does Direct Foreign Investment Influence Legislator Behavior?" *American Economic Review* 88, no. 4 (September 1998), pp. 1002–14.

Bradford, Scott. "Paying the Price: Final Goods Protection in OECD Countries." *Review of Economics and Statistics* 85, no. 1 (February 2003), pp. 24–37.

Cheh, John H. "United States Concessions in the Kennedy Round and Short-Run Labor Adjustment Costs." *Journal of International Economics* 4, no. 4 (November 1974), pp. 323–40.

Cline, William R. " 'Reciprocity': A New Approach to World Trade Policy." In *Trade Policy in the 1980s.* Edited by William R. Cline. Washington, DC: Institute for International Economics, 1983, pp. 121–58.

Corden, W. M. *Trade Policy and Economic Welfare.* Oxford: Clarendon Press, 1974.

Deardorff, Alan V. "Economic Effects of Quota and Tariff Reductions." In *The New GATT: Implications for the United States.* Edited by Susan M. Collins and Barry P. Bosworth. Washington, DC: Brookings Institution, 1994, pp. 7–39.

———. "Safeguards Policy and the Conservative Social Welfare Function." In *Protection and Competition in International Trade: Essays in Honor of W. M. Corden.* Edited by Henryk Kierzkowski. Oxford: Basil Blackwell, 1987, pp. 22–40.

Deardorff, Alan V., and Robert M. Stern. *The Michigan Model of World Production and Trade: Theory and Applications.* Cambridge, MA: MIT Press, 1986. Chapter 4.

Destler, I. M. *American Trade Politics.* 3rd ed. Washington, DC: Institute for International Economics, 1995.

Ellsworth, P. T., and J. Clark Leith. *The International Economy.* 6th ed. New York: Macmillan, 1984. Chapter 13.

Estimates of Producer and Consumer Subsidy Equivalents: Government Intervention in Agriculture. Edited by Alan J. Webb, Michael Lopez, and Renata Penn. Agriculture and Trade Analysis Division. Economic Research Service. U.S. Department of Agriculture. Statistical Bulletin No. 803. April 1990.

Finger, J. Michael; Merlinda D. Ingco; and Ulrich Reincke. *The Uruguay Round: Statistics on Tariff Concessions Given and Received.* Washington, DC: World Bank, 1996.

Gawande, Kishore, and Usree Bandyopadhyay. "Is Protection for Sale? Evidence on the Grossman-Helpman Theory of Endogenous Protection." *Review of Economics and Statistics* 82, no. 1 (February 2000), pp. 139–52.

"Globalisation and Its Critics: A Survey of Globalisation." *The Economist.* September 29, 2001 (following p. 52).

Hillman, Arye L. *The Political Economy of Protection.* Chur, Switzerland: Harwood Academic Publishers, 1989.

"In the Twilight of Doha," *The Economist,* July 29, 2006, pp. 63–64.

Irwin, Douglas A. "The GATT in Historical Perspective." *American Economic Review* 85, no. 2 (May 1995), pp. 323–28.

Krueger, Anne O. (ed.). *The Political Economy of Trade Protection.* National Bureau of Economic Research Project Report. Chicago: University of Chicago Press, 1996.

Krugman, Paul. "What Should Trade Negotiators Negotiate About?" *Journal of Economic Literature* 35, no. 1 (March 1997), pp. 113–20.

Madsen, Jakob B. "Trade Barriers and the Collapse of World Trade During the Great Depression." *Southern Economic Journal* 67, no. 4 (April 2001), pp. 848–68.

Magee, Christopher. "Administered Protection for Workers: An Analysis of the Trade Adjustment Assistance Program." *Journal of International Economics* 53, no. 1 (February 2001), pp. 105–25.

Magee, Stephen P., and Leslie Young. "Endogenous Protection in the United States, 1900–1984." In *U.S. Trade Policies in a Changing World Economy.* Edited by Robert M. Stern. Cambridge, MA: MIT Press, 1987, pp. 145–95.

Maggi, Giovanni, and Andres Rodriguez-Clare. "Import Penetration and the Politics of Trade Protection." *Journal of International Economics* 51, no. 2 (August 2000), pp. 287–304.

Mastel, Greg. "Why We Should Expand Trade Adjustment Assistance." *Challenge: The Magazine of Economic Affairs* 49, no. 4 (July–August 2006), pp. 42–57.

"Mini-Symposium on the Political Economy of International Market Access." *The World Economy* 15, no. 6 (November 1992), pp. 679–753.

Rodrik, Dani. "Political Economy of Trade Policy." In *Handbook of International Economics.* Vol. III. Edited by Gene M. Grossman and Kenneth Rogoff. Amsterdam: Elsevier, 1995. Chapter 28.

Smith, David. "Offshoring: Political Myths and Economic Reality." *The World Economy* 29, no. 3 (March 2006), pp. 249–56.

Stiglitz, Joseph E. *Globalization and Its Discontents.* New York: W. W. Norton & Company, 2002.

Trefler, Daniel. "Trade Liberalization and the Theory of Endogenous Protection: An Econometric Study of U.S. Import Policy." *Journal of Political Economy* 101, no. 1 (February 1993), pp. 138–60.

Vousden, Neil. *The Economics of Trade Protection.* Cambridge, England, and New York: Cambridge University Press, 1990.

CHAPTER 17

Aguilar, Linda M. "NAFTA: A Review of the Issues." Federal Reserve Bank of Chicago *Economic Perspectives* 7, no. 1 (January/February 1993), pp. 12–20.

Balassa, Bela. "Trade Creation and Trade Diversion in the European Common Market: An Appraisal of the Evidence." *Manchester School of Economic and Social Studies* 42, no. 2 (June 1974), pp. 93–135.

Brown, Drusilla K. "The Impact of a North American Free Trade Area: Applied General Equilibrium Models" with "Comments" by Timothy J. Kehoe and Robert Z. Lawrence. In *North American Free Trade: Assessing the Impact.* Edited by Nora Lustig, Barry P. Bosworth, and Robert Z. Lawrence. Washington, DC: Brookings Institution, 1992, pp. 26–68.

"Central and Eastern Europe: Assessing the Early Benefits of EU Membership." *IMF Survey*, November 20, 2006, pp. 331–34.

Eken, Sena. "Breakup of the East African Community." *Finance and Development* 16, no. 4 (December 1979), pp. 36–40.

Emerson, Michael, et al. *The Economics of 1992: The E.C. Commission's Assessment of the Economic Effects of Completing the Internal Market.* Oxford: Oxford University Press, 1988.

Gould, David M. "Has NAFTA Changed North American Trade?" Federal Reserve Bank of Dallas *Economic Review* (First Quarter 1998), pp. 12–23.

Hufbauer, Gary Clyde (ed.). *Europe 1992: An American Perspective.* Washington, DC: Brookings Institution, 1990.

Hufbauer, Gary Clyde, and Jeffrey J. Schott. *North American Free Trade: Issues and Recommendations.* Washington, DC: Institute for International Economics, 1992.

Karemera, David, and Kalu Ojah. "An Industrial Analysis of Trade Creation and Diversion Effects of NAFTA." *Journal of Economic Integration* 13, no. 3 (September 1998), pp. 400–25.

Kehoe, Patrick J., and Timothy J. Kehoe. "Capturing NAFTA's Impact with Applied General Equilibrium Models." Federal Reserve Bank of Minneapolis *Quarterly Review* (Spring 1994), pp. 17–34.

Limão, Nuno. "Preferential vs. Multilateral Trade Liberalization: Evidence and Open Questions." *World Trade Review* 5, no. 2 (July 2006), pp. 155–76.

Lipsey, Richard G. "The Theory of Customs Unions: A General Survey." *Economic Journal* 70, no. 279 (September 1960), pp. 496–513.

Meade, James E. *The Theory of Customs Unions.* Amsterdam: North-Holland, 1955.

Polak, Jacques J. "Is APEC a Natural Regional Trading Bloc? A Critique of the 'Gravity Model' of International Trade." *The World Economy* 19, no. 5 (September 1996), pp. 533–43.

Schipke, Alfred. "Building on CAFTA: How the Free Trade Pact Can Help Foster Central America's Economic Integration." *Finance and Development* 42, no. 4 (December 2005), pp. 30–33.

Sharer, Robert. "Trade: An Engine of Growth for Africa." *Finance and Development* 36, no. 4 (December 1999), pp. 26–29.

U.S. International Trade Commission. *International Economic Review* (November 1995), pp. 11–14.

———. *International Economic Review* (October/November 1996), pp. 22–26.

Viner, Jacob. *The Customs Union Issue.* New York: Carnegie Endowment for International Peace, 1950.

World Bank. *World Development Report 1996.* Oxford: Oxford University Press. 1996.

Yeager, Timothy J. *Institutions, Transition Economies, and Economic Development.* Boulder, CO: Westview Press. 1999.

CHAPTER 18

Appleyard, Dennis R. "The Terms of Trade between the United Kingdom and British India, 1858–1947." *Economic Development and Cultural Change* 54, no. 3 (April 2006), pp. 635–54.

Baldwin, Robert E. "Secular Movements in the Terms of Trade." *American Economic Review* 45, no. 2 (May 1955), pp. 259–69.

Bhagwati, Jagdish N. (ed.). *The New International Economic Order: The North-South Debate.* Cambridge, MA: MIT Press, 1977.

Burton, David; Wanda Tseng; and Kenneth Kang. "Asia's Winds of Change." *Finance and Development* 43, no. 2 (June 2006), pp. 8–13.

Cashin, Paul; Hong Liang; and C. John McDermott. "Do Commodity Price Shocks Last Too Long for Stabilization Schemes to Work?" *Finance and Development* 36, no. 3 (September 1999), pp. 40–43.

Chenery, Hollis B., and T. N. Srinivasan (eds.). *Handbook of Development Economics.* Vol. II. New York: North-Holland, 1989. (See especially Chapters 23, 24, and 31.)

Chow, Peter C. Y. "Causality between Export Growth and Industrial Development: Empirical Evidence for the NICs." *Journal of Development Economics* 26, no. 1 (June 1987), pp. 55–63.

Cottani, Joaquin A.; Domingo F. Cavallo; and M. Shahbaz Khan. "Real Exchange Rate Behavior and Economic Performance in LDCs." *Economic Development and Cultural Change* 39, no. 1 (October 1990), pp. 61–76.

Darity, William A., and Bobbie L. Horn. *The Loan Pushers: The Role of Commercial Banks in the International Debt Crisis.* Cambridge, MA: Ballinger, 1988.

Diakosavvas, Dimitris, and Pasquale L. Scandizzo. "Trends in the Terms of Trade of Primary Commodities, 1900–1982: The Controversy and Its Origins." *Economic Development and Cultural Change* 39, no. 2 (January 1991), pp. 231–64.

Eichengreen, Barry. "Restructuring Sovereign Debt." *Journal of Economic Perspectives* 17, no. 4 (Fall 2003), pp. 75–98.

"Escaping the Poverty Trap." In *The Least Developed Countries Report, 2002.* United Nations Conference on Trade and Development. Geneva: UNCTAD, 2002. pp. 103–17.

Edwards, Sebastian. "Openness, Trade Liberalization, and Growth in Developing Countries." *Journal of Economic Literature* 31, no. 3 (September 1993), pp. 1358–93.

Ellsworth, P. T. "The Terms of Trade between Primary Producing and Industrial Countries." *Inter-American Economic Affairs* 10, no. 1 (Summer 1956), pp. 47–65.

Fischer, Stanley, and Ishrat Husain. "Managing the Debt Crisis in the 1990s." *Finance and Development* 27, no. 2 (June 1990), pp. 24–27.

Frankel, Jeffrey A., and David Romer. "Does Trade Cause Growth?" *American Economic Review* 89, no. 3 (June 1999), pp. 379–99.

Grossman, Gene, and Elhanan Helpman. *Innovation and Growth in the Global Economy.* Cambridge, MA: MIT Press, 1991.

Hess, Peter, and Clark Ross. *Economic Development: Theories, Evidence, and Policies.* Fort Worth, TX: Dryden Press, 1997. Chapters 11 and 14.

Johnson, Harry G. *Economic Policies toward Less Developed Countries.* New York: Frederick A. Praeger, 1967.

Kenen, Peter B. "Organizing Debt Relief: The Need for a New Institution." *Journal of Economic Perspectives* 4, no. 1 (Winter 1990), pp. 7–18.

Kirchbach, F. von. "An Assessment of the LDC Export Performance from a Business and Product Perspective." Paper presented at the ITC Business Round Table. Third United Nations Conference on the Least Developed Countries. Brussels. May 16, 2001.

Krueger, Anne O. "The Effects of Trade Strategies on Growth." *Finance and Development* 20, no. 2 (June 1983), pp. 6–8.

———. "Trade Policy and Economic Development: How We Learn." *American Economic Review* 87, no. 1 (March 1997), pp. 1–22.

Krugman, Paul R. "Market-Based Debt Reduction Schemes." In *Analytical Issues in Debt.* Edited by Jacob A. Frenkel, Michael P. Dooley, and Peter Wickham. Washington, DC: International Monetary Fund, 1989, pp. 258–88.

Love, James. "Commodity Concentration and Export Earnings Instability: A Shift from Cross-Section to Time-Series Analysis." *Journal of Development Economics* 24, no. 2 (December 1986), pp. 239–48.

———. "Concentration and Instability: Again." *Journal of Development Economics* 33, no. 1 (July 1990), pp. 149–51.

MacBean, Alasdair I. *Export Instability and Economic Development.* Cambridge, MA: Harvard University Press, 1966.

Massell, Benton F. "Concentration and Instability Revisited." *Journal of Development Economics* 33, no. 1 (July 1990), pp. 145–47.

———. "Export Instability and Economic Structure." *American Economic Review* 60, no. 4 (September 1970), pp. 618–30.

Meier, Gerald M. *The International Economics of Development: Theory and Policy.* New York: Harper and Row, 1968.

Morgan, Theodore. "The Long-Run Terms of Trade between Agriculture and Manufacturing." *Economic Development and Cultural Change* 8, no. 1 (October 1959), pp. 1–23.

———. "Trends in Terms of Trade, and their Repercussions on Primary Producers." In *International Trade Theory in a Developing World.* Edited by R. F. Harrod and Douglas Hague. London: Macmillan, 1963, pp. 52–95.

Myint, H. "The 'Classical Theory' of International Trade and the Underdeveloped Countries." *Economic Journal* 68, no. 270 (June 1958), pp. 317–37.

"Point of View: Why Should Small Developing Countries Engage in the Global Trading System?" *Finance and Development* 42, no. 1 (March 2005), pp. 10–13.

Rodrik, Dani, and Arvind Subramanian. "The Primacy of Institutions (and What This Does and Does Not Mean)." *Finance and Development* 40, no. 2 (June 2003), pp. 31–34.

Romer, Paul M. "Increasing Returns and Long-Run Growth." *Journal of Political Economy* 94, no. 5 (October 1986), pp. 1002–37.

Santos-Paulino, Amelia, and A. P. Thirlwall. "Trade Liberalisation and Economic Performance in Developing Countries—Introduction." *Economic Journal* 114, no. 493 (February 2004), pp. F1–3.

Singer, Hans W. "Terms of Trade and Economic Development." In *The New Palgrave: A Dictionary of Economics.* Vol. 4. Edited by John Eatwell, Murray Milgate, and Peter Newman. London: Macmillan, 1987, pp. 626–28.

Singer, Hans W., and Javed A. Ansari. *Rich and Poor Countries: Consequences of International Economic Disorder.* 4th ed. London: Unwin Hyman, 1988.

Spraos, John. *Inequalising Trade: A Study of Traditional North/South Specialisation in the Context of Terms of Trade Concepts.* Oxford: Clarendon Press, 1983.

Streeten, Paul. "A Cool Look at 'Outward-Looking' Strategies for Development." *The World Economy* 5, no. 2 (September 1982), pp. 159–69.

Todaro, Michael P., and Stephen C. Smith. *Economic Development.* 8th ed. Boston: Addison-Wesley, 2003. Chapter 13.

Tyler, William G. "Growth and Export Expansion in Developing Countries: Some Empirical Evidence." *Journal of Development Economics* 9, no. 1 (August 1981), pp. 121–30.

United Nations. Department of Economic Affairs. *Relative Prices of Exports and Imports of Underdeveloped Countries.* Lake Success, NY: United Nations, 1949.

———. Economic Commission for Latin America. *The Economic Development of Latin America and Its Principal Problems.* Lake Success, NY: United Nations, 1949. (Written by Raul Prebisch.)

World Bank. *World Development Report 1987.* New York: Oxford University Press, 1987. (See especially Chapter 5.)

———. *World Development Report 1991.* New York: Oxford University Press, 1991. (See especially Chapter 5.)

CHAPTER 19

International Monetary Fund. *Balance of Payments Manual.* 4th ed. Washington, DC: IMF, 1977.

———. *Balance of Payments Statistics Yearbook.* Washington, DC: IMF, Annual.

Mann, Catherine L. "Is the U.S. Current Account Deficit Sustainable?" *Finance and Development* 37, no. 1 (March 2000), pp. 42–45.

Nawaz, Shuja. "Why the World Current Account Does Not Balance." *Finance and Development* 24, no. 3 (September 1987), pp. 43–45.

Ott, Mack. "Have U.S. Exports Been Larger Than Reported?" Federal Reserve Bank of St. Louis *Review* 70, no. 5 (September–October 1988), pp. 3–23.

U.S. Department of Commerce, Bureau of Economic Analysis. *Survey of Current Business.* January, April, July, and September issues annually.

Walter, Bruce C. "Quality Issues Affecting the Compilation of the U.S. Merchandise Trade Statistics." In *International Economic Transactions: Issues in Measurement and Empirical Research.* Edited by Peter Hooper and J. David Richardson. Chicago and London: University of Chicago Press, 1991, pp. 89–103.

CHAPTER 20

Chalupa, Karel V. "Foreign Currency Futures: Reducing Foreign Exchange Risk." Federal Reserve Bank of Chicago *Economic Perspectives* 6, no. 3 (Winter 1982), pp. 3–11.

Chrystal, K. Alec. "A Guide to Foreign Exchange Markets." Federal Reserve Bank of St. Louis *Review* 66, no. 3 (March 1984), pp. 5–18.

Fieleke, Norman S. "The Rise of the Foreign Currency Futures Market." Federal Reserve Bank of Boston *New England Economic Review* (March–April 1985), pp. 38–47.

Gendreau, Brian. "New Markets in Foreign Exchange." Federal Reserve Bank of Philadelphia *Business Review* (July/August 1984), pp. 3–12.

Jorion, Philippe. "Does Real Interest Parity Hold at Longer Maturities?" *Journal of International Economics* 40, no. 1/2 (February 1996), pp. 105–26.

Kasman, Bruce, and Charles Pigott. "Interest Rate Divergences among the Major Industrial Nations." Federal Reserve Bank of New York *Quarterly Review* 13, no. 3 (Autumn 1988), pp. 28–44.

Kubarych, Robert M. *Foreign Exchange Markets in the United States.* New York: Federal Reserve Bank of New York, 1978.

Machlup, Fritz. "The Theory of Foreign Exchanges." *Economica* 6, New Series (November 1939), pp. 375–97, and vol. 7 (February 1940), pp. 23–49. Reprinted in American Economic Association. *Readings in the Theory of International Trade.* Edited by Howard S. Ellis and Lloyd A. Metzler. Philadelphia: Blakiston, 1950, pp. 104–58.

McCormick, Frank. "Covered Interest Arbitrage: Unexploited Profits? Comment." *Journal of Political Economy* 87, no. 2 (April 1979), pp. 411–17.

McPartland, John W. "Foreign Exchange Trading and Settlement: Past and Present." *Chicago Fed Letter*, February 2006, pp. 1–4.

Rivera-Batiz, Francisco L., and Luis A. Rivera-Batiz. *International Finance and Open Economy Macroeconomics.* 2nd ed. New York: Macmillan, 1994. Chapters 1, 4–6.

Taylor, Mark P. "The Economics of Exchange Rates." *Journal of Economic Literature* 33, no. 1 (March 1995), pp. 13–47. (Pages 14–21 are particularly relevant for this chapter.)

CHAPTER 21

Aggarwal, Raj, and Andrea L. DeMaskey. "Cross-Hedging Currency Risks in Asian Emerging Markets Using Derivatives in Major Currencies." *Journal of Portfolio Management* 23, no. 3 (Spring 1997), pp. 88–95.

Bank for International Settlements. *Annual Reports.* Basle, Switzerland.

Bryan, Lowell, and Diana Farrell. *Market Unbound: Unleashing Global Capitalism.* New York: John Wiley and Sons, 1996.

Burghardt, Galen; Terry Belton; Morton Lane; Geoffrey Luce; and Rick McVey. *Eurodollar Futures and Options: Controlling Money Market Risk.* Chicago: Probus, 1991.

Dufey, Gunter, and Ian H. Giddy. *The International Money Market.* 2nd ed. Englewood Cliffs, NJ: Prentice-Hall, 1994.

Eng, Maximo, and Francis A. Lees. "Eurocurrency Centers." In *International Finance Handbook.* Vol. 1. Edited by Abraham M. George and Ian H. Giddy. New York: John Wiley and Sons, 1983. Section 3.6.

Gibson, Heather D. *The Eurocurrency Markets, Domestic Financial Policy and International Instability.* New York: St. Martin's Press, 1989.

Jochum, Christian, and Laura Kodres. "Does the Introduction of Futures on Emerging Market Currencies Destabilize the Underlying Currencies?" *International Monetary Fund Staff Papers* 45, no. 3 (September 1998), pp. 486–521.

Johnston, R. B. *The Economics of the Euro-Market: History, Theory and Policy.* New York: St. Martin's Press, 1982.

Kaufman, Herbert M. *Money and Banking.* Lexington, MA: D.C. Heath, 1992.

Kreicher, Lawrence L. "Eurodollar Arbitrage." Federal Reserve Bank of New York *Quarterly Review* 7, no. 2 (Summer 1982), pp. 10–22.

Kvasnicka, Joseph G. "Eurodollars—An Important Source of Funds for American Banks." In *Readings in International Finance.* 3rd ed. Edited by Joseph G. Kvasnicka. Chicago: Federal Reserve Bank of Chicago, 1986, pp. 165–76.

Magraw, Daniel. "Legal Aspects of International Bonds." In *International Finance Handbook.* Vol. 1. Edited by Abraham M. George and Ian H. Giddy. New York: John Wiley and Sons, 1983. Section 5.3.

Mayo, Herbert B. *Investments: An Introduction.* 5th ed. Fort Worth, TX: Dryden Press, 1997.

Mendelsohn, M. S. *Money on the Move: The Modern International Capital Market.* New York: McGraw-Hill, 1980.

Mendelson, Morris. "The Eurobond and Foreign Bond Markets." In *International Finance Handbook.* Vol. 1. Edited by Abraham M. George and Ian H. Giddy. New York: John Wiley and Sons, 1983. Section 5.1.

Shepherd, William F. *International Financial Integration: History, Theory and Applications in OECD Countries.* Aldershot, England: Averbury, 1994. Chapters 3–4.

Taylor, Alan M. "Global Finance: Past and Present." *Finance and Development* 41, no. 1 (March 2004), pp. 28–31.

CHAPTER 22

Black, Stanley W., and Michael K. Salemi. "FIML Estimation of the Dollar-Deutschemark Risk Premium in a Portfolio Model." *Journal of International Economics* 25, no. 3/4 (November 1988), pp. 205–24.

Branson, William H., and Dale W. Henderson. "The Specification and Influence of Asset Markets." In *Handbook of International Economics.* Vol. II. Edited by Ronald W. Jones and Peter B. Kenen. Amsterdam: North-Holland, 1985. Chapter 15.

Chinn, Menzie D., and Richard A. Meese. "Banking on Currency Forecasts: How Predictable Is Change in Money?" *Journal of International Economics* 38, no. 1/2 (February 1995), pp. 161–78.

Crespo-Cuaresmo, Jesús; Jarko Fidrmuc; and Ronald MacDonald. "The Monetary Approach to Exchange Rates in the CEECs." *The Economics of Transition* 13, no. 2 (April 2005), pp. 395–416.

Dominguez, Kathryn M., and Jeffrey A. Frankel. "Does Foreign Exchange Intervention Matter? The Portfolio Effect." *American Economic Review* 83, no. 4 (December 1993), pp. 1356–59.

Dornbusch, Rudiger. "Exchange Rate Economics: Where Do We Stand?" *Brookings Papers on Economic Activity,* no. 1 (1980), pp. 143–85.

———. "Expectations and Exchange Rate Dynamics." *Journal of Political Economy* 84, no. 6 (December 1976), pp. 1161–76.

Frankel, Jeffrey A. "Monetary and Portfolio-Balance Models of the Determination of Exchange Rates." In Jeffrey A. Frankel, *On Exchange Rates.* Cambridge, MA: MIT Press, 1993, pp. 95–115.

———. "Tests of Monetary and Portfolio Balance Models of Exchange Rate Determination." In *Exchange Rate Theory and Practice.* Edited by John F. O. Bilson and Richard C. Marston. Chicago: University of Chicago Press, 1984. Chapter 7.

Frankel, Jeffrey A., and Andrew K. Rose. "Empirical Research on Nominal Exchange Rates." In *Handbook of International Economics.* Vol. III. Edited by Gene M. Grossman and Kenneth Rogoff. Amsterdam: Elsevier, 1995. Chapter 33.

Frenkel, Jacob A. "A Monetary Approach to the Exchange Rate: Doctrinal Aspects and Empirical Evidence." In *The Economics of Exchange Rates.* Edited by Jacob A. Frenkel and Harry G. Johnson. Reading, MA: Addison-Wesley, 1978. Chapter 1.

Frenkel, Jacob A., and Michael L. Mussa. "Asset Markets, Exchange Rates and the Balance of Payments." In *Handbook of International Economics.* Vol. II. Edited by Ronald W. Jones and Peter B. Kenen. Amsterdam: North-Holland, 1985. Chapter 14.

Friedman, Milton (ed.). *Studies in the Quantity Theory of Money.* Chicago: University of Chicago Press, 1956.

Froyen, Richard T. *Macroeconomics: Theories and Policies.* 8th ed. Upper Saddle River, NJ: Pearson/Prentice Hall, 2005. Chapters 7 and 22.

Graham, Frank D. *Exchange, Prices and Production in Hyper-Inflation: Germany, 1920–1923.* Princeton, NJ: Princeton University Press, 1930.

Isard, Peter. *Exchange Rate Economics: Surveys of Economic Literature.* Cambridge, England: Cambridge University Press, 1995.

Levich, Richard H. "Empirical Studies of Exchange Rates: Price Behavior, Rate Determination and Market Efficiency." In *Handbook of International Economics.* Vol. II. Edited by Ronald W. Jones and Peter B. Kenen. Amsterdam: North-Holland, 1985. Chapter 19.

MacDonald, Ronald. "Exchange Rate Behaviour: Are Fundamentals Important?" *Economic Journal* 109, no. 459 (November 1999), pp. F673–91.

MacDonald, Ronald, and Ian W. Marsh. "On Fundamentals and Exchange Rates: A Casselian Perspective." *Review of Economics and Statistics* 79, no. 4 (November 1997), pp. 655–64.

MacDonald, Ronald, and Mark P. Taylor. "Exchange Rate Economics: A Survey." *International Monetary Fund Staff Papers* 39, no. 1 (March 1992), pp. 1–57.

———. "The Monetary Approach to the Exchange Rate: Rational Expectations, Long-Run Equilibrium, and Forecasting." *International Monetary Fund Staff Papers* 40, no. 1 (March 1993), pp. 89–107.

———. "The Monetary Model of the Exchange Rate: Long-Run Relationships, Short-Run Dynamics and How to Beat a Random Walk." *Journal of International Money and Finance* 13, no. 3 (June 1994), pp. 276–90.

Meese, Richard. "Currency Fluctuations in the Post-Bretton Woods Era." *Journal of Economic Perspectives* 4, no. 1 (Winter 1990), pp. 117–34.

Meese, Richard A., and Kenneth Rogoff. "Empirical Exchange Rate Models of the Seventies: Do They Fit Out of Sample?" *Journal of International Economics* 14, no. 1/2 (February 1983), pp. 3–24.

Melvin, Michael. *International Money and Finance.* 5th ed. New York: HarperCollins, 2000.

Mussa, Michael. "The Monetary Approach to the Balance of Payments." In *International Trade and Finance: Readings.* 2nd ed. Edited by Robert E. Baldwin and J. David Richardson. Boston: Little, Brown, 1981, pp. 368–73.

Rivera-Batiz, Francisco L., and Luis A. Rivera-Batiz. *International Finance and Open Economy Macroeconomics.* 2nd ed. New York: Macmillan, 1994. Chapters 19–20.

Rogoff, Kenneth. "Monetary Models of Dollar/Yen/Euro Nominal Exchange Rates: Dead or Undead?" *Economic Journal* 109, no. 459 (November 1999), pp. F655–59.

———. "The Purchasing Power Parity Puzzle." *Journal of Economic Literature* 34, no. 2 (June 1996), pp. 647–68.

Taylor, Mark. "The Economics of Exchange Rates." *Journal of Economic Literature* 33, no. 1 (March 1995), pp. 13–47.

Ujiie, Junichi. "A Stock Adjustment Approach to Monetary Policy and the Balance of Payments." In *The Economics of Exchange Rates.* Edited by Jacob A. Frenkel and Harry G. Johnson. Reading, MA: Addison-Wesley, 1978. Chapter 10.

CHAPTER 23

Alexander, Sidney S. "Effects of a Devaluation: A Simplified Synthesis of Elasticities and Absorption Approaches." *American Economic Review* 49, no. 1 (March 1959), pp. 22–42.

———. "Effects of a Devaluation on a Trade Balance." *International Monetary Fund Staff Papers* 3, no. 1 (April 1952), pp. 263–78.

Appleyard, Dennis R., and Alfred J. Field, Jr. "A Note on Teaching the Marshall-Lerner Condition." *Journal of Economic Education* 17, no. 1 (Winter 1986), pp. 52–57.

Backus, David K.; Patrick J. Kehoe; and Finn E. Kydland. "Dynamics of the Trade Balance and the Terms of Trade: The J-Curve?" *American Economic Review* 84, no. 1 (March 1994), pp. 84–103.

Bloomfield, Arthur I. *Monetary Policy under the International Gold Standard: 1880–1914.* New York: Federal Reserve Bank of New York, 1959.

Catão, Luis A., and Solomos N. Solomu. "Effective Exchange Rates and the Classical Gold Standard Adjustment." *American Economic Review* 95, no. 4 (September 2005), pp. 1259–75.

Cook, David, and Michael B. Devereux. "External Currency Pricing and the East Asian Crisis." *Journal of International Economics* 69, no. 1 (June 2006), pp. 37–63.

Devereux, Michael B., and Charles Engel. "Monetary Policy in the Open Economy Revisited: Price Setting and Exchange-Rate Flexibility." *Review of Economic Studies* 70 (4), no. 245 (October 2003), pp. 765–83.

Feenstra, Robert C.; Joseph E. Gagnon; and Michael M. Knetter. "Market Share and Exchange Rate Pass-Through in World Automobile Trade." *Journal of International Economics* 40, no. 1/2 (February 1996), pp. 187–207.

Goldstein, Morris, and Mohsin S. Khan. "Income and Price Effects in Foreign Trade." In *Handbook of International Economics.* Vol. II. Edited by Ronald W. Jones and Peter B. Kenen. Amsterdam: North-Holland, 1985. Chapter 20.

Gron, Anne, and Deborah L. Swenson. "Incomplete Exchange-Rate Pass-Through and Imperfect Competition: The Effect of Local Production." *American Economic Review* 86, no. 2 (May 1996), pp. 71–76.

Houthakker, Hendrik S., and Stephen P. Magee. "Income and Price Elasticities in World Trade." *Review of Economics and Statistics* 51, no. 2 (May 1969), pp. 111–25.

Klitgaard, Thomas. "Exchange Rates and Profit Margins: The Case of Japanese Exporters." Federal Reserve Bank of New York *Economic Policy Review* 5, no. 1 (April 1999), pp. 41–54.

Machlup, Fritz. "The Theory of Foreign Exchanges." *Economica* 6, New Series (November 1939), pp. 375–97, and vol. 7 (February 1940), pp. 23–49. Reprinted in American Economic Association. *Readings in the Theory of International Trade.* Edited by Howard S. Ellis and Lloyd A. Metzler. Philadelphia: Blakiston, 1950, pp. 104–58.

Marquez, Jaime. "Bilateral Trade Elasticities." *Review of Economics and Statistics* 72, no. 1 (February 1990), pp. 70–77.

Olivei, Govanni P. "Exchange Rates and the Prices of Manufacturing Products Imported into the United States." Federal Reserve Bank of Boston *New England Economic Review,* First Quarter 2002, pp. 3–18.

Orcutt, Guy H. "Measurement of Price Elasticities in International Trade." *Review of Economics and Statistics* 32, no. 2 (May 1950), pp. 117–32.

Robinson, Joan. "The Foreign Exchanges." In Joan Robinson, *Essays in the Theory of Employment.* 2nd ed. Oxford: Basil Blackwell, 1947, pp. 134–55.

Stern, Robert M.; Jonathan Francis; and Bruce Schumacher. *Price Elasticities in International Trade: An Annotated Bibliography.* London: Macmillan, 1975.

Yang, Jiawen. "Exchange Rate Pass-Through in U.S. Manufacturing Industries." *Review of Economics and Statistics* 79, no. 1 (February 1997), pp. 95–104.

CHAPTER 24

Baxter, Marianne. "International Trade and Business Cycles." In *Handbook of International Economics.* Vol. III. Edited by Gene M. Grossman and Kenneth Rogoff. Amsterdam: Elsevier, 1995. Chapter 35.

Bruce, Neil, and Douglas D. Purvis. "The Specification and Influence of Goods and Factor Markets in Open-Economy Macroeconomic Models." In *Handbook of International Economics.* Vol. II. Edited by Ronald W. Jones and Peter B. Kenen. Amsterdam: North-Holland, 1985. Chapter 16.

Canova, Fabio, and Gianni de Nicolo. "On the Sources of Business Cycles in the G-7." *Journal of International Economics* 59, no. 1 (January 2003), pp. 77–100.

Dornbusch, Rudiger. *Open Economy Macroeconomics.* New York: Basic Books, 1980.

Froyen, Richard T. *Macroeconomics: Theories and Policies.* 8th ed. Upper Saddle River, NJ: Pearson/Prentice Hall, 2005. Chapter 6.

Helliwell, John F., and Tim Padmore. "Empirical Studies of Macroeconomic Interdependence." In *Handbook of International Economics.* Vol. II. Edited by Ronald W. Jones and Peter B. Kenen. Amsterdam: North-Holland, 1985. Chapter 21.

Kenen, Peter B. "Macroeconomic Theory and Policy: How the Closed Economy Was Opened." In *Handbook of International Economics.* Vol. II. Edited by Ronald W. Jones and Peter B. Kenen. Amsterdam: North-Holland, 1985. Chapter 13.

Keynes, John Maynard. *The General Theory of Employment, Interest and Money.* New York: Harcourt, Brace, 1936.

Kim, Yoonbai. "Income Effects on the Trade Balance." *Review of Economics and Statistics* 78, no. 3 (August 1996), pp. 464–69.

Kose, M. Ayhan; Eswar S. Prasad; and Marco E. Terrones. "How Does Globalization Affect the Synchronization of Business Cycles?" *American Economic Review* 93, no. 2 (May 2003), pp. 57–62.

Machlup, Fritz. *International Trade and the National Income Multiplier.* Philadelphia: Blakiston, 1943.

Meade, James E. *The Theory of International Economic Policy.* Vol. I. *The Balance of Payments.* London: Oxford University Press, 1951. Part III.

Norton, Stefan C., and Don E. Schlagenhauf. "The Role of International Factors in the Business Cycle: A Multi-Country Study." *Journal of International Economics* 40, no. 1/2 (February 1996), pp. 85–104.

Swan, T. W. "Longer-Run Problems of the Balance of Payments." In *The Australian Economy: A Volume of Readings.* Edited by H.W. Arndt and W. M. Corden. Melbourne: F. W. Cheshire Press, 1963, pp. 384–95.

Tinbergen, Jan. *Economic Policy: Principles and Design.* 4th rev. printing. Amsterdam: North-Holland, 1967.

CHAPTER 25

Bonser-Neal, Catherine. "Does Central Bank Intervention Stabilize Foreign Exchange Rates?" Federal Reserve Bank of Kansas City *Economic Review* 81, no. 1 (First Quarter 1996), pp. 43–57.

Enoch, Charles, and Anne-Marie Gulde. "Are Currency Boards a Cure for All Monetary Problems?" *Finance and Development* 35, no. 4 (December 1998), pp. 40–43.

Fleming, J. Marcus. "Domestic Financial Policies under Fixed and under Floating Exchange Rates." *International Monetary Fund Staff Papers* 9, no. 3 (November 1962), pp. 369–79.

Frenkel, Jacob A., and Michael L. Mussa. "Asset Markets, Exchange Rates, and the Balance of Payments." In *Handbook of International Economics.* Vol. II. Edited by Ronald W. Jones and Peter B. Kenen. Amsterdam: North-Holland, 1985. Chapter 14.

Frenkel, Jacob A., and Assaf Razin. "The Mundell-Fleming Model a Quarter Century Later." *International Monetary Fund Staff Papers* 34, no. 4 (December 1987), pp. 567–620.

Froyen, Richard T. *Macroeconomics: Theories and Policies.* 8th ed. Upper Saddle River, NJ: Pearson/Prentice Hall, 2005. Chapters 7, 8, 16.

Kenen, Peter B. "Macroeconomic Theory and Policy: How the Closed Economy Was Opened." In *Handbook of International Economics.* Vol. II. Edited by Ronald W. Jones and Peter B. Kenen. Amsterdam: North-Holland, 1985. Chapter 13.

Mundell, Robert. "The Appropriate Use of Monetary and Fiscal Policy for Internal and External Stability." *International Monetary Fund Staff Papers* 9, no. 1 (March 1962), pp. 70–77.

———. "Capital Mobility and Stabilization Policy under Fixed and Flexible Exchange Rates." *Canadian Journal of Economics and Political Science* 29, no. 4 (November 1963), pp. 475–85.

———. *International Economics.* New York: Macmillan, 1968.

Mussa, Michael. "Macroeconomic Interdependence and the Exchange Rate Regime." In *International Economic Policy: Theory and Evidence.* Edited by Rudiger Dornbusch and Jacob A. Frenkel. Baltimore: Johns Hopkins University Press, 1979. pp. 160–204.

Taylor, Alan M. "Global Finance: Past and Present." *Finance and Development* 41, no. 1 (March 2004), pp. 28–31.

Tinbergen, Jan. *Economic Policy: Principles and Design.* 4th rev. printing. Amsterdam: North-Holland, 1967.

Willett, Thomas D., and Francisco Forte. "Interest Rate Policy and External Balance." *Quarterly Journal of Economics* 83, no. 2 (May 1969), pp. 242–62.

CHAPTER 26

Bergsten, C. Fred, and C. Randall Henning. *Global Economic Leadership and the Group of Seven.* Washington, DC: Institute for International Economics, 1996.

Coeuré, Benoît, and Jean Pisani-Ferry. "The Case against Benign Neglect of Exchange Rate Stability." *Finance and Development* 36, no. 3 (September 1999), pp. 5–8.

Cooper, Richard N. "Economic Interdependence and Coordination of Economic Policies." In *Handbook of International Economics.* Vol. II. Edited by Ronald W. Jones and Peter B. Kenen. Amsterdam: North-Holland, 1985. Chapter 23.

Dunn, Robert M., Jr. *The Many Disappointments of Flexible Exchange Rates.* Essays in International Finance No. 154. Princeton, NJ: International Finance Section, Princeton University, December 1983.

Fleming, J. Marcus. "Domestic Financial Policies under Fixed and under Floating Exchange Rates." *International Monetary Fund Staff Papers* 9, no. 3 (November 1962), pp. 369–79.

Friedman, Milton. "The Case for Flexible Exchange Rates." In Milton Friedman, *Essays in Positive Economics.* Chicago: University of Chicago Press, 1953, pp. 157–203.

Kenen, Peter B. "Macroeconomic Theory and Policy: How the Closed Economy Was Opened." In *Handbook of International Economics.* Vol. II. Edited by Ronald W. Jones and Peter B. Kenen. Amsterdam: North-Holland, 1985. Chapter 13.

Marston, Richard C. "Stabilization Policies in Open Economies." In *Handbook of International Economics.* Vol. II. Edited by Ronald W. Jones and Peter B. Kenen. Amsterdam: North-Holland, 1985. Chapter 17.

McCulloch, Rachel. "Macroeconomic Policy and Trade Performance: International Implications of U.S. Budget Deficits." In *Issues in U.S.-EC Trade Relations.* Edited by Robert E. Baldwin, Carl B. Hamilton, and André Sapir. Chicago: University of Chicago Press, 1988, pp. 349–68.

Mundell, Robert A. *International Economics.* New York: Macmillan, 1968. Chapters 17–18.

Rogers, John H. "Monetary Shocks and Real Exchange Rates." *Journal of International Economics* 49, no. 2 (December 1999), pp. 269–88.

Rivera-Batiz, Francisco L., and Luis A. Rivera-Batiz. *International Finance and Open Economy Macroeconomics.* 2nd ed. New York: Macmillan, 1994. Chapter 17.

Taylor, John B. "The Role of the Exchange Rate in Monetary-Policy Rules." *American Economic Review* 91, no. 2 (May 2001), pp. 263–67.

CHAPTER 27

Akerlof, George, and Janet Yellin. "Rational Models of Irrational Behavior." *American Economic Review* 77, no. 2 (May 1987), pp. 137–42.

Ball, Laurence, and N. Gregory Mankiw. "The NAIRU in Theory and Practice." *Journal of Economic Perspectives* 16, no. 4 (Fall 2002), pp. 115–36.

Blanchard, Olivier, and Justin Wolfers. "The Role of Shocks and Institutions in the Rise of European Unemployment: The Aggregate Evidence." *Economic Journal* 110, no. 462 (March 2000), pp. C1–33.

Bruce, Neil, and Douglas D. Purvis. "The Specification and Influence of Goods and Factor Markets in Open-Economy Macroeconomic Models." In *Handbook of International Economics.* Vol. II. Edited by Ronald W. Jones and Peter B. Kenen. Amsterdam: North-Holland, 1985. Chapter 16.

Darity, William, Jr., and Arthur H. Goldsmith. "Social Psychology, Unemployment and Macroeconomics." *Journal of Economic Perspectives* 10, no. 1 (Winter 1996), pp. 121–40.

Froyen, Richard T. *Macroeconomics: Theories and Policies.* 8th ed. Upper Saddle River, NJ: Pearson/Prentice Hall, 2005. Chapters 9–14.

Gordon, Robert J. *Macroeconomics.* 10th ed. Boston: Pearson/Addison Wesley. 2006. Chapters 7–9, 13–14, 17.

Maddock, Rodney, and Michael Carter. "A Child's Guide to Rational Expectations." *Journal of Economic Literature* 20, no. 1 (March 1982), pp. 39–51.

Mankiw, N. Gregory. "A Quick Refresher Course in Macroeconomics." *Journal of Economic Literature* 28, no. 4 (December 1990), pp. 1645–60.

Marston, Richard C. "Stabilization Policies in Open Economies." In *Handbook of International Economics.* Vol. II. Edited by Ronald W. Jones and Peter B. Kenen. Amsterdam: North-Holland, 1985. Chapter 17.

Stiglitz, Joseph. "Reflections on the Natural Rate Hypothesis." *Journal of Economic Perspectives* 11, no. 1 (Winter 1997), pp. 3–10.

Weiner, Stuart E. "Challenges to the Natural Rate Framework." Federal Reserve Bank of Kansas City *Economic Review* 80, no. 2 (Second Quarter 1995), pp. 19–25.

CHAPTER 28

Baxter, Marianne, and Alan C. Stockman. "Business Cycles and the Exchange-Rate Regime: Some International Evidence." *Journal of Monetary Economics* 23, no. 3 (May 1989), pp. 377–400.

Broda, Christian. "Terms of Trade and Exchange Rate Regimes in Developing Countries." *Journal of International Economics* 63, no. 1 (May 2004), pp. 31–58.

Broll, Udo, and Bernhard Eckwert. "Exchange Rate Volatility and International Trade." *Southern Economic Journal* 66, no. 1 (July 1999), pp. 178–85.

Calvo, Guillermo A., and Frederic S. Mishkin. "The Mirage of Exchange Rate Regimes for Emerging Market Countries." *Journal of Economic Perspectives* 17, no. 4 (Fall 2003), pp. 99–118.

Cooper, Richard N. *Currency Devaluation in Developing Countries.* Essays in International Finance No. 86. Princeton, NJ: International Finance Section, Princeton University, June 1971.

Cushman, David O. "U.S. Bilateral Trade Flows and Exchange Risk during the Floating Period." *Journal of International Economics* 24, no. 3/4 (May 1988), pp. 317–30.

Dornbusch, Rudiger. "Flexible Exchange Rates and Interdependence." *International Monetary Fund Staff Papers* 30, no. 1 (March 1983), pp. 3–30.

Flood, Robert P., and Nancy P. Marion. "Self-Fulfilling Risk Predictions: An Application to Speculative Attacks." *Journal of International Economics* 50, no. 1 (February 2000), pp. 245–68.

Friedman, Milton. "The Case for Flexible Exchange Rates." In Milton Friedman, *Essays in Positive Economics.* Chicago: University of Chicago Press, 1953, pp. 157–203.

Gagnon, Joseph E. "Exchange Rate Variability and the Level of International Trade." *Journal of International Economics* 34, no. 3/4 (May 1993), pp. 269–87.

Garber, Peter M., and Lars E. O. Svensson. "The Operation and Collapse of Fixed Exchange Rate Regimes." In *Handbook of International Economics.* Vol. III. Edited by Gene M. Grossman and Kenneth Rogoff. Amsterdam: Elsevier, 1995. Chapter 36.

Gulde, Anne-Marie. "The Role of the Currency Board in Bulgaria's Stabilization." *Finance and Development* 36, no. 3 (September 1999), pp. 36–39.

Gültekin, Bülent, and Kamîl Yilmaz. "The Currency Board Experience and the Alternatives for Turkey." Unpublished paper. Koç University. Istanbul.

Heller, H. Robert. "Optimal International Reserves." *Economic Journal* 76, no. 302 (June 1966), pp. 296–311.

Hooper, Peter, and Steven W. Kohlhagen. "The Effect of Exchange Rate Uncertainty on the Prices and Volume of International Trade." *Journal of International Economics* 8, no. 4 (November 1978), pp. 483–511.

Hutchison, Michael, and Carl E. Walsh. "Empirical Evidence on the Insulation Properties of Fixed and Flexible Exchange Rates: The Japanese Experience." *Journal of International Economics* 32, no. 3/4 (May 1992), pp. 241–63.

Ito, Takatoshi; Peter Isard; Steven Symanski; and Tamim Bayoumi. *Exchange Rate Movements and Their Impact on Trade and Investment in the APEC Region.* IMF Occasional Paper 145. Washington, DC: IMF, 1996. (Summarized in "Study Examines Exchange Rate Changes and Impact on APEC Trade and Investment," *IMF Survey,* Feb. 10, 1997, pp. 37–38.)

Korhonen, Iikka. "Currency Boards in the Baltic Countries: What Have We Learned?" Institute for Economies in Transition Papers No. 6. Bank of Finland. 1999.

Levy-Yeyati, Eduardo, and Federico Sturzenegger. "To Float or to Fix: Evidence on the Impact of Exchange Rate Regimes on Growth." *American Economic Review* 93, no. 4 (September 2003), pp. 1173–93.

McCulloch, Rachel. *Unexpected Real Consequences of Floating Exchange Rates.* Essays in International Finance No. 153. Princeton, NJ: International Finance Section, Princeton University, August 1983.

McKinnon, Ronald I. "Optimum Currency Areas." *American Economic Review* 53, no. 4 (September 1963), pp. 717–25.

Mundell, Robert A. "Currency Areas, Common Currencies, and EMU." *American Economic Review* 87, no. 2 (May 1997), pp. 214–16.

———. "A Theory of Optimum Currency Areas." *American Economic Review* 51, no. 4 (September 1961), pp. 657–65.

Taylor, Mark P. "The Economics of Exchange Rates." *Journal of Economic Literature* 33, no. 1 (March 1995), pp. 13–47.

Thursby, Jerry G., and Marie C. Thursby. "Bilateral Trade Flows, the Linder Hypothesis, and Exchange Risk." *Review of Economics and Statistics* 69, no. 3 (August 1987), pp. 488–95.

Tower, Edward, and Thomas D. Willett. *The Theory of Optimum Currency Areas and Exchange-Rate Flexibility.* Special Papers in International Economics No. 11. Princeton, NJ: International Finance Section, Princeton University, 1976.

Wang, Kai-li, and Christopher B. Barrett. "A New Look at the Trade Volume Effects of Real Exchange Rate Risk." Working Paper 2002-41. Department of Applied Economics and Management, Cornell University, November 2002.

Williamson, John. *What Role for Currency Boards?* Policy Analyses in International Economics No. 40. Washington, DC: Institute for International Economics, September 1995.

CHAPTER 29

Ahmed, Masood; Timothy Lane; and Marianne Schulze-Ghattas. "Refocusing IMF Conditionality." *Finance and Development* 38, no. 4 (December 2001), pp. 40–43.

Bergsten, C. Fred, and C. Randall Henning. *Global Economic Leadership and the Group of Seven.* Washington, DC: Institute for International Economics, 1996.

Black, Stanley W. "International Money and International Monetary Arrangements." In *Handbook of International Economics.* Vol. II. Edited by Ronald W. Jones and Peter B. Kenen. Amsterdam: North-Holland, 1985. Chapter 22.

Bloomfield, Arthur I. *Monetary Policy under the International Gold Standard: 1880–1914.* New York: Federal Reserve Bank of New York, 1959.

———. *Short-Term Capital Movements under the Pre-1914 Gold Standard.* Princeton Studies in International Finance No. 11. Princeton, NJ: International Finance Section, Princeton University, 1963.

Calvo, Guillermo A., and Enrique G. Mendoza. "Petty Crime and Cruel Punishment: Lessons from the Mexican Debacle." *American Economic Review* 86, no. 2 (May 1996), pp. 170–75.

Commission of the European Communities. *The European Monetary System.* European File No. 15/86. Luxembourg: Office for Official Publications of the European Communities, 1986.

Cooper, Richard N. "Economic Interdependence and Coordination of Economic Policies." In *Handbook of International Economics.* Vol II. Edited by Ronald W. Jones and Peter B. Kenen. Amsterdam: North-Holland, 1985. Chapter 23.

———. "Is There a Need for Reform?" In *International Trade and Finance: Readings.* 3rd ed. Edited by Robert E. Baldwin and J. David Richardson. Boston: Little, Brown, 1986, pp. 337–55.

Dunn, Robert M., Jr. *The Many Disappointments of Flexible Exchange Rates.* Essays in International Finance No. 154. Princeton, NJ: International Finance Section, Princeton University, December 1983.

Economic Report of the President, February 1999. Washington, DC: U.S. Government Printing Office, 1999. Chapter 7.

The ECU. 2nd ed. Periodical 5/1987. Luxembourg: Office for Official Publications of the European Communities, 1987.

Eichengreen, Barry. "European Monetary Unification." *Journal of Economic Literature* 31, no. 3 (September 1993), pp. 1321–57.

———. "A Review of Peter Isard's *Globalization and the International Financial System: What's Wrong and What Can Be Done?*" *Journal of Economic Literature* 44, no. 2 (June 2006), pp. 415–19.

———. *Toward a New International Financial Architecture: A Practical Post-Asia Agenda.* Washington, DC: Institute for International Economics, 1999.

Ellsworth, P. T., and J. Clark Leith. *The International Economy.* 6th ed. New York: Macmillan, 1984.

Frankel, Jeffrey A. "Recent Exchange-Rate Experience and Proposals for Reform." *American Economic Review* 86, no. 2 (May 1996), pp. 153–58.

Garber, Peter M., and Lars E. O. Svensson. "The Operation and Collapse of Fixed Exchange Rate Regimes." In *Handbook of International Economics.* Vol. III. Edited by Gene M. Grossman and Kenneth Rogoff. Amsterdam: Elsevier, 1995. Chapter 36.

Goldstein, Morris. "Whither the Exchange Rate System?" *Finance and Development* 21, no. 2 (June 1984), pp. 2–6.

IMF External Relations Department. "How the IMF Promotes Global Economic Stability: A Factsheet." Washington, DC. August 2006.

IMF Staff. "The Asian Crisis: Causes and Cures." *Finance and Development* 35, no. 2 (June 1998), pp. 18–21.

Issing, Otmar. "The Monetary Policy of the Eurosystem." *Finance and Development* 36, no. 1 (March 1999), pp. 18–21.

James, Harold. "From Grandmotherliness to Governance: The Evolution of IMF Conditionality." *Finance and Development* 35, no. 4 (December 1998), pp. 44–47.

Jennings, Thomas. "Dollarization: A Primer." U.S. International Trade Commission *International Economic Review,* April/May 2000, pp. 8–10.

Joyce, Joseph P. "The Asian Crisis and the IMF: New Problems, Old Solutions?" *The Journal of the Korean Economy* 1, no. 1 (Spring 2000), pp. 109–24.

———. "The IMF and Global Financial Crises." *Challenge: The Magazine of Economic Affairs* 43, no. 4 (July/August 2000), pp. 88–107.

Kenen, Peter B. *Ways to Reform Exchange-Rate Arrangements.* Reprints in International Finance No. 28. Princeton, NJ: International Finance Section, Princeton University, November 1994.

Krugman, Paul R. "Target Zones and Exchange Rate Dynamics." *Quarterly Journal of Economics* 106, no. 3 (August 1991), pp. 669–82.

Machlup, Fritz. *Plans for Reform of the International Monetary System.* Special Papers in International Economics No. 3. Revised. Princeton, NJ: International Finance Section, Princeton University, 1964.

———. *Remaking the International Monetary System: The Rio Agreement and Beyond.* Baltimore: Johns Hopkins University Press, 1968.

Machlup, Fritz, and Burton G. Malkiel (eds.). *International Monetary Arrangements: The Problem of Choice. Report of the Deliberations of an International Study Group of 32 Economists.* Princeton, NJ: International Finance Section, Princeton University, 1964.

McCulloch, Rachel. *Unexpected Real Consequences of Floating Exchange Rates.* Essays in International Finance No. 153. Princeton, NJ: International Finance Section, Princeton University, August 1983.

McKinnon, Ronald I. *An International Standard for Monetary Stabilization.* Washington, DC: Institute for International Economics, 1984.

———. "Monetary and Exchange Rate Policies for International Financial Stability: A Proposal." *Journal of Economic Perspectives* 2, no. 1 (Winter 1988), pp. 83–103.

Mundell, Robert. "Threat to Prosperity." *The Wall Street Journal,* Mar. 30, 2000, p. A30.

Peera, Nural. "The International Monetary System and the Less Developed Countries." In George Zis et al., *International Economics.* London: Longman, 1988, pp. 263–319.

Reinhart, Carmen M. "The Mirage of Floating Exchange Rates." *American Economic Review* 90, no. 2 (May 2000), pp. 65–70.

A Single Currency for Europe: Monetary and Real Impacts. Report of a conference organized by the Banco de Portugal and the Centre for Economic Policy Research in Estoril on January 16–18, 1992. London: Centre for Economic Policy Research, 1992.

Spahn, Paul Bernd. "The Tobin Tax and Exchange Rate Stability." *Finance and Development* 33, no. 2 (June 1996), pp. 24–27.

Stotsky, Janet G. "Why a Two-Tier Tobin Tax Won't Work." *Finance and Development* 33, no. 2 (June 1996), pp. 28–29.

Summers, Lawrence H. "International Financial Crises: Causes, Prevention, and Cures." *American Economic Review* 90, no. 2 (May 2000), pp. 1–16.

Svensson, Lars E. O. "An Interpretation of Recent Research on Exchange Rate Target Zones." *Journal of Economic Perspectives* 6, no. 4 (Fall 1992), pp. 119–44.

Swoboda, Alexander. "Reforming the International Financial Architecture." *Finance and Development* 36, no. 3 (September 1999), pp. 2–4.

Taylor, Mark P., and Lucio Sarno. "The Behavior of Real Exchange Rates during the Post-Bretton Woods Period." *Journal of International Economics* 46, no. 2 (December 1998), pp. 281–312.

Tobin, James. "A Currency Transactions Tax. Why and How." Paper presented at Conference on Globalization of Markets, CIDEI Universita "La Sapienza," Rome, Oct. 27–28, 1994. Revised version, January 1995.

———. "A Proposal for International Monetary Reform." *The Eastern Economic Journal* 4, no. 3/4 (July–October 1978), pp. 153–59.

Triffin, Robert. *The Evolution of the International Monetary System: Historical Reappraisal and Future Perspectives.* Princeton Studies in International Finance No. 12. Princeton, NJ: International Finance Section, Princeton University, 1964.

———. *Gold and the Dollar Crisis: The Future of Convertibility.* New Haven, CT: Yale University Press, 1960.

Tsiang, S. C. "Fluctuating Exchange Rates in Countries with Relatively Stable Economies." *International Monetary Fund Staff Papers* 7, no. 2 (October 1959), pp. 244–73.

Williamson, John. "The Case for Roughly Stabilizing the Real Value of the Dollar." *American Economic Review* 79, no. 2 (May 1989), pp. 41–45.

———. "Comment on McKinnon's Monetary Rule." *Journal of Economic Perspectives* 2, no. 1 (Winter 1988), pp. 113–19.

———. "Exchange Rate Management: The Role of Target Zones." *American Economic Review* 77, no. 2 (May 1987), pp. 200–04.

———. *The Exchange Rate System.* 2nd ed. Washington, DC: Institute for International Economics, 1985.

PHOTO CREDITS

PART 1

Page 15 © Brand X Pictures/PunchStock/DAL

PART 2

Page 63 RF/Corbis/DAL

PART 3

Page 171 PhotoLink/Getty Images/DAL

PART 4

Page 255 © Comstock/PunchStock/DAL

PART 5

Page 453 (top left) Ryan McVay/Getty Images/DAL
Page 453 (top right) Ryan McVay/Getty Images/DAL
Page 453 (bottom right) RF/Corbis/DAL
Page 453 (bottom left) PhotoLink/Getty Images/DAL

PART 6

Page 627 © Bran X Pictures/PunchStock/DAL

PART 7

Page 705 The Studio Dog/Getty Images/DAL

INDEX

Page numbers followed by n indicate material in footnotes and source notes.